The Philosophy of Law

GARLAND REFERENCE LIBRARY OF THE HUMANITIES (VOL. 1743)

The Philosophy of Law

An Encyclopedia

Editor

Christopher Berry Gray

GARLAND PUBLISHING, INC.
A MEMBER OF THE TAYLOR & FRANCIS GROUP
New York & London
1999

Library of Congress Cataloging-in-Publication Data

The philosophy of law : an encyclopedia / editor, Christopher Berry Gray.
        p.   cm. — (Garland reference library of the humanities ; vol. 1743)
   Includes bibliographical references and index.
    ISBN 0-8153-1344-6 (alk. paper)
    1. Law—Philosophy—Encyclopedias.   I. Gray, Christopher B.
   II. Series.
   K204.p49   1999   99-11065
   340′.1—dc21   CIP

Contents

Introduction

This book is a reference for the professions of law and philosophy, for individuals interested in legal theory and the issues with which it deals, and for students who will contend with formulating a philosophical conception of law and the values that lie at its foundation. The law is a means for controlling behavior and constructing the framework within which the quality of life is defined. There is, therefore, an increasing need to understand the principles upon which it is based. The best first step for gaining such an understanding is appeal to a comprehensive reference work—an encyclopedia—that can present the issues that constitute the philosophy of law fairly and point the interested reader to the means for further investigation.

Interest in philosophy of law thrives today around the world. New developments in law in both age-old and more recently established nations call for a good deal of philosophical reflection. New institutional and disciplinary contexts encourage that reflection and have further increased its range. New areas of employment for practitioners of philosophy and law have opened up. An encyclopedia of philosophy of law is an essential tool for investigating the field's conventions and current developments. This encyclopedia is organized around the historically significant legal cultures, schools, and persons, as well as around the systematic daily practice of law, in order to inspire and assist thought about legal issues and thereby aid such an investigation.

Philosophy of Law: An Encyclopedia covers virtually all topics under discussion in the recent literature in philosophy of law. Though the primary focus is upon issues relevant to a North America soon to enter the twenty-first century, coverage includes the international application of core issues, often following their historical development back to ancient sources. It is not a truism that both the public and the private remain significant in legal discourse, nor that narrowly defined legal practices are just as amenable to philosophical reflection as the grand topics. The encyclopedia reflects this awareness.

The broad scope of the volume is made possible by expert contributors, over three hundred men and women from over forty countries, nearly half of them working in philosophy and nearly half in the law, as judges, jurists, or jurisprudents. In addition, the contributions of scholars from related fields in the social sciences and humanities provide an even greater breadth of perspective. Although this is an English-language work, which suggests its readership and its serviceability, contributors to this volume were chosen with an eye toward surpassing regional narrowness. They were therefore encouraged to remain cognizant of the wide-ranging application of their topic to the philosophy of law today, since questions peculiar or current to any one legal system or constitutional instrument have no a priori determinative effect upon legal philosophy.

All of the contributors are participants in the debates in which the theorists of philosophy of law engage, and (as might be expected) each has a conceptual loyalty and an inclination to promote it. However, each was directed to be as even-handed in the treatment of his or her area as is possible, and the resulting work demonstrates the seriousness with which this instruction was taken. The reader can rely upon an academic objectivity rare in modern scholarship. The book presents a comprehensive picture of contemporary philosophy of law, including studies approximating doctrinal exposition of the law on one hand, and studies near to the philosophical ethics of society on the other. As is most desirable for the neophyte philosopher of law, most entries fall within these limits. The reader can rely upon the reportage and judgment of the contributors, who are among the current practitioners in the field of philosophy of law—its working professionals.

The reader is encouraged to browse at leisure. The titles of the majority of studies in the encyclopedia are drawn from the names of the issues under discussion as they would be recognized by practitioners of the law. In the study of law, specific activities are organized by jurisdiction, and the choice of entries in the encyclopedia was made with this in mind. For example, studies on public law issues (international and constitutional, criminal and administrative) stand alongside those concerning the private law (persons and property, contracts and tort).

However, when a burning inquiry is one's motive for opening the encyclopedia, a variety of tools are available to aid the search. The book is arranged alphabetically, but in order first to place a topic in a conceptual context, the Subject List by Topic at the beginning of the book should be consulted. The scope of one's investigation might expand as a result, but consciousness of related issues always leads to a more confident understanding of a topic of interest. For those readers interested in fundamental questions, such as the status and role of knowing and the normative assumptions of the law, the subject list will serve as a guide to investigation that lays the groundwork for understanding the rationales governing legal thinking.

The entries, for all their excellence, can be only starting points for learning. Research references follow each entry in order to carry cross-referencing beyond the confines of one volume. *See also* notes at the end of most entries lead to related topics in the encyclopedia, pointing the reader in a more specific way to study the interconnection of the principles of law and legal theory.

Such features—the alphabetical organization of the encyclopedia, its subject list and reference lists, as well as a comprehensive index—combine to facilitate inquiry: it is possible to satisfy very quickly the curiosity that first inspires the reader to draw the book from the shelf. However, this work was designed also to foster learning, to deal with issues many times over and from many points of view throughout the text. A topic is often considered once from the jurisdictional perspective in a particular locale, and again from the angle of a school of thought at some point in history; or first as the work of a prominent jurisprudent, and then as a concern for which normative and critical interpretation is offered. This is not evidence of redundancy, but of completeness, affording a well-rounded consideration of each issue and of the field as a whole.

Lest all this effort be expended to reinvent the wheel, however, a good deal of space is devoted to discussions of how these issues are dealt with in other places and at other times. Entries on current legal cultures (such as common law and civilian, European and Native American) mingle with treatments of other periods (whether Hellenistic or Sixteenth-Century or Federalist). Cutting across these issues are biographies of influential jurisprudents that include discussions of the schools or methods they launched. Several lengthy entries that provide basic factual information on the practice of legal philosophy in the modern era link these historical investigations to the aforementioned systematic essays.

Prospective users of the encyclopedia are scholars and practitioners in philosophy and in law, including undergraduates in arts and the law, as well as students in the many disciplines concerned with law, from literature to social work. Even a veteran in one of these disciplines, though a master of some areas within the scope of the philosophy of law, will profit from an introduction (or a reintroduction) to an area of study requiring the specialist's expert touch. It is hoped that readers will thereby gain a full appreciation of the complexity of law, and of the conceptual fabric that binds it.

In addition to support of this project by Garland Publishing and by my employer, Concordia University of Montreal, as well as by my family's patience, I gratefully acknowledge the Social Sciences and Humanities Research Council of Canada for funding many of its costs with a three-year research grant.

Christopher Berry Gray

Subject List by Topic

Realism, Legal
Sociological Jurisprudence
Liberal Philosophy of Law
Libertarian Philosophy of Law
Utilitarianism
Republican Philosophy of Law
Communitarian Philosophy of Law
Contractualist Philosophy of Law
Objectivist Philosophy of Law
Fascist Philosophy of Law
Decisionist Philosophy of Law
Action-Based Philosophy of Law
Exegetical School
Free Law Movement
Pragmatist Philosophy of Law
Institutionalist Philosophy of Law
Institutionalism, French
Array Theory
Chaos Theory
Hermeneutical Philosophy of Law
Phenomenological Philosophy of Law
Existential Philosophy of Law
Semiotic Philosophy of Law
Discourse Theory
Discourse Epistemology
Difference Theory
Feminist Philosophy of Law
Critical Legal Studies
Economics and Law
Anarchist Philosophy of Law
Marxist Philosophy of Law
Nihilist Philosophy of Law
Postmodern Philosophy of Law
Deconstructivist Philosophy of Law
Deriddean Jurisprudents
Radical Race, Class, and Gender Theory (Positionality)

Personages in Philosophy of Law

Ancient and Medieval
    Plato
    Aristotle
    Augustine
    Ulpian, Domitius
    Cicero, Marcus Tullius
    Isidore
    Anselm
    Maimonides
    Aquinas
    Mair, Thomas John (Major)
    Holdsworth, Richard

Modern British
    Hobbes, Thomas
    Locke, John

Hume, David
Scottish Enlightenment
Smith, Adam
Blackstone, William
Bentham Jeremy
Burke, Edmund
Austin, John
Spencer, Herbert

Modern European
Vico, Giambattista
Macchiavelli, Niccolò
Montaigne, Michel de
Montesquieu, Baron de
Lipsius, Justus
Grotius, Hugo
Pufendorf, Samuel
Spinoza, Baruch de
Leibniz, Gottfried Wilhelm
Beccaria, Cesare
Domat, Jean
Rousseau, Jean-Jacques
Kant, Immanuel
Fichte, Johann Gottlieb
Hegel, Georg Wilhelm Friedrich

Recent Anglo-American
Hutchinson, Thomas
Paine, Thomas
Founding Jurists, 1760–1800
Federal Jurists, 1800–1860
American Jurists, 1860–1960
Idealists, British
Holmes, Oliver Wendell, Jr.
Peirce, Charles Sanders
Pound, Roscoe
Dewey, John
Llewellyn, Karl Nickerson
Hohfeld, Wesley Newcombe
Lasswell/McDougal Collaboration
Fuller, Lon L.
Hart, Herbert Lionel Adolphus
Raz, Joseph
Posner, Richard Allen
Nozick, Robert
Rawls, John
Dworkin, Ronald
Finnis, John

Recent European
Jhering, Rudolf von
Savigny, Friedrich Carl von
Rosmini, Antonio
Nietzsche, Friedrich
Marx, Karl

Durkheim, Emile
Weber, Max
Kelsen, Hans
Radbruch, Gustav
Gurvitch, Georges
Scandinavian Realists
Bodenheimer, Edgar
Hayek, Friedrich von
Gény, François
Villey, Michel
Maritain, Jacques
Bobbio, Norberto
Cossio, Carlos
Betti, Emilio
Gadamer, Hans-Georg
Habermas, Jürgen
Husserl, Gerhart
Reinach, Adolph
Kaufmann, Felix
Kaufmann, Arthur
Pashukanis, Evgeny Bronislavovich
Petrazycki, Leon
Frankfurt School
Wróblewski, Jerzy
Wittgenstein, Ludwig
Foucault, Michel
Perelman, Chaïm
Luhmann, Niklas
Derrida, Jacques

Jurisdictional Philosophy of Law

Jurisdictions
Jurisdiction
Conflict of Laws
Comparative Law
Reception
Ecclesiastical Jurisdiction
International Jurisdiction
Institutional Jurisdiction
Public and Private Jurisdictions

Public Law Jurisdictions

Constitutional Jurisdiction
Constitutionalism
Constituting Acts
Community
Customary Law
Convention and Custom
Legality
Legitimacy
Authority

Justice in Contract
Gift
Hire
Sale
Negotiable Instruments
Agency (Mandate)
Ethics, Legal

Tort Jurisdiction
Torts
Fault
Causation
Products Liability
Harms
Personal Injury
Economic Loss
Corrective Justice
Damages
Punitive Damages
Liability, Protections from

Unjust Enrichment and Restitution

Systematic Philosophy of Law
Information in Philosophy of Law:
Study, Research, and Materials

Normativity
Axiology
Norms
Metanorms
Values
Standards
Validity
Logic, Deontic Legal
Artificial Intelligence
Game Theory
Aesthetics

Morality and Law
Goodness and Coherence
Is/Ought
Time and Imputation
Rights and Liberties
Powers and Rights
Natural Rights
Universal Rights
Abuse of Right
Obligation and Duty
Omissions
Imperfect Obligation
Prima Facie Obligation
Responsibility
Virtue

Contributors

Abbarno, John M.
Department of Philosophy
D'Youville College
Buffalo NY
Homelessness and Residency
Privacy

Abegg, Edmund
Philosophy Department
Edinboro University, Edinboro PA
Array Theory
Mobility Rights

Airaksinen, Timo
Department of Philosophy
University of Helsinki, Finland
Anarchist Philosophy of Law
Nihilism

Alexander, Larry
School of Law
University of San Diego, CA
State Action

Altman, Andrew
Department of Philosophy
George Washington University
Washington DC
Critical Legal Studies

Archard, David
Department of Moral Philosophy
University of St. Andrew's, Fife, Scotland
Parenting and Childrearing

Ardal, Pall S.
Department of Philosophy
Queen's University, Kingston ON
Desert

Arfa Mensia, Mokdad
Faculté des sciences humaines et sociales
Université des lettres, arts et sciences humains
Université de Tunis II, Tunisia
Islamic Philosophy of Law

Arfa Mensia, Mongia
Faculté des sciences humaines et sociales
Université des lettres, arts et sciences humains
Université de Tunis II, Tunisia
Islamic Philosophy of Law

Arnaud, André-Jean
Directeur de recherche
C.N.R.S., Paris, France
Role

Atienza, Manuel
Departamento de filosofia del derecho y
    derecho internacional privado
Universidad de Alicante, Spain
Southern European Philosophy of Law

Auxier, Randall E.
Department of Philosophy
Oklahoma City College, Oklahoma City OK
Order
Religion and Theology

Baker, Brenda M.
Department of Philosophy
University of Calgary, AL
Hart, Herbert Lionel Adolphus

Balaban, Oded
Department of Philosophy
University of Haifa, Israel
Ideology

Barden, Garrett
Philosophy Department
University College Cork
National University of Ireland
Legality

Barrett, Robert B.
Department of Philosophy
Washington University, St. Louis MO
Renaissance Philosophy of Law

Barretto, Vicente De Paulo
Universidade do Rio de Janeiro/
Universidade Gama Filho
Rio de Janeiro, Brazil
Tolerance

Baumrin, Bernard H.
Graduate School, Graduate Center
City University of New York, NY
Security

Beehler, Rodger
Department of Philosophy
University of Victoria, BC
Constituting Acts

Belliotti, Raymond Angelo
Department of Philosophy
State University of New York
Fredonia NY
Community
Decision-Making, Judicial
Justification

Bengoetxea, Joxerramon
Cour de Justice des Communautés
européennes, Luxembourg
Faculty of Law
University of the Basque Country
Donostia / San Sebastien, Spain
Institutional Jurisdiction
Nation and Nationalism

Bickenbach, Jerome E.
Department of Philosophy
Queen's University, Kingston ON
Ethics, Legal

Binswanger, Harry
The Ayn Rand Institute
New York NY
Objectivist Philosophy of Law

Bix, Brian
Quinnipiac Law School
Hamden CT
Dworkin, Ronald
Posner, Richard Allen
Raz, Joseph

Bjarup, Jes
Faculty of Law
Stockholms Universitet, Sweden
Northern European Philosophy of Law
Scandinavian Legal Realism

Black, Virginia
Department of Philosophy and Religious
 Studies
Pace University, Pleasantville NY
Dignity
Natural Law

Blatnik, Edward
School of Law
Columbia University, NY
Derridean Jurisprudents

Blegvad, Mogens
Copenhagen, Denmark
Social Philosophy

Bodéüs, Richard
Département de Philosophie
Université de Montréal, QC
Aristotle

Boetzkes, Elisabeth
Department of Philosophy
McMaster University, Hamilton ON
Pornography

Bohmer, Carole
Department of Sociology
Ohio State University, Columbus OH
Divorce and Marriage

Borsellino, Patrizia
Istituto di filosofia e sociologia del diritto
Università degli studi di Milano, Italy
Bobbio, Norberto
Norms

Bouchaert, Boudwijn
Faculteit der Rechtsgeleerheid
Universiteit Gent, Belgium
Exegetical School
Gény, François

Bowden, Thomas A.
Blum Yumkas Mailman Gutman and
    Dennick P.A.
Baltimore MD
Objectivist Philosophy of Law

Braybrooke, David
Departments of Government and Philosophy
University of Texas, Austin TX
Common Good

Brenkert, George G.
McDonough School of Business
Georgetown University, DC
Liberty

Brett, Nathan
Department of Philosophy
Dalhousie University, Halifax NS
Mercy and Forgiveness

Bridge, Michael G.
Norton, Rose
Kemson House, London, England
Sale

Brigham, John
Department of Political Science
University of Massachusetts, Amherst MA
Goods

Broekman, Jan M.
Centre de philosophie du droit
Katholische Universiteit Leuven, Belgium
Legalism

Bronaugh, Richard
Department of Philosophy
Talbot College, University of Western
    Ontario, London ON
Contractual Obligation
Ethics, Legal
Parties, Contractual

Brophy, Alfred L.
School of Law
Oklahoma City University, Oklahoma City
    OK
Slavery

Brown, Oscar James
Department of Philosophy
St. Thomas University, Fredericton NB
Aquinas, Thomas

Brudner, Alan
Faculty of Law
University of Toronto, ON
Mens Rea

Brühlmeier, Daniel
Baden, Switzerland
Smith, Adam

Brunk, Conrad G.
Department of Philosophy
Conrad Grebel College, Waterloo ON
Risk Assessment

Buckingham, Donald E.
Faculty of Law
University of Saskatchewan, Saskatoon SK
Ethics, Legal

Burgess-Jackson, Keith
Department of Philosophy and Humanities
University of Texas, Arlington TX
Negligence
Relevance
Sodomy

Burgh, Richard W.
Department of Philosophy
Rider University, Lawrenceville NJ
Aging

Carbone, June
School of Law
Santa Clara University, Santa Clara CA
Marriage Contract

Chapman, Bruce
Faculty of Law, University of Toronto, ON
Economics

Chemerinsky, Erwin
Law Center, University of Southern California
Los Angeles CA
Equality

Child, James W.
Department of Philosophy
Bowling Green State University
Bowling Green OH
Act Requirement
Deterrence, Strategic
Deterrent Rationale
Rebellion
Revolution
Superior Orders and Legitimate Authority

Christie, George C.
School of Law
Duke University, Durham NC
Obedience and Disobedience

Christman, John
Department of Philosophy, Virginia
Polytechnic Institute and State University,
Blacksburg VA
Autonomy

Christopher, Russell L.
School of Law
Columbia University, NY
Mistake and Ignorance
Self-Defense

Coady, C.A.J.
Department of Philosophy
University of Melbourne, Parkville
Victoria, Australia
Testimony and Expert Evidence

Cohen, Stanley A.
Senior Counsel
Human Rights Law Section
Department of Justice, Ottawa ON
Automatism
Prosecution, Private

Conklin, William E.
Faculty of Law, University of Windsor, ON
Authority
Constitutionalism

Connelly, Clare
School of Law
University of Glasgow, Scotland
Parties to Criminal Conduct

Cooper, David
Department of Philosophy
Northern Michigan University, Marquette MI
Difference Theory

Cooper, Katherine
New Hampshire Public Defenders Office
Manchester NH
Difference Theory

Cooter, Robert D.
Law School, University of California
Berkeley CA
Punitive Damages

Corrado, Michael L.
Law School, University of North Carolina
Chapel Hill NC
Defenses
Preventive Detention
Promulgation

Cotterrell, Roger B.M.
Faculty of Law, Queen Mary and Westfield
    College, University of London, England
Criminology
Gurvitch, Georges

Couture, Jocelyne
Département de philosophie
Université du Québec à Montréal, QC
Distributive Justice

Couture, Tony
Philosophy Department
University of Prince Edward Island
Charlottetown PEI
State

Cragg, A. Wesley
School of Business, and
    Department of Philosophy, York University
North York ON
Punishment
Sentencing

Cranor, Carl F.
Department of Philosophy
University of California, Riverside CA
Empirical Evidence

Cunha, Paolo Ferreira da
Instituto de Filosofia Luso-Brasileira
Catedra de Universidade Lusofona–Lisboa
Porto, Portugal
Isidore
Roman Philosophy of Law
Rosmini, Antonio
Treason

Dagger, Richard
Department of Political Science
Arizona State University, Tempe AZ
Restitutionary Rationale

Dais, Eugene E.
Faculty of Law
University of Calgary, AL
Hohfeld, Wesley Newcombe
Powers and Rights

Dalcourt, Gerard J.
Department of Philosophy
Seton Hall University, South Orange NJ
Finnis, John

D'Amato, Anthony
School of Law
Northwestern University, Chicago IL
Indeterminacy
Justice

Davis, Michael
Center for the Study of Ethics in the
    Professions
Illinois Institute of Technology, Chicago IL
Strict Liability
Wrongdoing and Right acting

Day, David C., Q.C.
Lewis, Day, Dawe and Burke
St. John's, Newfoundland
Affinity

DeCew, Judith Wagner
Philosophy Department
Clark University, Worcester MA
Discretion

DeMarco, C. Wesley
Department of Philosophy
Oklahoma City University, Oklahoma City
    OK
Character
Love

Di Lorenzo, Vincent
School of Law
St. John's University, Jamaica NY
Chaos Theory

Dillof, Anthony M.
Texas Wesleyan University
Fort Worth TX
Imputation and Exculpation

Di Norcia, Vincent
Department of Philosophy
University of Sudbury, ON
Commons

Dorsey, Gray L. (deceased)
School of Law
Washington University, St. Louis MO
Jurisculture

Doyle, James A.
Department of Philosophy
University of Bristol, UK
Rational Bargaining

Drysdale, John
Department of Sociology
Concordia University, Montreal QC
Weber, Max

Duff, David G.
Faculty of Law, University of Toronto, ON
Inheritance and Succession

Dunlap, William V.
Quinnipiac College School of Law
Hamden CT
Damages

Dwyer, Susan
Department of Philosophy
U.S. Naval Academy, Annapolis MD
Hate Literature

Elfstrom, Gerard A.
Department of Philosophy
Auburn University AL
Military Philosophy of Law

Ellin, Joseph
Department of Philosophy
Western Michigan University, Kalamazoo MI
Supererogation

Elliot, Robert
Philosophy Department
Sunshine Coast University College
Maroochydore South, Queensland, Australia
Intergenerational Justice

Eskridge, William N., Jr.
Georgetown University Law Center
Washington DC
Intent, Legislative

Finer, Joel Jay
Cleveland-Marshall College of Law
Cleveland State University, Cleveland OH
Confessions
Torture

Fischer, Norman
Department of Philosophy
Kent State University, Kent OH
Marxist Philosophy of Law

Francis, John G.
Department of Political Science
University of Utah, Salt Lake City UT
Eminent Domain and Takings

Francis, Leslie P.
College of Law
University of Utah, Salt Lake City UT
Eminent Domain and Takings
Liberal Philosophy of Law

Freeman, Samuel
Department of Philosophy
University of Pennsylvania, Philadelphia PA
Fundamental Rights
Rawls, John

French, Peter A.
Department of Philosophy
University of South Florida, St. Petersburg FL
Responsibility
Status

Frey, Raymond G.
Department of Philosophy
Bowling Green State University, Bowling
   Green OH
Omissions

Fridman, G.H.L., Q.C.
Faculty of Law
University of Western Ontario, London ON
Agency (Mandate)

Gaete, Rolando E.
Legal, Political and Social Sciences
South Bank University, London, England
Universal Rights

Gaitenby, Alan C.
Legal Studies
University of Massachusetts, Amherst MA
Artificial Intelligence and Networks

Gerber, Rudolph J., How.
Justice, Court of Appeals
State of Arizona, Division One, Phoenix AR
Insanity Defense

Ghirardi, Olsen A.
Academia Nacional de Derecho y Ciencias
   Sociales
Cordoba, Argentina
Epistemology in Law

Gil, Thomas
Institut für Philosophie
Technische Universität Berlin, Germany
Frankfurt School (Early)
Jhering, Rudolf von
Radbruch, Gustav

Gill, Emily R.
Department of Political Science
Bradley University, Peoria IL
Citizenship and Membership

Glenn, H. Patrick
Faculty of Law
McGill University, Montreal QC
Reception

Glenn, Richard A.
Department of Political Science
Millersville University, Millersville PA
Conscientious Objection

Glover, John
Faculty of Law
Monash University, Clayton, Victoria
   Australia
Unjust Enrichment and Restitution

Gochnauer, Myron
Faculty of Law
University of New Brunswick, Fredericton NB
Oaths

Goldstein, Gerald
Faculté de Droit
Université de Montréal, Montréal QC
Conflict of Laws

Goldstein, Laurence
Department of Philosophy
University of Hong Kong
Precedent

Goldsworthy, Jeffrey D.
Faculty of Law
Monash University, Clayton, Victoria
   Australia
Hayek, Friedrich von

Goyard-Fabre, Simone
Faculté de droit
Université de Caen (Emeritus); Centre de
philosophie de droit, Université de Paris II,
Paris, France
Domat, Jean

Grotius, Hugo
Pufendorf, Samuel
Western European Legal Culture in the
  Twentieth Century

Gracia, Jorge J.E.
Department of Philosophy
State University of New York, Buffalo NY
Latin American Philosophy of Law

Gray, Christopher B.
Department of Philosophy
Concordia University, Montreal QC
Estate and Patrimony
Included Offenses
Institutionalism, French
Nineteenth Century Philosophy of Law
Translations of Arnaud
Atienza
Goldstein, G.
Héleine
Neumann
Pohe-Topka
Renaut
Zanchini

Graydon, Charalee F.
Bishop and MacKenzie, Calgary AL
Rehabilitation and Habilitation Rationale

Grunebaum, James O.
Department of Philosophy
Buffalo State College, Buffalo NY
Ownership

Haarscher, Guy
Centre de philosophie du droit
Faculté de Philosophie et Lettres, Université
  Libre de Bruxelles
Belgium
Political Philosophy

Haber, Joram Graf
Division of Humanities
Bergen Community College, Paramus NJ
Professional Ethics
Psychiatry
Speech Acts

Haber, Lina Levit, M.D.
Spring Valley NY
Psychiatry

Hartney, Michael
Ottawa ON

Kelsen, Hans

Harwood, Sterling
Department of Philosophy
San Jose City College, San Jose CA
Exploitation
Is/ought Gap
Liability, Criminal
Paine, Thomas

Hassett, Joseph M.
Hogan and Hartson
Washington DC
Jury System

Héleine, François
Faculté de Droit
Université de Montréal, QC
Justice in Contract, Civilian

Henderson, Dan Fenno
Asian Law Program
School of Law, University of Washington
Seattle WA (Emeritus)
Hastings College of Law
University of California
San Francisco CA
Japanese and Asian Philosophy of Law

Henley, Kenneth
Department of Philosophy
Florida International University, Miami FL
Rule of Law

Hester, Thurman Lee, Jr.
Department of Philosophy
Oklahoma City University
Oklahoma City OK
Sovereignty

Heyman, Steven J.
Chicago-Kent College of Law
Illinois Institute of Technology, Chicago IL
Rescue in Tort and Criminal Law

Hiram, Hilary
School of Law
University of Glasgow, Scotland
Harms

Hogg, Michael M.
A.B. Freeman School of Business
Tulane University, New Orleans LA
Bankruptcy

Houlgate, Lawrence D.
Philosophy Department
California Polytechnic State University
  San Luis Obispo CA
Family Law

Hubbard, F. Patrick
School of Law
University of South Carolina, Columbia SC
Jury Trials

Hudson, Richard
Department of Commerce
Mount Allison University, Sackville NB
Cossio, Carlos
Husserl, Gerhart
Kaufmann, Felix
Phenomenology of Law
Reinach, Adolf

Hughes, William
Department of Philosophy
University of Guelph, ON
Conscience

Hunt, Alan
Department of Law
Carleton University, Ottawa ON
Foucault, Michel
Marx, Karl

Hunter, Graeme
Department of Philosophy
University of Ottawa, ON
Leibniz, Gottfried Wilhelm

Husak, Douglas N.
Department of Philosophy
Rutgers University, New Brunswick NJ
Drugs
Consent
Intent

Hyland, Richard
School of Law
Rutgers University, Camden NJ
Gift
Holmes, Oliver Wendell, Jr.
Spinoza, Baruch de

Inness, Julie
Department of Philosophy
Mount Holyoke College, South Hadley MA
Intimacy

Iturralde, Victoria
Teoria y Filosofia del Derecho
Facultad de Derecho
Universidad del Pais Vasco
  San Sebastian (Guipozooa)–Donostia, Spain
Civilian Philosophy of Law

Iwanicki, Jack
Philosophy Department
University of New Brunswick, Fredericton NB
Necessity

Jackson, Kevin T.
Graduate School of Business Administration
Fordham University, New York NY
International Jurisdiction

Jackson, Robert H.
Department of Political Science
University of British Columbia, Vancouver BC
Developing Countries

Jacobson, Arthur J.
Cardozo School of Law
Yeshiva University, New York NY
Luhmann, Niklas

Janda, Richard
Faculty of Law
McGill University, Montreal QC
Regulation

Jones, David H.
Department of Philosophy
College of William and Mary
Williamburg VA
Homicide

Kaptein, Hendrik
Faculteit van Rechtsgeleerheid
Universiteit van Amsterdam, Netherlands
Causation, Criminal
Fact and Law

Kastely, Amy H.
School of Law
St. Mary's University, San Antonio TX
Cicero, Marcus Tullius

Kazan, Patricia
Department of Philosophy
University of Toronto, ON
Novel Defenses

Kelley, Patrick J.
School of Law
Southern Illinois University, Carbondale IL
Causation, Tort Law

Kellogg, Frederic R.
Sabre Foundation
Washington DC
Jurisdiction
Natural Rights

Kerr, Ian R.
Faculty of Law, and Faculty of Information
   and Media Studies
University of Western Ontario, London ON
Fictions and Deemings

Kevelson, Roberta (deceased)
Department of Philosophy
College of William and Mary
Williamsburg VA
Pierce, Charles Sanders
Semiotic Philosophy of Law

Khan, Abrahim H.
Trinity College
University of Toronto, ON
Existentialist Philosophy of Law

Kingwell, Mark
Department of Humanities
University of Toronto, Scarborough ON
Civility
Liberality
Scottish Enlightenment

Kipnis, Kenneth
Department of Philosophy
University of Hawaii at Manoa, Honolulu HI
Plea Bargaining

Kitod, Teodros
Afro-American Studies
Harvard University, Cambridge MA
Self-Determination, Personal

Klinck, Dennis R.
Faculty of Law
McGill University, Montreal QC
Evidence

Koller, Peter
Institut für Rechtsphilosophie
Rechtssoziologie und Rechtsinformatik,
Karl-Franzens-Universität Graz, Austria

Acquisition and Transfer

Krajewski, Bruce
Department of English
Laurentian University, Sudbury ON
Gadamer, Hans-Georg
Hermeneutical Philosophy of Law

Kramer, Matthew H.
Department of Jurisprudence
Churchill College, Cambridge University
Cambridge, England
Deconstructionist Philosophy of Law
Truth

Kutz, Christopher Lee
Boalt Hall School of Law
University of California, Berkeley CA
Conspiracy

Lafrance, Guy
Département de philosophie
Université d'Ottawa, ON
Machiavelli, Niccolò
Translations of Goyard-Fabre

Lagerspetz, Eerik
Department of Philosophy and Social Sciences
University of Jyväskylä, Finland
Powers of Government

Lametti, David
Faculty of Law
McGill University, Montreal QC
Fragmentation of Ownership

Landesman, Bruce
Department of Philosophy
University of Utah, Salt Lake City UT
Liberal Philosophy of Law

La Torre, Massimo
Department of Law
European University Institute
San Domenico di Fiesole, Italia
Institutionalist Philosophy of Law

Laursen, John Christian
Department of Political Science
University of California, Riverside CA
Montaigne, Michel de
Skepticism

Leigh, Leonard H.
Criminal Cases Review Commission
Birmingham, England
Theft and Related Offenses

Leiter, Brian
School of Law
University of Texas, Austin TX
Realism, Legal

Lempereur, Alain Pekar
École supérieur des sciences économiques et
  commerciales
Graduate School of Management
Cergy-Pointoise, France
Arbitration
Dispute Resolution
Mediation, Criminal
Perelman, Chaïm

Levenbook, Barbara
Department of Philosophy and Religion
North Carolina State University, Raleigh NC
Disposition of Remains

Li, Kuo-Lee
Research Library, Law Library
McGill University, Montreal QC
Information on Philosophy of Law

Lind, Douglas
Department of Philosophy
University of Idaho, Moscow ID
Free Law Movement
Pragmatist Philosophy of Law

Lobban, Michael
Department of Law
Bruner University, Uxbridge, England
Blackstone, William

López Hernández, José
Departamento de Fundamentos del Orden
  Juridico
Facultad de derecho, Universidad de Murcia
Murcia, Spain
Purpose, Legislative

Lowery, Thomas J.
Department of Political Science
Brigham Young University, Provo UT
Convention and Custom
Plato

Lowy, Catherine
Centre for Public Policy
University of Melbourne, Carlton, Victoria
Australia
Action and Agency

Lucaites, John Louis
Department of Communications and Culture
Indiana University, Bloomington IN
Voice

Lucy, William N.R.
School of Law
University of Hull, England
Common Law Philosophy of Law

Luizzi, Vincent
Department of Philosophy
Southwest Texas State University
San Marcos TX
Value

Mabe, Alan R.
Department of Philosophy
Florida State University, Tallahassee FL
Standing

MacAdam, Jim
Department of Philosophy
Trent University, Peterborough ON
Rousseau, Jean-Jacques

Macdonald, Roderick A.
Faculty of Law
McGill University, Montreal QC
Natural Justice

Machan, Tibor R.
School of Business and Economics
Chapman University, Orange CA
Libertarian Philosophy of Law

Mackaay, Ejan
Faculté de droit
Université de Montréal, QC
Intellectual Property
Legislation and Codification

Macleod, Alistair M.
Department of Philosophy
Queen's University, Kingston ON
Efficiency

Marlin, Randal
Department of Philosophy
Carleton University, Ottawa ON
Actus Reus
Attempts

Marmor, Andrei
Tel Aviv University
Ramat Aviv, Tel Aviv, Israel
Interpretation

Martin, Bill
Department of Philosophy
DePaul University, Chicago IL
Derrida, Jacques

Mason, Sir Anthony, Hon.
Chief Justice
High Court of Australia, Sydney, N.S.W.
Australia
Research School of Social Sciences, Australian
    National University
Judicial Independence

Matsuo, Hiroshi
School of International and Business Law
Yokohama National University
Yokohama, Japan
Possession and Recovery

Matthews, Gareth B.
Department of Philosophy
University of Massachusetts, Amherst MA
Augustine

Mazzarese, Tecla
Istituto di Diritto Private e Processuale
Università di Pavia, Italy
Judicial Syllogism
Metanorms

McCrea, Adriana
Department of History
Dalhousie University, Halifax NS
Lipsius, Justus
Sixteenth-to-eighteenth Centuries Philosophy
    of Law

McGee, Glenn
Center for Bioethics
School of Medicine and Hospitals
University of Pennsylvania, Philadelphia PA
Euthanasia and Suicide

Medina, Vincente
Department of Philosophy
Seton Hall University, South Orange NJ
Decisionist Philosophy of Law
Social Contract

Melkevik, Bjarne
Faculté de droit
Université Laval, Québec QC
Aboriginal Legal Cultures
Chinese Philosophy of Law
Pashukanis, Evgeny Bronislavovich

Mellos, Koula
Department of Political Science
University of Ottawa, ON
Ecology and Environmental Sciences

Mendell, Mark
Department of Philosophy, Queens College
City University of New York, NY
American Jurists 1860–1960
Dewey, John

Merz, Jon
Center for Bioethics, School of Medicine and
    Hospitals
University of Pennsylvania, Philadelphia PA
Euthanasia and Suicide

Meyer, Linda
Quinnipiac School of Law, Hamden CT
Nietzsche, Friedrich

Mineau, André
Départment des Sciences réligieuses et
    d'éthique
Université du Québec à Rimouski, QC
Beccaria, Cesare

Moffat, Robert C.L.
Law Center
University of Florida, Gainesville FL
Fuller, Lon L.
Goodness and Coherence

Moles, Robert
School of Law
Australian National University, Canaberra
Australia
Austin, John

Moore, James
Department of Political Science
Concordia University, Montreal QC
Hume, David

Morales, Maria H.
Department of Philosophy
Florida State University, Tallahassee FL
Bentham, Jeremy
Hobbes, Thomas

Morse, Howard Newcomb
Faculty of Law
Pepperdine University, Malibu CA (retired)
War and War Trials

Moyer, David S.
Department of Anthropology
University of Victoria, BC
Anthropology

Murphy, Cornelius
Pittsburgh PA
Public and Private Jurisdictions

Nagan, Winston P.
College of Law
University of Florida, Gainesville FL
African Philosophy of Law
Lasswell/McDougal Collaboration
  (Configurative Philosophy of Law)

Narveson, Jan
Department of Philosophy
University of Waterloo, ON
Compliance

Nathanson, Stephen
Department of Philosophy and Religion
Northeastern University, Boston MA
Capital Punishment

Nederman, Cary J.
Department of Political Science
University of Arizona, Tucson AZ
Medieval Philosophy of Law

Nesteruk, Jeffrey
Department of Business Administration
Franklin and Marshall College, Lancaster PA
Secondary Rights

Neumann, Ulrich
Seminar für Rechtsphilosophie und
  Rechtossoziologie
Johann-Wolfgang-Goethe–Universität
Frankfurt am Main, Germany
Discourse Theory

Newman, Joel S.
School of Law
Wake Forest University, Winston-Salem NC
Taxation

Nickel, James W.
Department of Philosophy
University of Colorado, Boulder CO
Civil Rights
Due Process

Niggli, Marcel Alexander
Seminar Für Strafrecht
Universität Fribourg i. Ve.
Error, Deceit, and Disillusion

Norman, Wayne
Centre for Applied Ethics
University of Vancouver, BC
Minority, Ethnic, and Group Rights
Secession

Nunan, Richard
Department of Philosophy and Religious
  Studies
College of Charleston, SC
Legitimate Object of Contract

Oakley, John B.
School of Law
University of California, Davis CA
Bodenheimer, Edgar

Oldenquist, Andrew
Mershon Center
Ohio State University, Columbus OH
Retributive Rationale

Opalek, Kazimierz
Faculty of Law
University of Cracow, Poland
Wróblewski, Jerzy

Owen, David G.
Law School
University of South Carolina, Columbia SC
Products Liability

Pallard, Henri R.
Department of Law and Justice
Laurentian University, Sudbury ON
Cossio, Carlos
Husserl, Gerhart
Kaufmann, Felix
Phenomenology of Law
Reinach, Adolph
Translation of Vallançon

Palmer, Vernon V.
Law School
Tulane University, New Orleans LA
Fault

Pappu, S.S. Rama Rao
Department of Philosophy
Miami University, Oxford OH
Indian Philosophy of Law

Paquet, Gilles
Centre on Governance
Université d'Ottawa, ON
Economics and Law

Paroussis, Michel
Seminar für Rechtsphilosophie und
    Kirchenrecht
Albert-Ludwigs-Universität Freiburg
Freiburg im B., Germany
Discourse Epistemology
Standards

Partlett, David F.
School of Law
Vanderbilt University, Nashville TN
Liability, Protections from Civil

Passerin d'Entrèves, Maurizio
Department of Government
University of Manchester, England
Communitarian Philosophy of Law

Pastore, Baldassare
Dipartimento di Scienze Giuridiche
Università degli Studi di Ferrara, Italy
Betti, Emilio

Patterson, Dennis
School of Law
Rutgers University, Camden NJ
Llewellyn, Karl Nickerson
Wittgenstein, Ludwig

Pavcnik, Marijan
Law Faculty
University of Ljubljana, Slovenia
Abuse of Right

Payne, Dinah M.
Faculty of Management
University of New Orleans, LA
Bankruptcy

Peczenic, Aleksandr
Juridska Faculteten
Lunds Universitet, Lund, Sweden
Analogy
Coherence

Pencak, William
Department of History
Penn State University, State College PA
Federal Jurists 1800–1860, U.S.
Founding Jurists 1760–1800, U.S.
Hutchinson, Thomas
Sagas, Icelandic

Peruffo, Monika
Università di Milano
Biella, Italy
Metaphor and Symbol

Pestieau, Joseph
Département de philosophie
Collège de St.-Laurent, QC
Economics and Law

Piechowiak, Marek
Instytut Filozofii, Tadevsz Kotarbínski
    Pedagogical University,
Zielona Gora, Poland
Kaufmann, Arthur

Pietroski, Paul M.
Departments of Philosophy and Linguistics
University of Maryland, College Park MD
Prima Facie Obligation

Podgórecki, Adam
Department of Sociology
Carleton University, Ottawa ON
Petrazycki, Leon
Sociology of Law

Pohe-Topka, Denis
Faculté de Droit
Université Montesquieu (Bordeaux IV)
Pessac, France

Customary Law

Pompa, Leon
Department of Philosophy
University of Birmingham, Edgbaston,
Birmingham, England
Vico, Giambattista

Posner, Richard A., Hon.
Chief Justice
U.S. Court of Appeals, Seventh Circuit
Chicago IL
Corrective Justice

Preuss, Anthony
Department of Philosophy
Binghamton University, Binghamton NY
*Hellenic Philosophy of Law: Conceptual
  Framework*
*Hellenic Philosophy of Law:
  Primary Sources*

Primoratz, Igor
Department of Philosophy
Hebrew University, Jerusalem, Israel
Expressive Rationale
Mixed Rationales
Prostitution

Puntervold, Bente Bø
Faculty of Economics, Public Administration
  and Social Work
Oslo College, Olso, Norway
Asylum and Refugees

Quirk, Patrick
School of Law
Bond University, Gold Coast, Queensland,
Australia
Anselm
Hire

Rafferty, Nicholas
Faculty of Law
University of Calgary, AL
Economic Loss

Raikka, Juha
Department of Philosophy
University of Turku, Finland
Betrothal
Self-Determination, National

Reeve, Andrew
Department of Politics and International Studies
University of Warwick, Coventry, England
Franchise and Referendum
Lobbying

Rehg, William R.
Department of Philosophy
Saint Louis University, St. Louis MO
Habermas, Jürgen

Reidy, David A.
Department of Philosophy
Indiana State University, Indianapolis IN
Postmodern Philosophy of Law

Reimann, Matthias
School of Law
University of Michigan, Ann Arbor MI
Savigny, Friedrich Carl von

Renaut, Alain
Départment de philosophie, de morale, et de
  politique
Université de Paris–Sorbonne (Paris IV)
Paris, France
Fichte, Johann Gottlieb

Reynolds, Noel B.
Department of Political Science
Brigham Young University, Provo UT
Convention and Custom
Plato

Risser, David T.
Political Science Department
Millersville University, Millersville PA
Democratic Process
Violence and Oppression

Robinson, Ira
Department of Religion
Concordia University, Montreal QC
Maimonides

Robinson, Olivia F.
School of Law
University of Glasgow, Scotland
Ulpian, Domitius

Rossetti, Carlo
Sociology of Law
Istituto di Sociologia, Università degli Studi
  di Parma, Italy
Judicial Review

Rotenberg, Daniel L.
Law Center
University of Houston, TX
Entrapment

Rourke, Nancy
Center for Legal Reason, Windsor CA
Action-Based Philosophy of Law
Pound, Roscoe

Rowland, Tracey
Commonwealth Scholar
Gonville and Caius College
Cambridge, England
Private Law

Rudmin, Floyd W.
Psychology Department
University of Trousø, Norway
Property

Samu, Mihaly
Eotvos Lorand Tudomanyegyetem
Allam-Es Jogtudomanyi Kar
Budapest, Hungary
Axiology
Policy, Legal

Samuel, Geoffrey
Kent Law School
University of Kent at Canterbury, England
Comparative Law

Sarkowicz, Ryszard
Faculty of Law
Jagellonian University, Cracow, Poland
Objectivity

Schedler, George E.
Department of Philosophy
Southern Illinois University, Carbondale IL
Surrogacy

Schmaus, Warren
Department of Humanities
ITT Center, Illinois Institute of Technology
Chicago IL
Durkheim, Emile

Schött, Roland
Juridiska Institutionen
Lunds Universitet, Lund, Sweden
Burke, Edmund

Schulz, Lorenz
Seminar für Rechtsphilosophie
Institut für Kriminal Wissenschaften
Johann-Wolfgang-Goethe-Universität
Frankfurt am Main, Germany
Time and Imputation

Schumaker, Millard
Department of Religious Studies
Queen's University, Kingston ON
Imperfect Obligation

Scott, Stephen A.
Faculty of Law
McGill University, Montreal QC
Negotiable Instruments

Sellers, Mortimer N.S.
School of Law
University of Baltimore, MD
Republican Philosophy of Law

Shafer-Landau, Russell
Department of Philosophy
University of Kansas, Lawrence KS
Rights and Liberties

Sheldon, Mark
Department of Philosophy
Indiana University Northwest, Gary IN
Vengeance

Simmons, A. John
Department of Philosophy
University of Virginia, Charlottesville VA
Fairness
Locke, John
Political Obligation

Simon, Thomas W.
Department of Philosophy
Illinois State University, Normal IL
Radical Class, Gender, and Race Theories:
   Positionality

Slote, Michael
Department of Philosophy
University of Maryland, College Park MD
Virtue

Smith, J.C.
Faculty of Law
University of British Columbia, Vancouver BC
Obligation and Duty

Smith, Michael
Philosophy Program
Research School of Social Sciences, Australian
National University, Canberra, Australia
Morality and Law

Smith, Patricia G.
Department of Philosophy
Baruch College CUNY, NY
Feminist Philosophy of Law

Smith, Steven A.
St. Anne's College
Oxford, England
Freedom and Capacity of Contract

Soeteman, Arend
Faculteit der Rechtsgeleerdheid
Vrije Universiteit Amsterdam
Amsterdam, Netherlands
Logic, Deontic Legal

Stell, Lance K.
Department of Philosophy
Davidson College, Davidson NC
Dueling

Stevens, David
Faculty of Law
McGill University, Montreal QC
Trusts

Stevenson, Jack T.
University College
University of Toronto, ON
Monetary Power

Stone, Susanne Last
Cardozo School of Law
Yeshiva University, New York NY
Jewish Law

Suber, Peter
Department of Philosophy
Earlham College, Richmond IN
Amendment
Civil Disobedience
Paternalism
Self-Reference

Sumner, L. Wayne
Department of Philosophy
University of Toronto, ON
Utilitarianism

Superson, Anita M.
Department of Philosophy
University of Kentucky, Lexington KY
Sexual Abuse

Sweet, William
Department of Philosophy
St. Francis Xavier University, Antigonish NS
Idealists, British
Maritain, Jacques
Nozick, Robert
Spencer, Herbert

Sypnowich, Christine
Department of Philosophy
Queens University, Kingston ON
Socialist Philosophy of Law

Ten, C.L.
Department of Philosophy
Monash University, Clayton
Victoria, Australia
Criminalization

Thurschwell, Adam
Cleveland–Marshall College of Law
Cleveland State University
Cleveland OH
Aesthetics

Trentman, John A. (deceased)
Huron College
London ON
Holdsworth, Richard

Trigeaud, Jean-Marc
Centre de philosophie du droit
Faculté de droit, des sciences politiques
    des sciences économiques et de gestion
Université Montesquieu (Bordeaux IV)
Pessac, France
Persons, Identity of

Tuori, Kaarlo
Department of Public Law
University of Helsinki, Finland
Legitimacy

Tzitzis, Stamatios
Centre de philosophie du droit
Section de philosophie pénale, Université
    Panthéon–Assas (Paris II), Paris, France
Penal Law, Philosophy of

Valançon, François

Centre de philosophie du droit
Université Panthéon–Assas (Paris II), Paris
Villey, Michel

Vallentyne, Peter
Department of Philosophy
Virginia Commonwealth University
Richmond VA
Contractualist Philosophy of Law

van Dunné, Jan M.
Faculty of Law
Erasmus University Rotterdam
The Netherlands
Montesquieu, Baron de

Van Hoecke, Mark
European Academy of Legal Theory
Katholieke Universiteit Brussel, Belgium
Jurisprudence

Varga, Csaba
Legal Philosophy, Law Faculty
Péter Pázmany Catholic University of
   Hungary, Budapest, Hungary
*Central and Eastern European Philosophy of
   Law*
Codification
Ex Post Facto Legislation
History (Historicity of Law)
Ontology, Legal (Metaphysics)
Validity

Villa, Vittorio
Dipartimento di studi su politica, diritto e società
Università di studi di Palermo, Italy
Positivism, Legal

Viminitz, Paul
Department of Philosophy
University of Guelph, ON
Game Theory

von Hirsch, Andrew
Institute of Criminology
University of Cambridge, England
Incapacitative Rationale

Wardle, Lynn D.
J. Reuben Clark Law School
Brigham Young University, Provo UT
Abortion and Infanticide
Liaison

Warner, Richard

Law Center
University of Southern California
Los Angeles CA
Argumentation

Wein, Sheldon
Department of Philosophy
St. Mary University, Halifax NS
Human Rights

Weinstock, Daniel M.
Département de philosophie
Université de Montréal, QC
Kant, Immanuel

Weiss, Marcia J.
Department of Government and International
   Studies
Point Park College, Pittsburgh PA
Decision Making, Administrative
Personal Injury
Wrongful Life and Wrongful Death

Wellman, Carl
Philosophy Department
Washington University, St. Louis MO
Entrenchment

Wertheimer, Alan
Department of Political Science
University of Vermont, Burlington VT
Coercion

Weston, Nancy A.
Department of Philosophy
University of California at Berkeley
Hastings School of Law, San Francisco CA
Torts

Westra, Laura
Department of Philosophy
University of Windsor, ON
Terrorism

Willard, Andrew R.
School of Law
Yale University, New Haven CT
*Lasswell/McDougal Collaboration
   (Configurative Philosophy of Law)*

Winfield, Richard Dien
Department of Philosophy
University of Georgia, Athens GA
Hegel, Georg Wilhelm Friedrich

Wintgens, Luc J.
Law Faculty
Katholieke Universiteit Brussel
Keokelberg, Belgium
Fascist (National Socialist) Philosophy of Law

Wood, R. Neil
Department of Philosophy
University of Glasgow, Scotland
Mair (Major), John

Yhap, Jennifer L.
Centre d'Études anciennes
École Normale Superieure, Paris
Hellenistic Philosophy of Law

Zaibert, Leonardo A.
Department of Philosophy
State University of New York, Buffalo NY
Latin American Philosophy of Law

Zanchini di Castiglionchio, Francesco
Dipartimento di scienze giuridiche
Facoltà di Giurisprudenza
Università delgi Studi di Teramo, Italy
Avoccato di Rota Romana
Eccesiastical Jurisdiction

Ziegert, Klaus A.
Department of Jurisprudence
Faculty of Law, University of Sydney
Australia
Sociological Jurisprudence

Aboriginal Legal Cultures

The claims for recognition of Aboriginal legal cultures, for self-determination or political autonomy built on these cultures, for recognition of Aboriginal identity, differences, or authenticity, as an alternative or substitute to the established legal order of the state, today are challenging the legitimacy of modern legal philosophy. In this sense, we are the contemporary witnesses of an Aboriginal revolution. This revolution has produced, especially in the United States and Canada, an official legal recognition of Aboriginal legal cultures.

The Aboriginal or Indigenous peoples of the world are estimated to be 264 million, 4 percent of the world population in 1991. They are normally a minority, but in some situations Aboriginal people are a dominated majority. Typical examples of Aboriginal peoples are the Native or First Nations of North and South America, the Ainu of Japan, the Maori of New Zealand, the Aborigines of Australia, the "Hill-Peoples" of Asia, the "national minorities" in China, the Siberian peoples in Russia, and the Sami of Finno-Scandinavia. Nowadays it is recognized that these peoples have a legal inheritance as Aboriginal peoples and that this inheritance exists, to a greater or lesser degree, side by side with the dominant state law.

The term "Aboriginal legal" cultures refers to the legal inheritance of the Indigenous peoples of the world. In accordance with international Aboriginal or Indigenous law, an Aboriginal people or nation is comprised of the current descendants of the peoples who inhabited the territory of a country either wholly or partially, at the time when persons of a different culture or ethnic origin arrived there

from other parts of the world, overcame the Indigenous people, and, by conquest, settlement, or other means, reduced them to a nondominant or colonial situation. These descendants generally live more in conformity with their Aboriginal social, economic, and cultural customs and traditions than with the institutions of the country of which they now form a part.

Defining the concept of Aboriginal legal cultures is primarily a call for fact-finding. It expresses a positive conception of law promulgated by the Aboriginal people themselves in history, customs, folkways, and institutions, and so constitutes an object for scientific studies in anthropology, ethnology, history, and political or social sciences in general. It is thus outside the scope of legal philosophy. Current thinking in legal philosophy focuses on the philosophical patterns which govern Aboriginal legal culture and on the philosophy of accommodations between the latter and order. The extreme diversity of such philosophical patterns in the world's Aboriginal legal cultures excludes any systematic presentation in this inquiry. However, this discussion focuses on North American Native Nations and on the traditional philosophy which expresses their view about the foundation of law, the conception of rights, and the meaning of law.

North American Native legal cultures are founded on a spiritual and supranatural story which narrates the archetypical experience of beings from mythic times. The initial story of creation and the mythic experience of the tale of Aboriginal nations is designed as the Great Law, which promulgates an initial relation between the cosmos, nature, and the Native Nation. This spiritual aspect of Native North

American legal cultures serves thus to ensure the intersubjective embrace of common understanding and the mastery of human meaning and signification governing the cosmos, law, and the community of human beings.

It is the continued storytelling in historical times, by the members of the Aboriginal community, that is the framework in which the efficiency of this legal culture is established. The stories become real in the process of their telling, and, through maturity, the individual establishes his or her experience as an extension and thereby a confirmation of the initial story. It should be noted that this is a powerful method of binding one person to another and creating intersubjective, shared meaning. What is valued, then, in Aboriginal legal culture, is the community-bounded limits of experience.

It is in the concept of time, of time open to legal experience, that this community-bounded aspect of North American Native legal cultures first displays its limits. In contrast with the linear conception of legal modernity, the North American Native legal cultures promote a cyclical conception of time. The Native's traditional philosophy of law views the world in cyclical terms: time is a circle. This leads to a rejection of the categorization of law, and it suggests the methodological need to think the legal phenomena as inseparable from, or undifferentiated with, the cosmos, nature, and community.

The conception of rights, as well, in North American Native legal culture should be linked to the conception of "community authenticity." North American Native peoples drew their authenticity from the lands and the resources around them. They portrayed themselves as people who belonged and had communion with both nature and living creatures; hence their identification with the forest, the plains, the mountains, and the buffalo. The native worldview is a product of this internalized authenticity, which established their community as both physically and metaphysically an integral part of the natural order. In fact, for North American Native peoples, community authenticity exists as the parameter through which self-understanding is attained. In this way individual identities are subsumed under the collective whole, representing the sense of "us." In this context, the concept of "rights" remains philosophically controversial; it suggests, however, the individual obli-

gation to follow the rules of the community. Therefore, "rights" would be analogous with what the community finds predictable.

Another significant aspect of North American Native legal culture is that of legal meaning. In accordance with the argument developed above, this is a harmony-conception structured along the line of the relations between the community and the initial story. Both the concept of property and disputes, or abnormal behavior, require further elaboration.

Private ownership of land or resources was in fact alien to North American Native peoples. In general, the title of land is viewed as a gift given to all living creatures, to humans and fellow animals and plants. The original story of each one of the Native nations serves, however, to attribute, spiritually, specific land title to a Native community. It became their inheritance by a spiritual settling of one nation on a territory. The nation and the land are in fact conceived holistically as two sides of the whole. This conception of property thus includes the past and the future generations of the nation. Moreover, it raises the modern problem of the inalienability of land to other peoples because future generations cannot participate in any alienation.

There are, however, forms of private property or of mixed private-community property inside the community. These concern the harvest from fishing, hunting, or farming. The insistence on the survival of the community led to several different, complex systems intended to ensure a fair share for all the members of the community.

Conflict or abnormal behavior was, for most of the North American Native peoples, a collective affair, and it was conceived as a breach of harmony in the social order. We can, in many respects, observe the existence of "courts" in North American Native legal cultures. These would sometimes include mediation before the chief or the so-called medicine man, and, more frequently, the role of mediation by the elders. In this legal culture, the elders play an imminent role as the depositors and defenders of their people's story, and it seems natural to utilize their authority to settle conflicts. The settling of conflict is never a question of law or rights, but more a healing process intended to restore the broken harmony. The elders are guided by having privileged access to the story of their people and tend to rewrite the conflict or abnormal behavior in the light of this experience. The intention is to introduce the protagonist in a learning process about this story, their community, and about themselves. The conception of conflict resolution as a learning process implies an acceptance both of the tradition and of some remedy to heal offenses. In cases where healing is considered impossible, so that the conflict threatens the very core of the community, the sole solution offered would be the physical elimination of the wrongdoer, either by the death penalty or by ostracism.

North American Native legal culture offers insight into the structure of Aboriginal legal cultures in general. These have a holistic conception of law; accordingly, they are promulgated narratively and represent a community-bounded limit for legal experience. The fact that legal philosophy has not wanted to base its reflection on the presuppositions of this traditional philosophy, or traditional wisdom, is hardly surprising. Modern legal philosophy is more concerned with the question of accommodation.

A distinction should be made between factual and philosophical accommodation. Pure Aboriginal legal culture does not exist today, either in North America or in the rest of the world. All Aboriginal legal cultures have in fact changed with the contact and the intrusion of modern legal cultures, and many have simply disappeared. This contact has served to banish unacceptable practices such as warfare and slavery, although other practices continue to exist, such as the disadvantaged position of women in Aboriginal legal cultures. This factual accommodation process is found in legal history and in the morphology of existing Aboriginal legal systems, as in the tribal justice system in the United States. Therefore, the challenge for contemporary legal philosophy lies in the dialogue with Aboriginal legal cultures and in the creation of a place for them in modern legal systems.

This process of dialogue, or philosophical accommodation, has often been undertaken by non-Aboriginals. It has a long history in the philosophy of law, for example, in the sixteenth century, when the philosopher-theologians Francisco de Vitória, Francisco Suárez, and Bartholomé de Las Casas defended the rights of Native Americans as human rights; in the seventeenth and eighteenth centuries when the legal philosophers of the European Enlighten-ment, such as Samuel Pufendorf and Christian Wolff, entitled Native Americans as nations and thus recommended a practice based on treaties oriented to establish a system of Aboriginal political rights; in the nineteenth century when the first anthropologists such as Lewis H. Morgan and E. Burnett Tylor inscribed the Aboriginal legal cultures in a philosophical evolutionism, condemning them to simply be replaced with state law; and in the twentieth-century legal discourses of E. Adamson-Hoebel and Karl Llewellyn, who worked on the differences between Native American law and state law in order to prove the philosophical choices of American legal realism and their theses about the relation between social control and law. The result of these accommodation philosophies has been to view Aboriginal legal cultures in the light of human rights, of political rights, of an evolutionary scheme, or as concepts of Aboriginal rights. Today, we can observe this historical interpretation as revealing several implicit philosophical choices underlying contemporary legal and political discourses.

More important than the non-Aboriginal discourses is the contemporary Aboriginal process of accommodating their legal culture as an alternative or supplement to the dominant legal environment. Their task is to translate this legal cultural heritage in terms that respect both the cultural identity of an Aboriginal people and the inescapable horizon of modern law.

In the perspective of legal philosophy, it is not surprising to observe that many Aboriginal peoples have adopted a narrative approach to the inheritance of their legal culture. North American Native legal culture was an oral phenomenon that emerged from a mythic initial story and was enhanced through the history of the community. The new political narrative of Native law, found in Aboriginal political discourse and addressed to the community, is a discourse of identity. Aboriginal leaders know that crucial choices must be made; they know that their communities must accommodate themselves to new and altered patterns of existence. The new political narrative of Aboriginal legal culture works to ensure a basis of identity or of authenticity in these difficult processes, to establish a bridge between the new existence of Aboriginal peoples and the inherited legal cultures, and to rewrite the story of the legal culture inside new and altered sociopolitical patterns.

The new narrative of Aboriginal legal cultures, addressed to the non-Aboriginal, purports to convince the dominant societies in which they live to allow them space and time in order to continue to live and to develop as separate cultural entities. This new narrative stresses, therefore, the importance of a tenured land base and inherent Aboriginal rights as the contemporary expression of an Aboriginal legal culture.

The question of Aboriginal legal cultures is today one which explores the survival of distinct cultural entities. It is largely recognized that these legal cultures have the right to survival, but the question is how this can be achieved effectively in a world which is a global village in ongoing mutation.

References

Boldt, Menno, and J. Anthony Long, eds. *Quest for Justice: Aboriginal Peoples and Aboriginal Rights.* Toronto: University of Toronto Press, 1985.

Devlin, Richard F., ed. *First Nations Issues.* Toronto: Emond Montgomery Publications, 1991.

Hoebel, E. Adamson. *The Law of Primitive Man: A Study in Comparative Legal Dynamics.* Cambridge, MA: Harvard University Press, 1941.

Hoebel, E. Adamson, and Karl N. Llewellyn. *The Cheyenne Way: Conflict and Case Law in Primitive Jurisprudence.* Norman: University of Oklahoma Press, 1952.

Williams, Robert A., Jr. *The American Indian in Western Legal Thought: The Discourses of Conquest.* New York: Oxford University Press, 1990.

Bjarne Melkevik

See also COMMUNITY; CUSTOMARY LAW; SAGAS, ICELANDIC

Abortion and Infanticide

The protection that should be afforded the smallest and most vulnerable humans—the fetus in utero and the newborn infant—has been a matter of profound concern since antiquity. The Code of Hammurabi, Hittite law, and Old Testament Israelite law, for example, exacted monetary damages or other penalties for acts producing miscarriage, while the punishment for voluntary abortion among the Assyrians was impalement. Abortion was not consistently prohibited by law in the ancient world, but it was frequently, if inconsistently, condemned by ancient philosophers. Among the Greeks, Plato endorsed abortion only for women over forty years of age; Aristotle would allow abortion only before life entered the child (which he believed to occur at forty days for males and ninety days for females); Hippocrates forbade his followers to perform abortion except to expel an already-dead fetus. Yet exposure or killing of abnormal, deformed, and other unwanted children was generally tolerated in the ancient Near Eastern civilizations as well as among the Greeks and Romans.

In common law, abortion was criminally proscribed at least as early as the thirteenth century. Five centuries later William Blackstone summarized the status of the law regarding abortion in his *Commentaries on the Laws of England* as follows: "Life is the immediate gift of God, a right inherent by nature in every individual; and it begins in contemplation of law as soon as an infant is able to stir in the mother's womb. For if a woman is quick with child, and by her potion or otherwise, killeth it in her womb; or if anyone beat her, whereby the child dieth in her body, and she is delivered of a dead child; this, though not murder, was by the ancient law homicide or manslaughter. But the modern law doth not look upon this offense in quite so atrocious a light, but merely as a heinous misdemeanor."

The common law rule, eventually codified with exceptions excusing abortion when necessary to preserve the life (or health) of the mother, continued in Anglo-American law until the 1960s. Then, as medical advances substantially reduced the immediate risks to the mother from the abortion procedure, public debate over whether abortion should be allowed reignited.

In 1973 the United States Supreme Court decided *Roe v. Wade,* 410 U.S. 113 (1973), holding Texas' traditional abortion law unconstitutional on the ground that it infringed a woman's fundamental right of privacy, and declaring that the Constitution barred the states and federal government from preventing abortion before "viability." Since then, virtually no laws restricting abortion have been upheld in the United States, except public funding limitations, some informed consent provisions, some parental participation laws, and general medical regulation and reporting rules. While no other country has adopted an abortion policy as radically nonregulatory as the United States, several other countries have adopted milder versions of the privacy model.

However, most affluent civil law countries take a social-balancing approach to abortion policy, permitting restricted access to abortion (tight or loose restrictions depending on the jurisdiction) when the mother's circumstances are judged sufficiently difficult to overcome the presumed social interest in preserving prenatal life at the relevant stage of fetal development. In some poor, crowded countries lacking established tradition of protection for human rights, government policies encouraging or requiring abortion to enforce family size or population control policies have been adopted. In other countries where traditional religious influences (especially Catholic and Muslim) are strong, abortion is still prohibited except (possibly) when necessary to preserve the life of the mother.

The modern debate over whether abortion should be allowed raises many profound legal issues with significant moral and philosophical implications. One issue concerns "personhood": when in the process of biological development is a human being considered a "person" for purpose of receiving legal protection? One perspective identifies "personhood" with all living human beings, from the time of conception or implantation. The gist of this position is that from that point onward, a genetically autonomous human being exists, that all human life deserves basic human dignity, including legal protection against wanton destruction, regardless of age or condition, and that birth is a morally irrelevant demarcation for legal protection against killing human life. Another perspective argues that historically the unborn child has never been, and for practical reasons can never be, deemed a "person" in the whole sense, and that "personhood" is a social status that should be conferred only upon beings who have developed certain social capacities, such as sentience, cognition, and the capacity to interrelate, which all fetuses and neonates lack.

Gender equality issues also are implicated by the abortion controversy. Some feminists argue that abortion is necessary to give women equality with men, who, because they are not physically connected to the fetus, can easily abandon their offspring (and their responsibility to the female co-procreator who is carrying their child and who may be expected to accept the burden of raising the child). Others, however, argue that the Supreme Court abandoned women to the isolation of "privacy" by giving them the sole responsibility for reproductive decision making and eliminating any legal responsibility of the male co-procreator to participate in the abortion decision, thereby denying equality (solely on the basis of gender) to the fathers of unborn children. Some pro-life feminists argue that abortion is thinly disguised sexual exploitation of women, liberating women for more efficient use as sex objects of men. Relational feminists argue that abortion imposes a male model of relationships upon women who wish to nurture life rather than destroy it, who value relationships over rights and interdependence over "privacy," but who are coerced by their "liberation" to deny their own gender to satisfy the masculine model of independence, rights, and destructiveness.

Another gender equality issue concerns maternal-fetal conflicts and the hierarchy of valued humanity. Some commentators see an irreconcilable conflict between the interests of the fetus in not being destroyed and the interests of the woman in not being burdened with unwanted maternal responsibility and domestic subjugation. Others assert that the alleged "conflict" between the interests of mother and child is artificial, and that nondestructive alternatives (such as adoption) protect both interests. The practice of sex-selection abortion (still widespread in parts of the world), in which the fetus is destroyed if it is female but nurtured if it is male, also raises serious questions about whether permissive abortion enhances or erodes the status of women.

Another set of issues concern civil liberties. Libertarians oppose most government restriction upon individual choice, including, arguably, abortion restrictions. The extremely personal decision whether or not to have an abortion, they argue, should be made by the persons most immediately and directly affected. On the other hand, classic liberalism recognizes the duty of the state, as *parens patriae* (public guardian), to protect those who are most vulnerable, weak, and defenseless, including the unborn. They argue that the unborn are "others" whose rights justify some limit on individual action under Millian principles. "Right to life" advocates assert that the state's first duty is to protect the "right to life," while other civil libertarians argue that the "right to choose," that is, to make such intimate, personal decisions as whether to bear or beget a child, must always be protected against state compulsion.

Autonomy and social responsibility are themes often raised in the modern abortion debate. Some argue that the ability to control procreation, including access to abortion, is essential to individual autonomy and dignity, especially for women, in the modern world. Some argue that denial of abortion for a woman who has an unwanted pregnancy constitutes a totalitarian expropriation of her body, or that an unwanted fetus is a parasite upon the woman's body which she has the right to eliminate as a matter of basic self-protection and autonomy (the pregnant victim of rape being a prime example). It is urged by some that a pro-natalist policy is cruel to the unborn child in this day of war, pollution, pestilence, crime, and family disintegration, and irrational, if not suicidal, in this time of apparent overpopulation. Others argue that, in this day of effective and accessible contraception, the control-of-procreation argument does not justify abortion because the protected "choice" is whether or not to engage in sexual relations. Some pro-life advocates would allow abortions in the case of rape on the ground that the lack of maternal volition justifies an exception, while others argue that it is unjust to kill the child because of the crime of the father. Advocates of abortion restrictions assert that the balance of social interests mandates protecting all human beings, including the unborn, and proscribing all killing of innocent human life, including abortion, and that the solution to the distress of unwanted pregnancies is not to permit killing but to provide more adequate social services for needy unwed mothers. Some argue that the ethic of permissive abortion undermines the very foundation principles upon which individual freedom, political equality, and democratic government rest. Others see abortion restrictions as invasive of universal human rights.

The roles of religion and law, church and state, are also implicated in the abortion debate. Some view abortion as essentially a private, moral, or religious issue, which the state has no business regulating, and assert that it is an impermissible establishment of religion for the state to restrict abortion. Others assert that all law has a moral basis, that the religious content of laws restricting abortion is no greater than the religious content of laws prohibiting other forms of killing (such as murder), theft, perjury, or fraud, and view with concern attempts to exclude religious voices from a matter of such profound social importance.

Issues of federalism and separation of powers are also entangled in the contemporary abortion controversy. Virtually all of the permissive abortion policy in the United States has been created by federal judges, claiming to interpret the Constitution. Some critics see the abortion decisions as violative of basic principles of separation of powers and federalism— the exercise of political "will" (judicial legislation) rather than "judgment" by the judiciary, and improper federal encroachment upon the proper policy-making role of the state legislatures. Others assert that traditional limits on judicial policy-making by constitutional interpretation are outmoded and flawed, and that on an issue as basic as "personhood," and basic reproductive liberties, state by state, checkerboard policy-making is inconsistent with the need for national uniformity.

Historically, abortion and infanticide have been linked in both practice and concept. In Japan, for example, where both abortion and infanticide for socioeconomic reasons have been accepted for centuries, abortion, the more expensive and technically difficult method of disposing of unwanted children, was readily available to the elite, the court, the *daimyo,* the *samurai,* and rich merchants, while less expensive, simpler infanticide was practiced by the huge peasant class. In the West, there has been an inverse relationship between abortion and infanticide: historically, abortion was relatively rare because it entailed significant risk for the life of the pregnant woman (due to primitive abortion technology), while infanticide was discretely commonplace for centuries. However, when abortion technology improved, significantly reducing the immediate risks for the mother, abortion increased and infanticide decreased (though child abuse, the penumbra of infanticide, increased).

Historically, infanticide has been practiced for two purposes: to dispose of a handicapped or deformed child, and to dispose of a "normal" but unwanted child. In the ancient world and in medieval times, the birth of a deformed or apparently abnormal child was often judged an omen of bad things to come, or evidence of bad behavior or witchcraft of the mother. Hence, there was incentive to dispose of the child. Sometimes, abnormal-looking infants were deemed nonhuman, or possessed by evil spirits (changelings), or monsters, whom it was not immoral to kill. "Normal" children have been unwanted for two reasons: social and economic. Children socially unwanted have included children born out of wedlock, whose birth stigmatized (sometimes severely) the mother (and, at times, the father), and female babies born in times of severe gender discrimination when daughters were deemed social liabilities. Children unwanted for economic reasons have included those born during times of famine or other distress, females born into some ignorant societies that depend on physical labor, and children born at inconvenient times when child rearing would interfere with the immediate economic activities of the parent(s).

Prenatal screening and permissive abortion have reduced, but not eliminated, pressures for both categories of infanticide in many affluent countries today. However, infanticide still emerges in the debate over whether to withhold medical treatment from certain children, especially newly born infants who appear to be mentally handicapped. Some argue that it is tantamount to infanticide to allow parents or guardians to deny available, otherwise normally provided medical treatment simply because the infant is perceived to be "defective." Others argue that it is cruel not to let nature "take its course," and wrong to provide medical intervention simply because it is available. The role of "quality of life" considerations in making treatment decisions for children is fiercely contested.

Ultimately, both abortion and infanticide raise fundamental questions about the proper limits on (or duties of) humanity's power to kill immature forms of human life to avoid undesirable personal or societal burdens. The moral dilemmas are as old as knowledge of the mortal alternatives.

References

Dellapenna, J.W. "The History of Abortion: Technology, Morality, and the Law." *University of Pittsburgh Law Review* 40 (1979).

Dworkin, Ronald. *Life's Dominion: An Argument About Abortion, Euthanasia, and Individual Freedom.* New York: Knopf, 1993.

Ely, J.H. "The Wages of Crying Wolf: A Comment on *Roe v. Wade.*" *Yale Law Journal* 82 (1973), 920–949.

Glendon, Mary Ann. *Abortion and Divorce in Western Law.* Cambridge, MA: Harvard University Press, 1987.

Horan, Dennis J., Edward R. Grant, and Paige C. Cunningham, eds. *Abortion and the Constitution.* Washington DC: Georgetown University Press, 1987.

Mosely, K.L. "The History of Infanticide in Western Society." *Issues in Law and Medicine* 1 (1986), 345.

Noonan, John T., Jr. *A Private Choice, Abortion in America in the Seventies.* New York: Free Press, 1979.

Piers, Maria A. *Infanticide.* New York: Norton, 1978.

Wardle, L.D. " 'Crying Stones': A Comparison of Abortion in Japan and the United States." *New York Law School Journal of International and Comparative Law* 14 (1993), 183–259.

Wardle, Lynn D., and Mary Anne Q. Wood. *A Lawyer Looks at Abortion.* Provo UT: Brigham Young University Press, 1982.

Lynn D. Wardle

See also EUTHANASIA AND SUICIDE

Absolute Liability

See STRICT LIABILITY, CRIMINAL

Abuse of Right

Early liberal theory denied the possibility that a right could be abused. This was based on the principle *qui suo iure utitur neminem laedit,* and on the conclusion that the designation of an "abusive exercise of rights" is logically contradictory: one who exercises a right behaves in accordance with the law and his acts are permitted. The unlimitable nature of a right corresponds to economic and social competition: whoever achieves superiority in a certain area has the right to damage anyone else. The resulting damage is inevitable and legally allowed. It is not necessary to establish whether it was intended.

The theory of abuse of right first found a place within the framework of tort liability (subjective theory). The Austrian and German

Civil Codes each assert that a right is abused by someone who acts with fault and thereby damage is caused to someone else. A wider scope is covered by objective theories that consider the aim and social function of every right. This final aim is "outside" the right and "over" it. The direction of exercising a right is not set by the individual's will; instead, the aim ("spirit") of the right defines the direction of the conduct of the subject. The individual is liable not only when he behaves unlawfully (and does not have a legal basis) but also when he "incorrectly exercises a right." A similar standpoint is taken by mixed (objective-subjective) theories, which in addition to objective criteria require that the violator has encroached upon the right of someone else by fault.

With regard to the criteria proposed, the subjective theory ranges from the intentional to any other faulty action that is damaging to other rights-holders. This broadens the subjective theory and brings it closer to objective theories. Nevertheless, the subjective theory puts forward the holder's subjective relation to the exercise of the right and its consequences. The conduct is forbidden because it is not in accordance with the nature of the right, yet it is only forbidden if the subject can be reproached for faulty conduct.

The objective theory is more flexible. The criteria it applies are "open," allowing for adaptability in accord with changing social conditions (an objective-dynamic manner of interpretation). In this respect it goes much further than the subjective theory because it is not bound to the holder's faulty conduct, this being only one of the indices to abuse of the right.

In all theories, the main criteria are always of an objective nature. The objective theory uses subjective criteria like *animus nocendi* supplementarily. They are subjective to the extent that they require that the violator's attitude to the exercise of the right has to be established. The subjective theory is much less dynamic, since it always considers fault a condition sine qua non for the elements normatively constituting the abuse of right.

These elements are three. The basic assumption is that the subject starts out from a legally allowed abstract entitlement, and concretizes and materializes it in such a way that the conduct goes beyond the limits of entitlement. For instance, abuse of right takes place when the holder of a tenant's right puts off moving into a new house that is ready to be

lived in and thus makes it impossible for the owner to move into his own apartment, or when a party has a cart track on his land and uses it in such a way that the tracks get deeper and the water gathering in them flows onto a neighbor's land.

In these, lawful and unlawful elements mingle. The legality is sustained by the fact that the subject exercises a legally protected entitlement; the unlawfulness is sustained by recognition that the holder's conduct had gone beyond the legally allowed limits.

The second assumption is that a conflict of two rights has arisen and that they do not exclude each other. The conflict arises because two rights face each other and one of them is exercised in such a manner as to make it either partly or completely impossible to activate and realize the other one. Such a state of facts would occur if an uphill water beneficiary takes the water of a downhill user.

For abuse it is sufficient that the entitlement (demand) is enforced in a manner damaging to the other or is simply "making his situation more difficult." There is a conflict of rights because the subject of a duty still has the right to demand that the other party in the legal relationship stay within the limits of the right by choosing the less burdensome conduct among several possible ones and so enable the other party to achieve the advantages he is entitled to. Thus, a demand to cancel a contract should not be permitted if an improvement or later fulfilment is possible. A buyer cannot refuse to receive goods if their quality differs only slightly from the contractually agreed quality, but the buyer can demand a reduction in price.

Not every intrusion into somebody else's sphere can be considered an abuse, for it may be within the limits of legitimate criticism or competition. Nuisances are permitted if they do not go beyond the extent customary with respect to the nature and aim of the real estate and the local conditions. Thus, decisions have accepted that the interference is permitted when damage has been caused by a shadow falling over the crops of a neighboring lot. This legally empty (that is, uncertain) space can only be defined by relying upon the nature of the legally protected entitlement.

The third element is based on the claim that the rights are limited only by the equal rights of others. It follows from this interdependence of rights that in case a right is open as to its content, the holder must exercise it in such a manner that one's conduct does not go beyond the limit that allows someone else to exercise a right to qualitatively the same extent.

The social function of a right and its fulfillment can be used as criteria defining this. These include social benefit, normal and social fulfilment, insufficient entitled interest, aim of the legal relationship, and aim of the thing (object). Special weight is given to criteria of loyalty and good faith when dealing with local and business customs.

These criteria are not valid on the basis of their own authority, but are only legally binding when ordered by the lawgiver. If the criterion is not foreseen in the law, it can only be applied in a concrete case if the appropriate organ (the judge) so decides. When the content of the criterion is not evident from the text of the statute or of some other general legal act, but depends on social concepts of what is good and bad, lawful and unlawful, it is questionable how far such prohibition of abuse is legally binding. For example, under the pressure of certain economic interests, business morals conflict with the moral concepts of the social community. In this case, priority must be given to the morals of the social community, because the judge or other responsible government organ always has to determine the content of business morals, and whether this content is in accordance with the principles of the legal order.

Prohibition of the abuse of right is based on the law that is appropriate in terms of a civilization. The holder of the more (less) important right should get proportionately more (less), for example, when the owners of a working farm and of a holiday cottage are beneficiaries of the same water.

It is the duty of responsible government organs to act upon the request of the party involved or ex officio to limit the abused right, as well as to order reinstatement if it is possible. In addition, effective measures against abuse result from the refusal of legal protection as well as lack of recognition given to conduct going beyond the entitlement. The holder of a right may also be liable in tort. Only liability for damage caused by negligence can be found, unless the violator acts with intent to harm the other part (vexation). In this case, the conduct can be characterized as a civil offense, not an abuse of rights.

The prohibition of abuse is just one of the means leading to the socialization of law and right. Legislative intervention is necessary if a certain right is no longer in accord with the rule of law, for the prohibition of abuse can only bring it into line with someone else's right but cannot abolish it or give it a content that would significantly alter it. Otherwise there is danger that rights will not be taken seriously, will be unnecessarily narrowed, or even uncritically subordinated to "higher" aims and interests.

References

Association international du droit commercial et du droit des affaires; Group français. *Leasing: sociétés civiles professionelles, promotion immobiliere, ententes et abus de position dominante* (Leasing: Professional Firms, Realty, Understandings, and Abuse of Dominant Position). Paris: Sirey, 1967.

Bucher, E. *Das subjecktive Recht als Normsetzungsbefugnis* (Subjective Rights as Law Making Competency). Tübingen, Germany: Mohr, 1965.

Edmeades, Bernard. "Abuse of Right." *McGill Law Journal* 24 (1978), 136.

Koller, P. "A Conception of Moral Rights and Its Application to Property and Welfare State." *Ratio Juris* 5 (1992), 153–179.

Markovitch, M. *La théorie de l'abus de droit en droit comparé* (Theory of Abuse of Rights in Comparative Law). Paris: Librairie générale de droit et de jurisprudence, 1936.

Nino, C. *Rights*. Aldershot: Dartmouth, 1992.

Quero, Gilbert. *Contrats et abus de confiance: les rapports du droit civil et du droit penal* (Contracts and Abuse of Reliance: Civil and Penal Law). Paris: Cujas, 1961.

Raz, J. "On the Nature of Rights." *Mind* 93 (1984), 194–214.

Rotondi, M. *L'abus de droit* (Abuse of Right). Padova, Italy: CEDAM, 1979.

Saleilles, R. "De l'abus de droit." *Bulletin de la société d'études legislatives* (1905).

Schumaker, Millard. *Sharing Without Reckoning: Imperfect Right and the Norms of Reciprocity*. Walterloo ON: Wilfrid Lauier University Press, 1992.

Marijan Pavcnik

Acquisition and Transfer

Any social order aiming at a peaceful and expedient regulation of social life has to deal with the allocation of scarce goods. Thus, it has to provide rules determining the acquisition, use, and transfer of such goods. Even though such regulations do not necessarily presuppose rights in a strict sense, differentiated and large societies can hardly do without such rights. At any rate, modern occidental societies are in the habit of regulating the access to and participation in scarce goods by means of rights. This fact makes it possible to interpret every lawful acquisition, use, and transfer of goods as an acquisition, use, and transfer of rights.

Certain kinds of rights are considered transferrable, while some others are not. Nontransferrable rights can be divided into inalienable and functional rights. Most of what we call "human rights," particularly liberal and political basic rights, are considered *inalienable*. This view mainly rests on moral reasons resulting from requirements of justice. Efficiency cannot play a significant role here, because these rights are determined to define the initial conditions of social affairs from which considerations of efficiency ought to begin. The situation is different in the case of *functional* rights, which, according to contemporary views, contain all rights that confer public powers, as the powers of political authorities and state officials. The view that these rights ought not to be transferable is based on reasons of both justice and efficiency. If holders of public offices were free to transfer them to others by private transactions (for example, by bequeathing or selling them), it would be impossible to keep these offices open to all and secure their impartial performance. Additionally, many offices would come into the hands of incompetent people and a high degree of corruption would obstruct efficient execution.

If a transfer of rights is not excluded by sufficient reasons, several prima facie arguments are in favor of their transferability. An important moral argument results from the requirement of self-determination: only when rights are transferable are their possessors free to dispose of the things to which these rights entitle them. There is a further argument resting on considerations of efficiency: the transferability of rights by voluntary transactions is a much better means than any central distribution to achieve an optimal allocation of goods, since it provides people with the opportunity to exchange goods whenever doing so is in their mutual interest. The rights that form the

paradigm case of transferable rights are property rights.

In general, *property rights* are rights which endow particular individuals or collectives with a superior claim to dispose of certain (material or intellectual) things, a claim correlated with the duty of all others not to prevent those individuals or collectives from doing so. According to Jeremy Waldron, *private property* can be defined as a property where particular people (or small groups) have an exclusive, far-reaching, and durable right to dispose of certain things, a right that contains a number of more specific rights, including the right to possess and to use those things, and the right to transfer the property of them to others by voluntary acts of will. Property rights may be acquired either originally by *initial appropriation* of their first possessor, or derivatively through a *transfer* on the part of their previous bearer. As they always come into being by certain events, they are contingent rights which themselves are based on an inherent right, namely one's principal right to acquire and possess property.

The Original Acquisition of Property Rights

As far as the initial appropriation of natural resources is concerned, philosophers have developed various theories, two of which stand out: the occupation theory and the labor theory. The *occupation theory,* as discussed by Immanuel Kant and James Buchanan, maintains that one acquires a natural resource originally if one has actually taken possession of it and is able to defend it against others in the long run. Yet, since this theory starts from an initial state of affairs which itself results from completely accidental power relations and may contain significant inequalities, it is hardly acceptable from the viewpoint of justice. In contrast, as discussed by John Locke and Robert Nozick, the *labor theory* says that one acquires the property of a freestanding natural resource if one mixes one's own labor with it, provided that enough and as good is left for others. Yet this proviso turns out to be problematic. Taken literally, it excludes any and all exclusive, far-reaching, and permanent private property. In order to avoid this, the proviso must be interpreted very restrictively, for example, in the sense that one's appropriation of a thing must not worsen the position of others so that they are no longer able to use things of that kind. Understood in this way, however, the proviso allows almost unlimited inequalities, and is, therefore, incapable of securing a just distribution of property.

In a world in which almost all natural resources are actually in someone's possession, the problem of their original acquisition is a theoretical matter without practical importance. In this context, the *acquisition* of the products of human labor plays an important role. In modernity, the conviction that every human individual has an inherent *right to his or her labor force* and, consequently, also possesses a right to the products of his or her labor, has gained wide acceptance. Since, however, almost every human labor requires certain material resources in order to produce goods, the question arises as to when and to what extent one may acquire private property of such goods. A common view says that everyone who produces some things by using resources in his or her possession acquires an absolute private property of these things. Yet this view presupposes that the property of the resources under consideration is itself absolute. This may seem plausible under certain social conditions or with regard to particular things, but it is by no means always true.

In modern industrial societies, most economic goods are produced in contractual labor relations rather than being made by people themselves. As to the appropriation of these goods, one could take the view that an employer acquires an exclusive property right to all products of his or her employees, since the labor contract confers on him or her a right to the outcomes of their efforts. This leads to the problem of transfer.

The Transfer of Property Rights

Property rights are usually considered rights which include the right of their bearers to transfer them, at least to a certain extent, by contractual agreement or will to others who thereby acquire these rights. To be sure, there are various cases where such rights can be transmitted to others without an act of will of their previous bearers, for example, intestate succession or noncontractual transfers resulting from liabilities in delict or tort. This study, however, will deal only with the contractual transfer of property rights. One can take it for granted that, in principle, the opportunity of such transfers ought to exist, as it is necessary both for an efficient allocation of economic goods and for individual liberty.

In general, one can transfer a right only to the extent to which oneself possesses it. In general, it is also true that a state of affairs that emerges from another one through a (singular or repeated) transfer of rights may be considered legitimate only if the previous one was legitimate. But what requirements must be met by a proper contractual transfer? When and to what extent is it plausible to assume that contracts transform a legitimate state of affairs into another one which is legitimate as well?

A contractual transfer of property rights is *efficient* if and only if it is, under the prevailing initial conditions, to the benefit of all parties involved and has no significant negative external effects on others. Such a transfer may be called *just* if the transaction by which it is achieved (1) takes place under initial conditions that, as far as the contracting parties are concerned, conform to reasonable and widely accepted standards of justice, and (2) is performed in a way which leads, in all probability, to efficient results. A transaction which meets both conditions can be named *perfectly fair*. It seems plausible that a transaction must be perfectly fair to grant a transfer the legitimacy of which is beyond reasonable doubt.

In order for a transaction to be considered perfectly fair, it ought to satisfy a number of requirements, including the following: the contracting parties must be rational persons capable of ranking their preferences in consideration of their long-term interests and acting accordingly; each of these persons must consent to the agreement in his or her well-considered interest and in full knowledge of the relevant facts; each of the parties must agree on the contract voluntarily (which requires a more or less symmetrical power relationship between them); and their agreement must not have negative effects on third parties. In essence, these requirements correspond to the conditions that, according to economic theory, define a perfect, competitive market.

It is obvious, however, that contractual transactions taking place in real life conform with these requirements, if at all, only approximately. Thus, in order to make contractual transactions under real conditions possible, one must be satisfied with weaker requirements. For this reason, legal orders usually let valid contracts come into effect when responsible individuals reach an agreement without force and error. But these weaker requirements do, of course, not suffice to secure perfectly fair transactions. What they do guarantee is, in the best case, that contractual agreements are *rather fair*. Even if we assume that all transactions legally effective are rather fair, it is possible that a just initial state of affairs turns, step by step, through many small transfers into a state characterized by significant injustices. Yet the assumption that all effective transactions are rather fair is certainly too optimistic. There are rather good reasons to expect that a considerable number of these transactions are, more or less, unfair. In this case, however, it cannot be taken for granted that a just social structure tends to maintain itself without external intervention.

References

Ackerman, Bruce A., ed. *Economic Foundations of Property Law*. Boston: Little, Brown, 1975.
Buchanan, James M. *The Limits of Liberty*. Chicago: University of Chicago Press, 1975.
Nozick, Robert. *Anarchy, State, and Utopia*. New York: Basic Books, 1974.
Posner, Richard A. *Economic Analysis of Law*. Boston: Little, Brown, 1972. 3d ed., 1986.
Ryan, Alan. *Property and Political Theory*. Oxford: Blackwell, 1984.
Waldron, Jeremy. *The Right to Private Property*. Oxford: Clarendon Press, 1988.

Peter Koller

See also POSSESSION AND RECOVERY; PROPERTY

Act Requirement

A completed crime traditionally is said to have two essential parts: the actus reus and mens rea. The former is the human action or conduct which is the outward or behavioral manifestation of the crime. Lord Mansfield, in *R. v. Scofield* in 1784, averred that "so long as an act rests in bare intention . . . it is not punishable by our laws." The latest version of the *Model Penal Code* requires a voluntary act or an omission to perform a voluntary act as a prerequisite of guilt.

Why have an act requirement? The answer is that it is surely a requirement of a liberal system of law and may be a requirement of the rule of law altogether. For, without it, thoughts and what Lord Mansfield called "bare intentions" could be criminalized. One

has only to be reminded of the religious persecutions of the past or the totalitarian states of Nazi Germany and the Soviet Union to remember that, if one is not overly concerned with the niceties of justice, punishment for thoughts is quite possible and has been common throughout history. George Orwell, in *1984*, even invented a Newspeak word for it: *thought crime*.

The act requirement also prohibits prosecution for so-called crimes of status. For example, the Supreme Court of the United States, in *Robinson v. California*, decided that one cannot be guilty of the crime of being a "drug addict." This decision would equally disqualify racial, religious, or ethnic membership as crimes, as it would suffering from a disease or disability. Lastly, by banning crimes of status, the act requirement prevents a variety of common law "crimes" from being enforced. One no longer can be prosecuted for being a "common thief," a "common prostitute," or a "habitual drunkard."

Are there problems with crimes of status, including ones we might wish to accept as legitimate crimes? What about being the member of a terrorist organization, sworn to kill the head of state? Consider this difficult case: the Supreme Court of the United States, in *Powell v. Texas*, struggled with an instance of public drunkenness (the ordinance prohibited "being drunk in a public place"), questioning if the drunkenness did violate the act requirement and whether the drunkenness was innocuous. These examples indicate that the issue of status crimes is not all simple and clear-cut.

The act requirement also precludes prosecution of involuntary movements, muscle spasms, jerks, and the like. To cite Orwell again, certain sorts of nervous tics were considered facecrimes in Oceania and prosecuted fiercely, as was talking in one's sleep (if suitably seditious). Since under the act requirement these cases seem to be completely involuntary, it would appear that no act or even conduct has taken place. Thus, not even the rationality, let alone the morality of such prosecution, is clear. Even here, problem cases do arise. What do we do with Fain, the somnambulant gunman, in the famous Kentucky case *Fain v. Commonwealth?* If Fain really was sleeping when he fired the gun, he could not be acting, or so said the court. Yet Fain *shot* someone.

Lastly, the act requirement rejects the attribution of responsibility to those who have things happen to them. In *Eliza Lines,* a United States Supreme Court case, a ships officer was accused of deserting his post because he was washed overboard during a storm. This, says Justice Oliver Wendell Holmes, is "the difference between an act and no act."

Still, it is not clear just why the act is the paradigm entity for the attribution of responsibility. The nature of an act and of human action generally must be considered. The issue is not merely a definitional one or of philosophic interest only. There are several traditional legal problems surrounding the act requirement. One involves omissions. If an affirmative act is the paradigm for criminal liability, how can one be liable for not acting?

A standard account of an act for purposes of the act requirement in criminal law is that it be a "willed muscular contraction." This is John Austin's account, as it is Holmes' and John Stuart Mill's. This view of a criminal act has been roundly criticized by H.L.A. Hart, among others. Omissions, Hart says, are not muscular contractions of any sort, willed or otherwise. In this sense, they are nonevents.

A second, even more serious, problem for the act requirement is posed by negligence and strict liability. *Involuntary* actions, such as muscle spasms or movements while unconscious must be excluded if the act requirement is to mean anything. Yet *unintentional* action must be able to create liability in cases of negligence or strict liability, without throwing out the act requirement. That is, if I negligently run over an infant, such muscle spasms or movements while unconscious must be excluded if the act requirement is to mean anything. Yet unintentional action must be able to create liability in cases of negligence or strict liability, without throwing out the act requirement. How is this different from an involuntary act? The acts of driving, colliding, and killing are mine, and, based on a negligence doctrine, I can be held liable for them. But I cannot be held responsible if I lapse into unconsciousness at the wheel (so long as it is not through earlier fault of my own). Intuitively, we sense a difference between an unintentional and an involuntary act, but how can we explain it? In neither case was I guilty of performing the act of *intentionally running over someone,* let alone killing someone. What is the conceptual difference between unintentionally driving over an infant and the behavior of unconsciously doing so? Why should that conceptual difference make a moral and legal difference?

In a way similar to negligence, but totally dissimilar to involuntary acts, actions giving rise to strict liability are unintentional. If I am liable, under a strict liability statute, for harm done to persons by my explosive demolition work, it is assumed that the harm was unintentional. Yet I am responsible for the effects of the demolition, that is, of the effects of my act.

Some authors believe that contemporary action theory may clarify much about the act requirement. For example, one solution to the definition of an act might be to use Donald Davidson's notion that an act is *a doing intentional under some description.* This does not mean that the act must be done with mens rea or crimes of negligence would be problematic and strict liability crimes impossible. It does, however, require that the actor have some intention in carrying out the physical movements. Moreover, we could include omissions as the intentional carrying out of physical movements that omit required conduct. This allows us to include the cases of omissions, negligence, and strict liability and reject cases of status, involuntary movements, and natural occurrences.

Another approach might be indicated by Jonathan Bennett for whom "an act is an event that is an instance of agency." This has the attraction of diverting the debate to a ground far more familiar to the law, that is, one of competence, rationality, and grounds for the actor's (agent's) liability generally.

Although contemporary action theory has been, and will continue to be, helpful in explicating some of the issues surrounding the act requirement, it will not easily solve some of the most serious problems with the act requirement. Among the most perplexing are these: Is possession an act? If not, how is liability attributable? We do want to be able, at least conceptually, to speak of liability for certain kinds of status, even if on policy grounds we might prefer not to criminalize it. Membership in violent terrorist organizations or "criminal enterprises" are examples. Attempts and other inchoate crimes present special problems, as does speech as action. The act requirement and relative concepts promise to provide puzzlement to jurists and philosophers of law for quite a while.

References

American Institute of Law. *Model Penal Code and Commentaries*, Part I, sec. 1.01– 2.13. Philadelphia: American Institute of Law Press, 1985.

Bennett, Jonathan. *The Act Itself*. Oxford: Oxford University Press, 1995.

Child, James W. "Donald Davidson and Section 2.01 of the Model Penal Code." *Criminal Justice Ethics* (1992).

Davidson, Donald. *Essays on Actions and Events*. Oxford: Oxford University Press, 1980.

Duff, R.A. *Intention, Agency and Criminal Liability*. Oxford: Basil Blackwell, 1990.

Hart, H.L.A. *Punishment and Responsibility*. Oxford: Oxford University Press, 1968.

Williams, Glanville. *Criminal Law, The General Part*. 2d ed. London: Stevens, 1961.

James W. Child

See also ACTUS REUS

Action and Agency

These terms and their cognates in law, as elsewhere, are ambiguous, disambiguated by their context. This discussion focuses on two such common, but quite different, notions in law. In each case these are related to important conceptual underpinnings and philosophical controversies.

1. The first of the common understandings of agency in law is related to *action*. Agency in this sense is that which attributes an action to a person in such a way that there is an implication that the action is intentional. This is particularly important in the attribution of responsibility and the application of rules and sanctions to the agent.

Yet the contemporary philosophical understanding of agency is a more minimal one, taking agency in this sense only to indicate a relationship. Agency connects a person to an action in such a way that we may say of that person that the action is the action of that person. For many purposes it is important to establish under what description the action falls. One such purpose is to determine whether or not the action is intended by the agent. Agents themselves have different capacities with respect to knowledge, belief, desire, and interest that will have an effect on the description of the action. It will be these descriptions that will bring into play the notions of responsibility, blame, and punishment for the agent's actions. Thus an agent is one of whom it might be said he or she did it, with a further story being required for the purposes of relating the action to rules and the attribution of praise or blame.

The standard philosophical debates regarding this first sense of agency thus have to do with what description of an agent and an action is required sufficient for the attribution of intention, responsibility, praise, and blame.

2. The second common understanding of agency in law is dependent entirely on legal relations. Most broadly understood an agent is one who is in a position to change the legal situation of a person (the principal) with respect to some other legal entity. Here, it is important from a conceptual point of view to take into account the fact that an agent is not just one who does something for someone else, but one who does something for someone else with respect to the relationship that person has with some other party. In this broad sense, formal agencies are often created by legal instruments such as guardianship, contracts, wills, and trusts. Agencies which may be recognized by courts may not all be the consequence of such formal instruments; other relationships may also create agencies recognized by courts.

A narrow understanding of agency will only take into account as agencies, proper for the purposes of the law, those which affect the legal position of the principal by the making of contracts and the disposition of property. A discussion in a mode that is more conceptually oriented than those which rely on the traditional divisions of the law will require only that the agency relationship be present.

Whether or not the status of agent is dependent on the consent of the principal in a particular case and at a particular time may be a matter of dispute with respect to the substantive law. Nothing is implied with respect to whether an agency exists. This is the source of some central philosophical problems in determining what it is for someone to be an agent of someone else.

A philosophical account of agency in law in this second sense must deal with ethical dilemmas, most often in relation to the autonomy of the principal. The most difficult cases are those where the agent carries out the duties of agency on behalf of a never competent person (such as a child or mentally retarded person), or a no longer competent person (such as someone who is demented, or even dead). In the recent philosophical literature these problems have most widely been canvased in the biomedical context, but they apply equally elsewhere. In all these cases a central issue is whether autonomous decision making is transferable by means of agency or, alternatively, whether the legal fiction that suggests that this is the case is justifiable.

Some of the most philosophically controversial cases of agency are those which involve the application of the doctrine of substituted judgment. The doctrine requires that the agent (who in this case may be the court itself), in making a decision on behalf of the principal, substitute the principal's judgment for its own. This process involves the consideration of a complex conditional to the effect that if the principal were not incapacitated the principal would make a particular decision under the circumstances which the agent now faces. There are epistemological difficulties with respect to the basis on which the conditional is framed. Where there is evidence from the earlier part of a person's life as to their wishes with respect to specific future states of affairs, this is prima facie a less controversial matter. Evidence of this kind might come from so-called living wills regarding wishes concerning future specific medical treatments in the case of once competent, now incompetent, persons. It might also come from wills, properly speaking, that contain instructions to executors acting as agents of now dead testators, in this case for the disposition of property. In the absence of written instructions agents face a more difficult task in assembling evidence on the basis of which to substitute the judgment of the principal for their own. Thus, holders of powers of attorney for once competent, but now distant or incompetent, persons or the guardians of once competent and now incompetent, wards face more severe problems of assembling evidence from the scattered impressions of the verbal directions of the principal. For those principals who have not made their relevant desires express, there remains the possibility of constructing these desires by reference to primary goods as a (limited) set of markers of what anyone would want.

Some writers in the field have argued that the epistemological difficulties associated with agency as substituted judgment are such that agents ought to act only in the best interests of incompetent principals and that this should surely be the case where the principal has never been competent. To do otherwise is to maintain an untenable fiction that the decisions made on behalf of the principal by the agent are the principal's own. Others take this point further to argue that, even in the case of the once competent, there may be considerations which militate against taking seriously the expressed wishes of the competent person with respect to what should happen to a person who becomes incompetent. This point raises issues of personal identity in the philosophical literature. From the point of view of agency, the important question is who it is who is properly speaking the principal. One line of thought is that in some cases the person when competent and the spatiotemporally continuous incompetent person are sufficiently different in relevant ways not to constitute the same person and that agencies set up by them no longer apply. Even when there is no revision of the commonsense notion of personal identity, one may have doubts about the validity of agencies which relate to the no longer competent person we now have before us. It may be that the instructions which have been set up by the person when competent, for their current anticipated state, may no longer be appropriate to that state. These problems arise most acutely where there are issues of life and death, but may arise for any agency relationship involving a once competent, now incompetent, person.

Conceptualized very broadly, legal instruments of agency might be seen as creating agencies between the state and the polity. Wills, for instance, viewed in this way create the executor-as-agent who carries out the function not just between testator and beneficiary, with respect to the disposition of goods, but also carries out the agency function between state and polity for the same purpose. Agencies so broadly considered raise the analytical task of distinguishing between legal instruments which are precisely instruments of agency and legal instruments which are not. Unless we can distinguish between legal instruments of agency properly speaking, as well as all those legal instruments which mediate between the state and the polity, we will have too inclusive a conception of agency, one which does not give us any conceptual advantage in understanding third-party decision making distinguishable from the other activities of officials. This distinction may be achieved by requiring that the agency involve not just a mediation between the state and the polity, but that it also involve a primary instrument of agency to which the agency created between the state and the polity is secondary, as is the case with wills.

Philosophical as well as policy problems arise with respect to the trust placed in agents. The policy problems are addressed by the law in prescribing the scope and nature of fiduciary relationships and by establishing regulatory bodies, such as guardianship boards, charged with oversight of the agency function. Philosophical approaches range from the utilitarian, one expression of which is public choice theory, and the deontological, which includes the duties of trust amongst other absolute duties. Another and related arena of philosophical debate may arise between those who see trust through a humean lens, as a matter of habit or disposition, and those who take the kantian approach where the duty not to breach trust is the outcome of ratiocination. If the humean view is adopted, then it becomes important to provide opportunities for the exercise of both trusting and trustworthy behavior to entrench the habits relating to trust that are required for legal agencies to be efficacious as social tools.

References

Davidson, Donald. *Essays on Actions and Events*. Oxford: Oxford University Press, 1980.

Fridman, G.H.L. *The Law of Agency*. London: Butterworth, 1960. 6th ed., 1990.

Lowy, Catherine. "The Doctrine of Substituted Judgment in Medical Decision Making." *Bioethics* 2 (1989), 15–21.

Williams, Bernard. "Voluntary Acts and Responsible Agents." In *Making Sense of Humanity and Other Philosophical Papers,* 22–35. Cambridge: Cambridge University Press, 1995.

Catherine Lowy

See also AGENCY (MANDATE)

Action-based Philosophy of Law

Action theory is a methodology for grounding legal theory and practice in action, for developing legal processes grounded in an experimentalist, systemic jurisprudence. It is an evolutionary step beyond legal pragmatism, which has characterized twentieth-century jurisprudence. As developed to date, it begins from a base in a structurally distinguishable form of reason known as perspectivist reason. Perspectivist reason implies the need for a new theory of evidence and a new form of legal procedure. Close examination of events in actual law practice demonstrates that these innovations are warranted. The theory of evidence must go beyond the inductivism that has characterized twentieth-century law practice. To be adequate for use in a world of difference, the theory of evidence must account not only for facts or sense-based data but also for differences in the rationalistic element of human reason. It must account for the concepts actually in use and must assume that concepts can differ between any two reasoning agents. The correlated legal procedure must begin from the assumption that all humans are equal reasoning agents.

From the time of the Enlightenment until the pragmatists began working in the late 1800s, reason has been treated as universal, as beginning from the deep assumption that all humans think alike. The pragmatists fostered the understanding that each person sees the facts from a unique standpoint (empiricism). Beginning with works in the philosophy of science, such as those of Thomas Kuhn and E.A. Singer, Jr., philosophers began to recognize a need to take account of differences in how people think—in the rationalistic concepts in use. Perspectivist reason begins from the deep assumption that each human sees and thinks from a unique perspective. Legal theory and practice grounded in perspectivist reason necessarily differ significantly from that used in the twentieth century.

The most significant difference is that the trial will need to be restructured. The trial is commonly presented as a rational method for resolving disputes. The history of the trial reveals that the process emerged in its present form as a result of two great waves of rationalizing effort. The first wave of effort concerned the decision maker. Early medieval Europeans believed that God issued a judgment in a trial, but by the latter part of the medieval period a change took place. Scholars began to see the trial as seeking the judgment of man rather than that of God. The judgment was the product of human reason rather than of God's reason. The second great wave concerned the evidence to be considered by the decision maker.

As late as the Enlightenment, evidence presented at trial could still be the product of judicial torture. The belief was that the body spoke and would reveal its truth if properly questioned (meaning torture). That belief was abandoned. Now the American trial is considered rational because it is characterized by party presentation, meaning the parties decide what evidence to present, and the ability to make reasoned arguments. The evidence presented is thus rationalistic—the product of reason. To date, the trial process has not been rationalized in ways suited to those who are subject to law. For example, the trial still assumes that the primary decision that needs to be informed is that of the judge. The trial is not designed to treat the parties as equal reasoning beings, as fully participating members of the society that is governed by the law being made.

Legal theory and practice always assume some form of science: to do what is just, lawyers must know what is true. Pragmatism has been the philosophy of science used throughout the twentieth century. It is institutionalized in contemporary trial theory and practice. For example, when the *Federal Rules of Civil Procedure* were developed they were explicitly intended as a scientific system. Discovery was introduced in the early decades of this century and was seen as a method of enabling practicing lawyers to participate in the science of law. Practitioners could now discover the facts to be presented by the opposing side. In theory, discovery would encourage settlement and reduce litigation because the lawyers could get to the truth prior to trial.

To ensure impartiality under the assumption of perspectivist reason and to claim legitimacy, legal theory and practice need to be placed on a new operational base. The new technical base for the work of law must be grounded in action-based scientific methods. Law must be impartial and legitimate. Basing them in action corrects for the inherent bias of the judge as spectator. Scientific method has evolved over the course of the twentieth century in ways that the legal profession has only begun to absorb. Empirical or analytic science uses a process in which the spectator observes the subject of study under strictly controlled conditions. The method does not treat the subject of study as a participant in the scientific process. Most social scientific study of law has been performed in this mode. Methods of participant observation emerged in the social sciences because the scientist discovered a need to test both data and inferences from data with the humans being observed. Some social scientific study of law is being performed in this mode. The assumptions underlying contemporary legal procedure and built into current rules of court are a rough blend of these first two forms of scientific inquiry. Action-based scientific methods have begun to evolve in the last half of the twentieth century. They treat the "subject of study" as a social actor in his or her own light. The scientist must not only test data and inferences from data with the subject of study, the scientist must develop the scientific inquiry in ways necessary to inform the action which the social actor is undertaking. If the legal system is to become more effective than it currently is, it is essential to build legal theories and practices that embody this emphasis on informing the desired social action.

The approach assumes a new relationship between law and society. The legal pragmatists developed a view of law as an instrument of the social order. Their instrumentalist view displaced the nineteenth century view of law, which had become unacceptably metaphysical. Yet law does not govern its society from above (as in the twentieth-century instrumentalist approach) or outside of that society (as in the nineteenth-century metaphysical approach). It is within its society, a reciprocal and constitutive part of social life.

This methodology enables lawyers to identify aspects of their practice which do not fit within the confines of existing legal theories or their supporting practices. It enables the profession to develop theories and practices which are more adequately suited to the actual demands of practice.

References

Rourke, Nancy. *A Difference of Reason*. Lanham MD: University Press of America, 1997.

Nancy Rourke

Actus Reus

Actus reus is the overt conduct, proscribed by the criminal law, taking account of circumstances and consequences. It is said sometimes to be what is left over when one subtracts mentalist elements of culpability (mens rea), such as intention and foresight.

The courts and criminal law textbooks have treated the expression "actus reus" as a convenient shorthand for all the different components essential to a crime, apart from the mental elements of culpability grouped under the heading mens rea. To give a convenient example, contraction of a finger when it is on the trigger of a gun pointed at someone may involve a shooting and a killing of another person. If it does, and the shooting is intentional, then in the absence of special excuses or justifications, there is a crime of murder. It is useful to have a way of referring to elements of a crime other than intention, foresight, or other possible components of mens rea. If an element of the actus reus is missing, there is no corresponding crime, though there may be an attempt. If the victim does not die, there is no murder, however much there may have been an intention to kill.

Treatment of actus reus as a unified concept that always involves an act produces problems, for several reasons. One is that there are some crimes of omission, possession, or status offenses (for example, being a drug addict, in one controversial case) where there may be liability in the absence of any clear act. Another reason is that some crimes are defined in such a way that mental elements usually included in mens rea become part of the offense, or actus reus, itself. Carrying tools, innocent in itself, may become criminal if they are carried with intent to commit burglary. More radically, objection has been made that the actus reus concept is used to underscore the need, in a just criminal law system, for very different things which cannot all be reconciled, for example: (1) requirement of minimal controls and capacities for actions or omissions, (2) clear statement of what conduct will be treated as criminal, (3) requirement that no one should be criminally liable merely for contemplating or resolving to commit a crime; there must be some kind of overt execution of the resolve.

The adage associated with the term "actus reus" is the well-known *actus non facit reum nisi mens sit rea.* This has a long history in the common law of England. One translation, "an act does not make a person guilty unless the mind is guilty," already suggests that the phrase "actus reus" is not entirely coherent. If an act is guilty only by virtue of the guilty mind, how can the act still be guilty if the guilty mind is separated from it? If one translates *reus* as "harmful," then the adage ceases to be true. An act can be blameless but still harmful.

Not surprisingly, the exact meaning of the term "actus reus" has been the subject of much discussion. If one takes it to refer to the physical goings on that remain when all the mental components of an act are subtracted, then one would no longer have an "act." On other accounts, only mens rea (intention, knowledge, or negligence) is subtracted, leaving the minimal level of volition necessary for any act. But even minimal volition arguably involves some form of intention, so the contrast becomes unclear.

It has been argued that even more fundamental than intention or foresight is the requirement, in a just criminal law system, of the minimal mental elements associated with any voluntary action. Hence the argument that so-called "strict liability" offenses should admit of some exceptions. A person who suffers from sudden paralysis, or a reflex movement, or who is pushed from behind, may lack the minimal amount of control necessary for any act at all, and punishment would be unfair. H.L.A. Hart has noted that some benefit in the form of deterrence could be obtained from punishing such cases, because there would then no longer be any point to making dishonest claims of automatism or the like; but he argues that at least one strand in the justification for the act requirement lies in the greater predictability it gives to individuals concerning their own lives. Without such a requirement, the cost would be too great in terms of individual security, since no one, however concerned to obey the law, could then be sure of avoiding criminal penalties. The case of *R. v. Larsonneur,* 24 Criminal Appeals Reports 74 (1933), where a woman was forcibly brought from the Irish Free State to Holyhead in the United Kingdom and then convicted of contravening the *Aliens Order 1920,* has been rightly condemned for failing to respect the act requirement, even though she seemed to have tried to violate the spirit of the immigration laws and thus was not entirely blameless.

The analysis of acts is a matter of considerable controversy. John Austin, followed by Oliver Wendell Holmes, Jr., viewed genuine acts as limited to willed muscular movements, so that what in common parlance are called "killings" are not acts strictly speaking but involve genuine acts in the form of willed muscular contractions (of a finger over a trigger, for example) together with consequences (a gun firing and a person dying). One problem with this account, pointed out by Hart, is that people do not usually think of what muscles they will move; they, for example, just think of pulling the trigger. This may just be because some movements have become second nature, unlike the case where a new skill must be learned. Another problem is that this account is an open invitation to dissembling ways of speaking: "I did not shoot so-and-so; I just moved my finger muscle," could be said misleadingly by someone who shot and killed intentionally. Nevertheless, in the insistence on choice not chance, where culpability is concerned, there may well be some point in singling out for special attention so-called basic acts involving bodily movements. The question of proper action description has become a field of philosophical inquiry unto itself, involving intricate questions of reference and intentionality. Michael Moore has managed to revive interest in the Austin-Holmes view in a lively debate with Anthony Duff, who argues that some consequences and circumstances may be no less basic than muscular contractions.

Philosophical interest in action analysis goes beyond practical application to law, and it is unclear how much influence the former will have on the latter in the years ahead. Puzzles exist concerning cases where actus reus and mens rea do not coincide, and yet where a person seems to deserve punishment according to common sense. These may benefit from full-scale action analysis. Such cases include transferred mens rea, for example, where a person aims to kill one person but misses and kills another.

The future value of the term "actus reus" is on the whole uncertain. Characterization of inadvertent negligence in terms of acts is problematic, involving as it does a normative judgment of fault (ascription) not captured either in a physical description of an action or in mens rea as conceived by some writers. Specific discussions of actus reus are often found under headings such as attempts, automatism, conspiracy, dissociation, double jeopardy, duress, intention, foresight, mistake, negligence, provocation, recklessness, strict liability, voluntariness, and will.

Given the extensive use of the actus reus terminology, it seems unlikely to be abandoned overnight, but, in view of the difficul-

ties, some alternative discourse will no doubt be sought, perhaps in the light of what have been called agency versus welfare paradigms.

References

Clarkson, C.M.V., and H.M. Keating. *Criminal Law: Cases and Materials*. 3d ed. London: Sweet & Maxwell, 1994.

Fletcher, George P. *Rethinking Criminal Law*. Boston: Little, Brown, 1978.

Hart, H.L.A. *Punishment and Responsibility*. Oxford: Clarendon Press, 1968.

Moore, Michael. *Act and Crime*. Oxford: Clarendon Press, 1993.

Shute, Stephen, John Gardner, and Jeremy Horder, eds. *Action and Value in Criminal Law*. Oxford: Clarendon Press, 1993.

Stuart, Don. *Canadian Criminal Law: A Treatise*. Toronto: Carswell, 1982. 2d ed. 1987.

Randal Marlin

See also ATTEMPTS; MENS REA; STRICT LIABILITY, CRIMINAL

Administrative Decision Making

See DECISION MAKING, ADMINISTRATIVE

Admissibility

See RELEVANCE

Aesthetics

Aesthetics is the branch of philosophy that concerns the nature of the beautiful in art and nature, and the proper criteria for the judgment of beauty in these realms. Included within the field are the relationships among art, myth, religion, and language; the philosophical status of the individual arts; the status of aesthetic rationality; the nature of artistic creativity; the relationship of aesthetic production and interpretation to the social structure; the problem of aesthetic value and evaluation; and methodological questions concerning the interpretation of art.

A conundrum fundamental to the philosophy of beauty, first systematically articulated by Immanuel Kant, is of particular relevance to contemporary philosophy of law. First, although the aesthetic judgment of beauty is essentially rooted in subjective perception and its accompanying pleasure, the category of "the beautiful" pertains to the object perceived itself and not to its relation to the perceiving subject. (The "pleasing," by way of contrast, always implies "pleasing *to me.*") A similar problem is posed by the question whether judgments of the beautiful are subsumable under some general rule or law. Aesthetic experience teaches the negative—it does not follow from the fact that a particular nineteenth-century British landscape painting is beautiful, that nineteenth-century British art is beautiful, or that landscape painting is beautiful. In this sense aesthetic judgments are uncategorizably singular. However, the notion of aesthetic judgment itself seems to require the subsuming of a particular work under a general category—"the beautiful"—any definition of which will necessarily require rule-like criteria of general applicability.

These antithetical tendencies have determined an uneasy relationship between art and law. Like aesthetics, jurisprudence must reconcile the subjective and objective and general and particular dimensions of its domain, for example, in the tasks of legitimating the objectively binding force of law by reference to the subjective assent of the polity and reconciling the generality of legal rules with the particularity of cases to which they apply. Jurisprudence, however, has traditionally conceived this task as defending the legitimacy of objective and generally enforceable norms of conduct, the rule of law, while aesthetics is committed by virtue of its subject matter to the subjective and particular.

This tension has been evident from the beginning of Western philosophy and art. Plato argued that the ideal state would require censorship of the tragic poetry of his day, because poetry, by appealing to the subjective passions rather than the rational principle of its citizens, would lead them away from rather than toward the objective ideals of the true and the good as embodied in the laws of the state. His fears were not unwarranted, since a basic lesson of ancient tragedy is the failure of impersonal law to do justice to the subjective passion and uncategorizable particularity of human existence. In *Antigone,* for example, this failure takes the form of a confrontation between the demands of state law and the demands of a higher law based on the emotional bond and particularity of the blood relation. In *Oedipus Tyrranus,* it takes the form of the failure of the impersonal decree of a good and just sovereign—Oedipus the king—to do justice to a morally guiltless subject—Oedipus the finite, individual man. This critique of impersonal law as inadequate to do justice to the individual has been a consistent theme of literature about law, and the contradiction between the values of art and law reappears in the jurisprudential debates as well.

Aesthetics intersects with law and legal philosophy in four areas: methodologies of legal interpretation; humanistic critiques of law; legal regulation of the arts; and aesthetic critiques of legal works.

Aesthetics and Legal Interpretation

The most significant contribution of aesthetics to legal theory has been renewed reflection on the nature of legal interpretation. This development has been driven by the growing recognition that law and aesthetics are both fundamentally interpretive disciplines. An early and influential example of this genre is Hans-Georg Gadamer's *Truth and Method.* Beginning with a phenomenological analysis of aesthetic experience, he develops the thesis that all understanding is historically conditioned and interpretive, using judicial interpretation of an ancient law in light of the circumstances of the present case as one of his chief examples.

Attempts to apply lessons from aesthetic interpretive theory in support of normative theories of law and legal interpretation have proved more controversial. Some liberal legal philosophers have turned to principles of literary interpretation to defend a theory of law as an interpretive discipline capable of rendering just and determinate interpretive judgments. Others in the liberal tradition are less sanguine about the relevance of literary interpretation to legal interpretation, finding that the institutional settings and purposes of the two disciplines are too different to offer a sound basis for analogy. Critics of liberalism (particularly members of the Conference on Critical Legal Studies) draw more radical conclusions, arguing that the impartiality of liberal legal proceduralism is undermined by current theories of literary interpretation that demonstrate the inherent indeterminacy of all interpretation. Finally, deconstructive critics of law argue, echoing the ancient tragic poets, that the calculative and machine-like generality of the law is incompatible with the demand that it render particularized justice.

Humanistic Critiques of Law

Others argue that the relationship of law and art is cultural rather than methodological. Members of the law and literature and law and humanities movements emphasize the fact that law and art are both human artifacts with common roots in their larger culture. Humanistic in impulse, these schools arose largely in opposition to the increasing influence and perceived technocratic orientation of the law and economics movement. Adherents of the humanistic approach typically use literary texts to illuminate legal problems and ethical dilemmas, advocate a greater openness to narrative as an acceptable legal method, and criticize mechanistic views of law in favor of cultural and interpretive understandings.

Legal Regulation of the Arts

Aesthetic issues also arise in the legal regulation of the arts. Perhaps the most visible example has been the attempt to define "obscenity," a form of expression long exempted from constitutional protections afforded other forms of speech. The United States Supreme Court's current definition of obscenity requires a court to decide whether a particular work is "without serious literary, artistic, political, or scientific value," and similar considerations of aesthetic merit apply under parallel provisions of Canadian law, for example, *United States v. Miller,* 413 U.S. 15 (1973); *R. v. Butler,* 1 S.C.R. 452 (1992). Finding a workable definition has proved sufficiently difficult and controversial that works of literature like James Joyce's *Ulysses* and D.H. Lawrence's *Lady Chatterly's Lover* were banned for periods of time in the United States. The tension between aesthetic subjectivity and particularity and the objectivity and generality required by law is starkly captured in this area by United States Supreme Court Justice Potter Stewart's plaintive claim in *Jacobellis v. Ohio,* 378 U.S. 184, 197 (1964), that, although he was unable to articulate a satisfactory legal definition of obscenity, "I know it when I see it." Other areas of substantive law in which aesthetic questions arise include copyright and moral rights.

Aesthetic Critiques of Legal Works

Philosophical questions also arise in evaluating legal works, primarily judicial opinions, from an aesthetic perspective. The emphasis here is not on the "beauty" of an opinion in the usual sense but rather on the effectiveness of the aesthetic means used to achieve its goal, that is, on whether the rhetoric of the opinion is effectively persuasive. The question thus raised is the ancient one of the relationship of rhetorical persuasion to legal justification. Aesthetics overlaps with rhetoric in this regard.

References

Beardsley, Monroe C. *Aesthetics from Classical Greece to the Present: A Short History.* New York: Macmillan, 1965.

Derrida, Jacques. "Force of Law: The 'Mystical Foundation of Authority.'" In *Deconstruction and the Possibility of Justice,* 3–67. New York: Routledge, 1992.

Dworkin, Ronald. *Law's Empire.* Cambridge, MA: Belknap–Harvard University Press, 1986.

Gadamer, Hans-Georg. *Truth and Method.* Trans. Garrett Barden and John Cumming. New York: Crossroad, 1982.

Kant, Immanuel. *The Critique of Judgement.* Trans. James Creed Meredith. Oxford: Clarendon Press, 1952.

Kelman, Mark. *A Guide to Critical Legal Studies.* Cambridge, MA: Harvard University Press, 1987.

Lewis, Felice F. *Literature, Obscenity, and Law.* Carbondale: Southern Illinois University Press, 1976.

Posner, Richard A. *Law and Literature: A Misunderstood Relation.* Cambridge, MA: Harvard University Press, 1987.

Vernant, Jean-Pierre. *Myth and Tragedy in Ancient Greece.* New York: Zone Books, 1990.

White, James Boyd. *Justice as Translation: An Essay in Cultural and Legal Criticism.* Chicago: The University of Chicago Press, 1990.

Weisberg, Richard H. *Poethics: And Other Strategies of Law and Literature.* New York: Columbia University Press, 1992.

Adam Thurschwell

Affinity

As a legal term, "affinity" is, not infrequently, mentioned in conjunction with "consanguinity." In colloquial usage, according to *Black's Law Dictionary,* "affinity" sometimes embraces "consanguinity" in describing kindred relationships. Both "affinity" and "consanguinity" are, in juridical parlance, descriptive of human relationships.

According to *Wharton's Law Lexicon* and *Black's Law Dictionary*, "affinity" means, essentially, the "relationship by marriage between the husband and the blood relations of the (husband's) wife, and between the wife and the blood relations of the (wife's) husband." In contrast, consanguinity describes the "relation of persons descended from the same stock or common ancestor." A consanguine relationship may be lineal (ad infinitum), that is, either ascendant, between son and father and grandfather, or descendant, between son and grandson and great-grandson. A consanguine relationship may, instead, be collateral, such as subsists between a person descendant from the same stock or ancestor (uncle and nephew, for example) but not from each other, as obtains in lineal consanguine relationships.

Affinity and the permutations—that is, degrees—of affinity derive, according to *Dejardin v. Dejardin*, 2 W.W.R. 237 (1932) (Man. K.B., Macdonald C.J.K.B.), from "ancient origins," specifically, *Leviticus* in the Old Testament Scriptures. As subsequently developed in canon law (sometimes described as Christian and Judaic "ecclesiastical" or "church" law), the degrees of affinity assumed at least three personalities. First, there evolved "direct" affinity. This is the basic affinity concept and involves the relationship between (1) a husband and (2) his wife's blood relations, for example, between a husband and his wife's sister (who, by marriage of husband and wife, becomes the husband's sister-in-law). Second, there is "secondary" affinity, such as the relationship between (1) the sister of the wife (that is, a wife's relation) and (2) the brother of the husband (that is, a husband's relation), or vice versa. The third kind of affinity, "collateral" affinity, includes the relationship between (1) the wife, of the one part, and (2) relations of the husband's relations, of the other part, for example, between the wife and the wife of the husband's brother, or vice versa.

The degrees of affinity (like the degrees of consanguinity) eventually found expression in Archbishop Parker's Table of 1563, published, ever since, in the *Book of Common Prayer* of the Church of England. Moreover, the degrees of affinity (and of consanguinity) were recognized, interpreted, and applied as part of England's common law. Whether commencement of the recognition of the degrees, at common law, antedated or followed 1563, is unclear. Certain, however, is the enactment, both before and after 1563, in England of statutes addressing the impact of the prohibited degrees, particularly as pertained to matrimony.

Justification for most of the degrees of affinity (and consanguinity) are obscure. They apparently derived from taboos and beliefs that marriage within the degrees was a recipe for inbreeding of physically and/or mentally defective issue. In the context of contemporary scientific knowledge, these justifications are largely invalid.

The most significant legal impact of the degrees was on marriage. The degrees of affinity (and consanguinity) were regarded under canon law and, subsequently, common law, as representing relationships within which marriage was, at least in theory, prohibited. Thus, the degrees came to be known as the "prohibited degrees of marriage." Judicially, however, if persons were married (under canon law or, subsequently, under common law) within prohibited degrees, the marriage ceremony nonetheless created a valid—although voidable—marriage. A voidable marriage is a marriage that could, at the option of either spouse, be declared a nullity from the date a judicial declaration to that effect is made, as noted in *Elliott v. Gurr*, 2 Phill. Ecc. 16 (1812).

The *Marriage Act* (also known as *Lord Lyndhurst's Act*) enacted in England in 1835 altered the judicial interpretation of the impact of the prohibited degrees under canon and, subsequently, common law. The act provided that "all marriages which shall hereafter be celebrated between persons within the prohibited degrees of consanguinity or affinity shall be absolutely null and void to all intents and purposes whatsoever."

Solicitor B.L. Johnson summarizes in *Family Law* some of the common law and statutory consequences in England of the application of the prohibited degrees of affinity (and consanguinity):

If the parties are within the prohibited degrees, the marriage will be void in law, whatever ceremonies have been performed, and even though the parties were quite ignorant of their relationship. In some cases, if, after discovering their relationship, they continued living together, they would be guilty of the criminal offence of incest [in Canada, incest is an offence under *Criminal Code* s. 155]: but even if there were no breach of the criminal law, their marriage would be void, and both would be quite free at any time to contract a valid marriage with someone else. It might even be that the facts of the relationship only came to light after the death of one of them, and in that case, the survivor could not claim the rights of the surviving spouse on an intestacy, and the property of the one who had died would be distributed on the assumption that he had never married.

Comparable are the consequences under (public) criminal law and, affecting marriage and inheritance, under private law, in Canada, other Commonwealth countries, the United States, and elsewhere.

A relationship constituting affinity does not result per se from sexual relations or a conjugal relationship (a euphemism for "common law" marriage). A formal purported marriage between persons within the prohibited degrees is required to constitute affinity, as noted in *Restall (otherwise Love) v. Restall,* 45 T.L.R. 518 (1929).

The geographical and substantive extent to which the English common law and statute law on prohibited degrees of marriage settled in Canada's common law jurisdictions, or in other jurisdictions based on common law, is not entirely clear.

Because they affect capacity for, rather than procedural solemnization requirements of, marriage, the subject of prohibited degrees is the legislative responsibility of Parliament instead of the legislatures or legislative councils of the provinces or territories.

Capacity to marry between persons too closely related by marriage or blood has to a lesser or greater extent been proscribed by custom or law in most cultures. However, the "prohibition in our country," opines Fodden, "is wide-ranging. . . ." Based on Archbishop Parker's widely embracing Table of 1563, these prohibitions were modified by Parliament by the *Marriage Act* to permit marriage with a deceased wife's sister or niece and to permit marriage with a deceased husband's brother or nephew.

On 18 December 1991, the federal *Marriage (Prohibited Degrees) Act* came into force. The act codified the law in Canada respecting the prohibited degrees of marriage; expressly repealed previous federal legislation on the subject, namely, the *Marriage Act*

adopted in 1985; implicitly abrogated Archbishop Parker's Table of 1563; and provides for all "prohibitions in law in Canada against marriage by reason of the parties being related." Sections 2 to 5 of the act (in summary) provide as follows: (1) As a general rule, persons related by consanguinity, affinity, or adoption are not, by reason only of their relationship, prohibited from contracting a legally valid marriage with one another. (2) This general rule is subject to the exceptions that no person shall marry another person if (a) related lineally by consanguinity or adoption, or (b) related as brother and sister by adoption. Marriage between persons marrying within these degrees is void.

Legal proceedings requesting a declaration of annulment based on the prohibited degrees of marriage have rarely been brought in Canada's provinces or territories.

In Canada's only civil law jurisdiction, Province of Quebec, the prohibited degrees of marriage were, historically, provided for primarily by French law received into Quebec and by local Quebec jurisprudence until 1866; by the *Civil Code of Lower Canada* from 1866 to 31 December 1993; and by the *Civil Code of Quebec* from 1 January 1994.

John Brierley and Roderick Macdonald comment that the Civil Code has "not yet been amended to accord with the new federal law. . . . This lack of uniformity could give rise to a constitutional challenge should Quebec seek to enforce its more restrictive provisions, especially since the federal act claims to contain 'all of the prohibitions in law in Canada against marriage by reason of the parties being related.'"

References

Black's Law Dictionary. 4th ed. St. Paul MN: West, 1951.

Brierley, John E.C., and Roderick A. Macdonald, eds. *Quebec Civil Law: An Introduction to Quebec Private Law.* Toronto: Emond Montgomery, 1993.

Davies, Christine. *Family Law in Canada.* Toronto: Carswell, 1984.

Fodden, Simon, ed. *Canadian Family Law: Cases and Materials.* Toronto: Butterworth, 1977.

Johnson, B.L. *Family Law.* 2d ed. London: Sweet & Maxwell, 1965.

Marriage Act, S.C. 1882, c. 42; S.C. 1890, c. 36; R.S.C. 1906, c. 105; R.S.C. 1927, c.

127; S.C. 1932, c. 10; R.S.C. 1952, c. 176; R.S.C. 1970, c. M-5; R.S.C. 1985, c. M-2.

Marriage (Prohibited Degrees) Act. Legislative history: Bill S-14 (Hansard of Senate of Canada, Second Session, Thirty-fourth Parliament, 1989–1990): first reading, 1192; second reading, 1585, 1633; referred to Standing Senate Committee on Legal and Constitutional Affairs, 1633; 17th report (dated 07 June 1990) of Committee to Senate with proposed amendments to Bill S-14, 1865, 1871; third reading, 1872; message from Commons that Bill S-14 passed without amendments, 4856.

Wharton's Law-Lexicon. 8th ed. London: Stevens and Sons, 1889.

David C. Day

See also INHERITANCE AND SUCCESSION

African Philosophy of Law

Eighteenth- and nineteenth-century colonialism absorbed most of Africa into the sphere of Eurocentric sovereign hegemony. Since African sovereignty was absorbed into the political and juridical orbit of the colonial metropole, African law and jurisprudence became either consigned to a legal no-man's-land or came under the imperium of the dominant colonial paradigm, one that absorbed colonial possessions into the realm of metropolitan sovereignty. The dependent status of "local law" was subject to the supremacy of the law and control of the colonial power.

The colonial "dependent" state became the basic political and juridical unit of the postwar process of decolonialization, self-determination, independence, and "sovereignty." Indeed, the level of retention and reception of colonial law varied considerably, the results sometimes being progressive and innovative, and sometimes regressive and archaic. Additionally, the struggle for independence and self-determination often maintained as an implied datum the suspension of personal rights issues until the demon of alien rule had been exorcised. Finally, the jurisprudential import of these broad issues reflected the following outcomes of jurisprudential salience: (1) The jurisprudence of statism and "sovereignty" was imported. (2) Western legal culture in the form of the common law, the civil law, and attendant variations and mutations on these systems was imported and had uneven reception. (3) African forms of governance and law were relegated to the sphere of interest of anthropologists and social scientists. (4) African customary law, like constitutional and international law, generally held a dubious juridical status under the earlier version of the dominant paradigm (namely, austinian precepts of jurisprudence, positive morality), but at least some customary law was salvaged (a matter doubtless of juridical necessity), some traditional vestiges of authority were preserved (indirect rule) as a matter of colonial convenience, and some vestiges of sovereignty were recognized, especially treaties and concessionary agreements made between chiefs, potentates, and western interests, for certain limited purposes. (5) The struggle for decolonization predicated itself on the notion of "peoples" rights to self-determination, suggesting the pivotal political and juridical significance of "peoples" rights as opposed to colonial rights based on colonial state sovereignty. (6) African scholars and jurists were doubtlessly influenced by the prospect of using law to support the struggle for emancipation from colonial rule. African jurisprudential perspectives tied to "change" became pronounced in the continent-wide sphere as well as the international sphere generally. In part it became a force for influencing received paradigms of law, with the idea of "change," of "liberation," a kind of global jurisprudence of a "new" juridical deal. This was a jurisprudence of change and liberation, rather than a jurisprudence of conservation.

The actual position of the African state, says Ghai, in the context of the postcolonial world reflected four key factual issues. First, African states were weak from an international perspective and often became pawns of cold war politics. Second, African states had obscured the fact that their boundaries were a product of colonialism and that the "people" encased in those boundaries were not ethnically or economically or culturally homogenous. Third, the common base of political support of new Africa elites made them vulnerable to the ascendance of the military over the civilian authority. Fourth, issues of corruption, clientalism, and human rights abuse were vigorously insulated from international concern under the neo-austinian/neo-leninist incantation of sovereign equality. In other words,

African jurisprudence had to accommodate two contradictory trends. First, a claim for change and the transformation of the colonial public order system. This claim involved the undermining of the colonial state system, based on colonial precepts of sovereignty. Second, a claim that the "new" states be sovereign in almost exaggerated form. In effect, claims implied both a rejection of a status quo and a defense of a status quo. As a consequence, these claims had an important influence on the coherence and direction of African jurisprudence in the postcolonial world. Even more important for African jurisprudence was the reception of the austinian sovereignty precept in a form that in many instances seemed to either marginalize constitutional law or erode its efficacy to a level even less than the dubious status of positive morality it enjoyed under John Austin's scheme. In practice, then, African jurisprudence generated a close approximation to the traditional command theory of law. Indeed, even the marxist-leninist gloss on African jurisprudence would have a close correspondence with the austinian model.

The key doctrinal effort to collapse matters of international concern within the domestic jurisdiction and sovereignty of African states was also reflected in the formulation of so-called three generations of human rights and emphasizing the "third" generation prescriptions as "collective" rights, "fraternity" rights, and "solidarity" rights. These collective rights included the right to peace, a clean environment, and, most controversially, a right to development. At the back of this claim was an implicit recognition that new states were also weak states, and that the political economy of the cold war tended to entrench matters of economic and political dependence, as well as enhancing the potentials for external intervention. The antidote to this political reality was the emphasis on collective rights and the rights of weak, sovereign states.

Theoretical Trends in African Jurisprudence
T.O. Elias's classic work rejects the simple austinian command-sovereign formula for a more eclectic one based on ideas of rule and obligation. His central and testable idea is that one can separate coherently African law from African custom, a postulate in keeping with the traditional desire of positivism to separate law from morality.

Theorists like H.J. Simons and Yash Ghai have been more insistent that African law be seen in its socioeconomic and power context. Criticism of third world jurisprudence (pure or applied) argues that the approach is colored by an excessive preoccupation with ethnocentric variables and "historical assumptions." The recommended approach to African and third world jurisprudence is thus "explicitly historical and contextual."

Probably the most radical contextual approach to African jurisprudence is indicated in the writings of Francis Deng. Deng's *Tradition and Modernization: A Challenge for Law Among the Dinka of the Sudan* shares with Simons the commitment to the goal guidance of human rights standards, but it is radically contextual in locating Dinka law in the reality of African social process, more specifically, the relevant power process, the processes of affective loyalties, the processes of respect (equality, and so forth), wealth, well-being, and enlightenment, and so forth.

The contemporary jurisprudential landscape of Africa has been deeply affected by the international environment and the scope and character of human rights expectations. Moreover, the twilight of the cold war has forced a renewed and insistent pattern of popular demand for a new jurisprudence that defends and promotes a system of governance and constitutional order that is democratic, and structures a political economy of African governance that is more transparent, more accountable, and more sensitive to human rights. The crisis of human rights, development, and governance is also in its most basic sense a crisis of jurisprudence, constitutionalism, and the rule of law.

African Jurisprudence and the Twenty-First Century
The fundamental jurisprudential debate about law, legal culture, governance, and human rights in Africa poses two distinct possibilities. First, is the jurisprudence of a negative utopia. This means more than simply a rule of law denying jurisculture. It could possibly mean the evolution of a nonlaw body politic. The second possibility lies in the potentials of unfulfilled promise, that is, the possibility of a jurisprudence that honors and indeed celebrates the broadest identification with the *whole* human rights agenda and aspires in concrete terms to vindicate human dignity on the widest scale.

Regarding the pessimistic prospect, it has long been recognized that African legal scholars have been disenchanted with the capacity of governments to put themselves above the law and legal regulation. The most notorious failure has been the jurisprudence of constitutional expectation. This is the law that seeks to formalize and define the basic structures of governance in the modern state.

It may be parenthetically noted that the early African jurisprudence of the postwar period relating to basic or fundamental constitutional law anticipates in some measure modern forms of analytical positivism. Indeed, in the contexts of radical political transformations there is evidence of the actual prescription and application of some of its precepts. For example, in the context of South Africa, in the first *Harris* decision [*Harris v. The Minister of the Interior,* S.A., 528 A.D., 1951(2)], the Appellate Division of the South African Supreme Court rejected the simple version of Westminster-based parliamentary sovereignty precepts and invalidated a "purported" act of parliament taking so-called colored voters off the common voters roll. The decision anticipates H.L.A. Hart's restructuring of positivism by posing and answering the question: what is parliament? That is to say, before one can determine the validity of an act of parliament, one must know whether the act in question emanates from an organ recognized as parliament; hence, courts must clarify and prescribe the rules that recognize what parliament is and how it is to function if it is to be a parliament. Parliament, therefore, is recognized by rules of recognition criteria for validating what an act of parliament's efficacy actually is. For parliament to be parliament it must, as an institution, work according to a preexisting secondary rule of recognition. Thus, only if an act of parliament comes from an institution "recognized" as parliament would its acts be valid and enforceable. In this sense, the *Harris* case actually anticipates Hart's celebrated theory. It is arguable that in *Harris, II* [*The Minister of the Interior v. Harris,* S.A. 769 A.D., 1952(4)], the High Court of Parliament case is subject to a similar analytical explanation.

When Milton Obote engineered a coup in Uganda which purported to suspend the 1962 (Independence) Constitution and dismissed the President (the Kabaka) from office [*Uganda v. Commissioner of Prisons ex p. Matovu,* E.A. 514 (1966)], the court adopted the jurisprudence of Hans Kelsen (*Pure Theory of Law*), specifically that victorious revolutions or successful coup d'état are to be interpreted as procedures by which national legal order can be changed. That is to say, the court accepted the effectiveness of the new regime supported by the fact of acceptance by the people of Uganda. [Compare *R. v. Ndhlovu and Others,* 4 S.A. 515, (1968). Contrast *Madzimbamuto v. Lardner Burke,* 1 A.C. 645, (1969). The Pakistani case, *The State v. Dosso and Another* (PLD 1958, S.C. 533), which relied on Kelsen, may be contrasted with *Asma Jlani v. The Government of the Punjab* (PLD 1972, S.C. 139); compare also *Begum Nursrat Bhutto v. Chief of Army Staff* (PLD 1977, S.C. 657).]

This apparently was a high point in the jurisprudence of "legalism." African scholars have talked more recently and depressingly of constitutions without constitutional law and sometimes, with deep cynicism, of constitutions as "posters." Among the excuses for the failure of constitutional governance has been the charge that most African constitutions are "imposed," "alien," and "Western" artifacts. The replacement of constitutional expectations, allegedly rejected as "alien," has not meant African legal humanistic forms of legal culture and constitutional governance have replaced these "alien" artifacts. It has meant a reproduction of dictatorship that is alien to a few cultural traditions and not necessarily monopolized by any particular cultural tradition.

Forms of state that are inspired by collectivist-type ideological frames seek to monopolize the allocation of values according to criteria deemed expedient to those who control and regulate the apparatus of state. Those forms of state sensitive to democratic governance and buttressed by the legal culture values embedded in the Rule of Law do seek "monopoly" over all value processes, including power. Such governing forms thrive on the possibility of important value allocations, in terms of both production and distribution occurring outside formal governance structures.

The key jurisprudential elements of constitutive legal culture are preventive and architectural. A jurisprudence about basic law, especially constitutional law in its most elemental form, indicates mechanisms of political restraint and governing accountability. A primary function of the fundamental or the basic law of constitutional governance is "preventive politics." All systems of power relations from the global to the interpersonal contain an incipient capacity for overreaching or abusing power.

When the governing group rejects jurisprudential and constitutional law restraints on the exercise of power, it is also making the disguised claim to dispense with legal restraints on governance. Jurisprudence in this context must confront the central functions of legal culture that are both "preventive" and "architectural," that is to say, preventing the abuse of power and corruption and creating the architecture that permits both rational governance and the space for a civil society, rooted in popular sovereignty.

Perhaps the most disturbing outcome of the nonlaw body politic is the sociological conclusion, which suggests, regardless of "form," that in sub-Saharan Africa there are typologies of states operating under the relative insulation of sovereign equality doctrines as well as Article 2.7's domestic jurisdiction precept, that may be fairly characterized as "failed" states (Somalia), genocidal states (Rwanda, Burundi, Sudan), clientalist states (Zaire), terrorist states (Sudan, Libya), authoritarian states (Kenya, Nigeria, Sudan), anarchic states (Liberia, Rwanda, Zaire, Somalia), and Rule of Law–governed states (South Africa, Zimbawe, Namibia, and so forth).

The optimistic jurisprudential prospect is one rooted in the challenge Africa has presented to the world of informed jurisprudential discourse. The challenge that Africa poses is the challenge of a jurisprudence of human rights in its most comprehensive sense, one that integrates the perspectives of so-called first-, second-, and third-generation rights.

At the back of the African jurisprudence challenge is a major conceptual difference between the tradition of Western political philosophy and jurisprudence and that of African political philosophy and jurisprudence. Western perspectives remain strongly wedded to the core dualism between individual identity and that of the group (the state, the community, the society). African juridical perspectives have steadfastly sought to challenge the efficacy and essential validity of such a dichotomy. The precept is well expressed in a Tanzanian case, of *DPP v. Pete,* LRC (Const.) 533, 565 (1991):

The second important principle or characteristic to be borne in mind when interpreting our constitution is a corollary of the reality of coexistence of the individual and society, and also of the reality of the coexistence of rights and duties of the individual on the one hand and the collective of communitarian rights and duties of society on the other. In effect this existence means that the rights and duties of the individual are limited by the rights and duties of society, and vice versa.

The African term for this precept is *ubuntu,* and in the recent decision of the South African Constitutional Court, *State v. Makwanyune,* CCT/3/94 (6 June 1995), it served as the basis for some of the judges declaring South Africa's death penalty unconstitutional. Judge Langa explains in greater detail the practical meaning of the term:

An outstanding feature of ubuntu in a community sense is the value it puts on human life and dignity. The dominant theme of the culture is that the life of another person is at least as valuable as one's own. Respect for the dignity of every person is integral to this concept. During violent conflicts and times when violent crime is rife, distraught members of society [experience] the loss of ubuntu. Thus heinous crimes are the antithesis of ubuntu. Treatment that is cruel, inhuman and degrading is bereft of ubuntu.

The central idea implicit in these formulations is that jurisprudence that accords with social reality recognizes the ubiquitous facts of interaction, interdependence, and interdetermination; recognizes that legal interventions must be guided by some overriding goal values (in context of ubuntu, the overriding value of *mutual reciprocal* respect as the basis of a jurisprudence of human dignity. African jurisprudence is at a crossroads as we approach the twenty-first century, but important initiatives have already been launched from which the world may well witness a new African jurisprudence for a new age.

References

An-na-im, Abdullahi A., and Francis M. Deng. *Human Rights in Africa: Cross-Cultural Perspectives.* Washington, DC: Brookings Institute, 1990.

Cohen, Ronald, Goren Hyden, and Winston Nagan. *Human Rights and Governance in Africa.* Gainesville: University Press of Florida, 1993.

Deng, Francis M. *Tradition and Modernization: A Challenge for Law Among the Dinka of the Sudan.* 1971. Foreword by Harold D. Laswell. 2d ed. New Haven: Yale University Press, 1989.

Elias, T.O. *The Nature of African Customary Law.* Manchester: Manchester University Press, 1956.

Fortes, Meyer, and E.E. Evans-Pritchard. *African Political Systems.* 1940. London: Oxford University Press, 1966.

Ghai, Yash. *Law in the Political Economy of Public Enterprise.* Uppsala: Scandinavian Institute of African Studies, 1977.

Ghai, Yash, Robin Luckham, and Francis Snyder, eds. *The Political Economy of Law: A Third World Reader.* New Delhi: Oxford University Press, 1989.

Kelsen, Hans. *Pure Theory of Law.* Trans. Max Knight. Berkeley: University of California Press, 1967.

Simons, Harold Jack. *African Women: Their Legal Status in South Africa.* London: C. Hurst, 1968.

Winston P. Nagan

See also ABORIGINAL LEGAL CULTURES; CONVENTION AND CUSTOM; CUSTOMARY LAW

Agency (Mandate)

From a philosophical point of view, agency or mandate is concerned with the depersonalization of jural relationships. Acts in the law are performed by legal persons, who may be natural or artificial; such acts may affect the legal situation not only of the actors themselves but also of other legal persons. Conceptually and historically, law begins by looking at acts performed by one person directly with, against, or in respect of another. As a given legal system becomes more sophisticated, recognition is accorded to the notions of representation or delegation. That which can be done, factually and/or legally, by one person can eventually be done by another in the place or stead, and on behalf of the first person. There is no longer any necessity for direct physical or legal contact between the true parties to a legal act or transaction: the same result can be and is achieved through the agency of another legal person (even, in some systems, by one who would lack legal capacity to act on his or her own behalf).

An agent is the instrument of the one for whom the agent acts. Like a physical instrument or tool, the agent is subject to the direction and control of the person for whom the agent acts. Nevertheless it is accepted that some agents, by virtue of their special skills, for example, lawyers or brokers, must exercise a considerable degree of independence as regards the way they are to fulfill the function that has been delegated to them. At one and the same time, therefore, agents are subject to control but may be independent. Reconciling these two apparently contradictory aspects is one of the major tasks to be performed by the law governing agency. This is achieved by means of a network of duties that are implicit in the relationship between the agent and the person for whom the agent acts. Among these are duties of performance, for example, the duty to obey lawful commands or directions of the principal (the person for whom the agent acts), or the duty to execute the agency function with due care and skill, and duties of loyalty or fidelity, for example, the duty to act only in the interests of the principal and not to allow the agent's interest to conflict with those of the principal.

At all times, therefore, during the life of the agency relationship, whatever kind it may be, the principal is, in essence and in fact, the person for whom the agent acts, the alter ego of that person. This means that what the agent does, legally speaking, is regarded as having been done by the one for whom the agent acted. This is what Roman lawyers meant by the maxim *qui facit per alium facit per se.*

What is said above relates to agency as a legal concept. The term and the idea it enshrines are also relevant in nonlegal contexts. Representation or delegation can occur in respect of social obligations having no legal consequence or effect. Advanced legal systems, such as Roman law or the common law, have utilized the general notion of agency in a special way, so as to extend the range or scope of legal action. In doing so, legal systems have had to invoke certain concepts for the purpose of defining, analyzing, and applying agency. The most important of these are power and authority.

Every legal person is endowed with certain legal powers. What those are depends upon a particular legal system, and, frequently, on a particular time in the development of that legal system. Those legal powers are not necessarily coincident or congruent with a person's physical powers. The scope of legal powers is determined, inter alia, by what is termed legal capacity. Thus those under age or mentally incompetent may possess limited capacity to perform legal acts and, conversely, may be under limited liability if they perform acts that would involve someone with complete legal capacity in full liability. The law of agency of a legal system defines and delimits when and what legal powers of a person may be delegated. To the extent that the law allows, an agent is endowed with the legal powers of another person. In the nonlegal world any physical power may be delegated and exercised by a representative. In the legal world, however, only such legal powers as are prescribed by the law may be delegated to a representative.

The power that is entrusted to an agent is delineated by the term "authority." For legal purposes an agent can only legitimately perform, as the representative or delegate of another in such a way as to involve that other legally, such acts as are within the agent's authority. Whatever is done outside that authority is considered not to have been done for, or on behalf of, the person whom the agent represents. As such it does not bind that person in law. Nor can it be said philosophically that it binds that person. Neither in legal nor in nonlegal terms should and does something effected without authority count as anything done for or on behalf of another. The problem that has troubled the law for many years is the proper definition or explanation of what is within an agent's authority. This is the central issue of the law of agency in any legal system. Understandably it has caused the greatest difficulty for theorists and courts alike.

In the common law system it has been recognized and accepted that an agent's authority, which defines the powers that the agent may exercised on behalf of another, can exceed in scope and content the powers that have been entrusted to that agent in express terms by that other person. Sometimes such authority can be implied into the agency relationship by virtue of what is implicit in the oral or literal language used to create the relationship. Sometimes it is implied from the nature of the employment in which the agent is engaged and the kind of position that agent occupies. In these ways the express authority given an agent can be extended in certain ways and to certain lengths. Further extension is made possible by a doctrine referred to as "holding out." According to this, the authority of an agent can be enlarged (and even created where none was in existence before or otherwise) by conduct on the part of the person for whom the agent is alleged to act. This conduct leads those with whom the agent has dealt or in respect of whom has acted to believe that the agent was empowered or authorized to deal or act in this way. What is involved in such circumstances is, in effect, a kind of legal fiction. A person is treated as having in fact authorized another to act on the first person's behalf when that first person has done nothing of the kind. The rationale of this is sometimes commercial convenience, sometimes the need to make one person legally responsible for what another has done.

The legal concept of agency, therefore, could be regarded as an artificial construct of the law designed to achieve certain desirable ends or purposes, for example, to facilitate commercial transactions or to protect parties injuriously affected by others by providing a more financially responsible party to incur liability. This, it may be added, is especially useful, even necessary, when the person for whom the agent acts is not a natural but an artificial or juristic person, such as a corporation, which cannot act either physically or legally save through other, natural persons.

References

Bowstead, William. *Bowstead on Agency.* 1896. 16th ed. Ed. F.M.B. Reynolds. London: Sweet & Maxwell, 1996.

Dowrick, Francis. "The Relationship of Principal and Agent." *Modern Law Review* 17 (1954), 24.

Fridman, G.H.L. *Law of Agency.* 1960. 7th ed. London: Butterworth, 1996.

Holmes, Oliver Wendell. "Agency." *Harvard Law Review* 4 (1890), 345; 5 (189), 1.

Montrose, James. "The Basis of the Power of an Agent in Cases of Actual and Apparent Authority." *Canadian Bar Review* 16 (1938), 757.

Muller-Freienfels, Wolfgang. "Legal Relations in the Law of Agency." *American Journal of Comparative Law* 13 (1964), 193.

Powell, Raphael. *Law of Agency.* 1951. 2d ed. London: Pitman, 1960.

A

Seavey, Warren A. *Handbook of the Law of Agency*. St. Paul MN: West, 1964.
Stoljar, Samuel. *Law of Agency*. London: Sweet & Maxwell, 1961.

G.H.L. Fridman

See also ACTION AND AGENCY; CONTRACTUAL OBLIGATION

Aging

From the point of view of biomedical sciences, aging is a technological problem, the solution of which is understood in terms of forestalling the aging process. In this sense science has been remarkably successful. However, as more people live past sixty-five a new problem within the philosophy of law demands attention, namely, equality of treatment between generations. This problem appears within any context that involves the distribution of benefits or burdens between generations. Its most pronounced appearance involves the distribution of health care benefits among different age groups.

There is an important difference between age-group inequality and sex or race inequality that amplifies the philosophical issue underlying the problem of intergenerational equality. When comparing lives of persons for the purpose of evaluating equality of treatment, should a person who is aged be compared with a person who is young, or should their entire lives be compared? With respect to sex or race, if society treats people differently, this will result in differences over their complete lives. In contrast, on the assumption that the young will become old, if society treats age groups differently, it does not necessarily follow that this will result in inequalities between the complete lives of persons. Although the young may be granted a greater right to health care than the aged, over the entire course of their lives their rights may be equal—the diminished right in old age may be compensated by the augmented right in youth. Thus, if age groups are compared at a single slice of time, age-based allocation schemes may appear to violate equality in so far as resources are transferred away from the elderly to the young. In contrast, if whole or complete lives are compared, such allocation schemes may appear consistent with equality in so far as shares of resources over entire life spans may be equal. Hence, in evaluating intergenerational equal-

ity, should the focus be on comparing complete lives, taking into account all the good and bad things people receive, or should people's situations during their lives be compared?

Much can be said in favor of concentrating on complete lives. Suppose, for example, that there is one dialysis machine and the question is who is allowed to use it—a forty-year-old or an eighty-year-old? To give it to the eighty-year-old would appear unfair, since we would be denying the forty-year-old years of life that the eighty-year-old has already had. Equity would appear to demand that the forty-year-old be allowed the opportunity to live to eighty.

However, if justice is seen in terms of complete lives, then in principle extreme differences in the allocation of health care is tolerable so long as it is made good over complete lives. Thus, depriving treatment to a ninety-year-old with pneumonia would be acceptable if this deprivation were compensated by treatment he had received earlier in life. This consequence, however, is surely intolerable; the condition and experience of persons cannot be ignored during their lives. Consider two people: one has moderate pleasure throughout life, while the other experiences pleasure during the first half of life and pain during the second half. Assuming that the total amount of pleasure in their lives is the same, their lives could not be considered equal. Clearly the first life is preferable to the second.

The issue of intergenerational justice thus forces society to balance two competing conceptions of equality between people. Should priority be given to equalizing the complete lives of persons, or should priority be given to the person who experiences suffering during a period of their life? If priority is given to one, how much weight should be given to the other?

Asking the question in this way presupposes that a resolution to this conflict is possible by an appeal to abstract principles of justice. This assumption, however, has been called into question by those who argue that a morally acceptable scheme of intergenerational health care allocation is attainable only if there is a richer conception of the ideal of old age. It is argued that once this ideal exists there will be an understanding of the limits that the aged have on resources in the name of medical need, because the aged would need only those resources necessary to achieve that ideal. Once achieved, they would then need only those resources necessary to finish their years free of pain and avoidable suffering. On this model the conflict between generations would be obviated because the use of age as a criterion for allocation would be motivated out of respect for the fundamental need of the elderly to live out an adequate life.

There are many difficulties with this view. First, the concept of an "ideal of old age" is no less controversial than that of justice. Hence, rather than solving a problem, the controversy has simply been shifted to a different level. Second, should the ideal of old age be a concept that one chooses for oneself, or should it be a concept that is chosen for one? To constitute an age-based criterion, the state would have to specify the ideal and stipulate that the ideal has been achieved at a certain age. What is done with those who do not share the state's notion of the ideal or, contrary to the age stipulation, have not achieved the ideal? Are decisions to be made on a case-by-case basis? The question remains: who decides? If it is left to the individual, then an age-based criterion no longer exists. If it is left to the state, there will be the likely scenario of treatment withheld from individuals who have not, in their own eyes, achieved the ideal. Would such intrusion into the life of the individual be desirable or justifiable?

Thus, as the population continues to age, the conflict between the young and old will continue to grow. Another question remains: is it ever morally acceptable to resolve this conflict by using age as a criterion for distribution?

References

Callahan, D. *Setting Limits: Medical Goals in an Aging Society.* New York: Simon & Schuster, 1987.

Churchill, L. *Rationing Health Care in America: Perceptions and Principles in Practice.* Notre Dame: University of Notre Dame Press, 1987.

Daniels, N. *Am I My Parents' Keeper? An Essay on Justice between the Young and the Old.* New York: Oxford University Press, 1988.

Holmes, H., and L. Purdy, eds. *Feminist Perspectives in Medical Ethics.* Bloomington: Indiana University Press, 1992.

Jeckler, N., ed. *Aging and Ethics.* Totowa NJ: Humana Press, 1990.

Kilner, J. *Life on the Line.* Grand Rapids MI: Eerdmans, 1992.

McKerlie, D. "Equality Between Age Groups." *Philosophy and Public Affairs* 21 (1992).

Moody, H. *Ethics in an Aging Society.* Baltimore: Johns Hopkins University Press, 1992.

Richard W. Burgh

See also DISPOSITION OF REMAINS; EUTHANASIA AND SUICIDE; INHERITANCE AND SUCCESSION

Alternative Dispute Resolution

See DISPUTE RESOLUTION

Amendment

If the fundamental law, or constitution, of a nation cannot be changed by legal means, then it cannot adapt to changing circumstances; as the disparity with circumstances widens, the risk of revolution increases. Conversely, if it can be changed too easily, then the fundamental principles and institutions it establishes are at risk of being swept away by a majority momentarily enraptured with a new idea. An amendment clause permits fundamental change, courting the latter risk, but it makes that change difficult, courting the former. It aspires to capture the inconsistent virtues of stability and flexibility, protecting what the enacting generation thinks wise, but permitting future generations to think otherwise.

The mere existence of an amending clause in a constitution shows a belief that the fundamental law is a human contrivance subject to human refinement. Although it may be accompanied by affirmations of natural law, it is a sign of emergent positivism. It should not be a surprise, then, that the world's first explicit amending clause, in the Pennsylvania constitution of 1776, is a product of the Enlightenment.

Ordinary legislation can be changed by the body which made it. While this is often the case with constitutions, the amending body is rarely in continuing session. A special procedure, or body, or both, is needed to amend a constitution. Ordinary legislation embodies the policy decisions on which the majority ought to have its way. The constitution establishes more fundamental principles and institutions, including the procedures of ordinary legislation and limits on majoritarian power. If the power of ordinary legislation is exercised foolishly, no structural damage is done and its products may (in principle) be repealed or corrected the next day. If, however, the principles and institutions of the constitution are foolishly revised, then the channel of correction may itself have been removed or obstructed, and the only remedy may be a period in political purgatory while the nation establishes new, acceptable procedures.

When ordinary legislation conflicts with a constitutional rule, the latter takes priority. This legal priority is invariably yoked to a political difference: changing constitutional rules is procedurally more difficult than changing ordinary legislation. The legal and political differences occur together so that the more fundamental a rule or structure is, the more it is protected from hasty change. The risk, and opportunity, inherent in an amending procedure is that these basic rules and structures may still be swept away if a larger sort of consensus is obtained.

The political difficulty of constitutional amendment, when self-imposed by a people, is a form of self-paternalism. It is our method of protecting ourselves from our anticipated weak moments. When an amending clause is imposed by another people, for example, the 1946 Japanese amending clause by the Supreme Command for the Allied Powers, it can be an instrument of paternalism and political domination. Until 1982, the Canadian constitution could only be amended by the English Parliament; when England finally transferred this power to Canada, Canadians spoke of the "repatriation" of their constitution and of becoming for the first time sovereign in their own land.

Scholars and officials often view the constitutional amending power as an incident of sovereignty, and the amending body as the sovereign. This is clearly because the amending power is supreme within its legal system, even if not omnipotent. It is omnipotent as well if it can reach every rule, structure, or principle of the legal system. Scholars disagree on whether any amending power is legally omnipotent (and on what legal omnipotence is). There are always procedural limitations on the amending power, but some have alleged that substantive limitations may be implied and may even be irrevocable.

In the United States one substantive limitation is explicit: no amendment may deprive a state of its suffrage in the Senate without its consent. But it seems clear that with the consent of every state this provision could be repealed. Similarly, if the amending clause can amend itself, then all express and implied substantive limitations on the amending power might be overcome—with the exception of the limitation which prevents the amending power from imposing irrevocable limitations on itself.

References

Levinson, Sanford, ed. *Responding to Imperfection: The Theory and Practice of Constitutional Amendment.* Princeton: Princeton University Press, 1995.

Orfield, Lester Bernhardt. *Amending the Federal Constitution.* Ann Arbor: University of Michigan Press, 1942.

Suber, Peter. *The Paradox of Self-Amendment: A Study of Logic, Law, Omnipotence, and Change.* New York: Peter Lang, 1990.

Vile, John R. *Contemporary Questions Surrounding the Constitutional Amending Process.* Westport CT: Praeger, 1993.

Vose, Clement. *Constitutional Change: Amendment Politics and Supreme Court Litigation Since 1900.* Lexington MA: Lexington Books, 1972.

Peter Suber

See also CODIFICATION; LEGALITY; LEGISLATION AND CODIFICATION; SELF-REFERENCE

American Jurists, 1860–1960

The history of American jurisprudence and legal education has swung at various moments between formalism and antiformalism. The post–Civil War period began with a swing toward formalism, but it was not long before a major countermovement appeared: the beginnings of legal pragmatism, with its emphasis on action, practice, pluralism, inquiry, and experience. Legal pragmatists, and their offspring, the legal realists, attacked the myth of legal certainty and the narrow conception of legal reasoning inherent in legal formalism, in much the same way that philosophical pragmatists questioned their own tradition.

One American-born variety of formalism had an especially profound effect on the course of legal education and legal philosophy in America. In 1870 Christopher Columbus

Langdell inaugurated the deanship at Harvard Law School, and before long he and his successor, James Barr Ames, changed the way law was taught in this country. He reshaped the curriculum, introduced final exams, extended matriculation requirements from one to two and ultimately three years, and, most important, implemented the case method as the foundation of legal study. Langdell's theory of legal education was more original than the philosophical justification that lay behind it; a common law lawyer essentially, he drew on some of the insights of austinian analytical jurisprudence and the new positivistic trends in science and philosophy. Langdell wanted to treat the law as a science. Although the common law model suggested an unmanageable profusion of cases, Langdell argued that the law was in fact reducible to a few basic principles. Legal scientists had the task to identify those principles by making actual cases the primary sources for determining the state of the law with respect to any particular legal question. Legal doctrines grow slowly, and so legal scientists are not forced to engage in an analysis of every relevant case; a representative selection is sufficient for understanding the law and preserving its usefulness. The law becomes a science when legal scientists as legal philosophers furnish classificatory schemes to provide rational arrangements of legal concepts and relations.

John Chipman Gray (1839–1915) wrote one book of legal philosophy, *The Nature and Sources of the Law,* which ranks in its philosophical importance not far beneath Oliver Wendell Holmes' masterwork, *The Common Law.* Although Gray joins Holmes as one of the two great jurisprudential heroes for Jerome Frank, Karl Llewellyn, and the other legal realists, he is much more than that; he is a kind of American John Austin, but one whose analytical jurisprudence does not act as if legal concepts originated and developed outside legal history. He represents the positivistic branch of the American pragmatic legal tradition. He is closer to Austin than Holmes, certainly, but not as influenced as Holmes—or John Dewey—by historical jurisprudence, or the evolutionary controversy, or the increasing respect philosophers paid to the very idea of historical development.

Gray's choice for a title for his book was apt. Although he set out to distinguish the nature from the sources of the law, his distinctive contribution to jurisprudence lies in the way he defined the nature of the law in terms of its analytical scope, expanding the number of sources and narrowing the concept of law. Gray's strategy for defining the nature of the law was to present his theory against a background of three rival theories, Austin's command theory, Friedrich von Savigny's version of historical jurisprudence in which the law is identified with the folk wisdom of the people, and the common law lawyer's view that judges discover and declare the law but do not make it. All three deny what they should affirm, that, according to Gray, "the courts are the real authors of the Law" and not simply "mouthpieces" that express the authority behind the law.

Gray looked to the practical consequences of the adjudicatory process to justify his court-centered approach. Why, he wondered, does the law in one state often differ from the law in another when the cases on which they are based are nearly identical? The only difference, he concludes, is that different judges decided the cases. This implies that the nature of the law is determined by the courts. Gray's original contribution to jurisprudence lies in his belief that all considerations directly or indirectly relating to the law belong not to the nature of the law but to the sources of the law. Statutes, judicial precedents, opinions of experts, customs, and morality as well as equity, whose principles are often expressed in the form of public policy, must not be treated as positive law. The contents of this list were controversial, however; few theorists would object to identifying the last three as sources of the law, but not so the first two.

Before being elevated to the United States Supreme Court in 1932, Benjamin Cardozo (1870–1938), regarded as the premier state judge in America, was a common law judge whose opinions in several cases had become—and still are—part of the canon for law students. During the 1920s Cardozo wrote three short books; his jurisprudential reputation owes much to these extrajudicial writings. The first book, *The Nature of the Judicial Process,* has been the most influential of the three. Cardozo began his inquiry by identifying four methods of analyzing cases. They include (1) a method of philosophy in which judges reason by analogy and deduction to discern the logical basis of a legal principle; (2) a method of history or evolution, which traces a principle or concept's historical development for the purpose of illuminating past, present, and future; (3) a method of tradition, which considers the meaning of a principle in terms of the customs of the community and links legal standards and communal norms; and (4) a method of sociology, which allows judges to widen their discretionary field and appeal to considerations of social justice and welfare to help them determine what to do with principles. There are two impulses here, judicial innovation or experience and conservation or logic. The question is whether they can—or even need to—be reconciled in the pragmatic incrementalism he endorsed, a theory whose ultimate test is experience.

A renowned teacher and pioneer of the study of the law as a philosophical discipline, Morris R. Cohen (1880–1947) was the philosophical counterpart of Cardozo. He sought to make reason respectable in an age that celebrated experience by leavening the concept of experience with a deeper understanding of logic and scientific method. Cohen's commitment to rationalism in the law did not put him in the formalist's camp, since he refused to go back to the formalism of the previous century. His attack on legal formalism or absolutism did not presuppose the antimetaphysical bias and the narrow conception of logic that he attributed to the legal realists. Echoing Holmes, Gray, and Roscoe Pound, he assailed what he called the "phonograph theory of the judicial function," a theory that judges do not make the law, but find, interpret, apply, and pronounce the law in a mechanical way. He thought that his metaphysical "principle of polarity," a theory that opposites involve each other, could be brought to bear on legal problems, to help decision makers steer between extremes by incorporating the benefits to be found at each pole, such as the tension between rule and discretion.

Cohen also turned out highly respected articles in three areas of substantive law: property, contract, and criminal law. His purpose was not to extend the law in each of these areas, but to explore the analytical foundation of each by showing how it functions within a wider social, political, economic, ethical, and legal context. In his analysis of property law, for instance, he questions the meaningfulness of the traditional distinction between public and private law.

World War II marked the end of two decades in which legal realists were prominent in the legal academy. Their influential recommendations for legal reform provided some theoretical support for the rise of the administrative state during the 1930s, but they also had many critics, friendly critics such as Pound and Cohen, and critics in the natural law tradition, such as Lon L. Fuller and several Catholic legal theologians who worried that pragmatism and realism implied an abject positivism fueled by the fascism in much of Europe. These debates led to two important developments during the 1940s and 1950s.

1. Policy science became a stepchild of legal realism, which did not offer a constructive theory as part of its critique of conceptualism in law and legal theory. In their seminal 1943 article, "Legal Education and Public Policy," Harold Lasswell and Myres McDougal called for a comprehensive restructuring of the law school curriculum that would recognize the pervasive role of lawyers in the making of social policy. Lawyers, they argued, are always found in society's centers of power, corporate and governmental. Legal education must recognize that where there is power there are lawyers, either making policy or advising policymakers. They wanted traditional legal skills to be incorporated into a curriculum that integrated a value-oriented approach to the law by using the tools of the social sciences. Lasswell and McDougal thought that the social sciences should not simply be used to describe society's democratic values as accurately as possible, but should be used to identify goals and implement them through policy recommendations. The social sciences were to have a normative function in the legal arena.

2. The 1950s saw another response to the vestiges of realistic jurisprudence in the widespread use in the leading law schools of Henry M. Hart and Albert Sacks' book, *The Legal Process*. Designed for classroom use, their text and materials offered a theoretical framework for the law's place within the American polity, one which is relevant to the various areas of law. Legal realism and the activist legislatures and appellate courts of the New Deal had blurred the boundaries between substance and procedure; Hart and Sacks tried to bring that line back into focus. They tried to rescue the values they saw embedded in permanent principles of law through a process of "reasoned elaboration." Judges would then be able to rely on objective standards to make their legal determinations; judicial discretion would be based on

enduring principles. For Hart and Sacks, substantive rights derived from procedural rights. Herbert Wechsler's controversial search for general or "neutral principles" sprang from a process jurisprudence which could justify decisions that arrive at incorrect substantive results and could justify them on the grounds that respect for procedure is more effective in promoting the general welfare of the community.

References

Cardozo, Benjamin N. *The Growth of the Law.* New Haven: Yale University Press, 1924.

———. *The Nature of the Judicial Process.* New Haven: Yale University Press, 1921.

———. *The Paradoxes of Legal Science.* New York: Columbia University Press, 1928.

Cohen, Morris R. *Law and the Social Order: Essays in Legal Philosophy.* 1933. Reprint, Hamden CT: Archon Books, 1967.

———. *Reason and Law.* 1950. Reprint, New York: Collier Books, 1961.

Frank, Jerome. *Law and the Modern Mind.* New York: Brentano's, 1930; 6th ed., 1948. Reprint, Gloucester MA: Peter Smith, 1970.

Gray, John Chipman. *The Nature and Sources of the Law.* 1921. Reprint, Gloucester MA: Peter Smith, 1972.

Hart, Henry M., and Albert Sacks. *The Legal Process.* Cambridge MA: Harvard University Press, 1958.

Lasswell, Harold, and Myres McDougal. "Legal Education and Public Policy: Professional Training in the Public Interest." *Yale Law Journal* 52 (1943), 203–295.

Wechsler, Herbert. "Toward Neutral Principles of Constitutional Law." *Harvard Law Review* 73 (1959), 1–35.

Mark Mendell

See also HOLMES, OLIVER WENDELL JR.; PRAGMATIST PHILOSOPHY OF LAW; REALISM, LEGAL

Analogy

Statutory analogy (*analogia legis*) is the application of a statutory rule to a case that, viewed from the ordinary linguistic angle, is included in neither the core nor the periphery of the application area of the statute in question, but resembles the cases covered by this statute in essential respects.

Statutory analogy is employed in most legal systems, albeit it plays a greater role in the continental law than in the common law countries.

The relation of statutory analogy is not reflexive, since the set of cases regulated by a norm is not analogous to itself. Neither is it transitive: a case, C_1, can be analogous to those regulated by the norm in question, another case, C_2, analogous to C_1, and yet C_2 need not be analogous to the regulated cases.

Statutory analogy is justifiable by the principle "like should be treated alike" and thus by considerations of justice, universalisability, and coherence. One can logically reconstruct it as a generalization of a statutory prescription, but this theory is contestable because the judgment of analogy requires consideration of particular cases. Regarded as a procedure, statutory analogy implies an effort to achieve a "reflective equilibrium" of the generalized rule and particular judgments of analogy.

Statutory analogy is a traditional means to fill in so-called gaps (*lacunae*) in the law. A gap can occur in the literal sense of the statute or in the set of norms one obtains by interpreting the statute in the light of traditional legal methods. An *insufficiency gap* in a statute occurs when the statute does not regulate a given case. The "*genuine gaps*" (according to Zittelmann) are a special case. They occur when one cannot fill in the gap by employing a closure norm, such as "an action is permitted, if it is not explicitly forbidden by the law." The constitution stipulates, for example, that a certain statute should be enacted but the statute is, in fact, not enacted; or a statute stipulates that one can claim compensation but it does not specify who has to pay. The "*not genuine*" gaps occur when a closure rule is logically applicable but evaluatively inappropriate, often due to new economic or technological development. For example, when electrical current was discovered, the question occurred in several countries whether "milking the meter" should or should not be regarded as larceny. One should not confuse insufficiency gaps with so-called *axiological* gaps which occur when the statute regulates a given case in a morally unacceptable way.

To be sure, some jurists (notably Arthur Kaufmann) claim that the legal language in general has an analogical nature. Statutory analogy—implying a radical extension of the scope of application of the statutory prescription—must be distinguished, however, from the so-called *analogia intra legem* (analogy within the scope of the statute). Other jurists (for example, Alf Ross) reject the vague distinction between statutory analogy and extensive interpretation of a statute. The legal tradition uses this distinction, however; for example, statutory analogy in criminal law is to be employed more cautiously than extensive interpretation. By ignoring the distinction, a legal philosopher can thus unconsciously encourage an excessive use of analogy.

What is said about statutory analogy may be appropriately extended to the following modes of reasoning: "Law-analogy" (*analogia iuris*) or "legal induction" means that one applies a rule derived by generalizing several statutory prescriptions. "Legal institution analogy" means that a whole complex of rules in force in one field of law is applied to another field, for example, rules concerning sale are applicable to a donation. An argument similar to *analogia legis* is also applicable to radically extend the established *ratio decidendi* (reason for the decision) of a precedent.

When deciding not to reason by analogy, one can use the so-called *argumentum a contrario* (argument from the alternative). Statutory analogy and *argumentum a contrario* are, however, not complete reasons but mere argument forms, each supported by a different set of reasons. The following reasoning norms help one to make a choice between the use of analogy and *argumentum a contrario*.

Only relevant similarities between cases constitute a sufficient reason for conclusion by analogy. Judgments of relevance are justifiable by weighing and balancing of various reasons, often principles. Such a justification is based on the legal culture and tradition of the society. The tradition may change, yet the new elements can constitute a coherent evolution of the old. Relevant resemblances can concern many different things, such as persons, things, documents, rights, duties, circumstances concerning space and time, social effects of the application of the law to different cases, and, finally, the place of the cases in respective "stories" ("narratives"). The judgment of relevance is "finalist," that is, justifiable by a general principle expressing the *purpose* of the statute. Sometimes, analogy concerns a similarity of structure between two domains, that is, proportionality a:b = c:d.

One should not construe provisions establishing time limits by analogy. One should not construe provisions constituting exceptions from a general norm by analogy, unless strong reasons for assuming the opposite exist. The so-called principle of legality in penal law demands that no action should be regarded as a crime without statutory support and no penalty may be imposed without a statutory provision (*nullum crimen sine lege* [no crime without a statute]; *nulla poena sine lege* [no punishment without a statute]). In taxation law, the principle *nullum tributum sine lege* (no taxation without a statute) justifies the conclusion that one should apply analogy with restraint if it leads to increased taxation. The precise meaning of these restrictions is, however, debatable in many countries.

References

Frändberg, Åke. *Om analog användning av rättsnormer* (On Analogical Use of Legal Norms). Stockholm: Norstedts, 1973 (summary in English).

Kaufmann, Arthur. *Analogie und "Natur der Sache"; Zugleich ein Beitrag zur Lehre vom Typus.* 2d ed. Heidelberg: Decker und Müller, 1982. Trans. (1st ed.) Ilmar Tammelo as "Analogy and the Nature of Things; A Contribution to the Theory of Types." *Journal of the Indian Law Institute* 8 (1966), 358–401.

Nerhot, Patrick, ed. *Legal Knowledge and Analogy. Fragments of Legal Epistemology, Hermeneutics and Linguistics.* Dordrecht: Kluwer Academic Publishers, 1991.

Peczenik, Aleksander. "Analogia legis. Analogy from Statutes in Continental Law." In *Le Raisonnement Juridique. Proceedings of the World Congress for Legal and Social Philosophy,* ed. Hubert Hubien, 329–336. Brussels: Établissements Émile Bruylant, 1971.

Aleksander Peczenik

See also COHERENCE

Anarchist Philosophy of Law

The anarchist philosophy of law is a normative political theory according to which the state and all its institutions, supported by its laws, coercive power, and authority, are both violent and unjust. Moreover, according to this theory the state is not needed because people can live without it. Citizens should organize their social life spontaneously. Some anarchists are collectivists, some are egoists.

The first anarchist is William Godwin (1756–1836). The term "anarchism" is first used by Pierre-Joseph Proudhon (1809–1865) in France. Notable Russian anarchists are Michael Bakunin (1814–1876) and Peter Kropotkin (1842–1921). German Max Stirner (1806–1856) is well known for his egoism. Anarchism was first an ally and then a competitor of socialism. Karl Marx and his followers, like V.I. Lenin, were hostile to anarchism. The main difference is that the Marxist socialists wanted to gain the control of the capitalist state first and then dispose of it. They believed that the state would "wither away." Anarchists, on the contrary, thought that any state is necessarily evil. Any state involves intolerable violence so that the state cannot be utilized for any purpose whatsoever. Many anarchists, like Godwin, were also against all violence, although Bakunin was ready to accept a violent revolution. Leo Tolstoy (1829–1910), as an anarchist, was absolutely against violence. His main idea was Christian charity among people.

Anarchism is closely related to extreme liberalism or libertarianism. Some modern libertarians are anarchists, although the term is not used often in modern political philosophy, Robert Nozick's book *Anarchy, State, and Utopia* being an exception. The difference between libertarianism and anarchism is that the latter rejects even property as unjust, that is, anarchism is the more radical one of the two. Anarchism is not a rights-based view like libertarianism. People do not insist on their rights, according to anarchism, but they want to live a good and harmonious life. Another difference is historical. Anarchism is associated with socialism, unlike liberalism in the nineteenth century.

Anarchism has certain utopian features. Anarchists suppose that human nature cannot be evil and that the condition of nature, in Thomas Hobbes' sense, cannot be a mere violent chaos. On the contrary, the fact that human beings are violent is a result of the wrong education provided to them by the unjust state. Indeed, there is no reason to suppose that the disappearance of the state would lead to any harmful consequences. Human beings have enough benevolence, charity, and reason so that they are able to organize their lives on a spontaneous basis and be free and happy. They do not need laws.

Anarchism has another utopian feature which is not always noticed. This is its presupposed idea of the inherent nobility of the human mind and reason. We might call this optimism its aristocratic aspect, but the problem is that this word hints at some unjust privileges. However, every human being has a duty to be an independent, free, and yet responsible creator of the good human condition and a just society. Because there cannot be any power or authority above an individual, he or she is a sovereign individual. The responsibility is enormous, but an anarchist must believe in its reality.

Anarchism is utopian also in the sense that it is reluctant to answer the following practical question: the state, its institutions, and its laws are real. How are they supposed to become dismantled? This is an especially difficult question if the theory insists that the change from the state to anarchy must take place in a peaceful and just manner. It is difficult to believe that any democratic methods are sufficient. Anarchists do not pay much attention to this question. They seem to suppose that once the real nature of the state has been made evident the state will disappear and the real human nature will appear, making the spontaneous reorganization of social life possible. Anarchism is an end-state theory because it sketches the human condition after the state has already disappeared. A historical theory would give a description and explanation of the disappearance of the state. Marxism is a typical historical theory which does not pay much attention to the end-state. Liberalism and even libertarianism accept the state in some weak form, so that they arc not faced with this problem.

Anarchism contains an answer to Thomas Hobbes, who suggests in his *Leviathan* that without a sovereign power and his laws, supported by coercion, society would return to the state of nature. According to Hobbes, this condition is the worst possible one. It follows that any sovereign and his laws are better than the condition of nature and thus are justifiable and just. Hobbes' thinking seems to presuppose that human beings are egoists who are always eager to compete against each other. Once this starts there is no way of stopping them, until society collapses back to social chaos. The anarchists would not call such a situation anarchy—anarchy has a positive meaning to them. Anarchists say there is no reason to believe that Hobbes is right and that people can live together without a sovereign power.

Another influential background figure is Bernard Mandeville, whose satirical work *The Fable of the Bees* argues in 1714 that "private vices are public benefits." According to Mandeville, any state whose laws demand that its citizens be virtuous exists in suboptimal conditions. No society can be happy and prosperous if its members are law-abiding, good citizens. Mandeville's legacy is paradoxical, however, because the citizens need to be vicious in order to maximize the public good. The conclusion seems to be that no social organization can satisfy the demands of goodness and justice. Mandeville's view is difficult to interpret.

William Godwin's theory in his 1793 work *Political Justice* is clearly utopian. He believes in the principle that is usually called the "perfectibility of man," according to which the historical institutions of power distract human progress. Godwin says that human reason is ultimately omnipotent and where the truth is clearly visible it must finally prevail. The three methods of reform are literature, education, and political justice. He condemns all violence. Intellectual enlightenment will succeed if the reformers know how to promote it. For this people need to embrace civic duties, even if this means that they must reject the strong doctrine of rights, meaning "a full and complete power of either doing a thing or omitting it, without liability to animadversion or censure."

Emma Goldman (1869–1940) is the best known American anarchist. Her definition in her 1911 essay "Anarchism, What It Really Stands For" is as follows: "Anarchism: The philosophy of a new social order based on liberty unrestricted by man-made law; the theory that all forms of government rest on violence, and are therefore wrong and harmful, as well as unnecessary." She argues against all authority, including that of God and the state, by noticing, ironically, "[a]gain and again, man is nothing, the powers are everything." She argues against the idea that laws are needed to control crime: "Crime is naught but misdirected energy. So long as every institution of today, economic, political, social, and moral, conspires to misdirect human energy into wrong channels ... crime will be inevitable,

and all the laws and statutes can only increase, but never do away with, crime." These are typical anarchistic theses. Goldman also mistrusts the right to own property. This is a central theme already with Proudhon, who compares property to robbery.

In the philosophy of natural sciences Paul Feyerabend has made the idea of methodological anarchism fashionable through his 1988 book *Against Method*. According to his argument, anything goes in science, in the sense that no rules can be provided which would distinguish good from bad evidence. He uses the success of Galileo as an example. Galileo's evidence for the new heliocentric astronomical view was in fact weaker than that offered by his traditionalist rivals, who supported the geocentric view. Yet he used rhetoric and persuasion to support his own view. Of course later his theories were verified. According to Feyerabend, the lesson to learn is that the system of science and its official rules of evidence are unjustifiable. Scientists may use whatever data they like as evidence, even their dreams and prophecies. Natural science is an anarchistic enterprise. The same reasoning may be applied to legal studies as well.

References

Capouya, Emile, and Keitha Tompkins, eds. *The Essential Kropotkin*. New York: Liveright, 1975.

Cutler, Robert, ed. *From Out of the Dustbin, Michael Bakunin's Basic Writings, 1869–1871*. Ann Arbor: Ardis, 1985.

Joll, James. *The Anarchists*. Cambridge MA: Harvard University Press, 1980.

Pennock, J. Roland, and John W. Chapman, eds. *Anarchism, Nomos XIX*. New York: New York University Press, 1978.

Proudhon, P.-J. *What Is Property?* Trans. Benjamin Tucker. New York: Dover, 1970.

Sonn, Richard D. *Anarchism*. New York: Twayne, 1992.

Woodcock, George. *Anarchism, A History of Libertarian Ideas and Movements*. Cleveland: Meridian Books, 1970.

Timo Airaksinen

Anselm (1033/4–1109)

The monk, abbot, and archbishop St. Anselm of Canterbury is not known directly for any major works of legal philosophy, such as those produced by other scholastics (for example,

Thomas Aquinas' *Summa Theologiae*). Nevertheless, his contribution to philosophy, theology, and Church life left a lasting impression and earned him the title of "father of scholasticism." His mind has been likened by a modern biographer to a computer running an augustinian program on an aristotelian operating system. He played a significant role in preparing the ground for the later scholastics who, it has been claimed, "baptised Aristotle," thus reconciling classical Greek thought with Christian belief.

Anselm's two best-known works are the *Monologion* and the *Proslogion,* both of which concern themselves with proofs for the existence of God, independent of Scripture or divine revelation. The *Monologion* begins with the observation that things are unequal in perfection and that from this fact we may infer the existence of an absolute perfection in which the things of lesser perfection participate to a greater or lesser degree, for example, something is more or less just because it participates more or less in absolute justice. The argument is broadened by considering the fact of existence as a perfection that all things have in common. Such "existence" or "being-of-itself" in which all things participate must have a cause, and this is traceable back to the one single cause: God.

The *Proslogion* was an attempt to simplify the proof further by arguing, as a purely a priori demonstration, that since man can conceive of there being a God, and since God is a Being nothing greater than which can be conceived (that is, the greatest conceivable Being), it follows that God must exist both in the intellect of man and in reality. This must be so, for to exist in reality as well as in the mind is greater than to exist in the mind alone. The *Proslogion* also went on to show the attributes of God as goodness, justice, and truth existing in a single, perfect Being. Whereas the *Monologion* draws heavily on Augustine, the *Proslogion* is uniquely Anselm.

Anselm's argument for the existence of God has become known as the "ontological argument" and has divided great philosophers since it was first produced. (St. Bonaventure, René Descartes, Gottfried Leibniz, and G.W.F. Hegel each adopted it in a certain way, while St. Thomas Aquinas, John Locke, and Immanuel Kant rejected it.)

Anselm's reliance on reason in no way detracts from his firm faith in God. Indeed, along with Augustine, he saw reason as the servant of faith and was adamant that he did not seek understanding in order to believe (in God). Rather, he believed in order that he might understand. Gilson summarizes Anselm's approach when he says that understanding of faith presupposes faith.

Anselm's discussion of liberty and free choice is not only a reflection of his great learning and original thought but also of his singular commitment to the monastic lifestyle. For Anselm, true freedom (liberty) flowed only from self-effacement and rejection of worldly honor in favor of the eternal; paradoxically, then, true liberty arose only in those whom the world viewed as without liberty. Philosophically, Anselm took up the augustinian distinction between "free choice" and "liberty." Before the fall of Adam and Eve, man enjoyed both free choice and liberty; afterwards, however, liberty was lost in the sense that man retained his power of choice but lost the ability to exercise it in a free way. This necessitates God's intervention in the form of divine grace to restore man's liberty, which Anselm also described as man's natural inclination toward God and justice.

In the *Cur Deus Homo* (Why the God-Man?) he set forth his theory of redemption and rejected a widely held doctrine, namely that the devil has a claim on man. This major work has been described by Harold Berman as a "theology of law" due to its emphasis on the justice of God. According to Anselm, God's justice demands atonement for man's disobedience and finds expression in Jesus' death on the cross: only the God-Man could provide the acceptable and perfectly atoning sacrifice. God's justice requires satisfaction; his mercy provides it when he sends his Son. The concepts of purgatory and supererogatory works are said to have grown from this idea, which also mirrors to some degree the feudal criminal law tradition of penance and restitution as an alternative to revenge. Some authors link it to the more modern "retributive" theory of justice.

Anselm's other works include *De Veritate* (On Truth), *De Libertate* (On Liberty), and *De Casu Diaboli* (On the Fall of the Devil). Over four hundred of his letters have been preserved as well as Eadmer's biography *Vita Anselmi.* Anselm wrote only one work on a secular subject, the *De Grammatico,* which drew extensively on Aristotle and was meant as a student's introduction to syllogism and logic. Anselm was declared a Doctor of the Church in 1720.

References

Berman, Harold J. *Law and Revolution.* Cambridge MA: Harvard University Press, 1983.

Eadmer. *The Life of St. Anselm: Archbishop of Canterbury.* Ed. and trans. R.W. Southern. Oxford: Clarendon Press, 1972.

Hopkins, Jasper. *A Companion to the Study of St. Anselm.* Minneapolis: University of Minnesota Press, 1972.

Rule, M. *The Life and Times of St. Anselm.* London, 1883.

Schmitt, F.S. *Complete Works.* 5 vols. and index. Edinburgh: Edinburgh University Press, 1942.

Southern, R.W. *St. Anselm: A Portrait in a Landscape.* Cambridge: Cambridge University Press, 1990.

Patrick Quirk

Anthropology

The distinctive philosophical problems of the study of the anthropology of law arise from the variety of cultures that anthropologists study. These range from the simplest to the most complex on earth. The philosophical problems are not new. The essential issues were set out by Montesquieu in *De l'Esprit des Lois,* which was first published in 1748. In Chapter XI of Book XVIII he makes a distinction between what are generally considered the two simplest forms of human political organization. He writes: "One difference between savage peoples and barbarian peoples is that the former are small scattered nations which, for certain particular reasons, cannot unite, whereas barbarians are ordinarily small nations that can unite together. The former are usually hunting peoples; the latter pastoral peoples."

This use of the distinction between barbarians and savages continued into the nineteenth century and recurs in Lewis Henry Morgan's 1877 work *Ancient Society.* The distinction made by Montesquieu is astonishingly similar to the technical one made by anthropologists between *bands* and *tribes.* Tribes have pan-tribal mechanisms (sodalities) that link local groups. Bands do not. Most bands are hunting and/or gathering societies. Pastoralists and shifting cultivators tend to have tribal-level political organization. Particularly important is that these two types of societies are recognized as lacking centrality or some means of central coordination. Today one of the key questions of the philosophy of the anthropology of law is whether it is appropriate to argue that these uncentralized types of society have law. Montesquieu also addressed this question in Book XVIII, Chapter XII, "On civil laws among peoples who do not cultivate the land": "It is the division of lands that principally swells the civil code. In nations that have not been divided there will be very few laws. One can call the institutions of these people *mores* [*moeurs*] rather than *laws* (*lois*)." Clearly, Montesquieu reserves the term "law" for more complex societies and uses "custom" for simpler ones.

Though many cultural evolutionists agree with Montesquieu's general approach, a functional approach to law dominates much of the thinking of the anthropology of law. There is a strong ethical component to making the argument that all societies have some form of law. According to the proponents of this approach, to argue otherwise would be tantamount to saying that those societies labeled as not having law are backward, or worse, morally inferior. Considerable effort has been spent trying to frame a definition of law that is applicable to all, or nearly all, cultures.

The Cheyenne Way is a classical collaboration between a legal scholar, Karl Llewellyn, and an anthropologist, E. Adamson Hoebel. They used a case method approach to examine legal mechanisms in a tribal society. The next year Hoebel was able to assert with confidence that "there is law in primitive societies in the same sense as in ours." In *The Law of Primitive Man* Hoebel defines a legal norm: "A social norm is legal if its neglect or infraction is regularly met, in threat or in fact, by the application of physical force by an individual or group possessing the socially recognized privilege of so acting." This definition has exerted considerable influence on anthropologists, especially those not particularly interested in law.

In *Kapauku Papuans and Their Law,* Leopold Pospisil presented his four attributes of law: (1) the *attribute of authority*: "a decision to be legally relevant, or in other words to effect social control, has to be accepted by the parties to the dispute as a solution of the situation caused by their clash of interests"; (2) the *attribute of intention of universal application*; (3) the *attribute of obligatio*, "[which] has two directions—one going from the privileged party to the obligated one, which is called a right, and the other from the obligated party toward the privileged one, which is called a duty"; and (4) the *attribute of sanction*.

These definitions have been effective in including all (or nearly all) cultures so that all cultures may be viewed as having law. Their utility and strength derive from the original premise, that is, it is appropriate to frame a single definition of law for all cultures. However, this breadth comes at a price. Pospisil's definition may be so inclusive that many forms and types of behavior are included which, from a philosophical point of view, are probably not law. Pospisil is aware of this and later clearly states, perhaps inadvertently, the most serious objection to the universalistic approach:

> I would like to go even further and acknowledge the existence of legal systems in any organized group and their subgroups within the state. Consequently and ultimately, even a small grouping such as the American family has a legal system administered by the husband or wife, or both, as the case may be. Even there, in individual cases, the decisions and rules enforced by the family authorities may be contrary to the law of the state and might be deemed illegal. . . . To disregard such systems, as is often done in the writing of legal scholars, reflects not a cool scientific introspect but a moral value judgment that has its place in philosophy but not in the sociology or anthropology of law.

Universal definitions, with their priority on inclusiveness, tend to diminish the significance of the differences that do exist among the legal systems in societies of different levels of complexity. Further, being functional in nature, these definitions do not deal with change effectively and often lead to a neglect of historical perspective. In a technical sense, the problem lies with putting bands and tribes together with chiefdoms and states. There are fundamental political differences between these two types of systems: the latter have some form of genuine central authority and the former do

not. Ethical considerations arise when one type is embedded in the other. Today, most band and tribal societies are enclosed in one or more states. If both centralized and uncentralized systems are treated as equally valid at the group level, the possibility arises that some citizens of a single nation state have privileged access to a particular legal system and others do not. The reverse could also be true: some individuals, possibly minority group members, may have less opportunity of legal relief for wrongs committed against them by fellow group members or their leaders than members of the majority group have against their fellow group members and their leaders. The situation is even more complicated when there are large-scale migrations of refugees. To what degree must immigrants abandon practices that were considered essential in the original setting? Though all legal practices appear equal, do some have the right to displace others? An extremely contentious example of this problem is the issue of the legal status of female circumcision in refugee communities located outside the region where the practice is the norm. These ethical problems flow, in part, from a universalistic and functional definition of law. Initially, and on the surface, the desire to include all groups in a common definition appears progressive and empowering. The ethical conflicts and problems that flow from the approach are not initially apparent but, in retrospect, may be inevitable.

Another approach superficially similar to Montesquieu's is that of cultural evolutionism. This approach is not usually directly associated with the anthropology of law and tends to reserve law for those societies with some form of central authority that is capable of exercising legal authority. This approach includes states, proto-states, and most chiefdoms as having law but tends to exclude bands and most tribes. Bands and tribes possess institutions that carry out the functions that law does in more complex societies. These societies can be said to have proto-legal systems. This approach acknowledges a fundamental difference in kind and quality between legal and proto-legal systems. It also permits the discussion of history and evolutionary change. However, its evolutionary focus raises a number of ethical concerns at the outset. These concerns are often paramount at the present time. For many, evolutionary process implies progress or the moral superiority of the evolutionarily more "advanced" systems. To the cultural evolutionists, these arguments are akin to arguing that birds are morally superior to fish because, for the most part, they evolved later. The important issue is that there is a fundamental difference in kind. However, the ethical problem with this approach remains. The evolutionary view can be used to justify certain types of inequality and racism but may simultaneously be the more correct from a scientific point of view.

The emphasis on the universality of law continues. In her wide-ranging review of the anthropology of law, Sally Falk Moore unambiguously asserts: "No society is without law; *ergo*, there is no society outside the purview of the 'legal anthropologist.' . . . Not only does every society have law, but virtually all significant social institutions have a legal aspect." There is a strong case to be made for such a view but, as pointed out above, there are some potentially serious but largely ignored ethical consequences to such a functional, universalistic view.

References

Hoebel, E. Adamson. "Fundamental Legal Concepts as Applied in the Study of Primitive Law." *Yale Law Journal* 51 (1942), 951–966.

———. *The Law of Primitive Man*. Cambridge MA: Harvard University Press, 1954.

Llewellyn, Karl N., and E. Adamson Hoebel. *The Cheyenne Way*. Norman: University of Oklahoma Press, 1941.

Montesquieu. *De l'Esprit des Lois* (The Spirit of Laws). 1748. Paris: Garnier Frères, 1961.

———. *The Spirit of the Laws*. Trans. and ed. Anne M. Cohler, Basia Carolyn Miller, and Harold Samuel Stone. Cambridge: Cambridge University Press, 1989.

Moore, Sally Falk. *Law as Process: An Anthropological Approach*. London: Routledge & Kegan Paul, 1978.

Pospisil, Leopold. *Anthropology of Law: A Comparative Theory*. New Haven CT: HRAF Press, 1974.

———. *Kapauku Papuans and Their Law*. Yale University Publications in Anthropology, Number 54. New Haven: Yale University Department of Anthropology, 1958.

David S. Moyer

See also ABORIGINAL LEGAL CULTURES; AFRICAN PHILOSOPHY OF LAW; CUSTOMARY LAW

Aquinas, Thomas (1225–1274)

The theory of law of St. Thomas Aquinas is but one part, a profound and portentous part, of a panoramic and completely comprehensive metaphysical theology that is centered on the doctrines of divine creation and covenant (the law of Old and New Testaments). God's mind-will is at once the font of all existence and of any and all obligation or rules of right (*ius, lex*). Thus, the only adequate way to understand Aquinas' theory of law is, first and foremost, to place it properly: as a part of the dynamic economy of creation and salvation history. Aquinas' teaching on law is rooted in his doctrine of divine providence or God's government of his creation. Neither providence nor creation is to be found in the philosophy of Aristotle or, indeed, in any other classical philosopher, so that Aquinas' philosophy of law must be regarded as, at least contextually, Christian and theological—although not necessarily on that account antiphilosophical or even nonphilosophical.

For Aquinas it is of the very essence of law that it be a (1) duly promulgated, (2) the rational command (reason and will) of a (3) legitimate sovereign, and (4) aimed at promoting the public or common good. Law in the strict sense must meet each and all of these four fundamental requirements. Laws, however, are of different kinds and levels, hierarchically delineated by Aquinas.

Divine Law or Eternal Law (*Lex Divina, Lex Aeterna*)

The primary or archetypal analogate of any and all other levels of law is the eternal law of God, as the governing master mandate for the whole course of creation-history in all its aspects. Even (and especially) with respect to *human* destiny, divine law dominates decisively, and doubly so, as either "positive" divine law or "natural" divine law or, allowing for a large area of overlap, both together.

Positive Divine Law

Aquinas ordinarily refers simply to the *lex divina* without precise specification of its "positive" promulgation, which has been a source of some considerable confusion in regard to relating rightly eternal law, divine law, and natural law. However, in almost all contexts, it is clear that the term "divine law" refers to that *part* or *portion* of God's providential plan (eternal law) that is precisely promulgated by way of direct divine decree in God's revelation of divine wisdom and will in regard to human conduct, as in the prime paradigm of the Ten Commandments, as also in the magisterial moral doctrine of the Church. This portion of divine law, of course, obliges immediately only those human beings to whom it is immediately addressed, the community of the faithful or all true believers (*communio sanctorum*), although at least a part of positive divine law indirectly obliges all other humans as well to the extent of its overlap with divine "natural" law.

Natural Law *(Lex Naturalis, Ius Naturale, Rectitudo Naturalis)*

The natural (moral) law is that part or "participation" of God's governing providential plan (eternal law) that is, as it were, promulgated in the very creation of human nature as such, considered from the primary perspective of its intrinsic constitutional structure and, above all, its teleological dynamic as displayed at different levels of natural "instinct" (*inclinationes naturales*). Aquinas demonstrates a definite hierarchical order of rank of the different levels of natural instinct and the correlatively ranked levels of natural laws. The ladder of instincts indicates man's *passive* participation (shared by all animals) in the eternal law, while the ladder of corresponding natural laws calls man to close collaboration with his Creator's providential plan: a uniquely human and *active* participation in God's eternal law by way of free assent to the dictates of practical reason, the rational and legal transcription of the underlying dictates of the several natural appetites or inclinations.

At the lowest (and loosest) level of natural obligation, corresponding to the lowest level of instinct and the minimal human good, arises the natural law dictate of self-defense or the duty to protect, promote, and advance one's own individual security, especially as against aggression by others.

At a higher and relatively more binding level of natural obligation, associated with a more inclusive kind of instinct and a more expansive dimension of human good, arise those dictates of natural law enjoining intersexual copulation, in the comprehensive sense of a set of natural "family" obligations tending not merely to the production of offspring but also, and even more imperatively, to the complete upbringing or education of offspring in the context of conjugal community.

Still on the social level, although even more fully, there is that higher level of natural obligation for an even ampler human good corresponding to social instinct in the most comprehensive and uniquely human sense: the appetite for the political or public good, for justice and (by extension) any and all associated moral virtues.

Yet the fullest and highest human good, and thus also the highest imperatives of natural law, answering to the highest level of human appetite, is located by Aquinas in the area of intellectual appetite for *the* good of all human goods, the good of the human *mind,* which is precisely intellectual virtue and the knowledge of truth. Therefore, the very highest dictate of the natural law is the obligation to pursue and promote the truth, which translates easily enough for Aquinas into the absolute obligation to pursue and promote that true religion that teaches the truth about God, who alone is absolute and unqualified truth, absolute and unqualified good.

In view of the stringently hierarchical disposition and dynamic of the twin ladders of the levels of laws and instincts, it is the clear implication of Aquinas' doctrine that, in any case of conflict of different levels of natural laws or obligations, the superior, stricter, and stronger law prevails, at least in general, over any lower, lesser, and looser level of natural law.

Law of Nations *(Ius Gentium)*

What would today be termed "international law" is intermediately located in Aquinas' hierarchy: *ius gentium* lies between the quite general directives of the natural law and the much more pointed and concrete specifications (*determinationes*) of the civil law systems of the many varied civil societies. The intermediate location of the law of nations is reflected in the ambivalence of Aquinas' formulae for *ius gentium* in two different articles of his *Summa theologiae.* In *ST* 1–2.95.4, Aquinas adheres to the authority of Isidore's *Etymologies* and places *ius gentium* under and as part of human positive law ("*Dividitur ius positivum in ius gentium et ius civile.*"). However, in *ST* 2–2.57.3, Aquinas turns back, behind the Christian teachers, to the classical Roman law sources, such as the *Digest* of the Justinian Codex, and quotes with approval the formula of the jurist Gaius that places *ius gentium* much more under natural law: "*Quod . . . naturalis ratio inter omnes homines constituit, id apud omnes peraeque custoditur, vocaturque ius gentium.*"

Human (Positive) Law (*Lex Humana*)

Human law, in close conformity with the natural law, is utterly indispensable in order to spell out in some specific detail the concrete implications of the very general principles of natural law as they come to be actually applied, through the moral virtue and practical wisdom of legisprudence or jurisprudence, to the ever-shifting scenario of sociocultural history in all its manifold varieties.

Insofar as it is in line with the precepts of natural law, human law is also at the same stroke to be seen as a subspecies of God's eternal law, along with concomitant cogency or obligatory invigoration—so much so that any act of disobedience to human law is above all a serious sin against divine law. Despite that "deification" of human law, and despite its indispensability as a supplementary specification (*determinatio*) of the natural law, human law can come into conflict with natural law, in which case it could forfeit its binding power. Indeed, Aquinas expressly holds that, to the extent that it deviates from the dictates of divine law, a given human law is not "law" at all, certainly not in the strict or strong sense of the word. Since it may be law in *some* significant sense, it is seen by Aquinas as *perhaps* entailing an obligation of civil obedience, at least outwardly (*in foro externo*), even if not strictly binding in conscience (*in foro interno*). However, this is true only if overt obedience to a perverted "law" would probably produce more net social good than the evil likely to result from *dis*obedience.

On the other hand, some perverse human laws not only *may* be disobeyed but *must* be disobeyed, in accordance with the evangelical injunction (of divine *positive* law) that one ought to obey God rather than men. In the event of conflict of human law with divine *natural* law (that is *not* also encompassed by divine positive law), there also arises in some situations a right and even an obligation of disobedience; for example, in a case of conflict between a given human law and the require-

ments of the "common good," the pursuit and promotion of which is the primary precept of natural law at the high level of sociopolitical instinct. What, then, is the "common" public or political good? According to Aquinas it is ultimately *the* Good: God himself as the common telos or ultimate end of spiritual creatures, as well as *the* legislator of all laws of nature precisely as *laws* in the strictest sense. Thus, in a case of callous conflict between *the* common good (man's *ultimate* good) and any strictly secular "common good," the natural law dictates disobedience to any and all purely humanist or counterfeit constructs of the "common good" in favor of an absolute allegiance to the City of God (*Civitas Dei*) governed by the Creator of all existence and all obligation.

References

Aquinas, Thomas. *On Law, Morality, and Politics*. Ed. William P. Baumgarth and Richard J. Regan. Indianapolis IN: Hackett, 1988.

———. *On the Truth of the Catholic Faith*. Trans. A.C. Pegis et al. 5 vols. New York: Doubleday, 1955–1957. Reprinted (under title *Summa contra Gentiles*), Notre Dame: University of Notre Dame Press, 1975. (For the section on "Laws" see vol. 3, pt. II, pp. 114–164.)

Brown, Oscar J. *Natural Rectitude and Divine Law in Aquinas*. Toronto: Pontifical Institute of Mediaeval Studies, 1981.

Kalinowski, Georges. "Le fondement objectif du droit d'après la Somme théologique de St.-Thomas d'Aquin (The objective Basis of Law in St. Thomas Aquinas' *Summa theologiae*)." *Archives de philosophie de droit* 18 (1973), 59–75.

Oscar J. Brown

Arbitration

Arbitration is a process where binding, private decision making is accomplished by agents in relation to the dispute of their principals. Arbitrators stand at the *threshold* between the world of private liberty and that of public constraint, borrowing as hybrids from both realms. In a liberty/constraint loop, disputants *freely* grant their agents the power of *constraining* them. This loop is a challenge for arbitrators and an *opportunity to demonstrate strong ethical qualities.*

Act of Birth: The Disputants' Liberty and the Private Temptation

As private agents, arbitrators owe their presence to private citizens who conclude that they cannot reach, either by negotiation or mediation, a common solution on a legal contention; they can only agree on their disagreement. Yet, despite this unresolved difference, the disputants make a last attempt to remain together in control of *their* law, as far as possible: they appoint their adjudicators at their expense, and sometimes also designate the applicable norms, being national laws, trade usages *(lex mercatoria),* equity, and so forth. In advance—through an arbitration clause—or in the heat of a dispute, the parties sign this ultimate possible contract, entrusting agents with the task of bridging a detrimental gap.

Having as an *act of birth* a world of liberty that is defined by others, arbitrators are thus *delegates,* linked by the terms of their mandate. This is the private foundation of all arbitration. In all their posterior acts, arbitrators must remember that principals are loath to be disappropriated beyond necessity from their law; even more, by resort to arbitration, disputants express the will to be quickly reempowered, by an appropriate solution, of *all* the law.

Principals' binding mandate may, however, proportionally reduce the maneuvering space of invention for the arbitrators, especially for nonneutral arbitrators, who may remain excessively dependent on their respective principals. In the extreme case, it could prevent any decision: hence, the need to introduce in this mandate the arbitrator's power of constraint.

Act of Growth: The Disputants' Constraint and the Public Temptation

On this *constraint side,* in order to fulfill the expectations of their principals who demand a decision, arbitrators are asked to free themselves from the original subordination of their act of birth, and to somehow take the lead. In this emancipation from the foundation, as an act of *growth,* authority and power transfer takes place from the principals, who hope to benefit from it, to the agents. It is up to the arbitrators to use accurately this transfer.

Arbitrators are invited to peer at the public world of litigation, of imposed decisions, of stable judgments from *above.* They are no more working "under," but "over" their principals, to transcend their possibly narrow criteria and frames of reference. They are identified with figures of authority whose anticipated and sometimes feared decision is surrounded by an aura of respect, expertise, and legitimacy. Arbitrators are supposed to see "beyond" what the parties perceive, to reach deeper diagnoses on causes of conflicts and a more accurate prognosis on ways of overcoming them.

In any case, arbitrators also become *trustees,* linking their principals by their solution, as long as they do not revoke together the mandate. Of course, if a mutually satisfactory solution is found—one that restores the relationship—it will be executed spontaneously by both. If there is a winner and a loser, the latter will be imposed the arbitral sentence, after public *exequatur* and often without possible appeal.

The danger, though, in this imposed solution is to cross the "private/public" threshold too blatantly; to dodge the issue, so that the creators do not recognize their creatures any more, leaving the agents estranged from the arbitrators' practices and sentences: the mandate has been fulfilled somehow "beyond the claims" *(ultra petita).* Procedure may have been perceived as heavy and long, and bureaucratic costs as high. As for the decision, it may well be publicly held as truth, but be privately inappropriate, namely, if the parties are unable to work together in the future.

Beyond the Loop: The Arbitrators' Working Principles

Arbitrators are therefore acrobats of decision making who must find the best of both private origin and public seal. They must continue to keep in mind the two poles of the loop, optimizing the advantages of both. They must bring the law back to the parties, as much as possible, *and* lead it to an acceptable solution, cancelling the "under"/"over" distinction, making the law for the people and at the same time the people partisan of this law. In order to achieve this challenge, arbitrators must carry on strong *ethical qualities* and empathize with the needs of their principals.

As the maxim goes, arbitration is worth what the arbitrators are worth. Like judges, arbitrators' double role is to actually investigate and resolve legal controversies in the least biased way. They can only perform these tasks if, first, before starting, arbitrators are not affiliated to one of the parties (independence) and, second, they have not expressed publicly their opinion about the case (impartiality). The absence of conflict of interests and of *apriorisms* are such important virtues that they are often legally required; they become all the more indispensable when legal norms, at the request of disputants, are discarded to only refer to considerations of equity. Other qualities can also build an arbitration's *ethos,* that is, reputation: expertise in the field at stake, reasonable fees, swift and diligent work, imagination, self-questioning.

When the procedure has started, precisely because it is potentially supple, arbitrators must have as a communication rule not only to protect the *principle of the contradictory,* as legal procedure requires, but *to orient* it in the direction of a shared solution. Arbitrators must invite principals and counsels to expose to their counterparts their understanding of facts, laws, needs, and objectives, and to interact in a real dialogue, which improves their relationship. These exchanges are also opportunities for the arbitrators to value both versions, to insist on the realized progress, and to rephrase some elements in more positive ways, so that both parties can progressively conceive of the appropriate solutions themselves. Here, the more respect arbitrators get and show, the more authority they accumulate, which they can then reorientate to make principals work on their differences. Arbitrators' qualities are those of efficient negotiators: they must be able to actively listen to the parties, grasp their commonplaces, while convincing them all along with arguments that appeal to them. These qualities reinforce the persuasive power of arbitrators and increase the likelihood of having their sentence agreeable to both principals.

By combining openness to principals' needs and subtle authority on them, arbitrators balance permanently questioning and answering, while encouraging principals to do the same. The goal is to search for and find solutions that fulfill the requirements of both equity and justice, of the good and the right, where the relationship and the laws are enhanced. A real success of arbitration can be measured by the capacity for principals to state themselves the solution at the end of the process, before the arbitrators do, the latter having provided a ladder to get there, suggesting some of its outlines, but always letting the

parties appropriate it. The arbitrators' highest achievement is to transform their authority of threshold into an incentive for renewed freedom of contract, getting out of the loop, avoiding the use of constraint. They return the law to where it belongs, to the people.

References

Bazerman, M.H. "Norms of Distributive Justice in Interest Arbitration." *Industrial and Labor Relations Review* 38 (1985), 558–570.

Brett, J., S.B. Goldberg, and W.L. Ury. *Managing Conflict: The Strategy of Dispute Systems Design.* New York: McGraw-Hill, 1994.

Cohen, D. *Arbitrage et Société* (Arbitration and Society). Paris: Librairie générale du droit et de jurisprudence, 1993.

Elkouri, F., and E. Elkouri. *How Arbitration Works.* Washington, DC: Bureau of National Affairs, 1981.

Fouchard, P. *L'Arbitrage commercial international* (International Commercial Arbitration). Paris: Sirey, 1965.

Kassis, A. *Problèmes de Base de l'Arbitrage en Droit comparé et en Droit international* (Fundamental Issues Regarding Arbitration in Comparative and International Law). Paris: Librairie du droit et de jurisprudence, 1987.

Neale, M.A., and M.H. Bazerman. "The Role of Perspective-Taking Ability in Negotiating under Different Forms of Arbitration." *Industrial and Labor Relations Review* 36 (1983), 378–388.

Oppetit, B. "Sur le concept d'arbitrage" (The Concept of Arbitration). In *Mélanges Goldman,* 229–239. Paris: Litec, 1987.

Shapiro, D., and J. Brett. "Comparing Three Processes Underlying Judgments of Procedural Justice: A Field Study of Mediation and Arbitration." *Journal of Personality and Social Psychology* 65 (1993), 1167–1177.

Alain Pekar Lempereur

See also DISPUTE RESOLUTION; MEDIATION, CRIMINAL

Argumentation

The role of rules provides the distinctive feature of legal argumentation: legal reasoning is fundamentally constrained by the framework of legal rules within which it takes place. The key to understanding legal reasoning is understanding why rules play such a prominent role. The answer lies in the link between legal reasoning and democratic legitimacy.

A government is legitimate when (and only when) its citizens—at least most of them—have a prima facie obligation to obey it. Thus, the state may compel conformity only when citizens who live up to their obligations would voluntarily obey anyway, assuming they realize the obligation exists (and have the capacity to conform their behavior to recognized obligations). It is a mainstay of classical democratic theory that citizens have a prima facie general obligation to obey the state only when the state is appropriately responsive to the will of the citizens. Appropriate responsiveness requires that citizens exercise personal sovereignty by electing legislators that represent (in some sense) the views and preferences of their electorate. The judiciary—and this is the crucial point—requires special treatment because it is not representative. The judiciary must consist of impartial decision makers, where impartiality consists, in part, precisely in not favoring the views and preferences of any distinct group of citizens. Even when judges are elected, they are not supposed to represent the views and preferences of their electorate in the way required of legislators. How can nonrepresentative judicial decision makers achieve legitimacy in a representative democracy?

The answer of classical democratic theory is that legitimacy requires that courts decide exclusively on the basis of determinations of rights, permissions, and prohibitions. It is essential that the determinations are not merely arbitrary strictures but are instead the products of legitimate political processes. (Circularity here is avoidable as long as *judicial* legitimacy is defined by appeal to an independently definable notion of legitimacy for *non*judicial processes, such as legislation.) It is also a standard part of democratic theory that the determinations are to be made *prior* to their use to decide a legal issue; otherwise, citizens subject to such determinations will lack notice of what rights, permissions, and prohibitions are to govern their behavior. Authoritative legal materials encode such determinations. Authoritative legal materials consist of all common law decisions not overruled, all statutes and administrative law rulings still in force, and all constitutional provisions. Such materials enshrine the results of past political decisions, and courts are institutionally required to decide in light of authoritative materials.

Clearly, if courts decided solely in light of authoritative legal materials, they would decide exclusively on the basis of prior determinations of rights, permissions, and prohibitions. Equally clearly, however, courts have recourse to reasons not supplied by the authoritative legal materials. Even a cursory examination of the realities of adjudication makes this plain. Consider criminal negligence. The problem of defining the degree of negligence necessary for criminal liability arises primarily in cases of involuntary manslaughter, where it is clear that the crime requires a higher degree of negligence than civil liability requires. The requisite degree of negligence proves difficult to define. The *Model Penal Code* offers the following explanation:

> A person acts negligently with respect to a material element of an offense when he should be aware of a substantial and unjustifiable risk that the material element exists or will result from his conduct. The risk must be of such a nature and degree that the actor's failure to perceive it, considering the nature and purpose of his conduct and the circumstances known to him, involves a gross deviation from the standard of care that a reasonable person would observe in the actor's situation.

If one wants to learn what criminal negligence is, it is not much help to be told that it involves a "gross deviation." What degree of deviation is "gross?" This is tantamount to the question What degree of negligence is criminal? The *Model Penal Code* does not offer a noncircular definition of criminal negligence. What it offers is a summary of the features relevant to the application of the concept. So how does one learn to recognize those features? One learns by example—that is, by reading (or otherwise becoming acquainted with) cases in which the terms are used. One applies the various terms "gross deviation," "reasonable person," "substantial and unjustifiable risk" against a background of prior applications. A correct application must be relevantly like prior applications or a justifiable deviation from prior applications.

Such judgments of relevant likeness require a context, and the relevant context consists of the background moral and political culture in which the court is embedded. Our views about what counts as criminal negligence are linked in intricate and systematic ways to moral and political views—views about what degree of caution people typically should employ, about the extent to which the state can use the power of the criminal law to punish behavior, about what kind of behavior calls for criminal as opposed to civil sanctions, about the extent to which people have voluntary control over their actions, and so on. As we change the related views, we change what we count as criminal negligence. This is why a court, in determining what counts as criminal negligence, must reach beyond the authoritative legal materials.

These observations about criminal negligence illustrate a general truth; indeed, they reflect a general feature of language. Words do not have meaning in isolation. Words and the concepts they express generally stand in a network of relations to other words and concepts. Change the network of relations sufficiently, and the meanings of the words and redefine the concepts they express are changed. Legal terms and concepts are not somehow exempt from this fundamental feature of language. The network of words and concepts that guides our legal classifications and judgments does not conveniently divide itself into a "legal" and a "moral/political" part, where the latter part is somehow severable and can be discarded as one crosses into the courtroom.

United States v. Escamilla, 467 F2d 341 (4th Cir 1972) illustrates the point. The lower court convicted Escamilla of involuntary manslaughter for killing someone on T-3, "an island of glacial ice . . . which meanders slowly about the general area of the Arctic Ocean." The appeals court reversed, remarking that "[i]t would seem plain that what is negligent or grossly negligent conduct in the Eastern District of Virginia may not be negligent or grossly negligent on T-3 when it is remembered that T-3 has no governing authority, no police force, is relatively inaccessible to the rest of the world, lacks medical facilities and the dwellings thereon lack locks—in short, that absent self-restraint on the part of those stationed on T-3 and effectiveness of the group leader, T-3 is a place where no recognized means of law enforcement exist and each man looks to himself for the immediate enforce-

ment of his rights." The appeals court treats its holding in *Escamilla* as a justifiable deviation from its normal treatment of criminal negligence. Where does the court find its reasons for thinking that the deviation is justifiable? The appeal is to background moral and political views in light of which one is justified in looking to oneself for the "the immediate enforcement of [one's] rights" when "no recognized means of law enforcement exist." The entire decision depends crucially on reasons drawn from the background moral and political culture.

Some may object that the example is atypical since it involves a case for which there was no applicable precedent. Where precedent does apply, it should obviate the need to look outside the authoritative legal materials for legal reasons. The point to emphasize is that precedent simply represents a past interpretive judgment about what legal words and concepts mean, a judgment made with recourse to the background moral and political culture. Precedent represents a blend of the authoritative legal materials and the relevant moral and political culture. To find a source of legal reasons in precedent is to acknowledge, not to reject, the moral and political culture as a source of grounds for legal decisions.

The conclusion is inescapable: the background moral and political culture serves as an essential source of legal reasons. The problem is that this conclusion calls judicial legitimacy into question. Legitimacy, at least in the classical liberal conception, requires that courts base their decisions on prior determinations of rights, permissions, and prohibitions, determinations achieved by legitimate political processes. How can judicial decisions meet this demand when they rest essentially on grounds found in the background moral and political culture? What legitimate political process generated existing cultural views about rights, permissions, and prohibitions? Indeed, are there widely shared cultural views? Could our culture be characterized by widespread disagreement on fundamental moral and political matters?

This issue of judicial legitimacy is one focal point of jurisprudential discussions of legal reasoning. Some minimize the problem, claiming (quite dubiously) that courts only rarely reach out for reasons into the background moral and political culture. H.L.A. Hart, Lon Fuller, and Ronald Dworkin debate this claim.

At the other extreme, some, such as Joseph Singer, see courts as constantly employing background moral/political reasons and, on this ground, doubt the classical liberal legitimacy of such decisions. The broad middle ground between these extremes is home to a variety of views, among them Ronald Dworkin's and Steven Burton's. Dworkin contends that the courts' use of background reasons is consistent with the requirements of classical liberal legitimacy. Burton defends a similar claim but on quite different grounds, and argues that the requirement of *prior* determinations of rights, permissions, and prohibitions must be abandoned.

References

Altman, Andrew. *Critical Legal Studies: A Liberal Critique*. Princeton: Princeton University Press, 1990.

American Law Institute. *Model Penal Code and Commentaries*. Philadelphia: American Law Institute Press, 1985.

Burton, Steven. *Judging in Good Faith*. Cambridge: Cambridge University Press, 1992.

Dworkin, Ronald. *Law's Empire*. Cambridge MA: Harvard University Press, 1986.

———. *Taking Rights Seriously*. Cambridge MA: Harvard University Press, 1977.

Finnis, John. *Natural Law and Natural Rights*. Oxford: Clarendon Press, 1982.

Fuller, Lon L. "Positivism and Fidelity to Law—A Reply to Professor Hart." *Harvard Law Review* 71 (1958).

Hart, H.L.A. *The Concept of Law*. Oxford: Clarendon Press, 1961.

Raz, Joseph. *Practical Reason and Norms*. London: Hutchinson, 1975.

Singer, Joseph. "Legal Realism Now." *California Law Review* 76 (1988).

Warner, Richard. "Why Pragmatism?: The Puzzling Place of Pragmatism in Critical Theory." *University of Illinois Law Review* (1993).

Richard Warner

Aristotle (384–322 B.C.)

Aristotle is, after Plato, the first thinker in antiquity whose extant writings address all the main problems in the philosophy of law. He put foward a detailed theory of justice, discussed the foundations of civil and political society, criticized the various forms of a constitutional system of government, and examined, on the basis of extensive historical and anthropological research, all aspects of community life in a legal state.

Most of his doctrines on the subject are found in his *Politics, Nicomachean Ethics* (mainly in Book V, devoted to justice) and *Rhetoric* (in the chapters dealing with judicial proceedings).

Aristotle's thought had a profound and unrivaled influence throughout antiquity and the middle ages, during which time it inspired, among others, the Christian doctrines of Thomas Aquinas. Roger Bacon claimed that he would give up all the Latin jurisconsults for Aristotle's only book on justice. During the Renaissance, especially after Niccolò Machiavelli, new movements appeared which were often in very hostile opposition to Aristotle. Embraced by Jean Bodin, defended by Gottfried Leibniz against Thomas Hobbes and the contractualists, Aristotle influenced German theories of natural law until the eighteenth century, but has been thought of ever since as something of an antimodern thinker. His rediscovery by many contemporary thinkers (M. Villey, L. Strauss, E. Voegelin, J. Ritter, H. Kuhn, A. MacIntyre) is not without misunderstandings.

The interpretation of Aristotle's texts is often open to dispute, but there can be no ambiguity on the following points. Aristotle recommends a legal state, based on a system of public law, in order that "only the intellect rule," that is, in order to safeguard the practice of enlightened government from the whims of passion. Furthermore, he recognizes, seemingly without reservation, that justice is formally what the laws ordain, on the double proviso that they be in keeping with the principles of the constitution and that the constitution itself be righteous.

The first proviso, the "constitutionality of the laws," which jurists to this day uphold, corresponds to a rational requirement: the laws must be consistent with the political tendency (for example, republican) which forms the basis of the constitutional system in place. For Aristotle, however, such a requirement appears relative: this condition is compelling only if the political system itself is righteous. The principle of concordance does admit of infractions when it is done in order to redress a corrupt system. Aristotle criticized, from this point of view, the legislation of various cities that he had studied. In other words, it is not sufficient that a legislation be rational (that is, coherent with the constitution) for it to be commendable. Hence the second condition: in order for a law to promote justice, it must also be answerable to the principle of a righteous constitution. This higher principle of rectitude compels the constitutional system to serve the interests of all its citizens, rather than the interest of a ruling faction, be the latter the majority or a minority. Thus, for Aristotle, a majority which, in a democracy, subjugates a minority to serve its own interests leads to an unjustifiable popular despotism. For the end of the state would then be betrayed, given that this end consists in the well-being of all of its citizens, none of whom should become the instrument of another's happiness.

The theorists of natural law that subsequently used Aristotle as their authority have often tried to find universal norms capable of assessing what is just and of criticizing the law either in nature or in the principles of natural reason. This is today the case of philosophers unsatisfied with a narrow conception of legal positivism. Consider the case of a critique of laws which proceeds in the light of an interpretation of other more fundamental laws, which are themselves open to interpretation. Either this critique avoids normative jurisprudence, but then it is open to David Hume's objection regarding the "is" and "ought" distinction; or it inevitably becomes a matter of normative jurisprudence, as Ronald Dworkin believes, in which case the critique must look elsewhere than in positive law for its foundations.

Aristotle is alert to the problem, and at first sight his principle of the constitutionality of the law ranks him among the positivist supporters of an interpretative, as opposed to normative, jurisprudence. In Aristotle's opinion, therefore, the laws' shortcoming—due to their excessive generality—requires a hermeneutical remedy that will ensure equity. But this remedy, far from being a higher norm, or appealing to one, must express what the legislator's original intent was in writing the law and what his judgment would have been in this particular case, based upon the law itself and taking into account that the maxim the legislator follows is deficient by virtue of its generality. Similarly, all new laws must be based upon those fundamental rules that define the form of the constitutional system of government in place. Moreover, the principle of constitutional righteousness (that is, fundamental justice) is Aristotle's answer to Hume's objection, by appealing to a higher principle that disallows, in the name of justice, certain distorted forms of constitutional systems. Aristotle thus seems to follow a path which brings him close to the position of natural law theorists.

There are indications that Aristotle was heading in this direction. The "natural" is not for him what is characteristic of all laws; far from it. Legislation can by sheer convention, for example, decree as just what is in principle either unconcerned with or alien to nature (for instance, the weekly day of rest, the monetary standard, borders established by international treaty). Against the opinion of those for whom all law is conventional, the philosopher maintains the existence of a "natural" law, which he claims "has the same capacity everywhere," though it may vary from one positive legislation to another. Unfortunately, the substance of Aristotle's thought is not very clear on this matter. Does this entail that some universal unwritten law must inspire the different but analogous legislations adopted from one country to the next? It is possible, but scholars are hopelessly divided on this question. The following comments are therefore necessary in order to dispel some misunderstandings.

First of all, the idea of an unwritten natural law, which Aristotle endorses elsewhere as common to all people, even where neither community nor contract between men exists, seems to refer to a form of "law of peoples" (*jus gentium*). Implicitly yet universally recognized, this law, which is not peculiar to any one state, and which no state decrees for its own citizens, can sometimes be invoked in court against certain positive laws that appear to transgress it. As such, it does not have the status of a higher norm that should generate positive laws in the different legal communities. In short, it seems to be the source not of positive law, but precisely of what positive law does not ordain.

Furthermore, unlike classical rationalism, either kantian or neo-kantian (John Rawls), Aristotle does not consider deducing a priori his higher criterion of justice from universal principles of pure reason. The requirement of the common good is his criterion. This requirement is not to be understood exactly as the communitarian principle to which liberals object. No doubt the requirement in question leads Aristotle to assert the priority of whole (the state) over its parts (individuals or groups of individuals), but only in the sense that the preservation of the whole is the only guarantee of the well-being of the parts. The concern for the common good, which distinguishes good systems from bad, is here identical to that of excluding no citizen from the legislator's consideration and of deeming no citizen a mere instrument at the service of the interests of the ruling party.

However, as in the kantian perspective, there is a formal requirement. It makes no presumption as to the actual content of the positive laws that may fulfill it, and which in reality can be fulfilled by different constitutional systems (monarchic, aristocratic, republican). This possibilty is likely one of the essential points of Aristotle's thought. In other words, within the limits of higher justice, there is room for a variety of equally upright political systems and, hence, for a variety of positive legislation, all equally just without qualification in spite of their differences. Of course, within these limits, the question of which constitutional systems is best remains open. This question is not set at rest by the philosopher when he enumerates the main legislative dispositions to be decreed in the auspicious but very uncertain eventuality that all the preliminary conditions to the founding of a perfect state (geographic, climatic, demographic, economic, cultural conditions, and so forth) are fulfilled. This question has nothing to do with the question of law and justice pure and simple, which it assumes resolved. Rather, this question amounts to asking which system of government is preferable among those that can satisfy the requirement of higher justice, since many can satisfy it. Hence, by answering that the best system of government is always the one which, depending on the circumstances, is objectively best suited to those it rules, Aristotle does not in any way settle the question of justice.

The law, according to Aristotle, is partly a question of convention. However, he maintains in partial agreement with the contractualists, that the law cannot establish a just system if it remains blind to the imperative of the common good, although this imperative can be met by various systems of government. These facts are probably sufficient for an understanding of the sense in which Aristotle speaks of natural law. If the latter, as he

claims, is not immutable, it is precisely because just laws can vary according to constitutional systems, which come in many forms and may present an infinite number of individual characteristics. If, on the other hand, natural law is natural in that it has "the same capacity everywhere," this is precisely because these different laws have the virtue of always giving rise to a just state. Nothing in this thought implies a reference to a natural and transcendent norm that positive law should imitate, as seen in Plato. The law, Aristotle states elsewhere, imitates nothing at all.

Thus Aristotle has indeed stated a universal a priori principle of justice, but one that is not deduced from natural reason. It is rather based upon a conception of the end of the state, which consists in ensuring the well-being of all those who live in it. Furthermore, Aristotle does not hold an idea of "natural reason," which was later expounded by the stoics, and subsequently by the thomists who nevertheless claimed to draw their inspiration from aristotelianism. According to Aristotle, the principle of justice is not naturally etched in the minds of all the legislators, and if its scope remains universal, it nevertheless does not entail that it is the universal principle—even the implicit principle—of all those who legislate. It is only the principle of those who legislate correctly. It is not even, it seems, an absolute principle that one can oppose to the law without reservation, since for Aristotle the law, even when counter to nature, remains the law. If nature or the interest of all citizens suggests the need for an abrogation of a law, it does not sanction disobedience to this law, nor, more generally, revolutionary action. Aristotle is firmly opposed to revolutionary action, even against tyranny, and favors reforms without insurrection.

The antimodernism of Aristotle's position stems from the fact that universal liberty and universal equality are not the norms of the law. While for the moderns a law is worthy of its name if, and only if, it conforms to the principle that all men are free and equal, for Aristotle a law worthy of its name is confined to the relationship between men who are de facto free and equal. However, for Aristotle, no principle can establish a priori that all men are naturally free and equal. Unlike modern egalitarianism, Aristotle considers a posteriori the natural differences between men as so profound and sometimes so evident that they undermine all strictly lawful relationships between them. Contemporary thought, in particular feminist thinkers, are not about to forgive him this type of thesis. And his position concerning "natural slavery" is reputed to bear the stamp of a devious ideology. Aristotle's view is that some men possess a servile nature. Incapable of the foresight necessary to rule themselves, they are entirely dependent upon others, to whom they volunteer their manual labor in order to obtain sustenance. It is often forgotten that his judgment on this matter is coupled with a disavowal of purely legal and naturally unfounded slavery, which led the Greeks to institutionalize the right of the conqueror over the vanquished in war. Unlike the legal but inhumane measures that, for whatever reason, infringe upon certain subjects' capacity for autonomy, the willingness to recognize a servile nature partakes of the properly humanitarian concern to compensate for the incapacity of certain subjects for autonomy. The goal is to provide the latter with the authority they lack by nature in the person of an appropriate master who will care for them as if they were a part of himself. Justice is rendered, Aristotle believes, if, and only if, the interest of the naturally servile subject (a subject, therefore, made for serving) is assured in this way.

In spite of this, even the more just relations between a master and a slave are not, strictly speaking, legal relations; they are, rather, personal and based on friendship precisely because the de facto equality necessary to a legal relationship does not exist. Ultimately, for Aristotle as for the moderns, equality and liberty constitute principles of law, but in very different senses. Contrary to reality, the principle that all men are naturally equal and free cannot constitute for Aristotle the norm of the law. However, the principle that submits the law to a requirement of equality necessarily enters into the equation, since it is a matter of determining the relations between men who are equal and free in a righteous political society based on the law. Within these limits Aristotle's theory of justice continues to be of great interest.

First of all, on the political level, Aristotle is unwilling to believe that the law, and hence legislation, can determine the relationship between a monarch and his subjects, if the monarch has an undeniable superiority over his subjects, for the inequality between them entails that one gives everything and the others receive everything. Hence, the monarch and the subjects share nothing. Their relationship is consequently exempt from the principle of so-called distributive justice, which stipulates that each must receive according to one's due, or according to one's merit. However, the law decreed by the monarch for the subjects, who are more or less equal, institutes a legal relationship between these subjects, just like the one which the law institutes between men who are more or less equal in a nonmonarchical system. In this latter case, constitutional law itself conforms to the rules of distributive justice, which demands for each one's due, if each of the equal subjects is allotted an equal share of power. Political opposition, Aristotle believes, stems from a narrow egalitarianism, according to which equality in one respect is equivalent to equality pure and simple.

On the nonpolitical level, where it is a matter of distributing not power, honor, or office, but rather wealth or punishment, for example, the law also requires respect for equality. Justice, Aristotle believes, aims at making the benefits or penalties proportional to merit or need, that is, proportional to the capacity of the people that receive them. Taxation, for example, must be proportional to wealth, punishment proportional to offenses committed, social benefits proportional to poverty, rewards proportional to services rendered, and so on. In this way an egalitarianism that distributes the numerically identical benefits to each individual would constitute a form of injustice. Disregarding differences between individuals, it always assigns too much to one and too little to another. The aim of justice, on the contrary, is to correct excesses of this sort. Justice does not establish equality between individuals; rather, it determines the equality of relations that exist between individuals and what is due to them. Aristotle thinks justice is egalitarian in that it takes as exact equivalents, for example, two different levels of salary that remunerate two equally different services.

Distributive justice is therefore first and foremost attentive to the inequality of those who are entitled to some form of distribution (a baker and an architect whose salaries must be determined, for example). Similarly, "commutative" justice, which governs the exchange of goods, is first and foremost mindful of the inequality of the goods exchanged (a loaf of bread in exchange for a house, for example). On this point, justice requires that these goods be commensurable (determining the number of loaves needed for a house), and that is done by expressing it in some sort of monetary unit. Aristotle implies that the exchange value, the price, is normally determined in accordance with needs, which can naturally vary for certain goods but not for others. This allows for the resale of the goods acquired, at a profit or at a loss. Aristotle does not discuss the justice of these losses or gains; he is content to claim that a fair exchange requires obtaining as much as one gives—as much, in other words, equally.

Equality is, indeed, the key word of his theory on the various forms of justice and key concept of law. Unlike modern thinkers, however, Aristotle's theory resolutely turns its back on all the perspectives of egalitarianism.

References

Bodéüs, Richard. "Deux propositions aristotéliciennes sur le droit naturel chez les continentaux d'Amérique" (Two Aristotelean Conclusions on Natural Law for Native Peoples of the Americas). *Revue de métaphysique et de morale* 94 (1989), 369–389.

Everson, Stephen. "Aristotle on the Foundations of the State." *Political Studies* 36 (1988), 89–101.

Hamburger, M. *Morals and Law: The Growth of Aristotle's Legal Theory.* New Haven: Yale University Press, 1951.

Keyt, David. "Distributive Justice in Aristotle's *Ethics* and *Politics*." *Topoi*, 4 (1985), 23–45.

Keyt, David, and Fred Miller, Jr., eds. *A Companion to Aristotle's Politics.* Oxford: Blackwell, 1991.

Leyden, Walter von. *Aristotle on Equality and Justice.* London: Macmillan, 1985.

Lord, Carnes, and David O'Connor, eds. *Essays on the Foundations of Aristotle's Political Science.* Berkeley: University of California Press, 1991.

Salomon, Max. *Der Begriff der Gerechtigkeit bei Aristoteles* (Aristotle's Concept of Justice). New York: Arno, 1957.

Schroeder, Donald. "Aristotle on Law." *Polis* 4 (1981), 17–31.

Winthrop, Delba. "Aristotle and Theories of Justice." *American Political Science Review* 72 (1978), 1201–1217.

Yack, Bernard. "Natural Right and Aristotle's Understanding of Justice." *Political Theory* 18 (1990), 216–237.

Richard Bodéüs

Array Theory

Array theory is an effort to find common ground among supporters of liberalism, socialism, and libertarianism. Array theory proposes the establishment of a few cooperating polities rather than a single unitary political state. As such, it belongs to the family of theories of governmental structures that recommend federation, confederation, and alliances or leagues of nations. Array theory is distinct in that it does not argue for divisions based on religion or ethnicity or on such forms of government as monarchy, varieties of democracy, or aristocracy. Rather, array theory calls for polities to be differentiated by fundamental moral positions and for citizens to choose to live in the polity that they find morally most suitable. Moreover, citizens are permitted to migrate later to another polity, since over time they or the constitutions of their polities may change. The context of the array is that of an irremediable moral pluralism that is limited by shared values that motivate all parties to avoid oppression of citizens, support individual autonomy, and favor toleration. The proposal, then, is for something like a welfare or moderate socialist state, a liberal state, and a libertarian state. The size of the public sector and its role in supporting the well-being of citizens would thus be the main differentiating factor. This proposal, then, belongs to ideal theory, but there are also practical applications of its core values even if the array is not established.

Array theory arises in the context of the theories of John Rawls and Robert Nozick and their commentators.

Rawls' theory differentiates between the great variety of conceptions of the good and what he perceives to be the shared underlying justice—values from which we in our political culture can build a consensus on the basic principles which are to specify the terms of cooperation among free and equal citizens. Critics of Rawls have doubted that there are suitable shared justice-values and claim that conflicts are unresolvable for the foreseeable future, a situation which would prevent Rawls' consensus. At best there would remain what Rawls refers to as a *modus vivendi* agreement, one which each party will terminate when it judges that it can prevail over its opponents. More likely, many citizens will be sufficiently disaffected to reject this more precarious agreement and resort to some form of principled resistance to the laws of the state or to withdrawal from political participation. To counter any illegal resistance, government oppression will need to be established. This plight of the ideologically homeless is an embarrassment to Rawls' position, and it is at this point that the plural polities of the array model become relevant as a solution.

The voluntary associations in Nozick's ideal libertarian polity include those that happen to arise as a result of individual initiative. A voluntary community owns the land and wealth that it has justly acquired, but this wealth may or may not be adequate to sustain viability. There is no large-scale planning to insure that suitable alternatives are available for almost everyone, and more generally no one has a duty to help others. Since the dynamics of community membership are those of the market, no one has the right to be admitted to any association. The weak may not be admitted to a community devoted to sharing wealth. The contrast with array theory is clear, since the array proposal seeks to plan for and provide viable options. Array theory hopes, however, to find support among libertarians, since in the array they will be able to live in their preferred polity.

The basic values that underlie the array proposal are those of respect for others, toleration of diversity, and generosity motivated by a concern for the well-being of all others. Given the persistent moral pluralism assumed by this theory, the location of some shared values is essential as part of the justification for the array. The array theory requires a minimal respect leading to a willingness to forgo attacks on the person and property of others. Similarly, only a moderate capacity for toleration is needed, since the rejected ways of life are being practiced in another polity where they are not seen by those hostile to them. The required measure of generosity and charity is also modest. The libertarians need not support the ill and the poor who live in the array territory, but they must agree to the array grant of land for a welfare state where they will be cared for. Perhaps also they will need to make a one-time payment to the receiving polity

when one of their ill or disabled citizens emigrates. The libertarians may agree to this assistance, not because they agree that they have a duty to help others but because they find the cost of the array compromise acceptable given that most array inhabitants disagree with the libertarian view.

A minimal array government may be needed to handle defense of the array territory and issues of commerce and migration among member polities. Severe limitations on the scope of this government are required in order not to violate the integrity of the array states. Perhaps an array of states might function well without such a formal supranational government. A quasi-government akin to Nozick's might arise from limited multilateral treaties and accompanying conventions.

Critics of the array theory may first of all object that the array outcome represents failure, since the proper goal of political theory is to find grounds for a unitary state rather than to accede to fragmentation. In reply, the array theorist challenges nationalistic common sense, which always calls for unification or reunification and the avoidance of balkanization. A resolution that calls for cooperative separation is certainly not a failure and may represent an important success in a given situation.

Second, the critic may object that as the array functions, migration may lead to the overpopulation of one or more of the array states. Reapportionment of the land would seem to be the solution, but this process will doubtless be a troubled one if indeed member states agree to it at all. Again, the supporter of the array proposal may not have a simple answer here but only hopes that ways could be worked out to prevent the array from crashing. Of course, if one state does become the moral choice of almost everyone in the wider array, then the array can simply transform itself into this single state.

Third, in view of the trend toward a global economy, the ability of an array state to control its national economy in the name of a particular set of values (or ideology) may be severely limited. The most capable citizens may not be content with the relative poverty that may accompany the needed economic restrictions. Only the libertarian state would find itself at home in the hypercompetitive world economy. This difficulty, of course, is one that afflicts current nations, and replies to this objection would have to enter into complex specific issues. The array supporter would have to hope that this reply could justify some kind of economic independence.

The main objection, perhaps, is that the array proposal is utopian and completely impractical. This same objection, of course, applies to the theories of both Rawls and Nozick. But all of these theories attempt to deal with humans as they find them and hope to avoid being consigned to science-fiction scenarios. In any case, perhaps there is some useful role for what is, relatively speaking, utopian dreaming, which may provide us with wider horizons and deeper insight into our situation and its difficulties. Part of this deeper insight is reached through values clarification. For example, if only through contrast, issues of rights, restrictions, and privileges for Native Americans on reservations are illuminated by array theory, as discussed by Will Kymlicka. And at one level, at least, the array proposal is more practical than those of Rawls and Nozick, since it seems likely to gain support more easily in our morally pluralistic world. Finally, array values may help to promote a useful real-world partition of land or even encourage array-like emigration and immigration among a group of nearby states sharing some significant level of common culture. Rather than several states with radical and aggressive dissidents seeking to undermine their respective governments, we might encourage the states to differentiate to the needed degree so that dissidents would be content to migrate to a state where they will feel morally at home. "Voting with your feet" is an array value that can be useful, perhaps, in many situations outside a full and formal array of states.

The array theory offers a proposal that may or may not in the future be practical, but an understanding of moral pluralism and the array values furthers the task of values clarification and suggests, perhaps, solutions to some current problems among or within states.

References

Abegg, Edmund. "An Array Alternative to Rawlsian Consensus." Presented to Amintaphil meeting, 1990.
———. "An Array Model for the Consent of the Governed." Presented to the American Philosophical Association, Central Division meeting, May 1986.
Kymlicka, Will. *Liberalism, Community and Culture.* Oxford: Oxford University Press, 1989.
Nozick, Robert. *Anarchy, State, and Utopia.* New York: Basic Books, 1974.
Rawls, John. *Liberalism.* New York: Columbia University Press, 1993.

Edmund Abegg

Art
See AESTHETICS

Artificial Intelligence and Networks

Artificial intelligence in law includes the effort to model computer programs after practices of authoritative and professional legal actors, taking into account specific legal tasks, as well as theories of jurisprudence and computer science.

Computer science's early years were marked by great prophecy of replacing tasks of human thought and action with digital information processors. Artificial intelligence (AI) is that branch attempting to create software that mimics human cognitive and decision-making abilities. The disciplines of psychology, neurology, linguistics, philosophy, and mathematics provided foundations for theoretical models of human intelligence. Lofty early goals of AI research (for example, modeling the human brain) proved overly ambitious, and efforts were channeled to the still challenging project of emulating specific intelligent processes.

Central to this shift was the notion that intelligence can be conceptualized and ultimately realized in a distinct "sector of space-time (black box)"; an AI must stand alone, process input, make decisions, and learn. Positive, or formalist, legal theory aligns with AI in this sense, positing that law is embodied in another black box, one of rules from constitutions, statutes, administrative rulings and announcements, case opinions, and other authoritative texts.

Classical and connectionist AI legal expert systems have been constructed on positivist legal theory. Law provided AI with a body of knowledge and practice which had been compartmentalized by positivism, and distinguished from individual or social forces by adhering to the notion that law is the objective, yet "right," product of reasoned, rational, procedurally correct methods. Positive law, then, is a system of authoritative and procedural rules, expert knowledge as to the categorization and interpretation of rules and facts, and heuristics for applying rules to fact.

The two primary prongs of AI/law research are understanding and modeling aspects of legal reasoning and the construction of "smart" tools to aid legal workers. They are deeply interwoven, as the legal worker must function in an institutional world where actors behave pursuant to underlying assumptions of how law works, its nature, and what makes it right. Therefore, AI researchers utilize legal theory, yet question it vigorously, especially with respect to methods of reasoning and knowledge representation. To create software models of legal practices AI researchers systematically define legal terms and process components, their interrelations, and their role in case decisions. This rigor has led to a level of definitional specificity and process deconstruction not before attained in legal theory. AI researchers have attempted to do what social science has long struggled with: to test theories of law.

Classical AI legal expert systems use several reasoning methods: rule based, case based with hypotheticals, and hybrids which attempt to be sensitive to the open-textured nature of legal concepts. Their knowledge bases are drawn from legal texts and codes, established interpretations, and the iterative process of case disposition.

Rule-based systems assume that legal decisions, or at least parts of them, are the products of applying rules to fact pursuant to the experience of legal experts. They code the relevant knowledge of legal experts as heuristics, sequences of if-then statements, which consume certain case facts, producing weighted outcomes, not a computationally right, wrong, or final answer. Rules can conflict or be indeterminate; they also struggle with the open-textured nature of some legal concept. Therefore, to supplement the formal if-then structure of rule based systems, AI research attempted to fit reason and rules more loosely.

Case-based and hypothetical expert systems derive knowledge from case history, stare decisis, and legal texts and codes. They are data bases that have been coded by experts so as to represent a case's relevancy to supplied search terms, keywords, or most importantly other cases or legal doctrines. Systems design-ers assume legal reasoning is the "finding" of established legal principles and methodologies, as constructed by unfolding case law and stare decisis, and applying new cases to them.

Hypotheticals are used when a legal actor or decision maker cannot find a sufficiently relevant event in case law. The United States Supreme Court structures much of oral argument and discourse between bench and counsel upon hypotheticals. Justices use hypotheticals to query counsel as to the implications of counsel's view of the legal issue or principle at hand. The creative nature of this intelligent act poses one of AI's great challenges.

Machine learning and neural networks are at the forefront of AI connectionist efforts to better approach biological realism in intelligence. Connectionist AI systems have multiple processes occurring simultaneously, each linked, each enhanced or dampened by feedback representing the processes' usefulness to system function. Processes represent different parts of a single task (for example, legal information retrieval), and usefulness depends upon accuracy and user satisfaction.

Traditional expert systems are founded on the metaphor of mind as machine, processing inputs by adhering to established procedure and interpretation. The positivism of expert systems stakes a claim to knowledge in the abstract, without context other than relevant procedural norms and facts. Expert knowledge is the product of positive rules (i.e., sources of law), established and agreed upon interpretations of those rules, and their case-by-case application in a referential circle of reinforcement. Positivism is challenged because of just such a reliance on formal sources of rules and legal knowledge. Where positivists claimed that law comes from the formal black letter of statute or constitution, and the iteration of cases, others view law as creative, as environmentally situated, and legal reasoning as the contextually sensitive act of justifying what a legal actor does, not the discovery of truth or right reason.

Sensitivity to individual, social, cultural, and political context is central to other, antiformalist, theories of law (for example, realism-behavioralism, law and society, law and semiotics, law and economics, neo-natural law, critical legal studies, feminist jurisprudence). AI research and legal theory share concerns over the contingent nature of knowledge, the indeterminacy and malleability of language, and culture-bound constructs of power and right.

Interactionist theories of intelligence and action are inherently situated in a social/cultural/political context. Intelligence, like law, is not a distinct abstraction, or independent phenomenon, but rather is the dynamic interaction between individual and environment. AI research in law continues to utilize established methods (that is, rule based, case based) because aspects of legal practice are best positively construed and relatively context free; to model larger and more complex legal acts, however, will require the development of interactionist systems that incorporate those methods.

References

Carter, Licf. *Reason in Law*. New York: Harper Collins College Publishers, 1994.

Collins, H.M. *Artificial Experts*. Cambridge: Massachusetts Institute of Technology Press, 1991.

Crevier, Daniel. *AI: The Tumultuous History of the Search for Artificial Intelligence*. New York: Basic Books, 1993.

Gardner, Anne. *An AI Approach to Legal Reasoning*. Cambridge: Massachusetts Institute of Technology Press, 1987.

Murphy, Jeffrie G., and Jules G. Murphy. *The Philosophy of Law*. Boulder CO: Westview Press, 1990.

Narayanan, Ajit, and Mervyn Bennun, eds. *Law, Computer Science, and AI*. Norwood NJ: Ablex, 1991.

Rissland, Edwina. "Artificial Intelligence and Law: Stepping Stones to a Model of Legal Reasoning." *Yale Law Journal* 99 (1990), 1957.

Silverman, Alexander. *Mind, Machine, and Metaphor*. Boulder CO: Westview Press, 1993.

Way, Eileen Cornell. *Knowledge, Representation, and Metaphor*. Boston: Kluwer Academic Publishers, 1991.

Alan C. Gaitenby

Asian Philosophy of Law
See JAPANESE AND ASIAN PHILOSOPHY OF LAW

Asylum and Refugees
The right to apply for asylum is one of the basic human liberties in the *Universal Declaration of Human Rights* (Article 14), while the right to be granted asylum is, according to international law, up to the discretion of each nation-state. Few countries will deny that they have a moral responsibility to receive refugees and grant asylum, but the number of refugees that different countries feel obliged to receive varies. The 1951 Geneva Convention gives the signatories a legal obligation to abstain from returning asylum seekers to countries where they risk persecution or risk being sent to such countries (the nonrefoulement principle), and to investigate claims for asylum from those asylum seekers who are situated on their territory. The legal duties of the nation-state toward asylum seekers situated outside the territory of the state are, on the other hand, practically nonexistent. A more complicated question, legally as well as morally, is whether nation-states are entitled to prevent asylum seekers from reaching their borders as a means of limiting the number of claims for asylum that the states would otherwise be obliged to consider. This is precisely the overall goal of the asylum policy of the governments in the asylum-granting countries today. A range of legal measures are used to accomplish this. The implementation of many of these restrictive measures, as well as the dominating role of the state administrations in the policymaking in this field, raises legal as well as moral problems.

One fundamental question is whether the need of the foreigner for entry or residency, for reasons like starvation, persecution, unemployment, or political or social needs, may outweigh the "national interests" of the state to limit immigration. Would it be reasonable to demand that the number of asylum seekers each state receives be decided after a balancing of the capacity of the receiving state against the need of the persons in question? This would qualify the absolute sovereignty of the state to decide the entry requirements of aliens and thereby conflict with today's traditional legal thinking.

The Triple Role of Government in Asylum Policy
The laws passed by the legislature in the field of asylum and migration policies are often of a very general or procedural kind, leaving it to the state administration to give the laws "content." In this way, many of the lawmaking functions are passed over from the politicians

in the national assembly to the state administration. As a result, many important policy decisions involved in the lawmaking process are today made by the state administration. Later, when the laws are authorized, the political aspects are rephrased in a legal language, giving an appearance of political neutrality. When applications for asylum are denied by the immigration authorities, the rejections are justified by reference to the "requirements of the 1951 Refugee Convention," bypassing in silence that it is the same administration which has interpreted the requirements for refugee status in such a way that the cases in question do not satisfy the criteria.

The executive branch of government has not only the legislative functions just described, but certain judicial functions as well. One may say that the state administration to a certain degree also takes on the role of a judge when applications for asylum are turned down in the first instance and appeals are handled by the same bureaucracy at a higher level, as is quite often the case. To the extent that the governmental interpretation of the Geneva Convention is accepted by the judiciary when claims for asylum are brought to court, the state administration, as one of the parties of the trial, decides indirectly the outcome of the case. One may ask whether the separation of the legislative, judiciary, and executive powers is a fiction in the field of asylum policies.

Use of Legal Means to Limit States' Responsibility

According to the 1951 Geneva Convention, the number of asylum seekers that should be granted refugee status by the receiving state is limited only by the merit of each case. During recent years, however, countries have experienced a rising number of asylum seekers. According to United Nations High Commissioner for Refugees (UNHCR) statistics, the number of asylum seekers globally rose from less than one hundred thousand in 1983 to more than eight hundred thousand ten years later. These countries have tried to minimize the number of claims for asylum drastically by a redefining what constitutes a meritable case. From the point of view of the receiving states these measures have been successful in that the number of asylum seekers who are able to reach the asylum determination procedures in another country has been reduced dramatically in a few years. The total number of asy-

lum applications in the world was 849,000 in 1992, as against 500,000 in 1994; the number continued to fall in 1995 and 1996. Legal means used to limit the number of cases which "qualify for asylum" include (1) inventing new legal concepts, (2) limiting the scope of existing legal concepts, and (3) creating new legal obstacles.

1. States have designated as a "restricted zone" an area at the frontier; this geographical zone is regarded to be outside the territory where the obligations of the state under international law apply. Asylum seekers in these areas, usually in the transit area at international airports, may be refused access to refugee determination procedures or sent to another country, without their claim for asylum being investigated. According to the European Council on Refugees and Exiles, in spite of the fact that the term "is purely a matter of administrative practice," the states behave as if these areas are a legal entity outside the jurisdiction of the nation state.

The term "safe third country" is used either to indicate a country to which it is considered "safe" to return asylum seekers, or to indicate a country where it is unlikely that persecution takes place. Asylum claims from "safe" countries will be rejected automatically, without an individual judgment of each case. It is questionable whether the "safe country" concept is compatible with the general obligation to investigate each case individually.

2. Limitations of existing legal concepts include the requirement that a personal target recognize persecution and recognizing only governments as agents of persecution. People who are persecuted as members of a specific racial, national, or religious group are today defined as falling outside the scope of the refugee definition in the Geneva Convention. According to the UNHCR handbook, the "personal target requirement" is not a correct interpretation of the refugee convention. It is a sufficient requirement in order to obtain refugee status for the individual, to have a "well grounded fear that he will personally risk persecution upon return to the country he has fled." Only governments are recognized as agents of persecution. The governments of the asylum-granting countries now claim that only government-initiated or -controlled persecution counts as a requirement for refugee status according to the Geneva Convention. UNHCR does not agree: "Where serious discriminatory

or other offensive acts are committed by the local populace, they can be considered as persecution if they are knowingly tolerated by the authorities or if the authorities refuse, or prove unable, to offer effective protection."

3. One new legal obstacle is visa requirements to block the access to the asylum determination procedures. Visa requirements are imposed as conditions for entry on all nationals of countries that have previously been a source of a certain number of asylum seekers. Visa are not granted to applicants from these "asylum-producing countries." New legislation gives the transporting companies the responsibility to prevent the boarding of passengers without a valid visa and passport, regardless of the asylum claims from the passengers. Airplane and shipping personnel are through legal means forced to prevent refugees from leaving their country of persecution and to act in the role of immigration police. If these immigration control functions are not carried out effectively, the transporting company will have to pay heavy fines and/or the return expenses for the asylum seekers who are not admitted by the immigration officers. The fact that visa requirements and passport controls are carried out indiscriminately, regardless of the need of the refugee asylum seeker for protection, is highly objectionable. The fulfillment of universal moral rights is prevented by these legal means. Article 13 in the *Universal Declaration of Human Rights* states that "[e]veryone has the right to leave any country, including one's own, and to return to his country." From a legal point of view one may discuss whether this visa policy is compatible with Article 31 in the Geneva Convention, which pronounces that illegal entry shall not prevent an asylum seeker from getting his plea for asylum investigated. At present there is a considerable difference between the legal interpretation of several key concepts in the refugee convention given by the UNHCR, and the interpretation applied by the asylum-receiving countries. No international body has been given the authority to question the legal interpretation of the state procedure outside the national setting, so the legal interpretations of the refugee convention by the national immigration authorities remain unchallenged.

References

Barry, Brian, and Robert Goodin, eds. *Free Movement: Ethical Issues in the Transnational Migration of People and Money.* University Park: Penn State University Press, 1992.

Brown, Peter, and Henry Shue, eds. *Boundaries: National Autonomy and Its Limits.* Maryland Studies in Public Philosophy. Totowa NJ: Rowman and Littlefield, 1981.

European Council on Refugees and Exiles. *A European Refugee Policy in the Light of Established Principles.* London, 1994.

Gibney, Mark. *Open Borders? Closed Societies? The Ethical and Political Issues.* London: Greenwood Press, 1988.

Goodwin-Gill, Guy S. *The Refugee in International Law.* Oxford: Clarendon Press, 1989.

Hathaway, James C. *The Law of Refugee Status.* Toronto: Butterworth, 1991.

International Journal of Refugee Law. Quarterly. Oxford: Oxford University Press.

International Migration. Quarterly. Geneva: International Organization for Migration.

Joly, Daniele. *Refugees: Asylum in Europe?* Great Britain: Minority Rights Publications, 1992.

United Nations High Commissioner for Refugees. *The State of the World's Refugees: In Search of Solutions.* Oxford: Oxford University Press, 1995.

Bente Puntervold Bø

See also MOBILITY RIGHTS

Attempts

A person bent on crime may fail to accomplish the substantive crime and yet may still be guilty of a different crime, that of attempting to commit the main offense. Few would deny that many attempts deserve to be treated as crimes. The state of mind of the attempter can match the guilt of one who is successful in completing a similar offense. One person who shoots aiming to kill may fail only because of some chance occurrence, such as the bullet deflecting from a metal object in the victim's jacket pocket. It would be strange if the law were to ignore would-be murderers of this sort, and it does not.

Problems exist, however, in determining both the scope of punishment for attempts and its severity relative to that for corresponding completions. Disagreement about the rationale(s) for punishment has bearing on how attempts should be dealt with in law, though sometimes different theories converge on the same, or nearly the same, result. Since it is commonly felt that attempts should be treated less severely than corresponding completions, and practice usually reflects this feeling, discussion is often about reconciling theory with this practice. In the case of deterrence theory, for example, it might at first be thought that there should be no penalty for attempts, since punishment for the completed crime would also serve to deter someone from attempting the crime. However, it has been pointed out that punishment for attempts adds to the risk of criminal conduct, particularly in those cases where the risk of detection is small if the crime is successfully carried out. A lesser penalty for attempts also has a deterrence rationale in that it provides some incentive to abandon attempts; without the lesser penalty the offender may feel there is nothing to lose by continuing in cases where there appears to be a high probability that the criminal conduct has been detected.

Sometimes a theory of punishment, applied without modification to attempts, produces results that violate common sense. The area of criminal attempts is a useful touchstone for evaluating or refining theories of punishment.

A long-standing adage of law has it that *actus non facit reum nisi mens sit rea,* or in other words that an act does not make a person guilty in the absence of a guilty mind. The adage is useful for underscoring the fact that taking another's goods by mistake or accidentally killing another does not amount to crimes of theft or murder, respectively. In the case of attempts, what is missing is not the mens rea, or guilty mind, but the full actus reus, or criminal act. Should a guilty mind alone be punishable? Modern liberal societies, unlike some inquisitorial systems, are reluctant to allow the state to provide penal sanctions against what amounts to mere thought crimes alone. Reasons are not hard to find: intrusion into private life, greater possibility of error, difficulty of judging strength of intentions, curtailment of freedom of expression, and the expense of a huge potential increase in prosecutions. Some overt act, reflecting a criminal intention, is generally required for there to be a criminal attempt. In some cases, the absence of appropriate bodily movements might be treated as an overt act, as in the case of a pilot who ceases to control an aircraft with a view to allowing it to crash; alternatively, one might allow "overt omissions" of this sort to suffice.

An unresolved, and much-discussed, problem of criminal law theory is where to draw the line between outward behavior which reflects criminal intent that should be punishable as a crime and those manifestations of criminal intent that are sufficiently removed from a completed crime not to be fit subjects for punishment. Many cases fit the mold of a series of acts beginning with preparation and leading in a continuous line to completion. Dostoevsky's Raskolnikov revealed very early his intent to kill the pawnbroker when he sewed the axe-holder into his jacket. Most theorists would not treat this as an attempt, but would so treat his raising the axe in her presence, with intent to kill her. One reason is that between mere preparation and completed offense there may be plenty of opportunity to change one's mind. Another is that the intention at the preparation stage may not be firm.

The American Law Institute's *Model Penal Code* provides that for the crime of attempt there should be conduct which is a "substantial step" toward committing the offense, but it is not always clear what could count as such. As noted in *R. v. Eagleton,* 6 Cox C.C. 559, 571 (1859), at one time English law made the test of a criminal attempt whether the accused did the "last act" depending on himself in the series required to accomplish the criminal purpose. A modern-day example of such an act would be checking baggage containing a bomb timed to bring down an aircraft. Other suggested tests include that of "proximity" to completion or whether conduct reveals "unambiguously" the intent to commit crime. The English 1981 *Criminal Attempts Act* defined an attempt as doing something which is "more than merely preparatory" to committing an offense. The suitability of each test varies from case to case, and it is fairly predictable that controversy will continue, if not about the phrasing of the test (currently, the "substantial step" test is favored), then about the interpretation of that phrasing.

Not all attempts can adequately be thought of in terms of a break in some causal series leading to accomplishment of the substantial crime. In some cases an intended crime is thwarted because, although all the steps thought to be necessary by the accused are carried out, some misunderstanding means that success is impossble. For example, A succeeds in taking an umbrella, thinking it is B's, but in fact it is A's. Or A shoots at a wax effigy, believing it is B, whom he wants to kill. Analogous cases include attempting to pick a pocket which happens to be empty and poisoning someone with materials that are innocuous in the doses administered. Such cases are often discussed under the rubric "impossible attempts," although whether, or to what extent, something is "impossible" may depend on one's viewpoint. A burglar whose tools happen to be inadequate to crack a given safe or a poisoner who uses too small a dose of poison still makes use of means with a general tendency of effecting their purpose. Such persons are recognized threats to social order and are likely to be treated as guilty of an attempt. However, when the means used would be generally seen as totally inefficacious objectively, as with seeking to murder by voodoo, it would be unlikely that a criminal attempt either would or should be involved. This must be qualified: if the victim were one who believes in voodoo and were likely to suffer a fatal heart attack on being informed of the action, an attempt might justifiably be found, on the principle that in this case the overt act would now become a recognizable threat.

There is general agreement that one form of legally impossible attempt should not be criminal. That is the case where a person believes that his or her act is criminal when there is in fact no law against it. An example is engaging in adultery, believing it to be criminal in a given jurisdiction when it is not. If the system does not treat adultery as criminal, there can be little point in treating as criminal the attempt to do what the "offender" believes to be the crime of adultery. (The argument that people should be encouraged to respect the law is offset by arguments, first, that they should not be encouraged to respect what they believe to be the law when their belief is false and second, that such "encouragement" would be too costly, both in terms of consistent enforcement and in terms of maintaining popular support for the law when it would no doubt be seen as violating common sense.) By contrast, strong academic arguments have been advanced in support of criminalizing the act of attempting to handle stolen goods, notwithstanding that the goods might techni-

cally no longer be regarded as legally stolen by virtue of police having gained possession of them en route to trapping conspirators. These arguments were raised in opposition to the House of Lords decision in *Haughton v. Smith*, A.C. 476 (1975). The 1981 *Criminal Attempts Act* responded to these arguments by enacting that a person may be guilty of an attempt "even though the facts are such that the commission of the offence is impossible." The person's intent in such cases is to be judged in the light of the "facts of the case . . . as he believed them to be."

Opinion about attempts has, with limited usefulness, been characterized as divided between objectivists and subjectivists, the latter being more likely than the former to incriminate on the basis of criminal intention rather than accomplishment. The prime concern of the subjectivist is that people who are morally equally guilty should be punished equally, and that luck should not be allowed to make a difference because luck is morally irrelevant. The objectivist thinks that lucky outcomes may well provide for differences regarding whether, or how much, to punish, for a variety of possible reasons. Some early suggestions linked objectivism with variants of theories of retribution, revenge, denunciation, or expression, according to which the criminal law is seen as giving expression to justified resentment against a criminal on the part of victims and their sympathizers. Attempts can be expected to give rise to less resentment than corresponding completions. Some attempts might even cause more amusement than resentment, such as the nineteenth-century case of Lady Eldon attempting to smuggle "French" lace into England when, unknown to her, the lace had in fact been made in England.

That caution is needed in using the terms "objective" and "subjective" is suggested by the fact that Sir James Fitzjames Stephen, who explicitly supported a revenge justification for punishment, included in his proposed 1879 Draft Code a provision only recently achieved in England by subjectivist reformers: "Every one who, believing that a certain state of facts exists, does or omits an act the doing or omitting of which would if that state of facts existed be an attempt to commit an offence, attempts to commit that offence, although its commission in the manner proposed was by reason of the nonexistence of that state of facts at the time of the act impossible."

A different reason supporting the objectivist line involves an attack on the notion that luck should play no part in moral reckoning. Part of the argument is that although it is frequently a matter of luck whether people have the opportunity to face certain challenges, nevertheless we still praise or blame them for the kind of response they make to those challenges. As R.A. Duff has further argued, it makes a difference to our self-blame whether we actually murdered someone as distinct from trying and not succeeding. This sense of moral difference might give theoretical support for the distinction between attempts and completions that already exists in practice. Duff also notes, in line with the expressive theory of punishment, that failure to provide for a difference in penalties would convey the idea that actual causing of harm is unimportant.

A long-standing controversy exists on the question whether the minimum mens rea requirement for attempts should be stronger than that for a corresponding completion. One argument says no: if recklessness, acting with the conscious risk of causing injury, suffices for murder, then it should suffice also for criminal attempts when, but for some lucky circumstance, a person would be guilty of murder. Similarly with negligence, the acting or omitting to act in such a way as to risk causing injury, through culpable inadvertence to the risk. Risk for risk, why should the lucky escape punishment when there is equal culpability with the unlucky? Opposed to this reasoning is the argument that the word "attempt" implies direct intention to bring about what is proscribed, but such intention is absent in the cases of recklessness and negligence. The Supreme Court of Canada has, since *R. v. Ancio*, 1 S.C.R. 225 (1984), required direct intention as the mens rea of attempts. (An effect is said to be directly intended when it is consciously aimed at. It is indirectly, or obliquely, "intended" when the outcome is foreseen without being aimed at.) Some theorists would simply replace the word "attempt" by some other designation, such as "inchoate recklessness," to counter the verbal argument. Others have argued that actions are made up of physical and mental components and include results, so that the absence of results may be seen as a kind of deficiency. This deficiency in the chain of effects might be counterbalanced by a stronger element of mens rea, it has been argued, and thus a higher mens rea requirement for attempts has a theoretical rationale.

References

American Institute of Law. *Model Penal Code and Commentaries.* Philadelphia: American Institute of Law Press, 1985.

Ashworth, Andrew. "Criminal Attempts and the Role of Resulting Harm under the Code, and in the Common Law." *Rutgers Law Journal* 19 (1988), 726–772.

Clarkson, C.M.V., and H.M. Keating. *Criminal Law: Text and Materials.* 3d ed. London: Sweet and Maxwell, 1994.

Duff, R.A. *Intention, Agency and Criminal Liability.* Oxford: Basil Blackwell, 1990.

Fletcher, George. *Rethinking Criminal Law.* Boston: Little, Brown, 1978.

Hart, H.L.A. "The House of Lords on Attempting the Impossible." In *Essays in Jurisprudence and Philosophy,* ed. H.L.A. Hart. Oxford: Oxford University Press, 1983.

Marlin, Randal. "Attempts and the Criminal Law: Three Problems." *Ottawa Law Review* 8 (1976), 518–535.

Meehan, Eugene. *The Law of Criminal Attempt: A Treatise.* Calgary: Carswell, 1984.

Perkins, Rollin M., and Ronald Boyce. *Criminal Law.* 3d ed. Mineola NY: Foundation Press, 1982.

Smith, J.C., and Brian Hogan. *Criminal Law.* 7th ed. London: Butterworth, 1992.

Stephen, Sir James Fitzjames. *A History of the Criminal Law of England.* London: Macmillan, 1883.

Williams, Glanville. *Criminal Law: The General Part.* 2d ed. London: Stevens, 1961.

———. "Wrong Turnings on the Law of Attempt." *Criminal Law Review* (1991), 416–425.

Randal Marlin

See also CONSPIRACY; PARTIES TO CRIMINAL CONDUCT

Augustine (354–430)

Augustine of Hippo was the first great Christian philosopher and the most influential of the Latin Fathers of the Church. For well over eight centuries after his death, in fact until the influence of St. Thomas Aquinas (1225–1274) grew to a position of preeminence in Christendom, Augustine was the most important Christian philosopher. Virtually every medieval philosopher after him, including Aquinas, was strongly indebted to him, as were such early modern thinkers as René Descartes and Gottfried Leibniz.

Born in the North African town of Tagaste (modern Souk Ahras in eastern Algeria), Aurelius Augustinus lived almost all his life in Roman North Africa. As a student of rhetoric in Carthage he read Cicero's now lost dialogue, *Hortensius,* and came under the spell of philosophy. At first he was attracted to the Manichean sect. But when he went to Rome, he found the skepticism of the New Academy more attractive, and then, after moving to Milan, he joined a neo-platonic circle. Under the tutelage of Ambrose, Bishop of Milan, and the continuing influence of his mother, Monica, who had followed him to Italy, Augustine became a Christian convert and was baptized in 387.

After only five years in Italy, and soon after the death there of his mother, Augustine returned to North Africa, where he stayed until his own death forty-two years later. As a priest and then Bishop of Hippo he concerned himself with the great theological battles of his age. More than anyone else, he was responsible for defining the Christian heresies of Donatism, Pelagianism, and Manicheanism. His letters and treatises in condemnation of these heresies also made crucial contributions toward defining Christian orthodoxy.

Augustine's learning in philosophy came to him mainly through the writings of Cicero, who was not so much an original thinker as an elegant and urbane transmitter of the ideas and arguments of others. Augustine certainly knew several of Plato's dialogues and a significant body of neo-platonic literature. Among his philosophical predecessors it was clearly Plato he admired most.

Augustine's literary output was vast. Among his early writings, his *Against the Academicians, Soliloquies, On Free Choice of the Will,* and *Concerning the Teacher* are of special philosophical interest. Although nothing he wrote after he became a priest in 391 is a purely philosophical work, there are interesting and important philosophical passages in almost everything he wrote, including some of his sermons. His most famous works are his *Confessions* and *The City of God.* The latter work, written partly in response to pagan assertions that the sack of Rome in 410 was a response to its Christianization, became a kind of encyclopedia of knowledge for the early middle ages. Also important philosophically, as well as theologically, are his great treatise *The Trinity* and his *Literal Commentary on Genesis.*

Of the many philosophical and theological topics Augustine discussed, the following are of special interest to legal philosophers.

Intentionalism

In his *Commentary on the Lord's Sermon on the Mount* Augustine specifies these conditions as individually necessary and jointly sufficient for the commission of a sin: (1) entertaining an evil suggestion; (2) taking pleasure in the thought of doing the evil deed suggested; and (3) consenting to the evil deed. In this context, consent for Augustine is something like forming an intention to perform the action "consented to." Especially noteworthy in this analysis is the consequence that, while there is no sin without a relevant intention, there can be a sin without the intended action's ever being carried out.

Among later medieval philosophers Abelard is particularly Augustinian in his ethics. Augustine's influence was pervasive. The legal notion of mens rea is directly relevant to Augustine's idea of "consent to an evil suggestion."

Lying

Augustine wrote two whole treatises on lying, *On Lying* and *Against Lying.* In contrast to Plato, who in his *Republic* condones deception for political purposes, Augustine thought that every lie is a sin. However, Augustine does consider the intention of the liar and the circumstances in which the lie is told relevant in assessing the gravity of the sin. Moreover, he was acutely aware of the difficulty in saying exactly what constitutes telling a lie.

In general, Augustine thinks that telling a lie is (1) saying something one believes untrue that is also (2) actually untrue (3) with the intention of deceiving someone. But he considers cases that do not meet these conditions. Thus, he is inclined to say that someone who, intending to deceive, actually tells the truth, thinking that it is a falsehood, also counts as a liar. However, he never solves, even to his own satisfaction, all the puzzles that he created about lying.

Homocide and Suicide

According to Augustine in *City of God,* one has no "private right" to kill any human being, whether oneself or another, not even in self-defense. We are, however, not to be blamed for accidents that result in human death without our desiring it, so long as the actions we perform are in themselves good and lawful. As for actions performed in service of a state or monarch, one who "owes a duty of obedience to the giver of the command (to kill) does not himself kill; he is only an instrument, a sword in its user's hand." So in the right circumstances neither a state executioner nor a soldier in battle violates the divine commandment "Thou shalt not kill." As for suicide in particular, even the desire to avoid the pollution of rape does not justify suicide, according to Augustine. To one contemplating suicide at the threat of being raped, Augustine says there is no pollution, "if the lust belongs to another."

Political Legitimacy

Augustine's strong belief in the providence of God gives him confidence that every state, even the most evil one, in some way serves God's purpose. But it does not follow that any state, by its mere existence, or by the "earthly" circumstances of its founding, has even a prima facie claim to moral legitimacy.

Augustine's famous question in *City of God* "What are kingdoms, without justice, but gangs of criminals on a large scale?" might be taken to be suggesting that justice is a natural state of kingdoms. That would be a misreading. Augustine's view is certainly that good rulers "should extend their dominion far and wide, and that their reign should endure"; but he does not maintain that it is in any way natural to kingdoms to have good rulers. In fact, Augustine's doctrine of original sin suggests otherwise.

Punishment

Augustine's conception of punishment is basically retributive. Believing, then, that eternal suffering can be a just punishment for mortal sin, he quite understandably worries in *City of God* about how everlasting punishment can be just retribution for sins "which, however serious, were certainly committed in a short space of time." He argues that the period of the punishment need not be in temporal proportion to the time in which the offense was committed.

In *Protagoras* Plato had argued that it is irrational to punish someone on account of a past action, since a past action cannot be undone. Augustine, aware of this platonic tradition on punishment, if not this passage in particular, rejects the view. He does allow that it is sometimes appropriate to punish for remedial purposes, but his general view of punishment remains retributive.

Just War Theory

Augustine was certainly not the first thinker to suggest that certain requirements must be met for a war to be counted as a just war. The theory of just warfare—both the requirements that have to be satisfied for it to be the case that the war has been justly entered into (*ius ad bellum*) and also the requirements that must be satisfied for the war to have been conducted in a just manner (*ius in bello*)—were already well laid out by Cicero in his *De re publica*. Nor was Augustine even the first Christian to develop the idea of just warfare. Augustine's spiritual mentor, Ambrose, had already done that before him. Nevertheless, Augustine is often counted as the father of just war theory for the good reason that it is to him, rather than to Cicero or Ambrose, that later theorists harken back.

In his *Reply to Faustus the Manichean,* Augustine thinks that "the natural order, which seeks the peace of mankind, ordains that the monarch should have the power of undertaking war if he thinks it advisable." As we have already seen, the soldier is then like a sword in the monarch's hand and is not constrained by the divine command not to kill. However, the attitudes and intentions of the soldier are subject to moral scrutiny. "The real evils of war," Augustine writes, "are love of violence, revengeful cruelty, fierce and implacable enmity, wild resistance, and the lust of power" rather than "the death of someone, who will die in any case, that others may live in peaceful subjection."

References

Augustine. *Basic Writings of St. Augustine.* 2 vols. Ed. W. Oates. New York: Random House, 1948.

———. *A Select Library of the Nicene and Post-Nicene Fathers of the Christian Church.* First Series (1886–1888). Ed. P. Schaff. Reprinted, Grand Rapids MI: Eerdmans, 1971–1980.

Brown, Peter. *Augustine of Hippo*. Berkeley: University of California, 1967.

Christopher, Paul. "Saint Augustine and the Tradition of Just War." In *The Ethics of War and Peace*, Englewood Cliffs NJ: Prentice-Hall, 1994.

Kirwan, Christopher. *Augustine*. London: Routledge, 1989.

Gareth B. Matthews

Austin, John (1790–1859)

John Austin is the early-nineteenth-century legal theorist most widely known as a founding father of the school of "legal positivism." His work focused on laws relating to human conduct, and he excluded from his study those laws relating to inanimate matter (the laws of physics). He claimed that *all* of the laws with which he was concerned involved *commands, duties,* and *sanctions.* Each of those terms, he said, *signifies* the same notion—that of "law," *denotes* a different part of that notion, and *connotes* the residue (that is, each term brings with it by implication the other two). The major subdivision of law is into those *divine* and *human.* The latter is again subdivided into those of *positive law* and *positive morality.* This process of categorization is the basis for much debate in recent years concerning "the separation of law and morality."

This is the main distinction said to constitute the schools of legal positivism and those of natural law, and became the focus of debate in the 1960s between H.L.A. Hart at Oxford and Lon Fuller at Harvard. Positivists, it was said, define law without reference to moral factors, while natural lawyers define law by saying that accordance with moral principles is an essential characteristic of what counts as natural law (Harris 1980). Austin defined positive law in terms of the concepts of *sovereignty, subjection,* and *independent political community.* Because his categorizations distinguished law from morality and his definition of law did not involve moral factors, it seemed fairly safe to regard him as being an archetypal positivist.

However, he did go on to say that "[p]ositive law (or *jus*), positive morality (or *mos*), together with the principles which form the test of both, are the inseparably connected parts of a vast organic whole." He also went on to say: "But the circle embraced by the law of God, and which may be embraced to ad-vantage by positive morality, is larger than the circle which can be embraced to advantage by positive law. Inasmuch as the two circles have one and the same center, the whole of the region comprised by the latter is also comprised by the former." If these circles "have one and the same centre," then the area which they cover must be coextensive. Far from separating law and morality, Austin showed us how they work together. Far from *opposing* notions of natural law and positive law, Austin claimed to be an *adherent* of both. The former (which he went on to call "Divine" law) is based on the commands of God; the latter, on the commands of sovereigns. If there should be a conflict between the two, then one appealed to principles of utility to resolve the conflict. Because the sanctions which God can impose are greater than those which could be imposed by human lawgivers, it would be rational in certain circumstances to oppose the law of the state in order not to offend against the law of God. "[I]f human commands conflict with Divine Law, we ought to disobey the command which is enforced by the less powerful sanction."

In his later discussion of "judicial legislation" Austin discussed various ways in which morality both influences and limits the development of the law. He referred to the morality of the community, of the judicial and wider legal communities, and of the international community. Because his characterization of the law of the state was based on the political realities, he recognized that laws de jure but not de facto were really no laws at all, and that laws de facto but not de jure were to be seen as laws. The laws governing the relationship between states were matters of "international positive morality" rather than matters of law.

However, to know that something counts as positive law does not determine the question of how we should act. All we know is that it necessarily carries with it a duty (a legal duty). However, we know that there are also duties that arise from the existing morality of the community and from the Divine law or the ethical standards that we accept. To know which duty will prevail requires us to look at each of the duties in the light of the demands of the others.

Austin is often seen as an authoritarian person putting forward a very conservative view as to the nature of law. However, we often forget that he was part of that group which consisted of Jeremy Bentham and James and John Stuart Mill and which became known as the "philosophic radicals." When discussing the role of "judicial legislation," Austin said that we should not criticize the judges for doing what was absolutely necessary. "[I]nstead we should blame them for the timid, narrow, and piecemeal manner in which they have legislated, and for legislating under cover of vague and indefinite phrases, which would be censurable in any legislator."

Of precedent, he said: "Nothing indeed can be more natural, than that legislators, direct or judicial (especially if they be, narrowminded, timid and unskillful) should lean as much as they can on the examples set by their predecessors." He criticized the judges of the common law courts for not doing what they ought to have done, and modeled their rules and procedures to the growing exigencies of society, instead "of stupidly and sulkily adhering to the old and barbarous usages."

Austin taught at the new University of London from 1829 to 1833 and at the Inner Temple in 1834. He had brief periods of service with the British Criminal Law Commission during 1833, and for a short period as a Commissioner to the Royal Commission on Malta from 1836 to 1838. He otherwise lived in honorable poverty and tended his roses.

He published his opening lectures as *The Province of Jurisprudence Determined* in 1832. The larger two-volume work *Lectures on Jurisprudence or the Philosophy of Positive Law* was published posthumously by his wife, Sarah Austin, from his working papers. Originally published 1861–1863, the most frequently used version is the 1885 (fifth) edition, which was edited by Robert Campbell. Austin wrote a number of minor papers, the most widely known of which is "Plea for the Constitution."

References

Austin, John. *Lectures on Jurisprudence or the Philosophy of Positive Law*. Glashutten in Tanus: Auvermann, 1972.
———. *The Province of Jurisprudence Determined*. Cambridge: Cambridge University Press, 1995.
Hamburger, Joseph, and Lotte Hamburger. *Troubled Lives: John and Sarah Austin*. Toronto: University of Toronto Press, 1985.
Harris, J.W. *Legal Philosophies*. London: Butterworth, 1980.
Hart, H.L.A. *The Concept of Law*. Oxford: Oxford University Press, 1961.
———. "Positivism and the Separation of Law and Morals." *Harvard Law Review* 71 (1958), 598.
Moles, R.N. *Definition and Rule in Legal Theory*. Blackwell, 1987. Available at http://www.uniserve.edu.au.law/ under "books."
Morison, W.L. *John Austin*. Sevenoaks UK: Edward Arnold, 1982.
Rumble, W. *The Thought of John Austin*. London: Athlone Press, 1985.

Robert N. Moles

Authority

The concept of authority figures in the articulation, elaboration, and enforcement of legal discourse. Can one uncover a shared sense to the different contexts where "authority" is used in legal discourse and in the discourses of philosophers about legal discourse?

Authority arises from two contexts in legal philosophy. First, authority figures in legal reasoning. State officials justify their decisions in terms of the "authority" for their judgments and actions. Authority plays a part in differentiating constitutionally enacted instruments from unconstitutional ones. Even constitutional laws are sometimes said to be invalid or lacking in authority. The citizen is believed to be legally obligated to obey an authoritative instrument, whereas no such obligation is associated with acts which lack authority. Why is authority so important to obedience to the laws in a modern state? Why does authority make a text law? Why are judges, lawyers, police, and other juridical officials so preoccupied that one has authority to act in a certain manner? Lawyers, judges, and jurists often take these issues for granted, though the issues are critically important in the resolution of particular legal problems in a modern state.

A second context raises the term "authority." The authority of an official's action differentiates state-authorized violence from nonstate violence. Many people are imprisoned, their assets confiscated, their income taxed, their welfare payments terminated, and their bodies tortured authoritatively. When these acts are justified as authorized, official and citizen alike believe themselves constrained by the authoritative character of the acts. Authority compels the official to act in a certain manner, it is believed.

If authoritative, is there no limit to which a state official may intern or torture or execute the body of a resident? That is, is a detainee entitled, independent of authority, to certain minimum fairness, including minimum social and economic conditions, when officials claim to act under authoritative laws? Can the sense of authority, associated with a modern state, be displaced in favor of one which better respects the body of the resident in the state's territory?

Shifting to a slightly different context, political leaders often vie to represent the head of an authoritative structure. Whoever represents the head of an administrative structure, whether a prime minister, corporate president, union president, or other organizational leader, is obeyed. Indeed, civil wars erupt as leaders claim to represent the head of the authoritative structure of the state. More, in their rhetoric, jurists sometimes trace the authority or lack of authority in laws to one "founding father" rather than to another. The writings of the privileged "founding father" are revered as the source of all authoritative actions. Whichever group loses in the struggle to have a founding father recognized, that group may become the instrument of being "outlawed." Sometimes, ethnic cleansing follows.

Referring to both the first context of legal reasoning and the second context of the struggle for recognition as the head or "founding father" of a state, all juridical actions are rationally linked to a source or grounds or, ultimately, to a foundation external to the texts of judges and legislatures and external to political leaders. Through legal discourse, jurists struggle to represent the ultimate foundation. On close inspection, it seems that later jurists construct the foundation. Indeed, all authoritative actors presuppose that the authority of texts and actions dwells in a foundation situated external to the legal discourse. The foundation's externality to legal discourse is shrouded with a prehistory and an epistemological transcendence. The preexisting and transcendent foundation is inaccessible from within the trace of the grounds of juridical action. Put another way, the foundation is believed to be absent from the language of jurists; but jurists act as if the foundation exists. Why jurists presuppose the existence of an absent foundation is crucial to understanding the authority of a modern state.

The Romans associated authority with just such a foundation or grounds. The juristic belief that, supplemented with force, jurists could impartially and rationally link any state action with the external foundation aided the Romans to rule disparate linguistic and cultural groups who loyally deferred to the representers, whether the "founding fathers" or historically contingent institutions of the foundation such as the Senate. If a government official—administrator, army officer, judge, or emperor—acted without authority, the official acted *ultra vires* or beyond authoritative boundaries. The rational nexus of an official's action to the representers of the presupposed foundation lifted the jurist or judge above mere subjective whim into an objective, impersonal realm of legal reasoning. Such impersonal conduct contrasted with the later Greeks, such as Plato and Aristotle, who identified the foundation of a legal order with a personality. In Plato's *Republic* and *Laws*, philosopher kings, called the "Founders," grounded the just state. In Aristotle's *Ethics* and *Politics*, experience and practical wisdom privileged the founding statesmen of a just order. The Romans shifted the foundation from the personality to impersonal concepts. An *auctoritas* (quality of authority) was believed to transcend the wisdom, whims, biases, subjective values, opinions, and rhetoric of a personality.

Modern legal thought has continued the Roman association of authority with a foundation or final grounding. Initially, the foundation was believed to be located in the will of the founding authors of civil institutions. Thomas Hobbes, in the *Leviathan*, published in 1651, identified the foundation in a state of nature which he posited prior to a civil society. Authors in a state of nature agreed to devolve their authority to a representative, called the Leviathan, in whose name all civil institutions acted, according to Hobbes. Jean-Jacques Rousseau, in the *Social Contract*, published in 1762, argued that the founding authors shared a general will which transcended the individual wills of particular legislatures, judges, and citizens. In the case of both Hobbes and Rousseau, the foundation of civil society dwelt in a realm which preexists the experiences and languages of civil institutions. In a sense, the will of the foundational authors in a state of nature was invisible in that civil institutions could, at best, approximate the will of the whole.

At the turn of the nineteenth century, G.W.F. Hegel (1770–1831), in the *Phenome-*

nology of Spirit, published in 1807, and *Philosophy of Right,* published in 1821, associated the authority of a modern state with a series of experiential moments in Western culture. The deference to a foundation, external to citizen and judge, he argued, reflected merely one moment of human consciousness, a stoic moment best left with the Romans. The final moment of authority, he claimed, grows from a *Sittlichkeit* where the individual citizen, judge, and legislator feel immediately identified with the whole. Authority lies in the social, rather than external to it. Yet such a moment of immediacy is arguably an imaginary moment, which, like the state of nature, never existed as a historical contingency. Authoritative laws can, at best, re-present such a fictitious moment of immediacy.

During the nineteenth century, one finds legal theorists displacing the inaccessible will of transcendent authors with historically contingent authors. For Jeremy Bentham (1748–1832), for example, authority rested with the act of a sovereign legislature. However, even when Bentham focused upon the authority of such a legislature, he appealed to a transcendent concept, the "greatest good," as ultimately authorizing all legislative acts. When pressed, Bentham admitted that such a founding concept dwelt in a metaphysics without determinate particulars.

Hans Kelsen (1881–1973) took up the metaphysical context of the final source of authority in *The Pure Theory of Law* (1934). A law was a norm or "ought" as opposed to an "is," he claimed. However, all norms were differentiated from a single *Grundnorm,* which founded a system of norms. A norm was an act of will directed toward an external object. A *Grundnorm* was an act of thought without a further object. Absent a further object, the act of thought was a final, intrinsic "ought." Before a norm was posited, the jurist and citizen presupposed that one ought to obey the norm. The *Grundnorm* was presupposed before any jurist spoke or wrote. The *Grundnorm* even preexisted the founding text of a constitution, according to Kelsen. Jurists reasoned as if the unspoken and unwritten *Grundnorm* authorized all juridical acts.

More recent examinations of authority displace Kelsen's formalism with a self-described realism. In the *Concept of Law* published in 1961, H.L.A. Hart retrieved the genesis of authority from "unspoken judicial practices." In his earlier essays Hart referred to them as linguistic conventions. Once jurists recognize the foundation, called a rule of recognition, they justify the acts of all juridical persons in terms of a "rule of recognition," according to Hart. Hart transformed the social practices of judges into a epistemological function for legal reasoning. The act of recognition, though, occurred after judges and legislatures had posited primary rules. Once again, final grounds of authority are believed to preexist speech and writing. The key to authority, according to Hart, is that juridical officials effectively accept the foundation, even though the foundation is recognized after it has been taken for granted.

Heavily influenced by Hart, both Joseph Raz and Ronald Dworkin also associate legal authority with a justificatory project in the direction of an objectless foundation. In Raz's case, exclusionary reasons, first order reasons, second order reasons, closure reasons, the weight and strength of reasons, and reasons for action compose the metaphysics of authoritative action. In Dworkin's case, authority dwells in the arguments of an idealized knower, Hercules, and an idealized interpreter, Hermes, of the grand narrative of a legal discourse. Each judge, who plays a preeminent political role according to Dworkin, writes a never-ending chapter of the narrative. The chapter appeals to background arguments which institutional materials suggest. The justificatory narrative differentiates the force of a judge from the force of an armed thug. Like the utterances of the thug, though, the legal narrative is constructed from assumptions and conventions which the judge takes for granted. Once again, legal authority depends upon an external foundation, absent from language and consciousness until a judge, situated from an external vantage point, recognizes a principle of the foundation in past institutional materials.

A presupposed external grounding of posited laws finalizes the justificatory quest for authority. Without a final source or grounds for a statute or judgment or state action, the search for authority would lack a finality. Mere temporary fragments of an author's will, one would trace the authority of a civilly posited law to a statement about the grounds of one authored law to the statement of the grounds of another, and from that grounds to another ad infinitum. The authored statements would not apply to two or more events because there would be no ultimate source to act as a justificatory constraint upon the posit of a new "rule." Indeed, the judgments of jurists would be ruleless because, to be a rule, the rule must enclose at least two events. More, without an ultimate ground, one could not differentiate authoritative acts from raw barbaric force. To carry the finality necessary for an ultimate foundation, the final grounds or source must be understood differently from ordinarily posited rules and principles. Believed to be situated before legal discourse, jurists actually recognize the foundation after jurists reach their judgments. Gazing from afar, an image of the invisible foundation constrains all juridical actions.

The inaccessibility of the external situs of the foundation of laws carries a divine-like character. Jurists must conceive of the possibility of a foundation even if they never know or experience it. Its absence from spoken and written language forever postpones the moment of reaching the foundation. As a consequence, the authority of laws, associated with the external transcendent foundation, seems to collapse into that of modern natural law theory. For natural law theory also associates authority with a foundation which transcends all posited rules. The foundation of modern natural law theory shares the invisible character of the foundation of civilly posited laws in positivist theory. Without a presupposed absent foundation, situated in a metaphysics beyond juridical reasoning, civilly posited laws lose their authoritative character. Precisely because the absent foundation is the essential postulate of the modern legal discourse, authority can no longer be considered separate from a metaphysics, which postulates an a priori divine-like origin or end.

References

Arendt, Hannah. "What Is Authority?" In *Between Past and Present*, 91–141. New York: Meridian, 1961.

Conklin, William E. "The End of Judicial Review." In *Constitutional Review/*"Verfassungsgerichtsbarkeit." *Constitutionele Toetsing*, ed. Bert van Roermund, 33–54. Deventer, Netherlands: Kluwer Law and Taxation Publishers, 1993.

———. "The Invisible Author of Legal Authority." *Law and Critique* 7 (1996).

Derrida, Jacques. "Force of Law: The 'Mystical Foundation of Authority.'" *Cardozo Law Review* 11 (1990), 919–1045.

Dworkin, Ronald. *Law's Empire.* Boston: Harvard University Press, 1986.

Foucault, Michel. "Governmentality." In *The Foucault Effect: Studies in Governmentality,* ed. Graham Burchill, Colin Gordon, and Peter Miller, 87–104. Chicago: University of Chicago Press, 1991.

Hart, H.L.A. *The Concept of Law* (with a Postscript edited by Penelope A. Bulloch and Joseph Raz). 1961. 2d ed. Oxford: Clarendon Press, 1994.

Hegel, Georg Wilhelm Friedrich. *The Philosophy of Right.* Trans. T.M. Knox. Oxford: Oxford University Press, 1952.

Hobbes, Thomas. *A Dialogue between a Philosopher and a Student of the Common Laws of England.* Ed. and intro. Joseph Cropsey. Chicago: University of Chicago Press, 1971.

Kelsen, Hans. *The Pure Theory of Law.* Trans. Max Knight. Berkeley: University of California Press, 1970.

William E. Conklin

See also LEGITIMACY

Automatism

Automatism, strictly speaking, means action without conscious volition, or conduct of which the actor is not conscious. In essence, where automatism is present, the body becomes involved in actions that the mind does not control. According to *R. v. Cottle,* N.Z.L.R. 999, 1007 (C.A.) (1958), automatism results in a "temporary eclipse of consciousness that nevertheless leaves the person so affected able to exercise bodily movements."

It is a fundamental precept of our criminal law that an individual is responsible only for his or her conscious, intentional acts.

The criminal prohibition characteristically is comprised of both physical and mental elements, often referred to as the *actus reus* and the *mens rea,* respectively. As a general rule, before liability may ensue both elements must be present and proved.

In any consideration of automatism, attention is focused on the physical element or the *actus reus.* This element consists of the doing or commission of the prohibited act; that aspect may be satisfied by direct action, the creation of a prohibited state of affairs, or an omission to fulfill a legal duty. The prohibited conduct, however it is defined, must be willed or voluntary. (Some writers classify volition or voluntariness as part of the *actus reus,* while others view it as implicit in the mental element of crime.) It is a basic legal principle that the absence of volition is always a defense to a crime. In common law legal systems the general rule is that a defense proving that the act was involuntary entitles the accused to a complete and unqualified acquittal. The assertion that an act is involuntary, in this context, is equivalent to the contention that the act is automatistic. Hence the nomenclature, the defense of automatism.

Automatism as a legal defense is to be distinguished from the defense of insanity or mental disorder. Glanville Williams states that "automatism" has come to express "any abnormal state of consciousness (whether confusion, delusion or dissociation) that is regarded as incompatible with the existence of *mens rea,* while not amounting to insanity." The defense of insanity or not guilty by reason of mental disorder, unlike the automatism defense, does not yield a complete or unqualified acquittal when successfully invoked. Rather, the successful insanity defense characteristically results in indefinite confinement, subject to treatment and review before release is contemplated.

Another manner of comprehending the distinction between automatism and insanity is to regard both phenomena as subsets of a larger, more all-embracing conception of automatism. By this view, two categories of automatism exist: insane automatism (insanity) and noninsane automatism (automatism). For legal purposes, the point of differentiation between these two categories is whether the underlying condition giving rise to the misconduct is capable of constituting a "disease of the mind." ["Disease of the mind" is a legal, not a medical, term. It first obtained forensic significance in *M'Naghten's Case* (1843), 10 Cl. & Fin. 200.] If the underlying condition qualifies as a disease of the mind, then the only available defense is the limited or qualified defense of insanity (or insane automatism). In other words, when the automatistic condition stems from a disease of the mind that has rendered the accused insane, then the accused is not entitled to a full acquittal, but to a verdict of insanity, an example of which can be seen in *Bratty v. Attorney General for Northern Ireland,* A.C. 386 (1963).

Not surprisingly, many cases have arisen involving controversies as to whether a given condition should be characterized as constituting a disease of the mind. In general, such cases draw a distinction between a malfunctioning of the mind arising from some cause that is primarily internal to the accused, having its source in his psychological or emotional makeup, or in some organic pathology, and a malfunctioning of the mind that is the transient effect produced by some specific external factor, such as a blow to the head.

It is for the judge hearing the case to determine what mental conditions are encompassed within the term "disease of the mind" and whether there is any evidence that the accused suffered from an abnormal mental condition comprehended by that term. The evidence of medical experts called as witnesses with respect to the cause, nature, and symptoms of the abnormal mental condition from which the accused is alleged to suffer, and how that condition is viewed and characterized from the medical point of view, is regarded as highly relevant to the judicial determination of whether the condition constitutes a disease of the mind, although medical testimony is not determinative of that question.

Psychoses, dissociative states brought on by a "psychological blow," and any pathological condition (organic or otherwise) which effectively prevents an accused person from knowing the nature and quality of his acts are examples of conditions held to constitute a disease of the mind. By contrast, concussion, delirium brought on by the toxins of infection, hypoglycemia, and somnambulism have been used to validly found an automatism defense. However, the mere listing of what has been accepted as constituting a disease of the mind, and what has not, while of interest, must be recognized as being of only limited analytic utility.

"Disease of the mind," while not capable of precise definition, has been recognized as possessing a medical component as well as a legal or policy component. The medical component reflects the state of medical knowledge at a given time and essentially comprises the medical opinion as to how the mental condition in question in a given case is viewed or characterized medically. The legal or policy component relates to the scope of the exemption from criminal responsibility that is afforded by the mental condition in question and the need to protect the public by the control and treatment of persons who have caused serious harm while in a mentally disordered or disturbed state.

The legal or policy component of the disease of the mind inquiry has spawned two competing theories: the "continuing danger" theory and the "internal cause" theory.

The continuing danger approach has arisen as a result of an obiter dictum comment by Lord Denning in *Bratty* wherein he distinguishes insane and noninsane automatism as follows: "It seems to me that any mental disorder which has manifested itself in violence and is prone to recur is a disease of the mind. At any rate it is the sort of disease for which a person should be detained in hospital rather than be given an unqualified acquittal."

In short, this theory holds that any condition likely to present a recurring danger to the public should be treated as insanity. Critics of this theory doubt the ability of the medical profession to predict recurrent dangerousness. Also, eminent jurists have noted that the converse of Lord Denning's proposition is legally unsound, since holding that a serious mental disorder did not constitute a disease of the mind on the basis that it was unlikely to recur would be to exclude from the exemption from responsibility afforded by insanity those persons who by reason of a severe mental disorder were incapable of appreciating the nature and quality of their act, or of knowing that it was wrong.

By contrast, the internal cause theory suggests that a condition stemming from the psychological or emotional makeup of the accused, rather than some external factor, should lead to a finding of insanity. While this theory has gained a certain ascendancy in English and Canadian jurisprudence, it has been criticized as an unfounded development of the law and for the odd results that the external/internal dichotomy can produce. For example, in Canadian law, as a result of the decision in *Rabey v. R.*, 15 C.R. (3d), 225 S.C.C. (1980), it would appear that a psychological blow will not ground an automatism defense and must, if advanced, be regarded as constituting a disease of the mind. However, if the emotional shock is an extraordinary external event—one so intense as to remove it from the ordinary stresses and disappointments of life—the condition can possibly be regarded as automatistic within the authorities. Another example is furnished when a diabetic who has not eaten enough causes injury while suffering from a hypoglycemic episode. Under prevailing doctrine the result in such an instance is an insanity verdict, whereas the result may be an acquittal due to automatism when the episode is brought on as a result of the diabetic's taking insulin. These criticisms of the internal cause theory have some weight if that theory is viewed as the definitive answer to the disease of the mind inquiry. However, the better view is that the theory is merely an analytical tool that is not intended to have comprehensive scope.

Clearly, there are cases where neither of the two leading policy approaches will yield an inevitable result. Recurrent danger may not be present on the facts of a given case and the internal cause approach may not be readily applicable. Other competing policy considerations may have a role to play. Among these one might include the *in terrorem* argument that floodgates will open if a particular condition is recognized as amenable to a defense of automatism. Such an argument was advanced as a result of the controversial decision of the Supreme Court of Canada in *R. v. Daviault*, 33 C.R. (4th), 165 S.C.C. (1995), wherein voluntary extreme intoxication, producing a state akin to automatism, was recognized as providing an absolute defense to a charge of sexual assault (rape). The backlash against this decision proved so strong that the defense has since been removed by legislative amendment. Perhaps this development reflects a popular revulsion against exoneration in circumstances where the involuntary behavior in issue may be attributable to the individual's initial precipitating act(s) of negligence.

References

Colvin, E. *Principles of Criminal Law.* 2d ed. Toronto: Carswell, 1991.

Edwards, J.L.J. "Automatism and Criminal Responsibility." *Modern Law Review* 21 (1958), 375.

Fingarette, H. "The Concept of Mental Disease in Criminal Law Insanity Tests." *University of Chicago Law Review* 33 (1965–1966), 229.

Prevezer, S. "Automatism and Involuntary Conduct." *Criminal Law Review* (1958), 440.

Roth, M. "Modern Psychiatry and Neurology and the Problem of Responsibility." In

Mental Disorder and Criminal Responsibility, ed. S.J. Hucker, C. Webster, and M. Ben-Aron, 104–109. Toronto: Butterworth, 1981.

Whitlock, F.A. *Criminal Responsibility and Mental Illness.* 1963.

Williams, G. *Textbook of Criminal Law.* 2d ed. London: Sweet & Maxwell, 1983.

STANLEY A. COHEN

See also INSANITY DEFENSE; PSYCHIATRY

Autonomy

The etymology of "autonomy" (*auto-nomos*) indicates its general meaning: "self-rule." It generally refers to the conditions of agents (or a right relative to such conditions) whereby they have the capacity to form values, desires, and plans of their own, independent of manipulative interferences by others or by past or present conditions. The concept of autonomy has relevance for legal theory in several areas, including paternalism, use of the police power, privacy, and legal moralism. In order to explicate this concept more precisely, however, it is necessary to make several distinctions. First, autonomy should be distinguished from "liberty" or "freedom." The latter terms generally refer to the absence of constraining conditions restricting agents' actions. Paradigmatically, these constraining conditions exist outside the agent and physically prevent actions from being carried out (though the concept of freedom has been extended beyond that in many contexts). Autonomy refers to positive conditions concerning the agent's abilities to decide for himself or herself what values to adopt and what actions to take.

Second, one must distinguish political autonomy—a property of a state or society relating to its independence from other political bodies—from personal autonomy, a property of individual persons. Within the latter category (the subject of the present discussion), one can distinguish autonomy in a normative sense, as in "that policy does not show sufficient respect for citizens' autonomy," from autonomy in a descriptive sense, as in "mental illness and drug addiction destroyed her autonomy." The former usage refers to a right to be treated in a certain manner, while the latter refers to a set of personal and/or psychological characteristics that instantiate self-government in some sense. (Joel Feinberg subdivides normative and descriptive uses of the notion still further.)

At the individual level, autonomy must be distinguished from other related values attached to persons, such as dignity and well-being. While autonomy is an important component of these values, to be autonomous is separate from having dignity or self-respect, on the one hand, and enjoying general well-being, on the other. Issues of paternalism, for example, arise precisely because the exercise of individual self-determination—autonomy—can conflict with personal well-being, raising the question whether respect for autonomy should prevent others (or the state) from intervening to advance an agent's well-being against her or his will.

In its normative sense, autonomy can refer to a right to be treated in certain ways. This right can involve either the right that one's actual (or potential) psychological capacity to govern oneself not be disrupted or manipulated—that one not be hypnotized or brainwashed, for example; or that one be treated as if one possessed the psychological traits constitutive of autonomy. One's right to autonomy can be violated in this second sense even if one's actual mental capacities are left undisturbed but when insufficient respect for those capacities is not shown (for example, when one's personal decisions are preempted or disregarded).

As a (descriptive) set of psychological characteristics, autonomy refers to the ability of the person to be the true author of her or his own decisions, to be such that the actions that emanate from those decisions can be accurately ascribed to the person rather than to external forces or internal compulsion. At this level, autonomy can refer either to the person as a whole or to particular acts, decisions, or desires in particular. Whether referring to autonomous persons or autonomous desires (or decisions or acts), philosophers' accounts of autonomy have tended to be focused on the structural conditions of the person (or her desires, and so forth) at a particular time or to be focused on the causal history of those desires and beliefs. Whether structural or historical, conditions claimed to be necessary for autonomy have tended to cluster around three general areas: the rationality or cognitive competence of the person, the person's volitional control over her actions and will, and the authenticity of the values, preferences, and character traits that move the person to action.

One of the most influential approaches to the notion of autonomy was put forward by Gerald Dworkin, who claimed that a person is autonomous if he or she enjoys "authenticity" and "procedural independence." According to Dworkin, "[a] person is autonomous if he identifies with his desires, goals, and values [authenticity], and such identification is not influenced in ways which make the process of identification in some way alien to the individual [procedural independence]." This approach makes use of the assumption that a person is able to reflect on her or his desires and values from a higher order perspective. Hence, this approach has been labelled a "hierarchical" conception of autonomy (and of the person).

This view has been variously criticized (and indeed Dworkin revised his view in 1988). Writers have pointed out that people can be manipulated at the higher levels of reflection, just as they can be at the lower levels. Some have claimed also that the highest levels of reflection may not represent a "truer" or more authentic self at all. And finally, Christman has argued against the necessity, if not the coherence, of positing higher levels of desires and reflection, claiming that disapproval of one's lower order desires manifests simply a conflict of two desires.

These accounts have focused on what can be called "authenticity" conditions for autonomy—conditions referring to the status of the values and desires that move a person during his or her life. Berofsky and Meyers have jettisoned the requirement of authenticity (in this sense) altogether, arguing that as long as a person is competent (or rational in an appropriate sense) and in volitional control of herself (that is, does not suffer from debilitating pathologies), she is autonomous. Haworth has maintained that some procedural conditions of authenticity that are necessary for autonomy have nevertheless placed greater emphasis on the development of various cognitive, affective, and normative abilities that they claim are necessary for autonomy.

In addition to authenticity and cognitive competence, a condition of autonomy that is mentioned by relatively few philosophers, including Young, is the requirement of volitional control, the relative freedom from debilitating conditions that prevent an agent from turning otherwise authentic and rational desires into action. Phobias, neuroses, psychoses, and various other pathologies may inhibit an agent's ability to act on her authentic desires and hence fail in autonomy in a significant sense.

Autonomy in one of these senses has been recognized by many as an important if not basic human value, both in general and in relation to specific political and legal principles. There are many, as do Unger and Gilligan, however, who reject the idea that autonomy has basic or universal value or that it stands as an ideal of psychological development for women and men of all times and cultures. Questions remain, therefore, about whether autonomy can be characterized in a way that captures the basic normative claims made in its behalf but which is sensitive to the social, interrelated, and variable nature of the human agent.

References

Berofsky, Bernard. *Liberation from Self: A Theory of Personal Autonomy.* New York: Cambridge University Press, 1995.

Christman, John, ed. *The Inner Citadel: Essays on Individual Autonomy.* New York: Oxford University Press, 1989.

Dworkin, Gerald. "The Concept of Autonomy." In *The Inner Citadel: Essays on Individual Autonomy,* ed. J. Christman, 54–62. New York: Oxford University Press, 1989.

———. *The Theory and Practice of Autonomy.* Cambridge: Cambridge University Press, 1988.

Feinberg, Joel. *Harm to Self,* Vol. 3 of *The Moral Limits of the Criminal Law.* New York: Oxford University Press, 1986.

Gilligan, Carol. *In a Different Voice: Psychological Theory and Women's Development.* Cambridge MA: Harvard University Press, 1982.

Haworth, Lawrence. *Autonomy: An Essay in Philosophical Psychology and Ethics.* New Haven: Yale University Press, 1986.

Meyers, Diana T. *Self, Society and Personal Choice.* New York: Columbia University Press, 1989.

Unger, R.M. *Knowledge and Politics.* New York: Free Press, 1975.

Young, Robert. *Personal Autonomy: Beyond Negative and Positive Liberty.* New York: St. Martin's Press, 1986.

John Christman

See also LIBERTY; SELF-DETERMINATION, PERSONAL

Axiology

Axiology, one trend in modern philosophy, draws its theoretical antecedents from the thoughts of antiquity, since the explanations of philosophy include comments and claims about values. Axiological aspects came to the fore in the philosophy of the Enlightenment, in German philosophy (Immanuel Kant, Johann Fichte, Georg Hegel), and then in the axiological school and approaches to philosophy.

Legal theory also finds its antecedents in the philosophy of antiquity. Later the philosophy of the modern age applies its axiological theses in natural law. Under the influence of the neo-kantian legal philosophy, the definition of the values of law becomes a central category. Contemporary trends in legal philosophy do not ignore the problem of values.

Some legal philosophers consider the problem of values insoluble on account of the manifold and changing substance of values. This has given rise to abstract, formal explanations. The formal approach establishes the values of law irrespective of their substance; according to Hans Kelsen, legal values can be defined as formal values; the legal norm is itself the value of law. In addition, the view became accepted that there were no absolute values; the relative nature of legal values was stressed by Roscoe Pound. In today's legal theory an emphasis on the intuitive nature of legal values can frequently be found. Value is the consequence of the value-creating activity of men, the product of culture in the various spheres of social life, in production, education, regulation, religion, arts, and sciences. Besides the elaboration, assertion, and development of values, the deformation and destruction of values also has occurred; and the permanent contradiction between value and nonvalue has appeared in the various areas of social coexistence.

In many societies, despite their internal articulation of the system of particular values, values are interpreted narrowly in theory. Frequently artistic and scientific values are the only ones perceived, or moral values are emphasized alone. In view of this, the classification by G. Radbruch is significant. He separated individual, societal, and cultural values; one kind of values is the societal value incorporated in the law, in addition to the values which are manifest in the personality, as well as in the creative works of the arts and sciences. This description is fundamental, because it recognizes both the distinct nature of legal values and their distinction from moral values.

In the law, moral values naturally exercise an influence, but legal values cannot be identified with the moral ones; as a result of legal activity, separate legal values develop and exist sui generis. Legal value is not a natural or a spiritual idea, ideal, or moral principle, but a social category, objective, historic, and ontological. Consequently, legal value is not situated in the sphere of the spirit, which excludes reality, but is a reality which is the spritual and material achievement and regulator of human activity. Following T.I. Kohler and György Lukacs, value is a category of social reality and practice.

Finding the sui generis existence of legal value is accompanied by the conclusion that the legal norm is a value and that the law generally embodies values. The question arises: does the law represent a value in all circumstances? The historic fact can be established that the development of law represents progress over against conventional rules (customs, fetishes, taboos), the right of the strongest, and anarchy. Law is the result of the value-creating activity of a society, the achievement of legal culture. However, if we examine that later historical role of the law, we cannot give an unequivocal answer, because the contradiction between the creation and the destruction of value can be perceived also in the law, when legal values degenerate. That law is a value is especially doubtful in view of legal killings, cruelties, and inhumanities practiced within a legal framework. The social fact cannot be disregarded that the law sometimes exercises a harmful role. In other words, historical experience proves that under certain social conditions the law can also be a nonvalue.

The conclusion is that the law embodies a value as one achievement of culture, and that legal values exist; but this value does not play an exclusively positive role, does not exercise an influence as a value only, but is in certain historical circumstances a nonvalue. This peculiarity was seized upon by N. Hartmann and M. Scheler in their separation of positive and negative value. Legal institutions elaborated as a value can also be used in the service of non-values. In general, law being a value or a non-value is societally postulated and depends on the influence of the social environment.

The values of public life—equality, liberty, the protection of property, human rights—are embodied as separate values in the administration of justice, for instance, by equality before the law, civil rights, independence of the judiciary, the right to legal protection, adversarial procedure, directness, open hearings, and the institutionalization of appeal.

Lawyers' attitudes toward their responsibility can undo even the positive role of law. Even if no legal statute has been violated, the activity of the lawyer can be evaluated professionally and morally. This ethos of the legal profession is a decisive factor in the value-creating and value-asserting role of the law and lawyers.

References

Axtell, Guy. "Epistemic-Virtue Talk: The Reemergence of American Axiology." *Journal of Speculative Philosophy* 10 (1996), 172.

Bagolini, Luigi. "Value Judgments in Ethics and in Law." *Philosophical Quarterly* 1 (1951), 423–432.

Bahm, Archie. *Axiology, the Science of Values: Ethics, the Science of Oughtness.* Albuquerque NM: World Books, 1980.

Dror, Yehezkel. "Values and the Law." *Antioch Review* 17 (1957), 440–454.

Fuller, Lon L. "Human Purpose and Natural Law." *Journal of Philosophy* 53 (1956), 697–704.

Hatzimoysis, Anthony. "Ontology and Axiology." *Philosophy* 72 (1997), 293.

Saldanna, Nelson. "On the Origin of Law: Historical and Axiological Sides of the Problem." *Archiv für Rechts- und Sozialphilosophie* 55 (1969), 1–7.

Stevens, Gregory. "The Relations of Law and Obligation." *Proceedings of the American Catholic Philosophical Association* 29 (1955), 195–205.

Von Wright, Georg Henrik. "On Law and Morality: A Dialogue." *Ratio Juris* (1990), 321–330.

Wróblewski, Jerzy. "Evaluative Statements in Law: An Analytical Approach to Legal Axiology." *Rivista internazionale di filosifia del diritto* 58 (1981), 604–626.

Mihaly Samu

A

B

Bankruptcy

Congress designed Chapter 11 bankruptcy for debtors who might still be able to recover from the financial trouble that brought on incipient insolvency. Upon the debtor's filing of a Chapter 11 petition, the court issues a stay automatically to protect the debtor from "hounding" creditors. The debtor must submit a plan of reorganization, specifying how the debtor expects to return to maintain solvency. At this time, a creditor can raise an issue of good or bad faith filing. The courts utilize section 1112 of the bankruptcy code as a vehicle for dismissing a bankruptcy petition for cause, for example, bad faith. Among the myriad of situations involving bad faith intentions of the debtor, the three most common are tort claims, genuineness of the debt, and executory contracts.

In the area of unsatisfied tort claims, the payment of which would, in fact, render the debtor insolvent, the courts apply a good faith standard on a case-by-case basis. Since Chapter 11 does not require insolvency at the time of filing, a filing based on inability to pay tort claims does not violate the requirement of good faith.

The next category of suspect filings deals with the genuineness of the debtor's debts. Again, the issue is not the solvency of the debtor, but the validity of the debtor's debts, that is, debts that he cannot pay without becoming insolvent.

A final category of suspicious filings is in the form of executory contracts. Executory contracts may include leases, personal service contracts, and collective bargaining agreements. Two common threads run through these filings. First, if the executory contract would be too expensive for the debtor to complete the contract, the code allows the debtor some latitude to reject the executory contract. The case law describes "too expensive" as having a debilitating effect on the debtor's chances for successful reorganization. The second common thread is the filing of a dishonest, bad faith debtor who is merely seeking to rid himself of unwanted liabilities by defrauding his creditors.

A philosophical analysis of the decision to file Chapter 11 bankruptcy involves a moral assessment of motives and a review of the impacts on the stakeholders. In legal determinations based on the code, courts have used both legal and moral tools to formulate their reasoning. While debtors who file in bad faith gain several advantages, bad faith filings are detrimental to society.

The advantages associated with good faith filings are numerous. The protection of an automatic stay stops all attempts by creditors to collect their debts, thereby adding order and stability to the payment process. In many cases, the debtor-in-possession retains control and this allows management, who is most familiar with the debtor's problems, to make the financially challenged organization solvent. Financing arrangements may be made more readily available after a good faith Chapter 11 filing because those creditors would have a preferred standing vis-à-vis the other creditors. All this aggregates to aid the debtor in his reorganization and subsequent repayment of all creditors—the precise end that society has dictated.

The debtor must also review the negative consequences of filing Chapter 11. These range from full financial disclosure to a diminution of managerial control over the organization, through the court's and creditor's control over the reorganization plan. Additionally, such filings are expensive and time consuming for the debtor. The most paradoxical disadvantage to filing for reorganization bankruptcy is that the debtor, who may be left in possession, is the cause of the financial distress: the courts may be inviting further financial disaster by allowing the debtor to maintain control of the organization.

In conclusion, the philosophical issues presented are the motivations of good/bad faith filings, as well as the court's analysis of what constitutes such filings. The clearest statement of the complete philosophical question is: Who will pay?

References

In re: Johns-Manville Corp., 36 *Bankrupcty Review* 727 (1984).

In re: Plasmarc System, Inc., 18 *Bankruptcy Review* 306 (1982).

In re: Norco, Inc., 76 *Bankruptcy Review* 839 (1987).

Matter of Taylor, 103 *Bankruptcy Review* 511 (1989).

Matter of Truffles of Sarasota, Inc., 30 *Bankruptcy Review* 666 (1983).

Payne, Dinah, and M. Hogg. "Three Perspectives of Chapter 11 Bankruptcy: Legal, Managerial and Moral." *Journal of Business Ethics* 13 (1994), 21–30.

Dinah Payne
Michael Hogg

See also MONETARY POWER; SECONDARY RIGHTS; SECURITY

Beccaria, Cesare (1738–1794)

Born in Milan, Cesare Beccaria was a law professor and a top-ranking civil servant. His main work on the philosophy of law is his treatise *Dei delitti e delle pene,* originally published in Italian in 1764. According to Jean-Pierre Juillet, most subsequent editions have included changes in the order of chapters and paragraphs as introduced by André Morellet, in his French translation of 1766, for the purpose of enhancing the book's contribution to the struggle for penal law reformation. In this context, Beccaria's work soon became very popular, more so because it contributed new and important insights to the debate.

To Beccaria, the system of criminal law in eighteenth-century Europe had little to do with reason and wisdom, let alone humaneness. It had been shaped by traditions turning to obsolescence, by conflicting wills to power, by chance, by centuries of prejudice, abuse, and inhumanity. Nowadays, so he says, it is still plagued with arbitrariness, irregular process, and barbarian concepts of punishment. Given the stakes in terms of public life and happiness, the Enlightenment must be brought to bear on law as well as on any other aspect of the human experience.

In view of securing protection for their interests, so Beccaria says, human beings have agreed to transfer the smallest possible part of their natural freedom to a public sphere, on which they have implicitly vested the right to intervene against the effect of private passions. Laws are founded on the need to preserve this public "deposit" (Beccaria's term) of freedom insofar as it is beneficial to individuals, while such a need establishes the limits in which punishment must be circumscribed in order to be just. From this, Beccaria draws three principles: (1) Laws alone may ascribe punishment to particular offenses. (2) The sovereign is entitled to make general laws but not to judge on specific infractions. (3) Cruel punishments are disgusting, contrary to reason and justice, and useless. In the interest of justice, one must make sure also that laws are clear and carry predictable and equitable consequences for everyone. To achieve this, it is necessary that local judges, among whom there are too many "petty tyrants," content themselves with examining actions and refrain from interpreting the law.

Given that punishment makes sense, in terms of social utility, in relation to the amount of deterrence actually produced, it must be public, quick, and inevitable. These characters complete each other and allow for maximal dissuasive effects. For people, Beccaria says, are more likely to abstain from crime if they are threatened with moderate but certain penalties, rather than with cruelties theoretically extreme, but practically improbable. Furthermore, given that offenses can be measured in terms of damage caused to society, penalties must remain proportionate to the acts that they aim to suppress. For punishing different misdeeds in the same way amounts to leveling out their gravity and to blurring relevant moral distinctions in people's minds.

Generally speaking, and regardless of the logic according to which punishment must fit the crime, Beccaria argues for moderation, since lack of moderation is both counterproductive and inhumane.

For the same reasons, he also adopts a firm stance against judicial torture (which was to be abolished in France in 1780). He condemns such a practice not only as barbarian but also as inherently unjust, since it amounts to inflicting punishment on someone whose guilt is still to be proven, who must therefore be presumed innocent, and who might be so in reality. For the same reasons he dwells at length on his opposition to the death penalty, which cannot be, in his opinion, legally founded (although he provides for some very specific exceptions).

Partly original, partly a reflection of legal trends that had been developing for a while, Beccaria's main work has been widely read, commented upon, and used. It has constituted, therefore, a key contribution to the movement that led to the reformation of criminal law on the basis of an emerging ethic of human rights.

References

Beccaria, Cesare. *Des délits et des peines* (Crime and Punishment). Ed. and intro. Jean-Pierre Juillet. Paris: Flammarion, 1979.

André Mineau

Bentham, Jeremy (1748–1832)

Jeremy Bentham is one of the most important figures in the history of jurisprudence. Yet the extent of his contributions to legal and political theory, the complexity of his philosophical analyses, and the sophistication of his views are only now beginning to be appreciated. The sheer volume of Bentham's work is staggering and renders difficult a summary of his legal thought. Bentham remains the staunchest assailant of the common law tradition, which he denounced as the nemesis of progress and a copious fountain of human misery. To take its place, he constructed a positivist theory of law grounded on the following criteria: rationality, clarity, publicity, generality, comprehensiveness, and systematicity.

John Stuart Mill aptly referred to Bentham as "the great questioner of things established" and "the father of English innovation." With a zeal verging on obsessive, Bentham attacked the common law as William Blackstone defended it in his *Commentaries on the Laws of England*. According to Bentham, the methods of the common law are the root of law's inefficiency, rigidity, arbitrariness, obscurity, and inhumanity. A thick veil of tradition, mystery, formality, technicality, and jargon envelops the law.

Litigants face a maximum of confusion, vexation, delay, and expense; and the outcomes of legal processes are capricious and uncertain. The common law only serves the "sinister" (vested) interests of that "passive and enervate race," legal professionals. Common law practice, "ancestor-worship," is an apology for the status quo. The common law obstructs critical assessments of existing law by confounding what exists (law as it is) with what is right, reasonable, or just (law as it ought to be).

Bentham's legal positivism propels these criticisms. In his view, the true function of jurisprudence is not "expository," but "censorial." The censor must keep separate questions about law's existence and validity from questions about law's justification and morality. Censorial jurisprudence is a dynamic enterprise undertaken to improve legal systems. Considerations of improvement are moral considerations. The question is: What standard of value is required for improving the law? The common law's appeals to custom, tradition, "natural" rights and other "nonsensical" concepts for the development and justification of law conceals and sustains the consolidation of power in a ruling elite accountable to no one. This shroud of "fiction" is a cloak for despotism: it underlies an authoritarian conception of law, parasitic on the people's loss of independent judgment. Bentham called himself "the Luther of Jurisprudence."

The foundation of Bentham's constructive jurisprudence is the principle of utility, which should be "ruler of all things." The pivotal task of law is to establish the framework for social interaction, security, and general happiness. Like David Hume (whom Bentham greatly admired) and other positivists, Bentham believed that law is conventional, created by humans and for humans, notably for the satisfaction of our basic needs. The rationale for adhering to precedents ("dead men's views") lies not in their force as moral standards, but rather in their role in maintaining the security of people's expectations. Because security is key to social stability, the law must meet a stringent publicity standard. In addition, judicial activity must cease to be retroactive, as it is in the common law system. Bentham urged that the functions of judge and legislator be kept clearly distinct. Judges must apply general rules to particular cases. Their chief call is to balance competing interests by determining the relative weight of the parties' expectations, which always "follow the finger of the law." Judicial activity, which must respect precedent, is rigid and inescapably arbitrary, as "legislation." Legislators must flexibly frame general rules on the basis of their comprehensive view of society and of an appreciation of the requirements for the general good.

Bentham turned the traditional justification for the common law on its head. Blackstone had argued that this tradition combined two supreme virtues: respect for ancient wisdom and judicial ability to adjust law to new conditions. He was not a fan of parliamentary legislation or of statutory law, which he criticized as crude, uncompromising, and ultimately whimsical. Bentham's response is that in a nonarbitrary legal system all law issues from a sovereign legislator. Law properly so-called is the expression of the will of the legislative power, which is backed by sanctions. The only justification of law is utility—the maximization of happiness (pleasure) or the minimization of misery (pain). Only the principle of utility can be the foundation of a system whose end is "to rear the fabric of felicity by the hands of reason and of law." In this system, laws will be rational, clear, public, general, and systematically ordered rules. Among many others, Bentham coined the term "codification" to refer to the written and systematic ordering of laws in a comprehensive code—the "Pannomion." This code would contain all laws duly enacted by the legislative body, together with a brief account of their utilitarian rationale. Bentham acknowledged the herculean character of this project of "rationalization." Yet he believed that it would provide the basis for stable political life: it would force judges and legislators always to follow the dictates of utility; and it would enable citizens to obey the law willingly, rather than out of unreflective habit, intimidation, or fear. The restraint of officials committed to utility and an informed citizenry are true safeguards against tyranny.

References

Bentham, Jeremy. *A Fragment on Government.* 1776. Reprint, Cambridge: Cambridge University Press, 1988.

———. *An Introduction to the Principles of Morals and Legislation.* Ed. J.H. Burns and H.L.A. Hart. London: Athlone Press, 1970.

———. *Of Laws in General.* Ed. H.L.A. Hart. London: Athlone Press, 1970.

Harrison, Ross. *Bentham.* London: Routledge & Kegan Paul, 1983.

Hart, H.L.A. *Essays on Bentham: Studies in Jurisprudence and Political Theory.* Oxford: Clarendon Press, 1982.

Postema, Gerald. *Bentham and the Common Law Tradition.* Oxford: Clarendon Press, 1986.

Rosen, Frederick. *Jeremy Bentham and Representative Democracy: A Study of the "Constitutional Code."* Oxford: Clarendon Press, 1973.

Rosenblum, Nancy. *Bentham's Theory of the Modern State.* Cambridge MA: Harvard University Press, 1978.

Sample, Janet. *Bentham's Prison: A Study of the Panopticon Penitentiary.* Oxford: Clarendon Press, 1993.

Maria H. Morales

Betrothal

Betrothal (betrothement, engagement, marriage promise) is an event in which two persons promise to marry each other. The law on betrothal differs greatly between nations. At the very least, national laws usually answer questions concerning the marriage settlement, which can be made only by the engaged couple. In some legal systems there are norms to determine, for example, the (re)distribution of betrothal gifts should the engaged couple end their engagement.

There is little philosophical discussion that concerns directly and explicitly the subject of betrothal. However, much has been said about the issue in other contexts, including, first of all, the context of writings in philosophy of love. Perhaps the most interesting questions related to betrothal are the following two. First, is it conceptually meaningful to promise to love somebody? Second, who qualifies as a party to be engaged?

A person may well argue that engagement is a conceptually confusing event, since it does not seem to make sense to *promise to love* somebody. This view has several presuppositions. The main presupposition, of course, is that a promise to marry someone is a promise to love someone. This presupposition can easily be questioned, but no doubt we feel that marriage and love should have something to do with each other. Another presupposition of the view here is that one cannot promise to love someone. This view is tempting, since loving is not (note, on standard readings) a matter of free choice, so to say. Apparently, one can promise to make a business deal with someone next week, but how could anyone promise to love another person next week? Of course, there is no problem in promising to *try* to love another person. It is also unproblematic to *say* that a person promises to love somebody, but saying "I promise" does not always constitute a promise. If it is true that engagement is conceptually problematic, this may have interesting results when the moral significance of engagement is evaluated. If the whole event does not make sense conceptually, it may be questionable to assign blame for the termination of an engagement. The party who is left may be disappointed, but is anyone justified to expect that she or he will be loved because someone said so? If not, perhaps it should be stated that ending one's engagement can be morally wrong merely because in some cases it makes the other party sad. In his *The Agony of Legal Marriage* Pedro-Juan Viladrich discusses the connection between legal marriage and love.

Who qualifies as a party to be engaged? This is an important question, since it seems to have a direct bearing on the question of who qualifies as a party in marriage. Indeed, it is because we believe that engagement leads to marriage that we tend to think that not all persons qualify as a party. As such, there is no problem for anyone to say to another person that she or he promises to marry and perhaps to love the other person. A father could say this to his daughter and vice versa. A mother could say this to all her colleagues and colleagues could say this to her. Still, people in Western cultures do not normally think that a father and a daughter could be engaged to marry, nor that one person could be a party in an engagement of multiple couples. Can a woman be engaged to another woman, or a man to another man? Legal systems differ on this question, and so do people's viewpoints.

Those who oppose homosexual engagements oppose either homosexuality in general or homosexual engagements in particular. General arguments against homosexuality often have religious roots. A much discussed argument against homosexual engagement in particular is a view that to accept homosexual engagement is to accept homosexual marriage, which in turn is to accept the idea that homosexual couples are entitled to adopt children, and this is not a good result, as the well-being of children in such relationships, the argument goes, is not secured. Perhaps the strongest argument for a homosexual engagement is the point that homosexuals should have as much right to set up a family as heterosexuals, since sexual behavior is not a morally relevant property that should justify discrimination.

References

Beck, Ulrich, and Elisabeth Beck-Gernsheim. *The Normal Chaos of Love.* Cambridge: Polity Press, 1995.

Burgess, Ernest. *Courtship, Engagement, and Marriage.* Chicago: Lippincott, 1954.

———. *Engagement and Marriage.* Chicago: Lippincott, 1953.

Kuchler, Frances. *Law of Engagement and Marriage.* New York: Oceana: 1978.

Lear, Jonathan. *Love and Its Place in Nature.* New York: Noonday Press, 1990.

Rice, Lee C. "Homosexuality and Social Order." In *Philosophy of Sex,* ed. Alan Soble, 256–280. Totowa NJ: Rowman and Littlefield, 1980.

Viladrich, Pedro-Juan. *The Agony of Legal Marriage: An Introduction to the Basic Conceptual Elements of Matrimony.* Pamplona: University of Navarra Press, 1990.

Juha Raikka

See also DIVORCE AND MARRIAGE; FAMILY LAW; MARRIAGE CONTRACT

Betti, Emilio (1890–1968)

In the field of legal-philosophical twentieth-century studies Emilio Betti advances a general theory of interpretation concerning a reflection on hermeneutics. The Italian Romanist–philosopher considers interpretation as a fundamental category of legal knowledge. In the wake of the idealist-romanticist tradition, through neo-kantianism and phenomenology, he accepts Nicolai Hartmann's philosophy of values and tries to find the theoretical foundations of his methodology in this approach. Betti develops a methodological and critical hermeneutics regarding the *Geisteswissenschaften* (humane studies), antithetical to ontological hermeneutics. He attends to the rational control of the process of interpretation. The historicist conception of reality as a continuous process of objectivations of the mind, which present themselves in representative forms, constitutes the background of Betti's hermeneutical theory. The law takes root here.

Interpretation has a triadic form comprising the interpreter, the existence of an other mind, and its expression. Understanding demands transposition into another subjectivity that differs from the original one, and implies a requirement for objectivity: the interpreter's reconstruction of the meaning contained in representative forms has to correspond to their meaning-content as closely as possible. This requirement demands the subjectivity of the interpreter, but, as well, it holds to the solidity of the hermeneutical object. On this basis Betti constructs a model of legal interpretation.

The antinomy between subjectivity and objectivity leads to the dialectic emerging in any process of interpretation and lays the basis for a methodology that will guarantee correct results, in legal contexts and elsewhere, through the use of "hermeneutical canons." These are related both to the object (the hermeneutical autonomy of the object and immanence of the hermeneutical standard; the totality and coherence of hermeneutical evaluation) and to the subject (the actuality of understanding; the harmonization of understanding—hermeneutical correspondence of meaning). Through these canons objectivity in interpretation is achievable. In this perspective, Betti pays attention to the guidelines for interpretation in order to resolve the problem of the objective understanding of meaning, but he is still absorbed by the subject-object polarities of positivist epistemology.

Betti considers different kinds of interpretation (reproductive, recognitive, normative), each with its own principles. In legal contexts normative interpretation is used. This goes beyond the single task of the purely recognitive investigation of meaning. It has the task of adaptation, application, improvement, and providing guidelines for present activity. The legal order, for Betti, constitutes an organic unity, a totality coherent to itself. If the role of interpretation is to understand the norm in its intimate coherence, then proceeding by analogy constitutes the method to re-extract the maxims for decision that lead to self-integration of the legal order. Betti admits that the hermeneutical act is creative.

Realization of law is a shaping activity, aimed at recognizing and reconstructing the meaning to be attributed to representative forms defining the sources of legal evaluations, and retaining the efficiency of these evaluations in the life of a society. It is an inquiry into the interests at stake in order to concretize abstract legal norms. In this respect the Italian jurist gives to the legislator's intentions an important influence. In this way he maintains the specificity of legal interpretation and the relationship between legislative rationality and authority. However, by considering interpretation as the transposition of meaning from the original perspective of the author (the legislator) into the subjectivity of the interpreter, and alloting the interpreter the task of recognizing the intentions manifested in objectivations of the spirit of the author, Betti is still caught, at the same time, by psychologism and positivism. This did not allow him to be successful in the field of *general* hermeneutics.

Betti distinguishes the role of the historian of law from that of the lawyer, whose task is to apply the law, claiming (against the thinking of Hans-Georg Gadamer) the difference between recognition and application. Reference to the historicity of understanding is seen as a relapse into subjectivism.

Betti has stressed important hermeneutical problems, which are central in the contemporary debate. He systematically organized the wealth of traditional hermeneutical thought and was involved in an idealist-realist eclecticism. He also anticipated some results of the methodological thinking of contemporary legal hermeneutics. If questions concerning the conditions of validity of interpretations are a central aspect of hermeneutics, the contribution of Betti's legal philosophy is still relevant.

References

Betti, Emilio. *Die Hermeneutik als allgemeine Methodik der Geisteswissenschaften* (Hermeneutics as Comprehensive Methodology in Human Sciences). 1962. 2d ed. Tübingen: Mohr, 1972.

———. "Hermeneutics as the General Methodology of the Geisteswissenschaften." In *Contemporary Hermeneutics: Hermeneutics as Method, Philosophy and Critique*, ed. Josef Bleicher, 51–93. London: Routledge and Kegan Paul, 1980.

———. *Teoria generale dell'interpretazione* (General Theory of Interpretation). 1955. 2 vols. Ed. Giuliano Crifò. Milano: Giuffrè, 1990.

Emilio Betti e la scienza giuridica del Novecento (Emilio Betti and Nineteenth Century Legal Science). *Quaderni fiorentini per la storia del pensiero giuridico* 7 (1978).

Frosini, Vittorio, and Francesco Riccobono, eds. *L'ermeneutica giuridica di Emilio Betti* (Emilio Betti's Legal Hermeneutics). Milano: Giuffrè, 1994.

Gray, Christopher B. "Betti, Hermeneutic and the Suit at Law." *Archiv für Rechts- und Sozialphilosophie* 70 (1984), 138–143.

Griffero, Tonino. *Interpretare. La teoria di Emilio Betti e il suo contesto* (Interpretation: Emilio Betti's Theory in Context). Torino: Rosenberg e Sellier, 1988.

Grondin, Jean. "L'hermeneutique comme science rigoureuse selon Emilio Betti" (Hermeneutics as Strict Science for Emilio Betti) (1890–1968). *Archives de Philosophie* 53 (1990), 177–198.

Ingram, David. "The Historical Genesis of the Gadamer-Habermas Controversy." *Auslegung* 10 (1983), 86–151.

Noakes, Susan. "Emilio Betti's Debt to Vico." *New Vico Studies* 6 (1988), 51–57.

Studi in onere di Emilio Betti (Essays for Emilio Betti). 5 vols. Milano: Giuffré, 1970.

Zaccaria, Giuseppe. *Questioni di interpretazione* (Issues in Interpretation). Padova: Cedam, 1996.

Baldassare Pastore

Bill of Rights; Charter Rights

See ENTRENCHMENT

Blackstone, William (1723–1780)

Sir William Blackstone, jurist and author of a number of legal works, is best known for his *Commentaries on the Laws of England*, published in four volumes between 1765 and 1769, after his election as the first Vinerian Professor of Common Law in the University of Oxford in 1758. The work was based on a course of lectures first delivered in 1753, in which he aimed "to lay down a general and comprehensive plan of the laws of England" that would deduce their history and illustrate their leading rules and fundamental principles. The *Commentaries* was the single most important book on English law written in the eighteenth century and became essential reading for more than a century for both the budding lawyer and the cultivated gentleman. As a comprehensive overview of the common law, there had been nothing to rival it in scope and vision since *Bracton*.

The *Commentaries'* success can be attributed both to its style, which was elegant and readable, and to its structure, which showed that the common law was a scientific system no less worthy of academic study than Roman law. Blackstone wanted to portray English law as a coherent set of substantive rights and rules, rather than merely as the mass of fragmented procedures and precedents that was to be found in existing legal literature. Since the common law had no clear structure of its own, he borrowed from Roman law, being influenced in his arrangement in particular by Gothofredus' edition of Justinian's *Institutes*. The structure was well suited to accommodate those parts of the law where a body of substantive rules had emerged, such as the law of real property or crime. Blackstone had greater problems in accommodating those areas of law (such as contract) where rights were still largely bound up in procedure. Nevertheless, his efforts to rationalize the law acted as a spur to a series of other writers to compose treatises on different branches of the law, showing them to be based on clear and coherent principles.

Besides giving a concise and accurate summary of the law, Blackstone sought to show that there was a unifying principle that could explain its rules. To that end, he included a discussion of natural law in the introduction to the *Commentaries*. However, Blackstone was not a sophisticated theorist—much of his theorizing was borrowed from Burlamaqui—and the rationalist natural law set out at the start of the work was not used as an analytical tool elsewhere. The place of natural law in his thought seemed further diminished by the fact that he defined municipal law

B

in positivist terms, and said that in every constitution there was "a supreme, irresistible, absolute, uncontrolled authority." Some scholars have sought to explain the apparent contradiction in his position by pointing out that Blackstone (like his natural law predecessors) distinguished between natural laws and indifferent ones, which derived their authority from imposition, and by showing that the law which was dealt with in the *Commentaries* was for the most part indifferent and of positive origin. Others have suggested that Blackstone's positivistic view of the powers of the king-in-parliament was an uncontentious reflection of eighteenth-century reality, and that his use of natural law was merely intellectual decoration. Whatever his theoretical views, however, it is clear that Blackstone did not envisage an active and interventionist parliament. Indeed, he was highly suspicious of the impact of statute law on the common law.

The contradictions in Blackstone's position are best resolved by noting that the notions of custom and reason were more important to his common law thought than the continental natural law theorizing he invoked at the outset. In his view, the common law had emerged out of the customs of the people, as articulated by the judges, "the living oracles" of the law. The common law was natural because it had grown out of the needs of the English over a long period of time; it was rational because it could survive scrutiny not by the abstract reason of every subject, but the trained "artificial" reason of the lawyers. Blackstone's favored metaphor for the common law was thus "an old Gothic castle, erected in the days of chivalry, but fitted up for a modern inhabitant." It could only be understood by examining its history.

These views made Blackstone appear to many of his successors as a conservative apologist for a chaotic legal system much in need of reform. Jeremy Bentham in particular was able to attack the philosophical contradictions in Blackstone's introductory section: yet it may be doubted whether Bentham would have been able to develop his theories of law and law reform if the *Commentaries* had not been published.

References

Cairns, J.W. "Blackstone, an English Institutist: Legal Literature and the Rise of the Nation-State." *Oxford Journal of Legal Studies* 4 (1984), 318–360.

Hart, H.L.A. "Blackstone's Use of the Law of Nature." *Butterworth's South African Law Review* (1966), 169–174.

Kennedy, Duncan. "The Structure of Blackstone's Commentaries." *Buffalo Law Review* 28 (1979), 205–382.

Lieberman, David. *The Province of Legislation Determined.* Cambridge: Cambridge University Press, 1989.

Lobban, Michael. *The Common Law and English Jurisprudence 1760–1850.* Oxford: Clarendon Press, 1991.

Lucas, P. "Ex parte Sir William Blackstone, 'Plagiarist': A Note on Blackstone and Natural Law." *American Journal of Legal History* 7 (1963), 142–158.

Milson, S.F.C. "The Nature of Blackstone's Achievement." *Oxford Journal of Legal Studies* 1 (1981), 1–12.

Watson, Alan. "The Structure of Blackstone's Commentaries." *Yale Law Journal* 97 (1988), 795–821.

Michael Lobban

Bobbio, Norberto (1909–)

One of the most influential Italian intellectuals of the second half of this century, Norberto Bobbio, born in Turin, taught jurisprudence and political philosophy at the universities of Camerino, Siena, Padua, and Turin for over forty years. After the Second World War, he founded the school of Italian analytical legal positivism. He is the foremost legal and political theorist in Italy today. In 1984, he was made a Life Member of the Italian Senate.

Bobbio's first philosophical outlook was largely formed by Benedetto Croce's historicism as well as by the phenomenology of Edmund Husserl and Max Scheler and by the existentialism of Martin Heidegger and Karl Jaspers. In the mid-1940s he abandoned these philosophies to embrace a very different approach, influenced by logical positivism. Bobbio saw such an approach as being simultaneously rigorous, rationalistic, empirical, and ethically and politically committed. For these reasons this approach was suited to his own epistemological preferences, which have always been against the trends of what he has called the "Italian Ideology," that is congenitally speculative and idealistic in bias.

After World War II, these developments culminated in Bobbio being the founder of

Italian analytical legal positivism, an approach marked by an eclectic but fruitful attempt to graft a philosophical outlook—logical positivism—into the legal positivism of Hans Kelsen's pure theory of law.

In a first phase (1949–1965) Bobbio's theory of law was marked by his acceptance of Kelsen's interpretation of legal theory as a scientific, value-free form of legal study not concerned with the moral or political evaluation of law, nor with the sociological description of legal phenomena, but with the analysis of fundamental legal concepts and with the structure and logical interrelation of the elements of a legal system.

In Bobbio's opinion, many problems, which could not be solved by analyzing single legal rules, can be successfully addressed by elaborating a theory of legal systems. So, in his *Teoria dell'ordinamento giuridico,* Bobbio contended that the definition of law, as well as the distinction of law from other normative phenomena such as morals and customs, is possible only if the legal system is taken into consideration. There are no special features belonging to all legal rules and only to legal rules. A rule is legal because it belongs to a legal system; a system is legal because of the specific characteristics it has as a system.

This account of legal systems allowed Bobbio to acknowledge the existence of different types of legal rules. He refused Kelsen's reduction of all legal norms to duty- or sanction-imposing rules, taking into consideration the wide class of second-level rules (meta-rules), such as power-conferring rules, constitutive rules, and the like. The classification of different kinds of legal rules and the description of their interrelationship within legal systems has been one of Bobbio's main contributions to legal theory.

Toward the mid-1960s, Bobbio came to a major turning point in his interpretation of legal theory. It became clear that the two basic neo-positivistic philosophical assumptions at the root of Bobbio's outlook, namely the theory of discourse levels and the distinction between "is" and "ought" statements, were not consistent with Kelsen's interpretation of legal theory as a scientific endeavor. First, Bobbio distinguished between legal theory (jurisprudence) and the discussion of the method of legal theory (meta-jurisprudence). Second, he criticized Kelsen's meta-jurisprudence as prescriptive, thus not scientific at all because it did not aim at describing what jurists actually do but at prescribing what they should do. Third, Bobbio argued that Kelsen's doctrine of the basic norm, which gives unity and validity to a legal order, must rely on an ideological rather than a logical ground and for this reason cannot be the basis for a value-free science of law.

In this second phase (from 1965 onward) Bobbio thus acknowledged the prescriptive nature of the legal positivists' approach to law. Such an approach is not based on the desire to elaborate a scientific, value-free legal theory. Rather, the idea of a scientific description of the law is maintained by legal positivists because such an idea is logically required by the very notion of applying the law, which is central to the working of legal and political institutions based on the rule of law.

Since the 1970s, Bobbio has developed on the one hand a sociological theory aimed at describing the social functions of law; on the other hand he has increasingly devoted his studies to political theory. In his functional analysis of law, Bobbio has focused on the "promotional" function played by legal orders of developed countries, by stimulating desirable behaviors, mainly in economic and business activity, through positive sanctions such as subsidies, tax exemptions, and so on. This function is one of the characteristic features of the welfare state, defended by Bobbio, as opposed to the liberal minimal state.

In fact, liberalism defended by Bobbio is basically a doctrine of constitutional guarantees for individual freedom and civil rights, and not an economic theory of the free market.

Bobbio's main concern in political theory has always been that of reconciling the guarantees of the liberal-democratic state with the demands of socialists for greater equality. He suggests that socialists must rethink their goals of social equality in ways compatible with the institutional framework of liberal democracies. Representative democracy, he contends, has to be seen as a set of rules that cannot be given up if the risk of producing despotic regimes is to be avoided. Social rights, as the extension of civil and political rights, will be granted through the extension of representative democracy to the level of social life—to bureaucracies, to health and educational authorities, to the workplace, and so on.

Bobbio has consistently played a part in active political debate in many fields: politics and culture, the defense of human and civil rights, the problem of peace in the nuclear age. A major contribution by Bobbio to political theory has been to show the strict link between human rights, peace, and democracy.

References

Anderson, P. "The Affinities of Norberto Bobbio." *New Left Review* 170 (July–August 1988), 3–36.

Bobbio, Norberto. *Cosmopolitan Democracy: An Agenda for a New World Order.* Ed. Daniele Archangeli and David Held. Cambridge: Polity Press, 1995.

———. *Giusnaturalismo e positivismo giuridico* (Natural Law and Legal Positivism). Milano: Comunità, 1965.

———. *Studi per una teoria generale del diritto* (Studies Toward a General Theory of Law). Torino: Giappichelli, 1970.

———. *Teoria generale del diritto* (General Theory of Law). Torino: Giappichelli, 1993. Republication of *Teoria della norma giuridica* (Theory of Legal Norms), 1958, and *Teoria dell'ordinamento giuridica* (Theory of Legal Order), 1960.

Borsellino, Patrizia. "L'analogia nell logica del diritto: un contributo di Norberto Bobbio alla metodologia giuridica" (Analogy in Legal Logic: A Contribution by Norberto Bobbio to Legal Methodology). *Rivista internazionale di filosifia del diritto* 62 (1985), 3–39.

Chataway, Teresa. "Introduction to Norberto Bobbio." *Thesis Eleven* 48 (1997), 111.

Guastini, Riccardo. "I giuristi alla ricerca della scienza (Releggendo Bobbio)" (Jurists in Search of Science [Rereading Bobbio]). *Rivista internazionale di filosofia del diritto* 64 (1987), 179–195.

Lyubin, V. "Norberto Bobbio: Politics and Intellectuals." *Social Sciences* 24 (1993), 167.

Possenti, Vittorio. "Difficolta della filosofia pubblica (Riflessioni sul pensiero di Norberto Bobbio)" (Problems in Public Philosophy [Reflections on Norberto Bobbio's Thinking]). *Filosofia* 40 (1989), 151–174.

Sbarberi, Franco. "La formation de la théorie democratique chez Bobbio" (Origins of Democratic Theory in Bobbio). Trans. Jacques Rolland. *Archives de Philosophie* 57 (1994), 3–31.

Violi, Carlo, and Bruno Maiorca, eds. *Norberto Bobbio: 50 anni di studi* (Norberto Bobbio: 50 Years of Research). Milano: Angeli, 1984.

Violi, Carlo, and Bruno Maiorca. *Norberto Bobbio: bibliografico degli scritti 1984–1988 et su Norberto Bobbio* (Norberto Bobbio: Bibliography of Writings by author Norberto Bobbio 1984–1988). Milano: F. Angdil, 1990.

Patrizia Borsellino

Bodenheimer, Edgar (1908–1991)

Edgar Bodenheimer was a major contributor to the revival of natural law theory in the wake of World War II. His works were systematic as well as normative, renowned for their careful attention to historical sources and the clarity of their summaries of competing views. He drew on a wide range of disciplines, including modern psychoanalytic and anthropological theories, to defend the natural law tradition against positivistic arguments for a strict conceptual distinction between law and justice. His career spanned those of three contemporary giants of legal philosophy: Hans Kelsen (1881–1973), H.L.A. Hart (1907–1992), and Ronald Dworkin (1931–). He challenged each in articulating his own distinctive conception of the relevance of natural law to the validity and content of positive law.

Bodenheimer's jurisprudence was essentially dialectical: he did not reject conceptual analysis but subordinated it to the construction of a synthetic overview of the nature and function of law. He called for "an 'integrative' jurisprudence which would combine analytical studies of the law with sociological descriptions and an understanding of the value-components of legal ordering," rejecting "the dichotomy and tension between imperative and sociological approaches to the law" in favor of "a synthesis of analytic jurisprudence, realistic interpretations of psychological, social and cultural facts, and the valuable ingredients of the natural law doctrine."

Bodenheimer attacked Hart's analytical positivism as shortsighted. While he agreed with Hart that the natural conditions of social life and human psychology require any functional legal system to respect certain fundamental norms that Hart conceded could be viewed as the "minimum content" of natural law, Bodenheimer's conception of natural law was operational as well as structural. Bodenheimer argued for a "synthesis of order and justice" that would condition legal validity on "the elementary norms of natural law" not only when a written constitution has incorporated into the positive law abstract notions of justice, as with the "due process" clauses of the Fifth and Fourteenth amendments to the United States Constitution, but also independently of the positive law, provided that judges confine such extra-constitutional invalidation of positive law on natural law grounds to extreme cases of "monstrous, inhuman, and palpably unconscionable decrees." In more ordinary circumstances, he believed that the principal relevance of natural law theory was as a nonformal source of law to be used in interpreting and applying the positive law in doubtful cases. Although generally sympathetic to Dworkin's philosophical justification for consideration of arguments of justice in judicial decision making, Bodenheimer expressed strong disagreement on matters of detail, rejecting Dworkin's claim that in doubtful cases judges should give priority to arguments of individual rights over arguments of the common good.

For Bodenheimer justice was a synergistic ideal of social organization. A just state would protect both freedom and order and conceive of them as complementary political values, while demanding compromise at the margin where autonomy and efficiency might conflict. He emphatically rejected Kelsen's claim that justice was an irrational ideal and endorsed the view of Chaïm Perelman (1912–1984) that principles of justice could rationally be established and given legal application by a process of dialectical reasoning that would seek a constructive consensus among reasonable persons seeking to flourish both individually and communally within a given polity. As such, adjudication was to be conceived as culturally constrained but not value-neutral. Thus, Bodenheimer's understanding of the natural law tradition was one which legitimated judicial decisions that supplemented or interpreted the positive law in light of the fundamental purpose of law as a human artifact intended to organize society for the common good, the naturally determined needs and psychologies of any human population seeking to regulate the behavior of constituents in ways conducive to social efficiency but sensitive to individual differences and autonomy, and the received traditions of a particular society as to the appropri-

ate balance to be struck between individual freedom and social utility.

Bodenheimer was self-consciously aware that his desire to legitimate natural law as a component of contemporary legal theory was in part a reaction to the excesses of Nazi Germany, which he had personally experienced. A Jew born in Berlin, he emigrated to the United States in 1933 and held several positions as an attorney for the federal government before serving as a prosecutor at the Nuremberg trials. He taught law at the University of Utah from 1946 to 1966, and thereafter at the University of California at Davis.

References

Bodenheimer, Edgar. "Hart, Dworkin, and the Problem of Judicial Lawmaking Discretion." *Georgia Law Review* 11 (1977), 1143–1172.

———. *Jurisprudence: The Philosophy and Method of the Law.* 1962. Rev. ed. Cambridge MA: Harvard University Press, 1974.

———. "Modern Analytical Jurisprudence and the Limits of Its Usefulness." *University of Pennsylvania Law Review* 104 (1956), 1080–1086.

———. "Perelman's Contribution to Legal Methodology." *Northern Kentucky Law Review* 12 (1985), 391–417.

———. *Philosophy of Responsibility.* Littleton CO: Rothman, 1980.

———. *Power, Law, and Society.* New York: Crane Russak, 1973.

———. "Seventy-Five Years of Evolution of Legal Philosophy." *American Journal of Jurisprudence* 23 (1978), 181–211.

———. *Treatise on Justice.* New York: Philosophical Library, 1967.

The Reemergence of Natural Law Jurisprudence in Decisional Law. Symposium in Memory of Professor Edgar Bodenheimer. University of California at Davis Law Review 26, No. 3 (Spring 1993), 503.

John B. Oakley

Burial

See DISPOSITION OF REMAINS

Burke, Edmund (1729–1797)

Edmund Burke, English statesman and writer, of Irish descent, his father an attorney, his mother a Catholic, attended Trinity College, entered Parliament in 1765, but soon abandoned law as a profession and tried to make his mark in London on the literary arena. He published, in the 1750s, a satire, directed at Bolingbroke (*Vindication of Natural Society*), and in aesthetic theory (*Ideas of the Sublime and Beautiful*). With Oliver Goldsmith and a few others, he belonged to the original members of Johnson's Literary Club. Burke was an early exponent of the romantic movement, first to emerge in England, and indeed leader and inspiration for the school of the Lake Poets.

In politics, Burke's first appointment was a brief period under W.G. Hamilton, when the latter was chief secretary in Ireland. He then joined Lord Rockingham, one of the Whig magnates, whose secretary and advisor in commercial matters he became. During Rockingham's short premiership from 1765 to 1766, Burke, acting as whip, was instrumental in repealing the controversial Stamp Act, which levied a tax on the American colonies, and in trying to set to right some of the many corrupt practices of the England of the rotten boroughs. Later, after Rockingham's premature death, Burke found another patron in Lord Fitzwilliam. For many years he sat as member, most importantly for Bristol, in the House of Commons.

Burke's private life was later to be overshadowed by personal grief at the loss of his son, if not, as contemporary malice had it, by downright insanity. Ever present financial worries, much due to speculation together with his brother, and the breach of political friendships, such as with Charles James Fox, added to this. Burke had acquired an estate and, though of middle-class origin, lived the part of a representative of the natural aristocracy of his own teachings.

Burke never reached cabinet rank. Nonetheless, his political career had a tremendous impact. He became the European oracle of the antirevolutionary forces through his famous *Reflections on the Revolution in France*, published in 1790; George III is supposed to have said that the pamphlet version of this book should be read by every gentleman. In the same vein Burke attacked, in some of the latest outpourings of his seemingly never tiring energies, the "regicide peace" that in 1796 was being sought with the revolutionary government in Paris. On this issue of the French Revolution, Burke virtually caused the split of the Whig party, and he thereby laid the foundations of modern conservatism.

Just as vigorous was his defense of English liberties at home. With the accession of George III in 1760 things had changed. Unlike the predecessors of his house, the new king was trying to reassert the monarchy, which had tended to degenerate into a mere tool in the hands of the old Whigs. Thus, this defense of English liberties anew became a crucial task for those who, like Burke, had the protection of the results of the "Glorious Revolution" as an ultimate end in politics.

Was this defense of the principles of 1688 on Burke's part something more than what could have been expected from a representative of a vested interest? In the *Appeal from the New to the Old Whigs*, he argues for the coherence of his respective positions on the English and French revolutions. The English civic liberties, safeguarded by the delicate balance reached by the 1688–1689 settlement, were the product of history. The rights were organically grown, and as such something altogether different from the abstract and construed entities of the fanatics of the rights of men.

These historical rights were the inheritance of the American colonists as well, because they were Britons, once loyal subjects of the realm. Burke deplored that an irreparable breach had been brought about by an unwise and dangerous colonial policy, which eventually led to the loss of a considerable slice of England's possessions in the new world.

As far as India is concerned, it is more doubtful whether Burke's role in the impeachment of its governor, Warren Hastings, for his charges against the rajah of Benares in the monopolistic dealings of the East India Company, was exclusively inspired by the same care for local customs and institutions, or, for that matter, for natural law. On the contrary: ulterior motives on Burke's part cannot be ruled out.

Burke's recognition by posterity is a mixed affair. He was, of course, hailed by the advocates of reaction, not least in France. In Germany he was studied and revered by the "Hanoverian Whigs"; without explicitly giving Burke the spiritual credit for their teachings, Friedrich von Savigny, at any rate, and his colleagues of the historical school of law were in effect implementing his thoughts. Thereafter and up to our day, Burke has been claimed by, inter alia, utilitarian liberalism. Scornfully, Karl Marx summed him up as a "vulgar bourgeois." Burke has lately figured in the revival of natural law in the United States.

References

Burke, Edmund. *Reflections on the Revolution in France.* Ed. and intro. Conor Cruise O'Brien. Harmondsworth: Penguin, 1968.

Freeman, Michael. *Edmund Burke and the Critique of Political Radicalism.* Oxford: Blackwell, 1980.

Furniss, Tom. *Edmund Burke's Aesthetic Ideology.* Cambridge: Cambridge University Press, 1993.

Harris, Ian, ed. *Edmund Burke: Pre-Revolutionary Writings.* Cambridge: Cambridge University Press, 1993.

Kramnick, Isaac. *The Rage of Edmund Burke: Portrait of an Ambivalent Conservative.* New York: Basic Books, 1977.

Macpherson, C.B. *Burke.* Oxford: Oxford University Press, 1980.

O'Brien, Conor Cruise. *The Great Melody: A Thematic Biography and Commented Anthology of Edmund Burke.* Chicago: University of Chicago Press, 1992.

Stanlis, Peter J. *Edmund Burke and the Natural Law.* Lafayette LA: Huntington House, 1986.

Roland Schött

B

C

Capacity

See FREEDOM AND CAPACITY OF CONTRACT

Capital Punishment

While the death penalty has been imposed for many crimes, most debates about its morality focus on it as a punishment for murder. Many people support or oppose the death penalty as a matter of principle, but the complexity of the subject makes it unlikely that any single principle can show the death penalty to be justified or unjustified. To understand this, suppose that the principle "Everyone who kills deserves to die" were true. While it might seem to follow that the death penalty should be imposed, this is a mistake. If governments cannot determine guilt and innocence accurately, then it would be wrong to kill people convicted of murder, even if all murderers deserve to die. So, attention to factual questions about the reliability of judicial procedures is essential to reaching a reasonable judgment about capital punishment. Appealing to principles alone is not enough. Similarly, death penalty opponents often claim that because killing is wrong, governments that execute murderers are themselves guilty of murder. If these people believe that governments may legitimately go to war and that police officers may sometimes kill legitimately in the line of duty, then they cannot argue that all killings are morally the same. They need a more complex criterion to determine if and when killing by the state is morally justified.

The two central arguments for capital punishment appeal to deterrence and to justice. The deterrence argument claims that because people fear death more than imprisonment, the threat of capital punishment prevents people from committing murder more effectively than the threat of imprisonment. If correct, this would be a powerful argument because protecting innocent people's lives is an important moral value and a central duty of the state.

Many claim that the superior deterrent power of the death penalty is evident to common sense. They overlook several important facts, however. Murders are often committed without deliberation, and people who kill often do not consider particular punishments because they do not expect to be caught. Finally, fear of death is a less powerful motivator than the argument supposes. The risk of death often fails to deter people from actions like smoking cigarettes, climbing mountains, and driving fast in bad weather.

Most researchers who have studied the deterrent effects of the death penalty have not found its use to be correlated with lower homicide rates. The classic matching studies were done in the United States by T. Sellin. A study by I. Ehrlich claimed to show a correlation between executions and reductions in homicide, but its methodology has been severely criticized. Studies by W. Bowers and C. Peirce present evidence that executions actually increase homicide rates.

While studies yield conflicting results, it is possible to draw some relatively uncontroversial conclusions. Because killings have multiple causes, imposition of the death penalty by itself is unlikely to have a significant effect on homicide rates. Unemployment, availability of guns, and cultural attitudes all have a significant impact on the incidence of homicide. For this reason, the death penalty is unlikely to reduce homicide rates significantly.

The second major argument appeals to justice, claiming that death is the only just punishment for certain crimes; any lesser punishment for murder fails to do justice. One common argument for this view appeals to the *lex talionis* or "eye for an eye" principle. This principle, also called "equality retributivism," is most famously defended by Immanuel Kant, who argues that a just punishment treats the criminal as the criminal has treated the victim. Since murderers have killed their victims, they too should be killed.

There are serious problems with this principle. First, it conflicts with the widespread view that mitigating circumstances sometimes provide grounds for lesser punishments for murder. Second, the principle sanctions barbaric punishments. Killers who have raped or tortured their victims would have to be raped and tortured before death—not an appealing prospect, especially if one thinks about state personnel carrying out these tasks. Third, treating criminals as they treat their victims is often impossible or ludicrous. To see this, imagine using the "eye for an eye" principle to determine punishments for airplane hijackers, spies, prostitutes, or drug users.

More sophisticated retributivists argue for punishments that are proportional to crimes, not identical with them. For them, less serious crimes merit less severe punishments, while more serious crimes merit more severe punishments. This view is quite plausible, but it does not imply that the death penalty is necessary or justified. Given the seriousness of murder, it would be wrong to punish it lightly, but long-term imprisonment is not a lenient punishment. If it were the most severe punishment in a legal code, then murderers would be subject to a severe punishment that is the harshest treatment permitted by the code. The proportional retributivist's conception of justice permits but does not require the death penalty for murder.

Even if death penalty advocates could demonstrate that executing murderers is just in principle, they would have to confront two other problems in order to show the institution of capital punishment to be just.

First, they would have to show that the legal system can reliably identify murderers. All systems are imperfect, however, and innocent persons may be convicted, sentenced to die, and executed. As discussed in *In Spite of Innocence,* whatever justice might be achieved by executing murderers must be weighed against the injustice that could be done by executing innocent persons.

Second, if the law prescribes the execution of murderers who deserve to die and lesser punishments for those who do not, then the system must reliably distinguish between these two classes of people. Death penalty opponents deny that it can. They argue that decisions about which murderers should be executed are illegitimately influenced by irrelevant factors. Among these are the race of the victim and the criminal. Various studies in the United States provide evidence that death sentences are most likely in cases in which blacks kill whites. In *Furman v. Georgia* (1972), the U.S. Supreme Court rejected the death penalty as then administered because of its "arbitrary and capricious" imposition. Though the Court approved revised death penalty laws in *Gregg v. Georgia* (1976), many studies make a strong case for the continued influence of race on death sentences. Death penalty opponents also argue that sentences are illicitly influenced by the economic status and the low quality of legal defense for poor offenders.

As this brief review indicates, arriving at a reasonable view about the death penalty requires attention not only to moral principles but also to factual matters concerning the effects of punishment and the procedures by which people are tried and sentenced for murder.

References

Bedau, Hugo, ed. *The Death Penalty in America*. 3d ed. New York: Oxford University Press, 1982.

Nathanson, Stephen. *An Eye for an Eye? The Immorality of Punishing by Death*. Lanham, MD: Rowman and Littlefield, 1987.

Radelet, Michael, Hugo Bedau, and Constance Putnam. *In Spite of Innocence*. Boston: Northeastern University Press, 1992.

Sorrell, Tom. *Moral Theory and Capital Punishment*. New York: Blackwell, 1987.

van den Haag, Ernest. *Punishing Criminals*. New York: Harper and Row, 1975.

When the State Kills. London: Amnesty International, 1989.

Stephen Nathanson

See also HOMICIDE; PUNISHMENT

Catholic Philosophy of Law

See ECCLESIASTICAL JURISDICTION

Causation, Criminal

Acts or forbearances may be the causes of consequences contrary to criminal law. As legal security is of prime importance in criminal law, such causes and their consequences must be related according to general standards or rules of science and/or law. For example, drowning a person causes death and may lead to liability for murder or manslaughter, since a lack of oxygen is generally known and sometimes experienced to terminate life. Witchcraft was wrongly thought to cause plagues (though tests for witchcraft by immersion did cause death by drowning).

Responsibility for conduct and its causal consequences is a fundamental condition for an individual's sense of being a separate and self-respecting person. A fundamental condition for self-respect in victims is retribution by punishment against offenders who have caused them harm. Thus causation, as distinct from mere conditioning, is at the core of criminal law, based as it is upon responsibility and retribution. It is even thought that pre-socratic roots of causation in the law stem from retribution. Cause and effect are regarded, then, as analogous to offense and retribution, as "equal" and deeply related factors.

Though true conduct crimes are rare, problems of criminal causation mainly arise in connection with cases of murder, manslaughter, and related crimes. Also, causation is to be distinguished from other conditions for criminal conviction and their relationships, like violation of criminal law and criminal intent and/or guilt. Though human conduct is generally assumed to imply the absence of causally compelling internal or external factors like neural disorder or physical force, it may still be amenable to scientific explanation in causal terms. Such causation or even determinism does not touch upon the problem of causation in criminal law.

Causation as a condition for criminal liability must conform to stricter standards than causation in daily life and civil law, because it must comply with legal security against undeserved punishment. May such a conception be found in natural science as the paradigm of causal certainty? According to the predominant modern conception, influenced by David

Hume and John Stuart Mill, a cause is an *explanans* in a scientific law embedded in a theory which can be confirmed or falsified by empirical experiment. Causes are defined, then, as conditions stated by scientific explanations in terms of laws and theories.

Still, this kind of causal certainty may not suffice in criminal law. Scientific laws and theories identify causes and consequences defined by theoretical concepts, whereas criminal law is concerned with particular actions and events defined by legal notions and common sense. A scientific explanation of the plain fact of a punch in the face as a common cause of a bloody nose is both rather complicated and generally irrelevant in criminal law (as it is for most criminal purposes). Also, most criminal acts may not be experimentally repeated without grave consequences. Thus, the scientific paradigm of causal certainty cannot lead to certainty on causation in criminal law.

Analysis of causation in terms of conditions may still be important in criminal law. Such analysis cannot and need not be backed by scientific theory, as rules of commonsense experience or "recipes for action" may do here. Indeed, the first systematic analysis of causation in the law, developed in the nineteenth century, is a conditio sine qua non (CSQN) theory. J.L. Mackie suggested an INUS theory: a cause is an insufficient but necessary part of an unnecessary but sufficient condition for the consequence. Though undoubtedly an improvement upon the CSQN theory as a general analysis of causation, the INUS theory and its variants will not serve as explanations of causation in criminal law for at least two reasons.

First, such purely conditional conceptions cannot distinguish between relevant and irrelevant causes of criminal offenses. If a person drops a lighted cigar in the dry woods, the ensuing fire is caused by the person, not by the woods. Causation as necessary and/or sufficient condition is unlimited in principle both in time and space. Thus other criteria are needed for singling out relevant causes.

Second, and less important, criminal causation by human action may be assumed even if the conduct concerned is not a necessary and/or sufficient condition for the criminal offense. Two people may shoot a victim at the same time (alternative causation); somebody may have had a fatal heart attack even without threat by the offender (hypothetical causation). Most systems of criminal law assume causation in such cases.

Attempts at supplementing condition theories of causation by neutral space-time criteria like immediacy or proximity fail: a victim of murder may die because doctors were negligent, but the criminal offense is still the relevant cause. Conceptions of criminal causation must be normative in one or another sense. A criminal cause is something which disturbs the normal course of events, as known from rules of experience and rules of law. Causation depends, then, upon foreseeability, risk, criminal intent and/or guilt, and violation of criminal law. Thus speeding on the way to the spot of an accident may be regarded as the cause of that accident, even though speed was within legal limits when the accident occurred. A cause may be canceled by a *novus actus interveniens* (intervening new acts), for example, an abnormal event or independent conduct by a third party.

Central to such normative notions of causation are vague distinctions between conduct as such and conduct as cause of consequences. One may be said to have killed somebody or to have caused somebody's death by drowning. Both conduct and consequences of conduct are defined in terms of rules of law and common sense that leave room for different descriptions of the same course of events.

Foreseeability and risk as criteria for causation are related to commonsense conceptions of probability. "Rules of thumb" for action and causation may be true instead of just probable, for example, "Choking somebody leads to death." However, many such rules express probabilities, like "Poisoning somebody may lead to death." Also, there may be physical causation not covered by any probable "rule of thumb" and thus not constituting criminal causation, like ignorantly tapping an egg-shelled skull with fatal consequences.

Such commonsense probability is to be distinguished from probability in proof of criminal offenses. Most evidence of criminal offenses is circumstantial. Evidence, for example, a skeleton in a closet, may be causally related to murder by the defendant. Such causal relationships in proof may be stated in expert terms, relying on scientific knowledge of probabilities distinct from commonsense and legal standards determining criminal causation proper.

Causation as determined by rules of common sense and law seems to have lost its inde-

pendent status as a factual and "rock-bottom" condition for criminal conviction. Circular relationships may be found between causation and other conditions for criminal conviction, as they are partly defined in terms of each other. INUS or comparable causation in terms of scientific laws and theories may not even be a necessary condition for causation in criminal law. This leads to questions concerning the legal security of criminal causation as a more or less circular and normative notion.

References

Hart, H.L.A., and T. Honoré. *Causation in the Law.* 1959. Oxford: Clarendon Press, 1985.

Mackie, J.L. *The Cement of the Universe: A Study of Causation.* Oxford: Clarendon Press, 1974.

Shute, S., J. Gardner, and J. Hordner, eds. *Action and Value in Criminal Law.* Oxford: Clarendon Press, 1993.

Sosa, E., and M. Tooley, eds. *Causation.* Oxford: Oxford University Press, 1993.

Twining, W., and A. Stein, eds. *Evidence and Proof.* Dartmouth: Aldershot, 1992.

Hendrik Kaptein

Causation, Tort Law

Causation is an element in the plaintiff's case in every tort: in order to recover in any tort action, the plaintiff must plead and prove that the defendant's tortious conduct caused the plaintiff's injury. Difficult philosophical problems have been raised and discussed by the courts in determining the test or concept of cause-in-fact, in determining what constitutes adequate proof of cause-in-fact when the test seems to require proof of a counterfactual, and in defining and applying the concept of "proximate" or "legal" cause.

Cause-in-Fact

Courts have traditionally understood a "cause-in-fact" as a necessary condition. Consequently, they have explained that the test of causation is the sine qua non or "but for" test: in order to determine whether the defendant's tortious conduct was a cause-in-fact of the plaintiff's injury, one must determine whether the plaintiff's injury would have occurred without the defendant's tortious conduct (sine qua non—"without which, not"), or whether the plaintiff's injury would not have occurred "but for" the defendant's tortious conduct. In applying this test retroactively to the facts of the case, courts have asked this basic question: Had the defendant not acted tortiously, would the plaintiff still have been injured in the same way and to the same extent? The following example may be helpful. Plaintiff claims defendant was negligent in failing to signal for a left turn in front of oncoming traffic so that plaintiff's driver collided with defendant's turning car. If plaintiff's driver was not keeping a careful lookout and, therefore, would not have seen a turn signal had it been given, defendant's negligence was not a cause-in-fact of plaintiff's injury. That is so because, even if the defendant acted properly and gave an appropriate turn signal, the plaintiff would still have been injured in the same way and to the same extent.

Since the "but for" test proceeds by asking what would have happened had the defendant not acted tortiously, application of that test depends on a prior identification of the part of the defendant's conduct that was tortious. The test therefore easily accommodates omissions as causes. For example, the "but for" test would support a conclusion that a railroad's omission of a warning sign at a railroad crossing was the cause-in-fact of a plaintiff's collision with a train at that crossing because a trier of fact could conclude that the collision would not have happened had a warning sign been posted. Omissions can be causes under the "but for" test because the basic question under that test is a counterfactual one: What would have happened had the defendant acted properly?

Any necessary condition test of causation yields a number of causes for any particular event, including a number of human acts or omissions. The necessary condition test, therefore, cannot yield a single answer to the causation question, and there may be more than one tortfeasor whose tortious conduct is a cause-in-fact of the plaintiff's injury, since the conduct of each may be a necessary condition of the harm. They may, therefore, be considered concurrent causes. For example, Defendant One may park his truck, with its lights off, in a lane of traffic at night. Defendant Two, driving a car with the plaintiff as passenger, fails to keep a proper lookout and collides with the truck. The negligence of both Defendant One and Defendant Two may be a cause-in-fact of plaintiff's injury.

This last feature of the necessary condition test for causation poses a stumbling block for torts theorists who attempt to explain or justify tort liability by the appealingly simple principle that one who causes another harm ought to pay for it. The two most noteworthy attempts at such theories are by H.L.A. Hart and Tony Honoré in *Causation in the Law* and Richard Epstein in "A Theory of Strict Liability." To argue their theories successfully, the theorists must reject the necessary condition definition of causation. Hart and Honoré said that the commonsense notion of causation in human affairs includes a notion of deviation from the normal or usual course of events. Epstein said the notion of causation is limited to cases of a defendant's positive act directly causing harm to the plaintiff. Epstein objected to the hypothetical character of the "but for" test because, in his view, the causation question asks what did happen and the "but for" test asks what would have happened had things been otherwise. Consistent with this reasoning, Epstein claimed that omissions cannot be causes.

Patrick Kelley criticized both these attempts to construct an all-encompassing tort theory on a simple causation-justifies-compensation principle. He claimed that both theories distorted the ordinary notion of causation. Hart and Honoré imported into the concept of causation the extraneous notions of custom, habit, and expectations. Epstein mistakenly conceived of causation as an event rather than a relationship and therefore excluded from the notion of causation typical examples of it.

A recurring problem case—the "two fires" case—bedeviled a few courts and many tort theorists for a number of years. The problem was this: one fire, caused by Defendant One's negligence, joins another fire, either caused by Defendant Two's negligence or of unknown origin, and the combined fire burns down the plaintiff's house. Either fire alone would have done the job. Applying the "but for" test to each fire separately leads to the conclusion that neither fire was the cause of the harm because the house would have burned down anyway, from the other fire. An early theorist, Jeremiah Smith, rejected this result on policy grounds, saying it was unfair to let either or both defendants off under these circumstances. He therefore proposed a "substantial factor" test of causation to apply in such cases instead of the "but for" test. A more recent theorist has pro-

C

posed a more satisfactory explanation of the "two fires" case. Richard Wright stated that the fundamental notion of causation is this: something is a cause of a subsequent state of affairs if it is a necessary element of a set of conditions sufficient to bring about that state of affairs (the "necessary element of a sufficient set" test). In most cases, there is only one sufficient set of conditions, so the simple necessary condition test ordinarily works adequately as the test of causation. When there are two or more sufficient sets, however, as in the "two fires" case, the underlying, more basic test of causation must be used. A finding that each defendant "caused" the harm in the "two fires" case is thus not based on policy, as Jeremiah Smith thought, but on a concept of causation more fundamental than the simple concept of a necessary condition.

Proof of Counterfactuals in Cause-in-Fact

Some tort cases involving questions about the adequacy of proof of a causation raise the difficult problem of certainty in the proof of counterfactuals. Under the "but for" test of causation, the plaintiff's task is to prove a counterfactual: to establish what would have happened had the facts been different, that is, had the defendant behaved properly. One could plausibly argue that this can rarely be established with any degree of certainty. When a defendant's allegedly improper conduct is an omission, proof of causation may be particularly difficult.

Reynolds v. Texas and Pacific Railway Co. (1885), from the Louisiana Court of Appeals, is the leading case. In *Reynolds* the plaintiff was an obese woman passenger who went out into the darkness from a brightly lit sitting room to catch a train. Hurrying down unlit stairs that had no handrails to a narrow platform at the bottom, she made a misstep and pitched off the unlit platform. Defendant railroad company argued that its negligence in failing to light or handrail the stairs could not be determined with any certainty to be the cause of the plaintiff's injury, since the obese plaintiff might have suffered the same fate had the defendant lit and railed the stairs, and no one can tell for sure whether she would have fallen in that case. The court held that there was sufficient evidence of causation in this case because the defendant's negligence greatly multiplied the chances of this kind of an accident and was "of a character naturally leading

to its occurrence." The court would therefore consider "the natural and ordinary course of events, and not indulge in fanciful suppositions." In short, there is sufficient evidence to support a favorable conclusion on the counterfactual causation question if the evidence supports the following three findings: (1) the defendant's tortious conduct has the capacity to cause injuries like the plaintiff's injury; (2) the defendant's tortious conduct greatly increases the chances of injuries like the plaintiff's; and (3) the plaintiff's injury followed the defendant's tortious conduct.

Proximate or Legal Cause

The proximate cause requirement developed in the law of negligence during its formative years in the early nineteenth century. A typical early case involved a defendant railroad company that negligently delayed shipping wool from Syracuse to Albany. When the wool finally got to Albany, the railroad stored it in a warehouse, awaiting pickup. A sudden, extraordinary flood engulfed the warehouse and damaged the wool. The railroad was not negligent in storing the wool in that warehouse, but the wool would have been picked up, undamaged, before the flood, had the railroad not delayed in shipping it from Syracuse. The negligent delay in shipping was therefore obviously a cause-in-fact of the damage to the wool under the "but for" test. The court held that that negligence was a "remote" cause and not a proximate cause of the harm, however, because "it had ceased to operate as an active, efficient, and prevailing cause as soon as the wool had been carried beyond Syracuse." A recurring hypothetical used by theorists to explain proximate cause involves a defendant who gives a four-year-old child a loaded pistol. The child drops the pistol on her foot. The pistol does not discharge, but it does break several bones in the child's foot. Theorists agree that the defendant's negligence in giving the loaded pistol to the child is a cause-in-fact, but not a proximate cause of the child's injury.

Almost from the beginning, courts used two distinct tests of proximate cause—the "direct, continuous, uninterrupted sequence" test and some form of a foreseeability test. Early on, the foreseeability question was whether the harm to the plaintiff was a foreseeable consequence of the defendant's negligence; later, the foreseeability question was whether the plaintiff's injury was within the foreseeable risk of harm that made the defendant's conduct negligent.

The sequence test and the two foreseeability tests share a common problem. Each test seems so vague over such a large number of potential applications that in most problem cases the test is indeterminate. Each test could be used in the same case, plausibly, to support either a conclusion that the proximate cause test has been met or a conclusion that the proximate cause test has not been met. Moreover, cases that pose difficult problems for finding proximate cause under the direct sequence test can often be readily resolved in favor of proximate cause under a foreseeability test. Conversely, cases that pose difficult problems for finding proximate cause under a foreseeability test can often be readily resolved in favor of proximate cause under a direct sequence test. Since prior case law in most jurisdictions includes both "direct sequence" precedents and "foreseeability" precedents, courts may resolve problem cases by an unexplained choice to invoke either one or the other line of cases.

The proximate cause doctrine thus poses a twofold challenge: to the courts it poses a challenge to principled, coherent decision making; to scholars it poses a challenge in descriptive theory—how may one explain the results the courts themselves justify by reference to tests that are incurably indeterminate over a range of problem cases?

The natural place to start in responding to both challenges is to determine the purpose or justification for the proximate cause doctrine. Broadly speaking, legal theorists have given three different answers to that question. Depending on which answer they give, we can label these theorists the hard-core legal realists, the foreseeability theorists, and the purpose-of-the-rule theorists.

The leader of the hard-core legal realists, Leon Green, in his book on proximate cause, saw "proximate cause" as a label judges used to explain a host of different limitations on negligence liability, imposed by courts or juries, for a host of different, discrete public policies. This explanation is consistent with the position of those legal realists who contend that traditional judicial reasoning, using purportedly general legal principles, simply masks the various public policy judgments that are always the real reasons for judicial decisions.

The foreseeability theorists like Fowler Harper, Flemming James, and Oscar Gray posit that the purpose of the proximate cause doctrine is to limit liability for harm caused by a defendant's negligent conduct. Some limitation must be placed on the otherwise limitless liability for all harm caused in fact by a defendant's conduct. It makes sense to limit that liability to reasonably foreseeable harm, because reasonable foreseeability is the basis for negligence liability in the first place. The foreseeability standard for proximate cause thus reinforces the two basic policies Oliver Wendell Holmes said were reconciled in the negligence standard: it promises maximum deterrence of dangerous conduct, consistent with the general policy promoting freedom of action.

The purpose-of-the-rule theorists follow the basic position of Joseph Bingham, who argued that the proximate cause doctrine limited liability for the breach of a specific legal rule to harm caused by the hazard the rule was intended to prevent. Under this explanation, adopted by Patrick Kelley explicitly and Robert Keeton implicitly, the traditional example of proximate cause is explainable in the following way. The purpose of the rule against giving a loaded pistol to a young child is to prevent harm from the child's accidental or intentional shooting of the pistol. If the child is hurt because she dropped the gun on her foot, the harm does not result from the hazard the rule was intended to prevent, so there is no proximate cause there. This approach requires those adopting it to recognize that negligence is not a single, unitary standard but a general category that includes a number of very specific rules with specific purposes. Both Bingham and Kelley take that position, although Bingham says that the specific rules encompassed under the negligence category are legal rules set out by judges after the fact in the decision of individual cases, and Kelley says that the specific rules are preexisting community conventions that the courts later recognize as the basis for determining claims of wrong in negligence actions. Kelley goes on to argue that the proximate cause doctrine, understood in this way, helps answer this question: When is breach of a social convention, causing harm to another, nevertheless not a wrong to the person injured?

References
Bingham, Joseph W. "Some Suggestions Concerning 'Legal Cause' at Common Law."

Columbia Law Review 9 (1909), 16, 139.

Epstein, Richard. "A Theory of Strict Liability." *Journal of Legal Studies* 2 (1973), 151.

Green, Leon. *The Rationale of Proximate Cause*. 1927. Hackensack NJ: Rothman Reprints, 1976.

Harper, Fowler, Fleming James, and Oscar Gray. *The Law of Torts*. 2d ed. Vol. 4. Boston: Little, Brown, 1986.

Hart, H.L.A., and Tony Honoré. *Causation in the Law*. 2d ed. Oxford: Clarendon Press, 1985.

Keeton, Robert. *Legal Cause in the Law of Torts*. Columbus: Ohio State University Press, 1963.

Kelley, Patrick. "Causation and Justice: A Comment." *Washington University Law Quarterly* (1978), 635.

———. "Proximate Cause in Negligence Law: History, Theory, and the Present Darkness." *Washington University Law Quarterly* 69 (1991), 49.

Smith, Jeremiah. "Legal Cause in Actions of Tort." *Harvard Law Review* 25 (1911), 103.

Wright, Richard. "Causation in Tort Law." *California Law Review* 73 (1985), 1735.

Patrick J. Kelley

Central and Eastern European Philosophy of Law

Central and eastern European philosophy of law started its independent life in the second half of the nineteenth century by gradually distinguishing itself from the trends prevailing in the region, mainly German and Austrian ones, but also from French and Italian influence. Its formation bore the imprints of natural law, dominant in Europe at the time. In central Europe this was primarily transmitted through A. Martini's 1787 *Principles of Natural Law*. Immanuel Kant's and G.W.F. Hegel's philosophies contributed their influences. For his contemporaries, Hegel was the main symbol of philosophical protest against officialdom. He opposed the German historical school's respect for the past, with Gustav Hugo's *Natural Law* in 1798 as its first expression.

Under the guise of natural law, conservative ecclesiastical actions competed with enlightening secularization, feudal patriarchalism with contractual theories (designed for confirming or rejecting privileges), refutation of the *ius resistendi* (right of resistance) with approval of revolutionary republican ideas. Political use of a Christian natural law competed with the fashionable science of the law of reason, *Vernunftrecht*, launched in 1854 by Tivadar Pauler at Budapest. By that time, national languages had already gained ground in legal philosophy (for example, in Hungary in 1813), replacing Latin and German.

In central Europe, the last decades of the century signaled the formation of a positive social theory based on the idea of science. An artificially built view of history, rooted in the early developments of historical jurisprudence, appeared in Ágost Pulszky's reconsideration of Sir Henry Maine's *The Ancient Law* in his 1875 Hungarian translation in Budapest. Perhaps the most successful and lasting theory was the psychological theory of law proposed in 1900 by Leon N. Petrazycki, a professor in St. Petersburg at the time. Reasoning from the motives of human behavior, this theory based its explanation on the individual legal consciousness as a phenomenological fact.

The reactions were varied from flat refutation by arguments of natural law in 1897 by Sándor Esterházy at Kaschau to transformation by Tomás Garrigue Masaryk, professor at Prague in 1900. According to Masaryk, natural law has to be taken as an ethical maximum to be transformed into positive law as an ethical minimum. Felix Somló realized the need for reconciliation between positivism and moral considerations. Rudolf Stammler's theory of "just law" became the division line in 1902. The recognition of its unsustainability provided inspiration for seeking refuge either in axiology or in logical formalism, as did V.A. Saval'sky, 1908, in Moscow, Julius Moór, 1911, in Hungary, and P. Georgescu, 1939, in Romania. For this reason, laying the philosophy of the science of positive law on the value-free foundations of jurisprudence became a need of primary importance again. This project followed the patterns of John Austin in 1861 in London and Karl Bergbohm in 1892 in Leipzig.

In eastern Europe, in the region dominated by the Byzantine heritage, the orthodox variant of natural law represented the ideological framework. From the beginning of the nineteenth century, however, rival positions became more and more feverishly formulated within it. These reached from the kantianism of A.P. Kunitzyn, 1818, in St. Petersburg to the hegelianism of K.N. Niewolin, 1839, in Kiev. They included Italian-inspired national self-assertion through Simon Barnutiu, 1868, in Isai, to the positivism of Missir, 1904, in Romania. The ascetic mysticism reminiscent of early Christianity in V.S. Solovyev, 1897, and Leo Tolstoy's cry against violence in Russia, presented through I.A. Il'yn, 1910, were developed. In Russia proper, philosophy of law became accepted only in the last few years of the century. The textbooks of N.M. Korkunov and P. Redkin in St. Petersburg on the history of legal philosophy, as well as those of P.I. Novgorodtzev and E.N. Turbetzkoy in Moscow on natural law, exerted the main influence by their repeated editions.

A regional turning point in how to think about legal philosophy was provoked by the discussions related to Friedrich von Savigny's work and the historical school of law. These included U. Kollotay in Poland, a number of Serbs, Novgorodtzev in 1896, as well as A. Tamosaitis, 1929, in Lithuania. As to the trends born in Russia, the discussion of Solovyev and Petrazycki became the crystallizing point, determining the further development of legal-philosophical thought. Novogrodtzev, 1909, in Moscow, and A.S. Jashtshenko, 1912, in St. Petersburg, spoke to the former, while Trubetzkoy, 1901, and M.A. Reisner, 1908, addressed the latter in Moscow, as did M. Palienko, 1908, in Harkov, Venelin Ganev, 1904, in Sofia, J. Lande, 1916, in Krakow, and E. Tautro, 1925, in Warsaw.

In addition to this eastern European variety, the wave of scholars from the Balkans getting their doctorate degrees in law in Paris before World War I relied mainly on François Gény's revolutionary work *Méthode d'interprétation et sources en droit privé positif*. Gény's work generated interwar schools in Romania and Serbia through Mircea Djuvara, 1913, and Jivan Spassoyévitch, 1911, respectively.

The years preceding World War I signaled the launching of the so-called Vienna school in mastering and spreading philosophical positivism (issuing the journal *Zeitschrift für öffentliches Recht*, 1921–). Hans Kelsen's concept of the "pure theory of law" grew into an international trend followed by S. Rundstein in Poland, Leonidas Pitamic in Serbia, Vojtech Tuka in Slovakia. Almost simultaneously, a school in Brünn was formed, with their journal *Internationale Zeitschrift für Theorie des Rechts/Revue internationale de la théorie du droit*, 1926– . The Brünn school was begun by Frantisek Weyr, author of the "normative theory" based upon Schopenhauer's early concept of sufficient reason, Jaroslav Kallab (a student of W. Windelband's and H. Rickert's axiology), as well as Jaromír Sedlácek and Karel Englis. After the First World War, phenomenology and the analytical interest in aprioristic-deductivist realism also demanded ground in the work of N. Alexeev, 1918, in Russia, and Czeslaw Znamierowski, 1921, in Poznan.

Yet the interwar period was mainly shaped by generations which undertook the critical reconsideration of Kelsen's "pure theory of law." These included Djuvara, as a neo-kantian eclectic critical idealist in Bucharest, Ganev, who analyzed normative concepts as ideological tools for shaping the future in Sofia, Moór, who tried to reconcile positivism and natural law in Budapest, as well as Djordje Tasic in Belgrade, Ceko Torbov, a student of Leonard Nelson on kantian natural law in Sofia, Eugeniu Sperantia, an idealist in Cluj, Vladimír Kubeš, a disciple of Nicolai Hartmann in Brünn, and Jozsef Szabó, who all attempted to rationalize the irrational at Szeged. As a countereffect to the rigor of this purist defense against methodological syncretism, a number of synthetic philosophies were also born, with Toma Zivanovic, 1927, in Serbia, Barna Horváth's synoptic view with István Bibó in Szeged, and István Losonczy's neurophysiological realism at Pécs.

This flourishing was brought to an abrupt end by the Soviet Union, as the real winner of World War II, imposing its own regime on the region. With the liquidation of P.I. Stutshka, M.A. Reisner, and E.B. Pashukanis, A.J. Vishinsky's "socialist normativism" (1939) could no longer provide significant developments for legal philosophical thought. Although the entire region was destined to share the same fate, the tradition of analytical linguistico-logical theorizing in Poland proved to be strong enough to survive with outstanding journals (*Archivum Juridicum Cracoviense*, 1966– , *Studies in the Theory and Philosophy of Law*, 1986–), and magisterial oeuvres by Kazimierz Opalek, Jerzy Wróblewski, and Zygmunt Ziembinski. As for Hungary, less fortunate local traditions relied on neo-kantianism, which was easily swept away by Georg Lukács and his neophyte Mus-

C

covite comrades. Notwithstanding the devastating effects in the short run, the outcome grew into a scholarship with considerable historical and comparative interest, generating further reformist tendencies with the journal *Acta Juridica, 1959–* . This development led into an open-minded philosophizing on law in marxism with social-theoretical—and thanks to Lukács' late ontology of social being—even ontological pretensions, with Imre Szabó, Gyula Eörsi, and Vilmos Peschka. Marxist theories of law worthy of international attention were also formed in Serbia by Radomir Lukic, in Czechoslovakia by Viktor Knapp, and in Romania through the *Revue roumaine des Sciences juridiques, 1956–*, and by Anita M. Naschitz.

Today's endeavors, with the reintroduction of classical and contemporary trends from western Europe and the Americas, are mostly directed toward filling the vacuum left behind by the forced interruption of development. Identifying and reassessing national traditions meet the needs of contemporary synthesis and the necessity to reintegrate such neglected fields as natural law and, with theoretical foundations, the doctrinal study of law (*Rechtsdogmatik*). Sensibility toward philosophical issues and emphasis on historical and comparative approaches will surely survive the forced encounter with marxism. Hopefully the demand for interdisciplinary explanation (that is, an ontological reconstruction integrating macro-sociology, autopoietical systems theory, or cultural anthropology) can also survive as one of the characteristic traits and strengths of the central and eastern European philosophy of law.

References

Djuvara, Mircea. *Le fondement du phénomène juridique* (Foundations of Legal Experience). Paris: Sirey, 1913.

Eörsi, Gyula. *Comparative Civil (Private) Law. Law Types and Law Groups, the Road of Legal Development*. Budapest: Akadémiai Kiadó, 1979.

Horváth, Barna. *Rechtssoziologie* (Legal Sociology). *ARSP*, Beiheft 28. Berlin-Grunewald: Verlag für Staatswissenschaften und Geschichte, 1934.

Kubeš, Vladimìr, and Ota Weinberger, eds. *Die Brünner rechtstheoretische Schule* (The Brünn School of Legal Theory). Wien: Manz, 1980.

Lukic, Radomir. *Théorie de l'État et du Droit*. Philosophie du droit, Vol. 13 (Theory of State and Law). Paris: Dalloz, 1974.

Petrazycki, Leon N. *Law and Morality*. Trans. Hugh W. Babb. Intro. Nicolas Timasheff. Cambridge MA: Harvard University Press, 1955.

Somló, Felix. *Juristische Grundlehre* (Foundations of Law). Leipzig: Meiner, 1917.

Szabó, Imre. *Les fondements de la théorie du droit* (Foundations of Legal Theory). Budapest: Akadémiai Kiadó, 1973.

Varga, Csaba, ed. *Marxian Legal Theory*. The International Library of Essays in Law and Legal Theory, Schools 9. Aldershot: Dartmouth; New York: New York University Press, 1993.

Wróblewski, Jerzy. *The Judicial Application of Law*. Ed. Zenon Bankowski and Neil MacCormick. Law and Philosophy Library, Vol. 15. Dordrecht: Kluwer, 1992.

Csaba Varga

See also MARX, KARL; MARXIST PHILOSOPHY OF LAW; ONTOLOGY, LEGAL (METAPHYSICS)

Chaos Theory

Chaos theory is a new view of physical dynamics developed in the fields of physics and mathematics. Social scientists are exploring the usefulness of its principles for a better understanding of nonphysical dynamics, such as human dynamics. Chaos theory embraces the unpredictable nature of change. This results from several phenomena: complexity, the nonlinear character of change, sensitive dependence on initial conditions, and the aperiodic character of change.

Complexity rejects a reductionist view of causation. Instead, change is seen as resulting from the interaction of many forces. The existence and influence of forces vary over time, and the synergism produced from their interaction changes as well. The relationship between an effect and a cause or causes is also nonlinear in character, that is, not proportionate. This nonlinear relationship is seen as the norm rather than the exception. Sensitive dependence on initial conditions recognizes that a small initial change leads to a large difference in outcome over time. As a result, repetitions are not exact, and the outcomes will vary substantially as the time frame increases. Finally, equilibrium points are aperiodic in nature. This does not only refer to the onset and end of turbulence. It also refers to the result. Namely, there are many points, rather than one fixed point, at which an article undergoing change may settle. Despite the inherent unpredictability brought about by these phenomena, the result is not random outcomes. Some scientists believe there are forces that constrain outcomes to a general pattern—referred to as strange attractors. Others believe that in the midst of turbulence systems self-organize. In either view, order emerges in the end, not chaos.

These chaos principles are now being explored in a reexamination of both legal processes and the rules of law which emerge from such processes. This exploration of the science of chaos as a metaphor in the field of law is in its very early stages. The process of case law development has received the greatest attention. United States Supreme Court decision making has been similarly seen as unpredictable, in part due to the complexity of the judicial process. However, it is also seen as reflecting a pattern of sorts, in the form of epicycles. The Court's decision-making process is viewed as leading to no "final" answer to the issues of constitutional interpretation that come before it. However, this fluidity is thought to be a positive characteristic. Similarly, common law decision making in general is seen as both unpredictable and fluid, in fact in constant turbulence. Unpredictability exists in part from factual differences in each case, viewed through the lens of sensitive dependence on initial conditions. Unpredictability also exists in part because the rules which might be applied do not, and arguably should not, have smooth edges. Thus, principles do, and should, coexist with counterprinciples, and general rules with exceptions.

The turbulent nature of decision making in a case law context is understood to be a favorable characteristic when viewed through the lens of chaos theory. Just as chaos theorists see chaotic systems as more responsive to change and thus more stable in the long term, legal analysts have seen the turbulence in law, and its fundamental contradictions, as desirable characteristics. The tensions lead to a dynamic state of continuous renewal and repair.

The chaos metaphor has been applied not only to judicial decision making and evolution of the common law but also to the process of legislative decision making. A rejection of a reductionist view of the causes of legislative action has been advocated, and a recognition of complexity put in its place. A reductionist view, which characterizes theories such as pluralism and public choice, has dominated the field despite evidence of complexity in the case studies. Chaos theory provides a sense of order to the conflicting evidence of causes of legislative decisions found in past case studies. It also leads to reexamination of the likely effect reform efforts, such as campaign finance reforms, may have on legislative outcomes.

In addition to the legislative process itself, the outcomes of legislative choices have been studied in light of the teachings of chaos theory. These legislative outcomes reveal that legislative bodies embrace a pattern to address particular issues. In other words, this is a finding similar to the order uncovered by scientists, perhaps induced by strange attractors. However, the legislative pattern is not universal, unlike the pattern found in discrete physical structures. Moreover, within an adopted pattern there are variations in the details of enactments. This variation exists across legislative bodies, evidencing the aperiodic character of decision making. It also exists within a legislative body, evidencing what chaos theorists would call the fractal character of legislative dynamics.

Greater attention to principles of chaos theory, including complexity in human decisions, is required in the development of both legislative and judicial approaches, as well as specific rules. This is a matter that has received little attention to date. Some preliminary discussion has occurred. For example, fault-based divorce laws and exclusive-custody arrangements have been criticized as ignoring chaos theory's teachings—transitions between harmony and conflict, and sensitive dependence on initial conditions. In addition, mandatory disclosure rules imposed by corporate and securities law have been endorsed, in the face of doubts regarding market impact, based on the nonlinear character of causes and effects.

It is not clear where the teachings of chaos theory may lead legal analysts. Certainly, traditional viewpoints and legal requirements must be reexamined. For example, the common requirement of proof of causation as a prerequisite to the imposition of legal obligations or liability must be reconsidered in light of the complexity of physical changes and human decisions. Chaos theory may tell us that such a requirement, imposed in the past without a second thought, is impossible to prove in particular contexts and therefore the requirement must be modified or a new approach must be considered to reach desired outcomes.

References

Cunningham, Lawrence A. "From Random Walks to Chaotic Crashes: The Linear Genealogy of the Efficient Capital Market Hypothesis." *The George Washington Law Review* 62 (1994), 547–608.

Di Lorenzo, Vincent. "Legislative Chaos: An Exploratory Study." *Yale Law & Policy Review* 12 (1994), 425–485.

Gleick, James. *Chaos: Making A New Science.* New York: Viking, 1987.

Hayes, Andrew W. "An Introduction to Chaos and Law." *UMKC Law Review* 60 (1992), 751–773.

Lewin, Roger. *Complexity: Life at the Edge of Chaos.* New York: Maxwell Macmillan, 1992.

Murray, John S. "Improving Parent-Child Relationships Within the Divorced Family: A Call for Legal Reform." *University of Michigan Journal of Law Reform* 19 (1986), 563–600.

Reynolds, Glenn Harlan. "Chaos and the Court." *Columbia Law Review* 91 (1991), 110–117.

Scott, Robert E. "Chaos Theory and the Justice Paradox." *William & Mary Law Review* 35 (1993), 329–351.

Vincent Di Lorenzo

Character

Character is an issue for the law whenever the human element cannot be reduced to the impersonal devices of some mechanical procedure. Character, a reliable style of reasoning and action, a trained habit of perception and desire, becomes an explicit concern in (1) establishing liability, especially mens rea beyond actus reus; (2) considering pretrial release (ROR) and, increasingly, setting or denying bail; (3) considering diversion from prosecution; (4) the impaneling of jurors for criminal trial; (5) preparation of defense, such as insanity and irresistible impulse; (6) disposing or, decreasingly, sentencing; (7) recommending preventive detention or conditional release or parole for an offender; and (8) direct examination at trial, where the character of the witness in testimony, as well as that of the defendant, is at stake. Character is indirectly relevant in (9) findings and verdicts, since Anglo-American justice systems focus on the facts about particular occasions; according to rule 404 of the *Federal Rules of Evidence,* the dispositions of agents, however stable, may be prejudicial to defendants. While these systems are designed in theory to prohibit inferences from character—good or bad—to particular actions, character is pivotal at almost every significant juncture in legal practice.

An emphasis on character is an emphasis on who we are and who we should become, as opposed to an emphasis on acts or their consequences or intentions or rules. It is a stress on the settled dispositions from which intentions and actions spring, a stress on cultivated habits of thought and desire that shape our perceptions and choices. The traditional understanding of character is best articulated by Aristotle in his *Politics* and *Nicomachean Ethics,* to which these remarks will be limited.

In Book seven of *Ethics,* Aristotle outlines six main types of character. These are defined by the relative roles of reason and desire. When one's desires are reasonable, so that one genuinely wants and habitually seeks what is good, one's character is solid and excellent. This is virtue. On the other hand, when one's desires are base and reason is corrupted into mere cleverness in the service of those base wants, we have vice. In this firm but undesirable state of character, one typically fails to see anything *wrong* with one's desires or reasonings or acts. Vicious people have no regrets and are nearly impossible to change, according to Aristotle. Most, however, are neither virtuous nor vicious, but are somewhere in between. We know what is good or right, but our desires lure us in other directions. If reason generally prevails, and we act well after some inner struggle, we are "continent" or self-controlled. If untoward desires generally prevail, we are "incontinent" or lacking in self-control. These are somewhat wavering states of character, less stable than virtue or vice. Finally, Aristotle admits the possibility of two liminal types, in addition to virtue/vice and continence/incontinence. Best is the natural virtue beyond trained excellence called "godlike"—essentially off the scale of human possibilities, but persons do seem to appear every so often with such stellar goodness as to be beyond praise. Worst is what Aristotle calls brutishness (perhaps what we would call sociopathy)—typically due to morbidity or disease and, strictly speaking, beyond blame. Both are exceedingly rare.

Voluntary acts are subject to praise and blame. All chosen acts are voluntary, but not all voluntary acts are chosen. Children and some animals are capable of voluntary acts, which have their source of motion in the agent and involve knowledge of the relevant particulars. When we choose, we wish for some end, then deliberate about the means to that end; deliberation consists in making the largely indeterminate possibilities of choice become determinate. Then we decide among these determinate possibilities. Choice turns on reason, since it involves rational deliberation and rational wish, but it does not necessarily involve lengthy self-conscious debate. Evidence of such inner debate is evidence neither for nor against the presence of rational choice. Virtuous people choose what is right for its own sake without much fuss, take pleasure in it, and are to be praised; vicious people choose their bad acts, take pleasure in them, and should be blamed accordingly. Continent people struggle, but reason prevails in the end. Incontinent people do not, strictly speaking, choose, since the reason and knowledge that are present to them are not *engaged:* reason fails here to mesh with desire, so desire determines the act. While incontinent people do not really engage in rational choice, they still act voluntarily, are still appropriately blamed, still appropriately brought within the domain of legal sanction. Making voluntariness the locus of praise and blame solves the problem of how one might be held morally and legally liable for acts that are not, strictly speaking, chosen, or for single acts that are exceptions to patterns of decent character.

Virtuous people exhibit actions that skillfully hit the *mean* between extremes to be avoided. Excess and defect are vices; the mean is the point of virtue. This mean is not an arithmetic middle. It is itself a sort of extreme in the search for excellence, defined by a series of categories and approached by a sort of triangulation. The mean between ire and inirascibility is not a state of middling mildness, but precisely the ability to be angered by the appropriate people in the appropriate contexts in the appropriate ways at the appropriate times. Temperance (do not confuse with continence) is not a state where one is warmly pleased by bodily pleasures; it is the state of finding no pleasure at all in the wrong sorts of pleasures, and taking relish in the best pleasures *and* taking a moderate amount of pleasure in bodily things—but never at the wrong time or the wrong place or with the wrong people. The mean between fear and rash overconfidence is not a middling sort of confidence; courage is precisely the ability to sense what is dangerous, when fear is appropriate, and what actions, relative to one's actual abilities and the facts of a situation, are called for. The mean—the right act regarding the right person at the right time in the right context performed for the right reason—is relative to situation and character. It is cowardice for an expert swimmer to fear low waves and fail to aid a drowning child; it is rashness for a nonswimmer to leap in and try to save the child even though this is, *ceteris paribus,* the right thing to do. Since character shapes perception, we should not be surprised that a cowardly person typically sees the courageous option as rash (and vice versa), the stingy person typically sees the liberal course as prodigal, and so on. Legal systems can enshrine such confusions. Good laws are those that temper excesses and help train us to the mean.

Character is desirable and necessary in at least the following areas: (1) adjudication, where a seasoned sense of fairness is required for interpretation and judgment; (2) advocacy, since lawyers need virtue, as stated in their recommended oath of admission; (3) legislation, where good character allows a legislator to grasp genuine issues and articulate apt rules beyond the promptings of fickle opinion; (4) the execution and administration of law, where excellence of character affords canny application of legal rules to specific cases; and finally (5) the growth and development of law, which often requires morally courageous persons to act conscientiously and persuade by force of character.

In the classical tradition, ethics is part of politics, and politics focuses on legislation. Character formation, moral education, is the primary point of law. Most modern and postmodern movements have rejected this purpose. However, given its unavoidable reliance on virtue at so many points, a legal system that does not make the education of character a primary concern will be, according to the classical tradition, a system at odds with itself.

References

Aristotle. *Nicomachean Ethics*. Trans. T. Irwin. Indianapolis: Hackett, 1985.

———. *Politics*. Trans. E. Barker. New York: Oxford University Press, 1959.

Flanagan, O., et al. *Identity, Character, and Morality: Essays in Moral Psychology*. Cambridge MA: MIT Press, 1990.

French, P.A., et al. *Ethical Theory: Character and Virtue*. Notre Dame: University of Notre Dame Press, 1988.

Hobbes, T. *Leviathan*. Ed. C.B. McPherson. New York: Penguin, 1982.

Hogan, R. "Moral Conduct and Moral Character: A Psychological Perspective." *Psychological Bulletin* 79 (1973), 217–232.

Hume, D. *A Treatise of Human Nature*. Rev. Peter H. Nidditch. Oxford: Oxford University Press, 1981.

MacIntyre, A. *After Virtue*. Notre Dame: University of Notre Dame Press, 1984.

Malerstein, A.J. *A Piagetian Model of Character Structure*. New York: Human Sciences Press, 1982.

Slitskin, L.D. *Studies in Torah Judaism*. New York: Yeshiva University Press, 1969.

C. Wesley DeMarco

Charter Rights; Bill of Rights

See ENTRENCHMENT

Children

See PARENTING AND CHILDREARING

Chinese Philosophy of Law

In its more than three thousand years of history, Chinese philosophy has made significant contributions to world philosophy. A considerable body of important philosophical thought exists in the fields of science, ethics, politics, and legal philosophy. The classical period of Chinese legal philosophy took place within the Warring States era (fifth through third centuries B.C.). This was a time of war, massacre, social chaos, and political unrest, when the preoccupying question was how to conceptualize an adequate political and legal order. Two major legal philosophical doctrines that were destined to determine the course of Chinese legal philosophy emerged: the *ju chia* (confucianism) and the *fa chia* (legalism). Other philosophical schools such as taoism (or daoism), mohists, logicians, or the belatedly imported buddhist thought, largely became less preoccupied with legal philosophy.

In studying Chinese legal philosophy, two principal attributes should be noted. First, for China, legal method, legal science, legal profession, and adversary legal culture never occurred. The reason for this failure lies within the success of the Chinese legal philosophy.

Second, the realistic nature of Chinese philosophy should be emphasized. Chinese philosophy built itself on the image of man within reality, with no transcendent being to be worshipped. The absence of any metaphysics is one of its principal characteristics. The central question is humanity and how it perceives itself, as well as how humanity can master or consolidate with the surrounding reality. From the outset, Chinese legal philosophy was utilitarian (or utilitarian humanist), and particularly so with respect to confucianism and legalism, the two pillars of Chinese legal philosophy.

Confucianism and Legal Philosophy

Confucius (551–479 B.C.) is responsible both for molding Chinese civilization in general and Chinese legal philosophy in particular. Born of a noble but fairly poor family, Confucius (which is the Latinized form of the honorary title *K'ung Fu-tzu*; his family name was K'ung and his private name Ch'iu) raised Chinese thought to great heights. Confucius served in the state of Lu in his younger years as a magistrate and later became Minister of Justice, perhaps serving as a deputy Minister of Public Works somewhere in between. In all likelihood discharged because of his conservative attitude and his call for a return to ancient values, Confucius devoted the rest of his life to character building and training. His main ideas were recorded in *The Analects*.

Confucius was a conservative thinker. He lived in a very troubled period of Chinese history, and for him the only solution was to restore the values and rites of the ancient feudal order. The legal philosophy of confucianism can be summed up in its assumption of the fundamental goodness of human nature. If human nature is basically good, then everything should be done to restore and perfect this goodness, by being virtuous, observing rituals, and respecting propriety (*li*). The term *li* is central in confucian tradition and is an empirical reference to the body of customs already accepted by the sage-kings and the people, that is ancient taboos, and ceremonial and sacrificial observations. It therefore should never be associated with Western natural law doctrine.

Confucius says in *The Analects*: "If the people be led by laws, and uniformity sought to be given them by punishments, they will try to avoid the punishment, but have no sense of shame. If they be led by virtue, and uniformity sought to be given them by the rules of propriety (*li*), they will have the sense of shame, and moreover will become good." It followed that an order based on law and rights was for wicked, corrupt people and should be carefully avoided. Rather, the *li*, and especially the moral examples that they transmit, should be honored as a set of tradition-based relationships of honor and respect. Confucians refer to five relationships: between the (feudal) lord and the (family-chief) vassal, between father and son, between the old and the young, between husband and wife, and between friend and companion. In confucianism, these relationships are built upon the image of family affection, whereby the superior person loves the subordinate and the subordinate venerates the superior. This is also an expression of the cosmic order, since respecting *li* assures harmony, peace, and harvest, whereas not doing so results in disorder, calamity, and crime.

The confucian advocates a philosophical justification for the rule of man over man through love and honor. Social rituals, also called "rules of propriety," and the five social relationships mentioned above form the foundation of legality. Thus every problem of government, administration, military, and even international relations, is reduced to a problem of humanity, more precisely, a problem of choices, the degree of virtue, and the quality of the education of humanity. Its principal ideal, stated in *The Analects,* is that "[h]e who exercises government by means of virtue may be compared to the north polar star, which keeps its place and all the stars turn toward it." This is the foundation of the "superior man" doctrine of confucianism that he who governs not only should express goodness but should himself be good.

Confucianism as a legal philosophy can be characterized as largely antilegal. It is a doctrine of the rule of man over man, by way of a subtle control and paternalistic administration of customs that were traditionally accepted as good. It corresponds to the perspective that law (*Fa*) and rights were the invention of barbarians: whence the Chinese legend that *Fa* was invented by the tribal non-Chinese people Miao during the twenty-third century B.C.

The Legalists (*Fa Jia*)

If it is possible to speak of a legalist school, *Fa Jia* (literally: School of the Law), it should be kept in mind that this school was not founded by any master nor was it structured on any single philosophical teaching. Legalism was more of a movement, or a reaction against social disintegration and what the legalists considered to be confucian hypocrisy, than it was a hierarchical philosophical system. The legalists were mainly magistrates, ministers, or political advisors to the kings. Shang Yang (also known as Lord Shang), who died in 338 B.C., and Han Fei tzu or Master Han Fei, who lived from about 280 to 233 B.C., both personified legalist thought. Legalist philosophy was traditionally associated with the taoists (or daoists).

A singularity in Chinese civilization, the legalists not only refused to build on tradition or to restore the feudal order, but also refused to consider human nature as entirely good. The philosophical starting point for legalism is the duty to make a realistic analysis of situations, problems, and different alternatives as seen from the rulers' standpoint. Law (*Fa*) is the solution, providing the means, in the hands of the ruler, to govern and to obtain the desired results.

The legalists saw the law (*Fa*) as positive laws fixed beforehand by the ruler, to which everyone in the state, from the ruler himself down to the lowest public slave, was bound to submit; those who did not submit were subjected to sanctions of the most severe and cruel kind. Rather than being thought of as a concept, the law is seen as empirical: the ruler is master of society and the law is the concrete expression of this powerful, omnipotent will. Thus, the law must be absolute, not permitting any other expression of power that could alter this property.

In the hands of the ruler, the law is an instrument of power. The legalists insisted that the ruler could not administer society through virtue or goodness, as advocated by the confucians, but rather by means of the law. The law must therefore be published so that people are informed, but more important, it must control the administration that executes the law.

However, the cornerstone of legalist philosophy is the question of the efficiency of the law. Legalism is often designated as the "behaviorist science," in direct reference to its utilitarian character. The legalists, in fact, recommend that the ruler's law be situated empirically at the behavioral level of man. Moreover, legalism exploits human psychology in a twofold way, part subtle and part draconian. Since everyone is looking out for their own interests, the ruler should use rewards and punishments to rule. The rewards, such as military or administrative positions or honor, should be reserved for gifted persons and should serve to create a dependence on the ruler. Punishment, by the very fact that everybody fears it, should govern the people. Punishment must therefore be sufficiently astonishing, cruel, and draconian that almost everybody will, by fear, choose to obey the law. When punishment is necessary, not only should the criminal be punished, but also the family and village unit. Only by denouncing others could one save oneself.

The purpose of the legalists' legal philosophy is the *wu wei* (or "nonactivity"). It is a theme borrowed from taoism (or daoism), which refers to rule through nonactivity. Taoism teaches that the *Tao* (the Way) rests upon the spontaneous action of all things, and that therefore through nonactivity there is nothing which is not done. Translated into legal philosophy by the legalists, the ruler, conceived of as the *Tao* of nature, sits quietly in nonactivity above the *Tao* of man and dictates the actions of the people. It is possible for him to sit quietly because, according to the legalists, the *Tao* of man is within the law laid down by the ruler. Thus the law does all things, and the ruler can sit quietly and control the whole of society administratively. In fact, the nonactivity of the legalists foresees an interventionist policy that is administration and punishment to assure that the *Tao* of man is in concordance with the way (*Tao*) of the ruler and with will as promulgated by law.

Although the positive aspect of the law can be appreciated because it is written and published, and is developed after an analysis of a situation and goals, it is often the draconian side of the legalist punishment system that attracts attention. As far as legal philosophy is concerned, the legalist conception of law is entirely bureaucratic: it is an administrative and penal conception of law.

Cultural and Philosophical Symbiosis of Confucianism and Legalism

The legalist philosophies flourished in different states during the period of the Warring States. But it was the legalism in the state of Qin (or Chhin) which consolidated the movement's success and failure. Historically, legalist philosophy was practiced in Qin, with the result that Qin developed into the richest, best organized, and militarily strongest state. By applying legalist philosophy, the ruler of Qin, King Zheng (also known as Qin Shihuangdi) in 221 B.C. succeeded in conquering all the other states and went on to found the first Chinese empire. However, the Qin empire only lasted from 221 to 207 B.C. The Han dynasty, which ruled from 206 B.C. to A.D. 220, blamed its failure on legalism.

The ruthlessness of the unification of China, to say nothing of the mercilessness of the Qin regime, discredited legalist philosophy. The Han empire and its successors adopted confucianism as state ideology (and eventually as state religion). Later, on the advice of his confucian minister Tung Chung-shu, the Emperor Wu-ti, who lived from 140 to 87 B.C., banned all philosophical doctrines except confucianism. Other philosophical books (other than confucians') were burned, private "studies" were banned, and confucian philosophy was promulgated as the syllabus for the Mandarin examination system. Legalist philosophy was not dead; however, it entered into a symbiosis with confucianism, destined to define the Chinese legal mind to the present day.

The confucian philosophers and administrators soon discovered that the Chinese empire could not be governed with a system of good customs, righteousness, and sincerity: they were obliged to govern by law (*Fa*), and it was in this way that the symbiosis between the legalists' philosophy and confucianism occurred. The legalists had, in a way, "out-confucianed" the confucians with their insistence on an organized bureaucracy. Thus, a strictly legalist conception of *Fa* accompanied the "celestial bureaucracy" (that is, the confucian administrators) in the organization and administration of Chinese society. Ironically, the confucians and the legalists found themselves united in the ideal of a well-administered society. Where the confucians believed in the government of persons presumed to be morally "superior" (thanks to their confucian education) and the legalists believed in bureaucratic law from above, the symbiosis was found in the notion of government by superior men with paternalistic goodness on the one hand, and the means of bureaucratic law on the other.

In this way, a working division between *li* and *Fa*, between good customs/personal affections/rites, and the law, can be observed both in fact and in philosophy: *li* represents the honor of integrity and virtue and the signs of an honest man; *Fa* represents dishonor, corruption, and the necessity of state administration and of punishment.

An examination of ensuing confucian philosophy reveals many expressions of this symbiosis and of the dangers of falling into the realm of the law. The *Li Chi* (Record of Rites), put together in about 50 B.C., expressly states that "*li* does not reach down to the people, *hsing* [punishment or penal statutes] does not reach up to the great officers." Accordingly, the law is for the people and the *li* is for the upper class. This is similar to the classical confucian doctrine of the "superior men" (that is, the confucian upper class) who are considered to be above all law. Another testimony is the Thang code of the seventh century A.D., which specifically suggests that it is dangerous and ominous to leave the system of personal affections/social rites, or *li,* because "he who leaves *li* will fall into *hsing*" (punishment by the law).

In legal philosophical terms, this philosophical (and cultural) symbiosis provided the following framework for Chinese legal minds:

1. Law is seen as something evil or dishonorable.
2. Law is punishment and administration from above.
3. Law should be obeyed and should stipulate only duties.
4. Legal and social conflict should be "dissolved" (and never resolved) into the appropriate social relation.

Thus, according to this framework, every honest man should seek to avoid the legal domain. This cultural phenomenon of juridical rejection can be observed today in China as well as within the Chinese diaspora.

The Present Situation
Confucianism had been the unchallenged state ideology (and the Chinese state religion) up until modern times. In conjunction with legalist philosophy, confucianism determined the Chinese conception of law. Where confucianism was used in propaganda and education to form uniform obedient subjects and to dissolve social conflicts, legalism, on the other hand, was used to organize and administer, punish and repress any opposition to or usurpation of the established order. The former was the ideology, the latter the substance.

It is only in recent times that this system has been challenged. In 1911 the republican revolution established a modern system of statutes. This was also the case in 1949 during the maoist (or oriental communist) revolution.

The philosophical and cultural problems of present-day China are centered on the possibility and the necessity of establishing, for the first time in Chinese history, a real rule of law and rights. In this sense, the events on Tiananmen in June 1989 have been revealing.

References
Book of Lord Shang. Trans. J.J. Duyvendak. London: Probsthain, 1928.

Complete Works of Han Fei Tsu. 2 vols. Trans. Wen-Kouei Liao. London: Probsthain, 1939–1959.

Confucius. *Confucian Analects; The Great Learning and the Doctrine of the Mean.* Trans. James Legge. New York: Dover, 1971.

Dorsey, G. L. *Jurisculture,* Vol. 3, *China.* New Brunswick NJ:Transaction Publishers, 1993.

Fung Yu-Lan. *A History of Chinese Philosophy.* 2 vols. Princeton: Princeton University Press, 1952.

Han Fei Tzu. Basic Writings. Trans. Burton Watson. New York: Columbia University Press, 1964.

Needham, Joseph. *Science and Civilization in China,* Vol. 2, *History of Scientific Thought.* Cambridge: Cambridge University Press, 1962.

Bjarne Melkevik

See also ABORIGINAL LEGAL CULTURES; INDIAN PHILOSOPHY OF LAW; ISLAMIC PHILOSOPHY OF LAW; JAPANESE AND ASIAN PHILOSOPHY OF LAW

Cicero, MarcusTullius (106–43 B.C.)
The work of Marcus Tullius Cicero has significantly influenced modern Western law, legal theory, and legal practice. Cicero's numerous surviving philosophical texts, speeches, and

letters have been studied for centuries, through some times when they were held in high esteem and others when they were discounted as derivative or reactionary. His reputation as an outstanding lawyer, orator, and politician, which has also been subject to ebb and flow, has added to Cicero's influence as a model of engaged legal philosophy. Cicero's most lasting contribution has been his insistence on the connection between rhetoric and justice.

Cicero was born in Arpinum, then a small community some two or three days' travel from Rome. Cicero's family, the Tullii Cicerones, were an equestrian family who had been granted Roman citizenship, along with the rest of Arpinum, in 188 B.C. Although the Tullii Cicerones family enjoyed wealth and social privilege and had adopted the language and customs of Rome, they were still not part of the Roman aristocracy, and Cicero was the first person from his family and social class to hold high political office. As a young man, Cicero was educated in Greek rhetoric and philosophy, studying with teachers from the Academy, founded by Plato, and from the rival school of stoicism. Later, after working as an advocate for several years, Cicero traveled to Athens, where he studied with teachers associated with the Old Academy, and to Rhodes, where he continued his education in rhetoric and philosophy.

Writing as a prominent although oft-defeated political leader of the late Roman Republic, Cicero explored practical problems of politics and ethics and sought to engage others in their resolution. In the hundred years or so before Cicero's birth, Rome gained control of territories containing roughly one-fifth of the world's population. Although some conquered areas, like Arpinum, had been granted Roman citizenship and had adopted Roman customs, others actively resisted the Roman invaders; most spoke languages other than Latin and remained loyal to cultures that were quite different from the dominant Roman society. Much of Cicero's writing on law is concerned with what contemporary lawyers would term problems of justice in a society marked by conquest and difference.

The most important of Cicero's surviving writings on law are the dialogues *De Legibus* (c. 52–43 B.C.), *De Finiibus Bonorum et Malorum* (45 B.C.), *De Re Publica* (c. 54–51 B.C.), and *De Oratore* (57–55 B.C.), and the treatises *De Officiis* (46–44 B.C.) and *De Inventione* (c.

87 B.C.). Although Cicero's dialogues are not as well crafted or multilayered as Plato's, nevertheless the dialogue form is important to the expression of many of Cicero's ideas about law. The dialogue form allows discussion of competing values and ideas without the necessity for inappropriate resolution or unproductive simplification. One important theme in Cicero's writings on law is the importance of persuasion and refutation in a world of contested social goods and the related importance of thoughtful and responsible leaders. Through dialogue, Cicero both presents and demonstrates these ideas.

De Legibus, for example, is a discussion among characters named for Cicero's close friend Atticus, Cicero's brother Quintus, and Marcus Cicero himself, which occurs as the men walk on Cicero's family lands in Arpinum. The discussion first focuses on myth, with Atticus asserting that one must be able to discern fact from fiction and Cicero arguing that the distinction is not important, for so long as people talk and think about myths, the myths exist and have influence among us. This complex notion of truth and the power of narrative provides a rich introduction for the ensuing discussion of law, justice, and social order. Among other interesting ideas thrown out in the conversation is that valuing justice is a social practice, embedded in many languages and cultures, but the meaning of justice in a particular situation is often contested, and custom is not the sole authority for resolution of such disputes. In the dialogue, Cicero argues that people do not disagree about whether justice ought to be done, but rather whether one action or another is just in a particular situation: even villains, he asserts, either admit that they have committed a crime, or "invent some story of just anger to excuse its commission, and seek justification in some natural principle of right reason." The connection between persuasion and justice is developed and displayed in multiple and complex ways throughout Cicero's work on law.

References

Cicero, Marcus Tullius. *Works.* English and Latin. Loeb Classical Library. 27 vols. Cambridge MA: Harvard University Press, 1958–1979.

Enos, Richard Leo. *The Literate Mode of Cicero's Legal Rhetoric.* Carbondale: Southern Illinois University Press, 1988.

Frier, Bruce. *The Rise of the Roman Jurists: Studies in Cicero's Pro Caecina.* Princeton: Princeton University Press, 1985.

Habicht, Christian. *Cicero the Politician.* Baltimore: Johns Hopkins University Press, 1990.

MacKendrick, Paul Lachlan, and Karen Lee Singh. *The Philosophical Books of Cicero.* London: Duckworth, 1989.

Mitchell, Thomas. *Cicero the Senior Statesman.* New Haven: Yale University Press, 1991.

Rawson, Elizabeth. *Cicero: A Portrait.* Ithaca NY: Cornell University Press, 1983.

Wood, Neal. *Cicero's Social and Political Thought.* Berkeley: University of California Press, 1988.

Amy Kastely

Citizenship and Membership

Most would agree that the power to admit or exclude nonmembers is a key factor in the sovereignty of the political community. Continuing disagreement exists, however, as to how membership is to be measured. In *Graham v. Richardson,* 403 U.S. 365 (1971), the Supreme Court struck down legislation in two states that limited welfare payments to citizens or to legally resident aliens of fifteen years or more. Alienage, like nationality and race, is a suspect classification, and aliens are a "discrete and insular" minority for whom "heightened judicial solicitude is appropriate." Moreover, "[t]here can be no 'special public interest' in reserving for citizens tax revenues to which aliens have contributed on an equal basis with the residents of the state." In *Sugarman v. Dougall,* 413 U.S. 634, 647 (1973), however, although the same Court invalidated a New York law that confined to citizens employment in the competitive civil service, it simultaneously recognized the legitimacy of legislation that might require citizenship as a more narrowly defined qualification for office under the political community doctrine. "Such power inheres in the state by virtue of its obligation . . . 'to preserve the basic conception of a political community.'"

A variety of subsequent decisions have focused on the extent to which de facto decision making or policymaking authority constitutes governing. Supreme Court majorities have concluded that under this rubric, a citizenship qualification might be required for members of the New York state police force [*Foley v. Connelie,* 435 U.S. 291 (1978)], New York public school teachers who manifest no intention of applying for citizenship [*Ambach v. Norwick,* 441 U.S. 68 (1979)], and California deputy probation officers [*Cabell v. Chavez-Salido,* 454 U.S. 432 (1982)]. According to *Cabell,* "[t]he exclusion of aliens from basic governmental processes is not a deficiency in the democratic system but a necessary consequence of the community's process of political self-definition."

These cases center on the distinction between what *Cabell* labels the economic and the sovereign functions of government, and the disagreements focus upon how this distinction is made and whether or not it is made correctly. The legacy of *Graham* calls for strict scrutiny when states exclude aliens from the economic functions of government. Because aliens do not vote, they are not directly represented, and their interests are therefore more likely to be overridden by a democratic majority. Yet, according to *Ambach,* "[s]ome state functions are so bound up with the operation of the State as a governmental entity as to permit the exclusion from those functions of all persons who have not become part of the process of self-government." As stated in *Cabell,* the latter classification should ensure that truly important governmental functions be shared by "those having the 'fundamental legal bond of citizenship,'" resisting the interpretation that its true purpose is simply to prefer citizens over aliens, and to prefer them in situations where it is not the sovereign but really the economic functions of government that are at stake.

The question, then, is one of what purpose is served by the "fundamental legal bond of citizenship." The *Foley* majority voiced concern that strict scrutiny of all distinctions between citizens and aliens would obliterate these distinctions and thus lessen the value of citizenship: "The act of becoming a citizen is more than a ritual with no content beyond the fanfare of ceremony." Similarly, in *Ambach,* "[t]he distinction between citizens and aliens . . . is fundamental to the definition and government of a State." The context of the latter case was such that the Court here implicitly rejected any test of affinity or length of association with the United States, although it had emphasized this consideration when the economic functions of government were involved.

Cases involving the sovereign functions of government do not consider whether the alien's claim to participate in the political community grows stronger with the passage of time. Neither declarations of loyalty nor evidence of assimilation is sufficient; only actual naturalization counts. Whether the content of national values and traditions is defined substantively or is indeterminate, what matters is the act of commitment through a ritualized and deliberate act.

These considerations raise a number of issues for discussion. *Roberts v. United States Jaycees,* 468 U.S. 609 (1984), at 633, questioned whether the political community in its sovereign functions should operate as an "expressive association," for which the very formation "is the creation of a voice, and the selection of members is the definition of that voice." If so, exclusivity of membership may be protected regardless of whether the nature of the political community would change as a result of greater inclusiveness. There need be little or no distinguishable difference between citizen and alien in terms of the values and traditions they espouse. The existence of an identifiable political community with, according to *Sugarman,* "functions that go to the heart of representative government," however their definitions may be disputed, perhaps renders that community determinate in ways impossible if the political community simply included every person legally within the country's territory. To the extent, however, that the occupations at issue exemplify the economic functions of government, the political community is a commercial association, one whose activity enjoys minimal constitutional protection. Jobs represent goods, privileges, and advantages open to all, and membership carries no protected status.

Yet one can also argue that all legal residents are or should be potential members of the political community, not only in its economic functions but even in its sovereign ones. Michael Walzer argues that for special classes of resident aliens, admitted for work but barred from the civil and economic protections of citizenship, economic and material status cannot improve without an alteration in civic status. In other words, exclusion from membership in the political community in its sovereign functions may itself make a classification suspect and necessitate strict scrutiny when states exclude aliens from the economic

functions of government. Thus, although the community may determine that some will be excluded from its territory, arguably it should not decide that some individuals within its territory will be permanently excluded from its politics.

Other issues include cost-benefit considerations for inclusivity and exclusivity, the question of free public education for undocumented minors, and philosophical arguments for and against various admissions policies. For instance, Whelan considers liberal statist, liberal democratic, and liberal communitarian arguments against open admissions policies. Finally, issues of membership and citizenship also comprise state policies toward the members of subgroups within the nation state.

References

Gibney, Mark. *Open Borders? Closed Societies? The Ethical and Political Issues.* Westport CT: Greenwood Press, 1988.

———. *Strangers or Friends: Principles for a New Alien Admission Policy.* Westport CT: Greenwood Press, 1986.

Hull, Elizabeth. *Without Justice for All: The Constitutional Rights of Aliens.* Westport CT: Greenwood Press, 1985.

Kymlicka, Will. *Liberalism, Community and Culture.* Oxford: Clarendon Press, 1991.

Rosberg, Gerald M. "Aliens and Equal Protection: Why Not the Right to Vote?" *Michigan Law Review* 75 (1977), 1092–1136.

Shklar, Judith N. *American Citizenship: The Quest for Inclusion.* Cambridge MA: Harvard University Press, 1991.

Spinner, Jeff. *The Boundaries of Citizenship: Race, Ethnicity, and Nationality in the Liberal State.* Baltimore: Johns Hopkins University Press, 1994.

Tamir, Yael. *Liberal Nationalism.* Princeton: Princeton University Press, 1993.

Walzer, Michael. *Spheres of Justice: A Defense of Pluralism and Equality.* New York: Basic Books, 1983.

Emily R. Gill

See also ASYLUM AND REFUGEES; MINORITY, ETHIC, AND GROUP RIGHTS

Civil Disobedience

Civil disobedience is a form of protest in which protestors deliberately violate a law.

Classically, they violate the law they are protesting, such as segregation or draft laws, but sometimes they violate other laws that they find unobjectionable, such as trespass or traffic laws. Most activists who perform civil disobedience are scrupulously nonviolent and willingly accept legal penalties. The purpose of civil disobedience can be to publicize an unjust law or a just cause, to appeal to the conscience of the public, to force negotiation with recalcitrant officials, to "clog the machine" (in Henry David Thoreau's phrase) with political prisoners, to get into court where one can challenge the constitutionality of a law, to exculpate oneself or to put an end to one's personal complicity in the injustice which flows from obedience to unjust law—or some combination of these. While civil disobedience in a broad sense is as old as the Hebrew midwives' defiance of Pharaoh, most of the moral and legal theory surrounding it, as well as most of the instances in the street, have been inspired by Thoreau, Mohandas Gandhi, and Martin Luther King, Jr. In this article we will focus on the moral arguments for and against its use in a democracy.

Objection: Civil disobedience cannot be justified in a democracy. Unjust laws made by a democratic legislature can be changed by a democratic legislature. The existence of lawful channels of change makes civil disobedience unnecessary.

Reply: Thoreau, who performed civil disobedience in a democracy, argued that sometimes the constitution is the problem, not the solution. Moreover, legal channels can take too long, he argued, for he was born to live, not to lobby. His individualism gave him another answer: individuals are sovereign, especially in a democracy, and the government only holds its power by delegation from free individuals. Any individual may, then, elect to stand apart from the domain of law. King, who also performed civil disobedience in a democracy, asked us to look more closely at the legal channels of change. If they are open in theory, but closed or unfairly obstructed in practice, then the system is not democratic in the way needed to make civil disobedience unnecessary. Other activists have pointed out that if judicial review is one of the features of American democracy that is supposed to make civil disobedience unnecessary, then it ironically subverts this goal; to obtain standing to bring an unjust statute to court for review, of-

ten a plaintiff must be arrested for violating it. Finally, the Nuremberg principles require disobedience to national laws or orders which violate international law, an overriding duty even in (perhaps especially in) a democracy.

Objection: Even if civil disobedience is sometimes justified in a democracy, activists must first exhaust the legal channels of change and turn to disobedience only as a last resort.

Reply: Legal channels can never be "exhausted." Activists can always write another letter to their congressional delegation or to newspapers; they can always wait for another election and cast another vote. But justice delayed, King proclaimed, is justice denied. After a point, he argued, patience in fighting an injustice perpetuates the injustice, and this point had long since been passed in the 340-year struggle against segregation in America. In the tradition which justifies civil disobedience by appeal to higher law, legal niceties count for relatively little. If God trumps Caesar to justify disobedience to unjust law, then God can trump Caesar to permit this disobedience sooner rather than later. In this tradition, A.J. Muste argued that to use legal channels to fight unjust laws is to participate in an evil machine and to disguise dissent as conformity; this in turn corrupts the activist and discourages others by leading them to underestimate the numbers of their congeners.

Objection: We must obey the law under a contract with other members of our society. We have tacitly consented to the laws by residing in the state and enjoying its benefits.

Reply: Obviously this objection can be evaded by anyone who denies the social contract theory. Surprisingly, however, many disobedient activists affirm that theory, making this an objection they must answer. Socrates argues this objection to Crito who is encouraging him to disobey the law by escaping from prison before he is executed. Thoreau and Gandhi both reply (as part of larger, more complex replies) that those who object deeply to the injustices committed by the state can, and should, relinquish the benefits they receive from the state by living a life of voluntary simplicity and poverty; this form of sacrifice is in effect to revoke one's tacit consent to obey the law. Another of Thoreau's replies is that consent to join a society and obey its laws must always be express, and never tacit. Even for John Locke, whose social contract theory introduces the term "tacit consent," the theory permits disobedience, even revolution, if the state breaches its side of the contract. A reply from the natural law tradition, used by King, is that an unjust law is not even a law, but a perversion of law (Augustine, Aquinas). Hence, consent to obey the laws does not extend to unjust laws. A reply made by many blacks, women, and Native Americans is that the duty to obey is a matter of degree; if they are not fully enfranchised members of American society, then they are not fully bound by its laws.

Objection: What if everybody did it? Civil disobedience fails Immanuel Kant's universalizability test. Most critics prefer to press this objection as a slippery slope argument; the objection, then, has descriptive and normative versions. In the descriptive version, one predicts that the example of disobedience will be imitated, increasing lawlessness and tending toward anarchy. In the normative version, one notes that if disobedience is *justified* for one group whose moral beliefs condemn the law, then it is justified for any group similarly situated, which is a recipe for anarchy.

The first reply, offered in seriousness by Thoreau and Gandhi, is that anarchy is not so bad an outcome. In fact, both depict anarchy as an ideal form of society. However, both are willing to put off the anarchical utopia for another day and fight in the meantime for improved laws; consequently, this strand of their thinking is often overlooked. Another reply is a variation on the first. Anarchy may be bad, but despotism is worse (John Locke instead of Thomas Hobbes). If we face an iniquitous law, then we may permissibly disobey and risk anarchy in order to resist the tendency toward the greater evil of despotism. A.J. Muste extended this line of thinking to turn the slippery slope objection against itself. If we let the state conscript young men against their wills to fight immoral wars, then what will the state do next? For Muste, conscription puts us on a slippery slope toward despotism, and obedience would bring us to the bottom.

Utilitarians observe that disobedience and obedience may both be harmful. The slippery slope objection falsely assumes that the former sort of harm always outweighs the latter. In the case of an iniquitous law, the harm of disobedience can be the lesser evil. This utilitarian reply is sometimes found to coexist with a complementary deontological reply, for example in Thoreau: one simply must not lend one's weight to an unjust cause.

Ronald Dworkin replies, in effect, that the descriptive version of the argument is false and the normative version irrelevant. There is no evidence that civil disobedience, even when tolerated by legal officials, leads to an increase in lawlessness. Moreover, rights trump utility. Since (for Dworkin) there is a strong right to disobey certain kinds of unjust laws, and since the slippery slope argument points only to the disutility of disobedience, this is a case of a right in conflict with utility; hence the right to disobey must prevail.

The normative version of the slippery slope argument has little force if the criteria used by activists permit some but not all Disobedience. In Kant's language again, universalizability fails if the maxim of the action is "Disobey a law whenever you disapprove of it," but it can succeed if instead the maxim is "Disobey when obedience would cause more harm than disobedience," or "Disobey when a law is unjust in the following specific ways." It must be said that virtually all activists who practice civil disobedience follow criteria which endorse some, but not all, disobedience. King, for example, did not advocate indiscriminate disobedience; he advocated disobedience of unjust laws and obedience to the just. He articulated what he regarded as public, objective criteria that help us identify the unjust laws that may or must be disobeyed, as well as the just laws that must be obeyed. Any attempt to articulate the distinction between the two sorts of law is, in effect, an attempt to show that the slide down the slope can be halted, or that the maxim to disobey can be universalized.

King had a second reply, inspired by Gandhi: he deliberately made his example difficult to imitate. He pressed for negotiation before turning to disobedience; he underwent self-purification before every disobedient action; he accepted blows from police without retaliation; he accepted arrest and punishment. These tactical features of his actions had other purposes as well, but there is little doubt that they prevented onlookers from thinking that here was a criminal getting away with murder whose example could be imitated with profit.

The counterreply, made by Waldman and Storing, is that the example of the careful disobedient will be imitated by the careless and cannot be confined, especially if activists cloak their disobedient acts in the rhetoric of righteousness. If true, this instantly makes replies to the normative version of the slippery slope objection irrelevant. Caution in stating our criteria so that normatively we stop our slide far from the bottom does nothing to prevent the example from being misinterpreted or oversimplified by the less cautious. Scrupulosity in self-purification, courage in accepting blows, and sacrifice in accepting punishment do not stop the unscrupulous from being inspired by the example of disobedience as such.

One direct response, then, to the descriptive version held by Louis Waldman and Herbert J. Storing comes from John Rawls, who argued that civil disobedience can actually help to stabilize a community. It can be destabilizing if a very large number of people do it, but this rarely happens, and when only a few do it, it can have the beneficial and stabilizing effect of nudging a society closer to its shared vision of justice.

Thoreau and Richard Wasserstrom argue that while many in fact might be morally justified in disobeying, few in fact will actually disobey. For Thoreau and A.J. Muste, this inertia and docility in the general population are far larger problems than incipient anarchy.

Sometimes activists can point to the lawlessness of their opponents as the real concern. Thoreau claimed that the only harmful consequences of civil disobedience were triggered by the government's reaction to it. King painted white segregationists as the group most likely to precipitate anarchy, since it disobeyed desegregation laws without regard to their legitimacy or justice. Moreover, an activist need not be an anarchist to welcome widespread imitation. Thoreau ardently wished that all opponents of slavery would act on their convictions. He would regard a prediction of widespread imitation of his disobedience as an inducement to act, not as an objection. At this point, critics must be careful not to use the slippery slope objection inconsistently by predicting anarchy to those who fear it and inert indifference to those who fear that. On the other hand, activists who welcome imitation should probably do all they can to encourage this imitation; Thoreau did nothing of this kind until he wrote his extremely influential essay two years after he was arrested for withholding his poll tax.

References

Gandhi, Mohandas K. *Satyagraha in South Africa.* Trans. Valji Govindji Desai. Ahmedabad: Navajivan Publishing House, 1928.
Bedau, Hugo Adam, ed. *Civil Disobedience: Theory and Practice.* New York: Macmillan, 1969.
Harris, Paul, ed. *Civil Disobedience.* University Press of America, 1989.
King, Martin Luther, Jr. "Letter From Birmingham Jail." In *Why We Can't Wait,* ed. Martin Luther King, Jr., 76–95. New York: New American Library, 1964.
Thoreau, Henry David. *The Variorum Civil Disobedience.* Ed. Walter Harding. New York: Twayne, 1967.

Peter Suber

See also CONSCIENCE; CONSCIENTIOUS OBJECTION

Civil Rights

In the broadest sense, civil rights are simply rights protected by government. In this sense civil rights are general rights that states guarantee to their citizens through their constitution and laws. A more common contemporary usage, however, takes "civil rights" to be equality rights—constitutional and legislative norms that guarantee to minorities and women equal citizenship, equality before the law, nondiscrimination, and fair treatment. The struggle of African Americans to gain equality and escape segregation and second-class citizenship is referred to as "the Civil Rights Movement," and the legislation resulting from that struggle, such as the *Civil Rights Act of 1964,* bears the same name.

It is possible to contrast civil rights in the sense of equality rights with civil liberties. Civil liberties are constitutional liberties such as freedom of thought, speech, association, and assembly; civil rights are not mainly liberties but are rather protections against social and political inequality. Clearly, civil liberties such as freedom of expression and freedom of association can be used in ways that conflict with civil rights.

One philosophical issue about civil rights in the sense of equality rights concerns how they can be justified (or, at a deeper level, whether they can be justified). Consequentialist justifications point to the bad effects of segregation and second-class citizenship and to the likely good consequences of equal treatment. Segregation and discrimination resulted in blacks being concentrated at the bottom of the economic ladder, perpetuated stereotypes and prejudice, deprived black children of successful role models and damaged their self-esteem, and made understanding and cooperation between groups more difficult.

An alternative approach (although potentially complementary) emphasizes a claim to equal respect, equal citizenship, and fundamental fairness—and asserts that segregation, discrimination, and unequal rights are incompatible with these norms.

Another philosophical issue about civil rights concerns how we should understand the concept of discrimination. Prohibitions of discrimination apply to the allocations of important benefits, such as education and jobs, and forbid awarding or denying such benefits on grounds such as race, ethnicity, national origin, religion, or sex unless the use of these characteristics in particular circumstances is demonstrably legitimate and essential. This sort of antidiscrimination norm is presupposed by most condemnations of discrimination and is found in most civil rights legislation.

Many have attempted to broaden the antidiscrimination principle to cover institutional or structural discrimination, but such attempts remain controversial. A norm addressing institutional discrimination might attempt to cover unconscious discrimination, where people engage in discriminatory behavior out of habit without being aware of doing so; statistical discrimination, where a person or firm uses characteristics such as race or sex in allocations because those characteristics have some correlation to relevant characteristics such as education level or physical strength; discrimination based on customers' prejudices, where a company refuses to hire people with certain looks or beliefs because the company's customers are prejudiced against people with those looks or beliefs (these are sometimes called "reaction qualifications"); and hiring through personal connections, where a firm finds new employees by word-of-mouth advertising within the social networks of present employees. Perhaps the most difficult of all to bring within the concept of discrimination are allocative decisions that transmit the consequences of discrimination even though they are based on relevant considerations. For example, blacks who faced serious discrimination in education and employment in their childhoods may as a result have lower levels of education and job experience. A decision not to hire such a person at age forty for a senior position may be based solely on education and job experience, and hence may not be discriminatory in the standard sense; nevertheless, such decisions are the effects of earlier discrimination and perpetuate inequality for blacks.

Advocates of expanding our understanding of discrimination to include these sorts of actions argue that unless we do so legal prohibitions of discrimination will do little to end the unfair disadvantages that minorities and women face. Opponents of such expansions argue that they make discrimination extremely difficult to define and detect and that they make illegal certain actions that are frequently innocent and not based on prejudice.

There have also been extensive discussions concerning the nature and justification of affirmative action. Should it go beyond stopping discrimination, widespread advertising of positions, and record keeping by sex, race, and nationality? If so, are preferential policies part of it? Can it best be defended as compensation for past injustices, as a means to promoting utility through the elimination of harmful practices and distributions, or as a means to greater distributive justice in the future? Critics of affirmative action have preferred to call it "reverse discrimination" and have argued that it typically uses preferential policies that are deeply unfair to white males. They have also argued that affirmative action tends to stigmatize members of its target groups who are successful by suggesting that they gained their positions with less than the requisite amounts of merit.

References

Boxill, Bernard. *Blacks and Social Justice*. Totowa NJ: Rowman and Allenheld, 1984.

Cahn, Steven M., ed. *The Affirmative Action Debate*. New York: Routledge, 1995.

Ezorsky, Gertrude. *Racism and Justice: The Case for Affirmative Action*. Ithaca NY: Cornell University Press, 1991.

Grey, Thomas C. "Civil Rights and Civil Liberties: The Case of Discriminatory Verbal Harassment." *Social Philosophy and Policy* 8 (1991), 81.

Kymlicka, Will. *Multicultural Citizenship: A Liberal Theory of Minority Rights*. Oxford: Clarendon Press, 1995.

James W. Nickel

See also EQUALITY

Civilian Philosophy of Law

The expression "philosophy of law" emerged in continental Europe two centuries ago. Since its use became widespread it has been used to indicate diverse pieces of research, which, with the progress and greater articulation of studies, became increasingly different, with only their negative nature in common. These studies discuss matters which "surround" law and clarify notions which "bear relation" to law, but normally are not dealt with in express terms or are taken for granted by lawyers.

As Norberto Bobbio points out, searching for a definition of philosophy of law is a complete waste of time. Philosophy of law has been understood in two ways. First, it was understood as a branch of general philosophy, along with philosophy of nature, history, religion, art, and so forth. The most illustrative examples of this way of understanding it can be found in the teachings of Immanuel Kant and G.W.F. Hegel. This type of philosophy is a *Weltanschauung,* a view of the world which is mechanically applied to law. From this perspective, philosophy of law consists of accepting one or other of the many views of the world (for example, idealism, thomism, marxism, existentialism, and spiritualism); taking from the chosen view all its terms, concepts, and preconstituted principles; and then applying these in a systematic way to the problems of law and/or justice. So legal or judicial problems are no longer dealt with from legal experience, but from solutions that have already been provided to problems of a different nature.

The second way in which philosophy of law is understood is through the view taken by those who believe it is independent of philosophy in general. This way of understanding philosophy of law is not completely detached from philosophical knowledge, but its relative independence can be observed in two ways: first, it is not derived from a specific philosophical system but emerges directly from the analysis of legal reality; and, second, the conclusions which thinkers reach on each subject area are more than a "mere application of a series of principles from a foreign philosophical system." This perspective is what is commonly called *legal theory.* This theory does not assume preestablished conceptions of the world but rather specific conceptual problems which have emerged from the very heart of law. This modern way of conceiving philosophy of law in Europe is related to the philosophical conception of empiricism and of twentieth-century analytical philosophy.

The subjects which philosophers of law from the civil law tradition usually cover (although they use different terminology, something which illustrates different contents and concepts of law) are the following: (general) legal theory (or ontology of law), theory of justice (or legal axiology), and theory of legal science (gnoseology, or theory of legal knowledge).

(General) Legal Theory

To clarify what general legal theory is, we have to begin by analyzing the different meanings of the word "general." (The word "general" as linked to legal theory is used in French, Italian, and Spanish, although not in English.) First, there is the idea that general theory is a strong concept which designates "the conceptual study of law and which isolates the pure concepts used to describe any legal experience," or is the analysis of "general notions considered common to all legal systems." This is how Merkl views legal theory and it was he who coined this idea in 1874. Behind this way of viewing general legal theory is a way of thinking which maintains that all legal systems, wherever and whenever they occur, have characteristics in common which do not exist just by chance. However, this way of thinking means that certain characteristics, ones which do not appear in all legal systems (but which are characteristic of modern Western legal systems), are inappropriately generalized.

Second, there are those who talk about "general" theory to designate the principles and notions which are common not to all legal systems but to the different sectors of a specific legal system (for example, civil law, administrative law). For example, although the idea of "sale and purchase" is specific to civil law, the idea of "obligation" is common to all the different fields of law and is therefore something which can be dealt with as part of general legal theory.

Third, and especially in contemporary literature with an analytical linguistic tendency, "general" theory means "the analysis of a legal system under a structural and formal profile." In this third meaning for the general legal theory, the generality comes not from the fact that it is universally applicable to any legal system but from the fact that it ignores the normative content of the peculiar legal systems studied, and simply deals with its structure. For example, studying a country's positive constitutional law is different from trying to put its constitutional norms into a set type.

General legal theory should be limited to this last meaning. This view assumes that law is not just an isolated group of rules and regulations (and therefore each rule or regulation cannot be studied separately) but is part of a system: the legal system. This means that general legal theory is really the theory of legal systems and includes the following areas: (1) what a legal system comprises (the concept of rules and their classification); (2) its formation (the theory of sources of law); (3) problems of unity (validity and basic law), completeness (gaps and how they can be filled), and consistency (antinomies and how they can be eliminated); (4) the relationship between different systems (relationships of geographical proximity, relationships over time, and material relationships); and (5) interpretation of the law, that is, how the meaning shared by all norms of a specific type is determined once their specific content is left to one side.

Theory of Justice

The theory of justice is not preoccupied with *what* law is or *how* it is at a given moment in time, but examines what it *should be* like. So it does not refer to what law "is," but what it "ought to be." Thus it forms a part of legal ethics or the critical analysis of legal values.

The main guideline for this part of philosophy of law is the concept of "justice" understood as a set of values, goods, or interests which persons want to protect. When they decide to protect these values, they resort to a form of coexistence known as law. Theory of justice studies (1) the history of the different concepts of "justice"; (2) the systematic drawing up of a theory of legal values and a theory of human rights; and (3) the "justice" of different legal decisions, which implies developing a theory of the principles for the material criteria that all legal decisions use. In fact, if we take a step back and think about "justice," it is precisely because we want all the different legal decisions taken (whether they be constitutional, legislative, or judicial) to be fair (or just). That is why the development of a theory of principles as well as a theory of values implies the analysis of the aims of law, and with them an analysis of the most appropriate legal

model for obtaining the aim of "justice" in society.

Here, philosophy of law is considered as a subject with very little autonomy. Theory of justice can follow two very different fundamental types of discourse: First, it can explore normative or valorative doctrines of justice, that is, those valorations which criticize existing law and considerations of *iure condendo* (the foundations of law), and so forth. However, these discourses are normally included in the field of political philosophy and/or legal ethics. Second, it can pursue the logical analysis of value judgments, which is part of the specific field of meta-ethics.

Theory of Legal Science

Theory of legal science examines the intellectual procedures which lawyers follow when determining, interpreting, integrating, and conciliating the different norms of a legal system.

The aim of the theory of legal science is in relation to the juridical system that the theory studies. Thus, at least briefly, the so-considered main features of the civilian law tradition should be pointed out (although some of them are principally aspirations of legal science and do not belong to the valid legal systems). (1) Civilian law tradition stems from the Roman law. (2) It is a codified law, that is, the law is collected around a coherent and complete set of legal rules. (3) The main source of law is legislation; custom has a very secondary place, and precedents are not a source of law. (4) The previous characteristic involves a certain conception about the judge's task of applying the law: judicial reasoning is purely deductive (syllogistic) and, therefore, the judicial outcome has been considered as the unique correct solution to the problem posed. (5) There is a clear difference between private law and public law: the former deals with legal relations between subjects, as equals; the latter with legal relations between public authority and the subject. (6) There is a sharp difference between substantive law and procedural law. (7) It is usually said that its legal procedure is principally inquisitorial (in which professional magistrates deal with the whole case and there is no lay participation). In fact, whether the system is inquisitorial or adversarial depends on the kind of conflict at issue, for example, a civil or a penal procedure. (8) The judges are civil servants and have to pass several public examinations in order to reach the judicature.

As well, a small number of posts is reserved to distinguished jurists. (9) Judicial revision on the constitutionality of the statutes is maintained, by means of constitutional courts or by ordinary jurisdiction, depending on the country. (10) A basic feature of civilian legal systems has to do with the way that civilian lawyers think about their own juridical system. They believe that it is possible to build up a single, complete, coherent, and logical system of law to govern all the relationships of man to man, and that the human mind is able to think, work, and write it out.

The theory of legal science analyzes scientific-legal statements both in isolation and in their reciprocal relations. In the first of these analyses, the interpretation and application of the law is studied and, in the second, the logics and axiomatization of legal theories are studied, such as the alternatives to classical logic.

This theory considers the following aspects: (1) the description of the valid norms necessary to resolve a given case; (2) the interpretation of the norms in each branch of the law, their relationship with others when faced with the construction of institutions, and their systematization in a coherent whole; (3) the application of all the previous work to the resolution of specific cases in real life; (4) a critical reflection on legal science and the scientific activity of lawyers (here the "scientific nature" of legal science is analyzed); and (5) a comparative analysis with other social sciences and with the whole of current scientific knowledge. Hence, the theory of legal science is a legal epistemology and a critical theory of legal knowledge.

History of the Philosophy of Law

A different way of understanding philosophy of law is to regard it as a history of legal doctrines. This would involve analyzing each of the problems mentioned previously in a historical context. In this sense philosophy of law is not an independent subject. From a methodological viewpoint, the history of legal doctrines is no different from other general historiographic disciplines. From the point of view of the aim of research, it is impossible to draw a line between the history of legal doctrines and the history of other institutions.

References

Association of American Law Schools. *Science of Legal Method. Selected Essays by Various Authors*. New York: Augustus M. Kelley, 1969.

David, René, and John E.C. Brierley. *Major Legal Systems in the World Today*. Pt. 1: "The Romano-Germanic Family." London: Stevens, 1968; 2d ed., New York: Free Press, 1978.

Ehrman, H.W. "Civil Law Systems." In *Encyclopedia of the American Judicial System*, ed. Robert J. Janosik, vol. 2, 490–499. New York: Scribners, 1987.

Hampstead, L. of, and M.D.A. Freeman. *Lloyd's Introduction to Jurisprudence*. London: Sweet, 1985.

Mehrenn, A. von, and J.R. Gordley. *The Civil Law System: An Introduction to the Comparative Study of Law*. Boston: Little, Brown, 1977.

Merryman, J.H., and D.S. Clark. *Comparative Law: Western European and Latin American Legal Systems*. Indianapolis IN: Bobbs-Merrill, 1978.

La Philosophie du droit aujourd'hui (Philosophy of Law Today). *Archives de Philosophie du Droit*. Vol. 23. Paris: Sirey, 1988.

Prott, Lyndel V. "Judicial Reasoning in the Common Law and Code Law Systems." *Archiv für Rechts- und Sozialphilosophie* 64 (1978), 417–436.

Ryan, K.W. *An Introduction to the Civil Law*. Brisbane: The Law Book Company of Australasia, 1962.

Watson, A. *The Making of the Civilian Law*. Cambridge MA: Harvard University Press, 1981.

Victoria Iturralde

See also COMMON LAW PHILOSOPHY OF LAW; COMPARATIVE LAW

Civility

A virtue of citizens, typically defined as proper comportment toward fellow citizens and the common goods of a state, civility has played a central role in legal and political theory since at least the Renaissance and can be found in recognizable form in the work of earlier thinkers. Sometimes law is concurrently defined as a representation or codification of civility. Whether in neo-aristotelian, civic republican, or liberal terms, civility is central to any attempt to build substantive ethical commitments into the political-legal role of citizenship.

Historical Background

Perhaps the earliest defender of civility as a virtue of citizens was the Roman lawyer and orator Cicero, whose treatise *De re publica,* written in 51 B.C., introduced and defended notions of civic virtue, individualism, natural law, and common social good. Though no original thinker, drawing most of his ideas from Greek philosophers of greater genius, Cicero was an able popularizer and a brilliant rhetorician. (Quintilian called him the king of the law courts, and Jean-Jacques Rousseau labeled him "Prince of Eloquence.") Like his legal briefs, Cicero's philosophical works were ably argued, and he influenced, in turn, early Christian church fathers, republican humanists of the Renaissance, emerging early-modern liberals of central Europe and Britain, and reform-minded democrats of the French and Scottish Enlightenments.

Much of Cicero's political inspiration was provided by the peripatetic school, but he did not share Aristotle's idea that the state (*civitas*) should be an ethical crucible, a polis of like-minded virtuous men in common pursuit of justice. In contrast, Ciceronian justice, while insisting on civic commitment to the common good, incorporated the Roman notion that society is intended to protect the private property of law-abiding citizens (*cives*). The latter notion drew the approval of John Locke; the former, together with Cicero's hard-headedness as a practical politician in a volatile political context, coaxed regard from Niccolò Machiavelli.

Cicero does not use the word "civility" specifically in his works, but it is clear that his discussion of the civic virtues, especially *humanitas,* the fellow feeling which tempers acquisitiveness and private interest, vividly illustrates a citizen committed to the common good of civil society under the rule of law. Later republicans, including Machiavelli, would place this ideal at the center of their discussions of citizenship. Rousseau, echoing the earlier arguments, noted that all peoples face "the first duties of civility" in the early stages of social organization. Citizens have to abide by the social contract each of them has made, and make the efforts of participation and cooperation required for its success. Civility signals the creation of both authority and obligation.

The civic humanists of the Renaissance found Cicero's political vision congenial. For them, the political understanding of civility resonated with a newfound concern for matters of social comportment conceived more generally. Thus the new publisher's staple, the manners manual (for example, Della Casa's *Galateo*; Guazzo's *La civil conversatione*), was accepted as part of a continuum that included at its more serious end Baldassare Castiglione's *Il cortegiano* and even Machiavelli's *Il principe.* This link between civility in its political-legal meaning and the civility associated with manners is even sharper in the thought of certain Enlightenment thinkers, especially those associated with Joseph Addison's ideals of fellowship and conversation. In Augustan Scotland, especially, the idea of "polite society" became an active principle of social reform.

Lost here, arguably, is the specifically republican meaning of civility: the deep commitment to the public good. Replacing it is a stronger emphasis on self-interest and wealth acquisition, which, to be sure, is regulated by politeness but without the sense of shared ends and active participation in political association. This shift from civic to civil, from *polis* to politeness, marks the victory of laissez-faire liberal notions of political association over participatory republican ones. It also signals a move from the ethical monism of the ancient world, uneasily supported by later republicans, to the pluralism characteristic of modernity.

Contemporary Debates

Civility has recently become a focus for political theory once more, especially in the work of American thinkers whose tradition contains both liberal and republican elements.

According to John Rawls, for example, citizens have "a natural duty to civility" under conditions of fair distribution. Civility demands that they "not invoke the fault of social arrangements as a too-ready excuse for not complying with them, nor ... exploit loopholes in the rules to advance [their] interests." In later expansions and revisions of his original theory, Rawls clarifies his idea of civility, linking it with other virtues (fairness, tolerance, reasonableness) that characterize the members of a liberal state. In this expanded version, civility goes well beyond simply playing the game by the rules; civility is understood as the ability of citizens "to explain to one another on those fundamental questions [of justice] how the principles and policies they advocate and vote for can be supported by the political values of public reason." Civility therefore also "involves a willingness to listen to others and a fairmindedness in deciding when accommodations to their views should reasonably be made."

The duty to civility is moral, not legal. It concerns a shared commitment to a notion of citizenship that is rich, participatory, and vibrant. Such a concrete model of citizenship supports, through participation in the fora of public reason, the idea of justice as regulated interaction between reasonable people, each of whom finds his or her own reasons for upholding the society. Defended this way, civility begins to occupy a central role in the political discourse of legitimation. The emphasis on citizenly participation also means that political liberalism parallels in content (if not in derivation) the virtue-based accounts of citizenship found in the classical republican tradition that includes Machiavelli's *The Discourses* and, especially, Alexis de Tocqueville's *Democracy in America*.

Other "republican liberals"—for example, William Galston, Benjamin Barber, Stephen Macedo—have likewise sought to retain substance in liberalism by a focus on civility and other virtues of citizenship. Though these thinkers are cognizant of moral pluralism, and therefore do not pursue a fusion of ethical and political in the manner of neo-aristotelians, they nevertheless call for strength of ties between citizens that are stronger than those of classical liberalism's competing units of self-interest. Barber, for instance, calls civility the characteristic civic virtue of good democrats, and argues that strong community ties are required to commit such democrats to the active political participation necessary to exploring a common social good together.

But in thus stretching the ideas of democratic political theory to include "communitarian" values of fellow feeling, patriotism, neighborliness, and the like, such thinkers may extend past the boundaries of political liberalism. Focusing on the civic virtues may thus have the unexpected effect of undermining Immanuel Kant's priority of right over good that many think characteristic of liberalism. According to some critics, notably Michael Oakeshott, this merely indicates the inability of liberalism's "enterprise association" to take account of deeper ties of civility and "civil association," ties that in Oakeshott's hands begin to resemble again the classical republicanism of Cicero. (Significantly, Oakeshott uses the Roman vocabulary of *cives* and *civitas*, *lex* and *ius*.) Another sort of challenge comes from some feminist legal and political theorists, who object to the entire tradition of civic virtue—including centrally the virtue of civility—for its biases in favor of restrictive impartiality, reason conceived as hostile to affective thought, and abstract equality between citizens.

In response to these challenges, thinkers sympathetic to the priority of right have attempted to understand civility rather more abstractly, as a specifically *dialogic* virtue of citizens. Civility is viewed as a feature of a political conversation among citizens of diverse moral aspiration. As noted by James Fishkin, here we might conceive of a pluralistic society guided by a political culture of "participatory civility . . . where people learn to listen and respond on the merits [of arguments] in an atmosphere of mutual respect." An alternative offered by Mark Kingwell would be to defend civility as a two-sided "first virtue of dialogic citizens": dialogic self-restraint exercised on certain kinds of invidious or politically irrelevant arguments, combined with openness to the justice claims made by others. The success of these latest attempts to defend civility has not yet been fully assessed.

References

Barber, Benjamin. *Strong Democracy: Participatory Politics for a New Age*. Berkeley: University of California Press, 1984.

Fishkin, James. *The Dialogue of Justice*. New Haven: Yale University Press, 1992.

Galston, William. *Liberal Purposes: Goods, Virtues and Diversity in the Liberal State*. Cambridge: Cambridge University Press, 1991.

Green, Leslie. *The Authority of the State*. Oxford: Clarendon Press, 1988.

Kingwell, Mark. *A Civil Tongue: Justice, Dialogue and the Politics of Pluralism*. University Park: Penn State University Press, 1995.

Macedo, Stephen. *Liberal Virtues: Citizenship, Virtue, and Community in Liberal Constitutionalism*. Oxford: Clarendon Press, 1990.

Oakeshott, Michael. "On the Civil Condition." In *On Human Conduct*, ed.

Michael Oakeshott. Oxford: Oxford University Press, 1975.

Rawls, John. *Political Liberalism.* New York: Columbia University Press, 1993.

———. *A Theory of Justice.* Cambridge MA: Harvard University Press, 1971.

Mark Kingwell

Codification

Codification is a standard means for making the law public and available, as well as for recording the law in written texts. It is a tool known since the law's early development.

The fundamental task of codification in antiquity was the exclusion of any doubts in the presentation of the law, for example, the restoration by the Laws of Hammurabi of the validity of ancient traditions in accordance with the prevailing interests of the ruler, declaration of law as the common body of rules for the social game by the Laws of Twelve Tables (at least according to Titus Livius' legend of its origin), and also as the halt of law's previous development by the Codex Justinianus. In the medieval era, codification made possible the registration, recording, and uniform editing of the consolidated customs, adapted and brought up to date, prevailing in particular areas of customary law. In the modern era, the continued recording of recognized customs, the declaration of newly established national laws, the collection of an unambiguous body of law designated to be applicable by the sovereign power, as well as the activity of legal reform, often hidden and sometimes executed under the guise of restoring old-time conditions only ideologically postulated, have fallen within the domain of tasks for codification.

Earlier, the mere collection of portions of the law into qualitative summations proved to be enough for completing the task, without any structural renewal. However, on the European continent in the modern era, ending feudal disunity and division became the sine qua non for survival among competing empires and dynasties. In order to achieve this, the monarch had to organize a state army and its state financing separate from his own, as well as a bureaucratic institutional machinery to run them, which could function in an impersonal way to implant a far-reaching regulatory system. For the lucid arrangement and up-to-date handling of such a quantity of regulations, the old methods could not prove adequate. In other words, in the codification of continental Europe the quantitative collecting of legal material was replaced by their qualitative restructuring.

The genuine breakthrough was based on the idea of legality, the conceptualization of laws into a sequence of legal rights and duties, which translated the bourgeois view of society into the language of law, realized through complete structural reform, reestablishing and repositing of the whole body of law. This was accomplished by Enlightenment's bold demand for change, by the planning ethos characteristic of rationalism, by the refounding of natural law (by this time already opposed to feudalism), and, as to its methods, by taking the *more geometrico* (geometric manner) pattern from the axiomatic idea of the exact sciences (especially mathematics and physics). With the triumph of the idea of constructing *more geometrico,* the law became represented as a system having axiomatic logic as its ideal, replacing the chaotic mass of rules, disorderly and full of contradictions, built one upon the other by chance. The system was constructed as the well-ordered assembly of general principles, serving as foundation stones for the whole assemblage, general rules, specific rules, exceptions from the rules, and exceptions from the exceptions. All this was done in a code usually consisting of two parts, namely, the general part, which provided the directives for the entire legislation, and a special part, which offered regulation calibrated for standard situations (for example, individual contracts defined in civil law, or the legal facts that constitute a case in criminal law). Princely absolutism attempted to operate with casuistic precision (the General Law of Prussian Territory, 1791) but did not succeed. The Civil Code with which the French revolutionary renewal concluded (1804), then the Austrian (1811), the German (1897), and the Swiss (1907) codes of civil law, resulted in framing the influential bodies of the law on the European continent that are still in force today.

Codification meant new possibilities in the presentation of the law, as well as in its internal organization and structure. The germ of the claim for legal positivism was first formulated in the imperial codification of Justinian and, later, Frederick the Great: the embodiment of laws in a series of concepts; the development of its fundamental classifications and conceptual system, with an emphasis on prohibiting interpretation except before an extraordinary imperial committee; and, finally, the reduction of law (*ius*) to the body of enacted laws (*lex*), that is, the exclusive identification of law with the outcome of its formal enactment. However, the formative era's foundation of rules upon underlying general principles, in a consistently established system derived from the principles and based on the qualitative idea of codification, was soon lost in the rigid and exegetical application of the great civil codes. By the end of the nineteenth century, legal positivism was simplified to rule positivism or, more accurately, to statutory positivism.

In England, efforts of codification at the start advanced parallel to those in continental Europe. However, since legal unity was no longer in question and the judicial route to legal adaptation had been institutionalized at an early period, the idea of codification because of rational considerations did not take hold. Even in the United States codification proved to be successful primarily as the medium for legal transplant and for reform in the new state's institutions. The common law pattern of restructuring the law into a new systematic body, as opposed to the civil law pattern of codification, is based on the rearrangement of the legal materials. Thanks to the process of argumentation through precedents, general principles could become the source for the judges' considerations without any mediation by a code. Codification in the strict sense of the word was replaced by various substitutes, such as doctrinal codification (textbook writing, as the medium for nineteenth-century English legal export to the colonies; restatement of the law by private bodies with professional support, as the tool for the American approach to law in the twentieth century), the rearrangement of statutory law (consolidation), and the uniformization and unification of law.

Summing up, the code is a thoroughly organized body of rules covering a branch of legal regulation. From the ancient collections of law in Mesopotamia and China up to the general codes of the Nordic countries in the seventeenth and eighteenth centuries, the codes committed to one written body almost the entire system of law. From the later efforts at legal consolidation, from French absolutism until the present, codification has, instead, collected all the rules of a relatively independent area within individual branches of the law. Formerly it could be a recording of customs or a compilational collection or a proposal in a private work (for example, Werbőczy's *Tripartitum opus iuris*, 1514, which was successful in preserving Hungarian legal unity even after the country was divided in three). Private projects continue, for instance, in the recommended model codes of the Restatements of Law, which were meant for internal legal uniformization as well as for the codification of precedent law in the United States.

Today's codes are, in general, the products of legislative initiatives. In its modern forms, codification strives for a structure moving from the general to the specific, often introduced by a preamble stating its goals, and always having a statement of general principles as its foundation. The principles in the code are often formulated as a clause from which legal practice can generate new regulations, and can even erect new legal institutions.

As its name implies, compilation is a way of stating and arranging the applicable rules in chronological order as a written or printed collection, or as a mass of information stored on or in electronic data bases. This information is classified in accordance with the sources from which the legal provisions are taken, and eventually by topics. Until the formation of modern codes, most law books in the ancient, medieval, and modern era were only collections of the prevailing normative material—in some cases with textual corrections, which were meant mainly to exclude possible contradictions, to leave out the parts that had lost their validity due to desuetude, to remedy textual deteriorations caused by earlier copying, and sometimes to "correct" it, that is, revise it in order to satisfy current dominant interests. Modern compilations mostly do not revise, but keep the original structure of the legal sources elaborated in them. Sometimes the rationale of the minister who originally presented the bill is included, and in Nordic European states the preparatory material elaborated by scholarly and judicial committees (*travaux préparatoires*) are also included or attached to it.

References

Bayitch, S.A. "Codification in Modern Times." In *Civil Law in the Modern World,* ed. A.N. Yiannopoulos. Baton Rouge: Louisiana State University Press, 1965.

Cork, Charles M. The *American Codification Movement*. Westport CT: Greenwood Press, 1981.

Lang, M.E. C*odification in the British Empire and America*. Amsterdam: H.J. Paris, 1924.

Legrand, Pierre. "The Strange Power of Words: Codification Situated." *Tulane European and Civil Law Forum* 1 (1994), 1.

Sauvepanne, J. *Codified and Judge Made Law*. Amsterdam: North-Holland, 1982.

Schwartz, B. *The Code Napoleon and the Common-Law World*. New York: New York University Press, 1956.

Stoljar, S.J., ed. *Problems of Codification*. Canberra: Australian National University, 1977.

Tarello, Giovanni. *Le ideologie della codificazione nel secolo XVIII* (The Ideology of Codification in the 18th Century). Genova: Edizioni Culturali Internazionali, n.d.

Vanderlinden, Jacques. *Le concept de code en Europe occidentale du XIIIᵉ et XIXᵉ siècle* (The Concept of a Code in Western Europe in the 18th and 19th Centuries). Brussels: Editions de l'Institut de Sociologie de l'Université Libre, 1967.

Varga, Csaba. *Codification as a Socio-Historical Phenomenon*. Budapest: Akademiae Kiado, 1991.

Csaba Varga

See also LEGISLATION AND CODIFICATION

Coercion (Duress)

In Anglo-American criminal law, an act that would ordinarily constitute a punishable offense can be justified or excused under one of several accepted conditions, for example, self-defense, insanity, necessity, and coercion or duress. Although the law has traditionally distinguished coercion or duress from necessity, considering them together with necessity sharpens our understanding of coercion.

Consider the following examples:

1. Green, who had been subject to a series of homosexual rapes by fellow inmates, unsuccessfully sought help from the prison authorities. One day, on being told he would be raped that evening, he fled. He was captured and charged with escape. As noted in *State v. Green*, 470 S.W.2d 565 (1971), he claimed that he should be acquitted on grounds of *necessity*.

2. Lynch, in *Lynch v. Director of Public Prosecutions*, A.C. 633 (1975), claimed that he had been ordered by three members of the Irish Republican Army to drive a car to a place where they then shot and killed a policeman and that he had participated in the murder under *duress*.

3. Toscano, a chiropractor, was accused of conspiring in a scheme to defraud insurance companies. He argued in *State v. Toscano*, 378 A.2d 755 (1977), that the organizer of the scheme had *coerced* him into participating by threatening him and his family.

The demarcation between necessity and duress has traditionally reflected two different distinctions. First, in most cases of necessity (such as *Green*), a defendant responds to natural or social background factors that arguably make it reasonable to violate the law. In cases of coercion or duress (such as *Lynch* and *Toscano*), another party threatens the defendant with a harmful consequence if he should refuse to violate the law. Second, necessity has generally been understood as a justification (as is self-defense), which claims that the defendant has acted properly because violating the law is the "lesser evil," whereas duress has generally been regarded as an excuse (as is insanity), where the defendant concedes that the act is wrongful, but seeks to avoid the attribution of the act to the actor.

Given this, a theory of coercion or duress as a defense will answer two questions: (1) What kind of defense does coercion provide? Is it a justification or an excuse? (2) What constitutes coercion? When is it appropriate to say that a defendant has been coerced?

We typically say that a defendant has an excuse when the defendant is not acting voluntarily, that is, when he does not possess the appropriate mens rea. Although William Blackstone in his *Commentaries on the Laws of England* held that both necessity and duress involve the "want or defect of will," there is reason to think that defendants are acting with volition and rationally in most cases of necessity and in many cases of duress. In other cases, the judgment of defendants is so overborne by fear that they choose to succumb when they would, after calm reflection, choose not to do so; these defendents are thought to be acting without volition. There is no reason, however, to think that the second alternative was true in any of the cases noted previously. On the assumption that the defendant is acting voluntarily (in this limited sense), it could be stated that, like necessity, a coercion defense should be understood as justification, that is, should claim that it was permissible for the defendant to have chosen to commit the crime rather than endure the threatened action.

Understanding duress as a justification rather than an excuse helps in understanding several features of the law of duress. First, Anglo-American law has traditionally barred a duress defense to murder. If duress were an "excuse" (like insanity) grounded in the lack of volition of the defendant's act, there would be no reason to adopt such a view. If duress is considered a justification, it can be argued that it is not permissible to kill another person just to save one's own life. Second, courts have often refused to allow duress defenses unless there is the threat of present, imminent, and immediate death or serious bodily harm. If duress were an excuse, there is no reason to so limit the defense. Third, the law typically uses an "objective" standard of duress rather than a standard that appeals to the psychological state of the defendant. It claims that a defendant is coerced only when a person of "reasonable firmness" would have been unable to resist the threat, thus reinforcing the moral perspective of the defense of coercion.

If duress is a justification it does not follow that there is no important moral distinction between necessity and duress. We can distinguish between agent-neutral justifications and agent-relative justifications. An agent-neutral justification may require us to weigh impartially the interests of all affected parties. By contrast, an agent-relative justification allows us to place greater weight on our own interests or the interests of those to whom we have special relationships or obligations. From an agent-neutral perspective, one may not be justified in refusing to risk one's own life in order to save the lives of two strangers; from an agent-relative perspective, one is entitled to weigh one's own life more heavily than the lives of strangers. It could be stated that necessity provides an agent-neutral justification whereas duress or coercion constitutes an agent-relative justification. We do not say that a defendant is coerced by referring solely to empirical facts about his state of mind, but by arguing that he has an agent-relative justification for refusing to succumb to the threat. The claim that a defendant is coerced is a moral claim, not an empirical or psychological claim.

Whether duress or coercion is understood as a justification or an excuse, it is evident that the law has sometimes confused two questions: (1) *Did* the defendant act under duress? Was the defendant justified in committing the crime? (2) Should we *find* that the defendant acted under duress? Would it be best to acquit the defendant? To illustrate the confusion between these two questions, consider two special contexts in which coercion is offered as a defense. First, American courts have generally refused to allow intimidated witnesses to offer duress as a defense to a charge of contempt of court for refusing to testify, although prosecution witnesses are murdered with some frequency and the government runs an elaborate "witness protection program." Second, prisoners have generally not been able to offer necessity or duress as a defense to prison escape unless they turn themselves in to the authorities after having escaped, thereby putting themselves at risk to the same factors that motivated the original escape.

Society has a genuine interest in encouraging witnesses to testify and in limiting prison escape. In addition, because both situations present special epistemological problems with respect to the validation of the defenses, society may have to choose between (1) allowing a small number of valid necessity and duress claims while allowing numerous false claims and (2) excluding most false claims of necessity and duress but excluding many valid claims as well. Given this, it is entirely possible that considerations of social utility might well support a decision to choose (2) rather than (1).

Still, we should not confuse the claim that there are utilitarian reasons to reject a duress defense with the claim that the parties have not acted under duress. Moreover, a decision to sharply limit duress defenses raises a serious moral problem. The principle that it is especially wrong to convict the innocent is a cornerstone of our criminal justice system. If a defendant with a valid defense of necessity or duress is morally innocent of the crime, then severely limiting such defenses on utilitarian grounds gives rise to serious injustices. We would, in effect, be deciding that it is better that ten persons without valid defenses be punished than that one person with a valid defense be acquitted.

References

Fletcher, G. *Rethinking Criminal Law.* Boston: Little, Brown, 1978.

Greenawalt, K. "The Perplexing Borders of Justification and Excuse." *Columbia Law Review* 84 (1984), 1897.

Gross, H. *A Theory of Criminal Justice.* New York: Oxford University Press, 1979.

Wertheimer, A. *Coercion.* Princeton: Princeton University Press, 1987.

Alan Wertheimer

See also DEFENSES

Coherence

Jurists usually aim at presenting the law as a coherent system, but the concept of coherence is difficult to define precisely. According to Neil MacCormick's theory of normative coherence, legal principles support and explain a number of legal rules and make them coherent. Ronald Dworkin's theory of "integrity" is an example of a coherence in time, often called "narrative." Dworkin compares a judge with a coauthor of a chain novel produced by many persons. Each author sees to it that the additions made fit the already published fragments and the expectations of future ones. Similarly, each judge adapts legal interpretation to already established principles and institutional history of the law, as well as to expectations concerning its future development.

Logical consistency is a necessary but not sufficient condition of *synchronic* coherence, disregarding time. The more the statements belonging to a given (empirical, normative, or evaluative) theory approximate a perfect supportive structure, the more coherent the theory. Perfection of support depends on weighing and balancing of several criteria of coherence. Robert Alexy and Aleksander Peczenik distinguish between three kinds of criteria.

The first kind concerns the *supportive structure.* A deeper and broader support makes a theory more coherent. Ceteris paribus, the degree of coherence of a theory depends on how great is the number of sup-ported statements belonging to it; how long are the chains of reasons belonging to it; how great is the number of connections existing between various supportive chains belonging to the theory; and how many of the statements belonging to the theory are relevant in the type of reasoning the theory uses.

Another kind of criteria concerns *concepts.* Ceteris paribus, the degree of coherence of a single theory depends on how great is the number of universal statements belonging to it; how great is the number of general concepts belonging to it; and how high is the degree of generality of these concepts. Ceteris paribus, the degree of coherence between various theories depends on how great is the number of resemblances existing between concepts they use; how great is the number of conceptual cross-connections existing between them.

The third kind of criteria concerns the *subject matter* of the theory. Ceteris paribus, the degree of coherence of a theory depends on how great is the number of cases it covers; and how great is the number of fields of life it covers.

Logical consistency is not a necessary condition of *diachronic* coherence. Culture (including the law and science) changes continually. A new theory can be logically inconsistent with the old ones, yet it can constitute a coherent evolution of them. Actual laws, for example, inherit their validity from old laws, no longer valid. A new interpretation of the law must have support of the legal tradition, yet it implies a change of the tradition. Ceteris paribus, the degree of diachronic coherence of a culture depends on how many of its actual components (rules, data, theories, and so on) are justified and explained by the tradition of this culture, how long a time the tradition covers, and how much this justification approximates the best balance of the criteria of synchronic coherence. Legal theories, for example, that have their roots in Roman law cover the whole private law, have support of long and well-interconnected chains of arguments, and employ relatively general concepts; thus they are more coherent than theories with a limited history, scope, argumentation, and generality.

The relation between coherence and *truth* is complex and contested. Roughly speaking, truth is correspondence between beliefs and facts. By regarding a statement as true, one makes recourse to the external world, quite independently of the question of what constitutes the world. There is something in the world which makes a given statement true or false. The nonclassical theories of truth—consensus theory, coherence theory, and pragmatic theory—are criteria of truth.

Statements describing the enacted laws and legal practice can be true in the ordinary sense. Statements presenting an evaluative interpretation of the laws and practice cannot be literally true, but they claim rightness (correctness). The contested concept of rightness can be defined as follows. A legal interpretation is right (correct) if and only if it optimally fits both the institutional and moral tradition of the society. Coherence, consensus, and pragmatic success work as criteria of rightness.

References

Alexy, Robert, and Aleksander Peczenik. "The Concept of Coherence and Its Significance for Discursive Rationality." *Ratio Iuris* 3 (1991), 130–147.

Dworkin, Ronald. *Law's Empire*. London: Fontana Press, 1986.

Jackson, Bernard. *Law, Fact and Narrative Coherence*. Roby: Deborah Charles, 1988.

Krygier, Martin. "Law as Tradition." *Law and Philosophy* 5 (1986), 237–262.

MacCormick, Neil. "Coherence in Legal Justification." In *Theory of Legal Science,* ed. A. Peczenik, L. Lindahl, and B. v. Roermund, 235–251. Dordrecht: Reidel, 1984.

Aleksander Peczenik

See also GOODNESS AND COHERENCE

Collective Rights
See MINORITY, ETHNIC, AND GROUP RIGHTS

Common Good

St. Thomas Aquinas, expressing the core of natural law theory, says that genuine laws are ordained by reason to promote the common good. Here as elsewhere he invokes the common good without the least sense that it might require as much analysis and definition as other concepts that he struggles to clarify. How could he be so confident that its meaning would be obvious? In our day philosophers cannot help wondering how it deals with problems, now known to be intractable, about aggregating personal satisfactions (problems which have become familiar in the discussion of utilitarianism) or about aggregating personal preferences (problems which lead to various impossibility theorems, most famous among them Kenneth Arrow's).

The common good in natural law theory deals with these problems by avoiding them. Though Aquinas says that the happiness of any one person is subordinate to the "common happiness," promoting the common good is not a matter of maximizing an aggregative happiness score. There are for him no happiness scores for persons to sum up their satisfactions or utilities; thus there is no problem about aggregating such scores and no question, therefore, of an aggregative score sometimes maximizing only by making more of some people's happiness and less of others'. Nor does Aquinas consider the possibility of relying on personal preference orderings in lieu of happiness scores. The common good is not something that emerges from a function, paradox-free or otherwise (necessarily otherwise, according to Arrow), which combines personal preference orderings convincingly no matter how disparate they may be.

Nevertheless, the common good offers people through membership in a community their best chance of having happy lives, and with that their best chance of having lives that they prefer to what otherwise might befall them. It does this without guaranteeing that they will be spared all sacrifices. Hence it is not something that could be endorsed in a contract among self-interested agents to establish a society for mutual benefit, unless the contract precludes leaving whenever opportunities arise for improving one's position. (And how is it going to preclude that, if it can appeal only to self-interest, and the means of enforcing the contract are imperfect?) The common good is something sought in a community; to preserve the community in times of trouble, its members will be required to stay and die in its defense or make personal sacrifices less momentous.

Laws conscripting able-bodied men (and women) for military service or for labor in coal mines will thus derive on occasion from the common good. No doubt the service should not be made longer or more dangerous than necessary; even so, what about the common good justifies such sacrifices? To answer this question, assume a community already thriving or at least capable of becoming so. Conscriptive laws will figure in a larger set of laws that establish conditions for thriving.

The conditions may vary in detail. A community of hunter-gatherers will have laws different on the subject of private property from a community of independent subsistence farmers; a community that depends on a market to coordinate production—some of it industrial rather than agricultural—will have laws different again. There may be further variation in each of these categories. One community will have a set of laws that do no more to regulate the market than prohibit taking goods by force or fraud; another will have elaborate provisions for redistribution among citizens and among regions designed to offset what are taken to be inevitable imperfections in the market. Yet laws at any point in this range of variations may be justified by the common good, sometimes as options among a class of options all of which might serve, sometimes as deductions that adapt the pursuit of the common good to specific circumstances. In either case they must fit under principles that establish universal minimum conditions for communities in each case thriving by realizing the common good. For example, every community must have laws that maintain internal peace and laws that protect people from interference with their efforts to provide for their own needs. In the latter instance, every community must have the laws required to maintain a system that enlists personal efforts in production and distributes output to individual consumers efficiently enough on both sides for everyone to survive, at least in normal times, in health and decent comfort. Whether the market by itself provides such a system or whether it must be supplemented by governmental precautions against emergencies (in the Bible, Joseph's granaries) or, beyond these, by arrangements to cope with persistent unemployment are issues about means, not issues about fundamental principles. If they cannot be neatly settled, that does not imply any inadequacy or confusion in the standard of the common good.

A system for commodious living (the market itself, perhaps, with the laws essential as its preconditions, or the market with supplementary institutions), like the laws for maintaining internal peace, is in a sense defined by economists as a public good from which everyone in the community benefits without anyone consuming benefits that might otherwise go to other people. As such, the public goods cited answer to everyone's self-interest. However, the theory of the common good, accepting public goods as ingredients, does not suppose that is the only reason which people have for endorsing them or that only public goods of this type, which do answer to self-interest, are to be sought. On the contrary, fully developed attachment to the common good implies that people so attached rejoice in having laws and institutions that meet the needs of their fellow citizens. They rejoice, too, in the attachment of other citizens to the common good, not merely because it is useful to themselves to have those others so attached, but because they value the attainment through that attachment of virtue and happiness by the others. They rejoice, furthermore, in having the community as an instrument for their humane purposes and in living in a community in which they share commitment, attachment, and rejoicing with other members.

With such ingredients, the common good justifies laws against discrimination, though past theorists of natural law, insufficiently critical on this point, endorsed the subordination of women. If a census of the population discovers anyone who is being denied available provisions for needs and full development, that is a shortfall in realizing the common good. The common good has been all too often invoked uncritically in support of hierarchical structures of authority and class privilege. Judiciously applied, it would support having only as much hierarchy as is required for the community as a whole to thrive; that rules out (on occasion, with revolutionary implications) an idle or repressive elite. Yet the common good would justify having authorities to enforce positive, justifiable laws and accept having such laws enacted or decreed by people specially appointed to do so. Here, as elsewhere, its meaning is commonplace, but commonplace because it works successfully where attempts to improve on it sink under difficulties that they themselves create.

References

Aquinas, St. Thomas. *Summa Theologiae*, Pt. 1a2ae, QQ.90–92, 95–97; Pt. 2a2ae, QQ. 58, 6l. Blackfriars translation. London: Eyre and Spottiswoode, 1963.
Braybrooke, David, and Arthur P. Monahan. "Common Good." In *Encyclopedia of*

Ethics, vol. 1, ed. Lawrence C. Becker, 175–178. New York: Garland, 1992.

Finnis, John. "Community, Communities, and Common Good." In *Natural Law and Natural Rights*. Oxford: Clarendon Press, 1980.

Sen, Amartya K. *Collective Choice and Social Welfare*. San Francisco: Holden-Day, 1970.

David Braybrooke

See also NATURAL LAW; SOCIAL CONTRACT; UTILITARIANISM

Common Law Philosophy of Law

Philosophical thought about the common law is marked by two overlapping concerns. First, thinkers in this tradition are preoccupied with the nature of the common law as a system of law. They are interested in how this important body of judge-made, customary law—it is the basis of much of the Anglo-American law of contract, torts, property, and restitution—develops while maintaining some degree of coherence. This concern with the systematicity of the common law entails not only an interest in the forces that drive the development of this body of law but also a concern with the legitimacy of the changes brought about. For, since the common law changes and develops primarily as a consequence of judicial decisions as opposed to the lawmaking activities of democratically elected legislative bodies, questions about the legitimacy of this process abound. This concern with the legitimacy of the common law is often addressed in the classical English theory of the common law embodied in the work of, inter alios, Sir Edward Coke and Sir Matthew Hale. In modern jurisprudential thought, this concern has often been displaced by the general question of the citizen's duty to obey the law—common law or statute—without further specification.

Second, philosophical thought about the common law engages in the task of elucidating in depth the forces that drive the development of the law. This concern is most obviously manifest in the particular attention contemporary philosophers of the common law give to unearthing and debating the normative values that supposedly underpin particular segments of the common law, such as contract and tort. Instances of this contemporary work can be differentiated along two dimensions, one substantive, the other methodological.

The substantive dimension is by far the most obvious way in which contemporary philosophies of the common law come into conflict. These accounts often differ about the exact list of normative values said to underpin and drive the development of particular segments of the common law, as well as disagreeing about the status of those values (disagreeing, that is, about whether or not those values should be pursued). So, for example, philosophers of the common law disagree as to the whether or not the basis of contractual obligations is a matter of reliance or choice. The question for these scholars is twofold: are such obligations enforced because, inter alia, one party has freely done certain actions that trigger a convention of promising, or are they enforced because one party has reasonably relied upon the actions of the other? The different answers offered in response to this question are at least partially informed by competing accounts of the values thought to underpin this area of the law. Proponents of the "choice" answer hold that values such as individual liberty and autonomy inform and give sense to the doctrines of the law of contract, whereas proponents of the "reliance" answer hold that values of fairness, justice, and paternalistic concern for others also have a role. This kind of dispute also frequently arises in relation to the normative basis of particular segments of the law of tort.

Many philosophers of the common law engaged in disputes about the values said to underpin particular segments of the common law hold views that are modest and pluralistic. They are interested only in articulating and excavating the values that inform a particular segment of the common law (hence, their arguments are modest). They accept that different values may well inform different segments of the law (hence, they accept, more or less explicitly, that there is in this context a plurality of values). By contrast, the participants in this debate influenced by the Economic Analysis of Law (EAL) are both ambitious and monistic. They hold, ambitiously, that just about all the doctrines and segments of the common law are and should be informed by, monistically, one value (variously characterized as efficiency or wealth maximization). Finally, there are some accounts of the normative values said to inform the common law that are skeptical: they hold either that those values can never be made consistent one with another or that they are in some way objectionable.

The substantive differences between competing philosophies of the common law are differences about both the kinds and plausibility of the common law's underpinning values. Such differences could be resolved by a demonstration that the values in play were indeed compelling (or, in the case of skeptics, utterly lacking in weight). This step, which would run philosophers of the common law up against the most pressing and enduring question of moral and political philosophy, is rarely taken. Those who debate the basis of contractual obligations do not attempt to argue that the value of autonomy is more compelling than that of fairness, although proponents of EAL have attempted to demonstrate the morally compelling nature of notions of efficiency and wealth maximization. This particular dispute is one of the few instances of the substantive arguments made by philosophers of the common law being traced to their source within moral and political philosophy. It could not be said that the substantive arguments of EAL were strengthened as a result of this process.

Since philosophers of the common law are usually unwilling to take the step of attempting to justify the substantive claims they make within their natural habitat—which is, of course, the discourse of moral and political philosophy—then the dispute between them cannot be resolved at this level. However, some of these philosophers invoke a second strategy as a means of either commanding or criticizing an account of the common law's underpinning values. This strategy makes a claim about method. Like all such claims in the human and natural sciences, it prescribes certain means that must be employed to understand and explain the phenomenon in question, in this case, the common law or segments thereof. A simplified characterization of the methodological injunction most often invoked by philosophers of the common law is this: to understand or explain this area of social action one must capture the point, purpose, or value of that action as the participants in the activity (judges, practitioners, commentators, and citizens) themselves understand it. Within contemporary jurisprudence, this injunction is variously referred to as a manifestation of the "internal point of view," "the hermeneutic method" or as an instance of Max Weber's method of *verstehen* (grasping the point). Setting aside the genealogy of this injunction, it is plain to see what it amounts to in the hands of philosophers of the common law. It finds expression in the insistence that what participants (particularly judges) in the practices in question say about those practices must be taken extremely seriously. The philosopher of the common law must attend scrupulously to the detail of legal doctrine and in particular to the arguments of judicial decisions. When philosophers offer accounts of the values they think underpin the common law, they must surmount the methodologically inspired hurdle which holds that accounts succeed only if recognizable by participants in the practice. Furthermore, some philosophers insist upon a more demanding hurdle, namely, that the account be not merely recognizable by but also acceptable to participants.

Stating this methodological injunction takes us to the heart of the second dimension along which philosophies of the common law can be differentiated, for they can quite easily be distinguished according to the degree of respect they accord to this injunction. Some philosophies of the common law take the injunction very seriously. The fact that they do so does not guarantee that these accounts agree upon the nature and type of values said to underpin a particular segment of the common law. However, those who take the injunction seriously usually agree that other philosophers of the common law, particularly those influenced either by EAL or critical legal studies, do not take the injunction sufficiently seriously and are mistaken in so doing. It is thought that those influenced by EAL and critical legal studies take a dismissive attitude to the views of the participants about the point, purpose, or value of the practice. Nowhere is this dismissive attitude more obvious than in the supposedly scanty attention these scholars give to both the arguments of judicial decisions and the overall contours of legal doctrine.

Those philosophers of the common law who invoke the methodological injunction in order to distinguish between successful and unsuccessful accounts of the common law's underpinning values may, however, be disappointed. For this strategy is by no means certain to resolve the dispute between competing accounts, since it gives rise to a number of problems. Two are particularly pressing. First, proponents of this particular methodological injunction must at some point take steps to commend the conception of method it embraces. Even the most cursory glance at the literature of the philosophy of the human sciences shows that those seeking to explain and understand social action are faced with a plethora of competing methods. Therefore, it is not unreasonable to expect from those who seek to give accounts of segments of social action an attempt to justify their choice of method. This is something philosophers of the common law rarely do. Those who invoke the internal point of view or the hermeneutic method often do so solely because that approach has taken hold within mainstream jurisprudence. Unfortunately, the popularity of the method is not, without more, a compelling argument for its adoption.

The second problem concerns a snag that arises within the method itself. The methodological injunction holds that philosophies of the common law must characterize the point, purpose or value of that aspect of social action or some segment thereof in such a way as to capture the participants' understanding of it. If it is possible—and it surely is—that different participants in the practice can have different accounts of its point, purpose, or value, what is the philosopher to do? The philosopher could merely describe the plurality of views the participants have. In this case the report would be, for example, that some participants in the practice we know as tort law think the practice informed by the notion of corrective justice, whereas some think it informed by the notion of efficiency, and yet others hold that some conception of equality or distributive justice is in play. This option seems to reduce the philosopher's task to one of reportage. Alternatively, the philosopher could report the plurality of views the participants have and then move on to attempt to sort the wheat from the chaff, that is, could attempt to argue that one of the plurality of views about the point, purpose, or value of the practice held by participants is indeed better than the others. This move, however, takes the philosopher of the common law into the territory of moral and political philosophy, for in order to succeed in this task the philosopher will surely have to offer moral and political arguments as to why one participant's understanding of the practice is better than any others. As we noted

above, this is a domain into which philosophers of the common law are usually loath to enter. For the future, philosophers of the common law must both overcome this reluctance and strengthen their methodological arguments. It might be possible to look forward to a time in which philosophies of the common law are more closely connected with the arguments of political and moral philosophers, on the one hand, and the arguments of methodologists of the human sciences, on the other. Were this to occur, the philosophy of the common law will surely flourish as a meeting place for both methodological and normative arguments and as a context within which those arguments can be applied to a signifcant realm of social practices and institutions.

References

Atiyah, Patrick A. *Essays on Contract*. Oxford: Clarendon Press, 1986.

Balkin, Jack. "The Crystalline Structure of Legal Thought." *Rutgers Law Review* 39 (1986), 1–110.

Brudner, Alan. *The Unity of the Common Law*. Berkeley: University of California Press, 1995.

Coleman, Jules L. *Risks and Wrongs*. Cambridge: Cambridge University Press, 1992.

Fried, Charles. *Contract as Promise*. Cambridge MA: Harvard University Press, 1981.

Frug, Mary Joe. *Postmodern Legal Feminism*. New York: Routledge, 1992.

Kennedy, Duncan. "Form and Substance in Private Law Adjudication." *Harvard Law Review* 89 (1976), 1685–1778.

Posner, Richard. *The Economic Analysis of Law*. 4th ed. Boston: Little, Brown, 1992.

Postema, Gerald J. *Bentham and the Common Law Tradition*. Oxford: Clarendon Press, 1986.

Weinrib, Ernest J. *The Idea of Private Law*. Cambridge MA: Harvard University Press, 1995.

William N.R. Lucy

See also CIVILIAN PHILOSOPHY OF LAW; ECONOMICS; PRIVATE LAW

Commons

Given the confusion about the historic village commons, this article is designed to set the record straight about its communal ownership system, institutional and legal framework, and economic and environmental implications. Historically the commons referred to communally owned grazing pastures in the medieval European village. Rights of commons also applied to gathering firewood and peat and access to fisheries. This shows that communal ownership and its institutional structures were widely understood approaches to resource management. The system of communal ownership in grazing pastures developed in response to population increases and improved farming technology, and it lasted for centuries. The village designated certain fields as common grazing pastures, while arable land was privately owned by individual members of the community. The property rights in both cases were clear: communal ownership in the grazing, private in the arable. All village fields were regularly rotated from arable to grazing, thereby allowing mixed husbandry and sustaining the village's core resource, the land.

Communal ownership differs from free goods, private property right, and tribal ownership approaches. Villages did not treat their commons as an unlimited asset whose exploitation was free or costless and not in need of regulation. This would certainly have encouraged overgrazing and soon exhausted the village lands. However villagers, not being unintelligent, had better sense. Farmers, after all, are a canny lot when it comes to protecting their land. The villages then treated their grazing pastures as a communally owned limited asset in need of regulation, or communal property. In choosing communal ownership in grazing lands, they rejected the private property rights approach which they accepted respecting arable lands; for private ownership would have conferred ownership of a piece of the land, thereby allowing the owner to sell it at will. Communal ownership in contrast only conferred on members of the village community the right to use of common land. The village, in turn, maintained the asset owned by village members as grazing pasture, while it controlled the joint use of the land. Villages regulated the sale of lands. Under communal ownership a member could sell only his use right, not the land itself. Grazing rights were carefully regulated and overgrazing policed by officers of the village, for example, the reeve, usually by imposing a fine in the village court. Outsiders were excluded from enjoying com-

munal rights to use the village commons to graze their cattle. Indeed, new members could only be introduced by agreement of the village. In this other-excluding respect, communal ownership and private property were similar.

Communal ownership also differs sharply from tribal ownership, which is nonexclusive and neither defines nor regulates resources. Anyone may use tribal lands and resources. Thus overuse is a real possibility. Tribal ownership is appropriate, however, for small populations using relatively unproductive technologies, namely, systems that would not exhaust the tribal resource; but as population growth and more efficient technologies are introduced tribal ownership rights would offer no barrier to resource depletion and exhaustion. This in part explains what happened with the buffalo and the beaver in North America, and in the deforestation of central Africa. Communal ownership, in contrast, is an appropriate property rights system, since population increases and more productive technologies are deployed; it enables control and maintenance of the common resource. As a result the village commons mixed ownership system was more efficient and sustainable than the extant alternatives: free goods, tribal ownership, or purely communal or private ownership.

Communal ownership was reinforced by a supportive village institutional decision-making structure. Village officers regulated all aspects of the commons: its use, rotation of pasture and arable land, the number of cattle, and village membership. This system prevented overgrazing and sustained both commons and arable land for centuries. The village's institutional decision-making structure was proportional. Each member of the village had a vote in proportion to his share of the land. The proportion of the total herd allotted to each member for grazing on the commons also reflected his share of land. This system not only induced each member to participate in governing the commons so as to protect his stake, it also allowed members to form alliances as needed. This helped to prevent any one member from controlling the village and its resources. The village also regulated the sale of land and opposed land consolidation by any one member. Communal institutional structures in addition to ownership greatly reduced the number of transactions and the associated costs that would have been incurred if individual members privately owned the grazing pastures. It thereby reduced noncompliance and violations, significantly lowering the costs of resource management and agreement policing. Thus the commons system in many ways protected weaker members against stronger. Its institutional decision-making structure was not only democratic and egalitarian, it also reflected the ethical norm of recognizing stakeholder interests. It could only be changed by the agreement of at least three quarters of the votes of village members and was protected by parliamentary statute.

Only in the eighteenth century did the enclosure system gradually replace the commons system, with the help of a parliament controlled by the land-owning classes. Privately owned, enclosed fields were specialized solely as sheep pastures, in response to more productive clothmaking technology and rising market demand for wool. Enclosures yielded high short-term returns for their new, private owners from this specialized land use. In contrast to communal ownership and rotation, however, it acted as a positive feedback for single-use resource exploitation, thus hastening the exhaustion of the resource. The market responded by raising prices and inviting competing new products, such as cotton cloth. In the late twentieth century, however, markets combined with historically unprecedented productive technologies are approaching the limits of nature's capital stocks, in farming, fisheries, and forestry. So, as many have warned, the highly specialized, private ownership free market economy cannot be sustained.

In contrast, the village commons represented a more long-term model of an economy in which population, technology, and resources were interlinked in balanced fashion. It was so sustainedly productive that it formed the template for the institutional structure of the joint stock company, or modern firm. Indeed, communal ownership and corporate governance are similar inasmuch as voting rights and share of profits in each are proportional to asset shares of members. In addition, the old village and the early firm were similar in having a relatively small membership, requiring informal, small-scale management. The modern corporation, its management, and associated technologies are much larger in size and scale. Its extensive assets cannot be productively managed by a small, informal management group, or by the owners. Instead for-

mat, large-scale management, and multidivisional organization are required.

In conclusion, the legal regime of the commons was mixed, involving the civil law of property, village regulations and their enforcement, and quasi-constitutional provisions respecting institutional structure as enshrined in parliamentary statutes. The philosophical implications of the communal ownership system are interesting. First, it is not open to a single-factor model of law, based solely on sanction, contract, class power, or any other aspect of the law. Rather, the commons legal system was finely attuned to a democratic institutional structure and the interests of the communities it governed. The laws were comprehensible to the largely nonliterate village members who applied them. Furthermore, as a legal, political, economic, and social system it had a long-term productivity and staying power. Given that track record, communal ownership may again be a useful exemplar for environmental law and economics in democratic, pluralist societies.

References

Dahlman, Carl. *The Open Field System and Beyond.* Cambridge: Cambridge University Press, 1980.
Hardin, Garret. *Managing the Commons.* San Francisco: W.H. Freeman, 1977.

Vincent Di Norcia

Communitarian Philosophy of Law

Communitarianism is a doctrine in moral, legal, and political philosophy which holds that the individual can flourish as a moral being and as a political agent only within the context of a community.

The doctrine can be traced back to Aristotle (384–322 B.C.), who argued in the *Nicomachean Ethics* and in the *Politics* that moral and political virtue could be achieved only in the *polis,* and to G.W.F. Hegel (1770–1831), who in *The Philosophy of Right* stressed the importance of various forms of community, such as the family, the corporations, and the state, for the full realization of the moral and political capacities of human beings.

The communitarian doctrine has more recently been associated with the critique of two influential liberal traditions in moral, legal, and political philosophy, namely, utilitarianism and kantianism. Communitarian thinkers have criticized the conception of rationality and the understanding of human agency articulated by these two traditions, since they claim that utilitarianism reduces rationality to the instrumental calculation of costs and benefits and views the agent as a maximizer of utility, while kantianism conceives rationality in purely formal and procedural terms and considers the agent in abstraction from any concrete historical, social, or political context. In opposition to utilitarianism, communitarian thinkers have advocated a more substantive conception of rationality that emphasizes the role of reflection, deliberation, and rational evaluation, while in opposition to kantianism they have formulated a view of human agency that situates it in a concrete moral and political context and that stresses the constitutive role that communal aims and attachments assume for a situated self.

The communitarian doctrine has been articulated by a number of contemporary thinkers, such as Alasdair MacIntyre, Michael Sandel, Charles Taylor, Roberto Unger, and Michael Walzer. We may identify four central issues around which their critique of the liberal tradition in moral, legal, and political philosophy has focused: the liberal conception of the self, the liberal understanding of community, the nature and scope of distributive justice, and the priority of the right over the good.

Conception of the Self

The critique of the liberal conception of the self has been formulated most forcefully by Taylor, Sandel, and MacIntyre. Taylor has argued that much of contemporary liberal theory is based on an atomistic conception of the person and on a view of human agency that focuses almost exclusively on the will and on freedom of choice. Against the atomistic conception, expressed most clearly in the writings of Robert Nozick, as in *Anarchy, State, and Utopia,* Taylor has articulated and defended a relational and intersubjective conception of the self that stresses the social, cultural, historical, and linguistic constitution of personal identity. Against the voluntaristic conception of human agency, Taylor has formulated a cognitive conception that emphasizes the role of critical reflection, self-interpretation, and rational evaluation. Sandel has advanced a number of similar arguments, stressing the constitutive role of community in the forma-

tion of personal identity, showing the inadequacy of the disembodied and unencumbered conception of the self that underlies Rawls' theory of justice, and highlighting the cognitive dimensions of reflection and deliberation for a theory of human agency. MacIntyre, for his part, has defended a teleological conception of human nature and a contextualist view of human agency. According to the teleological conception, moral conduct is characterized not by the conscientious adherence to rules and principles (deontology), but by the exercise of the virtues that aim at the realization of the good. Such good may be attained through what MacIntyre calls the "narrative unity" of a human life. According to the contextualist view of human agency, agents cannot properly locate, interpret, and evaluate their actions except within the boundaries of a moral tradition or those of a moral community. For MacIntyre the great fault of the Enlightenment project of providing a rational foundation to morality and politics has been the rejection of both the teleological conception of human nature and the contextualist understanding of human agency, leaving agents with no criteria to adjudicate between competing values and without a moral context within which their actions could be rendered meaningful and coherent.

Conception of Community

The major advocate of a strong conception of community is MacIntyre, who has argued that the moral life and its attendant virtues can only flourish within local forms of community united around a shared conception of the good. One of the principal drawbacks of modern liberal theory, according to MacIntyre, is the absence of an adequate theory of community as constitutive of moral character and as the locus of moral practice. Both kantian and utilitarian moral theories fail in this respect, the former because of its abstract and formal conception of community, the latter because it views community in purely instrumental terms. Another strong advocate of community is Sandel, who has argued that community should be understood in a constitutive sense. He has distinguished between an instrumental, a sentimental, and a constitutive conception of community and has argued that only the third provides the basis for a politics centered on friendship, self-knowledge, and the cultivation of moral character. Walzer, for his part, has stressed the way in which community not only shapes moral character but is constitutive of our various conceptions of justice. According to him, the just distribution of social goods depends on the shared understandings that members have of these goods, and these understandings depend, in turn, on the nature of the community that members inhabit. For Walzer membership in a community is itself the most important good, since it shapes our understandings of social goods and determines our various conceptions of justice. Another important defender of community is Unger, who has formulated two distinct conceptions of community. The first, centered on the notion of "organic groups," aims at overcoming the antinomies of liberal thought, such as the opposition between reason and emotion, fact and value, individual and community. The theory of organic groups overcomes these antinomies by reconciling the particular and the universal within the context of an open and egalitarian community. The second formulation centers around the idea of "formative contexts" and attempts to overcome the strict opposition between autonomy and dependence and between piecemeal and revolutionary change. By revising the formative contexts and making them open to institutional change, such oppositions can be overcome and new forms of democratic community can be established.

Nature and Scope of Distributive Justice

The question of justice has been at the center of recent communitarian critiques. Walzer, Taylor, and Sandel have argued that the liberal conception of justice, especially the version articulated by John Rawls, is deficient in several respects. Walzer has maintained that there can be no single principle of distributive justice applicable to all social goods, but rather that different social goods ought to be distributed for different reasons and according to different criteria, which are derived from the different understandings that members have of the social goods themselves. Since for Walzer the most important good is membership in a political community, distributive principles must be specified in the light of a background conception of the nature and purpose of community and of the social goods that are attained through it. Taylor, on the other hand, has argued that modern liberal democratic societies operate on the basis of different and at times mutually exclusive principles of distributive justice, like rights, desert, need, membership, and contribution, and that we should therefore abandon the search for a single principle of distribution. Distributive arrangements should instead be based upon and evaluated by independent and mutually irreducible principles of distributive justice. Both Taylor and Walzer argue, moreover, that the search for a single overarching principle of distributive justice, applicable to different goods and across different spheres, appears plausible to contemporary liberals only because they start from the perspective of the autonomous self as bearer of rights, and proceed to frame the issue of distributive justice in terms of the conflicting rights-claims of sovereign individuals. If the framework adopted starts instead from a social conception of the individual and from the acknowledgment of the primacy of community, then it is possible to argue that principles of justice must be pluralistic in form, and that different principles of distributive justice articulate different conceptions of the good and different understandings of the value of human association. Sandel, for his part, has challenged the primacy of justice over the claims of community and has argued in favor of an understanding of politics that stresses the values of friendship, mutual knowledge, and the attainment of the common good. In his view Rawls' claim for the priority of justice over the common good can only be sustained if the parallel claim for the priority of the self over its ends is valid, and Sandel maintains that this conception of the person is incoherent because it fails to account for the constitutive role of our communal aims and attachments. By formulating an alternative conception of the person that takes into account these constitutive aims and attachments, Sandel claims that we may be governed by the common good rather than by the principles of right and justice. According to his communitarian conception of politics the claims of justice would still have a limited application, but they would no longer have primacy over the values of community or the requirements of the common good.

Priority of the Right over the Good

One of the central claims of Rawls' theory of justice in *A Theory of Justice* and *Political Liberalism* is that a just society does not seek to promote any specific conception of the good, but provides instead a neutral framework of basic rights and liberties within which individuals can pursue their own values and life-plans, consistent with a similar liberty for others. A just society must therefore be governed by principles that do not presuppose any particular conception of the good. What justifies these principles is that they conform to the concept of right, a moral category which is prior to the good and independent of it. The right is prior to the good, then, in the sense (1) that individual rights cannot be sacrificed for the sake of welfare or the general good; (2) that the principles of justice that specify these rights cannot be premised on any particular conception of the good, but must be independently derived from the concept of right. This strict priority of the right over the good has been questioned by Sandel, Taylor, and MacIntyre. Sandel has argued that the priority of the right over the good rests upon a conception of the self as always prior to its ends, values, and attachments, a conception that he finds implausible because we cannot conceive ourselves as wholly detached from our communal ends and values. To acknowledge the constitutive dimension of our communal ends means to challenge the strict priority of the right over the good and to question the neutrality of the principles of justice with respect to different conceptions of the good. Taylor, on the other hand, has maintained that every conception of the right and of justice presupposes a conception of the human good and of the good of human association. In his view Rawls' claim of the priority of right cannot be sustained, since it is itself premised on a prior conception of the human good (the exercise of free moral agency) and of the good of human association (securing the conditions for the full development and exercise of our moral powers). MacIntyre, for his part, has argued that there can be no neutral justification of principles of justice, since every conception of justice is located within a particular tradition and articulates its specific conception of the good. The good is thus always prior to the right and the question for him is whether the conception of the good articulated by the liberal democratic tradition can be shown to be rationally superior to others.

References

MacIntyre, Alasdair. *After Virtue.* Notre Dame: University of Notre Dame Press, 1981; 2d ed. 1984.

———. *Whose Justice? Which Rationality?* Notre Dame: University of Notre Dame Press, 1988.

Nozick, Robert. *Anarchy, State, and Utopia.* New York: Basic Books, 1974.

Rawls, John. *Political Liberalism.* New York: Columbia University Press, 1993.

———. *A Theory of Justice.* Cambridge MA: Harvard University Press, 1971.

Sandel, Michael. *Democracy's Discontent.* Cambridge MA: Harvard University Press, 1996.

———. *Liberalism and the Limits of Justice.* Cambridge: Cambridge University Press, 1982.

———, ed. *Liberalism and Its Critics.* New York: New York University Press, 1984.

Taylor, Charles. *Human Agency and Language.* Vol. 1 of *Philosophical Papers.* Cambridge: Cambridge University Press, 1985.

———. *Philosophy and the Human Sciences.* Vol. 2 of *Philosophical Papers.* Cambridge: Cambridge University Press, 1985.

———. *Sources of the Self.* Cambridge: Cambridge University Press, 1989.

Unger, Roberto M. *Knowledge and Politics.* New York: Free Press, 1975.

———. *Politics: A Work in Constructive Social Theory.* 3 vols. Cambridge: Cambridge University Press, 1987.

Walzer, Michael. *Spheres of Justice.* New York: Basic Books, 1983.

Maurizio Passerin d'Entrèves

Community

Throughout history, writers have argued that existential tension is at the heart of human experience: our yearning for intimate connection with others and the recognition that others are necessary for our identity and freedom coalesces uneasily with the fear and anxiety we experience as others approach. We simultaneously long for emotional attachment and yet are horrified that our individuality may evaporate once we achieve it. This disharmony may never be fully reconciled; we find ourselves instead making uneasy compromises and adjustments as we oscillate between the poles defined by "radical individuality" and "thorough immersion in community." This existential tension replicates itself at numerous levels including the nature of political organization and the purposes of law.

The existence of a community implies a group of people living in the same general locality who share certain interests and some degree of agreement on beliefs and values, who recognize mutual, reciprocal duties, who are bound together in a network of relationships, who enjoy a shared sense of membership and belonging, who exhibit a degree of solidarity with one another, and who thereby experience an identity which transcends the self.

At first blush it seems obvious that community is a prerequisite for constitutionality. Given two of the underlying themes of constitutionality, distinguishing a circumscribed group of people from the world as a whole ("self-determination and autonomy") and monopolizing justified force within that group ("exclusivity of coercive power"), a measure of commonality among constituents appears indispensable.

How much commonality is required for constitutionality? Is it sufficient to agree to form a legal structure ensuring only individuals' negative rights against force, fraud, and harm? Or must a constitutional community embody robust bonds of kinship, ethnicity, religious affiliation, clear understanding of a common good, and cooperative efforts to achieve a particular human telos?

Closely connected to these issues is a foundational question of constitutional law: Should the law aspire to be neutral among competing conceptions of the good? Or should law explicitly nurture and enforce the particular version of the good embodied by the community it defines?

Libertarianism, or classical liberalism, contends that the guarantees of individual political and civil liberties have priority over all collective notions of common purpose: the right is logically and morally prior to the good. All individuals have inviolable personal rights grounded in their equal worth and dignity. Thus constitutional law must remain neutral between competing notions of what is good in life or which particular way of life is morally best. Sometimes impartiality is presumed to require neutrality in the consequences of policies, sometimes it refers to the manner of justifying policies. Classical liberalism argues that each individual within the constitutional community is entitled to form and pursue his or her own conception of the good

life, provided that so doing does not transgress the freedom of others to do likewise. As such, classical liberalism explicitly endorses a slender theory of constitutional identification: the measure of community necessary to define a constitutional group is its common commitment to the priority of individualism as defined by negative rights and legal neutrality. While it is clear that individuals in such a constitutional order may mutually and voluntarily develop close communal bonds, such attachments are not perceived as prerequisites for constitutional identification.

Classical republicans argue that the strengthening of community should be the underlying aspiration of constitutional law. They embrace vigorous notions of civic virtue, a politically active citizenry, and social practices and traditions. The values of communal associations must be established in the public, constitutional domain. Law cannot be neutral, because some substantial conception of the good is required to inform its application. Republicans contend that communities exemplify distinctive social relationships, united by both necessity and personal solidarity, which transcend the isolated individualism of classical liberalism. Not all the relationships and attachments that partly constitute the self are voluntarily chosen. Such connections permit a healthy sense of membership that nurtures our identity as "social animals." Viewing liberals as preoccupied with the formal requirements and abstractness of law, an obsession that is partly responsible for the widespread estrangement and alienation in modern life, contemporary republicans focus on law's potential for nurturing communal life in concrete ways.

The debate between classical liberals and classical republicans on matters of law centers on two versions of constitutional community: a weak version in which members agree to remain at arm's length unless particular parties mutually agree to bind, and a strong version in which members acknowledge substantive antecedent bonds that define the life of citizens and the purpose of law. The strong version attaches intrinsic value to the community itself and to our relations with other members of the community, while the weak version attaches only instrumental value. Although it is unlikely that a classical liberal regime can retain an unadulterated allegiance to the weak version of community—since common history, shared culture, and the pressures of international politics will inevitably compel a thicker conception of law—it can still easily distinguish itself from classical republicanism. Classical liberalism is thus firmly planted near the individualistic pole of the continuum, while classical republicanism resides near the communitarian pole.

It should be clear that this dispute is a magnified version of the existential struggle each of us confronts daily. Individualism is necessary for full human development; it offers us a sense of specialness and uniqueness; it resonates our sense of personal dignity and freedom. Yet radical individualism isolates, alienates, and disintegrates human personality; it corrodes the soul and defeats the spirit. Community is necessary for support, security, and a sense of belonging; it fulfills our need for intimacy and elevates the human spirit. However, thorough immersion in community can suffocate, restrict, and prevent independence; it chokes possibilities for social transcendence and fosters stifling conformity.

Thus the hopes and fears of constitutional communities, as played out in the debate between classical liberals and classical republicans, reflect and reinforce our existential condition. Conceptual analysis cannot determine which version of community is logically required by constitutionalism. In fact, either version of community is compatible with constitutionalism, as are numerous other versions. Our collective resolutions of these matters help define our identities on the level of law, just as our temporary solutions to our personal existential crises help define the individuals we are and prefigure the people we might become.

References

Belliotti, Raymond A. *Seeking Identity.* Lawrence: University Press of Kansas, 1995.

Golding, Martin P. *Philosophy of Law.* Englewood Cliffs NJ: Prentice-Hall, 1975.

MacIntyre, Alasdair. *After Virtue.* Notre Dame: University of Notre Dame Press, 1981.

Narveson, Jan. *The Libertarian Idea.* Philadelphia: Temple University Press, 1988.

Nozick, Robert. *Anarchy, State, and Utopia.* New York: Basic Books, 1974.

Rawls, John. *A Theory of Justice.* Cambridge MA: Harvard University Press, 1971.

Sandel, Michael. *Liberalism and the Limits of Justice.* Cambridge: Cambridge University Press, 1982.

Taylor, Charles. *Sources of the Self.* Cambridge: Cambridge University Press, 1989.

Unger, Roberto M. *Politics.* Cambridge: Cambridge University Press, 1987.

Raymond Angelo Belliotti

See also COMMON GOOD; COMMONS; COMMUNITARIAN PHILOSOPHY OF LAW

Commutative Justice
See CORRECTIVE JUSTICE

Comparative Law

The contribution that comparative law, to date, has made directly to legal philosophy is relatively limited for a number of reasons. First, comparative lawyers have on the whole been more interested in the details of positive law than in the abstract questions of philosophy, and this has meant that most comparatists have all started from similar assumptions about the nature of law itself. Second, comparative law as a subject has distinguished itself only rarely from courses devoted either to the study of foreign legal systems or to overviews of the major legal families of the world. Third, comparative law has found itself, when not bound to the details of positive legal subjects, closely associated with the history of legal systems.

The weaknesses with respect to comparative law theory are not as such the result of an absence of literature, since contributions to legal knowledge by comparatists have ranked among the most elegant and insightful of legal writing. This tradition remains one of the striking features of the *International Encyclopedia of Comparative Law*. The sheer scholarship to be found in, say, Professor G. Treitel's comparative account of contract remedies is breathtaking and is matched only in its elegance by K. Zweigert and H. Kötz's introductory work to comparative law and to the comparative law of obligations.

Yet alongside the elegance there are some enduring weaknesses that have given rise to a parallel tradition in comparative legal writing that can at best be described as theoretically weak, from the need to justify comparative law by an appeal to its practical use. Is it really serious philosophy to imply that courses on comparative law would have had a civilizing influence on Napoleon or those who took Europe into the two world wars? Appeals to theory, rather than to practice, have fared little better. The idea of an international *Rechtswissenschaft* (jurisprudence) as a legitimating goal for comparative law can so easily betray, not so much a wish for a knowledge of difference, but a desire for intellectual imperialism. Other comparatists have turned their attention to the empirical or cultural underpinnings of legal systems in the hope of gaining insights into the functions of law or the values that they communicate. However, the logical difficulties of using empirical research as the basis for deriving philosophically normative ideas remains an obstacle.

These limitations in outlook should surprise few, since comparative lawyers often tend to be actively involved in the functions of mainstream national law as well. Indeed, as seen in *White v. Jones*, 2 A.C. 207 (1995), the good comparatist may even find the call of practice tempting on occasions. It might be possible to move outward from these more focused positions toward a theory of comparative law that encompasses the details of practical reasoning and conceptual analysis within a broader perspective that sees law, for example, in terms of a general theory that emphasizes difference. Thus, while legal theory is concerned with the general definition of law in terms of a principal function, comparative law looks at the function of law within specific legal traditions and the way these functions are performed. One danger with this kind of bottom-up approach is that, in scientific terms, it tends to make use of weak concepts with the result that J. Bell's "tradition as function notion," like Zweigert and Kötz's idea of legal "style," runs the risk of failing to connect with more comprehensive paradigms. A better understanding of science "can be obtained only by the invention and organisation of new concepts, and not by recourse to images, subjective impressions or universalising myths."

The fact is that comparative law remains plagued by the absence of any sustained theoretical reflection on the notion of comparison. What are the scientific goals of comparison in law? What is to be achieved, epistemologically, from comparing different courts, different cases, different legislative provisions, and so on? What is the theoretical basis of comparative law as a discipline? What is actually being compared when lawyers engage in comparison? Answers rarely connect with any major philosophical issue either within law itself or with respect to legal education or philosophy in general. Comparative law rarely seems a necessary part of any methodological, historical, or philosophical training in law.

In an otherwise perceptive piece on comparative contract law, Tony Weir specifically states that he has no theory to propound since it "is possible for us, like Hamlet, to tell a hawk from a handsaw, and to do so without a complete theory of aerial predators or an exhaustive inventory of the carpenter's toolbox." Of course, the antitheory or commonsense view is no less a statement of theory.

More problematic for comparative law is that the rejection of theory can lead to the idea that comparative law is nothing more or less than a methodology. The idea of "comparative law as method" is untenable, since a strict dichotomy between science and method is epistemologically dangerous. There is no science without method.

What links the two is the model, whose purpose is to relate the experience of the real world to an abstract scheme of elements and relations. Deduction as a method, for example, becomes explicable only when it relates to a structure whose transformations allow the discovery at one and the same time of general and particular propositions, together with solutions resulting from the transformations, within a framework where the direct study of all phenomena is impossible. The object of scientific thought is not the facts of the social world, for such facts cannot exist separately and have sense only in relation to a preexisting model; nor is it the scheme of thought or structure, since that would make the science exclusively and hermetically the object of its own discourse. The object of legal science is the model.

According to R. Sacco, comparative law has its role in relation to such models. The goal of legal comparison as a science is "to know the differences existing between legal models, and to contribute to knowledge of these models." Although the great codes were attempts to axiomatize legal knowledge in the manner of the *mos geometricus* (geometric method), no doubt legal models are different from scientific models. Yet legal knowledge can only be characterized from a methodological point of view by reference to a model. Law can only exist, then, as a scheme of knowledge, a genealogy of categories, and concepts which act as its object. What comparative law can do, through research into different models at different stages of development, is to help in the development of a legal epistemology by distinguishing from all the neighboring activities a distinct science of law to act as the object of this epistemology.

According to most legal philosophers, the model is a model of norms, which describes objects (norms, rules, relations, and so on) and which cannot be directly observed. Is knowledge of law knowledge of rules or, more metaphysically, norms? In other words, is legal knowledge propositional knowledge? Studies in artificial intelligence would suggest that such a rule-thesis is at best wanting; but there are, as yet, no alternatives to the rule model.

Here, then, is the philosophical task for comparative law: What is it to have knowledge of law? If legal knowledge is not propositional in form, might it be a matter of institutional structures, perhaps explicable through systems and (or) game theory? Comparative law can supply precedents. O. Kahn-Freund's perceptive introductory essay to K. Renner's volume and P. Stein's work on the history of the institutional system suggest new models consisting of relationships and elements that function at one and the same time in the world of fact and the world of law. No doubt such institutional models will not in themselves be enough for the epistemologist. However, at least comparative law is moving toward eliciting a model which might have the capacity to connect with the work of epistemologists.

References

Atias, C. *Épistémologie du droit* (Legal Epistemology). Paris: Presses Universitaires de France, 1994.

Bell, J. "Comparative Law and Legal Theory." In *Prescriptive Formality and Normative Rationality in Modern Legal Systems,* Ed. W. Krawietz, N. MacCormick, and G. Henrick von Wright. Berlin: Duncker & Humblot, 1995.

David, René, et al., eds. *International Encyclopedia of Comparative Law.* Tübingen: J.C.B. Mohr, 1973–1985.

Granger, G.-G. *La science et les sciences* (Science and the Sciences). Paris: Presses Universitaires de France, 1993.

Legrand, P. "Comparative Legal Studies and Commitment to Theory." *Modern Law Review* 58 (1995), 262.

Renner, K. *The Institutions of Private Law and Their Social Functions.* Trans. A. Schwarzschild. Intro. O. Kahn-Freund. London: Routledge, 1949.

Sacco, R. *La comparaison juridique au service de la connaissance du droit* (Comparative Law for Legal Understanding). Paris: Economica, 1991.

Samuel, G. *The Foundations of Legal Reasoning.* Antwerp: Maklu, 1994.

———. "Comparative Law Jurisprudence." *ICLQ* 4–5 (1998), 817.

Stein, P. *Character and Influence of Roman Civil Law.* London: Hambledon, 1988.

Treitel, G. *Remedies for Breach of Contract. A Comparative Account.* Oxford: Oxford University Press, 1988.

Van de Kerchove, M., and F. Ost. *Le droit ou les paradoxes du jeu* (Law and Game Paradoxes). Paris: Presses Universitaires de France, 1992.

Villa, V. *La science du droit* (The Science of Law). Trans. O. Nerhot and P. Nerhot. Paris: Librairie Générale de Droit et de Jurisprudence, 1990.

Weir, Tony. "Contracts in Rome and England." *Tulane Law Review* 66 (1992), 1615.

Zweigert, K., and H. Kötz. *An Introduction to Comparative Law.* 3d ed. Trans. Tony Weir. Oxford: Oxford University Press, 1999.

Geoffrey Samuel

See also CIVILIAN PHILOSOPHY OF LAW; COMMON LAW PHILOSOPHY OF LAW; CONFLICT OF LAWS

Compliance

Laws direct a set of people, those dwelling within the jurisdiction of the legal system in question, to perform or refrain from certain actions. Invariably, the persons in question, call them the citizens, though some noncitizens are often among those directed, might sometimes prefer not to do or to refrain as the law directs them. With that in mind, the law normally establishes various penalties for noncompliance, which it terms misperformance (offense, misdemeanor, crime, and so forth). The first question is, what is the correct description for the set of occasions on which the citizen (morally) ought to comply with the law? A second question arises: are there occasions on which the citizen positively ought not obey the law, when is it his "duty" to disobey, despite threats of punishment?

Views on both these questions have varied considerably. Here are what we may take to be the three basic options regarding the first one.

1. At one extreme, we have the view that the citizen's moral duty is to do his best to always to comply with the law, except only in cases where the law is indeterminate or inconsistent. Sometimes this position is qualified for cases of flagrantly unjust regimes.

2. Between that and the next view, we have the proposal that there is a "prima facie" obligation to obey the law. This means that the fact that x is required by law is regarded as conferring positive moral weight on the doing of x. Only if doing x conflicted with other moral requirments of greater "stringency" would one be justified in not doing x; and where doing x conflicts with a very strong moral obligation to the contrary, one would then be duty-bound to disobey this law. This "middle" view is probably the prevalent one among today's moral and legal philosophers.

3. At what would widely be regarded as the other extreme, it is pointed out that people ought always to do what is morally right, whether or not this coincides with the law: where the law is in the right, we are morally bound to obey; where it is wrong, however, we are not so bound, and in an important class of cases we are morally bound to disobey.

Certain arguments in the field dominate discussion. The case for the third view is straightforward. All law requires justification. The only noncontroversial justification is when it requires people to do what there is antecedently sufficient reason to require them to do, notably, to conform to fundamental moral requirements to respect life and limb and to respect others' liberty and property. However, these are things we ought to do anyway—there is no need for legislators' law to require this kind of behavior. Thus we ought to obey laws requiring these things because they are required by reason anyway. May law do anything further?

The classic answer, as stated by John Locke, is that it may not, for beyond that it infringes people's rights. Thus there is no prima facie reason to obey the law. At most there is a presumption that if something is illegal, there may be good reason why it should be, and the citizen should comply unless he has good reason to believe that the law has erred in the case at hand. At that point, the presumption is reversed: the citizen may, morally, and, in some cases of great importance, positively should, disobey the law. It is essential to realize, however, in this view self-interest is an entirely sufficient reason for not obeying erroneous law, and there is no need to protest in public courts of appeal.

The case against the first view is that there is no inherent reason why de facto law may not be unjust. Here we must distinguish two types of possible injustice. (a) One is where the law does what it has no business doing: requiring us to part our hair on the left, for example, or forbidding interracial marriage. (b) The more drastic cases, though, are ones in which the law arranges for the execution of innocent persons or requires citizens to do evil to others. The Nazi laws, some racist laws, and numerous others can be cited. Here the radical defense of the first view breaks down completely. If it is admitted that the law can be profoundly unjust, then to regard the law as morally authoritative is irrational.

One way out would be to modify the view somewhat, so as to read that we have an absolute obligation to obey all just laws. However, this could collapse the distinction between the first and third views; at a minimum, it makes the second the only plausible contender among views that espouse a basic obligation to obey the law.

This leaves the second and most popular view. The question here is what the force of "prima facie" is to be taken to be. Normally, to say that x is prima facie right is to say that unless some other moral requirement conflicts with x, then x is to be done. How do we read "moral requirement" for this purpose? This may define the distinction between the first and the second views. If the thesis is that only when you are morally *obligated* to do y, where y conflicts with x, are you permitted not to do x, then laws requiring us to part our hair on the left would be morally obligatory, for there is no moral obligation to part it on the right.

On the other hand, if what is meant is that requiring us to do x conflicts with a contrary moral *permission*, then the second view collapses into the third view. Morally, we are of course allowed to part our hair on the right. So if the law requires us to part it on the left, disobedience would be morally permitted, since the law has forbidden us to do something which morality allows us to do, and this, it may be held, it has no business doing.

Support for the principle of obedience to law has probably stemmed as much as anything from a concern for public "order." However, the question is whether this only means that citizens are, for instance, not to assault each other in the course of their daily lives, or something more. If more, then the question is whether the law is justified in imposing any other kind of order beyond whatever would emerge from the voluntary interactions of its citizens. This is a fundamental question of political philosophy, but it should be noted that the basic liberal tradition suggests that the answer is in the negative. And since the third view is sufficient to assure public order on moral terms, the current burden of proof would seem to rest on those who wish to support any stronger view.

Finally, any plausible defense of the second view will surely require appeal to such things as broadly democratic procedures in the fundamental lawmaking mechanism. If those procedures are conceived essentially along the lines of majority rule, then it is hard to see how they could prevent the creation of patently unjust law, nor why a community order desired by the majority should on that account be allowed to coerce the minority. The basically negative answer yielded by liberalism in the foregoing paragraph seems still to apply. On the whole, then, the currently most plausible view would seem to be the first.

References

Baumgarth, William P., and Richard J. Regan, eds. *Saint Thomas Aquinas on Law, Morality, and Politics*. Indianapolis IN: Hackett, 1988.

Buchanan, Allen. "Perfecting Imperfect Duties: Collective Action to Create Moral Obligations." *Business Ethics Quarterly* 6 (1996), 27–42.

Calhoun, Cheshire. "Kant and Compliance with Conventionalized Injustice." *Southern Journal of Philosophy* 32 (1994), 135–159.

Danielson, Peter. "Closing the Compliance Dilemma." In *Contractarianism and Rational Choice,* ed. Peter Vallentyne.

New York: Cambridge University Press, 1991.

Goerner, E.A., and Walter J. Thompson. "Politics and Coercion." *Political Theory* 24 (1996), 620–652.

Gold, Steven Jay. "Non-Voluntary Compliance." *Philosophy Research Archives* 14 (1988–89), 115–120.

Held, Virginia, Kai Nielsen, and Charles Parsons, eds. *Philosophy and Political Action.* New York: Oxford University Press, 1972.

Ishtiyaque, Haji. "The Compliance Problem." *Pacific Philosical Quarterly* 70 (1989), 105–121.

MacIntosh, Duncan. "Libertarian Agency and Rational Morality: Action-Theoretic Objections to Gauthier's Dispositional Solution of the Compliance Problem." *Southern Journal of Philosophy* 26 (1988), 499–525.

Murphy, Mark C. "Acceptance of Authority and the Duty to Comply with Just Institutions." *Philosophy and Public Affairs* 23 (1994), 271–277.

Jan Narveson

See also OBLIGATION AND DUTY; POLITICAL OBLIGATION; PRIMA FACIE OBLIGATION

Compound Damages

See PUNITIVE DAMAGES

Compound Offenses

See INCLUDED OFFENSES

Computers

See ARTIFICIAL INTELLIGENCE AND NETWORKS

Confessions

Involuntary confessions are excluded from evidence in trials throughout much of the world, for reasons relating to the search for truth and the revolting nature of coercive police practices. Says J.F. Steven in *A History of the Criminal Law of England:* "It is far pleasanter to sit comfortably in the shade rubbing red pepper into a poor devil's eyes than to go about in the sun hunting up evidence."

In the United States the exclusion of coerced confessions from criminal trials is based on the fifth and fourteenth amendments prohibitions of fundamentally unfair means of obtaining convictions, and of compulsory self-incrimination.

In *Brown v. Mississippi,* 297 U.S. 278 (1936), the first occasion for the Supreme Court to address confessions obtained by torture and used in state criminal trials, the police had repeatedly hung a suspect by a noose on a tree limb and whipped him with a belt to obtain a confession. The court reversed a conviction based on the ensuing confession, observing that the methods were "revolting to a sense of justice" and a "clear violation of due process." The court eventually came to hold that psychological methods of coercing a confession also rendered confessions inadmissible. Involuntary confessions are also inadmissible in Canada, the United Kingdom, and most of the civilized world. The traditional rule derives from *Ibrahim v. The King* (1914).

In countries that exclude confessions produced by duress, various reasons are given. These include:

- The profound transgression of human dignity and humanity involved in acts of torture and brutality against the individual.
- The unreliability of involuntary confessions. (Coercive methods that would tend to make only the guilty confess are not easily distinguishable from those that would make the innocent confess.)
- The fundamental nature of the right not to be compelled to condemn oneself out of one's own mouth (a violation of personal privacy and autonomy).
- In Anglo-Saxon jurisdictions, the notion that the system is accusatorial, not inquisitorial. (The burden is on the state to produce evidence of guilt, without compelling cooperation from the accused.)
- The importance of assuring that the police obey the law as they enforce the law.
- The denial to the police and prosecution of the fruits of unsavory practices, with the anticipated consequence of deterring such practices.

The argument has been made that not all confessions that are technically coerced are necessary unreliable. Thus Fred Inbau et al. have suggested that the test for admissibility should be whether or not the techniques used would tend to make an innocent person confess. This suggestion brings to mind the practice of torture in medieval, post–"trial by ordeal" Italy. Formal limits on torture were enacted, designed to assure that only "true confessions" were elicited. (At this time convictions could be obtained only by proof of a confession or by two witnesses to the crime.) Nevertheless, the practice soon degenerated into obtaining both true and false confessions.

In determining whether a suspect's will was overborne, courts consider the totality of the circumstances under which the interrogation has occurred: for example, as seen in *Spano v. New York,* 360 U.S. 315 (1959), the length of interrogation, whether it continued into the morning, the number of interrogators, whether any threats or promises were made, whether the suspect was permitted rest, food, and drink, and whether the police played on the suspect's sympathies or other emotions.

In the 1966 decision *Miranda v. Arizona,* 384 U.S. 436 (1966), the United States Supreme Court held that when a suspect is in custody the police, before interrogating the accused, must give certain prophylactic warnings. The accused must be told: "You have a right to remain silent, whatever you say can be used against you at trial; you have a right to representation by counsel before and during any questioning, if you cannot afford counsel one will be appointed to represent you." These warnings, known as the Miranda warnings, are designed to assure that the police will not exploit suspects' ignorance of their constitutional right not to be compelled to incriminate themselves and to alleviate the inherently coercive atmosphere of a police department interrogation room.

In the United Kingdom and Canada, the police are required to give similar cautions to a suspect and failure to do so will result in exclusion of a confession.

An issue that has occupied the courts is whether the subjective vulnerability of a suspect in custody, particularly a mental illness, that, together with police behavior, results in the overwhelming of the suspect's free will, should be considered in determining whether a confession by such suspect is inadmissible. In both the United States and Canada, as noted in *Colorado v. Connelly,* 479 U.S. 157 (1986), and *R. v Isequelia,* 1 All E.R. 77 (1975), the confession is admissible as long as the police were unaware of the suspect's vulnerable mental state and the police techniques were not, in and of themselves, objectively coercive.

Formal prohibitions against coercing confessions and formal rules against admitting coerced confessions into evidence do not assure that in fact convictions will not be obtained by the use of coerced confessions. Coercive police practices and police perjury as to interrogation techniques, while not invariable by any means, are still all too common in many countries, including Western democracies.

Regarding confessions in modern continental systems of criminal justice, such systems "place more reliance on the accused as a source of evidence than do common law systems. Though most continental systems now recognize the defendant's right to refuse to answer specific questions, they all permit questioning against the defendant's wishes, both before and during trial." Moreover, "continental provisions . . . do not preclude the admissibility of confessions obtained in violation of proper procedures."

In several Latin American countries, notwithstanding formal prohibitions against coercive interrogation techniques and, in some cases, exclusionary rules, involuntary confessions are routinely admitted.

As Justice Arthur J. Goldberg of the Supreme Court of the United States observed in *Escobedo v. Illinois,* 378 U.S. 478, 488–89 (1964): "We have learned the lesson of history, ancient and modern, that a system of criminal law enforcement which comes to depend on the 'confession' will, in the long run, be less reliable and more subject to abuses than a system which depends on extrinsic evidence independently secured through skillful investigation."

References

Inbau, Fred, John E. Reid, and Joseph P. Buckley. *Criminal Interrogation and Confessions.* 3d ed. Baltimore: William & Wilkins 1986.

Johnson, Sheri Lynn. "Confessions, Criminals and Community." *Harvard Civil Rights–Civil Liberties Law Review* 26 (1991), 327–411.

Kamisar, Yale. *Police Interrogation and Confessions.* Ann Arbor: University of Michigan Press, 1980.

———. "What Is an 'Involuntary' Confession? Some Comments on Inbau and Reid's *Criminal Interrogation and Confessions.*" *Rutgers Law Review* 17 (1963), 728.

Langbein, John H. "Torture and Plea Bargaining." *University of Chicago Law Review* 46 (1978), 3.

Maull, John, "The Exclusion of Coerced Confessions and the Regulation of Custodial Interrogation under the American Convention on Human Rights." *American Criminal Law Review* 32 (1994), 87–135.

Steven, J.F. *A History of the Criminal Law of England.* 1883. 3 vols. London: Routledge/Thoemmes, 1996.

Joel Jay Finer

See also DUE PROCESS; NATURAL JUSTICE; TORTURE

Configurative Philosophy of Law
See LASSWELL/McDOUGAL COLLABORATION

Confinement
See PREVENTIVE DETENTION

Conflict of Laws
Until the early twentieth century, doctrinal attempts to develop a complete system of private international law adhered to no specific philosophical approach.

Two philosophical approaches prevail: the *classical* school, European in origin, predominant worldwide, which merges several philosophies, especially natural law; and the *functionalist* school, with its European branch, plus a primarily American branch of *realist* positivism. In addition, a *sociological* strain claims that legal rules arise spontaneously out of the legal practice of entrepreneurs in international business (*lex mercatoria*). Jurisprudential debate goes on over its very existence and its legal character, but some states' case law and a number of international conventions recognize *lex mercatoria* and its standing as a source of law.

As well, hints of hegelian philosophy can be found in the enduring systems of private international law based on the nationality of persons, even though personalist doctrines precede this philosophy. Friedrich von Savigny, the founder of modern private international law, was influenced by this philosophy.

The *classical* school, represented by von Savigny and Henri Batiffol, took the essential objective of private international law to be the harmonizing of different legal systems, or "making them live together." The systems are put in contact when persons who belong to different systems create relations between themselves in the private order by their goods or their acts. The rules of private international law regulate the reception by one legal system of judgments coming from another. As a result, the classical jurists take the philosophical aspects of private international law to be a study of the philosophies supporting the *method* for reaching this objective of harmonization. This method consists in giving each type of situation an objective setting within a single legal order, by determining its "center of gravity" out of the connections it usually has. Doing this implies a level of abstraction higher than the level for the rules of private law applied to relations within only one system.

This classical doctrine derives from the philosophy of secular natural law. Savigny, for instance, builds his rules for resolving conflicts of laws directly upon "the nature of things," a notion akin to natural law. Analyzing the "nature" of the elements making up a situation lets one work out a rule of law pointing to the applicable system. As one example, the law of the place where a moveable is located determines the real rights in regard to that moveable.

Looking to natural law is also done when determining the legal status of a foreigner: one's legal personality is recognized in principle, but the foreigner's rights are not the same as those of nationals or of persons domiciled within the country. Similarly, public policy upholds the immutable principles of justice drawn from natural law in favor of the foreign person; but this operates in a given social milieu either by giving the foreigner rights he did not have in his country of origin, or by depriving him of these so as to ensure respect for the principle of equality, to satisfy the sense of local justice.

Natural law philosophy, this time in its voluntarist guise, finds expression also in the subjectivist theory of the autonomy of will. Because the parties have chosen one law, this is the choice which has effect: *pacta sunt servanda* (agreements must be kept). A prime role in law goes not to statutes, but to the person, whose liberty expresses itself in contractual provisions linking one to another independently of any municipal legal system. Such philosophy relates especially to individuals' legal acts (contracts, wills, prenuptial agreements). In most systems, however, this liberty is constrained by various techniques (the doctrine of *localization objective,* the doctrine concerning evasion of the law, and so forth).

Standing can be given to the circumstances of the case or to the vested rights in a foreigner in a similar way, by invoking the maxim *suum cuique tribuere* (render to each person what he is entitled to).

The classical theory runs up against the following criticism, however: the introduction of foreign law has to respect the logical unity of the legal order which receives it. This limitation appears in the *functionalist requirement* that the law to be applied is the one best realizing the objective of the court which hears it (that is, the doctrine of exception on grounds of public policy and its peremptory norms).

The classical doctrine is put into question by the *realist school,* as well, which is affiliated to Anglo-Saxon utilitarianism. Conflicts of law, in their view, are not abstract conflicts between systems of state law (their rejection of *Begriffsjurisprudenz,* conceptual jurisprudence) but are real conflicts between private interests (*Interessenjurisprudenz*) having to do with the human beings involved in a social context, which have to be resolved in an end-directed manner, by looking for specific social outcomes (Roscoe Pound). Among these is the aim of doing justice in the particular case while ignoring the aprioristic demands of legal naturalism (Savigny's "nature of things," and his safeguarding of vested rights), which the classical school insisted upon. American theories, especially those espoused by Brainerd Currie, have tried to integrate this analysis by taking into account the overall interests of states. These state interests are developed into policies whose application at the international level, by applying a single law to the particular case, has to be evaluated comparatively and in a functional manner by taking into consideration all the contacts with any interested state.

American case law has in large part taken its lead from this school by making pragmatic use of its suggestions. The results are mixed. The decisional outcomes are much more concrete, but the high level of uncertainty which this method brings in foreseeing the applicable law has been vigorously criticized, along with the injustices which result from it. Critics say that private benefit and state interest seldom

C

succeed in working out a conflict between rules; their recommendations are too general and too susceptible of contradictory interpretations.

Despite this, the realist school's ideas have supplied a new approach to classical theory and method; these ideas recently have succeeded in integrating the opposed school's relevant insights, either by rules which lead directly to concrete resolution as the parties wish (in effect, *material justice* in each case, or *social utility* for an institution, for example, the validity of a marriage) or by exceptions (through exemption clauses), without falling into the problems created by application of the American realist school's theories.

Finally, from the viewpoint of legal theory, the *normative positivism* of Hans Kelsen, which runs through the theories of many modern authors, Pierre Mayer and Werner Goldschmidt, for example, supplies quite adequate answers to some basic questions of private international law. According to it, the systematic and complete character of every "legal order," as it is formed out of a pyramid of express or implicit rules and of decisions basing their solutions on these two types of norms, is the core presupposition in most doctrines of private international law. This structure implies, then, at least on the level of rational content, a *virtually universal competence* on the part of every legal order, which is what stands as the source of the possibility for any conflict of laws.

This presupposition does not obviate the possibility that a judge in any state might take a solution either from a foreign legal system, or from the customary or conventional rules of international law often based on natural law, or even from unsystematized and incomplete sets of norms. Those are worked out in international business and known as the *lex mercatoria*; upon their occasional adoption, these become part of the legal orders which receive them. However, in the absence of a supranational judge, a judge can use only the rational content of the foreign norm, without making use of its imperative requirement.

Similarly, the dichotomy between a norm's validity and its effects, a deeply Kelsenian matter, is at the heart of private international law thinking.

References

Batiffol, Henri. *Aspects philosophiques du droit international privé* (Philosophical Aspects of Private International Law). Paris: Dalloz, 1956.

Borras, Alegria et al., eds. *E pluribus unum: Liber amicorum Georges A.L. Droz: On the Progressive Unification of Private International Law*. Boston: Martinus Nijhoff, 1996.

Cook, W.W. "The Logical and Legal Bases of the Conflict of Laws." *Yale Law Journal* 33 (1923), 457–488.

Currie, Brainerd. *Selected Essays on the Conflict of Laws*. Durham: Duke University Press, 1963.

Francescakis, Phocion. "Droit naturel et droit international privé" (Natural Law and Private International Law). In *Mélanges Maury*, Tome 1, 113–152. Paris: Dalloz, Sirey, 1960.

Goldman, Berthold. "Frontières du droit et lex mercatoria" (The Limits of Law and the Lex Mercatoria). *Archives de philosophie du droit* 9 (1964), 177–192.

Goldschmidt, Werner. "Système et philosophie du droit international privé" (Systems and Philosophy of Private International Law). *Revue critique de droit international privé* 44 (1955), 639–667; 45 (1956), 21–41, 223–244.

Graveson, Ronald Harry. "Philosophical Aspects of the English Conflict of Laws." *Law Quarterly Review* 78 (1962), 337–370.

Mayer, Pierre. *Droit international privé* (Private International Law). 4th ed. Paris: Montchrestien, 1991.

———. *La distinction entre règles et décisions et le droit international privé* (The Distinction Between Rules and Decisions in Private International Law). Paris: Dalloz, 1973.

Petersen, Hanne, and Heinrik Zahle, eds. *Legal Polycentricity: Consequences of Pluralism in Law*. Brookfield VT: Dartmouth, 1995.

Gerald Goldstein

See also COMPARATIVE LAW; REALISM, LEGAL

Conscience

The relationship between conscience and the law is intimate and intricate. It is intimate because both are essentially normative: both seek to bind us to act in certain ways and both speak to us in the language of rights and wrongs, liberties and duties. This closeness can obscure the fact that they are different in important ways. If we think of conscience as the voice of our deeply held moral convictions and of law as the expression of the political will of the state, we can see how the two must be different. First, the law typically prescribes penalties for disobedience, and these penalties are separate from the natural consequences of disobedience. However, conscience never prescribe penalties for disobedience: if we violate our conscience, we suffer self-imposed guilt rather than some extraneous penalty. Second, most of us believe that changes in the law should result from a political process that reflects the views of the majority, but no one seriously believes that conscience should be dictated by majority rule.

Ideally, the legal system we live under should match the voice of our conscience, in the sense that the law should never seek to force us to violate our conscience. In addition, it is important that this match should not arise because we have forced our conscience into conformity with the law but rather because the law respects our conscience. However, our deeply held moral convictions are always in a state of more or less gradual change as they are subjected to critical reflection arising out of internal tensions among them as well as challenges from without. These critical reflections are the source of a long-standing debate within legal philosophy that grapples with the question of the basis for, and limitations on, the moral duty to obey the law. The traditional natural law theory, following Thomas Aquinas, holds that the duty of legal obedience arises because valid positive law is part of the moral law ordained by God. In other words, the duty of legal obedience arises because the law is necessarily moral in nature. However, in the nineteenth century this view was challenged by John Austin and the legal positivists who held that laws are essentially the expressions of the will of a sovereign legislator, and that any coincidence with morality is, however desirable, merely a contingent and accidental feature of law. For the legal positivist, therefore, a separate argument for a duty of legal obedience must be provided. The argument presented by Austin was a utilitarian one: when the good that obedience to law produces outweighs the evils it also produces we have a duty of legal obedience; otherwise there is no such duty.

Contemporary debate on this question is dominated by the work of H.L.A. Hart and Joseph Raz. Following Austin's positivist approach, they hold that since legal systems are social institutions, they have a kind of factual existence that makes it conceptually inappropriate to treat them as part of morality. They therefore argue for a strict conceptual separation of law and morality. The leading critics of this separation thesis have been Lon Fuller, John Finnis, and Ronald Dworkin, all of whom hold that a legal system cannot be properly understood unless it is recognized as having a substantive ethical purpose. Thus, for contemporary legal philosophy the question is posed in the following way: does a correct understanding of the nature of law entail that law by its very nature has a moral quality that makes it worthy of obedience? The negative answer given by legal positivism seems at first glance to be much more plausible, since we are all aware that some laws and legal decisions in every legal system are unjust and that some legal systems embody large-scale injustices. The modern critics of positivism, however, do not deny that legal injustices occur, but claim that they are the exception to the rule, the rule being that there is always a moral presumption in favor of obedience to law. They argue that this presumption arises out of the very nature of law itself, since a legal system must, if it is to count as a legal system and not merely as a system of organized oppression by a government, embody certain features of justice or morality that make it *in general* worthy of obedience. They concede that no legal system ever embodies these features to an extent that can guarantee that legal injustices will never occur. But the onus is on anyone who would disobey a law to show that in the particular case the evil or injustice that obedience would cause is sufficiently great to justify overriding the presumption in favor of obedience. Legal positivists, of course, do not deny that conscience will sometimes justify breaking a law; they only want to deny that there is a general moral presumption in favor of obedience to the law.

The contemporary debate between the legal positivists and their critics seems to have reached a stalemate. The main protagonists seem to be divided not so much by their explicit views of the nature of law as by their implicit views of the nature of morality. According to utilitarianism, there is no inherent rightness or wrongness of an action; the right-ness or wrongness of an action is entirely a function of its consequences. When applied to the question of obedience to law utilitarianism requires us to compare the consequences of obedience and disobedience and to act in the way that will produce the best overall conse-quences. Consequently, a utilitarian cannot deny the legal positivist separation of law and morality. On the other hand, the kantian moral theory holds that morality must be un-derstood in terms of specific binding moral principles, such as those which assert the duty to keep our promises and the duty to respect human life. In this view, we have obligations that may run counter to the edicts of utilitari-anism. For example, we may hold that there are duties to our family or nation that override any utilitarian claim that more overall good would be achieved if we acted otherwise. In the end, then, the question of the relationship between law and conscience depends not so much on what we think about the law, but on whether we think our conscience speaks to us in nonutilitarian terms. Perhaps this question can only be resolved by each of us deciding for ourselves whether utilitarian considerations are sufficiently compelling to override the voice of our conscience.

References

Dworkin, Ronald. *Law's Empire.* Cambridge MA: Harvard University Press, 1986.

Dyzenhaus, David. *Hard Cases in Wicked Le-gal Systems: South African Law in the Perspective of Legal Philosophy.* Oxford: Clarendon Press, 1991.

Finnis, John. *Natural Law and Natural Rights.* Oxford: Clarendon Press, 1980.

Fuller, Lon L. *The Morality of Law.* New Haven: Yale University Press, 1964. Rev. ed. 1969.

Hart, H.L.A. *The Concept of Law.* Oxford: Clarendon Press, 1961.

Raz, Joseph. *The Authority of Law.* Oxford: Clarendon Press, 1979.

Shiner, Roger A. *Norm and Nature: The Movements of Legal Thought.* Oxford: Clarendon Press, 1992.

Waluchow, W.J. *Inclusive Legal Positivism.* Oxford: Clarendon Press, 1994.

William H. Hughes

See also CIVIL DISOBEDIENCE; CONSCIENTIOUS OBJECTION

Conscientious Objection

The term "conscientious objection" refers to religious, moral, or other principled opposi-tion to participation in a socially required ac-tivity. It need not refer to war. Yet, with the enormous impact of war on the modern world and the widespread government practice of military conscription, conscientious objection is usually understood to refer to military ser-vice. Thus, a conscientious objector is an indi-vidual whose religious or moral principles pro-hibit his or her participation or involvement in war. Since compelling persons to violate such principles is undesirable, particularly in a free society, lawmakers face a clash of values—the voice of the objector's conscience and the gov-ernment's claim that citizens have a duty, en-forceable by law, to contribute to the preserva-tion and security of the state.

Conscientious objection to war is as an-cient as war itself. One of the earliest docu-mented social theories that could be used to justify refusal of military service came from the sixth century B.C. Chinese philosopher Lao-tzu. Yet conscientious objection devel-oped primarily out of Christian pacifism in re-sponse to conscription. With little exception during the first three centuries of the Christian era, Christians espoused a conscientious objec-tion to participation in war on two grounds: their belief that the taking of human life under any circumstance was evil, and because mili-tary service was equated with idol worship and emperor sacrifices. The first known Chris-tian conscientious objector was Maximillan, a twenty-year-old from Numidia in North Africa, who refused to serve in the Roman mil-itary in A.D. 295 and was subsequently exe-cuted. However, when Christianity was offi-cially recognized as the state religion during the reign of the Roman Emperor Constantine (A.D. 306–337), the Church accepted the con-cept of a "just war" and religious objection to war became a minority current, supported by such small religious groups as the Albigensians in the twelfth century and the Anabaptists in the sixteenth century. However, since the Protestant Reformation, many religious sects (the Mennonites, the Amish, the Church of the Brethren, the Quakers, the Jehovah's Wit-nesses, and others) have insisted that war and violence contradict biblical principles.

While the focus has historically been on the religious objector, others have refused military service on secular grounds. These philosophical objections, supported by either political or private reasons, are based on a variety of sometimes conflicting moral principles. Charles Moskos and John Chambers refer to this as the "secularization of conscience": "the augmenting, indeed, near supplanting, of the old religious and communal grounds for objection by a new secular and often privatized base. . . ." In addition to their motivation for opposition, conscientious objectors can also be categorized according to the scope of their beliefs. "Absolute" objectors are opposed to all wars. "Selective" objectors are opposed only to particular conflicts. "Discretionary" objectors reject the use of certain weapons, primarily those of mass destruction (for example, nuclear weapons).

While each state's experience with this practice has been unique, two democracies in the modern era, Great Britain and the United States, have made more serious efforts at recognizing the legal provisions of conscientious objection. In Britain, the conscription Acts of Parliament in 1916, 1939, and 1948 included "conscience clauses." Individuals could object to military service on any grounds and were provided the opportunity to declare their beliefs to an independent civilian tribunal, and, if unsuccessful, to appear before an appellate tribunal. Britain also recognized the right not to perform civilian work that would assist the war effort. According to Mulford Sibley and Philip Jacob, the laws and regulations developed for conscientious objection in Great Britain during the early twentieth century "in terms of their concern and sensitivity for the individual conscience . . . were the most elaborate and far-reaching . . . in the world."

Conscientious objection to war is a longstanding tradition in America. Almost all of the original thirteen colonies recognized conscientious objection as a fundamental human right. As a matter of national policy, conscientious objection was introduced in 1789, when James Madison included in his proposal for a federal Bill of Rights: "[N]o person religiously scrupulous of bearing arms shall be compelled to render military service in person." While this provision was excluded from the final draft, Congress formally recognized conscientious objection in the early twentieth century. In 1917, Congress exempted members of "well recognized religious . . . organizations," such as "peace churches . . . [or] pacifist religious sect[s]." In 1940, the Universal Military Training and Service Act abolished all sectarian requirements to conscientious objection, mandating that objection had to be based on "religious training and belief." Yet, in the U.S. Supreme Court case of *United States v. Seeger,* 380 U.S. 163 (1965), it was decided that adherence to religious principles could not be the sole reason for granting conscientious objector status. Five years later, the Supreme Court, in *Welsh v. United States,* 398 U.S. 333 (1970), recognized that an individual's objection to war may "stem from . . . moral, ethical, or religious beliefs about what is right and wrong . . . and these beliefs [must] be held with the strength of traditional religious convictions."

Unique challenges to selective conscientious objection have arisen in recent years. While lawmakers may be willing to exclude persons whose religious or secular conscience prevents the taking of human life, it is much more problematic to exclude the individual who invokes the right to "choose" the wars in which he or she will participate. As a matter of public policy, most modern democracies that recognize conscientious objection have taken an "all or nothing" approach: objection is legitimate if and only if the individual condemns participation in all wars, and not simply certain "unjust" wars. In *Gillette v. United States,* 401 U.S. 437 (1971), for example, the U.S. Supreme Court denied conscientious objection status to those who did not object "to participation in war in any form" but only to particular "unjust" wars.

The problems raised by conscientious objection go to the very core of a citizen's relationship to the state. Nothing is more abhorrent in a democratic society than government forcing its citizens to violate deeply held principles. If government is the servant of the people, then it could be argued that the very idea of conscription is incompatible with free government. Indeed, compared to mandatory military service, with its inherent risk to one's life, all other "takings" (money, property, and so on) pale. Conscription is the ultimate demand placed on an individual by society. What other choice a person could make is more basic than that concerning when, if ever, one is justified in taking a human life?

Yet this independent moral choice is precisely what no government, dictatorial or democratic, can easily extend to its citizens, particularly in a time of war. In any form, conscientious objection is a direct challenge to the sovereignty of the state. Thus, government must be permitted to protect itself, and this normally includes the authority to conscript individuals for military service. Moreover, if one of the primary functions of the state is the security of its citizens, then one of the most basic civic duties is participation, either directly or indirectly, in the defense of the nation. Any individual who objects to this duty seeks to excuse himself or herself from the extreme hardships and heavy burdens of military service that all citizens are called upon to bear equally.

In Shakespeare's *The Life of Henry V,* the king, contemplating his sovereignty over *and* responsibility to his citizens, notes, "Every subject's duty is the King's, but every subject's soul is his own." This quote eloquently presents the basis for the conflict between one's obligation to contribute to collective self-defense and the demands of individuals' religious and/or moral convictions regarding the sanctity of human life. Conscientious objection has generated some of the most problematic conflicts between one's duty to the state and the demands of individual conscience.

References

Bay, Christian, and Charles C. Walker. *Civil Disobedience: Theory and Practice.* Montreal: Black Rose Books, 1975.

Moskos, Charles C., and John Whiteclay Chambers II, eds. *The New Conscientious Objection: From Sacred to Secular Expression.* New York: Oxford University Press, 1993.

Noone, Michael F. "Legal Aspects of Conscientious Objection: A Comparative Analysis." In *The New Conscientious Objection: From Sacred to Secular Expression,* ed. Charles C. Moskos and John Whiteclay Chambers II. New York: Oxford University Press, 1993.

Schlissel, Lillian, ed. *Conscience in America.* New York: Dutton, 1968.

Sibley, Mulford Q., and Philip E. Jacob. *Conscription of Conscience: The American State and the Conscientious Objector, 1940–1947.* Ithaca: Cornell University Press, 1952.

Richard A. Glenn

See also CIVIL DISOBEDIENCE; CONSCIENCE

Consent

Many legal philosophers accept the "volenti" maxim: *volenti fit non injuria* (no harm is done to one who has consented). There are at least two ways to understand this maxim. First, consent might negate the harm that a criminal offense would otherwise cause. According to this interpretation, broken bones are not harmful to a person who consents to a battery. Second, consent might justify the infliction of harm. According to this interpretation, broken bones are harmful to a person who consents to a battery, but the defendant who commits the offense does no wrong by inflicting the harm.

If the volenti maxim were consistently applied throughout all of the criminal law, as some theorists seemingly recommend, consent would be an effective defense to any criminal offense. For a variety of reasons, however, Anglo-American criminal law has not accepted the full implications of the volenti maxim. A few commentators reject the maxim altogether on the ground that crimes, unlike torts, are wrongs against the state, and thus cannot be authorized by the particular victim. This conception of criminality helps to explain why the victim's willingness to accept restitution or his subsequent condonation of the offense are not bars to liability.

Existing law neither totally accepts nor completely rejects the volenti maxim. In current practice, consent might preclude liability in any of three distinct ways. First, many criminal offenses are defined to include nonconsent as an element. Kidnapping and rape, for example, might be defined to require the absence of consent. In these cases, it is potentially misleading to describe consent as a defense; a defendant who acts with his victim's consent simply has not committed the crimes of kidnap or rape. If consent precludes liability on this ground, the prosecution must prove nonconsent beyond a reasonable doubt in order to gain a conviction. Second, some offenses that are not defined to include nonconsent as an element might contain special consent defenses that apply to them. The *Model Penal Code,* for example, contains a special consent defense applicable to a few offenses, such as bodily injury. Third, many criminal codes contain a general consent defense seemingly applicable to any offense. The *Model Penal Code,* for example, provides that consent is a defense if it "precludes the infliction of the harm or evil sought to be prevented by the law defining the offense."

The application of this provision can give rise to great controversy, insofar as it requires a judicial determination of the nature of the harm that a given offense is designed to prevent. If consent precludes liability on either of the latter two grounds, the burden of proving consent may be placed on the defendant.

Legal philosophers disagree about what consent is. A common assumption is that different accounts of the nature of consent need not be given for different offenses; one analysis of consent is adequate for all purposes. "Subjectivists" hold that consent is a mental state. They differ about the exact nature of the state of mind that consent is alleged to be; it might be an intention or an attitude, for example. Subjectivists hold that conduct or behavior is needed as evidence of consent but should not be confused with consent itself. "Objectivists," by way of contrast, believe that consent is conduct or behavior; consent is no more of a mental state than is a promise.

Consent need not be explicitly expressed, but is sometimes implied from the behavior of the victim. A theory of implied consent probably explains the "customary license" defense of many criminal codes. The *Model Penal Code*, for example, creates a defense when the defendant's conduct "was within a customary license or tolerance, neither expressly negatived by the person whose interest was infringed nor inconsistent with the purpose of the law defining the offense."

Many criminal codes also contain provisions that explicitly restrict the use of consent as a defense. Consent is generally not a defense to the infliction of serious bodily injury, including homicide, unless the serious injury falls within a range of special categories. Sports and games are the most widely recognized of these special categories.

Any limitations on the use of consent as a defense may appear unjustifiable when assessed from the perspective of the consenting "victim." Some commentators have objected to the infringement of autonomy that results from the law's unwillingness to allow persons to enlist the assistance of others in the commission of suicide, for example. According to this train of thought, one should be allowed to authorize others to help one attain any objective one is permitted to attain on one's own. Limitations on the use of consent, however, are typically supported on two grounds of public policy. First, there is good reason to be cautious about implicating other persons in dangerous forms of conduct. If a defendant were allowed to inflict a sadomasochistic beating on a consenting victim, for example, some theorists warn that the defendant's inhibitions against sadism may be weakened, to the detriment of nonconsenting victims. Second, there may be great difficulty in obtaining reliable evidence that the victim's consent is voluntary and effective, especially in the case of homicide. Thus some limitations on the scope of the consent defense are thought to be necessary.

Moreover, there are some offenses, frequently called paternalistic, that are designed to protect persons from harming themselves. Many commentators believe that the paternalistic coercion of sane adults is always unjustified. However, if such offenses are enacted, consent is not allowed as a defense. Much of the point of a law requiring the use of seat belts or forbidding the use of dangerous drugs, for example, would be undermined if liability were precluded by the consent of the driver or user.

In addition, a number of offenses have a social objective that cannot be reduced to the interests of an identifiable victim. In such cases, a consent defense would be peculiar or unintelligible. The commentaries to the *Model Penal Code* claim that "consent is not a factor" in such offenses as riot, prison escape, breach of the peace, bribery, and bigamy.

Regardless of the scope and limits of the defense of consent, all commentators agree that consent is effective only under certain conditions. Some theorists employ the concept of voluntariness to identify these conditions. In this context, as in others, it is very difficult to determine whether and under what circumstances consent is truly voluntary and thus effective. Some codes, including the *Model Penal Code*, provide a list of conditions under which consent is ineffective. These lists include immaturity or legal incompetency; thus consent is not a defense to statutory rape. In addition, consent is ineffective when it is induced by force, duress, or deception. Moreover, consent may be ineffective when a person is unable to make a reasonable judgment because of intoxication or some other kind of impairment.

Defendants may not be liable simply because they commit an offense without the consent of the victim. Typically, mistake about consent is a defense. Jurisdictions differ about whether and under what circumstances a mistake about consent must be reasonable in order to create a defense from criminal liability. This issue has given rise to enormous controversy in the context of rape.

Particularly troublesome, especially in the context of medical treatment, is the claim that consent is ineffective unless informed. There is considerable doubt about how much information about the nature and quality of a risk is required before consent is effective.

When consent does not preclude liability altogether, it may still have a significant impact on the administration of the criminal law. Consent may be important for whether police decide to arrest or prosecutors decide to charge. Moreover, consent can function as a mitigating factor to reduce the sentence that would otherwise be imposed.

References

American Law Institute. *Model Penal Code and Commentaries*. Philadelphia: American Law Institute Press, 1985.

Feinberg, Joel. *Harm to Others*. New York: Oxford University Press, 1984.

Fletcher, George. *Rethinking Criminal Law*. Boston: Little, Brown, 1978.

LaFave, Wayne, and Austin Scott. *Substantive Criminal Law*. St. Paul MN: West, 1986.

Robinson, Paul. *Criminal Law Defenses*. St. Paul MN: West, 1984.

Douglas N. Husak

See also CRIMINALIZATION; PATERNALISM

Conspiracy

The crime of conspiracy consists in an agreement to commit an unlawful act. The conspiratorial agreement is punishable whether or not the unlawful act is performed.

Scholars and judges alike have often deplored conspiracy law for its traditional role in suppressing dissident social and labor movements and for the unfettered prosecutorial discretion that flows from its loose and vague rules of evidence, venue, and joinder. Meanwhile, philosophical problems of definition and justification arise with regard to the highly anticipatory nature of the offense, liability for acts committed by co-conspirators, and the identification and individuation of particular conspiracies within large and complex criminal enterprises.

Conspiracy as an Inchoate Offense

Under conspiracy law, an individual may be held liable for agreeing to commit a statutory offense with another, while the simple declaration of intention to commit the same crime would not generally incur liability. The law of attempt requires substantial acts verging on actual commission. In contrast, although conspiracy law often requires some overt act in furtherance of the conspiracy, even very preparatory acts will suffice. This makes conspiracy law suspect with regard to the liberal requirement that criminal punishment be predicated upon consummated acts rather than mere intentions.

Courts and commentators have defended the anticipatory nature of conspiracy law on two main grounds: first, individuals who agree to commit crimes manifest their criminality more concretely and reliably than those who merely declare an intention, because of group pressure not to renege on an agreement; and second, the very existence of organized, criminally oriented groups constitutes a special and continuing danger to the public and to state authority. Thus, it is thought that groups are more likely both to commit and conceal crimes successfully, and to serve as potential platforms for future criminal activities.

Still, there is reason to worry that liability for unconsummated conspiracies is preemptive punishment. It is improper to jail individuals for mere likelihood that they will commit an offense not yet attempted, in part because of the uncertainty of behavioral predictions, and in part to preserve a wide sphere of individual liberty. These considerations do not evaporate in the case of aggregates of individuals. Perhaps some criminal agreements are so firm and well plotted that an attempt is sure to follow. But when that is true, it is in virtue of the particular qualities of the plot and plotters; it cannot follow from the mere existence of an agreement. Indeed, conspiratorial agreements are typically abstract constructs, inferred by a jury from circumstantial evidence, and so a very weak platform for strong predictive hypotheses.

Furthermore, if the real worry is criminal gangs and not agreements per se, then the task of deterring organized criminality can be met with enhanced penalties for criminal acts committed by structured groups, as under many European codes. Charging conspiracy only in the case of consummated crimes will also answer this purpose.

Conspirators' Liability for Substantive Offenses

A further peculiarity of conspiracy doctrine in U.S. federal law, as well as in many state jurisdictions (but not under the *Model Penal Code*), is that membership in a conspiracy can serve as a basis for holding one conspirator liable for substantive offenses committed by others in furtherance of the conspiracy, or as foreseeable products of it. In the case which gives this liability rule its name, *United States v. Pinkerton*, 328 U.S. 640 (1946), the defendant was convicted of several acts of illegal distilling committed by his brother. These offenses were committed while the defendant was in jail, without his aid, and indeed without his knowledge. The basis for liability was the brothers' conspiratorial relationship, on the principle that a conspiracy is a "partnership in crime" in which each conspirator acts as the agent of the others.

This justification for the Pinkerton rule, derived by analogy from agency law, is probably insupportable. Agency law holds principals civilly liable for the acts and agreements of their agents, even without the principals' authorization, in order to foster the reliability of contracts and to encourage principals to exercise additional control over their agents' conduct. Neither of these goals is present in the criminal law. Also, the agency law model of criminal partnership implies an egalitarianism that is probably as lacking in large-scale criminal enterprises as it is in large corporations. While it may be fair to hold criminal ringleaders liable for the acts of subordinates, there is little basis for holding the subordinates liable for the acts of their superiors, and less yet for holding them liable for the acts of co-conspirators of equal rank, over whom they exercise no control and from whom they extract no benefit.

Nonetheless, the Pinkerton rule is perhaps both less unfair and less anomalous than its eponymous case makes it appear. Very few cases involve as attenuated a relationship among the conspirators as did *Pinkerton*. Usually, the acts for which a conspirator is held liable have clearly been fostered by the conspiratorial agreement. In such cases a complicity charge would also provide a basis for liability. Also, the rule probably does deter organized criminal activity: if each conspirator is liable for the most serious acts of any other, those with potentially minor roles and smaller payoffs have less incentive to join groups and greater incentive to defect and cooperate with the prosecution. The imposition of derivative liability itself is thus less problematical than

the uniform severity of the penalties. The unfairness arising from this uniformity is exacerbated by the rigid sentencing guidelines under U.S. federal law.

Problems of Individuation and Scope

Many of the problems of derivative liability follow from the basic difficulty of individuating conspiracies. For example, as seen in *United States v. Bruno*, 308 U.S. 287 (1939), a set of drug retailers may deal exclusively with one set of distributors, but be indifferent about which smugglers the distributors deal with. The retailers may also know of other retailing clients of the distributors but have no interests in common with them. Under traditional conspiracy doctrine, all may be implicated within one conspiracy, and thus all subject to joint trial and liability for the acts of any others. Also, conspiracy law makes a procedural exception, admitting as evidence hearsay among conspirators, on the grounds that their agreement binds them to one another's testimony. These principles are defensible with respect to the distributors, who enjoy a community of interests with all parties, but there is probably no such relationship among retailers, or between retailers and smugglers. While it is true that the smugglers depend upon the ongoing success of some retailers, and vice versa, this form of commercial dependence does not constitute an agreement to pursue a common aim. This lack of an agreement undermines the basis for derivative liability and for the hearsay exception. Today, many cases involving dispersed networks of criminals are prosecuted under racketeering rather than conspiracy law. This change has further aggravated the problem of scope: racketeering laws base liability not upon a conspiratorial agreement, but instead upon the even broader and vaguer basis of participation in a criminal enterprise.

Scope problems also arise in the case of persons providing goods or services either innocent in themselves or widely available elsewhere. Is a sugar seller a member of a bootleg liquor conspiracy if he knowingly sells his product to the operator of a still [*United States v. Falcone*, 109 F.2d 579 (2d Cir. 1940), *aff'd*, 311 U.S. 205 (1940) (conviction reversed)]? Is the owner of a telephone answering service a member of a conspiracy to commit prostitution if many prostitutes use the service with his knowledge [*People v. Lauria*, 251 Cal. App.

2d 471 (1967) (conviction reversed)]? These cases indicate why a contribution's necessity to the success of a criminal venture has generally been rejected as a basis for the liability of the contributor. Necessity can be too broad a requirement, for essential aid might be too minor or too widely available to justify liability for the objectives of the whole enterprise. Necessity can also be too narrow a requirement, since an individual might be culpable in spite of a superfluous contribution.

Courts have instead taken a more discriminating approach to these problems, finding liability where the provider of the good or service in question has developed, in Judge Learned Hand's phrase, stated in *Falcone v. United States,* 109 F.2d 581 (1940), a significant "stake" in the criminal venture. In order to give content to the notion of a "stake," courts and legislatures have distinguished between intentional and mere knowing facilitation of a crime and between substantial and inconsequential aid; they have also emphasized the difference between the supply of intrinsically dangerous materials (for example, drugs or guns) and innocuous ones (sugar, answering services). These criteria help to identify a culpable intent given a normally legitimate provision of services. Most valuably, they spare legitimate businesses the great burden of policing their customers.

The courts' attempts to characterize individual intentions temper their tendency to deploy the conspiratorial agreement as a purely legal construct, based on patterns of behavior and commercial dependence. Because of the dual identity of conspiracies as legal constructs as well as structures of shared intentions, there may be no ultimate solution to the philosophical problems of responsibility and individuation they entail. Philosophically informed doctrinal solutions can, however, minimize the dangers of preemptive or vicarious punishment.

References

"Developments in the Law—Criminal Conspiracy." *Harvard Law Review* 72 (1959), 920–1008.
Fletcher, George P. *Rethinking Criminal Law.* Boston: Little, Brown, 1978.
Goldstein, Abraham. "Conspiracy to Defraud the United States." *Yale Law Journal* 68 (1959), 405–463.
Johnson, Phillip E. "The Unnecessary Crime of Conspiracy." *California Law Review* 61 (1973), 1137–1188.
Kadish, Sanford H. "Complicity, Cause and Blame: A Study in the Interpretation of Doctrine." *California Law Review* 73 (1985), 324–410.
Lafave, Wayne R., and Austin W. Scott, Jr. *Substantive Criminal Law.* St. Paul MN: West, 1986.
Lynch, Gerard E. "RICO: The Crime of Being a Criminal." *Columbia Law Review* 87 (1987), Pt. 1 and 2, 661–674; Pt. 3 and 4, 920–984.
Model Penal Code and Commentaries. Philadelphia: American Law Institute, 1985.
Sayre, Francis B. "Criminal Conspiracy." *Harvard Law Review* 35 (1922), 393–427.

Christopher Lee Kutz

See also ATTEMPTS; INTENT; PARTIES TO CRIMINAL CONDUCT

Constituting Acts

What constitutes law? What deserves description by the word "law"? How does it come to exist?

These are the most foundational questions in the philosophy of law, and they are not, as some have thought, merely "semantic" questions (akin to whether greyhound racing or Russian roulette may be classified as sport). They are ontological questions, asking whether anything exists that is law, and if something does, what gives rise to its existence.

The object of these questions is not the "physical laws" investigated by the natural sciences but the normative laws of conduct observed by human communities. The Greek city-state of Athens in the fifth and fourth centuries B.C. sought to achieve ordered relations among human beings by means of regulations whose justifying reasons were understood and accepted by all who were fully members of the community.

Our accepting much of ancient Greek practice while repudiating many of their particular judgments expresses a distinction fundamental to any consideration of what constitutes law: the distinction between procedures and the outcomes of procedures.

We recognize the difference between these two when we distinguish the constitutional laws of a society from its criminal prohibitions, property laws, tax laws, and so on. Both kinds of laws characterize a legal community, since without a procedure by means of which specific laws are instituted no particular regulations can acquire the status of law, while without employments of the procedure to institute specific regulations such a procedure is pointless. (Still, practices may be observed as among the customs or morals of a society long before they are recognized as law; instituting a practice as law may sometimes take the form simply of courts explicitly deeming it, at some datable moment in time, to have more than customary or moral status.)

It follows that the foundational constituting act giving rise to law is agreement on a procedure for instituting specific laws, a fact signaled by our describing such a procedure as "the constitution" of a legal community. Such agreement may be reached and expressed on some identifiable occasion, or emerge and reveal itself gradually over time. Whichever is the case, the questions next arising are who must be party to the constituting of such a procedure, and can any constituted procedure issue in law?

Some persons sidestep these questions by denying that any human procedure is necessary for law. Among the earliest conceptions of law is the idea that it is established by God's constituting the world and human beings. However, if God's commands are law for us because they enjoin what is right, then our being subject to them derives from a property they have other than the fact that they are God's commands, which jettisons any inherent connection of their law-creating contents to God.

Other persons deny any dependence of law upon God but still sidestep the question by claiming that nothing more is required for an act or forbearance to be law than its being what morality requires. Yet most human communities judge that much that is morally expected of persons is not law in their societies, and ought not to be law.

Still others have alleged that nothing regarding morality is required for acts or forbearances to be law. All we require for law is that someone constitute a regime of coercion that effectively subjects a populace to control. Yet our concept of law is precisely of a control which has authority in relation to those subject to it, not merely brute power over them. Enforcement of laws presupposes laws to be enforced. Accepting the need to enforce laws does not imply accepting that coercion constitutes law.

What, then, does constitute law? If we accept that appeals to law imply justification of what is claimed or sought, basic to justification between human beings is the achievement of justice between them. If this much is granted, we may argue that two things are minimally required for law: a just procedure for identifying rules of justice among human beings and just decisions reached by that procedure.

Who must be party to the agreement on what is a just procedure—all who are to be subject to it, or only some? Must the parties to the agreement be individuals, or may they be groups? Must they be presently living persons, or may they be past generations? Through what process of deliberation must agreement be reached? Furthermore, to what, exactly, must persons agree to constitute a system that is law? Finally, once constituted, by whom and how may the system be abrogated or reconstituted? These are among the basic questions surrounding the foundational constituting act, and the answers persons give to them disclose little consensus even in the self-described "democracies" of North America and Europe.

No decision procedure, including the most just, can guarantee that only just decisions will issue from it. Even the most just procedure will sometimes result in mistaken judgments about justice. Yet such judgments may be held to be law, even by those who think them mistaken, because they issue from a procedure judged to be the most just method of identifying what should be law in this community.

As Jean-Jacques Rousseau stressed, however, more is required than that the procedure be the most just that can at this time and place be identified. Deliberations according to the procedure must be governed throughout by the intention to identify and uphold justice for all who are subject to the procedure's outcomes. Deliberations must not be governed by self-regarding intentions to advance the interests of specific individuals or groups at the expense of the rest. Moreover, mistaken judgments must be corrected over time as they are recognized to be such.

Where persons judge that the constituted arrangements by which they are governed are not just, in design or actual workings, or are corrupted in their employment by self-aggrandizing factions or groups pursuing unjust objectives, these persons may deny that outcomes of this system are law in relation to them. They may concede that these regulations are effectively enforced against them and are even widely regarded as law by others. They may judge that these others either mistake or care nothing about the necessary constituents of law but confuse these, unknowingly or knowingly, with manipulation and predation.

Thus issues of the legitimacy, and so lawfulness, of a society's governing arrangements are never assuredly settled and may explode into violence even in communities whose overwhelming majority thought such questions long closed. Hence the permanent need to constitute and enact daily a form of government that can defensibly justify a claim to lawful authority, while educating citizens capable of judging alertly and reasonably that justification and practice. Even such a polity, however, cannot be wholly proof against unreason.

References

Locke, John. *Two Treatises of Government.* 1690. Ed. Peter Laslett. New York: New American Library, 1960.

Rousseau, Jean-Jacques. *Du Contrat Social.* 1762. Ed. Ronald Grimsley. Oxford: Clarendon Press, 1972.

Wills, Garry. *Inventing America.* New York: Vintage, 1978.

Rodger Beehler

See also CONSTITUTIONALISM; LEGITIMACY

Constitutionalism

Constitutionalism arises from a faint image of an external foundation which juridical agents believe constrains their official actions. Laws are believed to gain an objectivity if, first, a jurist abstracts a rule from the text of a particular judgment or statute and, second, if the jurist can rationally link that rule to a source which preexists and, indeed, transcends the immediate circumstances surrounding the application of the particular judgment or statute. If pressed, the jurist rationally traces the grounds or *ratio* of the rule to prior and hierarchically intermediate grounds and, from there, to final ultimate grounds beyond legal language. This hierarchy of sources and grounds is manifested through institutions on a pyramidal structure with a head or final institutional source at the pinnacle of the pyramid. In a federal state, two sets of pyramids, state and federal systems, are said to constitute the state's authoritative structure. The trace of the grounds of a rule to some institution in a lineage with the ultimate head of the pyramid encourages the impression that the laws have been enacted objectively. Although one can find such a concern with the objectivity of the legislation, adjudication, and application of laws with Plato, especially in his *Laws,* the rational and impartial trace of instruments to a chain of sources particularly distinguishes Roman law.

With Thomas Hobbes (1588–1679) and Georg Hegel (1770–1831), constitutionalism takes its modern color. Hobbes described a constitution beyond the whims of the particular leaders of the modern state. Hegel abstracted a juridical person from experiential beings and then described how a juridical person wills laws and institutions until the will emanates from a living whole, called the state. Both Hobbes and Hegel associated constitutionalism with pyramidal administrative structure. Legislation, regulations, judicial decisions, and, indeed, all juridical action, to be constitutional, must be enacted within the boundaries of action which juristic agents posit, with an intent posited by higher agents on the administrative pyramid. If a state official acts beyond such boundaries, however just or wise the action may seem, such an official acts *ultra vires* or "outside authority." If pressed, a juristic agent must be able to rationally link its action or legislation with the boundaries of the administrative pyramid. Although the linkage may be traced to the head of the pyramid, the final source of constitutionalism is usually described as "the Constitution." The constitution is believed to lay down procedures and, sometimes, substantive requirements which "constitute" legal validity. As long as a jurist can rationally link any particular rule with such an ultimate foundation, constitutionalism is believed to win, however philosophers, moralists, or political theorists might view the content of the rule.

What is the character of the foundation of a constitution? Here European thought seems to offer two responses. First, particularly with such 19th-century German theorists as Hegel and Friedrich von Savigny (1779–1861), the foundation of society is associated with *unwritten practices*. Texts merely offer indicia, not the source, of the constitution. With an unwritten constitution, no one institution authors any particular constitutional rule. As Antigone describes the unwritten constitution of Thebes, its unshakable traditions "live forever, from the first of time, and no one knows when they first saw the light." The source or foundation of the duties in an unwritten constitution lies internally within the shared values of citizens or, at least, within the conventions shared amongst jurists. The jurist makes conscious what has hitherto remained inarticulate in unwritten practices.

The practices of an unwritten constitution seem so real that, to use Hegel's term borrowed from Plato's *Laws,* they seem like a "second nature" with an uncontrollable objective character. Judge, legislator, and citizen identify immediately with the unwritten practices. The government of the day resigns if defeated in the British House of Commons on a no confidence motion, no questions asked. Unlike the authored constitution in the following discussion, representations do not mediate between jurists and the constitution. Much as Antigone experienced, someone who refuses to recognize the unwritten precepts will be treated as outside the law, as an outlaw, as an "other" to the legal order of a particular state. Constitutional discourse must either assimilate delinquents into the legal order or expel them. The impersonality of the unwritten constitution reinforces the assimilative process just as its impersonality colors the violence of the act of expulsion. So long as citizens share a common religion, language, gender, race, ethnic origins, and the like, the assimilative project may be highly unrecognizable. However, if diverse religious, linguistic, or social practices characterize a society, the violence of an unwritten constitutionalism lies bare for all to observe.

A second moment of constitutionalism arises with the American and French Revolutions. For here, the complaint was made that, however one believed oneself acting according to the long-standing practices of the unwritten constitution, George III early in his reign and Louis XVI acted as if their person embodied the constitution, as if there were no ultimate foundation which transcended their personalities. European jurists responded to such a personalization of the constitution by insisting that the "founding fathers" of a state authored a particular constitution. Thus, *authored texts,* rather than unwritten, shared traditions of a juristic elite, constituted the state's foundation.

The author of the written constitution takes two manifestations. First, Thomas Hobbes and Jean-Jacques Rousseau (1712–1778) redirect the concept of constitutionalism from conventions to authors whose texts are colored with the sanctity of the name "The Constitution." The authors of such a founding text resemble an unwritten constitution, unidentifiable in time and place. Hobbes and Rousseau locate the founding authors in a "state of nature." In Hobbes' case, the founding authors agree to be constrained by a make-believe representative, called the Leviathan, whose "actors" or juristic agents legislate in the name of the representative. In Rousseau's case, the authors in a fictitious state of nature contract to be bound by their general universal will that transcends the particular wills of citizens in a civil society. The will(s) of authors in a state of nature constitute the foundation of all laws in a civil society. With respect to both philosophers, all legislative and judicial acts are constitutionally valid and politically legitimate if a jurist can rationally link the acts to the covenants or general will of the founding authors situated prior to civil society. The invisible authors function to render the private acts of juristic agents in civil society impersonal, objective, and, therefore, constitutional.

The written constitution takes a second turn when the origins of a constitution are believed to be situated in the records of historically contingent authors rather than in the conventions or general will of invisible authors situated in a state of nature. Here, the search for the original intent of such historical authors takes two manifestations. The first manifestation occurred with the American Constitution or the French Declaration of the Rights of Man; jurists ground all legal doctrines in the original intent of the actual historical authors of such basic texts. For matters unforeseen by the authors, the jurist generalizes a political theory of the founding fathers and extends the principles of the theory to the configured circumstances before a contemporary judge. The founding fathers are believed to bind future legislatures and judges even though the historical authors did not specifically address the circumstances at issue.

C

The second manifestation of the historically contingent author occurred when Jeremy Bentham (1748–1832) and John Austin (1790–1859), among others, attributed constitutionalism to the rigid application of the enactments of a sovereign legislature. A.V. Dicey popularizes the theory. A legislature was described as sovereign if its authority to enact laws was unfettered. A sovereign legislature could not bind future legislatures. The only constraint was that the legislature comply with the proper manner and form requirements of what constituted an "enactment" and a "legislature." For example, an enactment might be defined as a text authorized by a majority of two-thirds of elected legislative members. In like vein, a "legislature" might be defined as being constituted from two houses of the legislature plus the consent of the head of state. If only one of the three institutions authored a text, the text failed to carry the authenticity of a "legislature." In the Benthamite moment of constitutionalism, in contrast with that of an unwritten constitution, one can locate the ultimate foundation of all civilly posited laws in a particular act of human creation contextualized at a particular time and place.

The constitutionalism of a modern state, as just outlined, presupposes that an external final source or ground constrains the acts of juristic agents. Without finality, a text cannot represent a rule: it may be continuously changed as if it were a textual fragment. Since World War II, the concept of constitutionalism has taken a third turn, which brings to consciousness the end point that legal positivism had hitherto presupposed. Hans Kelsen (1881–1973) probably made the most systematic study of such an end point in several of his works. The end point of constitutionalism, he argued, remains unauthored in that it is a presupposed *act of thought*. Although an act of will is directed toward an external object, an act of thought has no such directed object. Before a norm is posited, there must be a prior *Grundnorm* (basic norm) that one ought to obey the norm. The "act of thought" remains unrecognized until jurists, through their ratiocination of statutes and judicial decisions, transform their own historically contingent assumptions into an external justificatory grounding for reasoning. In *The Concept of Law,* H.L.A. Hart (1907–1993) described the unrecognized or "unstated judicial practices" as secondary to ordinarily posited rules. Once

recognized after they had been applied, the practices were stated as a "rule of recognition." Even Ronald Dworkin, who in *Law's Empire* privileges hermeneutics in legal reasoning, situates constitutionalism in an idealized realm of a single grand narrative that judges draw from their own justificatory arguments about the constitution. Dworkin situates the foundation of a constitution in the interpreter, not in the founding author, of texts.

A common theme characterizes this third moment of constitutionalism. Because the constitution is believed to be authored and because the act of any juristic agent must be traced to the will of such an author, it is crucial that all legislative enactments clearly state their author's intent. It is not surprising in this light that judges not infrequently hold an enactment constitutionally void because of its vagueness. After all, if the author's will counts for all, the author must use clear and unambiguous language in order that its surrogates understand the intent which the authored text represents. More, one must be able to identify the author's act of promulgation at a particular place and time. Constitutionalism in both its mode of the "will of the sovereign legislature" and the "will of the founding fathers" is caught in a web of interconnected texts. The lawyer must trace the intent of one historical author to that of a prior author situated higher on the pyramidal hierarchy until one reaches a final historically contingent author at the end point of constitutional reasoning.

During the 1970s and 1980s, both on the European continent and in Anglo-American legal scholarship, the objectivism and formalism of this third moment of constitutionalism came under attack. Hegel set the background for such a critical theory when he reoriented European thought to moments of an experienced consciousness. Max Horkheimer (1895–1973) and Theodor Adorno (1903–1969), along with other members of the Frankfurt School, identified how legal consciousness becomes reified in a modern legal system. Such a reification helped to explain the rise of instrumental rationality in totalitarian states. Instrumental legal reasoning assumed the givenness of its end point and thereby disguised how the social values in the ratiocination from one grounds to another and, ultimately, to a constitution, became ends. The means of constitutional analysis had become the end of a modern legal order. Hobbes and Rousseau,

Bentham and Austin, Kelsen and Dworkin assumed that the external situs of a transcendent foundation, hitherto associated with constitutionalism, objectified legislated enactments, even though the foundation itself was inaccessible. This objectivity of an external inaccessible foundation concealed the particular experiences of both interpreter and nonexpert. In *Truth and Method,* Hans-Georg Gadamer (1900–) particularly exposed the importance of the interpreter's environing world in constitutional discourse.

Jurists begin to reconsider the very concept of constitutionalism when they realize that, whether unwritten or written, whether authored by founding fathers or a transcendent source, juristic agents on the pyramidal organization of the state had supported heinous treatment of human subjects. The knowledge of the Holocaust finally brought into question the nature of constitutionalism after Auschwitz. Both unwritten constitutions, such as Germany's under Hitler or South Africa's under apartheid, and written constitutions, such as the Soviet Union's under Stalin, authorized the torture and death of millions of residents. Indeed, according to a United Nations' study, over nineteen million persons were killed between 1900 and 1991 in the struggle for the recognition of constitutional authority. The open exhibitions of torture, ethnic cleansing, concentration camps, and social destitution all implicitly and even explicitly authorized in the name of unwritten conventions, founding texts, or sovereign legislatures, have stigmatized the twentieth century. Even Dicey himself, the great constitutionalist of the British Constitution, understood constitutionalism in terms of a sovereign legislature and an "equality before the law," both of which contributed to the impartial administration of the legislature's posited rules. The content of legislated rules mattered little so long as the legislature had complied with the proper manner and form requirements.

Twentieth-century state barbarism has worked to reorient the theory of constitutionalism. First, constitutional theorists, influenced by Gadamer, have focused upon the importance of the interpreter of the texts of a sovereign legislature or the founding fathers. The objectivism of both the unwritten and authored constitutions has collapsed into a hermeneutics that places moral and political responsibility for state acts in the hands of the interpreter as much as in the authors of texts themselves. Second, strains of critical legal studies and feminist legal theory have exposed how constitutional discourse reifies the concrete lived experiences of particular subjects. Here, the objectivism of the unwritten and the authored constitutions, as well as the hermeneutics of the judicial interpreter, give way to a phenomenology of judicial reasoning. Third, departing from the experiential world of the interpreter and influenced by Charles Peirce (1839–1914) and Ferdinand de Saussure (1857–1913), theorists of constitutionalism have focused upon the web of signs that represents the concepts of a cognitive world. Configurations of signs construct the author, not the other way around. The fourth and final contemporary shift in the image of a constitution claims that the hierarchic administrative pyramid, so crucial to constitutionalism, emulates the well-known patriarchy of the western European family. More, the trace of the *ratios* of statutes and judicial decisions to some external transcendent author or concept, such as the "greatest good," manifests the voice associated with the male gender in western European culture. In particular, the authoritative configurations of signs construct an imaginary father in whose name all juridical officials write and speak. Constitutionalism thereby joins with authority to conceal the lived languages of all nonexperts, whatever the gender, ethnic origin, or race. The deference to presupposed external foundation of legal authority draws from a particular image of a constitution that has dominated modern legal discourses to the present day.

References

Conklin, William. *Images of a Constitution.* Toronto: University of Toronto Press, 1989. Reprint, 1993.

———. "The Legal Theory of Horkheimer and Adorno." *Windsor Yearbook of Access to Justice* 5 (1985), 230–257.

Dicey, A.V. *Introduction to the Study of the Law of the Constitution.* Intro. E.C.S. Wade. London: Macmillan, 1962.

Heuston, R.F.V. *Essays in Constitutional Law.* 1961. 2d ed. Oxford: Oxford University Press, 1964.

Kelsen, Hans. "The Function of a Constitution." In *Essays on Kelsen,* ed. R. Tur and William Twining. Oxford: Clarendon Press, 1986.

Lyotard, Jean-François. *The Differend: Phrases in Dispute*. Trans. Georges Van Den Abbeele. Minneapolis: University of Minnesota Press, 1983.

Plato. *Crito*. Trans. Hugh Tredennick. In *Collected Dialogues of Plato*, ed. Edith Hamilton and Huntington Cairns. Princeton: Princeton University Press, 1961.

Rawls, John. *A Theory of Justice*. Cambridge MA: Harvard University Press, 1971.

Sophocles. *Antigone*. Trans. Richard C. Jebb. Amsterdam: Servio, 1962.

Williams, Patricia. *The Alchemy of Race and Rights*. Cambridge: Harvard University Press, 1991.

William E. Conklin

Continental Philosophy of Law

See CIVILIAN PHILOSOPHY OF LAW

Contractual Obligation

Because not every promise or agreement will be legally enforced, it seems important to find some coherent and comprehensive theory to explain the ones that are. Central to the philosophically interesting body of law known as contracts (not under seal) is the question of their obligation. The issue exhibits a general debate over how positive obligations are to be grounded: whether they are given to oneself or how often they are imposed upon one from abroad. Without a general theory, "contract" would be nothing but a name for a large group, resembling a collection, of small laws (each narrowed presumably until coherence is achieved) for retail sales, insurance, land, services, trips by bus, and so forth. Several general theories of contractual obligation have been proposed, for example, will, reliance, bargain, efficiency, and justice.

The *will* theory focuses on what is intentionally undertaken by the party in the position of the promisor. In a bilateral contract each party, by definition, is both a promisor and promisee. If the promisor's subjectivity is sufficient to determine a contract's existence and content, then it is possible for a promisee's reliance, based on a different but reasonable understanding, to have been misplaced. The *reliance* theory, on the other hand, focuses on what has happened to the party in the position of someone taken to be a promisee. If this party's reliance itself were alone sufficient to determine a contract, then the promisor may face a suit that, given one's intentions, honestly comes as a surprise. Of course, if the promisee has not as yet relied, then there is no basis for an action. With either of these sometimes-advocated theories of contractual obligation, fairness seems to suffer. Objectivism is a way to determine contracts from the point of view of a reasonable third party. Logically, objectivism (along with subjectivism) disallows both parties from being right when they disagree about the contract, but it also allows (unlike subjectivism) for the finding of a contract that neither party had had in contemplation. That must seem, of course, a strange result. Normally, however, objectivism is suggested to help reliers when their understanding of the contract had been reasonable but different from the subjective intention of the promisor.

The *bargain* theory seeks to find the agreement that the parties made; what had someone offered and has someone accepted it? Ideally, parties who *have* an agreement are *in* agreement, because, as a matter of the logic of offer and acceptance, individuals cannot accept an offer they have not received and understood; indeed, in a bargain each has given up something to the other based upon a common understanding (at some level) of the undertaking. What each party gives in the creation of a contract is "consideration" for the promise of the other. To promise is to change one's moral position in a process that may change one's legal position too. In the case of bilateral contracts, the contractual nexus predates both performances and is grounded in the promises exchanged as consideration for each other. In the case of unilateral contracts, by definition, the offeree's performance *is* acceptance and so, as a logical matter, the contract comes to exist exactly when the offeree performs. If the offeree does not perform there is no breach, for he had not promised anything. When performance does occur, the offeror has then automatically promised what was tendered. The notion of a bargained-for agreement fits better the idea of a bilateral contract than it does the unilateral contract, so there is a problem of comprehensiveness for the bargain theory. Whether simple barters are contracts depends upon whether promising occurs when swaps are done—at best barters are unilateral.

A contract gives one a right to expect something from another person; this expectation need not induce reliance even if normally it would. Of course, gift promises—or any "bare" promise—would not, despite reliance, be enforced when a bargain is required. (Reliance cannot be cited by a relier as the consideration given to bring a contract into existence, for reliance, to be reliance, is placed upon an already existing contract.) At some level of abstraction, it is correct to say that "agreements" are contracts. Yet parties, making an agreement, are not always able to anticipate everything that might occur as they seek to act upon their bargain. So a question arises about how far *into* agreement parties must have been for a contract to exist and what terms exist to fill the gaps. Those who support a subjective approach will be reluctant to carry obligation beyond what can be (logically, reasonably) implied from what the parties actually intended as they contracted. The force of a subjective limitation will not be felt by the objective approach, where unthought-of obligations may be found for the parties to obey, perhaps, according to what distributive justice would require.

Not every agreement or bargain will be enforced at law. For example, despite offer and acceptance both parties were legal infants or insane at the time, or the contract promised the commission of a crime or entering into slavery. Such types of invalidation are typically based on concerns of morality and policy, but their role as limits upon contracting is no objection as such to the basic analysis found in the bargain theory. The theory itself is, of course, grounded in moral ideas about fidelity and—recognizing the exceptions—on the general importance to human life of seeing agreements kept. Because contracts attempt to order the hereafter in this fashion, basic to everything is the so-called expectation interest. Even if injuries suffered in reliance are morally more pressing for relief than loss of expectation (which need involve no real setback), the main point of contract law is not to protect reliance among people as such but to assist in the planning of one's affairs as they work their way into the future. To speak of the main point of contract law suggests that there are other grander theories of contractual obligation. As explanatory accounts these take the law to be coherent and purport to find a comprehensive basis for the law that is not dis-

closed upon on its face, for example, by the promise or the bargain. *Efficiency* analysis, for instance, would explain why agreements or promises are enforced (and some not enforced) by showing that the typical rules minimize waste and that different rules would run against this value. Such accounts are not designed as criticism of the law. Yet critics may accept a particular explanatory account but condemn the values thus exposed: one might point to the injustices that markets produce and urge interventions to improve the law on some basis other than economics. An apologist, on the other hand, might find that the law as explained secures the value of individual voluntary choice (which could ground the will theory) or even distributive justice as it stands.

References

Atiyah, Patrick. *The Rise and Fall of Freedom of Contract.* Oxford: Clarendon Press, 1979.

Collins, Hugh. *The Law of Contract.* London: Weidenfeld and Nicolson, 1986.

Fried, Charles. *Contract as Promise.* Cambridge MA: Harvard University Press, 1981.

Gordley, James. *The Philosophical Origins of Modern Contract Doctrine.* Oxford: Clarendon Press, 1991.

Kronman, Anthony T., and Richard A. Posner. *The Economics of Contract Law.* Boston: Little, Brown, 1979.

Richard Bronaugh

See also JUSTICE IN CONTRACT, CIVILIAN

Contractualist Philosophy of Law

Contractualist theory grounds moral permissibility or political legitimacy in social agreement. Contractarian (contractualist) moral or political theories hold that an action, practice, law, constitution, or social structure, is morally permissible, legitimate, or just if and only if it, or principles to which it conforms, would be agreed to by the members of society under certain specified conditions. The first comprehensive statement of contractarianism came in 1651 from Thomas Hobbes (1588–1679) in his *Leviathan;* he offered a contractarian justification for almost unlimited powers of the state. Other important historical figures associated with contractarianism include John Locke (1632–1704), Jean-Jacques

Rousseau (1712–1778), and Immanuel Kant (1724–1804). Since the publication of John Rawls' *A Theory of Justice* in 1971 there has been a significant renewal of interest (by economists, political scientists, and philosophers) in contractarian ethical and political theory. Other important recent contractarian authors include James Buchanan, David Gauthier, Jean Hampton, Gregory Kavka, Jürgen Habermas, and T.M. Scanlon.

Usually, contractarian theories are understood as normative theories about what makes things right or just. Sometimes, however, they are understood as metanormative claims about the meaning of rightness and justness. In addition, contractarian theories have been advocated as ethical theories of permissibility for the actions or practices of individuals, and as political theories of the legitimacy or justness of social structures (for example, legal systems). For the philosophy of law it is usually the latter that is relevant. Contractarian theories also vary as to whether they are direct (with the object of agreement being the object of moral assessment, for example, agreement on a specific legal structure) or indirect (with the object of agreement being rules for assessing the objects of assessment, for example, agreement on rules for assessing legal structures).

Contractarian theories differ in their specification of the circumstances under which agreement is to take place. Concerning the general structure of the choice situation, some of the main issues are: (1) What items are on the agenda? (2) What will happen if the parties do not agree (that is, what is the nonagreement outcome, for instance, a war of all against all)? (3) What are the dynamics of interaction in the choice situation (for example, are coalitions allowed)? (4) What is the principle of agreement (for instance, unanimity)?

Concerning the parties to the agreement, some of the main issues are: (1) Who are the parties in the choice situation (who counts as a member of society)? (2) What are the beliefs of the parties (for example, do they know what their position in society, their capacities, and their desires are, or is there a veil of ignorance)? (3) What are the desires of the parties like (for example, are they mutually unconcerned, envious, or care about fairness)? (4) How do they make choices (for example, are they utility maximizers)?

There are two broad approaches to the specifications of the circumstances of agreement. Hobbesian approaches provide realistic, morally neutral, specifications of the circumstances and attempt thereby to reduce morality to individual or collective rationality. Hobbes, Gauthier, Kavka, and Hampton are all in this tradition. Kantian approaches attempt to provide morally loaded specifications of the circumstances and thereby reject any attempt to reduce morality to pure prudential rationality. Rawls' veil of ignorance (blocking the parties' knowledge of their capacities and positions) is one such approach. The specification by Scanlon and Habermas that the parties are motivated by a desire to reach a fair and reasonable agreement is another sort of kantian approach.

Within the contractarian framework, then, there is a great variety of approaches, and there is debate about which sort of approach is the most plausible account. We shall now consider some external criticisms of the entire contractarian framework.

Contractarianism is sometimes charged with ignoring the interests of beings (such as animals, infants, and fetuses) that are not able to communicate linguistically, make commitments, and so on. Although some contractarian theories (such as Gauthier's) do ignore these interests, this is not an essential part of contractarianism. Some theories (such as Scanlon's) take these interests into account by allowing that trustees representing the interests of such beings are parties to the agreement.

A more fundamental criticism of contractarianism, often raised by marxists, feminists, and communitarians, is that it is individualistic. Contractarianism is indeed *normatively* individualistic, which is to say that it claims that the ultimate right-making features are features of individual people (namely, their consent), not irreducible features of collectivities. It does not, however, assume *ontogenetic* (or developmental) individualism, the view that denies that individual people are shaped and formed by the social context in which they find themselves. Nor does it assume *ontological* individualism, the view that individual persons are ontologically prior to society. Nor is contractarianism committed to the view that people are (inevitably or contingently) *egoistic* or materialistic in their desires (for example, caring only about the bundle of material goods that they control). Many contractarian theorists have made such assumptions, but such assumptions are not essential to contractarianism.

Of course, even if normative individualism is accepted, there is the further question of *what features* of individuals determine what is right and wrong. Contractarians claim that it is hypothetical consent, but rights theorists (such as libertarians) claim that it is nonviolation of rights (such as respecting actual agreements), utilitarians claim that it is promotion of welfare, and some feminists claim that it is concern for others. Even assuming that consent is normatively significant, why should we think that *hypothetical* consent has any normative force? (Is it morally permissible for you to take my car without asking me, just because I would have consented had you asked?) Given that most contemporary moral theorists are normative individualists, most of the external criticisms take the form of attacking the relevance of hypothetical consent. Responding to such criticisms is one of the main tasks that a contractarian must undertake.

References

Gauthier, David. *Morals by Agreement.* London: Oxford University Press, 1986.

Habermas, Jürgen. *Justification and Application: Remarks on Discourse Ethics.* Trans. Ciaran Cronin. Cambridge MA: MIT Press, 1993.

Hampton, Jean. *Hobbes and the Social Contract Tradition.* Cambridge MA: Cambridge University Press, 1986.

Kant, Immanuel. *Groundwork of the Metaphysics of Morals.* 1785. Ed. H.J. Patton. New York: Harper Torchbooks, 1958.

Kavka, Gregory. *Hobbesian Moral and Political Theory.* Princeton: Princeton University Press, 1986.

Locke, John. *The Second Treatise of Government.* 1690. Ed. Thomas Peardon. Indianapolis IN: Bobbs-Merrill, 1952.

Rousseau, Jean-Jacques. *Contrat Social.* 1762. In *Political Writings,* ed. C.E. Vaughan. Cambridge: Cambridge University Press, 1915.

Rawls, John. *Political Liberalism.* New York: Columbia University, 1993.

———. *A Theory of Justice.* Cambridge MA: Belknap–Harvard University Press, 1971.

Scanlon, T.M. "Contractualism and Utilitarianism." In *Utilitarianism and Beyond,* ed. Amartya Sen and Bernard Williams, 103–128. Cambridge MA: Cambridge University Press, 1982.

Peter Vallentyne

See also SOCIAL CONTRACT

C

Convention and Custom

Convention generally is best understood in contradistinction to nature. The former represents the claim that law is made exclusively by the human faculties, while the latter represents the notion that humans can simply follow objective moral truth that is in force everywhere for all humans at all times. The distinction has existed in Western legal theory since the earliest investigations into the character of law.

Convention generally can be divided into two categories, those of convention and custom. While both have been described as guides for regular behavior in societies, custom is described as tradition, a set of norms that have arisen through a history of practical experience in the process of fulfilling basic physical needs and wants. It is usually understood as the product of social interaction among all the individuals in a given society ("the people"), although traditionally recognized authorities of the society ("rulers") may have a disproportionate influence on the development of custom. Even then, custom in its purest form is the unconscious development of regular behavior into norms that are either prescriptive and proscriptive rules, including sanctions against violators, or nonprescriptive and nonproscriptive rules constituting practical expectations about social interaction—norms that might be rejected or modified if rationally examined in light of new circumstances, needs, and wants.

In the early development of many societies, customary norms were not understood as discursive rules of cause and consequence in practical life, but as moral imperatives that derive from a supernatural or divine source (often associated with rulers) and constitute philosophical or religious justification for social practices. They arise, however, to meet recurrent social difficulties and represent agreed guides for future interaction. Such norms may be primarily internal, as logical or intuitive cognitions within individuals, or they may be primarily external, expressed in the form of rewards and punishments imposed by others. Both can vary in intensity and viability according to the present importance of the social problem that the norm was intended to resolve. Custom, then, includes prescriptive and proscriptive norms of religious practice (as in ceremonial ritual), as well as norms coordinating the pursuits of needs and wants.

As a conscious distinction emerged between moral imperatives and human choice in the satisfaction of needs, wants, and beliefs—between imperative value and human fact—human systems of law became necessary, and legal theory required a more formal definition of law. Thus arose the distinction between law as unconscious conventional custom and law as a conscious conventional creation of social norms, the latter of which retained the distinction between law deriving exclusively from the will of rulers and law deriving from all the people in a particular society (conventionalism).

Convention is often viewed by natural law theorists as the exclusive will of rulers who hold power over subjects. Under this view of conventionalism, the interests of the rulers are the only guides for law, which likely results in the exploitation of subjects. This view of convention is called legal positivism, a distinct school of legal thought wherein law is called a mere social fact without any necessary connection to morality, and legal obligation is seen as rooted in fear of external coercion. However, convention need not constitute positivism.

Twentieth-century conventionalism has emphasized the conscious construction of legal systems based on empirical observations of factual and normative characteristics of human action. This brings to the forefront of legal theory the apparent dichotomy between law as a social fact, the positivist view, and law as objective normative truth, the natural law view, each of which favors a particular method of inquiry. Positivists rely on empirical observation of the relationship between law as the commanded will of rulers and the habit of obedience in their subjects, whereas natural law theorists focus on the examination of ideas to find objective or transcendent normative truth. Conventionalists rely on empirical observation to discover the factual *and* normative elements in human action associated with law, although such conventionalists as Thomas Hobbes have extended convention to a voluntary divine will responsible for creating a fixed factual nature.

The most recent theories of convention have attempted to reconcile legal positivism's purely factual interpretation of law with the purely normative interpretation of natural law theory through a theory of conventional coordination. Drawing from the social sciences, particularly economic theory as with Friedrich von Hayek, conventionalists begin with a description of human nature as fundamentally individual, motivated by desire, and able to make rational choices among options of fact and value, that is, to examine available choices of action and speculate about how to attain future objectives through foresight. Such cognitive behavior generates personal expectations for success in attaining individual ends. Reasonably certain expectations lead to action to attain those ends. However, when individuals act as such among others—which social interaction also may be a necessary characteristic of humans—a problem of coordination arises: pursuits of ends inevitably conflict. Law as convention provides a solution for coordinating these individual pursuits and, more important, interaction among human beings.

Conventional laws provide a society with the rule of law, a set of cognitive rules (internalized norms) that establish common rational expectations about social action upon which each individual or association of individuals can base plans for pursuing ends. Legal convention does not preclude voluntary collective action, but facilitates it just as well as individual action.

Conventionalism therefore resolves the apparent dichotomy between law as merely a fact of commands tied to sanctions against violators, and law as a transcendent moral truth, the interpretation or reality of which is problematic. Conventionalism is factual in that enforced legal rules are publicly known by all in the given society, and it is normative in the value each individual places on the peaceful pursuit of their own ends with reasonable expectations for success, which expectations are provided by legal rules coordinating the pursuits of numerous individuals. Thus, conventionalism creates obligation through agreement, avoiding legal positivism's potential tyranny of commands imposed by brute force and the political violence often involved in trying to impose an objective moral truth on an entire society.

This kind of law requires certain attributes in the character of law itself. First, that laws must be rules, not commands; that is, they must be contingent, requiring no necessary action for compliance but only prescribing direction in how to act if one acts. For example, a rule that requires driving on a given side of the road, if one chooses to drive, coordinates the actions of all drivers to arrive at their destinations. Under conventionalism, law dictates no means or ends but only how means will be used to attain ends.

While its rational character can be associated with abstract game theory, conventionalism attains normative force in a unanimous agreement among a set of individuals to follow legal rules that facilitate the peaceful voluntary pursuit of interests and principles. Such an agreement to rules constitutes an "internal morality" within individuals, which decreases the necessity for a positivistic external morality of sanctions against violators. For a set of such rules to exist, however, they must be (1) possible to follow; (2) known through publicity; (3) general, applying to everyone within the jurisdiction, and equally applied; (4) clear, coherent, and relatively stable; (5) prospective, and retrospective only when compensation can reasonably fulfill past expectations based on law; (6) enforced with certainty; (7) capable of resolution in disputes and reversible under constituted fundamental rules for adjudication and rule making when circumstances require it; and (8) subject to the consent of each subject of the law, which includes the availability of exit from the jurisdiction. These conventional characteristics of law attempt to define the conditions of unanimity, although preservation of the constituted fundamental agreement may require the tolerance of strong moral beliefs that go beyond these conditions.

References

Fuller, Lon L. *The Morality of Law.* New Haven: Yale University Press, 1969.

Kelly, J.M. *A Short History of Western Legal Theory.* New York: Oxford University Press, 1992.

Oakeshott, Michael. "The Rule of Law." In *On History and Other Essays.* Oxford: Basil Blackwell, 1983.

Postema, Gerald J. "Coordination and Convention at the Foundations of Law." *Journal of Legal Studies* 11 (January 1982), 165–203.

Reynolds, Noel B. "Grounding the Rule of Law" and "Law as Convention." *Ratio Juris* 2, no. 1 (March 1989), 1–16, 105–120.

Noel B. Reynolds
Thomas J. Lowery

See also CONTRACTUALIST PHILOSOPHY OF LAW; CUSTOMARY LAW; NATURAL LAW; POSITIVISM, LEGAL

C

Corrective Justice

The concept of corrective justice (equivalently, commutative or rectificatory justice) was formulated by Aristotle in Book V of the *Nicomachean Ethics,* was adopted in its aristotelian form by Thomas Aquinas, and has been revived in recent decades by influential figures in American jurisprudence who may or may not be indebted to Aristotle.

Aristotle explains that from the standpoint of corrective justice it does not matter whether a good man has defrauded or otherwise wronged a bad man, or vice versa. The law looks only to the character of the injury, treating the parties as equal before the law and thus considering only whether wrongful conduct by one has inflicted injury on the other. The judge tries to restore equality by imposing a penalty on the wrongdoer, thus nullifying the wrongdoer's gain so that the preexisting balance between the parties is, so far as possible, restored.

This spare concept contains two, possibly three or four, historically, politically, and philosophically significant features. The first is the idea of judging a dispute without regard to the character, merit, or social status of the disputants. This is a cornerstone of the modern idea of the rule of law, which existed in embryo in the ancient Greek idea, of which Aristotle's concept of corrective justice is in part the elaboration, of justice as a blind goddess—blind, that is, to the identity of the disputants as distinct from the character of the dispute. Although today we take for granted that adjudication should be "without respect to persons" (as the federal judicial oath puts it), this is not an inevitable or instinctual element of dispute resolution, and Aristotle's formulation of it is a notable milestone on the road to the modern conception of the rule of law.

The second notable feature of Aristotle's concept of corrective justice is the idea that for every wrong there should be a remedy that annuls it. The historical importance of this idea lies in the fact that, to the extent it is implemented, it makes the system of legal justice a more or less emotionally satisfactory substitute for vengeance by promising the victim of a wrong that the balance between him and the wrongdoer, which the wrong disturbed, will be righted.

Third, although it is unclear whether this is an organic part of the concept or merely a reflection of the privatized character of law enforcement in the Athens of Aristotle's time, corrective justice requires or presupposes a machinery of rectification that is activated by the victim himself (or his family). The remedy must run directly in favor of the victim (or his survivors), thus "buying off" the victim, who might otherwise seek revenge. Again, one sees corrective justice as a substitute for revenge. Publicly enforced criminal law is another substitute for revenge and, to the extent that it restores the balance between victim and criminal by annulling the latter's gain, whether pecuniary or psychic, from the act, the requirements of corrective justice would appear to be met. A public system of criminal law enforcement presupposes, however, a strong state. Early societies, having weak public institutions, often opted for a private system of law enforcement. Viewed historically, corrective justice is a phase or theory of law enforcement that is intermediate between the vengeance system of a stateless society and the publicly administered criminal justice system of a modern society.

A fourth possible element of the aristotelian concept, closely related to the third, is the idea that there must be ex post (after the fact) as well as ex ante (preventive) remedies for wrongful acts. Laws that punish speeding or unsuccessful attempts to commit crime, or that seek to deter crime by heavily punishing a small fraction of criminals in order to economize on the costs of law enforcement, or that require that dangerous activities be licensed, illustrate ex ante remedies. The award of damages for a tort or a breach of contract, and the imposition of punishment for a completed crime, illustrate ex post remedies. It is possible that Aristotle, in this respect anticipating Immanuel Kant, believed that corrective justice requires that if on a particular occasion a wrongdoer is not prevented or deterred, with the result that is a crime or other wrongful act is committed, the victim should be entitled to demand a remedy.

The third and fourth points together support, even if they do not necessarily entail, the idea already alluded to, of *private* law in the sense of a privately activated body of principles and remedies for maintaining the equilibrium among private persons by correcting wrongful disturbances of the equilibrium. Tort law and contract law, in which private persons seek legal redress for wrongful injuries to them, are familiar examples of private law. In a system of private law the only indispensable public officials are the judges—and even they may not be strictly necessary. Athenian "judges" were not public officials; they were akin to jurors.

Aristotle's concept of correct justice delineates important formal features of legal justice, but it is important to understand that they are indeed formal rather than substantive. The concept is not designed to indicate which acts are wrongful, or even to specify the details of the remedy. The definition of wrongs, in his theory of justice, belongs to the sphere of distributive justice, which determines entitlements. While corrective justice requires a remedy for the wrongful taking or destruction of an entitlement, it is not clear that the remedy must run in favor of the victim, and not be a public remedy that punishes the wrongdoer without providing any material compensation to the victim. Historically, and to some extent conceptually, corrective justice is linked to a private system of law enforcement, akin to our modern tort and contract law, but, strictly speaking, the institutional details, such as the choice between private and public officers, are, like the scope and definition of entitlements, distinct from corrective justice.

Recently, legal scholars such as Richard Epstein and legal philosophers such as Jules Coleman have tried to derive stronger conclusions from the concept of corrective justice than those suggested above. Epstein has argued that corrective justice requires that the dominant principle of tort liability be strict liability (liability without fault), since otherwise there will be many cases in which an injured person has no remedy for an injury inflicted by another person. Aristotle, however, requires rectification only when the injured person has been wronged, and if we may judge from the discussion of wrongful conduct in Section 8 of Book V of the *Nicomachean Ethics,* Aristotle himself would not have considered unintentional injuries, even when they were due to the injurer's negligence, to be wrongs requiring correction.

Coleman has raised the question whether a no-fault system of accident compensation, under which the victim of an accident may not be able to sue the injurer even if the latter was negligent, but is instead limited to seeking compensation from his own (first-party) insurer, is consistent with corrective justice. He concludes that it is, because he regards the essence of corrective justice as compensation of victims rather than the punishment or other sanctioning of injurers. He realizes that in so interpreting corrective justice he is departing from Aristotle's concept. Indeed, he is turning it on its head, since in a no-fault system the injurer is let off scot-free; there is no correction. Alternatively, however, no-fault might be viewed as a matter of redefining rights so that a negligent injurer is no longer deemed a wrongdoer. Since corrective justice in Aristotle's sense is about the adjudication and enforcement of whatever substantive rights people have rather than about what substantive rights they should have, such a redefinition is not problematic from the standpoint of corrective justice; hence no-fault does not violate Aristotle's concept. In contrast, a system of criminal punishment (arguably the system that we have today for most crimes) under which criminals are rarely punished, but when they are punished are punished very severely in recognition of the likelihood that they got away with many crimes before they were apprehended, may offend the aristotelian concept. Correction is sporadic; most wrongful acts are not followed by remedial action; most victims of crime get no relief at all.

It may be interesting to compare Aristotle's conception of corrective justice with other influential theories of justice. The closest is the retributive, which rests on a similar notion of disturbed equilibrium and bears a similar (though even closer) relation to justice as vengeance. Retribution, as distinguished from simple revenge, insists that the punishment equal the crime (an eye for an eye, not two eyes for one eye—unless possibly the victim had only one eye before his assailant put out the other one), but does not take a position on the equality of persons before the law or emphasize private-law remedies. The economic approach to law resembles the corrective-justice approach in insisting that there should be remedies (in effect, prices) for wrongs and that the law's principles apply equally to good and bad people; but it does not privilege ex post over ex ante remedies.

The foundational significance of Aristotle's concept cannot be doubted. Whether the concept has utility in dealing with contemporary issues of liability may, however, be questioned.

References

Aristotle. *Nichomachean Ethics*, Bk. V, Sec. 2–4, 8. In *The Complete Works of Aristotle: The Revised Oxford Translation*, vol. 2, ed., Jonathan Barnes, 1783–1787, 1791–1793. Princeton: Princeton University Press, 1985.

Coleman, Jules L. "Corrective Justice and Wrongful Gain." In *Markets, Morals and the Law*. Cambridge: Cambridge University Press, 1988.

———. *Risks and Wrongs*. Cambridge: Cambridge University Press, 1992.

"Corrective Justice and Formalism: The Care One Owes One's Neighbors." *Iowa Law Review* 77 (1992), 403.

Epstein, Richard A. "Nuisance Law: Corrective Justice and Its Utilitarian Constraints." *Journal of Legal Studies* 8 (1979), 49.

Hurd, Heidi M. "Corrective Injustice to Corrective Justice." *Notre Dame Law Review* 67 (1991), 51.

Posner, Richard A. "The Concept of Corrective Justice in Recent Theories of Tort Law." *Journal of Legal Studies* 10 (1981), 187.

———. *The Problems of Jurisprudence*. Cambridge MA: Harvard University Press, 1990.

Schwarz, Alan. "Responsibility and Tort Liability." *Ethics* 97 (1986). 270.

Weinrib, Ernest J. "Legal Formalism: On the Immanent Rationality of Law." *Yale Law Journal* 97 (1988), 950.

Richard A. Posner

See also DISTRIBUTIVE JUSTICE; TORTS

Cossio, Carlos (1902–1987)

The discipline of legal philosophy in Argentina owes much to the work of Carlos Cossio. However, Cossio's influence decreased substantially after he was removed in 1956 from his post as a professor at the National University of Buenos Aires by the military government which had overthrown the government of Juan Perón (1895–1974) the previous year.

Cossio's objective was to build a philosophy of the science of law; he wrote about the ontology of law, formal legal logic, transcendental legal logic, and the axiology of law. His first major work looks at the place of the *Grundnorm* (basic norm) in a pure theory of revolution. While remaining faithful to Hans Kelsen's normativism, he attempts to move beyond it in his most important work, *La Teoría egológica del Derecho y el Concepto jurídico de Libertad,* where he draws on Gerhart Husserl's conception of the transcendental ego to develop an egological theory of law.

An egological theory of law has as its object of knowledge the actions of people, human behavior. By looking to human experience—which itself arises in a cultural context—to explain law, Cossio believes that he can overcome the shortcomings of idealist and positivist theories of law and discover the objective meaning of legal concepts. In order to rise to the transcendental level, one must show how people relate to one another. Because constant originality and freedom characterize human action, it is only possible to have an existential understanding of human behavior in its intersubjective relationships.

This element of human experience cannot be discovered either by idealism, which simply uses a formal logic (which by definition limits itself to natural structures), or by positivism, which takes law as a natural object governed by the principle of causation. To Kelsen's analysis of the logical structure of norms, Cossio wants to add an axiological dimension by integrating the human experience into the science of law. Phenomenology is the philosophical methodology which can transcend the limits of idealism and realism and allow us to study legal objects as part of our cultural experience.

The legal world forms part of the cultural world, an axiological or value-laden world with its own distinct objects that differ from those found in the ideal, metaphysical, or natural worlds. The methods used to study objects in these worlds cannot be used in the cultural world: ideal objects are not real and do not have any value, natural objects can be experienced but do not have value, and metaphysical objects may have value but cannot be experienced. A new method that goes beyond the deductive method of formal objects and the empirical-deductive method of natural objects is required, one which grasps the significance of human experience in the constitution of the meaning of these cultural objects.

Three things characterize cultural objects: existence, experience, and value. Their existence is dependent upon the subject who gives them meaning and value, and they are thus constituted as cultural objects which can be experienced. The appropriate method is both empirical and dialectical. The axiological meaning and physical reality of the cultural objects form the poles of the dialectic that allows one to seize both the existential and normative dimensions of law.

Law is a normative concept which defines a certain conduct. Because we can know this behavior through understanding, legal evaluation is immanent to law. Its evaluation is not determinative because law is only positive justice; it does not seek to realize justice; it does not have justice as its goal.

The egological theory of law gives an essential place to the judge in the formation of law. The judge gives a legal meaning to reality. Legal experience lies within the evaluation of behavior by the judge.

For Cossio, the judicial decision is not an arbitrary result but is determined by the relevant norms or principles. On the one hand, legal rules circumscribe and delimit the range of possibilities open to the judge. On the other hand, the judge must also take into account the particular circumstances of the case when applying the dogmatic content of law to reality. The judge, however, is bound by the structure provided by the legislator; thus when faced with an unjust law, the judge may only choose the solution that is the least unjust. Order, security, and justice are to be used within the bounds determined by law.

Culture and its values form the basis of legal evaluation within Cossio's egological theory of law. However, the exact nature of these values remains undetermined and is never explained. It is unclear, on the one hand, why these values cannot be ideal or metaphysical objects, and on the other hand, how the introduction of the abstract concept of values adequately reflects social reality. Finally, the process by which culture and values are formed is never explained and it remains unclear why they should be the foundation of law.

References

Bernard, Brigitte. "From the Separation of Powers to the 'Gnoseology of Error'." *Fronesis* 1 (1994), 29–56.

Chiappini, Julio O. "La critica di Cossio et la escuela del derecho libre" (Cossio's Critique and the Free Law School). *Rivista internazionale di filosofia del diritto* 61 (1984), 195–204.

Cossio, Carlos. *El Derecho en el Derecho judicial* (Law Before the Courts). Colleccion Selecciones juridicas. 2d ed. Buenos Aires: Abeledo-Perrot, 1959.

———. "La norme et l'impératif chez Husserl. Nôtes analytiques pour en faire l'étude" (Norm and Order in Husserl. Notes for a Study). In *Melanges en honneur de Paul Roubier,* vol. 1, 145–198. Paris: Dalloz et Sirey, 1961.

———. "The Phenomenology of the Decision." Trans. Gordon Ireland. In *Latin-American Legal Philosophy.* The 20th Century Legal Philosophy Series, vol. 3. Cambridge MA: Harvard University Press, 1948.

———. *La Plenitud del Ordenamiento jurídico* (Total Legal Order). Biblioteca del Instituto Argentino de Filosofía jurídica y social. 2d ed. Buenos Aires: Editorial Losada, 1947.

———. *El Substrato filosófico de los Métodos interpretativos* (Philosophical Foundations of Interpretative Methods). Santa Fé: Imprenta de la Universidad Nacional del Litoral, 1940.

———. *Teoría de la Verdad jurídica.* Biblioteca del Instituto Argentino de Filosofía jurídica y social. Buenos Aires: Editorial Losada, 1954. Trans. as *La théorie de la vérité juridique.* 1954.

———. *La Teoría egológica del Derecho: Su Problema y sus Problemas* (Egological Legal Theory: Concept and Issues). Buenos Aires: Abeledo-Perrot, 1963.

———. *La Teoría egológica del Derecho y el Concepto jurídico de Libertad* (Egological Legal Theory and the Concept of Liberty in Law). Biblioteca del Instituto Argentino de Filosofía jurídica y social. Buenos Aires: Editorial Losada, 1944.

Doctor Carlos Cossio: Homenaje de la Universidad Nacional de Tucumán (Presentations at Tucumán National University). San Miguel de Tucumán, Argentina: La Universidad, 1989.

Duxbury, Neil. "Carlos Cossio and Egological Legal Philosophy." *Ratio Juris* 2 (1988), 3.

Machado, A.L. "Ontologie egologique et instrumentalité pratique" (Egological Ontology and Practical Instrumentity). *Rivista internazionale di filosofia del diritto* 4 (1974).

Pirela, Alberto e Serrano. "Prologomenos para el estudio de la teoria egologica" (Introduction to the Study of Egological Theory). *Anuario de filosofia* 2 (1969), 335–353; 3 (1970), 319–326; 4 (1971), 349–362.

Henri R. Pallard
Richard Hudson

Cost-Benefit Analysis
See RISK ASSESSMENT

Criminalization

What sorts of conduct should be made criminal? One major, and controversial, answer is provided by liberalism, which maintains that the criminal law may interfere only with conduct which harms others. Liberalism has often been criticized on the mistaken belief that it insists on there being an area of conduct, such as the consenting sexual acts of adults, which under no circumstances may be interfered with. Liberalism is essentially concerned about placing a limit on the kind of reasons that may be used to justify legal interference with conduct in any area. Interference is justified on the ground that conduct harms others, but not, for example, on the ground that it is disapproved of by the majority of society.

The liberal doctrine is at the center of a well-known debate between Patrick Devlin and H.L.A. Hart. Devlin believes that the criminal law may be used to enforce the shared morality of a society against conduct which violates this morality without directly harming other individuals. According to his thinking, a shared morality is essential to the very existence of a society: without it society will disintegrate. Many liberals, including Hart, accept the necessity of some shared morality. For example, it is acknowledged that no society can survive unless there are legal prohibitions, sustained by shared moral values, against such acts as murder, assault, and theft. However, there is, they argue, no evidence to show that unchecked deviations from society's shared morality in the areas of consenting adult sexual activities will destroy society. Moreover, in many contemporary societies it is doubtful that there is a consensus about what is right or wrong with respect to many sexual and other activities. In these areas it may be that what sustains society is the shared belief in tolerating different activities, just as religious toleration may be the shared value of people who believe in the truth of different religions.

Some liberals, while rejecting the arguments of Devlin, have extended liberalism in at least two directions. First, they allow varying degrees of paternalism in which the law protects individuals from harming themselves. The legal requirement that seat belts be used is often justified in paternalistic terms. Second, it is thought that the law may interfere with acts whose public performance, though not harmful to others or to the agents themselves, are offensive nuisances. Sexual acts between consenting adults in public places, with more or less captive audiences, may for this reason be legally prohibited, even if the same kinds of acts are permitted in the privacy of the home or in less accessible locations.

Once it is settled what sorts of conduct may be made criminal, the traditional view is that criminal liability requires both the performance of the forbidden act (actus reus or a guilty act) and certain mental states (mens rea, or a guilty mind). We are not liable simply for having untoward thoughts if we take no steps to realize them in our conduct. Criminal liability requires a voluntary act. Disputes about the actus reus center on how it is to be identified, whether it can really be distinguished from the mens rea of a crime, and whether it is in fact necessary for criminal liability.

Actus Reus

In the first alternative, the actus reus is simply the act shorn of its circumstances and results, for example, the stabbing or shooting in itself rather than in the totality of the circumstances in which it took place or in the resultant death. In this view, the act that constitutes the actus reus is only legally forbidden when it is committed in certain circumstances and with certain results. Thus the actus reus of a murder is the shooting that results in the death of the victim.

The claim that we cannot separate the actus reus from the mens rea is often made with respect to criminal attempts. The law prohibits not just murder, but also attempted murder. However, the crime of attempted murder does not have death as a result. In identifying the actus reus we need to distinguish, for example, between the shooting that was intended to kill but did not succeed and the shooting without such an intention. So it seems in the second alternative that the actus reus incorporates the mental element of intention, which is supposed to be the mens rea of the crime. However, the first alternative, which identifies the actus reus with the shooting, will treat the intention to kill not as part of the actus reus, but rather as the cause of the shooting, without which there is no attempted murder.

The requirement of actus reus has been called into question with respect to crimes involving omissions, in which no act has been performed. Omissions would have to be treated as negative acts if they are to satisfy the requirement. There are also offenses, such as the possession of drugs, in which persons are criminally liable not for any act, but for being in certain situations.

Mens Rea

Mens rea is the other component of criminal liability. Intentionally, knowingly, or recklessly harming someone satisfies the requirement of mens rea. In some cases negligence is also included in mens rea. There are, however, some crimes of strict or absolute liability in which criminal liability attaches to the mere performance of the prohibited act, irrespective of the mental state of the offender. In these cases mens rea is not necessary.

There are two main theories explaining the requirement of mens rea. According to the choice theory, we are liable for our conduct only when we have chosen it. This view is sometimes developed into the related view that our liability depends on our having the capacity and fair opportunity to conform to the demands of the law. The second main theory, the character theory, makes us criminally liable for the performance of forbidden acts only if our acts are expressions of bad characters.

According to the choice theory, the central cases of mens rea (when harm is inflicted on others intentionally, knowingly, or recklessly) are all cases in which offenders have chosen to act in harmful ways, as opposed to cases in which harm was accidentally inflicted. According to the character theory, other instances of mens rea (when harm is inflicted as an expression of bad character) are cases in which offenders harm as a result of their defective personalities. For example, when one steals or assaults, one shows a lack of concern for the interests of others and gives too great weight to one's own interests. On the other hand, when one harms others under duress, one's conduct does not display a bad character.

One objection usually raised against the choice theory is its alleged inability to explain our liability for negligent conduct. When we negligently harm others, there is no conscious risk-taking on our part, and so, in the ordinary sense, we cannot be said to have chosen to harm. Some advocates of the choice theory have accounted for our liability here in terms of our having the capacity and fair opportunity to avoid the law's prohibitions. Unlike the insane or the very young who lack the capacity to avoid certain harmful conduct, the negligent had the capacity to do so, but failed to exercise it. The difficulty here is whether we can recover from this account a sense of choice which connects with the notion of choice in the other cases of mens rea. It may be that the significance of choice has to be accounted for in terms of other values, such as the satisfactions gained when we exercise choice or the enhancement of our liberty and autonomy.

The notion of character also requires further analysis if the character theory is to avoid the objection that it cannot account for the liability of fully intentional wrongdoing which is "out of character." A bank clerk steals, but has a previously unblemished record of honest behavior, even in situations with many opportunities for undetected dishonesty. If character refers to a person's settled dispositions, then a single act against the grain does not reflect the character.

It is an interesting question whether one can give a unified account of the requirement of mens rea, and whether such an account will show that criminal liability is ultimately grounded in moral liability. Theorist B. Wootton has suggested that the requirement of mens rea obstructs the proper function of the criminal law in preventing socially harmful acts, and that a system of strict liability will best serve that function. We need to have a clear view about the requirement of mens rea and the values that it serves before we can respond to such radical proposals for changing the basis of criminalization.

References

Devlin, Patrick. *The Enforcement of Morals.* Oxford: Oxford University Press, 1965.

Feinberg, Joel. *The Moral Limits of the Criminal Law.* 4 vols. New York: Oxford University Press, 1984–1988.

Gorr, Michael, Jeffrie C. Murphy, and Douglas N. Husak. "Exchange: The Actus Reus Requirement." *Criminal Justice Ethics* 10 (1991), 11–36.

Hart, H.L.A. *Law, Liberty and Morality.* Oxford: Oxford University Press, 1963.

———. *Punishment and Responsibility.* Oxford: Clarendon Press, 1968.

Horder, Jeremy. "Criminal Culpability: The Possibility of a General Theory." *Law and Philosophy* 12 (1993), 193–215.

Paul, Ellen Frankel, Fred D. Miller Jr., and Jeffrey Paul, eds. *Crime, Culpability, and Remedy.* Oxford MA: Blackwell, 1990.

White, Alan R. *Grounds of Liability.* Oxford: Clarendon Press, 1985.

Wootton, B. *Crime and the Criminal Law.* London: Stevens, 1963. 2d ed. 1981.

C.L. Ten

See also ACT REQUIREMENT; ACTUS REUS; MENS REA; PATERNALISM; WRONGDOING AND RIGHT ACTING

Criminology

Criminology is the systematic study of crime, its causes, attribution, characteristics, and extent, and of the effectiveness of strategies for its control. From a perspective of legal theory, however, it may be understood as a compendium of theoretical knowledge reflecting an ongoing confrontation between the concepts of modern criminal law and persistent social and political demands for public order and personal security. Criminology owes its existence partly to a perceived inability of traditional legal doctrine to address the "crime problem" as an experienced social reality. The unifying characteristic of the criminological enterprise has been its effort to construct knowledge to inform and supplement the legal processes of crime control or to offer substitutes for them.

The origins of the term "criminology" remain obscure, but it gained currency from around 1890 to indicate a new science emerging from what had earlier been known as criminal anthropology. Conventionally, however, the founding of criminology is traced to the "classical school" associated with Cesare Beccaria, whose *Of Crimes and Punishments* proposed effective prevention and deterrence of crime by humane and measured legal treatment of the criminal as an essentially rational actor. Beccaria's ambiguous mix of retributive and utilitarian prescriptions marked the beginnings of the modern effort to translate systematically crime control policies into theoretically justified legal strategies.

Disillusionment with legal responses to crime led, however, by the end of the nineteenth century, to a displacement of classical approaches in favor of a view of the criminal as an abnormal being, *Homo criminalis,* fundamentally different from the ordinary citizen. The newly powerful "positivist" school sought to supplement or even replace orthodox legal emphases on classification of criminal acts with a scientific emphasis on classifying criminal types, characters, and propensities. Classical criminology's legal strategies of deterrence were thus confronted with a range of scientific strategies for neutralizing dangers posed by the criminal.

The transition from classicism to positivism in the history of criminology is complex, given the variety of positivist theoretical positions and the ambiguity of Beccaria's ideas. Yet the early evolution of the research field is one of intensifying effort to locate crime as an object amenable to measurement and prediction and having causes discoverable by science. Criminology thus emerged in an uneasy relationship with law; its significance given primarily by its utility in supporting legal institutions of criminal justice, but its autonomy arising from its claims to a scientific knowledge and practice competing with that of law.

This uneasy relationship has continued to the present. Late-nineteenth-century positivist criminology proposed various disciplinary alliances. Cesare Lombroso initially suggested biological bases of criminally as fundamental and popularized the idea of the "born criminal." Enrico Ferri's "criminal sociology," like earlier statistically oriented work by Adolphe Quetelet and others, emphasized environmental factors contributing to a social determination of crime. Criminology has continued to seek determining factors in criminality by reference to disciplines (especially biology, psychology, and psychiatry) bearing on the personal constitution of criminals as well as to those (especially sociology) examining the social environment of crime.

Despite the prevalence of medicolegal or psychiatric approaches in Britain until the 1960s and determined efforts, more generally in Western countries, to promote personality-based or genetic inheritance theories of criminality, sociological approaches have gradually achieved a particular prominence in academic research. With this development, however, the ambiguous intellectual status of criminology has become more apparent.

The importation of sociological insights suggested eventually that legal or moral concepts of "crime" as an object might be replaced by a more theoretically satisfactory sociological category of "deviance." Interactionist theory also questioned, to some extent, the assumed condemnatory attitudes which criminology had inherited from its legal and governmental "social control" origins. Sociological insights into deviant subcultures led to assertions of the need to understand such subcultures (perhaps in a value-neutral manner) rather than to condemn in the language of legal evaluation or administrative policy.

Inevitably also, the alliance of criminology with sociology led to a concern to understand criminality as, in part, a matter of interactions between the criminal actor and the criminal justice system. In such a perspective, crime might be seen as, in some sense, a product of this system, defined by and in relation to it. From the late 1960s the more radical forms of criminology paid as much attention to understanding the state's criminal justice structures as to examining patterns of criminal activity traditionally understood. Boundaries between criminology and sociology of law as research fields became blurred.

Along this route of broadening sociological inquiries a number of influential movements in thought can be identified, each of which has left an important legacy for contemporary criminology's eclectic theoretical outlook. Social ecology theory, maturing in the 1930s, established the idea that the destabilization of neighborhood organization might itself be criminogenic.

Edwin Sutherland's differential association theory offered a general theory of crime related especially to the learning opportunities presented by different social networks. Robert Merton's anomie theory related types of deviant behavior to different kinds of responses to tensions between social goals of "success" and social norms regulating the pursuit of such goals.

Suggesting the idea of socially induced tensions in individuals impelling them toward deviance, it provided inspiration for many such "strain theories" in contemporary criminology. Subcultural theory, emphasizing the significance of particular cultural networks in influencing operative social norms, opened up a variety of perspectives on the moral pluralism of contemporary societies.

The career of the sociology of deviance has inevitably mirrored sociology's own progress, eventually facing the need to reassess, in the face of apparently determining social structures, the nature of human agency in understanding criminal or other deviant conduct. David Matza's pivotal work *Delinquency and Drift* in 1964 portrayed delinquency in a context of the temporary loosening of social bonds, the individual drifting between conformity and nonconformity, choosing between them in an essentially undetermined manner.

This turn toward an emphasis on the fluidity of individual motivations appropriately reinforces the dangers of deterministic explanation. Radical criminology in the 1970s extended, in primarily marxist terms, early criminological arguments (for example, of Quetelet) that the causes of crime could be eliminated only by changing fundamental structures of society. From the 1980s, however, criminology discarded much of its radicalism and reconsidered some of its earlier explanatory ambitions. A sophisticated reflexive view of theory, recognizing the social and political conditions of its production and use, was sometimes advocated. "Realist" approaches emphasized the importance of addressing in practical terms the reality of individuals' experience and fear of crime. Renewed emphasis was placed on the study of prevention and control rather than ultimate causes of crime; a tendency mirroring in important respects the resurgence of "justice models" of punishment tracing some of their antecedents to the classical school of criminology.

In general it might be said that criminology has reaffirmed the ambiguity of its intellectual and institutional situation: seeking knowledge beyond the legal and administrative doctrines whose inadequacies created a space for it, yet tied ultimately to criteria of utility compatible with the assumptions embedded in those doctrines.

References

Beirne, P., ed. *The Origins and Growth of Criminology: Essays on Intellectual History, 1760–1945*. Aldershot: Dartmouth; New York: New York University Press, 1994.
Cullen, Francis T., and Velmer S. Burton Jr., eds. *Contemporary Criminological Theory*. Aldershot: Dartmouth; New York: New York University Press, 1994.
Maguire, M., R. Morgan, and R. Reiner, eds. *The Oxford Handbook of Criminology*. Oxford: Clarendon Press, 1994.
Nelken, D., ed. *The Futures of Criminology*. London: Sage, 1994.

Roger Cotterrell

See also SOCIOLOGICAL JURISPRUDENCE; SOCIOLOGY OF LAW

Critical Legal Studies

Critical legal studies (CLS) is an approach to law developed mainly in the United States during the 1970s and 1980s that questions the legitimacy of existing legal, political, and social institutions. CLS stems from the perspective of radical left-wing politics. Its proponents, called "crits," charge that Western-style liberal democracies are riddled with illegitimate hierarchies of power and privilege. Although influenced by marxism, crits generally reject as oversimplified the traditional class-based, marxist analysis of law and society. They assert that it is inadequate to conceive of law simply as an instrument of economic domination wielded by the capitalist class. And crits hold that the oppression of workers by capitalists is intertwined with the oppression of people of color by whites, of women by men, of children by adults, of students by teachers, and so on. CLS holds that law and legal institutions play an important role in creating and perpetuating these various forms of oppression. It also provides analyses and critiques of legal doctrines and principles with the aim of delegitimizing the law and the institutions that enact, enforce, and apply it.

The philosophical underpinnings of CLS were laid out in Roberto Unger's *Knowledge and Politics*. Unger presented a "total criticism" of liberalism, the dominant political philosophy of liberal democratic society. "Liberalism" refers here to the view that (1) each individual has a right to as much freedom as is compatible with equal freedom for everyone else, and (2) the rule of law is needed to protect the individual's freedom to pursue his or her own values and to preserve social order. In the liberal view, the rule of law supplants the rule of force and establishes the ground rules which everyone in society can accept despite their disagreement over values.

Unger argued that the liberal view unduly neglected the importance of community, rested on the unwarranted notion that values are subjective, and was riddled by inconsistencies. He claimed that the rule of law cannot possibly operate as the liberal intends: where individuals are free to develop and act on their own values, their disagreements about what is good and bad will reverberate in the legal arena and generate disagreements over how the law is to be interpreted. The rule of force will dictate whose interpretation is binding on society. Other crits followed Unger in criticizing the individualistic emphasis of liberalism and questioning the validity of the idea of the rule of law. Crits did not spend a great deal of time addressing basic philosophical questions about law and society. Instead, they devoted their scholarly energies to picking apart legal doctrines in order to reveal their arbitrariness and internal inconsistencies. Much of this work was modeled on Duncan Kennedy's pathbreaking essay "Form and Substance in Private Law Adjudication." Kennedy argued that substantive values played a role in determining the level of specificity in terms of which legal norms were formulated. In order to clarify the substantive values at stake, he developed two ideal-types, "individualism" and "altruism." The former valued self-reliance and tended to favor highly specific legal norms, while the latter valued solidarity and tended to favor more abstract norms. Kennedy argued that our legal system took neither individualism nor altruism to their logical conclusions: rather, it consisted of a patchwork of both specific and abstract norms, thereby reflecting both views but also arbitrarily truncating them.

Many crits followed Kennedy by using the models of individualism and altruism, or similar constructs, to show how norms and doctrines in specific areas of law both embodied and arbitrarily truncated underlying normative principles. Other crits employed a version of the approach to language known as "deconstruction." Following the deconstructionist idea that the meanings of all words are unstable and proliferate beyond the capacity of either the writer or reader to control, these crits claimed the legal rules had no inherent or fixed meanings. In the early years of CLS, whatever their specific methodology in analyzing law, crits generally agreed that the law suffered from a pervasive indeterminacy: there simply were no correct legal answers to the bulk of legal cases and controversies. As the legal realists had asserted decades earlier, crits insisted that judges needed to rely on their own values to arrive at decisions in the cases they heard. But unlike the realists, crits emphasized that pervasive legal indeterminacy meant that it was not law but politics that ruled in liberal society. And unlike the realists, who were mainly advocates of the expertise-based, administrative state, crits sought to foster a radical, egalitarian form of politics.

Many crits also pointed to the role that law played in making existing social, political, and economic arrangements appear natural, necessary, and good. They argued that human institutions and practices were thoroughly contingent and constructed, and that all such human constructions could be radically transformed, despite the aura of fixity that the law lent to them. Again, Unger was the philosophical leader of CLS in this regard, developing these ideas about contingency and proposing radical legal, political, and economic changes in his later work, *False Necessity*.

During the late 1980s, CLS began to undergo a process of fragmentation. Feminist legal thinkers, many of whom had earlier marched under the banner of CLS, began to break away, charging that Unger and his cohorts had a male bias in their views of law and society. Feminist jurisprudence now stands as a distinct approach to law. Other thinkers who were especially concerned with issues of race began to rally around the banner of critical race theory, arguing that the standard CLS analyses failed to articulate adequately the distinctive problems of racism and how law might be employed to combat those problems. Some proponents of critical race theory accused CLS of unjustifiably dismissing the importance of legal rights in the fight against racism.

The late 1980s also saw a noticeable moderation in the views of some crits, moving them closer to liberalism. Unger began calling his view "superliberalism," indicating that his earlier total criticism of liberalism had been abandoned. Where he had once rejected the possibility of the rule of law in a liberal society, the legal system he proposes in *False Ne-*

cessity explicitly relies on the rule of law without trying to eradicate the value disagreements characteristic of liberal society. Other crits, too, reassessed the earlier rejection of the liberal distinction between the rule of law and the rule of force. Instead of trying to deconstruct the distinction, they began to argue that the establishment of a rule of law requires dramatic changes to equalize power and privilege. Yet there remain crits whose allegiance is to deconstructionist methods and whose efforts are directed at dismantling the conceptual distinctions and categories essential to liberal thought.

Through its short history, CLS has been the subject of intense controversy. Its claims of pervasive legal indeterminacy have been rejected by mainstream thinkers, as have its assertions about the inconsistent and arbitrary character of legal rules. These controversies have not been restricted to the realm of theory. Many crits are professors at law schools in the United States, and they contend that some of their number have been blocked from appointment, or denied tenure, on account of their views.

The more radical, deconstructionist claims of crits are not plausible and will likely be abandoned by more and more thinkers as time goes on. Yet the more moderate claims have made solid contributions to our understanding of how political and ethical disagreements in society are reflected in the form and content of legal doctrine and argument.

Despite the opposition crits have elicited, the influence of CLS has spread beyond the United States and its law school faculties. In some form, CLS is bound to remain a presence in legal thought for years to come. The radical critique of law has had an important role in the Western legal tradition, and the need to fill that role will exist so long as society is open to charges of systemic injustice. Although critiques that focus on sexism or racism are likely to gain in importance, there will remain a place for the more general kind of critique of the law and society found in the work of the crits.

References

Altman, Andrew. *Critical Legal Studies: A Liberal Critique.* Princeton: Princeton University Press, 1990.

Boyle, James, ed. *Critical Legal Studies.* New York: New York University Press, 1992.

Habermas, Jürgen. *Between Facts and Norms: Contributions to a Discourse Theory of Law and Democracy.* Trans. William Regh. Cambridge MA: MIT Press, 1996.

Ingraw, David. "Dworkin, Habermas, and the CLS Movement on Moral Criticism in Law." *Philosophy and Social Criticism* (1990), 237–268.

Kairys, David, ed. *The Politics of Law: A Progressive Critique.* Rev. ed. New York: Pantheon, 1990.

Kennedy, Duncan. "Form and Substance in Private Law Adjudication." *Harvard Law Review* 89 (1976), 1685–1778.

Kramer, Matthew. *Critical Legal Theory and the Challenge of Feminism.* Lanham MD: Rowman and Littlefield, 1994.

Unger, Roberto. *The Critical Legal Studies Movement.* Cambridge MA: Harvard University Press, 1986.

———. *False Necessity: Anti-Necessitarian Social Theory in the Service of Radical Democracy.* New York: Cambridge University Press, 1987.

———. *Knowledge and Politics.* New York: Free Press, 1975.

Andrew Altman

See also DECONSTRUCTIONIST PHILOSOPHY OF LAW; INDETERMINACY; POSTMODERN PHILOSOPHY OF LAW

Customary Law

The spontaneous product of people's awareness, custom is one of the oldest formal sources of law. It was superseded by legislation, following the exegetical school's doctrine, contrary to the historical school, before being acknowledged more recently as one instrument for achieving legal pluralism.

From the Latin *consuetudo,* custom is a rule of law which slowly and spontaneously is distilled from the facts and practices habitually followed in a particular social milieu without any intervention by a legislator. It is distinguished from law that arises from the deliberate act of will of the legislative power.

The term is used synonymously with "unwritten law." It is distinct from "usage," the facts at the base of a customary rule that reflect a way of acting that is ancient, constant, well known, and common, and from "practice," which reflects any way of acting. Not to be confused with mores and folkways as inconsequential usages of daily living, custom is nonetheless the mores or usages which have legal force, which point out with certainty how someone should act and the conduct one should perform in one's social relations.

How is the passage from stable facts to rule of law to be justified? How can customary law follow from a behavior spontaneously reproduced a community, so that its members are required to repeat it? Its legal force has been explained by such phenomena as the interiorization of social constraint, reverence for what a large number do, or the dignity of tradition. Every community symbolizes its unity in a compelling way, with a system of values to be respected, by a body of usages thought to be good for harmony in social relations. For the facts able to be turned into customary law, civilian doctrine held to the Romano-canonical theory that required a material element and a psychological element.

The material element requires that usage has to be ancient and the result of the repeating of a large number of similar actions. It concerns usages and practices to which time has given its sheen. The psychological element is the *opinio juris seu necessitatis,* that is, the conviction among persons conforming to usage that they are acting because of an obligatory rule imposed on them as a rule of law.

In the positivist hypothesis of normative dependency, custom has legal force because that force is given by the law. This delegation, or *renvoi,* can be express or implicit. Many legislative texts look expressly to local usages concerning rural, even urban, property and to conventional usage for interpreting and filling contracts. Similarly, many international agreements refer to practice and the *lex mercatoria* for business law. To apply legal categories, such as "a good householder," a judge must give legal force to the ordinary conduct of a diligent and careful person. Much the same happens implicitly when the judge makes an estimate of fault.

Can custom have a legal force that is autonomous from positive law? Its autonomy relies on normative realism. Law must derive from experience and not from abstract concepts. To govern people, a norm must come not from the occasional and arbitrary will of an individual, but instead from the spontaneous development at the core of the nation. Persons in conflict seek out concrete justice with which they will agree and abide. Custom is the expression of direct democracy, while law is a construct by the people's representatives.

Hardly anyone today disagrees that custom can enter in without recourse to the legislator when there is a gap in the legislation: this is custom *praeter legem* or *secundum legem.* The Swiss civil code recognizes the authority of custom to fill legislative gaps. In France, no formal rule provides for a woman's ability to take her husband's name. The practice of letting notarial acts prove inheritance also derives from usages of notaries, not from a law.

The legal autonomy of custom is more forcefully confirmed by custom's preeminence over imperative law, custom *contra legem.* Thus, joint and several liability is presumed in commercial matters despite French civil law's suggestion that it is not presumed and cannot exist without express agreement. Again, this code requires a notarial act for the validity of a gift, clearly a matter of public order; but hand-to-hand gifts of moveables are still valid. The principle of equality among heirs, which was imposed by the civil code, had a difficult time superseding age-old customs in the Bearn and among Basques.

Particularly in the civil and penal law of newly established countries that were formerly colonized by Western powers does this phenomenon of contradiction stand out. In postcolonial countries the legislated law runs in competition with an ancestral law fitted to local lifestyles. Customary law made invisible by abrogation remains in force within collective attitudes and individual awareness. Abrogation by legal dogma does not abrogate society's conduct; legal monism cannot survive this fact. For example, in Syria, ten years after the law on responsibility was codified into European form in 1948, judges consciously continued to evaluate damages by the rules of the *dya* (village). African countries forbade polygamy, as well as the payment of dowry by the bride's parents. Thirty years later, they had to admit that polygamy was in fact accepted by them all, even those which had civil marriage. In some ethnic groups, such as the Krou (Wê, Bete, Dida), nonpayment of dowry continued to be a cause for dissolution of the marriage bond. In the face of survival by such legal pluralism, some legal systems (Senegal, Mali, Burkina-Fasso, Niger) installed a matrimonial option, between monogamy in civil marriage and polygamy in customary marriage.

Custom's resilience is especially notable in relation to real property, where the registration of property imposed by modern legal systems meant nothing to local chiefs and customary leaders in Africa, Asia, and Latin America. Family holdings remain governed by traditional rules with tools and concepts completely different from those of the West. Among some peoples in Africa, goods pass by inheritance from the maternal uncle to the surviving nephew under the norms of matriarchy, contrary to provisions of the civil codes in force.

Such lack of fit between the two legal orders is especially striking in penal law. In African and Asian countries, the evidentiary procedures imposed by European penal law have failed to expunge social facts native to local tradition, such as "previous offenses" in "witchcraft." In the absence of probable material evidence, modern penal law will declare an accused innocent of voluntary homicide, while in customary law the crime can be shown to have been committed due to supernatural and invisible powers whose secret only sorcerers and witches know. To penetrate these mysteries, traditional judges have recourse to an arsenal of devices unknown to modern law.

Decriminalization of abortion and adultery are contrary to the public order customary in Africa where procreation is the gift of God. Thus, among the Peuls, conjugal infidelity is not only a peremptory cause for dissolution of the conjugal bond, but even a cause for banishment from the group or for suicide. No alternative sanction can erase the shame and dishonor which attach to the unfaithful partner's family in this case.

A legal rule takes account of the human values of the people for which it is made. Experience shows that inappropriate normative rules can destroy cultural values. The applicable rule should give the group an awareness of its identity. Superimposing a foreign norm without adapting it to local realities has led to legal acculturation in the postcolonial countries.

References

Carbonnier, Jean. *Flexible droit* (Flexible Law). 7th ed. Paris: Presses universitaires de France, 1992.

Dumont, Louis. *Homo hierarchicus. An Essay on the Caste System.* Trans. Mark Sainebury. Chicago: University of Chicago Press, 1970.

El Hakim, J. *Le dommage de source delictuelle en droit musulman: survivance en droit syrien et lybanais* (Delictual Damages in Muslim Law: Continuity of Syrian and Lebanese Law). Paris: Librairie générale de droit et de jurisprudence, 1964.

Gény, François. *Methodes d'interpretation du droit et sources en droit privé; Critical Essay.* St. Paul MN: West, 1963.

Ghestin, Jacques, and Gilles Goubeaux. *Introduction générale du droit* (General Introduction to Law). 4th ed. Paris: Librairie générale du droit et de jurisprudence, 1994.

Gilissen, John. *La coutume* (Custom). Turn Hout, Belgium: Brepols, 1982.

Lebrun, A. *La coutume, ses sources, son authorité en droit privé* (Custom, Sources, and Force in Private Law). Paris: Librairie générale de droit et de jurisprudence, 1932.

Lingat, Robert. *Les sources du droit dans le systeme traditionnel de l'Inde* (Sources of Law in the Traditional Indian System). Paris: Mouton, 1967.

Stein, Peter. "Custom in Rome and Medieval Law." *Continuity and Change* 10 (1995), 337.

Vindogradoff, Paul. *Custom and Right.* Oslo: H. Aschenhoug, 1925.

Wilkinson, Don. "Marrying Law and Custom." *Alternative Law Journal* 20 (1995), 23.

Wolfke, Karol. *Custom in Present International Law.* Dordrecht: Martinus Nijhoff, 1993.

Denis Pohe-Topka

See also CONFLICT OF LAWS; CONVENTION AND CUSTOM

D

Damages

The question of damages concerns the *magnitude* of a defendant's liability, as distinct from liability *vel non,* the question of whether one will be held liable at all. "Damages" should also be distinguished from "damage," a term frequently used informally to describe the injury suffered by a plaintiff, whether or not compensable. Awards of damages are to be distinguished from nonpecuniary relief such as injunctions and declaratory judgments. Once the issue of liability *vel non* has been answered in the affirmative, it becomes necessary to determine the magnitude of the liability. The task of calculating damages can be burdensome but is relatively technical and straightforward, complicated primarily by choices between methods of valuation (for example, replacement cost, repair cost, and fair-market value) and between methods of depreciation. It is sometimes necessary to determine whether a particular category of damages is available to a plaintiff, but this issue is ordinarily subsumed within liability *vel non.*

The question of damages is primarily one of rectificatory justice. It necessarily also includes elements of distributive justice to the extent that it involves the redistribution of assets from a liable defendant to a successful plaintiff. When such redistribution can be justified under principles of rectificatory justice, no contentious issues of distributive justice are posed. In Robert Nozick's rights-based libertarian theory, however, any nonrectificatory redistributive role for the state would violate rights to private property. Utilitarians, on the other hand, might very well allow a judge to consider the effect of an award of damages on the future conduct of others, and thus weigh considerations of public interest and general welfare in addition to purely rectificatory demands. In Ronald Dworkin's view, the courts should be concerned with the preexisting rights of the disputants, not with promoting utilitarian social goals. In John Rawls' formulation, rectificatory justice is a function of justice as fairness, entailing an adjustment of outcomes based on a subjunctive calculation of hypothetical outcomes assuming that the liability-producing conduct had not occurred.

Three aspects of rectificatory justice are involved in the calculation of damages: compensation, forfeiture, and punishment. Compensation is a victim-oriented calculation designed to assure that the victim is no worse off than before the injury (assuming that money can adequately compensate for the loss of a limb or a loved one or a unique and irreplaceable possession). Forfeiture and punishment are wrongdoer-oriented and are directed at assuring that the wrongdoer is worse off (punishment) or at least no better off (forfeiture) than before the liability-producing behavior. All three are backward looking, basing calculations on the status quo ante, but punishment and forfeiture are also forward looking to the extent that they are designed to deter similar future behavior by the defendant (specific deterrence) and others (general deterrence). Compensation, too, has a forward-looking deterrence aspect, but whether this is an integral part of its function or an incidental side effect was the subject of a particularly controversial theoretical debate in nineteenth-century continental jurisprudence, and is today a matter of lively disputation.

The fault principle—that no one may be held liable for injury to another unless at fault in causing the injury—has long been an important, if often overstated, maxim of tort law. In recent decades, however, accident law has diluted the fault requirement to the point that relatively few negligent defendants (as opposed to insurance companies and vicariously responsible employers) pay damages personally. This has led to suggestions that compensation be justified not in terms of the personal ethical evaluation of the fault principle but by the considerations of social morality and utility that have led to the development of strict liability and no-fault compensation schemes, which in turn point toward the elimination of compensation for certain nonpecuniary injuries (for example, loss of consortium, emotional distress, and pain and suffering). To the extent that compensation is a natural corollary of the fault principle, however, compensation for these nonpecuniary losses may be unexceptionable.

Forfeiture, the least applied of the three approaches, is found mainly in cases involving business torts, particularly trademark or copyright infringement, where the plaintiff may not be able to prove injury but where the defendant has profited through the misappropriation of plaintiff's property. The theory of recovery is frequently characterized as unjust enrichment (a concept more closely identified with contract than with tort law), and the remedy is likely to take the form of an accounting and the disgorgement of profits generated by the misappropriation.

The punishment aspect is manifested in punitive (or exemplary or vindictive) damages for particularly outrageous or egregious behavior. The availability of punitive damages has long been one of the most controversial aspects of tort law, politically because it represents a deviation from the compensatory justification, and philosophically because it creates a tension between retribution, a noninstrumentalist moral concept of rectificatory justice, and deterrence, an instrumental goal related to distributive justice.

With the exception of products liability cases, punitive damages play a minor role in accident law. They are, however, employed frequently in cases of intentional torts, such as battery, false imprisonment, fraud, malicious prosecution, bad faith refusal of an insurer to settle within the policy limits, and defamation. While punitive damages are usually justified in terms of punishment and deterrence, it is far from clear that these goals are satisfied in the modern context of accidents. For example, who is punished or deterred when exemplary damages are imposed against a corporate employer guilty of no wrongdoing but held vicariously liable for the wrongdoing of an employee, or when a monopoly spreads the loss among its customers, or when the award is covered by insurance? Why should the payment of compensatory damages not already have provided an adequate deterrent? On the other hand, the imposition of punitive damages may emphasize the community's rejection or condemnation of practices that might otherwise be regarded as optional for those willing and able to pay for the harm their conduct causes. Nevertheless, if the purpose is indeed to punish a particular course of conduct, and if the concept is wrongdoer oriented (based on the defendant's wealth, rather than on the plaintiff's losses), then why should the damages go to the plaintiff, who has already been compensated for the injury, rather than into a public fund? How can one justify an award of punitive damages to more than one plaintiff for a single course of conduct (marketing an unreasonably dangerous product, for example)? Among the major criticisms of punitive damages are that to the extent they are punitive they infringe on the public functions of the criminal law, and to the extent that they are not punitive they are redundant or unjustifiable. To the extent that one rejects the public/private distinction in law, one may discount the former criticism. Guido Calabresi and Richard Posner respond to both criticisms with justifications of enhanced specific deterrence and market deterrence, respectively.

Some other vexatious issues became particularly contentious during the so-called tort reform movement of the 1980s and 1990s. The collateral-benefits problem asks, when all or part of a plaintiff's losses is paid for by a third party, such as an insurance company or the plaintiff's employer, should the benefit accrue to the plaintiff, the defendant, or the third party? As to the question of how to divide liability among multiple tortfeasors, the general rule has been that a tortfeasor is liable only for the injury he caused, if the multiple tortfeasors caused distinct and separate injuries or if there is a reasonable method of apportionment; otherwise, one defendant's share may be charged to other defendants, under theories of concert of action, joint and several liability, enterprise liability, or market-share liability. These theories of recovery have been criticized as violating the proportionality between a defendant's responsibility for an injury and his liability for damages; but as a historical matter, tort law has not apportioned damages proportionally to fault.

A verdict apparently designed solely or primarily to reward a sympathetic plaintiff at the expense of a wealthy corporate defendant or insurance company can pose a serious problem and cannot be justified under any principle of tort law, whether rectificatory or distributive; however, this should be viewed as an aberration to be controlled through rules of procedure rather than of substantive tort law. The effect of a plaintiff's negligence in causing his own injuries is dealt with in the duty to mitigate damages, the rule of avoidable consequences, and the doctrines of contributory and comparative negligence, all of which implicate questions of responsibility and accountability for one's own conduct. The contributory negligence rule long held that a plaintiff whose negligence contributed to his own injuries could not maintain an action against a defendant who had also negligently contributed to the injuries. This, a rule of liability *vel non*, has been largely supplanted by comparative negligence, a rule of damages, which reduces a contributorily negligent plaintiff's recovery by a factor proportional to the plaintiff's responsibility for his own injuries.

References

American Law Institute. *Restatement of the Law, Second, Torts*. 2d. ed. St. Paul MN: American Law Institute Publishers, 1965.

Buchanan, Allen. "Justice, Distributive." In *Encyclopedia of Ethics,* ed. Lawrence Becker, vol. 1, 655–661. New York: Garland, 1992.

Calabresi, Guido. *The Costs of Accidents, a Legal and Economic Analysis*. New Haven: Yale University Press, 1970.

Cottingham, John. "Justice, Rectificatory." In *Encyclopedia of Ethics,* ed. Lawrence Becker, vol. 1, 661–663. New York: Garland, 1992.

Dunlap, William V. "Reconciling Liability and Responsibility." *Archiv für Rechts- und Sozialphilosophie* 77 (1991), 153–175.

Dworkin, Ronald. *Taking Rights Seriously*. Cambridge MA: Harvard University Press, 1977.

Englard, Izhak. *The Philosophy of Tort Law*. Brookfield VT: Dartmouth, 1993.

Harper, Fowler, and James Fleming, Jr. *The Law of Torts*. 2d ed. Boston: Little, Brown, 1986.

Landes, William M., and Robert A. Posner. *The Economic Structure of Tort Law*. Cambridge MA: Harvard University Press, 1987.

Levine, Lawrence C., Julie A. Davies, and Edward J. Kionka. *A Torts Anthology*. N.p.: Anderson, 1993.

Nozick, Robert. *Anarchy, State, and Utopia*. New York: Basic Books, 1974.

Punitive Damages: Symposium Issue. Alabama Law Review 40 (1989), 687–1261.

Rawls, John. *A Theory of Justice*. Cambridge MA: Harvard University Press, 1971.

Shavell, Steven. *Economic Analysis of Accident Law*. Cambridge MA: Harvard University Press, 1987.

Smith, J.C. *Liability in Negligence*. Toronto: Carswell; London: Sweet & Maxwell, 1984.

William V. Dunlap

See also CORRECTIVE JUSTICE; ECONOMIC LOSS; PERSONAL INJURY; PUNITIVE DAMAGES

Death

See AGING; DISPOSITION OF REMAINS; EUTHANASIA AND SUICIDE

Death Penalty

See CAPITAL PUNISHMENT

Decision Making, Administrative

Multifunctional decision making, as administrative law, involves aspects of executive, legislative, and judicial functions, and seeks to reduce arbitrariness and unfairness in bureaucratic government through various regulations, thereby controlling the power of agencies and keeping a check on excesses and abuses.

Administrative agencies are the entities which deal with diverse social problems; they are flexible and have a limited scope of responsibility. Because of the narrow expanse of their power, agencies can develop expertise in a given area. Their standards of decision making are discretionary and can be tailored to fit a given situation. This inherent flexibility, however, has been criticized as permitting unchecked power and unrestrained government. In an effort to prevent excessive power, and yet permit agencies the flexibility necessary for their operation, the body of administrative law has developed to check overreaching and arbitrariness.

Administrative decision making involves informal as well as formal procedures. Informal or "notice and comment" rule making is wide-ranging in scope, involving notice, an opportunity for participation by interested persons, and the issuance of a statement of basis and purpose after consideration of public comments. Oral hearings are not required in informal rule-making procedures, and often procedures are not set down. Section 553 of the *Administrative Procedures Act,* however, permits interested persons to submit written or oral testimony at the discretion of the agency. Codification of proposed rules is contained in the *Code of Federal Regulations.*

Rule-making proceedings have become a popular method of formulating policy due to their efficiency and speed, placing all affected parties on notice of pending changes in regulatory policy and providing them with an opportunity to voice comments and objections prior to finalization of an agency's position on a given subject.

The inadequacy or absence of a record in informal rule-making proceedings, often supplemented by outside contacts with decision makers and staff members without documentation, leads to difficulties in judicial review. Formal rule making, or "rule making on the record," involves a trial-type hearing in which interested persons are given an opportunity to testify and cross-examine adverse witnesses before issuing a rule. Whether informal or formal rule making is required depends on the relevant statute or nature of the interest involved.

The adjudicative function of administrative agencies involves a determination of legal rights, duties, and obligations. When an agency wishes to obtain a binding determination that affects the legal rights of an individual, it must use legal principles and procedures traditionally associated with the judicial process. Most formal agency adjudications are preceded by staff investigations, which parallel civil "discovery," in which all relevant information useful to the decision makers is collected.

Administrative hearings, conducted by administrative law judges (ALJs), are generally less formal and more liberal than those in courts of law. Written evidence may be substituted for direct oral testimony, and there is a tendency throughout the hearing to favor the admission of questioned or challenged evidence, including hearsay. Like judges, ALJs decide both questions of fact and issues of law, limited to the evidence established on the record. They are empowered to issue subpoenas, administer oaths, make evidentiary rulings, and conduct hearings, but are not members of the federal judiciary. After making findings of fact, the ALJs recommend a decision that is sent to the board of review in the agency. There the ALJ's decision is reviewed and the result is adopted, altered, or reversed. The agency reviewing body may hear additional data or argument and alter the ALJ's findings and conclusions accordingly. Litigants must exhaust their administrative remedies through the agency's internal grievance procedure before judicial review of the agency's action is obtainable.

In its decision the agency explains its action and offers relevant factual and legal support for its rationale. In general, courts are willing to defer to an agency's expertise in policy decisions, law making, and interpretation, upholding administrative findings if the court determines that the agency examined the issues, reached its decision within the appropriate standards, and followed the required procedures. If the court finds the agency deficient in some respect, the case is generally remanded to the agency for further consideration, which may produce a change in the agency's decision or a better explanation or justification for it. An agency's decision will be set aside if the reviewing court determines that it is abusive, arbitrary, capricious, absent procedural due process, in excess of the agency's grant of power, or that there was a lack of substantial evidence on the record to support the agency's findings.

References

Aman, Alfred C., Jr. *Administrative Law in a Global Era.* Ithaca: Cornell University Press, 1992.

Davis, Kenneth Culp. *Administrative Law Text.* 3d ed. St. Paul MN: West, 1972.

———. *Discretionary Justice: A Preliminary*

Inquiry. Urbana: University of Illinois Press, 1979.

Gellhorn, Ernest, and Barry B. Boyer. *Administrative Law and Process in a Nutshell.* 2d ed. St. Paul MN: West, 1981.

Kerwin, Cornelius M. *Rulemaking: How Government Agencies Write Law and Make Policy.* Washington DC: Congressional Quarterly, 1994.

Robinson, Glen O. *American Bureaucracy: Public Choice and Public Law.* Ann Arbor: University of Michigan Press, 1991.

Marcia J. Weiss

See also EFFICIENCY; NATURAL JUSTICE; POLICY, LEGAL; RULE OF LAW

Decision Making, Judicial

Philosophical discussions of appellate decision making often attempt either to solidify or to unsettle the respective claims of legal formalism and legal realism. In its strictest form, legal formalism holds that judicial decision making is a rational, deductive process by which preexisting legal materials subsume particular legal disputes under their domain, thus permitting judges to infer the preexisting right answer to the case at bar. Under this view, judges are tightly constrained by the relevant legal materials which they apply. Legal formalism thus affirms a method of legal reasoning and justification that is uncontaminated by straightforward political and ideological dispute; a distinctive rationality that is immanent in legal materials; and a guiding normative vision, an intelligible moral order, that explains and justifies the bulk of received legal opinion but that retains the capacity to criticize and stigmatize small pockets of doctrine as mistakes.

Legal formalism invokes and sustains the rule of law (that set of logical requirements of justice which allegedly ensures notice to citizens of the law's demands), as well as consistency and objectivity in the law's application. Although it is highly improbable that any theorist has advanced the position in as uncompromising a version as sketched above, Christopher C. Langdell and Joseph Beale were two of the prime advocates of legal formalism in the late nineteenth and early twentieth centuries.

Critics of legal formalism charge that the view venerates lifeless abstractions and theoretical constructs at the expense of a robust understanding of social reality. By allegedly treating legal categories and classifications as if they were natural kinds and tacitly assuming that language embodied in legal materials is determinant, formalists misperceive the phenomenology of judicial decision making. Critics argue that formalists mask the necessary and inevitably contestable normative choices that judges in fact must make when selecting which general legal principles to apply to concrete cases and when determining how to apply them. Motivated by the desire to bring legal reasoning into the supposed objective realm of the natural sciences, thereby insulating judges from political conflict and sanctifying the rule of law, the formalists' vision may wrongly ignore the role of historical context and social reality in appellate decision making. Legal formalism, it is alleged, has pernicious social effects: it legitimates the political status quo and thereby confers normative approval on social inequalities.

In stark contrast to legal formalism, legal realism denies that judicial decision making can be fashioned from logical deduction. Realism was neither a monolithic school of thought nor a systematic jurisprudence; instead, it is better viewed as a set of attitudes about legal decision making. It emerged explicitly in the 1920s and reached its zenith in the 1930s and early 1940s. Karl Llewellyn, Jerome Frank, and Morris Cohen were representative figures.

Legal realism asserts that contradictory and conflicting decisions pervade the law. Under this view, concepts are not embedded in nature but are merely conventions of social life. Any set of legal facts is, according to realists, classifiable in an indefinite number of ways. All legal classifications are merely conventions motivated by the interests of various classes or individuals possessing a relative power advantage that translates into further social privilege. Instead of taking reality as a series of brute facts that humans discover through pure reason and perception, realists stress the role theory plays in characterizing reality. Such an approach denies the existence of ultimately objective or discoverable neutral meanings. Accordingly, in any nontrivial case, judges can advance several plausible competing general principles, which generate conflicting conclusions. Because of all this, no interpretation or application of language can be logically required by the language itself. Words are created, defined, and applied by people saturated by their social conditions and historical context. Each act of judicial interpretation is therefore an act of social and political choice. Accordingly, many realists were cognitive relativists while they simultaneously placed great faith in liberal, reformist values.

According to this view, judges' arguments are merely rationalizations, and not the true explanations, of their decisions. Judges necessarily manipulate precedent and other legal material after making decisions. That is, judges cannot use past legal doctrine as a treasure chest within which they will discover the antecedent right answer to the instant case; rather, it is only after they arrive at a decision on other grounds that they can consult past doctrine for supporting material. Accordingly, judges' private motives and values are fundamental to and necessary for understanding the legal conclusions they assert. To understand judicial decision making we must look at the behavior of judges, not abstract legal argument. Realists believe that considerations stemming from social needs and political conflict are more important to the development of law than logical propositions. Consequently, judges are constantly creating new law, not merely applying preexisting law.

Realists generally do not suspect that their descriptive account of judicial decision making is the result of a plethora of insidious or dishonest judges; rather, judges decide as they do because of the limitations of our language, logic, and normative concepts. Therefore, realists reject even the possibility that officials in complex legal systems could substantially comply with most elements of the rule of law.

There is a relationship between the adoption of a particular view of judicial decision making and the value judgment one makes about the political status quo. Historically, most legal realists had reformist aspirations. They perceived the political status quo as reactionary, anti-democratic, and partially the result of looking at law from a formalist perspective. Conceiving the law instrumentally, they were overwhelmingly concerned with the results of judicial decisions rather than with analyzing abstract legal reasoning. Most believed that values had a historical context and were not capable of determinate, eternal resolutions. Moreover, questions of value were

thought to arise not from an intellectual vacuum, but from political struggle and commitment. Accordingly, realists conspired to achieve necessary political reform by taking an important preliminary step: the debunking of traditional formalist pretensions in judicial decision making.

Critics of legal realism allege that realists accept and justify as inevitable an unwarranted amount of judicial discretion in most legal cases, thereby signaling free rein and overly broad powers to unelected officials. Moreover, the consequence of the relentless and all-pervasive attack realists advance against formalist pretensions may result in an impotent, effete skepticism that prohibits realists themselves from consistently developing a constructive program. Finally, it is charged that realism, despite its animating aspirations, ignores a crucial aspect of legal reality: the rational constraint that judges report and experience when making their decisions. Most judges believe and act on the assumption that the legal system is constituted by at least some of the virtues espoused by the rule of law, a reality which realists seem to ignore or deny. It would be peculiar if realists implicitly hold the view that judicial decision making can be understood independently of the meaning and values that judges who participate in the process attribute to it.

Ironically, extreme realists and extreme formalists share a suspicious assumption: the law is determinate and rational only if its identification and application are more or less mechanical. Moreover, formalism and realism are fueled by background theories that accept certain contestable dichotomies about the nature of language, rationality, and normative reasoning: either language is constituted by fixed meanings that allow natural classifications, demarcated spheres, and principled line drawing, or language is merely conventional and its users are always and inevitably reflecting particular interests or ideologies; either legal rationality is a deductive process, whereby sound argument involves general propositions subsuming particulars and yielding true conclusions, or legal rationality is contaminated with subjective value preferences, and rationalizations based on such preferences masquerade as logical arguments; either morality is justified foundationally by a metaphysical linchpin such as a normative order immanent in nature or a supreme being who embodies and defines goodness, or morality is yet another human artifact based on the conventions of culture, history, and contingent agreements.

Contemporary contributions to the discussion of appellate decision making include Ronald Dworkin's "law as integrity," Catharine MacKinnon's "feminism unmodified," Richard Posner's economic analysis, the critical legal studies movement, and critical race theory.

Dworkin's theory can be viewed as a sophisticated formalism. Avoiding most of the criticisms directed at crude formalism, Dworkin argues that appellate judges may appeal only to those political principles that they sincerely believe constitute the best coherent justification of law. Such principles embody the political rights of individuals. Thus, Dworkin agrees with the realist dogma that "law inevitably implicates politics" but only to the extent that law necessarily implicates political theory, as opposed to partisan politics. Judges, through a complicated interpretive process, must weave constitutional provisions, statutory demands, judicial precedents, and other legal materials into the best coherent justification of law. Once constructed, this justification, which is continually adjusted to fit new materials, is rich enough to decide all cases that arise for appellate judges. In principle, then, there is an antecedently existing right answer for all legal cases, and appellate judges never enjoy strong discretion. Accordingly, judicial decision making is constrained and the basic tenets of the rule of law are preserved.

MacKinnon's position is more of a critique of mainstream perceptions of law than it is a developed theory of judicial decision making. She stigmatizes the quest for universal legal rules and argues that such rules disproportionately project the aspirations of those males powerful enough to make the relevant decisions. According to this view, legal concepts are too often socially constructed from the situation of male domination and female subjugation. Through invocation of allegedly neutral standards of adjudication, striving for objectivity through manipulation of legal abstractions, and aperspectival rationality, sex differences come to be viewed as the justification for male power rather than the result of it. In contrast, the beginnings of a feminist approach to law depend on consciousness raising, result orientation, and appreciation and acceptance of paradox.

Posner's analysis is one of many versions of law and economics. He argues that the dominant goal of the legal system should be the maximization of wealth. His understanding of wealth includes the aggregate of the market values of all property held, as well as consumer and producer surplus. Such surplus values result when commercial entities and individuals hold certain properties because they affix higher values to those properties than the current market does. The goal of wealth maximization is an economic allocation in which products are under the ownership of their highest valuing user. According to this view, efficient economic behavior should be the criterion for choosing among legal rules.

Critical legal studies, a name given to a movement composed of heterogeneous thinkers, amplifies three legal realist themes: the radical indeterminacy of law, law's complicity in politics, and the ideological foundation of law. Unlike legal realists, however, critical legal scholars do not take solace in the social sciences, administrative agencies, or process-oriented jurisprudence. Instead, some critical scholars argue that we must disaggregate and eventually transcend liberal ideology itself, while others, such as Roberto Unger, advocate a superliberalism that facilitates, among other things, the destabilization of entrenched privileges and the judicial extension of pockets of doctrine outside the acknowledged core of law. Unger's chief goal is to recognize the contingency of our institutional and social arrangements and open them to transformation.

Critical race theory emerged in the 1980s and gained momentum in the 1990s. It is a self-consciously eclectic movement that borrows from and refines numerous traditions: marxism, classical liberalism, feminism, poststructuralism, critical legal theory, pragmatism, and nationalism. Critical race theory, however, embodies a number of common themes: it aspires to understand how traditional institutions and dominant normative discourses facilitate and systematize racial subordination; it critiques notions of neutrality, objectivity, and meritocracy, which mask the reality of racism by suggesting that racial subordination results from a series of random, individualized acts; it champions contextual and historical analyses of law; it takes as primary the collective experiential wisdom and critical reflections of those who have suffered from racism when analyzing law and societal

D

institutions; it accepts an interdisciplinary and eclectic outlook, a variety of traditions, methodological and theoretical suppositions that empower hitherto disenfranchised races; and it recognizes that racism is often found intertwined with other forms of political oppression.

Various forms of pragmatism also invigorate contemporary debates about judicial interpretation. Such forms argue that legal decision making is rational, although not fully determinate; legal decision making implicates ideological vision and is thus political all the way down, but it does not follow that it is irrational, merely subjective, or unconstrained. Both formalists and realists assume that the choices constituting the three dilemmas sketched above about the nature of language, rationality, and normative discourse are exhaustive, and thus define the range of possibilities. The acceptance of this fundamental assumption is what confers legitimacy and brio upon the formalist-realist debate. However, it is precisely the commitment to such dualities that much contemporary pragmatism calls into question. Such efforts aspire to expose the assumed polarities as inadequate and transformable.

References

Belliotti, Raymond A. *Justifying Law*. Philadelphia: Temple University Press, 1992.

Burton, Steven J. *Judging in Good Faith*. New York: Cambridge University Press, 1992.

Collins, Hugh. *Marxism and Law*. Oxford: Oxford University Press, 1984.

Dworkin, Ronald. *Law's Empire*. Cambridge MA: Harvard University Press, 1986.

Finnis, John. *Natural Law and Natural Rights*. New York: Oxford University Press, 1980.

Hart, H.L.A. *The Concept of Law*. Oxford: Clarendon Press, 1961.

MacKinnon, Catharine A. *Toward a Feminist Theory of the State*. Cambridge MA: Harvard University Press, 1989.

Posner, Richard A. *The Problems of Jurisprudence*. Cambridge MA: Harvard University Press, 1990.

Unger, Roberto M. *The Critical Legal Studies Movement*. Cambridge MA: Harvard University Press, 1986.

Raymond Angelo Belliotti

See also JUSTIFICATION; REALISM, LEGAL

Decisionist Philosophy of Law

Decisionists contend that certain problems (religious, moral, political, or legal) must be settled by virtue of an agent's capacity to render a decision during exceptional circumstances. The exception occurs when no objectively valid norms exist to guide action. At this point, therefore, they assume that only the capacity and willingness of the agent to act justifies the decision. Consequently, since the agent's decision is self-justified, it occurs in a normative vacuum. Decisionism is mainly associated with Carl Schmitt (1888–1985), who coined the term to describe his theory of sovereignty. Other decisionists are, for example, Jean Bodin (1530–1596), Thomas Hobbes (1588–1679), Juan Donoso Cortés (1809–1853), and Friedrich Nietzsche (1844–1900).

Nihilism

Because decisionism attempts to establish the validity of religious, moral, political, or legal norms upon an agent's decision, it is frequently characterized as a species of nihilism. However, if nihilism is defined as the rejection of all transcendent values, decisionism need not be nihilistic in this sense. For example, the "divine command" theory holds that the justification of moral rules depends on whether they conform to the will of God: the rightness or wrongness of an action is determined by God's decision. Accordingly, God's commands are universally valid for all people. On the contrary, by rejecting the validity of any transcendent value, someone such as Nietzsche embraces radical nihilism. For him, all values are perspectival: they are the result of people's will to power. Someone such as Thomas Hobbes, however, is not a nihilist in Friedrich Nietzsche's sense. He grounds the validity of moral, legal, and even religious values on the sovereign's power to enforce commands (decisions) on subjects. Thus Hobbes' decisionism avoids radical nihilism by postulating an all-powerful sovereign as the last court of appeal to settle value disputes among conflicting parties in society.

Law and Decision

While virtually absent from Anglo-American legal and political theories, the term "decisionism" is well known in the European continent. It is in continental jurisprudence and politics that decisionist theories have flourished. Decisionists maintain that a legal or political decision need not always be justified according to norms of adjudication within a given constitutional system. They contend that not all juridical and political problems can be effectively solved by appealing to legal or political principles or to free public discussion. For them, there are crucial moments in the life of a legal and political community when its representative(s) must act (contrary to the law if necessary) to salvage it. This is the so-called rule of exception or state of emergency. For example, when there is a real threat of either civil unrest (civil war) or foreign aggression, the sovereign may decide to suspend the constitution to restore order. From which it follows, according to Carl Schmitt, that "a sovereign is he who decides on the exception." During exceptional (abnormal) circumstances, a sovereign cannot appeal to valid norms to render a decision. This is because the validity of norms depends upon normal circumstances. For Schmitt, therefore, a sovereign's decision to declare a state of emergency is beyond normative justification. Consequently, his decision appears to be justified ex nihilo based just on the sovereign's power to impose his will on others.

Historical Background

The exception can be traced back to Jean Bodin, who recognized that one of the necessary conditions of sovereignty is the prerogative to decide in the last instance. The decisionist component is also present in the Hobbes' sovereign who has not only a monopoly to coerce, but, more important, a monopoly to decide the content of the law—including the content of canon law. In Donoso Cortés one finds an example of political decisionism: the sovereign decides to act against the anarchical forces of evil (those fomenting civil unrest) to preserve the stability and harmony of a given political community. For him, the choice is not between liberty and dictatorship, but rather between anarchy and order. He chooses dictatorship as the only way to contain civil unrest and therefore preserve order. For Schmitt, however, the role of the exception in law and politics is like the role of a miracle in traditional Catholic theology. A miracle is God's decision to suspend the laws of nature to intervene in world affairs and thereby reestablish Divine order. Likewise, when faced with civil unrest or foreign aggression, a sovereign decides to suspend the constitution and thereby re-establish public order.

Objections

Decisionists face a serious dilemma: Either they maintain that any decision is as good as any other (radical nihilism), or they postulate the existence of a sovereign who, by virtue of having a monopoly of power, imposes his decisions on others (authoritarianism). If one decides to accept the first horn of this dilemma, then one's decision is arbitrary. Why accept the first horn rather than the second one? On the other hand, if the second horn is accepted, then, according to Plato, the old Socratic question emerges: Is the sovereign's decision right because he commands it, or does he command it because it is right? Since some decisionists (for example, Hobbes and Schmitt) maintain that a sovereign's decision may be self-justified, they have no choice but to accept that a decision is right because it is commanded by one who has the power to enforce it. If this is so, they embrace the old dictum that *might makes right* (*Republic,* 338c). Others (for example, Bodin and Donoso Cortés) maintain that a decision is justified based on reason of state. That is, the sovereign's decision is justified as necessary to preserve a political community. Who, however, is to determine that a given political community should be preserved? The sovereign is to do so. Therefore, decisionists escape radical nihilism by embracing authoritarianism.

References

Bodin, Jean. *On Sovereignty.* Ed. and trans. Julian H. Franklin. New York: Cambridge University Press, 1992.

"Carl Schmitt." Ed. David Dyzenhaus. *The Canadian Journal of Law and Jurisprudence* 10.1 (Jan. 1997), 3–225.

Donoso Cortés, Juan. "Discurso Sobre La Dictadura." In *Obras Completas de Don Juan Donoso Cortés,* vol. 2. Madrid: Biblioteca de Autores Cristianos, 1946. Trans. as "The Church, The State, and Revolution." In *Catholic Political Thought 1789–1848,* ed. Béla Menczer. London: Burns Oates, 1952.

Hirst, Paul. "Carl Schmitt's Decisionism." *Telos* 72 (Summer 1987), 15–26.

Hobbes, Thomas. *Leviathan.* Ed. Richard Tuck. New York: Cambridge University Press, 1991.

Nietzsche, Friedrich. *The Will to Power.* Trans. Walter Kaufmann and R.J. Hollingdale. New York: Vintage Books, 1968.

D

Plato. *The Collected Dialogues of Plato.* Ed.
Edith Hamilton and Huntington Cairns.
Princeton: Princeton University Press,
1978.

Schmitt, Carl. *Political Theology: Four Chapters on the Concept of Sovereignty.* Trans.
George Schwab. Cambridge: MIT Press,
1985.

Schwab, George. *The Challenge of the Exception: An Introduction to the Political
Ideas of Carl Schmitt between 1921 &
1936.* 2d ed. New York: Greenwood
Press, 1989.

Wolin, Richard. "Carl Schmitt, Political Existentialism, and the Total State." In *The
Terms of Cultural Criticism: The Frankfurt School, Existentialism, Poststructuralism.* New York: Columbia University
Press, 1992.

Vincente Medina

Deconstructionist Philosophy of Law

Deconstruction is a substantive position and a method and is focused on the illogical workings of paradoxes in philosophy and in law. A deconstructive approach highlights the inescapable paradoxes at work in all areas of thought and existence. As a substantive position, it expounds the dynamic of every true paradox—the dynamic in which a proposition P is true if and only if it is not true—and explains why such a dynamic is to be found everywhere. As a method of reading, deconstruction consists in techniques of analysis and interpretation designed to facilitate the disclosure of paradoxes in specific texts.

Because deconstruction has undergone such widespread misrepresentation at the hands of its votaries and its critics, any suitable account has to begin by making clear what deconstruction is not. First, it is not skepticism of any sort—either nihilistic or relativistic. It does not nihilistically deny the existence of truth and meaning altogether, nor does it relativistically contend that truth and meaning emerge only as the products of mutable frameworks of interpretive assumptions. (Deconstructive analyses can combine with certain variants of the relativist position; but those analyses are not themselves such variants.) Second, deconstruction does not consist in showing that every text refers implicitly or explicitly to the fact of its own construction as a text.

Third, deconstructing a text does not amount to exposing the sordid motives or the sinister consequences associated with the production of the text. Fourth, deconstruction does not proceed as a claim about undecidability—a claim that the answers to myriad questions are strictly undecidable because the rules that govern the answers are ultimately unable to determine their own applications. (Again, deconstructive analyses can readily combine with such a claim, but they are distinct therefrom. Of course, when a state of undecidability arises because of the paradoxes involved in answering a certain question, the distinction between a deconstructive analysis and an undecidability-focused analysis will have broken down.)

A fifth and final caveat is especially important for legal theorists. A deconstructive approach does not highlight mere conflicts (like those frequently highlighted by ordinary legal discourse). Such an approach does not reside in the disclosure of tensions—tensions between conflicting ideals—that are to be solved only through arbitrary line-drawing or balancing. Nor does it reside in the disclosure of outright oppositions or trade-offs that are to be solved only through the arbitrary sacrifice of one ideal in favor of an opposing ideal. Nor, finally, does deconstruction reside in showing that categories that oppose each other are also partially constitutive of each other.

Deconstruction resides, instead, in the highlighting of full-blown paradoxes or antinomies. In order to understand the general structure of paradoxes, one should think about the most familiar and most accessible (though least important) type of paradox: the self-referential paradox. A sentence that consists in a proclamation of its own falsehood— "the present statement is false"—will be false if it is true, and true if it is false. In other words, it will be false if and only if it is true. We can extract and generalize the key principle at work in any such statement: whenever a proposition P is true if and only if it is not true, whenever a situation can be expressed as "P if and only if not-P," we confront the general whirling of a paradox. This general whirling in its myriad instantiations, with or without the element of explicit self-referentiality, is what lies at the focus of any deconstructive critique. (The reasons that we should expect this general whirling to appear everywhere are too complicated for the present discussion; they are expounded in Matthew Kramer's writings.)

How, then, does deconstructive philosophy differ from the approaches and positions with which it has been confused? First, instead of being equivalent to skepticism, it construes skepticism as merely one point or moment in the broader dynamic of "P if and only if not-P." If we let P stand for truth of every sort, then nihilism amounts to not-P. The task for a deconstructive analysis is to show that nihilism (not-P) is completely interwoven with the truth (P) that nihilism denies. Similarly, if we let P stand for any ultimate grounds of knowledge, then relativism amounts to not-P. The task for a deconstructive analysis is to show that relativism (not-P) is completely interwoven with the philosophical fundaments (P) that relativism denies. In short, far from amounting to either a nihilistic version or a relativistic version of skepticism, deconstructive philosophy presents a thoroughgoing critique of skeptical claims. Such claims, in the eyes of a deconstructive analyst, are no less problematic (and no more problematic) than the orthodox positions that loom as the bugbears of skeptical attacks.

Second, a focus on texts' references to their own textuality is at most a contingent step in a deconstructive critique. Such a focus is neither necessary nor sufficient for revealing the dynamic of "P if and only if not-P" at work in a given text. In fact, nothing in deconstructive philosophy suggests that references of the sort just mentioned will indeed be present in all or most texts.

Third, the deconstructive focus on paradoxes clearly does not amount to an unearthing of the seamier aspects of intellectual creations (in their origins or their consequences). A deconstructive approach is not necessarily denunciatory at all; and, insofar as it does engage in denunciation, it takes aim at paralogisms in reasoning rather than at moral lapses. Though a deconstructive encounter with a text can combine with a political or moral tirade, such an encounter per se is strictly analytical. Unless one makes the ridiculous assumption that paradoxes are somehow immoral, one will have no grounds for maintaining that deconstructive philosophy aims to highlight moral shortcomings in the texts and doctrines which it explores.

Fourth, deconstructive philosophy goes considerably beyond an analysis that focuses on undecidability (save when the undecidability obtains because of a paradoxical to-and-fro between untenable outcomes). To be sure, both a deconstructive analysis and an undecidability-focused analysis maintain that a straightforward choice between certain outcomes is not possible. However, the two analyses differ markedly in explaining the impossibility of a choice. For the approach focused on undecidability, the key factor is an utter lack of essential guidance. For the deconstructive approach, on the other hand, a straightforward choice is impossible because any choice will have negated itself and will thus have flipped itself into being the opposite choice (which will in turn have flipped back, and so forth ad infinitum). The truth of a chosen proposition entails its falsehood, and its falsehood entails its truth. Thus, for a deconstructive theorist, the problem is not a lack of guidance or is not only a lack of guidance; rather, the problem is that any guided decisions will have undone themselves by virtue of being what they are.

Fifth, and finally, a deconstructive analysis draws attention to a structure of thoroughgoing incompatibility and thoroughgoing entailment, not to a structure of partial incompatibility and not to a structure of incompatibility without entailment. In the dynamic of "P if and only if not-P," the values of truth and falsehood entirely exclude each other but also ineluctably entail each other. Those values are locked in a total conflict rather than in a manageable conflict that allows each to be balanced against the other; and, in the outright opposition between the values, each necessitates the other by dint of excluding it categorically.

Similarly, a deconstructive analysis does not highlight a partial interpenetration of categories—an interpenetration through which categories constitute each other in part as well as exclude each other. Instead, the deconstructive analyst draws attention to a complete (and hence unthinkable) interpenetration of conflicting categories. In the dynamic of "P if and only if not-P," the values of truth and falsehood have hollowed each other out unreservedly by requiring each other unreservedly. Each value is a wholly untenable option only because each one demands the other and thus demands a state of affairs that precludes its own emergence. Rather than partial interweaving along with total incompatibility, the structure of a true paradox, therefore, is one of total interweaving derived from total incompatibility.

In short, paradoxes are not simultaneous equations. That is, they do not leave any elements outside the structure of interpenetration that marks their categories; hence they do not leave any starting points that can be parlayed into "solutions." Paradoxes are thoroughly intractable problems, from which every exit has always returned upon itself. A method of reading that highlights paradoxes is thus as arduous as it is venturesome and rewarding.

References

Culler, Jonathan. *On Deconstruction*. Ithaca NY: Cornell University Press, 1982.

Derrida, Jacques. *Margins of Philosophy*. Trans. Alan Bass. Chicago: University of Chicago Press, 1982.

———. *Positions*. Trans. Alan Bass. Chicago: University of Chicago Press, 1981.

———. *Writing and Difference*. Trans. Alan Bass. Chicago: University of Chicago Press, 1978.

Kramer, Matthew. *Critical Legal Theory and the Challenge of Feminism*. Lanham MD: Rowman and Littlefield, 1994.

———. *Legal Theory, Political Theory, and Deconstruction: Against Rhadamanthus*. Bloomington: Indiana University Press, 1991.

Matthew H. Kramer

See also CRITICAL LEGAL STUDIES; DERRIDA, JACQUES; DERRIDEAN JURISPRUDENTS; INDETERMINACY; POSTMODERN PHILOSOPHY OF LAW; SELF-REFERENCE

Deemings

See FICTIONS AND DEEMINGS

Defenses

In a criminal prosecution it is up to the prosecution to prove the elements of the definition of the crime the defendant is charged with, and it is up to the defendant to raise and prove any defenses he may have. Strictly speaking, the word "defense" refers only to justifications, excuses, and other defense arguments that become relevant once the prosecution has made a prima facie case. In a looser sense, however, and in the sense to be used in this article, "defense" also refers to defense arguments aimed at throwing doubt upon the elements of the prosecution's case-in-chief. Using the term in this broader sense, we may distinguish *failure-of-proof defenses*, which are attacks upon the prosecution's case, from *affirmative defenses*, which become relevant only after the prosecution's case is established.

In the United States and other jurisdictions in the common law tradition the prosecution must prove the elements of the crime beyond a reasonable doubt, which means that a failure-of-proof defense will succeed if the fact finder believes that it raises a reasonable doubt about some element of the charge. The nature of the burden the defendant must carry in proving an affirmative defense varies from jurisdiction to jurisdiction. In some jurisdictions, for example, although the defendant must raise the issue of insanity, once it has been raised it becomes the burden of the prosecution to prove that the defendant was not insane.

Failure-of-Proof Defenses

The prosecutor must establish both the actus reus, or criminal act, and the culpability level (mens rea, or criminal mind) of the crime with which the defendant has been charged. If the prosecutor cannot establish that the act was voluntary and that it resulted in the harm that the law seeks to prevent, then the defendant may be said to have an actus reus defense. Aside from defenses that depend upon the fact that the defendant simply was not involved in the crime (*alibi defenses*), the defenses that the voluntary act requirement gives rise to are limited to certain well-established categories: reflex actions, unconscious movements, actions resulting from hypnotic suggestion, and (in some jurisdictions) automatistic behavior (*automatism*).

The *Model Penal Code* (MPC) recognizes four kinds of culpability with which an action may be performed: it may be done purposely, knowingly, recklessly, or negligently. Defenses having to do with culpability are, by and large, treated under the heading of *mistakes of fact*. Thus, a mistake of fact (or ignorance of a fact) may be inconsistent with the required purpose (or intent) or knowledge required by the definition of a crime, or, if the crime is one of recklessness or negligence may show that the defendant was mistaken about or not aware of facts that should have alerted him to the risk he was creating.

The most sophisticated approach to the mental aspect or culpability level is the so-called "element" approach, according to which the mental aspect must be considered separately for each separate element of the act. Thus, under the MPC approach, claiming that the prosecution has not established presence of the mental aspect or culpability level associated with *any* of the elements of the crime is a defense. If lack of consent, for example, is an element of battery, then if the crime of battery requires knowledge with respect to the lack of consent, even recklessness on the part of the defendant as to whether consent existed is not enough to convict. A simple belief in the existence of consent, even if unreasonable, means that the defendant is not guilty of the crime of battery.

It is also possible for the state to impose strict liability with respect to any element of a crime. That means that defendants' liabilities will not depend in any way upon their awareness of the presence of that element, or of the risk that their behavior will give rise to that element. In general, such crimes must be created by legislative action, and they are not looked upon favorably by commentators.

The element approach to culpability has brought a certain amount of clarity into the law of defenses. The common law, with one exception, treated the mens rea of a crime as a unitary whole and did not distinguish among the various states of mind that might accompany a single crime. The exception was for crimes of specific intent, wherein the common law distinguishes the general mens rea (intent, knowledge, negligence) with which the crime was committed from a further specified state of mind that accompanies the crime. Take, for example, the crime of assault with intent to rape, or the crime of assault upon someone known to be a police officer. In the first of these the intent to rape, and in the second the knowledge that the victim is a police officer, were said to be specific intent elements of the crimes.

This distinction between specific intent crimes and other crimes made a difference for the mistake defenses. In general, the common law recognized the defense of mistake only if the mistake was reasonable, a fact that created the logical oddity that although the required mens rea for a particular crime might be knowledge, a mere mistake (or lack of knowledge) would not constitute a defense; only a reasonable mistake would. But it was different for the specific intent of a crime, however: mere mistake, even if unreasonable, would there constitute a defense. Burglary, for example, is a specific intent crime; it consists of breaking into a dwelling at night with the intent to commit a felony. If one were to break into a dwelling at night with the intent of doing something that one mistakenly (and unreasonably) believed was not a felony, then one has not committed burglary, either in the common law or under the *Model Penal Code*.

Affirmative Defenses

Justifications and excuses are affirmative defenses. Together with the failure-of-proof defenses these make up what may be called the substantive defenses. In addition to these, there are other affirmative defenses that have nothing to do with the blameworthiness or accountability of the defendant; for example, a statute of limitations defense or one of the various sorts of immunity.

Justification

Sometimes violating the law may be the best course of action. No one should freeze to death in a blizzard because the law forbids him from breaking into a house nearby. A rule permitting one to choose the better course without penalty is a principle of justification. Standard justifications are self-defense, legal authority, and necessity.

Thus, it is permissible for a person to use force against another in *self-defense*, but only if the person defending herself reasonably believes that the person she uses force against has raised a threat of harm that can only be prevented by the use of that force. Various rules govern the proportionality of the force used to the harm to be prevented; deadly force may only be used to counter the threat of serious injury, and in some jurisdictions the defender must retreat if possible before using deadly force. A person also may be justified in using force to protect another person from harm, and may (to a limited extent) be justified in acting to protect property.

Things that would be crimes under other conditions will not be crimes if done with *legal authority,* in the course of enforcing the law. The police, for example, may use force where necessary to prevent a crime (the force must be in proportion to the crime to be prevented, of course) or to bring about the arrest of someone who has committed a crime. And an actor who breaks the law in order to bring about some greater good or lesser evil may be entitled to the defense of *necessity*. The person who breaks into someone else's mountain cabin during a snowstorm to avoid freezing to death, for example, has the justification of necessity. Necessity is not, however, a defense to murder, according to *R. v. Dudley and Stephens*, L.R. 14 Q.B.D. 273 (1884).

Excuse

We say that a person is morally justified when we think he has done the right thing; we excuse him when we think he did the wrong thing but had little choice in the circumstances. The law distinguished justification and excuse in roughly the same way: an excuse is a set of conditions in which a person of ordinary firmness would not have been able to comply with the law, even though it would have been better for all concerned if he had. Standard legal excuses are duress, intoxication, and insanity.

Ordinarily the defense of *duress* will be recognized only if there was a threat to kill or seriously injure the defendant or a close relative if the defendant did not commit the crime. Under the common law, duress was not a defense to crimes involving homicide; in some jurisdictions it is not a defense to crimes involving serious bodily harm. In a 1975 case involving the IRA, the British House of Lords extended the defense a bit, ruling that duress might excuse an accessory to murder; but in 1987 that case was overruled, and the common law rule reasserted.

Involuntary *intoxication* is ordinarily a defense; voluntary intoxication sometimes is. The better rule, and the rule of the MPC, is that voluntary intoxication, like involuntary intoxication, will excuse whenever, due to intoxication, the accused did not or could not have formed the mens rea required by the crime.

If the jurisdiction permits an *insanity defense* (and not all jurisdictions do), it will take one of a variety of forms, depending upon whether it takes into account both defects in cognitive capacity and defects in the capacity to control one's behavior, and upon whether it requires total or merely substantial impairment in these capacities.

Distinguishing Justification from Excuse

Following a long period in which the difference between justification and excuse had for all practical purposes disappeared, a vigorous theoretical discussion of the distinction began in the second half of this century with the work of writers like J.L. Austin and George Fletcher. Much of the discussion has centered on trying to find a theoretically sound basis for the distinction. The intuitive basis is this: A person is justified when she has done the right thing, everything considered. She is excused when, though she may have done the wrong thing, she is not blameworthy because she could not have done otherwise. The limits of this way of characterizing the distinction are reached rather quickly, and there has so far not been any very satisfactory resolution to the search for a sound principle.

Self-defense, for example, raises a number of problems. For one thing, killing another to save your own life may not be for the better. It certainly is not if all lives count the same, and it may not be if they count differently. Although it is considered a justification, therefore, it may not be the right thing to do in a given set of circumstances. Furthermore, the justification extends to cases in which one mistakenly believes one is under attack: these are cases in which self-defense clearly causes more harm than good, though the defender cannot know it at the time. Should these cases be treated as excuses rather than as justifications? What is the relevant moral difference between cases of actual self-defense and cases of mistaken self-defense? Perhaps they should all be treated as excuses. The problem is to decide whether the person who acts in self-defense does something praiseworthy (and so is justified), or whether he does something wrong but understandable, acting, as the MPC says, as a "person of ordinary firmness" would (and so should be excused). Similar problems plague other attempts to distinguish justification from excuse.

Mistake of Law

Sometimes a law contains a reference to another law. For example, it may prohibit all except those in certain legal categories from engaging in certain activities; to interpret such a law properly requires knowing whether or not one is in one of those categories. A mistake about the law in that case is very much like a mistake of fact, and should be a failure-of-proof defense under the same circumstances that would make a mistake of fact a defense. Most controversies over mistake of law, on the other hand, concern whether or not it should be a defense that someone was not aware of the very law he is being prosecuted under. In general, and with a few exceptions, the common law does not grant a defense under those circumstances. The reason has nothing to do with fairness or desert, but rather with the great difficulty of separating true claims from false claims; nothing is easier than to claim ignorance of the law. Indeed, most people are unaware of much of the criminal law under which they live, and to provide such a defense without limitations would be embarrassing to the legal system.

The Theory of Defenses

The aim of a theory of defenses is to bring all the substantive defenses together either under a single rationale or under a unified structure of rationales, or to show why it cannot be done. Although, as H.L.A. Hart argued, the point of the defenses need not be the same as the point of punishment itself, the fact is that theorizing in this area has tended to parallel theories of punishment. Any complete theory will address both (1) the question of the criterion, or mark, of the defenses; and (2) the moral basis of the theory.

A Criterion for the Defenses

William Blackstone wrote that all defenses could be reduced "to this single consideration: the want or defect of will." He believed that criminal liability required the concurrence of will and understanding, and distinguished four sorts of cases in which either the will or the concurrence was missing: (1) Cases in which there is no external harm traceable to an act of will of the defendant. This includes the actus reus defenses; it does not, apparently include cases of justification, which are treated by Blackstone as cases of external force (along with duress). (2) Cases of involuntariness, accident, or mistake, in which the understanding and will are both sound but did not cooperate in producing the prohibited result. This category includes most of the mens rea defenses, as well as the affirmative defenses of mistake. (3) Cases in which the accused is somehow deficient in the understanding of what he is doing. Blackstone included here the affirmative defenses of infancy, insanity, and intoxication. (4) Cases in which the prohibited act results from external force, including both the excuse of duress and the justifications of self-defense and necessity.

There is wide agreement about this point: what all defenses have in common is that in the circumstances the defendant did not freely choose to bring about the harm. It is somewhat misleading to think of free choice as a single notion in this context. However, the truth is that it captures two separate criteria: that the actor is not blameworthy unless he had real alternative choices, and that he is not blameworthy unless he actually intended or knew of the harm for which he is to be punished. If a person unknowingly runs over the neighbor's cat, he may well have had plenty of alternative choices: he could have refused to drive his car that morning; he could have taken other routes. What exculpates him in this case is not that he could not have done otherwise, but that he had no reason to think he should do otherwise. On the other hand, if he ran over the neighbor's cat deliberately because someone held a gun to his head and ordered him to do it, it is true that he intended to run over the cat; what exculpates him is that he had no real choice. An even better example may be the case in which the same actions take place under hypnosis.

This combination of criteria is captured by Hart: punishment is appropriate only if the defendant had the capacity to conform his behavior to the requirements of the law and a fair opportunity to do so. Not knowing that the cat was under the car, he may have had the capability not to run over it, but he lacked a fair opportunity to do so. One way of attempting to unite these two criteria theoretically would be to attempt to reduce them to considerations of efficiency: For one whose choices are limited by duress, natural catastrophe, or personal disability, the cost of complying with the law might be greater than we could require of a person of ordinary firmness; similarly, the cost of acquiring sufficient knowledge to avoid every mistake or accident would be enormous.

The Moral Basis of the Defenses

A utilitarian theory of punishment might be expected to generate a utilitarian theory of defenses, and a retributive theory of punishment a retributive theory of excuses. Various writers have pointed out, however, that mixed theories are possible, and we may, for example, conceive of the defenses as a limitation upon a utilitarian theory of punishment, a limitation rooted in retribution, or justice, or a theory of rights.

It was really Jeremy Bentham who brought the study of defenses to life with his attempt to show that they could be given a utilitarian justification. The aim of punishment, according to Bentham, is to reduce the costs of mischief, and no one ought to be punished when the punishment would not succeed in bringing about any good at all, or when the punishment would cost more than the good to be achieved (keeping in mind that punishment itself is "mischief"). Bentham listed four cases in which punishment did less good than harm: where there is no harmful act to be prevented; where punishment cannot prevent the act; where the punishment would be too expensive; and where punishment is unnecessary.

Although Bentham's study of defenses is one of the most important contributions ever made to the philosophical study of law, its faults are as great as its virtues. The primary utilitarian reason for punishing is to provide an example to others, so that they will not commit the same crime. The conclusion to draw from the fact that it is difficult to deter the intoxicated or the insane or those acting under duress, as Hart pointed out, is not necessarily that punishment is uncalled for in these cases. Even if they cannot be deterred themselves, it may be desirable to punish them so that others who *can* be deterred will be and to reduce the likelihood of someone falsely invoking one of those defenses. Hart intended the argument as a reductio ad absurdum, showing that the utilitarian account of defenses was defective.

Contemporary utilitarians who have undertaken to explain legal defenses are Richard Brandt in philosophy and Richard Posner in law. According to Brandt, the point of the criminal law is to encourage desirable character traits; the reason for the defenses is that acts performed under the defense-creating circumstances do not demonstrate any defect of character that can and should be corrected. For Posner, who approaches legal theory from an economic point of view, the point of the criminal law is to reduce the costs of crime, and a set of circumstances should be considered a defense only if harmful behavior in those circumstances cannot be deterred. Where behavior can be deterred, but only by increasing the penalty, it is a question of efficiency whether a defense should be granted or the penalty increased. Posner's response to Hart's *reductio* is thus to accept the conclusion.

Theories that see the right of the state to punish as something that has as a necessary condition the fact that the criminal deserves to be punished or that he has waived his right not to be punished will try to explain defenses as cases in which desert or waiver is absent. The strength of retributive theories of defenses lies in part in the weakness of the utilitarian theories. One of the great difficulties for such a theory is to explain why character traits should not serve as excuses. Clearly, doing the right thing is easier for some people than for others, and clearly, the difference is due in part to a difference in character. An avaricious person will have a harder time than a saintly person, an intemperate person a harder time than a person of moderate temperament. Character is not generally something we choose for ourselves; it is by and large beyond our control, even if we can influence it in small ways. It is determined by our background, upbringing, and genetic inheritance. It would seem to follow that the worse a person's character, the harder it will be for him to comply with the law, and the more inclined we should be to excuse him; whereas the better a person's character, the easier for him to follow the law, and the more inclined we should be to punish him for the smallest offenses.

References

American Law Institute. *Model Penal Code and Commentaries*. Philadelphia: American Law Institute Press, 1985.

Bentham, Jeremy. *Introduction to the Principles of Law and Morals*. Ed. J.H. Burns and H.L.A. Hart. London: Methuen, 1970.

Blackstone, William. *Commentaries on the Laws of England*. New York: Harper, 1852.

Brandt, Richard. "The Motivational Theory of Excuses." *Nomos* 27 (1985), 165–198.

Corrado, Michael, ed. *Justification and Excuse in the Criminal Law*. New York: Garland, 1994.

Dressler, Joshua. *Understanding Criminal Law*. New York: Matthew Bender, 1987.

Fletcher, George. *Rethinking Criminal Law*. Boston: Little, Brown, 1978.

Greenawalt, Kent. "The Perplexing Borders of Justification and Excuse." *Columbia Law Review* 84 (1984), 1897–1927.

Hart, H.L.A. *Punishment and Responsibility*. Oxford: Clarendon Press, 1968.

Moore, Michael. "Causation and the Excuses." *California Law Review* 73 (1985), 1091–1143.

———. "Choice, Character, and Excuse." *Social Philosophy and Policy* 7 (1990), 29–58.

Posner, Richard. "An Economic Theory of the Criminal Law." *Columbia Law Review* 85 (1985), 1193–1231.

Robinson, Paul. *Criminal Law Defenses*. St. Paul MN: West, 1984.

Michael L. Corrado

See also ACTUS REUS; COERCION (DURESS); INSANITY DEFENSE; JUSTIFICATION; MENS REA; NECESSITY; PROMULGATION; SELF-DEFENSE

Democratic Process

The term "democratic process" refers to the manner in which public policies, the most important of which is law, are produced in a democratic government. Perhaps the most significant feature of a democracy, a feature which distinguishes it from all nondemocratic forms of government, is the participation of the citizens in producing the laws that are binding on the entire community. This participatory feature is a defining characteristic of the democratic process and represents popular sovereignty in action. The participation of its citizens undergirds the legitimacy of a democratic government and supports the obligation of society's members to obey the law.

Participation can be direct, as in the government of fifth-century B.C. Athens, or indirect, as in modern representative democracies where citizens elect candidates on a periodic basis to serve in legislative bodies. In this age of large nation-states, representative rather than direct democracies predominate, and the democratic process most often operates within specific constitutional limits and constraints. The discussion here addresses the democratic process in contemporary representative and constitutional frameworks. It examines three problems regarding participation which have been raised and which cast doubt on the health and quality of the democratic process.

The first problem involves the way in which issues find their way onto the agendas of legislative and other political decision-making bodies. Political activity does not take place in a vacuum. It takes place within particular cultural, historical, and organizational contexts. Particularly in a democratic system where political freedoms, such as speech, press, and assembly are protected, the potential issues articulated will always outnumber those which become actual subjects for debate and resolution on the political agenda. In other words, potential issues struggle with one another for the attention of political decision makers. This struggle does not occur on an even playing field, however. As a function of unique cultural, historical, and organizational features, each political system has a characteristic bias favoring the inclusion of certain issues on the agenda and the exclusion or suppression of others.

E.E. Schattschneider has identified the kinds and levels of political party and interest group organization as primary factors in determining the particular bias of a political system. Since political issues reflect the various and competing interests of different groups or constituencies in a society, it matters a great deal which issues successfully make it onto the agenda and which do not. Groups whose interests are favored by the particular bias of a political system can become especially skilled at manipulating political conflict in a manner which further extends their already disproportionate influence on the content of the agenda. Steven Lukes has suggested that groups whose interests are extremely disfavored by the dominant agenda may be discouraged from even consciously formulating or articulating issues consistent with these interests. Although all of the members of a democratic community may possess equal constitutional rights to participate politically, the democratic process, due to agenda bias, may be incapable of representing all interests equitably.

Democracy is strongly associated, often even identified, with the rule of the majority. In classical democratic theory, the ability of the democratic process to represent the will of the majority through the decisions of elected officials is generally considered the very heart of popular sovereignty. However, the actual operation of the democratic process, particularly in the United States, suggests that it is primarily activated minorities, not majorities, that determine public policies. This divergence of practice from theory is a second problematic feature of democratic participation that deserves consideration.

In formulating public policies, the role of activated minorities, typically organized as interest groups, is seen most clearly if we look at the legislative process. On issues of specific policy, for example, agricultural subsidies, veteran benefits, or environmental regulation of particular industries, most members of the broad, politically active segment of society have no strong or clearly articulated preferences. It is rather those particular interest groups, that is, activated minorities, whose members are directly affected by a specific policy, that seek to influence the legislative outcome. Each policy area attracts its own unique constellation of interest groups. As we move from issue to issue, different and often conflicting groups come into play in the legislative process. The decentralized organization of modern legislatures around specialized committees having their own agendas and areas of expertise has facilitated an arrangement wherein particular groups develop long-standing and influential relationships with legislators who sit on the committees that handle matters important to them.

Robert Dahl has used the term "polyarchal democracy" to describe a system in which the number, size, and diversity of the minorities able to influence governmental decision making is extensive. If public policy formulation is primarily a process of bargaining and compromise between competing special interests, then perhaps what is missing in polyarchal democracy is a sufficient role for the common interest. The democratic process must allow groups representing special interests to play a role, but it must also provide ample opportunities for majority formation. Without such participatory opportunities, a democracy will be unable to generate the consensus on crucial issues necessary for some vision of the common interest and unable to move effectively to achieve the common goals of the whole community.

The third problem regarding democratic participation is raised by proponents of "elite" theory. This theory claims that society is divided into an elite minority possessing disproportionate power to influence public policy and a relatively powerless nonelite majority that has little or no significant role in policy formulation. Proponents of elite theory argue that electoral participation is largely a symbolic activity that only serves to foster the allegiance of the masses to the established order. Voting, then, is not a real exercise of power in the democratic process, but merely a device for choosing between competing elites who actually share a consensus on basic political and social values. According to this view, mainstream political parties do not offer the voters clear alternatives, but rather, espouse positions that fall well within the range of elite consensus. In addition, the interest group system is seen as stable and relatively impenetrable by new groups, particularly those perceived to be radical or those pursuing issues outside of the dominant agenda.

Peter Bachrach has used the term "democratic elitism" to refer to a political system in which representative and constitutional institutions and practices mask underlying oligarchical concentrations of power. Many theorists point to the wealth and political power of large corporations as a primary factor supporting the domination of elites in representative democracies. Not only can corporations bring tremendous resources to bear directly on the democratic process, but it is also claimed that their interests enjoy a preferred position in the prevailing power structures of most societies. This problem is compounded by the fact that corporate decision making remains, for the most part, outside the scope of democratic participation and accountability. A pressing question for democrats, which elite theory prompts, concerns those socioeconomic conditions under which a healthy and truly participatory democratic process can flourish. We must seriously examine whether societies in which large concentrations of wealth are outside the scope of democratic control or in which economic disparities between individual citizens are great can realize the full promise of democratic government.

References

Bachrach, Peter. *The Theory of Democratic Elitism*. Boston: Little, Brown, 1967.

Bachrach, Peter, and Aryeh Botwinick. *Power and Empowerment: A Radical Theory of Participatory Democracy*. Philadelphia: Temple University Press, 1992.

Barber, Benjamin. *Strong Democracy: Participatory Politics for a New Age*. Berkeley: University of California Press, 1984.

Dahl, Robert. *Dilemmas of Pluralist Democracy*. New Haven: Yale University Press, 1982.

———. *Preface to Democratic Theory*. Chicago: University of Chicago Press, 1956.

Fishkin, James. *Democracy and Deliberation: New Directions for Democratic Reform.* New Haven: Yale University Press, 1991.

Lukes, Steven. *Power: A Radical View.* London: Macmillan, 1977.

Madison, James. "Federalist #10." In *Hamilton, Madison, Jay: The Federalist Papers,* ed. Clinton Rossiter. New York: New American Library, 1961.

Pateman, Carole. *Participation and Democratic Theory.* Cambridge: Cambridge University Press, 1970.

Schattschneider, E.E. *The Semisovereign People: A Realist's View of Democracy in America.* New York: Holt, Rinehart and Winston, 1960.

David T. Risser

See also Franchise and Referendum; Lobbying

Deontic Logic
See Logic, Deontic Legal

Derrida, Jacques (1930–)

Although Jacques Derrida has not developed a "philosophy of law" in the ordinary sense of the term, he has in fact written a great deal concerning the concept of law. Derrida's writings on law may be said to fall into three general categories: (1) writing on the concept of law in the broadest sense, including, for example, the "law of genre"; (2) writing on the idea of the "law of the father," especially in connection with psychoanalysis; (3) writing that connects more directly with questions of justice, responsibility, right, and the state. The first two categories seem to be a great distance from more traditional discussions of legal philosophy, while even the third category of work does not deal directly with social institutions. However, there are close interrelations among these categories, and something like a "philosophy of law" emerges, at least on on the level of a metatheory.

Derrida's deconstruction of the "law of genre," wherein categories such as "philosophy" and "literature," for example, are seen as porous and interrelated, would seem to create insurmountable difficulties for any theory of law. After all, if the law (any system of laws) cannot categorically lay down the law, then what sense is there in speaking of law?

However, unlike Martin Heidegger, to whom his thought is often allied, Derrida does not argue that the open-endedness of categories means the end of thinking through categories. Instead, like Karl Marx, Derrida argues that there is something important to be learned by pushing categories to their limit and by viewing systems in terms of their margins or undersides. In particular, and very much on the material plane, Derrida is concerned with the fact that systems of laws are always established by actions that are themselves outside the systems they establish.

In terms of actual or potential legal structures, Derrida juggles three main claims, each seemingly at odds with the others. First, Derrida argues that justice must never be reduced to law or any actual or potential set of laws. Law can never be fully adequate to the demands of justice. This is for the reason that, in Derrida's view, the demands of justice are infinite, while law must operate in the realm of the finite. Furthermore, while any system of laws is, in Derrida's view, deconstructible, *justice itself* is that which is not deconstructible. (Indeed, Derrida has even argued that, therefore, deconstruction *is* justice.) However, and second, because people and societies do operate in the finite realm, actual decisions have to be made. The necessary inadequacy of law to justice is not a license for moral skepticism. Third, there is the problem of *exemplarity.* In some sense, this problem may be understood as the mediating issue between the first two claims. However, this mediation is also a deconstruction: on the one hand, the decision-making procedure in Western law relies heavily on the idea of the example, in the form of legal precedent and a history of case law; on the other hand, each case is different and brings something new to this history. Justice must be done both to the history of similar cases and to the particularity of the present case. Legal precedent would seem to generate something like a calculus, but, Derrida argues, justice can never issue from nor be reduced to such a calculus.

"Justice" as mere calculation, Derrida argues, is always akin and ultimately reduces itself to the mere "setting right" of things in the form of vengeance. While Derrida's argument encompasses other claims in the philosophy of law, for example H.L.A. Hart's, that legal reasoning must be open-ended and flexible, in order to allow consideration of new situations, his point is really quite different. For Derrida, there is never a point where the case is absolutely "closed," for justice in the past application of law is no more certain than is justice in the present case, as yet unprecedented. The ideal of justice-as-undeconstructible stands always as a metacritique of any possible approximation to justice through the application of law. As numerous commentators have pointed out (for example, Douglas Litowitz), Derrida's arguments in this regard share an affinity with Plato's and Immanuel Kant's. However, if one follows Derrida's actual argumentative moves, one sees that Derrida works more on the level of immanent critique, and that deconstruction reaches the level of (what Derrida calls) the "quasi-transcendental" by tunneling from within.

Of course, some systems of laws (and some social formations in general) may be so at odds with the pursuit of the ideal of justice that Derrida's metacritique only applies at the level of the whole. Derrida warns against an approach to such "'juridical voids,' as if it were a matter of filling in the blanks without re-doing things from top to bottom."

A number of legal theorists have pursued Derrida's arguments, including some associated with critical legal studies; among these, perhaps the most effective has been Drucilla Cornell.

References

Cornell, Drucilla. *Beyond Accommodation: Ethical Feminism, Deconstruction, and the Law.* London: Routledge, 1991.
———. "The Good, the Right, and the Possibility of Legal Interpretation." In *The Philosophy of the Limit,* ed. Drucilla Cornell, 91–115. London: Routledge, 1992.
Derrida, Jacques. "Before the Law." Trans. Avital Ronell and Christine Roulston. In *Derrida, Acts of Literature,* ed. Derek Attridge, 183–220. New York: Routledge, 1992.
———. "Declarations of Independence." Trans. Tom Keenan and Tom Pepper. *New Political Science* 15 (1986), 7–15.
———. "The Force of Law: The 'Mystical Foundation of Authority'." Trans. Mary Quaintance. In *Deconstruction and the Possibility of Justice,* special issue of *Cardozo Law Review* 11, no. 5–6 (July/August 1990), 920–1045.
———. "The Law of Genre." Trans. Avital Ronell. In *Derrida, Acts of Literature,* ed. Derek Attridge, 223–252. New York: Routledge, 1992.
———. *Specters of Marx. The State of the Debt, the Work of Mourning, and the New International.* Trans. Peggy Kamuf. London: Routledge, 1994.
Hart, H.L.A. *The Concept of Law.* Oxford: Oxford University Press, 1961.
Litowitz, Douglas. "Derrida on Law and Justice: Borrowing (Illicitly?) from Plato and Kant." *Canadian Journal of Law and Jurisprudence* 8 (1995), 325–346.

Bill Martin

See also CRITICAL LEGAL STUDIES; DECONSTRUCTIONIST PHILOSOPHY OF LAW; DERRIDEAN JURISPRUDENTS; INDETERMINACY; POSTMODERN PHILOSOPHY OF LAW

Derridean Jurisprudents

How can and should the thought and practice of Jacques Derrida (1930–), commonly labeled "deconstruction," be applied to legal contexts? Although legal scholars began employing deconstructionist techniques in the early 1980s, it was not until the late 1980s that this question was thematized and attempts were made to answer it. This entry will examine the two most systematic and influential of these attempts: J.M. Balkin's (1956–) and Drucilla Cornell's (1950–).

Balkin has been primarily concerned with how Derrida's work can be appropriated by those interested in the theory and practice of legal reasoning and/or rhetoric. To this end, he focuses his attention on Derrida's account of meaning. According to this account, there are two fundamental conditions of meaning: "iterable" signs and interpretive contexts. These conditions entail that it is impossible to fix the meaning of a sign once and for all. For neither is it possible to limit a sign to a single context, since its iterability is a necessary condition of its meaning anything at all; nor is it possible to fix the limits of any context, since contexts are delimited by norms that are themselves composed of signs. The upshot is not that meaning is completely indeterminate, but merely that meaning and communication take place within contexts that can be no more than relatively stable.

Balkin draws two main consequences from this account of meaning. The first concerns the precise nature of deconstructive argument itself. A deconstructive argument typically focuses on a particular conceptual opposition or oppositional hierarchy, for example, the public/private distinction. Balkin argues that such arguments rest on the view that "all conceptual oppositions can be understood as some form of nested opposition"; that is, as "a conceptual opposition in which the two terms possess simultaneous relationships of difference and similarity that are manifested as we consider them in different contexts of judgment." Hence, by recontextualizing the opposition in question, a deconstructive argument shows that the relationship between its two terms need not be conceived of in the "standard" manner or in the manner in which one's opponent conceives of it. Since judgments of similarity and difference are central to legal reasoning, this account of deconstructive argument enables us to see how it can be quite useful in legal contexts.

Second, Balkin develops a theory of "ideological drift" according to which "styles of legal argument, theories of jurisprudence, and theories of constitutional interpretation do not have a fixed normative or political valence. Their valence varies over time as they are applied and understood repeatedly in new contexts and situations." In addition to helping us understand the nature of legal argument in general, this theory enables us to see that deconstructive argument is itself subject to ideological drift. In other words, contrary to the widespread assumption that deconstruction has only progressive politico-juridical consequences, it actually has no particular practical consequences whatever. It is merely a particular style of rhetoric that can be wielded as successfully against just positions as against unjust positions; indeed, all positions are deconstructible.

Balkin is quick to realize, however, that if this were the final word on deconstructive argument, it could have no critical force. He thus argues that if it is to have such force, its users must allow that some positions are truer or more just than others, and that they can only do this by "postulating" transcendent values of truth and justice that exist "beyond" the constructed standards of truth and justice of particular communities. Balkin dubs this augmented version of deconstruction "transcendental deconstruction." With this reading of deconstruction, the goal of a deconstructive argument is to show that legal systems, doctrines, decisions, and so forth, are less just than other more just alternatives.

Although Cornell could accept much of Balkin's version of Derridean jurisprudence, her own version is informed by concerns quite foreign to Balkin's. First, she has a long-standing interest in and sees her own work as a continuation of the German idealist tradition's approach to ethico-politico-juridical issues. (Her conception of this tradition is quite broad, including both Immanuel Kant and Theodor Adorno in addition to G.W.F. Hegel, Johann Fichte, and F.W.J. Schelling.) The distinctive feature of this approach is its attempt to trace the boundary or limit between theoretical and practical reason. Cornell has been drawn to Derrida's work precisely because she views it as the most recent and most advanced such attempt. Derrida, in her view, has devised a strategy for navigating between the Scylla of Hegel's optimistic, yet "totalitarian" account of this limit and the Charybdis of Adorno's anti-totalitarian, yet pessimistic account of it. It is for these reasons that she renames deconstruction (with its negative overtones reminiscent of Adorno's "negative dialectics") "the philosophy of the limit."

At the same time, however, she has worked to develop a theory and program of radical feminist legal reform. This project rests on the view that Western society is so thoroughly suffused with "the law of the gender hierarchy"—the systematic privileging of the masculine over the feminine—that moderate, evolutionary legal reform cannot bring about *sustainable* improvements for women. Cornell holds that Derrida's "philosophy of the limit" is invaluable to this project precisely because it justifies and promotes the radical, utopian transformation of politico-juridical systems.

This result follows, she argues, from Derrida's account of the contextual nature of meaning. Since it is impossible to fix the boundaries of a context once and for all, and since a legal system is nothing more than a complicated context of interpretation and decision, it follows that legal systems cannot be rendered immune to radical transformation. Furthermore, not only are such contexts necessarily limited, but, more important, they are *limited* and *constituted by* that which they exclude. In the case of legal systems, this constitutive limit is nothing other than justice itself. In other words, since justice is an aporia that

D

must remain forever "unpresentable" or "to come," a given legal system cannot be fully just, and, as such, its radical transformation is justified and desirable. It is precisely in this way that Derrida enables us to avoid Hegel's "totalitarianism" without having to settle for Adorno's pessimism. In the specific case of "our" legal system, this "quasi-transcendental" account of justice as the limit of any system of positive law justifies and promotes attempts to radically transform this system by purging it of all traces of the gender hierarchy.

How is this purgation to be accomplished? Whereas Balkin would recommend deconstructive argument, Cornell places more emphasis on the second prong of Derrida's "double-gesture" (that is, dual strategy) for "transcending" such hierarchies: writing in a "new" way which attempts to avoid or at least minimize the use of rigid oppositional hierarchies and other features of "logocentric" discourse. She thus argues that overcoming the gender hierarchy requires us to "re-imagine" the feminine.

This said, she acknowledges that the philosophy of the limit requires supplementation by a more positive, constructive jurisprudence. As the preceding account of her interests and aims might lead one to expect, she suggests that the most appropriate supplement is a feminized version of John Rawls' kantian constructivism. Its centerpiece is the view that "the imaginary domain" ("the space for re-imagining who one is and who one seeks to become") is a minimum necessary condition of personhood.

References

Balkin, J.M. "Being Just with Deconstruction." *Social and Legal Studies* 3 (1994), 393–404.

———. "Ideological Drift and the Struggle over Meaning." *Connecticut Law Review* 25 (1993), 869.

———. "Nested Oppositions." *Yale Law Journal* 99 (1990), 1669.

———. "Transcendental Deconstruction, Transcendent Justice." *Michigan Law Review* 94 (1994), 1133.

Cornell, Drucilla. *The Imaginary Domain.* New York: Routledge, 1995.

———. *The Philosophy of the Limit.* New York: Routledge, 1992.

Derrida, Jacques. "Force of Law: 'The Mystical Foundation of Authority.'" *Cardozo Law Review* 11 (1990), 919.

———. *Limited Inc.* Evanston: Northwestern University Press, 1988.

Edward Blatnik

See also DECONSTRUCTIONIST PHILOSOPHY OF LAW; DERRIDA, JACQUES; INDETERMINACY; POSTMODERN PHILOSOPHY OF LAW

Desert

Suffering is in general an evil that ought to be, as far as possible, avoided or eradicated. Failure in sincere attempts to achieve this aim is a result of the fact that suffering is frequently found to be a necessary evil. Thus, painful surgery may have to be endured now to avoid greater suffering later.

There are other ways of justifying suffering than seeing it as the by-product of instrumentally valuable actions. For example, causing suffering may be deemed necessary to teach someone a lesson. The suffering itself is taken to have instrumental value. "Spare the rod and spoil the child" may be seen as the expression of this belief, although it can also be interpreted as a plea for corporal, as opposed to other, forms of punishment.

Two conditions are likely to be mentioned as foundations for deserved, and therefore justified, suffering: either the foolishness or the wickedness of the sufferer. "It served him right" and "He has only got himself to blame" attribute responsibility to the agent. However, it is not considered regrettable if the suffering is avoided. It is believed to be inherently better if the person can learn a lesson without suffering. If smoking tends to cause cancer, heavy smokers who get the disease perhaps have only themselves to blame, but no harm or injustice is necessarily done if these smokers live long, healthy lives. Foolishness does not demand suffering as an appropriate accompaniment.

When it is claimed that wickedness deserves punishment, the situation is different. "He deserves to suffer for it" suggests that the wicked ought to suffer. The expression is taken from the works of the eighteenth-century author Bishop Berkeley, who writes: "Upon considering or viewing together our notion of vice and that of misery there results a third, that of ill desert." The bishop writes as if the wicked ought to be miserable. However, "ill desert" is best regarded as a wider concept than that of deserving suffering. One may deserve well and ill, favorable and unfavorable treatment. If one's wickedness is extreme enough, killing may be thought too good for that person. It may also sometimes be seen as an act of mercy to kill a sentient being in order to prevent unnecessary suffering. To cause suffering deliberately, however, except as a necessary means to prevent greater suffering or to achieve some strikingly important good, is condemned as cruelty, the most abhorrent of vices.

The term "wickedness" is in general reserved for only extreme immorality, but moral guilt is a sufficient condition for justified punishment and for the severity of the punishment to fit the degree of moral wickedness displayed by the offense.

The belief in an essential connection between wickedness and suffering is built into the structure of our morality, as is shown by the way morality is taught and by the widespread view that suffering appropriate punishment wipes away a person's guilt. There is a certain tension between ill desert on the one hand and our duty to be forgiving, kind, and merciful on the other. Although ill desert is rejected in the attitude of a morally good person, a place may be found for appropriate suffering.

Retribution is sometimes confused with revenge, and it is certainly true that one who takes revenge on another often thinks that what he is doing to the other person is no more than what that person has asked for by his actions: "He has injured me (or my family) so he can expect to be hurt." But the important thing to remember is that the revenge is taken for an injury and not for an offense displaying wickedness. Ill desert is not necessarily connected with being a fit object for revenge. The person who believes in revenge need not be committed to any view about the fittingness between suffering and evil character. A person may in fact think well of those against whom she is committed to take revenge. Thus the person's only connection with the injury may be kinship with the perpetrator and in no way need the perpetrator be thought of as morally *deserving* of harm or suffering. In the case of revenge, it is the person harmed or someone closely related to that person who is required to impose the hard treatment on the one upon whom revenge is taken. Decisions regarding deserved punishment, on the other hand, are thought best left to impartial people who have not suffered because of the evil deed. Justice demands in both legal and nonlegal cases a certain detachment or distancing from the situation so that bias can be avoided.

A person of ill desert, we are told, has no claim to our pity, even if that person suffers because of it. However, the loss of a person's claim to pity does not entail that *we* may punish. We may lack the authority to do so. Although suffering pangs of conscience is often thought appropriate, this suffering is not to be equated with self-inflicted punishment. This is evident when we consider that the acute guilt feelings of the offender may lead to self-inflicted punishment or to the seeking of punishment from others. In the past, flagellation and other forms of self-torture were common among those who were most acutely aware of their sinfulness. Similarly, punishment by others is sometimes sought as a relief from having to live with one's conscience. People sometimes give themselves up to the authorities because they cannot bear their feelings of guilt. The guilt makes the person feel an outcast from the moral community and in seeking punishment, that person is seeking reestablishment in the community as an accepted member. Private suffering may not suffice to reestablish membership in the moral community. The suffering must be made public and visible to those whom it is meant to influence. If a person also submits to the decision of the authorities as to what form the suffering will take, this may be seen as an indication that one now accepts the standards violated by the offense. This social function of punishment as a ticket for readmission to society is undoubtedly important and may explain why it is considered unfair to make an offender suffer socially undesirable consequences after the punishment is completed, and to continue to hold against that person the offense for which he has been punished. The person has settled the score with the law that prescribes punishment for criminal actions, not for wicked character. Note carefully, however, that suffering as such does not wipe the *moral* slate clean. The acceptance by the criminal of the authority of the officers of the law to punish, and the belief that the law is just, are preconditions for the criminal's seeing the punishment as a morally deserved disgrace.

If the moral self-condemnation is justified and is a necessary means to moral reform, then the suffering caused by the punishment may be justified by its valuable consequences.

However, the moral retributivist, *leaning on the concept of ill desert,* holds a different view. To a retributivist, the suffering is justified whether or not it does anything to improve the person's character.

References

Ardal, P.S. "Does Anyone Ever Deserve to Suffer?" *The Queen's Quarterly* (Summer, 1984).

Beardsley, E. "A Plea for Deserts." *American Philosophical Quarterly* 6 (1969), 33.

Butler, Bishop Joseph. *Dissertation Upon the Nature of Virtue in Fifteen Sermons.* London: G. Bellson, 1949.

Cottingham, J.G. "Varieties of Retribution." *Philosophical Quarterly* 29 (1979), 238.

Davis, L.H. "They Deserve to Suffer." *Analysis* 32 (1972), 136.

Duff, R.A. *Trials and Punishments.* Cambridge: Cambridge University Press, 1986.

Fingarette, H. "Punishment and Suffering." American Philosophical Association Presidential Address, 1977.

Gross, H. "Culpability and Desert." In *Philosophy and the Criminal Law,* ed. R.A. Duff and N. Simmonds, 59. Wiesbaden: Steiner, 1984.

Morris, H. "Guilt and Suffering." In *Guilt and Innocence,* ed. H. Morris, 89. Riverside: University of California Press, 1976.

Winch, P. "Ethical Reward and Punishment." In *Ethics and Action,* ed. P. Winch. London: Routledge and Kegan Paul, 1972.

Pall S. Ardal

See also RETRIBUTIVE RATIONALE; VENGEANCE

Deterrence, Strategic

Deterrence in international affairs consists in obtaining compliance by threat. This very broad definition is usually further qualified by limiting threats to threats of force and to compliance with the desire not to be attacked. Thus, attacks are deterred by threatening (explicitly or tacitly) to extract a cost through military retaliation so great as to make the original attack not worthwhile. Conventional deterrence, that is, the threat to respond militarily using nonnuclear weapons is as old as recorded history. However, it was with the advent of nuclear weapons that deterrence took on both a strategic and moral significance dramatically disportionate to its old role. For now, one power could say to another power, "If you aggress upon me or my allies, my nuclear forces will destroy you as an organized society."

Three further things followed from this development. First, to destroy a society or even to use nuclear weapons at all in war would kill, maim, and injure millions or perhaps even hundreds of millions of people. Second, in all but the most unusual cases, for example, nuclear naval battles, the vast majority of those killed would be noncombatants. Thus, the moral stakes involved in nuclear deterrence are vast. Third, it is possible for two opposed powers to develop nuclear arsenals and, thus, for each to deter the other, creating the familiar mutual deterrence, accurately, if dramatically, described as the "balance of terror." Obviously, this is no mere theoretical construct but a realistic picture of the posture of the United States and the Soviet Union during the cold war.

It is fairly clear that the use of nuclear weapons in war does not directly violate international law, although some authorities have claimed that first use could be construed as a crime against humanity and that any use might have toxic or environmental effects that could indirectly violate a number of conventions and treaties. Nuclear deterrence, the threatened use of nuclear weapons in response to an unjustified attack, is on even stronger ground. Article 51 of the United Nations Charter justifies defensive war and does not exclude any means. It may be, however, that the threatened second strike (that is, a response to a nuclear first strike) might be more in the way of a reprisal than an act of self-defense. It would be a pure reprisal if no further military good could come of it for the nation striking second. It would be self-defense if damage from further war-waging by the original attacker could be mitigated. Clearly, a second strike could be both, in terms of motivation and of effect. Even if a second strike is deemed a pure reprisal, the laws of war might well permit it. All in all, there seems to be no doubt that the international law of war is highly tolerant of the use of nuclear weapons, especially for deterrent effect.

Modern moral sensibility and the moral interpretation of just war theory have not been so generous. There appears to be an ascending scale of moral justifiability beginning with an unprovoked aggressive use of nuclear weapons, a morally monstrous act. Next would come a preemptive strike where one power sincerely believed it was about to be attacked. Then comes a nuclear strike responding to a conventional attack by an adversary power. The United States and NATO have argued this to be justifiable and, through their influence, have managed to maintain its international legal permissibility. Then would come a retaliatory second strike responding to a first nuclear strike. Lastly, the most justifiable kind of use of nuclear weapons would seem to be a second strike directed at the attackers' remaining nuclear weapons (a so-called counterforce strike). Clearly, this kind of use is the most directly based upon self-defense.

Nonetheless, most moralists have argued that *any use* of nuclear weapons would be immoral. There are two primary reasons for this. Nuclear weapons cannot discriminate between combatants and noncombatants; many argue that the damage they would inflict upon innocent noncombatants would be so massive as to nullify any possible military advantage, even a morally legitimate one. Moreover, at least between powers with significant nuclear arsenals, the chance that use could be kept to one weapon, or even a few, in an exchange is small. It is sobering to realize that, at the height of the cold war, the United States and the Soviet Union each had approximately thirty thousand nuclear warheads of various types. Today, there are tens of thousands of nuclear warheads worldwide. According to Thomas Schelling, given these numbers and various game theoretic conditions attending some forms of nuclear readiness, nuclear war appears to be highly unstable and escalation a terrible risk. Therefore, the chances that the use of one weapon would lead to a full-scale nuclear war and catastrophic consequences seem high. For these reasons, most moralists have argued that the actual *use* of nuclear weapons would be immoral. Different opinions have been expressed by Paul Ramsey, David Gauthier, and James Child.

The primary philosophical battle has been fought over whether deterrent threats to use nuclear weapons are morally acceptable, even while the carrying out of those threats would not be. This issue seems to turn on what some commentators have defended as the *wrong intentions principle*, that is, it is wrong to intend to do that which it is wrong to do. Thus, since by hypothesis it is always wrong to use nuclear weapons, then it is wrong to intend to use nuclear weapons, even if only as a second strike deterrent. Others have argued that the deterrent threat "We will use our nuclear weapons only if you attack us" is a *conditional* one. Therefore, it is not immoral so long as the condition are unfulfilled and the threat not carried out. Thus, according to Gregory Kavka, a policy of nuclear deterrence can be morally acceptable while, paradoxically it would seem, the use of the arsenal that makes the policy possible would be immoral.

References

Akehurst, Michael. *A Modern Introduction to International Law.* 5th ed. London: George Allen and Unwin, 1984.

Child, James W. *Nuclear War: The Moral Dimension.* New Brunswick NJ: Transaction Press, 1986.

Finnis, John, Joseph Boyle, and Germain Grisez. *Nuclear Deterrence, Morality and Realism.* Oxford: Oxford University Press, 1987.

Gauthier, David. "Deterrence, Maximization and Rationality." *Ethics* 94 (1984), 474–495.

Johnson, James Turner. *Can Modern War Be Just?* New Haven: Yale University Press, 1984.

Kavka, Gregory. *Moral Paradoxes of Nuclear Deterrence.* Cambridge: Cambridge University Press, 1987.

Ramsey, Paul. *The Just War.* New York: Scribner, 1968.

Schelling, Thomas. *Arms and Influence.* New Haven: Yale University Press, 1966.

von Glahn, Gerhard. *Law Among Nations.* New York: Macmillan, 1981.

Walzer, Michael. *Just and Unjust Wars.* New York: Basic Books, 1977.

James W. Child

See also CONSCIENCE; CONSCIENTIOUS OBJECTION; INTERNATIONAL JURISDICTION; TERRORISM

Deterrent Rationale

One of the traditional theories of punishment is deterrence. The theory is that when effective social situations for inflicting punishment exist, people will commit fewer crimes, knowing that they will be punished if they do, or knowing at least that there is a high probability that they will be. Thus, the actual commission of the crime is not immediately and directly relevant to subsequent punishment. Instead, the issue is, what is necessary to prevent effectively future crimes of this sort? However, this claim leads immediately to the question Who is to be deterred? There are two possible answers. One is that the person who committed the crime is deterred by the actual punishment from committing similar crimes in the future. This is called specific deterrence. The other possible answer is that it is members of the public who are to be deterred by the threat of punishment made manifest in the offender's punishment. This is typically called general deterrence.

Deterrence of both kinds can be contrasted with the two other main theories of punishment. The first is not technically a theory of punishment at all. It is the reformative theory. That is, we put the criminal through a regime of *treatment* to correct criminal tendencies and prevent the offender from repeating the crime. The other main theory is the retributive theory, which holds that, as a morally appropriate thing for society to do, the offender *deserves* to be punished for the crime. Both kinds of deterrence share with reformation the feature of being wholly *prospective* and concerned with the *effects* of punishment. Moreover, either deterrence theory seems concerned only with the *efficacy* of punishment and not the *justice* of it. This, as we shall see, causes problems for the theory. The retributive theory, by contrast, is *retrospective* and concerned with the criminal's act and his state of mind, or mens rea, at the time of the act. It also seeks to do justice, with efficacy of prevention or deterrence, at most, a secondary issue.

There are a number of well-known arguments against each of these theories. One that is often launched against both specific and general deterrence is simply that they do not work. Care needs be taken with this argument, however, since high recidivism rates are often cited as an argument against general deterrence. This is not a cogent argument: all these rates show is that individual criminals are not deterred by punishment, that specific deterrence appears to fail to work.

The actual determination of the deterrent effects if any is, of course, an empirical question and a very sophisticated statistical one as well. Data are inconclusive, but C.L. Ten concludes in a survey of the literature that general deterrence seems to work, although just how effective it is remains obscure. Individual deterrence appears to be on even weaker ground.

Granting that deterrence works, it still faces formidable philosophical arguments. Some critics claim that general deterrence could justify punishing the innocent so long as the public believes them guilty, since the social effect is all that matters. Justice, according to this argument, is so intimately tied to retribution that, without it, social efficacy is our only criterion for the appropriateness of deterrence policies. Neither guilt nor innocence has any role, or so this critique goes.

Another related argument is that neither specific nor general deterrence can account for the appropriate proportion between the severity of the crime and the severity of the punishment. If we should find that capital punishment deters parking violations and light jail sentences deter murder, then, so this argument goes, we must accept such an apparently unjust regime of punishment or abandon deterrence. Only retribution, claims this view, can provide us the proportionality between offense and punishment required by justice.

It is worth noting that deterrence and reformative theories often seem to pull in opposite ways. To deter someone (at least the rational actor of decision theory), one would have to threaten to make that person suffer or at least make things less pleasant than they were before. Reformative theories are typically concerned with education, improving self-image, and generally treating offenders in a humane and supportive way.

There can be no doubt that the arguments against deterrence, both general and specific, are powerful. The best philosophic defense of deterrence theories is, probably, that equally compelling arguments exist against rival theories. Yet most authorities agree that a deterrence theory, if it is to withstand philosophical scrutiny, must be supplemented by some considerations of justice that cannot be accounted for merely by the social efficacy of deterring crime alone.

References

Duff, Anthony. *Trials and Punishments*. Cambridge: Cambridge University Press, 1985.

Garland, David. *Punishment and Modern Society: A Study in Social Theory*. Chicago: University of Chicago Press, 1990.

Hart, H.L.A. *Punishment and Responsibility.* Oxford: Oxford University Press, 1968.

Honderich, Ted. *Punishment: The Supposed Justifications.* Cambridge: Cambridge University Press, 1989.

Murphy, Jeffrey, ed. *Punishment and Rehabilitation.* Belmont CA: Wadsworth, 1973.

——. *Retribution, Justice and Therapy.* Dordrecht: Reidel, 1979.

Nathanson, Stephen. "Does It Matter If the Death Penalty Is Arbitrarily Administered?" *Philosophy and Public Affairs* 14 (1985), 149–164.

"Retributive Justice and Prior Offences." *Philosophical Forum* 18 (1986), 40–51.

Stuart, James D. "Deterrence, Desert and Drunk Driving." *Public Affairs Quarterly* 3 (1989), 105–115.

Ten, C.L. *Crime, Guilt and Punishment.* Oxford: Clarendon Press, 1987.

James W. Child

See also DESERT; REHABILITATION AND HABILITATION RATIONALE; RETRIBUTIVE RATIONALE

Developing Countries

Law in the ordinary meaning as a body of enforceable public rules is historically associated with the state or the church: Roman law, Byzantine law, (medieval) canon law, Islamic law, colonial law, criminal law, civil law, and so forth. Public law in this nonanthropological definition is an instrument of the civil state, which is basically a legal arrangement, and where there is no such state there is no such law.

In vast stretches of the developing world historically public law and civil states scarcely existed. Where there was a quasi-public law it was coextensive with the theocratic world of Islam: Islamic law. This was a belt of legal authority that extended from Morocco to Indonesia. Public law was transported to many places in Asia, Africa, and Oceania by European imperialism: it came with the colonial state. British colonies, for example, were under the sovereignty of Parliament and the administrative direction of the Colonial Office.

Most governments in developing countries inherited from the colonial power a legal order, which they adapted, with greater or lesser success, to their goals of self-government, nation-building, and economic development. As an alternative, they resorted to Is-

lamic law. Indigenous authorities, such as clan elders or tribal chiefs, were associated with a premodern past and were usually sidestepped. In many developing countries, particularly in Africa, the autonomous legal order of the former colonial government was not successfully carried over into the independence era. Colonial administrators were a guardian class of foreigners isolated from the surrounding society. African and Asian rulers, however, were creatures of that society. Most of these postcolonial governments lost autonomy when they were indigenized and became transfused with personalism, nepotism, and corruption. Indigenous social norms encroached upon the new state and its public laws. Political instability, violence, and even civil war often displaced law and order. In some places the civil condition disintegrated and a hobbesian state of nature supplanted the state of law. Whether a developing country's public philosophy is autocratic or democratic, socialist or capitalist, is not the most fundamental issue. The challenge for legal and political philosophy in developing countries today is reminiscent of what Thomas Hobbes confronted in England in the seventeenth century: lawlessness and internal war associated with dislocated or failed states. Theorists are again obliged by historical circumstances to reflect upon the requirements for instituting viable legal orders. The solution, however, cannot be the same because the world is entirely changed. A new philosophy of legal and political development is called for that can respond to new circumstances.

References
Brown, Bartram S. "Developing Countries in the International Trade Order." *Northern Illinois University Law Review* 14 (1994), 347.

Frankel, Tamar. "Knowledge Transfer: Suggestions for Developing Countries on the Receiving End." *Boston University International Law Journal* 13 (1995), 141.

Liu Wenzong. "Of the Human Rights." *Beijing Review* 39 (1996), 18.

McCarthy, Colin L. "Regional Integration of Developing Countries at Different Levels of Economic Development: Problems and Prospects." *Transnational Law and Contemporary Problems* 4 (1994), 1.

Minyersky, N., and L. Flah. "Adoption in the Developing Countries." *International Review of Contemporary Law* 2 (1989), 73.

Nygaard, Richard L. "A Bill of Rights for the Twenty-First Century." *Hastings Constitutional Law Quarterly* 21 (1994), 189.

Paysalian, Simon. "The United States and the Developing Countries in the 1990s." *University of Detroit Mercy Law Review* 73 (1996), 525.

Ramakrishna, Kilaparti. "Interest Articulation and Lawmaking in Global Warming Negotiations: Perspectives from Developing Countries." *Transnational Law and Contemporary Problems* 2 (1992), 153.

Robert H. Jackson

See also CUSTOMARY LAW

Dewey, John (1859–1952)

John Dewey was the most prominent philosopher in America in the first half of the twentieth century. Along with Charles Sanders Peirce and William James from the previous generation, he charted America's distinctive contribution to philosophy and reimagined many of its traditional problems and concerns by offering a fresh interpretation of experience. However, Dewey was the only philosophical pragmatist to study the law closely and thus best exemplifies the two main branches of the pragmatic tradition—philosophy and law. With his commitment to scientific method and the social sciences, he helped inspire legal realism, which in part grew out of legal pragmatism.

The law is discussed infrequently in Dewey's voluminous writings. He wrote no book in the area, only a few substantive articles, assorted reviews, and encyclopedia entries. Dewey's philosophy of law, spanning nearly a half century, may be organized around an account of the three most substantial essays he wrote on the law, essays which develop themes from his earliest ventures into legal theory.

In the most widely known essay, "Logical Method and Law," which was originally published in 1924, Dewey contrasts two theories of adjudication, his own theory on one side and rival theories on the other, in the hope of building a foundation for a more inclusive logical method grounded in legal experience. The "hunch" theory serves as an adjudicatory repository for outmoded theories. The logic judicial intuitionists subscribe to in their opinions is a logic of subsumption: all that judges have to do is find the appropriate rule (major premise) governing a particular set of facts

(minor premise) and then the judgment (the conclusion) will follow necessarily. Echoing Oliver Wendell Holmes, Jr., Dewey urges that a logic of "search and inquiry" replace a "logic of exposition" that values consistency for its own sake. His theory of adjudication accommodates change better than rival theories, and extends not only to the obvious changes in fact situations but, more importantly, to the method used to evaluate them. Although there is no guarantee that one will be able to deal successfully with hard cases, Dewey thinks the method tends to become better over time, because what does not work will either be abandoned or revamped.

The process starts with the presence of skepticism, not always well defined at first, which interrupts the continuity of legal experience. By analyzing "the total situation," one can define the problem and the available solutions with increasing precision. The goal is "to *find* statements, of general principle and of particular fact, which are worthy to serve as premises." The conclusion, which is more than a temporary expedient but something less than a definitive solution, will be a reasonably unified judgment that has been anticipated, sometimes vaguely, from early on in the process. Laws are nothing more than "working hypotheses" that must be tested according to practical standards. Dewey endorses "a logic *relative to consequences rather than to antecedents,* a logic of prediction of probabilities rather than one of deduction of certainties." He is not after "*theoretical* certainty" but "*practical* certainty," the logic that has the best chance of satisfying society's desire for "the maximum possible regularity in order to enable persons in planning their conduct to foresee the legal import of their acts." Premise and conclusion, antecedent and consequent, are viewed by Dewey as two aspects of the same process; the focus is on predicting the future in light of what is learned from experience.

Dewey's article on the historic background of corporate legal personality, published in 1926, qualifies as his only extended treatment of a substantive legal concept. At the time it was a leading statement in a debate that had long worried German, English, French, and American legal historians, theorists, and practitioners, with their theories of corporate fiction, concession, and real personality.

The problem of corporate personality involves determining what constitutes a legal agent and avoiding the controversies that arise out of disagreement over the scope of legal personality. Under what conditions does a corporate entity stand as a legal agent to which legal liability can be ascribed? Dewey applies his method, here associated with the pragmatism of Peirce, by analyzing logically and historically how extralegal considerations (metaphysical, theological, psychological, political, and ethical) have encumbered the concept of corporate legal personality. Extralegal considerations have a way of clinging to legal concepts; they make it difficult to appraise the distinctively legal ones. To determine what a concept means, one must be able to distinguish original motivations from subsequent ones. Characteristically, Dewey assails those accounts that assume that what makes an entity a person is some essence, a fixed form, which has antecedent existence and to which the facts must conform. What makes a corporation a legal person is that the law treats it as such; it has the rights and duties assigned to it by the courts, which, in the end, determine the reach of corporate agency with respect to individuals, other corporate entities, and the state. The idea of a corporation as a legal person requires a functional analysis.

Dewey's last major essay, "My Philosophy of Law," published in 1941, deals with questions that preoccupied him from the start of his jurisprudential career: questions about the sources, applications, and ends of the law, and how custom becomes law, as well as questions about the relationship between political and legal authority, and why the experimental approach is to be preferred over its historical rivals among the natural law lawyers (Thomas Aquinas, John Locke) and legal positivists (John Austin).

References

Dewey, John. "Corporate Legal Personality." In *Works of John Dewey: The Later Works, 1925–1953,* vol. 2, ed. Jo Ann Boydston, 22–43. Carbondale: Southern Illinois University Press, 1984.

———. "Logical Method and Law." In *Works of John Dewey: The Middle Works, 1899–1924,* vol. 15, ed. Jo Ann Boydston, 65–77. Carbondale: Southern Illinois University Press, 1983.

———. "My Philosophy of Law." In *Works of John Dewey: The Later Works, 1925–1953,* vol. 14, ed. Jo Ann Boydston, 115–22. Carbondale: Southern Illinois University Press, 1988.

———. "Nature and Reason in Law." In *Works of John Dewey: The Middle Works, 1899–1924,* vol. 7, ed. Jo Ann Boydston, 56–63. Carbondale: Southern Illinois University Press, 1979.

Frank, Jerome. "Modern and Ancient Legal Pragmatism—John Dewey & Co. vs. Aristotle." *Notre Dame Lawyer* 25 (1950), 207–257, 460–504.

Mendell, Mark. "Dewey and the Logic of Legal Reasoning." *Transactions of the Charles S. Peirce Society* 30 (1994), 575–635.

Patterson, Edwin. "Dewey's Theory of Valuation and the Law." In *John Dewey: Philosopher of Science and Freedom,* ed. Sidney Hook, 109–122. New York: Dial Press, 1950.

Mark Mendell

See also PRAGMATIST PHILOSOPHY OF LAW

Difference Theory

Abstract moral equality and real differences between people coexist uneasily in Western jurisprudence. Democratic legal traditions emphasize the "rule of law." To this end, there are principles of formal legality which stipulate that laws must be appropriately general, free of unfair retroactivity, free of internal contradiction and ambiguity, publicly promulgated, and easily accessible. There are principles of justice that regulate the application of law to particular cases. These characterize legal persons as free and equal rational beings with rights to legal due process and to equal treatment under the law. Thus, courts have major obligations to ensure that all parties in a dispute have an equal chance to voice their concerns and to ensure that laws are applied impartially. This emphasis in procedural law on impartial equal treatment has been enshrined in the equal protection clause of the Fourteenth Amendment to the Constitution of the United States.

In reality, however, differences between people have always been used to justify unequal treatment in the law. A typical example is the noncontroversial way in which the law discriminates against children by not allowing them to form enforceable contracts without the consent of a legal guardian. Since this kind of inequality protects children's interests, it is justified. If a similar kind of paternalistic protection is extended to adults, however, the resulting discrimination is controversial. For instance, it is difficult to see how using sex or race as a criterion for restricting voting rights can be in the interest of the group being restricted. The law must have clearly developed standards to help courts identify why some cases of unequal treatment are just, while other cases are unjust.

The Supreme Court established an early standard called "rational basis" review for interpreting cases under the equal protection clause. The Court held in *Gulf, C. & S.F. Ry. Co. v. Ellis*, 165 U.S. 150 (1897), that any deviation from equal treatment must be based on some reasonable ground that can justify treating people differently. For something to be a reasonable ground it must have a just and proper relationship to the purpose of the particular legislation. The Supreme Court has also developed other standards, such as intermediate scrutiny, for strict scrutiny, and so forth, to help evaluate the relationship between the goals of a regulation and the means used to achieve those goals. A long string of court rulings has expanded the application of the equal protection clause beyond its initial aim of protecting African Americans from arbitrary discrimination. For instance, the equal protection clause has been used to evaluate the reasonableness of gender-based legislation to make sure legal distinctions between men and women are not arbitrary. The courts have also used the equal protection clause to evaluate classifications like sex, race, sexual orientation, age, disabilities, class, legitimacy in birth, previous discrimination, and so forth. American jurisprudence continuously reevaluates the background liberal theory of equal protection that has been used to extend the universal and elastic language of the Fourteenth Amendment to other classifications.

Obviously, as the laws dealing with children illustrate, unequal treatment can be justified when differences are so great that it is unreasonable to think of people as free and equal adults. However, can a form of discrimination against adults be justified as a necessary means for giving substantive equal protection to those whose lifestyle happens to be different from that of average people? We can gain valuable insight into this question, if we consider some recent feminist criticisms of the attempt in the 1970s to give women equal legal standing with men. Feminists argue that because the legal status quo glorifies abstract universalist thinking, liberal attempts to extend equality amount to no more than formal adjustments that ignore the concrete reality of most women's lives. Since privileged white males have historically defined the baseline from which all considerations start, the background definitions of "gender" and "difference" are already biased in ways detrimental to the interests of most women. Thus, formal equal treatment merely perpetuates unfair advantages that are already built into the structure of the legal system itself. When legislation merely eliminates gender as a basis for discrimination and yet leaves the system's structure unchanged, then women as a class are stripped of gender-based protections but receive nothing in the way of substantive equality that can compensate for the lost protection. The logic behind this argument can be applied to other contexts as well. For instance, some African American feminists argue that the voice of mainstream feminism adopts the background agenda of privileged white women and ignores crucial racial and cultural differences that have greater impact on some women's lives than does gender. Others argue against the biased baseline of heterosexuality in mainstream feminism, and so forth.

The accusation that there is inherent bias in foundational definitions is referred to as the "standard man (or person) problem." This problem arises when a privileged powerful group assumes that its basic interests can adequately serve as a universal starting point or standard from which to evaluate matters of justice for all, no matter how different others might be. The standard person problem is endemic to the human situation since, as postmodern philosophers point out, existing legal structures "always already" presuppose a taken-for-granted background that reflects the sexual, racial, cultural, and other stereotypes of whatever privileged group controls the development of legal structures. All privileged groups are poorly situated for judging the discriminatory potential of their own legal structures.

In a multicultural world, the primary practical problem is to implement universal ideals (like moral equality) in ways that encourage us to properly respect concrete differences. For this reason, Jürgen Habermas argues that a complete ideal theory needs a "principle of appropriateness" to help determine when and how abstract ideals should be observed in different situations. This issue can be addressed from both a particularist and a universalist position.

Particularists think universalists fail to grasp the fact that, as stated by Michael Walzer, the only real "commonality of the human race is particularism." Thus, universalist principles deny reality because they fail to acknowledge that different groups are deeply embedded in incommensurable ways of life. Walzer's version of particularism tries to make room for all conceptions of justice that are found in various cultural groups or "tribes." He claims we have to accept the parochialism of every tribe; therefore, only one thin antiuniversal principle is possible, that of tribal "self-determination."

Universalists think that particularists fail to appreciate how easily people can accept forms of oppression when they bury their heads in the sands of their own perspective. Under particularism, choices among competing interpretations of justice seem to be arbitrary. When this is so, nothing is justifiable, so those who are different have no grounds for complaining that they are unjustly treated. Universalists argue that there is a practical need to construct transcendent universal forms of justice that can help us judge between benign and pernicious forms of inequality.

What is needed in the current debate is a way to construct a legitimate form of commonality among the different forms of life. In this context, "legitimate" means some form of reciprocity and mutual respect. One way to combine particularist and universalist concerns is to follow Onora O'Neill's reconstruction of Immanuel Kant's notion of "fellow workers." Under this conception, legal reform would start with people where we find them, acknowledge their differences, and encourage them to participate in rational, empathic dialogue to construct out of the materials of their different histories as good an account of mutual legal understanding as is possible.

As moral equals, all fellow workers have the right to equal substantive protection. Rather than assume that the law needs to protect only one standardized substantive version of needs, however, difference jurisprudence must find a way to make the equal protection clause sensitive to situational differences. Since the reality of difference entails that "standard persons" are not properly positioned to figure out by themselves how to give "different" groups the equal protection they need, moral equality requires everyone to participate in finding solutions to legal problems. Since principles protect at a variety of theoretical and conceptual levels, different groups must be represented in the deliberations at all levels of abstraction.

Every group wants those differences essential to their way of life protected by the law, so it is a mistake to think that universal equality necessarily implies the law should ignore concrete differences. On the contrary, a realistic understanding of moral equality entails that all forms of humanity (that do not oppress others) deserve equal protection, since, as particular expressions of our shared moral status, all forms have equal worth. Particularists are right, then, that we must "leave room" for all the tribes, but this is for universal reasons.

References

Crenshaw, Kimberlé. "Demarginalizing the Intersection of Race and Sex: A Black Feminist Critique of Antidiscrimination Doctrine, Feminist Theory, and Antiracist Politics." *University of Chicago Law Forum* 139 (1989), 139–167.

Farber, Daniel A., William N. Eskridge, Jr., and Philip P. Fricckey. "Gender Discrimination and Other Equal Protection Concerns." In *Cases and Materials on Constitutional Law,* 287–380. St. Paul MN: West, 1993.

Habermas, Jürgen. *Justification and Application: Remarks on Discourse Ethics.* Trans. Ciaran P. Cronin. Cambridge: MIT Press, 1993.

———. *Moral Consciousness and Communicative Action.* Trans. Christian Lenhardt and Shierry Weber Nicholsen. Cambridge: MIT Press, 1991.

MacKinnon, Catharine A. *Toward a Feminist Theory of the State.* Cambridge MA: Harvard University Press, 1989.

O'Neill, Onora. *Constructions of Reason: Explorations of Kant's Practical Philosophy.* Cambridge: Cambridge University Press, 1989.

Walzer, Michael. *Thick and Thin: Moral Argument at Home and Abroad.* Notre Dame: University of Notre Dame Press, 1994.

David Cooper
Katherine Cooper

D

See also Feminist Philosophy of Law; Radical Class, Gender, and Race Theories: Positionality

Dignity

Five concepts of dignity have coursed through history. All connect with legal provisions for dignity's attribution or maintenance, and all today remain in some recognizable form, even if attenuated: (1) a privileged dignity accorded to those filling high rank or engaging in noble deeds (Homer's heroes; the *dignitas* of the Roman patrician); (2) dignity connoting what one earns, or merits because of unusual virtuous character (stoic); (3) dignity because persons are autonomous beings; (4) dignity in one's worldly circumstances; (5) inherent moral worth.

The dominant contemporary usage encompasses a universalizable idea that no conditions whatsoever, worldly (slum dwelling) or internal (infancy, retardation), restrict the modal quality of inherent worth. Persons *as persons* are due respect just because they possess incommensurable dignity. From this follow searches for human remains, lengthy, costly, inconvenient, and unesthetic, such as for the bodies of American soldiers missing in action in Vietnam. The modern conception of dignity as unqualified inherent moral worth stems largely from the moral philosophy of Immanuel Kant (1724–1804): "So act as to treat humanity . . . as an end withal, never as a means only." To have inherent moral worth, or dignity, is to transcend being used by others for their ends. Here the notion of persons being ends in themselves can perfectly be identified with the notion of inherent worth and serves as an obvious connection to rights interpreted as achievable claims that persons are not to be treated like objects.

The ultimate ground for moral dignity, argued Kant, is our *autonomy,* echoing Samuel Pufendorf's (1632–1694) response that people deserve to be treated with respect and dignity because they contain "a principle of acting within themselves." Autonomy, however, cannot be a sufficient ground of dignity, for children, many elderly, retardates, and victims of traumas of various kinds are not autonomous; yet their natural dignity and rights remain intact precisely because these classes of persons need special attention to rights they cannot themselves enjoy or initiate.

The minimum that dignity demands is *civility* toward persons in any walk of life, disenfranchised or alienated, simply because they are persons. So besides its legal ramifications, dignity carries a deep moral imperative that whatever else may be true of a person or situation, respect is due that person.

In moral and legal contexts, dignity generally, but not exclusively, implies *equality of rights,* universalizing the moral principle that others' interests are as important to them as my interests are important to me. One can be unworthy of dignity in any of the above restrictive contexts, and even lack self-respect, while still possessing dignity as the respect due one as a human being, entitled to have one's basic interests equally considered.

The *rights* part of the formula encompasses at least the civil liberties. Whatever may be their disenabling, disliked, or dysfunctional personality, lifestyle, origins, or situation, everyone at least is a human being. Even if the purpose of these legally secured rights is only to exclude coercive interference with the reasonable inclinations of human beings, the basic liberties belong to everyone. As well, the procedural rights that accompany legal judgment, called natural justice, reflect the positivization of a presumption of innate dignity. Further, the right to be treated with dignity has itself become a legal right and not only interpreted as a body of basic rights. In the United States, the open variable called the Ninth Amendment has been used to secure this moral advance, placing it squarely within constitutional law.

The *equality* part of the formula that rights presuppose dignity implies that all individuals are incommensurably worthy in their own right. In one version or another, dignity has remained at the core of foundational social and legal values that mandate respect for the individual. Mary Ann Glendon speaks of "the dignity and uniqueness of every single human person [within] the social nature of human life." Autonomy, privacy, and the opportunity for self-development follow as rights. The antithesis is an excess of state protectionism, foreclosing on people's significant choices.

The abstract *individualism* implied by dignity is essential, for it carries with it the singular "each and every." If we limit dignity conceptually to the "concrete community," as in Nazi or communist law, or to membership in a group, then anyone not having a recognized position of service to the community, such as farmers, mothers, and officers, or not having a recognized group identity, such as a lone refugee who is banished or exiled, is no longer worthy of dignity. Law does not have to treat them as equals; their rights may be abridged or denied with justification if they obstruct useful means to collective ends.

Individualism is important for another reason. If under its own situational adversities, as in wartime, the state cannot treat people equally—if equal treatment under law is for a time inefficacious—dignity attributable to individuals remains unalloyed as a deep moral commitment between persons that can continue under adversity. Without a logically prior moral commitment, its legalization makes little sense. With such a commitment, its legal inefficacy can, for a time, be tolerated by those who understand the purpose behind its neglect.

Nonetheless, *social issues* like capital punishment, abortion, and euthanasia have, in the United States, been brought under the wing of the "innate dignity of the person." Supreme Court Justice Thurgood Marshall, writing for the minority in *Gregg v. Georgia*, 428 U.S. 153 (1976), affirmed "the basic concept of human dignity at the core of the Eighth Amendment." In his interpretation of the cruel and unusual punishment clause in the American Constitution, he wrote, "The objective in imposing [capital punishment] must be [consistent] with our respect for the dignity of . . . men. . . . [Capital punishment] has as its very basis the total denial of the wrongdoer's dignity and worth." Through 1984 in the United States, 136 cases invoking the dignity of the individual as a sine qua non of constitutionality occurred. In many of these cases, dignity converges heavily both on the idea of privacy and autonomy of the person and on equal protection of the laws as fundamental constitutional values precluding intrusion. Under the privacy rubric, the law mandates dignity of the family, of minors, of prisoners (for limits on cell and strip searches), and dignity against defamation of public figures "despite the first amendment guarantee of free speech. . . . [U]nless they spring from the Court's evolving understanding of human dignity," some have held these privacy considerations as hard to justify. The Fourth Amendment's "right of the people to be secure in their persons, houses, papers, and effects, against unreasonable searches and seizures" has notably and relevantly invoked dignity of the person.

"Dignity" seems to embrace both sides of the argument about whether laws and policies can, or even should, try to abolish lowly living conditions such as slums. If the state is the instrument for social remediation (if voluntary aid is not sufficient for the task), political coercion will continually manipulate everyone's dignity of free choice. If, on the other hand, the state allows unrelieved impoverishment, those whose social position is at the bottom of the scale or who suffer some serious disability, personal or social, will not be treated with equal dignity under law. Subtle positional evaluations can obstruct fair justice, while the same excesses of economic difference may allow justice to be bought.

Clearly this crucial social dilemma draws upon the idea of having dignity in one's worldly circumstances. Even here, however, the unqualified "dignity of the person" is the logically anterior idea and that on which moral and legal stress is laid. Without "equal dignity under law" as an inviolable, juridical source-norm, curing undignified worldly conditions would lack any justification.

The vagueness, the extended, sometimes inconsistent, usage, and the emotive appeal of the term "dignity" occasionally lend themselves to arguments on both sides of these issues. Jordan Paust, however, recognizes value and strength in the open-ended nature of this high-level abstraction. He claims its very generality allows for a dynamic development toward the *international* arena for which dignity is now universally expected and increasingly, copiously applied, as in the Strasbourg conventions, courts, and International Institute of Human Rights. The Aspen Institute for Humanistic Studies concluded that dignity is "the internationalization of human rights." Certainly we can argue that the vagueness of the concept facilitated the shift from the particulars of position to the unconditional morality of being human.

In time, dignity has operationalized itself in statutes, legal decisions, or policies that make its usage precise in an organizing jurisprudence. The German court in 1995 convicted a skinhead on grounds that hate speech is not legally protected because, the court argued, extended, public, prejudicial abuse violates the dignity of the person. The government of South Africa has announced that it is prohibiting capital punishment, on two grounds: the right to life and the right to dignity. Such important jural interpretations and later holdings looking to them as precedents, or even as potential constitutional language, help to concretize the ways in which dignity furnishes a powerful moral standard for law creation and judicial resolution.

References

Black, Virginia. "Losing and Keeping One's Dignity." *Natural Law: Goodrich Lecture Series*. Wabash College, Crawfordsville IN, March 1992.

Black, Virginia, ed. *Dignity as Natural Law*. *Vera Lex* (Historical and Philosophical Study of Natural Law and Right) 13, no. 1 and 2 (1993).

Glendon, Mary Ann. *Rights Talk*. New York: Free Press, 1991.

Kant, Immanuel. *Proper Self-Respect*. Trans. Louis Enfield. New York: Harper and Row, 1963.

Montgomery, John Warwick. *Human Rights and Human Dignity*. Grand Rapids MI: Zondervan Publishing House, 1986.

Paust, Jordan J. "Human Dignity as a Constitutional Right: A Jurisprudentially Based Inquiry into Criteria and Content." *Howard Law Journal* (Winter 1984).

Pico della Mirandola, Giovanni. "Oration on the Dignity of Man." In *The Renaissance Philosophy of Man*, ed. E. Cassirer, O. Kristeller, and J.H. Randall, Jr. Chicago: University of Chicago Press, 1956.

Skinner, B.F. *Beyond Freedom and Dignity*. New York: Knopf, 1972.

Virginia Black

See also NATURAL LAW

Diminished Capacity

See INSANITY DEFENSE

Discipline

See ORDER

Discourse Epistemology

Legal discourse epistemology is a theory about the unity and autonomy of law and legal thinking. Defining law as a socially institutionalized discourse requires that epistemic criteria must be developed for recognizing the juridical character of linguistic enunciations or social practices. The use of the term "legal discourse" has replaced to a large extent the former expressions "legal order" and "legal system," which represented a positivistic and normativistic way of legal thinking. Preference for the concept of legal discourse can be explained by the factual shift of interest in legal philosophy from the theory of norms to the theory of argumentative rationality and procedural justice. This methodological change in emphasis has led to the semantic clarification of the concepts of argumentation and practical rationality. The concept of discourse itself seems, however, to remain unreflected and to be used as self-evident.

Legal discourse epistemology contrasts with legal discourse theory; it is no longer concerned with the material or procedural correctness of normative statements, but with the formal classification of statements or actions as belonging to the social institution which we call law. From the point of view of the theory of argumentation, legal discourse is generally regarded as the only appropriate communicative medium, as the field for virtual realization of the presuppositions for the ideal speech situation, and of the rules for discursive ethics. In that sense, discourse means rational dialogue or speech. The main hypothesis of legal discourse epistemology is that legal discourse should no longer be conceived as a dialogical communicative structure, which links subjective reasons, but as an institutionalized epistemic entity. Up to a certain point one could argue that the two theories are complementary. Pragmatic theories of discourse investigate the modalities of argumentation as a central practice in the operation of legal discourse. Institutional epistemology, on the other hand, is concerned with discourse modalities as factual possibilities for discursive argumentation. This happens, however, not from the participant's perspective, but from an external point of view. The epistemological conception of discourse is a guide for skeptical observers of the discourse.

The roots for this kind of analytical approach are to be found in the French tradition of the history of science, represented mainly by Gaston Bachelard, Georges Canguilhem, and most importantly by Michel Foucault, who set down two paths for epistemology.

The first is the archeology of knowledge, concerned with the conditions for the formation of a given science. The second is the genealogy of knowledge, dealing with how rationality and power interact in civil society. In that last sense, authors like Jan Broekman and Peter Goodrich investigate the linguistic economy of power institutionalized in legal practices. Legal discourse epistemology provides, instead, an account of the formal aspects of discourse in the tradition of epistemic archeology. This transforms Foucault's investigation of historically closed knowledge formations into a study of the discursive regularities in legally significant operations as they are currently given. This epistemology is knowledge-centered, not science-centered; it does not identify the discourse with a given science, nor insist on giving formal criteria for justifying the "scientific" character of discursive enunciations. Instead of subordinating knowledge to an objective binary axiology ("scientific/not scientific"), one observes the discursive validation of rationality as an internal regularity of a conventional and contingent character. Discourses emerge around a central basic item (law, politics, economy, art, religion, science, sport, and so on) and produce truth by combining theoretical statements with their related practices. In that sense, discourses should be conceived as open records for classifying knowledge. They are characterized by historical discontinuity, communicative intersubjectivity, and time-dependent validation of truth.

As its methodological network, legal discourse epistemology points out first, those language-relevant factors that constitute the field for production of legal knowledge, and second, those social practices and stages through which the functions of law are perceived and are fulfilled. The phenomenology of legal discourse develops in this respect on two levels: first, on the production of a specific knowledge, and second, on the operationalizing of this knowledge in a functionally differentiated institution. Far from being just a class of normative propositions, law is constituted as an institution: it is legislative, jurisdictional, and executive stages and practices; and it is the sites and operations concerned with the production and maintenance of its knowledge. Both the application rules of specific juridical communicative practices and the material contents of legal science emerge and take shape in the relational network of institutional practices—those of legislation, judicial decision, administration, and legal research (legal dogmatics as well as legal theory), which respectively assume the functions of producing, reproducing, applying, and annotating the law and legal knowledge. Each partial field of legal operations constitutes a partial discourse. The general discourse, "law," can be abstracted only as a central reference from the operations that occur in all these peripheral and partial discourses.

Belonging to a discourse means that an enunciation possesses those specific features which distinguish it from not-discursive elements. These distinguishing marks constitute the analytical category of "discoursivity," which is an epistemic predicate expressing a specific affiliation of practical and linguistic actions. "Extradiscoursivity" is a counterattribute, which still remains epistemic but qualifies elements external to the discourse, that is, which belong either to other discourses than the discourse in question or to the epistemically open field of everyday practical actions and ordinary language. The significance of the distinction between discoursivity and extradiscoursivity becomes apparent when the composition of legal enunciations is examined. Taken as linguistic sentences, these consist of particular concepts but also make up part of whole texts. This forces the question whether the linguistics of discourse is homogeneous or not, whether the use of language for a given discourse automatically transforms the epistemic status of a term, utterance, or text. Discourses are the epistemological frame, institutionally existing, for an analysis of legal language. On the level of the text, analysis relies upon the conception of law as a discursive formation and not as a technical terminology. On the level of the sentence, it relies upon the conception of discursive enunciation, and not upon the conceptions of legal rule, logical (rational) proposition, or illocutionary speech act. On the lexical level, finally, it relies upon the understanding of legal concepts as discursive and not as normative concepts.

By focusing on enunciations, discourse analysis differs from semiotics, grammar, logic, or philosophy of language. Discoursivity operates as one epistemic function in the structure of the semiotic sequence. It is a supplementary aspect of the proposition, in addition to its linguistic correctness, its logical coher-

D

ence, or its illocutionary meaning-relevance. Discoursivity performs a pragmatic task: finding the enunciative character of a proposition depends on empirically observing the legal reality. A legal norm, a court verdict or an administrative decision, a jurisprudential treatise, or a legal theoretical survey represent four types of legal textuality. This means that these classes of enunciations are based on the appropriate institutions of legislation, adjudication, administration, jurisprudence, and legal theory. For institutional epistemology, they represent empirically ascertainable fields for production of juridical operations: they predetermine the existential presuppositions for all kinds of legal utterances and make possible the reproduction of legal discourse. This happens, first, because these stages, as conglomerates of social practices, occupy the position of central referents for the production of legal meaning. Second, their organizational structures provide discourse positions which allow the institutional participants in discourse to articulate their statements, propositions, or arguments. Third, they are the associative field that is needed for consistency among the concepts in discourse. Finally, they are a precondition for the concreteness of discursive enunciations, by supporting goal-oriented argumentative strategies. Referentiality, speaking position, conceptual associative field, and epistemic conjecture are the marks of discoursivity. They correspond to the four moments in the emergence of enunciations: formation of objects, of speaking subjects, of concepts, and of knowledge-strategy. On the nodal point of the enunciation meet all the factors of the discourse dynamics.

References

Broekman, Jan M. "Juristischer Diskurs und Rechtstheorie" (Legal Discourse and Legal Theory). *Rechtstheorie* 11 (1980), 17–46.

———. *Recht und Anthropologie* (Law and Anthropology). Freiburg: Alber, 1979.

Foucault, Michel. *The Archaeology of Knowledge*. London: Tavistock, 1972; New York: Pantheon Books, 1981.

Goodrich, Peter. *Legal Discourse. Studies in Linguistics, Rhetoric and Legal Analysis.* London: Macmillan, 1987.

Paroussis, Michel. *Theorie des juristischen Diskurses. Eine institutionelle Epistemologie des Rechts.* Berlin: Duncker und Humblot, 1995; English translation, *The Epistemology of Legal Discourse.* Dordrecht: Kluwer, 1997.

Michel Paroussis

Discourse Theory

Legal discourse theory is a normative theory of law. It treats the question whether the norms expressed in positive law can claim legitimacy as the "right" norms. Discourse theory deals with this question under the rubric of procedural criteria, not intrinsic criteria. According to the basic ideas of this theory, a legal norm is "correct" in the relevant sense if discourse about its legitimacy can reach consensus when carried out in ideal conditions.

Legal discourse theory is based on the general discourse theory worked out by Karl-Otto Apel and Jürgen Habermas, which, in the form developed by Habermas, was applied to the realm of legal norms first by Robert Alexy and later by Habermas himself.

General discourse theory claims that not only propositions but also norms have truth value. For both propositions and norms, truth makes sense not from the standpoint of agreement with an intended state of affairs (correspondence theory), but from that of its capacity for agreement (consensus theory). For both declarative and imperative propositions, disagreements arise over validity claims that resist grounding. Evidence for disagreements that have become problematic appears within discourse. The evidence concerns the validity claims of assertions, and so is dealt with in theoretical discourse; but clarifying the correctness of normative propositions is done, especially in practical discourse. Whether a proposition is correct is determined from the results of discourse, as is asserted by Habermas: "The determinant for the truth of propositions is their possible agreement with all others." Characteristically, this is not factual consensus, but consensus called for by being grounded in the strength of the best arguments. That the best arguments will be set forth is guaranteed by modeling discourse upon an ideal situation for speech. That speech situation is "ideal" in which communication is constrained either through external contingent influences or through directions that arise from the very structure of communication. These assumptions are guaranteed by a set of rules for discourse.

Even if, at its best, discourse designed on the ideal of these rules only approximates an actual discussion, still it is not a construct that is out of touch with life. For under each real discourse lies a commitment to the best arguments, and therewith a positing of the ideal discourse. This counterfactual positing has the character of an anticipation of the ideal speech situation that is truly at work in the real occurrence of communication and thus supplies a measure for testing every consensus reached in fact; the testing reveals whether the factual consensus presents an adequate indicator of a well-established consensus.

This criterion, set by discourse theory for truth in consensuses reached under ideal conditions, has the consequence for discourse ethics that, according to Habermas, "the only norms for which validity ought to be claimed are those which find (or could find) all parties in agreement as participants in a practical discourse." The assumption behind this is that the results that come from using this general norm on each discourse could be agreed to by all participants ("grounding by universalization").

This discourse ethic set out by Habermas for the realm of moral norms was extended to the realm of legal norms especially by Robert Alexy. The basis for legal discourse theory in the form set out by Alexy is the thesis that legal discourse is a sample in particular of practical discourse in general. It is dealt with as an instance of general practical discourse, since legal discussions are practical questions that are discussed as claims for rightness. In agreement with discourse theory in general, the criterion for right is formulated in a procedural way. This special treatment of practical discourse in general ought to control legal discourse as well, although its similarity to moral discourse is limited by reason of its dependence upon valid law.

From this attachment to valid law arise the specific rules of legal discourse, such as the rules for its semantic, its genetic, or its teleological expression in legal interpretation. The limits on legal discourse, and especially the importance of positive law in it, weakens the rules from practical discourses in general, since it often is not possible to work out their clear expression.

For Alexy, even courtroom discourses should be seen as an instance of practical discourse in general. It is not important that arguments by the parties to a suit are usually made in their own interests and not in order to search for truth together. All that is needed is that the parties attend to setting out rational arguments that are open to consensus.

Habermas has recently addressed once again the relation between legal argumentation and practical discourse. Earlier, legal argumentation was seen as disagreement in the form of courtroom disputes. The interaction by parties to the suit in terms of their own interests does not block recourse to the cooperative search for truth under which discourse stands. As to anything beyond this evaluation, the applicability of discourse models to legally institutionalized proceedings remains doubtful, as is noted by Habermas: "Discourse is not an institution, it is firmly counter-institutional."

Under the influence of Alexy's "theory of legal argumentation," Habermas broadened this appraisal and addressed legal argumentation in all its institutional expressions as an instance of practical discourse. Instead of a systematic treatment of discourse theory for law, Habermas commits himself afresh to a model that recognizes the autonomy of law over against morality, but also affirms the relevance of the discourse model for the legal order. This is done especially through his development of discourse principle "D" ("those norms for the details of practice are valid which all possible participants in rational discourse could agree to" under moral principles and, for the politico-legal order, under democratic principles).

While moral principle by itself can determine whether the results of carrying out a norm are acceptable to all participants, the legitimacy of legal norms stands within a broader spectrum of groundings. Democratic pursuit of legal outcomes as "a metaphysical source of legitimacy" gives foundation to the legality of legal norms not as a fully determinate result, but as one set of considerations that moves with an educated probability in the direction of rational outcomes. This supports the "fallible assumption, that results reached with procedural justice are more or less rational."

References

Alexy, Robert. "A Discourse-Theoretical Conception of Practical Reason." *Ratio Juris* 5 (1992), 231–251.

———. "Of Necessary Relations Between Law and Morality." *Ratio Juris* 2 (1989), 167–183.

———. *Theorie der juristischen Argumentation* (Theory of Argumentation in the

Law). Frankfurt: Suhrkamp, 1978; 2d ed. 1991.

Deflem, Mathieu. "Habermas, Modernity, and Law: A Bibliography." *Philosophy and Social Criticism* 20 (1994), 151–166.

Esparza, Jesus. "Logic and Rationality in the Legal Discourse." *Fronesis* 1 (1994), 115–138.

Guibentif, Pierre. "Approaching the Production of Law Through Habermas' Concept of Communicative Action." *Philosophy and Social Criticism* 20 (1994), 1–20.

Gunther, Klaus. "Critical Remarks on Robert Alexy's "Special-Case Thesis." *Ratio Juris* 6 (1993), 143–156.

Habermas, Jürgen. *Faktizitaet und Geltung. Beiträge zur Discurstheorie des Rechts und des demokratischen Rechtsstaats.* Frankfurt: Suhrkamp, 1992; 4th ed., 1994. Trans. William Regh as *Between Facts and Norms: Contributions to a Discourse Theory of Law and Democracy.* Cambridge: MIT Press, 1996.

———. "'Theorie der Gesellschaft oder Sozial-technologie?' Eine Auseinandersetzung mit Niklas Luhmann" (Theory of Community or Technology of Society? An Exchange with Niklas Luhmann), in *Theorie der Gesellschaft oder Sozialtechnologie?*, ed. J. Habermas and N. Luhmann, 142–290. Frankfurt: Suhrkamp, 1971.

———. *Theorie des kommunikativen Handelns.* Frankfurt: Suhrkamp, 1981. Trans. Thomas McCarthy as *The Theory of Communicative Action.* 2 vols. Boston: Beacon Press, 1984.

———. "Wahrheitstheorien" (Theories of Truth). In *Wirklichkeit und Reflexion. Festschrift für Walter Schulz zum 60. Geburtstag*, 211–265. 1973.

Mercedes, Iglesias. "Practical Reason in Habermas: Basis of Legitimacy in Law." *Revista di Filosofia* (Venezuela) 21 (1995), 143–161.

Van Hoecke, Mark, and François Ost. "Epistemological Perspectives in Legal Theory." *Ratio Juris* 6 (1993), 30–47.

Ulrich Neumann

See also DISCOURSE EPISTEMOLOGY

Discretion

Judicial discretion may concern judicial authority to make decisions, or the latitude judges have to affect outcomes with creativity, within or beyond legal standards. Alternative legal theories endorse widely divergent views on the scope of judicial discretion.

Natural law theorists, such as Thomas Aquinas and William Blackstone, believe law is an ordinance of reason dictated by God, binding everywhere at all times. Human laws are realizations of God's law; universal principles of morality and justice are built into the concept of law. The judge's task is to ascertain the relevant law and apply it to the facts of the case. The theory does not commit them to a mechanistic view; nevertheless, it implies no discretion. Law is clearly determined by reason. Once the correct law is discovered in enacted statutes or preexisting principles of justice reflected in them, application is straightforward.

Historical defenders of positivism include Jeremy Bentham and John Austin. For Bentham, a judge's role is to find law in legislated enactments. He allows that judges become involved in the process of making law but deems it inappropriate. Austin's nineteenth-century theory defines law as a command of a sovereign to political inferiors in the habit of obedience, with a sanction for noncompliance. Enforcement power determines a sovereign's ability to issue law, and all law is of human creation. Contrary to Bentham, Austin explicitly approves of judge-made law, under authority of the sovereign, describing it as "highly beneficial and absolutely necessary."

Early-twentieth-century theorists known as American legal realists defend a broader creative role for judges. Oliver Wendell Holmes rejects the formalist portrait of judicial adjudication, that judges survey and analytically discover the proper statutes and precedents governing a case, deciding deductively, with certainty and uniformity. Holmes believes judges do make law, should make law, and necessarily must make law because it is intrinsic to the very process of judging. Some realists emphasize judicial interpretation as determinative of law, and view all decisions as open, but feel decisions ought to be constrained by rational deliberation. The judge should (1) be impartial, (2) carefully survey all relevant alternatives and information, and (3) give a principled justifying opinion, even if it is a rationalization. Nevertheless, the basis of adjudication is always unspecified.

Extreme realists, including Jerome Frank, discount legal rules completely: "The rules are incidental, the decisions are the thing," according to Frank. Adjudication is always open, arbitrary, and political; there is no impartiality or neutrality. Statutes and precedents are only rough predictions of what judges will do. Subjective decision making is inevitable because judges have complete flexibility to reach beyond the law. The rule and fact skepticism associated with legal realism reappears in contemporary writings by critical legal studies (CLS) theorists in their focus on the indeterminacy of law. Duncan Kennedy and others argue that deep and extensive indeterminacy shows legal rules and doctrines are not, and cannot be, authoritative.

Reacting to the realist's freewheeling view of judicial power, H.L.A. Hart defends a refined positivism. Like earlier positivists, Hart divorces law and morality, basing the validity of law on source, not content. Hart believes application of relevant statutes is usually unproblematic. Nevertheless, he acknowledges there are penumbral cases, "debatable cases in which words are neither obviously applicable nor obviously ruled out." Where the meanings of words are vague, as is "vehicle" in his famous example, "No vehicles in the park," the judge must take responsibility for determining whether the words cover a particular case. In deciding whether baby carriages or skateboards are "vehicles," judges use discretion as judgment guided by rules, precedents, and their ordinary linguistic meanings. Despite Hart's detailed discussion of penumbral cases requiring discretion in interpreting vague terms, he is uncomfortable with a creative role for judges. He believes discretion is constrained by rules and the features of language. Most terms have a "core meaning," hence ambiguities of application are rare.

Lon Fuller embraces the positivists' stress on legal rules, yet is also influenced by realists. Fuller argues, against Hart, that ordinary language is frequently vague and ambiguity arises from many general legal phrases. Thus he grants judges an inescapable normative role. Fuller urges, however, that if judges view themselves as constrained not merely by legal language but also by the context of cases and the goals and purposes of legal rules, then many "hard" cases become easy to resolve. If the purpose of "No vehicles in the park" is to preserve a peaceful, quiet space, clearly baby carriages are not "vehicles" under the rule, whereas skateboards are. Fuller thus empha-

sizes the role of purpose in legal interpretation. When required, discretion can and should be constrained by the instrumental character of statutes and ordinances.

A theme in judicial decision making invoked to counteract broad discretion and subjectivity allowed and praised by legal realists and CLS scholars is originalism, the approach to constitutional adjudication that accords binding authority to the text of the constitution or the intentions of its adopters. As defended by Robert Bork, originalism urges that judges must merely apply the law as stated to the facts presented. The goal is to minimize judicial discretion, avoiding judicial activism so that unelected officials are not usurping the legislative function. However, whether one focuses on strict textual interpretation or the framers' intentions, there are serious difficulties with implementing originalism. The historical project of understanding vague wording or the intentions of original writers is difficult given inconsistent or indecisive evidence, and given multiple delegates at ratifying conventions with different intentions. Moreover, reading a provision without regard to its current social context, or deciding an issue the framers could not have foreseen due to technological advance, makes reliance on the text or intentions especially suspect.

Ronald Dworkin has suggested that the popularity of the doctrine of discretion is due to confusions about the concept. Arguing that the notion of discretion only makes sense in a context of restriction, where someone is charged with making decisions subject to authoritative standards, Dworkin first distinguishes two *weak* senses of the term "discretion." The first weak sense of discretion is used when a context is unclear or there is an issue of vagueness. The standards cannot be applied mechanistically, so one must use judgment to apply them. A second weak sense is used when determining who has the final word in a decision. An official in a hierarchy has this weak discretion when holding final authority to make a decision not subject to review or reversal by another.

One has discretion in the *strong* sense, according to Dworkin, when one is simply not bound by standards set by the relevant authority. One can have strong discretion and still recognize standards of rationality, fairness, or effectiveness. Moreover, having strong discretion does not imply one is immune from criticism, for one can exercise it stupidly, carelessly, or maliciously. In Dworkin's view, realists argue that judges have discretion in the second weak sense, because they view judges as the final arbiters of law. Positivists may refer to judicial discretion in the first weak sense, as Hart did, to maintain the role of judges in using judgment when words are vague. However, Dworkin maintains, positivists must also, at least sometimes, hold that judges have discretion in the strong sense when they cite standards other than rules that are not legally binding on the judges. In defending his contemporary version of natural law theory, Dworkin argues that judges never have discretion in the strong sense, for they have a duty to decide cases by discovering rights derived from rules or moral principles that are part of law and binding on the judges.

Views of adjudication that minimize discretion for judges have the advantage of being able to defend adjudication as consistent, uniform, and fair, values that support society's allegiance to the law. Those viewing adjudication as largely unconstrained confront questions surrounding the role of legal rules and the increased subjectivity of judicial decision making. Related difficulties include the problem of explaining why citizens should respect the law and the concerns that judge-made law is ex post facto and is incompatible with the role of judges as unelected officials in a democracy. Nevertheless, many see broad judicial discretion as an adjudicative reality that cannot be ignored.

References

Aquinas, St. Thomas. *Summa Theologica*. Ed. Anton C. Pegis. New York: Random House, 1945.

Austin, John. *The Province of Jurisprudence Determined*. Ed. Wilfrid E. Rumble. Cambridge: Cambridge University Press, 1995.

Bentham, Jeremy. *Of Laws in General*. Ed. H.L.A. Hart. London: Athlone Press, 1970.

Bork, Robert H. *The Tempting of America: The Political Seduction of the Law*. New York: Free Press, 1990.

Dworkin, Ronald. "The Model of Rules." *Taking Rights Seriously*. Cambridge MA: Harvard University Press, 1977.

Frank, Jerome. *Law and the Modern Mind*. New York: Doubleday, 1963.

Fuller, Lon. "Positivism and Fidelity to Law: A Reply to Professor Hart." *Harvard Law Review* 71 (1958), 593.

Hart, H.L.A. "Positivism and the Separation of Law and Morals." *Harvard Law Review* 71 (1958), 593.

Holmes, Oliver Wendell. "The Path of Law." *Harvard Law Review* 10 (1897), 457.

Kennedy, Duncan. "Freedom and Constraint in Adjudication: A Critical Phenomenology." *Journal of Legal Education* 36 (1986), 518.

Judith W. DeCew

See also JUDICIAL REVIEW; JUDICIAL SYLLOGISM

Disobedience
See OBEDIENCE AND DISOBEDIENCE

Disposition of Remains

Philosophers have taken two tacks in discussing acts respecting the dead. The first claims that such acts can be wrong on account of the deceased. The relevant philosophical discussions are of posthumous harm and posthumous rights violation. The second claims that such acts are wrong for more familiar reasons having to do with the living. Some think that the living can hold rights in dead bodies. Some think that corpses are precious symbols of humanity whose disrespect makes some treatments mistreatments.

Posthumous Harm

Suppose that people cease to exist after their deaths. Is it coherent to speak about harming people after they die? The two main objections are the "no subject" objection and the "existence condition" objection. The no subject objection holds that there is no subject to suffer the harm after death. The existence condition holds that existence at the time is a necessary condition for being harmed.

If harming is a causal condition that alters its object, and the object of the harm is the person, then both objections make perfect sense. By hypothesis, there is now no person, and no person's life, to be harmed. Though there is much support for this position in common sense, the two objections have counterintuitive consequences for killings. If a victim ceases to exist when killed, then either instantaneous killings do not harm their victims, or they do harm during the life of the victim and before the killing is done.

Common sense is notoriously unreliable. The concept of harm is both vague and ambiguous. Clarity can be achieved, Joel Feinberg suggests, by curing the vagueness in a way that stretches ordinary language. Once some such account is given, usually of a noncausal harm, philosophers who argue for the possibility of posthumous harm generally agree that the living person antemortem is the subject of the harm.

Most accounts of posthumous harm raise their own paradoxes. Feinberg holds that to harm is to invade or set back interests and that some interests can survive death. This view entails interests existing at a time without interest bearers. Barbara Levenbook holds that posthumous harm involves a loss, and this entails postulating losses when there are no existent losers.

Dorothy Grover holds that posthumous events can adversely affect what people accomplish, undermine the quality of decisions made, and generally have a serious noncausal effect upon the "quality of a person's life." Such a move pushes the controversy back one issue. Being harmed entails having something bad *for* one happen. Can events after one's death be good or bad *for* one? Some theories of well-being make it impossible that anything beyond the limits of a person's life (or a person's conscious experience) can be bad for that person; others do not.

Even if posthumous harm is possible, can a treatment of a corpse be posthumously harmful? Can anything done to one's corpse seriously undermine the quality of one's life? It is noteworthy that Feinberg does not include among surviving interests bodily privacy or modesty, nonmutilation, and not having one's body used without one's consent.

Posthumous Rights

Does it make sense to talk about rights of the dead, rights that operate posthumously, with regard to anything, let alone the disposal of corpses?

If rights protect interests or well-being, the same issues are raised with respect to posthumous rights as with posthumous harm. If rights reduce to relative duties, duties owed to someone, the no subject objection is relevant: how can there be a duty to one who does not then exist? If rights protect agency, analo-gous issues are raised about the limits of human agency with respect to biological life and about the coherence of talking about the agency of one who no longer exists.

Do sound moral principles justify recognizing posthumous rights? Loren Lomasky argues that they do. Carl Wellman argues that the rights of living persons are "proactive," imposing future duties. These duties, not any rights or interests, survive the rights-holders' deaths.

Partridge, too, justifies respecting the wishes of the deceased in terms independent of posthumous rights. He argues that such a practice protects the interests of the living to have posthumous influence while still alive. In reply, Wellman joins Feinberg in maintaining that these duties cannot be accounted for by appeal to "diffuse" social considerations, like the effects on institutional practices or the sensibilities of others. They would presumably say the same about Joan Callahan's suggestion that abstract virtues or values account for some moral duties to respect the wishes of the dead.

Callahan also suggests that the obligation to dispose of a deceased's property is owed to the heirs. Assuming that one's body is one's property, this view will account for a relative duty to dispose of a corpse in a certain way only when that corpse is willed to some person or institution.

Rights of the Living in the Bodies of the Dead

Can the living acquire rights over corpses? One view is that people have property or ownership rights over their own bodies. Suppose that these rights can be transferred, by gift or will, to others. Then the living can acquire property rights to corpses.

There is a long philosophical tradition, traceable to Hugo Grotius (1583–1645), but usually traced to John Locke (1632–1704), that people have property rights in their bodies. The assertion of ownership of one's body appears in G.W.F. Hegel (1770–1831), Arthur Schopenhauer (1788–1860), much of classic liberalism, and marxist studies. There is a longer tradition, dating back to the Old Testament and St. Paul, that we do not have property rights in our bodies, because human bodies are the property of God. Immanuel Kant (1724–1804), in *The Metaphysics of Morals and Lectures on Ethics*, denied that our bodies were our property and added that we have no liberty to sell or give away its parts as we please.

The coherence of self-ownership depends partly on one's view of personal identity. If one is one's body, there is no logically distinct owner, and the idea of ownership of one's body is incoherent.

Even if coherent, property is too complex to be helpful in describing the normative relation people have with their own bodies. Most analyses of property present it as a constellation of rights, liberties, and powers. The question is whether living persons have transferable rights to dispose of their bodies. One view is that persons have rights to dispose of (some) bodily parts: blood and other body fluids, one of a pair of organs. Are there, however, restrictions on what may be disposed of or the type of disposal? It is natural to suppose that no one can transfer a broader right or power or liberty than he or she possesses.

Alternatively, why not believe that the right evaporates at death, particularly if we assume only certain reasons for recognizing the right, like its role in developing a sense of the self?

Rights talk may be stronger than what can be morally justified. Perhaps what remains of me after death comes under different moral incidents and relations than what exists of me during my lifetime. I might have the power to create in others a duty to dispose of my dead body a certain way. Alternately, on the view that I am my body, my liberty-right to cause my body to be in certain places might be accompanied by a power to give other persons duties to deliver it when I can no longer move it.

Another view is that a dead body is like many other material things and that one can acquire property rights over it through whatever mechanisms are specified by a just theory of acquisition.

There is still the question of limitations. How do rights to dispose of corpses or duties to do so function in moral justification if some treatments of corpses are also posthumous harms? Honoring these rights or duties may cause social harm, as when corpses are unhygienic or profoundly offensive to the sensibilities of others. Limiting rights or duties may save lives or improve the quality of lives, as in organ transplantation or medical research. Commerce or entertainment may be promoted if rights or duties are further limited.

The Importance of Symbolism

Perhaps it is wrong to treat dead bodies in certain ways because such treatment fails to respect the dead human body as "a precious natural symbol of humanity."

While this view may seem initially appealing, the notion of respecting a symbol is opaque. There are conventional ways of respecting symbols, and there is enormous variation in cultural treatment of corpses. If respect for symbols is culturally determined, the view is inapplicable when cultural norms are in flux. That, arguably, is a good description of the current state in Western countries, where there are mixed reactions to claims made for harvesting cadaver organs and for using female cadavers to gestate fetuses.

One may not regard the respecting as conventional. What is needed, then, is a defense of the idea of nonconventional, cross-cultural respecting of symbols that specifies the relative weight of such respecting. Feinberg admits that respect for symbols must be balanced by other considerations and is prepared to find it outweighed, for example, where human lives can be saved by salvaging cadaver organs. However, a more general account is needed.

In any case, why should symbolism be respected? Is respecting the symbolism of dead bodies a way of respecting the dignity of persons? Is it, as Feinberg holds, a way of respecting sensibilities, of avoiding profound offense to others? If the answer to either question is affirmative, the disrespect view reduces to one of the others.

The field of bioethics contains the liveliest debates on the morality of treatments of corpses. In addition, the reader may wish to consult the literature on the ethics of organ transplantation and on pregnant cadavers gestating fetuses. Philosophical literature on a related topic, whether death is an evil, has implications for posthumous harm and posthumous rights in general.

References

Aristotle. *The Nicomachean Ethics*. Trans. Terence Irwin. Indianapolis: Hackett, 1985.

Callahan, Joan. "On Harming the Dead." *Ethics* 97 (1987), 341–1352.

Engelhardt, H. Tristram, Jr. *The Foundations of Bioethics*. New York: Oxford University Press, 1986.

Feinberg, Joel. *Harm to Others*. New York: Oxford University Press, 1984.

——. *Offense to Others*. New York: Oxford University Press, 1985.

Grover, Dorothy. "Posthumous Harm." *The Philosophical Quarterly* 39 (1989), 334–353.

Levenbook, Barbara. "Harming Someone after His Death." *Ethics* 94 (1984), 407–419.

Lomasky, Loren E. *Persons, Rights, and the Moral Community*. New York: Oxford University Press, 1987.

Pitcher, George. "The Misfortunes of the Dead." American *Philosophical Quarterly* 21 (1984), 183–188.

Wellman, Carl. *Real Rights*. New York: Oxford University Press, 1995.

Barbara Levenbook

Dispute Resolution

Problem-solving structures legal activities. Dispute resolution is its most obvious part, the *tip* of the legal iceberg. There are many subparts, that is, multiple ways of ending conflicts. Judicial decision making is of course the *top of the tip*. Yet, between nonconflictual legal resolution—the immersed part—and judicial resolution, there are also many intermediary stages: they are conceptualized as alternative dispute resolution. Beyond specific disputes and their resolution, other general techniques of problem solving are also available, through legislation. A large spectrum can then be studied: *infra, intra et supra disputationem*. Its various colors shed a different light on dispute resolution.

Infra Disputationem: The Immersed Part of Legal Resolution

Legal routines, like paying the rent, or legal projects, like drafting contracts, involve many nonproblematic, ready-at-hand answers. They stem from customary resolution processes, where people do not see legal problems at all or see them as *positive challenges,* that they solve spontaneously. This is the field of perceived social cooperation, of freedom as absence of constraint, of internalized norms, of self-regulatory behaviors, of legal obviousness and often of the unconsciousness of any resolution. It is marked by the coexistence of identities, with prevailing use of cooperative rhetorics, where differences between people are grasped as complementary.

Intra Disputationem: The Tip of Legal Resolution

Sometimes though, in the field of routines or projects, some major problem can emerge, which people may perceive this time as a real, acute, *negative impediment.* They feel bothered, shaken, or even attacked, that is, questioned to a variable extent. This is the field of progressive appearance of constraint and competition, which is experienced as problematic. The more people feel infringed upon, the more they try to retrieve some counteranswer that will feed their counterquestioning. A depository of reactions to acute problems is the legal corpus, which among others contains many "straight" answers and the correlative counteranswers. If some people have identified, even incorrectly, the source of questioning as a violation of some straight legal answer, they will call their conflict legal and summon the law and its counteranswers to solve it.

In this context of deep interactive questioning, a whole process of legal dispute resolution is brought into play. It will adopt two major forms: either it will confirm the emerging social competition that was just described—this is resolution in court, or it will try to resume immediately social cooperation—this is alternative dispute resolution. Whatever means, predominantly competitive or cooperative, the end is to restore cooperation.

Judicial Resolution

When a dispute occurs and is qualified as legal, the reflex is quickly to externalize law, which before was just in the shadow, as a preventive vaccine. The intuition is to transform it into a serum for conflicts, that is, a curative medicine which is clearly labeled legal. Lawyers as litigators pursue this path; they make the labeling even more precise in terms of legal categories. Representing their respective clients, they use competitive rhetorics against each other, questioning the other's resolution. Their rhetorics are more cooperative toward the judge, with the hope that the latter will identify with their own answers. After listening to both attorneys, a judge will come out with arguments to tell why "the law" prefers such solution.

Law is given back to the disputants, without being reached by them. At the trial, parties have their conflict taken over by legal professionals who seek an answer on their behalf. A judge's solution is finally imposed, and held as "truth" for all *(res iudicata . . .)*. If stating this answer—adjudicating—is not followed by spontaneous execution, forced resolution goes one step further: executive agents, like the police or bailiffs, will be summoned.

Once completed, judicial resolution is not necessarily perceived by many litigants as really satisfactory, even by winners. Something often remains missing. Part of the disputants' questioning has never been addressed in court, in the decision or during its execution. The disputants' frustration may even have increased: they won but did not get the respect they asked for or paid incredible fees; they lost and could not understand what actually happened; they were condemned but did not learn anything from the sentence. In a nutshell, simply assessing rights and sanctioning wrongs may not suffice to achieve full resolution.

Alternative Dispute Resolution
Because of the previously explained drawbacks of litigation and of its incapacity to appropriately fulfill people's needs, the idea has been to improve what could be accomplished out of court, *intra parietes,* between walls, among friends. There is indeed a vast continuum of possible actions to cope with conflicts: from direct or indirect negotiation, to arbitration, via conciliation and mediation. Though some major conflicts must remain within the court domain, in many other cases alternative dispute resolution can be utilized in disputants' interests.

Let us return to the beginning, the emerging conflict. No competitive escalation has yet taken place under the direction of legal professionals: contrasting legal categories, opposite rights and claims, have not been elaborated yet. There is still an opportunity to consider momentarily that the parties could tackle their problems themselves without a trial. If professional help is given to help resolve the conflict and to try to reverse its course now, some alternative solution may well benefit both disputants.

Instead of focusing on divisive positions, lawyers as negotiators (or mediators as neutrals) can ask the parties to investigate their shared interests, to work on their differences as possible opportunities for common gain, and hence to develop various options to reduce the existing gap between them. Rights as swords can be put aside for a while and kept as shields to be used later in the case no settlement is reached.

In such contexts, law is internalized as relational, as a network of rights and duties. It embodies a cooperative tool to build agreement and working relationships. Lawyers, who animate this process, become peacemakers and deal makers. They communicate through a rhetoric of joint problem solving, which intends to bring their clients closer to each other and not to keep them apart.

If these alternative paths do not seem practicable, that is, if parties cannot agree together on a solution to their dispute, they can still keep some of their freedom of choice in calling for an arbitrator, who at the threshold of litigation can impose a solution.

Supra Disputationem:
Recourse to Legislation
One last option should not be underestimated. It is particularly concerned with routines of dispute resolution which happen to have limited effects. If, for instance, some particular legal solutions, which are repeated over and over, cannot prevent the same problem from being raised again, with the same people—recidivism—or with others, problem solvers also need to question their usual techniques of resolution. If externalizing law in court or elsewhere does not help many people internalize it in their lives, law itself may need to be changed, as well as its level of action, which may require a shift from the particular to the general. Well thought out statutes, accompanied with appropriate financial means, can often prevent disputes from even arising. When they attack the general causes of conflicts—poverty, unemployment, deficient education—and not simply its consequences, these statutes will often be better solutions than the best formal or informal justice ever devised.

References
Abel, R. *The Politics of Informal Justice.* New York: Academic Press, 1982.
Arrow, K.J. et al., eds. *Barriers to Conflict Resolution.* New York: Norton, 1995.
Felstiner, W.L.F., R.L. Abel, and A. Sarat. "The Emergence and Transformation of Disputes: Naming, Blaming, Claiming. . . ." *Law & Society Review* 15 (1980–1981), 631–654.
Fisher, R., W. Ury, and B. Patton. *Getting to Yes.* New York: Penguin, 1982.

Goldberg, S.B., N.H. Rogers, and F.E.A. Sander. *Dispute Resolution: Negotiation, Mediation, and Other Processes.* Boston: Little, Brown, 1992.

Lempereur, A. *Legal Questioning and Problem-Solving.* Dissertation, Harvard University, 1995.

Maccoby, E., and R.H. Mnookin. *Dividing the Child: Social and Legal Dilemmas of Custody.* Cambridge MA: Harvard University Press, 1992.

Neale, M.A., and M.H. Bazerman. *Cognition and Rationality in Negotiation.* New York: Free Press, 1991.

Singer, L.R. *Settling Disputes: Conflict Resolution in Business, Families, and the Legal System.* Boulder CO: Westview Press, 1994.

Ury, W., J.M. Brett, and S.B. Goldberg. *Getting Disputes Resolved.* Cambridge MA : Harvard Program on Negotiation, 1993.

Alain Pekar Lempereur

See also ARBITRATION; MEDIATION, CRIMINAL

Distributive Justice

A key part of social justice, distributive justice aims at realizing to the greatest possible extent, and by means of the appropriate social institutions, a distribution that renders to each a fair share of social benefits and burdens. It is different from another, and arguably a derivative, part of social justice that simply aims at giving to each his own from justice conceived as being conformity to a society's particular legal arrangements. It is also different from justice conceived as a virtue and therefore as a property of individual actions. Influential competing theories of distributive justice are utilitarianism; John Rawls' "justice as fairness" and related theories such as those of Brian Barry, Ronald Dworkin, and Thomas Scanlon; rights based libertarian theories; and marxian-egalitarian theories.

Theories of distributive justice articulate, order, and justify what they variously take to be the principles of a just distribution. These principles are assessed as proposals for the quality of life, for their legitimacy as a political objective, or for their utility in determining political and economic policies. As standards of political legitimacy, principles of justice have a direct bearing on constitutional essentials often conceived as "the public reason" underlying legal institutions as well as legal decision making. In the task of articulating and ordering principles of justice, theories of justice face three questions.

1. *Who should benefit from the distribution?* For modern conceptions of justice in principle every member of a given society is in the scope of distributive justice. However, contractarian theories, which typically, but not invariably, conceive of a just society as a fair system of cooperation for mutual advantage tend in effect to exclude from the realm of justice those who are not engaged in mutually advantageous social interactions. Individuals or groups of individuals can be the direct beneficiaries of the distribution, but some utilitarian theories insist that justice requires the maximization of the overall good of society, in which case some individual (or groups of individuals) might not be better off as a result of what, on such conception, is a fair distribution. Theories of distributive justice seldom deal with justice between societies, though theories of global justice have recently been articulated.

2. *What should be distributed?* A functional distinction is often made between resources (or opportunities) and welfare. Although the extensional content of these categories is not sharply defined, education, civil and political rights, and freedom are frequently considered as resources, while wealth, income, health care, shelter, and other material goods are considered as welfare. Some argue that the distinction is spurious since, for a distribution of opportunities to be just, it should translate in a just allocation of welfare; others argue that only a fair distribution of resources can induce a permanent increase in welfare; still others argue that, welfare being a matter of subjective preferences and given a respect for individual differences, social justice should concentrate on providing opportunities for people to achieve whatever counts for them as well-being and a good life.

3. *What are the appropriate patterns of distribution?* Theories of distributive justice, depending on how egalitarian they are, fill differently the gap in the "to each according to his . . ." dictum. As a criterion for a just distribution among the subjects of justice, a focus on merit, desert, talents, and issues concerning the need for incentives tend to induce inegalitarian theories of justice, while a focus on needs and interests tends to allow for more

equality in distribution. There is no algorithm, however, since "to each according to his talents or merits" often arises as a principle countering inequalities originating in unjust discrimination or hereditary privileges, while "to each according to his needs or interests" is sometimes thought to open the door to inequalities resulting from the more or less expensive needs and interests of the subjects of justice.

Utilitarianism

This term refers to a cluster of theories which characteristically seek to resolve questions of distribution by reference to the overall utility of its consequences. "Utility" is a generic term for intrinsic goods ranging from mental states such as pleasure or happiness, to the realization of desires, preferences, and interests. Utilitarians are divided as to whether the greatest sum of utilities should consist in (1) the sum of the greatest amount of utility for each individual compatible with a similar amount for all (egalitarian utilitarianism), (2) the sum of the greatest amount of utility for a majority (average utilitarianism), or (3) the greatest overall sum of utility no matter how distributed (classical utilitarianism). The last two proposals have been criticized on the moral ground that they, in practice, allow the sacrificing of people for the sake of increasing utility. Utilitarians are also divided as to which institutional framework facilitates best these conceptions of utility maximization. Some think that private ownership of the means of production (capitalism) undermines utility maximization; others think that a strongly paternalistic state (welfare state) is required; and still some others think that the free market with limited intervention of the state (minimal state) allows best for the maximization of utilities. Many variations of these positions exist, which shows that utilitarianism is compatible with many divergent, and indeed often conflicting, conceptions of how societies are to be ordered.

Justice as Fairness

Deeply critical of utilitarianism, John Rawls' justice as fairness is a contractarian conception which finds its inspiration in Jean-Jacques Rousseau and Immanuel Kant; it prescribes an egalitarian distribution of "primary goods," described as what everyone needs in order to conceive and to realize a life plan. These are rights and liberties, opportunities and powers, income, wealth and self-respect. Rawls also articulates and defends a "difference principle" that shapes an overall pattern of distribution by stating that inequalities in distribution are permissible if and only if they work to the benefits of the least well-off members of society. Rawls' principles of justice are introduced by means of a hypothetical contractarian procedure of decision under a "veil of ignorance" (hence, "justice as fairness"). By contrast with utilitarian principles, Rawls' principles appeal neither to a measure of utilities nor to substantive subjective preferences.

In *Political Liberalism,* Rawls claims that his conception of justice is exclusively political, meaning that it is intended to shape the institutional framework of a constitutional (liberal) democracy, to give the extension and to secure the conditions of political rights in a tolerant and pluralist society; moreover, his conception of justice appeals for its justification to shared considered convictions about social organization of people in liberal pluralist societies. Some have thought—though this is a controversial matter—this in effect is a conservative turn, depriving political justice of tools for social criticism.

Rights-based Libertarian Theories of Justice

In their radical forms, these theories object to the very idea of distributive justice. They instead hold that what justice requires is a reinforcement of the individual rights to property and to freedom from coercion; according to Robert Nozick, distribution of wealth or taxation for redistributive purposes is admissible only for the purpose of rectifying past violations of property rights. Moderate libertarianism allows a limited redistributive role for the state, consisting in ensuring a safety net of minimal welfare services and providing certain public goods. Friedrich Hayek's moderate libertarianism is actually utilitarian (classical) and stems partly from an economic argument based on considerations related to the efficiency of the market. So conceived, the demands of social utility prevail, as it is typical in classical utilitarianism, over those of individual utilities. Such a libertarian response is that people who are granted the right to freely choose their frameworks of interaction will engage in rational economic behavior. No empirical evidence had been provided for this claim, however.

Marxian-Egalitarian Theories

These theories depart from marxist anti-moralism, which holds that distributive justice is a temporary means, since inequalities of wealth are the result of a deeper defect in the productive relations of class divided societies. Collective control, marxist antimoralists believe, along with the extensive abundance resulting from the development of the productive forces in advanced stages of communism, will end the need for distributive justice, as it will end the role of the state. More recently, marxian thinkers have articulated egalitarian conceptions of justice which concentrate on Karl Marx's deep criticism of capitalism and its injustices. Some have argued that Rawls' account is defective in its allowance for incentives and is insensitive to the problem of power relationships between individuals, most fundamentally rooted in differential ownership of productive property. However, two questions arise: whether marxian egalitarian principles of justice differ significantly from left-Rawlsian conceptions (marxian distinct political sociology apart), and whether there is a form of egalitarianism that is both reasonable and more egalitarian than that governed by the difference principle.

Contemporary theories of distributive justice have become increasingly sensitive, in the issues they consider and the methodology they adopt, to a cluster of social sciences ranging from political studies, economics, and law to social anthropology. As a result, theories of distributive justice have become a powerful framework for a comprehensive understanding of the body of institutions characteristic of constitutional democracies and perhaps beyond as well. Working from various conceptions of justice, they have brought to light the more or less implicit normativity of these institutions and have stressed the feasibility and reasonability of an overall normative appraisal and critique of social institutions and practices.

References

Barry, Brian. *Justice as Impartiality*. Oxford: Clarendon Press, 1995.

Cohen, G.A. "Incentives, Inequality and Community." *The Tanner Lectures on Human Values*, 13, 263–329. Salt Lake City: University of Utah Press, 1992.

Gauthier, David. *Morals by Agreement*. Oxford: Clarendon Press, 1986.

Hayek, Friedrich A. *Law, Legislation and Liberty*. Vols. 1–3. Chicago: University of Chicago Press, 1973–1979.

Nielsen, Kai. *Equality and Liberty: A Defense of Radical Equalitarianism*. Totowa NJ: Rowman and Allanheld, 1985.

Nozick, Robert. *Anarchy, State, and Utopia*. New York: Basic Books, 1974.

Rawls, John. *Political Liberalism*. New York: Columbia University Press, 1993.

———. *A Theory of Justice*. Cambridge MA: Harvard University Press, 1971.

Roemer, John. *Free to Lose*. Cambridge MA: Harvard University Press, 1988.

Sen, Amartya. *Inequality Re-Examined*. Cambridge MA: Harvard University Press, 1992.

Jocelyne Couture

See also CORRECTIVE JUSTICE; FAIRNESS

Divorce and Marriage

Following extensive changes in social attitudes and conditions, both the content of family law and its underlying philosophy have undergone significant developments in the last several decades in all Western countries. Virtually every aspect of the law has been questioned, from the nature of marriage to the basis for divorce. The general trend has been away from extensive state involvement in the marriage relationship and its dissolution and toward much greater private control by the parties themselves. While the doctrine of family privacy is an old one in family law, it has traditionally been used to limit intervention by the courts in intact families, sometimes with socially negative results, as in the reluctance to "interfere" in cases of domestic violence. Under current law, private ordering has been extended beyond this hands-off approach to intact marriage toward providing much greater freedom for individuals to arrange their personal lives as they see fit without being penalized by a "one size fits all" view of family law. As more and more people live together in nonmarital relationships, whether heterosexual or homosexual, some scholars have even questioned the necessity for the legal status of marriage, for example, Martha Fineman in *The Illusion of Equality*. Other principles of family law, once considered sacrosanct, have been abandoned and are now seen as quaint relics of a bygone era.

In its traditional concern to encourage marriage as a legal status, the law provided very little recognition for nonmarital relationships on the grounds that to do otherwise would be a violation of public policy. The limited recognition of the status of common law or putative marriage, did not provide any protection for those who did not "hold themselves out" as being legally married. That such an approach could lead to injustice and hardship did not prevent the law from punishing those who chose a "meretricious" relationship over the socially and legally acceptable status of marriage. All that has changed. Courts began in the early 1970s to apply various existing doctrines to the property distribution and support needs of those in nonmarital relationships. The most important case in the United States was *Marvin v. Marvin*, in which the court expressly rejected the view that legal recognition of a nonmarital relationship was tantamount to endorsing contracts for sexual services, as past decisions had asserted. Both contractual and equitable doctrines were recognized to be applicable in appropriate cases of nonmarital relationships. Courts in other common law countries have also used equitable doctrines, especially resultant and constructive trusts, to deal with the dissolution of nonmarital relationships (see, for example, H.A. Finlay and Rebecca Bailey-Harris' *Family Law in Australia*). Elsewhere, this legal recognition has come from the legislature. In Ontario, there is provision for support rights in certain heterosexual de facto relationships; in New South Wales, both property rights and limited spousal maintenance; and in Victoria, only property rights. For homosexual couples the option to marry legally is not available except in Scandinavia; the recognition of some rights in such relationships by the courts and legislatures is thus more important, though it is presently less forthcoming, except for limited rights in limited localities.

Family law is also following social change in its recognition that the traditional family of an income-earning husband, a dependent wife, and two or more children is no longer the statistical norm in any Western country. The legal definition of family has also broadened, for example, in zoning, in the determination of governmental benefits, and in the ability of homosexual couples to adopt.

Consistent with the both the recognition of nonmarital relationships and the broadening of the legal definition of the family is the blurring of distinctions between the legal status of legitimacy and illegitimacy. In the United States, recognition of the rights of illegitimate children came from a series of Supreme Court decisions mostly in the 1970s. These cases have served to provide illegitimate children with most of the benefits of legitimacy. In other countries, the process has been handled more neatly by legislation. In 1969 New Zealand abolished any legal distinctions between legitimate and illegitimate children; Australia followed suit between 1974 and 1978. However this change has been achieved, at a time when single motherhood is widespread in the West, illegitimacy as a stigmatized legal status seems both archaic and punitive.

The increased emphasis on private ordering is also obvious in the acceptance of agreements by couples entering and leaving marriage. Where previously any prenuptial agreement that mentioned the disposition of property on divorce was held to be invalid as conducive to divorce, courts have come to accept the current reality of divorce by allowing parties (in circumstances of full disclosure and equal legal advice) to negotiate the terms of their separation both before marriage and before divorce.

This recognition that both parties are equally capable to negotiate agreements is part of another recent change in focus in family law, that of gender equality, a legacy of the recent women's movement. This is also illustrated in a shift in support obligations from the husband only onto both parties. For example, in the United States, alimony can no longer constitutionally be awarded only by the husband, as decided in *Orr v. Orr*, but is based on considerations of need and contribution and is relatively rarely awarded at all. Child support is also an obligation of both parents. Gender equality is now the norm in the legal standards for awarding child custody. Maternal presumption has given way to the best interests of the child as a standard. How this general shift toward gender equality has worked out in practice has been the focus of much empirical research, some of which argues that the position of women has actually deteriorated as a result (see *Divorce Reform at the Crossroads* by Steven Sugarman and Herma Kay and *The Illusion of Equality* by Martha Fineman).

The final major change in state control of marriage comes in the change in the basis on which divorce is granted. Statutes in all common-law countries have moved from a fault-based system, which used a criminal analogy in which bad behavior provided the grounds for divorce, to a "no fault" system based on psychological concepts of behavior in which the law's role is not to prevent marital breakdown but to bury dead marriages. The individual or the couple, not the court, decides that the marriage is no longer viable. The couple, for the most part, also decides issues of property, support, and custody, with the courts available as a last resort to those who cannot come to an agreement on their own or with the help of lawyers or that recently much touted alternative, divorce mediation. The use of the courts is strongly discouraged and, despite the continued theoretical existence of the doctrine of *parens patriae* (public guardian), courts usually merely rubber stamp the agreement made by the parties.

The move to private ordering is, however, neither complete nor without its critics. Authorities are much more willing to intervene in cases of domestic violence and child abuse. The legislature has also found it necessary to step in to provide guidelines on which child support must be based, to counteract the trend to pay little or no support for children after the dissolution of a relationship. Despite these limited examples, the move to individual, rather than state, control of most aspects of family life seems to be here to stay for the foreseeable future. There has been too much social change in the family and too much emphasis on individual rights in other areas for it to be otherwise.

References

Bruch, Carol S. "Cohabitation in the Common Law Countries a Decade After Marvin: Settled In or Moving Ahead." *U.C. Davis Law Journal* 22 (1989), 717–757.

Clark, Homer H., Jr. *The Law of Domestic Relations in the United States*. St. Paul MN: West, 1988.

Fineman, Martha Albertson. *The Illusion of Equality*. Chicago: University of Chicago Press, 1991.

———. *The Neutered Mother, the Sexual Family*. New York: Routledge, 1995.

Finlay, H.A., and Rebecca J. Bailey-Harris. *Family Law in Australia*. 4th ed. Sydney: Butterworth, 1989.

Glendon, Mary Ann. *The Transformation of Family Law*. Chicago: University of Chicago Press, 1989.

Henaghan, Mark, and Bill Atkin, eds. *Family Law Policy in New Zealand*. Auckland: Oxford University Press, 1992.

Sugarman, Stephen D., and Herma Hill Kay, eds. *Divorce Reform at the Crossroads*. New Haven: Yale University Press, 1990.

Carol Bohmer

See also BETROTHAL; FAMILY LAW; HOMELESSNESS AND RESIDENCY; MARRIAGE CONTRACT; PARENTING AND CHILDREARING

Domat, Jean (1625–1696)

Jean Domat, jurisconsult and magistrate, is known mainly for his work on codification of law. Domat's thought is developed in three main works: his great book, the *Traité des lois*, published in the years between 1689 and 1694, with its long introduction, *Les lois civiles dans leur ordre naturel,* and *Les quatre livres du droit public,* which was posthumously published in 1697. (The latter two were reprinted from their Rémy edition in 1989 by Caen University and Vrin.) His raising of fundamental questions concerning the problems of law, and his opposition to the anthropologization of law initiated by Hugo Grotius, place him near Samuel Pufendorf, Cumberland, or John Locke. His influence on such great classical thinkers of the eighteenth century as Chancellor D'Aguesseau, Montesquieu, and Portalis, is far from negligible.

According to Domat, analysis of juridical notions proves clearly the powerful thesis that "all matters of law" obey the natural and the divine order. Indeed, his whole work is marked by the idea of natural law.

First, Domat condemns the crudeness of paganism and praises the merits of the Christian religion because it teaches that "the first principles established by God as foundations of the order of human society are the roots of all the rules of justice and equity." Like his friend Blaise Pascal, Domat affirms that man without God is a miserable being; there is felicity only in and with God. Consequently, life must be governed by a duty: obedience to the "law of love," which commands sociability.

Domat knows, however, that men do not always observe the rule of universal love. Like Augustine, he deplores the fact that self-esteem is stronger than mutual respect. However, the earthly City is not a place of exile. Divine natural laws cannot be eliminated from it. Indeed, there are two types of law: *immutable laws* and *arbitrary laws*; the question is knowing the proper relation between them for the goodness of human action and the proper organization of human societies. The first type is divine or natural, always just and everywhere absolute, universal and eternal; it expresses necessity governed by divine reason. From this derives a "natural obligation" that is deeper and stronger than the *vinculum juris* defined by positive laws. The second type of law draws from human decisions and will; it is made, in civil societies, by a legitimate authority that can alter and/or abolish them since they are relative and mutable. Domat does not think that the institutional rules by which normativity is introduced to human civil societies find their principle of existence and their justification in the decisional power of men. With a classical spirit, he thinks that, if civil laws are, as Grotius says, "human establisments," they are always liable to the transcendent order of divine law. Civil laws must obey the natural order.

This is why the idea of justice, which belongs, by its own essence, to God's infinite perfection, is the archetype of all positive laws. In this sense, civil laws indicate that, in "light of reason," obligation to society is the destiny of men. Domat, like Augustine (and before Jacques-Bénigne Bossuet), sees in them, as opposed to Jesuit deviations and to all future forms of positivism, the connection between temporal and spiritual orders.

In Domat's traditional vision of the world, however, philosophy of law is associated with the dictates of reason, not the least original of his tenets. Indeed, if civil and political laws find their regulative truth in the natural order willed by God, and their juridical value in the transcendent justice governing the universe, human reason is able to discover the paradigms of truth and value by its "natural light"; reason's main task is to transcribe the natural order onto the legal apparatus. Domat thinks, like Antoine Arnauld and his friends of Port-Royal, that reason has a powerful capacity of logic and organization. It follows that reason promotes systematization and codification of this legal apparatus. This is why Portalis, the writer of the French *Code civil*, takes Domat's system of law as a model. In it, natural order and rational order are joined together.

It would be a mistake to believe that Domat follows *more geometrico*, the deductive method. The rational order, he says, is not *"l'esprit de géométrie"* of which Pascal speaks; rather, it is *"l'esprit de finesse,"* which judge or magistrate applies in interpreting facts and situations, not only according to positive rules, but also in the light of natural and immutable laws of justice and equity. Accordingly, jurisdictional or jurisprudential work does not consist of the subsumption of particular cases under a general rule; it consists of thinking the foundation of their meaning before having recourse to positive rules. Natural law or the "spirit of laws" comes down from heaven and becomes the immanent principle of civil order. Consequently, justice, even in a corrupt world, is a road of redemption. Montesquieu, in his own philosophy of law, acknowledges this work of Domat.

References

Domat, Jean. *The Civil Law in Its Natural Order.* Ed. Luther S. Cushing. 2d London ed. Trans. William Strahan (1722). Boston: Little, Brown, 1861.

———. *Oeuvres de Domat* (Works of Domat). Ed. Joseph Rémy. Paris, 1828.

Goyard-Fabre, S. "César a besoin de Dieu ou la loi naturelle selon Jean Domat" (Caesar Needs God, or the Natural Law According to Jean Domat). In *L'État classique.* Paris: Vrin, 1996.

Goyard-Fabre, S. "La philosophie du droit de Jean Domat ou la convergence de l'ordre naturel et de l'ordre rationnel" (Jean Domat's Philosophy of Law: Convergence of Natural Order and Rational Order). In *La philosophie politique du XVIIe siècle.* Paris: Klincksieck, 1996.

———. "Montesquieu entre Domat et Portalis" (Montesquieu Between Domat and Portalis). *McGill Law Journal* 35 (1990), 715. Also in *Montesquieu: La nature, les lois, la liberté.* Paris: Presses universitaires de France, 1993.

Maspetiol, R. "Jean Domat: une doctrine de la loi et du droit public" (Jean Domat: His Doctrine of Legislation and Public Law). In *Estudios juridico-sociales, homenaje al Prof. L. Legaz y Lacambra,* vol. 2. Universidad de Santiago di Compostela, 1960.

Matteuci, N. *Jean Domat, un magistrato gi-ansenista* (Jean Domat, Jansenist Judge). Bologna: Il Mulino 1959.

Renoux-Zagamé, M.F. "Domat, le salut, le droit" (Domat, Salvation, and the Law). *Revue d'histoire des Facultés de droit et de la science juridique* 8 (1989).

Todescan, F. "Domat et les sources du droit" (Domat and the Sources of Law). *Archives de philosophie du droit* 17 (1982).

Voeltzel, R.F. *Jean Domat: essai de reconstitu-tion de sa philosophie juridique précédé de la biographie du jurisconsulte* (Jean Domat: Essay in Restoring His Philosophy of Law; with His Biography). Paris: Sidney, 1936.

Simone Goyard-Fabre

Donation

See GIFT

Drugs

Under existing law, a wide range of conduct involving various drugs—production, use, possession, distribution, and the like—is subjected to criminal liability under a variety of state and federal statutes. Many state statutes are modeled after the Comprehensive Drug Abuse Prevention and Control Act, more popularly known as the Controlled Substances Act of 1970. This act divides, drugs or controlled substances" into five "schedules." The criteria governing the assignment of a drug to a schedule are complex. The most important such criteria include the degree to which the drug has a potential for abuse, the extent to which the drug may lead to dependency, and whether the drug has or lacks an accepted medical use. Placement of a drug or substance in one schedule or another affects manufacturing quotas, import restrictions, dispensing limits, and criminal penalties for unlawful trafficking.

Any debate about what properties a substance must possess in order to qualify as a "drug" is unimportant for purposes of applying the act, since the act regulates drugs and controlled substances. In any event, tobacco and alcohol are explicitly exempted from regulation under the terms of this act.

The use of the criminal law to combat drug use is almost entirely a creation of the twentieth century. Although a number of states had previously enacted antidrug laws, federal action began with the Harrison Act in 1914, which was based on the federal taxing power. Prior to this time, persons were almost completely free to use, buy, sell, and advertise drugs without fear of prosecution. The general trend has been to place increasingly greater reliance on the criminal justice system to control drugs.

The case in favor of drug criminalization is more frequently assumed than explicitly defended. Clearly, any such defense must proceed on a drug-by-drug basis. From time to time, public opinion polls have identified some drug or another as our nation's greatest problem. The particular substance about which the public is most concerned—heroin, alcohol, marijuana, cocaine, crack, or tobacco—has changed from one historical period to another. Generally, drug use is thought to require criminal penalties because of the various harms that drug use causes both to users and to society. Some drugs pose unique harms to users because of their addictive properties. The link between drug use and criminality is often cited as a reason to continue present policy. Moreover, drug use is widely depicted as inherently immoral. In addition, some commentators allege that a change in the status quo would send the wrong message, implying state endorsement of drug use.

In recent years, many academics and a few politicians have joined in a movement calling for "drug decriminalization." This movement unites thinkers of very different political ideologies. The meaning of "decriminalization" is not entirely clear. Commentators differ about how they would change existing law and about what alternatives are most appropriate for which specific drugs. At one extreme some libertarians would replace the existing "criminal justice model" with a "free market" in all drugs, with a possible exception for the protection of children. More moderate proposals call for a "vice model" that removes criminal penalties for the use and possession of small quantities of drugs, while maintaining the ban on the sale of drugs. Some reformers would subject users to the kinds of regulations typically imposed for minor infractions such as motor vehicle violations. Several theorists would adopt a "medical model," so that drug abuse would be treated as a public health problem. Many commentators believe that social policy with respect to most or all illegal drugs should resemble present policy toward alcohol; laws forbidding drug use under given circumstances, such as while driving, would remain in place. Perhaps the only unifying theme of this diverse movement is that much less reliance should be placed on the criminal justice system to deal with the problems associated with drug use.

Legal philosophers who would change existing policy differ about why they regard decriminalization as an attractive option. Many can find no justification for the inconsistency between the treatment of alcohol and tobacco, on the one hand, and such drugs as marijuana, cocaine, and heroin, on the other. The sheer magnitude of the problem defies a criminal justice solution—over sixty million Americans admit to having used an illegal drug at some time in their lives, while approximately twenty-five million Americans do so each year.

Virtually all commentators are frustrated with the apparent inability of the criminal justice system to significantly reduce the problems associated with illegal drug use. They are persuaded that current policy is ineffective because levels of drug use have remained relatively stable despite massive efforts by the criminal justice system to curtail both supply and demand. Recalling the inability of the country to effectively control the consumption of alcohol during the era of prohibition, these commentators are convinced that the "war on drugs" cannot be won.

Many legal philosophers believe that heavy reliance on the use of the criminal justice system has actually exacerbated the social problems connected with drugs. They insist that current policy is counterproductive largely because of the opportunities for tremendous profits created by the existence of a black market in drugs. Most of the violence and property offenses associated with the drug trade are a consequence not of drug use itself, but of the illegality of drug use. Moreover, many of the health problems caused by drug use could be reduced if the manufacture and distribution of drugs were subjected to government supervision. Law enforcement has been involved in numerous scandals because of its central role in drug policy. Courts and jails have become clogged as a result of "get tough" policies toward drug offenders, at great expense to the public. The enforcement of drug laws has devastated minority communities and eroded civil liberties.

Other advocates of decriminalization adopt a principled objection to the punishment of drug offenders and are less inclined to emphasize the empirical failures of existing policy. Some legal philosophers believe that the drug war is unjust and should not be fought, regardless of whether or not victory is realistic. They are unconvinced that a principled case for the imposition of criminal penalties has been made. Some believe that drug use may actually be protected by a right similar to that which applies to personal decisions about the foods we eat and the clothes we wear. The problem is not simply that present punishments are too severe. More fundamentally, these commentators think that hundreds of thousands of persons have been punished for conduct that should be placed beyond the criminal sanction.

Defenders of current policy typically respond that any retreat from the use of criminal penalties is likely to bring about a substantial increase in drug use, with a corresponding growth in the myriad social problems that such use involves. While sometimes acknowledging the deficiencies of criminalization, they emphasize that a drastic change in direction would create too great a risk. In light of the current political climate in the United States, experimentation with various schemes of decriminalization is more likely to be explored in many European countries. Commentators should be especially interested in data from these countries about how rates of drug use are affected by the implementation of specific decriminalization strategies.

References

Husak, Douglas N. *Drugs and Rights*. Cambridge: Cambridge University Press, 1992.
Musto, David. *The American Disease: Origins of Narcotics Control*. New Haven: Yale University Press, 1973.
Nadelmann, Ethan. "Drugs: The Case for Legalization." *Science* 245 (September, 1989), 939.
Wilson, James Q. "Against the Legalization of Drugs." *Commentary* (February, 1990), 21.

Douglas N. Husak

See also CRIMINALIZATION; PATERNALISM

Due Process

Due process is a legal and political value, which in some areas has the status of legal right, prescribing fair, accurate, and humane procedures in the application of governmental laws, rules, and policies. This value is opposed to procedures or decisions that are arbitrary, capricious, legally unauthorized, discriminatory, unreasonable, careless, corrupt, or incompatible with the standards of a free society. Although due process is mainly a procedural value, in some cases its target may shift from the procedures used in a case to the rules or policies at work there. If these rules or policies themselves are deeply unfair, they too may be condemned as violating due process values. At this point we speak—somewhat paradoxically—of *substantive* due process. Neighboring ideas include formal justice, the rule of law, and equal protection of the law.

Due process rights include habeas corpus, the right to a fair trial in criminal and civil cases, the right against ex post facto laws and bills of attainder, the right against torture and cruel punishments, and the right to compensation for unlawful arrest or detention. These sorts of rights are found in many constitutional bills of rights, as well as in many international human rights documents and treaties. For example, the United Nations *International Covenant on Civil and Political Rights,* adopted in 1966, deals with due process rights mainly in Article 7, where it declares a right against "cruel, inhuman, or degrading treatment or punishment," and Article 9, where it declares rights to liberty and security of the person, against arbitrary arrest and detention, to be informed at the time of arrest of the reasons for one's arrest, to prompt indictment before a judge, to a prompt trial, to habeas corpus, and to an enforceable right to compensation for unlawful arrest or detention. Missing from this list is an adequate requirement that criminal trials be fair and impartial. Article 6.1 of the *European Convention on Human Rights,* adopted in 1952, is better on this issue: "In the determination of . . . any criminal charge against him, everyone is entitled to a fair and public hearing within a reasonable time by an independent and impartial tribunal established by law."

Criminal and civil trials are the natural home of due process values. In a criminal prosecution, due process requires an antecedently existing and knowable law defining the offense; accusation based on prima facie evidence; a fair, orderly, and public trial before an impartial body in which evidence is presented and in which the accused is assisted by competent legal counsel and has the opportunity to present, question, and challenge evidence; discharge unless found guilty; and, if found a punishment that is fair, not cruel, and based on and proportional to the crime. However, due process values are not restricted to criminal and civil trials; they apply as well to the application of rules and policies in areas such as the regulation and taxation of property, public assistance, unemployment insurance, workers' compensation, public employment, public education, and government licensing in various areas. Much of the contemporary debate about the scope of due process concerns how it should be applied in these areas.

Due process values are widely accepted— if not always respected—in the contemporary world, so philosophical questions about due process in recent decades have not generally taken the form of fundamental challenges to the justifiability of due process values. Philosophical inquiries have instead taken the following forms.

First, some writers have attempted to explain the nature of due process values in light of their history or in light of the complicated and central role that the due process clauses of the fifth and fourteenth amendments play in United States constitutional law.

Second, since a "due process explosion" extending the scope of due process requirements has occurred in the United States since 1970, a number of writers have discussed the appropriate scope, or areas of application, for due process values and rights. They have tried to identify the benefits and costs of extending formal due process requirements into new areas of governmental and private activity.

Third, many authors have attempted to explain the normative foundations of due process requirements. Attempts to justify the general value of due process, or particular due process rights, appeal to underlying values such as accuracy, fairness, and treating people in ways that respect their dignity. An approach emphasizing accuracy suggests that due process requirements such as trials and hearings are ways of ensuring that important benefits or burdens, such as criminal punishments or welfare payments, are distributed accurately in the sense that those whom the law identifies as entitled to or deserving such benefits or burdens actually receive them in a high percentage of cases. Of course, accuracy in this sense would have to be balanced against considerations of administrative cost and workability. Procedures that score high in terms of yielding correct results may nevertheless be unfair or fail to respect people's dignity.

An approach emphasizing fairness as the justification for due process requirements would recognize that an approach cannot be fair unless it is generally accurate and workable, but would emphasize that fairness requires more than this. Fair procedure in a legal or administrative system, one might say following John Rawls, is one that rational people could accept if they knew that they were going to be affected by the system, but did not know what role(s) they would play in that system. For example, they would not know, in the criminal context, whether they were going to be accused persons, judges, prosecutors, jurors, attorneys, or taxpayers fearful of crime and high court costs.

Another approach to justifying due process requirements might emphasize respecting the underlying dignity and humanity of the participants. This "dignitary" approach to due process imposes limits on how confessions and evidence can be obtained, how prisoners can be housed, clothed, and punished, and how long jurors can be sequestered.

If all three of these values underlie due process requirements, it is clear that they can conflict. This means that it will sometimes be unclear whether due process requires greater accuracy, greater fairness, or greater respect for the dignity and humanity of the parties involved.

References

Mashaw, Jerry L. *Due Process in the Administrative State*. New Haven: Yale University Press, 1985.

Miller, Charles A. "The Forest of Due Process of Law: The American Constitutional Tradition." In *Nomos XVIII: Due Process,* ed. J. Roland Pennock and John W. Chapman. New York: New York University Press, 1977.

Rawls, John. *A Theory of Justice*. Cambridge MA: Harvard University Press, 1971.

Rubin, Edward L. "Due Process and the Administrative State." *California Law Review* 72 (1984), 1044.

Scanlon, Thomas. "Due Process." In *Nomos XVIII: Due Process,* ed. J. Roland Pennock and John W. Chapman. New York: New York University Press, 1977.

James W. Nickel

See also DIGNITY; EQUALITY; FAIRNESS; NATURAL JUSTICE; RULE OF LAW

Dueling

A duel is combat between two persons, fought with deadly weapons, by prior agreement. The word derives from the Latin *duellum* (*bellum* and *duo,* war between two). By design, duelists fight with "cold blood" and in full possession of themselves rather than in the heat of passion or from necessity. A duelist might fight on his own behalf, because he had given fighting-offense or to exact personal retribution from an offender, or he might fight on behalf of another (for example, to defend a woman's honor, the interests of a political superior or of a nation) in which case, he would be a *champion* as well as a duelist.

Public duels have been fought since biblical times (David v. Goliath). Duels between knights (and other men who could claim the "privilege" on the basis of noble descent) enjoyed official approval until the fifteenth and sixteenth centuries. This enabled upper-class men to do in the name of honor what would bring down the wrath of the state on lesser sorts.

Private (and illegal) duels grew in popularity after public duels were forbidden, perhaps because of a belief that the remedies for reputation-damaging conduct (for instance, defamation) offered by a legal system could never provide satisfaction appropriate and sufficient to assuage a gentleman's wounded honor. The institution of private dueling rejected the state's pretense to monopolize vengeance for all injuries. The man of standing necessarily prized the opinion of his colleagues. Since their beliefs about him made his status real, he refused to surrender to the state the prerogative to determine how to defend his reputation for bravery. Among professional warriors and other men of consequence, it was regarded as inappropriate to prefer a court of law to the dueling field. The Enlightenment philosopher Immanuel Kant wrote that ". . . legislation cannot . . . wipe away the stain of suspicion of cowardice. . . ." Kant appreciated that dueling provided men of honor the opportunity to prove that they deserved their reputation for bravery, something that the law could not do. Remarkably, Kant invoked prepolitical rules of the "state of nature" to explain the normative pressures that constrained the choices of insulted military officers. Kant agreed that victorious duelists should be punished, but not as murderers, because death resulted from "a combat openly fought with the consent of both parties, even though they may have participated in it only reluctantly."

Kant's reasoning accurately reflected the attitudes of the Prussian Officer Corps. But kings tended to think otherwise. Thus Friedrich the Great opined, "I love brave officers, but executioners are something my army does not need." He prohibited it but grudgingly tolerated it in practice so long as it did not interfere with military discipline. The persistence of status-based dueling showed that an "officer and a gentleman" remained imperfectly subordinate to the law of the land.

Duels were usually carried out with some formality, in accordance with more or less elaborate prescriptions. Such prescriptions were often codified. Between the invention of the printing press and the late nineteenth century, more than five thousand works on dueling appeared worldwide.

In theory, the duelist's goal was not to inflict death, but to face it unafraid. The real world of duels was less sublime. Good men dueled for trivial reasons. Egged on by zealous colleagues, duelists fought contrary to their real convictions and better judgment. Rather than autonomy, duels often displayed heteronomy—the will to perform deadly acts from fear of social censure.

Dueling was not an idiosyncrasy of Western culture. It has a history in warrior-culture per se and in other settings that prized honor and bravery above all else. Its universality might be explained by an economic analysis of cultural practices. Such an analysis suggests that dueling is an efficient institutional arrangement in a subculture that prizes honor as a noninstrumental good.

Dueling was not considered a specific offense in English common law. Duelists who fought in public were charged with aggravated affray. Survivors of deadly combat faced murder charges. The rationale was provided by William Blackstone who argued that "the king and his courts are the *vindices injuriarum* (avengers of injustice), and will give to the

party wronged all the satisfaction he deserves." A man who killed another in a duel was a murderer because "both parties meet avowedly with an intent to murder; thinking it their duty, as gentlemen, and claiming it as their right, to wanton with their own lives and those of their fellow creatures; without any warrant or authority from any power either divine or human, but in direct contradiction to the laws both of God and man." Other English commentators rejected this characterization. J.F. Stephen approvingly cites the views of German jurists according to whom "[t]he offense of dueling presents itself neither as a breach of the public peace, nor as a usurpation by private violence of the public administration of justice, but as a punishable gambling with life and limb. . . . In a systematic view of the subject, dueling occupies in offenses against life and limb the same place as gambling relates to property."

In 1803, the Statutes of George III made dueling a specific offense, but apparently with little deterrent effect. In 1844, Prime Minister Peel revised the army pension statute to deny a benefice to the widows of duelists. The English duel went into decline thereafter, but proving a causal connection is not easy. The French *Edit des duels*, passed by Louis XIV in 1679, criminalized the duel, prescribed death for the principals, confiscated property, and deprived gentlemen of letter of nobility and Christian burial. However, the *code Napoleon* did not give dueling the status of a specific offense. The Prussian Law Code of 1794 (valid until 1851) prosecuted the duel as a statutory offense, but ostensibly dealt with resultant death or injury under the general categories of murder and assault. By contrast, Imperial Germany's penal code of 1871 treated both dueling and its bodily sequelae as a specific offenses. But it did so without great conviction. The code's dueling articles were prefaced by an explanatory paragraph that made dueling seem less a heinous crime and more a bad habit, the punishment for which had to take into some consideration the necessities of life.

Whether to make dueling a specific offense presented an interesting criminological puzzle that illustrates the limits of law. Treating a victorious duelist as a common murderer for successfully defending his honor against a willing colleague often resulted in jury nullification. However, creating a specific offense for dueling with lesser attendant penalties tacitly acknowledged that the law did not regard all premeditated killings alike, at least when the peculiar interests of gentlemen were at stake. Ending the duel proved beyond the law's power.

Like the refusal of potentially life-saving medical treatment, suicide, assisted suicide, and euthanasia, dueling forces consideration of the principled limits of personal liberty, the degree of jurisdiction the individual should have over his physical existence, particularly with regard to the principle that consenting adults should be free to risk their lives in any manner they choose so long as the protectable interests of nonconsenting others are not jeopardized. Unlike them, however, dueling is no longer a controversial issue, primarily because the conception of honor that supported it has virtually disappeared. Nevertheless, it remains an interesting (albeit theoretical) question of political philosophy and philosophy of law to explain what compelling rationale might be offered for prohibiting the duel that would not also rule out other well-accepted exercises of liberty.

References

Best, Geoffrey. *Honour Among Men and Nations: Transformations of an Idea.* Toronto: University of Toronto Press, 1982.

Kant, Immanuel. *The Metaphysical Elements of Justice.* Trans. J. Ladd. Indianapolis: Bobbs-Merrill, 1965.

McAleer, Kevin. *Dueling: The Cult of Honor in Fin-de-Siècle Germany.* Princeton: Princeton University Press, 1994.

Ny, Robert. *Masculinity and Male Codes of Honor in Modern France.* New York: Oxford University Press, 1993.

Pitt-Rivers, Julian. "Honor." In *International Encyclopedia of the Social Sciences.* New York: Macmillan, 1968.

Schwartz, Warren F., Keith Baxter, and David Ryan. "The Duel: Can These Gentlemen Be Acting Efficiently?" *Journal of Legal Studies* 3 (1984), 321–355.

Stell, Lance K. "Dueling and the Right to Life." *Ethics* 90, no. 1 (October 1979).

Stephen, J.F. *A History of the Criminal Law of England.* 3 vols. New York, 1883.

Wyatt-Brown, B. *Southern Honor: Ethics and Behavior in the Old South.* Oxford: Oxford University Press, 1982.

Lance K. Stell

Duress

See COERCION (DURESS)

Durkheim, Emile (1858–1917)

Emile Durkheim is considered one of the patron saints of sociology. His first major work, *The Division of Labor in Society,* published in 1893, concerns the causes and functions of legal and moral rules. Submitted as his dissertation in philosophy, this book draws on historical and comparative studies of the law to argue that labor specialization is giving rise to a new, "organic" type of social solidarity in modern societies. Thus, he concluded, specialization is not a dehumanizing force, but is in fact morally desirable.

According to Durkheim, the law is not the artificial creation of a legislator, instituted to oppose public mores: on the contrary, it is the very expression of these mores. Legal, moral, and religious rules all consist in collective representations, or states of the collective conscience. These collective beliefs, ideas, and sentiments he conceived as unconscious, unobservable mental entities, binding the individuals who share them into a society. This underlying social reality of shared beliefs could not be known through introspection. It could be studied only indirectly through its effects, which include written codes of law. Such codes then serve as observable signs or indicators of states of the collective conscience.

For Durkheim, this unobservable social reality includes feelings of social solidarity. There are two kinds of social solidarity, mechanical and organic. Mechanical solidarity characterizes the social relationships of relatively primitive, preliterate societies in which all people follow more or less the same way of life. Organic solidarity is characteristic of more modern societies that have a high degree of specialization. The name reflects an analogy with living things having specialized organs.

The presence of mechanical solidarity is indicated by what Durkheim called "repressive" or penal law. He argued for this relationship through his analysis of crime and punishment. Crime is an offense against collective sentiments that gives rise to collective indignation. Repressive law is the expression of these sentiments. The true function of the punishments spelled out in the law is to maintain these social sentiments among those not being punished. Of course, violations of moral rules also bring about collective indignation. Law is distinguished from morality, however, in terms of its more organized character. Crimes offend well-defined sentiments. Punishments are meted out by specific people or institutions according to well-defined practices. The sanctions attached to violations of moral rules, on the other hand, are applied in a more diffuse manner. Durkheim never considered those persons entrusted with enforcing the law as having interests conflicting with that of society at large, nor did he seem to investigate whether the sanctions specified by the law are ever actually applied.

Organic solidarity, on the other hand, is indicated by what Durkheim called "restitutive" law. This branch of the law spells out obligations that arise as a result of the division of labor. Durkheim is concerned specifically with domestic, contract, procedural, and administrative law, which are concerned with the regulation of specialized social functions and not with property law. The written laws, he thought, merely express relationships that arise spontaneously among people with specialized functions. Such rules of law, of course, are contained in the minds of only some members of society, and not in the collective representations of everyone.

Durkheim argued that the relative proportion in written codes of repressive and restitutive law provides evidence of the relative importance of the two corresponding types of social solidarity for keeping society together. The concomitant growth of restitutive law with increased specialization of labor was taken as evidence that specialization was giving rise to greater organic solidarity. It could be objected, of course, that the evidence in fact runs contrary to Durkheim's thesis, indicating that restitutive law is the older form of law and that the body of penal law is increasing. Such evidence, however, does not necessarily disprove his thesis that the division of labor gives rise to organic solidarity. It may instead undermine his assumptions about the connections between types of law and types of social solidarity. Also, Durkheim cited evidence that even if the penal law is still growing it regulates fewer types of activity than it did in the past, as it no longer controls such things as religious beliefs or manners of dress. Finally, in a paper published in 1901, "Two Laws of Penal Evolution" (translated in *Durkheim and the Law*), he argued for a trend away from very intense punishments, with deprivation of freedom alone becoming the normal type.

After 1901 Durkheim turned away from the study of comparative law and toward the study of ethnology. In his investigations of pre-literate societies, he hoped to come to understand the origins and formation of the collective representations of which our moral and legal rules, as well as our basic categories of thought, consist.

References

Durkheim, Emile. *The Division of Labor in Society*. 1893. Trans. W.D. Halls. New York: Free Press, 1984.
———. *Durkheim and the Law*. Ed. Steven Lukes and Andrew Scull. New York: St. Martin's Press, 1983.
Lukes, Steven. *Emile Durkheim: His Life and Work*. 1973. Stanford: Stanford University Press, 1985.
Schmaus, Warren. *Durkheim's Philosophy of Science and the Sociology of Knowledge: Creating an Intellectual Niche*. Chicago: University of Chicago Press, 1994.

Warren Schmaus

Duty

See OBLIGATION AND DUTY

Dworkin, Ronald (1931–)

Ronald Dworkin has been influential in the areas of legal theory and political theory since the late 1960s. For much of that time, he has been a professor at both New York University Law School and Oxford University (at Oxford, he took over the chair held by H.L.A. Hart).

In Dworkin's early writings, he challenged a particular view of legal positivism, a view which saw law as being comprised entirely of rules allowing discretion to judges in their decision making when the dispute before them was not covered by any existing rule. Dworkin offered an alternative vision of law, in which the resources for resolving disputes "according to law" were more numerous and varied, and the process of determining what the law required in a particular case was more subtle.

Dworkin argued that, along with rules, legal systems also contain principles. In his view, legal principles are moral propositions that are

D

stated in or implied by past official actions (statutes, judicial decisions, and constitutional provisions). In contrast with rules, principles do not act in an all-or-nothing fashion: that is, they can apply to a case without being dispositive. Rather, principles (for example, "One should not be able to profit from one's own wrong" and "One is held to intend all the foreseeable consequences of one's actions") have "weight" favoring one result; there can be—and often are—principles favoring contrary results on a single legal question.

Because there are (numerous) principles as well as rules, there will be few if any occasions where the law "runs out" and judges must decide the case without legal guidance; but at first glance, legal determinacy for Dworkin might seem to be undermined by the abundance of sometimes-contrary legal standards. This is not the case. According to Dworkin, judges consider a variety of theories regarding what the law requires in the area in question, rejecting those which do not adequately "fit" past official actions. Among the theories that adequately "fit," the judge chooses the one which best combines "fit" and moral value, making the law the best it can be. Two tenets of Dworkin's early writings were thus indirectly related: that law contains principles as well as rules, and that, for (nearly) all legal questions, there are unique right answers.

In his later works, Dworkin offered what he called "an interpretive approach" to law. (While Dworkin has said little about the relationship between his early writings and his later work, the later work is probably best seen as a reworking of earlier themes within a philosophically more sophisticated framework.) According to Dworkin, law is best understood through (and as) "constructive interpretation," interpretation that makes its object the best example of its genre that it can be. Constructive interpretation is both an imposition of form upon the object being interpreted (in the sense that the form may not be immediately apparent in the object) and a derivation of form from that object (in the sense that the interpreter is constrained by the object of interpretation).

The past actions of officials are the data to be interpreted constructively. In making the law, or an area of the law, the best it can be, the criteria Dworkin mentions most often are, as before, "fit" and moral value. (Dworkin also writes of "integrity," the belief that judges should decide cases in a way which makes the law more coherent, preferring interpretations which make the law more like the product of a single moral vision.) The judge's analysis remains much as it was in Dworkin's early writings: for some legal questions, the answer may seem easy because only one theory shows adequate "fit"; often, however, there will be alternative theories with adequate "fit." Among these, some will do better on "fit," others on moral value. In making comparisons among alternative theories, the relative weighting of "fit" and moral value will itself be an interpretive question and will vary from one legal area to another (for example, protecting expectations—having new decisions "fit" as well as possible with older ones—may be more important regarding estate or property law, while moral value may be more important than "fit" for civil liberties questions).

Dworkin's writings, both early and later, can be seen as attempts to come to terms with aspects of legal practice that are not easily explained within the confines of traditional legal positivism: for example, participants in the legal system regularly argue over even basic aspects of the legal system, not just over peripheral matters or the application of rules to borderline cases; even in landmark decisions and other decisions that appear to change or overrule settled law, judges write in terms of their decisions being required by, or at least consistent with, existing law; and even in the hardest cases, lawyers and judges speak as if there were already-existing unique right answers.

There is a wide and varied critical literature on Dworkin's jurisprudential writings. Among its themes are the following:

1. As to Dworkin's early writings, some commentators doubt that the distinction between rules and principles can be sustained, at least in the way Dworkin proposed; and some (for instance, Jules Coleman) argue that the existence of legal principles is not, as Dworkin claimed, inconsistent with legal positivism.

2. It is a common, if sharply contested, view in the philosophical literature that values are incommensurable (that is, that among alternative choices instantiating different values, one cannot say—it is nonsensical to say—that one is better than, worse than, or equal to the other), a position in the jurisprudential literature advocated by John Finnis and Joseph Raz, among others. If that position is correct,

Dworkin's thesis that (almost) all legal questions have unique right answers has grave difficulties. Dworkin's judge resolves legal disputes by comparing theories of what the law requires in the area, where one theory may be better as to the value of "fit," another better as a matter of moral value. If it does not make sense to speak of "right answers" (or "overall best alternative") when comparing options in terms of more than one value, then Dworkin's approach to judicial decision making will not work. (The debate on Dworkin and incommensurability is at an early stage and has developed along lines of how one proves commensurability or incommensurability, and which side has the burden of proof.)

3. It is not always clear what claims Dworkin has for his approach to law. There are times when he seems to be saying that the interpretive approach is all-encompassing, applying to anything one might want to say within legal practice, about individual legal systems or about law in general. Joseph Raz and H.L.A. Hart, among others, have argued that Dworkin's theory is primarily a theory about how judges should decide cases, and that there is both room for and need for an entirely different kind of theory, a general social theory about law. On occasion, Dworkin appears to concede some truth to that view.

4. Gerald Postema has argued that Dworkin's theory offers a "Protestant approach" to law, with every participant in the legal system having his or her own version of what the law requires, with everyone's view being more or less equally legitimate. The argument (which was also put forward, in different terms, by Robert Cover) is that such an approach is contrary to law's social and public nature.

5. Commentators have differed on the extent to which Dworkin's theory depends upon a holistic or coherence approach to truth and knowledge, and the extent to which it assumes metaphysical realism. Dworkin has been largely silent on these technical philosophical issues. Some commentators, including Michael Moore and Andrei Marmor, have argued that Dworkin's approach is built upon a faulty epistemology or metaphysics, or that parts of the theory are inconsistent with its basic philosophical structure.

References

Cohen, Marshall, ed. *Ronald Dworkin and Contemporary Jurisprudence*. London: Duckworth, 1984.

Dworkin, Ronald. *Law's Empire*. Cambridge MA: Harvard University Press, 1986.

———. *A Matter of Principle*. Cambridge MA: Harvard University Press, 1985.

———. *Taking Rights Seriously*. Cambridge MA: Harvard University Press, 1977.

Marmor, Andrei. *Interpretation and Legal Theory*. Oxford: Clarendon Press, 1992.

Symposium on *Law's Empire*. Law and Philosophy 6 (1987), 281–438.

Brian Bix

E

Ecclesiastical Jurisdiction

In the design of the new *Code of Canon Law,* jurisdiction in the wide sense is distinguished into the three sectors of legislative, executive or administrative, and judicial activity. This last taken by itself is called jurisdiction in a strict sense.

In its *strict,* public law sense, jurisdiction means the activity by which the organized group expresses itself in an official manner judicially, makes this judgment prevail by means of force, and preserves the order peculiar to its system of law. The group does this when someone harms another and the group must respond, or when a plaintiff brings a complaint about the system's response. In the Roman Catholic Church, this strict sense is the procedure designed for the part of this institution where practice is most firmly structured, where the canon law is in force.

In this institution, there is also a *broad* sense of jurisdiction. This refers to the power that ordinarily belongs to any church office-holder even without the strict power of ecclesiastical jurisdiction. The term applies especially to the mixed executive and legislative competence of popes and bishops called *summa imperii* (highest authority). Traditionally, in this case the expression designates the power of governing in general, and was usually called *potestas iurisdictionis seu regiminis* (the work of lawgiving or of directing), described by F.X. Wernz as "the public power of governing the baptized faithful to help them toward holiness and salvation, bestowed by the command of Christ or the mission assigned to the Church." In the 1983 *Code of Canon Law,* the legislator prefers simply the expression *potestas regiminis* as more precise and less open to misunderstanding.

Nonjurisdictional Offices

From jurisdiction in either sense must be distinguished the barely sketched hierarchy of offices to accomplish apostolic direction. This category of *potestas sacra* (sacred works) whose concept cannot be reduced to the idea of power lies on the conceptual margins of general public law. It involves *potestas ordinis* (the work of sanctifying) and *potestas magisterii* (the work of teaching). Jurisdiction, and this work of directing doctrine which belongs to the pope and bishops, lie near to each other. The latter uses nearly the same procedures and obligations as judicial activity. The distinction lies in the fact that the latter's judgments are binding on all, rather than being limited to a few interested parties. Good canonists like Hervada and Ciprotti keep these from being assimilated to jurisdictional power.

This distinction does not rely on the sacrament of orders, whose priority the canonical mission is required to respect. While priesthood is included in the work of sanctifying, that work constitutes a more diffuse power. It can be exercised not only within the narrow ambit of persons who hold full priesthood, but even by ordinary persons; these sometimes exercise extraordinary powers. In order better to achieve people's salvation, exercise of the *potestas ordinis* requires less responsibility for the care of souls by its minister, according to the Council of Trent's teaching on the *opus operatum* (that performing the action realizes the effects).

There are other legitimate powers that cannot be assimilated to jurisdiction. These derive from special statutes or exercises of authority, such as those regarding the location or the superior of a religious order. These cannot be considered as issuing from the public power of the Church, *potestas dominativa,* nor are they an exercise of jurisdiction. Provisions which lack any imperative content (for example, deterrents) are not jurisdictional, either, although they fully govern some legal subject.

Internal and External Forum

The distinction between the external and the internal forum of jurisdiction parallels the distinction between the power of jurisdiction and the power to govern. In the logic of the canonical system, jurisdiction in the internal forum focuses on responses, responses to the power of orders or to the power of governing. This focus demonstrates the central principle for distinguishing the two forums: that even the external is structured to be permeable by the internal, whenever pastoral concern for the individual's salvation is involved. This principle is filtered through the conceptual grid of the Christian community's practice, always present as relevant to the human legislator in forming positive law institutions.

The external forum is related to the central pastoral concern through its use of remedial clauses, as well. These moderate the rigor of clear requirements. In their place remedial clauses set up arrangements better able to achieve the chief value, which is people's salvation and the Gospel life. Innovation is always possible within the limits of the external forum's recognized principle: its dependence on the forum of conscience. This occurs, for example, when some third party acts instead of the one provided by the Church. This practice has left profound marks on the jurisdiction according to conscience (equity) in the common law, through its earlier influence upon the practice of ecclesiastical courts.

Ordinary and Delegated Jurisdiction

Clerics are authorized by reason of their sacrament to exercise jurisdiction as the power of governing; laypersons are authorized by the canons to work together in the canonical mission by assuming some church offices. Canon law presumes that the power of jurisdiction is given for exercise in the external forum.

Jurisdiction is usually defined in terms of the offices to which it is attached. Appropriated power exercised in one's own name is distinguished from vicarious power excercised in the name of someone else. Delegated power is distinct from both sorts of ordinary power; the holder of delegated power cannot act outside its delegated limits on pain of nullity.

In cases of error, when a group of persons falls under the (apparent) authority of an ecclesiastical official, that official's executive power is supplied automatically by law. This is in agreement with the practice of general public law as to the "authority in fact." The threefold governing power (legislative, executive, and judicial) is inserted into the new *Code of Canon Law* just at the point where delegated power is discussed.

Jurisdiction in History

It remains problematic today what jurisdiction in the strict sense really is, with no secure final answer to the long-standing debate. It is not settled that there is any relation between the area of *imperium* and that of *iurisdictio.* This relation between the container and its contents has been debated at least since the end of abstract natural law in the late Middle Ages, and its mitigation by the *volonté général* (general will) at work in the institutions of the French Revolution.

The changing history of this continuing problem of the relation between *potestas* and *iurisdictio* starts in classical Roman procedure. There, a modular structure distinguished two phases: a phase *in iure* (at law), before a magistrate pronouncing the law, sometimes without *imperium* and authorized to do no more than identify the legal maxim covering the concrete case; and a phase *apud iudicem* (before a judge) where a real and particular determination was given to a private citizen.

This distinction did not cease when the office of magistrate with *cognitio extra ordinem* (extraordinary authority) appears at the time of the empire, nor with the formation of the collections of barbarian law in the West. In this more confused period, jurisdiction remained a response to the continuing need for decisions in the political community. Jurisdiction did not depend absolutely and necessarily on "the form of the state," with the Roman pontiff and the Christian emperor at its summit, as the sole authorities vested with power to "make new laws or canons."

Greater awareness that judicial function is rooted in the people occurred with Charlemagne in France through the institution of the *scabini* ("law-finders" appointed with popular consent in each district to render judgment in lesser matters), or in southern Italy during the

Norman-Saxon middle kingdom. This awareness alternated with an explicit identification of jurisdiction with *summa potestas,* in feudal law and in the middle period of canon law, due to the influence of this rationale on Gregorian constitutive law. The idea remained firmly fixed in some authors, that jurisdiction had something to do with public law and was rooted in public power. Nonetheless there was no implicit identification of this *iurisdictio* with *imperium* since, as stated by the postglossator Azo (d. 1230), "the judge by power of office does not make law, but instead declares it." Ordinary judging was distinct from situations where a judgment of equity or a voluntary jurisdiction operated. There, the power was developed along with the content of law: "Governing *(imperare)* occurs, strictly, when a judge by power of his office supplies the law for a party, and rules in equity with nearly full authority."

The glossators took over explaining the notion of *iurisdictio* as "the faculty to declare what the law is, both the order already constituted and the law to be constructed through judgment." Their anonymous fragment is fully confirmed by Azo's definition: jurisdiction is "the public duty of stating with finality the law as it is to be upheld or as it is to be constructed with equity."

Judgment was fundamentally the attempt to reach a *just* solution in every case. Whether undiluted at the apex of the legal structure or modified by the intended effects and by the application of equity, the person authorized to make the decision was responsible primarily for doing justice. The judge is required to judge "in the name of Christ and holding only God before his eyes."

This call upon conscience did not remain intact in all phases of the *ancien régime,* nor did it come completely unscathed into the Gregorian era when, under the influence of the *Dictatus papae* (papal dictate), the system underwent a process of centralization analogous to that in the late Roman empire. A hierarchical conception of civil procedure was then dominant, inducing an analogous conception of canonical functions in the Church. Appeals to Rome increased, often too numerous to permit their serious consideration; and the system of delegated jurisdiction tended to expand, often requiring a consideration on the merits which did no more than frame the issue in a legally correct manner.

Church law, on this point also, is not far from Azo's definition above, which Placentinus in fact applied to "all judges" and which Ostiense, *fons et tuba iuris canonici,* took for granted in his definition. With Sixtus V, the Roman Congregation unfortunately came to absorb the competence of the Curia's courts under "extrajudicial appeal" against the administrative decrees (not the judicial sentences) of ordinaries; this brought about a system of recognizing appeals on predetermined subject matters, modeled on judicial administration in the royal absolutisms then prevailing, all of which did severe damage to the right of defense in proceedings under canon law.

In this hierarchical arrangement, it became more difficult to maintain the principle of the autonomy of jurisdiction, the judicial independence which is the basic constitutive element essential to contemporary systems of civil law. Still, some interpreters construed jurisdiction strictly, based on judges' absolute dependence on the two essential centers of *potestas sacra,* pope and bishops; this escaped the legal culture sufficiently to distinguish *imperium* from *iurisdictio.*

Autonomy of Jurisdiction

The problem is posed differently today, starting from the concepts clarified above. A function exercised "in the name of Christ" answers to no other authority than the forum of conscience. It is true that equivocation remains in some doctrinal positions contrary to the normative emphasis of the new *Code of Canon Law,* reinforcing old doubts about the autonomy of judicial practice from any other Church power. But this is out of step with a Church characterized by transition and moving toward re-establishing gradually the source for "stating the law" in the people of God as a whole, as expressed in the text surrounding canon 1420.

Today there is a rapid and final disappearance of the features of legal positivism. The French Revolution's introduction into modern procedures of the completely antitraditional idea that judges have no task but declaring the statutes gravely impaired their freedom of interpretation and was an obvious hindrance to the fulfillment of their duty to do justice.

These ideas, tied to the authoritarian vision of the Enlightenment and founded in the sheer utopia of a perfect code, are completely

E

ruled out by the general hermeneutical principle in canon 1752 and in the *Sacrae disciplinae leges* promulgated in 1983, which creates an absolute obligation on the interpreter to reconcile the *Code of Canon Law* with the principles of ecclesiology and, when that is not done, authorizing every appropriate equitable derogation.

Summarily between its two poles, one of a traditional legal system refined through history from which maxims of just decisions can be endlessly deduced, and the other pole a law for the act of faith residing in the creative responsibility of an individual judge's conscience, this extraordinary product of European culture that is canon law today lives facing its recent tradition, its proper rooting in equity and the internal forum.

References

Bassett. "Canon Law and the Common Law." *Hastings Law Journal* (1978), 1386.

Bertrams, W. "Natura iuridica fori interni Ecclesiae" (The Juridical Nature of the Internal Forum in the Church). *Periodica de re morali, canonica, liturgica* (1951), 307.

Betti, E. "La creazione del diritto nella 'jurisdictio' del pretore romano" (The Creating of Law in the "Jurisdiction" of the Roman Praetor). In *Studi in onore di Chiovenda*. Padova, 1927.

Ciprotti, P. "Sulle potestà della Chiesa" (On Power in the Church). *Archivio di diritto ecclesiastico* (1941), 49.

De Diego Llora, C. *Poder jurisdicional y funciòn de justicia en la Iglesia* (Jurisdictional Power and the Role of Justice in the Church). Pamplona, 1976.

De Luca, L. "Aequitas canonica et equity inglese alla luce del pensiero di C. Saint Germain" (*Aequitas canonica* and English Equity in the Thought of C. Saint Germain). *Ephemerides juris canonici* (1947), 46.

Hervada, J. *Elementos de derecho constitucional canonico* (Foundations of Canonical Constitutive Law). Pamplona, 1986.

Lefebvre, C. "Pouvoir judiciaire et pouvoir administratif en droit canonique" (Judicial Power and Administrative Power in Canon Law). *Ephemerides juris canonici* (1949), 330.

McIntyre, John. *Customary Law in the Corpus Juris Canonici*. San Francisco: Mellen Research University Press, 1990.

Onclin, W. "The Church Society and the Organisation of Its Powers." *The Jurist* (1967), 1.

Rouco Varela. "Le statut ontologique et épistémologique du droit canonique" (The Ontological and Epistemological Status of anon Law). *Revue des sciences philosophiques et théologiques* (1973), 225.

Vindogradoff, P. *Roman Law in Mediaeval Europe*. Oxford, 1929.

Wernz, F.X., and P. Vidal. *Ius canonicum. II. De personis*. Rome: Universitas Gregoriana, 1928.

Zanchini, F. *Chiesa e potere. Studi sul potere costituente nella Chiesa* (The Church and Power. A Study of Constitutive Power in the Church). Torino, 1992.

Francesco Zanchini di Castiglionchio

See also ISLAMIC PHILOSOPHY OF LAW; JEWISH PHILOSOPHY OF LAW

Ecology and Environmental Sciences

The term "ecology," derived from the Greek *oikos,* "habitat," and *logos,* "science," was first used by Ernst Haeckel, a German zoologist, in 1866 to designate the science which studies relations between living organisms in their natural habitat. Environmental sciences have emerged in more recent years as distinct disciplines, each defined by the nature and scope of its object of analysis. (Epidemiology, as an environmental science, is a medical science which focuses on transmissible disease-inducing parasites in populations, whereas urban planning is a social environmental science which focuses on patterns of economic and social activity in a space of concentrated human populations.) Ecology and environmental sciences have evolved in the context of scientific practices as sister disciplines with common assumptions about nature sharing their findings about the effect of human activity on natural processes. They draw from the specialized fields of biology, of geology and paleontology, and of physics and thermodynamics to pose and situate the interrelationships between life forms and their environment in the most comprehensive terms. Ecology and environmental sciences examine conditions of survival, reproduction, and dispersal of life within the planet's range of climatic and chemical environments; this involves inquiries into dynamics of ecosystems, energy flows, nutrient cycles, predation chains, species distribution, population dynamics, seasonal cycles, and so on. They also include an account of these processes as they are affected by human activity.

Ecology and environmental sciences share a broader philosophy, a relationship between reason and nature in which reason prescribes that action be one of conservation and preservation of nature. Such a view stands in stark opposition to a dualist conception prominent in various forms of modern thought. These various forms of dualism elevate human reason above nature and reduce nature to a passive object whose sole value is to provide a means with which humans achieve goals.

From the ecological and environmentalist perspective, the dualism underlying past and present patterns of activity has taken its toll on the environment by making demands that threaten the life-supporting capacity of the planet. One measure of the negative effects of such human activity on natural processes is pollution, of which there are many forms, each having different degrees of destructive potential on nature. Pollution is defined as human intervention in natural equilibria by the emission of toxic substances into the environment, which disturbs or prevents natural processes of evolution of the interconnected life forms in their habitat, the ecosystem, the most global and comprehensive being the biosphere. Of the life-threatening toxins the most serious are radioactive emissions. Chemical pollution has less immediate effect than nuclear pollution but in concentrated form is life threatening and severs the food chains and food webs of the ecosystem. Petrochemical products, emitted or spilled, are poisonous to many aquatic organisms. Plastic waste, although nontoxic, is a pollutant insofar as it is nonbiodegradable and has already acquired an extensive total mass.

Pollution is not an independent source of ecological disturbance. In its present forms, it is the effect of infrastructural technological growth and industrial expansion. For example, the increase of industrial power, permitted by the release of energy from fossil fuels and nuclear sources, threatens a thermodynamic disorder that would adversely affect the stability of vital natural cycles. Such factors of disturbance are posed not only in qualitative

terms, as in the case of nuclear technology and its destructive potential as such, but in quantitative terms. An ecological disproportion exists between the planet's resources in the light of its evolutionary capacities (including the rhythm of reproduction of ecosystems), on the one hand, and human demands on these resources, on the other hand. From the demands side, this disproportion applies not only to industrial expansion and technological growth but to the growth of human populations as well. The dynamics of human populations, unlike those of the nonhuman species, are posed in neo-malthusean terms insofar as the human pattern of growth does not encounter the same structural environmental resistance as do other species.

Ecological disorders of different forms and varying degrees of intensity are regarded as being the consequence of an anthropocentricism that grants privileges to humans without making them conditional on obligations and duties to preserve nature. The science of ecology joins a broader ecological philosophy in a rejection of the modernist dualism between human reason and nature, but from this concurrence there appears to emerge no consensus on what is to take the place of dualism. Proposals vary from a relation of stewardship, in which moral reason fixes responsibilities and duties to preserve and conserve nature in a viable state for future generations, to a relation in which reason fixes responsibilities and duties to preserve nature for nature's sake. A modified humanism prevails in the first form but wholly disappears in the second where reason is assimilated to nature.

For these two distinct and opposing ecological perspectives, the most contentious issue is that of rights and the bearer of rights. The humanist perspective, one exponent of which is John Passmore, derives rights from rational, moral agency and makes the human being the sole bearer of rights. The nonhumanist perspective, of which there are a number of variants, extends rights to nonhuman nature. A utilitarian variant, to which subscribe such thinkers as Joel Feinberg, derives rights from sentience, the capacity to suffer, and attributes rights to nonhuman animals. This view acknowledges the asymmetry between moral agents and nonhuman animals in regard to duties and obligations of bearers of rights. In this view, the asymmetry converts to an equitable balance by the accountability of human action where agents answer to the human community for their treatment of animals by means of agreed-upon judicial norms.

The holist, naturalist variant, with which the deep ecology of Arne Naess is associated, expands the notion of rights beyond moral agency and sentience to intrinsic value, which is posed as an attribute of all elements of being. Intrinsic value confers moral standing or relevance on a plant, river, or stream requiring respect from moral agency. In positive terms, such respect requires a recognition, acknowledgment, and an honoring of the integrity of animal and nonanimal nature. In negative terms, it implies a nonviolation of this integrity.

The attribution of intrinsic value has raised the problem seen by David Hume, the naturalistic fallacy of deriving value from fact. Among the various holist responses to the dualist thesis of fact-value dichotomy is a pragmatism inspired by John Dewey and by evolutionary biology. This pragmatism accords value and fact an interactive sense and casts them in dynamic relation to each other. In this conception, reason is integral to the activity that takes place in the organism's interaction with its environs. For naturalist pragmatism, the mutual effects of the dynamic interaction between self and environment reduces the fact-value antinomy to a dynamic unity.

These differing conceptions of rights and of bearers of rights give rise to new constellations and forms of community. The humanism that accords practical reason a protectorate role toward nature regards community as a cultural entity of shared values, including aesthetic values of conservation of nature. The humanist ethic poses rights of future and "possible" people in regards to the consequences of present action on the natural environment. Here, the criterion of rightness or wrongness of action toward nature, including legislated energy policies, is whether it tends to preserve nature in a state compatible with the flourishing of future peoples.

The naturalism that reverses the relation of primacy between reason and nature, and assimilates reason in nature, situates the human species in a community of nature. As a member species of nature, the human species has no special privileges in relation to other species. Community acquires a naturalistic sense of equal membership in a biotic community. In this naturalist, holist sense, community, itself, has rights as a biotic whole beyond those of any individual species member. These are collective rights which come to bear on action of any given species member that threatens the viability and flourishing of the whole. This form of naturalism first found expression in Aldo Leopold's concept of land as a fountain of energy flowing through a circuit of soils, plants, and animals. Food chains are regarded as the living channels which conduct energy upward and by death and decay return it to the soil. Here, the sole criterion of rightness or wrongness of an action is whether it tends to preserve the integrity, stability, and beauty of the biotic community.

A social awareness of ecological issues has emerged in the late twentieth century that goes beyond the community of scientists and philosophers. Citizen movements for a cleaner and safer environment are particularly active in North America and Europe, posing the question of ecology in political terms. They demand political resolution of such ecological issues as urban overcrowding, pollution, deforestation, and various other forms of natural despoliation that have direct effect on the quality of life. The issue of ecology may very well prove to be the force of unity among peoples around the globe.

References

Benthall, Jonathan, ed. *Ecology: The Shaping Enquiry*. London: Longman, 1972.

Feinberg, Joel. "The Rights of Animals and Unborn Generations." In *Philosophy and Environmental Crisis*, ed. William Blackstone, 43–68. Athens GA: Doubleday, 1972.

Leopold, Aldo. *A Sand County Almanac*. New York: Oxford University Press, 1966.

Naess, Arne. "Self-Realization in Mixed Communities of Human, Bears, Sheep and Wolves." *Inquiry* 22 (1979), 231–241.

Passmore, John. *Man's Responsibility for Nature: Ecological Problems and Western Traditions*. London: Duckworth, 1974.

Rambler, Mitchell, Lynn Margulis, and René Fester. *Global Ecology: Towards a Science of the Biosphere*. San Diego: Academic Press, 1989.

Worster, Donald. *Nature's Economy: The Roots of Ecology*. Garden City NY: Doubleday, 1979.

Koula Mellos

See also EMPIRICAL EVIDENCE

Economic Loss

With the expanding scope of the tort of negligence, a problem continuing to plague the courts has been the extent to which a defendant should be liable for purely economic loss suffered by a plaintiff as a result of the defendant's negligent conduct. In this context, purely economic loss means loss unaccompanied by any physical harm to the plaintiff, whether in the form of personal injury or property damage.

Writers have identified various situations in which purely economic loss may be incurred. These include cases involving (1) the liability of public authorities for the negligent exercise of their statutory powers, (2) negligent misrepresentations, (3) negligent performance of services, (4) negligent production of defective goods and structures, and (5) economic loss incurred in consequence of some physical damage suffered by a third party. Different policy considerations are involved in each of these enumerated categories, and it is impossible to divine a single unifying theory to explain the courts' approach to the recovery of purely economic loss. Many of the cases involve the appropriate demarcation between contractual and tortious liability. This discussion, however, centers upon the fifth category, sometimes referred to as "relational economic loss." The common law courts have applied a general exclusionary rule denying the recovery of such loss in most cases and, as a condition of liability, have demanded that the plaintiff suffer physical damage.

Part of the judicial reluctance to compensate a plaintiff for its purely economic loss stems from perceived differences between such loss and physical damage. There is the consequent determination that the recovery of purely economic loss should not be placed on the same footing as the recovery of physical damage, which is traditionally controlled by the broad concept of foreseeability. Above all, there is the pragmatic concern that a defendant would potentially be exposed to an indeterminate amount of liability to an indeterminate number of plaintiffs. As a result, more claims would be presented than could reasonably be handled by any judicial system. This would place an intolerable strain upon judicial resources as well as upon those of the individual defendant. Moreover, physical damage, at least in the form of personal injury, is regarded as more deserving of recompense than damage merely to financial interests.

It is difficult, however, to justify a rigid distinction between property damage and purely financial loss. The arguments in favor of drawing the distinction are again essentially ones of pragmatism and convenience. Property damage and personal injury are often combined in a single loss, and it is convenient to deal with both claims at the same time and under the same rules; conduct causing property damage typically poses at least a risk of personal injury; and, as the economists would say, property damage does constitute a true social loss rather than a mere transfer of wealth (somebody's economic loss being another's economic gain).

It is even harder to justify a distinction between purely economic loss and economic loss consequent upon physical damage suffered by the plaintiff. The latter loss is regularly recoverable. At best, the administrative costs involved in allowing a physically damaged plaintiff to add a claim for consequential economic loss are substantially lower than those that would be involved in allowing purely economic loss claimants to sue.

Relational claimants tend to fall within one of two classes: those who had no preexisting relationship with the party suffering physical damage and whose loss flowed from the general web of economic relationships in modern society, and those whose loss arose from an existing contractual relationship with the sufferer of the physical damage. The general denial of recovery stems from fears of imposing too much liability to too many plaintiffs. This fear is especially prevalent in the first class of claimant. It is based partly on a moral concern of imposing an extraordinary liability out of all proportion to the defendant's fault, which may consist of a momentary act of inadvertence.

The concern of restraining liability within some reasonable bounds is also informed by economic analysis. Thus, there is the judicial sentiment that the victims of such purely economic losses are better placed to predict their occurrence and magnitude and to protect themselves against such risks, whether by first-party insurance or self-insurance. In the case of contractual relational claimants, the exclusionary rule has the effect of encouraging those claimants to protect themselves by negotiating suitable contractual terms with the third party who suffers the physical damage. This approach "channels" the victims' eco-

E

nomic losses through the party suffering damage and thus reduces litigation costs.

On the other hand, the potential tortfeasor would find it difficult to obtain reasonable rates for liability insurance given the unpredictability of potential losses arising out of a single accident. Even if all potential tortfeasors were adequately covered by liability insurance, potential victims would still be advised to take out first-party insurance because of the number of accidents not caused by the fault of any party. This fact would encourage wasteful double insurance coverage.

Liability for relational economic loss is not required to achieve the deterrence goal of tort law, since the tortfeasor already has the incentive to take care so as to avoid physical damage to the third party.

If the tortfeasor is uninsured or underinsured and, consequently, is incapable of satisfying all of the claims brought against it, then, should relational claims potentially be available, physical damage claimants would have to share the tortfeasor's limited assets ratably with those relational claimants.

Another proposed advantage of the exclusionary rule is that it is certain and easy to apply through its creation of a "bright line" between liability and the denial of liability. It thus has the merit of reducing the volume of litigation and frees the courts from having to embark upon a case-by-case analysis to determine which relational claimants are worthy of compensation and which are not.

Many of the justifications for the exclusionary rule can be assailed, especially by those who do not share some of the basic economic assumptions underlying the rule. Proponents of such a broader approach would point to the fact that there is no rational distinction between purely economic loss on the one side and property damage and consequential economic loss on the other. They would also assert that huge losses might be inflicted even in a physical damage case and indeed a large number of plaintiffs may be involved. Further, the extent of liability, even in a physical damage case, has never borne any particular relation to the defendant's culpability. The law recognizes no gradations of moral fault in the tort of negligence.

At best, the restriction of liability to those suffering physical damage provides a pragmatic solution and a workable limitation on the specter of indeterminate liability.

References

Cane, Peter. *Tort Law and Economic Interests*. Oxford: Clarendon Press, 1991.

Cooper-Stephenson, Ken, and Elaine Gibson, eds. *Tort Theory*. North York, Ontario: Captus Press, 1993.

England, Izhak. *The Philosophy of Tort Law*. Aldershot: Dartmouth, 1993.

Feldthusen, Bruce. *Economic Negligence: The Recovery of Pure Economic Loss*. Toronto: Carswell Legal Publications, 1984. 3d ed. Toronto: Thomson Canada, 1994.

Furmston, Michael, ed. *The Law of Tort: Policies and Trends in Liability for Damage to Property and Economic Loss*. London: Duckworth, 1986.

Nicholas Rafferty

See also CORRECTIVE JUSTICE; TORTS

Economics

Where economics once focused almost exclusively on market actors and exchange, modern economic analysis now studies a much broader range of human interactions and social institutions. For example, economics is effectively used to analyze judges and the law, politicians and legislation, and bureaucrats and regulation, as well as the social interactions which take place between members of a family. It has also provided insight into choices as seemingly private as the decision to commit suicide and as essentially public as the decision on how to use shared symbols or language.

Thus, if economics is to be distinguished from the other social sciences, it is less by its subject matter and more by its general approach or methodology. Economics is a study of rational choice. It assumes, reasonably, that most resources are scarce relative to human wants and that individuals, organizations, and societies will constantly have to choose how best to allocate resources across competing uses. This assumption helps to label economics as "the dismal science," since it is so often the role of the economist to point to the limits of our opportunities and our need to choose.

The economic theory of rational choice vacillates between analyses which are purely descriptive, claiming only that persons or organizations behave (or will behave) in a certain way because they are for the most part rational, and those which are prescriptive, claiming that rational persons or organizations ought to behave in some particular way, at least if they are to maximize their ends. However, within the conventions of economics, the latter sort of normativity is usually thought to be minimal, since the choices which rationality is said to prescribe are always conditional on given ends, which are themselves not judged. On the other hand, critics of economic analysis see a much more substantive and controversial form of liberalism manifested in this equal treatment of ends, ends which might vary considerably in their relative worth. Moreover, these critics are also typically suspicious of the economist's method of accommodating the ends of different rational agents under the aspect of Pareto efficiency, as explained in the final section.

Rational Choice for an Agent

An economic agent, be it an organization or an individual, sets about maximizing its given ends in the following way. It considers bundles of goods for which the quantities of any possible pair of goods, say X and Y, vary within each bundle. The agent asks, for small changes in the quantities of goods X and Y, whether the increase in value (or utility) provided by having a higher quantity of good X in bundle A than bundle B is larger or smaller than the decrease in utility that is suffered in having a lower quantity of good Y. If the increase in utility in having an additional unit of X is larger than the decrease in utility in having one less unit of Y, then bundle A is said to be preferred to, or have more overall utility than, bundle B. A rational agent should be prepared, therefore, to trade the former for the latter. This process of comparison and trade between the bundles continues up to the point where the marginal increase in utility on adding the last unit of good X ceases to be larger than the marginal decrease in utility in subtracting the last unit of good Y. (There will be such a point if each good has diminishing marginal utility for the agent, that is, if the agent values each additional unit less than the previous one.) Any trades beyond this point will decrease overall utility because the loss of utility from the marginal change will exceed the gain. Thus, a rational economic agent, choosing over different bundles of goods, will tend to equate the marginal utilities of the different goods within a bundle, at least if the agent is maximizing overall value or utility.

Interpersonal Rational Choice

The different utility-maximizing choices of the various economic agents are coordinated with one another by prices, or the publicly observable terms of trade which exist between the different pairs of goods X and Y within an economy. These prices might be explicitly comparable monetary prices, as they are for goods available in different markets, but they need not be. They could be "shadow" or imputed prices in a nonmarket sector. Suppose, for example, that the price of choosing to go into the labor market to earn income is the time that one must give up at home with one's children. Suppose too that this opportunity cost of time is the same for all; it represents the real time which anyone needs to spend away from home and at work to do the job. As for any good, some economic agents will happily pay this price and others will not. However, in the final equilibrium brought about by the rational choices of different agents, all agents will have equalized the ratios of their marginal utilities for the goods (for example, labor market income and home child care), that is, how these utilities are ranked one against another, to the ratios of the market and nonmarket prices for these goods. If this were not so for some agent, then that agent would still want to substitute one good for another (for example, labor market income for child care, or vice versa) at the prevailing price and there would not be an equilibrium. Moreover, since these prices are the same for all agents, in equilibrium all agents must give the same ranking to the marginal utilities for these goods. Thus, in this way the price system is said by economists to induce the same value maximizing behavior (that is, equal marginal utilities for goods) across different agents that was described above as rational for a single agent.

Normative Assessment

An equilibrium that is achieved in this fashion, that is, through individually rational choices, coordinated by publicly observable prices, will (given certain other assumptions dealing mostly with the universality of markets) be Pareto efficient. This means that it will not be possible to introduce any further marginal reallocations of the goods to make someone in the economy better off without at the same time making someone else worse off. For economists (and many others) satisfaction of this Pareto efficiency norm is usually thought to be a necessary condition for an overall social optimum, even if it is not a sufficient one. Those who have reservations about even the necessity of the Pareto condition usually worry that it does not discriminate sufficiently with respect to given ends and that it might be incompatible with other norms reflecting concerns for equality and rights. (It should be noted that there is nothing in the Pareto condition by itself which precludes redistribution, wherein one person is made better off because another is made worse off; the Pareto condition only requires that we should make someone better off if we can do so without making another worse off.) These sorts of issues have generated a huge economic literature, known (since Kenneth Arrow used the phrase in 1951) as social choice theory, in which the mutual compatibility of various social norms, including the Pareto norm, is rigorously investigated with the aid of set theoretic logic.

References

Arrow, Kenneth J. *Social Choice and Individual Values.* New York: Wiley, 1951. 2d ed. New Haven: Yale, 1963.

Arrow, K.J., and Hahn, F.H. *General Competitive Analysis.* San Francisco: Holden-Day, 1971.

Becker, Gary S. *The Economic Approach to Human Behavior.* Chicago: University of Chicago Press, 1976.

———. *A Treatise on the Family.* Cambridge MA: Harvard University Press, 1991.

Mueller, Dennis C. *Public Choice II.* Cambridge: Cambridge University Press, 1989.

Posner, Richard A. *Economic Analysis of Law.* Boston: Little, Brown, 1972. 3d ed. Boston: Little, Brown, 1986.

Sen, Amartya. *Choice, Welfare and Measurement.* Cambridge: MIT Press, 1982.

Trebilcock, Michael J. *The Prospects for Reinventing Government.* Toronto: C.D. Howe Institute, 1994.

Bruce Chapman

See also ECONOMICS AND LAW; EFFICIENCY; POSNER, RICHARD ALLEN; RATIONAL BARGAINING

Economics and Law

"Economics and law" is a label denoting a way of looking at the world through lenses developed by compounding two systems of interpretation: the economic one and the legal one.

The first, economics, seeks to define the conditions for maximum efficiency under certain institutional and legal constraints taken as given, such as a regime of exclusive and transferable property rights and freedom of contract with provisions for the governance and enforcement of contracts. The second law seeks to develop the principles, rules, and procedures needed to provide orientation maps and ensure the orderly resolution of conflict in a community. Law and economics are obviously grafted onto a background of existing institutions that are both enabling and constraining, but legal and economic thinking transform these institutions and each other.

For quite a long time, these interpretation systems developed independently, but recently there has been a confluence of the two. There is no agreement yet about how the two systems might best merge. Three separate schools of thought have resolved the problem of developing a "law and economics" perspective in quite different ways.

The first is generally identified with the Chicago school. This is because of the importance of the contribution of economists and lawyers from the University of Chicago to the development of this approach and of the role of the *Journal of Law and Economics* and of the *Journal of Legal Studies,* both located at the university, in disseminating the ideas of this school of thought. It sees law as a handmaiden to economics: rules, conventions, and the like are contraptions designed or emerging to reduce the costs of transacting. Property rights and other broader social institutions are shaped in the long run by market forces.

The second school does not have as clear a center of gravity. It has an anthropological flavor and presents law as an echo of the fundamental values and customs of society. The legal system with its permanence, consistency, unity, and overall complementarity is seen as conferring identity, doing the classifying, the remembering, and the forgetting. In this context, law as an aspect of culture shapes economic organization. Of course, economics imposes its own constraints on culture, but it is also and, even more important, constrained by it.

The third school takes a more middle-of-the-road approach. For its protagonists, the legal-economic nexus is not given but is the result of a process of social learning. The legal order and the economic organization co-evolve: the legal framework necessary for the economy to operate is shaped historically by both the geotechnical constraints and the values of particular societies as experienced and interpreted by economics; this legal framework in turn is both enabling and constraining in the development of economic organizations. This school emphasizes the interactive process, law and economics jointly working out efficient solutions, rights and duties, power structure, and so forth.

The methodologies used by the three schools are of necessity quite different. The first school is unashamedly positivistic. It claims that economic rationality is a given and prevails and that the legal system that guarantees optimal results will emerge. Deductive reasoning is the preferred tool, and predictions are drawn from a fairly mechanistic conception of the economy. An interesting illustration of its modus operandi is Harold Demsetz's explanation of the emergence of property rights in the world of North American Indians. He explains how the growing commercial trade in fur led to the emergence of property rights in land as fur-bearing animals became valuable and, consequently, hunting grounds came to be worth patrolling. Even though the legal order may not always adapt as fast and as perfectly as the analyst would like, members of this school staunchly claim that in the long run it will. Temporary imperfections are explained away as ascribable to shocks and particular temporary circumstances. If and when the legal order does not materialize or does not ensure efficiency and sustainability, ad hoc rationalizations are provided. For instance, since the property rights system in the world of the North American Indians failed to ensure the maintenance of the stock of fur-bearing animals and led to depletion, John McManus has argued that overhunting was ascribable to a higher-order commitment to helping neighboring tribes in difficulty by allowing them to hunt for food and sustenance. This "good samaritan" element is then used to explain why the legal order failed to ensure an efficient use of the resource.

This "good samaritan" factor is, in a way, a concession to the second school of thought. While this school is almost equally strong in its deductive reasoning, it is less sanguine about making clear predictions. This is largely due to the fact that taking into account the broad array of values and mores and the vagaries of historical factors does not lead to generalizations about the nature of the economy. In line with the earlier reference to the fur trade in North America in the eighteenth and nineteenth centuries, the analysis of Abraham Rotstein shows how the nature of the fur trade was shaped by complex political and social arrangements that reflected the profound values of the North American Indians. The fur trade for Rotstein was completely determined by conventions that acted in lieu of a legal system. Law and conventions dominated and shaped the fur trade. Some studies pertaining to more modern times and societies have used the same line of argument. Edward Banfield and Robert Putnam have shown that certain types of normative orders may lead to more effective organization for economic growth and progess.

The third school uses a very different methodological strategy. Legal and economic elements are simultaneously cause and effect. The evolving legal and economic perspectives and the institutions and organizations embodying the tensions between the two perspectives are processes that do not readily lend themselves to prediction. Evolutionary processes are always emerging, and, while one may identify a drift in the institutional fabric, one cannot use the drift to predict an outcome. What this third school purports to provide is not explanations but an understanding of practices. In order to provide an explanation in a positivistic sense, one needs to be faced with repetitive and identical situations. In the face of unique emergent phenomena, the best that can be achieved is to make sense of the processes of evolutionary emergence. Warren Samuels is probably the most important name associated with this approach.

A fair amount of work has been done in each of these three traditions, but it can be said that the first school is clearly dominant at this time. Despite its reduction of law to the role of handmaiden, the Chicago school has succeeded in establishing a strong presence in most law schools. Moreover, some of the most important American scholars in this tradition have already been appointed to the bench. Their approach has also generated an immense literature purporting to explain most of the legal and institutional structures of governance from the emergence of the multinational firm

E

(McManus) to the economic institutions of capitalism (Oliver Williamson) to the rise of the Western world (Douglass North and Robert Thomas).

Intellectually, the second school has launched an extremely powerful attack on the "engineering" or "logisitic" foundations of the first school. It has challenged effectively the reductionist view the first school has promoted. Amartya Sen has been one of the most effective challengers. However, it is fair to say that the second school has not yet provided an alternative paradigm capable of guiding economic analysis.

Different philosophies of law are echoed in the juridprudence of various nations and have taken on different degrees of importance over time: (1) from the centrality of hierarchy and subordination of the *ancien régime* (*imperium*) that still defines the relationship between the citizen and the state, (2) to the centrality of egalitarian individual rights and the laissez-faire (*dominium*) that underpins the liberal exchange economy of the nineteenth century but also shapes contractual exchanges between and among citizens (3) to the centrality of the social legal framework that has emerged in the second half of the twentieth century and has been at the root of different forms of integration of communities via equity rules, redistributive provisions, and so on, in the recent past.

Those different philosophies are complementary: to the *dominium* and *imperium* of Roman law, twentieth-century society has added a whole new dimension since 1948 with the inclusion of social and economic rights in the Universal Declaration of Human Rights. It is clear that a pluralist fusion of the philosophies underpinning them is de facto shaping the fabric of our socioeconomies, through the courts, jurisprudence, the regulatory regime, and the ethos of our societies.

Such a pluralist philosophy of law is still emerging, but it has not yet reached a sufficient level of explicit coalescence to be effective in guiding economic thinking or public policy. What we have at this stage is nothing but an array of philosophical stances (utilitarianism, contractarianism, communitarianism, and so forth), each purporting to underpin a different economic perspective.

The third school, by choosing to emphasize the coevolutionary nature of the covenant between law and economics as embedded in institutions, the courts, and the rule-making processes, is both more all-encompassing but also less willing and able to provide predictions. Consequently, it has been able at best to introduce a new awareness about the emergent nature of the law-economics interface, of its congenital state of imperfection and disequilibrium, and of the possibility that at times either economics or law might be hegemonic. This has provided a deeper understanding of the dynamics of law and economics, but it is unlikely to provide the foundation for wide dissemination of the school's message.

Consequently, economics and law are almost condemned, for now at least, to be dominated by the first school, with the other two schools playing an important role as critics and ensuring that the excesses of economic imperialism are held in check.

References

Banfield, Edward C. *The Moral Basis of a Backward Society*. New York: Free Press, 1958.

Demsetz, Harold. "Toward a Theory of Property Rights." *American Economic Review* 57 (1967), 347–359.

McManus, John C. "An Economic Analysis of Indian Behaviour in the North American Fur Trade." *Journal of Economic History* 32 (1972), 36–53.

North, Douglass C., and Robert Paul Thomas. *The Rise of the Western World*. Cambridge: Cambridge University Press, 1973.

Oliver, J.M. *Law and Economics: An Introduction*. London: Allen & Unwin, 1979.

Putnam, Robert D. *Making Democracy Work*. Princeton: Princeton University Press, 1993.

Rotstein, Abraham. "The Fur Trade." *Western Canadian Journal of Anthropology* 3.1 (1972).

Samuels, Warren J., A. Allan Schmid, and James D. Shaffer. "An Evolutionary Approach to Law and Economics." In *Evolutionary Concepts in Contemporary Economics*, ed. Richard W. England, 93–110. Ann Arbor: University of Michigan Press, 1994.

Sen, Amartya. *On Ethics and Economics*. Oxford: Blackwell, 1987.

Williamson, Oliver E. *The Economic Institutions of Capitalism*. New York: Free Press, 1985.

Gilles Paquet
Joseph Pestieau

See also ECONOMICS; EFFICIENCY; POS-NER, RICHARD ALLEN; RATIONAL BARGAINING

Efficiency

At least five (and probably six) interpretations of "efficiency" need to be distinguished. The first describes the ordinary use of the term in a wide range of decision-making contexts. The other four (or five) incorporate technical definitions of various kinds.

1. As *ordinarily* employed, the term "efficiency" applies, paradigmatically, to the strategies devised by decision makers in pursuit of their ends (goals, objectives, and so forth). In this sense of the term, a strategy is "efficient" if it is an effective and economical means of achieving an end, whatever the end happens to be. Thus, the "efficiency" of a government's anti-inflation strategy depends crucially on how effective it is in reducing inflation and on how economical it is of the resources, material and human, at the disposal of the government.

2. The most common of the technical interpretations of the term "efficiency," and the one which is used most extensively in modern economic theory, is *Pareto optimality*. Efficiency in this sense applies, standardly, to states of affairs, not to the strategies which might, in given contexts, help to bring them about. A state of affairs SA^1, for example, the state of affairs constituted by a determinate distribution of a society's economic resources, is Pareto optimal if there in no alternative state of affairs (here, no alternative distribution of resources) that would improve the lot of at least one person without worsening the lot of others. Thus, in one of its most common applications, the allocation of resources effected by a free market is said to be Pareto optimal, and thus "efficient," when no further reallocation can be effected (for instance, through trade) that will make at least one person better off without making everyone worse off.

3. There is a second Paretian principle, the *Pareto superiority* principle, which permits strategies as well as states of affairs to be characterized as "efficient." In both applications, it calls for a comparison to be effected between two determinate states of affairs: an existing state of affairs and a contemplated state of affairs created by the transformation of the existing state by some strategy. Thus, a contemplated state of affairs SA^2 will be Pareto superior to an existing state of affairs SA^1 if at least one person will be better off and no one worse off in SA^2 than in SA^1. Since in these circumstances the *move* from SA^1 to SA^2 can be described as a Pareto superior move, there is an unproblematic sense in which the *strategy* that facilitates the transformation of SA^1 into SA^2 can also be represented as satisfying the Pareto superiority principle and therefore as "efficient."

4. Although the Pareto superiority principle permits judgments to be made about the efficiency of strategies, one of the conditions it imposes, namely, that no one's lot is to be worsened, is so demanding that some would-be Paretians have attempted to relax its stringency. Their reformulation of the Pareto principle is sometimes referred to the *Kaldor-Hicks compensation* principle. A state of affairs SA^2 is said to be Kaldor-Hicks efficient (in relation to a second state of affairs SA^1) if, despite the fact that it violates the Pareto superiority principle, for example, because at least one person is worse off in SA^2 than in SA^1, those who stand to benefit from the move from SA^1 to SA^2 *could* fully compensate anyone who is worse off in SA^2 for their loss and still be better off. The idea is not, of course, to require that compensation actually be paid—if it were, and if we disregard the costs associated with the provision of compensation, the Pareto superiority principle would be satisfied and the new principle would not be needed—but to make it possible for states of affairs (and strategies) to be characterized as efficient in the Kaldor-Hicks sense even when there are losers as well as gainers.

5. Efficiency is sometimes defined in terms of *"utility maximization."* An "efficient" strategy, in this view, is one which maximizes "utility"—either the utility of the individual decision maker or (in the case of social decision making) the utility of society as a whole. Efficient strategies always aim at a single end, the bringing about of states of affairs in which utility is maximized. Since "utility" can be defined in a variety of ways—in terms of pleasure, or happiness, or preference-satisfaction, or welfare, and so forth—there are as many versions of this account of efficiency as there are definitions of "utility." There is no essential connection, however, between any of these versions and "utilitarianism": utility maximization can be endorsed as the fundamental principle of morals and politics with-

out acceptance of any version of the utility maximization account of efficiency, and vice versa.

6. In the work of Richard Posner, one of the most important contributors to literature on the "economic analysis of law," it is *"wealth maximization"* and not economic efficiency in any of the senses indicated that law is said to promote. Wealth maximization is achieved, according to Posner, when resources of all kinds (including legal entitlements) are in the hands of those who value them most, which means that they are in the hands of those who are able and willing to pay the largest amount of money to have them. Considerable controversy surrounds the nature of the relationship between wealth maximization and both (a) utility maximization and (b) the various "efficiency" principles favored by Paretians. However, if Posner is correct in thinking that it differs from all of these and also correct in insisting that wealth-maximizing decisions serve the cause of "efficiency," then a sixth interpretation of the notion of efficiency must be added to the five already enumerated. When efficiency is seen as something we value, whether always or only under certain conditions, whether for its own sake or for the contribution it makes to the bringing about of states of affairs we value for their own sakes, then it is natural to ask whether efficiency can come into conflict with other values and how, if it can, such conflicts are to be resolved. It is widely assumed, for example, that the demands of efficiency and equity conflict and that when they do the problem presented by the conflict is a "trade-off" problem, the problem, that is, of determining *how far* each is to be accommodated, on the assumption that both must be accommodated to some degree.

It is not difficult to see how efficiency and equity might be thought to conflict in this way when any one of the various technical definitions of efficiency is adopted. In the case of the utility maximization and wealth maximization accounts, there is apt to be a systematic conflict between states of affairs in which utility (or wealth) is maximized and states of affairs in which there in an equitable distribution of the things people value. In the case of the Paretian accounts, there is apt to be a systematic conflict between states of affairs that qualify as Pareto efficient (in one or other of the three ways claimed by Paretians) and states of affairs in which the things people value are equitably distributed. In all such cases, it looks as though decision makers have to determine what the appropriate trade-offs between efficiency and equity considerations are to be if at least some weight is to be assigned to both.

However, when it comes to putative conflicts beween equity and efficiency as ordinarily understood, it is either incoherent or misleading to suppose that they have the shape of a trade-off problem. It is incoherent in all those cases in which there is an equity ingredient in the rationale for the ends served by efficient strategies, as there is, for example, when policymakers try to make the tax system an efficient instrument for the achievement of an equitable distribution of the tax burden. It is misleading in all those cases in which efficient strategies serve ends (and thus values) other than equity, because in such cases the real conflict is between equity and these *values* and not between equity and efficiency. For example, a strategy for reducing income differentials in society may be simultaneously an efficient means of achieving greater equity and an inefficient means of promoting rapid economic growth, in which case, policymakers may have to decide what the best trade-off would be between equity and *economic growth*. This, however, is not the same thing as a trade-off between equity and *efficiency*.

References

Buchanan, Allen. *Ethics, Efficiency and the Market.* Totowa NJ: Rowman and Allanheld, 1985.

Coase, Ronald E. "The Problem of Social Cost." *Journal of Law and Economics* 3 (1960).

Coleman, Jules. *Markets, Morals and the Law.* Cambridge: Cambridge University Press, 1988.

Dworkin, Ronald. "Why Efficiency?" *Hofstra Law Review* 8 (1980), 563–590.

Le Grand, Julian. "Equity versus Efficiency: The Elusive Tradeoff." *Ethics* 100 (1990), 554–568.

Macleod, A.M. "Efficiency as a Criterion of Public Policy." In *Contemporary Conceptions of Social Philosophy,* ed. S. Panou et al. Stuttgart: Franz Steiner, 1988.

Murphy, Jeffrie, and Jules Coleman. *The Philosophy of Law: An Introduction to Jurisprudence.* Totowa NJ: Rowman and Allanheld, 1984.

Okun, Arthur. *Equality and Efficiency: The Big Tradeoff.* Washington DC: Brookings Institution, 1975.

Posner, Richard. *The Economic Analysis of Law.* Boston: Little, Brown, 1973.

———. "Utilitarianism, Economics and Legal Theory." *Journal of Legal Studies* 8 (1979), 103.

Alistair M. Macleod

See also ECONOMICS; ECONOMICS AND LAW; POSNER, RICHARD ALLEN

Eminent Domain and Takings

Eminent domain is the power of the state to take property for public purposes, often coupled with the obligation to pay compensation. Generally viewed as a necessary feature of sovereignty, the power might appear to be the modern remnant of the medieval doctrine that all property is held subject to the power of a lord or monarch.

In the view of some historians, however, the origins of the modern-day doctrine are instead to be found in the development of a theory of representative government. The prerogative of the English kings to command provisions or to build fortifications, unlike the power of eminent domain, did not imply rights of compensation and did not extend to the acquisition of estates in land. The power of the British Parliament to take private land to build roads or sewers, on the other hand, was thought to be exercised only with the consent of the governed and with the requirement of compensation, thus precluding its arbitrary exercise. Likewise, the *Declaration of the Rights of Man and the Citizen,* promulgated by the French National Assembly in 1789, prescribed that property is a natural right and may be taken only by reason of public necessity, with just and predetermined compensation. Thus the modern doctrine of eminent domain principally represents a set of constraints on the government's ability to take property for the common good.

History

Hugo Grotius has been credited with inventing the term "eminent domain" with the publication of his *De Jure Belli ac Pacis Libri Tres* in 1646. Grotius appears to have developed the doctrine as part of a theory of limited property rights. In Grotius's view, God gave the world to mankind in common; the appropriation of rights to particular parcels is based on agreement to improve cultivation. The agreement intends, however, to depart as little as possible from "natural equity," and the rights thereby appropriated "are distributed to individual owners with a benign reservation in favor of the primitive right." Appropriated lands thus remain subject to rights of necessity and rights of innocent use (for example, passing through property without damaging it). Grotius coupled the eminent domain power of the king with this right of private necessity. Lawfully gained rights of citizens could be taken away by the king for "public advantage," particularly making and keeping peace, provided that "compensation from the public funds be made, if possible, to the one who has lost his right."

Grotius was much criticized for interpreting consent to be foundational to the right to property. In the *Second Treatise of Government,* published in 1690, John Locke attempted to justify property without reference to consent, but perhaps as a result did not have as clear a basis as Grotius for understanding limits to property rights. Locke argues that the right of first appropriation from the commons is subject to the provisions that property not be allowed to spoil and that there be enough and as good for all. The significance of these latter provisos has been hotly debated, from accounts such as Jeremy Waldron's that they imply a right to welfare, to libertarian views that they merely limit the initial acquisition of scarce resources. Some commentators attribute an absolutist theory of acquired property to Locke, giving the owner immunity from forced transfers, a theory which is inconsistent with the power of eminent domain. They find support for this view in Locke's account of usurpation and tyranny: "The Legislative acts against the Trust reposed in them, when they endeavour to invade the Property of the Subject. . . ." Others, relying on the provisos, see Locke as working with a limited right to property from the outset.

Writers in the utilitarian tradition likewise recognized the power of eminent domain, to the extent it maximizes the overall good. Jeremy Bentham's concern that property was an important basis for the security of expectations, for example, would have been traded off by utilitarians against the need to prevent holdouts from blocking a socially valuable project. The hegelian tradition of property as the self-actualization of the will, by contrast, provides a basis for viewing the exercise of the power as a metaphysical wrong. Because G.W.F. Hegel allows for contract, however, there is room even in the hegelian tradition for recognition of the power.

Contemporary Debates

There are echoes of these historical positions in present-day debates about eminent domain. For example, utilitarian discussions of when appropriation is beneficial are replicated in controversy over what public purposes support the takings power. The hegelian view is respected in the sense that it is more difficult to justify the state's taking uniquely personal property, such as a family homestead, than fungible land with principally economic value. Three areas of current debate warrant particular attention: what public purposes support use of the power of eminent domain, what kind of compensation is required, and when actions by the state that fall short of full assumption of ownership nonetheless amount to exercise of the power.

A standard limit on the power of eminent domain is that it be directed to public purposes. Initial defenders of eminent domain, such as Grotius, understood this as limited very stringently to cases of public necessity. From the nineteenth century on, public purposes have been construed more broadly, to include public works or other public benefits. Thus the state may take property to build public roads, to provide for the common defense, or to construct a reservoir. Under limited circumstances, the power of eminent domain may also be exercised on behalf of a private entity offering services to the public, such as a regulated utility. An area of particular controversy here is the extent to which the power may be used for redistributive ends, such as urban renewal projects. These projects have been controversial both for their redistributive aims and for the ways in which they have benefited private contractors.

The requirement that just compensation be paid is imposed to ensure that eminent domain does not impose unfair burdens on particular individuals. Unlike taxation, which spreads the costs of public works, state appropriation of property would place all the costs on affected owners, were compensation not required. The typical measure of compensation

in the United States is the property's fair market value at its highest and best use. This has the advantage of being objectively measurable in most cases, and of being a reasonable surrogate for what the owner would have received in a voluntary transaction. The fair market value measure is criticized, however, for generating windfall profits when the market has responded to advance speculation about a pending project and for undercompensation when an area has suffered diminishing maintenance and property values as a result of "precondemnation blight." It is also criticized for undercompensating the consequential losses to relocated businesses, such as the loss of "going concern" value caused by customers having to readjust. Finally, the market value approach is condemned for ignoring the unique value of particular holdings to individuals (the family homestead) or to entities (such as churches) that may use land for locations, improvements, or activities that do not find a ready market.

Perhaps the most controversial area of all is what counts as a taking in the first place. In the United States, the question of whether regulation is a taking has drawn the most fire, but this issue is really only a part of the more general problem of when government actions that affect property or property values warrant compensation. Beyond the core cases of outright assumption of title, government actions that have been alleged to be takings range widely indeed. In the United States, it is a taking if the government assumes any of the owner's rights to the land, such as by taking an easement; if the government invades property, even in a very minimal way, such as by laying television cable; or if the government imposes such an invasion on the owner's rightful use of land. Many forms of land use planning also have been argued to be takings, including zoning, historic preservation, and wetlands protection. These arguments have been met with some success in American courts, particularly when the regulation at issue eliminates all forms of economically valuable land use. Politicians on the right have been urging compensation whenever regulation reduces property values, a stance that critics contend would all but eliminate environmental protection statutes.

The difficulty for commentators has been whether a theoretically coherent doctrine of regulatory takings can be developed. One approach to this analytic task is conceptual, asking what is meant by a property right and when such a right has been abridged. This strategy is favored by proponents of the rule of law, who view bright line tests as important to the stability of expectations. It also is favored by American original intent theorists of constitutional interpretation, who believe that the conception of property in the Fifth Amendment has been clear from the outset. Although proponents of both of these (frequently overlapping) strategies tend to be conservatives who defend a sweeping understanding of regulatory takings, the historical evidence in the United States indicates that the Fifth Amendment takings clause originally applied only to outright assumption of title. The American idea of a regulatory taking appears instead to have originated in the early part of this century.

Another strategy for determining whether a regulation should be regarded as a taking is ad hoc balancing. A taking is identified, in the words of Justice Oliver Wendell Holmes, Jr., "when regulation goes too far," generally when regulation deprives the owner of all reasonable beneficial use of the property. This view, although dominant in American law since the 1920s and associated with pragmatism, has drawn criticism as unprincipled, as lacking articulated moral criteria for determining when a taking has occurred.

Utilitarian theorists argue for identifying takings based on the overall effect of policies on the general good. If uncompensated regulatory policies would generate such instability in expectations that socially important investment would be compromised, for example, compensation might be required. Utilitarian theorists who believe that efficiency is the good to be maximized, such as Richard Epstein, argue that determination of whether a taking has occurred should rest on analyzing the incentives created when the government can impose the burdens of its action on individuals without paying the costs. Other theorists of regulatory takings, according to Frank Michelman, have used John Rawls' account of justice as fairness to defend compensation when unfair burdens are imposed on individuals for the public good. The effort to draw principled lines with respect to when a taking has occurred remains an ongoing public policy issue in contemporary democracies.

References

Epstein, Richard. *Takings: Private Property and the Power of Eminent Domain.* Cambridge: Harvard University Press, 1985.

Fischel, William. *Regulatory Takings.* Cambridge: Harvard University Press, 1995.

Michelman, Frank. "Property, Utility, and Fairness: Comments on the Ethical Foundations of 'Just Compensation' Law." *Harvard Law Review* 80 (1967), 1165–1268.

Munzer, Steve. *A Theory of Property.* Cambridge: Cambridge University Press, 1990.

Nozick, Robert. *Anarchy, State, and Utopia.* New York: Basic Books, 1974.

Paul, Ellen Frankel, Fred D. Miller, Jr., and Jeffrey Paul, eds. *Property Rights.* Cambridge: Cambridge University Press, 1994.

Radin, Margaret Jane. *Reinterpreting Property.* Chicago: University of Chicago Press, 1993.

Stoebuck, William. "A General Theory of Eminent Domain." *Washington Law Review* 47 (1972), 553.

Waldron, Jeremy. *The Right to Private Property.* Oxford: Clarendon Press, 1988.

Yandle, Bruce, ed. *Land Rights: The 1990s' Property Rights Rebellion.* Lanham MD: Rowman and Littlefield, 1995.

John G. Francis
Leslie P. Francis

See also ESTATE AND PATRIMONY; OWNERSHIP; PROPERTY; STATE ACTION

Empirical Evidence

The use of scientific evidence in the law raises philosophic questions about the similarities and differences between the substantive burdens of proof in science and in the different areas of the law, about conceptions of philosophy of science, about the relationship between different areas of the law, for example, between the tort law and regulatory law and their roles in the legal system, and about who should have a proportionately greater role in assessing scientific evidence in a court of law in a democracy—judges or juries, or scientists themselves. At a minimum, general treatment of this topic would address the use of scientific evidence in the criminal, tort, and regulatory law. This discussion considers the use of scientific evidence in the common law of civil procedure and focuses mainly on toxic tort law, because it is in flux and because results here will have impact on other areas of the law.

Background philosophic issues that cannot be addressed concern philosophic conceptions of science and scientific evidence. There are considerable divergences between most academic and practicing lawyers' conceptions of science, scientists' conceptions of science, and philosophers' recent work in the philosophy of science, all of which open a number of research questions.

In common law in the United States prior to 1993, the dominant principle for admitting scientific evidence was articulated in a 1923 criminal case, *Frye v. United States*, 293 F. 1013–14 (1923). That court held that for novel scientific evidence or methodology to be admitted for consideration at trial it had to have "general acceptance" in the relevant scientific community, and courts have generally understood this to give scientists the major role in indicating what was "generally accepted" and, thus, what was admissible in law. In 1993, the U.S. Supreme Court in *Daubert v. Merrell-Dow Pharmaceuticals, Inc.*, 509 U.S. 579–601 (1993), rejected the *Frye* test, holding that in order to qualify as "scientific knowledge" an inference or assertion must be derived by the scientific method in order to establish evidentiary reliability and that the knowledge must be "relevant" to the facts of the case. A trial judge must serve a gatekeeping role to ensure that all scientific testimony or evidence is relevant and reliable. Finally, judges should screen the evidence for the reliability of the *procedure,* not the adversaries' substantive *conclusions.*

In considering scientific evidence, courts distinguish at least three levels of scientific results: (1) the theory or principle that supports factual conclusions drawn from evidence, (2) the general technique or procedure that produces the evidence in question, and (3) the particular practices that are utilized to obtain data. Sometimes a general theory is in dispute, for instance, whether lie detector tests are reliable; sometimes, even if it is sound, there is no agreed upon method for utilizing a general theory, for example, whether procedures for revealing unique DNA "fingerprints" are accurate; and sometimes a particular application of a theory may be in dispute, for example, whether a particular DNA match is correct.

Philosophic and legal issues arise at several different levels concerning the use of scientific evidence in the law. The *first level* concerns philosophical issues about the use of scientific evidence in a *particular area of the law,* for instance, the tort or criminal law.

Within this generic topic, the first issue is the quality and amount of evidence a moving party must provide in order to have evidence *admitted* to trial, evidence on which an expert can base his or her testimony. For admissibility, the focus is only on the moving party's evidence rather than on a comparison with the quality and quantity of an adversary's evidence. Typically, to satisfy this requirement a plaintiff must offer a "scintilla" of evidence. Second, the moving party must present *sufficient* evidence, compared with the evidence presented by an adversary, for a judge to permit a decision on the evidence to be decided by the finder of fact. Even if particular scientific testimony is deemed admissible, a court may still render a summary judgment or a directed verdict if the conclusions reached by the expert fail to establish a material issue of fact (when compared with the adversary's evidence) for the jury. Third, in a tort case once evidence is admitted and sufficient to permit the evidence to be decided by a fact finder, the plaintiff must *support each element* of a tort, including the cause-in-fact issue, by a "preponderance of the evidence." In a criminal trial, the state must support each of the elements of an offense, including any causation issues that are required, "beyond a reasonable doubt." Thus, the initial moving party in a trial (the plaintiff in a tort case, the state in a criminal case) must overcome admissibility, sufficiency, and burdens-of-persuasion hurdles on factual issues in order to prevail.

In a trial there are two kinds of mistaken outcomes—a defendant may mistakenly be held accountable (in the technical language of science this would be a legal "false positive" mistake) or a defendant may be erroneously exonerated (a legal "false negative"). The tort law's ultimate burden of persuasion and its procedural requirements suggest, roughly speaking, that it is equally concerned with avoiding both kinds of mistakes. By contrast, the criminal law's ultimate burden of persuasion and procedural requirements (suggested by the aphorism "It is better that ten guilty people go free than one innocent person be punished") suggests that it places a much greater emphasis on avoiding legal false positives than on avoiding legal false negatives.

Scientific standards of evidence tend to be designed (or have evolved) asymmetrically to prevent false positive mistakes (with a lesser concern about false negatives) in order to discourage overly enthusiastic scientists from too easily proclaiming their "discoveries," to prevent mistaken additions to the stock of scientific knowledge, and to prevent scientists from chasing research chimera.

The interaction between scientific and legal standards of evidence poses legal and philosophic problems for admissibility and for ultimate burden-of-proof questions. On one side of the admissibility debate are those who seek to ensure that legal decisions rest on evidence that would support a *firm* scientific judgment of causation and those who seek to make the law more responsive to science. In this view scientific judgments about causation are definitive and scientific evidence offered in torts should not be admitted into trial unless the evidence measures up to such standards. On the other side are authors with a somewhat more nuanced view, one sensitive to some of the incompatibilities between the legal and scientific burdens of proof. While this group accepts the importance of scientific support for causal claims, and while scientific evidence offers the hope of providing a neutral adjudication of factual issues, this group recognizes that scientific evidence can inadvertently predispose the factual inquiry because of the inclination to prevent factual false positives at the expense of factual false negatives. Unconscious adoption in the tort law of the scientific concern with false positives will result in a mistaken conception of "accurate" or "correct" decisions for torts law purposes.

The resolution of these issues by the law has important consequences for plaintiffs and defendants alike. A requirement that plaintiffs must have *firm* scientific evidence in support of their causal claims before such evidence is admitted will add to their initial burden of proof and prevent some meritorious cases being heard and going to a jury. Scientific uncertainties or weakness of evidence benefit defendants and strengthen their procedural advantages. A more nuanced assessment of scientific evidence may help preserve the present balance of interests between plaintiffs and defendants and produce a more nearly balanced number of false positives and false negatives, as is appropriate in torts.

The relationship between scientific and legal standards of evidence appears to be less problematic in the criminal law, because the *legal* concerns to avoid legal and factual false positives (exemplified by the state's typical burdens of proof in the American legal system) are in general reinforced by the scientific concerns to avoid scientific false positives.

A *second level* of concerns and somewhat more generic issues arise when one considers this question: Should the standards for the admission of scientific evidence in the aftermath of *Daubert* be different for the criminal law and for the tort law because of their different burdens of proof and procedures? If the standards for admitting scientific evidence are the same for the criminal and the tort law, this can lead to two different positions, neither of which may be fully satisfactory. On one hand, if firm scientific standards are required to admit scientific evidence of causation, then, as indicated previously, this will tend to disadvantage the moving parties (tort law plaintiffs and the state in the criminal law), but advantage defendants in both venues, for example, businesses and governmental agencies in product liability suits and criminal defendants. On the other hand, if more nuanced, and somewhat more liberal, admissibility standards are adopted for both areas of the law, this will tend to favor plaintiffs and further the aims of the tort law, but will disadvantage criminal defendants because the state will find it easier to introduce scientific evidence of the efficacy of new technologies or scientific findings, for example, of DNA techniques or lie detector tests.

A somewhat different approach would be to adopt admissibility rules more tailored for the particular areas of the law in which they were to be used. Thus, one might adopt somewhat less demanding admissibility standards for the civil law (given its procedures, overall burdens of proof, and aims) than one adopted for the criminal law (given its procedures, overall burdens of proof, and aims). This alternative would have different rules of evidence depending upon the area of the law, which lawyers and judges might not find as congenial as one set of rules of evidence common to both venues.

A *third level* of issues concerns interactions between different areas of the law and how treatment of scientific evidence might affect the interaction. This is particularly true of the administrative law—tort law interaction. Potentially toxic substances may come into commerce as products or into the environment as by-products of production, as contaminants or as pollutants, but they may or may not have been well tested scientifically for their toxicity. How stringent should the burdens of proof on scientific issues be for an administrative agency to remove such substances from commerce or to reduce exposure, and how stringent should the burdens of proof for scientific evidence be for recovery in the tort law? These are questions about the interactions between two different areas of the law, about the extent of administrative or tort law protections from potentially toxic substances, and about how different areas of the legal system should or should not work together to protect the population from harms it might suffer.

Finally, the *Daubert* decision appears to have modified the roles of scientists, judges, and juries in tort cases. Judges now have an explicit gatekeeping role for admitting evidence with perhaps less deference to scientists than might have been shown in the past, and judges exercising this power may preclude juries from hearing evidence that they once would have heard under older rules. Philosophically, what should be the proper roles of judges, juries, and scientists in a democratic society in contributing to the outcome of criminal and tort law cases in which scientific evidence is important?

References
Black, Bert. "A Unified Theory of Scientific Evidence." *Fordham Law Review* 56 (1988), 595–695.

Cranor, Carl. *Regulating Toxic Substances: A Philosophy of Science and the Law.* New York: Oxford University Press, 1993.

Faigman, David L., Elise Porter, and Michael J. Saks. "Check Your Crystal Ball at the Courthouse Door, Please: Exploring the Past, Understanding the Present, and Worrying about the Future of Scientific Evidence." *Cardozo Law Review* 15 (1994), 1799–1835.

Federal Judicial Center 1994. *Reference Manual on Scientific Evidence: Limitations and Potential.* Washington DC: Federal Judicial Center, 1994.

Giannelli, Paul C., and Edward J. Imwinkelried. *Scientific Evidence.* 2d ed. Charlottesville VA: Michie, 1993.

Green, Michael D. "Expert Witnesses and Sufficiency of Evidence in Toxic Substances Litigation: The Legacy of Agent Orange and Bendectin Litigation." *Northwestern University Law Review* 86 (1992), 643–699.

Sanders, Joseph. "Scientific Validity, Admissibility, and Mass Torts After Daubert." *Minnesota Law Review* 78 (1994), 1387–1441.

Strong, John William, ed. *McCormick on Evidence.* 4th ed. St. Paul MN: West, 1992.

Weinstein, Jack B., and Margaret A. Berger. *Weinstein's Evidence Manual: A Guide to the United States Rules Based on Weinstein's Evidence.* New York: Matthew Bender, 1987.

Carl F. Cranor

See also ECOLOGY AND ENVIRONMENTAL SCIENCES; TESTIMONY AND EXPERT EVIDENCE

Engagement
See BETROTHAL

Entrapment
Although entrapment is a criminal law trial defense, it derives from an improper police detection practice and thus is appropriately discussed under police enforcement. The police detection practice, which becomes entrapment when carried too far, has no official or even agreed upon name. It is sometimes loosely referred to as a "sting" or "undercover" operation; it is associated with the phrase *agent provocateur.* A descriptive label sometimes applied to it is "encouragement," because the police employ the practice against "victimless" crimes in which they simply feign being a victim and encourage the suspect, who when the crime is committed is arrested. Because it is often not a single event but a process, encouragement is often time-consuming, resource intensive, and tightly focused; it is not a technique that can be used randomly; and, in fact, the police customarily use it only against persons who, in one degree or another, are confirmed targets. Crimes which fall under the rubric "victimless" include sales of hard drugs, after hours liquor, and pornography; bribery; and solicitations by prostitutes and homosexuals. The range of options available to the police in any specific encouragement situation is

limited by the fact that to be effective the practice must simulate reality. Within the confines of reality there are choices, but if a police officer is too aggressive, too eager, or, sometimes, too relaxed, such a false move might alert the suspect. After all, suspects know the police use the encouragement detection-practice.

Whatever one may think of the idea of the police manufacturing crime so as to detect it, the basic policy justification viewed from a law enforcement perspective is necessity. No jurisdiction has outlawed the encouragement practice. The problem arises when the practice goes awry. This is where entrapment enters the picture. Although the United States Supreme Court in *Sorrells v. United States,* 287 U.S. 435 (1932), first decided that entrapment was a viable defense in federal criminal prosecutions, at least in the specific case then before it, the defense had been around in a few state courts for fifty years. The Court's decision, however, served as an impetus for state adoptions, although it was not until 1980 that the last state, Tennessee, joined the club. Although the Court was almost unanimous in its recognition of an entrapment defense, the Court split five to three on what it meant, where it came from, and what judicial procedures were relevant to its resolution. The majority decided that Congress, when it made possession and sale of liquor illegal under the National Prohibition Act, did not intend for a violation to occur when law enforcement officials entrapped, that is, encouraged an "otherwise innocent" person (or to state the same thing differently, a person not "predisposed") to commit a crime. Thus, entrapment was a matter of statutory construction and it resulted in no crime being committed by the suspect. Because of this approach, it seems obvious that every time a federal court confronts a different crime it must decide the relevance of entrapment for that crime; in fact, this seems not to be the case. Instead, entrapment is assumed to apply to all federal crimes. Two possible limitations, however, remain viable: first, the Supreme Court may disallow the defense in some instances, for example, when the crime is too heinous; second, Congress may expressly legislate the unavailability of the defense whenever it wants.

The concurring justices in *Sorrells* thought the majority's reading of the statute to be "strained and unwarranted. " Justice Felix Frankfurter later called it "sheer fiction" in *United States v. Sherman,* 356 U.S. 369, 379 (1958). Instead, the trio preferred an analysis based on public policy. To allow a defendant who was entrapped to be convicted would taint the purity of the courts. In *Russell v. United States,* 411 U.S. 423, 439 (1973), the minority justices emphasized a second policy argument: deterrence of police.

A short comparison of two approaches reveals that the majority's view is a subjective inquiry into a defendant's predisposition, based on statutory construction, and a question for the jury. The concurring approach focuses on an objective appraisal of police conduct, on public policy as the source, and on the court as decision maker. Since *Sorrells* the Court has decided several entrapment cases, each time reaffirming the subjective test; also, in almost every case there have been justices writing in support of the objective standard. Because neither version of entrapment is constitutionally rooted, the states are free to do as they will. As previously indicated all the states now have some form of the defense. Most, but by no means all, favor the subjective. Most commentators favor the objective; the trend of the law seems in this direction. English courts have consistently rejected the defense, for example, *Russell v. Sang,* 2 All E.R. 1222 (1997). As seen in *Russel v. Mack,* 67 C.R.(3d) 1 (1988), the Supreme Court of Canada adopted an objective entrapment standard based on the common law doctrine of abuse of process. The test provides that there is entrapment if (1) the police did not have reasonable suspicion that the suspect was engaging in criminal activity or were not making a bona fide inquiry or (2), if (1) is satisfied, if the police induced the crime rather than merely provided an opportunity to the suspect. The Court listed several relevant factors to help lower courts distinguish inducement from opportunity. Arguably, the approach is tentative. The Court, like the courts in the United States, seems to be searching for a solution.

Both of the basic standards, leaving aside for the moment the Canadian variation, have their imperfections. The subjective standard is flawed because of its concern not with what the defendant has done—his crime is conceded—but on what he might or might not have done. This raises questions concerning evidence as well as the ability of the jury to decide "otherwise innocence." The objective standard is imperfect because it allows guilty defendants to go free because the "constable has blundered"—even if the defendant is a notorious repeat offender.

As English law exemplifies, entrapment is not an inevitable criminal defense; but assuming it remains viable, there are several suggestions that may, or may not, improve it. One is to combine the two tests. In one respect this is almost accomplished when "otherwise innocence" of the subjective test is used in the objective test restricting the police so they may not encourage beyond the point that a "reasonable otherwise innocent" person would commit the crime. There is no reason, of course, for the objective test to be defined this way. Even when the objective test mimics the subjective, the other clear differences between the tests remain. The tests could be retained as separate standards, while allowing the defendant a defense if either one is not met, or allowing the defense only if both are not. Somewhat along this line, the United States Supreme Court has suggested that an objective limitation on police encouragement might coexist with subjective entrapment based on the constitution when the police activity is so egregious as to violate due process. Such a standard would have nationwide application. The Court has not decided a case on this ground and some federal courts are beginning to think the idea is a mere phantom. For a long time some federal courts have imposed a "reasonable suspicion" requirement on the police, which had to be met before encouragement was permissible. The Supreme Court has never required this. As previously mentioned, the encouragement practice is such that reasonable suspicion is usually present; but there are times when the suspicion may be too light or a police officer may be carried away with his or her own belief that the target is ripe. The Supreme Court of Canada has adopted this principle. Time will reveal its utility.

Although entrapment may not be a defense as in England, it nevertheless remains relevant to sentencing. On appeal an entrapped defendant may have his sentence reduced. In the United States some federal courts have taken the view that even when a defendant was not entrapped into committing the crime, he may have been entrapped into committing a more severe crime than was expected. If so, his sentence should be modified.

In England a judicial debate flourishes over whether entrapment may be considered a circumstance to be considered by the trial judge as part of "all the circumstances" to be weighed in determining the admissibility of evidence as it relates to the fairness of the trial procedure.

Both theoretically and operationally, entrapment is unsatisfactory. One major response is to abolish it. After all, one might argue, however extreme the encouragement, it has no logical bearing on either the evidence to be admitted or the crimes committed. This approach does not appeal to everyone. Perhaps encouragement should be abolished, carrying all of the entrapment baggage with it. If encouragement, however, is needed to detect the pervasive "victimless crime," abolition is senseless.

References

Jacobson v. United States, 112 S. Ct. 1535 (1992).
Choo, Andrew. "A Defence of Entrapment." *Modern Law Review* 53 (1990), 453.
Park, Roger. "The Entrapment Controversy." *Minnesota Law Review* 60 (1976), 163.
Stober, Michael. "The Limits of Police Provocation in Canada." *Criminal Law Quarterly* 34 (1992), 290.

Daniel L. Rotenberg

Entrenchment

In the technical sense, entrenchment refers to some limitation upon the legislative power to repeal or amend a right-conferring clause in a constitution. More broadly, entrenchment refers to any defense against an attempt to annul, suspend, or derogate from a constitutional right. Philosophers disagree about the possibility of limiting legislative power, the role of judicial review in constitutional law, what is internal to law, and the desirability of entrenching rights.

Is it logically possible to limit legislative power? John Austin defines law as the command of the sovereign. The sovereign is that person or body of persons that imposes commands, and thus duties, upon all other members of a society but is not subject to the commands of anyone else. To assert that legislative power could be legally limited is to imply that a sovereign could be subject to legal duties imposed by another and thus is not sovereign. Albert Venn Dicey echoes Austin when he asserts that the logical reason Parliament has failed to enact unchangeable laws is that a sovereign cannot, while remaining sovereign, restrict its own powers. H.L.A. Hart rejects Austin's command theory of law and distinguishes between duty-imposing and power-conferring legal rules. Thus, even the supreme legislative power could be limited by power-conferring rules that restrict its competence without implying that the legislature is bound in the sense of being subject to duties.

The question remains whether the entrenchment of rights is constitutionally possible. It is usual to distinguish between rigid and flexible constitutions, those in which the constitution cannot be changed by the usual legislative procedures and those in which no such limitation on legislative power exists. Hart points out that a written constitution may restrict the competence of the legislature, either by specifying the manner and form of legislation or by excluding certain matters from the scope of its legislative power. Thus, constitutional rights can be entrenched procedurally or substantively. For example, the United States Constitution entrenches its Bill of Rights by specifying a restrictive method of amendment, while the Basic Law of the Federal Republic of Germany prohibits any amendment to Article 1 in which human rights are acknowledged. On the other hand, Dicey and H.W.R. Wade have argued that the Parliament of the United Kingdom has unlimited legislative power. This suggests to many that entrenchment is possible only in a written constitution. This is not true.

Although both Canada and New Zealand have written constitutions, the Canadian Charter of Rights and Freedoms is entrenched by the Canadian Constitution Act of 1982 while the New Zealand Parliament is given unlimited power of constitutional change by the New Zealand Constitution Amendment Act of 1947, both acts of the United Kingdom Parliament pursuant to a largely unwritten constitution. Moreover, the distinction between written and unwritten constitutions is a matter of degree. Even Dicey recognized that the English constitution is partly written and partly unwritten, and the American legal realists argued that written law confers real rights only if applied in judicial practice. Therefore, whether constitutional rights are entrenched in some legal system depends upon the content of its constitution.

Assuming that Parliament does possess unlimited legislative power, an assumption that membership in the European Community may have undermined, could a bill of rights be entrenched in the constitution of the United Kingdom or in any similar legal system? Presumably Parliament could enact a bill of rights that included a provision specifying that this act could be repealed or amended only by a two-thirds vote. The crucial question is whether Parliament could thereby abdicate its power to repeal this act by the usual legislative procedures. Ivor Jennings argues that to deny this would be to declare the enactment of this bill of rights invalid, something no court granting the unlimited legislative power of Parliament could do. Wade replies that to declare invalid any attempt to repeal the bill of rights by the usual procedures is ruled out by the constitutional convention requiring judicial obedience to Parliament. Hart admits that, given the accepted rule of recognition, Parliament could not irrevocably withdraw the bill of rights from future legislation, but it could alter the manner and form of any subsequent repeal or amendment; to do so would not be to limit the legislative power of Parliament but to redefine Parliament by modifying its legislative procedures. Significantly, all the parties to this dispute agree that the issue hinges on whether the courts would or should declare invalid any repeal of the bill of rights enacted by a simple majority.

Thus, the entrenchment of rights presupposes judicial review of legislation; this in turn presupposes the division of legal powers, something impossible according to John Austin's theory of sovereignty. If each branch of government has only limited power, then each must obey another so that there is no sovereign. John Salmond replies that Austin confuses the limitation of power with its subordination. In theory Parliament has supreme legislative authority and the Crown has supreme executive authority, so that each is sovereign within its own sphere.

Not only is the division of powers presupposed by the entrenchment of constitutional rights, it indicates the attacks against which they need to be defended. Thus, the United Kingdom Bill of Rights of 1688 entrenched specified rights against the executive power by requiring the consent of Parliament to any action of the Crown that would suspend or infringe them. The First Amendment of the United States Constitution entrenches rights against the legislature by denying Congress the power to prohibit the free exercise of religion or to abridge the freedom of speech. In fact, these rights are doubly entrenched in United States constitutional law because the free exercise clause and the freedom of speech clause are themselves protected from legislative repeal or amendment by Article V, which requires a restrictive procedure to amend the Constitution. Moreover, these rights are strongly entrenched because the First Amendment provides that "Congress shall make no law" infringing them. Similar rights are only weakly entrenched in the Canadian Charter because "Parliament . . . may expressly declare in an Act of Parliament . . . that the Act or a provision thereof shall operate notwithstanding a provision in sections 2 or 7 to 15 of this Charter." Because the reality of such defenses against executive or legislative attacks on constitutional rights depends upon judicial review, one may wonder whether constitutional rights can be entrenched against the judiciary. The supremacy clause of the United States Constitution entrenches federal rights against the state courts, and the principle that lower courts are bound by the decisions of higher courts means that decisions by the Supreme Court entrench rights against the other federal courts. This reminds us that entrenchment presupposes that the principle *lex posterior derogat priori* (the later law takes precedence over the earlier) is limited by the principle *lex superior derogat inferiori* (the higher law takes precedence over the lower).

Even those who deny that sovereignty or the supreme legislative power can be legally limited in any way admit that both are subject to nonlegal limitations. Austin held that although no law can be illegal, it can be called unconstitutional if it conflicts with a principle of legislation that Parliament has habitually observed and that against a sovereign, constitutional conventions are enforced by merely moral sanctions. Similarly, Dicey distinguished between legal sovereignty, the power of lawmaking unrestricted by any legal limit, and political sovereignty, the body whose will is ultimately obeyed by the citizens of the state. Hence, there are both the possibility that constitutional rights could be entrenched externally, even if not within the legal system, and the danger that internal entrenchment may be ineffective unless reenforced by external entrenchment. The former is probably the case in the United Kingdom and the latter is exempli-

fied in nations where a bill of rights is ignored by those in power. However, how does one distinguish between what is internal and external to the law? Wade argues that the constitutional convention that confers legislative authority cannot be a legal rule because it is presupposed by legal validity, but Hart holds that the rule of recognition, although a social practice rule and the ground of law, is itself a legal rule. Although Hans Kelsen distinguishes between legal norm and political power, he insists that efficacy is a necessary condition of legal validity. Even though legal positivists separate law from morality, natural law theorists maintain that they are logically inseparable.

Granted the possibility of entrenching constitutional rights, there is the question of its desirability. Many condemn it as a constitutional straitjacket that renders the law excessively inflexible. Constitutional rights formulated in abstract language will require inequitable applications in unusual cases, and rights important in their time will exclude legislation needed under changing circumstances. In United States law, however, the strict scrutiny test under the due process clause provides for entrenching constitutional rights that can still be overridden when legislation is necessary for some compelling state interest. Many condemn the entrenchment of constitutional rights against the majority in an elected legislature as undemocratic. One reply is that political authority is grounded upon the protection of human rights rather than the consent of the citizens. A more moderate response is to argue that the entrenchment of at least some constitutional rights, such as the right to vote and the right to periodic elections, is necessary to preserve democratic institutions. Finally, some advocate democratic forms of entrenchment, for example, requiring a popular referendum to amend any rights-conferring clause in the constitution.

References

Austin, John. *The Province of Jurisprudence Determined*. New York: Burt Franklin, 1970.

Brookfield, F.M. "Parliamentary Supremacy and Constitutional Entrenchment: A Jurisprudential Approach." *Otago Law Review* 5 (1984), 603–634.

Dicey, A.V. *The Law of the Constitution*. 10th ed. London: Macmillan, 1959.

Hart, H.L.A. *The Concept of Law*. Oxford: Clarendon Press, 1961.

Wade, H.W.R. "The Basis of Legal Sovereignty." *Cambridge Law Journal* (1954), 172–197.

Carl Wellman

See also AMENDMENT; CONSTITUTIONALISM; HUMAN RIGHTS; JUDICIAL REVIEW; SELF-REFERENCE

Environment

See ECOLOGY AND ENVIRONMENTAL SCIENCES

Epistemology in Law

To understand epistemology in law, it is necessary to consider first the meaning of epistemology in general, and then to consider epistemology in law in particular. Many terms are used to define the study of the problem of knowledge. Among the specialists, one expression alone is not considered to be unanimously satisfactory and adequate for this purpose. The word "epistemology" has an ambiguous meaning. Its use began in the nineteenth century, but it appeared in French dictionaries only at the beginning of the twentieth century.

The different meanings of this word differ from country to country. In English-speaking countries the term "epistemology" is used as a synonym of theory of knowledge, and it applies to the study of the philosophical problems that refer to the nature, limits, and validity of knowledge. From this point of view, the term denotes a very general and broad meaning. In this respect, epistemology is distinct from philosophy of science; the philosophy of science studies the methods and goals of knowledge, while epistemology studies, in principle, knowledge itself, its sources, its criteria of evidence, and the problem of truth.

Meanwhile, in France, for example, the term "epistemology" refers to the discipline that studies the ways of knowledge and the critique of its results. It is taken in its etymological meaning, since it actually means the study of science. From this point of view, it has, contrary to its Anglo-Saxon sense, a rather narrow meaning.

The historical epistemologies have acquired special importance in virtue of the deep crises and revolutions experienced by different sciences; all this unrest became the basis for developing modifications and for giving birth to scientific theories. This growth has been reflected not only in the natural sciences, but also in understanding the problems faced by human sciences.

R. Blanché maintains that the two principal works that could be called epistemological in the nineteenth century are the work by Bernard Bolzano, entitled *Wissenschaftslehre* (published in 1837 and related to logical and mathematical formal sciences) and that by William Whewell, named *Philosophy of the Inductive Sciences* (published in 1840, and related to the sciences of nature).

This does not mean that the Greeks stated no problems of such a nature; but, it is in modern times, especially since René Descartes and John Locke, that the conditions of the possibility of knowledge and the problems set forth by human understanding are raised as a matter of fundamental importance.

In French thought, epistemology now maintains a certain philosophical character, a quality that vanished from Duhem to Bachelard; nowadays, it seems to have moved definitively from the hands of philosophers to those of scientists. Eventually, this process was able to give rise to regional epistemologies that differ from general epistemology.

The phenomenon that took place in the area of general epistemology occurred also, with more marked features, in the field of epistemology in law. On one hand, jurists do not seem to be prone to engage in a specialty of this nature, saying that not enough scientific material has been developed for that; on the other hand, the epistemologists have shown themselves rather reluctant to give attention to this specialty. Thus, legal science has been classified as a science so particular that insularity could be taken as its a natural attribute.

Christian Atias has dealt very clearly with the obstacles that have arisen in founding the science of law; but in the field of epistemology in law, another question has contributed to complicate its scheme of problems. Effectively, what is to be understood by the expression "legal dogmatics" has become the theme of an important discussion. This term meant the study which settles the object, method, and limits of legal science. It is imposible to develop the origin and history of the problem; but it must be noted that at present the philosophy of law is distinguished from the science of law. The latter, by virtue of studying legal dogmatics, is concerned with delimiting the scientific and philosophical scope of law, in view of the dogmatic character of the legal science. This means that jurists must discipline themselves to receive only the data that the present positive ordering offers as that which *is given*. The *dogmatic dimension* of legal science sets limits on the scientific and philosophical field of law. The scientist of law is satisfied to identify the positive ordering that he studies as something of unquestionable force. The dogmatic practitioner uses concepts which in the last analysis are not explained, but are received as something *given* that cannot be argued. Nevertheless, presently jurists try to transcend the traditional, purely dogmatic field and try to act as philosophers; or else they try to bring into their studies new elements that would lead to a more advanced concept of dogmatics.

Moreover, general epistemology or comparative epistemology, in spite of the specificity of the legal science, cannot be disdained when one approaches studies of epistemology in law. At first sight, a fundamental difference appears between the concepts developed by the sciences of nature and the ones produced by the legal sciences. The latter have as their object human action, human behavior. Their facts and acts just happen in time; they are historical. They are unique, since they take place only once and they occur in the field of human freedom. This shows, as a consequence, the impossibility of verifying experimentally the legal phenomena and of inducing their repetition, as occurs in the natural sciences.

In addition, epistemology in law is concerned with delimiting the pure concept of law and its fundamental forms. Thus, it is focused also on settling the concept of the legal norm, the legal subject, and so forth.

Expressions such as epistemology of law, fundamental theory of law, general theory of law, and gnoseology in law are used as synonyms. They include the philosophical side of the disciplines that have as their object the study of knowledge and method in the legal sciences.

The panorama is complicated by the co-existence of different schools where the specialists of legal thought are found. Thus, for example, the general theory of law and the analytic school of jurisprudence each maintain their own point of view with regard to the method and problems that legal dogmatics presents. The same thing happens with the neo-scholastic school.

Finally, each jurist and each legal philosopher generally adopts an original position within each school, which means that, in this field, it is necessary to judge very carefully and singularly the attitude of each author.

Epistemology in law could be defined as a critical reflection on the acquired legal knowledge and the ways of acquiring it. The word "critical" must be understood in its etymological meaning, that is, in the sense of *judging* the value of such knowledge. The history of the scientific problems and theories, dealt with from an epistemological point of view, frequently enlightens the critical reflection.

References
Atias, Christian. *Epistémologie juridique.* Paris: Presses Universitaires de France, 1985.

Barreau, Hervé. *L'épistémologie.* Paris: Presses Universitaires de France, 1990.

Conry, Edward J. "Metaphysical Jurisprudence: The Epistemology of Law." *American Business Law Journal* 33 (1996), 373, 691.

Guastini, Riccardo. "Problemi epistemologici del normativismo." In *Analisi e diritto,* ed. Paolo Comanduci and Riccardo Guastini, 177–192. Turin: Giappichelli, 1991.

MacCormick, Neil. *Legal Reasoning and Legal Theory.* Oxford: Clarendon Press, 1978.

Ost, F. "Dogmatique juridique et science interdisciplinaire du droit." *Rechtstheorie* 117 (1986), 89–110.

Peczenik, Aleksander. *The Basis of Legal Justification.* Lund, Sweden: Lund University Press, 1983.

Samuel, Geoffrey. "Epistemology and Legal Interests." *International Journal for the Semiotics of Law* 4 (1991), 309.

Teubner, Gunther. "How the Law Thinks: Toward a Constructivist Epistemology of Law." *Law and Society Review* 23 (1989), 727.

Williams, Susan H. "Feminist Legal Epistemology." *Berkeley Women's Law Journal* 8 (1993), 63.

Olsen A. Ghirardi

Equality

No value is more thoroughly entrenched in Western culture than is the notion of equality.

Even in an American society that sanctioned slavery and permitted women no rights, there were prominent declarations that "all men are created equal."

Equality was a central principle in the democracies of ancient Greece, according to Charles Abernathy. Euripides, for example, wrote that "nature gave men the law of equal rights." Plato and Aristotle both emphasized equality in their writings. Plato spoke of the political equality between men and women; Aristotle wrote of the need to treat all citizens equally. Yet both also said that those who were unequal deserved to be treated differently. Aristotle, for instance, described some people as being slaves by nature.

Modern notions of equality can be traced to the writings of philosophers such as Thomas Hobbes and John Locke. Both Hobbes and Locke believed that people in the state of nature were equal. All were equally free in the state of nature and thus all were endowed with the same natural rights. Jean-Jacques Rousseau wrote that "the social compact establishes among the citizens such an equality that they all pledge themselves under the same conditions and ought to enjoy the same rights. . . . The sovereign never has a right to burden one subject more than another, because then the matter becomes particular and the power is no longer competent." Immanuel Kant wrote of the need to treat all human beings equally as ends, not as means to other objectives. Writings such as these were highly influential in the revolutions that occurred in Europe and America in the eighteenth and nineteenth centuries.

Equality never has been understood as treating everyone under all circumstances the same. All philosophers who have dealt with equality have recognized that there are differences among people that, at times, require distinctions in laws. Aristotle defined equality as a requirement that "things that are alike should be treated alike, while things that are unalike should be treated unalike in proportion to their unalikeness."

Equality, therefore, is inherently an indeterminate concept; other concepts are necessary to decide when people are alike and when they are different. Peter Westen explained that in order to apply the requirement for equality it is necessary to determine in what respects people are similar and to decide which of these characteristics are relevant to the kind of treatment that they should receive. In other words,

external standards, not derivable from the concept of equality, are necessary to decide which inequalities are permissible and which are intolerable. Laurence Tribe noted that "[e]quality makes noncircular commands and imposes non-empty constraints only to the degree that we are willing to posit substantive ideals to guide collective choice."

However, the fact that equality as a concept is insufficient, by itself, does not, of course, show that it is unnecessary. Equality is morally necessary because it compels society and individuals within it to care about how people are treated in relation to one another. Equality is the only concept that commands that differences in treating people must be justified. It is the concept that forces society to consider how people are treated in relation to one another. Equality is descriptive in the sense that it is used to label the relative likeness or unalikeness in the status and treatment of people. Equality is normative in that it commands that unjustified differences in treatment be eliminated. Contemporary philosophers such as John Rawls have emphasized the concept of equality in their writings.

Equality also is a concept that is analytically necessary in that it creates a presumption that people should be treated alike and puts the burden on those who wish to discriminate to justify their actions. J. Coons, W. Clune, and S. Sugarman observe: "There is that enduring something which causes us to ask the state to make its case for distinguishing two humans, if it is to treat them differently; the state may make the case in a thousand ways and it must be assisted in this by presumptions galore, but make it it must."

In American constitutional law, as noted in *F.S. Royster Guano Co. v. Virginia,* 253 U.S. 412 (1920), all inequalities in government treatment must be justified as at least being rationally related to a legitimate government purpose. Some types of discrimination must be justified by a higher standard. For example, the Supreme Court consistently has ruled that classifications based on race and national origin must meet "strict scrutiny," that is, as noted in *Wygant v. Jackson Board of Education,* 476 U.S. 267 (1986), they must be proven to be necessary to achieve a compelling government purpose. In contrast, *Craig v. Boren,* 429 U.S. 190 (1976), states that gender discrimination must meet "intermediate scrutiny," that is, it must be shown to be substantially related to an

E

important government purpose. The Court says that these higher burdens are appropriate when discrimination is based on immutable characteristics because it is unfair to punish people for traits that they did not choose and cannot control. Also, the Court emphasizes the need for close scrutiny in areas where there is a history of discrimination that makes it likely that laws are based on stereotypes and not real differences among people.

Finally, the principle of equality is rhetorically necessary because it is a powerful symbol that helps to persuade people to safeguard rights that would otherwise go unprotected. Equality is a concept that has tremendous emotive force. Westen remarked that "arguments in the form of equality invariably place all opposing arguments on the defensive." Justice Robert Jackson, concurring in *Railway Express Agency v. New York,* 336 U.S. 106, 111–13 (1949), explained the importance of equality in protecting people against arbitrary government action:

> [T]here is no more effective practical guaranty against arbitrary and unreasonable government than to require that the principles of law which officials would impose upon a minority must be imposed generally. Conversely, nothing opens the door to arbitrary action so effectively as to allow those officials to pick and choose only a few to whom they will apply legislation and thus to escape the political retribution that might be visited upon them if larger numbers were affected.

Often commentators discussing equality will emphasize two different conceptions: one that focuses on equal treatment and the other that looks at equal results. The equal treatment approach focuses on whether the government is treating people equally without discrimination. If so, equal protection is provided, even if the results are unequal. The equal results approach emphasizes the outcomes of the government's actions. Both are supported in writings from philosophers and courts.

The choice between these two approaches is often crucial in determining results in particular cases. For example, a major issue of equal protection law is whether proving the discriminatory impact of a law is sufficient to establish an equal protection violation. Those who take the equal treatment approach, as seen in *Washington v. Davis,* 426 U.S. 229 (1976), would say that there is no violation of equal protection unless there is proof that the law had a discriminatory purpose. In contrast, those who take the equal results approach would say that there is an equal protection approach if a facially neutral law has a discriminatory impact.

Similarly, the debate over affirmative action, in part, concerns whether equal protection is about equal treatment or equal results. Opponents of affirmative action, for example, Justice Robert Jackson, concurring in *Adarand Constructors, Inc. v. Pena,* 115 S. Ct. 2097 (1995), argue that government must be color-blind and treat everyone the same, regardless of race or gender, in awarding benefits such as contracts or admission to schools. However, supporters of affirmative action, for example, Richard Lempert, argue that in light of the long history of race and gender discrimination, affirmative efforts are essential to eliminate inequality of results.

Because there is no fixed meaning to "equality," and because it is an essential attribute of any just society, the debate over its content will reflect key social problems in every generation and every culture.

References

Abernathy, Charles I. *The Idea of Equality: An Anthology.* Richmond VA: John Knox Press, 1959.

Coker, F. *Readings in Political Philosophy.* Rev. ed. New York: Macmillan, 1982.

Coons, J., W. Clune, and S. Sugarman. *Private Wealth and Public Education.* Cambridge MA: Belknap Press, 1970.

Foster, Sheila. "Difference and Equality: A Critical Assessment of the Concept of Diversity." *Wisconsin Law Review* (1993), 105.

Lempert, Richard. "The Force of Irony: On the Morality of Affirmative Action and *United Steelworkers v. Weber.*" *Ethics* 95 (1984), 86.

Ortiz, Daniel R. "The Myth of Intent in Equal Protection." *Stanford Law Review* 41 (1989), 1105.

Rawls, John. *A Theory of Justice.* Cambridge MA: Harvard University Press, 1971.

Rosenfeld, Michel. "Decoding *Richmond*; Affirmative Action and the Elusive Meaning of Constitutional Equality." *Michigan Law Review* 87 (1989), 1729.

Tribe, Laurence H. *American Constitutional Law.* Mineola NY: Foundation Press, 1978.

Westen, Peter. "The Empty Idea of Equality." *Harvard Law Review* 95 (1982), 537.

Erwin Chemerinsky

See also FAIRNESS; JUSTICE

Error, Deceit, and Illusion

Most systems of law depend in one way or another on the notion of truth, since justice is closely linked to truth. Correspondingly, deviance from truth is usually seen as negative and so are error, deceit, and illusion, all of which represent forms of deviance from or misrepresentation of truth. Yet, although in most systems of law error, deceit, and illusion are able to strongly influence the outcome of judicial processes, it is difficult to define what exactly needs to be taken into account and when one should do so. This is due to the fact that, contrary to law's assumptions, deception and self-deception constitute fundamental traits of human existence. As such they have not only negative but also positive aspects and, hence, they are largely neutral to morals.

While the notions of error and illusion denote involuntary deviance from truth, the term "deception" means an intentional or at least negligent misrepresentation of it. Error and illusion, in turn, are normally distinguished with regard to the intensity with which the erring person believes in the deviating views or conceptions. The notion of error denotes a misconception of reality, usually attributable to a defect in the organs of sense, which can be corrected easily and which the erring person will accept without great resistance, once the error is detected. Contrary to this, the term "illusion" signifies a strong and important deviance from truth that cannot be attributed to the organs of sense; the person under the illusion will not easily give it up, since the illusion is believed to be true. The presence of illusions, therefore, usually makes that person's mental health questionable.

However, the assumption of an independent and universally valid truth that can be discovered more or less easily, and which makes it possible to isolate and evaluate errors, illusions, and deception, is doubtful. On the conceptual level, indeterminacy prevails. The concept of truth itself is far from being very clear and, hence, second-level concepts like error, deceit, or illusion, which depend on it, remain vague in content. More problematic is that in the proper sense only those can err who judge already in conformity with humanity, as Ludwig Wittgenstein states. Error, illusion, and deception only make sense in relation to a common idea of truth. Where such an idea is absent, neither error nor deception is possible. As is apparent in the concepts of "ideology" or "illusion," too great a deviation from the acceptable political goals or the common idea of truth permits the concerned ideas or even the concerned person's mental health to become doubtful. Hence, truth, seen in this perspective, does not represent an objective category independent from the truth-seekers, but is rather akin to Friedrich Nietzsche's mobile army of metaphors. As such it constitutes one instance of the cardinal bond between the individual and the world of others. Both capacities, to deceive and to detect deception, develop through childhood and adult life, and very often the targets of deception are friends, rather than enemies. Both findings make sense only if we take into account that error, deception, and illusion presuppose a common point of reference (truth) from which to judge. Such a common basis can be found more readily among people who trust each other than among strangers or enemies.

Apart from these difficulties, it is the negative value commonly attributed to deviance from truth that is most problematic. As to deviance from truth targeted at others (deception), it seems clear that from a biological point of view such endeavor constitutes a natural and healthy activity. With regard to competition among genes and their carrier-phenotypes, deception cannot be viewed as an imperfection but should be seen as an efficient solution that humans and other primates have developed languages that exclude perfect clarity and that allow for an impressive amount of misunderstanding and deception. Deception can have negative effects on individuals or societies, but so can absolute truthfulness. The finding that deviance from truth concerning oneself (errors, illusions, self-deception) can have positive effects has led modern philosophy to differ from Immanuel Kant's absolute rebuttal of the noble lie. Hence, the fact that a speech act is true or not does not yet define it as morally right or wrong. However, the question whether self-deceptive behavior is a desirable goal or not, and how such behavior is possible, remains largely controversial.

Most systems of law take into account the ubiquity and moral neutrality of deviance from truth. Usually, it is not deception as such which is punishable, but only those instances of deceptive behavior that cause harm or damage to others (for example, fraud). Consequently, in situations where individuals are expected not to lie they are explicitly requested not to do so (for example, by oath). Similarly, deviance from truth without being induced by others is common and, hence, errors are judged to be relevant to the law only if their occurrence was not due to the erring person's negligence. By doing so, legal systems are able to define flexibly what counts as commonly grounded and shared truth.

Finally, the law itself might be viewed as a deceptive system. It purports to establish equality and to maintain a certain minimal standard of ethics and morals guaranteed to all members of a society. Yet one could believe the law to be just while also viewing it as an institution that untruthfully declares such goals in order to achieve a completely different purpose: the maintenance of a society's survival. Such a goal would be reached by promoting not equality but variance within a society and by limiting morals to a minimum. In this perspective, then, the law does not maintain equality but difference. Yet optimal results of cooperation are realized under trustful and stable conditions that are equal for all participants (tit for tat). Where short-term and long-term aims conflict, sincerity with regard to the latter may affect the former. Hence, if declared sincerely, the promotion of difference as a long-term purpose would lessen law's authority and individuals' (necessarily short-termed) disposition to cooperate. Thereby, it would lower a society's efficiency and reduce the probability of its survival instead of increasing or maintaining it. Hence, deceptive declarations concerning one's own behavior (or law's purpose, for that matter) can be necessary and effective to gain acceptance and establish short-term cooperation while maintaining completely different long-term purposes at the same time.

References

Alexander, Richard D. *The Biology of Moral Systems.* New York: Aldine de Gruyter, 1987.
Barnes, J.A. *A Pack of Lies: Towards a Sociology of Lying.* Cambridge: Cambridge University Press, 1994.
Flanagan, Owen. *Varieties of Moral Personality: Ethics and Psychological Realism.* Cambridge MA: Harvard University Press, 1991.
Goleman, Daniel. *Vital Lies, Simple Truths: The Psychology of Self-Deception.* New York: Touchstone, 1986.
Kuran, Timur. *Private Truths, Public Lies.* Cambridge MA: Harvard University Press, 1995.
Macy, Michael. "Backward-looking Social Control." *American Sociological Review* 58 (1993), 819–836.
McLaughlin, Brian P., and Amélie Oksenberg Rorty, eds. *Perspectives on Self-Deception.* Berkeley: University of California Press, 1988.
Niggli, M.A., and Marc Amstutz. "Recht als Amoral (Amoral Law)." *Archiv für Rechts- und Sozialphilosophie* 62 (1995), 11–31.
Rue, Loyal. *By the Grace of Guile: The Role of Deception in Natural History and Human Affairs.* New York: Oxford University Press, 1994.
Wittgenstein, Ludwig. *On Certainty.* Oxford: Blackwell, 1969.

Marcel Alexander Niggli

See also GAME THEORY; IDEOLOGY; RATIONAL BARGAINING; TRUTH

Estate and Patrimony

Estate and patrimony are the institutions that allow the ownership of goods and property rights to be exercised. Ownership and property rights presuppose the capacity to exercise them. Capacity presupposes some sort of relationship between things and persons, as well as among persons. Estate and patrimony supply that relation in the common law and the civilian law, respectively.

Estate is the institution by which real property can be held with legal authority by an owner. Estates hardly concern personal property, which is owned directly (similarly to civilian property, both moveable and immoveable, as noted in the ensuing discussion). The Conquest of 1066 put dominion over territory into the monarch's hands, so an owner's estate or authorization to deal with land was held only from the public authority.

These domains or tenures are held more or less fully, but never absolutely. They are all that can be owned, not the land. Constructed out of authorizations for a given period, "projected upon the plane of time," they are set up between the owner and the land. While ownership of land would have to be full or nil, ownership of estates can be multiple and simultaneous, although the estates can be exercised upon the land only one after another.

This characterization is ambiguous, since the term "estate" is also used to characterize the entirety of a person's holdings, real and personal, which is available for heirs or legatees upon death. This is a derivative usage, due to the momentary summing up of a deceased's holdings to be dealt with all at once.

Physical holding has the appearance of being an estate in the land. Possessing is evidence of an estate against other holders only; but neither this nor any other relation to an estate in land is absolute ownership of the estate against the world nor, even less, evidence for that. Remedies and not rights prevail: having a better estate, even without possession, gives a claim at law (called seizin) to possess. Title is the right to the remedy, namely, to the suit which might overcome an adverse physical possession and expel the disseisor. It is not a right to any particular outcome from the suit.

Estates are varied in several other ways. Depending on the fullness of the time for holding, the fullest estate is fee simple; the least full, and similar to the holding of personal property, are leasehold and tenancy, with estate for life and others as intermediate. Statutes and case law from the thirteenth century on have modified these.

The legal capacities for the actions that make up any estate can be located with different holders. There they may rest for different lengths of time, even forever. Typically, these capacities are classified as the rights to use, to benefit from, and to dispose of the same thing. Ordinary variations can be for one person to use the land, another to sell its air rights; one may use water to fish, another may use it for hydroelectric power.

Any one heir inherits only what estates remain or what remains of the estate after this dispersion. Since there is no ownership of the land, a fortiori no ownership of it remains after all of the interests in dealing with it have been disposed of from the "bundle" of interests which make up an estate.

The doctrine of estates is of judicial origin. Common lawyers opine that, usually, the entry of statute only mixes up its uses; doctrine steadfastly abjures rationalizing it.

Patrimony originates differently, as a creature of doctrine. Since the Conquest of 1066 just preceded the Glossators' restoration of a Roman law, the continental customs and the codes that organized them were given a less feudal and, putatively, a more conceptual standing than in England. The Roman ownership or *dominium* permitted a more focused reflection, which the nineteenth century provided by turning the commonplace term "patrimony" (*patrimoine, patrimonio, Vermögen*) into a term of art.

Citizens of republics, Roman or postrevolutionary, hold rights toward each other, and not only privileges from the ruler. Patrimony is the institution through which persons can have rights to own things in civilian legal systems. Each person has that capacity, one's own patrimony. A person has no more than one patrimony. No person has one way of holding moveables and another for holding immoveables. Even less likely is that any person would have different patrimonies for holding different groupings of things. The whole content of the patrimony is liable for debts.

Unlike estates, however, the patrimony as a capacity cannot be wholly lost. This is because, while estates are a device constructed as the object to be owned, the objects owned in patrimony are natural things; or at least they are goods, things so far as these are objects of interest. No multiplicity among the objects of property rights can multiply patrimonies.

The multiple exercises of property rights cannot be definitively detached from each other, nor from the whole patrimony. Particular things in patrimony may be made available to other persons, through the variety of special contracts. Not all of these separations may persist permanently, however, for then the owner could conceivably be left with nothing but a bare title. That is adjudged commercially to be a useless institution, and so not the intent of the law. However, that is indeed imaginable by conceiving civilian patrimony as a box which may still be owned even when the rights which are its contents are all gone; when the cluster of common law remedies which make up estate are all gone, on the contrary, nothing else remains.

The doctrinal problem for patrimony's unity corresponds, nonetheless, to common law's problem with leaseholds. Not being a freehold, this estate cannot be owned (and neither can the land, of course); but it bears on the land as ownership of personal property does upon its objects. The problem is how other estates can be simultaneous with leasehold, which reforming statutes have made no more conceivable.

Similarly, personal debts are among what is owned in patrimony, for they can be sold or have their income assigned like other things. Since they cannot be exercised in kind, however, there is no thing to be owned here, but only the right to something. So both things and rights are owned in patrimony. Patrimony is itself a right, the right to own things; and so it, too, is something which is owned. While patrimony as the right of a person is identifiable with that person as his or her unique identity, that is not true of the things owned, including patrimony. Those may be grouped or separated at will. Its unity is jeopardized.

The codes appear to construct many of these collections or universalities of goods for the same individual (trusts, unassimilated inheritances, pledges, to name a few). In effect, many individuals can have the same content to their patrimonies, and the same individuals can have many patrimonies.

The philosophical focus for dealing with these jurisprudential problems are the notions of personal identity to which each is related. Personhood is external (Thomas Hobbes' "author") and is fragmented (David Hume's percepts), constructed as a manifold; this is the context for British estates' multiplicity. Alternatively, personhood is self-unified idea (René Descartes) or will (Immanuel Kant), through Johann Fichte the source for continental patrimony. The current remedies for such deficiencies in the notions of personhood need to be turned toward remedying the incoherences in proprietary capacity, too, without losing the distinct institutional advantages which these several doctrines provide.

References

Aubry, C., and C. Rau. *Cours de droit civil français d'après la méthode de Zachariae* (The Study of French Civil Law according to Zachariae). 1838.

Burns, E.H. *Cheshire's Modern Law of Real Property.* 12th ed. London: Butterworth, 1976.

Ginossar, S. *Droit réel, propriété et créance; élaboration d'un système des droits patrimoniaux* (Real Rights, Property, and Obligation: A System of Patrimonial Rights). Paris: Librairie générale de droit et de jurisprudence, 1960.

Gray, C.B. "Patrimony." *Les Cahiers de droit* 22 (1981), 81–157.

Harris, D.R. "The Concept of Possession in English Law." In *Oxford Essays in Jurisprudence (First Series),* ed. A.G. Guest, 69. Oxford: Clarendon Press, 1961.

Honore, A.M. "Ownership." In *Oxford Essays in Jurisprudence (First Series),* ed. A.G. Guest, 107. Oxford: Clarendon Press, 1961.

Macdonald, Roderick A. "Reconceiving the Symbols of Property: Universalities, Interests and Other Heresies." *McGill Law Journal* 39 (1994), 761–812.

McClure, Lisa, Chantal Stebbins, and Gordon Goldberg. "The History of a Hunt for Simplicity and Coherence in the Field of 'Ownership', 'Possession', 'Property' and 'Title'." *Denning Law Journal* (1992), 103–136.

Merryman, J.H. "Ownership and Estates: Variations on a Theme by Lawson." *Tulane Law Review* 48 (1974), 916.

Rapports généraux au VIIe Congrès internationale de Droit comparatif [La transformation du patrimoine dans le droit civil moderne, Uppsala, 1966]. Stockholm: Almquist and Wiksel, 1967. [French report in *Revue trimestrielle de droit civil* 64 (1966), 185; Venezuelan, Polish, German, Belgian reports in monographs.]

Christopher B. Gray

See also FRAGMENTATION OF OWNERSHIP

Ethics, Legal

Legal ethics examines legal behavior as it arises from two distinct relationships, that between the legal profession itself and the public, and that between the individual lawyer and client, court, fellow lawyers, the general community, and even oneself.

At the level of the profession itself, legal ethics addresses a linkage between professional autonomy and the distinctive ethics of the profession. A profession claims, at a minimum, the authority to regulate its membership through controlling school admission and by setting and enforcing standards of professional competence. Typically, a profession will justify its status and monopoly by insisting that its membership alone is qualified to provide the specialized services called for by the public interest. This rationale may be called the "moral mandate" of a profession; it is the basis of its distinctive ethics.

The legal profession's moral mandate speaks to the central norms of the legal system, and in particular to the need for free and equal citizens to secure independent representation, counsel, and advocacy in those matters which fundamentally involve their role as citizens. Thus the legal profession is uniquely placed to call upon powerful political values for the justification of its professional authority. It is these values, and the accompanying need for a profession dedicated to their protection, that are embodied in canons of professional conduct and codes of ethics of bars and law societies.

The legal profession, familiar as it is with statute making, is comfortable regulating its affairs by means of legalistic codes. In Canada, and in particular the United States, codes of conduct have over the years shifted back and forth between being compendia of regulatory black-letter rules and being collections of aspirational ethical comments aimed to highlight the ideological underpinnings of the moral mandate. Rules of professional conduct typically include rules requiring lawyers to exhibit integrity in all aspects of their practice, to be competent, to advise clients candidly, to keep client confidences, to avoid conflicts of interest, and to act overall with propriety and uprightness.

The moral mandate of the profession has not gone unquestioned. In recent decades, especially in the United States, the literature on legal ethics has been dominated by critiques of professionalism. Those from the political right argue that the profession's monopolistic powers are unwarranted, should be dismantled and replaced by a more entrepreneurial, free-market approach. Critiques from the political left argue that professional powers are unjustified because they are antidemocratic and serve merely to entrench existing power structures.

Legal ethics at the level of individual relationships has been shaped by competing paradigms. In terms of the standard adversarial one, lawyering is thought to serve the interests of the client exclusively. This narrowly focused view of lawyers as merely zealous advocates, whatever the interests are, creates concern from a moral point of view and has attracted the most criticism. The adversarial view presumes that lawyers must act for a client as if everyone is potentially an adverse litigant and that all questions of justice can be decided only by a trial. This implies the lawyer's primary ethical obligations are confidentiality and to be zealous on a client's behalf. The first puts the lawyer under a special duty not to reveal information (subject to statutory exceptions), even if that impedes the pursuit of justice or conflicts with the lawyer's own values. The second obliges the lawyer to do everything, within the limits of the law, to further the client's interests against the world.

Recent writers have questioned whether the adversarial paradigm provides an adequate moral basis for the practice of law. The exclusive performance of adversarial lawyering may stunt one's moral discernment and judgment, and so be destructive to the moral character of the whole person. A more generous view of ethical lawyering envisions a vocation that integrates professional and social responsibilities with personal convictions. In any case, practice has never been exhaustively adversarial; there are many roles that lawyers always legitimately play that engage wider social interests.

Legal ethics also explores some of the inevitable tensions between the lawyer as professional and as businessperson. When law is understood exclusively as a money-making activity, the lawyer risks losing sight of the moral mandate of the profession. Lawyers must make a living, undeniably, but when the money being made in legal practice dominates a person's thinking, it is disruptive to the ideals of the profession and of an individual's self-respect and, to the degree that well-being depends upon this, to one's happiness as a lawyer. The business side of legal practice has traditionally been kept obscure because of the way it conflicts with the dignified image of the professional lawyer. The rejection of solicitation and aggressive advertising flows from this concern for professional image. Ethically, though, the more fundamental issue is whether the mere fact that a lawyer has entered into a commercial relationship with a client creates a conflict of interest for the lawyer that cannot be overcome.

The adversarial paradigm puts a high premium on the client's short-term transactional interests. The practice of law is more than this; it is profoundly social in nature. The lawyer's relationship with the client, though central, is but one of several relationships that raise

E

moral issues. Relationships with colleagues, with judges and other legal officers, and with the public at large create a wider moral context. Lawyers are moral consultants whether they like it or not; they should be appraised of the full range of their roles and responsibilities. Legal ethics, in short, goes far beyond the official codes of professional conduct and their interpretations.

Indeed, the profession has been transformed in the last few decades. The entrance of women and minorities into the legal profession is perhaps the most obvious demographic change; but there are other changes, resulting from economic, political, and technological factors, that have buffeted the profession. Throughout it all, the moral mandate of the legal profession—the provision of services that protect and enhance the role of citizen in the overall interest of the public—has remained the same. Its interpretation and application has had to keep pace with the moral sensibilities of the legal professionals of the time.

References

Buckingham, Donald, Jerome Bickenbach, Richard Bronaugh, and Bertha Wilson. *Legal Ethics in Canada.* Toronto: Harcourt Brace, 1996.

Freedman, Monroe H. *Understanding Lawyers' Ethics.* New York: Matthew Bender, 1990.

Kronman, A. "Practical Wisdom and Professional Character." *Social Philosophy and Policy* 4 (1986), 203–221.

Luban, David. *Lawyers and Justice: An Ethical Study.* Princeton: Princeton University Press, 1988.

———, ed. *The Good Lawyer.* Totowa NJ: Rowman and Allanheld, 1984.

Luizzi, Vincent. *A Case for Legal Ethics: Legal Ethics as a Source for a Universal Ethic.* Albany: State University of New York Press, 1993.

MacKenzie, Gavin. *Lawyers and Ethics: Professional Responsibility and Discipline.* Toronto: Carswell, 1993.

Mackie, Karl J. *Lawyers in Business and the Law Business.* London: Macmillan, 1989.

Simon, W. H. "The Ideology of Advocacy: Procedural Justice and Professional Ethics." *Wisconsin Bar Review* 29 (1978), 30.

Smith, Beverley G. *Professional Conduct for Canadian Lawyers* Toronto: Butterworth, 1989.

Wasserstrom, R. "Lawyers as Professionals, Some Moral Issues." *Human Rights* 5 (1975), 1.

Wilkins, David B. "Practical Wisdom for Practicing Lawyers: Separating Ideals from Ideology in Legal Ethics." *Harvard Law Review* 108 (1994), 458.

Donald E. Buckingham
Jerome E. Bickenbach
Richard Bronaugh

See also PROFESSIONAL ETHICS

Euthanasia and Suicide

Suicide, literally the killing of one's self, was a felony in British common law, but is not presently criminalized in any state in the United States. Euthanasia, literally "a good or happy death," has in the past twenty years been understood as the implementation of one of at least four kinds of practices. *Passive involuntary euthanasia* is the ending of someone's life, without their participation or consent, through the discontinuation of some means of life support (for example, a respirator or feedings). The assumption is that the means of support that would be discontinued are fundamentally artificial, and thus discontinuing these means is to allow "nature" to take its course. *Passive voluntary euthanasia* involves the consent and participation of the person in the discontinuation of some artificial means of support. Passive voluntary euthanasia differs from suicide in that the intent of the person is to control the timing and process of an already impending death from natural causes (due either to injury or disease), rather than to hasten or cause that death.

Active involuntary euthanasia, in contrast, resembles homicide in that there is no reliance on "natural" progression of illness—instead of omission, the parties to active euthanasia impose a technique known to hasten or bring about death, without the consent or participation of the party that is to be euthanized. However, active involuntary euthanasia potentially differs from homicide in that the intent to hasten death is in the service of a benevolent intent to make an already imminent death less agonizing. *Active voluntary euthanasia* is much like suicide, the willing participation of a person in an activity intended to end his or her own life, except that the person requires assistance of another to carry out the act. It is thus frequently termed "assisted suicide" or "physician-assisted suicide," to denote the patient's intent both to die and to bring about or control the timing and means of death through a positive act known to cause death.

Many have disputed the boundaries of these controversial practices. Physicians have disputed the idea that death is intended in active or passive practices that bring about the death of patients. Concerning the frequently used, so-called *passive* acts of omission or retraction of life-sustaining medical care, physicians note that the withholding or withdrawal of techniques is "medically appropriate," if the technique will not advance evaluation or therapy for a patient. The *withhold/withdraw decision,* some argue, in no way suggests an intent to end the patient's life, which acts would be forbidden both by the Hippocratic oath and by central tenets of the Judeo-Christian tradition. Physicians can thus argue that to think of such decisions as euthanasia misses the point that if a technique neither aids in a diagnosis that likely would lead to therapy nor is in itself therapeutic, it is inappropriate regardless of any subsequent decision about hastening or easing death. Similarly, physicians have utilized the doctrine of *double effect* to argue that even the active administration or prescription of a substance known to result in death is not assistance in suicide, as long as that outcome is not the one the physician intends, despite full knowledge or expectation of the likely effect. In this way, what might resemble assistance in suicide (active voluntary euthanasia) or the hastening of an incompetent patient's death (active involuntary euthanasia) is in fact only an unintentional or secondary by-product (double effect) of an action that has other primary therapeutic or palliative effects.

For those physicians, jurists, and patients who have endorsed policies and law that would legalize assisted suicide or other forms of euthanasia, significant jurisprudential obstacles present themselves. Two are worthy of note. First, to what extent is euthanasia defensible as a natural or derived right? Frequently this is construed as a "right to die." In cases of omission or retraction of therapy, it amounts to a right to refuse therapies that are not desired, for whatever reason. This right is recognized in U.S. law as a right to bodily integrity, and in medicolegal literature (particularly after important decisions in *Cruzan* and *Quinlan*) as a patient's right to *autonomy* in medical decision making at the end of life. Crucial to the question of when such discontinuation is a right, though, has been the competence of the patient to assert decision-making power. One way in which the problem of contemporaneous competence to refuse treatment has been handled is in the form of advance directives, written before the patient is cognitively compromised and unable to give consent, which specify patient wishes concerning withholding and withdrawal of care. In cases where the right to die would require positive action, such as the administration of a deadly dosage, the legal issue turns on what is required of others in the exercise of that right. Does the right to die suggest a responsibility for the state or physicians in much the same way a right to refuse treatment suggests a responsibility to cease and desist in the provision of that treatment? If not, the right to die amounts to a right to suicide, which could be protected either by a Supreme Court affirmation of state powers to legalize suicide or by recognizing the right to direct one's own health care as falling within the constitutional right to privacy. If the right to die is interpreted as a right to request assistance from others in dying, there must be a clearer articulation of what is presently a muddy issue: is one who aids and counsels suicide guilty of any crime where the commission of suicide is innocent of any violation of law? Some states have attempted to prosecute such attempts as homicide, even where patients requested assistance in suicide. In order that the right to die by positive clinical interventions is recognized, a concomitant right (and even responsibility) to aid in dying would need to be recognized in the constitutional, statutory, or common law.

The second problem with legalization of assisted suicide and euthanasia is the jurisprudential rationale for participation in such practices. While the Supreme Court has yet to take up this question, U.S. Circuit Courts of Appeals have ruled that state prohibitions against assistance in suicide are unconstitutional for reasons that suggest a significant problem in defining physician intent appropriately. In *Quill v. Vacco,* U.S.C.A. (2d Cir. 1996), the court ruled that the right to refuse treatment is legally the same as a right to hasten death. This, for reasons delineated above, would be troublesome to physicians who would aid patients in dying under a double-effect rationale, because it suggests an intent that they, as medical caregivers, do not endorse. More troublesome, though, is the effect of the collapsing of the distinction between desire to discontinue treatment and the desire to hasten death on the withhold/withdraw decision. If hastening death is always the intent in withdrawing treatments, as Justice Antonin Scalia argues in his concurring opinion cited by the Second Circuit, then physicians who discontinue treatments or forgo inappropriate treatments would always have to think of themselves as intending to hasten death, rather than as succumbing to the "natural causes" of patients' pathologies. Physicians may be unwilling to operate under the presumption that they intend to hasten death, and thus might be less willing to allow discontinuation of treatments. If, in the alternative, the Supreme Court rejects the Second Circuit rationale concerning a constitutional right to die, it might instead endorse the right to die via powers reserved to the state.

References

Moreno, Jonathan D., ed. *Arguing Euthanasia.* New York: Touchstone, 1995.

Thomasma, David C., and Glenn Graber. *Euthanasia: Toward an Ethical Social Policy.* New York: Continuum, 1990.

In re Quinlan, Supreme Court of New Jersey, 1976. 70 N.J. 10, 355 A.2d 647.

Glenn McGee
Jon Merz

Evidence

J.H. Wigmore defined judicial evidence as "[a]ny knowable fact or group of facts, not a legal or a logical principle, considered with a view to its being offered before a legal tribunal for the purpose of producing the effect of persuasion, positive or negative, on the part of the tribunal, as to the truth of a proposition, not of law or logic, on which the determination of the tribunal is to be asked." This definition, albeit nuanced, highlights the "truth-disclosing" aspect of judicial evidence. Other accounts of adjudication tell us that, as E.M. Morgan states, a "trial . . . is a proceeding not for the discovery of truth as such, but for the establishment of a basis of fact for the adjust-

ment of a dispute between litigants . . . ," or that what is at stake, according to W. Twining, is "legitimated conflict-resolution." "Truth," though important to this legitimation, is not the only value in play. Evidence law implicates as well "civil libertarian values" and "safeguards for persons suspected or accused of crimes"—in other words, aspects of "political morality."

According to Wigmore, one implication of this is a distinction between "evidence" and the "law of evidence." Evidence, per se, has been described as coextensive with "knowledge" (Jeremy Bentham, in Twining 1990: 341); some have argued that the rules of judicial evidence should embody, according to J.R. Gulson, "certain scientific principles or laws of Nature by which the process of verifying matter of fact is necessarily governed"; that, as noted by Wigmore, there is a "probative science." On the other hand, the "law of evidence," the actual rules governing admissibility, reflect not only these "principles of proof," but involve questions of "fairness" and "legality," according to N. Rescher and C.E. Joynt, as well as matters of efficiency or convenience. Any adequate theoretical account of the law of evidence must therefore consider not only ontology, epistemology, and logic but also social theory, theories of justice, and pragmatic factors, as well as how to mediate among the concerns suggested by these areas of inquiry.

Facts and Knowledge of Facts

Focusing on "evidence" as involving a fact-establishing or truth-disclosing process, however, one can identify several theoretical dimensions, implicit in Wigmore's definition: What is a "fact"? Are facts "knowable"? How are facts known? How do we get from a "knowable fact" to a further proposition? What is the nature of propositions, including their character as linguistic or semiotic phenomena? What do we understand by "truth" as opposed to falsity? What is the relationship of "persuasion" to truth?

The first of these, the "ontological" question, addresses the nature of "facts," ostensibly the primary or initial concern of evidence. This involves, for one thing, distinguishing "fact" from legal and logical principles (as well, as, for some purposes, from "opinion")—not always a straightforward matter, but one supposedly central to the relative functions of witnesses, juries, and judges in the trial process. The distinction suggests, for example, that there is such a thing as "brute" or "objective" fact, independent of the human observer's apprehension and assessment of it, an assumption that underlies what has been called by J.D. Jackson the empiricist account of evidence, an analysis exemplified by Gulson's statement that "[a] fact . . . [is] an existing reality of nature, capable of being ascertained by perception or intuition."

The latter part of this definition introduces the epistemological issue: that is, it addresses how "facts" are known, suggesting that a fact might exist apart from our knowledge of it. This idea in itself is problematic. Moreover, what is presented to a tribunal is seldom (apart from so-called real evidence, that is, the direct presentation of a material thing to the perceptions of the trier of fact) an immediately apprehensible phenomenon; it is usually a report by an observer/witness, that is, a *re*presentation (generally, but not necessarily, verbal) of such a phenomenon. In other words, the evidence is not, as Wigmore might be taken to imply, an objective fact, but a proposition—at best "something in the world" filtered through a witness's perception, memory semiotic resources, and biases. These biases would include not only personal predilections but also ways of looking at things given by cultural understandings, including the specific legal context in which the factual issue arises. To some extent, the law of evidence takes note of the epistemological issue, but not in ways that admit a radical skepticism. It questions the accuracy of *this witness's* knowledge and of the knowledge conveyed to the tribunal, under the heading of "credibility," and in such doctrines as hearsay. The law of evidence seems, however, perhaps for pragmatic reasons, to question neither the knowability of objective fact nor the "normativity" of the fact-constructing process.

It has been noted that the dominant, or rationalist, tradition in Anglo-American evidence law adopts a correspondence theory of truth, as reflected in assertions such as Gulson's that "[t]he truth of a proposition [of fact] consists in the correspondence or agreement of the language or assertion with the external reality." "Truth" and "falsehood" are arguably meaningless without such a reality against which a proposition can be tested. Recently, some writers (Jackson, for example)

have questioned the correspondence theory of truth, advocating instead a coherence theory: what validates evidence, or a theory about the "facts," is not its agreement with an external reality that can be known only through representations, but, rather, semiotic integrity or cohesiveness. An implication of such an account could be that "evidence" is not, as some would have it, "science," but a species of rhetoric. It may be not so much about "truth" as about persuasion, in terms of values and other culturally determined expectations.

The foregoing discussion has engaged three general issues: the ontological status of "facts," their immediate knowability, and knowledge of them through the mediation of witnesses.

Processes of Inference

A discussion of facts also implies another issue: the derivation of ulterior or secondary facts or propositions of fact from primary facts. This is the issue involved, although not comprehensively, in the distinction between "direct" and "circumstantial" evidence. The former is evidence of the very matter to be determined: in Wigmore's terminology, the evidentiary fact would be the same as the factual proposition "on which the determination of the tribunal was to be asked." The latter is evidence of a fact from whose existence some other fact and, ultimately, the very matter to be decided, can be inferred, the typical case that Wigmore's definition envisages.

This introduces another set of issues of theoretical interest in the law of evidence— those relating to reasoning and conclusion-drawing, the "logic" of evidence.

According to P. Tillers, *the* basic rule of evidence is the relevance rule: only relevant evidence is admissible. The concept of relevance requires not only some theory of rational connection (presumably much short of entailment) but also of degrees of relevance, and of relevance vis-à-vis countervailing concerns. Thus, does the law exclude "character evidence" because it is not relevant, or because it is not sufficiently relevant given its likely psychological effect on triers of fact? Is there an objective "science" of relevance, or, again, is relevance only, or largely, a matter of constructed, and thus relative, expectations?

A related inquiry is What is the nature of reasoning about evidence? A conventional answer, according to Wigmore, is that the process is inductive, in the sense that "a body of information can be evidence for another that goes *beyond* it in assertive content," as Rescher and Joynt state. This account has been questioned. Some argue that reasoning about evidence is syllogistic or deductive, the unenunciated major premise being provided from the trier of fact's "stock of previously acquired general information," in Gulson's words (or, where this is inadequate, by expert opinion). If so, then questions arise about the specific provenance and validity of that major premise; it is likely to be some cultural value, not an objectively valid "truth." This again would point to the relativistic and normative character of the "truth"-disclosing process.

Relativity, as discussed by Gulson, appears in another way in the drawing of inferences: "The connection between a principal fact and its evidentiary one is never more than a probable one; and since no number of probabilities can amount to more than a high degree of probability, no number of evidentiary facts . . . can . . . generate more than a high degree of probability of [the principal fact's] truth." Adding to the probabilistic character of the inferential process is the mediation of necessarily imperfect knowledge.

The element of probability in the process has generated debate as to the applicability of probability theory to evidentiary matters, including whether Pascalian (mathematical) or Baconian (nonmathematical) probability offers a better account. This inquiry may arise at the stage of relevancy ("given the existence of fact X, is it at all likely that fact Y also exists?"), but more frequently at the stage of assessing the sufficiency of evidence, that is, whether the evidence amounts to proof, tested against the applicable standard ("proof on a balance of probabilities," "proof beyond a reasonable doubt"). The existence of different standards (and of variation within those standards) implicitly recognizes the relativity affecting the process. Whether questions of relevancy and sufficiency of evidence can be resolved by "rigorous logical analysis" or by models provided by probability theory, or whether they are so complexly affected by subjective factors that they must simply be left to the appreciation of socially representative valuers remains unresolved.

According to Twining, a traditional understanding of the objective of the adjudication of questions of fact as being "to establish Truth by means of Reason in order to implement Justice under the Law" points to the foci of both a theory of evidence and its critique.

References

Cohen, L.J. *The Probable and the Provable.* Oxford: Clarendon Press, 1977.

Gulson, J.R. *The Philosophy of Proof.* London: Routledge, 1905. Reprint, Littleton CO: Rothman, 1990.

Jackson, B. *Law, Fact and Narrative Coherence.* Merseyside: Deborah Charles, 1989.

Jackson, J.D. "Two Methods of Proof in Criminal Procedure." *Modern Law Review* 51 (1988), 549.

Morgan, E.M. *Some Problems of Proof Under the Anglo-American System of Litigation.* New York: Columbia University Press, 1956.

Rescher, N., and C.E. Joynt. "Evidence in History and in the Law." *Journal of Philosophy* 56 (1959), 561.

Tillers, P. "Modern Theories of Relevancy." In *Evidence in Trials at Common Law,* ed. J.H. Wigmore and Peter Tillers. Boston: Little, Brown, 1983.

Twining, W. "Rationality and Scepticism in Judicial Proof: Some Signposts." *International Journal for the Semiotics of Law* 2 (1989), 69.

Twining, W. *Rethinking Evidence: Exploratory Essays.* Oxford: Blackwell, 1990.

Wigmore, J.H. *The Principles of Judicial Proof as Given by Logic, Psychology, and General Experience.* Boston: Little, Brown, 1913; 3d ed. 1937.

Dennis Klinck

See also ERROR, DECEIT, AND ILLUSION; RELEVANCE; SKEPTICISM; TESTIMONY AND EXPERT EVIDENCE; TRUTH

Ex Post Facto Legislation

Ex post facto legislation is regulation in a style which usually prescribes a negative sanction with punitive consequences in law for an action performed prior to the law's coming into force.

There is a technical, pragmatic, and, at the same time, deeply moral question hidden behind the decision as to whether it is allowable and whether it is worthwhile. For a long time law has permitted this; jurisprudence could only conclude that the retroactive effect of a rule is not excluded by any legal assumption. Its legal validity cannot be disturbed by the fact that it declares an act to have been a crime after the fact.

A decisive answer was first given on the European continent when criminal procedure was surrounded with legal guarantees. Recognition of the principles *nullum crimen sine lege* (no crime without legislation) and *nulla poena sine lege* (no punishment without legislation) expressly interdicted making a deed punishable or meting out a penal sanction without a prospective statutory decree. Some early modern constitutions excluded retrospectivity with moral overtones, for example, the Norwegian Constitution, and the 1784 New Hampshire Constitution: "Retrospective laws are highly injurious, oppressive, and unjust. No such laws, therefore, should be made, either for the decision of civil causes, or for the punishment of offences." The German Constitution (Grundgesetz) restricts this prohibition and limits it exclusively to substantive criminal law; German constitutional jurisprudence limits it further to cases no longer under adjudication, distinguishing the original from the nonoriginal retroactive effect. This is because analytical examination of the law embodied in precedents has proven long ago that judicial decisions which create a decision rule have an ex post facto effect as well.

Theoretically, since it is a means of social engineering, law is mostly prospective and makes use of regulation that links legal consequences to future events. As a program for social reform, trying to influence with prohibition and repression is less successful than offering a model for behavior that includes advantages because of being surrounded by positive sanctions. Opportunities protected by prospective regulation are needed for this.

Modern formal law is primarily the means for mediating relationships toward a network of ascriptions. Thus, it is of primary importance to provide regulations providing normative determinations for behavior. A secondary consideration is that inasmuch as the regulation is kept secret and does not become cognizable or available or bears a retroactive effect, it will not have the chance to influence the behavior law seeks.

Since the debate between H.L.A. Hart and Lon Fuller as to the conflict between Hitler and the SA (Sturmabteilung) for murdering its leaders in Nazi Germany, Anglo-American legal thought has seen legislation with retroactive effect as a moral dilemma and, according to Robert Summers, has made it a precondition that "the citizen will have a fair opportunity to obey the law." Overuse and abuse of a tool, however, is never the fault of the tool. According to Fuller, the same technical means can be used "to cure irregularities of form" under special and unavoidable circumstances.

This question was dramatically raised after World War II when, preparing for the Nuremberg and Tokyo trials, the victors had to consider retrospective prosecution and indictability for actions that were justifiable under domestic (respectively, German and Japanese) laws in force at the time. As discussed by Gustav Radbruch, they had to choose whether to use regulations with retroactive effect, or to employ natural law over the positive law, the dilemma of the contradiction between the "statutory no-law" (*gesetzliches Unrecht*) and the "supra-statutory law" (*übergesetzliches Recht*).

Recently, the collapse of communism raised the burning question in central and eastern Europe as to whether the legal processing of deeds instigated by former socialist states could finally begin or whether, because the passing of time had exceeded the time limits set by statutory decree, the long-persisting and cruel state crimes could avoid control by the rule of law. These acts ran against the penal codes applicable at the time but remained unprosecuted because of the state's complicity in their formal exclusion from prosecution, in some cases by a special classified decree. The Hungarian legislator in 1991 held that the illegal institutionalization of the state's machinery to abet avoidance of official criminal prosecution notionally excludes the start of the "tolling" period. The Hungarian Constitutional Court rejected this by reason of its own doctrinal construction of a "constitutional criminal law," that is, the primary need for legal security deriving from the constitutional principle of "the rule of law." A few years later, German and Czech laws, and the Czech Constitutional Court's assessment of the latter declared that lapse of time was a procedural question, which removed it from under the original prohibition against their retroactive force.

On the merits, however, neither law considered it justifiable to apply the limitation period, which presumes a rule of law, in conditions which actually deny any rule of law. The Czech Constitutional Court decision unambiguously declares:

> If we interpret the time passed since the commission of these crimes as a prescription period . . . this would be equivalent to confirming the "legal security" which the perpetrators had from the very beginning of their activity, and which was actually incorporated into their official immunity from prosecution. The "legal security" of the perpetrators, in this sense, would be equivalent to the legal insecurity of the citizens. . . . Any solution different than this would inevitably mean that the regime of totalitarian dictatorship receives a certification for its "rule of law"; this would create a dangerous precedent for the future. More precisely, this would confirm that crime can go unpunished, if and insofar as it is committed in mass proportions, is well-organized, lasts for a long time, and falls under the protection of state authorization.

References

Fuller, Lon L. *The Morality of Law*. New Haven: Yale University Press, 1964.

Golding, Martin P. "Retroactive Legislation and Restoration of the Rule of Law." *Annual Review of Law and Ethics* (1990), 128.

Gray, John Chipman. *The Nature and Sources of the Law*. 2d ed. 1921. New York: Macmillan, 1948.

Hart, H.L.A. "Positivism and the Separation of Law and Morals." *Harvard Law Review* 71 (1958), 593.

Lyons, David. *Ethics and the Rule of Law*. Cambridge: Cambridge University Press, 1984.

Radbruch, Gustav. *Rechtsphilosophie* (Philosophy of Law). 4th ed. 1946. Stuttgart: Koehler, 1950.

Somló, Felix. *Juristische Grundlehre* (Basic Law Doctrine). Leipzig: Meiner, 1917.

Summers, Robert S. *Lon L. Fuller*. London: Arnold, 1984.

Varga, Casaba, ed. *Coming to Terms with the Past under the Rule of Law: The German and the Czech Models*. Budapest: Windsor Klub, 1994.

———. *Transition to Rule of Law*. Budapest: Loránd Eötvös University Project on Comparative Legal Cultures, 1995.

Csaba Varga

See also PROMULGATION; RULE OF LAW

Exchange
See SALE

Exculpation
See IMPUTATION AND EXCULPATION

Exegetical School

The exegetical school of jurisprudence was predominant during the nineteenth century in France and Belgium. These two countries maintained the Napoleonic civil code without interruption. As a consequence, a homogeneous school of legal scholars was formed around a set of principles concerning the sources of law and statutory interpretation. This homogeneity was far less the case in other European continental countries such as Italy, Spain, and Germany, where a comprehensive civil code was introduced only toward the end of the century.

The exegetical school was first perceived as a school in 1899 by François Gény (1861–1959), who called the approach of the nineteenth-century French legal doctrine *la méthode traditionnelle* and criticized this approach vehemently in his famous work *Méthode d'interprétation et sources en droit privé positif*. The school owes its name to Emile Glasson, in his commemorative speech of the centenary of the civil code.

The origins of the exegetical school coincide with the enactment of the Napoleonic code in 1804. This event meant no less than a revolution concerning the sources of French law. Before the codification, legal sources were multiple, such as customary law, Roman law, royal decrees, urban law and judge-made law. This multiplicity allowed legal scholars and judges some intellectual discretion in the development of practical legal solutions. The promulgation of the code, however, was regarded by the legal scholars as a profound change of their mission. Under the regime of the code, it was the lawyers' task to put the code into operation by commenting and interpreting its provisions. In the further development of the exegetical school, three phases can be distinguished. In the period of formation (1804–1830), legal scholars, still educated under the ancien régime, remained predominant. Their works still attach much importance to the prerevolutionary sources of the code. Important authors of this period were Merlin, Toullier, Pierre-Joseph Proudhon, and Demante. Second, in the period of culmination (1830–1880), most authors followed the exegetical canon, as explained in the subsequent discussion. Here, the most famous legal scholars of nineteenth-century France and Belgium have to be mentioned: C. Aubry, F. Rau, Demolombe, Troplong, Laurent, and Mourlon. In the period of decline (1880–1900), several reputed authors deviated from the exegetical canons. Bufnoir for instance, devoted much attention in his teaching to comparative law and economics. Charles Beudant considered customary law as a full-fledged source of law. Raymond Saleilles was in favor of a less exegetical, and more flexible interpretation of the law. He wrote the preface to Gény's already mentioned famous work, which meant the beginning of the end of the school.

The theory of legal sources of the exegetical school was dominated by the conviction that the written law was by far the major source of the law. Most authors defined the law in a merely formal way, that is, the law as the expression of the will of the constitutionally competent body. To this, the older, more substantial notion of the law as a general rule of conduct had to give way. The written law was also regarded as the nearly exclusive source of the law. Article 4 of the Code Civil provided that incompleteness or obscurity of the statutes did not constitute an excuse for a denial of justice. According to the intent of the authors of the code, this article implied that the judge had to complete the written law with other sources, such as natural and customary law. Many authors of the exegetical school, however, taught that any action that had no base in a statute should be dismissed and that such a dismissal did not constitute a denial of justice.

All authors of the exegetical school expressed their faith in a suprapositive natural law, to which the legislator owed full respect. The philosophical origin of their natural law views varied greatly: some were of a Christian thomistic inspiration, others were lockean, still others were hegelian. Their allegiance to natural law, however, did not alter their unconditional recognition of the written law as the decisive source of positive law. The natural law was considered to be too vague to serve as a criterion for the practical decision of the judge. Natural law principles needed to be specified by the positive legislation. As most authors of the school thought that most natural law principles were elaborated in the civil code, positive law was nearly completely identified with natural law. In this respect, the exegetical school marks an important step between revolutionary natural law thinking of the French revolution and legal positivism of the beginning of the twentieth century. While the French revolutionaries regarded natural law as the most important source of law, which needed, however, the written law as its institutional expression, the authors of the exegetical school thought that the written law was the most important source of law, because it embodied natural law. This cleared the way for full legal positivism, which considers only positive law as real law, while natural law is assimilated with morals.

The authors of the school were also hostile to customary law and rejected the possibility that a statute could lose its validity through general contradictory practice (desuetude). Also, the role of precedent as a source of law was minimized. The emphasis was put on the role of the judge as a solver of legal conflicts. The judge was supposed to apply the principles embodied in the written law to facts. Precedents were in this respect of little use for other cases. The principles could be found in the legislation, whereas the facts differed so much from case to case that it was impossible to draw analogies between cases.

In spite of its name, suggesting a textual rigidity concerning statutory interpretation, the exegetical school allowed for a rich variety of methods of statutory interpretation. Although most authors stressed that clear texts did not require further explanation (*interpretatio cessat in claris*), they also recognized that often the texts of the civil code were ambivalent and that further research was needed to unveil the true intent of the legislator. To discover this true intent, several methods of interpretation were recommended. Thanks to several editions of the preparatory works of the civil code, which were complete and reliable, many authors made full use of the analysis of these editions in search of the real will of the legislator. The authors of the exegetical school made also full use of the so-called logical interpretation, which included arguments such as analogy, strict interpretation of exceptions, *a contrario* (by contrast) reasoning, and *a fortiori* (by excess) reasoning. Especially toward the end of the century, the authors increasingly used analogy to develop theoretical constructions, allowing for a wider application of the texts. Although much less elaborate, the French exegetical school can be compared in this respect with the German *Begriffsjurisprudenz* during the nineteenth century.

Concerning the internal structure of their works, two methods can be distinguished. In the older works from the first half of the century, the method of the *commentaire* was rigidly followed. The code was commented upon, article by article, and each article was related to other articles. In the second half of the century the method of the *traité* became popular. The author emancipated himself from the order of articles within the code and reorganized the legal materials around theoretical notions. The most famous authors of such a *traité* were C. Aubry and F. Rau, who taught for decades in Strasbourg and were inspired by German authors such as Zachariae. In many respects they deserve to be regarded as the founders of modern French jurisprudence.

References

Arnaud, A.J. *Les Juristes face à la société du XIXe siècle à nos jours* (Jurists and Society from the Nineteenth Century to the Present). Paris: Presses universitaires de France, 1975.

Aubry, C., and F. Rau. *Cours de Droit Civil Français* (The Study of French Civil Law). 6th ed. Paris: Marchal et Billard, 1897.

Bonnecase, J. *L'école de l'exégèse en droit civil* (The Exegetical School of Civil Law). Paris: E. de Brocard, 1924.

———. *La Faculté de Droit de Strassbourg. Ses maîtres et ses doctrines: Sa Contribution à la science juridique Française du dix-neuvième siècle* (The Strassbourg Law Faculty: Its Staff, Research, and Contribution to Nineteenth-Century French Legal Science). Toulouse: E. Privat, 1916.

Bouckaert, B. *De Exegetische School. Een kritische studie van de rechtsbronnen- en interpretatieleer bij de 19de eeuwse commentatoren van de Code Civil* (The Exegetical School: A Critical Study of the Legal Doctrine and Interpretation of Nineteenth-Century Commentary on the Civil Code). Antwerp: Kluwer, 1981.

Charmont, J., and C. Chausse. "Les interprètes du Code Civil" (The Civil Code's Interpreters). In *Le Code Civil: Livre du Centenaire*, vol. 2, 763–777. Paris: A. Rousseau, 1904.

Gény, F. *Méthode d'interprétation et Sources en droit privé positif* (Method of Interpretation and Sources of Positive Private Law). 2d ed. Paris: Librairie Générale de Droit et Jurisprudence, 1932.

Glasson, E. "Le centenaire du Code Civil" (Centennary of the Civil Code). *Dalloz Périodique,* supplément (1904).

Rémy, P. "Eloge de l'exégèse" (In Praise of Exegesis). *Droits* (1984), 115–123.

Boudwijn Bouckaert

Existentialist Philosophy of Law

The existentialist style of philosophizing flourishing in Europe around the 1940s and 1950s takes the self in its concrete human existence as its starting point and subject matter, instead of either the world or nature. In its lexicon, "existence" refers primarily to the human self conceived as relating itself to the world and experiencing in that relation tension, tragic conflicts, or deep inward suffering. The self initiates that relation by choosing its own courses of action, contrasted to drifting in its conduct with an impersonal public or institutionalized system of values. Choice is a crucial concept connected with this view of self. By exercising choice, the self in becoming transparent to itself begins to be aware of possibilities, which it is free to actualize, and of itself as being more than a mere thinking subject and as having a range of emotions, feelings, and moods.

Existential philosophers draw attention to this new way of viewing the human emotions and understanding by describing the various modes of concrete human existence. They rely on phenomenology as a method in their descriptive accounts; these accounts underscore the fact that humans are free to choose not only what to do on specific occasions but also what to value and how to live as part of their experiences of freedom. Recurrent themes in their writings further distinguish existentialist philosophy, which begins with the existent self. These include freedom, decision, responsibility, finitude, alienation, guilt, despair, and death. Though the style developed primarily among the French and Germans, the writings of the Spanish thinker Miguel de Unamuno and the Russian Nikolay Berdyaev show evidence of it.

Existentialists such as Jean-Paul Sartre, Albert Camus, Martin Heidegger, Karl Jaspers, Gabriel Marcel, Martin Buber, and Maurice Merleau-Ponty are diverse in their approach and choice of themes and in the extent of their reliance on Edmund Husserl's phenomenology. Though their styles indicate two strands of existentialism, all have for their intellectual ancestry Søren Kierkegaard and Friedrich Nietzsche whose writings stand as protests against the established order, oppose a universalizable or rule-governed morality, and connect truth with subjectivity or inwardness. These two nineteenth-century figures share a common cultural-religious situation against which they rebelled, a situation characterized by a social morality that was espoused by hegelian philosophy and endorsed by christendom. In fact, Nietzsche's reaction to his situation is a continuity on many points to the trend that Kierkegaard saw in its nascent phase.

Kierkegaard, prototype of the existential thinker and the first European thinker to carry the label of existentialism, urges a connection between life and thought. He employs in his writings the idea of individual or exceptional person (illustrated by the biblical personages Abraham and Job) as a major category in connection with the possibility for authentic human existence or with truth as inwardness. G.W.F. Hegel's system of philosophy, in Kierkegaard's estimate, reduced to absurdity the existing subject. For Kierkegaard, the subject has a reality that is its very own ethical reality and that it acquires through choosing itself and becoming responsible for its own condition. Kierkegaard's *Concluding Unscientific Postscript* and other writings depict possibilities for the self's own determination of itself (arousal and deepening of its self-consciousness) through three overlapping existent spheres: the aesthetic, the ethical, and the religious. These spheres suggest a development of the self to its full humanity and possibilities for existing at different levels of adequacy. At each level or sphere the self can exercise personal freedom and thereby occasion either deeper despair or lapse into its jejune self and thus shut itself up, as described in *Sickness Unto Death*, or *Concept of Anxiety*. The self has the possibility to break out from its shutupness or to be helped with its experiencing of a deeper despair in becoming truly human. Either possibility requires that the self moves toward transcendence, reliance on God's help, according to Kierkegaard. Theism is the capstone of Kierkegaard's thought. He is followed by Marcel and Buber as representatives of a theistic strand.

Nietzsche, in contrast, represents a nihilistic strand, which his axiomatic atheism reflects. He holds in *Good and Evil* and *Zarathustra* that humans are not bound to conventional morality, that they can choose a different set of values, and that they ought to so. Anyone who unthinkingly accepts moral opinions as if they were either facts or inevitable lives in bad faith, according to Nietzsche and to Sartre. For both of these thinkers, to realize that one is free to choose values is to become enlightened. Nietzsche's counsel is to remain true to the earth, to sweep away reliance on transcendence, for God is dead. Nietzsche's turn suggests a self-affirmation against the background of an absurd world that occasions an existential anguish, nihilism, or limiting situations of life. Jaspers and Heidegger are less pessimistic. In precisely the limiting situations, according to Jaspers, the reality of transcendence becomes open to the person; that is, there is an encompassing disclosure embracing both subject and object, which is different from either subjective attitude or from the subject-object pattern associated with technical knowledge. He tends toward nihilism by contending that transcendence speaks through a language of ciphers. Heidegger, too, discloses a similar tendency, even though he found Kierkegaard's edifying discourses profitable, by speaking of an anguish that leads to nothingness itself, which for him is, ultimately, being itself.

Awareness of being robbed of our "humanness" engenders in response an existentialist style of thinking or writing. This crisis looms in situations of conflicting cultural trends, stifling social norms, ideological repression—intellectual, moral, spiritual, or social—or with the pervasive triumph of science

E

and technology according to the analysis of Jaspers in *Man in the Modern Age*. In responding to our sense of malaise, alienation, and discontent, especially in the latter half of the twentieth century, existentialism has had a major impact in various disciplines: psychology, psychiatry, ethics, theology, and literature. The voices of legal minds such as that of Justice Oliver Wendell Holmes, Jr., and former Harvard Law School dean Roscoe Pound evidence a note of discontent with respect to the jural situation, especially the predominant influence of legal positivism vis-à-vis social controversies. The emergence of issues such as poverty, racism, minority rights, immigration, terrorism, and the harvesting and marketing of human organs for transplants has increased concern over values and the right of the legal subject as an existent individual. Implicit in the attempt to deal with these issues in a humane way is a recognition of the legal subject as a self that is conscious of making choices with respect to values that are meaningful to it.

Existential themes relevant to jurisprudence include absurdity, truth as ethical reality, and choice. Franz Kafka's *The Trial*, about a man suddenly dragged to the court who cannot discover the nature of the charge against him, states the problem of absurdity that a legal system raises, the anguish that comes to a mind threatened by the senselessness of a juridical process, and the importance of confronting that process at the core of our subjectivity. The challenge of jurisprudence, understood as a search for meaning and value in the law, requires broadening the focus of our intentionality to include consciousness of ourselves concerning real assent to final decisions and constitutional maxims, in the areas of justice and rights within community life. Put differently, the search for objective truth in a system of jurisprudence is to be found through a genuine subjectivity or inwardness requiring not merely intellectual assent but also passionate moral commitment, choice, and self-appropriation.

Current literature relating to jurisprudence discloses a tendency to annex the insights of existentialism, or the language of subjectivity. The Italian legal scholar Giorgio Del Vecchio in his 1956 work *Justice: An Historical and Philosophical Essay* holds that justice is a mode of consciousness reflecting a special kind of relationship between persons, and that in becoming aware of themselves the subjects are also aware of that which is not the subject. The subject or self is crucial also for critical legal studies, a new version of legal realism appearing in the last two decades and evidenced by Roberto M. Unger in *Knowledge and Politics*. This growing recognition of the existential subject with respect to human dignity is found also in 1976 by Judge John T. Noonan, Jr., in *Persons and Masks of the Law*. Finally, a case for the centrality of subjectivity with respect to appropriating legal meaning and value is made in 1988 by David Granfield in *The Inner Experience of Law: A Jurisprudence of Subjectivity*, which draws on Kierkegaard's insights about truth as subjectivity.

References

Collins, James. *The Existentialists*. Chicago: Gateway Edition, 1952.

Macquarrie, John. *Existentialism*. New York: Penguin Books, 1972.

Warnock, Mary. *Existentialism*. Oxford: Oxford University Press, 1970.

Abrahim H. Khan

Exploitation

There seems to be a consensus that exploitation is the taking of unfair advantage of the needs or problems of the innocent. A standard example would be luring a person unemployed through no fault of her own into prostitution by offering her money when no other source of money is available. Exploitation seems distinct from coercion, since exploitation can clearly involve offers that increase the options of the offeree, whereas coercion seems to reduce the options of the person coerced or at least make those coerced worse off.

There are at least three camps that disagree with the consensus. The first camp tries to show that exploitation involves a lack of reciprocity rather than unfairness. However, fairness seems to be such a broad concept that it can encompass reciprocity.

The second camp tries to show that exploitation involves degradation rather than unfairness. Again, fairness seems broad enough to cover the degradation involved in an undeserved lack of respect.

The third camp is by far the most important. It consists primarily of marxists who wish to use Karl Marx's concept of exploitation while interpreting Marx as avoiding any essential reliance on moral concepts. The idea of unfair advantage in the consensus' definition of exploitation is a moral concept. The nonmoral interpretation of Marx is important for many marxists, since they see morality as mere bourgeois morality, and ethic tainted by its genesis in the ruling class. Even some marxists have noted that this view of morality seems to commit an *ad hominem* or genetic fallacy. Many other marxists see Marx's use of moral terms as an endorsement of some morality other than bourgeois morality. So marxists need not insist on a completely nonmoral definition of exploitation. Marx's view of exploitation is based on the labor theory of value. The capitalist takes surplus value as profit from the value that the worker has put in the product or service through labor. Thus capitalists allegedly exploit every worker, since the capitalist takes out of the sale value that only the worker put into the product or service sold.

The marxist conception of exploitation is objectionable on at least two grounds. First, one could follow G.A. Cohen in rejecting Marx's labor theory of value as "a terrible incubus on progressive reflection about exploitation," although key capitalists such as Adam Smith also accept it. Second, Cohen's marxist alternative giving the capitalist no credit for the creation of value is objectionable. After all, capitalists choose investments, survey consumers' demands, organize production, defer consumption, raise more capital, oversee personnel departments, and so forth. N. Arnold and P. Warren counter that this is not work the capitalist does as a capitalist. This counterargument seems to fail for two reasons. First, Arnold and Warren give no reasons to sustain this extremely sharp distinction between the capitalist as laborer and the capitalist as capitalist. The examples of capitalist work above seem to be exactly the sort of entrepreneurial activity one expects capitalists to do. Arnold and Warren could argue that capitalists do not do all this activity themselves but hire others to do it. Many capitalists hire others to either do or help with this work. Even hiring or overseeing a personnel department is work. Arnold and Warren seem to reduce the capitalist as capitalist to a passive phantom who gets something for nothing. This reductionist and essentialist conception of the capitalist makes the capitalist too much of an apparition to allow Marx's portrayal of capi-

talists as the active oppressors of billions of people every day in a class struggle. Second, Arnold and Warren would lump capitalists together with the working class just to save the marxist concept of exploitation. However, the cost of this would be to undermine the fundamental class divisions, struggle, and conflict of Marx's view, for it would imply that we already have a virtually classless society under capitalism, since even the capitalists are essentially laborers in everything they do. It is the relationship to the means of production, not the amount of one's income, that categorizes a person as a capitalist or worker.

Exploitation is a key concept in philosophy of law because it is at the heart of the marxist understanding of the evil of capitalism, a system where the state and its laws are allegedly no more than crucial instruments of oppression. However, the concept of exploitation has a much broader use beyond marxism. It is an everyday concept of ordinary voters in a democracy, a concept that helps them decide a range of issues from whether the police are abusing their power, to whether the minimum wage should be raised, to whether surrogate motherhood contracts should be legally enforced, to whether we should wage a war on drugs. In these four areas, and many more, opportunism seems to lead some to exploit by preying on the needs and problems of others.

References

Arnold, N. Scott. "Equality and Exploitation in the Market Socialist Community." In *Economic Rights,* ed. Ellen Frankel Paul, Fred D. Miller, Jr., and Jeffrey Paul, 1–28. Cambridge: Cambridge University Press, 1992.

Cohen, G.A. "More on Exploitation and the Labor Theory of Value." *Inquiry* 26 (1983), 309–331.

Cohen, Howard. "Exploiting Police Authority." *Criminal Justice Ethics* 5 (1986), 23–31.

Feinberg, Joel. "Noncoercive Exploitation." In *Paternalism,* ed. Rolf Sartorius. Minneapolis: University of Minnesota Press, 1983.

Gorr, Michael J. *Coercion, Freedom and Exploitation.* New York: Peter Lang, 1989.

Marx, Karl. *Capital.* Vol. 1. Moscow: Progress Publishers, 1977.

Roemer, John E. *Free to Lose: An Introduction to Marxist Economic Philosophy.*

E

Cambridge MA: Harvard University Press, 1988.

Wertheimer, Alan. "Two Questions About Surrogacy and Exploitation." *Philosophy and Public Affairs* 21 (1992), 211–239.

Wood, Allen W. "Exploitation." In *The Just Society,* ed. Ellen Frankel Paul, Fred D. Miller, Jr., and Jeffrey Paul, 136–158. Cambridge: Cambridge University Press, 1995.

Young, Iris M. "Five Faces of Oppression." *Philosophical Forum* 19 (1988), 270–290.

Sterling Harwood

See also COERCION (DURESS)

Expressive Rationale for Punishment

Theories focusing on the expressive nature or function of punishment claim that punishment is not hard treatment (pain, suffering, deprivation) *simpliciter,* but conveys an important social message. The main varieties of expressionism in the philosophy of punishment (the term was introduced by A.J. Skillen) can best be set out in terms of two distinctions: descriptive/normative and extrinsic/intrinsic.

Descriptive and Normative Expressionism

One can *describe* or *analyze* punishment as expressive without thereby also justifying it as such. Joel Feinberg's influential paper is an example of a normatively neutral analysis of punishment as "a conventional device for the expression of attitudes of resentment and indignation, and of judgments of disapproval and reprobation, on the part either of the punishing authority himself or of those 'in whose name' the punishment is inflicted." In addition to deterrence and reform, punishment has some important functions that are made possible only by its expressive potential: vindication of the law, authoritative disavowal of the crime, symbolic nonacquiescence in it, and absolution of those who could otherwise be suspected of having committed it. On the other hand, one can also *justify* punishment as expressive.

Extrinsic and Intrinsic Expressionism

Normative expressionism has two varieties. One can justify punishment as expressive either by arguing that the expression has certain *effects* that justify it, or that it is appropriate and justified *in itself.* J.F. Stephen argues that

punishment expresses moral indignation at the crime committed and hatred of its perpetrator (this hatred being natural, healthy, and morally appropriate). It also ratifies these feelings, provides satisfaction for them, and makes sure they are not vented in socially unregulated and disruptive ways. This expressive function of punishment complements and reinforces its other main function, deterrence: disgrace involved in the condemnation deters.

In A.C. Ewing's "educative theory," punishment is both a symbol of the wickedness of crime and an expression of its emphatic moral condemnation by society. It has two aims: to help the criminal realize the wrongness of his act and change his ways, as well as to bring home to the public at large just how morally wrong crime is. Since the ultimate aim is crime prevention, the effect on the public is much more important than that on the criminal. Ewing sees this contribution of punishment to the moral education of the public as its main justification.

Extrinsic expressionism is actually a variety of utilitarianism and is therefore exposed to some of the standard arguments against it. The preferred aim of all theories of this type can under certain circumstances be achieved by merely apparent justice, such as "punishment" of the innocent; in such cases, these theories would justify such "punishment." Intrinsic expressionism would not, since it claims that punishment as the expression of society's emphatic moral condemnation of crime is appropriate and justified in itself. In expressing this condemnation, punishment vindicates the law that has been broken, reaffirms the right that has been violated, and demonstrates that its violation was indeed a crime. This must be distinguished from crime prevention, which is not inherent to punishment, but rather something distinct from it and achieved by means of it. The vindication of the law, reaffirmation of the right, and demonstration that the action was a crime *are* inherent to this punishment; we do not do that *by,* but *in* punishing. The relation of punishment to these tasks is not empirical and instrumental, but rather internal, conceptual. If there are to be rights sanctioned by the criminal law, if some actions are to be crimes, if there is to be criminal law at all, there must be punishment. Intrinsic expressionism offers a backward-looking justification of punishment and is therefore cognate to the retributive theory.

A standard objection to this type of expressionism is that it still has to be shown that society's condemnation should take the form of hard treatment. The reply to this would be that merely verbal condemnation is not likely to be fully understood and appreciated by the criminal, nor by the public at large. The radical dissimilarity and disproportion between the crime and society's condemnation of it would rather suggest that neither the crime, nor the right violated and the law broken, are taken very seriously.

R.A. Duff's theory of punishment straddles the extrinsic/intrinsic, utilitarian/retributive division. Punishment is expressive, retributive, and reformative. It conveys society's blame to the criminal. However, this blame has a goal: to bring about understanding and acceptance by the criminal of the blame and of punishment as its appropriate expression. That will bring remorse and acceptance of the hard treatment as self-imposed penance. This penance both assists and expresses for the criminal and for others his or her understanding of the wrongness of the crime, repentance, and desire for reform and reconciliation to the community and to the values flouted by the crime. Because the goal is not moral reform *simpliciter* (that could be achieved by nonrational methods, too), but rather moral reform of a rational and autonomous being (that is, the criminal's rational and autonomous understanding of the moral character of the crime), it can be achieved only by punishment that expresses appropriate, deserved blame. The goal of punishment is not a utilitarian one, but rather a goal internally and conceptually related to the sole means by which it can be achieved.

Duff's theory is an effective combination of backward- and forward-looking considerations and is therefore immune to the objections advanced against extrinsic expressionism. However, it does not convincingly explain why either fully repentant or hopelessly unrepentant criminals should be punished. Another recent expressionist theory, that of Andrew von Hirsch, has a more plausible answer to these questions. Punishment is primarily an expression of society's censure of crime. The censure addresses the victim and acknowledges that the hurt suffered is due to another's fault. It is also addressed to the criminal: it condemns the act and invites an appropriate moral response of the agent. However, unlike Duff, von Hirsch does not consider punishment a method of achieving such response. According to P.F. Strawson, condemnation is the appropriate "reactive attitude" to wrongdoing, and its expression is the appropriate retort, whether or not it will evoke the proper response on the part of the wrongdoer. It is justified intrinsically, rather than as a means of bringing about the desired response by the criminal. Finally, the condemnation addresses third parties: it gives them a moral reason for desisting from wrongdoing.

Such communication of judgment and feeling is inherent to discourse among moral agents. Since humans are imperfect moral agents, liable to be seriously tempted to break moral and legal rules, punishment has a preventive function, too: in addition to the moral reason for desisting it provides by expressing society's condemnation of crime, it also supplies a prudential reason for desisting by threatening hard treatment if one does not. This latter function is strictly secondary: it is not allowed to operate on its own in settling questions of the distribution of punishment. All such questions—who may and who ought to be punished, and how much—are answered in terms of appropriate, deserved censure. On the other hand, von Hirsch's two-pronged justification of punishment, unlike intrinsic expressionism, would allow the abolition of the institution of punishment if it were to prove inefficient as a means of crime prevention.

References

Duff, R.A. *Trials and Punishments*. Cambridge: Cambridge University Press, 1986.

Ewing, A.C. *The Morality of Punishment*. London: Kegan Paul, Trench, Trubner, 1929. Reprint, Montclair NJ: Patterson-Smith, 1970.

Feinberg, Joel. "The Expressive Function of Punishment." The *Monist* 49 (1965), 397–423. Reprinted in several anthologies, including *Philosophy of Law*. Ed. Joel Feinberg and Hyman Gross. 5th ed. Belmont CA: Wadsworth, 1995.

Kleinig, John. "Punishment and Moral Seriousness." *Israel Law Review* 25 (1991), 401–421.

Primoratz, Igor. "Punishment as Language." *Philosophy* 64 (1989), 187–205. Reprinted in *Philosophy of Law*. Ed. Joel Feinberg and Hyman Gross. 5th ed. Belmont CA: Wadsworth, 1995.

E

Skillen, A.J. "How to Say Things with Walls." *Philosophy* 55 (1980), 509–523.

Stephen, James Fitzjames. *A History of the Criminal Law of England*. Vol. 2. London: Macmillan, 1883.

Strawson, P.F. "Freedom and Resentment." *Proceedings of the British Academy* 48 (1962), 1–25. Reprinted in several anthologies, including Strawson's *Freedom and Resentment and Other Essays*. London: Methuen, 1974.

Von Hirsch, Andrew. *Censure and Sanctions*. Oxford: Clarendon Press, 1993.

Igor Primoratz

See also DETERRENT RATIONALE; MIXED RATIONALES; PUNISHMENT; RETRIBUTIVE RATIONALE

F

Facts and Law

Law seems to consist of norms and thus seems to be clearly different from facts. Such a simple distinction will not do, however. Many kinds of disputed relationships between facts and law are predominant in main themes in the philosophy of law, from adjudication to positivism versus natural law theory and the philosophy of punishment. Five of them may be most important. None of these interdependent relationships seems to allow for clear-cut separation of facts and law.

First, law is "petrified" in institutions, unlike morality and other systems of norms. In modern legal orders, there is some form of legislature, there is a body of administration, including police, and there are courts. Though legal institutions depend upon legal rules, their tangible qualities set them apart from "law in the books." Such institutions are factual parts of legal, political, and social reality. On the other hand, such institutional facts are different from "brute" facts not determined by rules, like trees and stars. Such conceptions are not limited to legal institutions like the police and the courts, though few if any institutions in modern society can be explained in exclusively nonlegal terms. Also, such institutions are generally thought to be amenable to functional or teleological explanation in terms of legal rules and principles. For example, explanations of what a legislature is will refer to the meanings, functions, or ends of legislature in society. Purely factual, causal explanations are not excluded, then, but are thought to be accessory. Thus a sociological or politicological explanation of changes in the legislature in terms of increasing representation by former administration officials, caused by their close relationships with politicians, may be interesting and important but may not replace functional or teleological explanation.

Second, general rules of law are to be applied to particular facts in reality, in conduct governed by rules of law and, ultimately, in adjudication. Though most lawful conduct will not be guided by rational consciousness of legal rules and their factual implications, increasing complexity of facts and legal rules requires increasing legal rationality. The world of facts is structured by legal rules: not all facts are relevant from a legal point of view. Specific cases or conflicts may further limit the realm of relevant facts. Also, facts must be interpreted in terms of relevant law, just as interpretation of law is partly determined by relevant facts. Indeed, most modern conceptions of adjudication reject formalism or conceptualism as implying strict relationships between legal rules and facts determining their application. More or less fruitful circular relationships between interpretation of legal rules and interpretation of facts have been suggested in hermeneutical and dialectical conceptions of adjudication. Other conceptions acknowledge such circularity, but stress distinctions between (circular, hermeneutical, dialectical) contexts of discovery and (logical) contexts of justification.

Third, law sets factual limits to and possibilities for action, comparable to physical and mental facts, dispositions, and risks. Factual threats and risks of punishment and other sanctions, like damages, determine at least part of lawful conduct, though such conduct cannot be based upon threats and risks of punishment only. Lawful behavior is in large part determined by tradition, custom, and social control. Citizens and officials may conscientiously try to obey and develop the law or they may just calculate risks in terms of self-interests and probability of legal sanctions. Constitutional, administrative, and civil law not only sanction misconduct but also create possibilities for action, like legislation and contract. Such lawful conduct may only be indirectly sanctioned by state force, if at all.

Fourth, facts about human beings and society make up at least part of the content of law. Law as we know it would not be needed if man were invulnerable, if natural resources were inexhaustible, and if human beings were completely reliable, among other factors. Such basic facts at least necessitate prohibition of manslaughter and protection of property and contract. As ought implies can, law and its administration need to conform to human possibilities and predilections. Thus nobody may be held legally responsible for conduct outside his powers. Also, law and its administration are partly determined by facts like ever-changing conceptions of the good and the right among citizens, by way of election for legislatures and by other political and social processes and developments.

Fifth, the facts of the world change as a consequence of all kinds of conduct in and according to the law. Law would make no sense if this could not be taken for granted. This is of course implicit in all relationships between facts and law. Criticism of law based upon marxism, critical legal studies, or other radical conceptions implies that this last point is overestimated, as it argues that law is essentially a by-product of underlying socioeconomic forces. Such criticism may also imply some kind of determinism and may deny free will as a basic presupposition of law and its administration.

Apart from such specific relationships, there remains the underlying abstract question whether law can be explained in terms of or even reduced to facts in one or another way. Legal positivism explains law in terms of kinds of facts, whereas natural law theories emphasize the normative or even moral character of law. Modern discussion on this started with the distinction between "is" and "ought." Related doubts on the status of anything not factual led to attempts to explain legal rules in terms of empirical facts. Such varieties of legal positivism, from John Austin in the nineteenth century to the Scandinavian school in the

twentieth century, are no longer held to be plausible. Varieties of American legal realism may also be interpreted as reductionist ("law is what judges do," though this is a slight simplification of realist conceptions), as may be varieties of critical legal studies ("law as exponent of underlying socioeconomic inequalities," a slight simplification again).

Contemporary debate takes it for granted that law cannot be completely reduced to facts in one or another way. Discussion between legal positivism, as expounded by H.L.A. Hart and others, and normative or even moral conceptions of law, like Ronald Dworkin's, center on the question of whether the existence and validity of legal rules and principles partly depend upon actual obedience or whether there may be legal principles not observed by anyone yet but valid in a sense, because they make up an as yet undiscovered part of the whole of the law.

John Finnis and other contemporary representatives of the natural law tradition stress the necessity of functional, teleological conceptions of law. For example, a judge cannot consistently conceive of the court's office as a set of purely factual occasions for instrumentalist or even self-interested use. Such "parasitic" use presupposes an antecedent legal teleological conception of the concept of a court and of law in general. This is closely related to the institutional nature of law mentioned previously.

Also, contemporary natural law theories stress the importance of human needs and qualities as essentially nonfactual, normative qualities determining part of the content of law. Such aristotelian conceptions of human beings and law are increasingly popular outside natural law traditions, too. They are fostered by general doubts about the sense of purely factual approaches to man and society.

References

Altman, A. *Critical Legal Studies: A Liberal Critique*. Princeton: Princeton University Press, 1989.

Dworkin, R.M. *Law's Empire*. Cambridge MA: Harvard University Press, 1986.

Finnis, J. *Natural Law and Natural Rights*. Oxford: Oxford University Press, 1980.

Fuller, L.L. *The Morality of Law*. 1964. New Haven: Yale University Press, 1969.

Hart, H.L.A. *The Concept of Law*. 1961. Oxford: Clarendon Press, 1994.

Nussbaum, M.C. "Human Functioning and Social Justice." *Political Theory* 20 (1992).

Searle, J.R. *The Construction of Social Reality.* New York: Free Press, 1995.

Weber, M. *Max Weber on Law in Economy and Society.* Ed. M. Rheinstein. Cambridge MA: Harvard University Press, 1969.

Winch, P. *The Idea of a Social Science and Its Relation to Philosophy.* London: Routledge and Kegan Paul, 1958.

Hendrik Kaptein

Fairness

A highly valued moral property of institutions, arrangements, and activities, fairness concerns the propriety of their distribution of benefits and burdens. The fairness of distributions can be at issue in either the distributive process, the outcome of the distributive process, or both; and the benefits or burdens whose distributions are evaluated in terms of fairness can range from the trivial (for instance, victory in a children's game) to the vitally important (for example, basic rights and duties, legal awards or punishments). In the philosophy of law, the concept of fairness has been most importantly employed in discussions of the justice of basic legal and political institutions, the evaluation of legal proceedings and decisions, and the analysis of the citizen's obligation to obey the law.

The Concept of Fairness

Fairness is one kind of right-ordering of distributive processes, and it is strongly associated with related virtues like equality, proportionality, impartiality, and justice. Questions about fairness typically arise in contexts involving social cooperation aimed at producing mutually beneficial results. What counts as fair in such contexts is generally relative to the specific context at issue, though fairness almost always involves treating people equally or treating them differently only in proportion to their relevant differences. Sometimes what makes an activity or process fair is determined by the point of pursuing the activity or by the "distributive intent." Thus, races or fights are fair when conducted so that the results (the benefits and burdens) will as far as possible reflect the abilities displayed by the contestants. Sometimes activities or processes are called fair or

unfair independent of their likelihood of producing a particular kind of outcome, as when a distributive process is said to be fair simply by virtue of being freely agreed to by all who are subject to it (for example, when parties determine distributive outcomes by freely subjecting themselves to an honest game of chance or to an acceptable arbitrator). In addition to distributive processes themselves, it is common to call both the outcomes of such processes and persons involved in the processes fair or unfair. However, these latter uses are normally linked to the fairness of the process, an unfair outcome being one that flows from an unfair process, and a fair person being one who is disposed to control or participate in distributive processes in ways that make them fair.

Social Justice

The basic structure of a society comprises its most important distributive institutions, including the legal and political practices that distribute to members their rights, duties, incomes, power, legal sanctions, compensations, and so forth. The justice or injustice of a society is most clearly revealed in the character of these distributive institutions; social justice, it has been argued, is best understood in terms of the related notion of fairness. The connection between fairness and justice is most explicitly affirmed in John Rawls' theory of "justice as fairness." Principles of justice are for Rawls a kind of fair compromise; these principles express the mutuality and noncoercive character of a true community. More specifically, if we imagine a fair initial situation in which free and equal persons bargain about the principles to guide the basic institutions of their society, the principles of justice are those which would be chosen. Justice can be thought of as the result of a hypothetical agreement among individuals who are fairly situated. The many critics of Rawls' important work have seldom attacked the connection between justice and fairness, concentrating rather on claims that neither the initial situation nor the resultant principles described by Rawls are in fact fair to all. More specific questions of legal justice have also been debated in these terms, such as the fairness of adversary versus inquisitorial systems or fault versus no-fault systems.

Legal Fairness

Fairness is an important virtue not only of legal systems and general legal principles but also of specific legal proceedings and decisions, such as trials, settlements, and awards. Legal proceedings should be subject to the constraints of procedural legal fairness. Procedural fairness is best understood as composed of three main elements. The first is control and decision making by a fair umpire or judge. A fair umpire must be a person or group, neutral in the case at issue, which acts in an unbiased and impartial fashion. The second element we may call a fair hearing. A fair hearing is one that encourages a full presentation to the umpire of the (lawfully obtained) relevant evidence and testimony. It may require "fair notice" of the proceedings, full disclosure, legal penalties for refusal to testify or withholding evidence, and so forth. The third element of procedural fairness is a fair decision. This need not be a "correct" decision, since the innocent can sometimes be convicted in even a genuinely fair trial. A fair decision must be rational and nonarbitrary (that is, based on an appropriate weighing of the full range of relevant data). In addition to their procedural fairness, legal proceedings are assessed according to the substantive fairness of their outcomes, as when punishment is said to be fair only if it "fits" the crime, or compensation for injury fair only if it makes the injured party as well off as before the injury.

Obligations of Fairness

Many philosophers in the twentieth century have argued that citizens can be understood to owe to one another obligations of fairness to obey the law and to do their parts within the legal order. The principle of fairness (or fair play) states that when persons are engaged in a mutually beneficial cooperative enterprise, involving rule-governed restrictions of liberty, those who have restricted their liberty to make possible the scheme's benefits have a right that other participants (who take these benefits) follow the rules as well. Participants in cooperative ventures have an obligation to refrain from unfairly "riding free" and taking advantage of the efforts of others. Insofar as the legal order can be characterized as a cooperative enterprise, then, those who accept the benefits of the "rule of law" are bound in fairness to obey the law. Libertarian critics of the principle of fairness have argued that it either sanctions tyrannical oppression of individuals by others engaged in cooperative activities or collapses into a principle of consent. Defenders of the principle of fairness have argued in response for a variety of modifications to or more explicit formulations of the principle, for instance, for a stricter understanding of "acceptance" of benefits or for limits on the kinds of benefits whose receipt can generate obligations.

References

Arneson, Richard J. "The Principle of Fairness and Free-Rider Problems." *Ethics* 92 (1982), 616–633.

Golding, Martin P. *Philosophy of Law*. Englewood Cliffs NJ: Prentice-Hall, 1975.

Klosko, George. *The Principle of Fairness and Political Obligation*. Lanham MD: Rowman and Littlefield, 1992.

Nozick, Robert. *Anarchy, State, and Utopia*. New York: Basic Books, 1974.

Rawls, John. "Justice as Fairness." *The Philosophical Review* 67 (1958), 164–194.

———. "Legal Obligation and the Duty of Fair Play." In *Law and Philosophy*, ed. S. Hook. New York: New York University Press, 1964.

———. *A Theory of Justice*. Cambridge MA: Harvard University Press, 1971.

Simmons, A. John. *Moral Principles and Political Obligations*. Princeton: Princeton University Press, 1979.

A. *John Simmons*

See also DISTRIBUTIVE JUSTICE; DUE PROCESS; EQUALITY; JUSTICE

Family Law

The central concern of the philosophy of family law is the moral evaluation of laws that affect or concern the family. Philosophical questions about family law are questions about the application of ethics or moral philosophy. Ethics deals with the most general normative questions (such as, what makes an action, law, or policy morally justifiable?), while the philosophy of family law deals with specific normative questions that arise when concern is directed toward laws pertaining to the family. Hence, the philosophy of family law can be defined as the discipline that is concerned with presenting normative principles or criteria and with applying these to ethical questions about laws that affect or concern the family.

There are six functions of laws that affect or concern the family: *penal* (for example, criminal statutes forbidding the sexual abuse of children), *remedial* (for example, tort laws that make parents liable for damage to the property of others caused by their child's vandalism), *regulatory* (for example, laws that set standards for child neglect), *private power-conferring* (for example, laws that confer on private persons the power to marry or to dissolve a marriage), *public power-conferring* (for example, laws that confer on trial courts the power to settle divorce and child custody disputes), and *benefit-burden distribution* (for example, laws that order the distribution of cash assistance or housing to families whose annual income falls below certain levels).

Philosophical questions about the family and family law can be arranged in a hierarchy. They fall schematically into three different levels:

General questions about the family: What is the family? What is the justification of the social practice of family in human society?

General questions about family law: What is the justification of family law? Why should we prefer a situation in which there are laws regulating the family to a situation in which there are no such laws?

Specific questions about family law:

1. Questions about marriage and divorce. For example, what is the justification of legal marriage? What is the justification of laws that confer special privileges and impose special liabilities on persons by virtue of their marital status? What is the justification of particular laws that regulate the conditons under which persons can dissolve their marriage?

2. Questions about procreation. For example, what is the justification of laws that restrict the liberty of persons to bear children? What is the justification of laws that restrict the liberty of persons to refrain from bearing children?

3. Questions about child custody decisions. For example, what is the justification of laws that confer the rights and duties of child custody on specific persons either when the child is born or at other times during the child's minority?

4. Questions about the limits and nature of the state's power to intervene in the parent-child relationship. For example, what is the justification of laws that restrict the liberty of parents to behave in certain ways toward their children? How should state power to intervene in child-rearing decisions be exercised?

Answers to many of the preceding questions reflect positions taken within traditional ethical theory. For example, answers to the question What is a family? have been largely ideological. A particular ideal or standard has been described and groups of men, women, and children who fail to meet this standard have been denied the legal status of "family," making them ineligible for significant benefits. Philosophers who take a natural law approach to ethical questions have maintained that the only groups that can be properly called families for purposes of legal recognition by the state are those in which group members are related by blood, marriage, or adoption. This is because these are the only relationships that are natural to the human species. Moreover, "marriages" between homosexuals ought not to be recognized by the state because such nonprocreative sexual relationships are "unnatural." Hence, because they cannot marry, homosexuals cannot form families, nor should they be allowed to adopt and rear children.

Natural rights theory, on the other hand, takes individual rights, especially the right to liberty, as fundamental. No act is morally wrong unless it violates someone's rights, and homosexual behavior between consenting adults violates no one's rights. If this is true, then it would be unjust to deny homosexuals the same private power to marry, to adopt children, and to form families that the state commonly extends to heterosexuals.

Utilitarians would take a middle ground in this debate. According to the utilitarian, the state should recognize only those family forms that promote the greatest good for all. Thus, if it can be shown that extending family status to nontraditional associations produces at least as much overall good as restricting the definition of family to traditional family forms, only then would it be permissible to recognize homosexual unions as families.

Perhaps the most persistent disputes in the philosophy of family law have been over the specific question of the conditions under which the state is justified in legally intervening in the family. Utilitarians would argue that the limits of the power that the state can legitimately exercise over the family are set by the consequences of legally restricting family autonomy. Several utilitarian-based principles justifying state intervention in the family have been proposed in recent literature, most of them used to justify intervention to prevent child abuse and neglect. The general utilitarian position is that coercive state intervention is justifiable only when a child is suffering, or there is a substantial likelihood that the child will imminently suffer a serious harm, and coercive intervention to alleviate the harm will be the least detrimental way of protecting the child. Objections to this principle have questioned the meaning of the word "harm" and have suggested that the principle may not justify enough state interference in parental child-rearing decisions. For example, some have proposed that the state can interfere in the family to protect the child from the failure of the parents to provide their child with appropriate moral training or an appropriate moral environment in the home, even if the child is not "harmed" in any discernible way. On the basis of this principle, children have sometimes been removed from the family home because the mother frequented taverns or the father was found out to be an atheist. Another supplement is a principle that says that the state is justified in compelling parents to support, maintain, and educate their children to the best of their ability and in a way that will give the child an opportunity to achieve the best life that the child is capable of achieving. This is not because the child will suffer harm if he does not receive this, but because he will not receive a benefit that the state regards as valuable. It is on this ground that laws compelling the education of children until they reach a certain age (for example, sixteen years) are justified. Debates over these issues engage the attention not only of scholars but the public and their representatives in state legislatures as well.

References

Blustein, Jeffrey. *Parents and Children: The Ethics of the Family*. New York: Oxford University Press, 1982.

Engels, Frederick. *The Origin of the Family, Private Property, and the State*. 1884. Chicago: C.H. Kerr, 1902.

Goldstein, Joseph, Abraham Solnit, and Anna Freud. *Beyond the Best Interests of the the Child*. New York: Free Press, 1973.

Houlgate, Laurence D. *The Child and the State: A Normative Theory of Juvenile Rights*. Baltimore: Johns Hopkins University Press, 1980.

———. *Family and State: The Philosophy of Family Law*. Totowa NJ: Rowman and Littlefield, 1988.

Lacey, W.K. *The Family in Classical Greece*. Ithaca: Cornell University Press, 1968.

LaFollette, Hugh. "Licensing Parents." *Philosophy and Public Affairs* 9 (1980).

O'Neill, Onora, and William Ruddick, eds. *Having Children*. Oxford: Oxford University Press, 1980.

Russell, Bertrand. *Marriage and Morals*. Garden City NY: Garden City Publications, 1929.

Wald, Michael S. "State Intervention on Behalf of 'Neglected' Children: A Search for Realistic Standards." *Stanford Law Review* 27 (April 1975).

Weitzman, Lenore. "Legal Regulation of Marriage: Tradition and Change." *California Law Review* 62 (1974).

Westmarck, Edward. *The History of Human Marriage*. 5th ed. 3 vols. London: Macmillan, 1921.

Lawrence D. Houlgate

See also DIVORCE AND MARRIAGE; LIAISON

Fascist (National Socialist) Philosophy of Law
Philosophical Foundations

It is sometimes thought that national socialism was a coherent philosophical system, relying on a worldview that was inspired by G.W.F. Hegel (1770–1831). If the influence of Hegel in national socialist thinking is undeniable, it must be remembered that most of the thinkers in national socialism were not philosophers, but lawyers. Therefore, they read and interpreted Hegel as lawyers. If some coherent philosophical system could be found in national socialism, it could be traced back to the concept of law and the conception of the state as described by Thomas Hobbes (1588–1679).

One of the basic issues in Hobbes' philosophical system is the unity of law and morality. This can be found in national socialist legal thinking: the legal and the moral order are one and the same, and the obligation to obey the law is an internal moral obligation. The transition from a purely legalistic liberal approach toward a moral concept of law implies at the same time a switch in the theory of law, concerning its sources as well as its interpretation. Theory of law, in short, becomes a theory of justice. Therefore, the national socialist state was qualified as a *"just"* state.

Hannah Arendt, according to Carl Schmitt, among others, is of the opinion that all state actions (and therefore, positive law to begin with) are presented as being in complete agreement with natural law, although the actions of the state are often completely arbitrary. Law is regarded as something immanent in nature, which can only be decoded by a few people, especially the leaders of the regime. This immanence of law can therefore be understood as a type of natural law. Law, being read in the existing reality, is transformed into positive law, which is perfectly in harmony with "discovered" law.

Because of this identification of law and morality, the state is the supreme incarnation of all values. There is no morality beyond the law of the state, only a normative vacuum.

Sources of Law

The absence of a coherent theory of the sources of law can be considered as being the main aspect of national socialist legal thinking. As a matter of fact, most of the legislation that was valid before 1933 in Germany (the year of the official installation of the Nazi regime) remained in force (except, for instance, the criminal code). The Nazis created little new legislation, in the formal sense. First of all, the Reichstag (parliament) had disabled itself. In doing so, it gave full power to Adolf Hitler and his government to take over the legislative task. Second, the period of 1933 through 1945, the year of the breakdown of the Nazi regime, was a relatively short period to create a large number of important, formal legal changes (although they were announced).

If in a formal sense the rule of law was respected, because existing legislation was still applied, it must be noted that the importance of individual norms, case-by-case decisions, the influence of the will of Hitler in the application of the law, and the influence of the party program seriously distorted the correct functioning of the rule of law.

The will of the leader, that is, Hitler, was the supreme source of law. In this sense, in case of conflict between a rule and his will, the latter had priority. If related to the philosophical presuppositions of Nazi thinking, the commands of the leader can be conceived of as a categorical imperative, in order to transform the state based on formal law into a state of the people. Here again, one sees the connection between law and morality in the conception of the sources of law.

The party program of the NSDAP (National Sozialistische Deutsche Arbeiterpartei) was another important source of law, though it was hardly more than a strange mixture of ideological slogans, lacking any coherence. Its official interpretation was the Führer's task and privilege. The state became an authoritarian, dictatorial state, functioning as an aim in itself. Finally, the national socialist ideology as expressed in the party program was put as a glass bell on the existing legal order, transforming it into a new system in which not the legal rule but the national socialist ideology prevailed. In this perspective, many authors agree in saying that national socialism was in fact hostile to law.

Anthropological Presuppositions

The Nazi state was built on strong racist presuppositions. The superiority of the Aryan race was the basic axiom of the racist doctrine that was uncritically accepted most of the time. The individual necessarily forms part of the state, the state being the appropriate space for personal perfection. However, apart from the fact that some races (for example, Jews) or parts of the population (for example, Gypsies) were considered inferior, the ethical respect of the human individual in general was denied. Not the individual but "the people" were the first and immediate fact, contrary to the hegelian conception according to which the existence of a popular community is mediated by the self-consciousness of free individuals. Only the group of people of which the individual is a part has an ontological value.

From one side, this ontological substance is determined by racial criteria, and, more precisely in Nazism, by anti-Semitism. In its authoritarian version, as Nazism proclamed it, a Jewish person is not a human being. On the other side, national socialism has a strong tendency to integrationism, though it implies a denial of the ethical value and moral autonomy of the individual person. The only true interpretation of human destiny comes from the popular community, of which the national socialist state is the emanation. Again, one sees, through these anthropological presuppositions, the strong link between law and morality in national socialism, in the sense that the state determines the ethical value of the individual.

Philosophy of Law and Legal Practice

As noted previously, national socialism was hostile to law. This can also be concluded once legal practice is taken into consideration. Two key concepts determined the approach to law: thinking in terms of concrete order and the "concrete-general concept."

The first concept means that reality contains its own order and that it precedes legal interference. As a consequence, any legal rule that was supposed not to be in accordance with this natural order could be adjusted through interpretation. Although this concept received no precise definition in the literature of that time, it was widely used to reinterpret law in terms of the national socialist ideology, in this sense that thinking (in terms of concrete order in legal practice) was promoted not as a method of application of the law, but as part of a theory of the sources of law.

The second concept that largely determined legal practice stemmed from the idea that legal concepts, like contract, property rights, and so forth, were general, and thus empty, concepts. Instead, as when thinking in terms of *concrete* order, a concrete-general concept was considered as the "totality of all its moments," thus being flexible at all moments and adaptable to all circumstances. The consequence of this preference for concreteness is that legal reasoning, instead of being based on *general* rules to be applied in a *neutral* way, was transformed in a highly arbitrary, ideological enterprise.

References

Arendt, Hannah. *The Origins of Totalitarianism*. 3d ed. New York: Harcourt, Brace and World, 1966.

Fränkel, Ernst. *The Dual State: A Contribution to the Theory of Dictatorship*. New York: Oxford University Press, 1941. 2d ed. New York: Octagon, 1969. 3d ed. 1980.

Kirchheimer, Otto. "The Legal Order of National Socialism." *Zeitschrift für Sozialforschung* 9 (1941), 456–475. 3d ed. 1980.

Maus, Ingeborg. *Bürgerliche Rechtstheorie und Fascismus. Zur Sozialen Function und actuellen Wirkung der Theorie Carl Schmitts* (Civil Jurisprudence and Fascism. The Social Function and Exercise of Carl Schmitt's Theory). Munich: Fink Verlag, 1976.

Neumann, Franz. *Behemoth: The Structure and Practice of National Socialism*. London: Oxford University Press, 1942. 2d ed. 1944.

Rottleutner, Hubert. "Die Substantialisierung des Formalrechts. Zur Rolle des Neuhegelianismus in der deutschen Jurisprudenz" (Giving Substance to Formal Law. Neohegelianism's Place in German Jurisprudence). In *Aktualität und Folgen der Philosophie Hegels*, ed. Otto Negt, 215–268. Frankfurt: Suhrkamp, 1971.

Wintgens, Luc, J. "Law and Morality: A Critical Relation." *Ratio Juris: An International Journal of Jurisprudence and Philosophy of Law* 4 (1991), 177–201.

Luc J. Wintgens

See also DECISIONIST PHILOSOPHY OF LAW

Fault

Evolution

Historically, tort systems in the West have vacillated between two principles of liability: fault and causation. Legal regimes have usually made the choice either to ground liability upon fault and make causation a separate question, or to disregard fault and make causation itself the basis of liability. No system has ever been purely causal or purely fault-based, but ancient and modern systems can be classified by the degree to which fault or causation is the dominant ground of liability.

The oldest liability systems were based upon strict liability. Such systems are found in the law of ancient Athens, Babylon, Rome under the Twelve Tables, various primitive legal systems, and in the English common law before liability for fault arose in the nineteenth century. The dominant reason for imposing liability was that a person or thing was in fact the author of an unlawful harm. The injurer could not be excused just because he was not at fault. Offended gods and religious taboos demanded punishment irrespective of fault, and the danger of clan violence—the clans reacting to results more than to faults—needed to be avoided. In certain societies the collectivity (the injurer and his kinsmen) bore responsibility for the unlawful act. Furthermore, rudimentary trial methods did not readily permit the gathering of facts about the injurer's state of mind or culpable intent. The ancient Athenians, for example, took the view that any homicide was unlawful, subjecting the perpetrator to the penalty of death or exile. Homicide was held in horror for religious reasons. The severe Athenian god admitted no excuse. Even deaths caused by animals or objects had to be purified by killing the animal or by flinging the object beyond the frontier of the city. In ancient law, strict liability responded to religious belief and social need.

Liability based on fault is the more recent and familiar notion in Western law. Its first appearance came centuries before the rise of the common law of England. The rise of fault can be traced to the jurists at the end of the Roman Republic, among them Quintus Mucius Scaevola, who, influenced by Greek ideas, introduced this requirement under the Aquilian action. In the process of becoming recognized, fault gradually undermined an older principle—the principle of unlawfulness (*injuria*). Thereafter, *injuria* became strongly associated with fault. Later, the Byzantines made an abstraction out of the notion of fault and thereby created an element distinct from the older notion of *injuria*. By the late seventeenth century French jurist Jean Domat proposed and articulated an all-inclusive principle of liability. To Domat belongs the intellectual credit for the Code Napoleon, Article 1382: "Every act of man which causes damage to another obliges the person at fault to make reparation." The principle "no liability without fault" became ascendant in the nineteenth century in all civil and common law systems, while strict liability became an exception relegated to certain special statutes or discrete pockets of the law.

Concept

Fault refers to deficient social conduct arising from a volitional act (intentional or negligent). The principle rests jointly upon an objective element (antisocial behavior) and the actor's subjective will, which either intends injury or causes it negligently. There is no fault unless both elements are intertwined.

Civil liability does not attach to an actor's mental state as such; the law does not sanction even dangerous intentions which have no harmful sequel. However, an actor's inability to form a legal intent, due to insanity or infancy, will avoid a finding of fault though the agent has caused harm to another. If liability is imposed upon the incapable in such circumstances, it will logically rest upon the principle of strict liability.

In determining which acts are blameworthy, the law has traditionally spoken of the care which society expects from an average reasonable person. This average care gives the appearance of a flat standard of responsibility, but average prudence is perhaps only the floor of the fault principle. There are gradative standards which may vary in exigency according to the profession, expertise, and representations of the actor. The demands of the fault principle have increased with technological advance and rising societal expectations and thus may approach the rigor of strict liability while seeming to be less exacting. The vigilance required of doctors has always been more exacting than any average prudence and skill; while cure is not guaranteed, care must be virtually error-free. Similarly product manufacturers, when judged under a negligence standard, must now maintain near perfect quality control.

The distinction between fault and strict liability has also become blurred for another reason. Courts in both civil law and common law countries, even as they professed their commitment to the principle of fault, have devised a number of procedural and evidentiary devices which are the equivalent of strict liability. The doctrine of *res ipsa loquitur* (the fact speaks for itself) is the most familiar illustration. The usual effect is to establish an inference of negligence, and this inference makes the case a judge or jury question though there has been no proof of fault offered by the plaintiff. This procedural device assists courts in lifting the standard of care up to the top notch. Another judicial technique has involved the use of strong presumptions of fault. In product liability cases, French courts not only have eliminated the need of plaintiffs to show the fault of manufacturers but also have denied manufacturers the opportunity to show their freedom from fault. This stride toward strict liability was taken by creating a conclusive presumption of fault.

A leading characteristic of liability based on fault is that it tailors responsibility to the circumstances of particular cases. Where the circumstances are novel, no prediction about liability can safely be made in advance. Whether the defendant was at fault in causing damage requires balancing opposed socioeconomic interests, including moral considerations, and it is the court (and/or the jury in the United States) which conducts this balancing. While traditional law perhaps reconciled these same factors by using the yardstick of the average, reasonable person *(bon père de famille)*, the modern tendency portrays the reasoning as a cost-benefit analysis wherein competing and conflicting interests are weighed. According to this approach, behavior is seen as blameworthy when the costs of that behavior outweigh its benefits. Conversely, it is blameless when benefits outweigh costs. In contrast to a statutory system of strict liability like workers' compensation, where the legislature has balanced the interests a priori and has used bright lines to establish the bounds of employer liability as well as employee compensation, court determinations of fault are based upon an elastic standard and after-the-fact appreciation of circumstances and reasonable levels of liability. The ability to shape responsibility to fit particular circumstances is perhaps the principal reason for the widespread belief that the principle is fair.

Another characteristic of the fault principle is the extension of this balancing process to the areas of causation and defenses. The principle reappears in the requirements of "proximate" causation. It is generally not enough to show a factual causal nexus, namely, that the defendant's conduct was a fact without which the injury would not have occurred. While causation may be sufficient under schemes of strict liability, fault regimes insist upon normative standards of causation that rule out liability for remote and unforeseeable consequences of the defendant's conduct. Likewise, fault-based defenses, such as contributory negligence or assumption of the risk, will be recognized, thus reducing the responsibility of the injurer and increasing freedom of action. Strict liability, by contrast, will tend to recognize only those defenses which negate or interrupt causation, such as an act of God and acts of third persons.

References

Becht, Arno C., and Frank W. Miller. *The Tort of Factual Causation in Negligence and Strict Liability Cases*. St. Louis: n.p., 1961.

Harper, Fowler V. "Liability Without Fault and Proximate Cause." *Michigan Law Review* 30 (1932), 1001.

Hart, H.L.A., and T. Honoré. *Causation in the Law*. 2d ed. 1984.

Keeton, Robert E., et al. *Prosser and Keeton on Torts*. 5th ed. St. Paul MN: West, 1984.

Malone, Wex S. "Ruminations on Cause-in-Fact." *Stanford Law Review* 9 (1956–1957), 30.

Nicholas, Barry. *Introduction to Roman Law*. Oxford: Clarendon Press, 1962.

Palmer, Vernon. "A General Theory of the Inner Structure of Strict Liability." *Tulane Law Review* 62 (1988), 1303.

———. "In Quest of a Strict Liability Standard under the Code." *Tulane Law Review* 56 (1982), 1317.

Winfield, Percy H. "The Myth of Absolute Liability." *Law Quarterly Review* 42 (1926), 37.

Zweigert, Konrad, and Hein Kötz. *An Introduction to Comparative Law*. Trans. T. Weir. 2d rev. ed. Oxford: Clarendon Press, 1987.

Vernon V. Palmer

See also CAUSATION, TORT LAW; TORTS

Federal Jurists, 1800–1860, U.S.

This "Golden Age" of jurisprudence adapted American constitutional law to promote economic development and national unity. Chief Justice Marshall and his cohorts developed an "instrumental" theory of law to subordinate states' rights to national authority and to permit industry and commerce to flourish at the expense of personal, local, and traditional rights.

John Marshall (1755–1835) served as chief justice of the United States from 1800 until 1835. Marshall's thought appears in a series of landmark decisions. *Marbury v. Madison*, 5 U.S. (1 Cranch) 137 (1803), established that the federal courts could declare acts of Congress unconstitutional. *McCulloch v. Maryland*, 17 U.S. (4 Wheat.) 316 (1819), confirmed the "implied" doctrine of congressional powers by holding the Bank of the United States constitutional. It also thereby upheld the supremacy of federal over state law. Ruling that the state of Maryland could not tax the National Bank, Marshall asserted that "the power to tax is the power to destroy."

McCulloch incidentally permitted the national government to facilitate economic development, as did several other Marshall decisions. *Gibbons v. Ogden,* 1 U.S. (23 Wheat.) (1824), forbade states from interfering with the flow of interstate commerce—New York had granted a monopoly to Robert Fulton and those he licensed to operate steamboats in its waters. *Dartmouth College v. Woodward,* 518 17 U.S. (4 Wheat.) (1819), recognized corporations, "invisible, intangible, and existing only in contemplation of law," as possessing legal rights. The constitution's clause protecting contracts applied to corporations, "fictional persons" as they soon became regarded, which meant they could do business without fear a state would renege on conditions included in corporate charters. Marshall's decision in *Cherokee Nation v. Georgia,* 30 U.S. (5 Pet.) 1 (1831), denied that treaties with Indian societies had the same status as those made with foreign nations. This prevented Native Americans from suing in federal courts when treaty-breaking whites seized their lands on the grounds the tribes did not possess legal standing as a collective body expansion.

Workers' rights came under court scrutiny during this period as well. Sixteen labor conspiracy trials followed in the wake of the 1806 Philadelphia *Cordwainers* case; efforts to organize workers collectively were considered conspiracies to deprive employers and nonorganized employees of their livelihoods. Even after a famous decision of the Massachusetts Supreme Court voiced by Chief Justice Lemuel Shaw (1781–1865) in *Commonwealth v. Hunt,* 4 Met. 45 Mass. 111 (1842), overturned this common law rule, courts hostile to labor had no shortage of means to combat unions—injunctions against real or potential disturbances of the peace being the most common. It was Shaw who wrote the decision in *Farwell v. The Boston and Worcester Railroad Co.,* 4 Met. 45 Mass. 49 (1842), that unless an employee could prove negligence, as in providing faulty equipment, injuries on the job must be attributed to a "fellow servant" and owners did not have to pay compensation.

Among a host of other procapital cases, *Vose v. Grant,* 15 Mass. 505 (1819), and *Spear v. Grant,* 16 Mass. 9 (1819), ensured limited liability for corporate stockholders; their loss in a corporate venture was limited by the amount of their investment. *Charles River Bridge Co. v. Warren Bridge Co.,* 36 U.S. (11 Pet.) 420 (1837), denied an "implied" contract existed between the state of Massachusetts and the Charles River Bridge Co. to an *exclusive* right to operate a bridge across that river. Financial harm to the older company was more than offset by the interest of "the whole community"; the community has "a right to require that the power of promoting their comfort and convenience, and of advancing the public propriety, by providing safe, convenient, and cheap ways for the transportation of produce, and the purposes of travel."

Economic development was also explicitly made a goal of law in the famous four-volume *Commentaries on American Law,* first published from 1826 to 1830 by Columbia College law professor James Kent (1763–1847), who had recently retired as Chancellor (head) of the state Court of Chancery. Kent's systematization of American legal practice took special consideration of the relationship of commercial law to both equity and common law. A legal modernizer, "the law" he codified was the law "known and received at Boston, New York, Philadelphia, Baltimore, Charleston, etc., and as proved by the judicial decisions in those respective states. . . . I shall *assume* what I say to be the law of every state."

The even greater commentaries of Joseph Story (1779–1845), Associate Justice of the United States Supreme Court (1811–1845), followed in the 1830s and 1840s. The titles of his volumes convey his comprehensive labor: *Bailments; On the Constitution; The Conflict of Laws; Equity Jurisprudence; Equity Pleading; Agency; Partnership; Bills of Exchange;* and *Promissory Notes.* Through these works and during his tenure as professor of law at Harvard College beginning in 1829, Story sought to justify philosophically and codify diverse laws to institute uniform commercial practices: "The law respecting negotiable instruments may be truly declared in the language of Cicero," he wrote, "to be in a great measure, not the law of a single country, but of the whole commercial world." He was unable, however, to persuade Congress to ratify a uniform federal commercial code.

The philosopher who best tied legal trends in the early-nineteenth-century United States to universal norms was German-born Francis Lieber (1798–1873). In his *Political Ethics,* Lieber took issue with Immanuel Kant that morality could be ideal only or known only intuitively. Rather, Lieber wrote of the increasing resemblances among the world's civilized na-

F

tions, which were leading humanity to higher levels of prosperity, happiness, and ethics. Lieber's own greatest contribution to law was *General Orders No. 100,* the code of war the Union adopted in 1863. It has been the basis for subsequent military codes throughout the world. Lieber's main point was that only military necessity could justify forms of combat that involved civilians, who along with the wounded and prisoners had to be treated as humanely as possible. The legality and morality with which a nation conducted war was also a sign of its civilized status.

Standing in opposition to the dominant nationalist jurisprudence was the states' rights philosophy of the South, most powerfully expressed in the writings of Vice President (1825–1832) and then South Carolina Senator (1832–1850) John C. Calhoun (1782–1850). Denying both human equality and the idea of natural rights, Calhoun insisted all rights were socially derived and every society required a class of working poor for any kind of civilization to flourish. If anything, the southern slaves were better cared for by paternalist masters than northern workers who were paid as little as possible and cast aside during slack periods. Calhoun also maintained that the United States was a compact among states, not among the people, and could be dissolved by the states when they no longer considered it beneficial. This, however, was a catastrophe he hoped to prevent through the doctrine of concurrent majority. Either the North or the South would be able to veto legislation—a dual executive was one possible means to this end—favored by the other section. This device would tend to unite "the most opposite and conflicting interests and to blend the whole in one common attachment for the country. . . . Each sees and feels that it can best promote its own prosperity by conciliating the good will and promoting the prosperity of the others." Only to the extent that nations ensured veto power for all significant concurrent majorities could they attain peace, civilization, and order.

Southern resistance to the triumph of commercial and industrial capitalism was swept away in 1865. Northern jurists, however, through their creative interpretation of the Constitution, which legalized practices required for economic development, had already provided the framework which made this triumph possible.

References

Freidel, Frank. *Francis Lieber, Nineteenth-Century Liberal.* Baton Rouge: Louisiana State University Press, 1947.

Haar, Charles M. *The Golden Age of American Law.* New York: George Braziller, 1965.

Holt, Wythe, ed. *Essays in Nineteenth-Century American Law.* Westport CT: Greenwood Press, 1976.

Horwitz, Morton. *The Transformation of American Law, 1780–1860.* Cambridge MA: Harvard University Press, 1977.

Newmyer, R. Kent. *The Supreme Court Under Marshall and Taney.* New York: Crowell, 1968.

Pound, Roscoe. *The Formative Era of American Law.* Boston: Little, Brown, 1938.

Spain, August O. *The Political Theory of John C. Calhoun.* New York: Buckman, 1951.

White, G. Edward. *The Marshall Court and Cultural Change, 1815–1835.* New York: Macmillan, 1988.

William Pencak

See also AMERICAN JURISTS, 1860–1960; FOUNDING JURISTS, 1760–1800, U.S.; JUDICIAL REVIEW; NINETEENTH-CENTURY PHILOSOPHY OF LAW

Feminist Philosophy of Law

An analysis and critique of law as a patriarchal institution, the feminist approach to legal theory began in the 1970s as a challenge to the exclusion and subordination of women. It is built on a history of feminist political philosophy and social activism that proliferated during the nineteenth and twentieth centuries.

Since the first women's rights conference at Seneca Falls, New York, in 1848, enormous changes have taken place in the lives and prospects of women. Much social progress has been made, and changes in law during the nineteenth and twentieth centuries reflect that progress. For example, during the 1840s, 1850s, and 1860s a series of legislative reforms, generally referred to as the married women's property acts, enhanced the legal capacity of women substantially by granting wives the legal power to make contracts, hold and convey property, and retain their separate earnings. While the practical effects of this legislation on the liberty of women should not be overrated (since in fact they were minimal), the formal barriers removed were nonetheless important. Similarly, in 1920 women were granted the right to vote. This had little immediate, practical effect on the lives of women, but in the long run the change is very important, for it began the long journey toward equal treatment and equal legal status.

Accomplishments of this kind reflect the early steps of the women's movement: the removal of formal barriers to the participation of women in the full range of human pursuits. The process has been a slow one, with many setbacks. Yet the accumulated accomplishments of the twentieth century are clearly visible if we compare the freedom, rights, and daily lives of contemporary women with that of women at the turn of the century.

During the 1970s and 1980s many legal barriers were confronted and dismantled. Beginning in 1971 with the case of *Reed v. Reed*, 404 U.S. 71 (1971), formal barriers to educational and occupational opportunities for women were deemed unconstitutional, a violation of the equal protection of law. Women at that time went to the law, assuming it to be neutral and objective, to fight for their rights to equal treatment. For a time the courts were responsive to equal protection arguments—so long as the target was a blatantly biased regulation or restriction, such as a flat ban on women's participation in an occupation. Soon, however, the courts proved resistant and traditional prejudices intractable, so feminist legal scholars began to examine legal structures more carefully. In the process, subtle issues regarding the implications and consequences, in fact the very meaning, of equal protection and justice for women as legal and moral equals of men have been raised. Exploring these issues is the object of feminist jurisprudence.

Examining the effect of law on the lived experience of women, feminist legal scholars found that law has regulated and restricted women's freedom rather than enhancing it. Law has reinforced social structures that promote the economic dependence of women on men by limiting their participation in the public sphere; it has impeded women's control over their own sexuality and reproduction, thus impairing their ability to define their own private lives. These limitations reflect the traditional patriarchal organization of society, which is mirrored in law.

The patriarchal world view has structured human life and social institutions since the beginning of civilization. The presumptions of this world view, considered so natural and inevitable until this century, are embedded and reinforced in legal structure and practice of all sorts. Since the patriarchal world view has been the predominant standard of life virtually without question until the latter half of the twentieth century, its presumptions have been all but invisible until recently. The idea that men appropriately control public life, that women are naturally domestic and subordinate, that men are innately aggressive, autonomous, and entitled to be free, while women are inherently nurturing, dependent, and should be cloistered and controlled by their husbands or fathers—in a word, that men are dominant and women subordinate— is still held by many individuals and groups. The implications of this idea are more pervasive and profound than we have yet been able to comprehend. So, even though many progressive and well-intentioned individuals reject the overt founding premise of patriarchy, the implications and effects of the world view still feel normal, natural, and inevitable. Identifying, exploring, and evaluating these implications and effects in law and legal institutions are the foci of feminist jurisprudence.

All feminism begins with the presumption that a patriarchal world is not good for women or fair to women—nor is it somehow ordained by nature or otherwise inevitable. On the contrary, patriarchal practices and institutions are unjust and oppressive and therefore should be corrected. The rejection of patriarchy is the one (and perhaps the only) point on which all feminists agree. It is also a distinguishing feature of feminism as a school of thought, since no other school of thought focuses on the critique of institutions and attitudes as patriarchal. Only feminism analyzes the patriarchal origin, nature, and effects of human attitudes, concepts, relations, and institutions, and criticizes them on that ground. Thus, the functional definition: feminist jurisprudence is the analysis and critique of law as a patriarchal institution.

This analysis and critique manifests itself in a variety of ways, owing partly to the range of issues it covers, and partly to divergence among feminists on virtually all points other than the rejection of patriarchy. As to the first, some feminists tend to concentrate on issues of particular concern to women, such as equal protection law; discrimination in educa-

F

tion, hiring, promotion, and pay; protection of reproductive freedom and other freedoms; protection from the harms of rape, sexual harassment, and spousal abuse; regulation of sexual and reproductive services, such as surrogate mother contracts, prostitution, and pornography; and patriarchal bias in law and adjudication. However, feminist analysis is appropriate to any area, concepts, relations, and institutions of law, and many legal theorists offer feminist critiques of standard legal categories such as contracts, property, and tort law. The issues covered by feminist jurisprudence are as wide ranging as the areas covered by law.

The other source of diversity within feminist jurisprudence is the broad range of theoretical approaches encompassed within it. It is well known and often noted that there is not one feminism, but many. Consequently, there are virtually as many approaches to feminist legal theory as there are to feminism in general. These views range from liberal feminist arguments that assume the current legal system can be adequately reformed to accommodate the goal of justice for all, to revolutionary critiques that regard the legal structure as inherently patriarchal. Many feminist approaches are associated with other political or analytical theories. For example, feminist analysis may be socialistic, marxist, liberal, communitarian, psychoanalytic, existentialist, postmodern, or pragmatic. In addition to these, radical and relational feminism are not associated with any other theories necessarily. Radical feminist jurisprudence, often associated with the work of Catharine MacKinnon (among others), is founded on the idea that gender itself is constructed on the presumption of male dominance and female subordination or objectification. This presumption is reflected in basic legal structures, which must be revised or dismantled to allow just institutions to grow in their place. Relational feminist jurisprudence follows the work of Carol Gilligan, which supposes a difference in male and female moral and psychological development, resulting in a difference in focus and approach to problem solving. In the relational view the "male" perspective is focused on justice and the abstract analysis of rights and fixed legal categories, while the "female" approach is more relational, contextual, and particular in its analysis, and is focused in terms of an "ethic of care." The deficiency of some legal institutions, it is argued, is that they fail to reflect the "female" perspective adequately. Thus, in contrast to a liberal feminist view that basically argues for treating all human beings alike, relational feminists argue that the differences should be acknowledged and honored in a way that disadvantages no particular group (and certainly not women). This is but one illustration of the diversity among feminist theories. Indeed, the only feature that all feminist views share is their common rejection of patriarchal relations and institutions. How the diverse versions of feminism characterize and critique these relations and institutions may vary widely.

By feminist standards this variety is a good thing rather than a problem. We should expect a diversity of perspectives on such a complex social institution as law. We do not need a final unified vision of society and gender to argue against oppression, disadvantage, domination, and discrimination. We do not need to know the nature of an ideal society or an ideal person so long as we know what prevents a society from being minimally good or prevents an individual from realizing the basic potentials of personhood. We do not need an ultimate vision when we have not yet met threshold conditions for a minimally just society. Many visions are possible and many theories are useful. Thus, the commitment to foster dialogue that allows the expression of diverse views and gives particular attention to eliciting views not usually heard is a unifying theme within feminist jurisprudence that attempts to represent the commonality of fundamental values appropriate to law without misrepresenting the plurality of experience appropriately addressed by it.

References

Bartlett, Katherine, and Rosanne Kennedy, eds. *Feminist Legal Theory: Readings in Law and Gender.* Boulder CO: Westview Press, 1991.

Bottomly, Anne, and Joanne Conaghan, eds. *Feminist Theory and Legal Strategy.* Oxford: Basil Blackwell, 1993.

Fineman, Martha, and Nancy Thomadson, eds. *At the Boundaries of Law: Feminism and Legal Theory.* New York: Routledge, 1991.

MacKinnon, Catharine. *Toward a Feminist Theory of the State.* Cambridge MA: Harvard University Press, 1989.

Minow, Martha. *Making All the Difference.* Ithaca: Cornell University Press, 1990.

Rhode, Deborah. *Justice and Gender: Sex Discrimination and the Law.* Cambridge MA: Harvard University Press, 1989.

Smith, Patricia. *Feminist Jurisprudence.* Oxford: Oxford University Press, 1993.

Tong, Rosemarie. *Women, Sex and the Law.* Totowa NJ: Rowman and Allenheld, 1984.

Patricia Smith

See also DIFFERENCE THEORY; RADICAL CLASS, GENDER, AND RACE THEORIES: POSITIONALITY

Fichte, Johann Gottlieb (1762–1814)

In his *Beiträge zur Berichtigung der Urtheile des Publicums über die französische Revolution* in 1793, nothing suggested Johann Gottlieb Fichte was likely to become an important philosopher of law. A defender of anarchist individualism, he made the state not an end but a means, and one soon to disappear. Obedience to laws required no right on the state's part to enforce them, but came from our imposing them on ourselves. So law was defined in terms of ethics and not of politics for the early Fichte: the human being has an absolute right to be free, since one has the duty to live morally and morality presupposes freedom. Thus natural rights preexist and go beyond any positive law. To think of any reason for needing the state means conceiving of the state of nature not as a situation of war but as a neutral condition: neither good not evil, human nature does not determine one necessarily to carry out moral demands. For Fichte in 1793, no deeper rationale was required to articulate the legal and the political more fully.

All this changed with publication of the *Grundlage des Naturrechts,* Fichte's principal work devoted to the problems of law. Its first part (1796) began with a "Deduction of Legal Concepts," which showed (1) that intersubjectivity is what constitutes subjectivity, that is, relation to the other underlies the relation to self or to consciousness, including moral consciousness: "Man becomes man only among men"; and (2) that law is the condition for intersubjectivity as the reciprocal recognition of liberty. There could no longer be any question of basing obedience to the law on moral conscience, since intersubjectivity as mediated by law precedes any consciousness; so law has to

be considered completely autonomous from morality.

A "deduction of the right to enforce laws" highlights this break with his anarchistic individualism of 1793 and its antipolitical consequences: if individual liberty cannot exist without legal community, this in turn presupposes the state, to which each person delegates the power to ensure respect for law. The state's indispensable enforcement leads directly to the separation of law and morality: because moral consciousness involves unconditional obligation and cannot be the basis for law (which involves only permissions), the science of law should not depend upon natural morality nor proceed as if human beings were evil. So the state, as the "institution of constraint," has the task of reaching an agreement among wills in a mechanical way, which never eliminates liberty.

The second part, on applied natural law (1797), lays down the political conditions for succeeding with law. Only enforcement coming from the general will could avoid violating liberty. However, when the human being is held to be perverse or egoistic, the general will does not come into being spontaneously; it has to be both brought to life and controlled by an institution. Fichte called this power of control the "ephorat," after the name of an institution in ancient Sparta. This institution itself is beyond control: the whole system, therefore, depends ultimately on the uprightness of the "ephors," who alone can guarantee the rule of law. How this group can be an exception to egoism Fichte recognizes as an aporia; he concedes that a perfect state is impossible "so long as pure reason does not appear on earth in person." All we can do, therefore, is to approach that ideal, which his *Sittenlehre* presents as a "duty" and as "the ultimate goal of every reasonable being."

The paradox and even drama of Fichte's philosophy thereafter consists in not holding to this basically kantian perspective of the unending approximation to a state conformed to law. From *Das geschlossene Handelsstaat* in 1800, Fichte tried at all costs to make incarnate in the real what remained, nonetheless, an idea. With this will to "move from concept to existence," in which is found "the primal error of socialism" according to the French philosopher Alain, Fichte crossed the gap which in 1796–1797 still separated his conception of the legal state as the "institution of enforcement," from the theory of the authoritarian or even totalitarian state to which his political writings from 1807 gave themselves over.

References

Breazeale, Daniel, and Tom Rockmore, eds. *New Perspectives on Fichte.* Atlantic Highlands NJ: Humanities Press International, 1996.

Fichte, Johann Gottlieb. *Gesaumtausgabe der Bayerischen akademie der Wissenschaften* (Complete Edition of the Bavarian Academy of Science). 26 vols. published, 36 planned. Ed. R. Lauth and H. Jacob. Stuttgart: Frommann-Holzboog-Wissenschaften, 1962– .

Hohler, Thomas. *Imagination and Reflection: Intersubjectivity, Fichte's Grundlage of 1794.* The Hague: Martinus Nijhoff, 1982.

Neuhouser, Frederick. *Fichte's Theory of Subjectivity.* Cambridge: Cambridge University Press, 1990.

Philonenko, Alexis. *La liberté humaine dans la philosophie de Fichte* (Human Freedom in Fichte's Philosophy). Paris: Vrin, 1990.

Radrizzani, Ives. *Vers la fondation de l'intersubjectivité chez Fichte* (Approaches to the Foundation of Intersubjectivity in Fichte). Paris: Vrin, 1993.

Renaut, Alain. *Le système du droit. Philosophie et droit dans la pensée de Fichte* (The System of Law. Philosophy and Law in the Thought of Fichte). Paris: Presses Universitaires de France, 1986.

VanManz, Hans-Georg. *Fairness und Vernunftrecht. Rawls' Versuch der prozeduralen Begründung einer gerechten Gesellschaftsordnung im Gegensatz zu ihrer Vernunftbestimmung bei Fichte* (Fairness and Conceptual Jurisprudence. Rawls' Development of a Procedural Foundation for a Just Social Order, in Contrast to Its Rational Meaning for Fichte). Hildesheim: Olms, 1992.

Alain Renaut

Fictions and Deemings

Many jurists have held that there are occasions when the application of an existing common law or statutory rule leads to an unjust result. In such cases it is said that judges are forced to make a difficult choice. Should the court be more concerned with following the established rule or with achieving what is thought to be a just result? One way out of the dilemma, according to some, is accomplished by the legal fiction.

Generally, a legal fiction is a false assumption of fact made by a court, as the basis for resolving a legal issue. Its purpose is to reconcile a specific legal result with an established rule of law. If no such rule precludes the desired result, there is no need for legal fictions; likewise if no particular result is desired. Legal fictions, it is said, provide a mechanism for preserving the established rule while ensuring a just outcome. Instead of ignoring or altering the rule, the judge refurbishes the facts of the case. By fictionalizing the facts, the rule is said to remain intact.

Roman Law

In the earliest period of ancient Rome the *ius civile* (civil law) was characterized by its rigidity. Once Rome expanded and as commercial interaction with foreigners increased, the simplicities and formalities of the *ius civile* became unsuitable for the new conditions of Roman life. Consequently, several legal fictions were developed to circumvent the strict results of the *ius civile*. These constructions were developed and employed by the praetor, an elected official whose role was to administer the law and to protect the civil rights of citizens. The praetor employed *fictio*, as Papinion put it, to "aid, supplement, or correct" the civil law.

An example of the Roman use of *fictio* is the *nasciturus* fiction. Roman law drew a basic distinction between *persona*, the bearer of rights and duties, and *res*, the object of rights and duties. As a legal state of being, *persona* began at birth and ended at death. All other states of being were considered *res*. In the formalistic period of ancient Rome, the unborn child, or *nasciturus,* was considered *res*. This led to certain problems in the law of succession. Sometimes an expecting father would die while his wife was pregnant. Since his child was not yet *persona,* and was therefore without rights, the child was unable to inherit despite being born only a few days after the father's death. This theoretical gap thwarted the father's donative intent. It created an obstacle for Roman jurists, who were too conservative to alter their entire system of law by including *nasciturus* into the category of *persona*. Instead, they resorted to a fictitious formula that "the unborn child shall be regarded as one already born." If the praetor prescribed the formula, the judge had no choice but to *pretend* that the child was already born. This allowed the fulfillment of the father's intentions. The child, once born, could then inherit despite the fact that it was not *in rerum natura* at the time of the device.

The *nasciturus* fiction illustrates the four main characteristics of the legal fiction as it occurred in Roman law: (1) A fact was assumed to exist, though in reality it did not; (2) The false assumption was made both deliberately and consciously; (3) The false assumption was indisputable; (4) The false assumption allowed an outcome otherwise unavailable under the strict law of the *ius civile*.

Early English Common Law

Like the Romans, William Blackstone (1723–1780) saw the fiction as "highly beneficial and useful." In his *Commentaries*, Blackstone painted a portrait of the fiction as a stairway that escalates modern British inhabitants of the legal castle above and beyond the moated ramparts of medieval law. Legal fictions like the bill of Middlesex and the writ of *quo minus*, Blackstone thought, were required to meet the growing needs of litigants; to help fasten new tiles to the older bricks of the legal castle. At the same time, Blackstone saw fictions as "one of those troublesome, but not dangerous, evils which have their root in the frame of our constitution." Fictions presented certain difficulties for legal classification. Still, Blackstone thought that legal fictions could never be extricated from the legal castle without making its halls utterly inaccessible.

Blackstone accepted the use of the procedural fiction by common law judges so long as it did not "extend to work an injury; its proper operation being to prevent a mischief, or remedy an inconvenience, that might result from a general rule of law." Blackstone thought that the function of legal fictions could be restricted to repairing the castle without actually rebuilding it. His preoccupation with the distinction between the form of law and its substance led him to believe that procedural fictions could be employed without affecting the substance of the law. Since he thought that judges could recognize what natural justice demanded in a particular case and could there-

fore limit the use of fictions to achieving equitable results, Blackstone believed that legal fictions had a home in law's castle.

Jeremy Bentham

Jeremy Bentham (1748–1832), Blackstone's jurisprudential nemesis, pinpointed a certain danger unrecognized by Blackstone and the Romans. Legal fictions might be used improperly by the judiciary. Rather than utilizing them strictly for procedural repair, lawyers and judges often employed fictions to reconstruct the substance of the legal castle. According to Bentham, the fiction "has never been employed to any purpose but the affording justification of something which otherwise would be unjustifiable." Bentham presented lawyers and judges with the following dilemma: "What you have done by way of the fiction—could you, or could you not, have done it without the fiction? If not, your fiction is a wicked lie: if yes, a foolish one."

Bentham's contempt lay in the fact that he saw the fiction as a tool for usurping the powers of parliament. Lawyers and judges use legal fictions only to dodge existing law. Bentham defined the legal fiction as a "wilful falsehood, having for its object the stealing of legislative power, by and for hands, which could not, or durst not, openly claim it,—and, but for the delusion thus produced, could not exercise it." Bentham wanted to rid the law of its fictions. He compared the fiction to a syphilis, "which runs in every vein, and carries with it into every part of the system the principle of rottenness."

Henry Sumner Maine

Sir Henry Sumner Maine (1822–1888), a near contemporary of Bentham, held a different view of the historical role of fictions in law: "We must, therefore, not suffer ourselves to be affected by the ridicule which Bentham pours on legal fictions wherever he meets them. To revile them as merely fraudulent is to betray ignorance of their particular office in the historical development of law." In *Ancient Law*, Maine provides a developmental view of legal history. Law and social order progress through several stages, starting with a primitive legal society, moving through a period of customary law until, finally, the law becomes codified. Law develops as society progresses. Consequently, certain instruments are required to achieve harmony between the law and the evanescent attitudes of a progressive society. Fictions are one such instrument which, according to Maine, "satisfy the desire for improvement, which is not quite wanting, at the same time that they do not offend the superstitious disrelish for change which is always present. At a particular stage of social progress they are invaluable expedients for overcoming the rigidity of law." For Maine, fictions are the most conservative method of achieving change in the law. He employed the expression "legal fiction" to signify "any assumption which conceals, or affects to conceal, the fact that a rule of law has undergone alteration, its letter remaining unchanged, its operation being modified. . . . The fact is . . . that the law has been wholly changed; the fiction is that it remains what it always was."

Ultimately, Maine saw fictions as a thing of the past. He did not agree with Bentham that the use of legal fictions must stand in opposition to the legislative process. According to Maine's evolutionary view, the instrumental application of fictions precedes a system of legislation in the natural course of things. Therefore, one need not worry that fictions usurp legislative authority. As legal systems become more progressive, they will naturally move away from the use of fictions, first to a system of equity and then to a comprehensive system of legislation.

Lon L. Fuller

Not everyone agrees with Maine that the role of legal fictions is merely historical. Lon Fuller (1902–1978), an adherent of the philosophy of Vaihinger (1852–1933), was intrigued with the idea that legal fictions are indispensable to legal thinking. In his *Legal Fictions,* Fuller devoted an entire chapter to that subject in an attempt to prove Maine wrong. Though an explicit use of legal fictions seems less frequent, Fuller believes that fictions continue to play a legitimate role in legal thinking.

According to Fuller, legal fictions represent the pathology of law. Fuller thought that the legal infirmities which compel our need for legal fictions will never vanish. This is because the fiction is a linguistic phenomenon; it is an affliction of language. Sometimes judges simply lack the conceptual and linguistic tools required to resolve a dispute in a novel situation. Fictions help "feel the way" toward a new principle when a judge is for the moment unable to see where it might lead. Fictions are persuasive where traditional analogical reasoning falls short. Fuller also recognizes other motives for dressing up new law as though it were a variety of the old. Fictions provide convenience and operate as a kind of shorthand when a judge wishes to fit a novel situation into an already established category. Fictions also function as shock absorbers when policies are introduced through the judiciary.

The Danger of Reification

Despite their purpose, Fuller and others since have recognized a certain risk in the use of fictions: sometimes we begin to believe in them. R.A. Samek calls this the *meta phenomenon*: "the human propensity to displace 'primary' with 'secondary' concerns, that is concerns about ends with concerns about means. The latter become perceived as primary, and distort the former in their own image." With persistent use the fiction acquires a life of its own. Once treated as real the fiction becomes dangerous and loses its utility. Remember that the supposed virtue of the fiction is that it leaves intact the irreconcilable rule of law by operating instead on the facts of the case—but this is not always so. When the fiction is applied alongside the doctrine of precedent, the irreconcilable rule is subject to erosion with each further use of the fiction. Confusion results about the existence of the very rule that the fiction meant to preserve.

This is precisely what has happened with the *nasciturus* fiction of Roman law. That fiction was first employed for no reason other than to square the donative intent of a father with the irreconcilable rule that personhood begins at birth. The *nasciturus* fiction has since been co-opted by Anglo-American courts. Through the guise of precedent, this fiction has crept not only into our succession laws but also across several other distinct areas of law. It has been unmindfully extended to tort law, so that newborn children can recover damages for prenatal injuries. The same fiction has recently been applied, almost automatically, in family law to grant injunctions in favor of the unborn. Whether or not we wish to applaud these outcomes, what has become apparent is that a broad and continuous application of the *nasciturus* fiction has resulted in confusion about the original rule that personhood begins at birth. Consequently, there now exists a dangerous inconsistency in the treatment of the unborn in private law compared to public law. One lesson to be learned from this is that fictions are wholly safe only when employed with a complete consciousness of their falsity. Without this awareness the danger of reification looms. Once fictions are perceived as real, the possibility for critical reflection about their use is lost.

Statutory Deemings
It is sometimes said that a legislative body will order the use of a fiction in a statutory enactment. This is said to occur when a statutory provision deems one thing to be another. A striking example can be found in the Abattoir Commission Act of South Africa, which provides that a karakul lamb shall be deemed not to be an animal. Besides fictions of identity, statutes employ fictions of quality (for example, a day shall be deemed to consist of ten hours), and fictions pertaining to the application of law (for example, this act shall be deemed to have come into operation on such and such a date).

Though these deemings seem incredible to the uninitiated, they are commonplace among lawyers and jurists. Most do not even regard them as fictions. In the law of South Africa, the karakul lamb *is not* an animal and no amount of zoological evidence could prove otherwise. Why? Simply because the statute says it is so. This illustrates not only the power accorded to the legislature but also the peculiar nature of law. As law students are told, things are different in the real world.

If a legislature has the power to create a world in which the Island of Minorca is part of London, one wonders why statutes are often written in such fictitious language. Why pretend one thing is another whenever one wishes to broaden the scope of a statute? Why not extend its scope directly? Some have argued that conservatism is the motive. Deemings conceal the real rule behind a fictitious facade, softening its harsh impact and creating the impression that the law remains unchanged. Others have held that fictitious language is used for economy of expression. J.J. Olivier disagrees on both counts, arguing that legislators are less concerned these days with the appearance of conservatism and that common sense indicates that fictitious language is a roundabout means of expression. Olivier thinks that fictitious language must be averted to avoid confusion similar to that generated by judicial fictions. He recom-

mends instead four distinct methods of achieving the same result: direct cross-reference, validating past acts, comparison, and stipulative definition.

The Call for Revival
Whether viewed as judicial constructs or as statutory provisions, legal fictions continue to thrive in our legal system. They are no longer an awkward patch on law's fabric of theory, as Fuller once described them. Yet, ironically, scholarly interest in them has faded considerably in the last century. Recognizing the dual nature of the fiction—indispensable on the one hand and dangerous on the other—a fistful of scholars have called for a revival of their study. However, a proper understanding of legal fictions demands more than the critical examination of their use. To know what a legal fiction is requires discernment about what counts in law as real. This calls for a revival of jurisprudence itself.

References
Bentham, J. *The Works of Jeremy Bentham.* Ed. J. Bowring. 1843.

Blackstone, W. *Commentaries on the Laws of England.* 1768.

Buckland, W.W. *Elementary Principles of the Roman Law.* Cambridge: Cambridge University Press, 1912.

Fuller, Lon L. *Legal Fictions.* Stanford: Stanford University Press, 1967.

Harmon, L. "Falling Off the Vine: Legal Fictions and the Doctrine of Substituted Judgment." *Yale Law Journal* 100 (1990), 1–71.

Maine, H.J.S. *Ancient Law: Its Connection with the Early History of Society and Its Relation to Modern Ideas.* 1878. London: Oxford University Press, 1931.

Olivier, J.J. *Legal Fictions in Practice and in Legal Science.* South Africa: Rotterdam University Press, 1975.

Samek, R.A. "Fictions and the Law." *University of Toronto Law Journal* 31 (1981), 290–317.

Ian R. Kerr

See also ERROR, DECEIT, AND ILLUSION; FACT AND LAW; TRUTH

Fighting
See DUELING

Finance
See MONETARY POWER; NEGOTIABLE
INSTRUMENTS

Finnis, John (1940–)
John Finnis developed a new version of the natural law theory that reduces or eliminates many points of contention between natural law theorists and legal positivists. He has also worked out its implications for various jurisprudential issues.

Having started from the thomistic theory of natural law, Finnis modified it considerably. He holds that through our experiences of life we come to know various self-evident basic goods: life, knowledge, play, aesthetic experience, friendship, practical reasonableness, and religion. Participating in them is what makes for a flourishing human life. The natural law is the objective principles concerning what must be done or avoided to achieve such a flourishing. Moral, political, and legal philosophers can develop theories about what these natural law principles are and how they apply under different conditions. Being all aware of the basic goods, we use the basic requirements of practical reasonableness to formulate whatever rules of moral conduct we need. For people to flourish, they have to belong to communities of various sorts, of which one of the most fundamental is the political community or state. It is a complete community, since it coordinates the activities of individuals, of families, and of every sort of intermediate association. Its purpose is to ensure the common good of the citizens, a set of conditions that will support their efforts for self-fulfillment.

Laws, in the primary and focal sense of the term, are rules made for a state, by a legally established authority, to coordinate the activities of all the individuals and groups in the state and to provide whatever sanctions and adjudicative institutions are appropriate, in order to achieve the common good. Terms like "law," "state," "sanctions," and "common good" are analogical and thus are instantiated more or less fully and in various ways. Every code of law will necessarily incorporate into itself a few natural law rules, like the prohibition of theft and murder, since they are indispensable for social order and give legal reasoning its backbone. Most laws, however, result from the authoritative choice of the legislators, who properly make their decisions on the basis of what is for the common good under existing conditions. Although an unjust law is, qua law, deficient, it is still a law. Citizens may even have a moral obligation to obey unjust laws, so as to maintain respect for law, although the more unjust a law is, the less of a moral obligation one has to obey it.

Rejecting various contemporary theories of justice, Finnis sees it as the basic requirements of practical rationality in regard to favoring and fostering the common good of one's communities. Thus, it is at the core of both personal and political obligations. Distributive justice deals with how we ought to share in the common stock and incidents (for example, natural resources, profits, taxes, and offices) of communal enterprise, while commutative justice is concerned with all other kinds of dealings between persons and groups.

Despite the widespread proclamation of bills of rights, which are pronounced inalienable, in practice contemporary government and elites do not recognize any absolute rights, that is, rights that are exceptionless. Finnis holds that humans do have, as humans, such rights. Respecting and enforcing these rights are a part of the common good of a state, which thus has a major role in moral as well as economic development. To the extent, then, that any theory of legal reasoning ignores such basic moral functions of the state, it is deficient.

Given human nature, sanctions are necessary to maintain the rule of law. Punishment is fundamentally a matter of commutative justice but should not be seen as primarily a means of self-defense by society. It provides vivid and continual lessons on the requirements of the common good and can help in the reformation of criminals, but it is above all retributive inasmuch as it restores a just balance of advantages between the criminals and the law-abiding populace.

Opponents have argued that Finnis's basic goods are neither incommensurable nor self-evident, that he reduces the common good to a mere aggregation of individual goods, that he overworks his notion of practical reasonableness, and that he weakens the natural law theory by trying to develop it independently of metaphysics and philosophical anthropology.

References
Finnis, John. "Natural Law and Legal Reasoning." In *Natural Law Theory: Con-*

temporary *Essays,* ed. Robert P. George, 134–157. Oxford: Clarendon Press, 1992.

———. *Natural Law and Natural Rights.* Oxford: Clarendon Press, 1980.

Fortin, Ernest L. "The New Rights Theory and the Natural Law." *Review of Politics* 44 (1982), 590–612.

MacCormick, Neil. "Natural Law and the Separation of Law and Morals." In *Natural Law Theory: Contemporary Essays,* ed. Robert P. George, 105–133. Oxford: Clarendon Press, 1992.

Pannier, Russell. "Finnis and the Commensurability of Goods." *The New Scholasticism* 61 (1987), 440–461.

Gerard J. Dalcourt

Forgiveness

See MERCY AND FORGIVENESS

Foucault, Michel (1926–1984)

Of one thing we can be sure, Foucault himself would have strenuously denied that his work had any intentional link to legal philosophy. Yet it undeniably has important implications for legal theory. Most directly he provides a damning, if indirect, critique of classical austinian positivism. This he captures dramatically in Volume 1 of *The History of Sexuality,* where he contends that "[i]n political thought and analysis we still have not cut off the head of the king."

In the period of absolutism, in which legal thought was dominated by the discourses of sovereignty, law functioned as orders of the sovereign. Such analyses, he insists in "Two Lectures," inhibit an understanding of the modern forms of power. Thus, he condemns liberalism for retaining the figure of the "monarchical sovereign" of eighteenth-century absolutism in the new guise of the "impersonal sovereignty of law." The continued retention of the concept of sovereignty in modern jurisprudence inhibits the ability to perceive the distinctive shift within modernity, from law to discipline. It it not so much that law disappears; rather, modern society is characterized by a legal discourse, manifest in legislation, grounded on a concept of public right that operates within a closely linked grid of disciplinary coercions, in which expert knowledge (of doctors, social workers, and so forth), rather than rules, is the bearer of the new disciplinarity.

He offers a suggestive account of the changing role of law in modernity in *The History of Sexuality:* "I do not mean to say that law fades into the background or that institutions of justice tend to disappear, but rather that the law operates more and more as a norm, and the judicial institution is increasingly incorporated into a continuum of apparatuses (medical, administrative, and so on) whose functions are for the most part regulatory." Here he suggests, first, a tendency that counterposes law and regulation, seeing the rise of administrative and technological regulation as signaling a decline of law. What, for Foucault, distinguishes the new forms of disciplinary power is that they function primarily by means of surveillance. As he stated in "Two Lectures," he views law as lacking the capacity "for the codification of a continuous surveillance." The second tendency views law as functioning increasingly as a "norm," that is, as general standards. This offers a now rather commonplace and one-sided account of the role of law as focused on the rise of open-ended standards creating an increased scope for judicial discretion.

More generally Foucault's thought involves a radical shift away from the traditional concerns of legal theory. In "Preface to History of Sexuality" he describes the general trajectory of his engagement with the link between law and power in the following terms:

> It was a matter not of studying the theory of penal law in itself, or the evolution of such and such penal institution, but of analysing the formation of a certain "punitive rationality." . . . Instead of seeking the explanation in a general conception of the Law, or in the evolving modes of industrial production . . . it seemed to me far wiser to look at the workings of Power.

Time and again he links law with the negative conception of power, a "juridico-discursive" conception of power, by which phrase he identifies all forms of law which specify "Thou shalt not . . . " prohibitions. In *The History of Sexuality* he predicts that "[w]e shall try to rid ourselves of a juridical and negative representation of power, and cease to conceive of it in terms of law, prohibition, liberty and sovereignty. . . . We must at the same time conceive of sex without the law, and power without the king." In "Two Lectures" he summarizes (emphasis added):

> In short, it is a question of orienting ourselves to a conception of power that *replaces the privilege of the law* with the viewpoint of the objective, the privilege of prohibition with the viewpoint of tactical efficacy, the privilege of sovereignty with the analysis of a multiple and mobile field of force relations, wherein far-reaching, but never completely stable, effects of domination are produced. The *strategical model* rather than the *model based on law.*

Thus, the thrust of Foucault's thought has devastating implications for the project of legal theory. Jurisprudence has continued to posit the viability of taking as its object of inquiry a conception of law as an autonomous field. To take Foucault seriously implies that today we must abandon the presupposition of the autonomy of law. In its place we must construct the project of legal theory as an inquiry into the interconnection of legal and other forms of regulation. In terms of his own texts the object of inquiry would need to be focused on the interaction of law and the new nonstate disciplinary mechanisms.

References

Ewald, François. "Norms, Discipline and the Law." In *Law and the Order of Culture,* ed. Robert Post. Berkeley: University of California Press, 1991.

Foucault, Michel. *Discipline and Punish: The Birth of the Prison.* London: Allen Lane, 1975; New York: Pantheon Books, 1977.

———. *The History of Sexuality.* Vol. 1, An Introduction. 1976. Trans. Robert Hurley. New York: Random House, 1978.

———. "Preface to History of Sexuality. Vol. 2. The Use of Pleasure." In *The Foucault Reader,* ed. Paul Rabinow, 333–339. New York: Pantheon Books, 1984.

———. "Two Lectures." In *Power/Knowledge: Selected Interviews and Other Writings 1972–1977,* ed. Colin Gordon, 78–108. Brighton: Harvester Press, 1980.

Hunt, Alan. "Foucault's Expulsion of Law: Towards a Retrieval." *Law and Social Inquiry* 17.1 (1992), 1–38.

Hunt, Alan, and Gary Wickham. *Foucault and Law: Towards a New Sociology of Law as Governance.* London: Pluto Press, 1994.

Palmer, Jerry, and Frank Pearce. "Legal Discourse and State Power: Foucault and the Juridical Relation." *International Journal of Sociology of Law* 11 (1983), 361–383.

Turkel, Gerald. "Michel Foucault: Law, Power, and Knowledge." *Journal of Law and Society* (1990), 170–193.

Alan Hunt

Founding Jurists, 1760–1800, U.S.

Creators of the government and political theory of the United States during the era of the American Revolution (1760–1800) are known as its founding fathers. The new nation presented its founders with a double challenge. On the one hand, as Thomas Paine wrote in his 1776 pamphlet *Common Sense*: "We have the power to begin the world over again" and establish "an asylum for mankind," as opposed to "an old world overrun with oppression," and become "the glory of the earth." A "novelty in the political world" which "had no model on the face of the globe" (*Federalist* No. 14), the United States charged itself with establishing a republic to challenge the monarchs and aristocrats who tyrannized over much of the globe. Yet on the other hand, the founders were acutely aware that if the United States did not ensure order through sound institutions that could provide "a republican remedy for the diseases most incident to republican government" (*Federalist* No. 10), America would join "the petty republics of Greece and Italy," of which "it is impossible to read the history . . . without feeling sensations of horror and disgust."

Participants in the Enlightenment, the founders insisted, along with Thomas Jefferson, in basing their republic on "the light of science," "the unbounded exercise of reason and freedom of opinion." "We exhibit," George Washington noted, "the astonishing and novel spectacle of a whole people deliberating calmly on what form of government will be most conducive to their happiness." Yet the founders drew heavily on English common law and the traditional rights of Englishmen, besides borrowing heavily from English theorist John Locke and Scottish "Common Sense" philosophers, when they universalized British thought and practice as the rights of humanity. Biblical examples of the ancient Hebrew polity, Greek and Roman republics of antiquity, and the city-states of Renaissance Italy also provided the historical evidence the founders used to construct institutions modeled to a large extent on their own British and colonial experience. Of French Enlightenment thinkers, Montesquieu's support for aristotelian mixed government made a far greater impression than Voltaire's witty deconstruction of all government, Jean-Jacques Rousseau's theory that government should reflect the undiluted "general will," or the confident belief in moral and material progress trumpeted by Condorcet and Claude-Adrian Helvetius.

While much of the founding fathers' political theory can be traced to various antecedents, they were also important innovators. The constitutional convention, where all the adult white males voted in a special election to choose representatives to approve a fundamental, written code of laws, was conceived as a reenactment of the passage from a state of nature to government theorized by John Locke in his *Second Treatise of Government*. Such a convention first ratified the Massachusetts Constitution of 1780 and later the United States Constitution of 1787.

Nearly every republic in the world has followed the United States in basing its legitimacy on a written constitution ratified by the people. This idea implies that government is subordinate to and derives its authority from "we, the people." Furthermore, government possesses only those powers granted by the people as necessary to protect liberty and promote the general welfare.

The world's new republics have also borrowed the United States' device of the Declaration of Independence, which justifies revolution. "All men are created equal" has been interpreted both collectively (all nations or groups of people have an equal right to govern themselves without outside interference) and individually (all individuals in a society should possess the same rights). The idea that equal rights are "inalienable" and inherent to "all men" was novel and unsettling in a world where different groups of people (clergy, nobles, city dwellers, peasants) possessed different rights granted by a sovereign through local charters and customs to which they were "subject." "The Age of the Democratic Revolution" turned "subjects" into "citizens."

At least four of the founding fathers made important individual contributions to legal philosophy. Thomas Jefferson (1743–1826), besides writing most of the Declaration of Independence, drafted the greater part of Virginia's precedent-setting legal code of 1776. It disestablished the church and decreed freedom of religion, abolished entail and primogeniture (thereby allowing intestate estates to be distributed as the owner wished), and liberalized a criminal law derived from England (where all felonies were theoretically, if seldom practically, punishable by death) in accordance with the enlightened penology of Cesare Beccaria, which limited executions to murderers and traitors. In the 1790s, as Secretary of State, Jefferson argued for a limited construction of the United States Constitution, emphasizing states' rights. In opposing the Alien and Sedition Acts of 1798, which made criticism of the federal government a crime, Jefferson joined with James Madison in sponsoring the Virginia and Kentucky Resolutions. They maintained that states could nullify laws they considered unconstitutional.

Jefferson advanced his theory of "strict construction" in opposition to the "implied powers" doctrine of Secretary of the Treasury Alexander Hamilton (1757–1804). Hamilton insisted that Article 1, Section 8 of the Constitution permitted Congress to pass "*all* laws" which were "necessary and proper" for carrying its enumerated powers into execution. If there were a "natural and obvious relation" between a constitutional power and "the end to which the measure relates as means"—such as the powers to tax and to coin and borrow money, and the creation of a Bank of the United States, which Jefferson denied—the law had to be constitutional or government would be paralyzed. It was for the courts, Hamilton argued in *Federalist* No. 78, to interpret the constitution and decide when a branch of government exceeded its bounds.

In addition to first putting forth the theory of judicial review in the United States, Hamilton challenged the laissez-faire economics of Adam Smith's 1776 treatise, *The Wealth of Nations*, with his own 1790 *Report on Manufactures* and *Report on the Public Credit*. He argued that the survival and success of the infant nation depended on active government development of the economy through tariffs, taxation, and investment (the last channeled through the Bank) to add a vig-

F

orous commercial and industrial sector to a predominantly agricultural country.

James Madison (1751–1836), noted as the "Father of the Constitution," initially favored a strong central government, and only changed his mind when he questioned Hamilton's economic policies. Commerce and cities bred corruption, mobs, and aristocrats, and sounded the death knell of republics. Previously, Madison had collaborated with Hamilton and John Jay in writing *The Federalist Papers,* the great defense of the new constitution. Madison's most important contribution was *Federalist* No. 10, in which he criticized the traditional assumption of political theorists that republics were best suited to small, homogeneous states. He argued instead that a large republic composed of diverse interests was far more likely to ensure stability and personal freedom than the short-lived, turbulent republics history had witnessed. Republics were prone to chaos because a majority faction (usually the poor) would despoil a minority (the rich) and open the door to anarchy or tyranny. The proliferation of geographic, economic, religious, and ethnic groups in the United States would prevent a majority from forming. Other factors would also preserve the republic. Checks and balances existed among the federal legislative, executive, and judicial powers. (This was *not* the traditional monarchical, aristocratic, and democratic elements of mixed government, since now all power came from the people.) Powers were separated between state and central governments, both of which added bills of rights to their constitutions to protect individual liberty. Madison himself drew up the United States Bill of Rights from a large number of suggestions.

Despite the United States' hopes to herald a new republican order for the world, the founding fathers were sure their creation would not endure forever. They predicted monarchy or aristocracy would succeed it once class differences became too great. John Adams (1735–1826) was the greatest of the pessimists who warned that America too would be taken over by either an aristocracy or the poor led by demagogues if a strong executive and balanced government did not check them both.

If Adams's insistence that Aristotle's mixed government could never become obsolete was unusual thinking among the founders, they all shared the belief that a republic's survival required a patriotic citizenry who put devotion to the general welfare above selfish pursuits. The idea that liberty is the right of the "individual"—a word unknown to the founders—to do as he or she pleases as long as others remain unharmed is a notion which only took hold in the mid-nineteenth century, when Adam Smith's economic theory became amalgamated with social Darwinism ("the survival of the fittest") and later versions of Jeffersonian limited government. The founders were republicans, not democrats. They designed a constitution to protect the populace from its own worst tendencies. The political theory they developed to justify their republic intelligently based legal philosophy on political praxis.

References

Bailyn, Bernard. *The Debate on the Constitution.* 2 vols. New York: Library of America, 1993.

Beeman, Richard, et al., eds. *Beyond Confederation: Origins of the Constitution and American National Identity.* Chapel Hill: University of North Carolina Press, 1987.

Greene, Jack P., ed. *The Reinterpretation of the American Revolution.* New York: Harper & Row, 1966.

White, Morton. *The Philosophy of the American Revolution.* New York: Oxford University Press, 1987.

Wood, Gordon S. *The Creation of the American Republic, 1776–1787.* Chapel Hill: University of North Carolina Press, 1969.

William Pencak

See also FEDERAL JURISTS, 1800–1860, U.S.; HUTCHINSON, THOMAS; PAINE, THOMAS; REPUBLICAN PHILOSOPHY OF LAW

Fragmentation of Ownership

In practice, the two major legal systems in the Western world—the common law of the Anglo-American legal world and the civil law of Roman-European legal traditions—allow for different persons to have different interests in the same property at the same time. Most often, this situation occurs in "property," land. In theory, this division of interests in the same property can be achieved in one of two ways: either one can divide or fragment interests at the level of *ownership itself,* thus creating two or more holders or "owners" of different "ownership" interests or "estates"; in such a division, estates are groupings of some of the various possible powers, rights, and duties that exist with respect to a property. Alternatively, one can preserve the singular and largest concept of ownership of property in one person while hiving off or "dismembering" *lesser real rights* and powers for the benefit of other persons. Although these dismembered rights, when added together, compose the whole of the ownership package or "bundle" of rights, they are not placed on the same conceptual level as ownership. The holder of a dismembered right merely has title to a specific real right comprising a set of rights, powers, and duties less than ownership. Often these lesser real rights contain all the powers necessary to effectively control the property; ownership of property and control thereof can thus be divorced.

Of these two alternative conceptual structures, the common law takes the first view, allowing the fragmentation of "ownership" through the doctrine of estates. The effect of this doctrine is that ownership is always fragmented in the common law; true *dominium,* or ownership in its fullest sense as the widest possible plenitude of powers over property, is nonexistent in practice in the common law. Rather, a number of people will own different estates, each characterized by different rights, powers, and duties, concurrently. The civil law opts for the latter approach, preserving ownership as an unfragmented concept but allowing certain rights to be subtracted, even to the point where under usufruct or emphyteusis most of the real rights in the ownership bundle are part of the title of the usufructuary or emphyteutic lessee, leaving the bare owner with few of the real rights normally attributed to ownership. Thus, while fragmentation of ownership as between owners only truly is achieved in the common law, the civil law in practice can tolerate largely similar divisions of rights, without attaching the label of ownership to the lesser interests.

The common law doctrine of estates has its origins in the history and evolution of the common law, particularly as it related to land law. Under a feudal structure, persons at differing levels of the hierarchy—monarchs, tenants-in-chief, lesser tenants, and serfs—shared distinct but concurrent types of estates in the land, all held ultimately by the Crown. The ability to hold these estates was predicated originally upon a web of mutual, correlative rights and obligations. As these various feudal obligations were shed or evolved into financial duties, and as land eventually was allowed to be inherited and alienated, the personal nature of the mutual obligations disappeared. Yet the idea that there could be contemporaneous ownership estates in land remained, and the various estates continued to evolve notwithstanding the removal of their original foundation. Thus it is that one owner can have a freehold estate, a fee simple, the most absolute ownership interest (though still held by the Crown or state), and another owner may have an estate limited to one's own lifetime, a life estate, on the very same property. To make matters even more complex, certain types of estates were not "legal" at all and were not recognized in the royal courts, but were "equitable" and recognized by the Lord Chancellor in the Court of Equity. Thus the legal estate in trust property is vested with the trustees, while the beneficial estate is held by the beneficiaries of the trust.

The modern civil law achieved many similar results by grafting a conceptual structure originally built on Roman law and practice onto societies which were shedding their feudal pasts. The traditional Roman institutions of fragmentation—real servitudes and rights of enjoyment such as usufruct, use, and emphyteusis—were not only reincorporated into modern civil codes, but the doctrinal writings surrounding these institutions in both Roman and civil law have influenced the common law's taxonomy of fragments, as well as its doctrinal discussions. The influence can go both ways: civil law jurisdictions have attempted to adopt the trust into their property law structures.

Fragmentation can be achieved over time. In the common law, certain estates can have temporal duration, vesting at different points in time, and allowing for the successive enjoyment of property rights. Thus a present estate holder may have only some future interest in a certain property, perhaps already vested or certain, or perhaps subject to some contingency. Estates may revert back to an original owner or may be transferred to some other person. The civil law likewise allows for such temporal fragmentation, also at the conceptual level of ownership, through the Roman law institution of fiduciary substitution, as well as through contingent ownership. Furthermore, both the common and civil law allow fragmentation through *co-ownership,* which allows more than one person to share the same interest in the same property at the same time in the same manner. Each system has specific rules governing the relations between and among co-owners.

Fragmentation can be achieved through the unilateral action of an owner or through agreement of parties. It is by this latter method that the creation of an interest in property borders the realm of contract. Thus in common law some types of leasehold interests create real rights while others are better dealt with through the law of contract; in civil law, leases are generally an example of contractual obligations, though emphyteutic leases are an enumerated dismemberment creating real rights. The same is true for a secondary group of real rights which attach to other rights: mortgages in the common law and hypothecs in the civil law. These institutions create certain limited real rights in specific property within the framework of a contractual agreement. Initially, a common law mortgage had the effect of transferring title to the mortgagee (lender), though some common law jurisdictions have begun to prevent this transfer, protecting the title of the mortgagor (borrower) while providing similar protection to the mortgagee. The civil law treats hypothecs as accessory real rights, limited real rights which attach to property through a *créance,* giving the hypothecary creditor (lender) some real security in the property, but always maintaining ownership in the hypothecary debtor (borrower).

It should be noted that fragmentation of ownership has applied mainly to real property, or immoveables in civilian terms; that is, land and those things attached to the land, such as buildings, plantations, and other works of some permanence. More recently, some fragmentation of less tangible property, such as monetary funds, has been achieved through more flexible institutions like the trust, and in the civil law, revised versions of the usufruct and substitution, as well as trusts.

There are a number of ways to explain or justify the fragmentation of ownership. In general, the various arguments and theories used to explain and justify private ownership can apply mutatis mutandis to allowing the frag-

mentation of ownership. A first group of arguments might be based on the idea of utility; allowing multiple interests, whether these are called ownership or something less than ownership, allows for the more effective or productive use of land whether measured in terms of individual benefit or overall benefit to society. A modern explanation of fragmentation might be based on an economic idea of utility, with utility being measured in terms of productivity or efficiency in use. Thus, allowing the ultimate owner to alienate part of the power and control over the property to someone else, to a usufructuary or a life tenant, for instance, could render the property more productive when the user is in a better position to exploit the land. Such an explanation might also help to justify fragmentation caused de facto by possession or occupancy: both the common and civil law recognize property rights created by adverse possession. These economic arguments do not always justify fragmentation; often the fragmentation of ownership results in interest holders with divergent interests as to the uses to which the land is put. Thus fragmentation might create incentive problems. With a usufruct or life interest, for example, the long-term preservation of the capital property (to the benefit of the holder of the ultimate ownership or reversionary interest) does not always coincide with its short-term exploitation (to the benefit of the present user); some rules requiring the care of the capital property are necessary.

The standard of measuring utility need not be economic. Historically, fragmenting ownership within the structure of feudalism allowed Norman conquerors to rule effectively over conquered England, at once rewarding their nobles and soldiers, without disrupting the existing social fabric, tied as it was to the land. In subsequent centuries, it allowed the monarchical system to survive and adapt: if a king owned the ultimate estate in all land, feudal incidents, and later taxes, could be collected. As centuries passed and the ownership by the Crown became less and less direct, the control over property was divorced from its theoretical ownership; this allowed for the freer alienation of land, laying the groundwork for a capitalist system where land, while still the most valuable type of property, was also a resource with exchange value. In all of these cases, the fact of fragmentation has served structural or systemic goals.

Other justifications might be based on more nonreductionist terms. One such argument might be based on the notion of distributive (or more precisely redistributive) justice: allowing fragmentation is a step toward equalizing an unequal distribution of land-based wealth by allowing some of the wealth generated by property to be shared by nonowners, particularly by those who have in fact created the wealth, such as life tenants and usufructuaries. Divorcing ownership of the property from its management allows for the dividing of the fruits. Other nonreductionist explanations based on personality or self-developmental theories of private property, when advanced in their classic form (such as those advanced by Hegel in *The Philosophy of Right*), fail to provide persuasive accounts for the fragmentation of ownership to the extent that they discuss ownership in an absolute and undivided manner, thus failing to account for multiple interests in the same property.

References

Brierley, J.E.C., and R.A. Macdonald, eds. *Quebec Civil Law.* Toronto: Emond Montgomery, 1991.
Lawson, F.H., and B. Rudden. *The Law of Property.* 2d ed. Oxford: Clarendon Press, 1982.
Simpson, A.W.B. *A History of the Land Law.* 2d ed. Oxford: Clarendon Press, 1986.
Terré, F., and P. Simler. *Droit civil: Les biens* (Civil Law: Goods). 4th ed. Paris: Dalloz, 1992.

David Lametti

See also ESTATE AND PATRIMONY; SECURITY

Franchise and Referendum

The franchise of a political community defines the persons who are entitled to vote in the determination of its affairs. In modern times, the franchise has become universal, meaning, usually, that all persons affected by the decisions of a legistaturc, or perhaps living within its jurisdiction, are entitled, through their possession of a vote, to contribute to determining the composition of the legislature or the laws enacted or policies adopted. The term is historically associated with freedom or privilege, a point which reflects the movement from an association between an entitlement conferred by the legal status of citizenship to the more modern assumption of universal entitlement, which renders the notion of privilege otiose. The association between enfranchisement and freedom rests on qualifying conditions: birth, wealth, freedom from the necessity to labor; in this sense, it is exclusive. Contemporary understandings, by contrast, begin from universal entitlement and variously exclude particular classes of persons—for example, those below a certain age, those suffering from mental impairment, and those found guilty of particular crimes. In general, the historical movement has been from a presumption of exclusion (so that possession of the franchise is indeed a privilege) to the presumption of inclusion (so that nonpossession has to be justified by specific reasons, such as felony).

The explanation of this change in presumption is partly that conceptions of democracy have shifted. In the ancient republics, the democratic element in the constitution was focused on the deliberative capacities of "the people"; hence citizenship was restricted to those who were thought to possess such abilities. This typically involved the exclusion of women, slaves, some groups of workmen, and foreigners. Critically, citizenship was linked to an ability and concern to pursue the common good of the city. Modern democracy, however, is not essentially deliberative: an individual's vote is used to choose who is to be a representative in a legislative assembly. Earlier discriminations between persons answered to the question Who is qualified to deliberate? These were replaced by other ideas: Who is qualified to choose? Who has an interest? Who is affected?

Of course, this contrast masks many nuances. In considering democracy, one has to ask who constitutes the political community—who, exactly, are the people? Hence the association of democracy with political equality is consistent with discrimination. The citizens of the ancient republics were to be treated as equal, and indeed might find their freedom in the collective determination of the laws by which they were to live, but the citizens were nevertheless considerably less numerous than the population of the empirical (as against political) community. The most compelling understanding of the normative component of contemporary democracy is also egalitarian and may be interpreted as one person, one vote. However, the emphasis has shifted from the possession of that vote as a privilege to possession of that vote as a right.

It is also important to acknowledge the obvious distinction between an equality of formal entitlement and an equality of substantive capacity. Many obstacles have been confronted on the road to effective universal suffrage: for example, in the absence of a secret ballot, the economically dependent were unlikely to be free to express their real political opinions through the ballot box. Registration mechanisms, literacy tests, opening hours of polling stations—all these can be used to put hurdles in the way of particular groups. The most significant legislation on these matters in the United States has been the Voting Rights Act. In the United Kingdom, the Representation of the People Act has similar importance.

The universal franchise is remarkably recent, but in many ways it is now taken for granted as a right. The entitlement it confers is to be part of the electorate, to participate in the choice of a representative, a legislature, a government, or a president. Even if democracy is associated with political equality, it is obvious that the electorate cannot be equal (in power) to the political elite thus chosen. Nevertheless, the idea of political equality has important implications for apportionment, for the geographical extent of constituences, and for the selection of a voting system. The plurality (or "first past the post") system is relatively uncommon in the political systems of the world, and supporters of rival proportional systems claim greater fidelity to the ideal of political equality.

It has been asserted, especially in modern times by Jean-Jacques Rousseau, that only direct democracy (that is, the determination of collective affairs by citizens themselves) is compatible with freedom. The practical impossibility of such an arrangement has usually been seen as overwhelming. However, the referendum offers a device for limited self-government. The constitutional status of referendums is varied. In some political systems, such as Switzerland, popular initiative is respected: if a sufficient number of qualified voters wish a question to be put, it must be. In others, such as the United Kingdom, a referendum is called by the government, usually when a particular issue is deeply threatening to the unity of the governing party. Not only do polities differ about who may call a referendum, but also they differ about the significance of the outcome. In some the result is binding, but in others it is not. Referendums have been seen as a device to supplement representative democracy by the direct expression of citizens' views on particular issues; and while critics have replied that referendums are expensive to organize, proponents have pointed to the technological changes that have made a voting button in each household's living room a realistic prospect. What has often been forgotten in this debate, however, is the close association between the merits of direct democracy and deliberation. The qualifications for citizenship in classical republics, noted above, were designed to ensure the capacity to deliberate, not merely the capacity to make "a choice." This tension, between the ability to contribute to reasoned debate and the ability to express an opinion, or an interest, underlies the history of democratic theory in general and the debate about the scope of the franchise in particular.

References

Birch, Anthony. *The Concepts and Theories of Modern Democracy.* London: Routledge, 1993.

Davidson, Chandler, and Bernard Grofman, eds. *Quiet Revolution in the South: The Impact of the 1965 Voting Rights Act 1965–1990.* Princeton: Princeton University Press, 1994.

Dunn, John, ed. *Democracy: The Unfinished Journey: 508 B.C. to 1993.* Oxford: Oxford University Press, corrected ed. 1993.

Held, David. *Models of Democracy.* Cambridge: Polity/Blackwell, 1987.

McLean, I. *Democracy and the New Technology.* Cambridge: Polity, 1989.

Reeve, Andrew, and Alan Ware. *Electoral Systems: A Comparative and Theoretical Introduction.* London: Routledge, 1992.

Rousseau, Jean-Jacques. *The Social Contract and Discourses.* Ed. G.D.H. Cole with additions by J.H. Brumfitt and John H. Hall. London: Dent, 1993.

Andrew Reeve

See also DEMOCRATIC PROCESS; LOBBYING

Frankfurt School (Early)

The "Critical Theory" of the so-called Frankfurt school, developed by a heterogeneous group of social scientists, is an interdisciplinary research program that integrates the main perspectives of a revised historical materialism, Sigmund Freud's psychoanalysis, and concrete empirical social research. Without Max Horkheimer, who was professor of social philosophy and the single director of the Social Research Institute in Frankfurt before emigrating in the 1930s to the United States, the Frankfurt school would not have been possible. He was the coordinating, organizing, integrating, and controlling figure. He was able to hold together a group of researchers that would otherwise have dispersed, insisting on some fundamental perspectives and always initiating new research projects.

The original idea of an "interdisciplinary materialism" was later substituted by a pessimistic philosophy of history interested in reconstructing how instrumental reason became universal in modern societies, eliminating other types of rationality. It is Jürgen Habermas who has found a way back to the original idea of an "interdisciplinary materialism," modifying radically the premises on which that idea had been based in the classical period of the "Critical Theory."

For the philosophy of law, two authors are especially important: Franz L. Neumann and Otto Kirchheimer. Franz Neumann, born in 1900, studied law in Breslau, Leipzig, and Frankfurt, where he became the assistant of Hugo Sinzheimer, one of the founding fathers of labor legislation in the Weimar Republic. As union lawyer in Berlin, he shared an office with E. Fraenkel and in 1932 became the legal adviser of the Social Democratic Party (SDP). In 1933 Neumann emigrated to London, where he studied political science at the London School of Economics with Harold Laski and Karl Mannheim, taking a doctorate degree in 1936 with the thesis *The Governance of the Rule of Law. An Investigation into the Relationship between Political Theories, the Legal System, and the Social Background in the Competitive Society* (an analysis of the modern European legal system's history and function, published in German in 1980 under the title *Die Herrschaft des Gesetzes*). He emigrated then to the United States and worked for the Institute of Social Research, mainly charged with organizational tasks, but finding the time to write his classical analysis of fascism, *Behemoth: The Structure and Practice of National Socialism,* that brought him a reputation in the international scientific community. From 1942 to 1945 he worked for the Office of Strategic Services in Washington and served as director of the German Research Sec-

tion in the State Department until 1947. In 1948 he became visiting professor and in 1950 full professor of Public Law and Government at Columbia University, helping to reorganize the Political Science Department of the Free University of Berlin. He died in 1954.

Neumann was able to combine his theoretical interests with practical legal expertise and a pragmatic approach to social and political problems, never losing contact with the concrete historical conditions and possibilities. Before 1933 he wrote on concrete political and legal matters from the viewpoint of a reform socialism that takes seriously the principle of democracy and the idea of the social welfare state. With the other members of the Institute of Social Research, Neumann shared the intention of developing and practicing a critical social theory in concrete historical analyses that takes into consideration economic, political, legal, and social realities without reductionisms and dogmatisms, even if his concrete analysis of German fascism as a form of a "totalitarian monopoly capitalism" marks a substantial difference between his own position and the "theory of state-capitalism" put forward by Frederick Pollock, Max Horkheimer, and Theodor Adorno.

More radical than Franz Neumann was Otto Kirchheimer. His background was similar to Neumann's. Born in 1905 of Jewish parentage, he studied law and politics. His doctoral dissertation at Bonn (with Carl Schmitt) contrasted the socialist and the bolshevik concepts of the state. Like Neumann, he participated in SDP affairs, lecturing in trade union schools and writing for such journals as *Die Gesellschaft* (an SDP journal) on the Weimar Constitution, the function of Parliament, bureaucracy and the legal system in bourgeois society, the role of the Social Democratic Party, and labor and criminal legislation. Forced to flee, he joined the Institute of Social Research in 1934 as a research associate in Paris, then in New York. In New York Kirchheimer was assigned the completion of the work George Rusche had begun on the relationship between penal practices and social trends. The result was published in 1939 under the title *Punishment and Social Structure.* Later he worked for different American institutions, and in 1961 he became professor of political science at Columbia University. He died in 1965.

Especially worthy of mention is Kirchheimer's study on the use of legal procedure

F

for political ends, *Political Justice,* which was published in 1961. Like Franz Neumann and Arkadij R.L. Gurland (the third research associate who wrote extensively on Nazism), Otto Kirchheimer focused on changes in legal, political, and economic institutions, offering an analysis of Nazism that differed from the one proposed by Horkheimer and Pollock, who had concentrated more on social psychology and mass culture.

The research program of a "critical social theory" of the early Frankfort school, based on an "interdisciplinary materialism," allowed different approaches and motivated very heterogeneous researchers and scholars who had a similar background but who found their own theoretical ways.

References

Jay, Martin. *The Dialectical Imagination: A History of the Frankfurt School and the Institute of Social Research 1923–1950.* Boston: Little, Brown, 1973.

Luthardt, W. "Bemerkungen zu Otto Kirchheimers Arbeiten bis 1933" (Notes on Otto Kirchheimer's Work Since 1933). In O. Kirchheimer, *Von der Weimarer Republik zum Faschismus: Die Auflösung der demokratischen Rechtsordnung,* 7–31. Frankfurt: Suhrkamp, 1976.

Schäfer, G. "Franz Neumanns *Behemoth* und die heutige Faschismusdiskussion" (Franz Neumann's *Behemoth* and Current Concern with Fascism). In F. Neumann, *Behemoth. Struktur und Praxis de Nationalsozialismus 1933–1944,* 665–776. Frankfurt: Fischer, 1984.

Scheuerman, Bill. "Critical Legal Studies in Germany: The Legacy of the Frankfurt School." *Constellations* 2 (1995), 286.

———. "Neumann versus Habermas: The Frankfurt School and the Case of the Rule of Law." *Praxis International* 13 (1993), 50.

Söllner, A. "Franz L. Neumann: Skizzen zu einer intellektuellen und politischen Biographie" (Franz L. Neumann: Sketch of an Intellectual and Political Biography). In F. L. Neumann, *Wirtschaft, Staat, Demokratie. Aufsätze 1930–1954,* 7–56. Frankfurt: Suhrkamp, 1978.

———. *Geschichte und Herrschaft. Studien zur materialistischen Sozialwissenschaft 1929–1942* (History and Authority. Essays on Materialistic Social Science 1929–1942). Frankfurt: Suhrkamp, 1979.

Wiggershaus, Rolf. *The Frankfurt School: Its History, Theories, and Political Significance.* Cambridge: MIT Press, 1994.

Thomas Gil

Free Law Movement

The free law movement (*Freirechtsbewegung*) was an influential, though short-lived, jurisprudential movement centered in Germany and Austria (and to a lesser extent France) during the first quarter of the twentieth century. Like its American counterpart, legal realism, the free law movement emerged in direct and critical response to certain formalistic tendencies that had flourished in nineteenth-century jurisprudence.

On the European continent, the dominant conception of law in the nineteenth century was a strict "positivist" jurisprudence often referred to as "pandectism." This jurisprudential approach emerged in part as a theoretical ratification of the codification movement that swept Europe in the nineteenth century. It also fell under the influence of those jurists, particularly from Germany, who sought to articulate a "jurisprudence of concepts" (*Begriffsjurisprudenz*), a vast, seamless network of legal concepts—rules, principles, and doctrine—which, viewed together as a harmonious whole, was said to reveal the systematic, conceptual unity of law over the centuries from the Roman Empire to nineteenth-century Europe. The pandectists claimed that the new nation-state civil codes contained the whole of the law (the entire conceptual system). They further maintained that when deciding cases courts should look no further and consult no sources outside the codes themselves. That is, they conceived of law as a logically closed system of axioms and corollaries, from which right outcomes in adjudication were said to flow, by logical deduction, from the generally applicable and definitionally complete legal rules and principles found in the civil codes. Law, from their point of view, was determinate, objective, uniform, and predictable, while judicial decision making was a mechanical, nondiscretionary process.

By the late nineteenth century a few European jurists began to question the goals and precepts of pandectism. Most important was Oskar Bulow (1837–1907), a German law professor, who argued as early as 1885 that not all law fits within the pandectist model of a codified set of rules ultimately derived from general, abstract principles. According to Bulow, judicial decision making does not follow the formal deductive structure the pandectists assume. Oftentimes legislative intent is indeterminate; sometimes courts must consult aspects of life beyond the confines of the codes; indeed, Bulow claimed, sometimes rules and principles found in formal sources of law, whether statutory or customary, are ambiguous or even contradictory. When such is the case, judges must exercise discretion, and effectively they make law. Yet most basically, Bulow charged that pandectism was an "exaggerated statutory cult" that grossly overstated the importance of written law. In his view, statutes and code provisions are unfinished legal thoughts that only come to have complete meaning when they are contested in daily human affairs and subjected to the deliberation of courts.

Bulow is generally considered the principal forerunner to, not a member of the free law school. His work provided an important stimulus to the free law movement which began at the turn of the twentieth century and whose central figures include Ernst Fuchs (German lawyer, 1859–1929), Johann Georg Gmelin (Austrian appellate judge), Eugen Ehrlich (Austrian law professor, 1862–1922), Hermann Kantorowicz (German law professor, 1877–1940), and François Gény (French law professor, 1861–1938). Following Bulow, these jurists began to characterize law as a function of social tendencies and ethical concerns. They stressed that determinacy in law is not principally a function of logical constraints, but the result of natural ordering through the free exercise of judicial power. The free law jurists saw adjudication as essentially an inductive and analogical process, where legal rules develop incrementally, like doctrines of experiential science, through the alignment and realignment of case law according to the facts presented by each new case. Within this process of case law development, they stressed the importance of "judicial personality," the essentially free and creative, yet practice-bound, dispositional state of the judge.

Most fundamentally, the free law jurists sought to free judges from all rules of interpretation aimed at yoking judicial decision making to the formal sources of written law. They argued that jurisprudential theories should acknowledge and describe the nature and limits of judicial freedom, not attempt to constrict judicial practice artificially. To that end, they stressed three points about adjudication: first, that it is inherently free and creative, involving a significant amount of discretionary lawmaking; second, that written law, from codes and statutes to precedent, is unavoidably incomplete and incapable of providing answers to all legal questions; and third, that all rules of legal construction, including those aimed at limiting the freedom of judges, involve implicit value judgments and the application of extralegal principles.

While these general precepts represent the shared perspectives of the free law jurists, individual members of the movement varied from one another considerably in their emphases and orientations. The most extreme version of free law theory, that begun by Ernst Fuchs and taken up by Johann Georg Gmelin, characterized judicial decision making as a subjective enterprise with very few formal limits. Fuchs maintained that no written law can possibly be so comprehensive as to cover every conceivable case. Since no written law can provide a decision rule for all possible cases, he reasoned that statutes and code provisions should not be read as establishing general legal rules. He claimed that statutory provisions should be read as "specific decisions," as decision rules extending only to those cases specifically and expressly addressed by the statutory language. Beyond those cases, courts should exercise a "truly free" method of decision—and in exercising that freedom, they should try, according to Fuchs, to issue decisions which stand in "harmony with a feeling for justice," a "feeling" drawn from "the personal character and substantial experience of the judge."

Justice Gmelin followed Fuchs in emphasizing the subjective and emotive side of judicial decision making. Gmelin recommended that judges abandon any pretense of detached objectivity by imagining that the interests at stake in the cases before them were their own. In this, judges should rely on their subjective emotional response. This was not, however, merely an appeal to personal preference. Gmelin believed in an inherent human sense of justice, a sentiment present in all people, only more finely tuned in the judge: "And finally, the judge is to point out the true direction of

F

the sense of justice implanted in all of us, like a magnetic needle, so to speak."

Yet beyond the actual practice of adjudication, Gmelin further thought that anyone with a cultivated sense of justice, whether judge or legal scholar, can evaluate and determine the rightness of judicial decisions. On the assumption that the sense of justice always takes priority over formal sources of law, he contended that decisions which rest on rational deductions from legislative intent are decided wrongly if they offend the subjective sense of justice. Similarly, courts err if they follow the formal letter of the law strictly when the subjective sense inclines toward equity, or when to do so would strike the subjective sense as "inhuman." Gmelin argued, in sum, that all judicial decisions which appear unsatisfactory to the intuitive sense of justice should be repudiated.

Other proponents of free law theory mollified its subjective orientation. Eugen Ehrlich stressed the importance of "the personality of the judge," yet he avoided the subjective intuitionism of Fuchs and Gmelin. Ehrlich saw adjudication as a creative, dynamic enterprise. He faulted pandectism, which he called "legal technicalism," for adhering too rigidly to written codes, and for thereby failing to apprehend all the factors involved in judicial decision making.

In addition to legislative sources, Ehrlich emphasized three factors that unavoidably influence judicial decision making. First, he argued that every rule of legal construction incorporates into judicial decision making certain value judgments, at the very least the normative assumption that a fair result obtains. Given this, he reproved the technicalists for claiming that their adjudicative method imposed no extralegal values. For if judges are to follow considerations of fairness in their interpretations of written law, then, according to Ehrlich, even the technical method itself allows for substantial judicial discretion.

Second, Ehrlich argued that every case must be viewed within its sociohistorical context. Courts should regard the facts of each case as "coefficients of social tendencies," and rest their decisions at least in part on those tendencies or social conditions prevailing at the time of decision. Ehrlich believed that openly acknowledging this sociohistorical aspect of law would allow judges to see that no legal rule is just absolutely and for all time,

thereby freeing them from the overly rigid adjudicatory fetters of technicalism.

Finally, and most important, Ehrlich emphasized "judicial personality." The freedom he saw inherent in judicial practice was not the subjective intuitionism of Fuchs and Gmelin, but a conservative freedom to responsibly develop and maintain a proper judicial personality. Ehrlich described that personality as one which considers all relevant factors, from written law to sociohistorical context, while regarding legal rules as "living energy." It is a personality that follows the strict letter of statutory or code provisions for what they provide, but no more. Beyond the express letter of the written law, Ehrlich's judge turned to the practice of adjudication itself, with the understanding that adjudicative excellence results from a personality fashioned and determined by what Ehrlich called the sense of justice which "grows out of the principles of juridical tradition." Emphatically declaring that "[t]here is no guaranty of justice except the personality of the judge," Ehrlich maintained that only by acknowledging judicial freedom can judges be held fully accountable for the injustice or arbitrariness of their decisions. Unlike technicalism, free law theory, according to Ehrlich, did not encourage judges to avoid taking responsibility for their rulings by appealing to a "fairness" underwritten by legal fictions, or by claiming that the result they reached was mandated by the intentions of the legislator. Ehrlich's judge was fully accountable, and his accountability resulted from his freedom. He was free to regard the facts of a case as "coefficients of social tendencies," to treat legal rules as "living energy," and to craft new rules of law in a creative, dynamic fashion. Yet these freedoms all fell under the responsibility of maintaining a proper judicial personality. Since that personality was fashioned objectively out of the principles of juridical tradition, the freedom Ehrlich saw inherent in judicial decision making was decidedly conservative.

Outside Germany and Austria the free law movement's principal proponent was François Gény, a French legal philosopher. Like Ehrlich, Gény regarded free law theory as a conservative approach to adjudication, not an appeal to subjectivity. In his view, the formal sources of law (statutes and custom) constitute the whole of the law to the extent they are unambiguous. However, he considered it a dangerous fiction to believe that a civil code could be so complete and comprehensive as to provide for the logical resolution of every legal issue. Accordingly, Gény argued that judicial practice must he understood as including a discretionary, legislative-type responsibility to "supplement" the formal sources of law. Claiming that this supplementary judicial discretion is "inherent in the very nature of the judicial function," he described it as allowing for "free research" into the nature of law under a set of practice-bound constraints that he modeled on the method of scientific discovery.

Gény called his version of free law theory, "free decision on the basis of scientific investigation." He saw judicial practice as resembling the discovery and application of scientific hypotheses insofar as it starts with the discovery of abstract legal concepts by inductive reasoning from the "nature of things" or from "objective realities," and then, by deductive inference, requires the application of those concepts in concrete cases. Like hypotheses of natural science, general legal rules abstracted from the "nature of things" were, for Gény, the critical "objective factors" in judicial decision making.

Gény thus considered the selection of the decision rule for a case to be the "peculiar" aspect of judicial decision making. Yet while he stressed, on the one hand, that judges enjoy inherent freedom to determine which general rule or principle of law should govern a case, he maintained, on the other, that the derivation of such general legal concepts must follow from what is apparent in the "nature of things." Inquiry into the "nature of things" revealed, to Gény, two ideals—justice and social utility—which he then posited as comprising the "ultimate standard" or "ends" of adjudication.

While Gény acknowledged that the ideals of justice and social utility are by themselves "nothing but empty forms," he gave them content by assuming three secondary principles which, he said, "animate the whole system of law." He identified these principles as "1. The principle of autonomous will. 2. The principle of public order or superior interest. 3. The principle of equilibrium of private interests." Combining the abstract ideals of justice and social utility with these three animating principles gave Gény a "scientific" method of free judicial research, which, in the final analysis, reduced all judicial decision making to a utilitarian balancing of interests. Freedom for judges to create legal rules in the context of judicial practice thus meant to him nothing more than a mechanical freedom to perform "a judicious comparison of all the interests involved, with a view to balancing them against each other in conformity with the interests of society."

The free law movement largely succeeded in discrediting pandectism. It also enjoyed a moderate degree of practical influence. For example, Section I of the Swiss Civil Code contains language, attributed to free law influence, extending permission to a judge to decide certain cases "according to the rules which he would lay down if he had himself to act as legislator." The free law movement did not, however, garner much general support for its approach to judicial decision making. It failed in part because each version of free law theory drifted toward one of two extremes—indeterminacy or absolutism. Implicit within the writings of those free law theorists like Fuchs and Gmelin, who argued for a truly free, unrestrained judicial discretion, was the belief that nearly all law is indeterminate. Those free law jurists who sought to avoid indeterminacy, such as Ehrlich and Gény, ultimately failed to show that adjudication is free and unrestrained. They disproved pandectism only by defining freedom in judicial practice in terms of specific methodological or interpretive criteria.

References

Bulow, Oskar. *Gesetz und Richteramt*. 1885. Trans. James E. Herget and Ingrid Wade as "Statutory Law and the Judicial Function." *American Journal of Legal History* 39 (1995), 71–94.

Ehrlich, Eugen. *Freie Rechtsfindung und freie Rechtswissenschaft*. 1903. Trans. Ernest Bruncken as "Judicial Freedom of Decision: Its Principles and Objects." In *Science of Legal Method: Selected Essays by Various Authors*, tr. Ernest Bruncken and Layton B. Register. New York: A.M. Kelley, 1969, 48–84.

Foulkes, Albert S. "On the German Free Law School (*Freirechtsschule*)." *Archiv für Rechts- und Sozialphilosophie* 55 (1969), 367.

Fuchs, Ernst. *Recht und Freiheit in unserer heutigen Justiz* (Law and Freedom in Contemporary Justice). Berlin: C. Heyman, 1908.

Gény, François. *Méthode d'interprétation et sources en droit privé positif: essai critique.* 2d ed. Paris: Librairie générale de droit et de jurisprudence, 1919. Trans. Jaro Mayda as *Method of Interpretation and Sources of Private Positive Law: Critical Essay.* 1963.

———. *Science et technique en droit privé positif. Nouvelle contribution à la critique de la méthode juridique* (Theory and Practice in Positive Private Law. A New Contribution to the Critique of Legal Methodology). 4 vols. Paris: Sirey, 1914–1924.

Gmelin, Johann Georg. *Quousque? Beitrage zur soziologischen Rechtsfindung.* Hanover: Helwing, 1910. Trans. in part by Ernest Bruncken as "Dialecticism and Technicality: The Need of Sociological Method." In *Science of Legal Method: Selected Essays by Various Authors,* ed. Ernest Bruncken and Layton B. Register, 85–145.

Herget, James E., and Stephen Wallace. "The German Free Law Movement as the Source of American Legal Realism." *Virginia Law Review* 73 (1987), 399–455.

Kantorowicz, Hermann. *Rechtswissenschaft und Soziologie* (Jurisprudence and Sociology). Tübingen: Mohr, 1911.

Mayda, Jaro. *François Gény and Modern Jurisprudence.* Baton Rouge: Louisiana State University Press, 1978.

Douglas Lind

See also EXEGETICAL SCHOOL; GÉNY, FRANÇOIS; REALISM, LEGAL

Freedom and Capacity of Contract

The ideal of freedom underlies two central principles of the law of contract in Western legal systems: (1) freedom *to* contract—the principle that contracting parties should be free to make contracts about any matter that they wish, and (2) freedom *of* contract—the principle that only freely made choices should give rise to contractual obligations. This study is about freedom of contract, although it should be noted at the outset that the two principles cannot always be separated neatly. Certain limits on freedom to contract, such as the unenforceability of self-enslavement contracts, although most naturally justified on substantive grounds (for example, that the subject matter of the contract is not morally valuable), are sometimes justified on the ground that they protect against force, fraud, and other freedom *of* contract concerns. The same justification has been put forward in respect of certain formal requirements of validity, such as the requirement that a contract to sell land be in writing or even the common law requirement of mutual consideration.

Importance

As an ideal, freedom of contract is defended on the same grounds upon which freedom generally is defended. Thus, for "rights-based" theorists inspired by Immanuel Kant, freedom of contract is one aspect of the right not to be used as a mere means for another person's ends. Freedom of contract is freedom from unconsented-to positive obligations. For other, teleological or "instrumental," theorists, freedom of contract is important because of the good that freedom promotes, be it wealth, utility, individual well-being or a particular distribution of resources. For an "economic" instrumentalist, for example, freedom of contract is important because only if contracts are freely made are they likely to be mutually beneficial and hence to increase social wealth.

Definition

The attempt to define a freely made agreement raises difficult conceptual problems, as is illustrated by the example of a contract signed at gunpoint. Such a contract is, literally, voluntary: the promisor had a choice between two alternatives and chose the more attractive alternative. The problem with the contract, it seems clear, is that it was made under pressure. Yet the mere existence of pressure cannot be sufficient to make an agreement involuntary. Traders in the marketplace are under pressure to sell if they wish to survive. The distinction that needs to be drawn, therefore, is between legitimate and illegitimate pressure.

Rights-based theorists define illegitimate pressure as an infringement or threatened infringement of a right. This approach is criticized for leaving unanswered the question of what rights individuals actually have, but, in response, the rights-based theorist can point out that defining individuals' rights is not strictly a task for contract law, since any transfer of resources, contractual or otherwise, is invalid if achieved through a threat. Instrumental approaches assess the legitimacy of pressure by asking whether enforcing the impugned agreement will promote the desired goal (for instance, wealth, well-being). This approach is criticized for resting on unproven empirical assumptions about the advantages and disadvantages of alternative rules, but, in response, the instrumentalist can point out that empirical issues are not a direct concern of legal theory. Neither instrumental nor rights-based approaches have had much to say about how improper pressure in the form of undue influence should be defined nor, despite much debate, had great success in explaining how the law does or should deal with the pressure created by a threatened breach of contract.

Capacity

For a contract to be freely made, the promisor not only must be free from improper pressure but must also have the mental capacities necessary to make free choices. The distinction between these two obstacles to freedom, one external (pressure), the other internal (incapacity), is not always recognized in the law. For example, in the common law of undue influence, courts do not distinguish between cases where the promisee improperly exerts pressure on the promisor and cases where the promisee is passive, the undue influence arising because of the promisor's internal disposition to rely on the promisee. In the standard case of incapacity, where the distinction is fairly clear, the promisor suffers a general incapacity such as minority, incompetency, or drunkenness. Little theoretical work has been done, at least by contract lawyers, to flesh out the notion of contractual capacity. According to a rights-based theory, a determination of incapacity would appear to reflect a conclusion that an individual lacks the mental capacities necessary to understand or exercise rights and thus to create a binding obligation. According to an instrumental approach, a determination of incapacity normally reflects a conclusion that the individual lacks the ability to act consistently in his or her own interests.

Standard form contracts are rarely discussed in the context of contractual capacity, but some of the issues they raise, in particular the issue of whether promisors should be held to terms that they cannot reasonably be expected to be aware of or to understand, are plausibly understood as capacity issues. It may not be coincidental, therefore, that in respect of both standard form contracts and contracts with parties who lack full capacity, most legal regimes adopt, in certain situations, a halfway position whereby the contract is unenforceable only to the extent that its terms are unfair. The assumption in these cases, it appears, is that the promisors are capable of making free choices, and thus ought to be allowed to contract, yet are not fully able to protect themselves, and thus ought to be protected against unfair terms. This concern for fair terms is significant because, while supported by ordinary intuitions, it does not fit easily into traditional rights-based or instrumental approaches. It is not obvious why a substantively unfair contract infringes a promisor's rights or is, for example, inefficient.

Monopoly

Difficult issues are raised by cases where, although external pressure has not been exerted and the promisor has full contractual capacity, the offeror is a monopolist. In rights-based approaches, the number of options open to a promisor is not significant, although it is important in most instrumental approaches. Economists, for example, dislike monopolies because monopolies normally reduce the number of wealth-enhancing exchanges concluded in a market. Aside from invalidating agreements that create or support monopolies, there is little that contract law, qua contract law, can do to prevent monopolies, but what it can and sometimes does do is to invalidate or at least rewrite contracts in which monopolists have charged exorbitant prices: thus a contract between a tugboat and a ship in danger is normally enforceable only insofar as the terms are fair. Here, again, substantive fairness is accorded independent value. Standard form contracts, it should be noted, are sometimes thought to reflect the abuse of monopolistic power, but in recent years there has been a wider appreciation that, while not unproblematic, standard forms are primarily a response to the high cost of individualized contracts in an age of mass contracting.

Mistake

A final factor to consider in determining whether a contract has been freely made is that of the adequacy of the information possessed by the contracting parties. It has been argued, from a rights-based perspective, that promises made under mistaken assumptions are not true promises and thus cannot support contractual obligations (though they may support noncontractual liability). The more natural conclusion, however, is that, as with adequacy of choice, adequacy of information is irrelevant in a rights-based approach to contract. Adequacy of information is, however, significant for an instrumentalist because an uninformed choice may not reflect the promisor's true interests. Whatever the value of adequate information, most legal regimes have weak disclosure requirements and rarely invalidate contracts because of mistaken assumptions. Active deception, such as fraud or misrepresentation, is a ground for relief, but such deception is a form of wrongdoing, analogous to duress. The instrumentalist's explanation of the law's approach is that requiring disclosure or permitting a broad defense of mistake will reduce the incentives to produce and acquire valuable information. That said, many theorists have argued for wider duties of disclosure, while others claim to find in the application, if not the articulation of the law, a refusal to allow parties to take advantage of ignorance and thus an implicit recognition of an ethic of cooperation.

References

Birks, Peter, and Nyuk Yin Chin. "On the Nature of Undue Influence." In *Good Faith and Fault in Contract Law,* ed. Jack Beatson and Daniel Friedmann. Oxford: Clarendon Press, 1995.

Epstein, Richard. "Unconscionability: A Critical Reappraisal." *Journal of Law and Economics* 18 (1975), 283.

Fried, Charles. *Contract as Promise.* Cambridge MA: Harvard University Press, 1981.

Gordley, James. "Equality in Exchange." *California Law Review* 69 (1981), 1587.

Kennedy, Duncan. "Distributive and Paternalist Motives in Contract and Tort Law." *Maryland LR* 41 (1982), 563.

Kronman, Anthony. "Contract Law and Distributive Justice." *Yale Law Journal* 89 (1980), 472.

Mazeaud, H., et al. *Leçons de Droit civil* (Studies in Civil Law). Bk. 2, Vol. 1. Paris: Editions Montchrestien, 1991.

Trebilcock, Michael. *The Limits of Freedom of Contract.* Cambridge MA: Harvard University Press, 1993.

Stephen A. Smith

See also COERCION (DURESS), JUSTICE IN CONTRACT, CIVILIAN; LEGITIMATE OBJECT OF CONTRACT; OBLIGATION AND DUTY

Fuller, Lon L. (1902–1978)

Lon L. Fuller, professor of jurisprudence at Harvard Law School from 1940 to 1970, is the best-known twentieth-century American exponent of secular natural law. Lon Fuller's highly original combination of sociological jurisprudence and natural law method manifests itself in conceptions of law, morality, and their interrelationships, which differ sharply from those conventional in the legal philosophy of the twentieth century. Fuller's devotion to Aristotle and his application of the methods of pragmatic philosophy lead him to focus on the human social processes that generate law and morality. Hence, he departs from traditional natural law approaches in that he develops almost no substantive content for his natural law thinking. Instead, he believes that attention to natural law process will ultimately have substantive consequences, although they would still be confined to the particular social setting in historical time.

Morality

Fuller begins his departure from conventional thinking in his approach to morality. First, he believes that the positivist effort to separate "is" and "ought" is ineffective, since the two interact in dynamic social settings and can therefore be separated only abstractly or in a purely analytical sense. Rather, he believes that moral duty can be understood *only* in its social context. Second, he adds a different sort of morality, of aspiration, which must be distinguished from the morality of duty. Third, he claims that morality must be separated in yet a different dimension as internal and external.

The social context in which he finds moral duty is the reciprocity growing out of the relations inherent in human social interaction, a notion that he takes from the pragmatic sociological theory known as symbolic interaction. Certain preconditions, to the extent they are realized, will optimize the reciprocity experienced: voluntariness of the agreement, reversibility of roles, and relative equivalence of the exchange. These preconditions are most representative of a society of free-market traders.

The morality of aspiration involves locating the pointer on the moral scale as a continuum between duty and aspiration. Too much duty characterizes a repressive society in which initiative and creativity are stifled. Too little duty produces a society in which persons are praised for carrying out the most basic social tasks, a self-esteem society.

External morality is the sort normally addressed in moral philosophy. Is an activity good? Is a behavior morally correct? In contrast, internal morality is actually a role or institutional morality, whose question is whether the activity under consideration is being carried out in accordance with the principles that constitute that activity. If not, the integrity of that institution will be impaired or even destroyed. For instance, a judge having private meetings with one of the parties in an adjudication breaks the internal rules of the process and calls into question the impartiality of the proceedings, thus undermining its integrity.

Law

Fuller sees the purpose of law as providing a framework for social interaction. He offers a nondefinition of law, as the enterprise of subjecting human conduct to the governance of rules. He consciously makes no mention of sanctions. The entire realm of legal powers derives its compliance from the fact that citizens derive benefits from following the law. Law allows citizens to enhance their freedom by making innovations possible in the structure of business and commerce as well as all aspects of everyday life. Ironically, Fuller sees law as more pervasive in social life than do the positivists.

Since the purpose of law is to provide a framework for social interaction, Fuller sees the possibility of compliance as a central feature of law. His "eight ways to fail to make law" violate the principles of legality by making compliance impossible. These principles require (1) that there must be rules; laws must be stated with some generality, neither ad hoc commands nor extensive use of managerial direction in government. The rules must be (2) promulgated; secret laws undermine the very heart of legality. Rules must also be (3) prospective, (4) noncontradictory, and (5) not so rapidly changed that behavior patterns cannot be adjusted. Rules must also be (6) reasonably clear; gibberish cannot be comprehended and therefore cannot be followed. Rules must

be (7) possible of performance. Finally, there must be (8) congruence between the rules as announced and the rules as applied, to avoid turning the legal system into nothing more than ad hoc commands.

Internal Morality of Law

Legality equates with law's capacity for enjoying legitimacy. Its principles of legality are its internal morality. (A law is unlikely to enjoy much legitimacy if it is unstated, unknown, or unclear.) This internal morality of law remains largely a morality of aspiration. Achievement of duty is only its minimal level; at the upper level, for outstanding achievements of legality, awards would be appropriate. Law is an enterprise that can be carried out with varying degrees of success; a legal system can half exist. How legal it is depends on the degree to which it complies with the principles of legality. Only complete failure to observe one of the principles of legality can result in a failure to make law.

An important point follows: the objective of attaining legitimacy means that the purpose of the principles of legality is not specific compliance with each principle, but the achievement of optimum overall legality. In some cases there may be trade-offs between one or more principles. For example, the greater the clarity, the more challenging the generality becomes. Retrospective legislation may be required to avoid the defeat of legitimate reliance expectations, for example, upon failure to promulgate new requirements for valid marriages. This example shows that the objective of legality is not the precise application of the legal enactment, but the furtherance of the aims held collectively by the society.

Law and Morality

Seeking legitimacy entails close attention to the moral aims of the society, lest tyrants claim legality as a pretext to justify retrospective warrants of execution. Consistency with the society's expectations of justice is necessary in order to have good compliance with the enforcement required of legality. Law too inconsistent with the moral expectations of society brings greater avoidance behavior, through failure to enforce the law consistently, selective prosecution, jury nullification, judicial leniency, and other means of avoidance that Fuller illustrates in his famous hypothetical "Case of the Speluncean Explorers."

H.L.A. Hart disputed Fuller's claim that the principles of legality are an internal morality of law, saying that the principles of legality are nothing more than guides to effective law. In *Anatomy of the Law,* writing for a general audience, Fuller attempts to clarify his point by employing a contrast between made law and implicit law. Legislation is a classic case of made law. Customary law is an example of implicit law. His attention is devoted to the made elements in implicit law and the implicit elements in made law. Legal positivists overlook the implicit elements in made law, exemplified by the principles of legality. Sociological approaches often ignore the made elements in implicit law; even apparently spontaneous legal orderings turn out to have many elements of deliberate and conscious decision making.

Fuller is almost entirely disinterested in speculating as to the content of an external morality of law. He does believe, however, that there is a connection between compliance with the internal morality of law and achievement in the domain of the external morality of law. Although not logically necessary, he believes that there is a tendency for the two to interact.

References

Fuller, Lon. *Anatomy of the Law.* New York: Frederick A. Praeger, 1968. Reprint, Westport CT: Greenwood Press, 1976.

———. "Collective Bargaining and the Arbitrator." *Wisconsin Law Review* (1963), 3–46.

———. "Irrigation and Tyranny." *Stanford Law Review* 17 (1965), 1021–1042.

———. *The Morality of Law.* New Haven: Yale University Press, 1964. Rev. ed., 1969.

———. *The Principles of Social Order.* Ed. Kenneth I. Winston. Durham NC: Duke University Press, 1981.

Moffat, Robert C.L. "Implicit Promise Keeping and Fuller's Internal Morality of Law." *Rechtstheorie* 11 (1991), 215–221.

———. "Obligation to Obey the Law: Substance and Procedure in the Thought of Lon Fuller." *International Journal of Applied Philosophy* 1 (1983), 33–49.

———. "The Perils of Positivism *or* Lon Fuller's Lesson on Looking at Law: Neither Science nor Mystery—Merely Method." *Harvard Journal of Law and Public Policy* 10 (1987), 295–348.

Summers, Robert S. *Lon L. Fuller.* Stanford: Stanford University Press, 1984.

Teachout, Peter Read. "The Soul of the Fugue: An Essay on Reading Fuller." *Minnesota Law Review* 70 (1986), 1073–1148.

Robert C.L. Moffat

See also GOODNESS AND COHERENCE

Fundamental Rights

Central to the liberal tradition is the idea that rights are not on a par and of equal significance. Certain rights protecting individual freedoms and the integrity of the person are more important than other rights and privileges of persons, and even powers of governments. These fundamental rights are in the first instance owed to persons, not to groups, and are owed to them all equally. The idea that there are such rights with a special weight originated with the natural law tradition. Certain rights were deemed "natural" in the sense that they were nonconventional, not a product of law or custom, but required by justice. They were also natural in that they were deemed knowable by "the natural light of reason," according to John Locke, pursuing commonsense methods of inquiry. Natural rights are now more commonly called "basic" or "fundamental."

Within liberalism, the primary function of fundamental rights has been to maintain the pluralism of different and often conflicting conceptions of the good, thereby ensuring the toleration of different religious and philosophical views and diverse ways of living. A different function of the idea of fundamental rights, in American law in particular, has been to secure economic relations of laissez-faire capitalism.

Rights easily overridden for other values and claims are not fundamental. The special weight assigned to fundamental rights exhibits their two central features. First, fundamental rights cannot be overridden by governmental laws or actions for the sake of others' likes and dislikes, or to promote efficiency, greater social welfare, or perfectionist values of culture. Fundamental rights, as a class, are then absolute with respect to other social values. This does not mean that any particular fundamental right is absolute or of greater significance than all the others. It means, rather, that a fundamental right should be limited or regulated only for the sake of protecting or maintaining others' rights or the scheme of basic rights. (For example, freedom of speech and expression can be limited, not because it is offensive or sacrilegious, but in order to protect people from bodily harm when speech is so incendiary that it rises to the level of incitement to riot or crime.)

The second way the special weight of fundamental rights is displayed is through their inalienability (an idea deriving from the social contract tradition). Inalienability means that rights cannot be given up freely by the person who has them. People cannot exchange or contract away their fundamental rights for the sake of greater perceived benefits. Fundamental rights, then, are unlike alienable property rights. John Locke, Jean-Jacques Rousseau, Immanuel Kant, and John Stuart Mill all held that one cannot sell himself into slavery. No court within a liberal constitution would recognize a contract where a person sought to alienate his constitutional rights. This does not mean people cannot forfeit some of their basic rights upon committing serious crimes. Criminal penalties can legitimately deprive people of certain fundamental rights (freedom of movement upon imprisonment, perhaps even the right to live assuming the death penalty is legitimate). However, involuntary forfeiture is not the same as voluntary alienation.

Libertarianism (for instance, of Robert Nozick, Ayn Rand) differs from liberalism in that it assigns absolute weight to freedom of contract and treats all rights as property rights that are completely alienable. In this sense, libertarians do not recognize fundamental rights as here defined, however much they might otherwise emphasize individual freedom.

Inalienability indicates that underlying the idea of fundamental rights is both an ideal of the person and an ideal of social relations among persons. Regarding this social ideal, a fixed tendency of the liberal tradition has been not simply to promote but also to maintain the freedom of all individuals, so as to ensure their equal civic status. The value of equality is then defined within liberalism primarily by reference to the idea of equality of basic rights. This social ideal of civic equality is supported by an ideal of persons as such being owed certain rights simply by virtue of having the capacities persons normally do, without regard to their racial, gender, or other group status. Within liberal thought traditionally, the capacities to reason and therewith plan and control one's actions, and the capacities to understand and comply with social norms and moral requirements, have been held sufficient to warrant the full array of basic rights.

Equality of fundamental rights is not a controversial notion within liberal and democratic thought. What is disputed is the kind and extent of rights that are to be deemed fundamental. Liberals generally agree that freedom of religion and, more generally, liberty of conscience—the right to decide basic questions of value and what gives life its meaning—are fundamental. Also, freedom of thought, speech, and expression, freedom of association, freedom of occupation and movement, and more generally the rights needed to maintain the integrity and freedom of the person to make important life decisions, are commonly accepted fundamental liberties (though theorists might disagree regarding the relative weight of these liberties). Rights to personal property are generally seen by liberals as among the rights needed to maintain the freedom and independence of the person. Classical liberalism (for example, of Friedrich von Hayek) differs from egalitarian views in emphasizing the fundamental status of individual property in productive resources, along with freedom of contract to buy and sell property rights, and rights of unlimited accumulation of property of all kinds. These extensive "economic rights" are allegedly needed to protect against government tyranny, and so are given protection from most legislative interferences and even regulations. By contrast, modern liberal egalitarian views (for example, John Rawls) assign fundamental status to equal rights of political participation, thereby incorporating democracy into liberalism. Democratic legislation is allowed far greater sway in economic matters than is recognized by classical liberals. To provide for the personal independence and self-respect of each citizen, egalitarian liberals might assign nearly fundamental status to a right to a social minimum of income and wealth, to be fixed by democratic decision.

In American constitutional law the Supreme Court has said in *Palko v. Conn.*, 302 U.S. 319, 325 (1937), that certain features of the federal Bill of Rights "represented the very essence of a scheme of ordered liberty, . . . principles of justice so rooted in the traditions and conscience of our people as to be ranked fundamental." These fundamental rights are the first priority in judicial review of legislation. The idea of fundamental rights is explicitly called upon by the Supreme Court to specify those federal constitutional guarantees that also apply to limit state and local governments; these rights are held to have been "incorporated" to apply to the states by the due process clause of the Fourteenth Amendment. Primary among fundamental constitutional rights are First Amendment freedoms of speech, press, religion, assembly, and petition, and most of the procedural rights protected by the fourth to the eighth amendments. Freedom of economic contract and rights of property were once treated by the judiciary as fundamental during the nation's first century and a half and were used to restrict federal and state authority to enact laws regulating property, workplace conditions, and commercial transactions. Since the decline of the doctrine of economic substantive due process in the 1930s, contract and property rights have lost their fundamental status for the most part. More recently, however, substantive due process has been revived to justify a fundamental right to privacy, therewith procreative freedom and a constitutional right of abortion. Moreover, protections against racial and gender discrimination have increasingly been construed as fundamental rights.

References

Hayek, Friedrich von. *The Constitution of Liberty*. 1960. Chicago: University of Chicago Press, 1978.

Locke, John. *Two Treatises of Government*. Cambridge: Cambridge University Press, 1988.

Mill, John Stuart. *On Liberty*. Cambridge: Cambridge University Press, 1989.

Nozick, Robert. *Anarchy, State, and Utopia*. New York: Basic Books, 1974.

Rawls, John. *A Theory of Justice*. Cambridge MA: Harvard University Press, 1971.

Samuel Freema

G

Gadamer, Hans-Georg (1900–)

Arguably the most significant German philosopher in the twentieth century, after Martin Heidegger (1889–1976), is Hans-Georg Gadamer. Gadamer was Heidegger's student for a time, though Gadamer is a philologist as well as a philosopher. Gadamer's first publications are on Plato and Aristotle. The early part of Gadamer's career, culminating in *Platos dialektische Ethik (Plato's Dialectical Ethics),* published in 1931, makes a case that Plato's is not a two-world theory—theory versus practice, or the forms (*paradigmata*) versus tangible phenomena—as many Plato scholars posit. Rather, a dialectical relationship is at work, so that there is not a world of ideas to which only gods have access and a world of phenomena reserved for human beings. This relationship is mediated, most importantly for Gadamer, by language.

It would be tempting to link cross-examinations in a courtroom to what goes in a Platonic dialogue, with one character claiming something that is then put to the test, questioned, the presupposition being that we are answerable for our words, responsible for them, obliged to be responsive. Thus the ethical dimension to Gadamer's book. Plato provides us with a world full of people being accountable for their words in the sense that the people who are questioned are asked to give reasons or causes. Throughout his works Gadamer highlights this back-and-forth movement of conversation as characteristic of thinking. However, a cross-examination situated in a courtroom would be a false analogy to what takes place in the Platonic dialogues, since the witnesses in court, though they present reasons and causes under questioning, are not free participants in dialogue, even on the obvious level of being unable to leave when they wish. In Plato's well-known aporetic dialogues, characters sometimes find themselves floundering under questioning and fleeing, such as in the *Euthyphro*. The constraints of the courtroom prevent speakers from such actions and put interlocutors in unequal positions. In a sense, witnesses are means to a greater end in the courtroom, something alien to the description of the dialogical situation in Gadamer's book, in which the "motive is not to secure the disclosure of [the] matter, but, rather, to enable the participants themselves to become manifest to each other in speaking about it. Thus, at bottom, such a conversation is made no less fruitful by the participants' inability to come to an agreement about the matter. . . ." The concern here is less practical (obtaining correct answers or winning the case) than ontological.

The direct link between legal matters and Gadamer's work appears in Gadamer's magnum opus, *Wahrheit und Methode (Truth and Method),* published in 1960, in a section titled "The Exemplary Significance of Legal Hermeneutics." In that section Gadamer asserts: "It is only in all its applications that the law becomes concrete. Thus the legal historian cannot be content to take the original application of the law as determining its original meaning." While Gadamer notes the importance of application for all sorts of interpretation, he sees it as an ongoing process, conditioned by new circumstances and situations, so that whenever the law speaks, it speaks differently. No one would imagine the proponent of "historically effected consciousness" (*wirkungsgeschichtliches Bewusstsein*) choosing the present over the past. In *Truth and Method*, Gadamer writes: "Someone who is seeking to understand the correct meaning of a law must first know the original one." Once again, Gadamer points to a dialogical relation, in which the past is seen in its continuity with the present. Those who promote the original intention of legal texts turn those texts into museum pieces to be preserved, thus deadening them, whereas Gadamer speaks of judges who, knowing the original law, are alive, aware of the new circumstances they must address to "define afresh the normative function of the law."

References

Dallmayr, Fred. "Hermeneutics and the Rule of Law." In *Legal Hermeneutics: History, Theory, and Practice*, ed. Gregory Leyh, 3–22. Berkeley: University of California Press, 1992.

Gadamer, Hans-Georg. *Gesammelte Werke* (Complete Works). 10 Vol. Tübingen: J.C.B. Mohr, 1985–1995.

———. *The Idea of the Good in Platonic-Aristotelian Philosophy*. Trans. P. Christopher Smith. New Haven: Yale University Press, 1986.

———. *Philosophical Hermeneutics*. Trans. David E. Linge. Berkeley: University of California Press, 1976.

———. *Plato's Dialectical Ethics: Phenomenological Interpretations Relating to the "Philebus."* Trans. Robert M. Wallace. New Haven: Yale University Press, 1991.

———. "Reply to Nicholas P. White." In *Platonic Writings, Platonic Readings*, ed. Charles L. Griswold, Jr., 258–266. New York: Routledge, 1988.

———. *Truth and Method*. 2d rev. ed. Trans. Joel Weinsheimer and Donald G. Marshall. New York: Crossroad, 1989.

Krajewski, Bruce. *Traveling with Hermes: Hermeneutics and Rhetoric*. Amherst: University of Massachusetts Press, 1992.

Michelfelder, Diane P. , and Richard E. Palmer, eds. *Dialogue and Deconstruction: The Gadamer-Derrida Encounter*. Albany: State University of New York Press, 1989.

Warnke, Georgia. *Justice and Interpretation*. Cambridge: MIT Press, 1992.

Bruce Krajewski

See also HERMENEUTICAL PHILOSOPHY OF LAW

Game Theory

Since it was first articulated by mathematician John von Neumann and economist Oskar Morgenstern in 1944, modern game theory has entered the canon of disciplines as diverse as international diplomacy and evolutionary biology. But it was only with R. Luce and H. Raiffa in 1957 that it reached the attention of ethicists, political philosophers, and philosophers of law.

Game theory is a subset of decision theory, according to which we are mutually disinterested, rational maximizers of the satisfaction of our well-ordered preferences. What game theory adds is that morality and politics are just intramental and extramental responses (respectively) to otherwise-dilemmatic patterns of *inter*activity.

In ethics and political philosophy game theory has become virtually synonymous with contractarianism. But since it aims at a complete and metaphysically neutral reduction of moral and political categories, it has found favor among positivists (both legal and logical) in general. Especially hostile to it, in turn, have been feminists and marxists, because concerns for children, future generations, the irremediably disabled—in short the interactively powerless—are relegated to the realm of the merely private.

Of these aforementioned "patterns" the most exhaustively reviewed has been the Prisoners' Dilemma (PD). Each of two partners in crime have been apprehended, isolated, and told she will serve two years if neither confesses, three if both confess, none if she unilaterally confesses, and five if she unilaterally keeps silent. There being no honor among thieves, each reasons that regardless of what the other does she had best confess—but similarly reasons the other.

Rehearsal of this eventuality prior to their arrest, would not have helped, for the more one convinces the other she will keep silent, all the more reason would there be for the first to defect on any agreement to do likewise. More generally, then, the gain in "expected utility" from mutual defection to mutual cooperation is the cooperative dividend—in this case an extra year of freedom each. And the challenge is to find a way to access that dividend.

The hobbesian (or externalist) solution, anticipated by Glaucon in *Republic*, is to institute a sovereign to lower the expected utility of defection so that each player now prefers to cooperate. However, in addition to such external mechanisms being (1) expensive, (2) corruptible, and (3) inadequate to account for uncoerced cooperation, (4) the act of instituting the sovereign itself presupposes a *meta*-sovereign, and so on ad infinitum. This "compliance" problem has become especially central to game theoretic critiques of *Leviathan,* for example, by David Gauthier, Gregory Kavka, and Jean Hampton.

To overcome all four difficulties Gauthier has proposed instead an *internalist* solution, according to which one adopts a translucent disposition to cooperate with those, but only those she has good grounds to believe will cooperate with her. Since she cannot be exploited by those without this disposition—and yet she can do considerably better than they can should she happen upon another similarly disposed—it should not surprise us that (or at least if) natural selection has rendered most of us just so "constrained."

Internalist game theory is currently being aided with tools borrowed from artificial intelligence (for example, Peter Danielson) to fine-tune the logic of such dispositions, and the insights provided are rapidly being applied across the philosophical landscape.

In most PDs the cooperative dividend is divisible; this gives rise to the bargaining dilemma. If severally you and I can produce one widget each, but together we can produce five, then, since it would be irrational for you not to settle for as little as two, it would be irrational for me to settle for less than three—but similarly reason you. So embedded within the logic of any bargaining "equilibrium"—that is, the split at which we would agree to settle—is a game of Chicken. (In Chicken, much as each would like the other to "chicken out" while she "stays the course," she would rather chicken out herself than neither doing so.) Unfortunately, a notion of equilibrium for Chicken has proven difficult to define let alone resolve.

Not surprisingly, however, given the enormous intellectual resources made available during the Cold War, considerable progress *has* been made toward understanding the logic of deterrence (for example, Gregory Kavka).

It is widely conceded that Thomas Hobbes erred in supposing that political liberties are indivisible and that civil society therefore demands their complete forfeiture. Provided each of us has something to offer (or

threaten to withhold), we are in a position to negotiate—and in an ongoing position to *renegotiate*—the rules for the distribution of the material and liberal dividends with which we are prepared to enter civil society and/or remain there. John Rawls invites us to negotiate this behind a "veil of ignorance" as to our particular natural and social endowments. However, we cannot be coaxed behind this veil without appeal to "fairness," and this would run afoul of game theory's commitment to full reduction. Joining Gauthier in offering versions of the lockean proviso for fixing on a baseline are Robert Nozick and Jan Narveson. For others, however, it is unclear that *any* principled baseline is required beyond "What's mine is what's useless to *you,* save by deferring to me for its deployment!"

There is no consensus on whether we are negotiating with or without our guns on the table. If the latter is true, then game theory's contribution to political economy begins only where recourse to violence lacks credibility. If the former is true, then it devolves to a subdiscipline of military science; that is, it anticipates what our respective bargaining positions *would* be had all parties spent their military resources, and then it proposes a distribution of the dividends of cooperation *and* of our not having actually spent those resources.

There has yet to be a comprehensive, canonical reduction of legal categories to game theoretic ones. But the program is clear. Substantive legal judgments will be adjudicated by procedural theorems generated from these as-yet-to-be-agreed-upon political axioms.

Thus, while internalism and its myriad applications flourish, externalism awaits the resolution of several foundational issues. Even if consensus on these is *not* forthcoming, game theory offers us a canonical language into which intractable philosophical differences can at least be rendered commensurable.

References

Campbell, R., and L. Sowden. *Paradoxes of Rationality and Cooperation: Prisoner's Dilemma and Newcomb's Problem.* Vancouver: University of British Columbia Press, 1985.

Danielson, Peter. *Artificial Morality.* New York: Routledge, 1993.

Gauthier, David. *Morals by Agreement.* Oxford: Clarendon Press, 1986.

Hampton, Jean. *Hobbes and the Social Con-*

tract Tradition. Cambridge: Cambridge University Press, 1986.

Kavka, Gregory. *Moral Paradoxes of Nuclear Deterrence.* Cambridge: Cambridge University Press, 1987.

Luce, R., and H. Raiffa. *Games and Decisions.* New York: Wiley, 1957.

Narveson, Jan. *The Libertarian Idea.* Philadelphia: Temple University Press, 1988.

Rapaport, Anatol, et al. *The 2 X 2 Game.* Ann Arbor: University of Michigan Press, 1976.

Vallentyne, Peter, ed. *Contractarians and Rational Choice: Essays on Gauthier.* Cambridge: Cambridge University Press, 1991.

von Neumann, J., and O. Morgenstern. *Theory of Games and Economic Behaviour.* Princeton: Princeton University Press, 1944.

Paul Viminitz

See also RATIONAL BARGAINING

Gény, François (1861–1959)

François Gény, a French jurist writing at the turn of the nineteenth century, was famous for his criticism of the strict and legalistic methods of the nineteenth-century exegetical school. He started his academic career in Algiers. In 1892 he was appointed to the University of Dijon and became ordinarius in civil law at the University of Nancy. Most of Gény's works concern legal theory. His first work, *Méthode d'interprétation et sources en droit privé positif* first published in 1899, was a big success on the academic market. In this book, Gény offers a systematic analysis and critique of the legal methods of his nineteenth-century colleagues, in order to develop an alternative view on legal sources and the role of the judge in lawmaking. Concerning statutory interpretation, Gény took a rather conservative point of view: statutes should be given the meaning that corresponds as truly as possible to the will of the legislator. In this respect, he distanced himself from the exegetical school, which put too much emphasis on textual interpretation, and from contemporary currents as well, which dissociated the meaning of a statute completely from the will of the legislator (for example, *Freie Rechtsschule* [the free law school], sociological jurisprudence).

Especially in his theory of legal sources, Gény's work meant a breakaway from the pre-dominant view. Beside statutory law, legal sources such as customary law and judge-made law, based on thorough scientific argumentation, should be fully recognized. In his view on customary law, Gény borrowed a lot from the German historical school. In order to be regarded as a full legal rule, a custom should be reflected by a general, public, and uninterrupted social practice, and be considered, by the people who practice it, as a binding rule.

Although a judge was not allowed to put aside explicitly a valid statute, as was the case with the famous "Judge Magnaud," Gény thought that judges had ample discretionary room for completing the law. He rejected the claim, however, that this would mean a government of judges or a return to the prerevolutionary practices of *les règlements d'arrêts.* In his creative role the judge had to rely on *la libre recherche scientifique,* that is, study of the intellectual, natural, and social data and social aspirations on which his decision had to be based.

In 1924 Gény published his *Science et technique en droit privé positif.* This work of fourteen hundred pages, which lacks the conciseness of the first, focuses more on the nature of legal science as such. His philosophical and methodological views expressed in *Science et technique* are rather eclectic and full of compromises between the major currents in the turbulent intellectual climate of the 1920s.

Gény propagated a wide notion of legal science, leaving plenty of room for interdisciplinary cooperation. For the sake of scientific seriousness, the legal scientist should consider different levels of relevant data in societies, which he calls the real and the historic given (*donnés réels, donnés historiques*). Further, the legal scientist should also study the underlying social aspirations of his time in order to elaborate a legal expression of them. The most important task in legal science, however, consisted of the rational given (*donné rationnel*). This encompassed the abstract aristotelian ideal of justice and the most general legal principles, such as respect for the human person and respect for marriages as stable unions. In this regard Gény defended a flexible notion of natural law against the positivistic views of contemporaneous authors such as Georges Ripert. With all these levels of data in mind, the legal scientist had to elaborate legal solutions with the help of a body of legal techniques, which Gény considered as more a means toward an end. As different legal techniques Gény distinguishes the "plastic" techniques, such as formalism in contracts and publicity of legal titles; the real categories in law, based on real features of social situations, such as the notion of quasi-contracts, or ius in re aliena; and the intellectual techniques, such as abstraction, systematization, and the development of legal fictions, such as legal entity.

François Gény was probably one of the most erudite legal theorists of his time. His knowledge of German and English legal literature was especially impressive. His legal theory is, however, too eclectic and not precise enough to tempt modern legal scholars. Nevertheless, Gény has won his place in the history of legal science by his sharp criticism of the strict and arid methods of nineteenth-century legal science.

References

Dabin, J., et al. *Le Centenaire du doyen François Gény* (The Centenary of Dean François Gény). Paris: Dalloz, 1963.

Sedlácek, J., et al. *L'oeuvre de François Gény, Recueil d'études sur les sources du droit en l'honneur de François Gény* (The Work of François Gény. A Collection of Studies on the Sources of Law in Honor of François Gény). 2 vols. Paris: Sirey, 1934.

Gény, F. *Méthode d'interprétation et sources en droit privé positif* (Method of Interpretation and Sources in Positive Private Law). 2d ed. Paris: Librairie Générale de Droit et Jurisprudence, 1932.

———. *Science et technique en droit privé positif. Nouvelle contribution à la critique de la Méthode juridique* (Theory and Practice in Private Positive Law. A New Contribution to the Critique of Legal Methodology). Paris: Sirey, 1924. (Trans. of pp. 155–159 and 169–176 from the 1st ed. as "Science of Legal Method" in *Modern Legal Philosophy*. Cambridge MA: Harvard University Press, 1917.)

Jones, Harry. "Modern Discussions of the Aims and the Methods of Legal Science." *Law Quarterly Review* 62 (1931), 67–73.

Pound, Roscoe. *Jurisprudence*. Pt. 1. St. Paul MN: West, 1959.

Whitecross Paton, George. *A Textbook of Jurisprudence*. Oxford: Clarendon Press, 1972.

Wortley, B.A. "François Gény." In *Modern Theories of Law*, ed. W.I. Jennings. Oxford: Oxford University Press, 1933.

Boudwijn Bouckaert

Gift

The law of gifts governs the enforceability and legal consequences of certain gratuitous transactions that are subject to the private law.

In daily usage, a variety of transactions are spoken of as gifts. These include the presents given to friends and close relatives on special occasions, transfers within the family to reduce taxes or as an advancement of inheritance, gifts between spouses, incentives given to good customers and to members of the sales force, awards made to employees upon retirement, and donations to charity. In many modern legal systems, however, these transactions are not all subject to the law of gifts to the same extent. For example, gifts of modest value (sometimes known as customary gifts) are often excluded from the scope of gift law. Due to their business context, incentives to customers and sales representatives may also not be considered to be gifts. Gifts between spouses are commonly governed by other rules. In some systems, special provision is made for remunerative gifts, which may include gifts given to employees upon retirement.

Gift law is principally concerned with transactions that, from the point of view of exchange and the marketplace, provide grounds for concern. These generally include larger gifts made within the family or for charitable purposes. Due to the largely protective purpose of gift law, the legal definition of the gift does not follow ordinary usage. In general, the legal definition combines four elements. The first is gratuitousness, which is variously defined as the absence of a quid pro quo or the lack of an obligation on the part of the donor. Second, there are subjective factors, including donative intent and agreement about the gratuitous character of the transaction. Third, in order to distinguish gifts from *mortis causa* (transfers that occur at death) such as those made under a will, a transaction is considered to be a gift only if it operates inter vivos. Finally, the transaction must involve a transfer of wealth, particularly of a property right, rather than a service or the conferring of other kinds of advantage.

When these four elements coincide, a number of consequences often ensue. In general, promises held to be gift promises are less likely to be judicially enforced than are those that are part of a bargain. In some systems, complex form requirements are mandated for the execution of a gift, and, if they are lacking, the gift may be held to be void. The capacity requirements for both making and, surprisingly, even for receiving a gift are often more restrictive than those imposed on parties to nongratuitous transactions. Some legal systems reduce the warranty obligations of the donor and, in certain circumstances, impose an obligation on the part of the donee to provide the donor with support. Furthermore, what the law characterizes as a gift may be revocable, even after it has been fully executed.

In a comparative perspective, gift law has received a variety of characterizations. In the common law, because executory gift promises are not enforceable as law, gifts generally are considered not from the point of view of obligation but rather as an aspect of property law, namely as a transfer of title without consideration, while the enforceability of gift promises is examined in equity. The legal systems derived from the French Civil Code tend to consider the gift and the last will and testament together as the two forms of *liberalité* (liberality). The Germanic legal systems, together with most recent civilian codifications, characterize the gift—not merely the accepted gift promise, but also the gift transfer itself—as a contract, for which particular rules are elaborated in the special part of contract law.

From the point of view of legal theory, one issue raised by the law of gifts is the extent to which a legal system should intervene in normative structures that are largely constituted outside the law. Much happens in society that is inappropriate for legal regulation. For example, a wedding guest must bring a gift, or send one within a year of the wedding; but the law does not enforce that obligation. Such obligations are governed by other norms and other enforcement mechanisms. In general, legal systems tend to regulate gifts only to the extent it is believed that those interested in the transaction need protection. Protection is thought to be necessary because gift giving is not based on self-interest to the same extent as

is exchange in the marketplace. For example, the appropriate limit for gifts to relatives or to charities is not clearly established, and prodigality may result if the donor's perception of the obligation is excessive.

In those civilian legal systems in which this risk is thought to be great (particularly in countries in which the Church has amassed great wealth on the basis of the generosity of its faithful) the law often intervenes to restrict gift giving, or at least to ensure the possibility of mature reflection. In other legal systems, the regulation of gift giving is left largely outside the law. One reason the common law places few restrictions on gift giving is to permit as broad a sphere as possible for the exercise of moral subjectivity. Legal systems in societies with extensive customary law occasionally leave the regulation of gift giving entirely to custom.

A further theoretical aspect of the law of gifts is that it reveals the limitations of the social vision that seems to be inherent in the law. Whether gift giving is carefully limited or largely ignored, the law tends to consider it to be an anomaly. From other perspectives, however, it becomes clear that gift giving plays a central role in social life. Anthropological research has found that both primitive and ancient societies have always been bound together by a culture of gift giving. Individuals in those societies are subject to obligations to give, to receive, and to reciprocate. Recent work in the social sciences suggests that activity outside the market is also essential to contemporary society, including such acts as the gift of life, dying for one's country, pleasure in work well done, team spirit, blood donations, charitable contributions, and even the art of conversation. In fact, much that matters in society is what we do for one another without monetary compensation. From this point of view, utilitarian exchange in the marketplace is a subsidiary activity, one that has as its goal the creation of the material conditions necessary for the gratuitous conferring of benefits.

Gift giving, by encouraging friendship and mutual reliance, is part of a pattern of social intercourse that differs from, and at times competes with, the one that inheres in the marketplace and that is protected by the law. Gift law thus demonstrates that legal norms play only a limited role in social relations. Yet, because the law so dominates our understanding of society, those social institutions that are not organized in terms of legal right, such as the giving of gifts, are often disregarded by legal theory or even considered by it to be superfluous.

References

Dawson, John. *Gifts and Promises*. New Haven: Yale University Press, 1980.

Godbout, Jacques T., and Alain Caillé. *L'esprit du don* (The Meaning of Gift). Paris: La découverte, 1992.

Hyde, Lewis. *The Gift*. New York: Vintage, 1983.

Hyland, Richard. "Gifts." In *The International Encyclopedia of Comparative Law*, Vol. 8, ed. R. David et al. Tübingen: J.C.B. Mohr (Paul Siebeck); Boston: Martinus Nijhoff, 1999.

Malinowski, Bronislaw. *Argonauts of the Western Pacific*. 1922. Reprinted, Prospect Heights IL: Waveland Press, 1984.

Mauss, Marcel. *The Gift*. Trans. W.D. Halls. London: Routledge, 1990.

Richard Hyland

Goodness and Coherence

The claim that laws which are procedurally good are more likely to be substantively good was associated most prominently with the late Lon Fuller. Fuller believes that there is a connection between compliance with the procedural morality of law and achievement of goodness in the substantive morality of law. His belief has sometimes been misconstrued as a claim that such a connection is logically necessary. That is not the case. However, he does believe that there is a tendency for the two to correlate.

There is significant objection to the idea that there is any sort of connection between internal (procedural) morality and external (substantive) morality. Both H.L.A. Hart and Ronald Dworkin are willing to accept Fuller's principles of legality as prudential concerns regarding the efficacy of law. However, they emphatically reject the notion that the principles of legality could be some kind of morality. Hart, for example, can see no reason why the greatest tyrant would not employ the principles of legality in order to make morally outrageous law more effective. These objections, however, cannot be evaluated without a deeper understanding of the background of Fuller's claim.

History of the Idea

The notion that there is some connection between coherence of the law and its moral goodness does not originate with Fuller. Indeed, he does not discuss the issue extensively. He seems to accept the notion from sources he finds influential. The earliest form of the claim appears in Plato's *Republic* with Socrates' rejection of Thrasymachos' claim that "[m]ight makes right, and justice is the interest of the stronger." In response, Socrates invites Thrasymachos to consider how a band of thieves will be able to maintain honor among themselves. Socrates believes that they will not be able to trust one another, because each will fear that the others may turn on him out of the same immoral greed that leads all of them to prey upon others. Socrates does not believe that the thief, lacking justice in his treatment of mankind, will have justice within himself. In the modern language of social psychology, Festinger would anticipate that the thieves would experience cognitive dissonance in their efforts to be honorable with one another but dishonorable with everyone else.

Fuller finds influential the idea that Lord Mansfield expresses as the common law working itself pure from case to case with principles drawn from the fount of justice. Fuller asks how it could it be possible for the common law process of justification to work, itself pure, toward a greater realization of iniquity. Fuller, of course, assumes that the judges who are engaged in the process of justification share reasonable agreement about the values that the law is pursuing and also share a sincere desire to reach rationally defensible conclusions. In this form, the claim is simply an expression of belief in the possibility of rational argumentation. In a similar vein, Justice Benjamin Cardozo concludes his famous lectures on *The Nature of the Judicial Process* with the testimony of his faith that the process of judicial justification in the long run will weed out errors and preserve the good that has been done.

These expressions illustrate the influences that help to shape Fuller's belief that coherent processes, the centerpiece of which is the process of justification, will tend to pull decisions in the direction of rightness. To evaluate that belief requires an examination both of the actual impacts that coherence has in real world situations and of what Fuller and his fellow advocates mean by goodness.

G

One presupposition that must be made clear is that any possible relationship between coherence and goodness assumes that there is at least basic agreement in the relevant moral community regarding the values that constitute goodness. Moreover, for coherence to help, the social values of justice must themselves be reasonably coherent. It would be possible to "work pure" toward more perfect justice only if there is a reasonably clear set of values for use in the process of justification. Only a reasonably coherent set of values allows decision makers to extrapolate with consistency in applying the values to new situations, thereby avoiding ad hoc decisions.

Advantages of Coherence

Assuming such agreement on fundamental values, what are the possible gains that might be produced through greater coherence? With greater coherence of values, new decisions should result in fewer inconsistencies. Moreover, decisions should more regularly be consistent with popular conceptions of justice. Indeed, the realization of goodness will be achieved more completely through coherence, since the absence of coherence is disorder. A rather dramatic example of the impact of the adoption of a consistent set of justice values is provided by imagining how Socrates' gang of thieves could become able to trust one another. If, instead of thieves, they are a band of rebels fighting for a revolutionary cause, they typically will trust each other with their lives. They are united by their revolutionary ideology, which provides them with a set of justice values that unites them against the rest of the world.

If those revolutionaries gain power, they would likely attempt to implement their new set of justice values. To the extent that they can appoint judges and administrators who share those values, they can allow them to make decisions based on their ideology and feel confident of the general outcome, because the decisions will be rationally drawn from those principles. To the extent that the people at large share the values of the revolutionary regime, the new regime will be aided by utilizing Fuller's principles of legality to help them make their law more coherent and obeyable. Making their law more accessible would allow their citizens to cooperate more fully with the laws of the new regime.

Disadvantages of Coherence

What if the population at large does not share the revolutionary values? Would the new regime benefit by making its law coherent and easily understood? If the revolutionary ideology is highly objectionable to the populace, employing the principles of legality would likely be counterproductive by encouraging evasion and resistance, because citizens have a clear idea of what the regime intends.

It is interesting to note that, where there is substantial resistance to the values of the regime, the principles of legality are typically violated quite systematically. For example, Hitler kept many laws secret. In a number of cases, he did not trust his subordinates to apply his laws and therefore required his ad hoc approval of enforcement.

In this negative sense, there seems to be a correlation between coherence and goodness in that coherence is of no benefit to the regime unless the audience finds the values of the regime at least tolerable. H.L.A. Hart would mislead them by advising that the regime can employ the principles of legality to make their laws more effective. Instead, the regime will find it necessary to rely on enforcement resources. Stalin and Hitler are prime examples of this technique of the massive use of enforcement resources. However, because such massive employment of force impoverishes society, the regime will normally find it prudent to try to convert the population to its revolutionary ideology as rapidly as possible. That is why reeducation programs are standard features of the revolutionary situation. To the extent that they can reeducate their populace to share their values, they will be able to reduce their use of enforcement resources and take advantage of the principles of legality to increase the effectiveness of their law. If people are able and willing to apply the law by themselves, then enforcement resources are much less significant.

Goodness

The notion of goodness implicated in the correlation between coherence and goodness causes problems for philosophers unfamiliar with sociological perspectives on morality. Quite naturally, philosophers think of ultimate standards of value. The goodness that tends to correlate with coherence is less troublesome if we think of social morality that changes with the growth of culture. More specifically, Fuller's emphasis on the principles of social order suggests that he would see goodness as solving the challenge of human social life with optimum success. In that same vein, Fuller's dynamic view of goodness is rather similar to Cardozo's. He sees justice as an emerging social conception that develops over time. Its content changes in response to many factors, including fresh moral insight from the advancing critique of existing social values or an emerging awareness of contradictions in the existing set of social values. In fact, Fuller's greatest hope is that the advance of knowledge will lead society to an improved understanding of justice.

Once variation in the content of goodness is admitted, the question arises of the possibility of success of propaganda or reeducation campaigns. Can the new regime reeducate people any way they wish? The reeducation campaigns in the former Soviet block countries seem to show that there are certain hard facts of existence and of human nature that limit the effective scope of such propaganda. However, within those limits, great variability in human society is clearly possible. Do all such theories of society stand on equal footing? Fuller believes that human societies have the capacity for invention of new institutions of social ordering, hence of evolving to an improved realization of justice. By the same token, it should be possible to compare past and present human societies to judge which ones work more successfully in solving the challenge of social living.

References

Cardozo, Benjamin. *The Nature of the Judicial Process*. New Haven: Yale University Press, 1921.

Dworkin, Ronald. "The Elusive Morality of Law." *Villanova Law Review* 10 (1965), 631–639.

———. "Philosophy, Morality, and Law: Observations Prompted by Professor Fuller's Novel Claim." *University of Pennsylvania Law Review* 113 (1965), 668.

Hart, H.L.A. "Book Review [of L. Fuller, *The Morality of Law* (1964)]." *Harvard Law Review* 78 (1965), 1281–1296.

———. "Positivism and the Separation of Law and Morals." *Harvard Law Review* 71 (1958), 593–629.

Fuller, Lon. "Human Interaction and the Law." *American Journal of Jurisprudence* 14 (1969), 1–36.

———. "Positivism and Fidelity to Law: A Reply to Professor Hart." *Harvard Law Review* 71 (1958), 630–672.

———. "A Reply to Professors Cohen and Dworkin." *Villanova Law Review* 10 (1965), 655–666.

Moffat, Robert C.L. "Coherence and Goodness." *Archiv für Rechts- und Sozialphilosophie* 5 (1968), 103–109.

———. "Lon Fuller: Natural Lawyer After All!" *American Journal of Jurisprudence* 26 (1981), 190–201.

Robert C.L. Moffat

See also FULLER, LON L; NORMS; VALUES

Goods

A form of personal property, this classic legal category organizes a part of the material world in sometimes archaic ways. Etymologically, the source is the Old English word *gòd*, a general adjective of commendation or appreciation. In law, the substantive plural form, *goods*, dates from the thirteenth century and includes those inanimate articles of furniture and personal effects that we possess. It is a catchall for tangible personal property. *Goods* may include our financial instruments, stocks, bonds, notes. And sometimes—always when linked with the related concept of chattel—*goods* includes livestock.

This distinction between possession of live things (those able to move) and simple material things is what gives us the term "livestock." The distinction also delineates the importance that forms of possession have in delineating the legal category of *goods*. "Chattel," from the French, refers to any species of property, except land, and is the more general reference. Land, as real property, indicates the traditional valuation at the heart of this area of law. Land was the first source of wealth and goods came later.

In law, the substantive singular form, a good, is not used. Economists, such as Harry Johnson in his theorem on value, "[d]efine a good as an object or service of which the consumer would choose to have more." In economics, the singular is necessary in order for the aggregation at the heart of demand to take place. However, in law the plural noun functions as an aggregate that cannot be broken down. In its aggregate form goods is the stuff of commercial transactions. Like the market itself, the form connotes a robust exchange. Thus, in efforts to regulate commercial transactions, a lawyer might say, "The sale of goods is regulated by the *Uniform Commercial Code*."

Goods raise philosophical questions in law to the extent that such basic matters as why things have value to people and which values are to be protected by government come to the fore. Political economy develops these questions as value theory, that aspect of economics which calculates demand. Here, economists work from the source of value in goods to more general theories of the market and market behavior. Adam Smith made the characteristics that give goods value a basis for the theory of demand. For John Stuart Mill, property in goods was the basis for his case for limited government intervention because "[n]o quantity of movable goods which a person can acquire by his labor prevents others from acquiring the like by the same means." The philosophical significance beyond economics lies, at least in part, in the social and etymological fact that goods are a physical embodiment of the metaphysical quality of good. In usage made popular by the political theorist Hannah Arendt, life as the highest good becomes a basic valuative tool. For marxists, material possession remains the determinative force at the heart of social theory.

In law, changing conceptions of our relationship to goods raise countless issues. Ownership seems more complex in an age of cultural diversity, since we acknowledge that the meaning of possession depends on culture. One recent study treats the artifacts sold by African immigrants on the streets of New York as authentic because of the context of the sale. As noted by Rosemary Coombe, even though they are made in China, the goods gain authenticity since they are sold by Songhay migrants from Niger. The legal category depends on the "cultural life" of goods. Political economies and markets constituted by law give goods their commercial significance. Since the legal meaning of goods is at the foundation of value theory, both goods and economic theory are highly susceptible to developments in the cultural life of the law.

We know goods in law through disputes over what is included in the category and hence protected. The protection of trademarks, or rights in a name like O.J. Simpson or Timberland, has consequences that tran-

scend the issue of whom the goods belong to and determines the level of profit. Indeed, according to observers such as Coombe, where the value of goods depends less on use or inherent quality than on the cultural cachet of the trademark, the legal definition of which goods are to be protected is increasingly important to their meaning. Perhaps it should be no surprise that we are beginning to hear discussion of a legal past, the traditional limits on the consumption of goods, or sumptuary law. These tracks refer to distinctive paradigmatic explorations.

Trends in law, such as the codification movement, influence how goods are seen by incorporating contemporary understandings. During the realist period in American law, according to William Twining, scholars such as Karl Llewellyn played a prominent role by linking the regulation of goods sought to more fluid norms of conventional practice rather than the rigid designations of title. In the *Uniform Commercial Code* (UCC), for which Llewellyn was largely responsible, this revision is at the heart of Chapter 2. Llewellyn's much discussed formulation meant to establish a functional basis for the sale of goods. Title theory asked when title passed from seller to buyer, a determination made more difficult by the modern context. In the UCC, matters such as risk and the availability of remedies are dealt with directly. With the influence of economic theory in law today, goods remain central in determinations of legal meaning for the philosophy of law. These determinations transcend issues of ownership much as the realists transcended title.

In the relationships by which law defines goods we find philosophical work at the center of social policy in such disparate areas as bankruptcy and sumptuary law. In the case of the law on bankruptcy, according to Donald Korobkin, scholars have recently noted that "the new corporate finance turns all claimants into 'stakeholders' with particular but not qualitatively different stakes." Here, the legal inquiry draws from an economic conception of claims. The traditional rehabilitative framework in bankruptcy has its base in a combination of old-fashioned morality and popular psychology, which drew on status relationships. The new economic models minimize status relationships in favor of autonomous actors with qualitatively interchangeable "stakes" in the system.

In the case of sumptuary law, the laws made for the purpose of restraining luxury or extravagance, laws reflect the desire for state regulation of the display and consumption of clothes, furniture, and food. Current inquiry has brought this seemingly archaic area to life and reminded scholars that the regulation of goods reveals action by the state in the constitution of class and other important relations. Although this role for law has become largely invisible, philosophical attention to the regulation of goods at the level of consumption leads to consideration of new ways in which law maintains disciplinary authority over our lives.

One of these is the psychological in law. In his book *Oedipus Lex,* Peter Goodrich draws our attention to what he calls "Autonomasia" or psychiatric harm and the English home. He offers the story of *Attia v. British Gas,* 2 All E.R. 455 [1987], as an anomalous introduction of psychiatric harm into the law; in this case the harm seeing one's home and goods burned up. This particular basis for recovery is somewhat anomalous as applied to goods. However, as Goodrich notes, the relevance of at least vernacular psychology to legal understandings of our relationship to all manner of possession has taken center stage in Anglo-American law. Now we recognize the construction of identity at least in part through our life with *goods*.

References

Arendt, Hannah. *The Human Condition.* Garden City NY: Doubleday, 1958.

Coombe, Rosemary. "The Cultural Life of Things." *American University Journal of International Law and Policy* 70 (1995), 791.

Goodrich, Peter. *Oedipus Lex.* Berkeley: University of California Press, 1995.

Hachamovich, Yifat. "One Law or the Other." *International Journal for Semiotics of Law* 3 (1990), 187.

Hunt, Alan. *Sumptuary Law.* Forthcoming.

Johnson, Harry. "Demand Theory Further Revisited *or* Goods Are Goods." *Economica* 25 (1958), 149.

Korobkin, Donald R. "Rehabilitating Values: A Jurisprudence of Bankruptcy." *Columbia Law Review* 91 (1991), 717.

Mill, John Stuart. *Principles of Political Economy.* New York: D. Appleton, 1884.

Smith, Adam. *An Inquiry into the Nature and Causes of the Wealth of Nations.* 2 vols. Ed. E. Cannon. London: Methuen, 1961.

Twining, William. *Karl Llewellyn and the Realist Movement.* Norman: University of Oklahoma Press, 1973.

John Brigham

See also OWNERSHIP; PROPERTY

Grotius, Hugo (1583–1645)

Hugo Grotius (Hugo de Groot) was born in Delft, Holland, in 1583, and was educated by his father. At the University of Leiden, he studied mathematics, philosophy, poetry, and jurisprudence. He became a barrister and, in 1605, he wrote his first work, the *De jure praedae commentarius*, legal advice in a maritime case. In 1707, he was named historiographer of the United Provinces and became General Fiscal Advocate for Holland and Zealand. A perfect functionary, he had also a very happy domestic life with his wife, Mary van Reigesberg.

However, political events—the English drive for hegemony on the seas, Spanish and Portugese trading ambitions, and, mainly, religious intolerance in his own country between Arminians and Gomarists (a new version of the quarrel between Pelagius and Saint Augustine)—decided otherwise for him. Since he was a friend of Jon van Oldenbarnevelt, the leading statesman of the United Provinces, he was condemned to a lifetime prison sentence and confiscation of his goods: at the age of 36, he was incarcerated in the fortress of Louvestein. After the first difficult months of a prisoner's life, his wife, Mary, who pondered the means of his escape, could visit him and bring him some books. One day in 1621, Grotius, hidden in a book trunk, recovered his liberty.

Now began a difficult period of exile and poverty. In Paris, King Louis XIII granted him a pension, but it was meager and irregularly paid. Grotius again took his pen and his books and wrote his magistral work on *De jure belli ac pacis,* published in 1625. Louis XIII accepted the homage of the book, but he did not reward the author; the Court of Rome (the Holy Office) placed the book on the Index; the sales were mediocre. However, Grotius's name was pronounced in all the European courts.

In 1635, the young Queen Christina of Sweden promoted Grotius counsellor of her court and ambassador in Paris. But his task was politically delicate and poisoned by religious problems. In 1645, Grotius left Paris and, via Holland, went to Stockholm, where Queen Christina received him very generously. He died on the boat she had offered him, in a tempest the night of August 28, 1645.

Grotius's work includes various spheres: literature, theology, history, and jurisprudence. In all his writings, however, the same preoccupation is expressed: a very high conception of justice and peace. His greatest book, *De jure belli ac pacis*, shows why and how the peace of the world must be constructed by juridical means.

Its first edition, *De jure belli ac pacis libri tres, in quibus jus naturae et gentium item juris publici praecipua explicantur* (Three Books on the Law of War and Peace, in which the Precepts of Natural Law, The Law of Peoples, and the Public Law Are Developed), is an *in quarto* of 786 pages with sixteen preliminary sheets. In this voluminous work, Grotius wants to elaborate a rational and systematic "science of right." In the long *Prolegomena*, he determines his working method: it shall have the rigor of deductive process as in mathematics, and it shall require a *certus ordo* (certain order) like the Cartesian method. Such a paradigm of rationality removes speculative dogmatism, scholastic *disputatio* (disputation), and empirical observation: Grotius reasons in abstract and general terms and he obeys demonstrative logic. This is why it is necessary to give clear and precise definitions at the beginning of the jurisprudential system.

The definition of the term *jus* is particularly important. But it is not easy because if the word *jus* connotes traditionally the *justum* (that which is just) or, more exactly, "that which is not injust," it indicates also either "a moral quality of a person" (a subjective right) or the *lex* as obligatory rule (the objective law). In this latter case, we must distinguish *jus naturale* (natural obligation) and *jus voluntarium* (contractual obligation). According to Grotius, the natural right, proved either a priori by universal sociability, or a posteriori by the *consensus gentium* (agreement of humankind), is the central motive of the jurisprudential system. Indeed, natural right is a *dictamen rationis,* universal, obligatory, and immutable: even if God did not exist *(etiamsi daremus Deus non esse),* natural right should be what it is. That does not mean the perfect laicization of the juridical sphere—Grotius makes a hypothesis and does not state a thesis—but indicates Grotius's desire to renew the

conception of law and, especially, of the law of war and peace. In this project, the distinction between *jus naturale* and *jus voluntarium* has a great importance: indeed, even if the defense of his own life is legitimate and proceeds from natural law (that is why "authorities generally assign to wars justifiable causes, defense, recovery, and property, and punishment")—volitional or positive law must rule the "formal public war." The originality of Grotius's doctrine is to insist on the "competence" of the positive rule of law to regulate and control the phenomena of war. Consequently, in the traditional *jus belli* (just war), Grotius distinguishes the *jus ad bellum* (right *to* war) and the *jus in bello* (law *in* war). On the one hand, the "just war" is allowed only under formal conditions: war must be confined within the limits of a just cause. On the other hand, war not only obeys moral conditions but, first of all, juridical demands: before the hostilities, a formal declaration of war is necessary; during the war, ruses and perfidy are imperatively prohibited; after the hostilities, treaties of peace and conventions impose inviolable promises on belligerents.

On this basis, Grotius elaborates a theory of positive *jus gentium* of which the fundamental principle is *Pacta sunt servanda* (agreement must be kept). Sometimes, this law of nations, being a positive law, diverges from natural law; but, in conformity to the moral obligation imposed by natural right, the law of nations includes an appeal to the conscience of sovereigns and a series of *temperamenta* (or moderations) to avoid "unnecessary suffering." So, juridical and moral obligations intertwine and compound in order that, in the *jus gentium*, rationalist and naturalist imperatives together lead to peace.

In Grotius's work, *justitia belli* (the justness of war) constitutes the central question, at the same time juridical, moral, and philosophical. The use of brute force, says Grotius, is undignified in a truly human world. It is why he thinks that the laws of war and peace must broaden to the *humani generis societas* (community of human beings): because they are founded in reason, they must take on a universal dimension.

By his rationalist process and universalist purpose, Grotius appears to be a modern thinker. However, in spite of the insistence with which many commentators present Grotius as "the father of international law," his theory of "the just war" and, more generally, his doctrine of law do not offer an answer to contemporary problems. Grotius is a thinker between two ages. In his century, he could not elaborate a treatise on international law in its modern sense; after Erasmus, Gentilis, or Suárez, he thinks in the manner of a classical humanist: he shows how much the means of law, answering to the *dictamina rationis* (dictates of reason), are important not only to rule and humanize war, but also to substitute order and justice for brute force. They open the path to peace and announce the great hope of public world law. However, even if Grotius puts the defense of the liberty of states before the ecclesiastical power, he remains closer to the past than to the future. In a scholastic vein, he develops throughout his work the strong and secular thesis of the *justitia belli*: the justice, norm, and aim of juridical order is also the noblest humanistic purpose.

References

Boukema, H.J.M. "Grotius' Concept of Law." *Archiv für Rechts- und Sozialphilosophie* 69 (1983), 68–73.

Chroust, Anton-Hermann. "Hugo Grotius and the Scholastic Natural Law Tradition." *The New Scholasticism* 17 (1943), 101–133.

Costigan, Richard F. "A Rationalist Critique of Grotius." *Revue de l'Université d'Ottawa* 33 (1963).

Edwards, C. "The Law of Nature in the Thought of Hugo Grotius." *Journal of Politics* 32 (1970), 784–807.

Grotius, Hugo. *De jure belli ac pacis libri tres*. 1625. Trans. A.C. Campbell (1901) as *The Rights of War and Peace, including the Law of Nature and of Nations*. Reprint, Hyperion, 1993. Trans. Francis W. Kelsey of prefatory text as *Prolegomena to the Law of War and Peace*. New York: Liberal Arts Press, 1957.

———. *De jure praedae commentarius* (Commentary on the Law of Prize and Booty). 1605. Reprint, Buffalo NY: W.S. Hein, 1950.

———. "Mare liberum" (The Freedom of the Seas, or the right which belongs to the Dutch to take part in the East India trade). 1609. In *De jure praedae commentarius* (Commentary on the Law of Prize and Booty), reprint, Ayer (Arno), 1972.

Hodges, Donald Clark. "Grotius on the Law of War." *Modern Schoolman* 34 (1956), 36–44.

Saint Léger, J. *The "etiamsi daremus" of Hugo Grotius*. Rome: Pontificum Athenaeum Internationale "Angelicum," 1962.

Scott, Jonathan. "The Law of War: Grotius, Sidney, Locke and the Political Theory of Rebellion." *History of Political Thought* 13 (1992), 565–585.

Tuck, Richard. *Natural Rights Theories: Their Origin and Development*. New York: Cambridge University Press, 1982.

Simone Goyard-Fabre

Group Rights

See MINORITY, ETHNIC, AND GROUP RIGHTS

Gurvitch, Georges (1894–1965)

Georges Gurvitch's legal theory seeks in a highly original way to integrate legal philosophy and legal sociology. It offers one of the most intricate and sophisticated modern theories of legal pluralism, challenging all conceptions of a unitary source of law in sovereign authority or moral absolutes. Its elaboration of the concept of social law extends the concerns of legal analysis beyond the activities of legislative and judicial agencies of the state, encouraging a legal perspective favoring decentralization and the flexible coordination of systems of autonomous regulation of social groups.

Gurvitch grew up in Russia, where he studied and taught philosophy and participated in the 1917 revolution. Disillusioned about prospects there for a pluralistic and democratic society, he left Russia in 1920 and settled in Paris in 1925. Apart from wartime years in the United States, he taught in France until the end of his career. His philosophical outlook, originally influenced by Edmund Husserl's and Max Scheler's phenomenology and Henri Bergson's intuitionism, was gradually adapted to serve his growing sociological interests. He became the leading French sociological theorist of his era and succeeded to Emile Durkheim's chair at the Sorbonne. His work has been described by his sociological contemporary Pitirim Sorokin as "one of the most original and significant sociological systems of our time."

In two major books published in the early 1930s Gurvitch explored the idea of social law as a law of integration and cooperation. Far from being imposed by sovereign command, social law finds its authority as positive law in social interaction itself. In *Le temps présent et l'idée du droit social* he identifies emerging social law in industrial collective bargaining practices, national economic regulation, and new institutions of international law. His *L'idée du droit social* surveys, with great erudition, legal theories from Hugo Grotius and Gottfried Leibniz to Duguit and Hauriou in search of antecedents of and influences on the idea of social law.

Gurvitch sought to detach legal thinking from its fixation with the legal processes of the modern centralized state and to suggest a far more complex and fluid legal state of affairs, in which emergent sources of legal authority compete with each other at many levels of experience. He portrayed law as an intricate plurality of forms of normative regulation. In *Sociology of Law,* his only major work on law published in English, he elaborated in full the theory of legal pluralism partly expressed in his earlier analyses.

Emphasizing social rather than political sources of law, Gurvitch extends Petrazycki's ideas by treating law as a socially guaranteed correlation between claims and obligations. Influenced partly by phenomenology, he developed a theory of immediate jural experience, seeing this as the foundation of the varied social forms and expressions of law. Different kinds of law (for example, social law) express different forms of sociality—ways in which individuals interact socially and relate to their collective life. Law in this basic sense derives its sanction from the character of the sociality to which it relates. Complex frameworks of law (for example, trade union law or family law) are expressions of the combination, in actual social groups, of such abstract forms of sociality, and so of kinds of law corresponding to them. Finally, "all-inclusive" societies are microcosms of such social groups and give rise to entire systems of law (for example, feudal law, bourgeois law, American law, French law).

In addition to the plurality of kinds, frameworks, and systems of law, related to the variety of patterns of social life, Gurvitch analyzes a "vertical" pluralism of law in terms of its degrees of organization and formal expression. Thus, law may be organized or unorganized, fixed in advance, formulated flexibly to deal with problems as they arise, or experienced merely intuitively.

Gurvitch's writings are largely unconcerned with causal explanation or historical specificity. They offer an entirely general, elaborate conceptual framework for analysis of any legal environment. Jural experience, as conceptualized by Gurvitch, presents to the sociologist the normative facts underpinning law and at the same time confirms for the legal philosopher the moral intuitions that ground legal interpretation and evaluation. Thus, legal philosophy and sociology appear as inseparable partners in analyzing law's social reality.

Despite its abstraction, Gurvitch's legal theory has clear moral and political implications. Throughout his career he was committed to political decentralization, moral and political pluralism, and democratic socialism. He saw social law as expressing a form of sociality—community—which usually held out the best prospects for individual autonomy, active solidarity, and democratic organization in a world torn between possibilities of totalitarianism, on the one hand, and anarchistic individualism, on the other.

Gurvitch's ideas on social law are part of a significant heritage of legal thought outside the liberal mainstream. The relative neglect of his pluralist theory has been traced to the complexity and abstraction of its classifications and to the belief that pluralist conceptions of law are inapplicable to the centralized, monistic legal systems of contemporary Western societies. Resistance to his ideas may also be due, as J.-G. Belley has argued, to the fact that they question fundamental assumptions of much professional legal thought, especially about law's rational bases, the sources of its authority, and the forms of knowledge that it entails. Yet Gurvitch's work may offer valuable partial resources for contemporary legal inquiry. Its pluralistic outlook gains in relevance insofar as Western law becomes more transnational and international, and movements such as those of communitarianism, nationalism, and regionalism provoke fresh debates about the legal authority of the nation-state and the legal organization of collective life.

References

Belley, J.-G. "Georges Gurvitch et les professionnels de la pensée juridique" (Georges Gurvitch and Professional Jurists). *Droit et Société* 4 (1986), 353–371.

Gurvitch, G. *L'expérience juridique et la philosophie pluraliste du droit* (Juristic Experience and Pluralistic Philosophy of Law). Paris: Pedone, 1935.

———. *L'idée du droit social* (The Concept of Social Law). 1932. Aalen: Scientia Verlag, 1972.

———. *Le temps présent et l'idée du droit social* (The Concept of Social Law Today). Paris: Vrin, 1931.

———. *Sociology of Law.* 1942. London: Routledge, 1973.

MacDonald, P. "The Legal Sociology of Georges Gurvitch." *British Journal of Law and Society* 6 (1979), 24–52.

Swedberg, R. *Sociology as Disenchantment: The Evolution of the Work of Georges Gurvitch.* Atlantic Highlands NJ: Humanities Press International, 1982.

Roger Cotterrell

See also SOCIOLOGICAL JURISPRUDENCE; SOCIOLOGY OF LAW

H

Habermas, Jürgen (1929–)

The legal philosophy of Jürgen Habermas finds its mature expression in his *Faktizität und Geltung (Between Facts and Norms)*. Specifically, *Faktizität und Geltung* elaborates a normative theory of law and democracy that takes into account the social and institutional realities of complex, pluralistic societies.

Habermas's central thesis is that the rule of law is internally related to deliberative democracy, in the sense that the legitimacy of the constitutional state depends upon the quality of the citizens' participation in the democratic process of lawmaking. In terms of the history of ideas, this thesis attempts to overcome the split between "liberal" theories, which emphasize the protection of individual liberty through basic rights (for instance, John Locke and, more recently, Friedrich von Hayek), and "civic-republican" theories, which stress participation in self-governance or "popular sovereignty" (for example, Jean-Jacques Rousseau, Hannah Arendt, and Frank Michelman). The argument itself draws upon a sociologically informed reading of modern societies as both ideologically pluralistic and functionally differentiated into spheres of competitive or instrumental action, such as the capitalist market economy. In this context, positive law, and in particular individual rights, have the function of stabilizing behavioral expectations, and thus coordinating social action, without recourse to substantive agreements in worldview, religious outlook, and so on. Here Habermas puts a sociological twist on Immanuel Kant's analysis of the formal properties of law as a mode of regulating external behavior. That is, legally defined rights carve out areas in which individuals are free, not only to pursue private preferences but also to develop their own distinct identities and cultural memberships without interference and without being required to justify themselves to the legal community.

The above considerations ground the first half of Habermas's argument: the very "medium" of law is constituted by equal rights of individual liberty (or negative rights), along with the membership rights and due process rights required for these to be effective. Such rights make up the "private autonomy" of citizens as free and equal members of a legal community. However, this private autonomy would be incomplete if citizens themselves had no capacity to further define and shape individual rights. Indeed, as various twentieth-century struggles over rights show, private autonomy would mean little without rights of political participation that allow citizens themselves to define what counts as "equal" and what counts as "unequal." To be legitimate, then, a legal order must simultaneously secure both the private and the political, or "public" autonomy of its members. This internal relation between the two types of autonomy accounts for rights as regulating citizens' "horizontal" relations with one another; it is only in a subsequent step that Habermas brings in the state as a necessary sanctioning and administering power for an effective system of rights.

Habermas's account of the exercise of public autonomy in deliberative politics attempts to do justice to the complexity of contemporary societies. Thus political discourse involves several types of discourse, distinguished according to the type of issue and mode of questioning, and it takes place across a number of social and institutional levels. By distinguishing between *types of discourse*, Habermas avoids an overly moralistic view that would define legitimacy simply in relation to justice, or respect for persons. Legitimate laws should also be pragmatically expedient, they should be compatible with a community's values and collective identity, and they should represent a fair compromise of the particular interests at stake. By distinguishing different *social and institutional levels* of political discourse, Habermas recognizes the complexities of the political process. Ultimately, legitimate lawmaking must be rooted in broadly dispersed public discourses open to all citizens. The ideas and inputs generated by such an informal public sphere usually cannot be directly translated into political programs and laws, however, but must be institutionally channeled and focused in representative deliberative bodies such as Parliament or Congress. Hence a viable democratic process must be sustained at a number of points: in the voluntary associations and informal fora where citizens can articulate and discuss their concerns, in the various intermediate institutions that should sensitively pick up and transmit such concerns to official decision-making bodies, as well as in the decision-making procedures themselves. At this point Habermas's theory of democracy opens on a critical sociological analysis of the use and abuse of power in the political process.

Habermas frames his entire analysis of law and democracy in terms of a "proceduralist paradigm" of law. Here "paradigm of law" refers to a loose set of background assumptions about law in relation to its social context and possibilities. At the core of the proceduralist paradigm is the internal relation between individual liberty and democratic participation. Once one grasps this internal relation, one can find fresh solutions to a number of conundrums in legal and political theory. Here Habermas hopes to show how philosophical analysis can usefully inform other disciplines, most notably jurisprudence and the sociology of law. More specifically, he suggests how the proceduralist paradigm can help overcome a number of stalemated debates in the United States and Germany, such as jurisprudential debates about judicial decision-making, the role of the Supreme Court, and the separation of powers; debates over the welfare state; and debates within feminist legal theory and politics.

References

Habermas, Jürgen. *Between Facts and Norms: Contributions to a Discourse Theory of Law and Democracy.* Trans. William Rehg. Cambridge: MIT Press, 1996.

———. "Law and Morality." Trans. Kenneth Baynes. In *The Tanner Lectures on Human Values,* vol. 8, ed. Sterling M. McMurrin, 217–279. Salt Lake City: University of Utah Press; Cambridge: Cambridge University Press, 1988.

———. "Reply to Participants in a Symposium." In *Symposium on the Legal Theory of Jürgen Habermas,* ed. Michel Rosenfeld et al. *Cardozo Law Review* 17 (1996), 767, 1417.

———. *The Structural Transformation of the Public Sphere: An Inquiry into a Category of Bourgeois Society.* Trans. Thomas Burger and Frederick Lawrence. Cambridge: MIT Press, 1989.

———. "Struggles for Recognition in the Democratic Constitutional State." Trans. Shierry Weber Nicholsen. In *Multiculturalism: Examining the Politics of Recognition,* ed. Amy Gutmann. 107–148. Princeton: Princeton University Press, 1994.

———. *The Theory of Communicative Action.* 2 vols. Trans. Thomas McCarthy. Boston: Beacon, 1984, 1987.

William Rehg

Harms

Harms in tort may be defined as loss, injury, or damage sustained in breach of an obligation and caused either by an intentional act or by an omission to act. While common law imposes delictual liability for certain harms caused by the negligent acts or omissions of one person toward another, it does not impose liability in respect of every kind of harm that can be sustained. Conversely, some kinds of acts or omissions are considered serious enough to require intervention in the public interest and liability may be imposed, either additionally or alternatively, by statutory provisions (for example, in relation to employment or the safe operation of a business) and the criminal law. Harms which are the result of intentional acts or omissions may be both actionable in civil law and prosecuted as crimes, the clearest example being assault. Economic loss, product liability, and losses arising either in relation to property or *ex contractu* (on the contract) will not be considered here, nor will any statutory duties imposed by particular jurisdictions. Rather, this entry focuses on the conceptual justifications for imposing liability for harms caused to persons by other persons in tort and the ways in which this determines which harms fall, or ought to fall, into the category of delictual, as distinct from statutory or criminal, liability for personal harm.

Conceptually, harms may be classified in four ways: physical, emotional, moral, and economic. Which of those categories a particular harm belongs within is a matter of some difficulty and some types of claims may, of course, belong to more than one. Several criteria have been put forward as relevant in classifying a particular harm in one or more of those four ways. These involve different kinds of criteria and conceptual overlap, but a brief discussion will bring several issues come into focus in relation to how and when certain types of delictual claim are actionable.

Until the emergence of a system of public prosecution, there could be no procedural distinction between a crime and a delict, or a public and a private wrong. In general, this meant that there was no distinction between public and private wrongs. Although some acts were reserved as the right of the Crown to prosecute—mainly treason, murder, and rape—the onus was otherwise on the individual harmed to raise an action against the wrongful party and was considered a matter for individual action in either the local or ecclesiastical courts, depending on the nature of the particular act. The development of a centralized state legal system entailed the recognition of an increasing number of acts and omissions as being sufficiently serious to constitute an offense to the public as a whole and, therefore, classifiable as criminal and a decreased emphasis on some types of wrong as being an essentially private matter concerning only the individuals involved. As a corollary, only the state may now exercise coercion in relation to those acts or omissions considered to be such.

A distinction between punishment and reparation developed alongside the development of a centralized system of justice. Prior to this, remedies were obtained by the wronged individual and usually involved the payment of money with little distinction as to whether it was a fine or compensation. The emergence of

the distinction was largely due to a combination of both the reception of Roman law in Europe from the fifteenth century onwards and the influence of natural law thinkers. Hugo Grotius, for example, wrote in *De jure belli ac pacis* that a wrong was "every fault . . . which is in conflict with what men ought to do, either generally or by reason of a special quality" and that from such a fault "if damage has been caused, an obligation arises naturally, namely that it should be made good." Punishment came to be reserved to the state in enforcing the criminal law, while the reparation or compensation of persons harmed by the negligent acts or omissions of others remained within the power of private citizens.

This distinction focuses on the extent to which a harm is inflicted willfully. Under the modern law, those harms which are inflicted willfully or recklessly will be a matter for the criminal law (although they may also be torts), but the test for civil liability is negligence. Compensation alone, and not punishment, is therefore available to the wronged or injured party. While damages are awarded to compensate only for losses suffered, some jurisdictions also, however, permit punitive damages to be claimed in order to express disapproval of the defendant's negligence and to deter others from similar acts.

At a different level of analysis is the question of the purpose or purposes which the law is to serve. At one end of the theoretical spectrum, the rules of delictual liability are seen as a mechanism which operates to allocate risks and losses as a function of maximizing the efficient operation of the market, according to Richard Posner. At the other, corrective justice requires that the purpose of the law is to restore equilibrium between the parties involved so that private law, according to Ernest Weinrib, "looks neither to the litigants individually nor to the interests of the community as a whole, but to a bipolar relationship of liability."

Crucial to whether any type of injury or loss is actionable is the issue of the actual type and extent of the harm suffered. In general, in common law there is no duty in relation to harms caused by moral or social harms, and no delictual liability arising in using hurtful language toward another person, unless it can be classified as coming within the scope of, for example, the law of defamation or incitement to racial hatred. Likewise, no delictual liability arises from a simple failure by parents to provide certain items for enjoyment by a child, unless such failure amounts to an actual injury. An act or omission is not necessarily delictual because it is wrong in the moral sense, but rather because it constitutes a harm, harm being understood as losses. An actual loss capable of quantification must, therefore, have been suffered. Although nominal damages may exceptionally be awarded to signify simply that a legal duty has been breached, losses must generally be quantifiable in monetary terms. Damages for pain and suffering are, of course, symbolic, since no actual price corresponds to an injury, but these damages are seen, nonetheless, as corresponding to a verifiable injury proven by established theories of both causation and proximity. Thus there has been no successful action for injury caused by pornography due to the difficulty in proving that a harm has been caused to a particular plaintiff. In addition, causation is not the only issue invoked; the importance of other, conflicting interests may be seen as outweighing the seriousness of the harm. For example, proof of harm was balanced against the right to free speech in *Memoirs v. Massachusetts,* 383 U.S. 413 (1966), where it was stated that "[t]he First Amendment demands more than a horrible example or two of the perpetrator of a crime of sexual violence, in whose pocket is found a pornographic book, before it allows the Nation to be saddled with a regime of censorship." The problem appears to be one of whether pornography is a cause, rather than merely a symptom, of violence.

Whether the harm is inflicted willfully or negligently toward a person to whom the wrongdoer owes a duty, damages will be awarded, provided that it can be shown that an actual loss was sustained. Economic loss will not be dealt with in this section. Emotional injuries or "nervous shock," while subject to more stringent tests of proximity, can be seen in much the same way as physical injuries. Unless there has also been a crime, the state has no interest in raising an action either on behalf of the injured person or in the public interest and will provide only the mechanisms by which civil judgments can be enforced. Whether the purpose of the law is market efficiency or corrective justice, physical or mental harm is quantifiable in terms of actual or estimated loss, both in relation to pain and suffering and to the expenses resulting from it. Thus, in terms of all

three criteria, bodily and mental harms are the most doctrinally straightforward.

Acts or omissions which do not tend to come within the scope of delictual liability are those which can be seen as involving primarily moral issues and imposing obligations not only that appear to go beyond concepts of reasonable foreseeability but that would impose a duty to compensate in situations where fault cannot readily be attributed. It may, however, be so attributed in some cases and in some jurisdictions. For example, an action of wrongful life is incompetent in most but not all jurisdictions; that is, a child born with physical or mental abnormalities is rarely able to claim damages from his or her parents on the sole basis that they caused him or her to be born at all. Actions of wrongful life brought by parents against doctors, on the other hand, are generally competent; that is, damages are recoverable for the pain and suffering and the costs of rearing a child caused by, for example, a doctor's negligence in performing a sterilization procedure that results in pregnancy. Similarly, there is no legal duty under U.K. law to rescue a person in danger or to refrain from invading his or her privacy, but such acts or omissions are deemed to constitute harms in the United States.

References

Coleman, Jules L. "Moral Theories of Torts: Their Scope and Limits." *Law and Philosophy* 1 (1982); 2 (1983).

Easton, Susan M. *The Problem of Pornography: Regulation and the Right to Free Speech.* London: Routledge, 1994.

Feinberg, J. *Harm to Others: The Moral Limits of the Criminal Law.* Vol. 1. New York: Oxford University Press, 1984.

Hadden, T. "Contract, Tort and Crime: The Forms of Legal Thought." *Law Quarterly Review* 87 (1971), 240.

Mason, J.K., and R.A. McCall-Smith. *Law and Medical Ethics.* 4th ed. London: Butterworth, 1994.

Muncie, J., and E. McLaughlin, eds. *The Problem of Crime,* London: Sage/OU, 1996.

Posner, Richard. "A Theory of Negligence." *Journal of Legal Studies* 1 (1972).

Rogers, W.V.H. *Winfeld and Jolowicz on Tort.* 14th ed. London: Sweet and Maxwell, 1994.

Walker, D.M. *Delict.* Edinburgh: W. Green and Son, 1981.

Weinrib, Ernest J. *The Idea of Private Law.* Cambridge MA: Harvard University Press, 1995.

Winfeld, P. "The Foundation of Tortious Liability." *Criminal Law Journal* 7 (1939), 111.

Hilary Hiram

See also ECONOMIC LOSS; PRODUCTS LIABILITY; PUBLIC AND PRIVATE JURISDICTIONS; PUNITIVE DAMAGES; RELEVANCE; WRONGFUL LIFE AND WRONGFUL DEATH

Hart, Herbert Lionel Adolphus (1907–1992)

Herbert Lionel Adolphus Hart reinvigorated legal philosophy as a major area of philosophical inquiry by bringing the methods of analytical philosophy to bear systematically on the clarification and critical examination of the nature of legal systems, their role in society, and many established legal doctrines and practices. First in Greats at Oxford in 1929, Hart was called to the bar in 1932 and spent eight years as a chancery barrister. A fellow and tutor in philosophy at New College, Oxford, he held the chair of jurisprudence from 1952 to 1968 at University College and was principal of Brasenose College at Oxford 1973–1978.

Hart's 1953 inaugural lecture, "Definition and Theory in Jurisprudence," and his paper "Are There Any Natural Rights?" published in 1955 demonstrated immediately the wisdom of his appointment. In the former, a fresh approach to questions of definition and meaning of legal terms is provided by looking at how we use such language in ordering our real-life legal and political affairs. Legal language is often used nondescriptively, to draw legal conclusions, render verdicts, or claim rights, and we need to understand its functioning in these contexts if we are to understand its sense. "Are There Any Natural Rights?" made skillful use of traditional philosophical methods by arguing ingeniously to a natural right to be free as a presupposition of our moral rights talk. Hart claims that there is a close connection between possessing a moral right and having a justification for the exercise of certain choices that permit control over the freedom of others. Thus the existence of moral rights presupposes that people have an equal right to be free that cannot be circumscribed without justification. The paper's argument shows a talent for synthesizing a variety of situations under a single illuminating set of principles, and the argument remains richly suggestive, even although the "protected choice" model of rights it advocates has met with criticism.

Hart's most important contribution to legal theory was his seminal analysis in 1961 of the distinctive character and mode of regulation of modern systems of law in *The Concept of Law.* This defended a sophisticated form of legal positivism. Hart's own conception of law arose out of dissatisfaction with John Austin's analysis of law as a set of general commands, issued by a political superior or sovereign and enforced by the threat of penalties, which were habitually obeyed by a populace as a whole. In an elegant and penetrating analysis, Hart shows that Austin's account of law cannot explain central features of standard legal systems. It cannot explain the origination of law through common law or the variety of contributions to social life that law makes through the provision of rules conferring private and public powers, in addition to rules prohibiting actions. Austin's notion of a sovereign as the source of all law and subject to none ignores the fact that sovereignty is an office or position within a legal system, which acquires its supreme lawmaking powers by virtue of certain high-level power-conferring rules in that system.

Hart proposes that law is a complex form of rule-governed or normative behavior. Understanding how rules identify and regulate standards of conduct is central to his account of law. Rule-governed behavior has an essential internal aspect, consisting in the fact that the rules are perceived by those accepting them as constituting certain standards of correctness or reasonableness in conduct, and as warranting certain normative responses such as demands for conformity and criticisms of deviations from the rules. Because rules are normative, they are of the right type to help in analyzing many normative relations at work in legal systems—for instance, having rights or entitlements, being authorized to act, being under a legal obligation, and possessing certain powers. Law is not just a method of social control or ordering, but a particular way of ordering human communities by the provision of rules or standards of behavior for the guidance of the citizenry. A legal system is best understood as a combination of two kinds of rules, primary rules and secondary rules, and the dynamic interplay between these. Although Hart's account of primary and secondary rules contains serious ambiguities, the account is valuable in developing the idea that law involves a tiered structure of rules operating at different levels, in which second (higher) order rules provide the machinery for the official identification, administration, and enforcement of first (lower) order rules in the system. The principal secondary rules identified by Hart are rules of change, rules of adjudication, and, most important, the rule of recognition, which specifies criteria for the conclusive identification and scope of primary rules. Hart's model illuminates many features of law, including the institutionalized and conventional character of a legal as compared with a moral order, the critical role of official judgment in the law, how legal validity is determined by reference to higher order criteria in the system, and how the rule of recognition serves to create a unified system of laws.

A major implication of Hart's analysis is that the fundamental secondary rules of any legal system exist insofar as they are effectively adopted as customary normative practices by judicial and other officials, and in this way the existence of a legal system is a matter of fact rather than evaluation. There are empirical tests for the existence of a legal system, although, of course, the facts in question will be complex social facts about rule-governed and rule-constituted behavior. Hart agrees with the positivist tradition that the existence of law is always a conceptually distinct question from that of its moral merit or demerit. A more detailed defense of the separability of issues of legality and morality is given by Hart in his essay "Positivism and the Separation of Law and Morals," as part of a celebrated debate with Lon Fuller.

Some elements in the argument of *The Concept of Law* have been widely criticized. These include the way in which the distinction between primary and secondary rules is drawn, the account of a single supreme rule of recognition for each legal system, and Hart's attempt to defend the idea of law as a system of rules against legal realist accounts of law emphasizing the importance of judicial activity in law determination. Hart's account of judicial reasoning is too narrowly and linguistically framed and does not recognize the diversity or range of substantial questions of an institutional, social policy, or evaluative kind that judges may be obligated to consider in reaching judgments about what is the law. Many legal theorists (Jules Coleman, Kent Greenawalt, Graham Hughes, Philip Soper, Joseph Raz, Rolf Sartorius) have contributed to the subsequent development of a more sophisticated positivist account of the nature of judicial reasoning which retains elements from Hart, most notably Neil MacCormick and Wil Waluchow.

The most serious critical challenge to both the content and the philosophical approach of *The Concept of Law* has been posed by Hart's successor to the chair of jurisprudence in Oxford, Ronald Dworkin. In "The Model of Rules" and other articles reprinted in *Taking Rights Seriously*, Dworkin argues that the body of law incorporates moral principles along with rules, that these moral principles do not acquire their legal standing by satisfying some rule of recognition (by pedigree) or by the exercise of judicial discretion, and that even in hard cases judges have a duty to uncover morally defensible rights existing in the law, and so lack strong discretion. Dworkin's criticism exposes unclarities about the structural integrity of Hart's model of law and the supreme place of the rule of recognition in it. It also implies that Hart's account of judicial reasoning underestimates the role there of a variety of types of normative standard in addition to rules, and their relations to broader moral and political community values. In *Law's Empire*, Dworkin argues that both judicial and philosophical theorizing about law should be understood as exercises in constructive interpretation, which seek a structure of values and principles that will represent that practice in its most defensible light. Dworkin tries to recast Hart's analysis of law as a normative enterprise of justifying law as convention, but, as Hart argues in a "Postscript" to a revised edition of *The Concept of Law*, to do so confuses the kind of descriptive-explanatory account of the characteristic features of legal systems given in *The Concept of Law* with an internal exercise in judicial interpretation.

Hart's philosophical writing displayed an incisive no-nonsense intelligence along with a respect for our commonsense understandings of ourselves and the world. He found the techniques of ordinary language philosophy, particularly as practiced by Gilbert Ryle and

J.L. Austin, well suited to his philosophical aims, and made skillful use of these in developing powerful explanatory and critical analyses of central ideas in Anglo-American law, especially tort law and criminal law. Two important contributions of this kind are to be found in *Causation in the Law,* written with A.M. Honoré, and in *Punishment and Responsibility,* a collection of reprinted papers on conceptual and normative claims about action and responsibility-attribution in criminal law.

Causation in the Law gives a masterful appraisal of classical philosophical accounts of causation in terms of universal laws and necessary connection, and argues that particular causal judgments in ordinary life, history, and the law take their sense from quite different ideas latent in ordinary thought. These include the central ideas of making a change in the world through human action, seeking an explanation for occurrences which are puzzling because they are in some way departures from the norm, the contrast between a cause and standing conditions, and the role of voluntary action in breaking the chain of causation. Hart's and Honoré's account of causation draws on the purposes for which we use causal language in daily life, namely for understanding and controlling events and for determining questions of personal responsibility and liability. They defend their general analysis by means of a richly detailed discussion of uses of "cause" and cognate notions, such as inducing wrongful acts, contributory negligence, foreseeability, and risk, in various branches of law.

In *Punishment and Responsibility* Hart examines several traditional criminal law doctrines about voluntary actions and mental conditions of responsibility, and he shows how they create mistaken or distorted pictures of what it is like to act or to be responsible and answerable for one's actions. He aims to show that our use in the law of the concepts of action and responsibility is continuous with and shares common purposes with the use of these concepts in everyday thought and language, and that the latter context provides a good resource for developing plausible accounts of these important notions. Hart is also concerned to defend our practice of determining responsibility as part of our daily interactions with others and of criminal liability determination. He argues both against

those who think personal responsibility is undermined by determinism and those who think that a practice of responsibility-attribution requires a retributivist justification of punishment. Hart's discussions of the justifiability of punishment show a comprehensive and subtle understanding of the complexities of a social institution such as punishment. A schema for addressing various distinct questions that will be part of an overall defense of the institution is admirably laid out in his 1959 paper "Prolegomenon to the Principles of Punishment."

Despite the mid-century conventional wisdom that analytical philosophy should eschew value judgments and moral commitments, Hart's philosophical attention was never confined to purely conceptual questions, but was alive to deeper concerns not only about the overriding aims and purposes of legal practices and principles but also how these could usefully contribute to a society that promoted individual welfare and individual liberty. Throughout his work there is an implicit understanding that the tools of philosophical analysis can be of value in defining, clarifying, and reasoning clearheadedly to answers to moral questions. This understanding is made explicit in his famous debate with Patrick Devlin about the legitimacy of using the criminal law to enforce a society's moral beliefs, particularly its beliefs about sexual morality. Hart's Oxford lectures, published in 1963 as *Law, Liberty and Morality,* are notable for being one of the first ventures of a philosopher as a philosophical moralist into the field of substantial moral-political debate since the advent of logical positivism in Anglo-American philosophy. One virtue of the book is the clarification it provides by situating the issues under debate in an illuminating framework. Hart distinguishes several different kinds of questions—factual, conceptual or analytical, and moral—that can be raised about the connections between morality and law, and he further distinguishes two very different referents for "morality" in this context. We might be referring to the set of moral beliefs actually accepted by a society (its positive morality), or we might be talking about that set of moral principles which, whether accepted or not, could survive a reasoned critical examination (critical morality). Thus, whether a society is justified in enforcing its moral beliefs (its positive morality) through the use of the criminal

H

law is a question of justification or critical morality about the enforcement of a society's positive morality. On the critical moral question, Hart endorses the spirit of John Stuart Mill's principle in *On Liberty* that the criminal law should prohibit only conduct that is harmful to others and that, therefore, the fact that a kind of behavior is viewed as seriously immoral by society is not, of itself, sufficient reason to prohibit it by criminal sanctions. Hart's defense of the "harm principle" is modulated to sanction limited roles for paternalism and protection of standards of public decency as grounds of prohibition of conduct, but is defended vigorously against the arguments of two important legal moralists, Judge James Fitzjames Stephens in 1873 in his *Liberty, Equality, Fraternity* and Lord Devlin in *The Enforcement of Morals* in 1959. *Law, Liberty and Morality* is one of the significant twentieth-century defenses of liberal values in relation to criminal law.

Hart admired Jeremy Bentham's enormous body of work as a rich source of penetrating criticism and constructive argument, and as unusual in combining insightful generalization about broad principles with an eye for precise detail in applications. Bentham's writing was informed by an acute understanding of how language can be a source of misconceptions and mystification, and how vested interests and authority can cloak the defects of established institutions. Hart wrote numerous papers conveying the subtlety and contemporary relevance of Bentham's ideas on topics such as sovereignty, legal rights, legal powers, duty, and obligation. These were collected together in his *Essays on Bentham* in 1982. Hart also worked steadily with J.H. Burns on the demanding project of bringing out improved editions of Bentham's works, and during the 1970s editions of Bentham's *Of Laws in General, An Introduction to the Principles of Morals and Legislation,* and a *Comment on the Commentaries* and a *Fragment on Government* were published.

In addition, Hart was interested in the governing ideas of other jurisprudential and political traditions than his own, particularly those in the United States and Scandinavia. He explored critically the jurisprudence of Oliver Wendell Holmes, Jr., Lon Fuller, Hans Kelsen, Alf Ross, and von Jhering, and later John Rawls' theory of justice and Ronald Dworkin's conception of law.

References

Dworkin, Ronald. *Law's Empire*. Cambridge MA: Harvard University Press, 1986.

———. "The Model of Rules." *University of Chicago Law Review* 35 (1967), 14. Reprinted in *Taking Rights Seriously*. London: Duckworth, 1977.

Hart, H.L.A. *The Concept of Law*. Oxford: Clarendon Press, 1961. 2d ed. Oxford: Clarendon Press, 1994.

———. *Essays in Jurisprudence and Philosophy*. Oxford: Clarendon Press, 1983.

———. *Essays on Bentham*. Oxford: Clarendon Press, 1982.

———. *Law, Liberty and Morality*. Oxford: Clarendon Press, 1963.

———. "Positivism and the Separation of Law and Morals." *Harvard Law Review* 81 (1958), 598.

———. *Punishment and Responsibility*. Oxford: Clarendon Press, 1967.

Hart, H.L.A., and A.M. Honoré. *Causation in the Law*. Oxford: Clarendon Press, 1959.

MacCormick, Neil. *H.L.A. Hart*. Stanford: Stanford University Press, 1981.

———. *Legal Reasoning and Legal Theory*. Oxford: Clarendon Press, 1978.

Waluchow, W.J. *Inclusive Legal Positivism*. Oxford: Clarendon Press, 1994.

Brenda M. Baker

See also LIABILITY, CRIMINAL; MORALITY AND LAW

Hate Literature

The publication and dissemination of material that expresses or incites hatred against persons on the basis of their skin color, gender, religion, ethnic origin, or nationality pose theoretical and pragmatic challenges in legal regimes committed to the equality of all persons and to stringent protections on freedom of expression. Hate literature arguably threatens equality, but it is contentful expression. The central question of principle is whether the restriction of hate literature is ever justified. Three approaches may be discerned. Some theorists look to existing constitutionally permissible restrictions on free speech, especially on "fighting words" and libel, and contend that to the extent that hate literature resembles them, it falls outside the scope of protected speech. Others examine the reasons underlying the protection of freedom of expression and argue that because the interests so served (for example, pursuit of truth, self-fulfillment) are not at stake in the expression of hate, such material may be permissibly restricted. Finally, an emerging view is that hate literature is a form of discriminatory conduct that serves to construct and maintain social and political inequality.

The central pragmatic questions concern the specific objectives of antihate literature legislation, its efficacy in meeting those objectives, and how such laws are to be framed. Hate literature is just one dimension of racial and other forms of prejudice, so its prohibition is unlikely to eliminate such discrimination. However, if such literature is a primary source of racist, sexist, and xenophobic attitudes and beliefs, then antihate measures might serve to stem the spread of such ideas. Some also argue that antihate literature laws are required to makes explicit a state's commitment to equality.

Several worries about the enforcement of antihate literature legislation cast doubt on its efficacy. Empirical evidence concerning the effects of the Race Relations Act in Great Britain and the application of campus speech codes in the United States indicate that laws prohibiting expressions of hate work against, rather than for, the minorities whose interests they are thought to protect. Together with the claim that hate speech directed at members of dominant groups is not harmful, this has led some scholars to suggest that hate speech restrictions should apply exclusively to the expression of members of those dominant groups. However, this asymmetry would itself violate various guarantees to equal protection under the law. In addition, it is dubious whether such laws are the most effective way to combat racism, sexism, and the like. First, because the prosecution of hate mongers provides a public forum in which they can air views that otherwise might only reach a small minority, it is argued that hateful opinions garner greater credibility. Second, there is the danger that adoption of antihate laws will engender complacency and prevent the development of more costly educational and other means of combating discrimination. Third, antihate laws only target public speech and are therefore powerless against the private dissemination of hate literature. A final practical problem concerns the legal definition of hate literature: it must be (1) explicit enough to avoid charges of vagueness and to allow for the effective application, (2) broad enough to capture most of the material that promulgates hate, yet (3) narrow enough not to capture what is otherwise taken to be protected speech. These desiderata are clearly in tension with one another, and we might predict that any definition which satisfied them would deter only the most blatant forms of hate literature; committed racists may resort to more subtle expressions of their hatred.

Partly in response to two international treaties [the International Convention for the Elimination of All Forms of Racial Discrimination (CRED) and the International Covenant on Civil and Political Rights (ICCPR)], many countries, including Canada, Great Britain, France, and the Netherlands, but with the notable exception of the United States, have adopted antihate laws. Both criminal and civil remedies are provided for. In the United States, no federal law specifically targets hate literature. However, a majority of states have some form of antihate legislation, and several universities have instituted campus speech codes. None of these, however, have withstood constitutional challenges. [See *R.A.V. v. The City of St. Paul,* 112 S. Ct. 2538 (1992), and *Doe v. University of Michigan,* 721 F. Supp. 852 (E.D. Mich. 1989).]

In those jurisdictions in which hate literature is constitutionally prohibited we might predict the extension of such restrictions to other forms of expression that threaten equality. For example, it is arguable that the Canadian Supreme Court's 1992 decision in *R. v. Butler,* 1 S.C.R. 452 (1992), upholding the constitutionality of criminal obscenity provisions, was made possible in the light of its finding in *R. v. Keegstra,* 2 W.W.R. 1, 43 S.C.C. (1991), that section 319(2) of the *Canadian Criminal Code* prohibiting hate propaganda does not unjustifiably infringe the right to free speech. In contrast, proposed civil rights legislation against pornography in the United States has been uniformly unsuccessful, as noted in *American Booksellers Association v. Hudnut,* 771 F.2d 323 (1985). More generally, in the face of increasing ethnic and racial conflict around the globe, there is pressure to examine more closely the feasibility and desirability of legal measures concerning hate literature.

References

Coliver, Sandra, ed. *Striking a Balance. Hate Speech, Freedom of Expression and Non-*

Discrimination. Article 19, London; Human Rights Centre, University of Essex, 1992.

Delgado, R. "Words that Wound: A Tort Action for Racial Insults, Epithets, and Name-Calling." *Harvard Civil Rights–Civil Liberties Law Review* 17 (1982), 133.

International Covenant on Civil and Political Rights. General Assembly resolution 2200 A (XXI) of 16 December 1966; entered into force 23 March 1976.

International Convention on the Elimination of All Forms of Racial Discrimination. General Assembly resolution 2106 A (XX) of 21 December 1965; entered into force 4 January 1969.

Kretzmer, D. "Freedom of Speech and Racism." *Cardozo Law Review* 8 (1987), 445.

Matsuda, Mari. "Public Response to Racist Speech: Considering the Victim's Story." *Michigan Law Review* 87 (1989), 2320.

Race Relations Act, 1976, ch. 74 §70 (amending *Public Order Act,* 1936, I Edw. 8&1 Geo. 6,§2).

Sunstein, Cass. *Democracy and the Problem of Free Speech.* New York: Free Press, 1994.

Susan Dwyer

See also PORNOGRAPHY

Hayek, Friedrich von (1899–1992)

Friedrich von Hayek was an internationally renowned economist whose interest in the interrelationships between prosperity, free markets, liberty, and law led to a distinctive reformulation of classical liberalism. Hayek argued that "negative" liberty, or freedom from coercion, is the most important and fundamental of all goods. It protects the individual from being used by others as a tool and is a necessary condition for moral responsibility and genuine moral virtue. It is also essential to free markets, which maximize material well-being, including that of the least well-off members of society. Free markets maximize the utilization of the knowledge, inspiration, and creativity of individuals, which central planners are much less able to harness; this enhances the complexity of economic activity and stimulates experimentation, which, when successful, enables societies to adapt productively to unpredictable changes.

Negative liberty depends on the legal protection of a "private sphere" of individual autonomy. Law is therefore a necessary condition for freedom, rather than a threat to it. The private sphere must include individual rights to own or control property and to enter into binding contracts. However, in general its content cannot be exhaustively deduced from abstract political principles: our understanding of it must develop as we learn from experience.

In delimiting the private sphere, the form of the law is a more immediate concern than its content. Formal qualities distinguish law, used to coordinate a society of individuals pursuing their own freely chosen goals, from commands, used to direct an organization pursuing collective goals. The government of a free society is an organization, which must use commands to direct its employees; but it should use only laws to coordinate the activities of citizens. Hayek's discussion of the formal qualities which distinguish laws from commands has helped to clarify the idea of the "rule of law."

The most important formal quality of law is abstractness. Law is concerned with means, not ends: it should be aimed, not at achieving particular goals chosen by the lawmaker, but at prescribing conditions with which individuals must comply in pursuing their goals. Furthermore, it should not be aimed at particular individuals or groups, but apply equally to everyone who is similarly situated. By increasing the likelihood that lawmakers will be bound by their own laws, these requirements of generality and equality make it less likely that laws will unduly restrict liberty. They also make it more difficult for law to be used to coerce particular individuals. Discrimination disguised in a law which appears to satisfy these requirements can be exposed by asking whether majorities of both those regulated and those not regulated by the law accept that it is reasonable.

Another formal quality essential to the rule of law is predictability, which requires that laws be public, prospective, certain, inflexible, and applied in particular cases regardless of circumstances unknowable in advance. However, this does not mean that law must consist only of rules and not of general principles. Law can include principles which are generalizations implicit in explicit rules, but not the constantly changing policies of particular governments.

Hayek once recommended the codification of law in statutory form, on the ground that the judicial lawmaking and flexibility which characterize common law are less compatible with the rule of law. However, he later reversed this assessment, partly because of his disillusionment with the legislative process, which he depicted as an unprincipled auction in which selfish interest groups seek special privileges. The common law, derived from evolving community practices, is less able to be used by powerful interest groups to direct society toward their goals. Nevertheless, Hayek conceded that legislation can be useful in filling gaps, correcting errors, or introducing innovations in the law. When judges confront legal gaps or uncertainties, they must explicate principles previously only implicit in the law. In doing so, they should attempt to maximize the fulfillment of citizen's expectations; this is to a large extent a matter of trial and error, another point in favor of common rather than statute law.

Hayek strongly opposed the idea of "social" or "distributive" justice. Justice concerns only the rules and procedures which regulate the actions of individuals, and not their overall, collectively unintended outcome. Individuals cannot be held morally responsible for that outcome failing to resemble some distributive pattern thought to be desirable. Moreover, such patterns can be achieved only by governmental command and not by law. Compulsory egalitarianism is incompatible with the rule of law.

Critics on the left have attacked Hayek's focus on "negative" liberty and the virtues of the free market. Those more in sympathy with his political agenda have questioned the consistency of his epistemological and ethical premises, and the adequacy of the formal qualities of law to delimit and protect the liberties at the heart of that agenda. They argue that liberalism needs a more substantive theory of rights.

References

Barry, N. *Hayek's Social and Economic Philosophy*. London: Macmillan, 1979.

Gray, J.N. *Hayek on Liberty*. 2d ed. Oxford: Oxford University Press, 1986.

Hayek, F.A. von. *The Constitution of Liberty*. Chicago: University of Chicago Press, 1960.

———. *Law, Legislation and Liberty*. 3 vols. Chicago: University of Chicago Press, 1973–1979.

Kukathas, C. *Hayek and Modern Liberalism*. Oxford: Oxford University Press, 1989.

Jeffrey Goldsworthy

Hegel, Georg Wilhelm Friedrich (1770–1831)

Georg Wilhelm Friedrich Hegel's contribution to the philosophy of law resides as much in his comprehensive conception of the different spheres of right as in his analysis of legal institutions. Unlike his ancient and liberal predecessors, Hegel attempts to free ethics from all foundations, recognizing that so long as conduct is legitimated by according with privileged givens or by issuing from privileged procedures of construction, normative validity derives from an assumed ground that can never enjoy the same validity it confers. Although Hegel's polemic against foundations has led many to misconstrue him as a historicist who has no ethics, Hegel instead concludes that valid conduct can be nothing other than self-determined, for only freedom escapes determination by external factors. Accordingly, Hegel adamantly repudiates the historical school of law and maintains that ethics must proceed as a philosophy of right, conceiving the reality of freedom in all its different institutional spheres.

Hegel addresses this task most comprehensively in his *Philosophy of Right,* first published in 1821, arguing that self-determination consists not in the natural capacity of choice privileged by liberal theory, but rather in a self-ordered system of different enacted interactions wherein individuals engage in artificial, objectively recognized modes of freedom that can only be exercised within the intersubjective practices they compose. Within these interactions, whose participants exercise rights reciprocally respected by one another, agents can achieve genuine self-determination, where their own acts of will determine both their ends and the form of agency they exercise. Although these interactions are not given by nature, but arise in history and, in Hegel's estimation, have developed most fully in the postclassical era, they still have a universal character that sets the standard for judging the legitimacy of modern institutions.

Consequently, for Hegel, conceiving what law ought to be revolves around determining both what forms of self-determination require legal enforcement and what spheres of right provide the context for legal institutions themselves. Hegel conceives self-determination to fall into three fundamental forms: abstract right (the basic freedom in which individuals determine themselves as property owners, precluding enslavement and enabling themselves to enjoy other rights), morality (in which agents hold each other accountable for acting on conscience with good purposes and intentions), and ethical community (in which individuals interact in recognition of rights and duties that they enjoy as members of three different associations: the family, civil society, and the state). Unlike recent communitarian thinkers, Hegel neither historicizes ethical community as a contingent convention nor absolutizes it as the exclusive context of objectively valid conduct. He instead recognizes that household, social, and political rights, as dimensions of freedom, have an unconditioned universality requiring specific institutions and that individuals cannot exercise these rights unless their freedoms as property owners and moral subjects are already respected.

Hegel's account of property relations might seem particularly apt for making sense of tort law, given how he ascribes to property entitlements a normativity logically prior to provisos of distributive justice rooted in family, society, and state. Nevertheless, Hegel actually situates law and the legal process within civil society, after abstract right, morality, the family, and the market. Hegel thereby acknowledges that unless conventions have arisen enabling individuals to exercise their property rights, moral responsibility, family freedom, and economic autonomy, individuals will be prevented from enjoying the universality and equality of legal standing. Moreover, by conceiving legality within ethical community, whose rights and duties are operative only within an institutional framework already embodying them, Hegel allows for desuetude and for how law has its binding character only where legal subjects already predominantly interact in recognition of its authority.

By placing legality in civil society and not in the state, Hegel might seem to go astray, especially since he emphasizes how law posits right. Nonetheless, this positing should not be identified with the legislation of a political sovereign, because law's positing of right can take the form of common law, codification can be undertaken by courts and scholars, and law applies to citizens and noncitizens alike, either domestically or on an international plane. In the first instance, law's positing is simply a public proclamation that has legitimacy by giving externally enforceable right a recognized universal and objective determination, which right lacks under conditions of customary compliance. Although what law legitimately promulgates are the rights already entailed in property, family, and economic relations, legal promulgation adds positive qualifications to their content, stipulating, for example, certain formalities for valid contract and marriage, as well as specific punishments and compensations.

In order to have the objectivity and universality that right requires, Hegel argues, law must be made accessible to all legal subjects by codification in as nontechnical a language as possible. Reliance on common law and judicial precedent is an inadequate substitute, leaving the content of law deficiently indeterminate. By the same token, due process must enable all participants to follow legal proceedings and have their rights upheld through judicious determination of the facts and an authoritative application of the law. Since determining the facts of the case requires no legal expertise and court decisions should respect the subjective freedom of the accused, Hegel argues in behalf of trial by jury, where decision by one's peers allows one's will to be represented in the verdict. All these requirements of court procedure are matters of right for legal subjects and therefore the norms of due process should be posited in legal form as well.

The distinction Hegel draws between malicious and nonmalicious wrong in his treatment of abstract right provides the basis for distinguishing between civil and criminal law and for comprehending why inadvertent violations of person and property require compensation, whereas crime warrants not only compensation when victims suffer loss, but punishment, even if no harm results. As Hegel argues, nonmalicious wrong lies in the particular injury to the property rights of the victim, whereas malicious wrong lies in the universal wrong consisting in the criminal's express willing against the rights of others. Hence, while the particular injury in nonmalicious wrong can be remedied by equivalent compensation, the universal wrong in crime is only counteracted by restricting the will of the criminal, which is where that wrong resides. Incarceration is thus the rational form of punishment, and punishment is due even in cases of attempted crime that result in no particular damage or injury. In the context of civil society, where civil and criminal law promulgate how nonmalicious and malicious wrongs should be treated, the determination of punishment, Hegel argues, must further take into account the offense to legality of malicious law-breaking, as well as the strength of the social order to withstand particular crimes, which may call for softening punishments. In no case, however, can deterrence or rehabilitation be the primary rationale for punishment, since both entail withdrawing recognition of the freedom and responsibility of the criminal.

Hegel supplements these features of legality when he addresses the institutions of political freedom, where statutory legislation and constitutionality come into play. Because the different spheres of right must be united through an activity of self-determination, rather than rest on grounds external to freedom, self-government must preside over prepolitical institutions, including the legal institutions of civil society. Although the supremacy of politics involves partially restricting prepolitical rights so that they do not undercut political freedom, Hegel maintains that no contradiction arises because individuals cannot enjoy equal political opportunity unless their other freedoms are upheld. For this reason, the legal system of civil society is a precondition of self-government, and the founding of an effective, just constitution is not a unilateral political act, but a culmination of the historical process in which all the institutions of freedom arise.

Hegel comprehends that constitutionality requires a division of powers where the legislature only formulates statutes that do not become law until the sovereign authorizes them and hands their implementation over to the executive branch. However, in violation of his own commitment to the exclusive authority of freedom, Hegel makes the sovereign a hereditary monarch, characterizes the legislature as an estate assembly in which estate membership rests partially on birthright and confers political privileges, and subordinates the estate assembly to the tutelage of the monarch. Combined with Hegel's restriction of the family to heterosexual monogamy in which the wife is restricted to domestic affairs and the husband represents the household in civil society and the state, these measures undercut the upholding of right in which Hegel himself exclusively

grounds the authority of legality. Accordingly, Hegel's *Philosophy of Right* calls for critique, not on Karl Marx's terms of abolishing state, civil society, and the family to recapture the natural liberty of human species being, but in terms of eliminating the inconsistencies that mar Hegel's attempt to conceive law's empire as the reality of self-determination.

References

Berman, Robert Bruce. *Categorial Justification: Normative Argumentation in Hegel's Practical Philosophy* Albany: State University of New York Press, 1997.

Brudner, Alan. *The Unity of the Common Law: Studies in Hegelian Jurisprudence.* Berkeley: University of California Press, 1995.

Foster, M.B. *The Political Philosophies of Plato and Hegel.* Oxford: Oxford University Press, 1968.

Hegel, G.W.F. *Elements of the Philosophy of Right.* Ed. Allen W. Wood. Trans. H.B. Nisbet. Cambridge: Cambridge University Press, 1991.

Hegel and Legal Theory. Cardozo Law Review 10, 5–6 (March/April 1989).

Nicholson, Peter P. "Hegel on Crime." *History of Political Thought* 3 (1982), 103–121.

Weinrib, Ernest J. *The Idea of Private Law.* Cambridge MA: Harvard University Press, 1995.

Winfield, Richard Dien. *Law in Civil Society.* Lawrence: University Press of Kansas, 1994.

Richard Dien Winfield

Hellenic Philosophy of Law: Conceptual Framework

Suppose that the fundamental questions for philosophy of law are What is law? and From what sources does law come into being? On that basis, the pre-Platonic hellenic tradition provides exceptionally ambiguous answers, because there is no early hellenic word that could be unambiguously translated "law," and because there is no general agreement about the sources of whatever in Greek culture could be called "law" or "justice.

Modern legal theory presupposes that existing law has one or more of four sources: legislation, judicial decisions serving as precedents for a body of case law (common law), a written constitution, the writings of legal scholars. Written constitutions were envisioned by philosophers like Plato and Aristotle but did not exist before their time. There was no written scholarly legal tradition in classical Greece, nor was there a common law tradition as that is understood in the English-speaking world (at least), where earlier decisions of competent courts are regarded as prima facie binding on later courts in the jurisdiction. In reality, classical hellenic practice was "agonistic" in character: an individual having a grievance against another would present his (rarely, her) case before the appropriate official, the "defendant" would present the defense in reply, and the official, or a group, who could call a panel of judges or a jury, would decide what ought to be done in this case. Decisions of this kind were not regarded as precedent setting, except to the extent that some later plaintiff or defendant might argue that one ought, in principle, be consistent from one case to the next. Thus the "courts" tended to resolve individual conflicts without generating positive law.

That leaves us with "legislation" as a source of law, and certainly there was legislation; a crucial question for those who discuss "law" and "justice" in the classical hellenic period is whether there is some ground or basis for legislation—a divine sanction, age-old customs, mutual self-interest, or something else—or if legislation is an originative, creative act of the legislator. If legislation is as arbitrary as the decisions of judges/juries, then would it not be as variable, mutable, as those decisions?

We may approach an understanding of the hellenic answers to questions like these by a look at the Greek concepts that resemble, in some way or other, the English-language concept of "law." If we were to try to translate the word "law" into classical Greek, we would find that there are several words that might be appropriate in varied contexts: *nomos, themis, dikê, graphê,* and *archê.*

ΔΙΚΗ

Dikê in the earlier writers such as Homer is proper procedure, the practice of divine kings, that which is right as opposed to that which is compelled, and the judgment that is reached by kings. The verb *dikazô* means to sit in judgment (in the active) or to plead one's case (in

the middle). *Dikê* may refer to a private lawsuit, or the object of a case brought to judgment, whether punishment for crime, penalty, atonement, or restitution. A person who is *dikaios* is observant of customs and rules, a well-ordered, civilized, righteous person. As a more developed system of law comes about, the *dikaios* is also one who is equitable, legally punctilious, fair, just. Thus the abstract noun *dikaiosunê* may be translated either "righteousness" or "justice." By the time of Herodotus, at least, "injustice" or "unrighteousness" (*adikia*) is of roughly two sorts: *pleonexia,* getting more than one's fair share, and *anomia,* not following proper procedure.

Perhaps we can trace a categorization of *hubris* or *adikia* into more than one class, including *pleonexia,* back to Solon. Erik Wolf discusses *dikê* and *themis* first as deities; that is probably misleading. Although *dikê* is personified by Hesiod and others, she is undoubtedly a relatively late addition to the pantheon. Etymologically, *dikê* is "that which is said," like the later *logos.*

ΘΕΜΙΣ

An alternative Homeric concept is that of *themis. Themis* is literally that which is laid down or established (from the verb *tithêmi*). *Themistes* are not only the customary and accepted social rules but also, importantly, the decrees of gods and oracles. *Themis* is also the name of the goddess of law and order, the mother of the Seasons and the Fates. The concept came first, obviously. The Homeric Zeus passes along to the kings (*basileis*) the task of preserving customary usages; *themitos* is that which is in accord with the divine and human usage. Later, the related words *thesmos* and *thesmia* refer to written decisions in court cases. In Athenian law, at least, the *themothetai* are those who write down the decisions. The ordinances written down by Draco, the older codification of Athenian law, are called *thesmoi.*

ΝΕΜΩ, ΝΕΜΕΣΙΣ, ΝΟΜΟΣ

The verb *nemô* means "deal out," "dispense"; in Homer it is often the gods who are distributing good and bad items to human beings. The abstract noun built on this verb, *nemesis,* in Homer indicates righteous indignation, especially of the gods, and retribution for disobedience of divine will. But another development of the verb *nemô* is into the noun *nomos,* that which is in habitual practice, use, or possession. *Nomos* as usage and custom begins in Hesiod: Zeus has ordained this *nomos,* that animals eat each other, but to human beings he gave *dikê,* to argue their case before each other. Soon the word is used of statute or ordinance (as well as of a melody, incidentally). We may see the fundamental tension in the concept of *nomos* by looking at the verb formed from it, *nomizô*: *nomizô* means to use customarily, make common use of, or practice, but also to enact, as a law; in another set of senses, *nomizô* means to acknowledge, consider as, esteem, hold in honor, believe. Similarly *nomismata* are customs and usages, but also legal rights; *nomismata* are whatever is sanctioned by current or established usage, custom, institution; especially current coin; *nomisma* is also full legal measure. The codification of the laws by Solon include what the Athenians called *nomoi.*

As a group, Draco, Solon, Zaleucus, Pittacus, Demonax, Charondas, and others were called "lawgivers," *nomothetes,* charged with writing down the *nomoi* of their cities. These *nomoi* might be grouped into four categories: tort laws, family laws, public laws, and procedural laws. Draco and the others did not write "constitutions" of their cities; they produced, perhaps, something resembling a summary of part of a civil and criminal code. The process of developing written laws, legislation, remains a central concern of most classical Greek communities throughout antiquity. One city that apparently did not write down its *nomoi* was Sparta; it seemed to operate on the basis of traditional, oral, and customary practice into the fifth century.

Once some "laws" were written down, it was possible to argue that some laws, and possibly more important and superseding laws, had not been written down, and perhaps could not be written down ultimately, since they were not of human fabrication. The most famous pre-Platonic assertion of the priority of "unwritten laws" is in Sophocles' *Antigone,* where it is asserted that the unwritten laws are divine and are the source of human (written) laws. We may compare a fragment of Pherecydes, a late-sixth-century thinker: "From the marriage of Heaven and Earth were born *nomoi* for gods and human beings." However, some argued that unwritten laws are in fact natural, rather than divine, and when combined with the notion that some people have a superior nature, the idea may lead to a defense of tyranny. So by the end of the fifth century B.C., as noted in *Philosophy Before Socrates,* the Athenians passed a decree that, according to Andocides, "[t]he magistrates must not make use of unwritten law."

In the fifth century B.C. and later, philosophers and statesmen debated the relationship between *nomos* and *phusis*—as we might say, between "law" or "custom" on the one hand, and "nature" on the other. The debate was partially thematized by reference to "justice" (*dikê*): is justice "conventional" or "natural." A partisan of *phusis* might claim that we can discover what is just by observing the behavior of human beings, while a partisan of *nomos* might claim that justice might be discovered by finding out the opinions of people concerning justice or by taking a vote. A partisan of nature might emphasize the natural power of unusual individuals, or general laws of nature, like self-preservation or desire for pleasure, and give those normative force, while a partisan of *nomos* might argue that only *nomos* differentiates human from bestial existence, that everyone should support *nomos* for their own protection and self-interest.

ΓΡΑΦΗ

Another word that may often be translated "law" is *graphê.* While the primary etymological sense of the word *graphê* would be "representation by means of lines; drawing, delineation, that which is drawn, picture; writing, art of writing, that which is written," it can also mean a "written law." However, in Athenian law, from Solon onward, a *graphê* has a very special sense: prior to Solon, it seems, "criminal" cases could be brought only by the victim or, in the case of murder, by a member of the victim's family. Such accusations, plaints, were known as *dikai.* Athenian law allowed persons not themselves victims of crimes to bring charges against those they believed should be punished; that was done by a *graphê,* or "bill of indictment in a public prosecution."

ΑΡΧΗ

A mention of *archê* is useful. *Archê* is "beginning, origin, first principle," but also "rule, sovereignty, dominion, political office." Hellenic philosophers are much more apt to think about the meaning of *archê* than about any of the concepts already discussed: about origins

H

and authority, than about that which is said (*dikê*), posited (*themis*), or allotted (*nomos*). As Aristotle defines the term in *Metaphysics*, *archê* is a starting point in any of several ways, but also "that by whose choice that which is moved is moved and that which changes changes, e.g., the magistracies in cities, and oligarchies and monarchies and tyrannies are called *archai*, and so are the arts." That, however, takes us from philosophy of law to political philosophy.

References

Cartledge, P., P. Millett, and S. Todd, eds. *Nomos*. Cambridge: Cambridge University Press, 1990.

Ehrenberg, Victor. *Die Rechtsidee im Frühen Griechentum* (The Idea of Law in Early Greek Society). Darmstadt: Wissenschaftlichen Buchgesellschaft, 1966.

Gagarin, Michael. *Early Greek Law*. Berkeley: University of California Press, 1986.

Havelock, Erik. *The Greek Concept of Justice*. Cambridge MA: Harvard University Press 1978.

Jones, J. Walter. *The Law and Legal Theory of the Greeks*. Oxford: Oxford University Press, 1956.

Lloyd-Jones, Hugh. *The Justice of Zeus*. Berkeley: University of California Press, 1971.

McKirahan, Richard D., Jr. *Philosophy Before Socrates*. Indianapolis: Hackett, 1994.

Wolf, Erik. *Griechisches Rechtsdenken* (The Greek Doctrine of Law). Frankfurt: Vittorio Klostermann, 1950–1956.

Anthony Preus

See also ARISTOTLE; HELLENISTIC PHILOSOPHY OF LAW; PLATO; ROMAN PHILOSOPHY OF LAW

Hellenic Philosophy of Law: Primary Sources

"[N]either the Greeks, nor any society speaking and thinking in their language, ever showed the smallest capacity for producing a philosophy of law," said Sir Henry Sumner Maine. Yet Erik Wolf wrote four sizeable volumes on *Griechisches Rechtsdenken (The Greek Doctrine of Law)*, without getting as far as Plato's major works on law. Maine is right to this extent, that the classical Greeks did not produce what English-language scholars of the philosophy of law would call a clear

example of a treatise on the philosophy of law. Plato's *Republic* and *Laws* deal with "justice" (*dikaiosynê*) and the appropriate legislation for an ideal state; Aristotle's *Politics* is more nearly a treatise of political science than an exposition of philosophy of law. However, Wolf and the many others who have written on the history of law and the philosophy of law have plenty of material to discuss; if a philosophy of law, a *Rechtsdenken*, is the fundamental intellectual framework for legal practice and legislation, then the Hellenes certainly had that; one could hardly find a more self-consciously litigious and political society.

Homer

Justice may be distinguished into "procedural" and "substantive"; written laws may codify either, but tend to emphasize substantive justice. Before there were written laws, procedure was much more emphasized; according to Erik Havelock, oral tradition is reflected in the Homeric poems, where justice is "a procedure, not a principle or any set of principles. It is arrived at by a process of negotiation between contending parties carried out rhetorically." *Iliad,* describing the shield of Achilles, includes a description of a mediated dispute; the language is quite ambiguous, so any interpretation is open to criticism. There is a plaintiff asking for blood money, a defendant claiming to have paid it already, a circle of elders serving as judges/jury, and heralds holding back the crowd. Some plural group *dikazon* argue their respective cases or give judgment, and there is a pile of gold to be awarded to the one who most justly "says *dikê*," that is, pleads his case or gives judgment. We may suppose that the gold has been taken from the defendant, that the plaintiff is trying to get it, the defendant to get it back, and that the elders will decide on the basis of what is said. That is an example of the sort of procedure of negotiation envisaged by the Homeric poems. It is on the basis of those descriptions, we may suppose, that Anaxagoras says, according to Diogenes Laertius, that "Homer's poetry is about virtue and justice."

Hesiod

Hesiod speaks of justice (*dikê*) at some length in *Works and Days*. Dikê sits at the right hand of Zeus: those who deal justly are rewarded by Zeus, and those who do not are punished. Her sister Eunomia has the job of straightening out crooked judges. Hesiodic *dikê* is not a system of rules; it is proper procedure, the accepted method of resolving disputes. Where Homer uses the word *themis*, Hesiod in this passage and elsewhere in *Works and Days* uses *nomos* to denominate the judgments of Zeus. We may compare the *Hymn to Hermes*, a late sixth-century work, which describes legal procedure as occurring among the gods, in that Zeus resolves a conflict between Hermes and Apollo. This is represented as if it were a paradigmatic case of "justice."

Solon, reformer of Athenian law, describes a procedural justice: "I achieved these things by combining force with justice; I wrote laws (*thesmoi*) for both lowly and noble fitting justice appropriately to each person." Solon fixed penalties for various torts, codified family law, instituted the public suit (γραφή), regulated state religious rites, and bolstered his economic reforms with a range of legislation. Like all other early lawgivers that we know, Solon also concerned himself with the regularization of judicial procedure. For Solon, Dikê brings the truth to light, Dikê has her appointed time.

Philosophers

Turning to the canonical philosophers, the fragment of Anaximander bases its analysis on the notion of justice: Anaximander says that the source (*archê*) for everything that comes into being is the "indefinite," and it is into the indefinite that everything is ultimately destroyed "according to necessity, for they pay penalty (*dikê*) and retribution (*tisis*) to each other for their injustice (*adikia*) according to the ordering of time." We have here the concept of a cosmic justice leading to punishments and rectifications among everything that exists. (For a discussion of the legal implications of the fragment, see *Anaximander and the Origins of Greek Cosmology* by Charles Kahn.)

This idea of justice as a universal reciprocity among entities may also be found in the Pythagorean tradition. Aristotle tells us in the *Metaphysics* (985b23, 1073b21) and *Nicomachean Ethics* (1132b21) that the Pythagoreans defined justice as reciprocity, that Pythagorean justice is an attribute of numbers. The aristotelian author of the *Magna Moralia* assures us that justice is *not* an equally equal number" (*arithmos isakis isos*). Incidentally, Pythagoras may well have derived some of his philosophy from his acquaintance with Egypt-

ian thought and practice; later Greeks believed that Egyptian philosophy centered on two issues: the nature of God (or gods) and justice. Diogenes Laertius cites Manetho's *On the Egyptian Philosophy* for the idea that the Egyptians attributed their much-admired legal system to the intervention of Hermes. Pythagorean legal philosophy, in partial imitation of a notion of Egyptian law, is said to have attempted to achieve social stability. See, for example, Isocrates, *Busiris*. Plato's *Republic* and *Laws* stand squarely within the Pythagorean tradition in respect to the centrality of mathematical analysis and to the desirability of social stability.

Heraclitus takes from Anaximander (and no doubt others) the idea of law as a central reality of the cosmos and develops it in several ways, reapplying his developed notion to human social practices. The cosmic role of Dikê in Heraclitus may be well seen in "[t]he Sun will not go out of his measures; if not, the Furies, ministers of Dikê, will find him out." However, Dikê is bound up in the world of flux and opposition: "It is necessary to know that war is common, Dikê is strife, and all things come into being according to strife and necessity," and "They would not know the name of Dikê if these things did not exist." (Presumably "these things" can be defined as injustices.) Dikê is not really ultimate: "To God all things are beautiful and good and just (*dikaia*), but to people some things are unjust and others just." Still, that divine relativity should not comfort evildoers: "The person in highest opinion knows opined things, and keeps them; and indeed Dikê will seize fabricators and witnesses of falsehoods."

Beside the somewhat personalized Dikê, Heraclitus posits a divine Nomos: "It is necessary for those who speak intelligently (ξὺν νόωι—*sun nooi*) to be strong in intelligence (ξυνοι—*sunoi*) of all things, just as a city in the law (*nomoi*) and much stronger. For all human things are nourished by one law (*nomos*), the divine; for it is strong as much as it wants and is sufficient for all and is still left over. Even though divine Law is "sufficient," nevertheless "[t]he people ought to fight for the *nomos* just as much as for the city wall." Politically the *nomos* may represent just about any constitution, including a monarchy: "It is also *nomos* to obey the wish of one."

Parmenides, the founder of the Eleatic school of philosophy, is not normally thought of as contributing to concepts of justice, but he does use the figures of Dikê and Themis in ways that indicate a reliance upon notions of "justice" and "right" as support for his ontological position. For example, in the Proem of his poem, much-penalizing Dikê holds the keys for the gates to the way to the goddess who will tell him the truth about everything. When the goddess addresses him, she tells him, "No evil fate (*kakê moira*) has sent you this way, but right and justice *(themis te dikê te)*." Later, "being" is held not only in logical bond, but also "Dikê has never loosed the fetters of being to allow it to become or perish, but holds it fast." And again, "[t]herefore it is right (*themis*) that what is should not be imperfect."

Empedocle, too, uses these concepts in a poetic way. For example, in an invocation to the muse he asks her to bring "whatever is *themis* for ephemeral beings to hear." In another place, he talks of the generation of individual living beings through the advent of a soul into the material world, and destruction by their departure: "Whenever they arrive in the *aither* mixed so as to form a man or one of the wild beasts or bushes or birds, that is when they speak of coming into being; and whenever they are separated, that is called the ill-starred fate of death. They do not call it as is right (*themis*), but I myself too assent to their convention (*nomos*)." He uses *nomos* in a quite extended sense: "But what is lawful (*nomimon*) for all extends far through the wide-ruling *aither* and through the immense glare." According to Aristotle in *Rhetoric* (1373b6), this fragment refers to the injustice of killing living things.

The case of Democritus is a bit complex, since there are two seemingly separate sides of his thought. One side is his ontological theory, the theory of atomism, that everything is really composed of atoms, and all sensory attributes are conventional and appearances. He uses the word *nomos* to express this idea: "[B]y convention (*nomoi*) colored, by convention sweet, by convention bitter, but in reality, atoms and void." The other side of his thought is a collection of moral observations, without any overwhelming basis in the atomism. In that mode he says things like "People who are controlled by money cannot ever be just," or "Just desire is to strive without violence of noble things." The conventionalism of his position is often striking: "One ought punish those who do in-

justice as much as possible and not let them go; for that sort of thing is just and good, and not to do that is unjust and bad." However, sometimes he says things that are quite perceptive: "As things are now arranged, there is no way for rulers to be protected from being unjustly treated, even if they are very good people. . . . Things should be organized so that if someone does no injustice, even if he severely examines those who do injustice, he should not come under their control; a statute (*thesmos*) should protect those who do just things."

According to the interpretation in *The Presocratic Philosophers*, Democritus

> expresses the view . . . that the well-being of the state should be the paramount consideration. But this, as other fragments . . . make clear, depends on the voluntary public-spiritedness of its citizens. Law can only be of benefit, if people are willing to obey it. . . . An external constraint, it cannot on its own prevent their "sinning in secret." Hence Democritus' interest in the inner, psychological motives for right conduct in "conviction, understanding and knowledge" in the sanctions of a guilty conscience, in "respect for oneself"—and not just for other people's opinion—as a "law for the soul." Hence, too, his interest in remedies for antisocial attitudes, such as envy which can lead to civil strife and so to the ruin of the whole community. By following the advice of fragment 191 [Be content with what one has], Democritus' reader might not only put himself into better spirits; he might also become less of a menace to his fellow-citizens. In thus encouraging a certain civic virtue, Democritus was carrying on the work of poets and moralists before him.

Dramatists

We should add a word about the philosophy of law in the early Greek dramatists. (For an extended discussion, see Erik Havelock's *The Greek Concept of Justice*.) In several plays, notably Aeschylus' *Eumenides*, Sophocles' *Oedipus at Colonus*, and Euripides' *Suppliants*, we have representations of trials on the stage. The *Eumenides* emphasizes justice as due process, and as a compromise settlement; Aeschylus' *Choephoroi* emphasizes the reciprocal justice of retribution, an idea that also drives his *Agamemnon*. The legal implications of Sophocles' *Oedipus the King* are well known; we should also remember his *Ajax, Electra, Antigone, Philoctetes,* and *Oedipus at Colonus.* In all of these plays Sophocles explores the interplay of *dikê, themis,* and *nomos* in relationship to the will of the individual in the context of the larger religious and political concerns. Henry Sumner Maine thought that the Greeks did not produce a philosophy of law because, as he says in context, they did not consider the problem of free will. One may discover in later literature that Sophocles, at any rate, did indeed consider the limitations on the freedom of the individual from just about every angle. In a way, the oeuvre of Sophocles provides just exactly the philosophy of law that Maine thought was not there. Whatever is not supplied by Aeschylus and Sophocles is provided by Euripides. For example, in his *Suppliants* he writes: "When laws are written down, the poor and the rich have equal justice."

Historians

The historians, too, consider the legal implications of historical processes. When Herodotus discusses King Deioces the Mede, he describes him as beginning by dispensing justice in the old-fashioned way, but when Deioces becomes king he insists (like Euripides?) on written laws. Herodotus also discusses in books two and six the legal theories of the twelve kings of Egypt and the legal arrangements of Glaucus of Sparta, contrasts the notions of justice ascribed to Xerxes and Artabanus, and explores the legal theories of Cadmus of Cos in book seven. Thucydides, in response to challenges of traditional concepts of justice, pursues a profound study of the role of law in human affairs. Especially in the famous "speeches," the debates presented in dramatic form, Thucydides represents contrasting concepts of justice and the rule of law. An example is the debate between Cleon and Diodotus in book three, known as the "Melian Dialogue," in which the Athenians assert that "decisions about justice are made in human discussions only when both sides are under equal compulsion; but when one side is stronger, it gets as much as it can, and the weak must accept that." The Melians reply, "[A] plea of justice and fairness should do some good for a person who has fallen into danger, if he can win over his judges. . . . If you should ever stumble, you might receive a terrible punishment and be an example to others."

Sophists

It is notorious that Plato tends to represent the sophists in a bad light, yet we can derive from them, and from their fragments, a serious consideration of the foundations of civil society and of law. For example, the representation of Protagoras in the *Protagoras* includes a long speech in which human survival is ascribed, ultimately, to the sense of shame (*aides*) and justice (*dikê*), upon which civil society must be based. While Socrates subsequently ties Protagoras into dialectical knots in the dialogue, nothing that is said really refutes Protagoras' major points in that speech, undoubtedly because Plato would not have been seriously in disagreement with those points.

Gorgias, in the dialogue of the same name, is represented as teaching a technique of argumentation, but not teaching people to be just, dramatically represented by the rejection of justice by Callicles, one of Gorgias' students. Yet in the remaining fragments of Gorgias' works he often appeals to concepts of law and justice. For example, in his *Epitaphios,* he praises the war dead for, among other things, their "justice," which in this context would be obedience to law. In his *Praise of Helen* he argues that Helen was the victim of Paris, even if not by force but by persuasion, or if it was under influence of an emotion of love, her flight was forgivable, since we also forgive those who disobey the law under force of the emotion of fear. In his *Palamedes,* he again at least relies on a concept of law and justice in order to work the defense.

The critical sophistic text is a collection of longish fragments of Antiphon found on papyrus in Egypt (available in English in R.K. Sprague's *The Older Sophists*). Antiphon argues that "justice consists in not transgressing the *nomoi* of the city in which one enjoys citizenship." So one should think about justice when there are witnesses present, but otherwise follow the demands of nature: "For the demands of the laws are artificial, but the demands of nature are necessary." If *nomos* and *phusis* are in conflict, one is in greater danger violating natural law than legislated law. In another fragment Antiphon argues that providing evidence against someone in court is never a good idea, since if the evidence is false, it is unjust, and if the evidence is true, you are harming the person against whom you testify, and that person will be out to get you afterwards: "The administration of law and justice and arbitration with a view to a final settlement are all contrary to justice. For helping one set of people harms another."

Classical Greek writers before Plato used the common understanding of the concepts of *themis, dikê,* and *nomos* as presuppositions of religious, cosmological, dramatic, poetic, historical, philosophical, and other writings. It is possible to derive a hellenic "philosophy of law" from the legal practices of the Greek city-states, especially of Athens about which we know most, but also from an examination of the assumptions about the leading concepts that we find in literary and philosophical works.

We learn that Greek writers before Plato were concerned with equitable procedure and distribution of goods, with the possibility that there might be cosmic or transcendent sources of justice, that Zeus or other deities might be concerned with the rules by which civil society operates and might actually ultimately enforce those rules via divine sanctions. Eventually dramatists and philosophers come to concern themselves with issues of personal responsibility, of volitional capacity to obey legislated law, or even to follow the course that is most to one's own advantage.

Many authors have noticed that, although classical Greece has many varied influences on the development of Western civilization, there are exceedingly few examples of ancient Greek legislation that have persisted into the modern era. We might say that modern Western law is a combination of Roman and Germanic (including Anglo-Saxon common law) legal traditions with a healthy admixture of Jewish law via the influence of the Bible. Thus we may expect that philosophical reflections on the nature of law, from the modern point of view, will attempt to penetrate at least one of those traditions. At the same time, philosophical examinations of the nature of *themis, dikê,* and *nomos* will seem somewhat alien, or beside the point to modern Western thinkers, because they are grounded on a legal system that is so different. Thus the most profound recent investigations of classical Greek law have utilized the techniques of legal anthropology, treating the classical Greeks, quite properly, not as "Western," but as members of a distinctly different and, to us, alien culture. Very possibly the greatest affinities with Hellenic theories of law would be found in Egyptian culture, from one point of view, and in Hindu (vedantic) considerations of law, from another point of view. If the comments in this article tend to make hellenic thought about law less alien, to that extent they are not entirely trustworthy.

References

Havelock, Erik. *The Greek Concept of Justice.* Cambridge MA: Harvard University Press, 1978.

Kahn, Charles. *Anaximander and the Origins of Greek Cosmology.* New York: Columbia University Press, 1960.

Kirk, G.S., J.E. Raven, and M. Schofield. *The Presocratic Philosophers.* Cambridge: Cambridge University Press, 1983.

MacDowell, Douglas M. *The Law in Classical Athens.* Ithaca: Cornell University Press, 1978.

———. *Spartan Law.* Edinburgh: Scottish Academic Press, 1986.

Maine, Sir Henry Sumner. *Ancient Law.* London, 1906.

Ostwald, Martin. *From Popular Sovereignty to the Sovereignty of Law.* Berkeley: University of California Press, 1986.

Sprague, R.K. *The Older Sophists.* Columbia: University of South Carolina Press, 1972.

Todd, S.C. *The Shape of Athenian Law.* Oxford: Oxford University Press 1993.

Wolf, Erik. *Griechisches Rechtsdenken* (The Greeks' Consideration of Law). 4 vols. Frankfurt: Vittorio Klostermann, 1950 (*Vorsokratiker und Frühe Dichter* (Presocratics and Early Poets)), 1952 (*Rechtsphilosophie und Rechtsdichtung im Zeitalter der Sophistik* (Philosophy and Pronouncements on Law in the Sophistic Era)), 1954 (*Rechtsphilosophie der Sokratik und Rechtsdichtung der alten Komödie* (Socratic Philosophy of Law and the Presentation of Law in Older Comedies)), 1956 (*Die Umformung des Rechtsgedankes durch Historik und Rhetorik* (The Elemental Forms of Legal Thought in History and Rhetoric)).

Anthony Preus

See also ARISTOTLE; HELLENISTIC PHILOSOPHY OF LAW; PLATO; ROMAN PHILOSOPHY OF LAW

Hellenistic Philosophy of Law

Hellenism is a form of civilization whose foundation lies in the Greek city-states of the fifth and fourth centuries B.C. and whose ensemble comprises Greek forms of language and practice. Geographically, hellenism extends to include the Mediterranean basin wheresoever Greek colonization has implanted, this fact taken separately from the local population's political or cultural participation therein. Historiographically, hellenistic law had its origins in the period which dates from Alexander's rise to power as king of Macedonia in 338 B.C. and extended until the Roman conquest of Greece in 146 B.C. As such, hellenism has particular reference to the spread of Greek culture by the armies of Alexander. However, equally, the term "hellenism" serves to indicate the assimilation of Greek culture by Rome; and by virtue of its dissemination throughout the Roman Empire it can be argued that hellenism as a characteristic form of thought and culture remained active until the fall of Rome and the collapse of the Western Empire in A.D. 476.

Greek Law

Greek law is the product of two major and nearly coincident factors, the founding of the Greek city-state, or *polis,* and the invention of the Greek alphabet. Invention of an alphabetical form and its distinct language (*logos*) corresponds to the city's establishment solely upon human reason (*logismos*). The city is organized as a substantive reality, a real nature independent of the individual will, whose perdurance withstands the effect of time. This contrasts to jurisprudential organization upon rules of parentage (the clan) or of religious authority (the priesthood).

For Greek "politics," polity (*politeia*) signifies a technique or practical reflection upon the city and its citizenry whose end is the rule of good order (*eunomia*). This fact is evidenced in a form of *logos* particular to the social realm, that of law (*nomos*). It is only after the constitution of Cleisthenes (sixth century B.C.) and the successful defense of Greece by Athens against the Persian invaders (490 and 480–479 B.C.) that the term *nomos* becomes the usual denomination of law. Greek law is subject to the difficulty that, since it derives from human reason and is by nature a cognitive activity, a standard of recognition is needed to identify its object, justice. Its background is the metaphysical antinomy of nature (*phusis*) and law (*nomos*) derived from the eleatic philosophies. What is, is unitary, nature; diversity exists only in language, in hu-

man belief. Law, thus detached from its ontological ground, must seek a new basis of rational justice.

These questions were clearly and brilliantly formulated by the sophists, the most celebrated being Protagoras (ca. 485–410 B.C.), the proponent of relativism and the dictum "Man is the measure of all things." The sophist response to the central difficulty of Greek jurisprudence is achieved through substitution, the replacement of the sphere of nature by the sphere of human convention. The stoic and epicurean schools, contemporary with the Alexandrian conquests and monarchies, no doubt the leading representatives of hellenistic philosophy, feature two developments of Greek jurisprudence that have remained influential to this day: the stoic doctrine of natural law and the epicurean doctrine of valid law.

Stoics

Founded by Zeno of Citium (335–263 B.C.) at the Stoa Poikile, a public hall in Athens, the school's history falls into three distinct periods: the early Stoa from its foundation to the first half of the second century B.C.; the middle Stoa to the first century B.C.; and the late Stoa under the Roman Empire. The stoics are the first great systematizers of philosophy and are responsible for the institution of the tripartite division of philosophy into logic comprising knowledge and rhetoric, physics comprising ontology and theology, and ethics comprising economics and politics. Regarding ethics and jurisprudence, the principal figures belong to the early Stoa, Zeno and Chrysippus (ca. 280–207 B.C.), the author of a work entitled *On Law.* At large, stoicism can be viewed as the attempt to reconcile the exigency of nature posited by the eleatic philosophies with the requirement of a standard of recognition consonant with legal reasoning proffered by the sophists. They accomplished this end in two ways: first, the metaphysical way, or the derivation of human reason from nature; and, second, the anthropological way, or the development of the notion of kinship (*oikeiòsis*) among members of a kind or species.

The Metaphysical Way

Stoic metaphysics is fundamentally materialist and biological in nature, the universe being the instance of divine principles of organic unity. Defined as the "Living Animal," nature is the totality of matter animated by immanent principles of life called spermatic reasons; these reasons are themselves manifestations of the element of fire, the active principle of movement and thought. Stoic philosophy admits a threefold acceptation of reality: it is nature or divine providence; it is fire or the principle of movement and thought; and it is animal or the principle of life.

Humans partake in divine reason through the *hègemonikon*, the ruling part of the human soul. A physical reality, human reason depends for its efficacy on the principle of the compresence of substance, the action of body which is everywhere present to another body. Reason is at once an act of the soul, the cause of knowledge, as well as a material substance continuous with nature.

Human reason is also substantively constituted in universal reason, the totality of which is divine providence itself. Nature is a divinity whose parts are distributed in view of the perfection of the whole: it is a cause, whose operation by immanent law or providence ensures the orderly passage from beginning to end, from lesser perfection to greater perfection. Divine providence is the founding cause, and also the totality of causes, one domain being the active principle or spermatic reason present in each particular soul. To the unity of nature affirmed by the eleatic philosophies, the stoic philosophy responds with the notion of totality, that is, the identification of each part with the whole.

The stoic philosophy derives human reasoning from nature, finally, by genetic considerations. In virtue of the doctrine of the living animal, the stoics conceive relations between the divine and human orders as direct and particular, in contradistinction from the general and removed relations of earlier Greek philosophies. Rather than a mechanical model of craft and pattern, the stoics suggest a community of body and soul, the immediate sympathetic union of like parts, and of parts with the whole.

There ensue five principal consequences:

1. The objectivity of stoic knowledge. The stoics are objective cognitivists, that is to say, the task of human reason is to conceive the objectively real in nature. Knowledge, then, is the agreement of one's mental concepts with nature, wisdom consisting in the consent (*katalèpsis*) of reason. Regarding the epistemology of law, the stoics adhere to the doctrine of ethical objectivism, which holds that the truth of an ethical or legal statement is independent of the speaker.

2. The stoic prescriptiveness. By virtue of the concept of divine providence, the stoics are able to elaborate an ontological basis for the normativeness of ethics and law. Unlike the early Greek philosophies, which conceived providence in anthropomorphic and especially retributive terms, hellenistic stoicism introduces an impersonal and naturalist concept of providence: it is the purposeful and necessary elaboration of the divine plan, the agency of which admits neither chance nor plea. As such, the stoics may be called the founders of prescriptiveness, the elucidation of universal laws inscribed in nature. According to H. Von Arnim, Chrysippus states: "Law is king of all things human and divine. Law must preside over what is honorable and base, as ruler and as guide, and thus be the standard of what is just and unjust, prescribing to animals whose nature is political what they should do; and prohibiting them from what they should not do." Law, then, is a substantive reality whose actuality consists in the provision of norms. Human law is the awareness and application of reason in its prescriptive and practical employment.

3. The stoic standard of recognition. As noted, this difficulty belongs to the antinomy *phusis-nomos* known to early Greek law. At large, the stoic response consists in the notion of equity, formal and material. Formal equity is founded on the existence and prescriptions of written law, an effect seen most clearly in the classification of the kinds of law (for instance, civil law, criminal law, administrative law, and their attendant subdivisions). Within these classifications may be found the entirety of legal prescriptions: its procedure, positive structure, and measures of sanction. Material equity, on the other hand, is based on the deduction of human norms from the existence of natural norms, for example, the respect of personal property in virtue of the distribution of parts within the whole of nature. Formal equity and material equity harmonize inasmuch as formal equity clarifies material equity (the public and institutional expression of justice), while material equity corrects and perfects formal equity through the apprehension of rationally approved norms (justice by moral rectitude).

4. The stoic individualism. In the stoic philosophy, the world is composed of individ-

uals of which no two are exactly alike; each individual is the recipient of a quality proper to itself *(idiôs poion),* which defines its essential nature. Background to this doctrine may be found in the stoic logic, which maintains that all judgments bear on simple subjects, for example, "Socrates," "this man," "a man," and the relations pertaining thereto. Natural rights are, therefore, both inalienable (impossible to assign) and imprescriptible (impossible to void by legislative or judicial order). Counterbalancing the determinism of providence, the stoic philosophy affirms the dignity and freedom of the individual based on the notion of proper quality, the materiality of which substantiates the legal rights of the individual.

5. The pedagogical role of law. An ethical rationalism, the stoic philosophy conceives law as the provision of means for the attainment of virtue, the supreme Good. Risen to the level of perfection, the stoic sage is eminently just upon taking cognizance of the internal causes of things, their commands and prohibitions. Law, then, has an essentially pedagogical function that teaches the true ends of human action as instructed by nature.

*The Anthropological Way
of Kinship* (Oikeiòsis)
As a supplement to the metaphysical way, kinship provides the stoic philosophy with a notion which is analyzable into its empirical effects. The term *oikeiòsis* means familiarity with oneself; it is the instinctive familiarity and affection which commences at birth. There ensues a familiarity or kinship with the family, also instinctive in nature. At maturity this instinct becomes fully rational and comprises a wide range of subjects well known to oneself, for example, the city-state and its citizenry. Finally kinship's widest extension extends to every other human as knowable in principle, the members of a region, race, or creed. The image of concentric circles is apt, for it suggests the primacy of the inner experience for the comprehension of the whole.

There ensue two important consequences at variance with early Greek law, namely, the diminished role of the Greek city-state and the evolutive aspect of the stoic philosophy of law. In stoic literature, the *polis* is not the especial instance of ethics and law; instead, the stoic sage is typically represented as inhabiting an ideal universe the generality of which precludes attachment to a familial city-state. One can say that the *polis,* substantial ground of Greek jurisprudence, is forthwith relegated to the role of one mode of legal existence. Second, middle stoics such as Antiochus of Ascalon (ca. 130–68 B.C.) and Arius Didymus (first century B.C.) emphasize the evolutive aspect of legal reasoning, its causal development from the rules of parenthood to the rules of rational deliberation both formal and material. Stoic jurisprudence forsakes, therefore, the distinction in kind between the political (social and rational activities of the city state) and the familial (private household management or *oikonomia*) understood by early Greek jurisprudence and realized in their polity.

In sum, the Stoa is both a continuation of and an original contribution to Greek jurisprudence: a continuation because it accepts the tradition of rationalism and objectivity common to early Greek law; but an original contribution insofar as it sets forth a new notion, providence, the normativeness of which resolves the *phusis-nomos* antinomy received from the eleatic tradition.

Epicureans

With Epicurus of Samos (ca. 342–271 B.C.) hellenistic philosophy rejoins the positivism of the sophists while yet differing from them in its results. The epicurean philosophy is divided into three parts: the axiomatic part called "canonice," physics, and ethics. The canonice enumerates four kinds of evidence for the ascertainment of truth, three of which are sensory and one nonsensory. The three sensory kinds are passion, pleasure, and pain; sensation, the immediate impressions of the five senses; and "prenotion," the acquired evidence of sensation. The fourth kind of evidence is reflection *(epibolè),* the intuitive grasp of things in their essential nature. Epicurean philosophy is therefore an intuitive empiricism that regards the immediate perception as the basis of knowledge. Meanwhile, general statements concerning experience are subject to a method of falsifiability *(ouk antimarturèsis),* the verification of which depends on testing and confirming other knowledge that stands in close logical relations to the subject matter in hand.

Taught within the tranquil air of the school's garden *(kèpos),* epicureanism is of a different temper from the prescriptive theology of the Stoa. This difference is clearly marked in epicurean physics. First, Epicurus rehabilitates the ionian atomism, which conceives the universe as constituted of atoms, the matter and substance of reality. Infinite in number, each atom is uniform, unchanging, and eternal. The void is a noncorporeal existence which fills the space between atoms. It follows that the visible world is only one world among many in kind and number. As such, the epicurean philosophy is content to observe the present disposition of things; its rules of inquiry seek only to eliminate error, for example, the presence of incongruous elements, as well as to establish the conditions under which observation does confirm fact.

Second, Epicurus inveighs against the determinism of stoic providence; this position follows from a consideration of the infinity of the atoms and their eternal movement. In the creation of worlds, the atoms coalesce according to shape and size, this movement freely granted by virtue of an intrinsic declension from their original position. Thus epicureanism rejects the notion of causality as intrinsic necessary connection, preferring instead the notion of cause as the simple presence of changes found together, their sequence or variation. Also, Epicurus denies that voluntary human action can be construed in terms of an antecedent cause which, once given, is the necessary and sufficient condition for producing a specified effect. Instead, Epicurus suggests the doctrine of the plurality of causes, which maintains that one event can be the result of many different causes, for example, a headache from illness, bad eyesight, or even hunger. Epicurus rejects, therefore, the stoic necessitarianism that understands universal antecedent causes as determining of human action.

Finally, Epicurus defends against an eschatological view of life. The human soul is a kind of matter that actualizes the body in sensation and movement; at death the atoms of the soul disperse and sensation ceases immediately. Ignoring the notion of divine reason, epicureanism seeks to ground human existence on principles of perception, in particular the measurement of pleasure and pain. As such, the epicurean philosophy is not concerned with what ought to be (a basic ought statement) but rather with what is (an account of fact). The stoic normative laws of nature, the inviolable principles which govern reality, are henceforth banished from the garden.

At large, the epicurean philosophy wishes to free humanity from the fear of death, discomfort, retribution of the gods, and natural catastrophe. In so doing, Epicurus elaborates a positive philosophy of law that separates the norms of justice from the norms of law. Unlike the stoic natural law, which subsumes the human order under the divine, epicurean jurisprudence is a humanism whose discourse is centered on human actuality. For instruction Epicurus turns to the passionate and instinctive parts of the human soul as explanatory of action, their veracity being assured upon grounds of simplicity and immediacy. Using a method of psychogenetic analysis, Epicurus is thus able to clarify the factors which condition the institution of law: in the natural state human existence is selfish, cruel, and susceptible to error; it is also particular, disparate, and irregular. Law, then, is the corrective to human nature insofar as it founds community, order, and security. A positive reality, law serves to rectify the harmful tendencies inherent in human nature. This is the anthropological basis of epicurean jurisprudence.

Five important consequences follow:

1. The remedial role of law. In epicurean jurisprudence, the basic fact of human existence is fear, whether it pertains to the potential harm suffered at the hands of others or the punishment for harm committed against others. The role of law is therefore remedial. Epicurus states: "The laws exist for the sake of the wise, not that they may not do wrong, but that they may not suffer it." Law is the *pharmakon* of human nature, a palliative, whose actuality consists in the establishment of commutative rules of justice.

2. The epicurean intuitivism. Justice is a "prenotion"; it originates in a spontaneous perception of the danger of murder and enjoins from engaging in mutually harmful actions as disadvantageous to life. Epicurus observes: "The justice which arises from nature is a pledge of mutual advantage to restrain men from harming one another and save them from being harmed." Hellenistic epicureanism is therefore remarkable insofar as it adheres to the doctrine of ethical intuitivism, the view which holds that humans are capable of discerning right action from wrong by means of direct and immediate perceptions rather than as the result of rational reflection. To this extent, the epicurean philosophy is an important departure from early Greek law insofar as it denies the rationalist presupposition. Meanwhile, law intervenes at a later stage in order

to ensure that the prenotion of justice is uniformally observed.

3. The epicurean standard of recognition. Epicurean jurisprudence is a remarkably original and influential doctrine of valid law. In order to grasp this significance it is necessary to recall its basic empiricist presupposition: unless the truth of sensation be accepted, all knowledge is impossible and the world remains unknowable. Sensation is evidenced in pleasure and pain, their knowledge confirmable by quantitative units of intensity and duration rather than by qualitative differences of kind. The doctrine of natural kinds thus eschewed, and the conventionalism of Antiphon disallowed by virtue of an ethical intuitivism, Epicurus suggests a standard of recognition which habilitates the legal judgment as valid and binding based on the notion of utility, a real quality of the human act. Epicureanism is, then, the first school of philosophy to operate a clear conceptual distinction between just law (whether natural or conventional) and the positive act of law (law which states the rational calculus of the useful and the harmful). As such, epicurean jurisprudence is not a doctrine that implies the derivation of law from justice; for just as Epicurus denies the notion of intrinsic and necessary connection in the physical order, so, too, he denies a similar connection between the norms of justice and the norms of law in the human order. This positivism is well illustrated in the laws pertaining to the treatment of animals, for while Epicurus does not extend the notion of justice to include other species due to a lack of mutual comprehension, it is nonetheless clear that the notion of valid law requires that these laws adhere to certain principles of legality, that is, of usefulness, else they would not suffice as law. Thus Epicurus resolves the traditional antinomy of *phusis* and *nomos* by introducing a new notion, that of valid law, whose ground lies in the objective content and calculus of utility.

4. The epicurean instrumentalism. Regarding the epistemology of law, epicurean jurisprudence assumes an instrumentalist position that conceives the legal act in the manner of an explanatory tool or calculating device whose operation is effective on empirical observations. Instrumentalism admits different and even competing interpretations of a law based on circumstances, an epistemological stance which agrees with the epicurean analysis of causation and its doctrine of the plural-ity of causes for a given effect. In consequence there ensues the relativization of Greek polity and jurisprudence; first conceived as a substantial existence, the city-state is forthwith referred to the category of relative existents.

5. Epicurus and the social compact. The term "social compact" (*synthèkè*) signifies the establishment of the city-state based on mutual agreement rather than on force. Consensual in nature, epicurean jurisprudence does not involve a conflict between collective and individual interests. Its compact proffers neither a rule of subjection (the condition of being under a superior power) nor a rule of libertarianism (the doctrine of the freedom of the will). As such, the epicurean social contract is neither an arbitrary convention nor a necessary deduction from the norms of nature; instead, the compact is a psychological fact which comes into existence when there is a meeting of minds (*consensus ad idem*), the application of which produces a set of mutual legal acts. Furthermore, the epicurean genealogy of law conceives the compact as an originative principle, the existence of which founds the stability, evidence, and obligation of legal norms. In particular, the compact ensures the objective basis of obligation insofar as legal reflection may conceive a prenotion whose actuality is predictive; for example, the failure to satisfy the legal duty to pay taxes renders more likely certain forms of harm. Epicurean jurisprudence teaches, then, a sociology of law that clarifies legal norms and institutions within the perspective of a historical process, the apprehension of an observable verified reality.

In sum, the epicurean philosophy of law introduces a new and remarkably current doctrine of valid law. Empiricist by nature and instrumentalist by reflection, Epicurus teaches a positivism that denies both the conventionalism of early Greek law and the necessitarianism of hellenistic stoicism, placing in their stead the rational calculus of utility and the consensus of the social contract.

Neoplatonism

The term "hellenism" also extends to an influential school of philosophy active during the middle and late Roman Empire that began in Rome with its foundation by Plotinus (A.D. 205–269/70) and terminated with the closing of the Academy of Athens by Justinian in A.D. 529. It is a commonplace among historians to say that hellenism ignores the political and legal branches of philosophy admonishing instead to "live unknown" in the world. However, this period of late antiquity is replete with works bearing on legal philosophy if understood in a critical as distinct from ideological sense, for example, Damascius' (ca. A.D. 460–538) commentary on *Alcibiades 1* on the realization of the essentially political nature of human existence, and Simplicius' (sixth century A.D.) commentary on the *Manual* of Epictetus, which may contain a subtle attack on Justinian and Christianity.

To begin, there is the communitarian thesis, which affirms a homology between personal thought and public expression; there results both the ability to communicate among ourselves and the communal life (*koinònikon zòon*). In the *Prolegomena,* according to A. Busse, Olympiodorus (sixth century A.D.) observes that, the end of human existence being to live in common society, nature has provided humanity with the faculty of language in order to signify reality, for just as it would not be possible to lead a social life without the common use of words, so, too, it would not be possible for peoples with different laws to live together under one political rule. According to Busse, this teaching is constant in neoplatonism, for example, in Elias' (sixth century A.D.) *In Porphyrii Isagogen Commentaria,* on the intrinsic relation of human nature and language, and in Philoponus' (sixth century A.D.) *In Aristotelis Categorias Commentarium,* on the human community and the common attribution of words to designate realities, semantic activity thus realizing human nature as a social being. Following up the early Greek reflection on reason and law, neoplatonism is the first school of philosophy to found the science of law upon an especially linguistic basis.

As regards jurisprudence, the powers of the soul are analyzed in two parts. The first is the cognitive part whose result is theoretical knowledge, the source of declarative statement *(logos apofantikos),* and the second is the vital part whose result is practical knowledge, the source of all other forms of statement, for example, wish, question, and command. The neoplatonists conceive law to partake in the vital powers of the soul, ascribing to jurisprudence a practical knowledge whose realization through choice and deliberation is similar to providential rule. This utilization of law and providence clarifies two distinct but interrelated aspects of neo-platonic jurisprudence, namely the pedagogical and the political.

Concerning the pedagogical aspect, neoplatonism admits two kinds of productive activity. One kind inspires the respondent to be like the agent, this effect seen most clearly in the case of the pupil who aspires to be like the teacher in knowledge and virtue *(mimèsis)*. A second kind does not have the imitative effect, for example, the work of sculpture not causing its public to produce a like work. The role of pedagogy is important in neo-platonism insofar as it provides the anthropological and semantic basis for the foundation of the city-state. The lawgiver is like a teacher whose task is to improve the lives and practices of the citizenry through the promulgation of laws; the laws are the communicative matter necessary for the formation of universals in the soul that are univocal and that realize the human essence to live in society. Several examples serve to illustrate this relation between pedagogy and jurisprudence in the neo-platonic philosophy. First, Plotinus affirms that the role of the philosopher consists in imparting both a theoretical and a practical knowledge, the former kind realized in daily lessons taught by means of *diatribe,* a procedure of examination by question and answer, and the latter kind realized through governance, for example, his appointment as legal guardian and trustee of the children of many of his aristocratic friends, a charge which he fulfilled most ably and conscientiously. Second, Plotinus had hoped to found a new city based on its association with his school, and, while never realized due to a lack of political support, his plan illustrates well the fundamental role of pedagogy within the neo-platonic reflection on law.

Concerning the political aspect, the neoplatonists maintain that the rule of law constitutes a first step toward the perfection of human essence and society. This effect is clearly stated in the treatise entitled *On Virtues,* wherein Plotinus affirms two kinds of virtue: a superior virtue, which is intellectual and whose object is the forms and the One, the supreme ground of existence, and an inferior virtue, which is practical and whose object is human conduct. Once again the neo-platonists conceive the imitative relation as founding the city-state insofar as law, a practical knowledge, qualifies the human soul to exist in the image of the divine *(homoiòsis theò)*. In deliberation, the practical virtues attain to a semblance of rationality, an illuminated reflection upon superior virtue, which rehabilitates the city-state as divine, that is, as a universal principle communicable with each of its parts. A rationalism, neo-platonism yet surpasses the secularism and anthropology of Greek law, whether positive or naturalist. One can say that with neoplatonism, hellenistic philosophy reaches its penultimate expression and foresees a new era in jurisprudence, the philosophy of St. Augustine and the city of God.

References

Armstrong, A.H. *The Cambridge History of Later Greek and Early Medieval Philosophy*. Cambridge: Cambridge University Press, 1967.

Bailey, Cyril. *The Greek Atomists and Epicurus*. Oxford: Oxford University Press, 1928.

Busse, A. *Commentaria in Aristotelem Graeca* (Greek Commentaries on Aristotle). 1863–1891.

Goldschmidt, Victor. "La théorie épicurienne du droit" (The Epicurean Theory of Law). In *Science and Speculation*, ed. J. Barnes et al. Cambridge: Cambridge University Press, 1982.

Laks, André, and Malcolm Schofield. *Justice and Generosity. Studies in Hellenistic Social and Poltical Philosophy. Proceedings of the Sixth Symposium Hellenisticum*. Cambridge: Cambridge University Press, 1995.

Maffi, Alberto. "Chroniques" (Updates). *Revue historique de droit français et étranger* 66.1 (1988), 96–132.

O'Meara, Dominic. "Vie politique et divinisation dans la philosophie néoplatonicienne" (Political Life and Becoming Divine in Neoplatonic Philosophy). In *Sophiès Maiètores Chercheurs de sagesse. Hommage à Jean Pépin*, ed. Marie-Odile Goulet-Cazé et al., 501–510. Série Antiquité 131. Paris: Institut d'Etudes Augustiniennes, 1992.

Ostwald, M. *Nomos and the Beginnings of the Athenian Democracy*. Oxford: Oxford University Press, 1969.

de Romilly, Jacqueline. *La loi dans la pensée grecque des origines à Aristote* (Law in Greek Thought from Its Origins to Aristotle). Paris: Belles Lettres, 1971.

Schofield, M. *The Stoic Idea of the City*. Cambridge: Cambridge University Press, 1991.

Von Arnim, H. *Stoicorum veterum fragmenta* (SVF) (Fragments from the Ancient Stoics). 4 vols. 1921–1924.

Usener, H. *Epicurea*. 1887.

Jennifer L. Yhap

See also ARISTOTLE; HELLENIC PHILOSOPHY OF LAW; PLATO

Hermeneutical Philosophy of Law

The term "hermeneutical" derives from the Greek verb *hermeneuein*, generally translated "to interpret." To study hermeneutics is to study the history of interpretation, which would include legal interpretation. Hermeneutics is the theory and practice of interpretation. As Hans-Georg Gadamer has mentioned in his famous work *Wahrheit und Methode (Truth and Method)*, first published in 1960, legal interpretation is paradigmatic for hermeneutics.

In *Hermeneutics Ancient and Modern*, Gerald Bruns says that "hermeneutics is a loose and baggy monster, or anyhow a less than fully disciplined body of thinking whose inventory of topics spreads out over many different historical, cultural, and intellectual contexts." Hermeneutics stretches back at least as far as the allegorical interpretations of Homer (see Robert Lamberton's *Homer the Theologian*) to early interpretations of the Hebrew Bible and the gospels, which would include midrash, and figures like Philo of Alexandria, Origen, and Augustine of Hippo. Bruns's book is exemplary for providing a sense of the range, historical and topical, of hermeneutics. From a legal perspective, hermeneutics involves coming to understand texts like Deuteronomy, investigating Renaissance glossators (for example, Ian Maclean's *Interpretation and Meaning in the Renaissance: The Case of Law*), and thinking through the questions that animate current legal discussions, such as those about original intent. Given the almost universal scope of hermeneutics, it would seem wrongheaded to speak of it as a school, and it is certainly not a methodology, at least not in the twentieth century since Martin Heidegger. Rather, for hermeneutics, the law is a matter for thinking. In fact, Gadamer claims that the law is exemplary of what it means to understand and to interpret just about anything.

Hermeneutics has always been about the weird and the problematic, what the ancients called *skandala*, stumbling blocks or snares. Things which scandalize us, texts which seem nonsensical, offensive, bizarre, unmanageable, as well as unimaginable—these have always been the lightning rods for hermeneutics. Such texts make for situations that call out for interpretation. However, distinctions between plain and complex happen to depend on context as well as content, so that even the most lucid ancient text might seem perplexing in a contemporary context, one in which interpreters do not share similar presuppositions, nor even, as Ludwig Wittgenstein would say, the same form of life. Hermeneutics is partly about trying to overcome that kind of historical alienation, perhaps in some instances by asking how one might live an old form of life, or adjust oneself in accordance with an old law, so that the living is the answer to What is your understanding of this law? In *The Sages,* Ephraim Urbach puts it this way: "[C]ustoms are unwritten laws (*agraphoi nomoi*), the decisions approved by men of old, not inscribed on monuments nor on leaves of paper, which the moth destroys, but on the souls of those who are partners in the same citizenship." Hermeneutics enters the picture when the question is about those who are not partners in the same citizenship. As Bruns puts it, "[The] community does not need to be a community of readers or interpreters—one does not have to be a reader of the law in order to be bound by it, in fact one need not even be aware of the law in order to stand under its jurisdiction." Think here of Franz Kafka's stories about the law.

Urbach's comment suggests the old hermeneutical distinction between the letter and the spirit of the law, one of which is dead, mute, the other alive, answering, embodied, soulful. We could call this distinction the difference between a grammatical reading of the law and a rhetorical one, where rhetoric means attentiveness to the situation at hand, and speaking to it. The question then becomes How does the legal text speak to the situation at hand? or What might a new application of the law look like? What often troubles people about legal interpretation is the occasional disjunction between the words of the text and the manifestation of the words in another context, their application, their coming alive, so to speak. A good literary example of this (allowing for a helpful temporary conflation of prophecy and law) might be *Macbeth* and the ways in which the witches' words, bizarre as they seem (particularly unlikely examples of words having

any connections with Macbeth's reality), come alive, and prove to be true: "[N]one of woman born/Shall harm Macbeth"; "Macbeth shall never vanquish'd be until/Great Birnan wood to high Dunsinane hill/Shall come against him." Like a good literalist, Macbeth takes comfort in the impossibility of these words, though they sound vaguely law-like ("Thou shalt not" becomes "He shall not"). Who could have imagined their application, let alone their ferocity? Macbeth had thought the conversation with the witches over, once he believed he had understood and had attributed timelessness to their words. Who would not be captivated by the witches' part of the conversation? The point of hermeneutics is that the conversation is ongoing, unanchored, suffused with temporality, with no one having the last word. The truth of the witches' words *happens*. Macbeth's attempt to take possession of the meaning of the witches' words shows his desire to put an end to them, to show that they do not possess him, to remind himself and others that their authority resides in their deadness and impossibility for ever happening. Call Macbeth a strict constructionist, one who learns not a lesson about the ambiguity of language, for ambiguity is not the issue, but one about language as such: that words recur in unpredictable contexts.

Macbeth's is one way out of wildness. It is a version of an attempt at establishing a base, a foundation, that can provide security for interpretation, or at least reduce the plurality of interpretations. Legal interpretation has its own Macbeths who seek to improve law by cognitive cleansing, by ever more subtle refinements in assertions, propositions, definitions, and principles and conceptions of justice, whereas hermeneutics foregrounds the rhetorical nature of the law, its situatedness. One of the main proponents of this kind of rhetorical reading of the law has been Peter Goodrich. Following Jacques Derrida's antifoundational reading of law in his essay on Kafka's "Before the Law," Goodrich has also insisted on a hermeneutics of law that does not privilege law's origins: "That origin is hidden, distant, and dark. It is the logos, the source of oracle of law that our authors variously name as God, nature, time immemorial. . . . Just as the constitution binds invisibly—it is simply 'how things are'—so the discourse of law remembers and repeats an ideal that is ever elsewhere, an origin or absolute other into whose face we may never look." The legal community wishes for people to forget this groundlessness, the human construction of the law in its concrete practices, its re-establishing of itself from within its activities, some of which are quite violent, others of which bar the public from participation, since the legal community often insists upon professional qualifications to participate in its discourse. This strategy materializes in efforts to remind people of what cannot be remembered—law's origin(s). Nonetheless, Goodrich seems to acknowledge the success of the legal community's pointing to the aura and mystery surrounding law's genesis, thus putting the law out of question.

The primacy of questioning in hermeneutics works against hierophantic descriptions of law and undermines efforts at situating the law in dogmatic contexts, such as the way the law appears in its rituals (for example, the activities of the courtroom). An excellent example of this undoing of legal auras and dogmatism appears in a 1933 film called *I'm No Angel,* in which Mae West's character represents herself at her trial and handles the cross-examinations with the skill of a ribald Socrates, cutting through the overbearing maleness in the room, winning over the judge and the jury so that the law that day could see as a woman.

Those who believe in the sanctity and autonomy of the law might be dismissive about thinking through the law as it appears outside its institutional contexts, in literature and on film, and in a form that does not attempt to mimic legalistic discourse, but the hermeneutical point here is that our understanding of the law takes shape in many places, not only in a lawyer's office, a courtroom, or a law school class. Hermeneutics tends to be unruly and transgressive, partly by insisting on its universality. It contemplates "themes out of school," for it is neither school nor methodology. According to Goodrich, the law might fear fiction, given that the law institutes itself through fictions that it tries to suppress: "Law is a literature which denies its literary qualities. It is a play of words which asserts an absolute seriousness; it is a genre of rhetoric which represses moments of invention or of fiction. . . ."

References

Bruns, Gerald. *Hermeneutics Ancient and Modern.* New Haven: Yale University Press, 1992.

———. "The Problem of Figuration in Antiquity." In *Hermeneutics: Questions and Prospects,* ed. Gary Shapiro and Alan Sica, 147–164. Amherst: University of Massachusetts Press, 1984.

Gadamer, Hans-Georg. *Truth and Method.* 2d rev. ed. Trans. Joel Weinsheimer and Donald G. Marshall. New York: Crossroad, 1989.

Goodrich, Peter. *Oedipus Lex: Psychoanalysis, History, Law.* Berkeley: University of California Press, 1995.

———. "Of Law and Forgetting: Literature, Ethics, and Legal Judgment." *Arachne: An Interdisciplinary Journal of Language and Literature* 1 (1994), 198–230.

Krajewski, Bruce. *Traveling with Hermes: Hermeneutics and Rhetoric.* Amherst: University of Massachusetts Press, 1992.

Leyh, Gregory, ed. *Legal Hermeneutics: History, Theory, and Practice.* Berkeley: University of California Press, 1992.

Mueller-Vollmer, Kurt, ed. *The Hermeneutics Reader.* New York: Continuum, 1985.

Palmer, Richard E. *Hermeneutics: Interpretation Theory in Schleiermacher, Dilthey, Heidegger, and Gadamer.* Evanston IL: Northwestern University Press, 1969.

Smith, P. Christopher. *Hermeneutics and Human Finitude.* New York: Fordham University Press, 1991.

Warnke, Georgia. *Justice and Interpretation.* Cambridge: MIT Press, 1992.

Bruce Krajewski

See also BETTI, EMILIO; CONSTITUTIONALISM; GADAMER, HANS-GEORG

Hire

The philosophical issues surrounding the contract of hire mirror those surrounding contract generally. Nevertheless, the particular features of hire have led to special difficulties not encountered to the same extent in general contract.

In modern law there are essentially four types of contract which could be identified as contracts of "hire": (1) the hire of goods to be used by the hirer (*locatio rei*), (2) the hire of personal services or labor (*locatio operis faciendi*), (3) the hire of services to be performed on the thing delivered (*locatio custodiae*), and (4) hire involving the carriage of goods for reward (*locatio operis mercium vehendarium*).

In circumstances (1), (3), and (4) the concept "hire" relates to what is generally defined as a bailment for reward. Circumstance (2) is dealt with separately.

Hire of Goods

Bailment is the transfer of possession of goods, for a purpose, with the agreement that when the purpose is fulfilled, the goods will be returned or otherwise disposed of. The parties to such a transaction are typically known as "bailor" and "bailee." Hiring of goods is to be distinguished from mere borrowing in that hire is always for a price, a stipend, or additional recompense, while borrowing is merely gratuitous.

Various terms have been used to describe a bailment for reward including "hiring," "lending," "letting," "renting," "lease," "chattel lease," "operating lease," "finance lease," "charter," and "charter party." The latter two occur most frequently when the subject of the bailment contract is a boat or ship. "Employment" and "hire" are often used interchangeably when discussing the hire of persons or labor for reward, although "employment" generally has a more enlarged meaning than "hire," as discussed later.

Unless the contract provides otherwise, certain duties attach to a contract of hire. In the case of the hire of goods to be used by the hirer *(locatio rei)*, these duties include an obligation on the hirer to give to the hiree uninterrupted possession, to warn of any defects inherent in the goods, and to keep the subject goods in suitable condition for the purposes of bailment. The hiree then has the duty to take reasonable care of the goods, to pay the price of the hire, and to return possession of the goods at the appointed time. Certain types of bailee have traditionally been subject to a higher standard of care than normal, for example, innkeepers and common carriers. In the case of hire of services to be performed on the thing transferred *(locatio custodiae)*, the principal duties on the hirer are to enable the worker to perform the contracted task and to pay the agreed price.

The transferring of possession, but not ownership (title), to the hiree lies at the center of hire as compared with a contract of sale. Contracts of sale and bailment are thus, in one sense, mutually exclusive as bailment is a transfer of possession, whereas sale involves a transfer of ownership. Which of these has occurred is usually determined by scrutinizing the intention of the parties involved and the forms of property which they hold before and after the transaction. The modern contract of hire purchase in a sense "falls between" bailment and sale, since it covers the situation wherein the hiree takes possession (but not ownership), coupled with an option to purchase or take ownership at the end of or during the period of hire. It is in effect a system of sale with deferred payment. In such cases rental rates are structured so as to amortize the cost of the product over the period of the hire purchase.

In modern times the contract of hire of goods has been more commonly described as a chattel lease and has become widespread in the commercial world under this name. The terms "finance lease" and "operating lease" have also entered common parlance as subcategories of the chattel lease; the former is in essence a financing tool in which the lessor's retention of ownership is only nominal (that is, it is a legal retention and as a practical matter the lessee is regarded as "owning" the chattel), while the latter is used generally for equipment which is hired to a number of different lessees, in turn, over the life of the chattel. There has been some discussion as to whether a transfer of ownership under a chattel lease leaves the new owner free to dispossess the lessee. As yet there is no clear solution to this problem, though some commentators have argued that the Roman law principle that "sale breaks hire" should be used to resolve the difficulty.

Hire of Personal Services or Labor

In its narrowest sense, the hiring of work and labor extends to a very few situations in which the hire is connected with the manufacture or repair of chattels, such as the hiring of a tailor to make clothes or of a jeweler to set gems. This may or may not involve the bailment and contract of sale issues discussed previously. The term "hire" has also, however, developed a broad meaning which ranges over all kinds of employment. Early conceptions of the hire of labor were subsumed under the rubric of the law of master and servant. This relationship had its roots in Roman law and supported a complex system of rights and responsibilities in circumstances that were centered on a particular household or enterprise (often agricultural) and were paternalistic in nature.

The designation "master" or "servant" usually assumed a comprehensive lifetime commitment. The master's rights extended to disciplining the servant and carried with it a responsibility for the servant's welfare. Certain restraints were also placed upon the master's power to terminate the relationship at will.

As economies developed, so too did a contractual theory of employment. This led on the one hand to increased freedom to bargain for wages and conditions and on the other hand to abuses due to an inequality in that same bargaining power. Jurisprudential schools which deal especially with the contract of employment would include democratic theory, contractualism, critical legal theory, economics and law, marxism, and communitarianism.

References

Goode, Roy. *Commercial Law*. London: Penguin, 1982.

Palmer, Norman E. *Bailment*. 1979. 2d ed. Sydney: Law Book Company, 1991.

Palmer, Norman E., and Ewan McKendrick, eds. *Interests in Goods*. London: Lloyd's of London Press, 1993.

Patrick Quirk

History (Historicity of Law)

History is one of the main poles of relationship to law. By historicity of law one means not only the purely internal and technical components of the law's individual instruments but also the embeddedness of legal phenomena in contexts of development; that is, the concrete *hic et nunc* (here and now) of their explanation within the paradigm of challenge and response, as Arnold Toynbee termed it. On the other hand, historicity emphasizes the factor of traditions in legal development. In the modern era three currents of legal thinking focused on such historical inquiries: the historical school of law (*historische Rechtsschule*) in Germany, historical jurisprudence in England, and marxism—which was born between the former two but developed its full display in the recent past. All three currents were variations of the dominant evolutionism, bringing the idea of legal evolution into focus, according to Peter Stein, an "assumption that changes in the law followed a predetermined sequence of states parallel to stages of social evolution."

The historical school of law was formed at the beginning of the nineteenth century in opposition to German efforts at reforming civil law through codification. It intended to prove that law was something other, and more, than the mere product of legislation and that its contents were not governed by the allegedly universal nature of man but rather by the particular character of the society to which it was applied. "Statutes are not the only sources of juristic truth," announced Gustav Hugo's program; and Friedrich Carl von Savigny, inspired by Edmund Burke's conservatism and J.G. Herder's concept of nation, described law as "the common conviction of the people, the kindred consciousness of an inward necessity, excluding all notion of an accidental and arbitrary origin," which was developed "by internal silently operating powers, not by the arbitrary will of a lawgiver." Startled by the romantic terminology of *Volkgeist*, the famous "popular spirit," its critics declared Savigny's school to be nonphilosophical, a- and antihistorical, having recourse to biologistic mystification and actualizing the past. Yet, in the light of today's complex historico-sociological and anthropological reconstruction of the factors and processes of legal change, it can rather be interpreted as an early and sensible description.

Historical jurisprudence was born at Cambridge from Sir Henry Maine's lecturing efforts at providing a proper legal theory for his students; this would meet the requirements of a positivist scientific ideal but would overcome Jeremy Bentham's and John Austin's speculative and unjustifiable stance in which law was just the command of the sovereign. He found both example and analogy in Sir Charles Lyell's 1830 study of geology, according to which changes in the earth's surface were not caused by periodic and unpredictable, sudden catastrophes, but were rather the result of regular physical forces in constant but gradual, and almost imperceptible, change. Ironically enough, neither the evolutionary line he portrayed in "From Status to Contract" nor the fiction, the equity, and the legislation he had defined as the three successive instruments of legal change proved to be sustainable. The lasting effect of his 1861 classic *The Ancient Law* was that it provided an analytical framework to approaches that later became known as legal anthropology and legal sociology.

Marxism forged a genuine principle from historicity by taking evolutionism seriously. "The anatomy of men holds a key to the anatomy of the ape": Marx's 1857 thesis from his *Grundrisse der Kritik der politischen Ökonomie* throws light upon his belief that the question on the nature of the open, latent potentialities inherent in the paths of development can only be answered retrospectively as assessed from the perfected state actually achieved. It is exclusively this perfected state that offers criteria for defining what the meaning of the perspectives on development has been. Today's theories are opposed to this. By respecting the principle of historicity, they do not construe any sequence of events as embodiments of the laws (or teleologies) of any philosophy of history.

According to Frederic William Maitland, "[h]istory involves comparison." Comparative approaches showed that (1) law lives its own life to a considerable extent, largely independent of its direct conditions, and that (2) it develops mostly by following its own inertia through borrowing from alien patterns, as noted by Alan Watson.

Today's more differentiated knowledge about law suggests these claims: (1) Law is composed not only of rules, nor merely of rules and principles. In solving social conflicts, law, through an intermediate filter, is primarily a culture of mediation (in the philosophical sense of *Vermittlung*) with its own sensibility, conceptualization, ways of channeling, and skills of handling. It provides a medium for having recourse to principles and rules in the resolution of conflicts, through which the principles and rules referred to in the procedure obtain their standardized (that is, interpretable and justifiable) significance and meaning in the given culture. (2) This very culture is historical, as it is carried on by human praxis traditionalized from the past, reconventionalizing conventions through their continuous reactualization. (3) Therefore, neither immobility nor leaps in development can be characteristic of law. Furthermore, this is why neither following external patterns nor purely internal development can be characteristic, exclusively. Any of these extremes can at most only be dreamed about. What is actually achieved is necessarily the outcome of a compromise. (4) This compromise is historical by definition. It is aimed at providing a pragmatic response, and it can only do this through relying on the memory of the past or the experience of others, as processed and filtered through its own medium (informed by its world-concept, ide-

ologies, utopias, and so forth). It has to be used, not understood. Therefore, to talk about its *mis*understanding could only prove the *mis*perception of the basic setting. "Je prend mon bien où je le trouve (I take my value where I find it)," said Molière's character, since the only thing that matters is not What is it made from? but What is made from it? (5) Throughout its life, the multifactorial character of law becomes one of the sources of this multifactoriality itself. Enacted rules (legislation), patterns enforced by authoritative decisions (precedent), and behaviors accepted as legal by the community (customs) compete with each other as practical components of law, in a constant maelstrom to determine what will prevail as the law in the given society. Overcoming others can only be temporary, and the struggle for domination will continue. Yet the law's actual composition can be reshaped from either side. (6) Positive law is exposed to modification by alternative strategies: through formal (textual) amendments and/or by changing its contextual environment. (7) In a historical perspective, all effects cumulate and finally will conclude with a change in law.

References

Maitland, F.W. "Why the History of English Law Is Not Written." In *Collected Papers*, vol. 1, ed. H.A.L. Fisher. Cambridge: Cambridge University Press, 1911.

Savigny, F.C. von. *On the Vocation of Our Age for Legislation and Jurisprudence*. 1814. Trans. Abraham Hayward. London, 1831.

Schott, Clausdieter. "Einfachheit als Leitbild des Rechts und der Gesetzgebung" (Simplicity as Criterion for Law and Legislation). *Zeitschrift für Neuere Rechtsgeschichte* 5 (1983), 121–146.

Stein, Peter. "The Tasks of Historical Jurisprudence." In *The Legal Mind: Essays for Tony Honoré*, ed. Neil MacCormick and Peter Birks, 293–305. Oxford: Oxford University Press, 1986.

Van Der Merwe, Derek. "Regulae iuris and the Axiomatisation of the Law in the Sixteenth and Early Seventeenth Centuries." *Tydskrif vir die Suid-Afrikaanse Reg/Journal of South African Law* (Johannesburg) (1987/8), 286–302.

Varga, Csaba. "Law as History?" 1986. In *Law and Philosophy*, Philosophiae Iuris

Series, ed. Csaba Varga, 477–484. Budapest: Loránd Eötvös University Project on Comparative Legal Cultures, 1994.

———. *Theory of Judicial Process: The Establishment of Facts.* Budapest: Akadémiai Kaidó, 1995.

———, ed. *Comparative Legal Cultures.* The International Library of Essays in Law and Legal Theory: Legal Cultures, 1. Aldershot: Dartmouth; New York: New York University Press, 1992.

Watson, Alan. "Comparative Law and Legal Change." *Cambridge Law Journal* 37 (1978), 313–336.

Csaba Varga

See also NINETEENTH-CENTURY PHILOSOPHY OF LAW; ONTOLOGY, LEGAL (METAPHYSICS); SOCIOLOGY OF LAW

Hobbes, Thomas (1588–1679)

An understanding of Thomas Hobbes' legal theory requires some familiarity with the contractarian foundation of his political philosophy. On this foundation rest Hobbes' conventionalist conception of the laws of nature, his procedural account of justice, and his formalist model of adjudication. These views place Hobbes squarely in the positivist tradition. Nonetheless, there are legitimate questions about the role of natural law in his thought.

To justify absolute sovereignty and the preservation of existing institutions, Hobbes used the *contractarian* devices of a state of nature and a social compact. For Hobbes, the state of nature leads to a state of war. To avoid this condition, individuals (hypothetically) agree on nineteen "articles of peace": the laws of nature. These laws are general rules that constitute the normative basis of society. They are "natural" in that they conform to reason. However, Hobbes rejected the classical natural law understanding of natural laws as immutable, rational principles independent of society. The laws of nature are *conventional*: they result from an agreement to avoid the miserable state of nature. Moreover, they are contingent on certain characteristics of human nature (equality, the desire for peace and commodious living) and of the world (scarce resources).

Two other features of Hobbes' legal theory warrant labeling it positivist. First, Hobbes' primary definition of justice is *procedural*. According to his command theory of law, all laws issue from a sovereign with authority to enforce their compliance. The sovereign's will defines the meaning of "just." By definition, then, positive law is just. The laws of nature are products of reason rather than of sovereignty and, hence, "laws" only in a derivative sense. Second, for Hobbes, there is no necessary connection between morality and law. He distinguished between the justice of laws and their goodness, which depends on whether they advance the fundamental human interests that the laws of nature specify. However, a bad law is still a law. The primary definition of "justice" captures this formal feature of positive law.

Yet Hobbes advances another account of justice, different from the procedural one. The third law of nature, which he calls "the fountain and original of justice," prescribes the performance of (private) covenants independently of the sovereign's will. The rationale for this natural law is clear: if nothing binds individuals in the state of nature, then the transition to the commonwealth appears impossible. The problem is that in the state of nature individuals would seem to be bound by a type of "natural" justice, which is logically prior to positive justice. Any such understanding of justice clashes with the positivist thrust of Hobbes' overall legal theory.

The solution of this puzzle hinges on ascertaining the precise role of natural law in Hobbes' practical philosophy. Arguably, in an intermediate state between the "war of all against all" and the commonwealth, individuals agree to accept the bindingness of the laws of nature. The need to postulate this intermediate state supports a more refined understanding of Hobbes' legal philosophy as a historical transition from natural law theory to legal positivism. Despite this refinement, the preponderance of positivist elements in Hobbes' thought is undeniable. In his view, even the effectiveness of natural law depends on the existence of positive law. And unlike lockean citizens, hobbesian subjects can never appeal to natural law to justify challenges to the positive justice that positive law embodies. Only the sovereign's interpretation of the laws of nature is authoritative.

This reading is consistent with Hobbes' *formalist* model of adjudication. According to Hobbes, judges determine what the law is by reference to the sovereign's written or unwritten declarations. The process of adjudication consists in the application of these general rules or precepts to particular cases. Hobbes recognized that rules always require interpretation and maintained that the sovereign's intent serves as the chief constraint on judicial interpretive activity. When such intent is unclear, contradictory, or (apparently) iniquitous, judges must rely on equity. However, neither the inescapability of interpretation nor the occasional appeal to equity undermines law's formality. Hobbes believed that sovereign power and judicial impartiality suffice to preserve the character of law as a stable conventional system of positive legal rules for peace and cooperation. The (rational) sovereign will guarantee that the laws of nature are "contained" in the civil law and, therefore, that the civil law is rational. Such later positivists as Bentham and H.L.A. Hart challenged this view. From their perspective, Hobbes demystified natural law at the expense of mystifying its positive counterpart.

References

Gauthier, David. *The Logic of 'Leviathan.'* Oxford: Clarendon Press, 1969.

———. "Thomas Hobbes and the Contractarian Theory of Law." *Canadian Journal of Philosophy* Suppl. 16 (1990), 5–34.

Hampton, Jean. *Hobbes and the Social Contract Tradition.* New York: Cambridge University Press, 1986.

Hobbes, Thomas. *The Elements of Law, Natural and Politic.* 1640. Ed. Frederick Toennies. 2d ed. M.M. Goldsmith. London: Cambridge University Press, 1928.

———. *Leviathan.* 1651. Ed. C.B. Macpherson. Harmondsworth: Penguin, 1968.

Kavka, Gregory. *Hobbesian Moral and Political Theory.* Princeton: Princeton University Press, 1986.

———. "Right Reason and Natural Law in Hobbes's Ethics." *The Monist* 66 (1983), 120–133.

State, S.A. *Thomas Hobbes and the Debate Over Natural Law and Religion.* New York: Garland, 1991.

Tuck, Richard. *Natural Rights Theories: Their Origin and Development.* New York: Cambridge University Press, 1982.

Warrender, Howard. *The Political Philosophy of Hobbes.* Oxford: Clarendon Press, 1957.

Maria H. Morales

Hohfeld, Wesley Newcombe (1879–1918)

Wesley Newcombe Hohfeld was graduated cum laude in 1904 from the Harvard Law School. After practicing with a San Francisco law firm for only a year, he was offered a partnership. This he turned down for a career in legal teaching and legal research, first at the Stanford Law School from 1905 to 1914 and then at the Yale Law School until his death just four years later.

His philosophic contribution is a scheme of rights published in a mere 114 pages (originally appearing in the 1913 and 1917 volumes of the *Yale Law Journal*), entitled "Some Fundamental Legal Conceptions as Applied in Judicial Reasoning." This scheme, although it was in preliminary form and its argument is still widely criticized, provided the insight into rights that places him as the leading analytic jurist of the twentieth century, following Jeremy Bentham (1748–1832) and John Austin (1790–1859).

Unlike them, however, Hohfeld rejected the formalist conception of law and its pedigree test: duties and rights as valid deductions from commands validly issuing from a sovereign to its subjects. In this conception, a liberty is not a right in law until one person, A, risks an unauthorized interference with the liberty of another person, B. Until then every person has the duty not to interfere with the general liberty that the silence of legal commands permits everyone. Only the judicial finding that no command imposes a duty on A to act in a certain way in relation to B brings liberty into the law as a legal right of A.

However, this formalism, Hohfeld observed, recognizes only the unlawful relation as a legal relation, and thus prima facie ignores other legal relations, especially the lawful relation. For Hohfeld, however, a rule that *permits* an act by A in relation to B is just as real a rule in law as a rule that *prohibits* an act. This permitted act is what Hohfeld calls a liberty (or privilege) right of A to do or not to do the act. B has a "no-right" (an awkward term Hohfeld innovated) and not a duty not to interfere with it. This lawful relation of liberty-no-right entails not merely the absence of a duty on A and the absence of a (claim) right for B, but it is the alternative relation to the unlawful relation in which A's duty is correlative to B's (claim) right.

The two other correlative relations of rights typically obscured are power-liability and immunity-disability. The eight conceptions (atoms, building blocks, and so on) also relate as opposites. Others have added the relation of contradictories. Together they constitute a rights scheme in which any two persons as to certain acts have clusters, aggregates, or bundles of various conceptions of rights in relation to each other.

Hohfeld's ambition was that the rights scheme would not only reveal what judges do in fact, apart from what they say they do, but as a result of this realism would also improve judicial reasoning in the following ways. It would clarify the term "rights" by exposing confusions in its usage. This exposure would then force judges openly to justify on grounds of justice and policy the different jural relations or conceptions of rights they apply, and to do so in a terminology not calculated to mislead. In particular, they would have to justify publicly the merits of their choice between (1) the unlawful relation: prohibiting or permitting unilateral interferences with liberty by imposing or not imposing a duty on the acting party only, and (2) the lawful relation: permitting bilateral interferences with liberty by imposing no-rights on both parties, whether they act or not, to interfere with the liberty of the other party. Finally, he ambitiously suggested, the scheme would serve to discern common principles of justice and policy underlying various jural problems, thus rendering the issues of a case so precise that, so to speak, they would answer themselves.

His ambitious point invites the most skepticism. However, a plausible case can be made at least partly in its defense. Once it is seen that judges must always choose between the unlawful relation and the lawful relation, and cannot formally deny the legal existence of the latter, rights issues can be stated more precisely in terms of competing arguments of justice and policy. Only then are judges likely to genuinely agree on the arguments; and if they so agree, then it appears as if merely ascertaining the facts of what would otherwise have been a hard case answers the issues.

Hohfeld recognized, as many of his critics still do not, that his rights scheme, as an analytic aid, is only a necessary and not a sufficient condition of sound judicial reasoning. The scheme does not in itself include the scientific and practical phases of the law that would provide reasons to justify major premises. Still, Hohfeld had the ambitious hope that the

"deeper the analysis, the greater becomes one's perception of the fundamental unity and harmony in the law." He never made it clear how his scheme could do this, however. At best, his scheme can serve as a meta-language for translating diverse notions of rights into a common language, and this language can perhaps facilitate an overlapping consensus on what (we now know) are otherwise the always at least partly opposed justificatory grounds of justice (or right) and policy (or good).

Also still controversial about the scheme are the words most apt to denote its eight conceptions, as well as the scheme's applicability beyond private law (to include equity, criminal law and public law, constitutional law, conflict of laws, and the law of nations) and its utility for lawyers and judges who typically resist its analytic rigor for looser language and thought. Had Hohfeld not died prematurely, it is interesting to speculate whether he would have satisfied these and other omissions and criticisms. Nonetheless, some eight decades later, it is widely agreed, Hohfeld's rights scheme has no serious rival as the place to start to understand more deeply and critically the nature, purpose, and limits of rights talk.

References

Hohfeld, Wesley Newcombe. *Fundamental Legal Conceptions as Applied in Judicial Reasoning.* Ed. Walter Wheeler Cook. New Haven: Yale University Press, 1919. Reprint, with a new Foreword by Arthur L. Corbin, 1946.

Hudson, Stephen D., and Douglas N. Husak. "Legal Rights: How Useful Is Hohfeldian Analysis?" *Philosophical Studies* 37 (1980), 45.

Perry, Thomas D. "A Paradigm of Philosophy: Hohfeld on Legal Rights." *American Philosophical Quarterly* 14 (1977), 41.

Radin, Max. "A Restatement of Hohfeld." *Harvard Law Review* 51(1937–38), 1141.

Eugene E. Dais

See also POWERS AND RIGHTS

Holdsworth, Richard (1590–1649)

One could scarcely claim that Richard Holdsworth was a major philosopher. He was a theologian and a notable preacher, university and college teacher, and administrator at Cambridge. Yet he was a very good philosopher and, more to the point here, a significant indicator of important trends in natural law thinking in the late scholastic period. In his thought one sees very clearly an emphasis that had been gaining in importance from the late middle ages in the philosophy of law and ethics. This is what one might call a "linguistic turn," a turning away from locating the foundations for natural law in external nature to looking for these foundations in the way the mind works, as this is primarily exemplified in language and the deep structure of language. In this emphasis we can see a parallel to other trends in the history of philosophy generally in the late middle ages, Renaissance, and (what we have been taught to call) "early modern philosophy." These trends also reflect growing concern about the challenges of skeptics and a growing doubt about what external nature in and of itself can teach us.

Before considering some details of Holdsworth's theory of natural law, it is important to recount in a very brief way something of his history and his place in the thought and society of his times. Holdsworth must remain something of a puzzle to people who see standard stereotypes in seventeenth-century English history. He was a famous puritan preacher, an aristotelian philosopher with a wide knowledge of and appreciation for late scholasticism, and (to the dismay of some who had supported and promoted him) when the troubles of the civil war period came, an outspoken royalist. He was first and foremost a theologian.

Although Holdsworth was first known as a "puritan" preacher, one of the primary themes running through his thought was his rejection of some of the main doctrines of puritanism in its calvinistic form, and in this he foreshadows the thought of the Cambridge platonists, several of whom were his students or colleagues at Emmanuel College, Cambridge. He believed that while the fall of humankind had baneful effects indeed, such that we all are by nature sinners and need God's help to become justified or righteous in his sight, all was not lost, especially all was not lost from an epistemological point of view. As rational beings we retain some *vestigiae,* tracks or traces, not only of speculative knowledge but also of knowledge of the moral law.

Holdsworth thought these traces of God's own image in us, in spite of the Fall, have left every human being with "vestiges" of knowledge of the moral law that are chiefly to be located in our capacity for language use and learning a language. Here is where we can find the *lumen naturale,* which enlightens our consciences to recover some sort of innate knowledge of law and morals. In all this he builds on a long medieval tradition of contrasting mental language with written and spoken language. (Indeed, the distinction goes back to Aristotle and was particularly adumbrated by Augustine.) These discussions can also be seen as significantly foreshadowing certain influential movements in modern linguistics and philosophy of language, especially the positions of the so-called transformational grammarians and their doctrines about universal grammar and the deep structure of language, theories particularly associated with Noam Chomsky. In this linguistic turn we see another example of a general tendency in late scholasticism, the tendency to internalize order, to shift emphasis from looking for order in the external world to looking for order within, in the workings of the mind as they are reflected in the use of language. Thus, Holdsworth finds the foundation for natural law in what he calls *natura integra,* integral nature or pure nature, which is not to be found in external nature but within us. Of course, this "integral nature" is itself a normative concept, an ideal left to us through the workings of rational language.

What he was doing can be seen especially clearly in the importance he attached to an old argument going back to Aristotle, but of increasing importance in late scholastic thought, the "bad names" argument. According to Aristotle, some terms simply designate something blameworthy and are as good as an insult to anyone who understands them. Thus, nobody praises someone for being a liar or a murderer. The description, by its logical implications, is as good as an insult. Given the general linguistic theory alluded to previously, this is not only true for those who understand English words like "liar"; it is built into the very deep structure of language. Holdsworth even manages to get this idea into a small treatise he wrote about university education where he warns students who are in danger of turning into rakehells that they should heed the fact that they do not like being called rakehells; "rakehell" is itself logically a bad name. In ways like this law is ultimately based on linguistics.

References

Holdsworth, Richard. *Praelectiones Theologicae* (Theological Preambles). Ed. Richard Pearson. London: Jacobi Flesher, 1661.

Trentman, John A. "The Authorship of Directions for a Student in the University." *Transactions of the Cambridge Bibliographical Society* VII (1978), 170–183.

———. "Richard Holdsworth and the Natural Law: An Early Linguistic Turn." *Vera Lex* 8.2 (1988), 7–10.

———. "Scholasticism in the Seventeenth Century." In *Cambridge History of Later Medieval Philosophy,* ed. N. Kretzmann, A. Kenny, and J. Pinborg, 818–838. Cambridge: Cambridge University Press, 1982.

John A. Trentman

Holmes, Oliver Wendell, Jr. (1841–1935)

Oliver Wendell Holmes, Jr., the most renowned figure in the history of American law, left his stamp on American jurisprudence as a forerunner of legal realism and an early proponent of the economic analysis of law. In addition, it has been suggested that Holmes was a legal positivist, a utilitarian, a pragmatist, and a nietzschean nihilist. Despite frequent commentary, there is still no consensus about how best to characterize his thought.

Holmes was born in 1841 into a distinguished Bostonian family. He was a childhood friend of William and Henry James and Henry Adams and was acquainted with Ralph Waldo Emerson. Upon graduation from Harvard College, Holmes enlisted in the Union army and was thrice grievously wounded. After graduating from Harvard Law School, Holmes participated in the Metaphysical Club, whose members included the founders of philosophical pragmatism, Charles Sanders Peirce and William James. In 1881, Holmes published *The Common Law,* which is sometimes mentioned as the best book ever written about American law. Two years later, Holmes was appointed to the Supreme Judicial Court of Massachusetts. While a justice, he published "The Path of the Law," one of the most inspired texts in the law review literature. At the age of 61 Holmes was appointed to the United States Supreme Court, on which he served until 1932. He died in 1935 without issue and left a considerable portion of his estate to the federal government, which, as the Oliver Wendell Holmes Devise, has been used to fund a history of the Supreme Court.

Holmes' legal thought is important both for its substance and the rhetorical form of its presentation. It is almost exclusively concerned with the question of the proper role of the courts in modern society. However, his thought has not been convincingly reconstructed as a systematic whole, despite a number of impressive recent attempts to do so. Instead, Holmes' thought has influenced American legal theory through its aphorisms, which have been frequently cited by proponents of differing jurisprudential theories.

Holmes conceived of two limits on judicial lawmaking. The first arises from the proper relationship between the law and morality. Holmes sought to protect the particular concerns of the law from the encroachment of morality, and particularly from the natural law thesis that there are universal moral norms for which the law is to provide a state sanction. Law, in Holmes' view, is properly limited to maintaining the framework of social institutions so that individuals may pursue their own conceptions of moral value. Holmes' own view of morality is difficult to discern. It seems to consist principally in two elements: a notion of duty and a belief about the meaning of life. Holmes derived his notion of duty from something akin to fate—from an individual's situation and station in life. For example, Holmes believed that a soldier's duty in wartime is, most frequently, blind obedience to orders. Holmes' conception of meaning in life was influenced by the pragmatists. A life project is meaningful when we imbue it with meaning, which we do to the fullest when we conceive of unattainable goals and attempt to pursue them. For Holmes, the task of the law is to provide individuals with the space necessary for the realization of their goals.

Holmes emphasized the distinction between the legal and moral orders by suggesting that the law, in contrast to morality, might best be defined from the perspective of a "bad man," as a simple prediction of how the courts would decide a particular case. Holmes' theory of contractual obligation demonstrates the distinction in exemplary fashion. First, in Holmes' view, the law enforces a promise only when the promise is supported by a bargained-for consideration—in other words, only when societal confidence in the institution of contract would be diminished if there were no sanction for the breach. Second, Holmes insisted that contract law is concerned only with external facts and objectively verifiable conduct, not with the subjective motives that characterize moral reflection. Thus, Holmes rejected any attempt to ascertain whether the parties' minds actually met, and proposed instead an objective interpretation of party communications. Finally, in Holmes' view, a breach of contract does not necessarily constitute a moral wrong. A breach implies simply that the nonperforming party agrees to compensate the aggrieved party for the damages suffered. Holmes has been cited in support of the theory of efficient breach—the idea that a party should breach when it would maximize wealth. The law-and-economics theorists suggest that, once damages are paid, no moral issues remain. For Holmes, however, the fact that the law differs from morality means that an individual contemplating breach still must resolve the value questions.

Holmes derived a second limitation to judicial lawmaking from his conception of the proper relationship between the courts and the legislature. Holmes rejected the view, prevalent on the Supreme Court during much of his tenure there, that the role of the courts is to test the rationality of the legislative process. Instead, he believed that, as far as social legislation is concerned, the courts should defer to the political process. This principle dictated two seemingly contradictory tenets in Holmes' opinions. First, Holmes, frequently in dissent, refused to invoke the due process clause to strike down social legislation. In Holmes' social darwinist conception, society benefits from legislation sponsored by the dominant interests—those that have obtained electoral success. He also believed that rules of law should receive sympathetic interpretation in light of the policies and purposes they were designed to achieve. To this end, he recommended the use of the social sciences. However, Holmes preferred to leave the instrumental use of the law to the legislature. He believed that the courts should not make law, except interstitially, and thus recommended judicial restraint. The legal realists expanded Holmes' position to suggest that the law is instrumental social science, even when applied by the courts.

The second aspect of Holmes' seemingly contradictory approach to state legislation was his view, again expressed often as a dissenting voice, that the state may regulate speech only under quite limited conditions, notably when the speech presents a clear and present danger of immediate violence or of interference with established institutions. For the electoral process to select the fittest government, free trade in ideas (the phrase is from Holmes) must be protected from undue state interference.

Holmes presented his thought in a distinctive rhetorical form. He never attempted to elaborate his ideas about the law in a systematic fashion. Instead, he perfected an oracular style, distilling his arguments into single phrases of great oratorical power. Those who have endeavored to put Holmes' thought to work have been left with little alternative but to mine his prose for the brilliant epigrams it contains. This aspect of Holmes' manner may be related to his belief that an individual's preferences are, in the end, arbitrary and that nothing really can be demonstrated by reasoned argument.

References

Gilmore, G. *The Death of Contract.* Columbus: Ohio State University Press, 1974.

Grey, T. "Holmes and Legal Pragmatism." *Stanford Law Review* 41 (1989), 787–870.

Holmes, O. *The Common Law.* 1881. Ed. M. Howe. Boston: Little, Brown, 1963.

———. "The Path of the Law." *Harvard Law Review* 10 (1897), 457–478.

Howe, M. *Justice Oliver Wendell Holmes.* 2 vols. Cambridge MA: Belknap–Harvard University Press, 1957–1963.

Luban, D. "Justice Holmes and the Metaphysics of Judicial Restraint." *Duke Law Journal* 44 (1994), 449–523.

Pohlman, H. *Justice Oliver Wendell Holmes and Utilitarian Jurisprudence.* Cambridge MA: Harvard University Press, 1984.

Posner, R., ed. *The Essential Holmes.* Chicago: University of Chicago Press, 1992.

White, G. *Justice Oliver Wendell Holmes: Law and the Inner Self.* Oxford: Oxford University Press, 1993.

Richard Hyland

Homelessness and Residency

Intrusions, defamation, and assaults against privacy reflect the economics and the technology of the day. The issue of homelessness and altered families has refocused the limits of privacy rights claims.

The homeless are people who do not rent, own, or dwell for an extended time in one place. Their fragile economics sustains their social crisis, and they remain on the streets. Its membership is generally divided into three classifications: (1) families and single parents, (2) those with substance addiction (drugs and/or alcohol), and (3) the mentally ill. A common problem with such a diverse population is identification for a correct count to determine the effectiveness of programs.

There is no agreed upon number of homeless in the United States, although social scientists and coalition advocates present figures ranging from modest to high. Social scientist Peter Rossi's method of identification estimates a population of 350,000 to 500,000, while advocates record 2 million to 3 million. The causes of homelessness are (1) the gentrification of urban areas that rendered displacement of the poor from low-rent rooms, (2) an increased population with less capacity to meet the increased demands for skillful employment, and (3) the changes in release and admission/commission policies of mental health facilities. This group has been in double jeopardy, released without monitored care. E. Fuller Torrey criticizes the libertarian attitude for bringing about this condition by supporting patient choices. The mentally ill homeless have perished in the streets for the sake of their rights. Efforts have been made to change this. In 1993, the New York State Supreme Court ruled that hospitals have an obligation to the discharged mental patients only if they have a home willing to accept them.

Through the 1960s and 1990s, courts adjudicated cases resulting from antihomelessness legislation. Enforced city ordinances that banned panhandling, bathing, sleeping, and washing in public spaces were viewed as a punishment of homeless people. Justice White, in *Powell v. Texas*, 492 U.S. 680, cited a violation of the Eighth Amendment when ordinances that punish people for their involuntary status were enforced. The general trend to penalize the homeless for sleeping, bathing, or panhandling is unconstitutional. Were Judith Thomson's view correct, the homeless would have no claims to privacy since they have no property. The Congress initiated the McKinney Homeless Assistance Act in 1987 and a stronger, more comprehensive edition followed in 1994. Families and children are given higher priority.

The federal surplus property program supplements the McKinney Act with unused government property for residences. They receive skill training in computers, planting tools, and parenting techniques so that their children may imagine alternative lifestyles. Resistance is expressed in some communities by rezoning this kind of property. The courts will again have a role in shaping the solution to this condition. Residences such as these create a different profile for homelessness, one that constructs life plans from economic strife. The transformation can reclaim the homeless as a contributing force to society.

References

Rossi, Peter. *Down and Out in America.* Chicago: University of Chicago Press, 1989.

Thomson, Judith Jarvis. "The Right to Privacy." *Philosophy and Public Affairs* 4 (1975), 295–314.

John M. Abbarno

See also INTIMACY; PRIVACY

Homicide

The law of homicide reflects the universally accepted moral belief that the killing of one human being by another human being constitutes the most serious kind of harm that can be done to a person. All killings are unlawful and criminal unless there are circumstances that make them legally justified or excusable.

The general definition of homicide is the killing of a human being by the act or omission of another human being; this definition excludes both suicide and killing of animals. Homicide requires that the perpetrator's act or omission cause the death of the victim, and traditionally death was defined as the cessation of breathing and heartbeat. Since current medical technology is able to maintain cardiorespiratory functioning in a person who is brain-dead, many legal systems have adopted new definitions that recognize that death has occurred whenever there is irreversible cessation of either cardiorespiratory function or brain function.

Although there are important variations in the way that homicides are classified, many modern legal systems recognize the following categories: justifiable homicide, excusable homicide, murder, and manslaughter. The underlying rationale for this classification becomes clearer once each category is defined and examples of each kind of offense are provided. The definitions used here reflect common law, statutory language, and *Model Penal Code* provisions, as appropriate.

Justifiable Homicide

Homicide is justifiable if it is either commanded or authorized by law; some examples are a member of the armed forces killing an enemy in time of war, a police officer killing a fugitive from justice, or an executioner carrying out a legally valid death sentence.

Excusable Homicide

Homicide is excusable if it is committed accidentally by a person who is engaged in a lawful act without negligence or an intention to hurt, or if it is done in self-defense based on a reasonable belief that deadly force is necessary.

Both justifiable and excusable homicide are lawful and carry no criminal liability. The justification for this can be understood in the light of some of the generally recognized purposes of criminal law. For example, no valid retributive ("just deserts") purpose would be served by punishing soldiers and police who in the course of duty kill someone; they do not deserve punishment and the social condemnation it implies. Likewise, persons who kill accidentally without negligence or malice do not deserve to be punished; their conduct does not reflect either ill will or disregard for life that would deserve social condemnation. Likewise, no valid deterrent purpose would be served by punishing members of the military and the police who kill in the course of conscientiously discharging their duties, and it would be highly undesirable to interfere with individual liberty of citizens to the extent that would be required to prevent or greatly reduce the incidence of innocent and accidental homicide that is now excusable. Finally, there is no need to assuage the feelings of revenge, resentment, or indignation on the part of the families of victims of justifiable or excusable homicides, since such feelings are misplaced.

In sharp contrast with the first two categories, all homicides classified as either murder or manslaughter are unlawful and carry some degree of criminal liability because pun-

ishing them furthers the legitimate goals of criminal law.

Murder

In common law murder is defined as unlawful killing of one person by another "with malice aforethought," an expression that is still used in many legal systems. However, it is a misleading expression in the context of modern understanding of the law of murder, because it is not strictly necessary that the perpetrator act with malice in an ordinary sense (hatred, spite, or ill will). For example, many legal systems consider mercy killing or euthanasia to be murder. It is not necessary that one act "aforethought" (with premeditation or planning); in many legal systems it is sufficient that the killing was intentional even without any forethought. Indeed, felony murder need be neither intentional nor premeditated. The state of much (though not all) current legal thinking in the United States about murder is indicated in the following classification, beginning with the most serious offense.

First-degree or capital murder is (1) unlawful killing, (2) of one person by another, that is (3) intentional and (4) premeditated and deliberate. A clear example of first-degree murder would be a husband killing his wife in order to collect her life insurance benefits. Some legal systems stipulate certain aggravating circumstances (for example, killing for hire, multiple victims, or killing a police officer) that are required for the imposition of the death penalty. A very plausible explanation for the special seriousness attached to first-degree murder is the great degree of control over their conduct and the surrounding circumstances that perpetrators display, control which in turn gives them the ability and opportunity to avoid the extreme harm of killing the victim. The high degree of control exercised by perpetrators in turn justifies an appropriately severe penalty. Giving these perpetrators their just deserts demands it, because there are likely others who may be potential perpetrators and would be deterred by severe penalties, and because only a severe punishment is likely to assuage the understandable feelings of revenge, resentment, and indignation suffered by the families of victims.

Second-degree or noncapital murder is the same as first-degree murder except that it is not premeditated and deliberate. The distinction between first- and second-degree murder further supports the view that it is the perpetrators' degree of control over their conduct and circumstances that best explains the difference in the degree of seriousness of various crimes of homicide.

Felony murder is (1) killing of one person by another (2) in the course of the commission of a felony that involves reckless disregard for life or limb; (3) although the commission of the felony must be intentional, (4) the killing that occurs as a result need not be either intentional or premeditated. An example would be the killing of a store clerk in the course of a robbery.

Manslaughter

Manslaughter is a distinct offense, not a degree of murder.

Voluntary manslaughter is (1) the unlawful killing (2) of one person by another that is (3) intentional, (4) the result of adequate provocation, (5) committed in the heat of passion, and (6) there is a causal connection between the provocation, the passion, and the killing. For example, person A is highly insulted by the remarks of person B and kills B in a sudden fit of rage. At work here is a commonsense psychological assumption that persons can be provoked to such an extent that they suddenly and temporarily lose control over their conduct and act out of extreme emotion before there has been time to cool off and regain their ordinary powers of judgment. It is important to notice that voluntary manslaughter is intentional, not accidental, and that the entire basis for treating it less seriously than murder is the perpetrator's lack of control.

Involuntary manslaughter is (1) the unlawful killing (2) of one person by another that is either (3) the causal result of the commission of an unlawful but nonfelonious act, (4) due to culpable negligence, or (5) due to an omission or failure to perform a legal duty (criminal omission). Involuntary manslaughter does not involve intentional killing.

The definition of involuntary manslaughter is untidy because it is designed to cover all unlawful homicides not covered by murder or voluntary manslaughter, and these differ greatly from each other. For example, it lumps together unlawful acts that accidentally result in killing with acts which would otherwise be lawful except for the fact that they cause a killing in a manner that involves a degree negligence or recklessness that constitutes "a wanton disregard of human life." Both kinds of acts involve an element of culpability, but they differ in the kind of culpability they exhibit.

Two kinds of involuntary manslaughter that deserve particular mention are vehicular homicide and criminal omission. *Vehicular homicide* is the negligent killing of another person while operating a motor vehicle (motorcycle, aircraft, and so forth) that has become so prevalent in modern life. *Criminal omission* is (1) the failure to act in a way that would save the life of another person (thus the death is "due to," that is, its occurrence can be explained by, the failure to act), (2) the person has a legal duty to act, and (3) it is possible for the person to act. In the United States there are only four grounds recognized for an affirmative legal duty to save life: a statutory duty (for example, one spouse must provide for the necessary food, clothing, and medical care of the other spouse), status or relationship in common law (for example, parents have the duty to prevent physical harm to their children), duty arising from contract (for example, a nurse is hired to care for a patient), and voluntary assumption of the responsibility for care (for example, a grandmother volunteers to care for her grandchild). This contrasts sharply with most European countries, which recognize a broad legal duty to render aid to someone whose life is in serious danger and provide criminal penalties for failure to honor it.

References

American Law Institute. *Model Penal Code and Commentaries*. Philadelphia: American Law Institute Press, 1985.

Devine, Philip E. *The Ethics of Homicide*. Ithaca: Cornell University Press, 1978.

Gross, Hyman. *A Theory of Criminal Justice*. New York: Oxford University Press, 1979.

Kleinig, John. "Good Samaritanism." *Philosophy and Public Affairs* 5 (1975).

Klotter, John C. *Criminal Law*. 3d ed. Cincinnati: Anderson, 1990.

LaFave, Wayne R., and Austin W. Scott, Jr. *Handbook on Criminal Law*. St. Paul MN: West, 1986.

Williams, Glanville. *The Sanctity of Life and the Criminal Law*. New York: Knopf, 1957.

David H. Jones

See also ABORTION AND INFANTICIDE; CAPITAL PUNISHMENT; EUTHANASIA AND SUICIDE; PARTIES TO CRIMINAL CONDUCT

H

Homosexuality
See SODOMY

Human Rights

Human rights are widely understood as being those moral or natural rights held by all (and only) humans and which we hold just in virtue of being human. The term has great normative appeal, and almost everyone would now agree, albeit for substantially different reasons, that for a state to violate the human rights of those it governs is for it to do them a grave moral wrong. The widespread agreement among different types of theorists about the value of human rights stems from the fact that human rights are meant to express the minimum standard of conduct a state and its agencies must meet in the treatment of those over whom they exercise control.

In general terms, to say that someone has a right to something (or to perform some action) is to claim that it would be wrong to deprive them of that thing (or to keep them from performing that action) even if so depriving them would, on the whole, make society better off. Rights, to use Ronald Dworkin's helpful phrase, serve as trumps on social goals. If society wants to attain some goal by doing X and I have a right that X not be done, then I may use my right to stop society from doing X, that is, to trump society's would-be X-ing. Rights serve as side constraints, to use Robert Nozick's term, on legitimate ways of accomplishing things. When a society seeks to accomplish something, it is morally constrained to adopt only those means which do not violate anyone's rights. Human rights, being rights held by all humans, impose side constraints on the way any society can go about its business in a morally legitimate manner.

Because all humans have whatever human rights morality provides people simply in virtue of their being human, it seems clear that every legal system should make provisions to ensure that governments and their agencies do not violate anyone's human rights. However, not all governments have been willing to pass legislation or introduce constitutional instruments protecting all human rights. Consequently, a major practical problem has been how to ensure that human rights (construed as moral rights held by humans) become legal rights. In response to this problem, since World War II a series of international charters, covenants, conventions, and declarations has been promulgated stating what human rights individuals have. (Among the most important of these instruments are the United Nations Charter; the Universal Declaration of Human Rights; the International Covenant on Economic, Social, and Cultural Rights; and the International Covenant on Civil and Political Rights. These are supplemented by various regional documents, such as the Council of Europe Convention for the Protection of Human Rights and Fundamental Freedoms and the African Charter on Human and Peoples' Rights, as well as documents which deal with special issues, such as the Convention on the Prevention and Punishment of the Crime of Genocide, the International Convention on the Suppression and Punishment of the Crime of Apartheid, and the Declaration on the Rights of Mentally Retarded Persons. For a more complete account of these instruments, see *Human Rights* by Winston Langley. These and other documents state the minimum standards which nation states must meet in their treatment of individuals and groups, and these documents have done much to limit the cruel and degrading treatment inflicted on humans by their governments. A variety of efforts have been made to enforce adherence to these codes of conduct. For instance, international courts (such as the World Court, the International Court of Human Rights, and the European Court of Human Rights) have labored both to interpret these documents and to enforce compliance with them. Furthermore, independent agencies such as Amnesty International have worked to uncover human rights abuses and to bring public pressure on governments to ensure compliance.

Some have objected to the idea of human rights on the grounds that they are a Western invention based on an atomistic conception of the individual. This is mistaken. Basic human rights express a minimum standard that decent political institutions, whether they be founded on Western ideals or not, must meet. The principles of global justice tend to be expressed in terms of internationally protected human rights because these are the rights individuals have in virtue of being members of a universal human community. We have these rights because we are human, not because we are members of any particular state or national group. If we think of human rights as those moral or natural rights held by all and only humans just in virtue of their being human, then these rights will be seen to be independent of our conventional or legal rights and will serve as a standpoint from which to critically evaluate the moral status of specific legal systems and the provisions they make to ensure that each person's human rights are protected. Of course, in one sense the term "human right" is unfortunate, simply because it is not our being human that is morally relevant. Were there a nonhuman species on this planet with relevant characteristics, other than being *Homo sapiens,* similar to ours, they would be worthy of the same concern and respect as all humans are.

Jeremy Bentham, the founder of utilitarianism and an early legal positivist, is notorious for having opposed the idea that there are any natural rights because this seemed to involve conceiving of nature as creating or supporting moral imperatives, something Bentham thought absurd. Hence his famous claim in *Anarchical Fallacies* that "natural rights is simple nonsense: natural and imprescriptible rights, rhetorical nonsense—nonsense upon stilts." Bentham's view is that rights exist only when law creates them. However, like all good utilitarians, Bentham would applaud the substantial extent to which international law has been strengthened in the last half of the twentieth century in the aid of creating, promoting, and protecting human rights (understood as legal rights each of us has under international law).

Typical human rights (such as the right not to be tortured) consist of a hohfeldian liberty (in this case, to avoid or resist torture) together with a hohfeldian claim against the government (that it not torture you), combined with a hohfeldian immunity (against both the government and oneself) that this right not be altered (even with one's permission). Libertarians are inclined to advance philosophic arguments against the idea that sane adults ever should have immunities against themselves imposed on them. (Unlikely though it is that someone might want to be tortured, we should not interfere with the individual's judgment on this matter.) Whatever the merits of this position, the enormous practical advantage of defining human rights to include an immunity against oneself giving up those rights is obvious. Inalienable human rights—rights which one cannot forgo at will—do not allow evil governments to disingenuously claim that those whose rights they are violating have abandoned those rights.

References

Amnesty International. *Amnesty International Report.* London: Amnesty International Publications (annual).

Langley, Winston E., ed. *Human Rights: Sixty Major Instruments Introduced, Reprinted, and Indexed.* Jefferson NC: McFarland, 1992.

Nardin, Terry. *Law, Morality, and the Relations of States.* Princeton: Princeton University Press, 1983.

Shute, Stephen, and Susan Hurley, eds. *On Human Rights: The Oxford Amnesty Lectures 1993.* New York: Basic Books, 1993.

Sumner, L.W. *The Moral Foundations of Rights.* New York: Oxford University Press, 1987.

Sheldon Wein

See also Entrenchment; Fundamental Rights; Powers and Rights; Rights and Liberties

H

Hume, David (1711–1776)

Hume's philosophy of law may be found in his 1740 *A Treatise of Human Nature,* Book III, Part II, and in his 1751 work *An Enquiry Concerning the Principles of Morals,* Section III and Appendix II; from 1777, Appendix III. His understanding of law and justice, of rights and obligations, was perceived by his contemporaries (by James Balfour and Thomas Reid, among others) to have been inspired by the ideas of philosophers, ancient and modern, of an epicurean and skeptical persuasion. Like those philosophers (Epicurus, Horace, Pierre Gassendi, Pierre Bayle), Hume discovered the origin of law in a convention to abstain from the possessions of others. In the absence of such a convention, humankind must remain in a state of nature: in conditions of poverty, weakness, and insecurity. There is no natural remedy for these conditions in human reason or in the power of the human will or in the natural sociability of humankind. The natural avarice and ambition of humans can only be restrained artificially, by a convention or agreement of judgments that it is useful to oneself and to others to live in accordance with laws or general rules. Such rules determine the rights of property owners; they specify the conditions in which promises oblige; they fix the objects of allegiance to governments. Utility, Hume declared following Horace, is the mother of justice and equity.

Duncan Forbes and Knud Haakonssen have described Hume's philosophy of law as "a modern theory of natural law" or as a position which mediates between scholastic natural law theories and modern natural rights theories. The characterization of Hume's philosophy of law as a natural law theory must be qualified very substantially. Hume's description of the conventions of property, promise keeping, and allegiance to government as "laws of nature" was designed to underline the extraordinary utility of these conventions for life in society. But Hugo Grotius, Samuel Pufendorf, and other modern natural jurists identified the reduction of laws of nature to considerations of utility to be the very position they were arguing against in their treatises of natural jurisprudence. And while Hume's account of the origin of justice and property, the rights of property, and so forth, in the *Treatise* may be seen to have followed the intellectual agenda of Pufendorf and his annotators, Hume's arguments appear to have been worked out in opposition to natural law and natural rights theories. Hume denied that there was a foundation for law in the nature of things. He argued, against John Locke and others, that no natural right of property can be discovered in the activity of laboring or producing: the connection between persons and things is never a necessary connection, it is at best a contingent and separable connection; this is why rights of property must be determined artificially, by conventions and by general rules. The theory favored by early modern natural rights theorists, that government has its origin in an original contract or in the consent, express or tacit, of subjects, was also rejected by Hume; he found no evidence in history or in the experience of the founding of governments of an original contract or consent. He argued instead that governments have their origin in conquest or usurpation, that the authority of government derives from the opinion of subjects that government is useful and in their interest. Wise legislators will so order the institutions of government that politicians will recognize that it is in their own interest to conduct the government in a manner consistent with the interest of the public or with public utility.

The centrality of the principle of utility in Hume's understanding of law and legislation might suggest that Hume's legal philosophy was a precursor of the utilitarianism of Jeremy Bentham and his followers. According to Douglas Long, it seems clear, however, that Bentham understood the principle of utility very differently from Hume, and was puzzled by Hume's more skeptical (and, Bentham thought, sentimental) approach to moral and legal judgments. Hume did not imagine that the consequences of individual actions could be calculated, nor did he believe that the general or greatest happiness could be achieved by legislation. The utility of the conventions of social life may be discovered only in experience of the advantages and disadvantages which have followed from these conventions in the past. In this respect Hume's understanding of law may be recognized to have been an empirical or experimental understanding of law and legal reasoning. His philosophy of law was neither a natural law theory nor a utilitarian theory; it was a conventional understanding of law inspired by the ideas of the epicureans and the skeptics but grounded more securely than their theories upon reasoning based on experience.

References

Forbes, Duncan. *Hume's Philosophical Politics*. Cambridge: Cambridge University Press, 1975.

Haakonssen, Knud. *Natural Law and Moral Philosophy. From Grotius to the Scottish Enlightenment*. Cambridge: Cambridge University Press, 1996.

———. *The Science of a Legislator. The Natural Jurisprudence of David Hume and Adam Smith*. Cambridge: Cambridge University Press, 1981.

Hayek, F.A. "The Legal and Political Philosophy of David Hume." In *Hume: A Collection of Critical Essays,* ed. V.C. Chappell, 335–360. New York: Anchor Books, 1966.

Long, Douglas. "'Utility' and the 'Utility Principle': Hume, Smith, Bentham, Mill." *Utilitas* 2 (1990), 12–39.

Moore, James. "Hume's Theory of Justice and Property." *Political Studies* 24 (1976), 103–119.

Stewart M.A., and John P. Wright, eds. *Hume and Hume's Connexions*. With essays by Moore, Darwall, and Westerman. Edinburgh: Edinburgh University Press, 1994.

James Moore

Husserl, Gerhart (1893–1973)

Gerhart Husserl, the son of Edmund Husserl (1859–1938), who was the founder of the phenomenological movement, emigrated to the United States after he was fired in 1933 from his position as a professor of law in Germany for being a "non-Aryan." He taught at the National University Law School and was a founding member of *Philosophy and Phenomenological Research*. He published several articles in English, but his most important work is in German. In the 1950s, Husserl returned to Germany, continued his teaching and research in comparative and Anglo-American law, and also became very active in the reform of legal education.

His interest in the basic structure of law led to questions about legal personality, property, the relationship of substantive to procedural law, and especially the temporal structure of law. While he raised issues mainly in the area of civil law, he also drew upon other areas of the law, such as international and criminal law and the foundations of law. Husserl believed that comparative law—comparisons of Anglo-American to continental law or of modern law to the law of earlier periods in Europe—was particularly helpful for understanding basic legal structures.

Husserl was not really a member of any particular philosophical school; yet he took his own work to be phenomenological and he often referred to his father's writings. Like other legal theorists practicing phenomenology, he believed we should grasp the a priori structures underlying legal phenomena by describing the givens of legal situations without imposing preconceived notions on them. His phenomenology is quite consonant with the movement's motto of returning to the things themselves.

Husserl thought that legal science was a special science based on a particular region of a priori probabilities. It then becomes the task of philosophy of law to work out a system of fundamental concepts that would found this science. He himself worked on broad legal concepts, such as the legal object, legal subjects versus legal persons, time and law, world and law, justice, property, and the promise.

Husserl's discussion of justice reflects the phenomenologist's concern to base analysis on the a priori structure of the object. He believed that justice is not an ontological entity possessing some independent existence; rather, it is an attribute, an attitude of the mind, an expression of equality between two things. Justice is the equality which is based on the *eidos,* or essence, of the objects compared and not on their externality, homogeneity, or similarity—and the essence of equality is justice.

It then becomes the task of the community of law to allow the transcendental ideal of justice to work itself out in the real world. Law is supposed to safeguard the essential equality of all persons and not to remedy social inequalities, redistribute wealth, or reform the social order. Because the ideal of justice is transcendentally grounded, Husserl would argue that his distinction between formal or essential equality and material or existential equality is impervious to Karl Marx's criticism that the former cannot exist without the latter and that such distinctions ultimately serve the interests of the dominant class.

According to Husserl, the gradual process of rationalization of social life results in the rise and development of the legal order. He holds that, when law is viewed as a social institution, it becomes readily apparent that there is a historical rationality working itself out in human existence. This conception of the historical development of law and community and of their relationship is similar to ideas developed by Friedrich von Savigny (1779–1861) and the historical school of jurisprudence and to the distinction between community and society put forward by Ferdinand Tönnies (1855–1936).

The community plays an important role in the realization of justice because the just person is one who acts as a representative of the community and whose decision is valid throughout the community. Husserl arrives at this universal validity by transposing Immanuel Kant's categorical imperative from the individual into the social sphere, giving it the same transcendental validity.

The notions of community, justice, and law are intertwined in Husserl's thought; law appears within the community, and the task of the legal community is to ensure the reality and effectiveness of justice in the social world. Just action defines a community of law as one governed by the principles of justice. These find their expression in the constitution of the state. As the material realization of the transcendental idea of justice, the constitution thus poses legal restraints on the activity of the state; the dictator then becomes one who simply refuses to admit that legal restraints exist. However, it may be argued that the institution of law knows no legal restraints and that the transcendental restraints that Husserl would impose on the law cannot be legal restraints.

References

Husserl, Gerhart. *Person, Sache, Verhalten: Zwei phänomenologische Studien* (Person, Thing, Limit: Two Phenomenological Studies). Frankfurt: Vittorio Klostermann, 1969.
———. *Recht und Welt: Rechtsphilosophische Abhandlungen* (Law and World: Studies in Philosophy of Law). Juristische Abhandlungen, Band 1. Frankfurt: Vittorio Klostermann, 1964.
———. *Recht und Zeit: Fünf rechtsphilosophische Essays* (Law and Time: Five Essays of Philosophy of Law). Frankfurt: Vittorio Klostermann, 1955.
———. *Der Rechtsgegenstand: Rechtslogische Studien zu einen Theorie des Eigentums* (Polarity in Law: Studies in Legal Logic Toward a Theory of Property). Berlin: Springer, 1933.
Würtenberger, Thomas, ed. *Phänomenologie, Rechtsphilosophie, Jurisprudenz. Festschrift für Gerhart Husserl zum 75. Geburtstag* (Phenomenology, Philosophy of Law, Jurisprudence: Essays in Honor of Gerhart Husserl on his 75th Birthday). Frankfurt: Vittorio Klostermann, 1969.

Henri R. Pallard
Richard Hudson

See also PHENOMENOLOGY OF LAW

Hutchinson, Thomas (1711–1780)

Conservative defender of natural and customary law against the natural rights theorists of the American Revolution, Thomas Hutchinson served as lieutenant governor (1757–1770), chief justice (1760–1770), and governor (1770–1774) of the British province of Massachusetts Bay during the turbulent era preceding the American Revolution. He articulated in his writings and decisions from the bench a conservative philosophy of law to counter colonial resistance to British taxation and trade regulation. His philosophy antici-pated Edmund Burke's response to the French Revolution.

Hutchinson insisted government existed to fulfill natural law and further "the happiness of every individual, so far as it is consistent with the safety of the whole." Those who violently sought to change government had to violate natural law when they harmed innocent people. While no government perfectly enforced natural law, it was best approximated through fidelity to whatever traditional practices and institutions a given society had evolved over time. "No prince in Asia," Hutchinson wrote, "has a right to deprive me of my natural liberties by compelling me to become his subject, but if for the sake of his protection I become and continue his subject, I have as much submitted my natural rights to his government there, although I have parted with more of them than I should have in Europe."

Hutchinson thus denounced the Massachusetts revolutionaries' theory, derived from John Locke, that government was established to guarantee people the "natural" rights of life, liberty, and property. "All that is said of natural contracts is . . . merely ideal," Hutchinson argued. Any state which insisted on preserving them intact would be a "mere rope of sand" where "every individual has a right to judge when the acts of government are just and unjust and to submit accordingly." Hence, there was "no instance of government from the creation of the world established upon such fundamentals."

Hutchinson further insisted that, paradoxically, revolutionary governments pretending to be founded on the popular will and natural rights theory were worse than others: "If individuals or particular parts of governments may resist whenever they shall apprehend themselves aggrieved, instead of order and peace and a state of security, we may expect tumults, wars, and a general state of danger." Only tyranny could halt the anarchy, and Hutchinson predicted the two would alternate amid the fatuous rhetoric of a revolutionary age.

The most cogent opponent of the political theory of the American Revolution, Hutchinson justified continued British rule based on the general happiness of the colonies under the historically evolved, though philosophically undeveloped, political and legal system British Americans had traditionally enjoyed. He thus opposed British as well as American attempts to insist that "there must be a line" drawn between colonial liberty and parliamentary sovereignty. Custom was flexible and evolving. It could only be preserved if it were *not* defined. Hutchinson thus opposed British administrators who also sought to redefine the imperial relationship by insisting the colonists were "virtually" represented in Parliament and thus retained their natural rights. Fellow loyalists who hoped to reform the empire by establishing an American Parliament met Hutchinson's scorn as well. Institutional tinkering could not restore a once-healthy balance in which liberty and power had coexisted and flourished through limited tensions.

References

Bailyn, Bernard. *The Ordeal of Thomas Hutchinson*. Cambridge MA: Harvard University Press, 1974.

Pencak, William. *America's Burke: The Mind of Thomas Hutchinson*. Lanham MD: University Press of America, 1982.

William Pencak

See also FOUNDING JURISTS, 1760–1800, U.S.

H

I

Idealists, British

The British idealists were philosophers and social reformers whose work inspired progressive legislation in Great Britain (and, though to a lesser degree, throughout its Commonwealth) from the mid-nineteenth century until the beginning of World War II. The main figures were Thomas Hill Green (1836–1882) and Edward Caird (1835–1908) and, in a second generation, Bernard Bosanquet (1848–1923), David G. Ritchie (1853–1903), Henry Jones (1852–1922), John Watson (1847–1939), Francis Herbert Bradley (1846–1924), and Richard Burdon Haldane (1856–1928).

Called "idealists" because of their view that social relations and institutions were not ultimately material phenomena, but best understood as existing at the level of human consciousness, their work shows both a strong influence of G.W.F. Hegel and an important debt to Immanuel Kant and to the classical Greek thought of Plato and Aristotle. Although the movement is sometimes regarded as socially conservative, many of its major representatives were counted among the radical wing of the British Liberal Party, and several became leading figures in the British Labour Party.

British idealism sought to present an alternative to the then-dominant utilitarian positivist and natural law theories. While all would agree that "the law" is a set of "general rules" enforced by the state, the idealist saw the law as based on neither individual consent or a social contract nor the command of a sovereign, but as an expression of what Bosanquet called the "real" or general will and a product of natural development in human social life. (This notion of a "general will" has, however, been subject to much criticism.) Law,

then, has a teleological and a rational character. Idealists also tended to an organic view of society and argued that, largely because of their underlying individualism, utilitarians and natural rights theorists could not adequately account for the obligatory character of law.

For several of the idealists, a central problem with positivism was that the activity of the law in regulating, coordinating, and arbitrating social life was purely "external" and need not be part of the "living system" of individuals and institutions that it presumed to control. Moreover, since both law and morality had, as their respective ends, the common good, and since social and political institutions were held to represent this good (albeit imperfectly), legal rights and obligations were not separated from the moral, and the idealists saw no ultimate separation of law and morality. (This controversial view has been criticized, particularly by L.T. Hobhouse and J.A. Hobson.) Still, their account of law is quite distinct from a classical natural law approach, and idealists demurred from views that the aim of law was to govern or enforce moral duty and that, to be law, a system or statute had to satisfy a "higher law" or external moral standard.

Although law employs compulsion and restraint, it was considered to be "positive" in that it provided the material conditions for liberty, the functioning of social institutions, and the development of individual moral character. Unlike some prior liberal views, then, idealism held that there was no incompatibility between liberty and the law; the coercive character of law does not displace the individual will, but allows it to have a clearer and more fruitful expression. According to Bosanquet, law and compulsion were necessary to self-realization and to social life, and there was little to be gained by an a priori limitation of the law. Yet resort to law could legitimately be invoked only once certain moral criteria were met. (Some critics have noted a tension between the kantian and hegelian tendencies implicit in these criteria.)

Still, while law was seen as necessary to the promotion of the common good, it could not make a person good, and social progress could sometimes be better achieved by volunteer action. Many of Green's and Caird's students were actively involved in social reform (for example, Toynbee Hall, the Charity Organization Society, and the Christian Social Union) in the late nineteenth and early twentieth century, and Bosanquet's wife, Helen, played a leading role in the preparation of the majority report of the Royal Commission on the Poor Laws (1905–1909).

Since law was impossible without the enforcement power of the state, and since rights had to be "recognized" in law, there could be no rights against the state. Nevertheless, the idealists sometimes (though, arguably, incorrectly) have been seen as maintaining a natural rights perspective. Green and, later, Ritchie might be read as allowing that some rights were based on the nature of the individual as a moral person. However, all held that the moral person was necessarily a social being, and such rights were neither absolute and inalienable nor meaningful apart from social life. Again, while it was generally acknowledged that, where social institutions were fundamentally corrupt, there could be a duty to resist, there was no right to rebellion.

In the main (with, perhaps, the exception of Bradley), the idealists followed Kant in adopting a retributivist view of punishment. Acts set precedents, and thus wrongful acts must be "annulled" and "publicly undone" and there must be an additional "act" which "negates" the bad will of the offender. Reformation as the primary end of punishment treated individuals as less than responsible and free beings, and a deterrence model would violate the respect due them as moral persons. In fact, like Kant, Bosanquet held that a criminal has "a right to punishment."

Although many of the later idealists considered that the state (identified with the nation state) was absolute, they did not exclude the possibility of an organized system of international law. The conditions for an effective recognition and enforcement of such law were, they thought, absent at that moment—although some held out hope that proposal of a League of Nations reflected the beginnings of a genuine human community and might provide a mechanism by which multinational action could be accomplished.

In the last twenty years there has been a renewed interest in idealist political philosophy, and this, along with similarities to some of the recent work of Ronald Dworkin, suggests more attention may be given to idealist philosophy of law.

References

Bosanquet, Bernard. *The Philosophical Theory of the State*. 1899. 4th ed. London: Macmillan, 1923.

Green, Thomas Hill. *Lectures on the Principles of Political Obligation, and Other Writings*. Ed. Paul Harris and John Morrow. Cambridge: Cambridge University Press, 1986.

Nicholson, Peter P. *The Political Philosophy of the British Idealists: Selected Studies*. Cambridge: Cambridge University Press, 1990.

Ritchie, David G. *Natural Rights*. London, 1895.

Sweet, William. "Law and Liberty in J.S. Mill and Bernard Bosanquet." In *The Social Power of Ideas*, ed. C. Peden and Y. Hudson. Lewiston NY: Edwin Mellen Press, 1995.

———. *The Social Ontology of Rights in the Political Thought of Bernard Bosanquet*. Lanham MD: University Press of America, 1996.

Vincent, Andrew, and Raymond Plant. *Philosophy, Politics and Citizenship: The Life and Thought of the British Idealists*. Oxford: Basil Blackwell, 1984.

William Sweet

Ideology

The term "ideology" was coined by Destutt de Tracy in 1796 to refer to a science about the formation of ideas, mainly oriented to the analysis of error, masking, and concealing, attributes that have been affixed to the meaning of ideology in all its historical turns. The reference here is to those approaches regarded as "critique to ideology," which constitute a secondary, reflective level, in which ideologies are the subject of analysis. On their own level, ideologies are espoused or rejected just as ideals are.

Ideology can be characterized as (1) a system of ideas and beliefs, generally with political relevance, that confuses knowledge and valuation. Ideology mixes "is" with "ought" issues. It asserts that something is, or is being done, and simultaneously asserts that something ought to be, or ought to be done. For this reason, ideological discussions blur the difference between values or facts. (2) Ideology is also a justification that remains indifferent to the goal it serves, whether the goal be a specific legislation, political measure, or juridical verdict. Thus, to understand ideology, it is necessary to distinguish between acts and their justifications.

We see, then, that ideology differs from *knowledge, valuation,* and *practical thinking.* The purely cognitive attitude seeks to describe and explain the object of knowledge, for example, the sum of all the positive laws. The *valuative attitude* consists of taking a stand for or against the object of valuation. *Practical thinking* means applying values to facts, while maintaining a clear distinction between the two. For instance, legislators cannot pass effective laws unless their prior assessment of conditions and consequences is as objective as possible.

Are ideologies merely convenient lies, or do they genuinely satisfy some human need? Traditionally, there are two answers to the question.

First, ideology is primarily a need for lawmakers, rulers, and judges. For the ruled, ideology is a lie that succeeds as long as the ruled do not realize that rulers manipulate ideology to advance political goals. Ideology is a lie because it pretends to be knowledge but it is not. Thus, Theodor Geiger calls it "pseudotheory." Believers are misled, because ideology is harmful for them. Ideology runs contrary to the deepest interests and values of the people; if this were not so, there would be no need to tell them lies. The Frankfurt school believed that disillusion is possible, as in psychoanalysis, because of man's lack of self-consciousness. This approach underlies Plato's theory of the state. Deficient regimes, like democracy, are based on lack of knowledge, and even the ideal state is based on lies, which are necessary to persuade citizens to accept the privileges of a ruling class. For Nic-

colò Machiavelli, the ruler is unable to explain his calculations to the people. This approach has two versions: the positive version asserts that enlightened leaders must sometimes be duplicitous in order to further the well-being of their subjects; the negative version asserts that ideology is bad for people and must be exposed for what it is.

Second, ideology is a need for the ruled. It is not a lie but a justification based on manipulating the values of those who consume the ideological message. It is an expression of their social being. This approach has been called "sociology of knowledge" by Karl Mannheim. As socially conditioned ideas, ideologies are neither true nor false. Politics neither needs, produces, nor imposes ideology upon people from outside. It merely takes ideology into account. Politicians pay attention to prevailing social values. The legislator tells people what they want to hear. The public never actually supports a specific law, policy, or political decision, but supports, rather, the arguments that justify these actions. According to this premise, the ruled do not want to be disillusioned. They cling to their ideologies in the face of all contrary evidence. According to Karl Marx, people need illusion.

According to the first answer, the unmasking of ideology reveals the true intentions of those who offer it. According to the second, ideology reveals the social milieu of those who believe in it. Besides, since ideology does directly concern policy and law, but only their justifications, it is true, for both answers, that the same ideology can be claimed by two opposite policies, and the same policy justified by two opposing ideologies.

The way the "is" and the "ought" are mixed determines the distinction between kinds of ideology. There are two kinds of ideologies. *Transcendent* ideology speaks in the name of a transempiric reality; it approves or rejects a present in the name of a future, or it presents an "ought" as if it were an "is." *Immanent* ideology, of positivistic lineage, justifies the present, closing the doors to any alternative to the prevalent values, exhibiting given facts as if they were an "ought." It is an anti-ideological ideology. It is supported, for instance, by those who decline to distinguish between knowledge and valuation, assuming that values can be deduced from facts.

Supporters of ideologies vehemently oppose their adversaries and do not recognize their own postures as ideological. Daniel Bell, for example, attacks ideology as if it were always transcendent, proclaiming the end of ideologies. However, he himself offered an anti-ideological ideology, one that justified the cold war.

In recent years there has been renewed interest in ideology, especially in the fields of literary and cultural studies. Generally, their project is to unmask the many kinds of power relations which are assumed, a priori, to inhabit or to shape discursive and cultural practices.

References

Balaban, Oded. *Politics and Ideology: A Philosophical Approach.* Hampshire UK: Avebury, 1995.

Bell, Daniel. *The End of Ideology.* 2d ed. New York: Collier, 1962.

Fukuyama, Francis. "The End of History?" *The National Interest* 16 (1989), 3–18.

Geiger, Theodor. *Ideologie und Wahrheit* (Ideology and Truth). Berlin: Hermann Luchterhand, 1968.

Machiavelli, Niccolò. *The Discourses of Niccolò Machiavelli.* Ed. W. Stark. Pt. 5.1, Bk. 1, no. 11–12. London: Routledge and Kegan Paul, 1950.

Mannheim, Karl. *Ideology and Utopia.* New York: Harcourt, Brace, and World, 1936.

Marx, Karl, and Frederick Engels. "The German Ideology." In *Collected Works,* vol. 6. London: Lawrence and Wishart, 1976.

Oded Balaban

See also ERROR, DECEIT, AND ILLUSION; MARXIST PHILOSOPHY OF LAW

Ignorance
See MISTAKE AND IGNORANCE

Immunity
See POWERS AND RIGHTS

Imperfect Obligation

Ulpian's *Epitomé* (ca. A.D. 320) reports that Roman laws, and by extension obligations and rights, are of three sorts: *perfect* laws, which both provide penalties for violations and invalidate unlawful acts; *almost perfect* laws (*minus quam perfectae*), which provide penalties but do not invalidate what was done unlawfully; and *imperfect* laws, which merely require or forbid but neither stipulate penalties nor invalidate. Later, this threefold division was simplified so that laws, obligations, and rights were considered to be perfect if they included a penalty (often called a "sanction") and imperfect if they did not.

John Austin (1790–1859) argued that so-called imperfect laws are not laws at all but merely "counsels" because enforceability is a necessary component of a law. His argument has mostly carried the day, and the distinction is only rarely used in contemporary jurisprudence. Nevertheless, contemporary law does include some imperfect obligations. For example, many jurisdictions require everyone to report suspected cases of child abuse but provide penalties for failing to so report only in the case of certain professionals. Contrary to Austin, these imperfect laws are not entirely without effect: their violation might be brought forward, for example, in civil suits.

Moral obligations as such, insofar as they are not also legal or quasi-legal obligations, never include penalties; and so some writers see legal obligation as *perfect* and moral obligation as *imperfect*. Because moral obligation cannot be enforced, it is sometimes said that while perfect obligations carry with them correlated rights, imperfect obligations do not give rise to any rights at all. It is sometimes also claimed that the realm of the *perfect* is the realm of justice (whether moral or legal), while the realm of the *imperfect* is the realm of unrequited love, or charity.

The perfect/imperfect distinction is also understood in several other ways. Some obligations are said to be *imperfect* because they are phrased so vaguely that they do not make clear exactly what is demanded, while other obligations are much more precise and hence more *perfect*. Speed limits for automobiles are in this sense precisely defined, while the obligation of public officials to fulfill their duties responsibly and with diligence is much less precise.

Gaius (ca. second century A.D.) claimed that in Roman law some contracts are entered *stricti juris* but others are governed by the less precise idea of good faith and require the exercise of discretion to achieve fairness. It is sometimes observed that obligations that are imperfect by virtue of vagueness allow discretion in their discharge, while perfect obligations stipulate much more precisely what must be done.

Yet another tradition goes back to the Middle Stoa in ancient Greek philosophy and was popularized by Cicero (103–43 B.C.) in his *De officiis*. This tradition points out that most laws and moral codes require not perfection, but a somewhat lesser standard of conduct. Hence, these codes are only imperfect approximations of genuinely moral life. Cicero refers to ideal law and morality as *officium perfectum* and to lesser accommodations as *offica media*. In this sense, all legal systems are imperfect; we say, "Law is a blunt instrument."

The use of the perfect/imperfect distinction was most common in the eighteenth century, and Immanuel Kant (1724–1804) used it more extensively and creatively than did anyone else. Recently, quite a few moral philosophers (but very few legal philosophers) have reintroduced the distinction in their work, often referring to Kant. This has sometimes been the source of confusion, because the exact meanings of the terms have not always been specified clearly.

References

Austin, John. *The Province of Jurisprudence Determined.* 1832. London: Weidenfeld and Nicholson, 1971.

Campbell, T.D. "Perfect and Imperfect Obligations." *Modern Schoolman* 52 (1975), 285–294.

Kant, Immanuel. *Metaphysik der Sitten.* 1897. Trans. Mary Gregor as *The Metaphysics of Morals.* Cambridge: Cambridge University Press, 1991.

Schumaker, Millard. *Sharing Without Reckoning: Imperfect Right and the Norms of Reciprocity.* Waterloo ON: Wilfrid Laurier University Press, 1992.

Millard Schumaker

See also OBLIGATION AND DUTY; PRIMA FACIE OBLIGATION

Imputation and Exculpation

A person may be liable for an offense even if that person has not strictly satisfied all of the offense's elements. Similarly, a person may not be liable even if all the elements have been strictly satisfied. Imputation and exculpation are the means by which a person's guilt may be so established or avoided.

The criminal law contains a number of general doctrines that allow an element of an offense to be imputed to a person in cases where the element has not been strictly satisfied by that person. Complicity is a prime example of such a doctrine. In most jurisdictions, a person acting with the requisite mens rea, or state of mind, may be guilty of an offense requiring certain conduct if, rather than engaging in the conduct itself, the person merely facilitates, promotes, or solicits another's engaging in the conduct. Thus, accomplices may be convicted for the acts of the principal; conspirators may be convicted for acts of their co-conspirators. Another example of an imputation doctrine is the doctrine of transferred intent. Under this doctrine, an intent to cause a particular result will be imputed a person if that person intended to cause a sufficiently similar and related result.

Imputation doctrines, such as complicity and transferred intent, are useful devices for modifying and enlarging liability for a broad range of crimes without altering the definition of each individual crime. In general, imputation doctrines will be defensible to the extent they permit liability in conditions that are analogous to the occurrence of the imputed element, significantly increase deterrence, or enable prosecutors to overcome specific fact-finding limitations that juries may have.

Imputation doctrines, however, may be controversial because they allow for criminal liability under conditions that are not obviously the moral equivalent of the actual occurrence of the imputed element. For example, under some versions of the felony-murder rule, an accomplice in the commission of a dangerous felony may be found guilty of murder where a killing is committed by another accomplice in furtherance of the felony. Thus, the driver of a getaway car for a bank robbery in which a patron is killed may be found guilty of murder even though the driver neither caused nor intended the bank patron to die. Some would argue that it is unduly harsh, and inconsistent with general principles of criminal culpability, to treat the driver as a murderer merely based on his participation in the robbery. In response, the felony-murder rule is sometimes defended on (1) the retributive ground that a killing in the course of a felony is the natural and probable consequence of the felony for which the participants in the felony should be held accountable, or (2) the utilitarian ground that the rule deters felonies or killings in the course of felonies. Perhaps because these justifications rest on overly broad generalizations about felonies and the psychology of felons, the felony-murder rule has been abolished in England and Canada [English Homicide Act of 1957; *R. v. Vaillancourt*, 2 S.C.R. 636 (1987 Can.)]. The *Model Penal Code* also rejects the rule in favor of a mere presumption that felons recklessly endanger the lives of others. Nevertheless, the felony-murder rule in some form continues to exist in most United States jurisdictions.

Other common criminal law doctrines may also be conceptualized as imputations: the intent to engage in a criminal act may be imputed to a person whose intoxication prevented the formation of the intent where the intoxication was self-induced; the causing of a prohibited result may be imputed to a person based on the omission of an act in certain circumstances; intentions and actions may be imputed to nonhuman entities such as corporations. Sometimes it is unclear whether a legal rule should be conceptualized as an implicit imputation. The offenses of possession of burglary tools and possession of narcotics may be thought to implicitly impute to the possessor the intent to use these items in a socially harmful way. Possession of items so closely identified with criminal activity, however, may be thought to be so unnerving to the community as to be wrongful in its own right.

Exculpation is the converse of imputation. A person may be exculpated, that is, held not liable for the offense, even if that person has satisfied all the elements of the offense where a defense applies to that person. Insanity and self-defense are examples of common defenses. Thus, for example, a person who has satisfied the elements of murder by intentionally causing the death of another may be held not guilty of murder if the person was acting in self-defense or was insane at the time of the killing.

Exculpatory rules in criminal law operate differently than those relating to liability in two important respects. First, the prosecution in a criminal case typically is not required to prove beyond a reasonable doubt that an exculpatory rule does not apply to the defendant. Rather, the defendant bears the burden of proving the applicability of an exculpatory rule. This significant procedural distinction places pressure on the legal system to clearly identify when a fact exculpates, as opposed to when it merely shows that an element of the offense has not been satisfied. Is a defendant charged with murder required to show that she was subject to extreme emotional disturbance, which would render her liable for no more than manslaughter, or must the prosecution, in order to obtain a conviction for murder, show that the defendant was not subject to extreme emotional disturbance? Although conventions have developed settling these questions, there is no single general theory that adequately explains these conventions. Guideposts for assigning burdens, however, include intuitive judgments concerning what is prima facie wrongful or stigmatizing, which falls to the prosecution to prove, versus what excuses or mitigates, which falls to the defendant. Also relevant are more practical considerations, such as whether the prosecution or the defense typically has superior access to the relevant evidence and so is better suited to carry the burden.

Second, some exculpatory doctrines are not subject to imputation. Consider the case of a minor who commits a theft with the aid of an adult accomplice. As noted previously, under the doctrine of complicity, the act of theft will be imputed to the adult accomplice. In contrast, the minor's age, which will exculpate the minor of criminal liability, will not likewise be imputed to the adult. Thus, the adult accomplice, and only the accomplice, will be guilty of theft. The justification for not imputing the exculpatory fact while imputing the inculpatory act turns on our sense of moral responsibility. A theft has occurred for which the accomplice is felt to be partially responsible and the minor is felt to be excused. The doctrines of imputation and exculpation are devices that allow these moral intuitions to be expressed within the framework of the criminal law.

References

American Law Institute. *Model Penal Code and Commentaries*. Philadelphia: American Law Institute Press, 1985.

Cole, Kevin. "Killings During Crime: Toward a Discriminating Theory of Strict Liability." *American Criminal Law Review* 28 (1991), 73.

Fletcher, George P. *Rethinking Criminal Law*. Boston: Little, Brown, 1978.

Jeffries, John, Jr. "Defenses, Presumptions, and Burdens of Proof in the Criminal Law." *Yale Law Review* 88 (1979), 1325.

Robinson, Paul H. "Imputed Criminal Liability." *Yale Law Journal* 93 (1984), 609.

Smith, K.J.L. *A Modern Treatise on the Law of Criminal Complicity.* Oxford: Clarendon Press, 1991.

Wells, Celia. *Corporations and Criminal Responsibility.* Oxford: Clarendon Press, 1993.

Anthony M. Diloff

See also FICTIONS AND DEEMINGS; LIABILITY, CRIMINAL; PARTIES TO CRIMINAL CONDUCT

Incapacitative Rationale

Incapacitation is the idea of simple restraint: of rendering a convicted offender incapable, for a period of time, of offending again. Whereas rehabilitative and deterrent strategies seek to make the offender less criminally inclined, incapacitation presupposes no such change. Instead, obstacles are interposed to impede the person's carrying out whatever criminal inclinations he or she may have. Usually, the obstacle is the walls of a prison, but other incapacitative techniques are possible, such as exile or house arrest.

Incapacitation has usually been sought through predicting the offender's likelihood of reoffending. Those deemed more likely to reoffend are to be restrained—for example, by imposition of a prison term, or of a term of longer duration than they otherwise would receive. Traditionally, sentencing statutes have authorized such a strategy. The *Model Penal Code,* for example, permits an offender to be imprisoned if "there is undue risk that [he or she] will commit another crime." However, some recent legislation has sought to restrict reliance upon such predictive judgments. The 1991 English sentencing statute, for example, makes crime-seriousness the ordinary criterion for the sentence and permits extension of sentence on grounds of dangerousness only when serious prospective harm is involved. The 1988 Swedish sentencing law is still more restrictive of the use of prediction in sentencing.

Incapacitation seems most readily defensible on utilitarian assumptions. It would be necessary merely to establish the effectiveness of the strategy, in the sense that the aggregate benefits (crimes prevented) exceed the aggregate human costs (most notably, the added prison time for offenders). Even this utilitarian criterion of effectiveness, however, is not easily met in practice—because of the difficulty of establishing a significant net impact on crime rates.

It has for several decades been possible to devise prediction instruments having a modest capacity to forecast recidivism. Certain facts about offenders, for example, their previous criminal records and drug habits, are to a limited extent indicative of increased likelihood of recidivism. Taking a particular potential recidivist out of circulation, however, will not necessarily affect the overall crime rate. The net impact on crime would depend on such difficult-to-estimate factors as the potential length of the confined offender's residual criminal career, the number of remaining potential offenders, and the potential offenders' inducements to "replace" the criminal activities associated with confined offenders.

If a purely utilitarian perspective is not assumed, incapacitative strategies are open to challenge on a variety of fairness grounds. One problem derives from the tendency of forecasts of criminality to overpredict. Although statistical forecasting methods can identify groups of offenders having higher than average probabilities of recidivism, these methods show a disturbing incidence of "false positives": many of those classified as potential recidivists will, in fact, not be found to offend again. The rate of false positives is particularly high—as much as two false positives for every true recidivist—when forecasting serious criminality (for instance, violence). Ostensibly, the offender classified as dangerous is being confined to prevent him from infringing the rights of others. Depending on the extent of the overprediction, those offenders would not have committed that infringement—and are confined merely because people *like* them offend again, and the prediction instrument cannot specify which of them would actually do so. It should be noted, however, that the false-positive argument is only a conditional challenge to the incapacitative sentence: concern about false positives would diminish to the extent it were possible to predict more accurately.

A more fundamental objection to incapacitation strategies concerns their conflict with the requirements of proportionality. Punishment is a "moralizing" sanction, in the sense that it imposes its deprivations in a manner that conveys censure. Since punishment involves censure, its quantum should, arguably, fairly reflect *how wrong* the conduct is—that is, how serious it is. Proportionate sentences are designed to reflect the conduct's seriousness, whereas sentences based on prediction do not. To the extent that future offending can be forecast at all, the predictive criteria usually have little to do with the degree of reprehensibleness of the current offense. Instead, those criteria tend to reflect such ulterior matters as the number of previous arrests, age at first conviction, and so forth.

It has been suggested that the conflict with proportionality would be reduced if the predictive judgments were constrained within bounds set by the seriousness of the crime. Those bounds would be designed to prevent incapacitation from involving "excessive" disproportion of sentence. Such a strategy, however, may encounter a fairness/effectiveness tradeoff. Imposing longer sentences on high-risk offenders, if capable of affecting crime rates at all, is apt to do so only when substantial extra confinement is involved. Lengthy extra confinement will, however, infringe proportionality to a great degree. Shorter periods of added restraint may be somewhat less morally objectionable on grounds of disproportion but are not likely to have much impact on crime.

An alternative incapacitative strategy is that of "general" incapacitation. Here, no prediction of individual dangerousness is involved: penalties are scaled on other grounds, for example, according to the relative seriousness of crimes. However, to the extent incarceration is used as the penalty for the more serious crimes, there will be an incapacitative effect: those confined cannot commit crimes against citizens on the outside, during the term of confinement. If the magnitude of the penalty scale (that is, its overall degree of punitiveness) is also decided on other grounds—for example, that of desert—then the incapacitative impact becomes a mere side effect. Matters are otherwise, however, if the scale's magnitude is decided in part on incapacitative grounds. Suppose the penalty scale is increased in overall severity by 25 percent, for instance, in order to lengthen prescribed prison terms and thus augment the incapacitative effect. Then the objection can be made that such a scheme bypasses the moral agency of those confined: that offenders are being treated as though they were incapable of moral choice, much as incarcerated dangerous animals are.

References

American Law Institute. *Model Penal Code and Commentaries.* Philadelphia: American Law Institute Press, 1985.

Ashworth, Andrew. *Sentencing and Criminal Justice.* 2d ed. London: Weidenfeld & Nicholson, 1995.

Jareborg, Nils. "The Swedish Sentencing Reform." In *The Politics of Sentencing Reform,* ed. C.M.V. Clarkson and R. Morgan, 95–123. Oxford: Oxford University Press, 1995.

von Hirsch, Andrew. *Censure and Sanctions.* Oxford: Oxford University Press, 1993.

von Hirsch, Andrew, and Andrew Ashworth, eds. *Principled Sentencing.* Boston: Northeastern University Press, 1992.

Andrew von Hirsch

See also MOBILITY RIGHTS; PREVENTIVE DETENTION; PUNISHMENT

Inchoate Offenses

See ATTEMPTS

Included Offenses

The offense related to an offense principally charged, for which conviction is permitted instead of the principal offense, is known as an included offense. This is also known as a lesser included, necessarily included, or compound offense. Examples are conviction of manslaughter instead of murder, second-degree murder for first, assault for robbery (but not theft for robbery) or for sexual assault, and sexual assault for rape.

Retrial, conviction, acquittal, or dismissal for the same offense does not concern a different, included offense; these are known as double jeopardy for the same charge, conviction, or punishment. Not included are attempts, although these are involved in committing any offense. Not so called are criminal offenses of strict liability, which remain as an included actus reus after evidence of intent or knowledge is set aside, nor are multiple crimes arising from the same set of facts and parties, whether tried together and called joinder, or tried successively in the same or in different jurisdictions. Examples such as extortion in one region that is tried again as gangsterism in another, trafficking, transporting, and possessing the same contraband, even "driving impaired" for driving drunk where differently defined: these do not constitute included offenses, although among judges there are disagreements.

Included offenses are offenses all of whose elements are included among the elements that constitute another offense. Included offenses are also described as a part of a full offense, as having fewer of the essential elements that comprise the full offense, as an incomplete set from among the complete set of elements, as lesser than that greater one. This last metaphor does not refer to the lesser moral iniquity or legal seriousness of the offense, although frequently that lesser degree is also the case. This is shown by the fact that offenses both for indictment and for summary conviction may be reduced to their included offenses.

Convictions for lesser included offenses are sought in situations where evidence for commission of the complete set of elements in the greater offense is dubious or difficult to obtain, while evidence for the lesser set of elements is more available or is less costly to obtain. This situation is similar to the circumstances in which plea bargaining is used.

The acceptance of and the limitations upon included offenses are related to legal values. These values relate to differing evaluations of the benefits of refusing to accept lesser convictions. The outcome is "all or nothing," namely, conviction of the full offense or no conviction of any offense at all. These values are akin to ones that relate to procedural safeguards generally.

Favoring the acceptance of included offenses are values of social justice, that is, of protection for citizens and of retribution for the wrongdoer. The public is not protected by the release of persons who harmed others, nor is its interest in upholding its announced restrictions upon behavior. Better to convict for something lesser, than for juries to refuse to convict at all upon something greater. Offenders will not then be rewarded for their lack of competence.

In favor of limiting or abandoning included offenses are the values of individual justice. Allowing conviction for a crime of which one was not accused, because of defective proof of the elements in another crime's actus reus, appears to violate the principle of "no punishment without crime." Convicting for proven criminal intent, despite failure to prove the other elements, appears to violate the principle of "no crime without a law." As well, introducing such a charge upon the failure of another charge violates the right to due process, in particular, the notice of a charge and the opportunity to prepare and present a reply to it.

Acceptance, however, also protects offenders, namely, from juries that would rather convict for a dubiously proven, greater offense than allow complete escape. Conversely, the individual justice of not convicting beyond the evidence for an offense is indispensable to continuing public support for law.

Individuals' rights are not protected by some of the procedural settings for charging included crimes. The included charge may be made along with the original charge but, alternatively, the prosecution may amend its charge at any point. The judge may do so *proprio motu* (on his or her own initiative). This extends all the way up to the time that the case is sent to jury for verdict. Failure to allow for notice, preparation, and defense, however, would surely make a guilty verdict liable to reversal on appeal.

Alternatively, requiring that an included charge be made at the opening could induce a jury either to convict of only that crime, while sufficient evidence for the principal charge is available, or to convict of it when insufficient evidence of either has been put forward.

The doctrine of included offenses has both subjective and objective contexts for its employment. These relate to the mens rea and the actus reus of offenses, respectively. The subjective context relates to the characterization of some crimes as ones of general intent and others of specific intent. The distinction is drawn in terms of capacity: an offender may have the capacity only for a general intent, for example to assault, which may be insufficient for the specific intent needed, for example, to rob or to rape. The categories in which this distinction is drawn have been criticized as being incoherent in the light of the capacity needed for a behavior to be characterized as an actus reus of any sort at all and as overstepping judicial boundaries. The categories continue, nonetheless, to be employed.

The objective setting for included offenses has to do with the characterization of the actus reus in which the offense is putatively included. There is judicial agreement, although it is often blurred, that what constitutes the full offense cannot be the prosecutor's charge. The charge cannot include rape and murder as one offense, of which either is an included part. It is not so clear that the prosecutor's charge may not include together assault with a prohibited weapon and possession of a prohibited weapon. What must be shown is that the elements are necessarily related and not only accidentally combined.

The philosophical issues which remain are several. Given that the metaphors in which this doctrine is expressed, of "inclusion" "part/whole," "greater/lesser," of the "substance/accidentals" of the offense, cannot be taken at face value, the investigation of just how one offense includes another at all must be undertaken. Neither extension to all its instances nor comprehension (intension) of all its elements is a sufficient analysis. As well, whether this inclusion can be reduced to arbitrary drafting, or is conceivable in terms of the elements of conduct being necessarily included one within another, appears to be a challenge even when the crime is of statutory origin; this is a new setting for the natural/positive law interplay. Furthermore, a premium which may be unpayable is placed upon the ability to individualize actions, in order to discriminate which are the arbitrary additions and which fall necessarily within the including offense. Finally, the metaphors in which this doctrine is expressed are refreshed with each new philosophical psychology, whether hydraulic or computational or libertarian.

References

Blair, C.R. "Constitutional Limitations on the Lesser Included Offense Doctrine." *American Criminal Law Review* 21 (1984), 445.

"Criminal Procedure—Recognizing the Jury's Province to Consider the Lesser Included Offense: *State* v. *Ogden*." *Oregon Law Review* 58 (1980), 572.

Ettinger, J.L. "In Search of a Reasoned Approach to the Lesser Included Offense." *Brooklyn Law Review* 50 (1984), 191.

Gray, Christopher B. "'The Substance of the Offense': Included Crimes and the Philosophy of Substance." *Les Cahiers de Droit* 29 (1988), 795–805.

Hamrick, Tracy L. "Looking at Lesser Included Offenses on an 'All or Nothing' Basis: *State* v. *Bullard* and the Sporting Approach to Criminal Justice." *North Carolina Law Review* 69 (1991), 1470–1483.

"Jury Deliberations and the Lesser-Included Offense Rule: Getting the Courts Back in Step." *University of California at Davis Law Review* 23 (1990), 375.

Mascolo, E.G. "Procedural Due Process and the Lesser-Included Offense Doctrine." *Albany Law Review* 50 (1986), 263–304.

Williams, Glanville. "Included Offenses." *Journal of Criminal Law* 55 (1991), 234–253.

Christopher B. Gray

See also ACTUS REUS; IMPUTATION AND EXCULPATION; PARTIES TO CRIMINAL CONDUCT

Indeterminacy

A practical definition of law is that it is society's attempt to shape and regulate human conduct by means of signs, signals, and words, backed by the force of the state. Signs, signals, and words do not "hook onto" the real world by themselves; they must be interpreted and applied by the people who want to obey them and by the judicial system that wants to enforce them. Accordingly, the legal system is preoccupied with matters of interpretation. Indeed, some scholars assert that law is solely a matter of interpretation, that there is no such thing as the plain meaning of a word or signal. Consider one of the clearest possible signals: the familiar traffic signal light. Does red always mean "stop" and green always mean "go"? What if the red light is stuck; must automobiles stop and wait at the intersection for hours until it is repaired? A British firefighters' union called for a work slowdown; it instructed its drivers to stop at red lights even on the way to a fire. The relevant statute provided simply that "all vehicles" must stop at the red traffic signal. A court held that "common sense" did not require fire engines to comply with the traffic signal. However, the court was unable to explain its apparent departure from plain meaning.

Are any words plain enough to hook onto the real world without the need for interpretation? Proper names would seem to serve this function. Plato, in his early and neglected dialogue, *Cratylus*, speculated if the name Homer was the name of a particular definite person, a noun like "tree" was similarly the name of a particular and definite object. There could be many objects satisfying the term "tree" just as there could be many persons answering to the name Homer. Early in the twentieth century Bertrand Russell contributed the second significant analysis of indeterminacy and nominalism. Russell contended that a proper name is not a "word" at all. Unlike proper names, words can have indeterminate applications, and some (like "a square circle") no application at all.

As an example of an indeterminate application, Hilary Putnam asks of the seemingly plain word "tree," whether the number of trees is Canada is odd or even. Apart from the practical difficulty of counting all the trees, no answer is possible because of indeterminacy. Should bushes or hedges count as trees? Is a sapling a tree? Does an elm tree in a V-shape count as one tree or two? If your answer is one because it has the same root, would you apply the single-root theory to the banyan tree, whose roots drop down from the ends of its branches forming many other banyan trees, all of which are interconnected?

H.L.A. Hart has suggested that each word has a "core" incontrovertible meaning as well as indeterminate "penumbral" meanings. A maple tree is clearly a tree, but bushes and hedges are within the penumbra of the word "tree." Yet Hart's distinction can itself be problematic in some cases. Consider the word "persons" in the Fourteenth Amendment to the U.S. Constitution, which grants to "persons" due process and equal protection of the law. Courts have held that corporations are "persons" within the meaning of this provision. Recent American decisions have held that a fetus less than three months old is not a person, but a fetus more than six months old is very nearly a person. Hart's core/penumbra distinction does not appear to help in interpreting whether the word "persons" applies to corporations or fetuses.

The third and most recent philosophical development of indeterminacy began in 1960 with Willard Quine's work on radical translation. Quine argued that a linguist who is compiling a dictionary of an alien culture cannot be sure that the translations are correct. Although the linguist may translate the native word "gavagai" as "rabbit," there is no way to prove that what the linguist means by the word "rabbit" is what the natives mean. By extension we can never prove that any meaning we give to a word is the same meaning assigned to that word by any other person, even in our own culture; the other person might have a radically different conception. Yet we and the other person usually "get along" in daily life making the assumption that there is a commonality of meanings, and in practice this seems to work without too many rude surprises.

The large majority of lawyers and judges today appear to regard themselves as moderate formalists. They accept Russell and Hart, but are unwilling to go so far as Quine. Moderate formalists believe that words have core meanings, and that most words do not give rise to problems of interpretation in most cases. Indeed, they view most cases as "easy cases" that do not require interpretation of the applicable legal rules. To be sure, the "easy cases" are not appellate court cases in which attorneys and courts struggle over the application of various rules of law to the facts of the case. However, appellate court cases are a minute fraction of the cases that arise in everyday life. Most "easy cases" are not litigated.

It is difficult to describe even one "easy case." Recall that a red traffic signal can be problematic in some situations. One attempt to describe an easy case was the suggestion that a homeowner who eats ice cream in the privacy of her home cannot possibly be contravening any law, no matter how the law is interpreted. Consider, however, the following radical change of context: she deliberately eats the ice cream in front of a child who is starving. Here, eating the ice cream would violate the law against child abuse.

Lawyers earn their living by disputing the meanings of words, questioning whether a statute really applies to their client's situation. If a case involves a great deal of money, one side will surely argue that certain rules of law apply to the case and the other side will just as surely argue that those same rules of law, properly interpreted, do not apply. Lawyers will seek additional facts in order to reinterpret the context, either clarifying or casting further doubt upon whether the alleged rules of law apply to the case. As the argument proceeds, the very words in contention may appear to the judge or decision maker to become increasingly vague, ambiguous, and indeterminate. The fact that a judge decides the case for the parties does not settle the meaning of the words. In the next case, the facts will necessarily be different, and a new cycle of disputed interpretation and application could begin.

Is it possible that the "easy cases" of everyday life are only easy because no one wants to spend the time and money to litigate them? Can an easy case become a hard case simply by litigating it? Or does the infusion of additional financial resources eventually reach diminishing returns? Do most cases halt at some level of determinacy and resist any further attempts to be unraveled? These are the present philosophical battle lines; answers so far have been, well, indeterminate.

References

D'Amato, Anthony. "Pragmatic Indeterminacy." *Northwestern Law Review* 85 (1990), 148–189.
Kress, Kenneth. "Legal Indeterminacy." *California Law Review* 77 (1989), 283–337.
Quine, Willard Van Orman. *Word and Object.* Cambridge: MIT Press, 1960.

Anthony D'Amato

See also CRITICAL LEGAL STUDIES; DECONSTRUCTIONIST PHILOSOPHY OF LAW

Indian, North American
See ABORIGINAL LEGAL CULTURES

Indian Philosophy of Law

The Sanskrit word *dharma* is the nearest equivalent of the word "law." Dharma, however, means not only law, but also religion, morality, equity, custom, usage, virtue, disposition to justice, and most importantly, duty. Dharma connotes all these meanings because traditional Indian thought believes that life is one whole and any separation, for example, of the legal from the moral, the customary from the religious, is artificial. Dharma is also considered one among the four "human aims" (*purushārthas*), the other three being *artha* (material well-being), *kāma* (sexual desire), and *moksha* (spiritual liberation). For three thousand years, until the introduction of "law" by the British in the eighteenth century, Indian society was governed by dharma. Law and legality have not completely replaced ancient dharma in contemporary Indian society.

Indian jurists have written volumes on What is dharma? Dharma, it is stated, is eternal and is embedded in nature. Being eternal, dharma is not a human or divine creation. Dharma is a matter of discovery. In our investigation into dharma, we discover not only the dharma (laws) of nature but also the social

dharma (duty, obligation) of individuals and classes. The dharmas (laws) of nature and society are fixed. Indian society is divided into *varnas* or castes, each *varna* having its own dharma or duties (*varṇa-dharma*). Indian thought also divides life into four stages (*āshramas*), consisting of celibacy, householder, forest dweller, and the renouncer, and each stage of life, except the renouncer, has fixed dharmas. In addition, there are dharmas fixed for the roles people play, like wife, husband, and citizen.

There are three aspects of dharma. They are *āchāra, vyavahāra,* and *prāyaschitta. Āchāra* consists of ethicosocial rules and regulations that govern the day-to-day conduct of individuals, castes, and life stages (*āshramas*). *Vyavahāra* consists of the legal administration of justice, and *prāyaschitta* deals with the religious sin and its expiation. The kings administer justice according to their understanding of dharma; in case of doubt, they consult the learned pundits. Indian thought does not empower the kings with absolute sovereign power. Dharma, which is the "sovereign of the sovereigns," does not confer powers, it imposes duties and disabilities on kings. Kings do not have the power of legislation, but only the power to issue ordinances to administer dharma.

Dharma, which is eternal, is manifested in the Śruti and Smṛti literature of India. According to Manu, the greatest Indian lawgiver, the sources of dharma are (1) Śruti, which is the "revealed scripture" consisting of the four Vedas (3000–600 B.C.); (2) Smṛti, "remembered scripture" or tradition (600 B.C.–A.D. 800), consisting of Epics, Purāṇas, and the Dharma Śāstras; (3) Sadāchāra, or custom; and (4) "inner contentment," or conscience. Among these four sources of dharma, śruti, or scriptures, takes precedence over smṛti, or tradition, and tradition over sadāchāra, or custom; when all the three sources are silent, one should be guided by one's own conscience. Although the Vedas (śruti), being revealed scriptures, are the final court of appeal in all juristic matters, they contain scant legal material, and therefore Indian jurists refer to the Vedas very infrequently in the administration of justice.

Legal material in the Smṛti literature is contained in the Dharma Sutras (600–100 B.C.), which are written in aphoristic form by ancient sages like Gautama, Apasthambha, Baudhāyana, and Vasistha. Dharma Śāstras (100 B.C.–A.D. 800), written by eminent jurists like Manu, Yājñyavalkya, Nārada, Kātyāyana, and Bṛhaspati, are longer treatises and more juridical in nature and contain clear formulation of the duties and obligations of different *varnas*, the duties of the king, legislative procedures, family law and contract law, property and torts law, and procedures for the administration of justice.

Of all the *Dharma Sūtra* and *Dharma Śāstras,* the most celebrated juridical work was written by Manu called the *Manu Smṛti. Manu Smṛti* is the most important treatise in Indian jurisprudence and deals exhaustively with the duties of different castes, the duties of individuals in different stages of life, the duties of the king, eighteen types of disputes and their resolution, punishment, and penance for various kinds of sin, and so on. Manu and Yājñyavalkya were followed by juristic commentators who wrote "digests" or "treatises" on dharma. The commentarial tradition continued untill the British introduction of English law into India. Some of the prominent *Dharma Śāstra* commentators were Vachaspati Misra, Raghunandana, Kumarila, and Nilakantha.

The interpretative works on *Dharma Śāstras* are not interpretations of a single work, but the interpretation of the entire literature in the form of digests or treatises. As interpretation is impossible without a theory of hermeneutics, we find many hermeneutic insights in these writings, which discuss issues like the meaning of a word, the meaning of a text, whether the import of the *Dharma Śāstras* is the formulation of injunctions (*vidhi*) and prohibitions *(niṣedha)*, whether Vedic injunctions are self-validating, how to resolve conflicts between texts, and so on. In addition, we find in these texts attempts to deduce the particular from the general, the statute law from dharma, and the living law from the statute law.

The Muslim rule of India from the eleventh to the sixteenth century did not change the dharma-based legal system of India. Attempts to interfere in Hindu dharma have resulted in people clinging more to their ancient dharma. This accounts for the fact that treatises on dharma and interpretative works continued to be written during the Muslim rule.

When the British rule was instituted in Indian territories, Western conceptions of law and legal institutions were established. In the absence of the old kings' courts in British Indian territories, the British judges, from the eighteenth century, have acted as interpreters of dharma to settle disputes. The early British rulers did not intend to interfere, but only interpret, the *śāstra* and customs. Some British judges have read the *Dharma Śāstras* and digests, consulted the pundits, and have arrived at *legal* solutions to disputes. When an aggrieved party felt that a British judge had erred in interpreting dharma, they have appealed to a higher British court, some cases going all the way to the Privy Council. Interpreting dharma by a British judge with a *legal* background and appealing a dispute through the hierarchy of British courts, introduced into ancient Indian dharma elements of (1) certainty, (2) precedent, and (3) legality to dharma. Once the people started accepting the British judges' decisions as binding, the British became emboldened and some activistic governors-general started legislating. Thus, Governor-General Lord William Bentinck (1928–1935) in 1929 abolished through legislation the practice of *suttee* or burning of widows "for the good of mankind," and in 1956 the British permitted the remarriage of widows. In 1935 the British Parliament enacted the "Government of India Act," and in 1937 legislative councils in British Indian provinces were established, giving power to elected people's representatives to legislate. We thus find even in pre-independence India the origins of lawmaking through legislation by the Indian people.

On January 26, 1950, India became a democratic republic and has adopted a constitution which establishes a liberal polity and a legal system with an independent judiciary, a parliamentary system of democracy, and a civil bureaucracy and military subservient to the elected representatives. The Indian Constitution aims to create an open society based upon the principles of individual rights, emphasizing the contract model of relations among individuals. It provides for the creation of a secular state with freedom of conscience in religious matters.

Although the present Constitution of India and its legal system have survived for nearly five decades, the anguish of the Indian legal and political system is the anguish of the seeds of western political and legal ideas taking roots in the ancient dharma soil. The liberal Constitution of India is based on a philosophy of rights, dharma is a philosophy of obligations; liberalism stresses individualism, dharma stresses community; liberalism is oriented toward a contract society, dharma supports a status-based society; liberalism stresses individual freedom of choice, dharma stresses the duties of the individuals; liberalism stresses equality, dharma stresses a "separate but equal" principle; liberalism is secular, and dharma is sacred. Although liberalism and dharma have opposing legal philosophies, a liberal legal system was able to survive in Indian society because Indian thought is founded on "both-and" and not "either-or" logic. Western liberalism, therefore, has not eliminated ancient dharma, it lives side by side with dharma. Contemporary Indian society is both liberal and dharmic: liberal at the statute level but dharmic at the level of living law. Ancient Indian philosophy divides reality into *vyāvahārika* (empirical, phenomenal) and *paramārthika* (transcendental, noumenal). It is no exaggeration to say that contemporary Indian society follows dharma at the *paramārthika* level and is guided by the Constitution at the *vyāvahārika* level.

References

Austin, Granville. *The Indian Constitution: Cornerstone of a Nation.* Oxford: Clarendon Press, 1978.
Banerjee, A.C. *The Constitutional History of India.* Delhi: Macmillan, 1978.
Dharma Sastras: Brhaspati, Manu, Narada. Trans. in the Sacred Books of the East series. Vols. 25 and 32. Oxford, 1886, 1887. Reprint, Delhi: Motilal Banrsidass, 1964, 1966.
Dharma Sutras: Apastambha, Gautama, Baudha. Trans. in the Sacred Books of the East series. Vols. 2 and 7. Oxford, 1897. Reprint, Delhi: Motilal Banrsidass, 1965.
Jain, M.P. *Indian Constitutional Law.* Bombay: M.M. Tripathi, 1978.
Kane, P.V. *History of Dharmasastra.* 5 vols. Poona: Bhandarkar Oriental Research Institute, 1930–1962.

S.S. Rama Rao Pappu

See also ABORIGINAL LEGAL CULTURES; ISLAMIC PHILOSOPHY OF LAW; JAPANESE AND ASIAN PHILOSOPHY OF LAW

Information on Philosophy of Law: Study, Research, and Materials

Philosophy of law directly affects the material output of the legal enterprise. What we regard as sources of law (the legitimate object of study and research), what are their form and content as well as their normative value and functions in the legal process, and so ultimately whether they get published or not, are all influenced by our philosophical view of law. Conversely, the materials and objects available for legal study and research decisively shape the form, substance, and vision of one's jurisprudential thinking and materially affect the authority and persuasiveness of propositions and actions.

Yet this evaluation of the significance of jurisprudence is not readily accepted. At one extreme, philosophy of law is dismissed as armchair abstract speculation. At another, its particularistic and imperialistic claim for the complete truth in normative jurisprudence is seriously contested.

Philosophy of Law in Legal Study and Practice

Legal education in North America, as in England, was traditionally the by-product of apprenticeship supplemented, or occasionally displaced by, tutorials and lectures offered by judges or practitioners in schools organized by the legal profession. Since legal training/education was brought into the mainstream of the liberal arts university and popularized by Christopher Langdell's case-method teaching, the philosophical approach to law and law teaching has struggled to assert its place in law schools. The Round Table on Jurisprudence and Legal History of the Association of American Law Schools at the Thirty-Seventh Annual Meeting in Chicago, December 29, 1939, is one of the earliest attempts at the issues. University law teachers, as the relatively younger members, were under considerable pressure to legitimize their academic status by vigorously engaging in theoretical study and critical analysis of the subject matter of their learning and at the same time to distance themselves from the strong vocationalism of the legal profession. For this purpose, jurisprudence appeared to be an appropriate and effective vehicle for them to achieve full academic partnership.

The question respecting the importance of jurisprudence in university legal education ultimately focuses more on its role and significance to the practice of law than its study and research. The rules, principles, and standards used both for guiding one's own conduct and for other-regarding criticism, as well as for the taking of committed political action, are referred to as "the internal point of view of law." Jurists, judges, and legal practitioners by virtue of their formal legal training and professional responsibility cannot help belonging to its elite group known as the "interpretive community," whose collective internal viewpoint exerts a direct and powerful influence on law's formation and transformation. As well, the category of "hard cases" in contrast to "easy cases," also as conceived by H.L.A. Hart, involves decisions, mainly judicial, where rules are neither clear nor determinate in meaning or in application, where different principles compete for primacy and control, or where value judgments are in conflict among practitioners.

In both these instances, theory and practice in law are inextricably linked; there is no sharp distinction between what the law is and what it ought to be; authoritative and effective decisions and politicized normative commitments and actions in both the legal world and the social fields forever interact and mutually shape. Even the most routine and mundane tasks of law practice become philosophically and politically informed. These views are particularly compelling at the international level, where courts, general or specialized, are accorded a less important status and role, and where treaties, especially those of a multilateral nature, often are drafted deliberately in general and vague terms and thus susceptible to divergent interpretations and applications. In order to play an active and relevant role, international lawyers are advised to conceive "cases" in a much broader sense to include all authoritative and effective decisions in the entire normative process.

The expectations and communications of value-impacting decisions of individuals, groups, and institutions in the broad social context are no less internal than those of the legal elite. Normative guidance must be sought from actions and communications of a normative nature of all citizens individually or collectively manifested in the public domain. If governmental bodies, collectivities, and individuals are all legitimate participants in the legal process, wielding varying degrees of effective power and normative command and persuasion, then the distinctness of law as a "discipline-effect" phenomenon would be much less source-based or focused on lawmaking entities.

Legal Philosophy in the Law Schools

One preliminary question is whether jurisprudence should be taught as a credit course, separately in law schools, in joint degrees, or in other disciplines, compulsory or optional, as opposed to having it incorporated in courses on substantive law or in some sort of an introductory course to law, such as "the foundations of law" and treated at a time considered most appropriate by the teacher in the course of teaching. Undoubtedly, this latter form of presentation does have the value-added advantage of saving time, and, above all, enhancing the practical relevance of theoretical approach to the study of law. A counterargument stresses that "the inclusion of a detailed and exclusively analytical treatment of particular legal concepts such as right, duty, personality, and ownership may impair the balance and structure of a jurisprudence course which aims to encourage the student to view law from many contrasting aspects (including sociological, analytical, and ethical viewpoints) and achieve a balance between these approaches."

University legal education was introduced at a time when faith in positivist legal thinking and the fetishism of legal formalism and the pure law prevailed. With the langdellian approach firmly entrenched at Harvard Law School, a leader in American legal education, the case-method and its highly inductive, analogy-saturated socratic style of question and answer virtually swept the entire scene of Anglo-American legal education. In most common law countries, law practice was and admittedly still is mainly pragmatic, technical, and case oriented. However, the twentieth century witnessed a cornucopia of innovative jurisprudential thinking and ideas. All made serious attempts to transform the way law was taught through either curriculum reform or imaginative research. Examples were the American legal realist's advocacy for clinical training, the configurative jurisprudence of policy science at the Yale Law School, Columbia University's sociological jurisprudence, Chicago Law School's law and economics, and the critical strand of the Harvard scholarship. Conceptual jurisprudence proved remarkably resilient under constant attacks and criticism, however. Among many reasons are the cogency in analytic skills of the case method, and the lasting authority and effectiveness of positive law. Perhaps the most damaging weakness of many new jurisprudential theories was their

I

conspicuous lack of a comprehensive theoretical framework and a coherent body of thought, which not only manifest the internal points of view of citizens as participants in the legal process but also make sense of the accounts of detached external observers and the behaviors of Oliver Wendell Holmes' "bad man."

The most reliable and official sources for ascertaining the nature and content of courses on jurisprudence or philosophy of law are course synopses and outlines published in calendars, syllabuses, and similar materials issued by law schools, philosophy departments, and related disciplines, as well as courses offered in joint degree programs by the law faculty and the philosophy department. *The Guide to Legal Studies in Europe* is the most comprehensive basic tool for identifying European universities offering courses on jurisprudence or related subjects as well as their nature and level. The *Lawasia Directory of Law Courses* in the Asia and West Pacific regions is another useful tool.

Among the jurists, philosophers, schools of thought, and jurisprudential concepts and issues, there are undoubtedly favorites and weighted authorities. For example, according to the surveys conducted in Great Britain in 1973 and 1984 and published, respectively, in the 1974–1975 *Journal of the Society of Public Teachers of Law,* and the 1985–1986 volume of *Legal Studies,* H.L.A. Hart, John Austin, Ronald Dworkin, Lon Fuller, Hans Kelsen, Karl Llewellyn, and Roscoe Pound stood out. The favored schools are also within expectation. These include legal positivism, natural law, marxist theory, and sociological jurisprudence. Works of the philosophers of law mentioned above are also the preferred texts, along with the distinctly important text of John Rawls' *A Theory of Justice* and the historically favored *Lloyd's Introduction to Jurisprudence.* While these surveys aptly describe the state of the teaching of jurisprudence in British universities, the situation would be somewhat different in the United States, Canada, and in other common law jurisdictions, and certainly in the civil law countries of Europe.

Many landmark publications and seminal texts in the field of philosophy of law are in fact authored by nonlaw scholars. Most, if not all, of postmodern theories of law, the "law and" jurisprudence, such as law and economics, law and literature, critical legal studies, and autopoiesis of law, draw heavily on the ideas and insights of the related or not so related nonlaw disciplines. Many law schools have started to recruit or invite teachers from other disciplines to join in giving courses on jurisprudence. Of particular significance are the many and increasing number of joint degree programs on philosophy of law offered by the law faculty and the department of philosophy.

Legal Philosophy in Non–Law School Faculties

Teaching and study of philosophy of law in the departments of philosophy in university is widely accepted as an integral and legitimate part of the teaching and study of philosophy. Therefore, there is neither need nor desire on the part of philosophers, political scientists, and sociologists to engage in strategic discourses of self-justification for engaging in normative scholarship, as teachers in law schools must do. It is perfectly normal that few writings regarding the study and teaching of philosophy of law in the broader university are found in any indices to philosophical or related literature. This is confirmed by the marked lack of references of this nature in *Teaching Philosophy,* a journal dealing specifically with theoretical issues on the teaching of philosophy, the nature of curricula, courses, and pedagogy as well as interdisciplinary courses with philosophical content.

Scholarship and Scholars in Philosophy of Law

Legal theory and legal scholarship are intimately linked. Legal positivism and conceptual jurisprudence spawned and sustained the orthodoxy of an expository tradition. The atomistic and deconstructive approach of the realists threw serious doubts on the value of legal treatises. Yet the realist-influenced casebooks brought to a fine art the inclusion of the "snippet" from philosophy, sociology, or economics. The neoconceptualists have yet to fully revive the importance and vigor of doctrinal writing. Searching for "cases on all fours" becomes the new faith. Compiling casebooks and annotated statutes have started to unduly preoccupy and overtax the intellectual elites of the law. Recording and digesting judicial decisions by topics have become the major concern of commercial entities, increasingly mechanized and empowered by computer. Increasingly, the responsibility of systematizing and clarifying the law has also been taken over by commercial entities. Loose-leaf becomes a predominant form of publishing, not only materials in regulatory fields but also traditional doctrinal texts; and a continuing stream of new cases, legislative enactments, and other documents forever updates its content. It has been suggested that with the West Publishing Company's indiscriminate publication of cases and the marked increase in electronic legal databases and in searching and correlating texts by facts and/or keywords, a new version of "mechanical jurisprudence" threatens to emerge, which espouses not only the automation of legal reasoning but also the idea that a computer dispenses objective "technical" legal justice: a scenario which would be highly antithetical to legal scholarship, however differently one would conceptualize the law in a digital world. Fortunately, it seems that the decline of the expository orthodoxy and the commercialization of law identifying and clarifying functions may have helped liberate the creative and imaginative potential of jurists and philosophers. Scholarly writings on jurisprudence have since flourished; countless monographs have been published. The expository works which continue to prevail in some areas have become more self-conscious and sophisticated. Even the so-called practical doctrinal scholarship has moved away from its narrow and unreflective tradition characterizing the earlier version of the expository orthodoxy.

Like their counterparts in other academic disciplines, teachers or researchers active in philosophy of law also pursue their common interest and share ideas by means of institutional arrangements and organized activities. These collective entities not only frequently publish or sponsor the publication of the intellectual output of members' joint intellectual efforts, but may also serve as funding agents. Among those either devoted exclusively to or having a keen interest in philosophy of law, there is first of all the International Association for Philosophy of Law and Social Philosophy (known as the IVR, from the German version of its name, the *Internationale Vereinigung für Rechts- und Sozialphilosophie*) and its six dozen national branches. Many other learned societies, including especially those in closely related fields, such as sociology and law, social philosophy, and political philoso-

phy, which have a keen interest in legal philosophy, have also been founded at the regional (for example, the North American Society for Social Philosophy), national (for example, the Committee on Law and Philosophy of the American Philosophical Association, and the Canadian Society for Political Philosophy and Philosophy of Law), and local level (for example, the good number of research centers or institutes in philosophy of law established either within or affiliated with various universities: Paris and Brussels, Caen and Bordeaux, Oñati and Bologna, Graz and Frankfurt). Publications such as the *Directory of American Philosophers* and its companion volume, the *International Directory of Philosophy and Philosophers,* are specifically designed to provide information respecting organizations, universities, institutes, societies, publications, journals, publishers, as well as faculty and their specialities, student enrollment, and degrees offered. Philosophy of law teachers as well as those having particular interest in the subject can be easily identified by using the subject index found in directories of law teachers in Canada and in the United States. Searching these and university catalogs is now feasible online.

Postgraduate Study in Philosophy of Law
Another aspect of scholarly research in jurisprudence is postgraduate study. Increasingly, jurisprudence has become a legitimate thesis topic for master or doctoral degrees in law or other related fields and has been frequently so chosen. Presumably, most law schools and departments of philosophy which offer postgraduate studies are readily accessible to qualified candidates for such a pursuit. University calendars found in the reference department of university libraries or law libraries are the best sources for information in this respect. However, occasionally the theoretical study of law at the postgraduate level is especially promoted and publicized in journals of jurisprudence, philosophy, or other closely related fields. Due to its highly interdisciplinary nature, philosophy of law has become a favorite subject for postgraduate degrees or other special programs offered jointly by the faculty of law and the department of philosophy. Other sectors of the university often participate in such joint endeavors as well. For example, there are the joint degree program in law and philosophy at the University of Pennsylvania

I

and the special program in philosophy of law at the University of Western Ontario. There is also the annual European Erasmus Seminar on Legal Theory organized by the Katholieke Universiteit Brussel and the Facultés Universitaires Saint-Louis in Brussels since 1989. These latter two universities, together with the European Association for the Teaching of Legal Theory, also founded a European Academy of Legal Theory that offers a master's degree in legal theory and funds the European award for legal theory.

General dissertation abstracts and bibliographies of theses, international, national, or local in scope should be consulted to identity theses on jurisprudence. Examples of current publications of this kind include *Dissertation Abstracts International: Series A, Humanities and Social Sciences,* the *Index to Theses with Abstracts Accepted for Higher Degrees by the Universities of Great Britain and Ireland and the Council for National Academic Awards,* and Canadian theses published by the National Library of Canada. *Index to Law School Theses and Dissertations,* by Sanford R. Silverburg, in 1995 covers American law schools only. Hein's *Legal Theses and Dissertations* Microfiche Project is the latest of such sources.

Funding for Study and Research in Philosophy of Law

Funding is better understood in the context of funding for legal education and for the general social sciences and humanities programs of which law study used to be a neglected part. Since funding of legal education in universities was also caught in the polemics between academic lawyers and the bar and squeezed by government's reluctance to subsidize vocational training of which a highly lucrative profession claims control, funding of innovative legal research has become much more challenging. A number of such projects and programs were either stillborn or aborted before having had a chance to develop. The few notable exceptions, such as the Law and Economics at Chicago, the Policy Science Jurisprudence at Yale, and the Critical Legal Studies at Harvard are all funded by certain farsighted intellectual commitments and enjoy strong institutional support. Since the 1980s in both Canada and England, the general climate of opinion strongly favors applied research. This is reflected in funding policies for areas

such as sociolegal studies, where a high priority is given to policy-oriented works. Funds for "pure" or "fundamental" research are hard to find. While there are both historical and contemporary reasons for the paucity of funding of theoretical legal research, persuasive arguments nevertheless have been made.

New and imaginative funding schemes for research and publication of jurisprudential research are possible. With the increasing appreciation of the relationship of legal scholarship to the profession, learned societies may be established and developed into a viable mechanism for promoting and supporting theoretical legal scholarship. For example, in Canada, the Osgoode Society promotes research in legal history, and, in England, the Socio-Legal Studies Association signifies the coming of age of a particular interdisciplinary idea. A good number of jurisprudential titles have been either regularly or occasionally published by learned societies in the field.

Facing the shortage of special funding sources, academic scholars of jurisprudence have to resort to general granting agencies for support. There are a number of such bodies whose purview of interest covers the promotion of theoretical legal research. The publications and directories listed in the publications section (funding), which follows this discussion and which are widely available in university libraries, should be consulted. The subject index of these publications includes specific headings such as "law," "jurisprudence," "legal theory," "philosophy of law," or simply "philosophy."

Publications in Philosophy of Law

Legal texts of a jurisprudential nature can be readily identified in universities' catalogues and periodical indices using either the term "jurisprudence," "philosophy of law," or "legal theory." Many of the progressive and postmodern legal thoughts have made their way into the subject headings used in periodical indices: for example, headings such as sociological jurisprudence, economic jurisprudence, law and politics, critical legal studies, critical race theory, and feminism. University presses are predominant publishers of works on philosophy of law, and Oxford University Press is outstanding among them in both quantity and quality. Learned societies also sponsor the publication of such works. Commercial establishments which have published and will publish quality philosophical works are not difficult to identify. In this respect, past record is a useful guide, though insistence on subsidizing the publication of such works by that of practical texts remains an important concern. Law book publishing is still controlled by a few leading publishing houses. Unfortunately, they have a firm, rigid, and very narrow idea about what constitutes a law book.

There are many journals specially devoted to theoretical legal scholarship. Some have their interest clearly indicated in the title of the journals. Others are specifically intended to promote a particular school of thought and are very polemical. It bears special emphasis that law reviews of a general nature, especially those published by elite law schools and learned societies, are among the best sources for jurisprudential writings. As a matter of fact, it is this very dedication which has attracted the attention of the opponents of theoretical scholarship, caused members of the legal community to spill much ink over "the growing disjunction between legal education and the legal profession," and generated some renewed heated debates on the subject. It would be a fair description of the present state of the enterprise of law to say that in all its three constitutive components, that is, laws, research, and materials, we are in a world of polyjuriality (legal pluralism) rich in competing value beliefs, divergent in approaches and methodology, and open and inclusive in sources and materials.

The magnitude of periodical articles is even more impressive. Many thousands of titles have been identified by simply searching under the heading "jurisprudence" or "philosophy of law" in the *Index to Legal Periodicals, Current Law Index, Index to Foreign Legal Periodicals, Index to Canadian Legal Periodical Literature,* and the *Index to Canadian Legal Literature.* For example, from January 1926 to September 1928, the *Index to Legal Periodicals,* one of the most scholarly indexes, lists forty-two titles, while from September 1988 to August 1990, the number increases to more than three hundred. The first volume of the *Index to Foreign Legal Periodicals* lists five hundred titles for the three years 1960–1962, whereas close to three hundred have been found in the 1994 volume alone. Many of these articles are also found in bibliographies and indices published in law-related fields, such as those given in the fol-

lowing paragraph. Few legal subjects match the literature on philosophy of law in richness and diversity.

There is no comprehensive and up-to-date bibliography on philosophy of law, let alone one systematically organized with easily accessible topical subdivisions. Dias' *A Bibliography of Jurisprudence,* which predates the postmodern legal movements, is designed as a companion volume to his work on jurisprudence. Fortunately, it is a standard feature of scholarly publications to include an extensive list of new literature on the chosen subject matter. This is true also for collections of essays in honor of distinguished legal philosophers. Comprehensive bibliographies on particular schools of law or legal thought have been published, for example, A.J. Trevino's *The Sociology of Law: A Bibliography of Theoretical Literature* (Rochester: Schenkman Books, 1994) and R.W. Buaman's *Critical Legal Studies: A Guide to the Literature* (Scranton, PA, and Boulder, CO: Westview Press, 1996). For a short period early this century, the *American Political Science Review* and the *American Journal of Jurisprudence* published lists of titles available in this area. Both the book review section and the new books received section in periodicals in the field of the philosophy of law are good sources for new publications. Of particular interest is the *Current Legal Theory: International Journal for the Theory of Law and Its Documentation,* which since 1983 has offered a biennial full international bibliography covering not only all recent publications in the major languages but also in less known languages, providing an English translation of the title and an abstract. In general, most comprehensive bibliographies of law include sections on philosophy of law and related subjects. *Law Books in Print,* which publishes titles in English throughout the world, contains a good number of current titles under the heading "jurisprudence." A few monographic series are given in the Series List section of *Law Books in Print.*

It should be pointed out that for serious researchers even journals on philosophy and other law-related subjects should not be ignored. To tap the intellectual resources of this nature, special subject bibliographies and indices, especially those in the field of philosophy, social sciences, and humanities should be consulted. Titles such as *Bibliographie de la philosophie (Bibliography of Philosophy),*

Repertoire bibliographique de la philosophie (International Philosophical Bibliography), Philosophical Books, and *Philosophers' Index* should not be missed. There are also a number of retrospective bibliographies of philosophy. Above all, a good number of readily available periodicals are devoted specifically to the study and research of jurisprudence. These are provided in the publications (journals) section which follows this discussion. (Journals of interdisciplinary studies of specific subjects are excluded.) Perhaps it would be appropriate to note that information of a legal nature, including that pertinent to the study and research of philosophy of law, is increasingly being published on the Internet. It would be highly desirable that one be adequately prepared to explore cyberspace.

Collections in Philosophy of Law

To ensure that faculty members and researchers are well informed of new and innovative thoughts on jurisprudence, university law libraries must strengthen their collections on legal philosophy and vigorously promote them. The librarian's law is the most comprehensive imaginable. Librarians by virtue of their professional responsibility must be prepared to harness all potential sources of intrinsic authority in a world of polycentric normativity and to tap compelling legal rationality across jurisdictions.

To fulfill their optimal responsibility in this crucial respect, university law libraries must be prepared to extend their responsibility of collecting research materials much beyond the traditional sources of law as notoriously typified by those of a positive law nature, and to break with the primacy given to "primary" over "secondary" sources. The unrepresentative nature of judicial decisions in the total scheme of dispute resolution and lawmaking and the disproportionate authority accorded them are widely criticized. That legislation is contingent, partisan, and unduly influenced by special interests is common knowledge. The rationality of legislation in juridification must be critically evaluated. For this there are Fuller's unwritten rules as well as yet-to-be-formulated principles, including Dworkin's principles of political morality. For a broader conception of law and of legal materials, William Twining is particularly articulate and outspoken. While deploring the overconcentration in libraries of materials of positive law

and vocational texts, he explicitly points out the lack of, among other primary legal documents, records of all institutions specialized to law, be these governmental, "para-statal," or private. The factum of appellate courts as well as lawyers' documents are conspicuously missed in library collections.

In search of a new paradigm and perspective in collections development, one may even read A.W.B. Simpson's historiographical works and others in the same genre as important counterparts to law reports. It is perhaps an overexaggeration that lawyers who aspire to be architects rather than mere working masons should fill their bookshelves with books of classical literature rather than law reports. Yet this is the very tenet of the teaching of the "law and literature" strand of postmodernism. As mentioned previously, it is particularly apt to conceive of case law in broad terms in international law. The "incidents" theory is an interesting and innovative idea there. It is no less compelling to define cases in domestic law in equally generous terms. An innovative interdisciplinary approach to law calls for juridification on the basis of authoritative and effective decisions informed by enlightened political morality in the entire lawmaking and application process.

Kuo-Lee Li

ANNEX A: Funding

Annual Register of Grant Support. Chicago: Marquis Academic Media, Marquis Who's Who, 1969– .

Awards Almanac: An International Guide to Career, Research, and Education Funds. Detroit; London; Washington DC: St. James Press, 1995.

Canadian Directory to Foundations. 6th ed. Toronto: Canadian Centre for Philanthropy, 1985.

Cantrell, Karen. *Funding for Law: Legal Education, Research and Study, Law School Fellowships and Interships, Grants for Legal Research.* Phoenix: Oryx Press, 1991.

Coleman, William E. *Grants in the Humanities: A Scholar's Guide to Funding Sources.* 2d ed. New York: Neal-Schuman Publishers, 1984.

Directory of Grants in the Humanities. Phoenix: Oryx Press, 1986– .

Directory of Research Grants. Scottsdale AZ: Oryx Press, 1975– .

Faculty Grants Directory: Funding Sources for the Humanities, Social Sciences, and the Arts—With Special Focus on Religion and Theology. Pittsburgh PA: Association of Theological Schools in the United States and Canada, 1992– .

Federal Government Funding Sources: A Practical Guide for the Social Sciences. Ottawa: Social Science Federation of Canada, 1993.

The Foundation Grants Index. New York: The Foundation Center, 1971.

The Grants Register. Chicago: St. James Press, 1969– .

Krathwohl, David R. How to Prepare a Research Proposal: Guidelines for Funding and Dissertations in the Social and Behavioral Sciences. 3d ed. Syracuse: Syracuse University Press, 1988.

Krickau-Richter, Lieselotte. EC Research Funding: 3rd Framework Programme: A Guide for Applicants. 3d rev. ed. Brussels: Commission of the European Communities, 1992.

Policy Grants Directory. Urbana IL: Policy Studies Organization, 1977– .

Ries, Joanne B. Applying for Research Funding: Getting Started and Getting Funded. Thousand Oaks CA: Sage, 1995.

ANNEX B: Journals (Current)

American Journal of Jurisprudence. Notre Dame: Notre Dame Law School, 1956– .

Archiv für Rechts- und Sozialphilosophie = Archives de philosophie du droit et de sociologie juridique = Archives for Legal Philosophy and Social Philosophy. Wiesbaden: Franz Steiner, 1907/1908.

Ars Interpretandi: Journal of Legal Hermeneutics. Padua: CEDEM, 1996– .

Australian Journal of Law and Society. Sydney: School of Law, Macquarie University, 1982– .

Cambridge Studies in Philosophy and Public Policy. Cambridge: Cambridge University Press, 1988– .

Canadian Journal of Law and Jurisprudence. London ON: University of Western Ontario, 1988– .

Canadian Journal of Law and Society = Revue canadienne de droit et société. Montreal: Université de Québec à Montréal, Département des sciences juridiques, 1994– .

Columbia Journal of Law and Social Problems. New York: Columbia Law School, 1965– .

Continuity and Change: A Journal of Social Structure, Law, and Demography in Past Societies. Cambridge: Cambridge University Press, 1986– .

Current Legal Theory: International Journal for the Theory of Law and Its Documentation. Tilburg, Netherlands: Tilburg University Press, 1983– .

Droit et société (Law and Society). Paris: Librarie générale de droit et de jurisprudence, 1985– .

Droits: revue française de theorie juridique (Rights: French Review of Legal Theory). Paris: PUF, 1985.

Ethics: An International Journal of Social, Political, and Legal Philosophy. Chicago: University of Chicago Press, 1938– .

Faxue Zazhi (Journal of Jurisprudence). Beijing: Beijing Jurisprudence Society (text in Chinese).

Harvard Journal of Law and Policy. Cambridge MA: Harvard Society for Law and Public Policy, 1985– .

International Journal for the Semiotics of Law. Merseyside: Deborah Charles, 1988– .

International Journal of the Sociology of Law. London: Academic Press, 1979– .

Journal of Christian Jurisprudence. Virginia Beach VA: Regent University, School of Law and Government, 1980– .

Journal of Law and Religion. St. Paul MN: Hamline University, School of Law, 1983– .

Journal of Law and Society. Oxford: Blackwell, 1982– .

Journal of Legal Pluralism and Unofficial Law. Published by the Foundation for the Journal of Legal Pluralism in association with the African Studies Centre, UCLA, 1981(?)– .

Journal of Legal Studies. Chicago: University of Chicago Law School, 1972–(?).

Law and Critique; Journal of Critical Legal Studies. Liverpool: Deborah Charles, 1991– .

Law and History Review. Ithaca: Cornell Law School, 1983.

Law and Philosophy. Dordrecht; Boston: Kluwer, 1982– .

Law and Policy. Oxford: Blackwell, 1979– .

Law and Social Inquiry: Journal of the American Bar Foundation. Chicago: University of Chicago Press, 1976– .

Law and Society Review. Amherst: Law and Society Association, Hampshire House, University of Massachusetts, 1966– .

Law and State. Tubingen: Institut fur wissenschaftliche Zusammenarbeit, 1970– .

Legal Studies (Society of Public Teachers of Law). London: Butterworth, 1947– .

Legal Theory. Cambridge: Cambridge University Press, 1995– .

Oxford Journal of Legal Studies. Oxford: Oxford University Press, 1981– .

Oxford Socio-Legal Studies. Oxford: Clarendon Press; New York: Oxford University Press, 1979– .

Ratio Juris. Oxford: Basil Blackwell, 1988– .

Research in Law and Economics. Greenwich CT: JAI Press, 1979– .

Res Publica; A Journal of Legal and Social Philosophy. Liverpool: Deborah Charles, 1991– .

Social and Legal Studies. London: Sage, 1992– .

Social Philosophy and Policy. Bowling Green OH: Social Philosophy and Policy Center, Bowling Green State University, 1983– .

Studies in Law, Politics and Society. Greenwich CT: JAI Press, 1990– .

Studies in Social Philosophy and Policy. Bowling Green OH: Social Philosophy and Policy Center, Bowling Green University, 1983– .

Vera Lex. Pleasantville NY: Natural Law Society, 1980– .

Windor Review of Legal and Social Issues. Windsor: Faculty of Law, University of Windsor, 1989– .

Yale Journal of Law and Feminism. New Haven: Yale University, Faculty of Law, 1989– .

Yale Journal of Law and Humanities. New Haven: Yale University, Faculty of Law, 1988– .

Annex C: Monographic Series (Current)

After the Law. New York: Routledge, 1992– .

Amherst Series in Law, Jurisprudence, and Social Thought. Ann Arbor: University of Michigan Press, 1991– .

Applied Legal Philosophy (series). Brookfield VT: Dartmouth, 1991– .

Archives de philosophie du droit (Archives of Philosophy of Law). Nouv. Ser. Paris: Sirey, 1952– .

Bibliothèque de philosophie comparée: philosophie du droit (Library of Comparative Philosophy: Philosophy of Law). Bordeaux: Editions Biere, 1985– .

Cambridge Studies in Philosophy and Law. Cambridge: Cambridge University Press, 1991– .

Collection "Philosophie du droit" (Collection "Philosophy of Law") (series). Paris: Dalloz, 1953– .

Critic of Institutions. Gen. ed. Roberta Kevelson. New York: Peter Lang, 1994– .

Dickenson Series in Philosophy. Belmont CA: Dickenson, 1965– .

Hamlyn Lectures. London: Stevens, 1949– .

Law and Philosophy Library. Dordrecht; Boston: Kluwer Academic Publishers, 1985– .

Law in Context. London: Weidenfeld and Nicolson, 1970– .

Legal Semiotics Monographs. Merseyside: Deborah Charles, 1988– .

Nomos. Cambridge MA: Harvard University Press, 1958– .

Oxford Readings in Philosophy. Oxford: Oxford University Press, 1967– .

Philosophy, Social Theory, and the Rule of Law. Berkeley: University of California Press, 1994– .

Prentice-Hall Foundation of Philosophy Series. Englewood Cliffs NJ: Prentice-Hall, 1963– .

Round Table on Law and Semiotics. Ed. Roberta Kevelson. Center for Semiotic Research in Law, Government, and Economics, Pennsylvania State University, 1987– (publisher varies).

Studies in Moral, Political and Legal Philosophy. Princeton: Princeton University Press, 1984– .

ANNEX D: Legal Schooling: Monographs

Law and Learning: Report to the Social Sciences and Humanities Research Council of Canada by the Consultative Group on Research and Education in Law. Ottawa: Social Sciences and Humanities Research Council of Canada, 1983.

Legal Education in Canada: Reports and Background Papers of a National Conference on Legal Education. Winnipeg: October 23–26, 1985. Ed. Roy J. Matas and Deborah J. McCawley. Montreal: Federation of Law Societies of Canada, 1987.

Lloyd's Introduction to Jurisprudence. 6th ed. Ed. M.D.A. Freeman. London: Sweet & Maxwell, 1994.

Lasswell, Harold D., and Myres S. McDougal. *Jurisprudence for a Free Society: Studies in Law, Science and Policy.* New Haven: New Haven Press, 1992.

Posner, Richard A. *Overcoming Law.* Cambridge MA: Harvard University Press, 1995.

Stevens, Robert. *Law School: Legal Education in America from the 1850s to the 1980s.* Chapel Hill: University of North Carolina Press, 1983.

Legal Schooling: Journals

Barnett, Hilaire A., and Dianna M. Yach. "The Teaching of Jurisprudence and Legal Theory in British Universities and Polytechnics." *Legal Studies* 5 (1985), 151–171.

Coase, R. H. "Law and Economics at Chicago." *Journal of Law and Economics* 36 (1993), 239.

Cotterrell, R.B.M., and J.C. Woodliffe. "The Teaching of Jurisprudence in British Universities." *Society of Public Teachers of Law Journal* 13 (1974–1975), 73–89.

Epstein, William. "Contemporary Philosophy and Legal Education." *Legal Studies Forum* 9 (1985), 307–328.

Folsom, Ralph H. "Reflections After Teaching Anglo-American Legal Theory: Dean Pierre Azard Memorial Symposium." *San Diego Law Review* 19 (1982), 289–296.

Kavanagh, Patrick. "A Foundation Course for the Law School Curriculum: History and Philosophy of Law." *Australian Journal of Law and Society* 5 (1988), 133–152.

Lasswell, H.D., and M.S. McDougal. "Legal Education and Public Policy: Professional Training in the Public Interest." *Yale Law Journal* 52 (1943), 203–295.

"Legal Theory and Legal Education." *Yale Law Journal* 79 (1970), 1153–1178.

Priest, George L. "Social Science Theory and Legal Education: The Law School as University." *Journal of Legal Education* 33 (1983), 437–441.

"Symposium [on] Comparative Legal Theory: A Meeting of East and West." *Connecticut Journal of International Law* 6 (1991), 295–410.

Weeramantry, C.G. "Jurisprudence in the Third World Law School: A Blueprint." *Melanesian Law Journal* 10 (1982), 136–150.

I

Inheritance and Succession

Broadly understood, the terms "inheritance" and "succession" may be defined as the acquisition of property rights by one person upon the death of another. Consequently, unlike the word "bequest" (which refers to the donative aspect of property transferred at death under the terms of a will), inheritance and succession concern the receipt of property transferred at death whether pursuant to the will of the deceased person or by the operation of law.

As such, the subject of inheritance involves three distinct situations: (1) the acquisition of property pursuant to the will of a deceased person, (2) the acquisition of property by the operation of law where the deceased person leaves no will (dies intestate), and (3) the acquisition of property by the operation of law in circumstances where legal rules override the express terms of the deceased person's will. Differing views on each of these forms of acquisition reflect opposing conceptions of private property and contrasting assumptions as to the nature and scope of interpersonal bonds and obligations.

Inheritance and Testamentary Freedom

Perhaps the most prominent justification for inheritance regards a person's right to inherit property as a derivative right based on a more fundamental right to bequeath one's property to whomever one chooses (subject to claims of spouses and dependents, which are considered later in this discussion). To the extent that a right to bequeath property according to one's will is regarded as a necessary incident of private property, the right of a designated beneficiary to inherit or succeed to this property must be acknowledged as essential to the full expression of the transferor's property rights.

Whether and to what extent private property should include a right of bequest is, of course, a matter of considerable dispute. At one extreme, it is argued that bequest and inheritance are entirely extraneous to the essential character of private property on the grounds that property rights attach to living persons alone, whereas bequest and inheritance apply only to property that ceases to have an owner upon the death of the proprietor. (See sources discussed in Ronald Chester's *Inheritance, Wealth, and Society*.) On this basis, some maintain that strict limits on allowable inheritances may be justified without concern about any possible infringement of private property rights. Indeed, the U.S. Supreme Court has accepted this view, upholding estate and inheritance taxes on the ground that rights to bequeath and inherit property are mere civil rights, created by positive law, not natural rights to which positive laws must defer.

At the opposite pole, libertarians typically consider an unlimited right to bequeath property at death as an essential element of private property. For some, this feature is inherent in the very idea of private property, which by definition is presumed to include exclusive rights of possession, use, and disposition both during the owner's lifetime and at death. For others, this characteristic depends upon John Locke's justification for private property, according to which private appropriation of a previously unowned thing is said to establish a "permanent bequeathable property right" in the thing, provided that no person is made any worse off by the act of appropriation. To the extent that private property contributes to economic efficiency, individual autonomy and political liberty, this "lockean proviso" is generally assumed to be satisfied.

In contrast to each of these positions, a third approach affirms the rights to bequeath and inherit as integral to an appropriate conception of private property, while also emphasizing that these and other property rights are not unlimited. John Stuart Mill, for example, regards these rights as "part of the idea of private property," but also as "fit subjects for regulation" on the utilitarian grounds of "general expediency." Similarly, while John Rawls recognizes rights of bequest and inheritance within his framework of a "property-owning democracy," these rights may be restricted to satisfy the so-called difference principle (to promote the advantage of the least well-off) and to ensure fair equality of opportunity and the fair value of political liberty. In each case, these philosophers advocate progressive taxes on amounts received either by inheritance or by gift in order to encourage property owners to distribute their wealth more widely and to limit concentrations of unearned wealth and power.

To fully examine the strengths and weaknesses of each of these arguments is impossible within the scope of this brief overview. Nonetheless, there are several reasons why some version of the third approach is likely to be most persuasive. With respect to the first argument, that property rights end with the death of the proprietor, one can respond that this conclusion disregards the owner's expectations and downplays the practical and philosophical similarities between gifts and bequests. To the extent that expected restrictions on one's ability to transfer property at death necessarily affects one's freedom to deal with this property during life (for example, since gifts must be made while one is alive in order to avoid restrictions on transfers at death), it is difficult to argue that the right to bequeath can be limited without also limiting the owner's property rights during his or her lifetime. Further, to distinguish between gifts made on one's deathbed and transfers intended to come into effect at one's death seems artificial. Indeed, since the legal and philosophical basis for the transfer of property rights is properly understood to be the abstract will of the transferor (as expressed in the form of a contract, gift, or bequest) as opposed to this person's actual will at any moment in time (so that a gift or contract persists despite a change in the transferor's mind), any ethical distinction between gifts and bequests must be regarded as suspect.

With respect to the second argument, that private property includes an unlimited right of bequest, two responses are in order. First, to assert this characteristic as part of the definition of private property is merely to assume a particular conception of private property, without any explanation as to why this conception is ethically more appealing than any other. Second, while libertarians are able to provide convincing reasons why "permanent bequeathable property rights" are preferable to a state of primitive communism in which property rights are wholly absent, they fail to explain why this rigid conception of private property should be preferred to other conceptions of private property according to which rights to bequeath and inherit are justifiably limited in order to further particular ends of distributive justice. Whether these ends are utilitarian, rawlsian, or ultimately pluralistic, the principles of bequest and inheritance that they suggest are likely to be much more convincing, according to David Duff, than that of a "permanent bequeathable property right."

Intestacy

Where a person dies intestate, there is no formal will by which his or her testamentary intentions are expressed. In this situation, therefore, it might seem that succession rights cannot be based on a primary right of bequest on the part of the deceased. Indeed, for this very reason Mill, among others, suggested that the property of persons who die intestate should generally revert to the state. Instead, however, statutory rules typically create a set of succession rights for persons to whom the deceased might reasonably have been expected to bequeath property under a will.

These rights necessarily reflect prevailing social norms regarding the kinds of attachments that persons typically recognize at death. Not surprisingly, therefore, throughout much of the nineteenth century common law systems in Britain and North America stipulated that the property of a person who died intestate should descend to the eldest son. In the twentieth century, however, recognition of sexual equality has led to the abolition of gender biases and a distinct preference for spousal rights. Nonetheless, traditional conceptions of the family continue to influence statutory definitions of the word "spouse," which are generally restricted to married persons of the opposite sex.

As a practical matter these "statutory wills" can be defended on the grounds that they provide a convenient alternative to the effort and expense required to draft a "custom-made" will, and that it would be unfair to deprive persons of all influence on the distribution of their property at death merely because they failed to effect a formal will. Philosophically, therefore, the justification for this form of inheritance is essentially the same as it is where the will of the deceased person is actually expressed. Even though the recipient acquires property by the operation of law rather than pursuant to the express will of the deceased person, the recipient's basic right to inherit this property derives from the prior right of the deceased to dispose of his or her property at death.

Spouses and Dependents

While laws governing intestate succession are designed to approximate people's intentions regarding the disposition of their property at death, laws establishing minimum claims on the part of spouses and dependents apply notwithstanding the deceased person's intentions. As a result, unlike inheritance pursuant to the will of a deceased person or inheritance by operation of law in cases of intestacy, this third kind of inheritance requires a different philosophical justification from that supporting the deceased's rights of bequest.

Historically, this justification was based mainly on deceased persons' obligations to care for their children and other dependents. John Locke, for example, argued that children had natural rights to inherit the goods of their parents based on the "natural duty" of the parents "to preserve what they have begotten." Likewise, the traditional right of dower, which entitled a widow to a life interest in one-third of her deceased husband's estate, recognized the economic dependency of female spouses within a patriarchal society.

While legal rules continue to protect dependent children and spouses by allowing them (as well as other dependents) to apply to a court for a share of the deceased person's estate in order to provide for their support, family law reforms have eliminated the gender biases that formerly governed a spouse's entitlement to support. In addition, legal recognition of marriage as an equal partnership has led to the introduction of further spousal rights to an equal share of this partnership's property ("net family property") at death. In each case, therefore, changing social assumptions with respect to the nature of the family and the personal obligations of parents and spouses have resulted in different limits on the scope of testamentary freedom.

References

Ascher, Mark L. "Curtailing Inherited Wealth." *Michigan Law Review* 89 (1990), 69.

Chester, Ronald. *Inheritance, Wealth, and Society.* Bloomington: Indiana University Press, 1982.

Duff, David G. "Taxing Inherited Wealth: A Philosophical Argument." *Canadian Journal of Law and Jurisprudence* 6 (1993), 3.

Haslett, D.W. "Is Inheritance Justified?" *Philosophy and Public Affairs* 15 (1986), 122.

Levy, Michael B. "Liberal Equality and Inherited Wealth." *Political Theory* 11 (1983), 545.

Locke, John. *Two Treatises of Government.* 1698. Ed. Peter Laslett. Cambridge: Cambridge University Press, 1988.

Mill, John Stuart. *Principles of Political Economy.* 1848. Ed. David Winch. London: Penguin Books, 1970.

Nozick, Robert. *Anarchy, State, and Utopia.* New York: Basic Books, 1974.

Rawls, John. *A Theory of Justice.* Cambridge MA: Harvard University Press, 1971.

Tullock, Gordon. "Inheritance Justified." *Journal of Law and Economics* 14 (1971), 65.

David G. Duff

See also PROPERTY; TAXATION

Injury

See PERSONAL INJURY

Insanity Defense

The modern insanity defense in the Anglo-American world derives from a bizarre English trial in 1843. Daniel M'Naghten, a Glasgow woodworker suffering from delusions of persecution, felt that Sir Robert Peel, the British Prime Minister, the Jesuits, and the Pope were all conspiring against him. Unable to get at the Jesuits or the Pope, he came to London intending to assassinate Peel. His plan would have succeeded but for the fact that Peel chose to ride in Queen Victoria's carriage because of her absence from the city, while Drummond, his secretary, rode in the carriage normally occupied by Peel. Believing that the Prime Minister was riding in his own carriage, M'Naghten shot Drummond and was charged with the first-degree murder of Drummond, who "languished, and languishing, did die."

M'Naghten's trial developed into a battle between medical knowledge and ancient legal authority. The prosecutor opened with a learned background on criminal insanity. The defense relied in large part on Dr. Isaac Ray's scholarly *Medical Jurisprudence of Insanity,* published in 1838, containing medical views on the weakness of the current right-wrong test.

The defense proposed Ray's medical model of responsibility to replace the existing "right-wrong" test. The jury was told that the human mind is not compartmentalized and that a defect in one aspect of the personality could affect other areas.

Lord Chief Justice Tindal practically directed a verdict for the accused. "I cannot help remarking," he commented to the jury, "that the whole of the medical evidence is on one side, and that there is no part of it which leaves any doubt in the mind." Instead of directing a verdict he gave the case to the jurors who found the defendant not guilty on the ground of insanity. M'Naghten was committed to a mental institution, where he later died.

Queen Victoria thereafter wrote a letter to Peel expressing her dissatisfaction with the administration of the insanity defense. The fifteen judges of the common law courts convened in extraordinary session to answer complex questions on the status of criminal responsibility in England. Lord Chief Justice Tindal, responding for fourteen of the fifteen judges, articulated what has come to be known as the M'Naghten rule. Tindal wrote: ". . . we have to submit our opinion to be, that the jury ought to be told in all cases that every man is to be presumed to be sane, and to possess a sufficient degree of reason to be responsible for his crimes, until the contrary be proved, that, at the time of the committing of the act, the party accused was labouring under such a defect of reason, from disease of the mind as not to know the nature and quality of the act he was doing, or if he did know it, that he did not know he was doing what was wrong."

The judge's response influenced the law for nearly the entire English-speaking world since his day. The rule formally established the defense as a legal excuse, "not guilty by reason of insanity" (NGRI). In response to Ray's attempt to substitute a medical model for a legal one, the English judges sought to establish new criteria for what they considered a legal rather than medical problem.

The M'Naghten rule was adopted by the courts of the British Isles, excepting Scotland, and by then-existing states of the United States, except New Hampshire. In the ensuing century, despite advances made by psychiatry, the rule has remained substantially unchanged until the mid-twentieth century. It has colored most trials of the criminally insane in courts embracing the Anglo-American legal system. It remains the sole test of criminal responsibility in approximately one-third of the United States. In some states the rule is supplemented by the irresistible impulse test. Courts in some of the jurisdictions which adhere to M'Naghten have expressed dissatisfaction with it but refuse to discard it, usually concluding that such a change must come from the legislature.

M'Naghten's emphasis on cognition reflects a rationalist era. At this time cognition was seen as the highest function of the personality. Philosophers draining the cartesian dregs of the period speculated that the mind controlled bodily behavior like an angel driving a machine. Not surprisingly, the rule concluded that an individual who knows right from wrong has all rational powers intact and is capable of governing behavior.

Today, psychology has largely rejected the primacy of cognition. The theory of partial insanity or monomania—that a person could be sane in all other respects and yet have a cognitive delusion—has also yielded to a more modern theory of the integrated psyche. Psychologists as diverse as Sigmund Freud, Carl Jung, Carl Rogers, and B.F. Skinner maintain that cognition is not the sole or even the principal controlling function of the psyche. Volition, impulse, the subconscious, or the environment may each at times overpower cognition. The psyche is now often seen as integrated rather than compartmentalized, as "openness to experience" rather than as primarily cognitive. As a result, and in seeming contradiction to M'Naghten, insanity may factually inhere in quiet, controlled behavior, not only in visually bizarre craziness affecting cognition.

Other objections to the M'Naghten rule reside in the view that it reflects a minimalistic policy regarding irresponsible people because it fails to adequately identify all disabled persons who deserve to be excused from criminal responsibility. The test calls for total impairment: the accused must not know at all. This traditional hallmark of "total" insanity sets a narrow standard. Few persons are total madmen; insanity is usually a matter of degree. M'Naghten's single-track emphasis on the cognitive aspect of the personality, however, recognizes no degrees. The defendant either knows right from wrong or does not; all or nothing is the only choice the jury is given.

Ennui over the proliferation of insanity tests has spawned the proposal to abolish the insanity defense completely. Some scholars and part of the public have urged the abolition of the defense not merely for its own sake but as a first step toward abolishing all mens rea from criminal law, prompting competing theories on the relationship between mens rea and insanity. Mens rea, or "criminal intent," tech-

nically refers to the actor's mental state which, together with his physical act, constitute a crime. These mental elements, as defined by the *Model Penal Code* and by most modern criminal codes, basically appear in four "diminishing" (hence diminishing responsibility) forms: (1) "intentionally," acting toward a conscious criminal goal; (2) "knowingly," acting with the awareness of the circumstances surrounding the act; (3) "recklessly," acting with a conscious disregard of dangerous results known to be likely to occur; and (4) "negligently," acting without awareness of risk. Any one of these four mental states constitutes the mens rea of a crime.

Absence of all of these four mental states means that no crime has been committed, in effect, that a bodily movement occurred independently of the mind's acquiescence. A proven absence of mens rea thus establishes a claim of innocence; that is, despite performance of the forbidden act, there is no crime at all. The presence of a lower culpable mental state indicates, in effect, diminished responsibility.

Insanity can be seen as both a failure-of-proof defense and an excuse defense. As a failure-of-proof defense, insanity can be seen as a specific instance of partial responsibility or diminished capacity. When there are lesser degrees of culpability, as in the case of homicide crimes, mental defects may reduce liability to a lesser degree of the original offense because the more culpable mental state cannot be proven. However, there is nothing partial about the insanity defense in its other role as an excuse. As an excuse to a crime, insanity under M'Naghten either overrides the required statutory element or it does not: with insanity taken as an excuse culpability is not diminished, for the defendant is either competent or not.

Recent efforts have proliferated to redefine the insanity test, in part for criticism as being too narrow, overemphasizing the cognitive aspect of personality and artificially restricting the scope of expert testimony. There seems little doubt that the M'Naghten formulation embodied intellectualistic psychology. Delusional insanity seems to have been the chief, if not the only, kind of insanity the judges had in mind, since their view was that insanity was a defect in the intellectual-perceptual faculties. The test arose from a case involving delusion and at a time when delusion was sine qua non of insanity. In 1955, the American Law Institute (ALI) proposed an alternative standard as part of its *Model Penal Code*. During the last few years, a new series of developments suggests a reversal of this more liberal trend and a move back toward and even beyond M'Naghten. These developments include recent recommendations of the American Bar Association and the American Psychiatric Association, a recently passed federal statute, 18 U.S.C. 17(a) (1986), and a recently passed California statute, Cal. Penal Code, sec. 25(b), all of which seek to narrow the number of insanity acquittals.

During the late 1970s, twenty-four states altered their NGRI defenses to make them more restrictive. Since the 1982 *Hinckley* verdict, seven jurisdictions restricted the definition and use of the insanity defense. Four changed to the M'Naghten standard from the ALI test or a supplemented form of M'Naghten, two restricted use of insanity by barring its use to negate mens rea or its use as an excuse to certain offenses, and one repealed the insanity plea entirely.

The American federal government has recently adopted its first NGRI statute, which authorizes the NGRI finding only when "the defendant, as a result of severe mental disease or defect, was unable to appreciate the nature and quality or the wrongfulness of his acts." This standard parallels M'Naghten in that it directs attention to the capacity to understand the nature, quality, and wrongfulness of the crime; it is broader than M'Naghten because of its replacement of "know" with "appreciate."

Another recent modification of the defense provides for a special verdict of "guilty but mentally ill" (GBMI). The Attorney General's Task Force on Violent Crime recommended this approach in its final report, and several states have enacted legislation to this effect. This reform leaves the existing defense of insanity intact but permits the GBMI verdict as an alternative where a defendant suffers from a mental illness not so serious as to qualify for legal insanity. It is intended to be an addition to the insanity scenario rather than a replacement.

References

American Law Institute. *Model Penal Code and Commentaries*. Philadelphia: American Law Institute Press, 1985.

Biggs, J. *The Guilty Mind*. 1955. New York: Harcourt, Brace, 1955.

Callahan, Mayer, and Steadman. "Insanity Defense Reforms in the United States-Post-Hinckley." *Mental and Physical Disabilities Law Reporter* 54 (1987), 11.

Fingarette, Herbert. *The Meaning of Criminal Insanity*. Berkeley: University of California Press, 1972.

Gerber, Rudolph. *The Insanity Defense*. Port Washington, NY: Associated Faculty Press, 1984.

Glueck, Sheldon. *Mental Disorder and the Criminal Law*. Boston: Little, Brown, 1925.

Goldstein, Abraham. *The Insanity Defense*. New Haven: Yale University Press, 1967.

The Queen v. Daniel M'Naghten, 4 State Trials, N.S. 847, 924 (1843).

United States v. Hinckley, Crim. No. 81-306 (D.D.C. June 21, 1982).

Wexler, H. "Redefining the Insanity Problem." *George Washington Law Review* 53 (1985), 528.

Wingo. "Squaring M'Naghten with Precedent—An Historical Note." *Southern California Law Review* 26 (1974), 26.

Winslade, William J., and Judith Wilson Ross. *The Insanity Plea*. Scribner, 1983.

Rudolph J. Gerber

See also DEFENSES; LIABILITY, CRIMINAL; MENS REA

Institutional Jurisprudence

Jurisdictions can be approached from an institutional perspective in different ways. *Iuris dictio*, stating the law, is a function entrusted to certain organs or bodies, namely, judicial institutions, and consists in determining (declaring, interpreting) and applying the law in the instant case. There is a wide variety of organs or bodies entrusted with litigation. Indeed, jurisdiction as the sociolegal job of declaring the law and authoritatively settling a dispute is unthinkable without litigation, without the existence of institutions entrusted with that job, or without rules and procedures monitoring the action. Leaving aside institutions whose function is to litigate, that is, to plead for a special solution to the instant case, in the interest of a party or of the public—solicitors, barristers, attorneys, procurators—and leaving aside special agencies set up as alternatives to litigation—ombudspersons, arbitrators, or mediators—courts and tribunals are the typical law-applying institutions. For the purposes of applying and declaring the law a special case of practical reasoning is used, that is, institutional legal reasoning, and special procedures exist which are highly institutionalized. Law is a highly institutionalized normative system. Jurisdictional institutions declare and develop the law in their judgments and contribute to this intensive institutionalization. They do so by means of legal interpretation and legal reasoning, which is a special case of normative or practical reasoning used in the justification of law-applying and law-interpreting decisions of judicial institutions. Legal reasoning is to a large extent institutional reasoning not only because it is the official reasoning of judicial institutions but also because there are, on the one hand, relatively detailed substantive rules that must be applied as established premises and, on the other hand, procedural rules and standards of necessary application that regulate the jurisdictional game. On top of this, judicial institutions develop principles which order the law into a system and guide the different forms of reasoning from rules and standards by legal agents.

It is impossible to give a universal definition of courts and tribunals, but certain common traits can be identified: their authority is grounded on the constitution, their intervention is obligatory, having the power and the duty (1) to inquire into the facts of the legal conflict which they are asked to resolve, (2) to establish the relevant facts, and (3) to consider arguments put forward by the parties to the dispute and to adjudicate by declaring and applying the law in the case by means of a judgment, thus instantiating the legal order in the concrete case. Jurisdictional institutions and their members, the judges, enjoy a certain degree of organizational self-management and personal and professional independence, and yet they often mirror the social conditions and political realities of their territory and their environment. They are state agencies with authority to give an official solution to a legal dispute. Their decisions can be enforced by means of state authority and apply the valid law of their state which often includes law of suprastate origin, for example, European Community law. Courts of first instance will normally settle the factual aspect of the conflict and will deal with clear cases in a quasi-administrative manner, and higher courts will deal with the technical legal questions of hard cases in a discursive but authoritative way, contributing to the development of the law. In all legal systems, supreme court decisions are binding in practice on the lower courts. Thus, a hierarchical organization of legal doctrine obtains in jurisdictional institutions: they declare and reshape the law. The question has been highly debated to what extent they create new law or they merely reinterpret existing law. While some judicial models emphasize the role of jurisdictional institutions as the mouth of the law, as Montesquieu put it, other models encourage judges to engage in social reform and use their institution as a political alternative.

These institutions might be more or less complex according to their internal rules of procedure (particularly those concerning access to justice: information, standing, cost, representation), their composition (namely, whether they are single judge courts or chambers or panels of judges) and organization (registrars, court officials, and so forth), their working methods and the existence or not of control mechanisms to evaluate their work, the existence or not of a jury, the participation or not of laypersons, whether they are state, regional, or federal courts, whether they are trial courts, appellate courts, courts of last resort, and so forth. They may operate in general areas or in specific areas of the law: administrative, labor law, and industrial relations; social security and employment; tax law, trade law, and restrictive practices; maritime law; and constitutional law. Thus, in Germany one finds ordinary jurisdiction, labor jurisdiction, administrative jurisdiction, social jurisdiction, tax jurisdiction with their respective state and federal courts, a special patent jurisdiction, and state and federal constitutional courts. Besides, suprastate law, like the law of the European Communities or the European Convention for the Protection of Human Rights and Fundamental Freedoms, or even international law are applied by the all of these and ultimately by special suprastate courts. In suprastate jurisdictional institutions further elements need to be considered; for example, in the Court of Justice of the European Communities, besides the judicial institution proper composed of thirteen judges, there are six advocates general, a peculiar institution which presents to the court independent opinions for the solution of a case, there is a complex registry for relationships with the parties, divided in nine language sections, there is a translation service staffed by lawyers, an interpretation service, a computer service, and a research and documentation service composed of lawyer-consultants from the different legal systems. Another peculiar institution is the European Commission of Human Rights, which, until recently, worked as a first examination and filter of the cases that reached the European Court of Human Rights. In cases where some specialization is expected from courts of general jurisdiction, special mechanisms of assistance and cooperation can be devised. Such is the case for the European Communities system of requests from Member State courts for preliminary rulings by the European Court of Justice on the interpretation and validity of Community law. Similar mechanisms exist for constitutional law. In these situations it is important to be able to define the institutions that are to cooperate. Criteria for the identification of judicial institutions have been developed by the Court of Justice: they are constituted by law according to certain instituting rules (rules of adjudication) giving these organs competences and authority to solve disputes between parties toward whom they are neutral; these disputes have to be solved by applying legal norms, themselves recognized as valid according to the rules of recognition of the state of these courts. Cooperation between different jurisdictional institutions can also obtain by means of an appeal against a court of last instance before a constitutional or a suprastate court, such as the European Court of Human Rights. Jurisdictional institutions in western Europe are thus undergoing a thorough transformation toward institutional complexity, specialization, and pluralism, and reshaping the very concept of "state" and the relation between law and state, a trend which might spread out to other parts of the world.

References

Aarnio, A., R. Alexy, and A. Peczenik. "The Foundation of Legal Reasoning." *Rechtstheorie* 2, 3, 4 (1981).

Glaser, Cyril, and Simon Roberts, eds. *Dispute Resolution: Civil Justice and Its Alternatives. Modern Law Review* (special issue), 56 (1993).

Hart, H.L.A. *The Concept of Law.* Oxford: Clarendon Press, 1961.

MacCormick, Neil, and Ota Weinberger. *Institutional Theory of Law.* Dordrecht: D. Reidel, 1986.

La sentenza in Europa. Metodo, tecnica e stile (Legal Judgment in Europe. Method, Means and Style). Padova: Università degli studi di Ferrara, 1985.

Wróblewski, Jerzy. *The Judicial Application of Law.* Dordrecht: Kluwer, 1992.

Joxerramon Bengoetxea

See also INSTITUTIONALISM, FRENCH; INSTITUTIONALIST PHILOSOPHY OF LAW

Institutionalism, French

French institutionalism is a tradition of jurisprudence and social thought during the first half of the twentieth century characterized by its juridical description of legal groupings as institutions. Primarily the work of Maurice Hauriou (1856–1929), it is continued by Georges Renard (1876–1944) and Joseph Thomas Delos (1891–1974).

Late-nineteenth-century jurisprudence was driven by sociologists' enthusiasm for groups' reality. This succeeded to the paramouncy of will theory in law, that is, the determination of private relations by contract, and of public relations by general will, dialectical will, or imperative command.

Gabriel Tarde's social imitation led Maurice Hauriou to understand that social reality evokes law to remedy its lacks. Emile Durkheim's social organicism led Leon Duguit, by contrast, to say that society demands strict liability regimes, and order over rights. Hauriou's institutionalism and Duguit's social positivism were the chief continental competitors in jurisprudence during the first quarter of the twentieth century.

Maurice Hauriou initiated institutional method with *La science sociale traditionnelle* (*Tradition in Social Science. Studies of Social Movement*) in 1896 and *Leçons sur le mouvement social* in 1899. He developed its doctrine while dean of law at the University of Toulouse in twelve editions of his *Précis de droit administratif* (*Precis of Administrative Law*) (1892–1933), two of his *Principes de droit public* (*Principles of Public Law*) in 1910 and 1916, and two of his *Précis de droit constitutionnel* (*Precis of Constitutional Law*) in 1923 and 1929. To practitioners, he was better known for three volumes of *La jurispru-*

dence administrative (*Administrative Caselaw*), his commentaries on decisions by the Conseil d'État's emerging role in forming French administrative law. To theorists, his set of later essays published in 1933 in *Aux sources de droit; le pouvoir, l'ordre et la liberté,* mostly translated in Joseph Albert Broderick's *The French Institutionalists,* is nearly the sole entry point.

While Hauriou early on did not eschew the conceit of a "hydraulics" favored by positivists for social movement, he made reason and choice one of its levers. Similarly, "tradition" in social science gives momentum not as a limp public opinion, but as the assertion of reason in law.

The core of social and legal development, however, is the institution. Institutions are the public presences persisting in society and in law. They are called institutions because groups and procedures are instituted or founded. Founding is but one of the factual moments which law acts upon. Factual social milieux have normative force, since they are founded with an idea of task; the idea is founded, then is realized by organizing social powers into organs, and endures through members' manifesting community by activating legal procedures.

Idea is neither the classical metaphysical form of a being nor the empiricist conscious concept of a purpose. Idea is the directive idea of Henri Bergson's vitalism or, better, the physician Claude Bernard's, for whom a person's thriving follows an observable dynamic, born with and peculiar to him or her.

The legal phenomena of the factual organization (organic individuality) are enhanced when its participants become conscious of its task, modify it, and intend to pursue it (moral personality). Contract and delict, corporation and trust, syndical groups, and nation as the peak of civil society are so described.

The institution's diversity leads it to set limits, procedural and substantive, upon its own power for the sake of its project (legal personality). Law is not absent from the organizing and disciplining earlier in institutional history, but law as itself an institution is achieved only with the state. State as an institution is not assimilable to society or nation, because it is defined by sovereignty. No more a minimal state nor anarchical than it is absolute, its sovereign law is indispensable but responsive; its role is not to initiate but to "redeem" the inevitable abuses among what is created by the economic and political strata ("tissues") of the social institution. Law responds, in Hugo Grotius' phrase, that social personality is a "social whole of personalities" whose individual rights take precedence. Law is reason which not only recognizes the directive idea but formulates its procedures into a separation of powers which "auto-limit" each other.

Georges Renard studied Hauriou and, as social activist and public law professor at Nancy, developed institutionalism into the legal philosophy that Hauriou always denied, by the thomistic linkage he also disclaimed. The institution makes up all of law, not just an occasional presence in it; finality makes up its idea. Renard applied institutionalism to the rest of property, family, and then international law. Renard made legal personality into a category contrasted with individuality similarly to Jacques Maritain and Emmanuel Mounier.

Joseph Delos, as Renard's Dominican confrere, did not dismiss the thomistic philosophizing of institutionalism. Delos restored the sociological investigation of administrative subsidiary, however, and expanded its application in international relations. National institutions are socially faulted if they do not achieve legal institutionalization under international law, instead of iterating their narrowness within national law.

A refugee from national socialism's law, Delos brought institutionalism to the first graduates from Laval University's social science school, and their "Quiet Revolution" of the 1950s out of Quebec's ethnic closure. Institutionalism's adoption by Carl Schmitt was less happy, as by Italian positivist Santi Romano with Iberian jurists and their Latin American scholars in train. The influence upon them and French jurists is represented in several collections of essays.

Institutionalism can clarify jural dispute over corrective justice or strict liability in the private law, over administration by statute or by experts in public law, and over non–nationally based sovereignties with their informal and multiple sources of law in the emerging international order.

References

Beaud, Olivier. "Hauriou et le droit naturel" (Hauriou and Natural Law). *Revue d'histoire des facultés de droit et de science juridique* 7 (1988), 123–138.

Broderick, Joseph Albert, ed. *The French Institutionalists*. Trans. Mary Welling. Intro. Miriam Theresa Rooney. Cambridge MA: Harvard University Press, 1970.

Delos, Joseph T. *Le problème de la civilisation: La nation* (The Question of Civilization: The Nation). Montreal: Arbre, 1944.

———. *La société internationale et les principes du droit public* (International Society and the Principles of Public Law). 1929. 2d ed. Paris: Sirey, 1950.

———. "La théorie de l'institution" (Theory of Institution). *Archives de philosophie du droit et de sociologie juridique* 1 (1931), 87–153.

Gray, Christopher Berry. *The Methodology of Maurice Hauriou* (thesis). Ann Arbor MI: University Microfilms International, 1970; portions in *Rechtstheorie* 14 (1983), 401–417; 15 (1984), 256–267; 25 (1994), 335–365.

Mélanges Maurice Hauriou (Essays for Maurice Hauriou). Paris: Librairie du Recueil Sirey, 1929.

Melkevik, Bjarne. "Pasukanis: une lecture marxiste de Maurice Hauriou" (Pashukanis' Marxist Reading of Maurice Hauriou). *Revue d'histoire des facultés de droit et de science juridique* 8 (1989), 295–301.

La pensée du doyen Maurice Hauriou et son influence (The Thought of Dean Maurice Hauriou and Its Influence). Paris: Editions A. Pedone, 1969; *Annales de la faculté de droit de et des sciences économiques de Toulouse* 16 (1968).

Renard, Georges. "De l'institution à la conception analogique du droit" (From Institution to an Analogical Notion of Law). *Archives de philosophie du droit et de sociologie juridique* 5 (1935), 80–145.

———. *Introduction philosophique de l'étude du droit* (Philosophical Introduction to the Study of Law). 3 vols. Paris: Sirey, 1924–1928.

———. *La philosophie de l'institution* (Philosophy of Institution). Paris: Sirey, 1939.

———. *La théorie de l'institution: Essai d'ontologie juridique* (Theory of Institution: An Essay in Legal Ontology). Paris: Sirey, 1930.

Rodriguez-Arias Bustamante, Lino. "La teoria institucional del derecho" (The Institutional Theory of Law). *Anales de catedra Francisco Suarez* 12 (1972), 37–64.

Schild, Wolfgang. "Die Institutionentheorie Maurice Haurious" (The Institutional Theory of Maurice Hauriou). *Österreichische Zeitschrift für öffentliches Recht* 25 (1974) 3–21.

Sfez, Lucien. *Essai sur la contribution du doyen Hauriou au droit administratif français* (A Study of the Contribution to Administrative Law by Dean Maurice Hauriou). Pref. Jean Rivero. Foreword by André Hauriou. Paris: Pichon et Durand-Auzias, 1966.

Tanguay, Yann. "L'institution dans l'oeuvre de Maurice Hauriou; Actualité d'une doctrine" (Institution in the Work of Maurice Hauriou: The Present Status of the Doctrine). *Revue de droit public et de la science politique* 107 (1991) 61–79.

Christopher B. Gray

See also INSTITUTIONALIST PHILOSOPHY OF LAW

Institutionalist Philosophy of Law

Legal institutionalism is a current of thought that forms part of the "revolt against formalism" that came after the end of the nineteenth century. This is true of both the "classical" institutionalism associated with the names of Santi Romano and Maurice Hauriou and of the more recent neoinstitutionalist theories put forward by Ota Weinberger and Neil MacCormick. Institutionalism is one of the attempts to find a way out of the many problems created by a narrow conception of law as basically a command from the political "superior" or the state, and of legal science as a purely logical and systematic exercise about norms and "institutions." The legal positivism that allows no recourse to strong normative arguments (if they are moral or political) and ridicules any reference to or even consideration of a social context into which legal norms are placed, is responded to from various quarters by claiming the normative and hence also legal value of social facts. One of those quarters, and one of the least radical and most epistemologically aware among them, is legal institutionalism.

There are three versions of "classical" institutionalism, two of them, so to speak, "legitimate" and one more or less "illegitimate," in the sense that its allocation specifically to the institutionalist camp is controversial. The two "legitimate" versions are a French one and an Italian one, represented by the work of Maurice Hauriou and Santi Romano, respectively. The third version, the "illegitimate" one, is German represented by the work of Carl Schmitt, particularly in a period from the early 1930s to the mid-1940s, also dubbed *Konkretes Ordnungsdenken (Doctrine of Concrete Order)*. It may be significant, and is certainly suggestive, that all three of those mentioned are scholars of public and constitutional law. Perhaps institutionalism is an answer to questions felt more urgently in the area of public law, such as the need for integration of individuals into collective structures, for stability in intersubjective relations, and for legitimacy of political authority.

For all the diversity among the three "classical" versions of institutionalism, some common features may also be noted. For all these theories, the law shares the features of sociality, "ordinamentality," and "plurality." That is, law is seen first and foremost as closely connected with society, so that for some institutionalists the two terms become synonymous; it is then conceived of as an "order," as organization; finally, it is "plural," in the sense that it is not believed that in a given territorial context there is only one system of norms consistent and closed in on itself, but that there are several legal systems interconnected with each other.

The two "legitimate" theories of the institutions, as we have said, are those of Hauriou and Romano; there are, however, some important differences between them. For Hauriou the institution is in some sense prior to law. An institution, he asserts, is a "concept of a work or undertaking" set up and lasting legally in a social environment. For Romano, by contrast, law and institution coincide. "Every legal order," writes the Italian jurist, "is an institution, and conversely every institution is a legal order: the equation between the two concepts is necessary and absolute." For Hauriou, further, the institutions as such are constitutional and representative in nature, that is, they must bring about, albeit on a minor scale, a sort of state based on the rule of law; the idea was heavily criticized by Romano, who sees in it a confusion of the descriptive level proper to the "scientist" (and hence the legal theoretician) and the prescriptive one appropriate to the moralist and politician (foreign to "legal science"). Ac-

cording to Hauriou the constitutive features of the institution are the accomplishment of an idea of social action, the existence of an organized power to accomplish that, and the social acceptance of the idea; Romano instead identifies these features as a plurality of subjects, an organization linking them, and a norm-creating power that is an expression of the organization. Hauriou's theory, influenced by Henri Bergson's vitalism, sometimes looks like a political philosophy; Romano's, entirely within the positive law tradition and influenced if anything by Otto von Gierke *(Genossenschaftstheorie)*, fits into the domain of sociology. For Hauriou, indeed, the ideal element is the determining feature; moreover, he does not seem prepared to accept just any sort of "idea of undertaking" as the normative core of the institution, but only one that expresses the principles of the rule of law. For Romano, more realistically or, if you wish, cynically, even the mafia is an institution; what matters is the organization's level of elaboration, its evolutionary stage and its effectiveness.

As far as the "illegitimate" version of institutionalism goes, its features are sketched in a more or less occasional piece by Schmitt, *Über die drei Arten des rechtswissenschaftlichen Denkens (Three Types of Thought in Legal Theory)* of 1934; here, the institution is sharply counterposed to the norm and, instead, reconciled with "decision." The institution dealt with in *Konkretes Ordnungsdenken (Concrete Thinking About Order)* is an organic rather than contractual community, into which the individuals fit as parts of a whole they cannot transcend, the regulation of which is inherent in the organism itself, and thus needs no norms (abstract and general), but is manifested in the members' expressions of life and finally (or better, primarily) in the decision of individuals that have a privileged contact with the community. This sort of institutionalism repudiates normativism, regarding conventional rules as suspect, as being universalizable measures (even if limited to a particular "case in point"), and as explicit reasons for action in relation to which individuals may exercise their reflective capacities. Schmitt accordingly uses institutionalism as an ideological justification for the decisionism which is the actual end point of so-called *Konkretes Ordnungsdenken*. Clearly neither Hauriou nor Romano is a decisionist; the latter even remains tied to a rationalist and, in Hauriou's case, radically democratic worldview; this is not the case with Schmitt's work, whose guiding theme is anti-Enlightenment, irrationalist, and antiliberal.

Let us now consider neo-institutionalism. This is the joint product of Neil MacCormick and Ota Weinberger, the outcome of two mutually convergent traditions of thought: the analytical jurisprudence as renewed by H.L.A. Hart (of whom MacCormick was a student) and the "pure theory of law" in the critical, heterodox version offered by the Czech Frantisek Weyr, a great friend of Hans Kelsen, who dedicated to him the book *Der soziologische und der juristische Staatsbegriff (The Sociological and Juridical Concept of the State)* and a lecturer in Brno Law Faculty (where Weinberger received his legal education). Despite some (sometimes considerable) differences in philosophical approach between MacCormick and Weinberger, some common features of new institutionalism may be identified. First, there is a general antireductionist attitude. This is evident, first, in the ontological sphere, so that social reality is not seen as entirely reducible to material space-time reality (as instead affirmed by the Scandinavian realists like Olivecrona), and a distinction is drawn between "brute facts" and "institutional facts" (with reference to a proposal by the philosopher John Searle). Second, law is not reduced to a series of norms, even if systematized among themselves, but the definition of the concept of law is held to have to take acount of other features, too, like the spheres of action made possible by norms, and principles of action expressed in particular social contexts that inspired those norms and direct their application for good or ill. Nor is there an obsessively prescriptivist view of the norms; it is instead held that norms not only restrict but sometimes also extend human beings' sphere of action. Thanks to "institutions" (contract, property, marriage, and so forth), human beings, says MacCormick, are capable of increasing the number of facts existing in the world without necessarily increasing the number of physically existing objects. However, neo-institutionalism is also and especially a *methodological liberalism* (that is, *antireductionism*); so that legal concepts are not for it reducible to structures representing norms or prescriptions, to mere tools in the hands of a dogmatist (as realists like Alf Ross wanted it). Other common features are *antiprescriptivism,* for which norms cannot be reduced to imperatives, commands, or direct prescriptions of behavior, and a *moderate legal positivism,* for which, while the law is conceived as a product of the will of human beings and not of entities beyond conscious involvement of humans, the possibility is accepted of norms not explicitly laid down by the legislator. Another common feature, despite some hesitation in this connection by MacCormick, seems to be a meta-ethical noncognitivism, it being affirmed that while law is capable of being known (once the norms are posited), the same cannot be said for (critical) morality, and law and morality are seen as clearly separate spheres.

In relation to "classical" institutionalism, neo-institutionalism is much more methodogogically refined. Yet there is considerable affinity between the two versions. Romano, for instance, would share both the ontological and the methodological antireductionism, would without too much hesitation accept a nonprescriptivist view of law, and would not draw back from defining the separation of law and morality; he, too, could without difficulty be labeled as a "moderate legal positivist." Nonetheless, there are important differences. There are at least two of these. For MacCormick and Weinberger, "institution" is equivalent mainly to "institutional facts"; for Romano, it is equivalent to "society." Obviously, not every "institutional fact" constitutes a "society" (consider, for instance, a contract). Romano endeavors at one point of his theoretical trajectory to base the "ought" (the validity of norms) on the "is" (their efficacy); the distinction between the two categories in neo-institutionalism is instead clear and unequivocal. The price for this is, however, a little too much obscurity and ambiguity: how can one, for instance, accept the idea of "institutional fact," without adopting the concept of "constitutive norm," that is, the idea of rules ("ought") producing some kind of reality (an "is"), which is so opposed by Weinberger? In the last analysis, Romano's "classical" version, however less philosophically refined, is more consistent with the more recent institutionalist theories.

References

Hauriou, Maurice. *Aux sources du droit; le pouvoir, l'ordre, et la liberté.* Paris: Bloud et Gay, 1933.

———. *Précis de droit constitutionnel.* 2d ed. Paris: Sirey, 1929.

LaTorre, Massimo. "Institutionalism Old and New." *Ratio Juris* 6 (1993), 190–201.

MacCormick, Neil, and Ota Weinberger. *An Institutional Theory of Law.* Dordrecht: D. Reidel, 1986.

Romano, Santi. *Frammenti di un dizionario giuridico.* 2d ed. Milano, 1983.

———. *L'ordinamento giuridico.* 1918. 3d ed. Firenze, 1977.

Schmitt, Carl. *Über die drei Arten des rechtswissenschaftlichen Denkens.* Hamburg, Hanseatische Verlagsanstalt, 1934.

Weinberger, Ota. *Law, Institution, and Legal Politics.* Dordrecht: Kluwer, 1991.

Massimo La Torre

See also INSTITUTIONAL JURISPRUDENCE; INSTITUTIONALISM, FRENCH

Integrity

See COHERENCE; DWORKIN, RONALD

Intellectual Property

Intellectual property denotes a variety of rights that protect applications of ideas and information which has commercial value. Patent, industrial design, copyright and trademark are the most important such rights. Intellectual property is not itself a legal term, although it is used in names such as the United Nations' World Intellectual Property Organization.

Intellectual property rights confer upon one or more individuals a limited right to control an intangible object and to stop others from using or trading that object in particular ways. These rights are normally granted to the creator of the intangible object the rights are designed to protect. The rationale is that the return to be earned on trading the creations so protected will encourage creators to develop ideas, products, and creations, and put them in a form suitable for public consumption or enjoyment; negatively, one may fear that creators will hesitate to engage in inventive activity or to make the fruits thereof public, where, in the absence of such rights, anyone can copy them and profit without having to incur the cost of discovery.

Like ordinary property rights, intellectual property rights are normally transferable, but contrary to them, they exist for a limited period only: around twenty years for patent, the life of the author plus fifty or seventy years for copyright. The classical intellectual property rights operate in separate spheres. Patent is available for industrial inventions. Copyright covers artistic, cultural, and literary creations. Trademarks are designed to protect the holder's commercial reputation, which in the public eye is associated with that mark, against depreciation through imitation by others.

All intellectual property rights protect some intangible object, and hence can be said to protect information or ideas. None of them, however, protects abstract ideas as such, as in mathematical formulae, scientific theories or plots of literary creations. In each case, a particular expression, design, or embodiment is protected. The ideas themselves cannot be appropriated; they are part of what in this field is called the public domain. It is not always easy to determine, for an invention, a new design, or an artistic creation, what belongs to the public domain and what to the protected embodiment or expression. The plot of a film, for instance, is not protected (by copyright), but the dialogues written for it are. Did the computer game K.C. Munchkin illegally borrow protected elements (a maze, pursuers and pursued with the ability to eat one another, power pills producing reversal in the pursuit, and so on) from the Pac-Man game? Or were these common elements of what makes up a maze game, and hence unprotected ideas? Much actual litigation concerns questions such as these.

Most intellectual property rights are based nowadays on statutes and international treaties, explicitly setting out their rules of operation. Such is the case of patent, industrial design copyright, trademark and of the newer rights of plant breeders and semiconductor chip manufacturers. But there remains some intellectual property that is protected only by fuzzier case law rules. This is true of trade secrets and of other valuable commercial information—a firm's goodwill, know-how, or commercial strategies—which are protected by case law regarding abuse of confidential information, passing off, and unfair competition.

Intellectual property rights originated in privileges granted by emperors, kings, and princes from the Renaissance onward. They were conferred to reward creative effort or special skills, but also for reasons less respectable in modern eyes, such as censorship (in the case of book printers' monopolies), reg-

I

ulation of industry, and providing revenue for the emperor, king or prince.

Are modern intellectual property rights, as the name suggests, a species of ordinary property rights, institutions that make markets possible? Or are they privileges in modern guise, fruits of "rent-seeking" not sustainable in the market?

The privileged ancestry does not in itself provide an answer to those questions. Surprisingly, economists are not able to answer them either. Economic theory and historical studies convincingly show how important well-defined and secure ordinary property rights are to economic development, because of the incentives they create and the decentralized decision-making they entail. One may surmise that those factors carry over into the field of intellectual property. The complicating factor is that intellectual property rights, by reserving an intangible object to one person, exclude others from it, while most advances in science, technology, and social organization are built upon earlier information, which requires information to flow freely. Monopolies of any sort in information slow down the accumulation of knowledge. The right that rewards the first innovator at the same time inhibits followers who might better the original idea. How does one count the inventions and creations that might have been or judge whether they did not come about because rights were too weak or, on the contrary, forbiddingly strong? No way has yet been found to determine scientifically whether intellectual property rights in fact stimulate discovery and creation.

The view that creators should have an unlimited natural right in their discoveries does not square with existing intellectual property rights. All existing intellectual property rights show a compromise between the reward through exclusivity for those who have created something and the free flow of information favouring later creators who may compete with them. The compromise varies from right to right.

Patent is a very strong right. It allows the holder to prohibit others from using the patented invention, even where they discovered it independently. The counterpart to the strong right is that to be patentable, the invention must exhibit objective novelty (measured against worldwide knowledge) and it must not be obvious to someone of the same trade. The right is granted upon request only and for a short period. A description of the patented invention is made public.

Copyright is a weaker right. It protects only the particular expression in which the creator has cast his or her ideas. The expression may not be copied, translated, or adapted, but use itself is not regulated. An independently developed similar expression is subject to a new copyright unrelated to the earlier copyright. The counterpart to this relatively weak right is the low level of originality required, meaning essentially that the creator must have some distinct input and must not have taken the creation from other sources. The right is granted for a long period; it need not be requested but arises automatically out of the act of creation. There is no obligation to publish.

As for trade secret, in general one may keep commercial ideas or trade practices to oneself. The law gives modest protection against disloyal disclosure of such information. But once the information becomes common knowledge, even through disloyal acts, no protection is available. If one sells products that embody secret information, there is no protection against competitors' reverse engineering those products to get to the secret.

Trademarks are names or other distinctive marks designating commercial products or services. Trademarks improve the functioning of markets, in that they allow consumers to select products on the basis of qualities that are not directly observable at the time of the purchase, but have become associated with those marks. Trademarks, while allowing the owner to stop others from using them, are not monopolistic, as the aforementioned rights are. Anyone can invent a new name and give it commercial value by providing consistently good products or service. There is, therefore, no reason to limit the protection of a trademark in time, unless the mark loses its distinctive character by becoming part of ordinary language, as in xerox-copy or band-aid in North American English. Existing legislation embodies these principles.

The progressive expansion of information technology into all walks of life is believed to strain intellectual property rights. Inventions in software take the form of small steps which may well fail to reach the level of novelty required for a patent. Copying, on the Internet in particular, is so easy that the natural barriers that made copyright effective in earlier days appear to dissolve; piracy is decried as rampant.

What rights should be available for lesser inventions? Given the compromise that intellectual property rights involve, one would like to find the answer under a Rawlsian type veil of ignorance. A place where such a condition might be approximated would be an association for sharing ideas amongst creators, all of whom are now discoverers of ideas, now borrowers of ideas discovered by others. In adopting rules governing the conditions under which a member may borrow ideas from other members, the association would not skew the solution either way. Antitrust legislation may, however, stand in the way of such associations.

The alleged piracy problem raises the question of who should build and enforce the "fences" protecting exclusive rights. Normally that task falls to the right's holder. It creates the incentive to invent new fences and new institutions to enforce them. Making the government assume that enforcement role risks transforming intellectual property into stifling privileges of earlier ages.

References

Branscomb, Anne Wells. *Who Owns Information: From Privacy to Public Access.* New York: Basic Books, 1994.

Ginsburg, Jane C. "A Tale of Two Copyrights: Literary Property in Revolutionary France and America." *Tulane Law Review* 64 (1990), 991–1031. Reproduced in *Of Authors and Origins: Essays on Copyright Law,* ed. Brad Sherman and Alain Strowel, 131–158. Oxford: Clarendon Press, 1994.

Kitch, Edmund W. "The Nature and Function of the Patent System." *Journal of Law and Economics* 20 (1977), 265–290.

Landes, William M., and Richard A. Posner. "An Economic Analysis of Copyright Law." *Journal of Legal Studies* 18 (1989), 325–363.

———. "Trademark Law: An Economic Perspective." *Journal of Law and Economics* 30 (1987), 265–309.

Machlup, Fritz, and Edith T. Penrose. "The Patent Controversy in the Nineteenth Century." *Journal of Economic History* 10 (1950), 1–29.

Plant, Arnold. *The New Commerce in Ideas and Intellectual Property.* London: University of London, 1953.

Rose, Mark. *Authors and Owners: The Invention of Copyright.* Cambridge MA: Harvard University Press, 1993.

Strowel, Alain. *Droit d'auteur et copyright—Divergences et convergences—Étude de droit comparé.* Bruxelles: Bruylant; Paris: L.G.D.J., 1993.

Toward a Third Intellectual Property Paradigm. Columbia Law Review (special issue) 94 (1994), 2307–2677.

Ejan Mackaay

Intent

The philosophical and the legal literature about intention rarely intersect. Philosophers have been largely interested in the ontological status of intentions and their place within a theory of mind. Legal theorists have been more concerned to identify the conditions under which an act is intentional or unintentional. To accomplish this objective, they have not tended to believe that they must resolve the deeper philosophical questions about the nature of intentions.

Intention is important to the criminal law primarily because action that intentionally brings about a harm is thought to be the paradigm of culpable action. A person who intentionally kills or intentionally injures is widely believed to be more blameworthy and deserving of a more severe punishment than a person who performs these acts unintentionally. The most serious offenses for which persons deserve the most severe punishments—murder, for example—frequently require intention. This clear connection between intention and culpability has led to a disagreement about whether the concept of intention is partly ascriptive or wholly descriptive. Does a judgment of whether a person is responsible for something affect an assessment of what that person did intentionally? On the other hand, does an assessment of what a person did intentionally simply describe an inner state or process that is independent of a judgment of responsibility?

Despite the centrality of the concept of intention, criminal theorists lack a clear account of its meaning, and disagree about whether its meaning in the criminal law differs from its meaning in ordinary usage. The problem surfaces in at least three contexts. First, what does it mean to perform an act intentionally? The locution "Person D performed action A intentionally" cannot be analyzed without imposing some constraints on how to interpret the action variable "A." According to accounts of action inspired by Donald Davidson, all actions are intentional under some description: if D performed A, then there must be some description under which D did A intentionally. The account of action endorsed by most criminal theorists, however, simply construes an action as a bodily movement and supposes that these bodily movements are voluntary actions when they are caused by volitions. A theory of action must be invoked to settle these issues.

Second, what does it mean to intend to perform an action in the future? An analysis of "D does A with the intention to do B" is required to interpret statutes that prohibit doing some act with a further intention. Burglary, for example, is defined in the common law as a breaking and entering of the dwelling house of another at night with the intent to commit a felony therein. In terminology that has given rise to much confusion, the further intention to do B has sometimes been called a "specific intention," to contrast with the alleged "general intention" to do A. How does this further intention differ from a hope or expectation?

Third, what does it mean to bring about the consequence of an action intentionally; how should "brings about the consequence of A intentionally" be analyzed? This question has stimulated the greatest interest from courts and philosophical commentators. Presumably, D's action A intentionally brings about whatever consequences he wants or desires to occur, and these consequences constitute his aim or objective in performing A. However, does D intentionally bring about those consequences, which he foresees will occur, even when he does not want or desire them? This dispute is about whether what Jeremy Bentham called "oblique intentions," in contrast to "direct intentions," are really a kind of intention at all. Suppose that a defendant is aware that a victim will be killed if he burns down a house. If he sets the fire in order to collect the insurance he has taken on the structure, and not because he wants or desires to cause death, does he intend to kill, and thus commit murder, simply because he foresees that his action will cause someone to die? If so, must the defendant have foreseen a consequence with practical certainty, or does foresight of a high degree of probability suffice for that consequence to

have been brought about intentionally? Courts and commentators divide over this issue.

In order to avoid such difficulties, the *Model Penal Code* and most of the state criminal codes that have followed it have all but abandoned the use of the concept of intention. If intention is so ambiguous and troublesome, why not replace it with comparatively clear concepts such as purpose and knowledge? A person brings about a consequence *purposely* when his conscious object is to cause that consequence. A person brings about a consequence *knowingly* when he is practically certain that his action will cause that consequence. If this reform is adopted, one need not take a stance on whether those results that are brought about knowingly are brought about intentionally. Murder, for example, need not be defined to require an intentional killing. Instead, murder might be defined as a purposeful killing, or (as in the *Model Penal Code*) to include killings performed either purposely or knowingly. One of the most significant questions in drafting a statute or a whole criminal code is to determine whether to follow the *Model Penal Code* in this respect and to delete reference to intention.

If the concept of intention is retained in criminal statutes and theorists decide that the agent has not killed intentionally simply because he foresaw that his act would cause death, there is room for doubt about whether the most serious offenses, such as murder, should continue to require intention. Why should intention be the paradigm of culpability? Legal philosophers have brought many different kinds of challenges to the centrality of intention. If intention is agreed to be so important, should not all crimes—or at least, all serious crimes—require it? Why are there kinds of culpability or mens rea other than intention? Many offenses can be committed even though a defendant does not intentionally cause harm but is merely reckless about whether that harm will occur. Offenses that may be committed recklessly at least require that a defendant is conscious of the risk that his action will cause harm. Even more controversial are offenses that may be committed with mere negligence. These offenses impose criminal liability when the defendant should have been aware of the risk that his conduct would result in harm—that is, when a reasonable person in the defendant's situation would have been aware of the risk—even though the defendant himself may have been unaware of that risk. The most controversial offenses are those of "strict liability" that require no culpability at all. To the extent that they are persuaded that intention is the paradigm culpable state and that culpability is essential to criminal liability, theorists are likely to oppose the punishment of persons whose mental state diverges further and further from intention.

A different question about the importance of intention can be raised by theorists who inquire why motives are so widely believed to be immaterial to criminal liability. Do not motives as well as intentions affect the blameworthiness of defendants? Given that intentions are so hard to distinguish from motives, why should the criminal law be so preoccupied with the former and so totally uninterested in the latter?

In addition, the centrality of intention can be challenged by noting that the criminal law occasionally accepts a number of substitutes for intention. A few of these have been widely discredited. Most jurisdictions have replaced "objective" standards of intention with a "subjective" standard. That is, a defendant is no longer taken to have intended what a reasonable person in his circumstances would have intended. Instead, the trend has been to seek to ascertain the actual mental state of the particular defendant. However, other substitutes for intention have persisted; sometimes a crime that generally requires an intention can be committed despite the absence of the appropriate intention. Two such devices are noteworthy. The first is the "felony-murder rule." According to the least qualified version of this rule, a person is deemed to have intended to kill, and thus is guilty of murder, whenever death results from his commission of a felony.

The second device is the "doctrine of transferred intent." According to this doctrine, a defendant who intends to harm Vl, but accidentally harms V2, is treated as intentionally harming V2. The justifiability of both these devices is subject to dispute.

A number of theorists have concluded that intention should not be so central to the criminal law. Some of these reservations about intention have arisen from the practical difficulties of proving that a defendant acted intentionally. Other reservations derive from a view about the function or purpose of the criminal law. If the criminal law is designed to deter harmful conduct, why should it be so important whether a harm is brought about intentionally or unintentionally? Following Barbara Wootton, some theorists have proposed that all offenses should become instances of "strict liability." Although this sweeping proposal has gained few adherents, there is little consensus as to exactly why it is objectionable. H.L.A. Hart has emphasized that the implementation of this proposal would result in the loss of control over whether persons would incur criminal liability and thus would undermine planning and predictability in human affairs. Although this response is clearly correct, it does not seem to capture why theorists are so convinced that mental states in general and intention in particular should be used in the definitions of serious offenses. What is required is a theory of culpability, a justification for regarding intention as the paradigm culpable state, and a reason to conclude that persons should be punished only for those acts for which they are culpable.

Although philosophers have contested the general significance of intention to the criminal law, a number of important questions about intention arise in the context of particular offenses. Which offenses should require intention, and which can be committed despite the absence of intention? The acts prohibited by some statutes necessarily require intention; it seems impossible to "bribe" or to "kidnap," for example, without intending to do so. In many other cases, however, there is controversy about the degree of culpability that should be required to give rise to liability. Rape is one such example. Should a defendant be liable for rape when he consciously disregards the risk that consent has not been given, or must he actually know that his victim has not consented? Possessory offenses are another example. Should they require an intention to possess the proscribed item, or should recklessness be sufficient to give rise to liability?

Disagreement has long been expressed about whether liability for the various inchoate offenses should require intention (construed as purpose). Consider liability for a criminal attempt. Is the degree of culpability required for an attempt to commit a given crime identical to the degree of culpability that is required to commit that crime? If so, D attempts to murder V when he tries to perform an action that he foresees will kill V, even though his purpose is not to cause V to die. But perhaps a criminal attempt requires an intention (that is, a purpose) to commit the completed offense, even though the completed offense requires no such intention. If to attempt to commit a crime is to try to commit that crime, then it would seem that attempts necessarily require purpose. Much the same question arises in the context of conspiracy or solicitations. If D performs an act that he knows will encourage E to commit a crime, is D liable for solicitation, even though his purpose in performing the act was to make money and not to encourage E? These are only a few of the examples involving disputes about whether the definitions of particular offenses should include or dispense with intention.

References

American Law Institute. *Model Penal Code and Commentaries*. Philadelphia: American Law Institute Press, 1985.

Bentham, Jeremy. *An Introduction to the Principles of Morals and Legislation*. Ed. J.H. Burns and H.L.A. Hart. London: Athlone Press, 1970.

Davidson, Donald. *Essays on Actions and Events*. Oxford: Clarendon Press; New York: Oxford University Press, 1980.

Duff, R.A. *Intention, Agency and Criminal Liability*. Oxford: Blackwell, 1990.

Hart, H.L.A. *Punishment and Responsibility*. Oxford: Clarendon Press, 1968.

Kenny, Anthony. "Intention and Purpose." *Journal of Philosophy* 63 (1966), 642.

Mele, Alfred. "Recent Work on Intentional Action." *American Philosophical Quarterly* 29 (1992), 199.

Moore, Michael. *Act and Crime*. Oxford: Clarendon Press, 1993.

Norrie, Alan. *Crime, Reason and History*. London: Weidenfeld and Nicolson, 1993.

Simons, Kenneth. "Rethinking Mental States." *Boston University Law Review* 72 (1992), 463.

Wootton, Barbara. *Crime and the Criminal Law*. 2d ed. London: Stevens, 1981.

Douglas N. Husak

See also ACT REQUIREMENT; MENS REA; NEGLIGENCE, CRIMINAL

Intent, Legislative

Theorists of statutory interpretation believe that judges and administrators should implement or at least be sensitive to the "legislative intent." This bromide conceals difficult issues of interpretation and meaning.

The simplest meaning of the term looks to "specific intent": how would the enacting legislators have answered the interpretive issue before the court or agency? When the statute is recent and the issue uncontroversial, one may readily enough discern the legislature's specific intent—usually because the statute's text clearly answers the question. Justice Oliver Wendell Holmes, Jr., of the U.S. Supreme Court and many notable British jurists maintain that the only admissible source of evidence as to the legislature's specific intent is the text of the statute. It is only the text that the legislature enacts, and in the United States it is only the text that both chambers of Congress agree to and that is presented to the president for signature.

On the other hand, extrinsic materials, including committee reports and floor debates, can provide useful context for evaluating ambiguous textual directives. If I tell you the pot of gold must be sought in "Cambridge," the text of my directive is ambiguous, but the ambiguity can be readily resolved by knowing that I was residing in Massachusetts rather than England when I uttered the directive. Where the statutory text is ambiguous, American courts and more recently the British House of Lords are willing to examine extrinsic legislative materials that shed light on the particular issue.

Inquiries into specific intent become more intractable, and less productive, for divisive issues and for those not anticipated by the legislature. Where the issue itself aroused controversy, there may be no discoverable specific intent, because there was no consensus on the issue. The text will usually be ambiguous, and extrinsic materials will either be as ambiguous as the text or will point in contradictory directions. The fictive quality of legislative intent becomes most apparent in such instances. Likewise, where the issue was not clearly anticipated by the legislature, there is by definition no discoverable legislative intent. How should the interpreter proceed in these cases?

Where the specific intent of the legislature is in doubt, the interpreter might set her inquiry at the legislature's "general intent." What was the overall goal or purpose of the statute? Which interpretation then best advances that purpose or the proper balance of purposes? The same evidence consulted to figure specific intent should also be consulted to determine general intent. Indeed, the extrinsic materials that should be viewed cautiously when inquiring after specific intent may be most useful when inquiring after general intent.

The most famous case of statutory interpretation in the United States during the last generation is *Weber v. Steelworkers*. 443 U.S. 193 (1979). The issue was whether the Civil Rights Act of 1964's prohibition against race "discrimination" in the workplace prevents an employer from adopting an affirmative action plan to remedy past discrimination against people of color. The Court held not. A dissenting opinion lampooned the majority for violating what the dissenting jurists considered "smoking guns" evidencing a clear intent by Congress to disallow all forms of race discrimination, including remedial discrimination for the benefit of disadvantaged racial groups. A closer reading of the evidence suggests, however, that the precise issue was not before Congress, because legislators assumed that the nondiscrimination norm would soon lead to workplace equality, which it unhappily did not. Because Congress did not focus on the precise issue and because its assumptions were undone, the Court was right to examine the more general intent of the legislature, namely, to rectify gross economic inequality among the races.

References

Dworkin, Ronald. *Law's Empire*. Oxford: Oxford University Press, 1986.

Eskridge, William N., Jr. *Dynamic Statutory Interpretation*. Cambridge MA: Harvard University Press, 1994.

Eskridge, William N., Jr., and Philip P. Frickey. *Legislation: Statutes and the Creation of Public Policy*. 2d ed. Minneapolis: West, 1994.

Hart, Henry M., Jr., and Albert Sacks. *The Legal Process: Basic Problems in the Making and Application of Law*. 1958. Ed. William N. Eskridge, Jr., and Philip P. Frickey. Mineola NY: Foundation Press, 1994.

Holmes, Oliver Wendell, Jr. "The Theory of Legal Interpretation." *Harvard Law Review* 12 (1899), 419.

Pound, Roscoe. "Spurious Interpretation." *Columbia Law Review* 7 (1907), 379.

Radin, Max. "Statutory Interpretation." *Harvard Law Review* 43 (1930), 870–871.

William N. Eskridge, Jr.

Intergenerational Justice

It may seem self-evident that those requirements of justice which limit our permissible acts affecting our contemporaries likewise limit our permissible acts affecting future people. Reflection suggests that this is not straightforwardly so, subject to two qualifications. First, some members of future generations, our grandchildren for instance, are for a time our contemporaries. Second, some of our acts affecting future generations may be unjust but indirectly so. Where some present act results in impaired life chances for future people, it may be unjust on account of what we owe to our contemporaries. So, our contemporaries may strive to ensure that their great great grandchildren flourish, and our contrary efforts may involve injustice to the former. There is otherwise a distinctive philosophical problem in the idea of intergenerational justice, namely, the "nonidentity problem."

The nonidentity problem is best introduced by the specific example of a couple who decide to have a child. They discover that procreating now will result in a child with a particular deformity, which, while not rendering its life not worth living, will cause it considerable discomfort. Delaying conception would ensure that the resultant child has no deformity. Considerations of justice do not obviously compel a choice here. If they procreate now, the resultant child enjoys a life worth living, and there seems no injustice in that. If they delay conception, they do not thereby improve conditions for the child they would have had were they to have procreated earlier. There is no particular child who could be conceived earlier with a deformity, and later without a deformity. There are two possible children, only one of which becomes actual. Each has a life worth living, and the choice is between that particular life or no life at all.

It is assumed that the procreative choices of the parents determine the identity of the child they end up having. This assumption rests on the claim that an individual's identity is partly determined by its origin, including its original genotype, which claim does not entail that subsequent changes to genetic structure alter identity, and also on facts about fertilization and meiosis. Altering the timing of conception will alter origin, including original genotype, and so will result in different individuals coming into existence that would have otherwise come into existence. The claim concerning origin may be strenghtened by the claim that (personal) identity is also partly determined by psychological makeup, that is, by the beliefs, memories, attitudes, preferences, and the like, which constitute an individual's psychology. The timing of an individual's birth will partly determine resultant psychological makeup, and hence (personal) identity.

Just as the parents' choice determines the identity of their child, so, too, our choices collectively determine the identity of members of future generations. Similarly, it is difficult to see how justice compels a choice in favor of one set of future individuals as opposed to some other, subject to the proviso that life for members of each set is worth living. The nonidentity problem is metaphysical, not epistemic. It should not be confused with the argument that the requirements of justice toward future generations are weakened by our ignorance of what they will like, of what their needs and preferences will be. This epistemic argument can be blunted by appeal to certain constants in human biological, and perhaps social, nature. The metaphysical argument is, however, apparently more decisive. Yet it supports a conclusion, that we owe less as a matter of justice to future people than we do even to our distant contemporaries, which clashes with the views which many people have on intergenerational justice. These views are evident, for instance, in appeals to the rights of future generations found in many environmentalist positions.

The nonidentity problem weakens the requirements of intergenerational justice for that large range of cases where the present generation determines the identity of future people. There may, however, be cases where there is no such determination. Imagine a present person who plants a bomb timed to explode some generations hence. Here the action seems unlikely to contribute to determining the identities of the individuals who will be harmed when the bomb explodes. The present act is directly unjust to those to whom it in the future causes harm. There may be less catastophic outcomes flowing from present acts which harm, while not determining the identity of, future people.

One response to the nonidentity problem is to urge that justice may be owed to groups as well as to individuals. Allegedly, the requirements of intergenerational justice are not weakened by the fact that a given future generation is constituted by one set of individuals rather than another. While the requirements of justice are often spelled out in terms of what is owed to groups, this is misleading. Although it is convenient to speak this way, not least of all because injustices to individuals are frequently related to their membership of particular groups, it is difficult to see how one could treat a group unjustly without at the same time treating some individual member of the group unjustly. This response to the nonidentity problem assumes that this is possible and so is less than credible.

Another response is to argue that there are rights that members of future generations have which entitle them to demand, so to speak, of their predecessors more than a life worth living. Consider John Locke's proviso on the acquisition of property from nature that such acquisitions leave as much and as good for others. Present use of natural resources which degrades the land and which pollutes air, oceans, and waterways is an acquisition of natural resources that apparently violates the proviso. If the proviso specifies something akin to a property right, we might say that justice, which requires that rights be respected, requires also that we avoid the actualization of future individuals in circumstances where there is no access to clean air and water, and to undegraded land. Other putative rights, such as the right to self-development, might play a similar functional role. This style of argument will strike some as odd: it implies that it is unjust to bring into existence certain individuals whose lives are well worth living and who are glad that they, and not other individuals, were actualized.

Another way in which justice might enter into our deliberations about future generations is as an ideal in some perfectionist vision of human life. Some in the present will want material and social conditions to prevail in the future in which just institutions and just conduct flourish. Their concern is not that they themselves act justly toward future people in advocating those policies which produce such conditions; they might, for instance, accept the argument for comparatively limited requirements of intergenerational justice based on the nonidentity problem. Rather, their concern is, like consequentialists, to promote a certain value.

References

Barry, Brian, and Richard Sikora. *Obligations to Future Generations*. Philadelphia: Temple University Press, 1978.

De-Shalit, Avner. "Community and the Rights of Future Generations: A Reply to Robert Elliot." *Journal of Applied Philosophy* 9 (1992), 105–115.

Elliot, Robert. "Libertarian Justice, Locke's Proviso and Future Generations." *Journal of Applied Philosophy* 3 (1986), 217–227.

Heyd, David. *Genethics*. Berkeley: University of California Press, 1992.

Parfit, Derek. *Reasons and Persons*. Oxford: Clarendon Press, 1984.

Rawls, John. *A Theory of Justice*. Oxford: Clarendon Press, 1972.

Routley, Richard, and Val Routley. "Nuclear Energy and Obligations to the Future." *Inquiry* (1978), 133–179.

Woodward, James. "The Non-Identity Problem." *Ethics* 96 (1986), 804–831.

Robert Elliot

See also ECOLOGY AND ENVIRONMENTAL SCIENCES

International Jurisdiction

International jurisdiction refers to the competence of international tribunals and national courts to impose responsibility for acts or omissions pursuant to international law. An international tribunal may be defined as a tribunal which deals with legal issues not handled by a particular national jurisdiction.

International tribunals which exercise international jurisdiction include the International Court of Justice (ICJ), the Court of Justice of European Communities, the European Court of Human Rights and the Inter-American Court of Human Rights. Each of these courts exercises jurisdiction over the parties only by virtue of their consent. This is referred to as contentious, or consensual, jurisdiction. The courts' enforcement authority is limited to the agreement of the parties to comply with their decisions. The decisions of these courts and decisions from national courts resolving issues of international law are contained in International Law Reports.

Critics say the exercise of consensual jurisdiction becomes specious in practice because the parties can manipulate the courts' jurisdiction in self-serving ways. For instance, a party may deny that an international court has jurisdiction when a ruling is anticipated to go against them. A notable instance in which this occurred was the United States' denial of the ICJ's jurisdiction in the Nicaragua case involving allegations that the Central Intelligence Agency mined Nicaragua's ports. In support of its position that the court had no jurisdiction, the United States claimed that a declaration in which it originally accepted compulsory jurisdiction of the Permanent Court of Justice (the ICJ's predecessor) had never attained legal force and effect. The United States had also attempted to repudiate the court's jurisdiction by giving notice to the court that its compulsory jurisdiction would not apply to disputes pertaining to events in Central America. Nevertheless, the ICJ held that it properly had jurisdiction in the Nicaraguan case. The United States, in turn, declined to participate in the court's subsequent proceedings in the case.

Proponents say that due to the nature of international politics, consensual jurisdiction may be imperfect, yet it is at least an appropriate means of preserving respect for national sovereignty.

The International Military Tribunal at Nuremberg was established by the London Charter in 1945 for the prosecution of "Crimes Against the Peace," "War Crimes," and "Crimes Against Humanity" perpetrated in Europe during World War II. The following year an international military tribunal was established in Tokyo for prosecuting principal war criminals in the Asian theater. The exercise of international jurisdiction by the Nuremberg tribunal raises several controversial issues that bear on the very nature of the rule of law. Although both critics and supporters of the trial agreed that the Nazis brought before the tribunal were guilty of horrendous moral offenses, there is a question whether the court could justifiably try and punish them for international legal offenses. Critics of the trial advanced the following arguments: (1) there was an inadequate legal basis for the trial, since the charter instituting the tribunal did not define what a war of aggression was (thus violating the principle of "no crime without a law") and the court applied retroactive law to the defendants; (2) the tribunal was not impartial and amounted to political revenge by the victors over the vanquished, since it was impaneled exclusively by judges from the Allied countries; (3) a summary execution of the defendants would have been preferable since it would not have involved the pretense of a juridic proceeding under the rule of law. Supporters of the trial, however, maintained that (1) the international community had sufficiently outlawed aggressive war, war crimes, and crimes against humanity by means of extant international treaties and agreements; (2) though belonging to the Allied powers, the judges were in fact reasonably impartial as evidenced by their decision to acquit some defendants and to only impose the death sentence on the most culpable defendants; (3) granted that the trial may have involved less than perfect conformity to an ideal rule of law, on balance it was better than either lawless summary execution or a refusal to assert international legal jurisdiction over the Nazis would have been.

More recently, the War Crimes Tribunal for the former Yugoslavia has been established by the United Nations to prosecute individuals charged with war crimes committed during the Serbian onslaught of Bosnia in 1992.

National tribunals are sometimes accorded authority under domestic law to decide questions of international law. For instance, the Alien Tort Claims Act gives United States federal courts jurisdiction in lawsuits by an alien in tort for violations of the law of nations. In *Filartiga v. Pena-Irala,* 630 F.2d 876 (2d Cir. 1980), the U.S. Court of Appeals for the Second Circuit was faced with the jurisdictional issue of whether a foreign government's torture of its own nationals is violative of the "law of nations," that is, customary international law. The court held that sufficient international consensus existed to render the right not to be tortured by officials of one's own government a universalizable norm. The court argued that "[t]orture is viewed with universal abhorrence; the prohibition of torture by international consensus and express international accords is clear and unambiguous; and 'for purposes of civil liability, the torturer has become—like the pirate and the slave trader before him—*hostis humani generis,* an enemy of all mankind.'" In addition, the court stated that "[i]f the courts . . . are to adhere to the consensus of the community of humankind, any remedy they fashion must recognize that this case concerns an act so monstrous as to make its perpetrator an outlaw around the globe." Included in the sources of international law upon which the court based its decision was Article 5 of the Universal Declaration of Human Rights. The court indicated that the right to freedom from torture "has become

part of customary international law, as evidenced and defined by the Universal Declaration . . . which states, in the plainest of terms, 'no one shall be subjected to torture.' "

Critics hold that foreign governments are immune from civil liability except for a narrow class of actions: those in which a government has either consented to be sued or waived its sovereign immunity. Thus, they argue that national courts lack jurisdiction to hear most cases involving international legal violations by governments and their officials. Proponents, however, say that when cases involve deprivations of basic international human rights, foreign governments ought not to be able to avail themselves of the sovereign immunity defense. By violating nonderogable *jus cogens* (mandatory) norms, it is argued, a state is contravening the international community's collective will, and therefore cannot be performing a sovereign act entitled to immunity and has waived its right to claim that defense.

The jurisdiction of national courts over businesses from other countries is another critical issue in international law. A frequent matter of international dispute concerns the issue of whether a country can require a foreign company to defend lawsuits within its own territory. Generally, courts within each nation have jurisdiction over foreign business entities present in the country that are conducting business, just as they have jurisdiction over any domestic company. The businesses' presence is deemed to constitute consent to the jurisdiction of the courts of that country to handle cases in which they are named as a party.

References

Brownlie, Ian. *Principles of Public International Law.* Oxford: Harvard University Press, 1990.

Jackson, Robert H. "The Rule of Law Among Nations." *American Bar Association Journal* 31 (June 1945), 290–294.

Kelsen, Hans. "Will the Judgement in the Nuremberg Trial Constitute a Precedent in International Law?" *The International Law Quarterly* 1, no. 2 (Summer 1947), 153–171.

Mendelsohn, John. "Trial by Document: The Problem of Due Process for War Criminals at Nuremberg." *Prologue* 7, no. 4 (Winter 1975), 227–234.

Princz v. Federal Republic of Germany, 26 F3d 1166 (D.C. Cir. 1994).

Kevin T. Jackson

See also Jurisdiction; War and War Trials

Interpretation

Law, literature, history, theology, and other disciplines share a common interest in the interpretation of texts. Judges and lawyers, like historians and literary critics, face texts they have to understand, and this understanding is, at least in part, an interpretative activity. This common interest in the concept of interpretation, shared by such diverse disciplines, suggests that a general theory of interpretation is called for. Despite the diversity of purposes and context, interpretation is a unique intellectual activity worth exploring.

It is generally conceded that the concept of interpretation is closely related to the concept of meaning. Interpretation is, by and large, an explanation of the meaning of its object. This shared starting point, however, opens the door for considerable controversy about the kind of meaning in question, its point, and its limits. Generally speaking, a theory of interpretation should be expected to provide answers to at least three kinds of questions: What are the possible objects of interpretation? Namely, what are the kind of objects capable of bearing a certain meaning? Are these only products of communicative acts, such as texts and works of art, or perhaps just about any object one can tell a story about. Second, there is the question about the point of interpretation, that is, what makes a certain explanation, or understanding of an object, interpretative? Are there any limits on the kinds of understanding that can count as an interpretation of a text, for example, a certain degree of fit? What should an interpretation fit with—the text? What are its author's intentions? What are the interpreter's own interests and concerns? Finally, a theory of interpretation should also provide answers to the questions concerning the possibilities of truth and knowledge in this field. Are there correct and incorrect interpretations? Are there any objective truths about interpretations?

There are basically four main models of a general theory of interpretation. The oldest, perhaps, maintains that interpretation consists in the retrieval of the author's intentions.

This simple model has a considerable advantage over other theories, in that it renders interpretation objective in principle. Interpretation, according to this intentionalist model, is confined to a kind of factual inquiry, facts concerning the actual intentions of people, namely, the authors of the texts in question. The author's intention model, however, is generally regarded as very unsatisfactory. The practice of interpretation in such realms as literature and law does not support it; nor is it supported by a critical reflection on the nature of interpretation and, particularly, the complexities involved with the notion of "author's intention."

Among those who reject the author's intention model, some reach the opposite conclusion: interpretation, they say, is really not different from invention. There is nothing in the texts themselves that can constrain an interpretation of them. This skeptical model is closely associated, though not identical with the deconstruction school in literary theory. Between these two extremes, two further models have been developed in recent years: the constructive model of interpretation and the positivist model. One of the disputes among these two models concerns the question whether all understanding of texts is interpretative. According to the constructive model, the answer is affirmative, while interpretation is only the exception to the standard way of understanding texts and language according to the positivist model. Both models agree, however, that interpretations are partly evaluative and normative. Interpretation is not only a matter of discovery, but of evaluation and judgment as well. The kind of evaluations involved, and their relations to other aspects of understanding language and texts, forms further ground of controversy between these two models.

These and similar positions about the general concept of interpretation have considerable implications for legal theory and legal practice. Judges are expected to interpret certain kinds of texts, like statutes, constitutional provisions, and precedents. How are they to identify those texts as such, however? What are the criteria for the identification of certain texts as the appropriate objects of interpretation? Assuming that we have identified the relevant texts, can we assume that those texts substantially constrain their possible interpretations? If we think that texts themselves do not constrain the interpretation in any significant way, what is the basis of the legitimacy of judicial interpretations of statutes and constitutional provisions? Does interpretation differ at all from invention, and if not, is it reasonable and warranted that judges invent the law?

These conceptual and political concerns about the interpretative activities of lawyers and judges have always formed part of jurisprudence. Viewing them from the vantage point of a general theory of interpretation, however, is a fairly recent development. Since the early 1980s interpretation has become one of the main intellectual paradigms of legal philosophy. Like the interest in rules during the 1960s, and legal principles during the 1970s, much of legal theorizing since the 1980s has being built around the concept of interpretation. In one important respect, however, interpretation turned out to be a much more ambitious paradigm: it is not only a subject matter legal philosophers are interested in, but according to some influential scholars, interpretation is also a general method, a meta-theory of legal theory. According to this view, not only the legal practice is interpretative throughout, but legal theory, too. Ronald Dworkin, for instance, presented the interpretative attitude to legal theory as a rival to the analytical approach to jurisprudence.

It has been one of the central assumptions of the analytical school in legal philosophy, that a clear distinction can be drawn between the philosophical question What is law? and the lawyer's question What is the law on this or that matter? and between these two and the moral question What should the law be?

Dworkin's interpretative theory of law challenges these conceptual distinctions. Accounting for the concept of law, he claims, is inevitably tied up with considerations about what the law is there to settle. Law, Dworkin maintains, is not only an interpretative enterprise, but must also be accounted for by the very same methods employed by the participants; both theorists and practitioners are engaged in one and the same kind of reasoning, namely, in an attempt to impose the best interpretation on the practice they encounter. Thus the concept of law and the justification of its particular requirements can no longer be seen as two separate issues.

One of the main themes in dispute among legal philosophers since the early 1980s is whether this interpretative turn in legal philosophy is a turn for the better or worse. Dworkin's methodological turn seems to support an antipositivist stance in legal theory, as it challenges the conceptual distinction between what the law is and what the law should be. However, his model is subject to controversy among positivists and antipositivists alike. For Dworkin's school, interpretation is the paradigm of legal scholarship; for his opponents, interpretation is only the exception to the standard, preinterpretative understanding of texts and social practices.

References

Dworkin, Ronald. *Law's Empire*. London: Fontana Press, 1986.

Fish, Stanley. *Doing What Comes Naturally*. Oxford: Clarendon Press, 1989.

Marmor, Andrei. *Interpretation and Legal Theory*. Oxford: Clarendon Press, 1992.

———, ed. *Law and Interpretation: Essays in Legal Philosophy*. Oxford: Clarendon Press, 1995.

Mitchell, W.J.T., ed. *The Politics of Interpretation*. Chicago: University of Chicago Press, 1982.

Moore, Michael. "The Interpretative Turn in Modern Theory: A Turn for the Worse?" *Stanford Law Review* 41 (1989), 871–957.

Andrei Marmor

See also DECONSTRUCTIONIST PHILOSOPHY OF LAW; HERMENEUTICAL PHILOSOPHY OF LAW; INTENT

Intimacy

Privacy critics look at privacy law and see only confusion. From William Prosser to Hyman Gross, the right to privacy has been criticized as "pernicious" and "a malformation of constitutional law." The rationale for these criticisms is simple to discover. One need only consider that the United States constitutional right to privacy alone has been invoked to protect child rearing, family relationships, procreation, marriage, the home, contraception, and abortion. As for the tort of privacy, it has been used to protect against intrusion, to guard reputations, and to maintain personal seclusion. Looking over the extraordinary breadth of privacy rulings, they appear to lack any underlying unity. It seems that privacy rulings are concerned with unrelated matters: the security and seclusion of the home, the desire to conceal embarrassing personal facts, property claims, procreation, and family relationships. At first view, privacy appears to protect nothing more than diverse autonomy issues, lacking any conceptual or moral core that would justify its special legal protection. Rather than focusing on the impossible task of gathering together these heterogeneous issues under the rubric "privacy," we should focus on protecting an agent's claim to autonomy or liberty.

Yet is privacy as formless a concept as has been claimed? Intimacy theorists suggest that privacy protects a realm of individual autonomy with respect to emotional intimacy. Looking at privacy rulings from the perspective of intimacy, homogeneity is discovered rather than heterogeneity. In constitutional privacy rulings, for example, the U.S. Supreme Court repeatedly mentions intimacy as a crucial distinguishing factor. From citing the "intimate marital relation" in *Griswold v. Connecticut,* 381 U.S. 478 (1965), to acknowledging the intimacy of the home in *Stanley v. Georgia,* 394 U.S. 557 (1969), to showing regard for a woman's "intimate personal decision" in *Roe v. Wade,* 410 U.S. 113 (1973), the Court has stressed the relationship between privacy and intimacy. In *Paris Adult Theatre I v. Slayton,* 410 U.S. 49 (1973), the Court suggests that the right to privacy protects decisions about "personal intimacies." Looking to tort privacy rulings, theorists such as Samuel Warren, Louis Brandeis, and Edward Bloustein suggest that privacy protects one's "inviolate personality" or "human dignity." In a classic case such as *De May v. Roberts,* the privacy violation developed because the defendant had gained access to the "intimacies of childbirth," to use Bloustein's evocative phrase—accessing childbirth being intimate because it involves access to both childbirth and a woman's undressed body, forms of access that touch the closest of emotional ties. More generally, the tort of privacy developed from Warren and Brandeis's desire to regulate intimate access and information. For Warren and Brandeis, an individual could not possess an "inviolate personality" unless one had control over access to the "domestic circle" and "private life" and control over information that is "whispered in the closet," such as information about "the details of sexual relations." Stepping back from tort and constitutional privacy, intimacy-based privacy theorists, such as Ferdinand Schoeman and Julie Inness, argue that privacy law is unified due to its underlying concern to protect a realm of intimacy, including a person's control over intimate decisions about access to oneself and one's fundamental life choices. Protecting such a realm enables the person to construct one's own self and personal relationships free from manipulation, scrutiny, or adverse judgment.

For the intimacy-based privacy theorist, privacy law is intensely important due to the protection it extends to an interest that many people understand as crucial for human happiness. Protecting privacy clearly depends on whether one can locate its conceptual core, a core that is understood to possess a value that demands distinct protection. As stated by Warren and Brandeis, intimacy-based accounts of privacy locate such a core in the fact that the individual's "inviolate personality" can sustain "spiritual" wrongs when denied freedom with respect to crafting one's individuality and close emotional relationships. Privacy violations damage a person's "own feelings" since they fail to acknowledge the person's autonomy with respect to one's emotional life. As the Court noted in *Roberts v. United States Jaycees,* 468 U.S. 609 (198A), intimate activities embody the fact that we all depend on the "emotional enrichment of close ties with others." People need to develop close emotional ties with not only the self but also friends, family members, and sexual partners; privacy protects a domain which provides fertile soil for such emotional ties. Privacy claims cannot be reduced to liberty claims without loss, for people place a distinct value on protection of autonomy with respect to intimacy. From protecting a personal diary, guarding the home, or allowing for contraceptive use in marriage, privacy acknowledges that people are emotional as well as rational beings, needing protection for their relationships to both self and other. Although the concerns of Estelle Griswold, Samuel Warren, and Louis Brandeis may appear unrelated, they shared a common desire to protect the agent's "inviolate personality" with respect to intimacy.

References

Bloustein, Edward. "Privacy as an Aspect of Human Dignity: An Answer to Dean Prosser." *New York University Law Review* 39 (1964), 962–1007.

Gross, Hyman. "The Concept of Privacy." *New York University Law Review* 42 (1967), 34–54.

Inness, Julie. *Privacy, Intimacy, and Isolation.* New York: Oxford University Press, 1992.

Prosser, William. "Privacy." *California Law Review* 48 (1960), 383–422.

Schoeman, Ferdinand, ed. *Philosophical Dimensions of Privacy: An Anthology.* New York: Cambridge University Press, 1984.

Warren, Samuel, and Louis Brandeis. "The Right to Privacy." *Harvard Law Review* 4 (1890), 193–220.

Julie Inness

See also PRIVACY

Is/Ought Gap

The allegation of a gap in reasoning from purely descriptive premises (is) to a prescriptive conclusion (ought) is often called the central problem in moral philosophy. A descriptive claim purports to state only facts, as distinct from evaluations. A prescriptive claim recommends an act or policy and thus involves evaluation. The claimed existence of the is/ought gap is called Hume's Law, since David Hume was evidently the first to articulate the problem in book three of his *Treatise.* Controversy surrounds Hume's position, however. Some claim the is/ought gap seems merely Hume's afterthought to another discussion, and suggest that Hume did not imply that the is/ought gap is insurmountable; others suggest that Hume thought exactly that. There surely is an is/ought gap in many arguments. For example, "Slavery is legal. Therefore, slavery morally ought to be allowed." The problem is whether every moral argument either has an is/ought gap or else relies on prescriptions in its premises. The latter is a problem because so many moral skeptics and relativists work to deny any moral prescription in any premise. A bridge to the is/ought gap would frustrate moral skeptics and relativists because the bridge would make morality depend purely on facts and deductive logic, which is as objective and grounded in knowledge as any argument can get.

The is/ought gap is a misnomer, since there are obvious cases where the gap is bridged. For example, consider "Serial killing is immoral. Therefore, you ought not to become a serial killer." Or "It is wrong to kill any human. Therefore, you ought not to kill any Greek." The premises use "is," but they are not purely descriptive claims. The real problem is to move validly from purely descriptive premises to prescriptive conclusions. Of course, the whole of the premises can be greater than the sum of their parts. Each premise can be purely descriptive, but the set of premises could have more than descriptive import. The premises can have a synergy that works to imply a prescriptive conclusion. To deny this possibility is to commit the fallacy of composition, to insist that whatever is true of each premise (pure descriptiveness) must be true of the set of premises considered as a whole (that the set is purely descriptive). Fine candidates for examples where the is/ought gap seems bridged include "Dynamite is dangerous to use. Therefore, you ought to be at least a little careful when using dynamite"; and "Torturing children randomly is no more than gratuitous suffering. Therefore, you ought not torture children randomly"; and "To kill a man just to watch him die is needless. Therefore, you ought not kill a man just to watch him die."

Another approach to solving the problem suggests there is no more of an is/ought gap than there is an is/is gap. For example, one might never be able to deduce truths of psychology from truths of biology, or truths of biology from truths of chemistry, or truths of chemistry from truths of physics. Still, if we find no conceptual trouble in moving from claims of chemistry to claims of biology, for instance, we should by parity of reasoning remain similarly untroubled about moving from pure descriptions to prescriptions. There are other logical moves besides valid deduction.

The is/ought gap concerns philosophy of law in both major and minor problems. A major problem is the debate between natural law and legal positivism. The existence of an insurmountable is/ought gap would favor the legal positivists, since they deny any necessary connections between law and morals. Many legal positivists see law as a matter of sociological fact (is) which need not connect with morals (ought). However, if the is/ought gap can be bridged, that would favor the natural lawyers, since they affirm some necessary connection between law and morals. A natural lawyer might be able to use such a bridge to argue "X is a law. Therefore, X ought to be obeyed." A minor problem concerning the is/ought gap is the tort doctrine of *res ipsa loquitur* (that is, the thing speaks for itself). The doctrine holds that negligent care over some events simply is so obvious that there ought to be some liability to remedy these events. For example, if the ordinary opening of a bottle of soda leads it to explode in one's face, the bottle's manufacturer has tort liability under the doctrine.

References

Brink, David O. *Moral Realism and the Foundations of Ethics*. Cambridge: Cambridge University Press, 1989.

Garofalo, Bruno. "A Note on the 'Is/Ought' Problem in Hume's Ethical Writings." *Journal of Value Inquiry* 19 (1985), 311–318.

Hare, Richard Mervyn. *The Language of Morals*. Oxford: Clarendon Press, 1952.

Hudson, W.D, ed. "The Is/Ought Question." In *A Collection of Papers on the Central Problem in Moral Philosophy*. New York: St. Martin's Press, 1969.

Karmo, Toomas. "Some Valid (But No Sound) Arguments Trivially Span the 'Is'-'Ought' Gap." *Mind* 97 (1988), 252–257.

Prior, A.N. *Logic and the Basis of Ethics*. Oxford: Clarendon Press, 1949.

Schultz, Janice L. " 'Ought'-Judgments: A Descriptivist Analysis from a Thomistic Perspective." *The New Scholasticism* 61 (1987), 400–426.

Silvers, Anita, and Sterling Harwood. "Moral Reasoning." In *Critical Thinking*, ed. Brooke Noel Moore and Richard Parker, 3d ed., 363–367. Mountain View CA: Mayfield Publishing, 1992.

von Wright, George Henrik. "Is and Ought." In *Man, Law and Modern Forms of Life*, ed. Eugenio Bulygin, 263–281. Dordrecht: Reidel, 1985.

Yang, Shu-Tung. "Moral Reasoning. A Discussion with John Searle Concerning 'Is' and 'Ought'." *The Philosophical Review* (Taiwan) 11 (1988), 81–106.

Sterling Harwood

See also FACTS AND LAW

Isidore (550–636)

Isidore, Bishop of Seville, as scholar and statesman involved himself in the crisis over elective monarchy among Visigoths in the Iberian Peninsula. His philosophy of law reflects classical heritage and practical life.

Isidore of Seville received the episcopate from his brother, St. Leander, who had participated in efforts for the political unification of the country, and had a prominent role in converting the king (and his people) from the Arian heresy to Christian orthodoxy. Isidore continued this role by presiding at the Second (619) and Fourth (633) Councils of Toledo and influencing their texts.

Isidore's contribution to the philosophy of law was a reinterpretation of some points of the philosophy of Roman law, a strong position about juridical legitimation of power, and a new conception of the role of the governed, chiefly concerning their relations with the government. Although his paternity is seldom recognized, Isidore fathered most of the Western tradition about some points of natural law, its position on tyranny in the exercise of power, and one family of systems concerning the protection of rights.

Isidore was not a legalist. "Law" (*ius*) is derived from "just" (*iustum*); this etymology approximates the conception of Roman law fixed by Ulpian. This law, *ius*, can be materialized either in laws (*lex;* derivation attributed to *legendo,* to read), or in customs (*consuetudo*; from *communis usu*s, common practice). Isidore reminds us that laws can be divine or human. The latter are based on custom and the former on nature. The difference between the different laws of various nations is due to the existence of manifold customs. Isidore explains the reason for written Roman law: the Roman people could no longer bear their magistrates, who had deceived them; so the Law of the Twelve Tables was written to make the rule public and to avoid the corruption and errors of the weak.

The important question concerning the reason and provenance of laws did not escape him: law has to keep in consideration every individual in society, both victims and criminals. It must be honest, just, possible, and clear, according to nature and to national custom, locally and temporally appropriate, and designed for the common good.

The internal logic of Isidore's theory may seem to dissolve because of its openness to his religious environment: the presence of divine law, not always compatible with the structure of his system; or the idea that all norm systems based on reason (law or custom) are law. This reveals the syncretism then current.

His idea of the real and objective protection of persons, a fundamental basis for the "Iberian way" of liberty, is present in Isidore's idea of natural law. Isidore maintains that marriage, procreation and education are natural institutions, following Ulpian's lead. However, he substitutes much more material rights for the stoic principle that natural law is common to people and animals: liberty, and the common property of everything not possessed individually, is limited by individual appropriation. This is the principle that private property is a social good. He supports a right to the return of what is loaned and a right to self-defense. Isidore also extends natural rights to any "similar things." In this, he did follow his time, by including in natural law the duties of obedience toward God, parents, or the nation, despite his classical source in Pomponius.

This clarification in natural law, reaffirmed by the Decree of Gratian, clarifies also the concept of *ius gentium,* which for Isidore is already an international law. In public law, the acts of Councils reveal more than their theoretical tracts do. The legacy for one powerful theory in political law is laid by the phrase *Rex eris si recte facias, si non facias non eris.* (You are king if you behave correctly, if you do not you are king no more.) While not an original discovery, being already present in Roman thought, and echoing Horace, it becomes the slogan for a new age on the Iberian peninsula, and the seed for its concrete, material freedom. Legitimation of title and exercise, and theories of tyrannicide, have been germinating ever since. The deposition of incompetent and despotic kings was, as a consequence, perfectly natural after this doctrine, and took place several times.

References

Albert, Bat-Shiva. "Isidore of Seville: His Attitude Toward Judaism and His Impact on Early Medieval Canon Law." *Jewish Quarterly Review* 80 (1990), 207

Bourret, J.C.E. *L'Ecole chrétienne de Séville sous la monarchie des Visigoths* (The Christian School of Seville Under the Visigoth Kingdom). Paris, 1855.

Bravo Lira, Bernardino. "Derechos Politicos y Civiles en España, Portugal y America Latina. Apuntes para una Historia por hacer" (Political and Civil Rights in Spain, Portugal and Latin America. Notes Toward a History). In *Poder y respeto a las personas en Iberoamerica,* 35–68. Valparaiso: Universidad Catolica de Valparaiso, 1989.

Brehaut, Ernest. *An Encyclopedist of the Dark Ages: Isidore of Seville.* New York: B. Franklin, 1964.

Cunha, Paulo Ferreira da. "Do Direito Clássico ao Direito Medieval. O papel de S. Isidoro de Sevilha na supervivência do Direito Romano e na criação do Direito Ibérico" (From Classical Law to Modern. St. Isidore of Seville on the Survival of Roman Law and the Crisis of Iberian Law). In *Para uma História Constitucional do Direito Português,* 93–113. Coimbra, 1995.

Fontaine, J. *Isidore de Séville et la culture classique dans l'Espagne Wisigothique* (Isidore of Seville and Classical Culture in Visigoth Spain). Paris, 1959.

———. *Tradition et actualité chez Isidore de Seville* (Isidore of Seville: Tradition and Modernity). London: Variorum Reprints, 1988.

Isidore of Seville. *History of the Kings of the Goths, Vandals and Suevi.* 2 rev. ed. Trans. Guido Donini and Gordon B. Ford, Jr. Leiden: E.J. Brill, 1970.

Montoro Ballesteros, Alberto. "Raíces medievales de la protección de los derechos humanos" (Medieval Roots for the Protection of Human Rights). *Anuario de Derechos Humanos* (Madrid) 6 (1990), 85–147.

Sejourne, Paul. *Le dernier Père de l'Eglise, Saint Isidore de Seville. Son rôle dans l'histoire du Droit Canonique* (The Last Father of the Church: St. Isidore of Seville and His Role in the History of Canon Law). Paris, 1929.

Paulo Ferreira da Cunha

Islamic Philosophy of Law

Law and its principles is a study which Islamic scholars have pursued deeply. This article describes their study of the law briefly, sketches how philosophers have treated it, and analyzes some aspects. Only the classical period is treated, before Islamic jurisprudence felt the influence of Western legislation. The nineteenth century saw the movement by reformers who sought a return to pure Islam, starting from first principles; they were opposed by modernists, who looked for a reform based on the demands of modern life. During the twentieth century, a more or less complete adoption of modern law took place, with its constitutional and social content.

Law and Legal Principles

In Islam the science of law is called *fiqh*. *Fiqh* deals with both the public and private dimensions of life, and so contains both ritual (*'ibâdât*) and social (*mu'âmalât*) practices and extends to all parts of the law.

Usûl al-fiqh (the sources of law) is the science of legal principles, the methodology of legal reasoning; it studies the arguments or formal grounds for legal rules. For most jurisprudential schools, there are four principles: the Koran, the words and deeds of the Prophet (Sunna), the consensus *(ijmâ)*, and reasoning by analogy *(qiyâs)*. At various times, account has also been taken of informed personal opinion or intelligent decision (*ra'y*), public utility (*maslaha*), and the purposes of law (*maqâsid*).

The legal traditions in orthodox Islam (Sunnism) are Hanafism, Malkism, Shafiism, Hanbalism, and Zahirism. The nonorthodox schools are Kharijisme and Shi'ism, which founded law and legal principles on different theories of legitimate power. So law remains closely linked to politics. From origins as living schools these doctrines were institutionalized into well-established formulae on the basis that only traditional teachers have the privilege to employ *ijtihâd* (personal efforts at independent legal reasoning by the jurist). Since the tenth century, when this notion was made into an unquestionable dogma, which is usually called the "closing of the door of *ijtihâd*," what has dominated has been imitation of these teachers.

The arrangement of classical contents under *ash'arite* theological obedience by al Ghazali (d. 1111) in his *Mustasfâ* can be used. Since each law has a definition and a structure and has a relation to the legislator who sets it, to whomever applies it, to the actions it concerns, and to whatever motivates or causes it, law has the following arrangement.

Statute

Statutes are the words of the legislator under religious law, addressed to a person who has obligations (*taklîf*) and which characterizes his actions. If a statute imposes an action and a sanction for disobedience, it is (1) a prescription (*wujûb*) or, if no sanction, (2) an affirmative counsel (*nadb*). If it imposes an abstention with sanction, it is (3) a proscription (*hurma*); and if without sanction, (4) it is a negative counsel (*karâha*). Finally, the agent may be left with liberty to choose, and this is (5) a permission (*ibâha*).

Evidence

Evidence includes the verses of the Koran, the Sunna, and unanimous agreement (*ijmâ*) by the community (Umma).

Procedures

Procedures are the means through which evidence establishes laws by drawing one from another. Procedures are binding in order to ensure validity. This is where *qiyâs* (analogy) and *'illa* (the reason for legal characterization) are treated.

Ijtihâd

This is the fact of making the greatest possible effort to discern the precepts of the law. *Mujtahid,* the person who makes the effort, needs a good knowledge of the sources of law—the Koran, Sunna, and the consensus. This person judges through one's own opinion in contrast to the mere imitator who is content to take prescriptions from the *mujtahid* without their reasons (*dalîl*).

Philosophers and Law

Falâsafa are the Arab-Muslim philosophers who look to hellenic and hellenistic culture to think through the issues arising within their community. This is how they deal with *fiqh,* although the major classical divisions of philosophy are not usually fitted to such legal study. Ibn Rushd (Averroes, d. 1198), the Commentator on Aristotle, exemplifies the joining of philosophical understanding to Islamic law and legal principles. His book *Bidayat al-mujtahíd wa nihâyat al-muqtasid* reorganizes malikite law according to reason so as to make *ijtihâd* accessible. He also recapitulated the *Mustasfâ* of Ghazâlî by highlighting its technical materials. Before Averroes, al-Fârabî (d. 950) developed *fiqh* and laid out its philosophical groundwork. In his book outlining the sciences, *Ihsâ' al-'ulûm,* he names politics among the philosophical sciences and, within that, two sciences: *kalâm* (theology) and *fiqh*. Within politics, these take on a philosophical stature. Fârâbî defines *fiqh* as the science by which a person becomes able to discern the value of things, and to determine the order of values when that has not been defined by the first legislator, but in agreement with those so defined and their intention. This discourse is set within political philosophy which, as for Plato, has as its purpose to characterize the good city ruled by the philosopher-king and how to achieve it. In this, religion has the political role of expressing in an imaginative representation accessible to citizens the truths grasped intellectually by the philosopher. Legal philosophy is part of political philosophy; legal philosophy alone can determine universal theories and practices and the best ways to achieve them in the city. Fârâbî clearly substitutes philosophical truths for the traditional principles of law.

Philosophical Aspects

Whether Islamic law is a source of inspiration or is a set of positive legal norms is often discussed. The basic point is that law and religion are intimately associated. Beneath *fiqh* lies the idea that every act falls under a prescription of the legislator, each with its own evidence so that another can be drawn by analogy when needed.

The liberty found in *fiqh* and in *usûl al-fiqh* should not be overlooked. First of all, disagreements are often legitimate, as noted by Ibn Khaldun in *Muqaddima*. This can be seen in *ijtihâd,* where a saying of the Prophet is often repeated: "A judge is rewarded once when mistaken, and twice when he is right." The *mujtahid* is not, then, infallible. Such decision has the validity of an opinion (*zann*), because legal "truth" on any question does not belong to one judgment only. The logical dimension of true or false judgment is distinguished from the dimension of legal responsibility, of innocence or guilt. Once at this level, one is forbidden just to follow another's judgment on the *mujtahid,* but is required to reach one's own conclusion. The nonprofessional, on the contrary, is required to consult someone learned, who provides a legal opinion (*fatwâ*). As well, one can choose freely which tradition to follow.

To exemplify the philosophical issues, the relations between Islamic disciplines of religion *(Ilm al-kalâm,* rational theology), law, and the principles of law can be noted. The "principles of religion" is frequently taken as a universal theoretical science setting down religious principles in terms of their rationality, which the particular practical sciences of law and its principles take as true without demonstration. The principles of law can rightly be seen as an Islamic philosophy of law, and theology as a philosophical discipline treating with autonomous rationality such first-order questions as free and necessitated human acts and their good or evil moral character, along with their axiological foundation, which moves between objectivist ethics and subjectivist ethics, divine or human.

In the objectivist ethics of Mu'tazilism, actions themselves are characterized as good or evil. Reason can reach this ethical reality, and humans are by nature in the state of having obligations (*taklîf*) even before the advent of religious law. Religious law for the most part confirms rational axiology. Legal prescriptions can be explained by their objective cause (*ta'lît*). A parallel can be drawn between moral demands and legal requirements, as noted by Abd al-Jabbâr in *Sharh al-usûl al-khamsa.*

In the ethical subjectivism of Ash'arism, it is the will of God, subject to no objective good and evil, which dictates what to do. This depends on no ethical or legal order prior to the law. In the absence of religious law, moral values have for their criterion personal interest and pleasure. Legal requirements in their essential definition are purely the expression of the law's discourse, expressing no moral character intrinsic to an action. So reason can never grasp this order by itself, without or outside the religious law.

Clearly the definitions of the five legal standards vary to the extent that scholars affirm or deny ethical realism. For Mu'tazilites, for example, an obligatory action is one for which its agent necessarily merits praise for performing or blame for refusing. For Ash'arites, obligation is only what is imposed by the law, with a mere possibility for reward or punishment, and so God remains free. Based on the axiological neutrality of actions, Ash'arites say that the starting point for deciding a case according to law must always be the absence of legal requirement (*nafy aslî, barâ'a asliyya,* the primal condition of noncharacterization of actions), unless there is a prescription from written sources or analogical reasoning, while always following the principle to avoid what is harmful to persons (*nafy al-haraj*). Law becomes the exception, which results in enlarging the domain of what is permitted. For Mu'tazilism, if there is no legal requirement, any action must be considered in terms of its objective ethical requirements, if any.

References

Anderson, N. *The Study of Islamic Law.* Ann Arbor: University of Michigan Press, 1977.

Coulson, N.J. *A History of Islamic Law.* Edinburgh: University Press, 1964.

Faruki, K. *Islamic Jurisprudence.* Karachi: Pakistan Publishing House, 1962.

Goldziher, I. *Muslim Studies.* Trans. S.M. Stern. Vol. 2. Chicago: Aldine Publishing, 1971.

Khadduri, M. *Islamic Jurisprudence.* Baltimore, 1961.

Laghmani, S. *Eléments d'Histoire de la Philosophie du droit.* T.1. Tunis: Presses de l'Université de Tunis, 1993.

Masud, M.Kh. *Islamic Legal Philosophy: A Study of . . . Shâtibî's Life and Thought.* Islamabad: Islamabad Research Institute, 1977.

Schacht, J. *An Introduction to Islamic Law.* Oxford: Clarendon Press, 1964.

———. "Islamic Religious Law." In *The Legacy of Islam.* Oxford: Clarendon Press, 1974.

Shehata, Shafiq T. *Études de droit musulman.* Paris: Presses Universitaires de France, 1971–1973.

Shuafi Aui, Mohammad ibn Idruis. *Islamic Jurisprudence,* trans. Majid Khadduri. Baltimore: Johns Hopkins University Press, 1961.

Moqdad Arfa Mensia
Mongia Arfa Mensia

J

Japanese and Asian Philosophy of Law

By the end of the isolation policy of the Tokugawa Shogunate (1603–1868), Japan had developed an effective power structure, a system of administration, and a system of justice, including dispute settlement and redressing crimes. However, whether the Tokugawa Shogunate had "law" poses a question of definition. If we include administration based on nonjusticiable regulations and orders (that is, "do as you are told" law) in our definition of "law," the Tokugawa had a considerable body of law. Indeed, the term "law" is, even in today's discourse, often used to reflect administration of the nonjusticiable sort, as well as to refer to rights-enforcing, justiciable law required by a modern rule of law. Justiciable law is based on rules applicable to all equally, rules which create rights enforceable in independent courts with due process, the help of lawyers, and, notably, enforcement by suits initiated by citizens (that is, enforcement from the bottom up through an independent judiciary, rather than administration imposed from the top down by officials issuing "do as you are told" orders to the subjects).

Much can be said for using two words: one, "law," for justiciable rules, and another, "administration," for top-down orders. This is simply because law and administration are significantly different ways of wielding state power. If we limit "law" to justiciable law, then Japan before 1868 had precious little, if any, such "law," but it did have a command system of administrative orders (by "do as you are told" law) congenial to the sinic, disciplinary philosophy of governance as opposed to a rule of law.

The point that is critical to an understanding of the traditional Japanese philoso-phy of governance without law is this. The sinic philosophy, borrowed, adapted, and used by the Japanese from at least the seventh century onward, did not include even the idea of law, which the western heritage takes for granted as a universal category. For western jurisprudence, law is reified, external, transcendental, and given from above. Its idea of law arises first from the Bible and Christianity where all are equal before God; law is sourced outside of persons, given by God and transcendent, extant, reified, valid, univerally applicable equally to all. The prototype is the Ten Commandments. The basic category of law was later spread over human affairs by the Romans and natural law and positive law, as well as by private law and public law schisms that later appeared with the emergence of the modern state. Independent courts followed after Montesquieu, and the American constitution added judicial review of governmental acts to complete what is now the rule of law regime widely identified with western legal philosophy but largely unknown in the sinic culture embraced by Japan up to the Meiji Restoration (1868), which destroyed the old Shogunate and revived the Imperial government in the name of the Emperor. A rule of law was not put in place until the postwar Showa constitution (1947).

The major issue of Japanese philosophy, raised by the foregoing discussion, is: How was traditional Japan governed without western-style law, lawsuits, and lawyers operating in independent courts? What was the substitute for "law"?

Japan's system of governance was adopted and adapted over a period of more than two millennia from Chinese culture and philosophy; especially important were elements drawn from the sinic family culture and developed over the centuries from the thought attributed originally to Confucius (K'ung Ch'iu, 531–479? B.C.) but developed centuries later by Chu Hsi (1130–1200) into a neo-confucianism, which became the orthodox ideology of the rulers in China and Korea, as well as in Japan, for centuries right up to the twentieth century. Chu Hsi's philosophy was known in the Tokugawa period as Shushijzaku and sponsored by the descendants of Hayashi Razan (1583–1657). These hereditary, neo-confucian scholars operated a training school for samurai in Edo (named Shoheiko), in turn supported by Shoguns for twelve generations, though neo-confucianism was not adopted officially as the orthodox philosophy of the Shogunate until 1790.

The content of neo-confucianism, as interpreted for the Tokugawa, had metaphysical and religious aspects, but its essential core was a political and ethical system based on authority and hierarchy suitable for maintenance of the Shogunate in power. One hierarchy ranked social classes in accordance with their worth in society: warriors, farmers, merchants, and artisans (Shi-no-sho-ko). Another hierarchy ranked persons in familial relations: father over son (or lord over servant), man over wife (or male over female), older brother over younger, and friend to friend. These neo-confucian social and ethical principles supported a power structure in society based on unquestioning subordination of inferior to superior, making for an efficient disciplinary system to administer the country. The genius of the system was the total delegation of responsibility, without recourse, right down to the smallest social unit, the family. The head of the family spoke for all its members, who did not exist as individuals in contemplation of the administration.

The delegation to village and family authorities of the duties of compliance made the "do as you are told" orders especially effective, because enforcement was left to those who knew and cared about each other. It was more a social governance than a legal regime enforced by police and officials.

However, the sinic confucian model of governance, though sensitive, communitarian, and efficient, was a regime based on authority (without recourse), on order and discipline, and on duties, not rights. Notably it was a system based on systemic inequality. Needless to

say this Japanese time-honored approach to social order presents a stark contrast to a modern western regime of law and equality based on justiciable rights.

In this Japanese system the channeling of behavior (as a leading function of western law) was achieved by interpersonal didactic guidance from the authority figures and by moral intuition imparted by the orthodox ideology to the underlings. By permeating the society down to the head of the household, the Japanese traditional disciplinary system without justiciable law had a built-in value system: unquestionable loyalty to the masters (Samurai, husbands, older brothers, and such) and subordination of the member to the group interest. These few principles can be seen as akin to "natural law." The exercise of authority at the ultimate level of the village and family solved also the jurisprudential problem of equity (or individuation). Social authorities uninhibited by rules could simply fit the orders to the circumstances. There was no spurious equality demanded by rules of law, nor were there imperatives to treat unequal people equally. It was, however, a human rule fraught with the risk of condoning might as right. Unconvincing as it may seem, the theory was that authority goes with wisdom and virtue of the confucian family heads and other superiors.

In sum, here was a system of social discipline bereft completely of external, transcendent law, imposed on all alike for the channeling of behavior. Instead, acceptable behavior was specified by the superiors and adjusted by the interpersonal give-and-take.

In dispute settlement as well, the system functioned tolerably, it seems, without justiciable law, not even a glimmering of it except perhaps in the sole area of the assessing of penalties for specific crimes once the criminal was apprehended. All disputes were settled between the parties by conciliation or mediation of social superiors, but not heard by them as a matter of the petitioner's right, rather as a matter of the superior's grace; if the settlement process foundered, he did not adjudicate but instead instructed. What is important here is to understand, however, that in traditional society, there was nothing resembling a court, or a lawyer, or a right. Thus, mediated dispute settlement was all there was; it was "mainstream" dispute resolution, and not the "alternative" dispute resolution (ADR), which has sprung up in America recently. Both the channeling of behavior and settling of disputes were essentially a matter of sociology, not law, in traditional Japan.

The essential sociality of this whole system of channeling social behavior and settling disputes was dependent on interaction man to man, and the guidance and agreed settlements were evoked from within the interacting parties themselves, not imposed or required by applying external rules of law, nor adjudication.

A system of governance based on interaction of superiors and inferiors to generate ad hoc, tailor-made guidance of behavior from day to day was not readily understood by early western observers. Some of the best were missionaries and diplomats, and instinctively, it seems, they discussed sinic governance in hometown legal terms, referring to courts, lawyers, and adjudication without realizing that the processs and roles they were observing lacked the essential elements of "law."

It is to the credit of Meiji leaders, on whom fell the task of modernizing Japan, that they soon came to realize that their confucian system of social discipline was not apt for the commercial industrial society which they hoped to create in a nineteenth-century quest for national security against colonial powers. So the project they embarked upon to import a full set of western legal codes and to superimpose it on the tenacious customs of two hundred and fifty years of national isolation turned out to be one of the great episodes of comparative jurisprudence. Unfortunately, the enormity of the task, the complexity of social, cultural, and philosophical differences, and the inscrutability of it all in the Japanese language has obscured the true dimensions of the historic enterprise, unique perhaps in scale and complexity.

Bibliographies on the Japanese philosophy of law are scarce, especially in western languages. P. Granet and Joseph Needham were among the first to correct the early scholars' tendency to "translate backwards" into Chinese and Japanese governance the western legal concepts and institutions, which in fact were so basic to their instinct that they did not notice that the differences were fundamental, not just cosmetic or of detail.

References

Granet, P. *La Pensée Chinoise* (Chinese Thought). Paris: Renaissance du Livre, 1934.

Henderson, Dan Fenno. *Conciliation and Japanese Law: Tokugawa and Modern.* 2 vols. Tokyo: University of Tokyo Press, 1965.

Needham, Joseph. *Science and Civilization in China.* Vol. 11. Cambridge: Cambridge University Press, 1956.

Northrup, F.S.C. "The Mediational Approach Theory of Law in American Realism." *Virginia Law Review* 44 (1958), 357.

Ryosuke, Ishii. *Japanese Legislation in the Meiji Era.* Tokyo: Pan-Pacific Press, 1958.

Stephens, Thomas B. *Order and Discipline in China: The Shanghai Mixed Court 1911–27.* Seattle: University of Washington, 1992.

Dan Fenno Henderson

See also: CHINESE PHILOSOPHY OF LAW; INDIAN PHILOSOPHY OF LAW

Jewish Law

The Jewish legal system, known as the "halakhah" (from the root *halakh,* to go), is a comprehensive, transnational system of law that is over three thousand years old. The concept of law in the Jewish legal system is extremely broad. It includes not only those subjects found in modern legal systems, such as laws of familial and personal status, civil law, criminal law, and national and international relationships, but also matters of ritual, ceremonial, moral, and cultic obligation. Although some of these laws are inoperative today, due to the loss of political sovereignty and the destruction of the Temple, the remainder of the law continues to apply and develop despite the absence of the framework of a state and of a supreme court. Thus, law is not defined in national-territorial terms.

Religious Character of Jewish Law

Although the halakhah distinguishes between matters of ritual law and civil law, it does not recognize the modern distinction between secular and religious law. The norms regulating societal obligations are derived from the same sources and subject to the same methods of legal reasoning, legal classification, sanctions, and binding force as those regulating obligations to God. This integration of law and religion poses a challenge for the application of modern jurisprudential models to the Jewish legal system. Several contemporary scholars have applied positivist models to Jewish law. According to Menachem Elon, Jewish law is composed of the sources of law and means of creating and developing law recognized by the legal system, the ultimate authority of which is divine command. In contrast, José Faur argues that the covenant established between God and the people of Israel is the source of the authority of the law. As in other models of a social contract between subjects and sovereign, the result of the covenant is the creation of a new sovereign authority, the law, to which both parties are subject. These and other theories of Jewish law correspond only partially with general theories of jurisprudence.

Structure of Jewish Law

Although modern critical scholarship understands the halakhah as a developmental phenomenon, according to classical rabbinic legal theory, Jewish law originated in the revelation by God to Moses of the written and oral law in a historical event at Mount Sinai. The written law consists of the commandments, positive and negative, found in the Torah (the Five Books of Moses). The oral law consists of laws handed down through the oral tradition; interpretations of the written law, including those that are linked to scripture by the application of rabbinic hermeneutics, an elaborate system of interpretation known as *midrash* (from the root *darash*, to inquire and implying inquiry into scripture); and logical deduction. In addition, the oral law tradition includes rabbinic decrees and enactments to preserve and enhance the law and customs ratified by the legislative authorities. Rabbinic jurisprudence also distinguishes between laws considered scriptural (of the Torah) and those deemed rabbinic (of the scholars). Both scriptural and rabbinic law are obligatory, but ordinarily there is greater lenity in the treatment of rabbinic law. The precise classification of scriptural and rabbinic law is the subject of internal disagreement that can only be resolved through analysis of the legal sources.

The oral law tradition is now found in the "Mishnah," a record of the legal debates and decisions of the rabbinic teachers known as *tannaim* and edited by Rabbi Judah Ha-Nasi in about 220 C.E., and in the Palestinian and Babylonian "Talmuds," the records of the debates

and decisions of the rabbinic teachers known as *amoraim* (ca. 220–500 C.E.). Scriptural law is also known and transmitted through the oral law tradition found in the Talmud. The close of the Babylonian Talmud marks the close of the oral law tradition. According to rabbinic legal theory, the Babylonian Talmud was accepted by all of Israel and its statements of the law are final and authoritative.

In the posttalmudic period, judicial application of the law to new circumstances is found in the vast *responsa* literature, which functions as the case law of the halakhic system. New legislation continues through local rabbinical enactments (*takkanot*). Normative, standard practice is also communicated and elaborated through the posttalmudic codes, each with its own spheres of geographic influence, the most prominent of which are the twelfth-century Mishneh Torah of Maimonides and the sixteenth-century Shulhan Arukh of Rabbi Joseph Caro. Despite initial opposition to the codes, on the ground that they codified individual opinion and impeded the tradition of full and free inquiry into the authoritative legal sources, the codes eventually won acceptance because they provided a significant unifying and stabilizing force in an otherwise decentralized legal system.

Nature of the Halakhic Process

The cornerstone of rabbinic jurisprudence is that the revelation of the law at Sinai was exhaustive and thus no further substantive revelation, either abrogating or amending the law, is possible. The judges (halakhic scholars) of each succeeding generation are authorized to apply the law and decide disputes about the law in accordance with accepted methods of halakhic methodology and the principle of majority rule. Although scriptural law cannot be abrogated, the rabbis have authority to suspend such law temporarily in emergency circumstances or in order to reinforce general observance of the law.

The most debated issue in contemporary analyses of Jewish law is the degree of openness of the legal system to human choice-making, consistent with its divinely revealed nature. This subject touches on a variety of important and discrete subissues, including the role of divine authorial intention in the halakhic process; the objectivity of the law; the role of formal procedure in leading to a conclusive, binding resolution of a legal dispute; and the internal openness of the halakhah to a plurality of answers to a legal question.

Although rabbinic literature is devoid of systematic theory, the Babylonian Talmud addresses these issues obliquely in two famous stories. One tells of the dispute between the majority of the sages and a dissenting rabbi about a matter of ritual purity. A heavenly voice confirms the legal opinion of the dissenter. Nonetheless, the sages rule that "it [the Torah] is not in heaven." The Torah itself instructs that, after the revelation at Sinai, disputes must be decided by majority rule. The other tells of the heavenly voice that eventually mediated between the conflicting legal opinions of the schools of Hillel and Shammai by proclaiming, "[T]hese and these [both] are the words of the Living God."

In commenting on these and other talmudic passages, later rabbinic authorities divide over the nature of halakhic methodology. Their solutions are often linked to differing views of the revelatory process itself. According to some sources, all the laws in *all their detail* were revealed to Moses at Sinai. The judge's role is limited to the rediscovery of the law through the rigorous application of halakhic reasoning. The consensus-building process of majority resolution has the potential to yield greater substantive accuracy and reflects the objective truth, depriving dissenting opinions of further validity, except for conceptual and didactic purposes. The principle of majority rule is sometimes characterized as a guarantee of the objective truth of the law that emerges as binding.

The more prevalent view is that *multiple normative truths* are possible, a view often linked to a conception of the revelation either as consisting only of general principles or as containing a series of decisional options that provide a basis for prohibiting or permitting conduct. Therefore, halakhic determination lacks absolute finality and the halakhah contains rules for its own resolution and modification. Yet another model stresses the concept of the *authority of the professional* community entrusted with the elaboration of the law. God's will is satisfied by reasoned interpretation of the law in accordance with the accepted rules of halakhic methodology, even if the result is substantively erroneous and thus fails to reflect abstract divine truth. In this view, halakhic determination is a formal process that must be faithful solely to its own internal procedures.

A second question is whether pluralism is a possible and even desirable feature of the law at the legal level. Rabbinic sources often attribute legal pluralism to external historic circumstances, especially the loss of a centralized juridical authority. From the internal perspective, the halakhah exhibits a marked preference for uniformity in behavior and legal stability and implies that the goal of the halakhic process is to reach one final, binding determination. Nonetheless, the Talmud does on occasion adopt two conflicting opinions and transforms both into valid legal norms, suggesting that there is no one uniquely correct answer to all legal questions.

Autonomy of Jewish Law

A central jurisprudential issue is the degree to which Jewish law is open to values that are extrahalakhic or expressed in nonnormative form. As the exclusive, legal concretization of the Jewish religion, the halakhah is, in theory, autonomous and self-sufficient. The halakhah itself stipulates that legal norms may not be derived exclusively from the *aggadah*—the ethical and anecdotal teachings of the tannaite and amoraic rabbis. In theory, these and other spiritual systems, whether ethical, mystical, or philosophic, may illuminate the deeper purpose of the law but may not determine halakhic norms. Modern scholarly investigation into the history of the halakhah debate the extent to which aggadic, mystical, and even extraneous philosophic sources nonetheless influenced the rulings of individual halakhists or, especially in the case of the aggadah, served as the basis for legal rulings.

The relationship between law and morality in the halakhic system poses a similar problem. The concept of a divinely revealed legal order implies that the divine law incorporates a transcendent morality that cannot be obviated or overridden by human speculation. The question remains, however, whether the halakhah recognizes an inherent, universal, human morality that may serve as a minimum standard in the interpretation of the law or even as an independent source of law. In the Pentateuch and prophetic literature, law and morality are treated as a single, indivisible entity. By the tannaite period, the existence of a gap between enforceable legal norms and desirable, although nonenforceable, behavior was recognized. The rabbis dealt with this gap in several ways, including the recognition of a category of equitable or supralegal behavior that is sometimes treated as unenforceable and at other times becomes assimilated into the realm of law. Indeed, the Babylonian Talmud ascribes the destruction of Jerusalem to the failure to act "beyond the line of the law." Whether this ethical realm complements the halakhah or is, in fact, part of the corpus of the halakhah itself is a matter of debate. Several contemporary scholars argue that the halakhah contains not only rules, but principles and ideals, such as "in the interest of peace" and "for the benefit of society," that are either expressed in scripture or discernible in the accumulation of the halakhic corpus. These principles and ideals not only shape decision making and legislation but may also serve as a direct source of law.

References

Elon, Menachem. *Jewish Law: History, Sources, Principles*. Philadelphia: Jewish Publication Society, 1994.

Faur, José. "The Fundamental Principles of Jewish Jurisprudence." *New York University Journal of International Law and Politics* 12 (1979), 225–235.

Jackson, Bernard, ed. "The Philosophy of Jewish Law (I)." In *Jewish Law Annual* 6 (1987), 3–175. Boston: Institute of Jewish Law, Boston University School of Law.

———. "The Philosophy of Jewish Law (II)." In *Jewish Law Annual* 7 (1988), 5–251. Boston: Institute of Jewish Law, Boston University School of Law.

Kirschenbaum, Aaron. *Beyond Equity: Halakhic Aspirationism in Jewish Civil Law*. New York: Ktav, 1989.

Schonberg, David, and Phyllis Holman Weisbard. *Jewish Law: Bibliography of Sources and Scholarship in English*. Littleton CT: Rothman, 1989.

Silberg, Moshe. *Talmudic Law and the Modern State*. New York: Burning Bush Press, 1973.

Stone, Suzanne Last. "In Pursuit of the Countertext: The Turn to the Jewish Legal Model in Contemporary American Legal Theory." *Harvard Law Review* 106 (1993), 813–894.

Suzanne Last Stone

See also ECCLESIASTICAL JURISDICTION; ISLAMIC PHILOSOPHY OF LAW; JUDICIAL REVIEW

Jhering, Rudolph von (1818–1892)

Rudolph von Jhering was born in 1818 in Aurich and died in 1892 in Göttingen. He was professor of law at different universities: Basel (1845), Rostock (1846), Kiel (1848), Giessen (1852), Vienna (1868), and Göttingen (1872).

His main works are *Der Geist des römischen Rechts auf den Stufen seiner Entwicklung* in three parts (The Spirit of Roman Law in the Different Stages of its Development, 1852–1865); *Der Zweck im Recht* in two volumes (Finality in Law, 1877–1884); *Der Besitzwille* (The Will of Possession, 1889); *Der Kampf ums Recht* (The Struggle for Law, 1872); different satirical papers collected in *Scherz und Ernst in der Jurisprudenz* (Hilarity and Seriousness in Jurisprudence, 1884); and several monographical treatises and essays published in the *Jahrbücher für civilrechtliche Dogmatik,* which he founded with Gerber in 1857.

Before his conversion to the "teleological jurisprudence" ("interests jurisprudence," *Interessenjurisprudenz*), he was a representative of "conceptual jurisprudence" (*Begriffsjurisprudenz*): a methodological understanding of law as a system of concepts perfectly coherent and logically well ordered. In the first volume of *Der Geist des römischen Rechts,* Jhering characterizes the essence of the *Begriffsjurisprudenz* when he affirms the productivity and generating power of concepts that join each other, creating new ones, and contribute in that way to the "constructive" proliferation of law by itself.

Later Jhering opposed such a formalistic conception of law, demonstrating the teleological structure of law. Law is something human beings have developed in order to protect social life and in order to attain certain goals, so that it cannot be conceived independently from such goals. The essential finality of the legal system shifted to the center of attention in *Der Zweck im Recht* and the occasional writing in *Der Kampf ums Recht,* whose title reminds one of Darwin's "struggle for life." Law enforcement is viewed now as something more than the mere formal operation of subsuming special cases under existing norms. The legal system not being a closed system providing solutions for every possible problematic case, Jhering stresses the creative performance by the agents who apply it to certain concrete real social needs and in specific controversial contexts where there are struggles, conflicts, disputes, and problems to be solved by and through the law. The law is a product of the human will and an instrument through which people implement and realize their will and their interests. Law is purposive; the purpose or goal of law, the end in view, its aim (*der Zweck*) creates it. Law is an instrument of society dependent on and determined by the goals human agents have. Jhering's teleological arguments have a certain similarity to Auguste Comte's sociological positivism, Jeremy Bentham's utilitarianism, Charles Darwin's evolutionism, and Friedrich Nietzsche's genealogical reconstruction of moral systems.

In *Scherz und Ernst* he criticizes the logicism he had defended in *Der Geist des römischen Rechts*. However, even in this early work Jhering had interpreted the legal system as a manifestation of the Roman spirit and will (*Volksgeist*), anticipating many ideas of the later conception, a conception that remains ambivalent and contains many obscurities.

References

Behrends, O., ed. *Rudolf von Jhering: Beiträge und Zeugnisse* (Rudolf von Jhering: Claims and Proofs). Göttingen: Wallstein, 1993.

Gromitsaris, A. *Theorie der Rechtsnormen bei Rudolf von Jhering* (Theory of Legal Norms According to Rudolph von Jhering). Berlin: Duncker-Humblot, 1989.

Jhering, Rudolph von. *L'esprit du droit romain dans les diverses phases de son développement* (The Spirit of Roman Law in Its Different Phases of Development). Trans. O. van Meulenaere. 4 vols. Paris: Marescq, 1886–1888.

———. *Etudes complementaires de l'esprit du droit romain* (Further Studies on the Spirit of Roman Law). Paris: n.p., 1880–1882.

———. *Law in Daily Life*. Trans. Henry Goudy. Oxford: Clarendon Press, 1904.

———. *Oeuvres choisis* (Selected Writings). Trans. O. van Meulenaere. 2 vols. Paris: Marescq, 1903.

———. *The Struggle for Law*. Trans. John L. Lalor from 3d German ed. Chicago: Callahan, 1879.

Muller, F. Max. "Review of Rudolph von Jhering." In *Last Essays: Essays on Language, Folklore, and Other Essays*. 1st series. New York: Longsmans, Green, 1901.

Smith, Munroe. "Rudolph von Jhering, 1818–1892." In *A General View of European Legal History, and Other Papers of Munroe Smith*. New York: Columbia University Press, 1927.

Wieacker, F. *Rudolf von Jhering*. Stuttgart: Köhler, 1968.

Wolf, E. *Große Rechtsdenker der deutschen Geistesgeschichte* (Great Philosophers of Law in German Cultural History). Tübingen: J.C.B. Mohr, 1944.

Thomas Gil

Judicial Independence

The concept of judicial independence is linked to the doctrine of the separation of powers. Aristotle and John Locke identified the division between the legislative and executive powers of the state. However, it was Montesquieu who recognized, in his *Spirit of the Laws*, that an independent judiciary adjudicating legal disputes exercised a judicial power that was distinct from legislative and executive powers. His view that the separation of powers was an essential element of democratic government became influential and led to the incorporation of the separation of powers in the United States Constitution.

The effect of the separation of powers in the three different branches of government is to prevent any one branch from dominating the exercise of governmental powers. The separation creates a system of checks and balances that confines each branch to its legitimate role.

In this scheme, the function of the judiciary is vitally important because it adjudicates upon the legality of the acts of the organs of government and decides disputes between government and citizen. To achieve these objects and to maintain public confidence in the administration of justice, the judiciary must be independent.

Historically, judges were appointed and removed by the executive. However, acceptance of the concept of judicial independence required that judges should be immune from coercion, threat, or influence by the executive. So, in order to protect judicial independence, it became accepted that judges should be appointed for life or until retirement upon reaching a specified age and that they could not be removed otherwise than by resolution of the legislature in consequence of proved misbehavior or incapacity.

More recently, it has been recognized in various jurisdictions that the protection of judicial independence calls for more than protection against arbitrary removal. Entitlement to reasonable remuneration, the provision of adequate resources, and judicial control of court premises, expenditure, staff, and facilities are now seen as essential safeguards against executive coercion, interference, or influence, though this view is resisted in some jurisdictions.

Once it was acknowledged that the exercise of judicial power was not mechanistic, the legitimacy of its exercise by nonelected judges became an issue. On what basis could the performance of the judicial function by nonelected judges be reconciled with democratic principles? That issue loomed larger under federal constitutions that established legislatures and executives with limited powers and conferred power on the judges to review statutes for invalidity. The issue came into even clearer focus once guarantees of fundamental rights were entrenched so that the judges were authorized to invalidate statutes on the ground that they violated fundamental rights. The theoretical justification urged for the exercise of these powers by a nonelected judiciary is the necessity for neutral independent adjudication.

Various expedients were adopted to resolve the issue of legitimacy. One was the election of judges. Another approach was to provide for executive appointment with the advice and consent of the legislature. So, in the United States, the Senate discharges that function, and, in doing so, the Senate Judiciary Committee conducts confirmation hearings in which a nominee for federal judicial appointment is examined. In jurisdictions in which the Westminster system prevails, the executive generally appoints the judges without legislative oversight. In those jurisdictions, the theoretical response on the issue of legitimacy is that because the executive is elected by the people, the judges are indirectly appointed by the people.

The practical justification for executive appointment is that popular election of judges has been thought to politicize the judiciary and compromise judicial independence and quality, thereby damaging public confidence in the judiciary. So, despite the problem of democratic legitimacy, executive appointment prevails because it serves the object of the doctrine of separation of powers.

However, executive appointment carries with it the risk that the executive may appoint as judges persons who will serve its interests. In order to guard against this possibility, several different procedures have been advocated—and sometimes adopted—to make the process of appointment more open. These procedures range from confirmation hearings to consultation with, or appointment by, representative bodies.

In jurisdictions where simple executive appointment prevails, support for such procedures is gaining ground. That is because individual judges bring to the judicial function varying judicial approaches. Each judge has a legal philosophy, a view of the role of the court, and an attitude toward precedent. The procedures mentioned achieve openness and may well result in the appointment of able and independent judges.

The principal problems associated with judicial independence in advanced societies have arisen in relation to termination of appointment and accountability. Underlying these problems is a fundamental question which has not been resolved: Is judicial power capable of precise definition? The absence of precise definition explains ambiguities inherent in the concept of judicial independence. Does the concept apply to magistrates and members of tribunals standing outside the orthodox court system? Historically, judicial independence was associated with judges of superior courts, rather than with magistrates and tribunal members, no doubt because they performed some administrative functions or because their functions were not thought to be judicial. There are signs of a windshift in thinking, however, due to the emergence of a more expansive view of what constitutes adjudication in relation to rights and interests. Thus, the Universal Declaration on Judicial Independence calls for the preservation of the independence of judicial officers and members of tribunals.

The application of judicial independence presents difficulties for legislatures and governments that wish to restructure courts and tribunals in the public interest, when restructuring involves the abolition of courts or tribunals. Is tenured appointment an obstacle to that outcome? Is tenured appointment an obstacle if the appointee is not appointed to another court or tribunal because the appointee lacks the qualities or experience for such an appointment? Questions of this kind have arisen in Australia, and they involve a tension between the need to preserve judicial independence by eliminating the possibility of arbitrary removal by indirect means and the desirability of preserving the freedom of the legislature to make necessary reforms.

Like problems have arisen in connection with judicial accountability and the establishment of tribunals to inquire into judicial misconduct. Traditional procedures for the removal by legislatures of judges for proved misbehavior or incapacity are unsuited for lesser disciplinary purposes. So, in some jurisdictions, tribunals have been established with jurisdiction to entertain complaints of judicial misconduct and to report to the legislature in the case of serious misconduct or to reprimand in other cases. These measures, taken in the name of accountability, have been criticized on the ground that they compromise judicial independence. In other jurisdictions, informal arrangements exist whereby such complaints are dealt with by the presiding judge or other judges. That approach has also been criticized on the score that it threatens the equality of judges and detracts from judicial independence.

Another issue is the tendency of legislatures to entrust judges with executive functions. Such functions may be incompatible with the exercise of judicial power and may involve judges in political controversy that, it has been thought, is damaging to judicial independence. Although the judiciary cannot be immune from controversy, controversy should be avoided as far as it is possible to do so. That is why most judges refrain from participating in public debate.

References

Blackstone, William. *Commentaries on the Laws of England.* (1765) Vol. 1, 257–269; (1768) Vol. 33, 22–25.
Locke, John. *Two Treatises of Government.* Ed. P. Laslett. London: Cambridge University Press, 1988.
Mason, Sir Anthony. "Judicial Independence and the Separation of Powers—Some Problems Old and New." *University of British Columbia Law Review* 24 (1990), 345–346.
McGarvie, R.D. "The Foundations of Judicial Independence in a Modern Democracy." *Journal of Judicial Administration* (1991).
Montesquieu. *The Spirit of the Laws.* 1748. Bk. 11, ch. 3–6.
Nicholson, R.D. "Judicial Independence and Accountability: Can They Co-exist?" *Australian Law Journal* 67 (1993), 404–426.
Ramseyer, J.M. "The Puzzling (In)dependence of Courts: A Comparative Approach." *Journal of Legal Studies* 23 (1994), 721.
Shetreet, S. "The Limits of Judicial Accountability." *University of New South Wales Law Journal* 11 (1987), 4.
Vile, M.J.C. *Constitutionalism and the Separation of Powers.* Oxford: Clarendon Press, 1967.

Sir Anthony Mason

See also JUDICIAL REVIEW; POWERS OF GOVERNMENT

Judicial Review

Judicial review, the review of legislative and executive action by an independent judiciary entrusted to enforce the U.S. Constitution, is a distinctly American institution. While the idea is very ancient, it was revived in the 1600s, in opposition to the will of the English Crown at a time when legislature and court alike were perceived as the voices of reason.

In South Africa's 1961 constitution, by contrast, section 59 (2) expressly provided that, with very few exceptions, "no court of law shall be competent to enquire into or pronounce upon the validity of any Act passed by Parliament." Exclusion of judicial review from Nazi Germany's system of government was one main reason for the crimes that were perpetrated, because it made officials mere instruments of the Führer's will.

In a judicial review system, judges are not "subjected to the law," that is, bound by the absolute supremacy of the state law, as when the legal review exercised by administrative tribunals is limited to evaluating the legitimacy of acts by agents of the state, as in France and Germany until the *Grundgesetz* (Basic Law) and the constitutional reforms which took place in Europe after World War II. Separation between the jurisdiction of ordinary courts and of administrative tribunals reflects a system where constitutional questions are exclusively in the keeping of the state and its government, rather than in the keeping of the courts. This legal and political order stands on a philosophy of public law that confers an absolute priority on the state. Indeed, philosophers in this tradition usually consider states rather than constitutions to be the centerpiece and source in philosophy of law.

Republican Argument

United States

The tenet that judicial review is a creation of the U.S. Constitution, because the judges are the guardians of its supremacy, was a factor of the greatest importance to the United States. Leaders of postrevolutionary opinion argued that "the federal judiciary may be truly said to have neither force nor will but merely judgment," and so could be "trusted to serve as an intermediate body between the people and the legislature." The emphasis on understanding and judgment as its fundamental feature suggests that the framers saw it as an organ of reflection, as the philosophical arm of government.

The brief period around the 1800s was crucial. It was then that the designers of the American constitutional structure treated federal judges as the guardians of the deepest commitments of the American society. The Supreme Court in *Marbury v. Madison*, 5 U.S. (1 Cranch) 137 (1803), asserted the power to review the constitutional validity of actions taken by coordinate branches of the national government as discussed in *Martin v. Hunter's Lessee*, 14 U.S. (1 Wheat.) 304 (1816). Judicial review was established firmly, entrenched, and finally recognized by Congress in the course of the events of 1866–1877, after a long debate. The meaning of judicial activity shifted from the review of regularity of acts of Congress or Parliament according to procedural rules and common law precedents, to a reconstruction of the law in terms of principles established by the Constitution, as decided in *Cohen v. Virginia*, 19 U.S. (6 Wheat.) 214, 494 (1821).

Rome

The judges working in a judicial review system are in many respects similar to the jureconsults in the classic civilizations and ancient Israel, or the Lozi judges Max Gluckman sees so similar to American justices. In republican Rome, jureconsults were the interpreters of the law, the authors of *interpretatio juris* and the creators of the forms of action. They were the "oracles of the law," the voice of legal wisdom. Then the creation of the empire, and the establishment of the imperial chancery, incorporated jureconsults into a bureaucratic order. *Interpretatio juris* (interpretation of the law) became the emperor's grant, *ex authoritate,* as from its author. Jurists were expected to give their opinions on imperial laws. The Roman republic was seen as a model of civil and legal virtue in the debates in seventeenth-century England and even in America.

Israel

The paramount model of a free and just regime was not Rome but ancient Israel, the *Respublica Hebraeorum* (the republic of the Hebrews). There the interpretation of the law was not in the hands of a caste of priests. It was open to study, learning, and wisdom. Jurists were free representatives of their communities, their schools, and their synagogues. The doctors of the law were not members of a bureaucratic order. This is a fundamental feature of that trend of the ancient Yahwistic puritanism which looked at the law as the center of a multiplicity of communities tied to one another by the exegesis of the law and the study of the jurisprudence created by interpretation. Exegesis, not the edict, is the instrument of government and of the formation of laws. A regime which endeavored to reconstruct social and political relations in terms of rules of law decided each case according to the fundamental meanings of the principles and the values they entail, not as a mechanical application of the enacted positive laws. It was a system of government which did not recognize the state, kings, and princes. The highest source of the law was the language of God, interpreted as a legal language, not as the esoteric preserve of a caste of magicians and priests.

England

Recovery of the "Ancient Jews' Republic" offered a new model. It meant a departure from the Roman-Christian tradition, and its Christology, which constituted the model of legitimation for centuries, and from the notion of the source of the law that this tradition had forged. The model of the imperial and papal chancery became the source of royal law, which is to say of state law and the supremacy of the state. An executive power, the king, was jointly the master of the law.

In the seventeenth century the great constitutional discussions debated on theological models, as John Locke's discussion of Cardinal Bellarmino testifies. Furthermore, John Selden and Hugo Grotius, especially in his discussion of Paul, argue that public authority is under the obligation to construct the law assuming the highest principles and concept of justice as the guiding light. The purpose of law is to advance the fundamental values of justice, not to negate them.

Puritanism
The rediscovery of the ancient sacred texts in the rise of Puritanism was a rediscovery of Judaism. This is the typical characteristic which distinguishes Lutheranism and Calvinism, and all other reformed churches, which looked fundamentally at the New Testament as their ideal model, from the movement which looked at the Pentateuch and the Jewish books and treatises.

This view meant a shift away from Edward Coke's, Holt's, and seventeenth-century judges' technical notion that the basis of the court's authority was the king's prerogative of justice. This is the purported ground of Coke's tremendous claims in mandamus, and it is the ground upon which one hundred years later, and after two successful revolutions against the prerogative, Holt sought to rest certiorari and mandamus, in saying that "no court can be intended exempt from the superintendency of the king in the court of B.R."

This is an attitude typical of an elite of lawyers, of judges, and of philosophers of law, who had embraced republican ideals. The republican movement was defeated in England. However, the great constitutional debates, and the ideas which took shape, provided the ideal center of American constitutional jurisprudence. It is not clear to what extent the framers envisaged the Supreme Court as an instrument of coordination of the judicial system or as the key element of the protection of the supremacy of the Constitution.

Democratic Argument
Between the judge's discretion to interpret the constitution and democracy there is perpetual tension. Democracy is a delicate balance between majority rule and certain fundamental values. The democratic problem, however, intensifies in a legal system such as that of the United States, which has a formal written constitution that guarantees judicial review of the constitutionality of statutes. Exclusive judicial control would entail "enormous vices" and undermine the Constitution. Among those vices is the danger, warned against most recently by Justice Powell in *Goldwater v. Carter,* 444 U.S. 996 (1979), of having the Supreme Court closely "oversee the very constitutional process used to reverse its decisions."

The resort to amendment, to constitutional politics as opposed to constitutional law, should be taken as a sign that the legal system has come to a point of discontinuity, a point at which something less radical than revolution, but distinctly more radical than ordinary evolution, is required. The criteria of appropriateness for amendment surely must not be elaborated or enforced by courts. As L.H. Tribe writes, the merit of a constitutional amendment is a true "political question," a matter that the Constitution addresses, but that it nevertheless commits to judicially unreviewable resolution by the political branches of government. In this respect, political branches have responsibility for some sort of political, principled decision making, as noted in *Bell v. Hood,* 327 U.S. 678, 884 (1946), and *Baker v. Carr,* 369 U.S. 186 (1962).

Constitutional politics in the amendment process is a safeguard erected against the monopoly of the determination of policy by judges, which would contradict the basic democratic principle according to which policy in a democratic regime is determined by the people through their representatives. The "democratic argument" is that adjudication in the hard cases is undemocratic because policy is determined by the judge and not by the people, as required in a democracy. The argument is that in a democratic regime, policy is established by an elected body, not by the court.

The amendment process protects the representative system of government from arbitrary intrusions by the judicial supervision processes into the policy-making capacities that the Constitution confers on the executive and legislative branches of government as elected bodies. The problem is to protect the amendment process from obstruction by the very tribunals whose interpretation of the Constitution an amendment may be designed to overturn. When faced with challenges to ratification procedures approved by Congress, deference or judicial abstention from substantive review of constitutional amendment supervision would be necessary.

Philosophical Argument
This attitude brings the judges to reflect upon the general and universal premises of the law and offers a justification of it in terms of the constitutional values, principles, and standards from which rights and duties must be drawn and alone can be legitimated. A philosophical quest is thus an inherent feature of judicial review.

The doctrine that the list of enumerated rights, in the Bill of Rights, does not exhaust the number of rights which are possible and the corollary—that in principle there are unstated rights—are typical features of legal philosophy in a judicial review system. The hermeneutical interpretation of "judgment" leads the judges, while they are considering parliamentary acts, to search for a specific form of justification in accordance with the integrity of general principles, standards, rules, and values, and to the body of interpretations, case law, or jurisprudence the judges have evolved in their interpretative work on the Constitution and legislation. Free judicial decisions are essential to prevent only outcasts from being deprived of the so-called open-ended fundamental rights. Judicial decisions are equally important to protect the constitutionality of rights, eventually letting the "people" decide if the rights are fundamental, before a right can be abridged by a decision maker who may remain hidden.

Judicial review is a philosophical tradition created by philosopher-judges, and it is perhaps the most important philosophical-legal tradition of the last two centuries. It was a revolution achieved by the judges, rather than by university philosophers. It is for this reason that, in Europe, those who studied academic philosophy of law and political theory discovered judicial review and realized its importance for democracy so late.

References

Bryce, J. *Studies in History and Jurisprudence.* Oxford: Oxford University Press, 1901.
Burt, R. "Inventing Judicial Review: Israel and America." *Cardozo Law Review* (1989), 2010–2097.
Cohn, H. "Faithful Interpretation: Three Dimensions." *Mishpatim* 5 (1976), 6–7.
Duncan-Derret, J. "Law and Society in Jesus's World." In *Aufstieg und Niedergang der römischen Welt,* ed. H. Temporini and W. Haase, 478–564. New York: De Gruyter, 1982.
Jaffe, L.G., and E. Henderson. "Judicial Review and the Rule of Law: Historical Origins." *Law Quarterly Review* 7 (1956), 945.
Selden, J. *De Synedris et Praefecturibus Juridicis Veterum Ebreorum* (The Lawmaking Assemblies and Officers of the Ancient Hebrews). Frankfurt: Schirey, 1696.
Tierney, B. *Church Law and Constitutional Thought in the Middle Ages.* London: Variorum Reprints, 1979.
Tribe, L.H. "A Constitution We Are Amending: In Defense of a Restrained Judicial Role." *Harvard Law Review* 97 (1983–84), 433–445.

Carlo Giuseppe Rossetti

See also JUDICIAL INDEPENDENCE; POWERS OF GOVERNMENT; REPUBLICAN PHILOSOPHY OF LAW

Judicial Syllogism
Definition
By "judicial syllogism" is usually meant the logical schema to which judicial decisions are assumed to conform. Thus, judicial syllogism provides the key concept of the logical-deductive view according to which the norm of the case is a logical consequence following from a legal premise, that is, the statement expressing the legal norm(s) to be applied to the case at issue, and a factual premise, that is, the statement expressing the reconstruction of the fact(s) of the case at issue. In other words, judicial syllogism is the logical form according to which the norm of the case is taken to be the conclusion of a logical inference, where the legal statement and the factual statement on which the judicial decision is based stand for the major and the minor premise, respectively.

Such a logical reconstruction is traditionally said to be of great relevance in grounding and showing the rational nature of judicial decision making. Actually, to maintain the logical-deductive nature of judicial decisions (that is, to argue that they can be accounted for in terms of judicial syllogism) is usually taken to be the same as to maintain their rational nature.

Despite its long-lasting and widespread consensus, this tenet of the rationality of judicial decisions because of their logical-deductive nature is far from being as simple and plain as it might appear. In fact, both their logical-deductive nature and the equation between such a presumed nature and rationality are doubtful.

Logical Nature of Judicial Decisions

From an epistemological point of view, it is to be remarked that the premises (both the legal and the factual one) upon which the norm of the case is based are constitutive in character, not declarative. Both the legal and the factual statement are the result of an act of decision by the judicial decision maker. Such an epistemological remark has a logical bearing insofar as the objective character ascribed to the logical schema of judicial syllogism is revealed to be specious, because the premises of such a logical inference are the result of unavoidably subjective choices.

From a logical point of view—obvious as it may sound—it should be noted that the validity of the norm of the case is the result of an act of deliberation by the judicial decision maker; and, undoubtedly, to decide is not to deduce. That is the core of Hans Kelsen's later view of law and logic, which is usually disclaimed as obvious, but in opposition to which no strong theoretical counterargument has yet been put forward.

Rationality in Judicial Decisions

The traditional view of judicial syllogism is being replaced by two different views, each along with its own peculiar form of rationalism. One may be termed the "renewed view," qualified as a sort of "revised" or "emended" rationalism. The other, in its turn, may be termed the "skeptical view," and the form of rationalism which characterizes it may be qualified as "critical."

The renewed view is achieving an ever increasing consensus. Such a view does acknowledge that judicial syllogism provides an oversimplified conceptual schema, which cannot properly account for the complexity of the procedures by which the judicial decision maker comes to select the legal and the factual data on which the norm of the case will be based. Nevertheless, it firmly claims that such a conceptual schema still provides the ultimate rational constraint for judicial decision mak-

ing since, according to it, the legal and the factual premises grounding a judicial decision are made explicit and hence are liable to intersubjective control.

The rarely supported skeptical view takes seriously the heuristic limits on judicial syllogism, but also maintains that the importance of such limits cannot be confined by resorting to the distinction between the context of discovery and the context of justification. That is so because of the difficulty in drawing a clear-cut boundary between the two contexts when judicial matters are at issue. Moreover, if such a distinction is to be given any relevance at all, then it is the context of discovery and not the context of justification that has the prominent role for understanding the variety of legal mechanisms through which judicial decisions are to be taken.

References

Aarnio, Aulis, and Neil MacCormick, eds. *Legal Reasoning.* 2 vols. Aldershot: Dartmouth, 1992.

Alchourrón, Carlos Eduardo, and Eugenio Bulygin. *Normative Systems.* Wien: Springer Verlag, 1971.

Gottlieb, Gidon. *The Logic of Choice.* London: Allen and Unwin, 1968.

Kelsen, Hans. "Recht und Logik." *Neues Forum* 12 (1965), 421–425 and 495–500. Trans. "Law and Logic." In Hans Kelsen, *Essays in Legal and Moral Philosophy,* 228–256. Dordrecht: Reidel, 1973.

Mazzarese, Tecla. "Fuzzy Logic and Judicial Decision-Making: A New Perspective on the Alleged Norm-Irrationalism." *Informatica e diritto* 18 (1993), 2d vol., 13–36.

Wasserstrom, Richard A. *The Judicial Decision: Toward a Theory of Legal Justification.* Stanford: Stanford University Press, 1961.

Wróblewski, Jerzy. *The Judicial Application of Law.* Ed. Zeno Bankowski and Neil MacCormick. Dordrecht: Reidel, 1992.

———. "Legal Syllogism and Rationality." *Rechtstheorie* 5 (1974), 33–46.

Tecla Mazzarese

Jurisculture

Jurisculture is the relationship of fundamental ideas to the structure, processes, and policies of societies. The subject has been addressed, in the past fifty years, in the context of the conflicts that have prevented the United Nations from functioning as intended. John Gaddis is representative of most North American scholars, who ignored the role of ideas and attributed national conflicts to geopolitics, social forces, or psychology. Adda Bozeman, a notable exception, argued that societies rest on cultures and national differences are to be explained by cultural differences. Jurisculture adds that cultures and societies rest on philosophical premises. Myres McDougal and Harold Lasswell, on the basis of a new philosophical premise, argued that cooperation at the world level can be achieved despite cultural differences. F.S.C. Northrop and Gray Dorsey, who coined the term "jurisculture," reconsidered philosophical premises for the purpose of reconciling cultural differences.

The Charter of the United Nations specifies that members shall be nation-states. According to Dorsey, the modern nation-state emerged from the settlements ending the Thirty Years War, in 1648. Its philosophical premises are that the universe is rationally ordered and that human beings possess reason, which enables them to know that order. Human sovereignty replaced the divine sovereignty of the middle ages. Over the succeeding centuries, nation-state institutions moved toward democracy, private property, and a market economy, as well as legally protected civil rights. Europeans believed their view of physical and human nature to be universal, exclusive truth. Islamic infidels and those who believed other strange things, in lands newly discovered by Europeans, could not be permitted to control natural resources or to govern people. Through colonialism, European outmigration, and the prestige of modern science and technology, nation-state institutions were, at the beginning of the twentieth century, close to being universal paradigms.

Following the Bolshevik revolution in 1917, a new entity, which Dorsey calls the party-state, was created, based on marxist-leninist philosophical premises. These premises are that order is constantly emerging from dialectical material processes, that human beings are material and develop consciousness from experience, and that only Communist party members, who have revolutionary experience, have true consciousness. It followed that all activities of every person should be controlled by the Communist party. Institutions developed in the Soviet Union in the interwar years were dictatorship instead of democracy, state ownership and a command economy instead of private property and a market economy, and censorship/surveillance/terror instead of legally protected civil rights.

When the United Nations was created, in 1945, the western democracies failed to realize that the Soviet Union had been, and the countries of Eastern Europe soon would be, reorganized according to the party-state model. Peoples that were dependent under colonialism were eager to become independent, but they did not aspire to become nation-states. The idea system of the nation-states had touched them oppressively, traditional idea systems were still alive except among western-educated elites, and the support of the party-states provided justification for old and new forms of totalitarianism. Efforts of western democracies to keep the peace and to assist in the development of newly independent states seldom succeeded.

Taking into account differing cultures and idea systems of member states was helpful in understanding why the United Nations seldom functioned as intended. However, if the problems of war, want, and injustice were to be addressed at the world level, actions had to be changed—in spite of cultural differences or by reconciling cultural differences. Both approaches required reconsideration of the philosophical premises of societies.

McDougal and Lasswell, immediately after the war, developed at Yale Law School the theory of a "world public order" (world society) premised on a view of human nature stated by Lasswell and Abraham Kaplan in an analysis made during the war for the purpose of generating strategy and tactics of propaganda. According to Lasswell and Kaplan, human beings are actors, who desire "values" (goods) such as wealth, power, and respect, who can know the present distribution of these goods, and who can calculate what actions of self and others will be needed to produce a desired redistribution.

The change from reason to self-serving actions as the essence of human nature shifts the basis of society from contract to manipulation. Rational beings agree to cooperate for the common good and the common defense in accordance with a set of common principles. Pursuit of individual advantage in ways that conflict with common ends is disapproved or prohibited on a scale from bad faith to treason. The nation-state acts at the world level on behalf of its nationals. In contrast, self-serving actors are specified to participate individually, and on their own behalf, in a "world social process," even though they may be acting in concert with those "with whom they share cultural sentiments." Self-serving actors use information cognitively to understand a situation and manipulatively to "persuade" others to act in ways that will result in a distribution of goods desired by the manipulator. This "integrative approach" is the heart of the McDougal-Lasswell "policy science."

McDougal and Lasswell implicitly assumed that a critical mass of individuals in the world would prefer a fair and just distribution of goods instead of seeking to maximize their own shares. They declared their own preference for an egalitarian-democratic distribution, which they called a "world public order of human dignity." They also asserted that the peoples all over the world are committed (at least rhetorically) to such a distribution. The world public order of human dignity would be created when executives, legislators, judges, bureaucrats, and influential private sector persons—persuaded by the right kind of scholars—acted in ways that would achieve an egalitarian-democratic distribution of the world's goods. The McDougal-Lasswell "policy science" approach grew into a subculture of its own, now known as the New Haven school of international law.

Northrop, a Yale philosopher who moved from the college to the law school shortly after the war, sought to understand the causal relation between philosophical premises and the norms of culture and societies. In *The Meeting of East and West* he argued that different epistemologies caused the differences between western societies and eastern (Chinese and Indian) societies. *Ideological Differences and World Order,* edited by Northrop, explored whether any philosophical premise, or cultural principle, is common to all the societies of the contemporary world. In *Philosophical Anthropology and Practical Politics,* using recent neurological research, Northrop presented the theory that physiological epistemic correlates of basic ideas and postulates become trapped in neural nets that fire or inhibit motor neurons. Accordingly, he said that society is based not upon agreements between rational beings, or upon manipulations that produce (shifting) alliances of coinciding interests, but upon the possession of the same set of neural nets.

Northrop's epistemological determinism was unsatisfactory to Dorsey, a student of Northrop who had written the final chapter in *Ideological Differences.* He undertook the study of the organization and regulation of societies in different times, places, and civilizations. In the first three volumes of his *Jurisculture* series, he presents his findings and conclusions with respect to Greece and Rome, India, and China, respectively. Dorsey says that human beings form societies for the practical purposes of survival and well-being, not to live by philosophical truth, as Plato would have it. However, since human beings live in the world as they understand it to be, the organization and regulation of the auxiliary and complementary activities that constitute society is necessarily done in terms of the meanings, values, and purposes of the believed reality which is their common consciousness. In his view, that believed reality is composed of fundamental ideas that have seeped pervasively into the consciousness of a large number of persons over a long period of time. Ideas he considers fundamental are those concerning the world, human nature, what is most worth having, how we know, and who can know.

References

Bozeman, Adda B. *Politics and Culture in International History.* Princeton: Princeton University Press, 1960.

Dorsey, Gray L. *Beyond the United Nations: Changing Discourse in International Politics and Law.* Lanham MD: University Press of America, 1986.

———. *Jurisculture.* New Brunswick NJ: Transaction Publishers, vol. 1, 1989, vol. 2, 1990, vol. 3, 1993.

———. "The State, Communism, and International Law." *Washington University Law Quarterly* (1955), 1–39.

Gaddis, John Lewis. "The Tragedy of Cold War History." *Foreign Affairs* 73 (1994), 142–153.

Lasswell, Harold D., and Abraham Kaplan. *Power and Society.* New Haven: Yale University Press, 1950.

McDougal, Myres S. *Studies in World Public Order.* New Haven: Yale University Press, 1960.

McDougal, Myres S., and Harold D. Lasswell. "The Identification and Appraisal of

Diverse Systems of Public Order."
American Journal of International Law
53 (1959), 1–29.

Northrop, F.S.C. *The Meeting of East and
West.* New York: Macmillan, 1946.

———. *Philosophical Anthropology and
Practical Politics.* New York: Macmillan,
1960.

Northrop, F.S.C., ed. *Ideological Differences
and World Order.* New Haven: Yale University Press, 1949.

Gray L. Dorsey

See also CONFIGURATIVE PHILOSOPHY OF LAW;
CONFLICT OF LAWS

Jurisdiction

Jurisdiction (*juris* being the genetive of *jus*;
diction, the act of saying) is the general term
defining the scope and limitation of the power
of a legal official or institution to interpret and
apply the law authoritatively.

Jurisdiction is also known as the competence of courts of law. Although now derived
from delegated state power rooted in constitution and enactment, jurisdiction was in the
middle ages more akin to a proprietary right,
often bound up with the tenure of land. Legal
jurisdiction was one of several bonds through
which a tenant was bound to a lord; English
law of the thirteenth century seems to have admitted the broad rule that every lord with tenants enough to form a court could, so far as
the king was concerned, hold a court of and
for his tenants. Against this tradition the influential Henry de Bracton, himself a royal justice, asserted the principle that all jurisdiction
derives from the king's sovereign power.

Long prior to the influence of land tenure
and medieval communities, jurisdiction derived from Roman law and legal organization.
The Roman republic replaced the ancient
monarchy with the three institutions of magistrates, Senate, and assemblies, with magistracies having full power within a given sphere,
subject to certain conditions, including legislation. A magistracy concerning private law, the
praetorship, was created in 367 B.C., and numerous magistracies with discrete functions
eventually proliferated, each with the prerogative of stating the law within its jurisdiction.

It might be said that the modern concept
of jurisdiction by subject matter was anticipated by the Roman magistracies, and that the
notion of dividing governmental jurisdiction
by territory and community (to the extent not
already recognized by Roman law) was anticipated by medieval practices.

In the modern era, the notion of jurisdiction has become critical both to legitimation
and limitation of public power. Thus jurisdiction is generally defined according to particular governing bodies and the particular laws
that they adopt and enforce. For example, in
the United States the jurisdiction of the federal
government and courts is distinct from that of
the several states and the local counties, cities,
and towns within the states. Jurisdiction over
certain classes of legal disputes may overlap,
giving rise to rules and practices of deference
and the resolution of conflicts.

Jurisdiction has historically influenced
substantive law, and likewise also legal theory.
A lawsuit commonly begins with a jurisdictional statement, and it is the nature of such a
statement to implicate the competence of a
court through a description of the substantive
nature of the case. This was accomplished
from the earliest common law tradition by the
"forms of action." To a considerable degree,
the substantive law administered in a given
form of action grew up independently of that
administered in other forms. "So great is the
ascendancy of the Law of Actions in the infancy of Courts of Justice," wrote Sir Henry
Maine, "that substantive law has at first the
look of being gradually secreted in the inter-
stices of procedure."

Although use of the forms was formally
abolished in the nineteenth century, F.W. Maitland could say at the beginning of the twentieth
that "[t]he forms of action we have buried,
but they still rule us from their graves." He
showed, for example, that the twofold division
of private remedial law into tort and contract
was better understood as the residue of the old
forms of action, shaped by jurisdictional battles, than any logical necessity.

Oliver Wendell Holmes took the matter to
a broader conclusion. Focusing also on the origin of substantive law in ancient procedure, he
criticized the positivist jurisprudential theory
found in John Austin's *Lectures on Jurisprudence* and eventually questioned whether there
existed any logical necessity in the fundamental
legal concepts of duty and right. Holmes's famous treatise, *The Common Law,* while primarily outlining a general theory of liability,
treats law itself as less a system of formal logic

than of historically determined areas of inquiry. He came to understand modern legal logic and classification as both the residue of ancient procedure and, as its replacement, a revised methodology of determining and limiting legal inquiry, indeed as a new and more accessible jurisdictional language, replacing the forms of action but not fundamentally unlike them in origin and operation.

Thus it can be argued that all legal concepts, including even the notion of fundamental constitutional right, operate as jurisdictional statements. They are precedentially determined areas of inquiry, rather than a priori decalogical truths. For Holmes, understanding them as such was the only path to avoid judicial legislation under the illusion of interpreting permanent or foundational principles.

References

Austin, John. *Lectures on Jurisprudence.* London: John Murray, 1869.

Bracton, Henry de. *On the Laws and Customs of England.* Trans. Thorne. Cambridge MA: Belknap–Harvard University Press, 1968.

Holmes, O.W. "Codes, and the Arrangement of the Law." *American Law Review 5* (October 1870), 1–13.

———. *The Common Law.* Boston: Little, Brown, 1881.

Kellogg, F.R. "Legal Philosophy in the Temple of Doom: Pragmatism's Response to Critical Legal Studies." *Tulane Law Review 65* (1990), 31–46.

Maine, H.S., Sir. *Early Law and Custom.* London: John Murray, 1891.

Maitland, F.W. *The Forms of Action at Common Law.* 1909. Cambridge: Cambridge University Press, 1971.

Pollock, F., and F.W. Maitland. *History of English Law.* Cambridge: Cambridge University Press, 1968.

Frederic R. Kellogg

See also CONFLICT OF LAWS; ECCLESIASTICAL JURISDICTION; STANDING

Jurisprudence
Definition

In its broad sense "jurisprudence" could be defined as a *critical external reflection on law.* "External" in this definition means: not from the internal point of view of the doctrinal analysis of the law within one specific legal system. In the common law countries, however, "jurisprudence" traditionally meant knowledge of cases and their doctrinal import. (In fact, the French word *jurisprudence* just means "case law.") It was only in the nineteenth century that it acquired the meaning of the theory or science of law in general. Jurisprudence in the Anglo-Saxon sense encompasses continental European legal theory and part of its legal philosophy.

Theory/Philosophy

In the continental European tradition a distinction is made between the term "legal theory" on one hand and "legal philosophy" on the other. Here, "legal theory" covers the analytical and methodological part of jurisprudence (for example, analysis of legal concepts, interpretation of law), whereas the term "legal philosophy" is generally used for the normative, ideological jurisprudential discussions of law in general (for example, the debate between legal positivism and jusnaturalism, as natural law theory was often named in the past, and today on the continent).

Legal theory in this sense is, as a rule, considered to be (1) a positive science of law, (2) being as much as possible "objective," value-free, and not normative, (3) analyzing, from an external point of view, problems which are common to all, or most, legal systems, and (4) for which regularly a pluri- or interdisciplinary method is used. Legal philosophy, for its part, is considered to be general philosophy, applied to law. In the continental European tradition "legal philosophy" also covers large parts of what in the Anglo-Saxon tradition is called "political philosophy."

The distinction between legal theory and legal philosophy is not a clear-cut one, as the starting points, the methods, and the fields covered are neither fully complementary nor mutually exclusory. "Legal theory" sometimes is used in a very broad sense, thus encompassing legal philosophy, but also other (external) approaches to law, such as legal sociology, economic analysis of law, legal anthropology, and the like (see, for example, the master's course on legal theory offered by the European Academy of Legal Theory since 1992, the international bibliographical journal *Current Legal Theory* since 1983, or the American journal *Legal Theory* since 1995, in which "analytical jurisprudence" and "normative jurisprudence" are titles for only parts of the fields covered by "legal theory"). When used in a broad sense, "legal philosophy" may also cover the whole field of legal theory.

The distinction between legal theory as "science of law" (or as "analytical jurisprudence") on one hand and the normative methodological study of law on the other, is, as such, partly determined by philosophical theories and debates over the last two centuries (positivism/natural law, analytical philosophy/metaphysics, empiricism/normativism, pluralism/dogmatism, and so forth).

History

Legal theory, with its emphasis on (value-neutral) analysis, has its roots in the nineteenth-century European reaction against traditional metaphysical jusnaturalistic theories, and, on the continent, also in a reaction against the black letter approach to statutory interpretation, which was at that time often only recently codified. In England this movement had started with Jeremy Bentham and John Austin, who can be considered to be the founders of Anglo-American positivism. One main scholar in this movement in continental Europe was Hans Kelsen (1881–1973), who worked out a theoretical approach to law which was purely analytical and strictly separated from any normative point of view. Topics discussed were mainly the analysis of legal concepts, of legal norms, of legal systems, and the methodology of law. In the course of the last decades of the twentieth century the belief in the possibility of constructing completely value-free legal theories decreased dramatically. Today, in legal theory, emphasis lies on *distinguishing* values from empirical and analytical facts and theories, rather than trying to exclude them completely from the analysis, as Kelsen did.

Metaphysical approaches within legal philosophy, for its part, have considerably declined in the course of the twentieth century. For a long time the opposition between positivistic and jusnaturalistic theories has been the core of the philosophical debate. In the second half of the twentieth century this traditional opposition has, to a large extent, been overcome. In the mold of postmodernism the belief in grand theories was lost. Mainstream approaches at the end of the twentieth century are, to a large extent, deconstructing traditional constructs and beliefs (for example, feminist jurisprudence, critical legal studies, legal semiotics). In

the pluralist Western societies there is a growing lack of a common worldview, which makes it very difficult to rely upon, or to construct, a common set of values. On the other hand, "natural law" has partly been concretized in the form of, and in fact replaced by, international human rights treaties. "Natural law" thus, paradoxically, became part of positive law. In combination with the above mentioned decline of the belief in (the possibility of) completely value-free analysis, this has resulted in the weakening of strict positivistic approaches. Moreover, in the legal philosophical debate there has been a shift from discussing the content of values to discussing the framework and the procedures for this value discussion (argumentation theory: Chaïm Perelman, Robert Alexy; communication theory: Jürgen Habermas; theory of justice: John Rawls; interpretation theory: Ronald Dworkin). The main question discussed is not What is the ultimate good? but How do we determine nowadays the best possible solution, the value to be preferred in a concrete discussion? The debate is about a structure for discussing values, rather than about the construction of value systems as such.

Fields

Legal theory, as the analytical part of jurisprudence, has four different fields of research:

1. Analysis of law: concept of law in general; legal norm; legal system; legal concepts; functions of law; sources of law.
2. Methodology of law: theory of legislation; adjudication of the law (interpretation, gaps, antinomies, argumentation).
3. Theory of science; epistemology and methodology of legal doctrine.
4. Analysis of the ideological content of the law: values which are not explicitly propounded and ideologies hidden in legislation, in court decisions, and in doctrinal analysis of law.

Legal theory has both a theoretical and a practical goal. On one hand it answers a theoretical need by explaining the phenomenon of law and by reducing its complexity through a globalizing, systemic approach. On the other hand, legal theory answers practical needs in that it helps to improve the methodology of legal technique and legal practice, that is, the methodology of statutory interpretation, legislative technique, and legal concepts and constructs as used and developed in legal practice and in legal doctrine.

Legal philosophy, as the normative part of jurisprudence, partly focuses on the same legal phenomenon, but from another point of view. In practice emphasis lies on problems concerning the legitimation of the law, the relationship between law and morals, the content of legal values such as "justice," "equity," "equality," "legal security," "fairness," and the like.

Methodology

As legal philosophy is nothing else than general philosophy applied to law, it uses the same methodology as philosophy in general. Legal theory, for its part, lays an emphasis on plural and interdisciplinary approaches, in addition to the more traditional analytical methodology. The birth and growth, especially in the twentieth century, of numerous new disciplines and approaches studying law from a specific perspective, created the need for a "coordinating discipline" being able to integrate two or more of these approaches into one systemic whole. Logical, psychological, semiotic, anthropological, sociological, and economic approaches have been useful for throwing a new light on legal phenomena, thus offering new insights. However, the reality is more complex. It is more than just psychology or just economy, or just history, or just argumentation, and so on. For the future a growing need for such interdisciplinary research can be expected. Such an interdisciplinary synthesis raises many epistemological and methodological problems. The one-dimensional alternative, however, often raises still more epistemological questions.

References

Alexy, Robert, and Ralf Dreier. "The Concept of Jurisprudence." *Ratio Juris* 3 (1990), 1–13.

Bergel, Jean-Louis. *Théorie générale du droit* (General Theory of Law). Paris: Dalloz, 1985. 2d ed., 1989.

Cotterrell, Roger. *The Politics of Jurisprudence: A Critical Introduction to Legal Philosophy*. London: Butterworth, 1989.

Dreier, Ralf. *Was ist und wozu Allgemeine Rechtstheorie?* (What and Whither the General Theory of Law?) Tübingen: Mohr, 1975.

Herget, James. *American Jurisprudence 1870–1970*. Houston: Rice University Press, 1990.

Lloyd of Hampstead, and M.D.A. Freeman. *Lloyd's Introduction to Jurisprudence*. 1959. London: Stevens and Sons, 1995.

Minda, A. "The Jurisprudential Movements of the 1980's." *Ohio State Law Journal* 50 (1989), 599.

Peczenik, Alexander et al., eds. *Theory of Legal Science*. Dordrecht: Reidel, 1984.

Prakash Sinha, Surya. *What Is Law? The Differing Theories of Jurisprudence*. New York: Paragon House, 1989.

Van Hoecke, Mark. *What Is Legal Theory?* Leuven (Louvain): Acco, 1985.

Van Hoecke, Mark, and François Ost. "Epistemological Perspectives in Legal Theory." *Ratio Juris* 6 (1993), 30–47.

Mark Van Hoecke

See also CIVILIAN PHILOSOPHY OF LAW; EPISTEMOLOGY IN LAW

Jury System

The jury arguably constitutes the most direct exercise of government power by citizens since the demise of the Athenian city-state. No other institution of government affords such direct power to citizens. The requirement of a jury trial in criminal cases, as provided for in the Sixth Amendment to the United States Constitution, interposes the judgment of citizens between the state and the accused. A recurring issue that sheds considerable light on the origin and nature of the jury is that of whether a juror is disqualified by reason of pretrial knowledge of the facts at issue. In recent celebrated criminal trials in the United States, such as those involving O.J. Simpson, Oliver North, and the various Watergate figures, it has generally been assumed that a juror's prior knowledge of the events at issue is a bar to jury service.

This notion is completely at odds with the original idea that the jury should be drawn from those most likely to know the facts. This early view of the jury is reflected in the 1374 statement of Chief Justice Belknap that the court should not proceed to determine who owns a parcel of land if, among the potential jurors, it "does not see six, or at least five, men of the hundred where the tenements are, to inform the others who are further away." In other words, the jurors were not only to weigh the evidence provided by witnesses, but were to bring their own knowledge to bear as well.

The importance of a local jury, composed of members of the vicinity or "vicinage" of the alleged crime, served a second purpose. The right of the jury to rely on its own knowledge buttresses its independence. The jury's knowledge of facts unknown to the king's judges is a basis for independent action to protect popular conceptions of fairness against encroachment by the central government. This relationship is illustrated by the classic decision in *Bushell's Case* (1670), the trial of Bushell and others for allegedly violating their duty as jurors at the trial of the Quakers William Penn and William Meade on charges of unlawful assembly. As jurors in the prior trial, Bushell and his codefendants initially refused to convict the defendants of unlawful assembly, but would find them only "guilty of speaking in Gracechurch Street." When the trial judge insisted on a verdict of guilty or not guilty on the charge of unlawful assembly, Bushell and his fellows returned a verdict of not guilty, and then were themselves prosecuted for doing so. In reversing their conviction, Chief Justice Vaughan insisted that the jury could not be required to accept the judge's view of the facts because the judge knows only what he has heard from the evidence given in court, whereas the jury may know matters of their own private knowledge of which the judge knows nothing.

These ideas played an important role in the debate surrounding the adoption of the American Constitution, in which antifederalists, with an eye on the refusal of colonial juries to convict their neighbors of alleged crimes against the king, insisted on a requirement that the criminal jury be drawn from the vicinage of the alleged crime.

Beginning with the celebrated treason trial of Aaron Burr in 1807 and continuing throughout the nineteenth century, the law gradually developed to define the requisite impartiality of a juror in terms that permitted knowledge of the events at issue so long as any opinion founded on such knowledge was not so strongly held that it could not give way to the evidence and argument presented in court. Since the time of the Watergate trials in the 1970s, the pendulum has swung in the direction of excluding jurors with even a passing knowledge of important public events. More recently, in the Oliver North case, the trial judge automatically eliminated potential jurors who had done no more than see or read about North's testimony before Congress. Excluding such potential jurors, and thus relegating the role of juror to the least informed candidates, may ultimately undermine the reliability, and thus the credibility, of the jury system.

Another fundamental philosophical question that goes to the heart of the jury's function is the question whether the jury's verdict must be unanimous. The requirement of unanimity seems to be coeval with the jury itself. Frederick Pollock and Frederic William Maitland observed that, "[f]rom the moment when our records begin, we seem to see a strong desire for unanimity." The role of the jury as the inscrutable "voice of the countryside" seems to require that it speak with a single voice, a requirement likely enforced by the medieval idea of the unity of truth.

The requirement of unanimity was little questioned until mid-twentieth century. Then, in 1967, England authorized nonunanimous verdicts in criminal cases. In 1972, the United States Supreme Court ruled that state, though not federal, criminal juries need not be unanimous in noncapital cases.

The departure from the requirement of unanimity seems also to be a departure from the ideal that jurors will not act as representatives of a particular interest (of race, class, gender, or region) and simply vote his or her "interest," but will endeavor to bring his or her particular perspective to bear upon what, through deliberation, will ultimately be a unanimous view. Harry Kalven and Hans Zeisel's classic study, *The American Jury,* found that, even where unanimity was required, the ultimate verdict was the same as the verdict on the first ballot in ninety percent of the cases. Proponents of departing from the unanimity standard cite this as an indication that doing away with unanimity has only a limited practical effect. However, the Kalven and Zeisel study also shows that, ten percent of the time, the original minority succeeds in changing the majority view. It may be wondered whether the short-term advantages of eliminating the unanimity requirement ultimately undercuts the reliability—and, again, the credibility—of the jury system.

References

Abramson, Jeffrey. *We, the Jury: The Jury System and the Ideal of Democracy.* New York: Basic Books, 1994.

Kalven, Harry J., and Hans Zeisel. *The American Jury.* Chicago: University of Chicago Press, 1970.

Pollock, Frederick, and Frederic W. Maitland. *History of English Law.* Cambridge: Cambridge University Press, 1959.

Joseph M. Hassett

Jury Trials

The trial jury has received relatively little attention as a topic in legal philosophy, understandably, given the fact that most Western liberal democracies do not use the institution to a substantial extent. If one views these societies as reasonably just, the jury does not appear to be necessary for a just society. On the other hand, the jury plays a significant role in some countries, especially in the United States.

Trial juries in the United States usually consist of from six to twelve members. Each trial jury is an ad hoc group assembled for the purpose of serving in a single trial. After the trial, that jury is dissolved and there is no continuing identifiable entity to be blamed or questioned. The jury pool is selected by using a broad-based listing of citizens in a defined geographic area, thus ensuring it is at least a prima facie fair decision maker in that it is democratic, egalitarian, and "representative." The jury for a particular trial is selected to ensure the neutrality and minimal competence of each juror; jurors are excluded by the trial judge "for cause," and trials are postponed or moved to secure a more neutral pool. In some states, a limited number of jurors can also be "peremptorily" excluded by each side.

The range of decisions entrusted to trial juries include both "factual" disputes and a wide range of "normative" determinations. Criminal juries often make normative decisions in determining whether a "reasonable doubt" of guilt exists. In some jurisdictions they have a crucial role in determining whether a murderer will be sentenced to death or to life imprisonment. Civil juries make normative decisions, since they decide such questions as whether a party acted "reasonably" or whether a punitive award of some amount of money is appropriate.

Juries also have the power to nullify the law by simply ignoring the judge's instructions concerning the law and imposing their own view of what the law should be. Because of the prohibition of "double jeopardy" in criminal matters, this power of jury nullification is virtually unlimited where "not guilty" verdicts are involved. In civil matters, the trial judge or appellate court has the power to overrule a jury verdict, but this judicial power is normally limited to extreme cases.

This power of jury nullification is effective because the jury functions as an "aresponsible" decision maker. To the extent that it gives decisions ad hoc in character, deliberates in secret, and does not give reasons for its decisions, it is not "responsible" in the ways that a legislative, administrative, or judicial body would be.

On the other hand, the jury is subject to a variety of checks. First, the jury is shaped and limited through the selection process, which is designed to limit the possibility of bias. Second, the rules of evidence are designed in part to ensure fairness and rationality by limiting the information that will be made available to the jury. Third, the process of jury selection and of the trial are designed to impress upon the jurors the nature and importance of their task. Fourth, some courts utilize interrogatories or special verdicts to force juries to be more specific about the nature and basis of their decisions. Fifth, the trial judge and appellate courts usually have the power in civil cases to "trump" the jury's decision where the decision is "unreasonable," by such means as granting a new trial or deciding the case themselves. Finally, the courts and the legislatures have the power to change the substantive legal rules applicable to particular disputes.

The traditional critiques of the jury can be viewed in terms of a series of arguments and counterarguments concerning the competence of the jury and the effectiveness of the checks summarized above.

1. Factual Complexity. *The jury does not possess either the specific knowledge of an expert in the subject area of dispute or the general experience of a judge in evaluating disputed facts.* The traditional responses to this criticism are (a) the collective powers of twelve jurors are normally sufficient for the task; (b) empirical studies support this view; (c) a single judge is no better equipped to handle such disputes; (d) resolving disputes about facts often involves interrelated normative dimensions that should be addressed by the jury; and (e) the jury is necessary to provide a check on the tyranny of experts or special interests.

2. Legal Complexity. *Juries do not know and cannot understand the law because they are given the applicable legal rules in the form of instructions by the trial judge, often orally, often long and complicated.* The traditional reply to this criticism is (a) that the collective approach results in a reasonably acceptable level of understanding, (b) that the legal issues often involve a normative component that the jury should address, and (c) that legal doctrine should be capable of being expressed in terms that people can understand and apply with only "common sense" as a guide.

3. Costs Versus Benefits. *The jury involves a number of costs: financial costs, delay, errors, and unpredictability of decisions by an ad hoc, aresponsible decision maker. The wide range of civil disputes in the United States resolved without a jury, including "equitable" actions, many federal civil rights actions, and patent disputes, suggests that its benefits are nonexistent or overrated.* The response is twofold. First, there is disagreement concerning the extent, if any, to which the jury system involves these costs more than alternative systems do. Second, defenders contend that the benefits are worth the costs, including (a) the quality of collective decision making; (b) the symbolic and other possible benefits of citizen decision making, particularly given the pluralistic nature of our society and the resulting difficulty in value agreement where normative decisions are involved; (c) the beneficial impact on the jurors themselves; and (d) the usefulness of jury verdicts in shaping negotiated settlements, which usefulness may not be obvious when the per case financial costs and benefits of juries are assessed.

4. Bias and Prejudice. *The jury's "black box" characteristics provide an opportunity for the exercise of improper bias and prejudice, including racial or class prejudice, excessive sympathy for injured victims, and intolerance of the expression of disfavored views.* Responses are (a) the case for prejudice has not been empirically demonstrated; (b) the concept of improper prejudice or bias is unclear and contentious given the necessary normative quality of jury decisions; (c) to the extent that improprieties can be identified, these improprieties can and should be corrected on a case-by-case or category-by-category basis; (d) the potential improprieties involved in jury decision making are less, or at least no greater, than those involved in other parts of the system (for example, in the exercise of prosecutorial discretion) or in alternative decision-making systems (for example, an individual judge may be pressured to decide a case in a particular way or may consistently exhibit a particular bias); (e) the discretion given to the jury provides a limit on the state in criminal matters because of the possibility of jury nullification; and (f) ad hoc aresponsible "black box" decision makers serve an important function in cases where the facts and/or the proper normative decision cannot be determined and/or articulated in terms of stated reasons acceptable in a pluralistic society.

The resolution of the debate about the utility of the trial jury ultimately is reduced to a political issue: is trial by jury, whether in its present form or in a somewhat "reformed" nature, preferable to alternative systems like bench trials, arbitration, or legislation as a method of resolving a particular type of dispute? The defense of the jury is premised on the position that law is itself a community activity and that two central issues in constructing legal institutions are (1) the definition of the relevant community and (2) the method to be used in identifying that community's concerns and choices. Choices between aristocracy and democracy, localism versus centralism, experts versus ordinary citizens, and aresponsible versus responsible decision makers involve these two issues. These choices are complex because they are partly dependent upon such diverse factors as the nature of the decision involved, the quality of the ordinary local citizens involved, and the ability to choose a different local community where there is dissatisfaction with the local situation. Moreover, since individual citizens can often have an impact on their local community, some of these factors are not objective "givens" in the evaluative process. For example, a strong role for local citizens in decision making can affect the quality of the citizens' ability to exercise their legal power of decision.

Localism, egalitarianism, and aresponsibility involve substantial risks of intolerance, ineptitude, and other ills. (Moreover, moving to another community is not a meaningful choice for many people.) The federal courts have imposed clear limits on the power of local juries where First Amendment values may be threatened by local jury intolerance. Specific legislative limits, called "tort reform," on the power of juries to award damages to persons injured by "wrongdoing" have been adopted or are currently being considered, as well. Their proponents tend to be "repeat players" in the tort process, businesses which tend to be sued repeatedly and thus have a long-term interest in the "rules of the game." Their opponents tend to be plaintiffs' attorneys and "public interest" groups, since past victims are not "repeat players" and future victims are not an easily definable class.

One such "reform" proposal is to limit the dollar amount of compensatory and/or punitive damages that a jury can award for medical malpractice or for injuries from a defective product. Such limits have been attacked as an unconstitutional denial of the right to trial by jury. Some state supreme courts have upheld such attacks, relying on the language of their state constitutions, which can be viewed in terms of protecting the role of the jury as a reflection of community views.

Another proposal limits the jury by restricting its power to define wrongful conduct. For example, the jury will be prohibited from "second-guessing" experts in determining whether a product is reasonably safe or whether a professional acted reasonably in performing a service. In evaluating such proposals, it is still helpful to phrase the issue in terms of the proper role of a localized, egalitarian approach to direct citizen decision making. The political arguments concerning these tort *reforms* often parallel the earlier analysis of the arguments for and against *retention* of the jury.

References

Abramson, Jeffrey. *We, the Jury: The Jury System and the Ideal of Democracy.* New York: Basic Books, 1994.

Adler, Stephen J. *The Jury: Trial and Error in the American Courtroom.* New York: Times Books, 1994.

Daniels, Stephen, and Joanne Martin. *Civil Juries and the Politics of Reform.* Evanston: Northwestern University Press, 1995.

Hans, Valerie P., and Neil Vidmar. *Judging the Jury.* New York: Plenum Press, 1986.

Kalven, Harry, Jr., and Hans Zeisel. *The American Jury.* Boston: Little, Brown, 1966.

Moore, Lloyd E. *The Jury: Tool of Kings, Palladium of Liberty.* 2d ed. Cincinnati: Anderson, 1988.

Simon, Rita J. *The Jury: Its Role in American Society.* Lexington KY: Lexington Books, 1980.

Vidmar, Neil, ed. "Is the Jury Competent?" *Law and Contemporary Problems* 53.4 (1989).

F. Patrick Hubbard

Justice

The usefulness of invoking "justice" as a standard for criticizing law is a matter of everyday observation. If someone claims that a given legislative enactment or judicial decision is unjust, the typical response is not "What do you mean by 'unjust'?" but rather "Why do you think it is unjust?" This reflects the fact that most people seem to have a fairly developed sense of injustice, one that they are willing to use as a (presumptively) shared criterion for arguing about statutes or rulings. Although the term "unjust" is surely broad and vaguely contoured, in normal discourse it is not considered vacuous.

Let us first consider the application of "justice" to legislation and later turn to adjudication. Justice is certainly not part of the criteria of validity of legislation. Parliaments are free to enact laws of their own choice, although many states require that the statutes comport with the state's constitution. Constitutions do not contain a "justice clause" that would serve to invalidate laws that are not just; to have such a clause would be to make the judiciary into a superlegislature (for it would be the task of the judiciary to determine which laws are just). Hence the test of constitutionality of a statute is not a justice test.

To be sure, under William Blackstone's conception of law, there are certain kinds of legislative enactments that are so blatantly unjust that Blackstone would deny them the status of "law," such as laws that command people to do the impossible. However, Blackstone's conception with its overtones of natural law has not survived to the modern era. Today, any law enacted by the legislature is a "law," leaving the citizenry with the limited choice of either criticizing a given statute as unjust or opposing the reelection of the legislators who enacted it.

Since legislation is primarily devoted to the general allocation of valued goods in a society, "justice" is an appropriate critique of such legislation. For, as David Hume pointed out, claims of justice arise because of the competition for scarce goods in a society. In evaluating particular statutes, we are operating within the general rubric of "distributive justice." However, political theorists and moral philosophers through the ages have painted with a broader brush. They have attempted to consider the most general types of legislative allocations that would spell out the structure of a just society. Plato would assign people to permanent stations in life according to their natural talents as ascertained in their childhood. The immobile, stratified society of Plato's *Republic* may strike some observers as just, as Plato intended, and others as the opposite of justice—Karl Popper called it totalitarian. In the nineteenth century, Henry Sidgwick claimed that a just society would give every person what he or she deserved. Individuals' just deserts might be measured by their moral virtue, their productive efforts, their capacities, and so on. In the same century, Karl Marx allocated social goods to each person "according to his needs." However, Ayn Rand, among others, effectively showed that measurements based on desert or need would have to be carried out by governing bureaucrats who would have neither the perspicacity nor the empathy for fair measurement, and hence would employ subjective criteria that would attract partisan influence, if not corruption.

John Rawls in 1971 argued, contrary to Plato, that in a just society everyone should have equal opportunity to be considered for all jobs and government positions. In what he termed "the difference principle," Rawls prescribed the redistribution of society's goods by taxing the wealthiest persons just to the point where their continued productivity will remain motivated, and redistributing the taxed wealth to society's poorest persons. To some extent, Rawls' position is reflected in the "progressive income tax" policy of some states. John Stuart Mill had argued in the nineteenth century that a flat percentage rate tax was required by justice: the poor and rich man alike would be assessed, say, a 15 percent tax on income. A progressive income tax, in contrast, might assess the poor man 10 percent and the rich man 20 percent. This progressivity would result in a "transfer payment" from rich to poor, much the same as Rawls' "difference principle." (There is in a sense a transfer payment under Mill's scheme as well, because the rich person pays more dollars to the government than the poor person. However, Mill argued that since the government protects everyone's assets—internally through the legal system and externally through the army—the rich person, having more assets to be protected, should pay more dollars to the government.) In certain present-day societies where the caste system or where second-class citizenship for women operate to make it impossible for a large group of people to become wealthy by their own efforts, Rawls' redistribution system might well serve the interests of aggregate justice by compensating the permanently poor groups; but in societies where people have (relatively) equal access to economic betterment, John Stuart Mill's system might seem more just. Otherwise, those people who worked hard will be taxed in order to support those who are poor because they have chosen not to work hard. To be sure, there are some people with physical or mental disabilities who may have wanted to work hard but were unable to do so. Fairness arguably requires taxing the more fortunate persons in society in order to help the handicapped (although Friedrich Nietzsche would have disagreed). Disabled persons aside, Rawls' "difference principle" has seemed to some observers to be an unjust recipe for penalizing productivity and rewarding laziness.

While questions such as whether a flat tax or a progressive tax is more just may never be finally settled, there is a certain utility in discussing such questions in terms of justice, if only because it steers the debate toward foundational issues. A similar payoff can result from critiques of judicial decisions in terms of justice. Nearly every writer agrees that justice is a goal of law and that law should strive to attain justice. Yet when it comes to particular cases, the widespread acceptance of positivism in twentieth-century jurisprudence has led to great skepticism about whether justice should be a concern of the practicing lawyer. Hans Kelsen has attacked "justice" arguments as supererogatory, because justice in the courtroom consists precisely in applying legal rules to the facts of a case. Kelsen argued that there is no such thing as justice apart from strict adherence to the rules of law. Kelsen was of course aware that a given rule of law itself could be said to be unjust, but relegated such contentions to the spheres of religion and social metaphysics. The point was made more colloquially decades ago in a first-year class at the Harvard Law School. A student asked, "But sir, is that just?" and the professor replied, "If it's justice you're looking for, you should have gone to divinity school."

However, on the issue of the place of justice in the law, positivist theory seems fatally incomplete for the reason that strict adherence to the rules of law—Kelsen's prescription for legal justice—is only possible if one is given a set of rules and instructions for applying them to a fixed set of facts. The fact is that, in nearly every contested case, opposing lawyers will challenge the applicability to the facts of a given set of legal rules, the uncertainty as to what the facts are, and the question of which particular rules should be chosen from among many relevant statutes and precedents. Hence the judge or other decision maker has three tasks: what legal rules to adopt, what version of the facts to apply the rules to, and whether those rules are indeed applicable. None of these questions can be decided mechanically or by resort to the command of the legislature (which itself would have to be "interpreted"). As a result, most judges make their choices by considering what, in the circumstances, would be most fair and most just to the contesting parties. In this way, justice becomes part of nearly every case (excluding only the distinct minority of cases where the judge, for reasons of politics or personal interest, decides to ignore justice).

The argument that justice is part of the law—and not simply a commentary upon the law—is an unintended consequence of positivism. Positivists have managed to convince most legal observers and practitioners that rules of law have no necessary moral content, that rules are merely the whims of legislators or judges issued in the form of commands. In brief, rules of law are facts, not values. This does not mean that legal rules can be ignored; they must be, and are, taken into account in every case because they form part of the topography of the case. However, getting from the rules to a decision involves taking a normative step. The judge must decide which party, in light of the legal rules and facts and all the other circumstances, ought to win. Since the rules of law are themselves value-free, they cannot give rise to an "ought." Hence the "ought" must be superimposed by the judge upon the rules of law and the facts of the case. Thus, by performing the (useful) theoretical work of stripping all value from rules of law, positivism has in effect invited justice to play a necessary role in all judicial decision making.

References

D'Amato, Anthony. "On the Connection Between Law and Justice." *University of California at Davis Law Review* 28 (1993), 527.

Kelsen, Hans. *What Is Justice?* Berkeley: University of California Press, 1957.

Rand, Ayn. *Atlas Shrugged.* New York: Signet, 1942.

Rawls, John. *A Theory of Justice.* Cambridge MA: Belknap–Harvard University Press, 1971.

Anthony D'Amato

See also CORRECTIVE JUSTICE; DISTRIBUTIVE JUSTICE

Justice in Contract, Civilian

Early philosophy of contract in the civilian codes of Napoleon (1806) and of Lower Canada (1866) made autonomy of the individual will the source of private obligation, as freedom of the collective will was for public obligation. However, exercise of liberty can lead to legally intolerable subjection. Since only the law can give legal force to the contractual parties' obligating of themselves, it is also open for the law to remedy this. In a society rife with social and economic inequalities, this is no small task; education alone is not enough. As in some common law practice, current civil code revisions in North America, notably in Canada (1993), can be used to exemplify how civilian law can make justice its basic imperative, and courts the means of achieving that goal.

This project remains supplementary to will, however, in order to preserve contract as the valuable tool forged over the centuries of human interaction that it is. According to the *Civil Code of Québec* [CCQ], sec. 9, "[I]n the exercise of civil rights, derogations may be made from those rules of this Code which supplement intention (*volonté*), but not from those of public order."

Legislation

The legislator might have stopped with mandating *good faith* in every contractual relation.

According to the CCQ, "Every person is bound to exercise his civil rights in good faith." This is "objective" good faith, that is, intending behavior like that usually required from a person considered to be acting in good faith. This would be simplest; but it risks not reaching all dimensions of conduct, such as *abuse of right* without malice. The legislator preferred to offer judges a set of tools bringing together good faith, abuse of right, and equity. As noted in the CCQ, "[N]o right may be exercised with the intent of injuring another or in an excessive and unreasonable manner which is contrary to the requirements of good faith. . . . The parties shall conduct themselves in good faith both at the time the obligation is created and at the time it is performed or extinguished." Their requirements are ordered cumulatively, so that each must be satisfied before invoking the next.

In these texts is reinforced the recognition that rights provide no more than a reasonable exercise of their entitlements. Good faith is formulated as normal behavior in contract so that, while dropping its peerage, it gains in efficacy.

Equity remains the tool of last recourse in judges' hands. Beyond what good faith and normal usage demand, equity enters to correct disproportions coming not from the parties' behavior, but from the economic circumstances. Proportionality in what is exchanged depends not on agreements, but on circumstances apart from any act of will.

The better to ensure contractual justice and to control inequality, in a society where knowledge, wealth, and power are badly skewed, the legislator has also called upon *public order*. Particular practices are forbidden (for example, abusive clauses), exploitation is sometimes deemed (for example, in lesion), providing information is made an obligation (for example, in consumer contracts), to ensure that economic inequality does not become injustice. As well, judges have the power to determine that what the law requires is, in fact, of public order even when it appears to be neutral (virtual public order).

Finally, the legislator has looked for persons related to the contract's outcome. *Third-party immunity* is no longer presumed. The circle of persons obliged on the contract is widened to include those with benefits (for example, inheritance of contracts accessory to property) and burdens (for example, upon successive dealers in a product, as well as administrators usually protected by corporate anonymity) outside the normal ambit of the contract. The chain for providers of goods and services is followed across their chain of contracts, and the stipulations of the strongest and most crafty are no longer the decisive factors.

Courts

Courts are the ones to exercise this search for contractual justice, using the legislative tools set before them to control contractual behavior; good faith, equity, and nonabusive exercise are their specialized panoply to ensure equality in transacting. The texts set the tone; the judges must be relied upon to make them effective and, with this aim, to make use of their wide power of *evaluation*. In most of the numerous instances, two features are constant: (1) the parties cannot make up their own criteria for good faith, but must use those recognized in the democratic society they inhabit— not good faith in one party's own estimation, but according to the social norm that is accepted; (2) the concept of good faith in the case law goes further than does abuse of right—a party cannot be heard to claim that it has just done all the law requires.

In seeking contractual justice, courts might have been content to control behavior by *canceling* contracts or finding *damages and interest*. The legislator did not limit them to this, but provided some power to *remake* a contract. Making it deficiently need not lead to nullity, but, alternatively, to its continuing with a *reduction* in the burdens on its victim. Executing it deficiently need not dissolve it or bring damages with interest, but can bring a reduction in the corresponding obligation of the party who suffered the breach. Judges are left to make reductions at their discretion in view of all the relevant circumstances.

Even beyond reducing the contractual requirements, the court can alter the contract's *content and modalities* in view of the ability to pay or receipt of its benefits in consumer contracts, loans, and contracts by minors or protected persons. The judge is put in control over the contract's worth; more than judging between parties, the judge has become an actor on the socioeconomic field, ensuring it is worthwhile to keep the contractual bond going.

Still more bold is the judge's ability to use all means available at law to set the contractual obligation in motion, even to require *execution in kind*. This power looks not only for its basis to the texts giving plaintiffs the right to demand that their contract be executed, according to the CCQ, "in full, properly and without delay," but also to the principle of stability of contracts in order to make cancellation the exceptional means for ending a contractual breach. While the *injunctive procedure* for obtaining specific performance is hampered by special rules, with some daring and imagination judges can put it to good use upon contracts.

This direction in contracts puts new values in opposition to others: justice, to liberty; completion of contracts, to their stability; remaking obligations, to judicial neutrality. Whatever the back-and-forth in this direction, parties must accustom themselves to thinking about the virtual party in every contract: its judge. Here especially is the venue for contractual ethics.

References

Coipel, Michel. "La liberté contractuelle et la conciliation optimale du juste et de l'utile" (Contractual Liberty and the Optimal Agreement of the Just and the Useful). *Revue juridique Thémis* 24 (1990), 485–504.

Diosdi, Gyorgy. *Contract in Roman Law, from the Twelve Tables to Glossators.* Trans. F. Szabo. Budapest: Academai Kiado, 1981.

Heleine, François. "Le droit des obligations. Une double préoccupation des tribunaux: contrôler les comportements; s'adapter au droit nouveau" (The Law of Obligations. The Courts' Twofold Concern: Governing Conduct, Adapting to New Law). In *Le nouveau code civil du Québec: un bilan,* 27–51. Montréal: Wilson et Lafleur, 1995.

Honoré, Tony. *Making Laws Bind: Essays Legal and Philosophical.* Oxford: Clarendon Press and Oxford University Press, 1987.

Leclerc, Ginette. "La bonne foi dans l'exécution des contrats." *McGill Law Journal* 37 (1992), 1071–1109.

Lefebvre, Brigitte. "La bonne foi dans la formation du contrat" (Good Faith in Contract Formation). *McGill Law Journal* 37 (1992), 1053–1069.

Lindgren, Ralph. *Horizons of Justice.* New York: Peter Lang, 1996.

Masse, Claude. "Développements récents en matière de lésion et d'équité contractuelle" (Recent Developments in Lesion and Contractual Equity). *Congrès annuel du Barreau du Québec* 1990, 169–189.

Perret, Louis. "Une philosophie nouvelle des contrats fondée sur l'idée de justice contractuelle" (A New Philosophy of Contract: The Idea of Contractual Justice). *Revue générale du droit* 11 (1980), 538–601.

Pineau, Jean. "La philosophie générale du code civil" (The Overall Philosophy of the Civil Code). In *Journées Maximilien-Caron, 1992,* 269–291. Montreal: Thémis, 1993.

Sur les notions du contrat (Ideas of Contract). *Archives de philosophie du droit* 13 (Paris: Sirey, 1968).

François Heleine

See also CONTRACTUAL OBLIGATION; FREEDOM AND CAPACITY OF CONTRACT; JUSTICE

Justification

Because law is the most powerful instrument of social control, its institutions, procedures, and coercive functions are continually under rigorous scrutiny. The parts of a legal system must demonstrate their validity, justness, and rationality. The demand for legal justification is responsive to perceived problems about official authority. Thus, numerous recurring questions trouble legal theorists: What establishes the moral legitimacy of a legal system? How do particular laws earn the right to rule citizens? Can we rationally demonstrate the validity of a system of punishment? In the United States, is there any noncircular argument supporting the institution of judicial review?

This essay focuses on only one such question: Are the arguments embodied in appellate decisions rationally defensible? On the other hand, are they merely question-begging reflections of judges' subjective preferences?

Legal realists provide one of the main sources of skepticism about appellate decision when they claim that judges are not compelled by extant legal doctrine when arriving at their legal conclusions, but are instead moved by intuition, subjective preferences, moral and political ideologies, even their own immediate psychological moods. Judges decide cases on such bases not because they are irresponsible or lack integrity. These internal inclinations and attitudes may be dimly understood even by judges themselves; but decision makers must choose conclusions from their own vantage points because legal doctrine is too indeterminate to compel particular conclusions of its own.

Traditionalists who argue in favor of the rational justification of appellate decision making often respond to such skeptics by relying on a classic distinction between the context of discovery and the context of justification. Mainstream scientists and legalists contend that there is a difference between the procedures, motivations, and ways by which we discover various truths, and the justifications and explanations by which we demonstrate these discoveries to be truths. Our rational beliefs that a proposition is true, it is argued, are not necessarily linked with the ways that the proposition was discovered. Thus, we could agree, at least in part, with legal skeptics about the phenomenon of discovery but still insist that legal justification is a function of the persuasiveness of the arguments, reasons, and supporting legal material advanced by a judge.

Skeptics, whether in the form of critical legal scholars, radical feminists, critical race theorists, or marxists, can rejoin that their criticism of judicial justification runs much deeper: there is no justification of truth beyond motivations, ways, and procedures employed within a practice to discover truths. The traditional distinction between discovery and justification is fraudulent because it is grounded on the familiar, and ultimately incomprehensible, belief that there can be an Archimedean point by which to judge the claims emerging from our constrained interpretations.

Traditionalists can respond in a variety of ways. Some attempt to demonstrate that an Archimedean point is available and is, indeed, presupposed by rational discourse itself. Others argue that the rational justification of appellate decision need not invoke an Archimedean point.

Thus, neo-pragmatists point out that once inside the enterprise of normative debate, once we are actually arguing for and evaluating moral and legal conclusions, we all presuppose that some claims are better than others, that some are right and others wrong. The arguments we advance to support our favored normative conclusions are not supported by different esoteric arguments that claim that our

conclusions are objectively validated from a privileged Archimedean point. Normative justification is thus constituted by theoretical explanations that are rational not necessarily because they are grounded by the view from nowhere, but because they include self-correcting aspects that put any claim in jeopardy, though not all claims at once.

Accordingly, judicial decisions are justified if the reasons and arguments advanced by the judge are adequate to establish the answer to the case at bar. Moreover, the soundness of judicial justifications should not be sharply distinguished from what socially passes for acceptable legal arguments, and the correctness of legal propositions is partially determined by whether sound legal justifications can be given for them. Judicial rationality is grounded not in the psychological moods of officials but in the ongoing process of public criticism generated as particular decisions are subjected to public scrutiny, to examination by higher review courts, and to tests provided by subsequent cases with similar fact patterns.

This modest view of legal justification is compatible with a host of claims usually associated with skeptics: it admits the contingency and contestability of judicial arguments and legal conclusions; it acknowledges the presence of several conflicting legal ideologies in extant doctrine; it understands that judges internalize law's institutional history and possess tacit knowledge of how to decide cases; and it agrees that political dispute is unavoidable in a pluralistic society. Nevertheless, unless one clings to the view that validation from an Archimedean point is necessary for sound decision making, all of the above are compatible with legal justification. In this fashion, the neo-pragmatist strategy turns the skeptics' charge against them: it is skeptics who implicitly subscribe to the necessity of an Archimedean point for rational validation.

Unless one embraces some version of natural law theory, however, there is no necessary logical connection between legal and moral justification. There is a distinction between what the law requires and what justifies a judicial decision. Thus, an appellate decision may be justified internally, from within the processes of a particular, reasonably just legal system and the demands of a specific body of legal material, but still be morally unjustified.

What is a judge to do under such circumstances? Perhaps this is the best answer: judges are obligated to decide cases in accord with legal justification, but the scope of this obligation is bounded. Judges are justified in not applying settled law only after making the determination that inordinate substantive injustice would occur if the settled law is applied; no other institutional justifications (for example, that the rules, principles, and policies that support the settled law are themselves morally justified and ignoring them in extraordinary cases will do them significant damage, or that the legal system as a whole is morally justified and will be damaged more by ignoring the law's requirements than the good that is produced, or harm prevented, in the instant case) can be persuasively offered for applying the law; and there is no less drastic means of resolving the problem.

References

Belliotti, Raymond A. *Justifying Law*. Philadelphia: Temple University Press, 1992.

Bernstein, Richard. *Beyond Objectivism and Relativism*. Philadelphia: University of Pennsylvania Press, 1988.

Dworkin, Ronald. *Law's Empire*. Cambridge MA: Harvard University Press, 1986.

Frank, Jerome. *Law and the Modern Mind*. 1930. Garden City NY: Anchor Books, 1963.

Golding, Martin P. *Legal Reasoning*. New York: Knopf, 1984.

Kelman, Mark. *A Guide to Critical Legal Studies*. Cambridge MA: Harvard University Press, 1987.

Kuhn, Thomas. *The Structure of Scientific Revolutions*. 2d ed. Chicago: University of Chicago Press, 1970.

Lyons, David. "Justification and Judicial Responsbility." *California Law Review* 72 (1984), 178.

Pennock, J. Roland, and John W. Chapman, eds. *Justification. Nomos* XXVIII. New York: New York University Press, 1986.

Wasserstrom, Richard. *The Judicial Decision*. Stanford: Stanford University Press, 1961.

Raymond Angelo Belliotti

See also DECISION MAKING, JUDICIAL